June 25–30, 2016
Singapore

Association for
Computing Machinery

Advancing Computing as a Science & Profession

MobiSys'16

Proceedings of the 14th Annual International Conference on
Mobile Systems, Applications, and Services

Sponsored by:

ACM SIGMOBILE

In-cooperation with:

ACM SIGOPS

Supported by:

Singapore Exhibition & Convention Bureau, National Science Foundation, Singapore Management University, Hewlett Packard Enterprise, Facebook, Google, IBM Reserarch, LARC, Microsoft, Naver, TATA Consultancy Services, and VISA Research

Association for
Computing Machinery

Advancing Computing as a Science & Profession

The Association for Computing Machinery
2 Penn Plaza, Suite 701
New York, New York 10121-0701

ISBN: 978-1-4503-4269-8 (Digital)

ISBN: 978-1-4503-4608-5 (Print)

Additional copies may be ordered prepaid from:

ACM Order Department
PO Box 30777
New York, NY 10087-0777, USA

Phone: 1-800-342-6626 (USA and Canada)
+1-212-626-0500 (Global)
Fax: +1-212-944-1318
E-mail: acmhelp@acm.org
Hours of Operation: 8:30 am – 4:30 pm ET

Printed in the USA

General Chairs' Welcome

We take great pleasure, as general chairs, to welcome you to Singapore to attend the 14th International Conference on Mobile Systems, Applications, and Services -- MobiSys'16. MobiSys has, since its inception in 2003, been the premier venue for world-leading research in mobile systems.

We are delighted that the steering committee, led by Victor Bahl, agreed to let us bring the conference to Singapore this year. This is the first time the conference has come to South Asia and we are deeply honoured to be chosen to do so, especially as this edition coincides with the 20th anniversary of ACM SIGMOBILE.

Running a successful conference, first and foremost, requires a stellar program of excellent research papers. We are delighted that the program committee, led by Sharad Agarwal and Cecilia Mascolo as program committee chairs, has done a fantastic job in selecting 31 excellent papers from a submission pool of 197 submissions. We are also very grateful to Sharad and Cecilia for their constant and excellent help in improving all aspects of the MobiSys program, which also includes a special session to honor some luminaries who are proud recipients of SIGMOBILE's first "Test of Time" paper awards.

This year's edition of MobiSys continues the tradition of having multiple workshops, which allow our community to explore emerging and evolving topics in smaller, focused interactions. Our workshops chairs, Nicholas Lane, Eduardo Cuervo and Yunxin Liu, deserve special credit for coordinating 8 different workshops (including our first Women's workshop), spread across 2 days.

For this iteration of MobiSys, we are delighted to introduce two innovations. First, we developed a mobile application, for both iOS and Android, to improve the engagement with and between MobiSys attendees. This conference app uses location and sensing technologies to intelligently provide attendees with games, quizzes, program information, and the ability to chat with fellow attendees. We would like to thank Ignatius Tan and his entire engineering team comprising Ritesh Kumar, Tran Anh Quan, Tieu Thi Thanh Chau, William Tan, Le Hai Son, Huynh Quang Trung, Aniket Pujara, John Lee, Jeena Sebastian, and Prakhar Vishnoi for developing, testing, deploying, and maintaining the conference application. In addition, we would like to thank Sharad Agarwal, Stefan Sariou, and Alec Wolman for helping us integrate the Microsoft Research Embedded Social Software Development Kit into the app. We would also like to thank all our internal and external testers for their feedback that helped to improve the app.

Second, we wanted to greatly increase the number of student attendees at MobiSys, with a special emphasis on students from our regional neighborhood and various parts of Asia. To do this, we created a special symposium called the Asian Students' Symposium on Emerging Technologies (ASSET) that will run from June 23-June 25th, right before the main conference. ASSET was designed to help students with their research and presentation skills, allow them the opportunity to present and discuss research with distinguished researchers, and to increase and improve their peer networks. We would like to humbly thank Youngki Lee, JeongGil Ko, Tadashi Okoshi, and Jie Xiong for helping us to organise ASSET. In addition, we would like to thank Suman Banerjee, Romit Roy Chowdhury, Nigel Davis, and Lin Zhong for generously volunteering their time and agreeing to be speakers at ASSET.

In addition to ASSET, we also increased the demo and poster session to a two day event with up to 150 presenters. This allowed many additional students to present their work at MobiSys. We would like to thank Landon Cox, Yutaka Arakawa, Xia Zhou, and Robert LiKamwa for managing the expanded demo/poster session.

This year, we have been fortunate to receive amazing sponsorship support from academic, governmental, and industrial sources. This allowed us to sponsor at least 80 students to attend MobiSys -- students that otherwise would not have been able to attend. We would first like to thank our main sponsors, the ACM and ACM SIGMOBILE for making this conference possible. In addition, we would like to thank Singapore Tourism Board (STB), Suntec Convention Centre, LiveLabs Urban Lifestyle Innovation Platform (LiveLabs), Information Technology Research Academy (ITRA), National Science Foundation (NSF), Hewlett Packard Enterprises, Facebook, Google, Microsoft Research, Visa Research, Living Analytics Research Centre (LARC), School of Information Systems at Singapore Management University (SIS), IBM Research, Tata Consultancy Services (TCS), and Naver Labs for their generous support that made these student scholarships possible. We also would like to thank Pei Zhang, Vinayak Naik, and Christos Efstratiou for managing the entire scholarship application process in a very competent and seamless way.

Running all of these events requires an entire team of 'heroes'--unsung volunteers who help manage the chaos and madness that every conference like ours must face. We would like to extend our heartfelt thanks to our entire local arrangements team, led by Youngki Lee, and ably assisted by our colleagues, Huang Sipei and Luar Shu Hui. Special thanks also to our colleagues Jonathan Wang (Finance) and Kazae Quek (Registration), who have gone well beyond their nominal designations and helped out in so many different ways. This team of battle-hardened veteran is being helped by so many enthusiastic student volunteers, ably coordinated by Mun Choon Chan, Salil Kanhere and Azeem Khan. We owe all of them a big thanks for making MobiSys a seamless and enjoyable experience for all our guests.

The reason that most people know about the events taking place at MobiSys is because of the publicity efforts and the website. In this regard, we are very grateful to our publicity chairs Moustafa Youssef, and Tamer Nadeem for sending out numerous publicity emails. In addition, we would like to thank Tadashi Okoshi for his amazing social media publicity efforts that created engaging publicity channels that was not utilised heavily previously. We also want to express our sincere thanks to Kasthuri Jayarajah and Inseok Hwang for being amazing webmasters who were willing and able to update the website as soon as changes were required -- which was quite frequently at some points in time.

Finally, we would like to thank everyone, including our volunteers and especially the authors who submitted paper, poster, and demo submissions for making MobiSys a very successful event. On behalf of the entire organising team, we would like to welcome you to Singapore and we hope that you have an amazing experience here!

Archan Misra & Rajesh Krishna Balan
MobiSys'16 General Chairs
Singapore Management University

Message from the Program Chairs

It is our great pleasure to bring you the proceedings for the 14th ACM Conference on Mobile Systems, Applications, and Services (ACM MobiSys 2016). We hope you enjoy this technical material behind the conference that attracts a diverse set of attendees from both academia and industry and is a leading venue for publications and idea exchange on mobile systems. ACM MobiSys 2016 has a highly selective, single-track program featuring research related to mobile systems and applications. It is an ideal venue to address research challenges facing the design, development, deployment, use, and fundamental limits of these systems.

Our paper review process this year was highly selective. Out of 197 submissions, the technical program committee accepted only 31 for publication and presentation as full papers, yielding an acceptance rate around 15.73%. Submitted papers underwent a rigorous, multistage review process. First, we checked all submissions for compliance, general quality, and topic match. We administratively rejected those not meeting our submission criteria. We assigned 3 reviewers to papers that survived this stage from the program committee and the external review committee. At the conclusion of this stage, those papers where none of the reviewers recommended acceptance were rejected. We then assigned at least 2 additional reviewers from the program committee to papers that survived, thus totaling at least 5 reviews per paper. An online discussion phase then ensued, resulting in the PC recommending 59 papers for discussion at the PC meeting. The PC meeting was held in person in St. Augustine, FL, USA, the day before ACM HotMobile 2016. At the conclusion of the PC meeting, we tentatively accepted 31 papers to the conference. All tentatively accepted papers were assigned shepherds to help ensure that the authors produce a final manuscript that satisfactorily addresses reviewer comments. All shepherded papers were ultimately accepted to the conference.

Our program this year covers an exciting set of topics including operating systems, transport, networking, sensing, security and privacy. It also includes a poster/demo session, a panel, and keynote speakers.

Putting together the program of ACM MobiSys 2016 was a team effort. We thank the General Chairs, Professors Rajesh Krishna Balan and Archan Misra, for supporting us and forming and driving the rest of the organizing committee. We thank all authors for submitting their work to the conference. Our special thanks go out to the program committee and external review committee members for the monumental amount of work in producing over 800 reviews. We thank ACM and the other members of the organizing committee for all the logistical arrangements that made it possible to bring this program to you. Our thanks also go out to the ACM MobiSys Steering Committee for trusting us to produce the 2016 program. Last but not least, we thank the conference attendees for their patronage of the conference and for making it a successful meeting place for multiple communities and a catalyst for discussions and creative exchange.

We hope that you will find this program interesting and thought-provoking and that the conference will provide you with a valuable opportunity to share ideas with other researchers and practitioners from institutions around the world.

Sharad Agarwal, *Microsoft*

Cecilia Mascolo, *University of Cambridge*

ACM MobiSys 2016 Program Co-Chairs

Table of Contents

Session IV: Transit and Mapping

Session Chair: Robin Kravets *(University of Illinois at Urbana-Champaign)*

Session V: No More Leaks

Session Chair: Ben Greenstein *(Google)*

Session VI: Better Mobile Interfaces

Session Chair: Inseok Hwang *(IBM Research)*

Session VII: Small and Large Scale Networking

Session Chair: Xia Zhou *(Dartmouth College)*

2016 MobiSys Organization

General Chairs: Rajesh Balan *(Singapore Management University)*
Archan Misra *(Singapore Management University)*

Program Chairs: Sharad Agarwal *(Microsoft)*
Cecilia Mascolo *(University of Cambridge)*

Workshop Chairs: Nicholas Lane *(Bell Labs)*
Eduardo Cuervo *(Microsoft)*
Yunxin Liu *(Microsoft)*

Poster/Demo/Video Chairs: Landon Cox *(Duke University)*
Yutaka Arakawa *(NAIST)*
Xia Zhou *(Dartmouth College)*
Robert LiKamWa *(Rice University)*

Local Arrangements Chairs: Youngki Lee (Lead) *(Singapore Management University)*
Sipei Huang *(Singapore Management University)*
Shu Hui Luar *(Singapore Management University)*

Publicity Chairs: Tamer Nadeem *(Old Dominion University)*
Tadashi Okoshi *(Keio University)*
Moustafa Youssef *(Egypt-Japan University of Science and Technology)*

Publication Chair: Jie Xiong *(Singapore Management University)*

Treasurer & Registration Chairs: Jonathan Wang *(Singapore Management University)*
Kazae Quek *(Singapore Management University)*

Web Chairs: Inseok Hwang *(IBM Research)*
Kasthuri Jayarajah *(Singapore Management University)*

Student Scholarship Chairs: Christos Efstratiou *(University of Kent)*
Vinayak Naik *(IIIT Delhi)*
Pei Zhang *(Carnegie Mellon University)*

Student Volunteers Chairs: Mun Choon Chan *(National University of Singapore)*
Salil Kanhere *(University of New South Wales)*
Azeem Javed Khan *(Oriental Institute of Management)*

Steering Committee Chair: Victor Bahl *(Microsoft Research)*

Program Committee: Mary Baker *(HP Labs)*
Aruna Balasubramanian *(Stony Brook University)*
Geoffrey Challen *(University at Buffalo)*
Jennifer Yingying Chen *(Stevens Insitute of Technology)*
Landon Cox *(Duke University)*
Eduardo Cuervo *(Microsoft)*
Nigel Davies *(Lancaster University)*
Jakob Eriksson *(University of Illinois at Chicago)*
Jason Flinn *(University of Michigan)*
Deepak Ganesan *(University of Massachussetts)*
Ben Greenstein *(Google)*
Marco Gruteser *(Rutgers University)*
Jeremy Gummeson *(Disney)*
Polly Huang *(National Taiwan University)*
Minkyong Kim *(IBM Research)*
Robin Kravets *(University of Illinois, UC)*
Nicholas Lane *(Bell Labs)*
Youngki Lee *(Singapore Management University)*
Qin *(*Christine*)* Lv *(University of Colorado, Boulder)*
Z. Morley Mao *(University of Michigan)*
Lama Nachman *(Intel)*
Vishnu Navda *(Microsoft)*
Giovanni Pau *(UPMC - LIP6)*
Ardalan Amiri Sani *(University of California, Irvine)*
Lenin Ravindranath Sivalingam *(Microsoft)*
Junehwa Song *(KAIST)*
Jia Wang *(AT&T)*
Kamin Whitehouse *(University of Virginia)*
Ying Zhang *(HP Labs)*
Xia Zhou *(Dartmouth College)*

External Review Committee:

Yuvraj Agarwal *(Carnegie Mellon University)*
Jeremy Andrus *(Apple)*
Nilanjan Banerjee *(University of Maryland)*
Alastair Beresford *(University of Cambridge)*
Jeremy Blackburn *(Telefonica Research)*
Mun Choon Chan *(National University of Singapore)*
Kuan-Ta Chen *(Academia Sinica)*
Hao-Hua Chu *(National Taiwan University)*
David Chu *(Microsoft)*
Sarah Clinch *(Lancaster University)*
Mark Corner *(University of Massachussetts Amherst)*
Nicola Dell *(Cornell Tech)*
Christos Efstratiou *(University of Kent)*
Shyam Gollakota *(University of Washington)*
Y. Charlie Hu *(Purdue University)*
Wenjun Hu *(Yale University)*
Inseok Hwang *(IBM Research)*
Puneet Jain *(HP Labs)*
Fahim Kawsar *(Bell Labs)*
David Kotz *(Dartmouth College)*
Sung-Ju Lee *(KAIST)*
Kyunghan Lee *(UNIST)*
Ilias Leontiadis *(Telefonica Research)*
Justin Manweiler *(IBM Research)*
Mahesh Marina *(University of Edinburgh)*
Richard P. Martin *(Rutgers University)*
Mirco Musolesi *(University College London)*
Tadashi Okoshi *(Keio University)*
Abhinav Pathak *(Apple)*
Matthai Philipose *(Microsoft)*
Kiran Rachuri *(Samsung Research)*
Bozidar Radunovic *(Microsoft)*
Silvia Santini *(TU Dresden)*
Stefan Saroiu *(Microsoft)*
Souvik Sen *(Google)*
Kannan Srinivasan *(The Ohio State University)*
Emmanuel Munguia Tapia *(Intel*
Sasu Tarkoma *(University of Helsinki)*
Alec Wolman *(Microsoft)*
Guoliang Xing *(Michigan State University)*

MobiSys'16 Sponsors & Supporters List

Sponsors:

Venue Partner:

Academic Partner:

Held in:

Supported by:

Platinum Supporter:

Gold Supporter:

Silver Supporter:

Hewlett Packard Enterprise

Bronze Supporters:

facebook

Google

IBM Research

LARC Living Analytics Research Centre

Microsoft

NAVER

TATA Consultancy Services

VISA Research

LiveLabs: Building In-Situ Mobile Sensing & Behavioural Experimentation TestBeds

Kasthuri Jayarajah, Rajesh Krishna Balan, Meera Radhakrishnan,
Archan Misra, and Youngki Lee
School of Information Systems, Singapore Management University
{kasthurij.2014,meeralakshm.2014}@phdis.smu.edu.sg, {rajesh,youngkilee,archanm}@smu.edu.sg

ABSTRACT

In this paper, we present *LiveLabs*, a first-of-its-kind testbed that is deployed across a university campus, convention centre, and resort island and collects real-time attributes such as location, group context etc., from hundreds of opt-in participants. These venues, data, and participants are then made available for running rich *human-centric behavioural experiments* that could test new *mobile sensing* infrastructure, applications, analytics, or more social-science type hypotheses that influence and then observe actual user behaviour. We share case studies of how researchers from around the world have and are using *LiveLabs*, and our experiences and lessons learned from building, maintaining, and expanding *LiveLabs* over the last three years.

Keywords

Mobile Sensing; Experimentation; Testbed

1. INTRODUCTION

A key desire for many mobile computing researchers is the opportunity to test their hypotheses, systems, and techniques on real users in real environments in realistic ways. However, making this happen is hard: in particular, you need to recruit participants, secure an environment where such participants will exhibit natural behavior, and finally, put in all the instrumentation necessary to accurately trigger your experiment as well as to collect the data needed to evaluate the effectiveness of the experiment. All of these steps are hard, painful, and sometimes impossible to do.

For example, recruiting participants can take many man-months of work to manage recruitment calls, screen the responses for suitability, engage with suitable candidates to collect demographics data, and to keep them interested and informed about the experiments, and finally, follow up with payment and other paperwork, where necessary. Next, securing a suitable test environment can also take many man-months as the venue owner needs to be convinced that running experiments in their venue is acceptable. For example, even at universities, this may involve long negotiations with the facilities management staff as well as the institutional review board. Finally, instrumenting the environment is strenuous as some types of useful experiment data, such as where the participants went or who they were with, is hard to capture without in-environment sensors. As such, experimenters often resort to instrumenting a mobile application and asking the participants to download that app and run it. However, this limits the types of data that can be collected and also the participant pool – as the app may only work on Android for example.

In this paper, we describe our multi-year effort to provide an in-situ real-time behavioural experimentation testbed, called *LiveLabs*, that can be used by researchers to run rich *human-centric mobile sensing & behavioural trials* in realistic settings. In particular, *LiveLabs* provides three testbeds at: our university (*SMU*), a convention centre (*Suntec*), and a resort island (*Resort*[1]). These provide real-time attributes about participants at each venue, such as location and group membership, and additionally, at *SMU*, a large and diverse fully opted-in and IRB-approved participant pool that can receive, as mobile notifications, and react to real-time in-situ experimental stimulus. *LiveLabs* can also be used at all 3 venues, *SMU*, *Suntec*, *Resort*, to test novel mobile sensing applications, infrastructure, analytics, and other research ideas and prototypes.

LiveLabs has been actively developed for the last 3 years[2] by over 90 people, and leverages many deep technology components such as server-side location tracking [26, 60], dynamic group [50] and queue detection [42], energy efficient mobile data collection software [7], and a very usable and intuitive UI. In the rest of this paper, we briefly describe the main *LiveLabs* components and showcase its integrated use for various behavioural studies.

Building *LiveLabs* required this effort level as we had to develop, implement, *harden*, and *maintain* many different novel pieces of technologies that could work with minimal maintenance across Android, iOS, laptops, etc. We also had to secure the necessary funding, hire the right people, convince our venue partners to deploy *LiveLabs*, and most importantly, *convince participants and researchers* to join and use *LiveLabs*. This last point needs to be stressed as forming a stable test and user population was much harder than we thought. Indeed, to overcome these challenges, we had to change our lab structure – from a standard research lab into more of a startup with separate roles and personnel for research, production, maintenance, client management, administration, and participant recruitment. For example, technology developed by our researchers is never integrated into *LiveLabs* directly; instead it is handed over to the production team to re-implement correctly – i.e. hardened and made maintenance-friendly.

LiveLabs has been described previously [8, 35], however, this is the first presentation of the full end-to-end system along with

MobiSys '16, June 25–30, 2016, Singapore.
© 2016 ACM. ISBN 978-1-4503-4269-8/16/06. . . $15.00
DOI: **http://dx.doi.org/10.1145/2906388.2906400**

[1]Venue intentionally anonymized

[2]Through generous support by Singapore's National Research Foundation http://www.nrf.gov.sg/

detailed usage results. Specifically, we focus on how *LiveLabs* allows researchers to run innovative in-situ real-time human-centric behavioural studies. We will describe the experiment types that *LiveLabs* supports and show how this improves on the state-of-the-art. We then present numerous case studies showing how *LiveLabs* has been successfully used for various experiments. The main contributions that we make in this paper are as follows:

- We present, to our best knowledge, a first-of-its-kind, available-for-use testbed specifically tailored towards in-situ, real-time mobile sensing & human-centric behavioural experiments.
- We describe how *LiveLabs* uses well-established experimentation methodologies that allow both social science and technology researchers to test new and innovative multi-disciplinary ideas in mobile sensing, real-time analytics, behavioural studies, marketing methods, and other related domains.
- We present the various *LiveLabs* building blocks, showing how deep technology components, such as location sensing, couple with a rich, yet intuitive, UI to provide a complete end-to-end experimentation platform.
- Finally, we present case studies showing how *LiveLabs* has been used to investigate various research hypotheses by many different groups of researchers. *LiveLabs* has been operational since January 2015 at *SMU* and since June 2015 at both *Suntec* and *Resort*. As of May 2016, $\approx$ 4,000 undergraduates have signed up as *LiveLabs* participants at *SMU*; at *Resort*, $\approx$ 27,000 members of the public have downloaded the resort's publicly available (Android and iOS) smartphone application that incorporates our technology.

LiveLabs is available for use, for free, by any researcher[3].

2. DESIGNING LIVELABS

Designing and conducting unbiased behavioural experiments is a highly complicated process that involves recruiting the right participant pool to running minimally biased experiments. For minimum bias, subjects should be placed in natural environments where nothing is artificial – i.e., they are using their own devices and interacting in normal ways with their friends and others around them. In this setup, you then want to inject a stimulus and observe how the subject pool behaves (or how some system behaves if you are testing a technology component). It is this kind of natural test environment that *LiveLabs* was built to provide. A natural environment allows for running truly innovative experiments that go far beyond the constraints of a standard user study where the experiments are usually not realistic, e.g. "shopping" simulations done inside a lab, and the subjects are biased as they are aware that they are part of an experiment, e.g., the experimenter is present.

2.1 Design Goals

The two main design goals of *LiveLabs* were:

1. **Rewarding & Safe for Participants:** *LiveLabs* requires the active participation of either students or members of the public to be successful. Thus, it is important that being a part of the testbed is seen as both *useful* and *safe* to all the participants. We describe our privacy mechanisms in Section 2.2 and our attempts to make *LiveLabs* useful in Section 6.3.

2. **Useful for Technology & Behavioural Researchers:** The second major goal of *LiveLabs* is to make it useful for multiple types of experiments. For example, *LiveLabs* should support systems-type experiments that require installing and testing new sensors or forms of data collection, new sensing algorithms, or types of real-time analytics. In addition, *LiveLabs* should also support behavioural-type experiments where the participants are provided some kind of stimulus, via an in-app notification for example, followed by observation of their reaction to that stimulus.

   To support both types of experiments, *LiveLabs* must thus be *flexible* to support multiple experiment types, *easy to modify* to add new functionality, and *easy to use for experiments* even by non computer-scientists. We describe in Section 3 the main components and implementation of *LiveLabs* that allows us to satisfy these design criteria.

2.2 Privacy Considerations

A key *LiveLabs* design goal is to achieve a useful tradeoff between maintaining user privacy while still supporting useful context-aware experiments. For example, *LiveLabs* could average the locations of all users in a large area and store just one location for all of them. However, experiments that require identifying the locations of specific people such as "Send a coupon only to people at Table 23" cannot be run if the averaging has removed the required fidelity.

Hence, we decided to anonymise all collected data without performing any kind of aggregation or reduction that preserves privacy at the expense of data fidelity. We created a unified framework (Section 3), where all data is processed by an anonymisation sub-component that 1-way hashes all personally identifiable information. The raw data is then removed and only anonymised data is retained. In addition, during participant sign up, we explicitly state how we collect and anonymise all data including demographics information and regular uploads of sensor and app usage data from their smartphones as well as location data from infrastructure sensors. The entire *LiveLabs* participant data and consent handling procedures have been approved by both the university's *Institutional Review Board (IRB)*, and legal department who deemed our procedures to be in compliance with Singapore's *Personal Data Protection Act*[4] data privacy regulations.

However, even with these procedures in place, it is possible for a malicious hacker, with access to all the *LiveLabs* databases, to identify specific individuals as we use a consistent hashing scheme. We are leaving, as future work for both ourselves and for any interested systems privacy researchers, the development of better privacy schemes that can protect against more attacks, and still allow *LiveLabs* to provide the level of context-driven personalized experimentation that it currently supports.

3. IMPLEMENTING LIVELABS

To achieve the goals in Section 2, *LiveLabs* needs to overcome the following technical challenges. First, sensor data has to be collected without imposing unacceptable privacy or energy concerns for the participants. Next, accurate and useful contextual triggers have to be provided from the data collected (e.g., accurate activity detection from inertial sensing data from participant smartphones). Then, a powerful yet easy to use interface to describe experiments that *LiveLabs* can run has to be designed. This is particularly important, and hard, as a large number of experimenters are not computer scientists and have limited experience and patience with complicated IT systems. Finally, *LiveLabs* needs to provide detailed experiment results that can be used by experimenters to understand and improve their experiments. This is surprisingly non-trivial as

[3] `http://is.gd/livelabs` to test a sandboxed version for yourself

[4] https://www.pdpc.gov.sg/legislation-and-guidelines/overview

running experiments in real-world spaces introduces errors, e.g., the computed location of a participant can be wrong, that need to be accounted for in the experiment reports. We describe how we solve these challenges in the rest of this section.

3.1 Architecture Overview

The *LiveLabs* architecture is shown in Figure 1. The process flow is as follows: (i) Participants sign up for *LiveLabs* and install the *LiveLabs* Service app on their personal iOS or Android phones. (ii) The service apps running on each phone along with the environmental sensors, Wi-Fi in particular, regularly upload raw data to the *LiveLabs* data collection service. The data is anonymised and then processed to generate real-time contextual information about the participants. (iii) In parallel, experimenters provide experiments using the *LiveLabs* experiment specification user interface. (iv) For each approved experiment, the *LiveLabs* experiment engine checks when the experiment should run based on the dates and times provided by the experimenter. When the experiment needs to run, the experiment engine contacts the analytics engine to retrieve a list of participants that match the specified contextual triggers. (v) The experiment engine then sends the treatment, as a notification, SMS, or rich message to a specific *LiveLabs* app, to each matched participant. (vi) The experiment engine monitors what each participant did after a treatment was sent to them. (vii) The anonymised responses are sent to the experimenter for analysis and improvements. To achieve this entire logical flow, *LiveLabs* builds on multiple technical components, which we describe next.

Content	Android	iOS	Information Recorded
Accessibility	Yes	No	Accessibility Event, App Name, Package Name, Event Class
Battery	Yes	Yes	Battery level
Calendar	Yes	Yes	Title, Notes, Location, Dates
Call Logs	Yes	Yes	Last_Dialed_Number
Contact	Yes	Yes	First/Middle/Last Name
Location	Yes	Yes	x, y Coordinates
Program State	Yes	Yes	State
System Settings	Yes	Yes	App Version, Language, Carrier, Phone No, IMEI, Mac Address, Device Name, Signal Strength
System Log	Yes	Yes	ASLMessageID, Level, PID, Facility, Sender, Message
Wifi Trace	Yes	Yes	Action, BSSID, *RSSI*
Bluetooth	Yes	No	State
External Media	Yes	No	Media state
Installed Apps	Yes	No	Package Name
Network State	Yes	No	Data Source, Data Type
Profile State	Yes	No	Possible Actions
Cell Tower	Yes	No	Cell ID (CID), Location Area Identity (LAC), Primary Scrambling Code (PSC)
Sensor Data	Yes	No	Accelerometer, Gyroscope, Light, Pressure, Rotation

The collectible data changes with each OS version update, e.g. iOS 6 vs 7. This table lists the maximum data we can collect from each OS.

Table 1: Contextual Data Collected: Android vs. iOS

3.2 Collecting Data

Collecting Data From Participants: A key *LiveLabs* component is the *LiveLabs* Service app for both Android 4+ and iOS 6+. As stated earlier, we do not provide any devices to the participants – instead participants install the *LiveLabs* app on their primary smartphone. This decision was made to reduce the testbed bias as we strongly believed that you could only observe natural behaviour when participants were using their own devices and data plans.

The data collected by the *LiveLabs* Service app depends on the OS and the current data collection policy. For example, we are able to collect more data on Android versus iOS – See Table 1 for details. However, a key lesson learned early on was that participants were extremely sensitive to any extra smartphone power drain or heat generation caused by our data collection routines and that they would quickly uninstall the *LiveLabs* app, leave the pool, and also speak negatively about *LiveLabs* to their friends.

Hence, we extensively measured the power drain of various sensors both individually and when they were used together (key results are presented in Balan et al. [7]), and created energy profiles for various sensors and sampling frequencies. We then added policy support into the *LiveLabs* service app to allow the data collection policy to be dynamically updated, e.g. which sensors to collect data from, at what sampling rates, for how long, etc. All data collected is compressed, and stored as files on the participants phone with quotas determining how much data to store before overwriting. The data is uploaded to the *LiveLabs* Analytics Engine whenever the phone is using Wi-Fi to eliminate any cellular data charges. After uploading, the data is cleared from the participants phone.

To achieve the highest participant satisfaction, the default policy is to introduce no additional power drain by collecting no data at all. However, based on experiment requirements, we can and do turn on phone sensors, e.g. inertial sensors to detect current activity, for a few hours, at most, per day.

Collecting Data From The Environment: In addition to phone data, *LiveLabs* also collects data from the environment. In particular, we collect Wi-Fi signal strengths of every connected device directly from the Wi-Fi infrastructure.

Data Anonymiser: All data collected, from either phones or the environment, is processed by our anonymisation service before it enters any *LiveLabs* data store. This service uses a consistent 1-way hashing function to hash any personally identifiable information in the data, such as MAC addresses, email ids, user ids, names and numbers. In addition, any data that was collected unintentionally, e.g. data that is not required by any existing data store, is discarded. The raw data that enters the anonymisation service is discarded and only the hashed data is stored.

3.3 LiveLabs Context Services

Another key component of *LiveLabs* is the analytics engine that processes the data collected from smartphones and environments to generate the contextual information used to trigger experiments and to understand their effectiveness. This engine uses contextual data generated by numerous pieces of prior work built by the *LiveLabs* research team over the last few years. We briefly describe the key prior work below:

Location Service: A key *LiveLabs* contextual trigger is the current location of all participants. The challenge was to obtain these locations with both high accuracy and high recall, both indoors and outdoors. To achieve both goals, we decided to collect raw signal strength data directly from the commercial Cisco or Aruba Wi-Fi controllers used at each venue. This is because collecting data from phones consumes energy about which our participants are sensitive to. Also, as many devices are either not part of *LiveLabs* or run OSs that don't allow client-side Wi-Fi sniffing (e.g., iOS), this results in data sparsity. In contrast, collecting data from the infrastructure allowed us to track every device that connects to the Wi-Fi infrastructure – even those not part of *LiveLabs*. Note: every device that connects to the Wi-Fi infrastructure at each venue has agreed to this tracking as part of the sign-on agreement. In addition, for devices that are not part of *LiveLabs*, the system tracks them as hashed entities with no additional knowledge about them.

We use fingerprint maps and a RADAR-inspired [5] solution to convert the raw data from the controllers into precise locations of

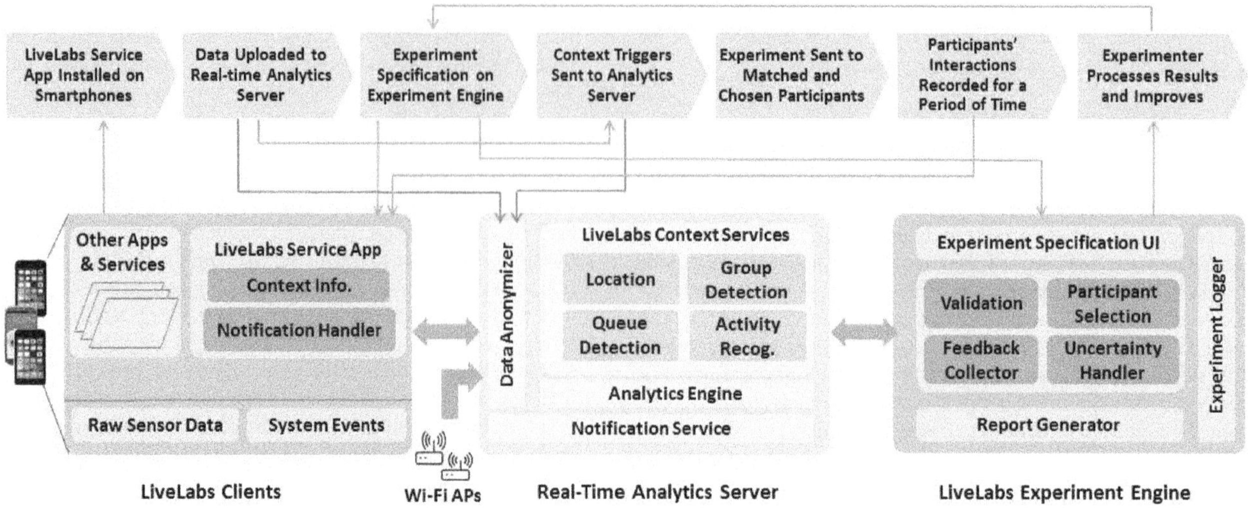

Figure 1: *LiveLabs* Architecture

every device at each venue. In the process, we discovered unique challenges of doing this type of server-side localisation and refined our system to overcome these challenges. Nairan et al. [60] describes our solutions to these challenges and provides detailed performance results for our system. Overall, our location system has been operational at *SMU* since August, 2013 and at both *Suntec* and *Resort* since June 2015. It tracks, as of May 2016, ≈19,000 unique devices per day across all venues. At *SMU*, location results are updated every 1-2 minutes with a 6-8 meter accuracy.

Group Detection Service: We leveraged the fact that our location system tracks every device, whether they are *LiveLabs* participants or not, to build a dynamic group membership system called *GruMon* [50]. This system combines the location traces of every device detected in the environment with probabilistic analysis to identify devices that are *moving together with intent* – i.e., they are interacting with each other and thus in the same group. This is particularly hard in crowded places such as our university campus where tens or hundreds of people can be physically co-located in the same area, such as the campus food court, even though they are not interacting with each other. We have deployed *GruMon* at SMU since August 2014, and the other venues since June 2015, and provided the ability to select participants based on the size of the groups they are in.

Group membership is important as our recent results [22] showed that the behaviour of a group, in terms of how long they spend in places and where they are likely to go next, is very different when compared to the behaviour of individuals. In addition, different sized groups, e.g small 2 person groups versus large 7 person groups, behave quite differently from each other as well. Hence, we believe, with corroboration from our psychology and marketing peers, that controlling for group membership is important when trying to understand the reactions of individuals to any kind of stimulus. As far as we know, *LiveLabs* is the only testbed that allows researchers to dynamically target different sized groups in an easy and non-invasive manner.

Queue Detection Service: In crowded places, such as *SMU*, queues can form dynamically at ATM machines, food stalls etc. To detect these dynamic queues, we built *QueueVadis* [42] that uses sensor data collected from participants' phones to detect the wait and service times of queues. We then combine the data from multiple phones to create an overall view of the current wait and service times of all current queues across the campus. *QueueVadis* employs a two-tier classification approach for detecting individual-level queuing episodes using the locomotive signature of short bursts of shuffling forward between periods of standing. We showed, via numerous experiments in both Singapore and Japan, that it produces accurate values irrespective of queue shapes and even if participants join or leave the queues prematurely. We also showed that only a fraction of the people standing in a queue need to generate the data for it to work. Currently, we use *QueueVadis* only for special experiments as the need to actively collect data from participants' phones prevent it from being an always-on service.

Activity Recognition Service: Finally, we have also developed a number of activity detection solutions that can detect what the participant is doing from the inertial sensor data collected from their phones and, more recently, smartwatches. For example, *A3R* [59] that detects standing, walking, sitting, and other basic activities as well as *Annapurna* [52, 51] which detects eating activities. Similar to *QueueVadis* above, we do not offer these activity detectors as a standard service, and use them only on a case-by-case basis, as they require active data collection from the participants' phones.

3.4 LiveLabs Experiment Engine

The final component of *LiveLabs* is the experiment engine. This component receives experiments from experimenters through a GUI-driven entry process, validates, schedules, and selects the right participants for any given experiment, executes the experiment, and provides the experimenter with data that can be used to validate the efficacy of the experiment.

Experiment Specification (UI): Figure 2 shows part of the experimenter UI. This UI portion allows experimenters to select the contextual triggers, e.g., the precise location in the top left area and the group membership criteria in the top right, for their experiment. Overall, the UI was developed and refined over many months with various experimenters to be easy to use, yet powerful enough to specify all experiment details, such as the number of control versus treatment participants and the actual intervention sent when the experiment runs. The *LiveLabs* UI can be accessed at `http://is.gd/livelabs` and sample experiments can be created in this sandbox environment.

Experiment Validation: Currently, all new experiments entered through the non-sandbox UI portal must be approved by a *LiveLabs* director, who will receive email reminders, before the experiment can be executed. This is to ensure that every experiment is non-damaging to our participants, e.g., the experiment does not spam participants with junk messages or try to steal their personal data, as a bad user experience will affect our participant retention rate.

Participant Selection: Once an experiment has been approved, it gets scheduled according to the date and time selected by the experimenter. When the scheduled date and time occur, the participant selection component will query the analytics engine to ask for a list of participants who currently match the contextual triggers specified by the experiment. The analytics engine continuously queries its up-to-date databases and returns a list of all participants that match the triggers. The selection component then partitions this list into control and treatment groups based on the experiment specifications. If the size of any group is smaller than the minimum required size, the experiment is delayed until the appropriate minimum sizes are reached. If the sizes are sufficient, the selection component sends the list of treatment participants to the notification service along with the content to send as specified by the experiment. The experiment continues until either enough participants, as specified by the maximum required size criteria, have received the treatment or the experiment time window has expired.

***LiveLabs* Notification Service**: This component uses existing push notification services provided by Google (GCM [18]) and Apple (APNS [4]) to send the experiment content to the selected participants' phones. On the participants phone, the messages are routed either to the *LiveLabs* service app which then displays them as a notification or to another *LiveLabs* app as shown in Figure 3. The last time each *LiveLabs* app on a participants phone connected to a *LiveLabs* service is recorded in specific databases and used to check if specific participants can receive rich messages.

Experiment Logger: The experiment logger activates every time an experiment is executed. It retrieves and stores the location and context updates by every participant in that experiment, for both treatment and control groups, for a configurable period.

Collecting User Feedback: When an experiment is sent to a participant, the experiment logger could decide to turn on specific data collectors, e.g collect inertial data to generate activity information, on that participants phone. If so, an updated policy is sent to the phone. In addition, the experimenter can also specify a post-experiment survey, to collect qualitative feedback, that will be sent to each participant, after the experiment concludes, as a link in a notification message.

Context Uncertainty Handler: A hidden *LiveLabs* bias is that the trigger events are derived from noisy sensor data. For example, the location system has an average 6 to 8 meter error with all the other analytics services having their own specific errors. Thus the participants chosen by *LiveLabs* can include people who do not satisfy the experiment criteria. Quantifying this error, which can never be eliminated as every sensing system will have errors, is an active area of research. Currently, we developed models that combine the errors generated by the low level sensors into probabilities that can be used by experimenters to understand and improve the accuracy of their experiments. For example, we use the notion of overlap regions to determine the probability that a chosen participant pool was actually located where the system thought they were [37]. In addition, we use models to suggest whether the minimum participant numbers need to be increased to reduce the uncertainty caused by the underlying sensing systems [36]. For example, choosing only 2 participants will lead to a large probabilistic selection error if room-level location accuracy is required.

Report Generator: Finally, the experiment engine will generate a detailed post-experiment spreadsheet containing information such as the timestamp and location where every participant received the experiment, along with the timestamp and location where they saw any notification, clicked any link, opened any *LiveLabs* app, and activated any *LiveLabs* app features. Example reports can be seen at the *LiveLabs* sandbox portal at `http://is.gd/livelabs` under "Experiment List".

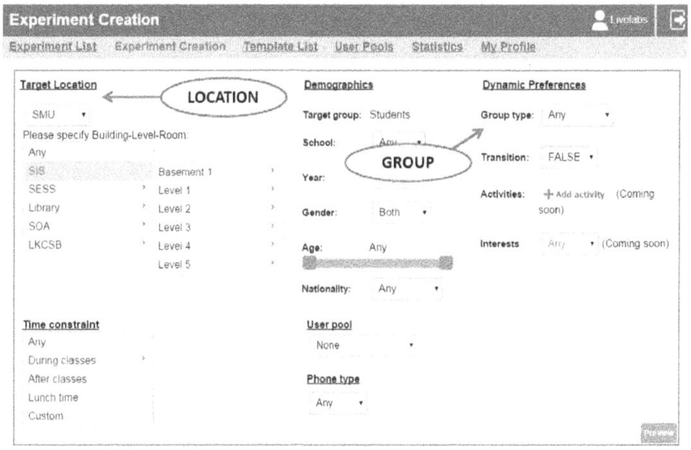

Figure 2: Expt. Specification UI – Context Selection

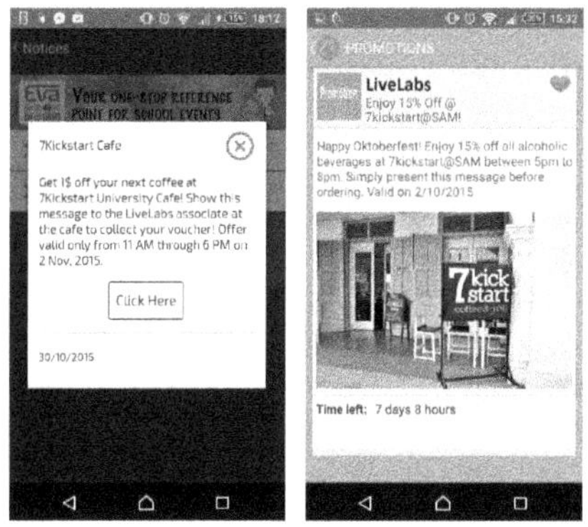

Figure 3: Treatments as Seen on a Participant's Phone

3.5 Current LiveLabs Testbeds & Status

Table 2 shows an overview of the three testbeds where *LiveLabs* is deployed. These testbeds are *SMU* – our entire university campus, *Resort* – a popular outdoor resort island in Singapore, and *Suntec* – a large and popular convention centre. At all three venues, we have deployed our infrastructure sensors, that track device movements using Wi-Fi, along with the real-time analytics solutions. At both *SMU* and *Resort*, we also engage with participants who install our mobile apps, built by *LiveLabs* for *SMU* and by enhancing the existing *resort-specific* app for *Resort*. We then provide researchers and marketing personnel with the portals and ability to run behavioural trials on these participants. Currently, *Suntec* does not have any participants; however that will change when the conference app (Section 4.1.2) is deployed for MobiSys 2016 and future conferences.

Most of the *LiveLabs* back-end systems are built using PHP with some components built using Java and JSP. PostgreSQL is used for most databases along with MongoDB to store unprocessed location data. We also built and maintain two campus-specific apps to help participant retention – an app to provide promotional content, and another to provide event information. We are currently building a third app that will be used during MobiSys 2016.

Testbed	Type	Size / meters^2	Floors	Participant No.	Collecting Data?	Real-Time Analytics?	Experiment Engine?	Operational From
SMU†	University Campus	70,000	30 (5 bldgs)	4,000	Infra. & Phone	Yes	Yes	Jan 2015
Resort	Resort Island	14,000	1 (Outdoor)	26,950	Infra. & Phone	Yes	Yes	Jun 2015
Suntec♭	Convention Centre	20,000	5 (1 bldg)	N/A♯	Infra. Only	Yes	No	Jun 2015

† **http://www.smu.edu.sg**, ♭ **http://www.suntecsingapore.com**
♯As of April, 2016, the deployment at Suntec is infrastructure-based only with no registered, opt-in participants.

Table 2: Summary Of Testbeds

LiveLabs is maintained by a team of full-time professional developers who ensure that all core systems and apps are always working and available. In addition, we have a separate team of outreach and administration personnel who manage, maintain, and increase the participant pool. Separately, our research staff, Ph.D. students, postdocs, and faculty, design, prototype, and test the next set of *LiveLabs* improvements such as new sensing modules and better uncertainty handling. Once these new features are stable and deemed of value to experimenters, they are handed over to the professional developers to integrate into the main system as a core feature. Overall, about 90 people, including students, faculty, developers, post-docs, interns, admin staff, have helped to build *LiveLabs*.

3.6 What Can LiveLabs Be Used For?

LiveLabs can be used to test the following: (1) *Mobile Sensing*– hardware or software sensors that can be easily installed/deployed and used to monitor some aspect of human behaviour, (2) *Mobile Analytics*– algorithms, policies, and analytics that work on human-generated location and contextual data, (3) *Mobile Applications*– any Android or iOS application that does not require root access, and finally, (4) *Behavioural Trials*– experiments that interact with humans in real environments in real-time using contextual triggers and phone-based notifications. We provide examples of the systems experiments in Section 4 and the behavioural experiments in Section 5.

3.7 Limitations of LiveLabs

LiveLabs was designed and optimised for experiments that can be triggered on a participant's smartphone – either through an app that the participant willingly downloads or an SMS. This works well for experiments that require the participant to see a coupon or a message, run an app, or answer a survey etc.

A limitation of *LiveLabs* is that it does not, yet, integrate with social media data such as Facebook or Twitter. We are investigating ways to integrate social media feeds as the context they describe does not necessarily match the physical environment that *LiveLabs* operates in. Related to this, *LiveLabs* cannot be used to trigger experiments that require data that either *LiveLabs* does not collect (e.g., mental well-being status of a user), or cannot infer accurately (e.g., centimeter-level locations).

Another limitation is that the *LiveLabs* contextual data feeds may be limited by practical considerations such as participants uploading minimal data or by the accuracy and latency of the Wi-Fi data collected from the commercial Wi-Fi controllers. Also, experiments that require rich media, such as promotion coupons with images, can only be sent to participants who have voluntarily installed the appropriate *LiveLabs* app that can receive the rich content. By default, the *LiveLabs* service app can only receive plain content.

Finally, *LiveLabs* does not facilitate *responsive* surveying where experimenters immediately react and adapt the experiment. In addition, unlike lab settings, *LiveLabs* does not isolate participants – their response times are thus not guaranteed and may be influenced by non-experiment real-world stimulus.

Image from http://www.suntecsingapore.com/advertise-at-suntec/the-big-picture

Figure 4: Large Public Display at *Suntec*

4. RUNNING EXPERIMENTS

We now describe how *LiveLabs* has enabled research in Systems and the Social Sciences.

4.1 Using LiveLabs For Systems Research

A key use case for *LiveLabs* is to help test new technology. In fact, the context services that we described in Section 3.3 were all incubated as part of *LiveLabs*. We are actively improving *LiveLabs* with extensions to our environmental sensing by adding BLE-based fine-grained localization[46], context sensing capabilities with occupancy detection[39], emotion sensing [21], GPU-based vision sensing [20], privacy violations detection [25], improved power management for OLED displays [55, 54], support for wearable devices that can be used to detect eating [51], shopping [45] etc. Also, the ability to perform additional experiment types with support for social network-based experiments [23], trajectory-based recommendation systems [24], and audio log-based experiments. Finally, we have hosted interns from PhoneLab [38], KAIST, Wisconsin, and PEC, and have started the tech transfer process to setup a similar testbed at UMASS Amherst. We welcome and offer other researchers the chance to test their technologies in our campus. We now present two upcoming systems experiments that could only be done on a testbed like *LiveLabs*.

4.1.1 Real-Time Contextually-Aware Public Displays

One of our venues, *Suntec*, uses large public displays, as shown in Figure 4, throughout their premises. As part of a joint study with professors and a Ph.D. student from Lancaster University, we plan to investigate how to use these displays to engage more effectively with customers using the premises. One key idea is to use contextual information collected from our real-time sensors to automatically display relevant information to customers passing by the displays; for example showing the location of a meeting to a business user or providing information about shopping promotions to a customer heading towards the mall. In addition, we plan to add interactive sensors, such as the Kinect [33], to some screens to allow customers to interact with the screen in useful ways. Finally, we plan to identify techniques to partition the screen space of a really large screen, such as the one shown in Figure 4, between multiple users located in the same proximity.

4.1.2 Gamification of Conference Programmes

As part of the MobiSys 2016 conference [1], which will be held at *Suntec*, *LiveLabs*, together with researchers from Microsoft Re-

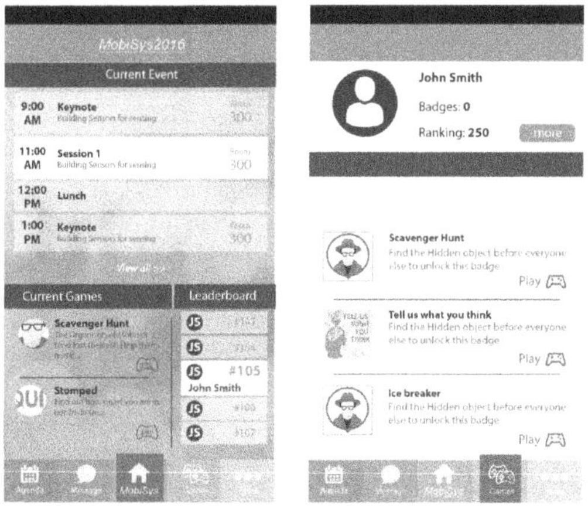

Figure 5: MobiSys 2016 Conference Application

search Redmond, are exploring the use of a mobile iOS and Android app to improve the interactive quality of the conference through gamification and other social networking features. The key features of the app include smart friend finding, using the *LiveLabs* location service, contextually-triggered games, notifications, and other experiments using a modified version of the *LiveLabs* experiment engine, continuous engagement through creative games, points, leaderboards, and badges using technology built for the *SMU* apps, and social interaction during talks and other events using a technology called Microsoft Research Embedded Social Software Development Kit Service [34] from MSR Redmond. Figure 5 shows how the current app prototype [5] looks like; the reception from our initial testers has been very positive. We will report on the success of the app at MobiSys in a future article and we hope to use this conference app at other academic conferences, such as MOBICOM and SIGCOMM, as well as trade shows and consumer events run at *Suntec*.

4.2 In-Situ Behavioural Studies

Creating a natural experiment environment for running behavioural studies, without cutting corners or introducing additional bias, is extremely challenging. In this section, we review how conventional experiments are usually performed and then we describe how *LiveLabs* improves on various aspects of the experimentation process. We also discuss how we reduce the experimentation bias as much as possible. In Section 5, we provide case studies of experiments that we have run with colleagues from around the world cutting across various disciplines such as marketing, psychology and computer science.

4.2.1 Existing Experimentation Process

Currently, running experiments requires the following common steps. First, experimenters design the experiment. In this stage, they decide the scale of the study, the target participant demographics and recruitment locations, experiment methodology, e.g survey, focus group, shadowing etc., prepare the survey instruments and related material depending on the chosen methodology, set aside the necessary budget for incentives, prepare and clear IRB approvals, and perform any other necessary preliminary steps. Second, experimenters start recruiting participants. During this process, the experimenters usually contact every interested participant to explain the purpose and process of the experiments, and to collect any necessary demographics and personal details for controlling or analysing the study results, processing payments etc. Third, the experiments are conducted with the twin goals of achieving reliable/meaningful responses while reducing as much bias as possible. However, achieving both goals usually requires an experienced experimenter – indeed, many studies are re-done as either valid responses were not collected or unintended biases were introduced into the study. Finally, experimenters analyse the responses and other data to draw useful conclusions. Usually, their responses will be a mix of quantitative, e.g., precise response times, and qualitative, e.g., free form questions, data.

4.2.2 How LiveLabs Improves The Process

We now describe how *LiveLabs* improves on the conventional experimentation process.

Step 1: Experiment Design. The key *LiveLabs* innovation is allowing experimenters to easily use contextual inputs as experiment triggers. For example, in conventional studies, the control and treatment groups are usually manually determined and pre-assigned by the experimenters. With *LiveLabs*, treatment groups can be dynamically assigned, at no additional cost, using various contexts.

In addition, *LiveLabs* allows experiments that are almost impossible to do, without excessive bias, in a lab setting. For example, *LiveLabs* can support experiments such as "Send a survey to the participants *only* when they are with 3 or more people". We list the full set of *LiveLabs* experiment conditions in Section 4.3.

Based on the experimenter requirements, *LiveLabs* currently supports the following experiment designs: *Simple Control and Treatment*: a single treatment along with the size of the treatment and control groups, *Multiple Treatment*: multiple treatments that are sent concurrently to distinct participant pools with the same contextual triggers), and *Chained Conditions*: a series of treatments that are sent to the same set of selected participants in sequence. In all cases, *LiveLabs* will select the control and treatment pools using the specified contextual triggers. The experiment continues to run until the minimum pool size is met or the experiment expires.

Step 2: Participant Recruitment. *LiveLabs* greatly simplifies this process for an experimenter by providing a large, demographically diverse pool of opted-in participants belonging to multiple majors, gender, etc.,. If the experiment requires data or permissions beyond what the participants have agreed to, *LiveLabs* will send a new agreement. In many cases, the participants have already provided sufficient consent as the experiments usually involve sending a notification to the phone or collecting raw sensor data.

LiveLabs uses a team of dedicated staff to actively recruit and retain participants. To sign up, participants must provide explicit consent, basic demographics information, and then install the main *LiveLabs* service app – this serves as both an app store for participants to obtain other *LiveLabs* apps as well as a conduit that allows *LiveLabs* to collect data from the participants' smartphone and to send treatments to the participants. The participants are incentivised to sign up through bonuses, periodic promotions and, most importantly, compelling apps, e.g., a campus events app, that they could not obtain otherwise. In addition, we make it clear that their data is kept private and that this is benefiting research. We discuss the recruitment process in more detail, along with our challenges, in Section 6.3. An advantage of this centralised approach is that our large pool of participants don't actually know *what* experiments will be sent to them or *why*. Thus, every participant's reaction to notifications, survey requests, or other experimental content is quite natural.

Step 3: Conducting Experiments. After an experimenter submits an experiment, it is validated by senior *LiveLabs* staff. An experimenter is allowed to run experiments that send a simple notification (e.g., a link to a survey, an SMS, or a rich message like

[5] Videos available at **http://is.gd/mobisys16app**

sending a visually appealing campus store discount coupon to a *LiveLabs* promotions app) to a participant's smartphone. Currently, we have developed rich apps that can handle promotions, events, and micro-tasks. The *LiveLabs* experiment engine (Section 3) will execute the experiment at the correct time), with a participant set that matches the experiment's contextual triggers, and then send the experiment content to those participants.

Note: the above is the standard setup for conducting social-science type experiments where a stimulus is sent to the participant and the reactions observed. *LiveLabs* can also be used to test the efficacy of various sensing and/or other technologies. In this case, the technology will be deployed to participants, via an app, and *LiveLabs* will collect both the necessary data from the app and appropriate ground truth, using environmental sensors etc., to allow the technology to be evaluated.

Step 4: Results Analysis. A key benefit of *LiveLabs* is that it is able to collect rigorous post-intervention data through data collected from the participants' phones and environmental sensing. As such, we can provide experimenters with detailed reports on the efficacy of their experiments. For example, we can tell them when and where a particular promotion was received by a participant, where the participant actually viewed the promotion, and where they actually clicked the redeem button, along with the time taken to transition between each phase. This type of precise data is very hard to obtain, without bias, in a lab setting, and almost impossible in a real-world environment.

Note: we never reveal personally identifiable information to any experimenter or allow them to interact with participants directly. For example, experimenters only receive details such as "Participant 1110010 (Gender: Male) from Economics Year 3 saw the promotion at 11.33 a.m. at Level 3, Building A". This level of detail, after discussions with various experimenters, was deemed suitable as it provides sufficient details while hiding the identities of participants from non-malicious experimenters – we use strict admission control to detect and remove malicious experimenters. If an experimenter requires personally identifiable information, additional consent from each participant will be required.

Context Triggers	Replicate	Extend	Innovate
Static Contexts			
Demographics	No	Yes	Yes
Participant Pool	No	Yes	Yes
Dynamic Contexts			
Location			
Building-level	Yes	Yes	Yes
Floor-level	No	Yes	Yes
Room-level	No	No	Yes
Location Transitions	No	Yes	Yes
Time	Yes	Yes	Yes
Group Status	No	No	Yes
Queue Status	No	No	Yes
Activities (e.g., *walking*)	No	No	Yes
Interests (e.g., *web history*)	No	No	Yes

The replicate entries were derived from actual prior work [14, 16]. Extend and Innovate were influenced / designed by our social science colleagues – based on the state of research in their respective fields.

Table 3: Experiment Use Cases and Context Triggers

4.3 LiveLabs Experiment Use Cases

We designed *LiveLabs* for three experiment use cases: (1) *Replicate*: where an experimenter re-runs an existing experiment on *LiveLabs* to benefit from the lower setup cost and high fidelity *LiveLabs* test environment. (2) *Extend*: where an experimenter runs standard experiments but at higher fidelity because of the unique capabilities of *LiveLabs*. For example, instead of sending a standard marketing message to the entire subject pool, use *LiveLabs* to target students at specific locations on campus. Finally, (3) *Innovate*: where an experimenter uses *LiveLabs* to create new and innovative experiments that push the research boundary. For example, a psychologist is generating new insights into mental well-being by using *LiveLabs* to send targeted surveys to participants based on their interactions with people around them. The key *LiveLabs* features that allow this are the dynamic tracking of a person's interactions with other people using the *GruMon* group detection system [50] and the ability to intervene exactly when certain triggers occur in the natural world without the participant being interrupted by the research team – previously the survey would have been administered to the participants by a research assistant.

Table 3 shows the context triggers that *LiveLabs* can support for the three experiment cases. Note: *LiveLabs* is constantly adding new features, sensing modalities, and contextual triggers, both developed in-house and from other research groups worldwide, that allow us to expand the range of experiments – especially the *Innovate* kind.

5. BEHAVIOURAL EXP. CASE STUDIES

In this section, we show how *LiveLabs* allows experimenters to **replicate** traditional experiments faster and with less effort, **extend** existing experiments in interesting ways, and finally, and most importantly, to **innovate** and create completely new and previously impossible-to-do high research-value experiments.

5.1 Replicating Existing Experiments

We replicated two classic psychology experiments with the help of a SMU psychology faculty and a Temple university marketing faculty. As stated in Table 3, *Replicate* type experiments do not depend on real-time context triggers, but they help establish the *representativeness* and *sufficiency* of the size of our participant pool.

Bystander Apathy [29]: We replicated a classic phenomena, where the presence of others inhibits helping behaviour, described in Garcia et al. [16]. Our results are completely consistent with both the original work as well as a follow up study [15] that showed that bystanders could either increase or decrease the helping behaviour depending on where the bystander's attention was focused. To replicate this study, we sent a survey, similar to the original study [16], that asked participants what percentage of their annual earnings, after graduation, would they be willing to donate to charity along with questions regarding their group context. The survey questions and responses are available at `http://tinyurl.com/bystandersurvey`.

Foot-in-the-Door Technique [14]: We demonstrate through *LiveLabs*, that it is possible to replicate this type of classical study [14] which examines a highly influential, compliance technique where an individual agrees to a large request only because they were first asked and agreed to a modest request. To do this, we created a control group which was asked for a large favor, a donation amount to create literacy programs for blue collar workers in Singapore, and a treatment group that was asked of a moderate favor, to sign a petition asking for more literacy programs for workers in Singapore, followed by the same large favor. The survey questions and responses are available at `http://tinyurl.com/fitdsurvey`.

5.2 Extending Experiments In New Ways

Many social science experiments involve *priming* and administering surveys to score participants along some behavioural or attitudinal trait such as psychometric scales etc. We show how *LiveLabs* has *extended* such techniques in new ways.

Priming Effects: This study, being run by an ESSEC business school marketing faculty, tries to understand how different types of text, either deliberative or implemental [17], would subliminally affect where a participant would go next. We do this by sending a specific passage, written in either deliberative or implemental tone, to participants at specific locations on campus and then observing where they stayed after being subjected to the treatment. *LiveLabs* extends this experiment by allowing precise location triggers, e.g. "send only when they enter the library", with non-invasive and accurate server-side monitoring of where the participants went to, e.g., did they pick a central or peripheral location in the library, after receiving and interacting with the text passage.

Promotion Framing: Another study run by the ESSEC faculty investigates how the framing of a promotion, e.g. offering an instant promotion versus one that is available after a delay, and the group context of a person impacts the redemption rate. Specifically, they hypothesize that the people who are alone are more likely to redeem the delayed promotion due to the effect of cognitive fluency. Further, the study also investigates whether the presence of strong or weak group ties when the participant receives the promotion is also a moderating factor in redeeming the offer. *LiveLabs's* Group Detection Service enables this experiment by providing continuous monitoring of the participants' group context, as well as quantified measures of tie strength through historical analysis of the participants' co-location with others [23].

Opinion Leadership Study: A research team from Carnegie Mellon, Temple, and Emory universities is using *LiveLabs* to understand the role of leaders in groups – with the hypothesis that sending promotional content to the group leader, compared to other group members, will lead to better redemption rates. *LiveLabs* extended this study in the following ways: (1) the location traces collected by *LiveLabs* Location Service were used to generate models of who the leaders or followers for any group might be – validated by a opinion leadership scale survey, and (2) *LiveLabs's* Group Detection Service allows those pre-identified leaders to be interacted with only when they are in groups. In particular, first part could have been done previously, but the second part is a new capability. Previously, they would have relied on self-reports of the identified group leaders to discover what they might have done or deployed shadowers to follow the leaders. These are now unnecessary as *LiveLabs* enables scalable, unobtrusive, and real time observations – allowing experimenters to use, with minimal effort, specific triggering conditions and to obtain accurate and non-invasive feedback on where and what the participants did.

Group-Aware Marketing: *LiveLabs* is being used by marketing faculty from Arizona State University to test group-aware marketing strategies where participants would receive *group-aware*, or *generic* promotional content depending on whether they were in a group or alone. Their hypothesis is that sending group-aware promotions to people in a group results in higher redemption rates compared to generic promotions. This type of experiment is only possible, with minimal bias, using *LiveLabs* due to its dynamic location and group detection capabilities.

5.3 Innovating Experiment Designs

We now describe high-value experiments that could *only* be executed on *LiveLabs*.

Tracking The Spread Of Malware: One of our SMU computer science colleagues is using *LiveLabs* to track the spread of malware. In the first phase, they used *LiveLabs* to recruit participants for the study, via a survey. In the second phase, they plan to use *LiveLabs* Location and Group Detection Services to understand the physical context of participants at the time they receive "deceptive" messages that ask them to click on unknown web URLs – clicking on these URLs will trigger a malware that sends messages to friends in their phone contact lists. The new insights that *LiveLabs* provides is a deep understanding of the physical context of the participants at the time when they receive the malware message, clicked on or discarded the message, and their reaction when they learned that they had been deceived. Note: the experimenters will clearly explain to every participant about the deception and what they should have done as part of the debriefing process. The study was approved by the full IRB board. In addition, the experimenters had to convince the *LiveLabs* directors that the study was not going to harm the participants.

Survey Mode	Response Rate
Paper-based	22% [49]
Web	17 - 20 % [49], 18% [27]
Mail	24.2% [27]
SMS	22.5% [6]
LiveLabs	21.85 - 34.27% (non-exam periods), 12.07 - 17.62 % (exam periods)

Table 4: Comparison Of Response Rates

Experiment	Subjects	Viewed Exp.	Did Exp.
Bystander Apathy	454	100 (22.0%)	80 (80%)
Foot-in-the-Door	561	88 (15.7%)	69 (78.41%)
Priming Effects	303	76 (25.08%)	70 (92.10%)
Promotion Framing	426	160 (37.55%)	146 (91.25%)
Opinion Leadership	778	171 (21.97%)	170 (99.41%)
Group-Aware Marketing	58	13 (22.4%)	7 (53.8%)
Malware Spread	286	46 (16.08%)	43 (93.48%)
Personality Traits†	302	100%	100%

† This study used a separately recruited participant pool

Table 5: Summary Of Experiments

Personality Traits Study: Most personality studies in Psychology rely on self-reported data. However, self-reported data confounds *situation selection* with *situation perception*. Situation selection refers to the association between personality traits and objective situational attributes such as the number of people you are interacting with etc. Situation perception refers to the association between personality traits with subjective situational features such as their reaction to a red banner etc. Both variables are needed to understand how people experience a situation. However, self-reports make it impossible to distinguish selection from perception.

A SMU social psychology faculty is using *LiveLabs* to send surveys ($\approx$ 400 surveys have been sent as of publication time) to known introverts and extroverts, identified a-prior through in lab interviews, at various times and locations. The survey data, which provides the situation perception, is then combined with the *LiveLabs* Group Detection Service to accurately identify the situation selection, e.g. who is around them and who they interacted with, when they answered the survey. Thus *LiveLabs* provides a previously unrealisable ability to capture both the situation selection and perception simultaneously in a real world setting.

5.4 Success Metrics

In this section, we evaluate *LiveLabs* in terms of how it compares with traditional methods such as pencil-and-paper, web (e.g via Mechanical Turk), mail, and SMS surveys. We focus on two key survey success metrics – response rates and non-response bias [49]. In addition, we investigate the ability of *LiveLabs* to replicate results from conventional modes of experimentation.

Response Rate: In Table 4, we compare response rates previously reported for other modes of delivery against *LiveLabs*. We note that *LiveLabs* achieves comparable response rates, in addition to offering benefits such as real-time context-awareness. Further, we also note that the response rate is sensitive to the time period that

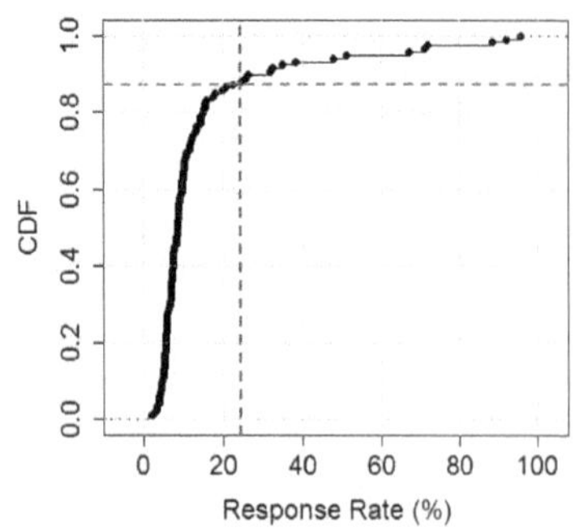

Figure 6: Notification Response Rate (118 Android Users)

the surveys/promotions were sent out; we observe that the overall response rate was consistent at around 20-30% prior to the exam week, and dropped to 12-17% during the exam week.

Table 5 shows the response rate for each of the case study experiments – all the rates are comparable or higher than other approaches. In addition, participants respond to *LiveLabs* with more frequency than other phone notifications. To determine this, we analysed the phone data collected from 118 *LiveLabs* Android users, between Aug 2014 and Jan 2015, and determined that those users clicked on only 14.29% on average ($sd = 17.77\%$) of the notifications they received whereas the average view rate observed with *LiveLabs* was much higher at 24.38%. Figure 6 plots the CDF of the response rates for all those users. It shows that over 87% of the users responded to less than 24.38% of their notifications.

In Table 6, we summarize the response rates of experiments/trials run as part of the *LiveLabs* deployment at *Resort*. The testbed has been used to run many promotional campaigns, 5 so far, across a wide demography comprising of all island visitors with the *Resort-specific* app installed. Interestingly, compared to SMU, the viewing rate is much higher at a lower redemption rate. Overall, *LiveLabs* achieves a better redemption rate (≈4.3%) compared to the SMS-based mobile coupon redemption study (3.2%) reported in Andrews et al. [3], for an Asian population similar to ours.

Campaign	Subjects	Viewed Promo.	Redeemed Promo.
Early Bird Campaigns	3534	2457 (69.5%)	151 (6.15%)
Normal Campaigns	1265	863 (68.2%)	58 (6.72%)

Table 6: Summary Of Campaigns at *Resort*

Non-Response Bias: This is a critical survey flaw [49] where survey respondents are statistically different from the non-respondents in terms of demographics or attitudinal variables. To detect this bias, we separated the response and non-response rates by gender and school. We observed, similar to prior studies [49], that the women response rates were higher than men. However, and more importantly, we did not observe any significant difference in the demographics of respondents and non-respondents in terms of their school or year of study. Table 7 shows the response rate for all our studies broken down by our six schools. The percentages were not statistically different (using the Kolmogorov-Smirnov test), with $D = 0.33$ in all cases with $p-$values between 0.893 and 0.931.

Efficacy of Replicating Results: For the Bystander Apathy Study, our results, shown in Table 8, reinforce the original [29] and follow-up studies [15] in that individuals were less likely to help, donate in this case, when surrounded by people. However, if those people were not strangers, i.e., they were part of the same group, they were more likely to help.

Likewise, for the Foot-in-the-Door Study, similar to the original study [14], we observed a statistically significant increase in willingness to donate in treatment group individuals who agreed to the moderate favor, compared to those that did not. Table 9 presents these results with $t-$statistic=2.8945, and $p-$value=0.0111 for the difference in means test.

We do not provide results for the *Extend* or *Innovate* experiments as they are still ongoing and yet to be published. In addition, no baselines for comparison exist due to their originality.

6. KEY LESSONS LEARNED

We summarize here some of our main lessons learned as part of building and maintaining *LiveLabs*.

6.1 Deploying a Testbed Is Hard!

We initially envisioned [8, 35], deploying four separate testbeds, at SMU, *Resort*, an Airport, and a Mall, by the first half of 2015. However, as of May 2016, *LiveLabs* has only been deployed at *SMU*, *Resort*, and partially at a replacement venue *Suntec*. A key reason was our gross underestimation of the effort, especially to agree on legal terms and generate convincing use cases, to deploy at commercial venues. Even at SMU, we learned that deploying at such unprecedented scales, e.g., a user pool in the thousands, is hard as supporting this large pool also meant supporting any software releases for month across heterogeneous devices and OSs. To address these challenges, we transformed from a standard research lab to a multi-faceted startup-like environment with dedicated staff and students handling research, software engineering, business development, participant recruitment, and administration separately.

6.2 Should Academics Be Doing This?

LiveLabs is supported by a large government research grant that allows us to hire the large full-time staff needed to build and support *LiveLabs*, and to offer it for free to other researchers. However, is this model sustainable, replicable elsewhere, and something academics should even try to do? Regarding sustainability, even though *LiveLabs* is currently fully funded, moving forward, we plan to offer membership tiers for organisations that run multiple experiments as well as charge a nominal per-experiment fee. These revenue streams will help pay for the full-time staff and any incentives needed to recruit participants.

The question of replicability and academic interest are inter-related as the interest drives the replication and vice versa to some extent. Over the last few years, numerous large multi-site testbeds such as PlanetLab [12], EmuLab [13] and GENI [10] have been proposed and successfully built. All of these testbeds were for core networking research use as that was of high interest to the research community. In all these cases, the testbeds were supported by both government grants, through the United States National Science Foundation (NSF), and by companies such as Intel for PlanetLab, Cisco for EmuLab etc. Hence, there are numerous examples of initiatives obtaining the resources needed to scale smaller testbeds into larger multi-site multi-country initiatives.

Our view is that academics should definitely strive to build compelling testbeds for various domains, such as mobile sensing, human interaction, energy solutions etc., as they will have a very large positive impact on the greater research community. However, creating testbeds is only partially about creating new technology solutions. Most of the time will be spent elsewhere – obtaining funding, hiring the right people, managing administrative requirements, recruiting, and retaining clients, experimenters, and participants, and building hardened solutions or prototypes for clients, participants etc. All of these additional tasks make building the testbed similar to running a startup — indeed we learned that we needed to convert our research lab effectively into a startup. Hence, building a testbed

	% of Respondents From That School						% of Non-Respondents From That School					
	Acc.	Bus.	Econ	IS	Law	So.Sc.	Acc.	Bus.	Econ.	IS	Law	So.Sc.
Promotion Framing	15.0	32.8	10.0	26.4	4.2	11.4	14.4	40.8	12.4	19.5	5.2	7.7
Opinion Leadership	15.7	31.4	11.4	27.7	3.7	10.1	16.8	36.4	9.2	23.7	6.1	7.8
Bystander Apathy	15.0	30.0	13.7	32.5	1.3	7.5	13.9	34.5	8.4	27.3	7.6	8.3
Foot-in-the-door	11.6	31.8	13.0	28.9	1.5	13.2	15.6	38.3	9.5	23.2	6.5	6.9
Group-Aware Marketing	0	40.0	20.0	20.0	20.0	0	18.5	35.2	11.1	22.3	7.4	5.5
Priming Effects	15.7	31.6	10.5	28.7	3.5	10.0	16.3	41.0	11.3	20.1	5.4	5.9

Table 7: School-wise % of Respondents vs Non-respondents (Acc = Accountancy, Bus = Business, So.Sc = Social Sciences)

Condition	Garcia et al. [16]	People around in past 1 hr	With friends in past 1 hr	With friends currently
1 person, neutral controls	4.2 (1.6)	2.67 (1.03)	2 (0.63)	2.28 (1.01)
Group of 10	3.9 (1.5)	2.43 (1.01)	2.42 (1.00)	2.43 (1.03)
Group of 30	3.6 (1.3)	2.36 (1.08)	3.25 (1.71)	2.55 (1.21)
Trend	*Inhibiting*	*Inhibiting*	*Increasing*	*Increasing*

Table 8: Comparison of Mean Charity Contributions of Garcia et al. [16] against *LiveLabs* Results

requires faculty who want to have a large impact on how research is evaluated in their fields, and are willing to effectively run a startup.

Group	Amount Willing to Donate, mean (std.dev)
Control	3.655 (3.265)
Treatment (Yes to modest request)	4.276 (3.011)
Treatment (No to modest request)	1.5 (2.204)

Table 9: Foot-in-the-Door Replication Experiment

6.3 The Challenge of Participant Retention

Maintaining a stable participant pool is our biggest challenge as using the standard approach of regular monetary incentives fails when the absolute dollar amount to keep incentivising 4,000+ participants is very large, and participants start dropping out rapidly when the incentives stop. We thus started providing unique functionality that *only LiveLabs* participants could enjoy – in this case, two campus-specific apps that we build and maintain for campus promotions and events tracking respectively. These apps have little research value but are key *LiveLabs* components that require a dedicated development team to provide support and regular new features to keep participant interest high.

We managed to build a reasonably large & stable participant pool, e.g. > 4,000 sign ups with $\approx$ 700 users actively using *LiveLabs* and running experiments, using these strategies; (1) provide a small monetary incentive ($10) to new participants, (2) run regular contests (e.g., lucky draws), during lull periods, to keep interest levels up, (3) refine and promote our exclusive applications that solve specific and compelling student needs, and (4) run experiments that offer interesting promotions/incentives to participants.

6.4 What Did We Do Wrong?

In this paper, we present, mostly, what we did right based on the final design. However, there were quite a few things that we did wrong – some quite obvious in hindsight. These include:

Believing that Phone Data Is Key: We initially assumed that most of our data would come from participants' phones. However, we quickly learned that energy consumption was *the* dominant factor for participants staying in *LiveLabs*. In addition, the large variety of phones such as iOS, multiple versions of Android, meant that our data collection was not consistent even among our participant pool. Eventually, we re-focused on collecting most of our data from infrastructure sensors instead, e.g., Wi-Fi, BLE, interaction points such as displays. Indeed, all the behavioural experiments described in Section 5 use only data collected from environmental sensors as that was the only data sensor that was common across all participants. Currently, due to energy concerns, our current default setup is to turn off all data collection from phones unless needed – very different from how we initially envisioned *LiveLabs* operating.

Assuming that Others Would Use Our Cool Mobile Sensing Solutions: We also believed our colleagues would use our novel mobile sensing solutions, such as group and activity detection as experiment triggers. However, our non computer-science colleagues did not know how to include these dynamic triggers into their current experiment methodologies. As such neither queuing nor activity detection was used by any of our case studies.

Our current approach is to provide familiar contextual triggers, such as location, time, demographics, interests etc., and slowly introduce new concepts, such as groups, queuing status, current activity etc., to them. We believe that our colleagues, with more *LiveLabs* experience, will integrate our novel new inputs to create new and innovative experiment designs. In addition, they will also tell us what new inputs they need to drive their research forward. This is already bearing fruits as one group of social researchers from Emory, Temple, and CMU, is already using our group detector, and suggesting improvements to it, to perform novel leader-follower type experiments (Section 5).

Hiring the Right Person is Crucial!: Finally, building a testbed is like running a startup where you need to hire talented people who are also *innovative*, *adaptable*, and *flexible* as their job scope / tasks can and will change often – sometimes daily. For example, our engineering staff frequently help out as advocates at participant recruitment fairs, and our admin staff also help to test engineering products. We learned to avoid hiring solely to fill specific work requirements as those requirements can and do change rapidly.

6.5 Future Work

In this section, we present our future work plan to address concerns raised by experimenters and to improve the overall testbed.

6.5.1 Experiment Scheduling & Fairness

Running concurrent experiments on *LiveLabs* raises an interesting scheduling problem as it may induce *participant fatigue* caused by receiving multiple treatments within a short period and this could deteriorate the quality of responses. While running three concurrent experiments, we observed that the participants chosen for the experiments had a 78% overlap and amongst those who responded there was a 58% overlap. In addition, we learnt that we also needed to maintain *fairness* – i.e. experiments with contradictory outcomes should not be run with overlapping participants within a short time period of each other. For example, scheduling an experiment which promoted soft drinks after one that promoted healthy living, with some overlapped participants. Currently, we interview all researchers to identify what they are testing for and what conditions would create bias. We then manually add the required exclusions to *LiveLabs* to maintain fairness.

To reduce the effect of fatigue and bias, we plan to integrate recent techniques [43, 31, 32] that predict the best times to interrupt participants as well as build mechanisms to allow experimenters to specify the amount of experiment overlap, if any, they can accept.

6.5.2 Uncertainty Handling

One of the questions we received from some of our colleagues was "What is the error in the results?". As discussed in Section 3.4, this is an active area of research. In particular, we are working with our colleagues, with machine learning and statistics expertise, to develop models to propagate the errors at every level of the system, in the form of error distributions, upwards where it is finally combined, using weighted distribution merging techniques, to create a final error distribution for the overall experiment. However, this is preliminary work that is promising but not usable yet.

7. RELATED WORK

Behavioural Experimentation: EmotionSense [44] used a rule-based logic inference engine which allowed social scientists to declare contexts, e.g., emotions, location and activity, relevant to their experiments. Social fMRI [2] combined rich smartphone data collection with intervention capabilities for a small family setting. More recently, Vivo [19] proposed to integrate smartphone-based crowdsensing with IoT to improve context analytics. *LiveLabs* is similar in vision but much larger in scale – in terms of venue provided, experiment types, and participant pool.

Mobile and Wireless Testbeds: PhoneLab [38] is the most similar to *LiveLabs* and provides custom Android smartphones to hundreds of university students to study and experiment with various smartphone technologies. SmartLab [28] built an open cloud of smartphones to conduct various mobile systems research. Wireless testbeds such as ORBIT [47] and WISEBED [11] allow testing of network protocols and technologies in laboratory settings, as opposed to simulations, whereas TFA [9] provided a city-scale mesh-networking testbed. The Santander testbed [48], is a large-scale IoT testbed geared towards smart city-type applications such as transport tracking and waste management. Mobilyzer [40] is a library for network measurements that can be seamlessly integrated with any app. *LiveLabs* differs from these testbeds by providing the opportunity to study completely natural human behaviour – i.e., the participants are using their own devices and are interacted with discretely – i.e. they don't know why they received any particular notification. In addition, *LiveLabs* provides a platform that allow numerous research disciplines to innovate within their research areas. The panOULU WLAN testbed [41] is a city-scale, municipal wireless network, started with the goal of providing open and free internet to all. Although technically different to *LiveLabs*, it uses an academia-industry-government relationship model that is economically viable and plausible for testbeds such as *LiveLabs*.

Smartphone Sensing-based Studies: In Wang et al. [57, 58], the authors use smartphone-based sensing to derive mental well-being and other behavioural insights. NetSense [53] distributed instrumented smartphones to several hundred incoming freshman undergraduate students. Device Analyzer [56] is an Android App that collects a broad range of smartphone usage statistics, primarily as a means for personal analytics. This is one of the largest such deployments with over 33,000 contributors spread across the world. Smartphone-based *Experience Sampling Methods* [30] is also a popular method to query participants, in real-time, based on contextual triggers. *LiveLabs* differs in that it is a complete testbed that focuses on a broad range of experiments from a diverse set of experimenters. In particular, many of these previous works could be re-run on *LiveLabs*.

8. ACKNOWLEDGEMENTS

We sincerely thank our shepherd Geoffrey Challen for providing excellent iterative feedback that greatly improved our paper. We also thank the anonymous reviewers for their valuable feedback. This research is supported by the National Research Foundation, Prime Minister's Office, Singapore under its IDM Futures Funding Initiative and partially by the Singapore Ministry of Education's Academic Research Fund Tier 2 under research grant MOE2011-T2-1001. Kasthuri Jayarajah is supported by an A*STAR Graduate Scholarship. Any opinions, findings, conclusions or recommendations expressed in this material are those of the authors and do not necessarily reflect the views of the granting agencies or Singapore Management University.

LiveLabs has been built by the efforts of multiple people over the years. The authors would like to humbly thank all current staff and students (as of May 1st 2016), namely Jonathan Wang, Sipei Huang, Kazae Quek, Luar Shu Hui (Admin), Francis Lim, Thannermalai Lakshmanan (Outreach), Ignatius Tan (PM), Tan Kiat Wee, Jeena Sebastian, Ritesh Kumar, Swetha Gottipati, John Lee, Tran Anh Quan, Le Hai Son, Aniket Pujara, Tieu Thi Thanh Chau, Prakhar Vishnoi, Huynh Quang Trunh, Arpita Chopra (Engineering), and Sougata Sen, Joseph Chan, Amit Sharma, Huynh Nguyen Loc, Huynh Nguyen Phan Sinh, Nguyen Huy Hoang Huy, Tran Huy Vu (Ph.D. Students), Vigneshwaran Subbaraju, Thivya Kandappu, Nikita Jaiman, Randy Daratan, Bharat Dwivedi, Desmond Koh (LiveLabs associates), Jiang Lingxiao, Jie Xiong (Faculty). In addition, we also humbly thank our former colleagues who helped build up *LiveLabs*. These include Narayan Ramasubbu (Faculty), Azeem Khan, Trun Tuan Luong, Lu Yu, Rijurekha Sen, Rajya Lakshmi Lella, Xiaonan Guo (Postdocs), Yvonne Mok, Daphanie Tay, Foo Zhi Yu (Admin), Walter Dumo, Kenneth Fu (Outreach), Vivienne Tan (PM), Le Gia Hai, Nguyen Vu Nhat Minh, Harisankar Krishnaswamy, Vikash Ranjan, Koh Quee Boon, Tadashi Okoshi, Sharib Anis, Nikunj Handa (Engineering), Kartik Muralidharan, Nguyen Huynh (Ph.D. Students), Shriguru Nayak, Kuldeep Kulshreshtha, (LiveLabs Associates), Chetna Vig, Joshua Tan, Kok Kiat Han, Nishant Saini, Rahul Majethia, Saharsh Tibrewal, Deepankar Tyagi, Abhinav Kumar, Varun Gandhi, Satayadip Chakraborti, Gomatam Prasanth, Ananda Krishna, Aryan, Praveen Kumar, Nakul Gulati, Changhun Lee, Yeo Guo Kuan, Clarence Koh, Zaman Lantra, Gihan Hettiarachchi, Amila Jayawickrama (Undergraduate Interns), and Anudipa Maiti, Nairan Zhang, Savina Singla (Ph.D. Interns).

9. CONCLUSION

We presented *LiveLabs*, a large testbed for conducting in-situ real-time mobile behavioural experiments. *LiveLabs* uses many deep technology components to create an environment where innovative and important insights into human behaviour can be deeply understood. We showed how researchers, from many different disciplines around the world are already using *LiveLabs* to generate those new insights. In addition, *LiveLabs* can also be used to test many different technology components – especially those in the mobile sensing, analytics, privacy, and applications domains. Finally, *LiveLabs* is free to use and open to any researcher – visit `http://is.gd/livelabs` for details.

10. REFERENCES

[1] MobiSys 2016,The 14th International Conference on Mobile Systems, Applications and Services. `http://www.sigmobile.org/mobisys/2016`. Accessed on 30th April 2016.

[2] Nadav Aharony, Wei Pan, Cory Ip, Inas Khayal, and Alex Pentland. Social fMRI: Investigating and Shaping Social Mechanisms in the Real World. *Pervasive and Mobile Computing*, 7(6):643–659, Dec. 2011.

[3] Michelle Andrews, Xueming Luo, Zheng Fang, and Anindya Ghose. Mobile Ad Effectiveness: Hyper-Contextual Targeting with Crowdedness. *Marketing Science*, 35(2):218–233, 2016.

[4] Apple Developers. Apple Push Notification Service. `https://developer.apple.com/library/ios/documentation/NetworkingInternet/Conceptual/RemoteNotificationsPG/Chapters/ApplePushService.html`. Accessed on 24th April 2016.

[5] Paramvir Bahl and Venkata N. Padmanabhan. RADAR: An In-building RF-based User Location and Tracking System. *Proceedings of the 19th Annual Joint Conference of the IEEE Computer and Communications Societies (INFOCOM 2000)*, 2000.

[6] George Balabanis, Vincent-Wayne Mitchell, and Sarah Heinonen-Mavrovouniotis. SMS-based surveys: strategies to improve participation. *International Journal of Advertising*, 26(3):369–385, 2007.

[7] Rajesh Krishna Balan, Youngki Lee, Tan Kiat Wee, and Archan Misra. The challenge of continuous mobile context sensing. *Proceedings of the Sixth International Conference on Communication Systems and Networks (COMSNETS'14)*, 2014.

[8] Rajesh Krishna Balan, Archan Misra, and Youngki Lee. LiveLabs: Building an In-situ Real-time Mobile Experimentation Testbed. *Proceedings of the 15th Workshop on Mobile Computing Systems and Applications (HotMobile '14)*, 2014.

[9] Oscar Bejarano, Stanislav Miskovic, Ehsan Aryafar, and Edward W. Knightly. TFA: A Large Scale Urban Mesh Network for Social and Network Research. *Proceedings of the 2010 ACM workshop on Wireless of the students, by the students, for the students (ACM S3'10)*, 2010.

[10] Mark Berman, Jeffrey S Chase, Lawrence Landweber, Akihiro Nakao, Max Ott, Dipankar Raychaudhuri, Robert Ricci, and Ivan Seskar. GENI: A federated testbed for innovative network experiments. *Computer Networks*, 61:5–23, 2014.

[11] Ioannis Chatzigiannakis, Stefan Fischer, Christos Koninis, Georgios Mylonas, and Dennis Pfisterer. WISEBED: An Open Large-Scale Wireless Sensor Network Testbed. *Sensor Applications, Experimentation, and Logistics*, volume 29 of *Lecture Notes of the Institute for Computer Sciences, Social Informatics and Telecommunications Engineering*, pages 68–87. 2010.

[12] Brent Chun, David Culler, Timothy Roscoe, Andy Bavier, Larry Peterson, Mike Wawrzoniak, and Mic Bowman. Planetlab: an overlay testbed for broad-coverage services. *ACM SIGCOMM Computer Communication Review*, 33(3):3–12, 2003.

[13] R Fish, M Flickinger, and J Lepreau. Mobile emulab: A robotic wireless and sensor network testbed. *Proceedings of the 25th IEEE International Conference on Computer and Communications (INFOCOM 2006)*, 2006.

[14] Jonathan L Freedman and Scott C Fraser. Compliance without pressure: the foot-in-the-door technique. *Journal of personality and social psychology*, 4(2):195, 1966.

[15] Stephen M Garcia, Kimberlee Weaver, John M Darley, and Bryan T Spence. Dual effects of implicit bystanders: Inhibiting vs. facilitating helping behavior. *Journal of Consumer Psychology*, 19(2):215–224, 2009.

[16] Stephen M Garcia, Kim Weaver, Gordon B Moskowitz, and John M Darley. Crowded minds: the implicit bystander effect. *Journal of personality and social psychology*, 83(4):843, 2002.

[17] Peter M Gollwitzer, Heinz Heckhausen, and Birgit Steller. Deliberative and implemental mind-sets: Cognitive tuning toward congruous thoughts and information. *Journal of Personality and Social Psychology*, 59(6):1119, 1990.

[18] Google Developers. Google Cloud Messaging. `https://developers.google.com/cloud-messaging`. Accessed on 24th April 2016.

[19] Andreea Hossmann-Picu, Zan Li, Zhongliang Zhao, Torsten Braun, Constantinos Marios Angelopoulos, Orestis Evangelatos, José Rolim, Michela Papandrea, Kamini Garg, Silvia Giordano, Aristide C.Y. Tossou, Christos Dimitrakakis, and Aikaterini Mitrokotsa. Synergistic User -> Context Analytics. *ICT Innovations 2015*, volume 399 of *Advances in Intelligent Systems and Computing*, pages 163–172, 2016.

[20] Loc N. Huynh, Rajesh Krishna Balan, and Youngki Lee. DeepSense : A GPU-based Deep Convolutional Neural Network Framework on Commodity Mobile Devices. *Proceedings of the 2nd Workshop on Wearable Systems and Applications (WearSys'16) collocated with MobiSys'16*, 2016.

[21] Sinh Huynh, Youngki Lee, Taiwoo Park, and Rajesh Krishna Balan. Jasper: Sensing Gamers' Emotions Using Physiological Sensors. *Proceedings of the 3rd Workshop on on Mobile Gaming (MobiGames'16) collocated with MobiSys'16*, 2016.

[22] Kasthuri Jayarajah, Youngki Lee, Archan Misra, and Rajesh Krishna Balan. Need Accurate User Behaviour?: Pay Attention to Groups! *Proceedings of the 2015 ACM International Joint Conference on Pervasive and Ubiquitous Computing (UbiComp '15)*, 2015.

[23] Kasthuri Jayarajah, Archan Misra, Xiao-Wen Ruan, and Ee Peng Lim. Event Detection: Exploiting Socio-Physical Interactions in Physical Spaces. *Proceedings of the 2015 IEEE/ACM International Conference on Advances in Social Networks Analysis and Mining (ASONAM'15)*, 2015.

[24] Thivya Kandappu, Archan Misra, Nikita Jaiman, Randy Tandriansyah, Shih-Fen Cheng, Cen Chen, Hoong Chuin Lau, Deepthi Chander, and Koustuv Dasgupta. Ta$ker v3: Deployment of, and Insights from, Campus-based Mobile Crowdsourcing. *Under review for the 2016 ACM International Joint Conference on Pervasive and Ubiquitous Computing (UbiComp'16)*, 2016.

[25] Joseph Chan Joo Keng, Tan Kiat Wee, Lingxiao Jiang, and Rajesh Krishna Balan. The Case for Mobile Forensics of Private Data Leaks: Towards Large-scale User-oriented Privacy Protection. *Proceedings of the 4th Asia-Pacific Workshop on Systems (APSys '13)*, 2013.

[26] Azeem Javed Khan, Vikash Ranjan, Trung-Tuan Luong,

Rajesh Krishan Balan, and Archan Misra. Experiences with performance tradeoffs in practical, continuous indoor localization. *Proceedings of the 14th IEEE International Symposium and Workshops on a World of Wireless, Mobile and Multimedia Networks (WoWMoM'13)*, 2013.

[27] Nojin Kwak, Barry Radler, et al. A comparison between mail and web surveys: Response pattern, respondent profile, and data quality. *Journal Of Official Statistics-Stockholm*, 18(2):257–274, 2002.

[28] Georgios Larkou, Panayiotis Andreou, Andreas Konstantinidis, and Demetrios Zeinalipour-Yazti. SmartLab: Empowering Mobile Computing Research through an Open Smartphone Cloud. *ERCIM News 93, Special theme: Mobile Computing*, page 18. 2013.

[29] Bibb Latané and John M Darley. Bystander "Apathy". *American Scientist*, 57(2):244–268, 1969.

[30] Neal Lathia, Kiran K. Rachuri, Cecilia Mascolo, and Peter J. Rentfrow. Contextual Dissonance: Design Bias in Sensor-based Experience Sampling Methods. *Proceedings of the 2013 ACM International Joint Conference on Pervasive and Ubiquitous Computing (UbiComp '13)*, 2013.

[31] Abhinav Mehrotra, Mirco Musolesi, Robert Hendley, and Veljko Pejovic. Designing Content-driven Intelligent Notification Mechanisms for Mobile Applications. *Proceedings of the 2015 ACM International Joint Conference on Pervasive and Ubiquitous Computing (UbiComp '15)*, 2015.

[32] Abhinav Mehrotra, Jo Vermeulen, Veljko Pejovic, and Mirco Musolesi. Ask, but Don'T Interrupt: The Case for Interruptibility-aware Mobile Experience Sampling. *Proceedings of 4th ACM Workshop on Mobile Systems for Computational Social Science (MCSS'15) collocated with UbiComp/ISWC'15*, 2015.

[33] Microsoft Developers. Microsoft: Kinect for Windows. `http://www.kinectforwindows.org/`. Accessed on 24th April 2016.

[34] Microsoft Research Redmond. Microsoft Research Embedded Social Software Development Kit. Using pre-release version. Accessed on 29th April 2016.

[35] Archan Misra and Rajesh Krishna Balan. LiveLabs: Initial Reflections on Building a Large-scale Mobile Behavioral Experimentation Testbed. *SIGMOBILE Mobile Computing Communications Review*, 17(4):47–59, Dec. 2013.

[36] Kartik Muralidharan. *Enabling Real-Time In Situ Context-Based Experimentation to Observe User Behaviour.* PhD thesis, Technical report, Singapore Management University, 2015.

[37] Kartik Muralidharan, Srinivasan Seshan, Narayan Ramasubbu, and Rajesh Krishna Balan. Handling Location Uncertainty in Event Driven Experimentation. *Proceedings of the 8th ACM International Conference on Distributed Event-Based Systems (DEBS '14)*, 2014.

[38] Anandatirtha Nandugudi, Anudipa Maiti, Taeyeon Ki, Fatih Bulut, Murat Demirbas, Tevfik Kosar, Chunming Qiao, Steven Y. Ko, and Geoffrey Challen. PhoneLab: A Large Programmable Smartphone Testbed. *Proceedings of First International Workshop on Sensing and Big Data Mining (SENSEMINE'13)*, 2013.

[39] Huy Hoang Nguyen, Nakul Gulati, Youngki Lee, and Rajesh Krishna Balan. Real-time Detection Of Seat Occupancy & Hogging. *Proceedings of the 2015 International Workshop on Internet of Things towards Applications (IoT-App) collocated with SenSys'15*, 2015.

[40] Ashkan Nikravesh, Hongyi Yao, Shichang Xu, David Choffnes, and Z. Morley Mao. Mobilyzer: An Open Platform for Controllable Mobile Network Measurements. *Proceedings of the 13th Annual International Conference on Mobile Systems, Applications, and Services (MobiSys '15)*, 2015.

[41] Timo Ojala, Jukka Orajärvi, Katriina Puhakka, Ilari Heikkinen, and Juhani Heikka. panOULU: Triple Helix Driven Municipal Wireless Network Providing Open and Free Internet Access. *Proceedings of the 5th International Conference on Communities and Technologies (C&T '11)*, 2011.

[42] Tadashi Okoshi, Yu Lu, Chetna Vig, Youngki Lee, Rajesh Krishna Balan, and Archan Misra. QueueVadis: Queuing Analytics Using Smartphones. *Proceedings of the 14th International Conference on Information Processing in Sensor Networks (IPSN '15)*, 2015.

[43] Tadashi Okoshi, Jin Nakazawa, and Hideyuki Tokuda. Attelia: Reducing User's Cognitive Load due to Interruptive Notifications on Smart Phones. *Proceedings of the 2015 IEEE International Conference on Pervasive Computing and Communications (PerCom'15)*, 2015.

[44] Kiran K. Rachuri, Mirco Musolesi, Cecilia Mascolo, Peter J. Rentfrow, Chris Longworth, and Andrius Aucinas. EmotionSense: A Mobile Phones Based Adaptive Platform for Experimental Social Psychology Research. *Proceedings of the 12th ACM international conference on Ubiquitous computing (UbiComp '10)*, 2010.

[45] Meera Radhakrishnan, Sharanya Eswaran, Archan Misra, Deepthi Chander, and Koustuv Dasgupta. IRIS: Tapping Wearable Sensing to Capture In-Store Retail Insights on Shoppers. *Proceedings of the 2016 IEEE International Conference on Pervasive Computing and Communications (PerCom'16)*, 2016.

[46] Meera Radhakrishnan, Archan Misra, Rajesh Krishna Balan, and Youngki Lee. Smartphones & BLE Services: Empirical Insights. *Proceedings of the 2015 IEEE 12th International Conference on Mobile Ad Hoc and Sensor Systems (MASS'15)*, 2015.

[47] D. Raychaudhuri, I. Seskar, M. Ott, S. Ganu, K. Ramachandran, H. Kremo, R. Siracusa, H. Liu, and M. Singh. Overview of the ORBIT radio grid testbed for evaluation of next-generation wireless network protocols. *Proceedings of the IEEE Wireless Communications and Networking Conference (WCNC'05)*, 2005.

[48] Luis Sanchez, Luis Muñoz, Jose Antonio Galache, Pablo Sotres, Juan R. Santana, Veronica Gutierrez, Rajiv Ramdhany, Alex Gluhak, Srdjan Krco, Evangelos Theodoridis, and Dennis Pfisterer. SmartSantander: IoT experimentation over a smart city testbed. *Computer Networks*, 61:217 – 238, 2014. Special issue on Future Internet Testbeds - Part I.

[49] Linda J. Sax, Shannon K. Gilmartin, and Alyssa N. Bryant. Assessing Response Rates and Nonresponse Bias in Web and Paper Surveys. *Research in Higher Education*, 44(4):409–432, 2003.

[50] Rijurekha Sen, Youngki Lee, Kasthuri Jayarajah, Archan Misra, and Rajesh Krishna Balan. GruMon: Fast and Accurate Group Monitoring for Heterogeneous Urban

Spaces. *Proceedings of the 12th ACM Conference on Embedded Network Sensor Systems (SenSys '14)*, 2014.

[51] Sougata Sen, Vigneshwaran Subbaraju, Youngki Lee, Rajesh Krishna Balan, and Archan Misra. Annapurna: Smartwatch based Food Diary & Eating Analytics. *Under review for the 14th ACM Conference on Embedded Networked Sensor Systems (SenSys'16)*, 2016.

[52] Sougata Sen, Vignesh Subbaraju, Archan Misra, Rajesh Krishna Balan, and Youngki Lee. The case for smartwatch-based diet monitoring. *Proceedings of 2015 IEEE International Conference on Pervasive Computing and Communication Workshops (WristSense'15)*, 2015.

[53] Aaron Striegel, Shu Liu, Lei Meng, Christian Poellabauer, David Hachen, and Omar Lizardo. Lessons Learned from the Netsense Smartphone Study. *Proceedings of the 5th ACM Workshop on HotPlanet (HotPlanet '13)*, 2013.

[54] Kiat Wee Tan, Eduardo Cuervo, and Rajesh Krishna Balan. FOCUSVR: Effective & Usable VR Display Power Management. *Under review for the 14th ACM Conference on Embedded Networked Sensor Systems (SenSys'16)*, 2016.

[55] Kiat Wee Tan, Tadashi Okoshi, Archan Misra, and Rajesh Krishna Balan. FOCUS: A Usable & Effective Approach to OLED Display Power Management. *Proceedings of the 2013 ACM International Joint Conference on Pervasive and Ubiquitous Computing*, UbiComp '13, 2013.

[56] Daniel T. Wagner, Daniel R. Thomas, Alastair R. Beresford, and Andrew Rice. Device Analyzer: A Privacy-aware Platform to Support Research on the Android Ecosystem. *Proceedings of the 8th ACM Conference on Security & Privacy in Wireless and Mobile Networks (WiSec '15)*, 2015.

[57] Rui Wang, Fanglin Chen, Zhenyu Chen, Tianxing Li, Gabriella Harari, Stefanie Tignor, Xia Zhou, Dror Ben-Zeev, and Andrew T. Campbell. StudentLife: Assessing Mental Health, Academic Performance and Behavioral Trends of College Students Using Smartphones. *Proceedings of the 2014 ACM International Joint Conference on Pervasive and Ubiquitous Computing (UbiComp '14)*, 2014.

[58] Rui Wang, Gabriella Harari, Peilin Hao, Xia Zhou, and Andrew T. Campbell. SmartGPA: How Smartphones Can Assess and Predict Academic Performance of College Students. *Proceedings of the 2015 ACM International Joint Conference on Pervasive and Ubiquitous Computing (UbiComp '15)*, 2015.

[59] Zhixian Yan, Vigneshwaran Subbaraju, Dipanjan Chakraborty, Archan Misra, and Karl Aberer. Energy-Efficient Continuous Activity Recognition on Mobile Phones: An Activity-Adaptive Approach. *Proceedings of the 2012 16th Annual International Symposium on Wearable Computers (ISWC '12)*, 2012.

[60] Nairan Zhang, Rajesh Krishna Balan, Archan Misra, and Youngki Lee. Practical Indoor Localisation In Commercial Buildings. *Under review for the 14th ACM Conference on Embedded Networked Sensor Systems (SenSys'16)*, 2016.

Platypus — Indoor Localization and Identification through Sensing Electric Potential Changes in Human Bodies

Tobias Grosse-Puppendahl[1], Xavier Dellangnol[2], Christian Hatzfeld[2], Biying Fu[3], Mario Kupnik[2], Arjan Kuijper[2,3], Matthias R. Hastall[4], James Scott[1], Marco Gruteser[5]
[1]Microsoft Research, 21 Station Road, CB1 2FB Cambridge, UK,
{tgp,jws}@microsoft.com
[2]Technische Universität Darmstadt, Karolinenplatz 5, 64283 Darmstadt, Germany,
xdell@live.fr, {c.hatzfeld,kupnik}@emk.tu-darmstadt.de
[3]Fraunhofer IGD, Fraunhoferstr. 5, 64283 Darmstadt, Germany,
{biying.fu,arjan.kuijper}@igd.fraunhofer.de
[4]TU Dortmund University, Emil-Figge-Str. 50, 44227 Dortmund, Germany,
matthias.hastall@tu-dortmund.de
[5]WINLAB, Rutgers University, New Jersey 08902, USA,
gruteser@winlab.rutgers.edu

ABSTRACT

Platypus is the first system to localize and identify people by remotely and passively sensing changes in their body electric potential which occur naturally during walking. While it uses three or more electric potential sensors with a maximum range of 2 m, as a tag-free system it does not require the user to carry any special hardware. We describe the physical principles behind body electric potential changes, and a predictive mathematical model of how this affects a passive electric field sensor. By inverting this model and combining data from sensors, we infer a method for localizing people and experimentally demonstrate a median localization error of 0.16 m. We also use the model to remotely infer the change in body electric potential with a mean error of 8.8 % compared to direct contact-based measurements. We show how the reconstructed body electric potential differs from person to person and thereby how to perform identification. Based on short walking sequences of 5 s, we identify four users with an accuracy of 94 %, and 30 users with an accuracy of 75 %. We demonstrate that identification features are valid over multiple days, though change with footwear.

Categories and Subject Descriptors

H.5.m [**Information Interfaces and Presentation (I.7)**]: Miscellaneous

Keywords

localization; identification; capacitive sensing; electric potential sensing

MobiSys '16, June 25–30, 2016, Singapore.

DOI: http://dx.doi.org/10.1145/2906388.2906402

1. INTRODUCTION

Localizing and identifying humans in indoor spaces has been a challenging problem in mobile and pervasive computing for many years [56, 39, 32]. Applications in valuable domains like home automation [30], institutional care [60], and personalized energy metering [64] rely on localization and identification information.

Ideally, such a system should be "tag free", so that the users at home or in an office environment are not required to carry any particular hardware. Existing tag-free approaches have relied on sensing various properties of humans such as sounds they make [22], heat emissions [42] or the effect of the body on RF signals [1, 36]. In our system we remotely sense a different underlying quantity: the electric potential carried by the human body. Unlike existing capacitive sensing systems that actively generate an electric field to sense people [57, 9], we passively *observe* naturally occurring electric field changes, similarly to platypuses when hunting underwater preys [16].

As people move, their bodies' electric potential changes when interacting with the environment. The most significant changes occur through two means: static charging explained by the triboelectric effect [10], and changes in capacitive coupling to the environment as one's feet move towards and away from the floor during walking [17]. With Platypus, we remotely infer body electric potential changes at distances up to 2 m using a distributed grid of passive electric field sensors. Requiring at least three sensors, we have developed a method of inferring both the location of the body and the characteristic signature pattern of electric potential changes that occurs when walking, which permits identification of users.

The contribution of this paper is the introduction of Platypus, a novel use of electric field sensing that supports both localization and user differentiation:

- We localize a person observing the ambient electric field, further reconstruct body electric potential change, and extract a signature for identification.

- We detail the physical principles behind Platypus, the mathematical models and working prototype hardware.
- Based on detailed experiments, we show that Platypus achieves a median localization error of 16 cm for a walking user.
- We experimentally validate Platypus's ability to recognize users based on their signature of electric potential changes during walking; we observe an average accuracy of 94 % for 4 users and 75 % for 30 users.

2. BACKGROUND & RELATED WORK

2.1 Localization & Identification Systems

Indoor localization and identification systems can be divided into *tag-dependent* and *tag-free* [32, 35, 39, 56]. Tag-free systems, including Platypus, do not limit who is monitored to those with tags, or require specific behaviour (carrying the tag). We therefore focus on other tag-free systems as comparisons for Platypus.

Camera-based systems [60], including depth [62] cameras, can localize people accurately (error < 1 cm) as well as identify them with face and/or body shape recognition. However, privacy and security concerns make them unsuitable for some environments [31]. Similar concerns may be raised when using an array of microphones to recognize human activities (e.g. talking or opening a door). These can be realized with techniques such as time difference of arrival [7] and may also require classification of sounds [22].

Infrared sensors have been used as binary [52] as well as analog [26, 41, 42] sources for localization. The modality is a low-power, low-cost solution [42] that can even track multiple targets [63], and potentially perform identification by gait analysis [65]. Pressure-sensitive or capacitive localization systems use sensors deployed underneath the floor or integrated in furniture [8, 9, 51, 57]. The effort of installing such systems is large, as changes to existing flooring are required [9].

Various RF-based tag-free localization methods have been presented, using ultra-wideband radar [48], radio tomography [61], RSSI fingerprinting [2], WiFi Doppler [47] and FMCW-modulated radar [1]. Recent systems have leveraged Wi-Fi for vital sign detection [36] or to recognize spoken words [58].

Identification and room-level localization has been demonstrated by ultrasonic distance sensors used to measure the height of occupants, e.g. as they walk through doors [28, 54]. Compared to these weak biometric factors related to body height and movements, we investigate an even more temporary factor that changes with footwear and clothing. This can be regarded as a privacy advantage, allowing to identify a person for as long as the same shoes are worn.

Our system Platypus uses changes in body electric potential due to walking, which is a different underlying physical mechanism to any above. This modality has a particular set of trade-offs. It is passive, requiring no injection of e.g. RF or audio into the environment. Like PIR, camera and audio systems, it cannot operate through walls, in contrast to RF systems [47]. While active capacitive techniques are susceptible to high-frequency noise, Platypus as a passive system has a cut-off frequency of less than 10 Hz. Higher frequency components, e.g. injected by power-lines [15] or switch-mode power supplies [34], have a limited effect on the operation of Platypus. Other appliances like fluorescent lamps, gas ovens, and electro-magnetic motors emit lower frequency electric fields that can inject noise [34].

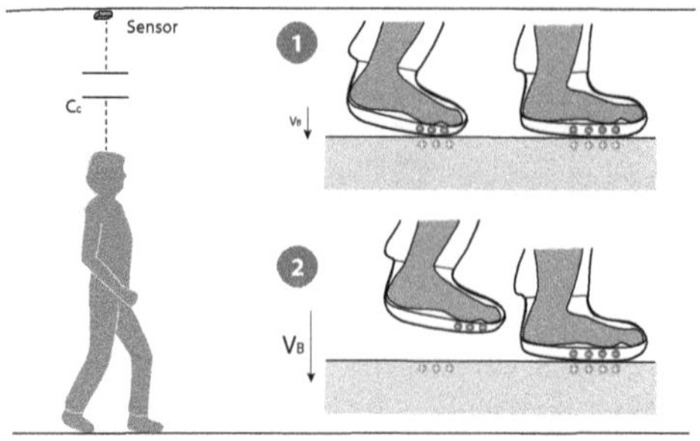

Figure 1: Platypus uses a passive electric field sensor to sense changes in a body electric potential due to (1) triboelectric charging, and (2) capacitance changes.

Passive electric field sensing has been used to measure body electric potential in body-attached [14, 49] as well as stationary applications [13, 45]. Cohn et al. investigated the technique as a low-power replacement for accelerometers by measuring the body electric potential with a wrist-worn node. The approach allows for motion recognition, and similar to Rekimoto et al. [49], enables the sensing of footsteps which induce a large change in body electric potential. Stationary approaches include sensing of electric potential changes through step variations [33]. Different to sensing the body electric potential, the capacitive coupling to the environment can be measured with active techniques, as shown by Haescher et al. [23].

2.2 Electric Potential of the Human Body

Every object in our environment carries electric charge, which gives rise to differences in electric potential between objects. Considering humans, changes in electric potential occur internally, caused by heartbeats or muscle movements, or body-wide changes, for example when walking. With Platypus, we focus on sensing the body-wide change in human body electric potential. While walking with shoes, two physical phenomena cause the most variation in the body electric potential: changes in charge explained by the triboelectric effect and capacitance variations (see Figure 1).

As a shoe comes into contact with the ground, the soles and the flooring material become charged through contact. This effect, known as triboelectric effect, is a matter of common experience, such as rubbing one's hair with a balloon [29, 38, 50]. Recombination and leaking phenomena, such as current circulating through the soles, oppose the accumulation of charge Q, leading to a saturation effect [17]. When walking, the capacitive coupling C between body and grounded objects in the environment changes, mostly due to the variations in distance between the sole of the foot and the floor. When the person lifts a foot, this distance is raised, the capacitive coupling to ground decreases, and the body electric potential V increases since $V = Q/C$. The inverse happens when the foot is put back down. A regular walking motion therefore results in a periodic variation of body electric potential [17] (Figure 3).

2.3 Measuring Ambient Electric Potentials

Low-frequency electric fields can be measured with various devices, for instance field mills [4], electro-optic sensors [27]

Figure 2: Custom sensor board, integrating an electric potential sensor from Plessey Semiconductors [44].

or induction probes [37]. The latter are the simplest to build and use outside of a laboratory [5]. A basic induction probe consists of an amplifier connected to an electrode on which the ambient electric field induces a weak charge. The electrode eventually discharges through the amplifier's finite input impedance, which makes this apparatus unable to measure static electric fields. Rekimoto [49] and Kurita [33] built their own induction probes to sense the influence of human activity on the ambient electric field. Due to the passive approach and the low operating frequencies, EPS were realized with a power consumption of $6.6\,\mu W$ [14]. A similar sensor with very large input impedance (about $10^{15}\,\Omega$), large bandwidth (mHz to MHz) and low noise [5] was designed at the University of Sussex [13, 19, 25]. This device is known as an *electric potential sensor* (EPS) and commercially available under the name *electric potential integrated circuit* (EPIC) [44].

3. SYSTEM OVERVIEW

Platypus exploits natural changes in human body electric potential to provide localization and identification. It relies on electric potential sensors attached high on walls or on ceilings that are sensitive enough to be used up to 2 m to a person. A minimum of three sensors allows us to estimate the position of a person and, based on this information, the change in body electric potential occurring when stepping. In typical installations however, we use two rectangular cells composed of six sensors to increase performance. The body electric potential exhibits a characteristic pattern enabling us to distinguish people from each other, using a movement sequence of approximately 5 s.

We integrated a Plessey EPIC sensor [44] on a custom peripheral board (Figure 2) to measure the ambient electric potential. The board provides a bipolar power supply as well as an operational amplifier (OPA2322) for voltage level translation (33 mW total power consumption per sensor). We connect an array of up to six sensors to an OpenCapSense board [20], which conducts 50 analog-to-digital conversions each second, and performs digital filtering to remove mains hum.

Figure 3 (bottom) depicts a walking activity underneath four sensors attached to the ceiling in a rectangular configuration. The amplitude of a sensor signal increases when the person moves closer to the sensor (e.g. sensor 4) and vice versa. Two other important effects play into this measurement, however: (1) the charge carried on the body and (2) the change in coupling to the environment. Using an EPS, we are not able to distinguish between these two effects and we base our observations on the combination of both: the body electric potential. This can be observed in Figure 3 (top), which shows a direct body voltage measurement from a voltmeter attached to a walking person. It can be seen that the charge carried on the body increases slowly to a saturation point (effect 1). The steps taken by a person

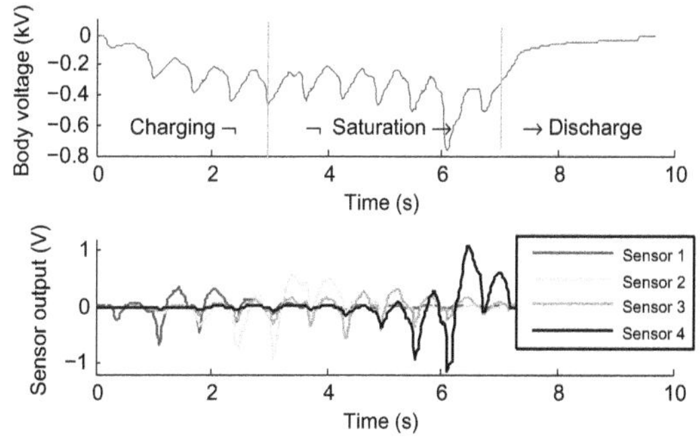

Figure 3: The top plot represents a contact-based measurement of absolute body electric potential. When walking, the potential gradually increases up to a saturation point, while exhibiting peaks when a foot is lifted. An array of four sensors (bottom) detects these changes, with highest amplitude as the walker passes under them.

influence the environmental coupling and lead to recurring peaks (effect 2). When the person stops walking, the charge decreases within a couple of seconds.

In order to make meaningful assumptions about a person's position and change in body electric potential, it is necessary to describe them based on the physical principles of the sensing modality. We do so by introducing a model that predicts how sensor values change when a human affects the ambient electric field. By inverting the model, we can derive a person's position from a set of real sensor readings. Once this position is known, the change in body electric potential can be reconstructed. We show that this change is specific for a person, and that it can leverage identification using an SVM classifier with a feature set extracted from a short walking sequence (typ. 5 s).

4. MODELING THE SENSOR RESPONSE

We now derive a forward (or predictive) model that estimates sensor values based on a person's location and body electric potential. This forward model enables us to understand how human movements are reflected in our sensor signals. The model also acts as a means to validate our assumptions on reconstructing body electric potential and localization by matching model predictions with experimental data. Let us first consider the dynamic sensor response to a changing input.

An EPS can be modelled using a resistor and a capacitor, in combination with an ideal voltage follower, as shown in the right part of Figure 4 [13]. Recall that a voltage follower is an amplifier with a gain of 1, it simply follows the voltage at its input, which is connected to the sensing electrode. By using the amplifier, the electrode is decoupled from the sensing circuit, enabling it to adapt to changes in the ambient electric field.

The voltage follower's output is v_S. Its input capacitance and resistance are explicitly represented by C_{in} and R_{in}, respectively. As for the electric field generated by a human body, it is equivalent to a voltage source v_B coupled to the sensor through a very small capacitance C_C, usually less than 100 fF. In human movement sensing applications, the distance between the person and the sensor is typically in the meter range, which results in a weak coupling ($C_C \ll C_{in}$) [45].

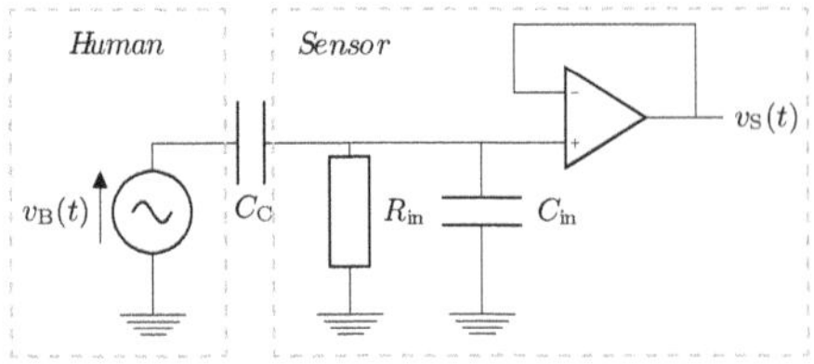

Figure 4: Electric potential sensor represented by an equivalent circuit (adapted from [13]). v_b represents the changing body electric potential, whereas C_C is the coupling capacitance which changes with the body-to-sensor distance.

When the person moves relatively to the EPS, C_C is not a constant but depends on the body-to-sensor distance d. In order to simplify the notation, d is considered a function of time $d(t)$ in the following, and the coupling capacitance is written $C_C(t)$. Analyzing the circuit yields

$$v_S'(t)[C_C(t) + C_{in}] + v_S(t)[C_C'(t) + 1/R_{in}] = \frac{d}{dt}[C_C(t)v_B(t)] \, . \quad (1)$$

We can solve (1) for the sensor output v_S by assuming that $C_C(t) \ll C_{in}$ and $C_C'(t) \ll 1/R_{in}$ for all t. These assumptions are justified in weak coupling situations with a high input impedance sensor such as the EPIC. Additionally, we introduce a first-order low-pass filter with impulse response $h_1(t)$ (time constant $\tau_1 = R_{in}C_{in}$), and a first-order high-pass filter with impulse response $h_2(t)$ (cutoff frequency typically in the mHz range). The first filter simplifies the expression, and the second models the effect of the passive components integrated in the EPS [46]. The output of an EPS is finally

$$v_S(t) = R_{in}h_1(t) * h_2(t) * \left(\frac{d}{dt}[C_C(t)v_B(t)]\right) \, . \quad (2)$$

With this equation, we are able to predict a sensor output based on the two variables of coupling capacitance and body voltage.

4.1 Coupling Capacitances

We now take a closer look on how coupling capacitances are related to a person's distance to a sensor. To derive the coupling capacitance C_C, we start with a point charge approximation [11], in which $C_C(d) \propto 1/d^2$. We generalize this slightly to $C_C(d) \propto 1/d^\alpha$ where a constant α is the distance exponent, to account for deviations from the point charge approximation [53, 21]. In the far field/weak coupling case, there must be a lower limit d_{min} to the distance corresponding to an upper limit $C_{C,max}$ to the coupling capacitance, so that

$$C_C(d) = C_{C,max}\left(\frac{d_{min}}{d}\right)^\alpha \, . \quad (3)$$

Placing the sensors on a room's ceiling (or at the top of walls) ensures that there is a minimum distance of about 0.5 m to 1 m between the ceiling and the top of the person's head. This point approximates the participant's position, assuming the human body is perfectly conducting at low frequencies [18]. With an electrode of about 1 cm^2, the point charge approximation is justified, at least on the sensor side.

Knowing that the sensors are on the ceiling, the constant minimum height between the top of the person's head and the sensors is defined as

$$H = \text{ceiling height} - \text{person's height}. \quad (4)$$

We introduce the simplification that the coordinates of a person may only vary in two dimensions. Let $(x(t), y(t), z(t))$ be the person's coordinates at time t, and (x_S, y_S, z_S) the coordinates of a sensor. The $z = 0$ plane is the space where the top of the person's head moves. This allows to write the Euclidean distance between the head and the sensor, and define the minimum distance $d_{min} = H$. The final coupling capacitance is

$$C_C(t) = \frac{C_{C,max}H^\alpha}{\left([x(t) - x_S]^2 + [y(t) - y_S]^2 + H^2\right)^{\alpha/2}} \, . \quad (5)$$

4.2 Complete Forward Model

We described models for the EPIC sensor (2) and the body to sensor coupling (5). Each element of the measurement situation (Figure 1) is known. Let us synthesize this knowledge in a complete forward model.

For further derivations, it will be useful to separate the filters' responses in (2) from the rest of the expression. The filtered signal is the derivative of a product, that may be expressed as a sum thanks to the product rule. The two elements of this sum are

$$\Psi_a(t) = R_{in}C_C(t)v_B'(t), \text{ and} \quad (6)$$

$$\Psi_b(t) = R_{in}C_C'(t)v_B(t) \, . \quad (7)$$

With the coupling capacitance (5), the expressions of $\Psi_a(t)$ (6) and $\Psi_b(t)$ (7) can be inferred. Let us focus on Ψ_a, which is related to the change in body electric potential, for example caused by stepping:

$$\Psi_a(t) = \frac{R_{in}C_{C,max}H^\alpha v_B'(t)}{\left([x(t) - x_S]^2 + [y(t) - y_S]^2 + H^2\right)^{\alpha/2}} \, . \quad (8)$$

The signals that compose the response of an EPIC are filtered versions of Ψ_a and Ψ_b, which is noted $\psi_a(t) = h_1(t) * h_2(t) * \Psi_a(t)$ and $\psi_b(t) = h_1(t) * h_2(t) * \Psi_b(t)$.

To complete the forward model, an experimental phenomenon is considered: the sensor placement within the room influences the amplitude of the output. For instance, an EPS has a strong coupling to the environment when placed close to a wall. If this coupling increases the circuit's input impedance, the amplitude of the sensor output is decreased. Let this effect be approximated by a simple dimensionless factor, the *calibration constant* K. Including the partial components ψ_a, ψ_b and the calibration constant, the expression

$$v_S(t) = K\left[\psi_a(t) + \psi_b(t)\right] \, . \quad (9)$$

describes the output of an EPIC, depending on the body's position and electric potential.

The measurement result is a filtered combination of the body electric potential, its derivative, the position and the speed. This is a new formulation of an old observation. As Aronoff et al. [3] already noted in 1965, the variable electric field generated by a walking human being is a combination of two effects: the variable electric potential (due to stepping) of a static body, and the static electric potential of a moving body. This corresponds exactly to the two components

Ψ_a and Ψ_b, which will be called respectively the *stepping component* and the *movement component*. By extension, ψ_a and ψ_b bear the same designation.

5. APPLYING THE MODEL

After having derived a forward model, which enables us to predict sensor values based on a person's location and body electric potential, we now invert the model. The inverse model allows us to analyze sensor data and estimate a person's location. Based on the localization, we reconstruct the person's change in body electric potential used for identification. Being aware of the simplifications introduced in our model, we also gain a better understanding of possible effects on localization and identification performance.

5.1 Localization

As described in the forward model, each raw sensor signal $v_S(t)$ consists of two components. Contrary to the movement component $\psi_b(t)$, the stepping component $\psi_a(t)$ is very distinct and enables us to estimate the location of a person. However, the two components of (9) are superposed in the raw sensor signal and can hardly be separated in the time domain. By band-pass filtering $v_S(t)$ around a realistic stepping frequency of 1 to 2.5 Hz [43], we obtain the *estimated stepping component* $\hat{\psi}_a$. Another simplification we introduce is that the filtering simply attenuates the fundamental of the real signal Ψ_a without distorting it. Thus, the estimated stepping component is

$$\hat{\psi}_a(t) \approx GK\Psi_a(t) = GKR_{in}C_C(t){v_B}'(t) \ , \quad (10)$$

with G a constant that represents the combined gain of the measurement and the processing filter at the stepping frequency.

We combine the output of several sensors to localize the person. A *sensor pair* with sensors S_i and S_j performs two independent electric field measurements. The parameters and signals specific to a sensor S_i will be noted in the following with the index i, e.g. C_{Ci} is the coupling capacitance between the body and sensor S_i. The filtered output of a sensor S_i is

$$\hat{\psi}_{ai}(t) \approx \frac{GK_iR_{in}C_{C,max}H^\alpha {v_B}'(t)}{([x(t)-x_{Si}]^2+[y(t)-y_{Si}]^2+H^2)^{\alpha/2}} \ , \quad (11)$$

When detecting a peak in two sensor signals, we can compare the ratio between them, corrected with the calibration factors (assumed to be known) and take the α-th root. The ratio has the advantage of eliminating $C_{C,max}$, which is difficult to estimate in general. Assuming that the EPS have the same characteristics, and that the signals are processed by the same filter, R_{in} and G are also eliminated. Lastly, ${v_B}'(t)$ disappears in the ratio, and the obtained function is purely dependent on the position. The α-th root cancels the $1/d^\alpha$ proportionality of the electric field. We call the resulting function *estimated distance ratio*, and note it $\hat{\Delta}_{ij}$ for the sensor pair (S_i, S_j):

$$\hat{\Delta}_{ij}(t) = \sqrt[\alpha]{\frac{K_j\hat{\psi}_{ai}(t)}{K_i\hat{\psi}_{aj}(t)}} \approx \Delta_{ij}(t) \ . \quad (12)$$

The actual *distance ratio* Δ_{ij} is given by

$$\Delta_{ij}(t) = \sqrt{\frac{[x(t)-x_{Sj}]^2+[y(t)-y_{Sj}]^2+H^2}{[x(t)-x_{Si}]^2+[y(t)-y_{Si}]^2+H^2}} \ . \quad (13)$$

The parameters of Δ_{ij} are the sensors' coordinates, which are known, the ceiling to head distance H and the distance exponent α, that can be estimated. There are two unknowns x and y with only one equation, and a single sensor pair is still not sufficient to find the person's coordinates.

Similarly to RF-based systems that use propagation models for trilateration [12], at least three estimated distance ratios such as (12) are needed to find the person's coordinates with no sign ambiguity. In a non-ideal case, the system of three or more equations must be optimized to find the coordinates that minimize the error, i.e. the person's estimated position.

Our basic installation consists of four sensors organized in a rectangular *sensor cell*, which provides four distance ratios. A larger area can be covered by installing more sensor cells. In that case, the first step of localization is to find in which cell the sum of signal amplitudes is the strongest. Optimizing the coordinates based on the distance ratios is then accomplished within this cell only.

5.2 Body Electric Potential Change

The information about a person's location enables us to inverse another step presented in the forward model (Section 4.2) in order to derive the change in the body electric potential. The change in body electric potential is a powerful modality, which will later help us to identify a person. Once the person's position has been estimated, the equation of the stepping component for an individual sensor (11) can be solved for the derivative of the body electric potential:

$${v_B}'(t) \approx \hat{v}'_B(t) = \frac{\hat{\psi}_{ai}(t)d_i(t)^\alpha}{K_iA} \ , \quad (14)$$

where $d_i(t)$ is the Euclidean distance between the person and sensor S_i, and

$$A = GR_{in}C_{C,max}H^\alpha \ . \quad (15)$$

The individual estimates $\hat{v}'_B(t)$ (14) are combined by taking the weighted average over all sensors. In the following evaluation, we compare combining the predictions based on distance and equal weights.

If a reference measurement of the body electric potential is available, the error between the estimated and the real ${v_B}'$ can be used as a cost to find an optimized value for A. Without a measurement, A is set arbitrarily and scales linearly to the real body electric potential.

5.3 Identification

During our experiments, it became obvious that body electric potential changes are very distinct for different people when taking a step. Reasons can be seen in a number of properties related to a human being, in particular gait cadence, but also footwear, synthetic materials worn, or body height. These properties contribute to a characteristic charging and coupling behaviour.

In the following we use the term *step signature* for a window of reconstructed body electric potential change around a step. We experimentally determined a window size of 0.72 ms as suitable to not interfere with the following step.

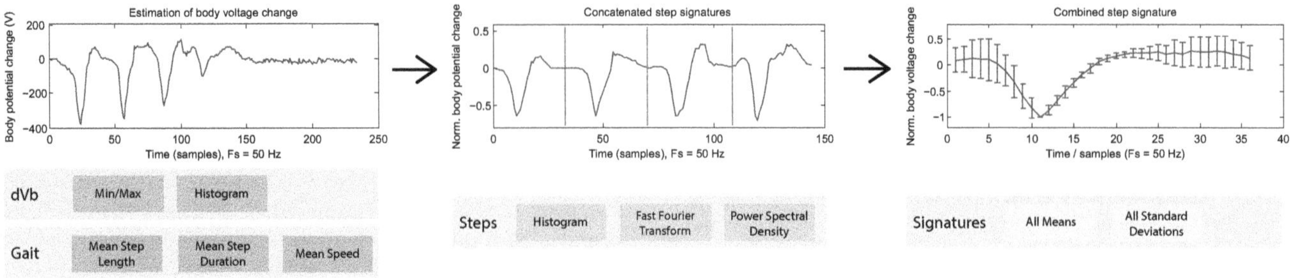

Figure 5: The feature extraction process for identification results in four feature sets: (1) *dVb* body electric potential, (2) *gait*-related, (3) a sequence of normalized *steps*, and (4) the combined and normalized step *signatures*.

Figure 5 shows an overview of the feature extraction process. Here, the negative peaks correspond to a user lifting the foot off the ground.

Although the step signatures may be of different amplitudes due to accumulation or decumulation of body charge, their shape remains quite constant. Therefore, the step signatures are normalized to a common scaling. In order to retrieve the frequency characteristics of all step signatures, we multiply each step signature by a Hamming window and concatenate them into one time-series, shown in the middle diagram of Figure 5. Based on this concatenated series of steps, we compute the Fast Fourier Transform (FFT), the Power Spectral Density (PSD), and a histogram.

The third diagram in Figure 5 depicts an overlay of all step signatures. We compute the mean step signature, as well as the standard deviation. All samples from both means and standard deviations are used as features. Based on the estimated electric potential and the localization, we also extract a few features that are typical in gait analysis [6]. We compute the mean step length and mean step duration to determine the gait cadence. Due to the fixed model parameter H (head to ceiling height), we currently do not take features like up- and down displacement into account.

6. EVALUATION

To evaluate Platypus, we collected a dataset in a controlled setting. The dataset comprises sensor measurements and a ground truth for localization and identification. We also recorded the human body electric potential to complete our dataset.

6.1 Test Setup and Participants

The data was collected in a room at Fraunhofer IGD (Darmstadt, Germany). The test room was approximately 16 m^2, with a metallic false ceiling 2.62 m high and a bare concrete floor. A sensor array of 2.5 m long by 2 m wide was installed on the ceiling. The array consisted of two rectangular sensor cells (i.e. six sensors), with each sensor at least 50 cm away from any wall. Markings on the floor materialized the limits of the covered area, the cell centers (for calibration) and start/stop points for the participants (Figure 6).

Thirty participants, all researchers and students at Fraunhofer IGD and TU Darmstadt, were involved in the experiment. The sample was predominantly male (three females), young (min. 16, max. 36, mean 28 years old) and tall (min. 1.60 m, max. 1.92 m, mean 1.79 m). All participants were asked to wear closed casual shoes for the experiment to minimize the effect of different types of footwear.

Figure 6: Setup of the model evaluation experiment. Left: six ceiling-mounted sensors arranged at the corners of two rectangular cells, and acquisition board. Right: marks on the floor defining the two sensor cells and the start/end locations of the walking paths. The sensors are located vertically above the sensor cells' corners, marked by black dots.

The participants were asked to walk on specific paths in the area covered the sensor array. For the position ground truth, we used a Kinect V2 [40]. Prior evaluation [62] has shown that this device has an accuracy in the range 1 mm to 10 mm, which is sufficient for evaluating our system. Ground truth for body electric potential was acquired using a high-impedance volt meter (model 820, Trek Inc.), connected to one wrist with a conductive strap.

6.2 Experimental Factors

Possible experimental factors were derived from the physical room situation, the participants' properties, the data processing scheme, and pre-tests of the system. The factors that depend on the physical situation are (1) room properties (flooring and ceiling material, ceiling height), (2) proximity of the sensors to room walls, and (3) presence of large grounded objects in the room. The participants' properties include (4) height, weight, footwear, and (5) walking speed. Data processing factors include (6) calibration constants K, (7) electric field distance exponent α and the (8) head to sensor distance H. This distance H is assumed as data processing factor, since it is not feasible to measure or estimate the body height of a person in the intended applications.

Room properties (1) and (2) are fixed for each room and installation, they are also assumed fixed in this first experiment. The presence of grounded objects is systematically varied with a grounded metal cart (1 m high, 1.2 m long and 0.5 m wide) placed in a corner of the localization area in half of all experimental runs. The properties of the participants (4) are generally random and are not systematically varied in the experiment. Walking speed (5) is included as a nominal factor, asking participants to walk normally or slowly.

Two data processing factors were varied in the experiment, namely K and α. The calibration constants K used for estimating the distance ratio in (12) were either from an individual calibration for each test person or taken from a standard calibration performed by the second author. Pretests showed that $\alpha \approx 2.5$ could be a better choice than the theoretical $\alpha = 2$ as a value for the electric field distance exponent. This factor was evaluated on three levels. Head-to-ceiling-distance H showed no effect in the pre-tests. Therefore, H was calculated with the ceiling height using an average statue of 1.72 m [55].

This led to a 2 2 2 3 full factorial design with the factors walking speed, presence of grounded object, type of calibration (individual or standard) and the value of α. Only (speed object) treatments needed an actual experiment, since all data processing factors could be varied in the calculations afterwards. Four repetitions per test person (i.e. 16 trajectories) were conducted.

For each participant, a series of eight trajectories with random start and stop points (see Fig. 6) and random speeds was drawn. The speeds were picked without replacement from a set of four "normal" and four "slow", to get a random order of speeds but always four normal walks and four slow ones. A similar series of eight start/stop/speed sets was picked for the tests with the grounded object present (eliminating the stop point 21, which was blocked by the object). Additionally, a calibration routine (100 steps in each cell) was performed by participants, to look at the effect of using individual calibration constants K rather than a system-wide calibration. The experiment lasted about 20 min per person and the results were analysed with SPSS version 22.

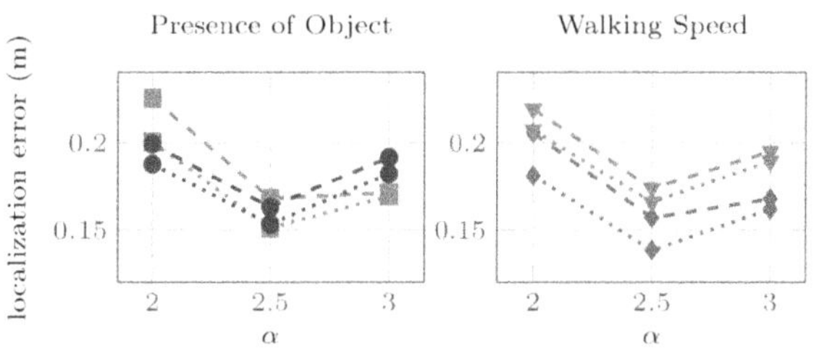

Figure 7: Interactions of α values on median localization error plots with object (left, square data points indicate object present, circles no object present) and walking speed (right, triangles indicate normal speed, diamonds slow speed). Calibration level is marked with dotted lines (standard) and dashed lines (individual).

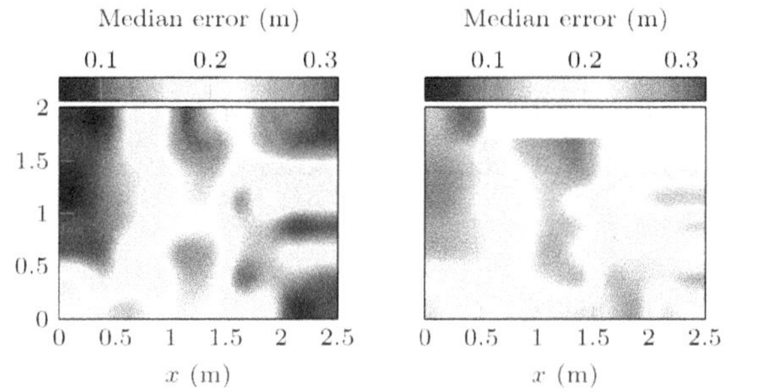

Figure 8: Median localization error over the covered area, without any object present (left) and with a grounded metallic cart in the top right corner (right). Because the cart was in the way, no trajectories entered the white zone. In both maps, the median error is largest at the border between the two cells ($x = 1.25$ m).

6.3 Localization Results

The localization error is calculated for detection i in the recording according to

$$\epsilon_i = \sqrt{(x_K[k_i] - x_P[k_i])^2 + (y_K[k_i] - y_P[k_i])^2}\,, \quad (16)$$

where k_i are the discrete samples when signal peaks were detected, and the subscripts K and P indicate the true coordinates measured by the Kinect and the estimates given by the Platypus, respectively. The errors from all trajectories of a test person with the same treatment are pooled and the median is used as localization error measure for this treatment. This leads to 24 localization errors for each person, corresponding to the 24 treatments and 720 results in total.

We used linear regression to test the assumptions of negligible effects of test person height and weight as well as shoe size. Analysis shows a lack of significance for all participants' properties (height: $R^2 = 0.007$, $p = 0.657$; weight: $R^2 = 0.015$, $p = 0.525$; shoe size: $R^2 = 0.001$, $p = 0.902$). We therefore conclude that Platypus's localization errors are not sensitive to these factors.

Further analysis is based on a repeated-measures analysis of variance (ANOVA). From the total variation of this data set, 19.81 % can be attributed to the variations between participants. These variations cannot be described any further, but can be explained by individual properties of the participants not accounted for (e.g. clothing). The model above can explain 32.42 % of the variation, whereas 47.77 % are non-systematic variations. Given our ANOVA results, we derive the systematic variance and the reliability of this information.

A significant effect ($p < 0.001$) with medium size (i.e. accounting for about 10 % of the total variance) is found for the value of the electric field exponent α. As Figure 7 shows, the value $\alpha = 2.5$ gives much better results than the theoretical $\alpha = 2$. Further analysis showed that $\alpha = 2.5$ performs the best regardless of calibration level, walking speed, or the presence/absence of the grounded object. In the remaining we thus assume $\alpha = 2.5$.

On the other hand, although there is a significant effect ($p < 0.001$) of the calibration factor (with the standard calibration performing *better than individual*), the effect size is too small to have a relevant impact for the design of the system. We observed that calibration constants differ only in a very small range between participants, but in a much larger way depending on the positioning of the sensors, i.e. the room characteristics. Therefore, a standard calibration for each installation is sufficient for the use of Platypus, and future results refer to the standard calibration only.

The second largest effect ($p < 0.001$), albeit with small size (i.e. explaining about 1 % of the total variance), is observed for the walking speed factor. Slower walking speeds lead to smaller errors. We attribute this effect to a better performance of the separation of movement and stepping components by filtering, since the movement component has a lower frequency for slow movements. Due to the small ef-

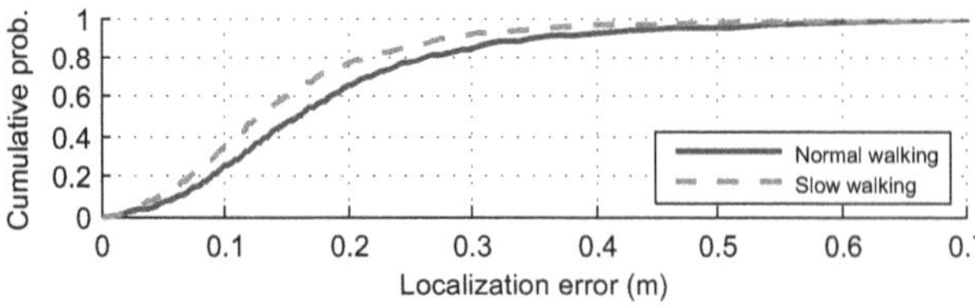

Figure 9: Cumulative distribution of localization error: The median error is 0.16 m for normal walking and 0.13 m for slow walking. 95 % of errors are under 0.36 m (slow walking) and 0.47 m (normal walking).

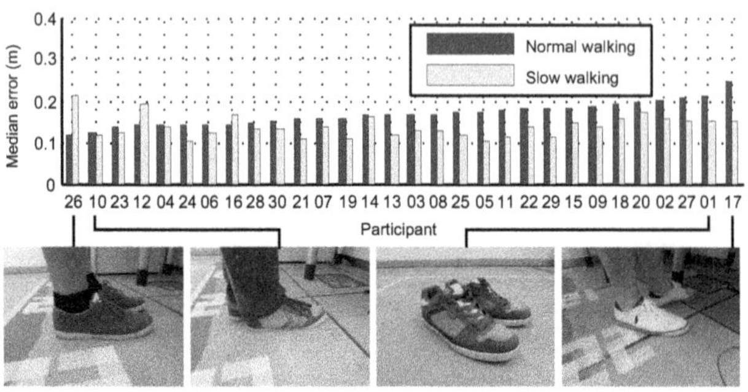

Figure 10: Localization median errors per user: the error shows no correlation with shoe size and body weight.

fect size, the error difference is in an acceptable range and we consider Platypus usable for both slow and normal walking speeds.

Overall, Platypus's localization error in this experimental configuration was found to have a median of 0.16 m for normal walking speed and 0.13 m for slow walking speeds (Figure 9). The ANOVA shows no significant effect of the metallic object on the localization error ($p = 0.640$, $\eta^2 = 0.0003$). We therefore conclude that Platypus is not adversely affected by static conductive objects. This is illustrated in Figure 8 which shows that locations close to the conducting object were not subject to high localization error. Figure 8 also illustrates that a 2 m by 1.25 m cell size of Platypus sensors leads to acceptable localization performance across the whole space. The user-dependent median localization errors are depicted in Figure 10. No correlation between shoe size and body weight with regard to the localization error could be observed.

6.4 Body Electric Potential Change

When a user's position, and thus the distance to a sensor, is known, it is possible to reconstruct the change in body electric potential using our model. To evaluate this, we compare the true change in body electric potential to the estimated change in body electric potential.

For a number of N discrete sampling points, we calculate the normalized root-mean-square error (NRMSE). The absolute RMSE can only provide limited insights, as the maximum and minimum body electric potential differ greatly from user to user:

$$\text{NRMSE} = \frac{1}{\max v'_\text{B} - \min v'_\text{B}} \sqrt{\frac{\sum_{t=1}^{N} (\hat{v}'_{\text{B},t} - v'_{\text{B},t})^2}{N}}. \quad (17)$$

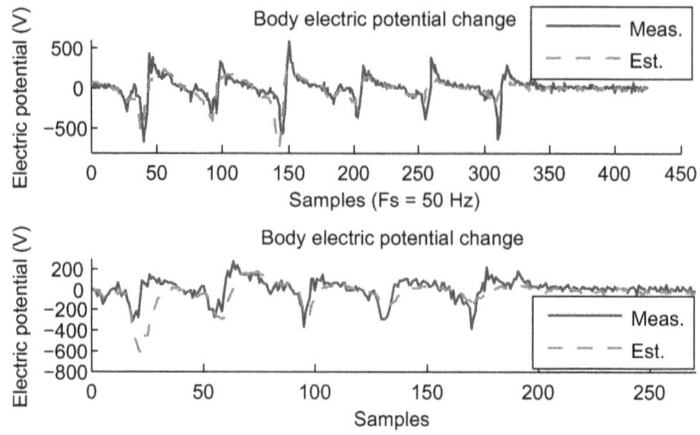

Figure 11: Top: Good estimate of body electric potential change with a NRMSE of 0.07. Bottom: Bad estimate with an NRMSE of 0.16.

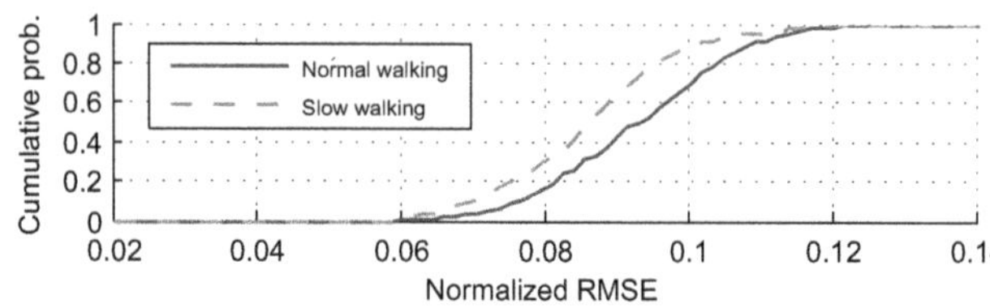

Figure 12: The body electric potential change estimation is most accurate for slow walking speeds. The NRMSE increases for normal walking speeds.

Figure 11 shows two examples of body electric potential change estimates and their ground truths. It can be seen that the estimates provide a good impression of the real change in body electric potential. However, as the stepping component $\hat{\psi}_{\text{a}i}(t)$ is determined by band-pass filtering the sensor signals, some high-frequency features cannot be estimated. This results in smoother peaks for the estimated body electric potential change.

Fusing the estimates for body electric potential change can be achieved by summing up each sensor's prediction with equal weights. Using this technique, we achieve a mean NRMSE for slow walking of 0.085 ($\sigma = 0.012$), which shifts to 0.091 ($\sigma = 0.013$) for normal walking. Figure 12 shows the distribution of NRMSE for equal weighting. Assuming that the sensors closer to the person better estimate the change in body electric potential, we can also use the distances $d_i(t)^\alpha$ as weights. However, this results in a lower quality estimation, with a mean NRMSE of 0.098 ($\sigma = 0.018$) for slow walking, and 0.116 ($\sigma = 0.029$) for normal walking. The main reason can be seen in imprecise separation of stepping and movement component Ψ_a and Ψ_b. By applying equal weights, the influences of movement-related errors tend to cancel each other out as a person's distance to the sensors both increases and decreases.

6.5 Identification

To evaluate the identification performance based on location and body electric potential change we employ the feature sets introduced in 5.3. We use a standard SVM classifier (libSVM, RBF kernel, normalization) integrated in the WEKA framework [24]. The feature extraction is performed on a window comprising the whole trajectory of a partici-

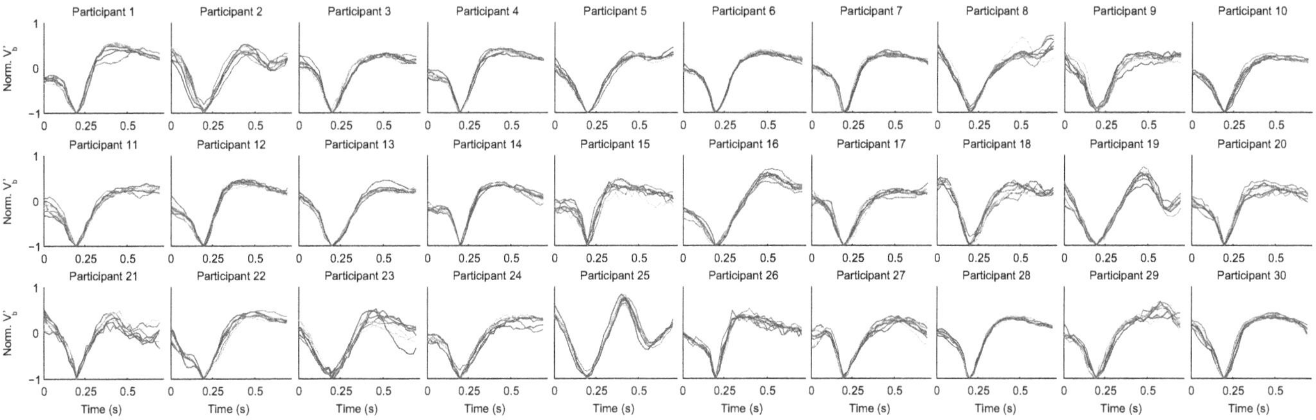

Figure 13: The estimated body electric potential changes when taking a step (step signatures) differ from user to user and represent a discriminative measure for classification. The amplitudes depend on the actually carried charge and require normalization.

Normal Walking	dVb	Gait	Steps	Signatures
dVb	49.3 %	56.2 %	65.6 %	**77.0 %**
Gait	-	29.0 %	48.8 %	65.6 %
Steps	-	-	47.2 %	70.1 %
Signatures	-	-	-	65.8 %
All sets	74.7 %			
Slow Walking	dVb	Gait	Steps	Signatures
dVb	55.1 %	64.2 %	**73.6 %**	69.6 %
Gait	-	35.1 %	59.2 %	63.6 %
Steps	-	-	51.1 %	63.6 %
Signatures	-	-	-	62.9 %
All sets	73.0 %			

Table 1: F-measures for identification of 30 participants walking with normal speeds (4-fold cross validation, 8 samples per participant).

pant (usually less than 5 s). Our identification is based on 30 participants, eight random trajectories with two movement speeds (240 windows for each speed). As a measure of classification performance, we apply the F-measure (or F1 score) which combines the measures of precision and recall.

First, we take a closer look on the four feature sets, containing information on body electric potential change (dVb), gait features (gait), steps (steps), and step signatures (signatures). We evaluate each single feature set and combinations between two feature sets. Each participant's dataset contains 2 x 8 randomized trajectories for slow and normal walking. The two walking speeds were first evaluated separately in a 4-fold cross validation, as listed in Table 1.

Combining all feature sets yields in an F-measure of 73.5% for slow walking and 74.7% for normal walking (average accuracy 75.0 %). It is conceivable that the feature set containing step signatures provides most discriminative data. Figure 13 depicts all extracted step signatures for the 30 participants. The most significant differences in the step signatures can certainly be seen in the rise and fall times of the signal (user 10, user 26). Also, the standard variance between consecutive steps differs greatly (user 21, user 7). Confusions in classification could be observed for very similar step signatures (user 15, user 1) or very irregular signatures (user 21).

The gait features provided least discriminative data. We believe that this can be attributed to the rather short trajectory, which did not allow the participants to move with a regular cadence. Also, the dataset contains people with very similar body height and physical condition, which leads to a very similar step pattern. The feature set comprising absolute change in body electric potential provided discriminative features and performed second best. A cross-validation between the data for each movement speed showed that the extracted features, especially the step signature, are inherently different. This leads to the conclusion that a user identification must be based on the natural movement pattern and does not generalize over multiple speeds.

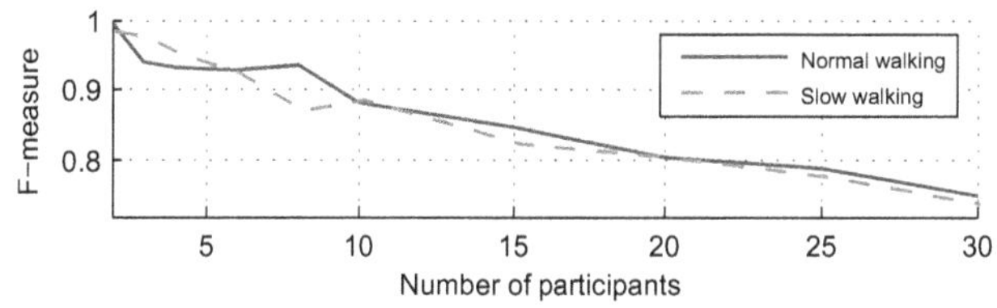

Figure 14: Identification accuracy compared to the number of people in the dataset.

In the following, we evaluate the influence of a different number of participants on the classification result. We conducted 10 repetitions on a 4-fold cross validation for a set of N randomly drawn participants. The results shown in Figure 14 indicate that two participants can be distinguished almost perfectly. The performance degrades with the number of people. Only slight differences in classification performance could be observed for walking slowly and normally.

7. CORRIDOR EXPERIMENT

We deployed Platypus in a corridor to evaluate a more realistic environment with less movement constraints. We recorded a dataset that contains sensor data and ground truth concerning walking four discrete paths along the corridor, as well as the participants' identities, covering multiple days. The questions we would like to answer with this experiment are whether participants can be reliably recognized even on different days and how different types of footwear influence the identification. We also evaluate whether Platypus is able to classify which path down the corridor was taken.

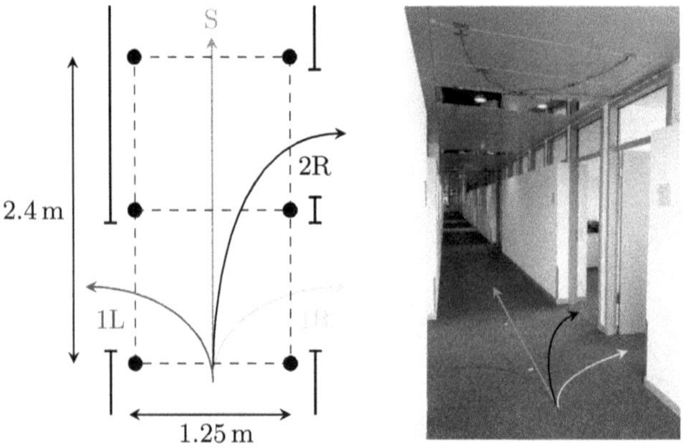

Figure 15: Left: Corridor experiment setup with six sensors (black circles) and four possible paths. Right: The deployment with sensors mounted to the ceiling.

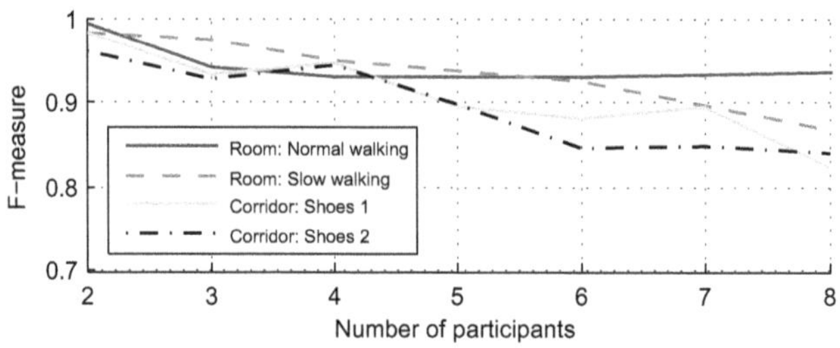

Figure 16: The classification performance of the corridor deployment evaluated on two different days compared to the controlled room experiment. Participants wore the same footwear on the two days.

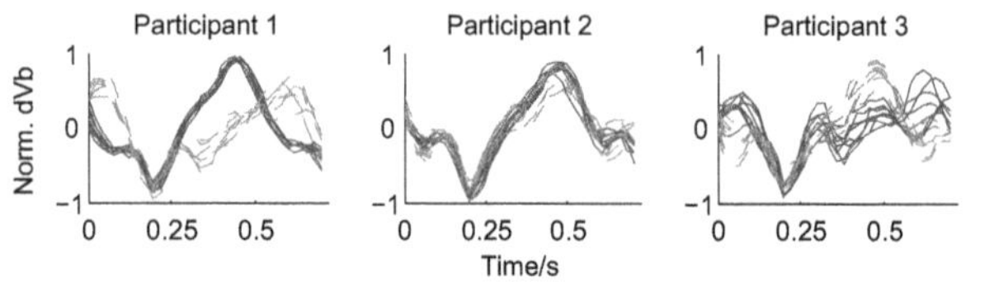

Figure 17: Most step signatures of participants changed when wearing different footwear. Few of them generated similar signatures, as shown in the middle plot.

7.1 Setup & Participants

We conducted this evaluation in a semi-controlled manner. Six sensors were installed on the ceiling of an office corridor with three doors (Figure 15). In contrast to the first experiment, a synthetic carpet covered the floor. We asked the participants to start walking about 2 m away from the sensing area, then to enter one of the three rooms or keep going through the corridor. To avoid hampering the participants' movements with a wrist strap and a cable, the body electric potential was not measured. Since the people went out of line of sight through doors, positioning by Kinect was not reliable for this test. Thus, the ground truth for localization was limited to discrete paths (end of the corridor or one of the three rooms).

For each participant, the experiment comprised four sessions. In the first session, the person walked eight times through the corridor and four times through each door, for a total of 20 measurements. The paths were taken in a random order, different for each session. The second session was similar to the first, with a second pair of shoes (all shoes were the participants' own). In the third and fourth sessions, we repeated the procedure of the two first sessions using the same shoes, but different clothes, on another day. The participants were not asked to choose any particular type of shoes, or to walk in any particular way.

We had 8 participants (6 male, 2 female), between 20 and 52 years old (average 32 years old). Similar to the first experiment, the participants were relatively tall (min. 1.67 m, max. 2 m, mean 1.79 m). All participants were researchers and students at Fraunhofer IGD and TU Darmstadt.

7.2 Persistence of Identification Features

One central aim of the experiment was to find out whether there are similarities in the features that could identify people independently of their footwear. The results are based on an SVM classifier as in the first evaluation (libSVM, RBF kernel, normalization).

To evaluate the feasibility of recognizing a user after a certain time, we asked the participants to perform the experiment on two days, with a gap of one to five days. We validated the data based on eight straight trajectories, using data from one day for training, and the other day for validation (and vice-versa). To evaluate the performance depending on the number of people, we conducted 10 repetitions for a set of N random participants. The results are shown in Figure 16 and compared to data from the previous room experiment with the corridor experiment. For eight participants, we yield an average F-measure of 83.59 % (accuracy 83.6 %) in the corridor, which is less than the first room experiment for the same amount of participants (90.21 %). This can be attributed to the less controlled manner in which the experiment was carried out (no control over shoes, changed clothing, more freedom of movement).

Another question we investigated is whether it is possible to recognize a returning user with a different pair of shoes. Therefore, we combined data recorded on two days and used one pair of shoes for training, and the other for evaluation (and vice-versa). For eight users, the results indicate a poor average F-measure of just 26.15 %. We attribute this to differences in step signatures due to materials which influence contact charging, and different sole thicknesses which result in a different capacitive coupling to the floor (Figure 17).

For application developers, it is especially vital to know how many training samples are required to achieve a certain identification performance. For each number of training samples and number of people, we trained the classifier with 100 randomly drawn permutations containing straight

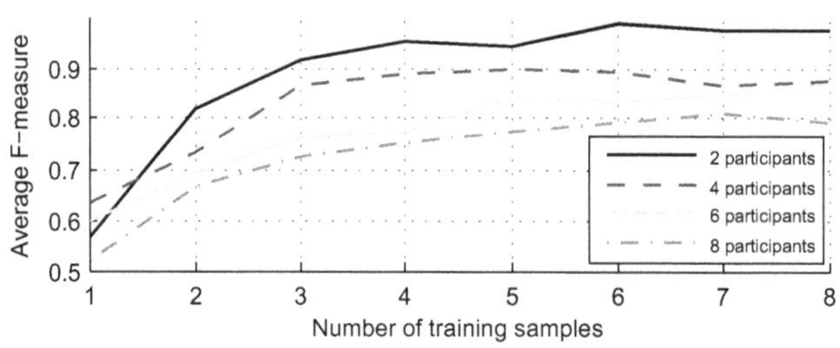

Figure 18: The identification performance stabilizes after 3-6 training samples of a 2.4 m walk.

	Recognized as			
	S	**1L**	**1R**	**2R**
S	244	3	9	0
1L	0	127	0	1
1R	0	4	119	5
2R	0	3	3	122

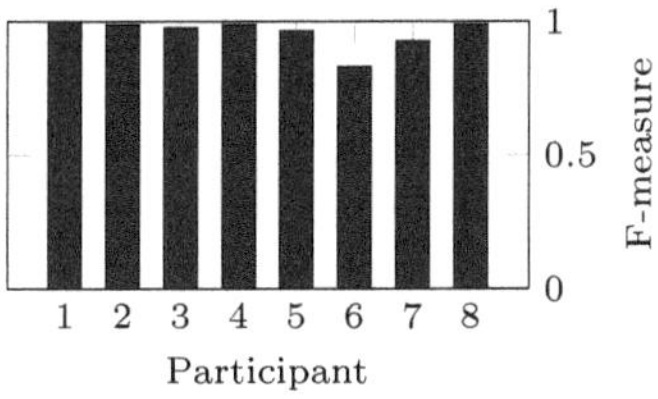

Figure 19: Left: confusion matrix for the trajectory classification. The four trajectories are noted as S (straight), 1L (first door, left of the corridor), 1R (first door, right) and 2R (second door, right). Right: average F-measure of path classification per participant.

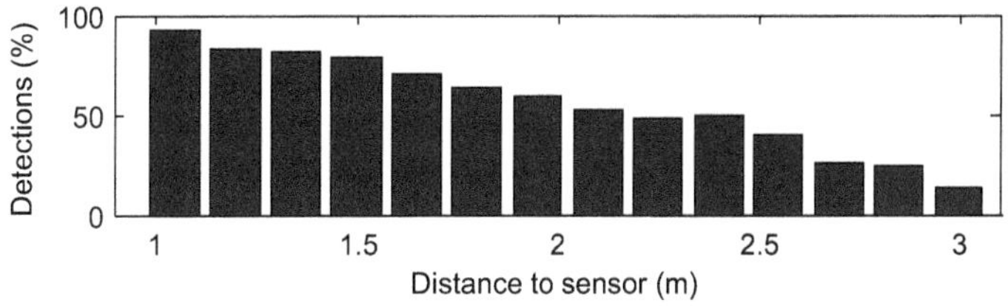

Figure 20: The rate of successful Platypus detections compared to distance, when a footstep occurs. The histogram starts at 1 m distance to account for head-to-ceiling height.

trajectories from day 1. We evaluated the trained classifier instances with all 8 straight trajectories recorded on day 2 (Figure 18). The results show that the classification performance stabilizes quickly for a small amount of users. Considering eight users, a stable performance is achieved after 5-6 training samples of a 2.4 m walk.

7.3 Trajectory Classification

Besides identification, we investigate how well Platypus recognizes one of the four possible paths taken within the corridor. We applied dynamic time warping (DTW) for classification [59], with the localization events as time series. As reference templates, we defined four mean paths based on all recorded trajectories.

Over all recordings, the classification accuracy reaches 95.6 %. The confusion matrix can be seen in Figure 19 (left). The F-measure by participant is shown in Figure 19 (right), and the average over all trajectories and all participants is 95.7 %. While the classification performance is almost perfect for many users, we observed a poor recognition accuracy for participant 6 (50 %) on one day and with one pair of shoes. This inaccuracy was not observed during the second day of measurement with the same shoes.

8. LIMITATIONS

Our experiments have shown that Platypus operates without the need for person-specific sensor calibration, and that it is independent of the user's height/weight/clothing as well as the presence or absence of grounded electrical objects in the environment. However, person-specific model training is still required, and identification of users depends on wearing the same footwear.

The experimental deployments are relatively dense (grid size from 1.2 m to 2 m) which is challenging when scaling to larger spaces. Figure 20 depicts the sensing range achieved using our current hardware and signal processing, and shows that the underlying electric field sensing does work at longer distances. In order to create more sparse deployments and lower the cost of Playtpus, future work can explore ways of increasing this range, for example by employing multiple analog frontends with different gain levels. This would also enable different topologies than grids - e.g. by arranging multiple sensors in a ceiling lamp.

Although smaller grounded objects do not affect the localization accuracy, we found that walls have a very strong coupling to users. This leads to an attenuated signal when person-to-wall distances are less than 30 cm, which could create blind spots in a deployed Platypus system near walls. A modified capacitive coupling model that not only includes the person-to-sensor coupling, but also the person-to-wall coupling, can potentially overcome this issue.

9. SUMMARY & FUTURE WORK

We introduced Platypus, a tag-free system to localize a person and to extract a signature pattern for identification. It is based on a novel use of electric field sensing to remotely infer a person's body electric potential changes. Our experiments have shown that using a 6-sensor array covering an area of 2 m by 2.5 m, Platypus can perform localization with a median error of 0.16 m while walking, and identification of 30 persons with an average accuracy of 75 % in a controlled setting. While the sensor density is high, the passive operation enables sensor designs with very low power consumption. Platypus incorporates a mathematical model which uses data from remote passive electric potential sensors to infer a human body electric potential, with a normalized root-mean-square error of 9.1 %. In a further, less constrained experiment, Platypus could identify 8 walking people with an average accuracy of 83.6 % using different days for training and testing. Depending on the number of users, Platypus's classification performance stabilizes after 3-6 training trajectories.

Some future work has already been described in the previous seciton. Other future work includes model refinements, most importantly the elimination of simplifications like stepping and movement component separation. We aim to analyse correlations between sensor signals that occur due to stepping, and are caused to a lesser extent by the movement component. This may lead to better localization and identification performance. Moreover, future model extensions include the localization and identification of multiple people, which would require distinguishing between multiple superposed signals. To avoid the installation of more sensors, we believe that our work towards identification can help separate the person-dependent signals.

We believe that remote passive sensing of electrical potential changes in the body is a promising technique that can be applied to other scenarios than we have so far addressed. Applications could include recognition of touch interactions with objects or other people in the environment, emergency situation recognition such as epileptic fits, as well as gait and gesture recognition.

Acknowledgements

We would like to thank Robert Prance and Daniel Roggen, University of Sussex, for initial explorations that inspired this work.

10. REFERENCES

[1] F. Adib, Z. Kabelac, D. Katabi, and R.C. Miller. 3D tracking via body radio reflections. In *Proceedings of the 11th USENIX Conference on Networked Systems Design and Implementation*, NSDI'14, pages 317–329, Berkeley, CA, USA, 2014. USENIX Association.

[2] H. Aly and M. Youssef. An analysis of device-free and device-based wifi-localization systems. *Int. J. Ambient Comput. Intell.*, 6(1):1–19, 2014.

[3] A.D. Aronoff, W.H. Boghosian, and H.A. Jenkinson. Electrostatic means for intrusion detection and ranging. Technical report, DTIC Document, 1965.

[4] A. Aydin, P.B. Stiffell, R.J. Prance, and H. Prance. A high sensitivity calibrated electric field meter based on the electric potential sensor. *Meas. Sci. Technol.*, 21, 2010.

[5] S.T. Beardsmore-Rust. *Remote applications of electric potential sensors in electrically unshielded environments.* PhD thesis, University of Sussex, 2010.

[6] C. BenAbdelkader, R. Cutler, and L. Davis. Person identification using automatic height and stride estimation. In *Pattern Recognition, 2002. Proceedings. 16th International Conference on*, volume 4, pages 377–380 vol.4, 2002.

[7] M.S. Brandstein and H.F. Silverman. A practical methodology for speech source localization with microphone arrays. *Computer Speech and Language*, 11(2):91–126, 1997.

[8] A. Bränzel, C. Holz, D. Hoffmann, D. Schmidt, M. Knaust, P. Lühne, R. Meusel, S. Richter, and P. Baudisch. Gravityspace: Tracking users and their poses in a smart room using a pressure-sensing floor. In *Proceedings of the SIGCHI Conference on Human Factors in Computing Systems*, CHI '13, pages 725–734, New York, NY, USA, 2013. ACM.

[9] A. Braun, H. Heggen, and R. Wichert. Capfloor - a flexible capacitive indoor localization system. In S. Chessa and S. Knauth, editors, *Evaluating AAL Systems Through Competitive Benchmarking. Indoor Localization and Tracking*, volume 309 of *Communications in Computer and Information Science*, pages 26–35. Springer Berlin Heidelberg, 2012.

[10] G.S.P. Castle. Contact charging between insulators. *Journal of Electrostatics*, 40/41:13–20, 1997.

[11] J. Chang, A.J. Kelly, and J.M. Crowley. *Handbook of Electrostatic Processes.* Marcel Dekker, Inc., 1995.

[12] K. Chintalapudi, A. Padmanabha Iyer, and V.N. Padmanabhan. Indoor localization without the pain. In *Proceedings of the Sixteenth Annual International Conference on Mobile Computing and Networking*, MobiCom '10, pages 173–184, New York, NY, USA, 2010. ACM.

[13] A.J. Clippingdale. *The sensing of spatial electrical potential.* PhD thesis, University of Sussex, 1993.

[14] G. Cohn, S. Gupta, T. Lee, D. Morris, J.R. Smith, M.S. Reynolds, D.S. Tan, and S.N. Patel. An ultra-low-power human body motion sensor using static electric field sensing. In *Proceedings of the 2012 ACM Conference on Ubiquitous Computing*, UbiComp '12, pages 99–102, New York, NY, USA, 2012. ACM.

[15] Gabe Cohn, Daniel Morris, Shwetak Patel, and Desney Tan. Humantenna: using the body as an antenna for real-time whole-body interaction. In *CHI '12*, pages 1901–1910, 2012.

[16] N. U. Czech-Damal, G. Dehnhardt, P. Manger, and W. Hanke. Passive electroreception in aquatic mammals. *Journal of Comparative Physiology A*, 199(6):555–563, 2013.

[17] T. Ficker. Electrification of human body by walking. *Journal of Electrostatics*, 64:10–16, 2006.

[18] S. Gabriel, R.W. Lau, and C. Gabriel. The dielectric properties of biological tissues: II. Measurements in the frequency range 10 Hz to 20 GHz. *Physics in Medicine and Biology*, 41(11):2251–2269, 1996.

[19] W. Gebrial, R. J. Prance, C.J. Harland, and T.D. Clark. Noninvasive imaging using an array of electric potential sensors. *Review of Scientific Instruments*, 77(6), 2006.

[20] T. Grosse-Puppendahl, Y. Berghoefer, A Braun, R. Wimmer, and A Kuijper. Opencapsense: A rapid prototyping toolkit for pervasive interaction using capacitive sensing. In *Pervasive Computing and Communications (PerCom), 2013 IEEE International Conference on*, pages 152–159, March 2013.

[21] T. Grosse-Puppendahl, A. Braun, F. Kamieth, and A. Kuijper. Swiss-Cheese Extended: An Object Recognition Method for Ubiquitous Interfaces based on Capacitive Proximity Sensing. In *CHI '13*, pages 1401–1410, 2013.

[22] Y. Guo and M. Hazas. Localising speech, footsteps and other sounds using resource-constrained devices. In *10th International Conference on Information Processing in Sensor Networks (IPSN)*, pages 330–341, 2011.

[23] Marian Haescher, Denys J. C. Matthies, Gerald Bieber, and Bodo Urban. Capwalk: A capacitive recognition of walking-based activities as a wearable assistive technology. In *Proceedings of the 8th ACM International Conference on PErvasive Technologies Related to Assistive Environments*, PETRA '15, pages 35:1–35:8, New York, NY, USA, 2015. ACM.

[24] M. Hall, E. Frank, G. Holmes, B. Pfahringer, P. Reutemann, and I.H. Witten. The weka data mining software: An update. *SIGKDD Explorations*, 11(1), 2009.

[25] C.J. Harland, T.D. Clark, and R.J. Prance. Electric potential probes - new directions in the remote sensing of the human body. *Measurement Science and Technology*, 13(2):163–169, 2002.

[26] D. Hauschildt and N. Kirchhof. Advances in thermal infrared localization: Challenges and solutions. In *2010 International Conference on Indoor Positioning and Indoor Navigation*, pages 1–8, 2010.

[27] K. Hidaka. Electric field and voltage measurement by using electro-optic sensor. In *Eleventh International Symposium on High Voltage Engineering*, volume 2, pages 1–14, 1999.

[28] T.W. Hnat, E. Griffiths, R. Dawson, and K. Whitehouse. Doorjamb: Unobtrusive room-level tracking of people in homes using doorway sensors. In *Proceedings of the 10th ACM Conference on Embedded Network Sensor Systems*, SenSys '12, pages 309–322, New York, NY, USA, 2012. ACM.

[29] P.M. Ireland. The role of changing contact in sliding triboelectrification. *Journal of Physics D: Applied Physics*, 41(2), 2008.

[30] C.D. Kidd, R. Orr, G.D. Abowd, C.G. Atkeson, I.A. Essa, B. MacIntyre, E. Mynatt, T.E. Starner, and W. Newstetter. The aware home: A living laboratory for ubiquitous computing research. In *Cooperative Buildings. Integrating Information, Organizations, and Architecture*, volume 1670 of *Lecture Notes in Computer Science*, pages 191–198. Springer Berlin Heidelberg, 1999.

[31] F. Kirchbuchner, T. Grosse-Puppendahl, M.R. Hastall, M. Distler, and A. Kuijper. Ambient intelligence from senior citizens' perspectives: Understanding privacy concerns, technology acceptance, and expectations. In *Ambient Intelligence*, volume 9425 of *Lecture Notes in Computer Science*, pages 48–59. Springer International Publishing, 2015.

[32] T. Kivimäki, T. Vuorela, P. Peltola, and J. Vanhala. A review on device-free passive indoor positioning methods. *International Journal of Smart Home*, 8(1):71–91, 2014.

[33] K. Kurita, R. Takizawa, and H. Kumon. Detection of human walking motion based on measurement system of current generated by electrostatic induction. In *ICCAS-SICE, 2009*, pages 5485–5488, 2009.

[34] G. Laput, C. Yang, R. Xiao, A. Sample, and C. Harrison. Em-sense: Touch recognition of uninstrumented, electrical and electromechanical objects. In *Proceedings of the 28th Annual ACM Symposium on User Interface Software & Technology*, UIST '15, pages 157–166, New York, NY, USA, 2015. ACM.

[35] H. Liu, H. Darabi, P. Banerjee, and J. Liu. Survey of wireless indoor positioning techniques and systems. *IEEE Transactions on Systems, Man, and Cybernetics, Part C: Applications and Reviews*, 37(6):1067–1080, 2007.

[36] J. Liu, Y. Wang, Y. Chen, J. Yang, X. Chen, and J. Cheng. Tracking vital signs during sleep leveraging off-the-shelf wifi. In *Proceedings of the 16th ACM International Symposium on Mobile Ad Hoc Networking and Computing*, pages 267–276. ACM, 2015.

[37] P. Llovera, P. Molinié, A. Soria, and A. Quijano. Measurements of electrostatic potentials and electric fields in some industrial applications: Basic principles. *Journal of Electrostatics*, 67(2/3):457–461, 2009.

[38] J. Lowell and A.C. Rose-Innes. Contact electrification. *Advances in Physics*, 29(6):947–1023, 1980.

[39] R. Mautz. Indoor positioning technologies. ETH Zurich, 2012. Habilitation thesis.

[40] Microsoft. Kinect for Windows features. http://www.microsoft.com/en-us/kinectforwindows/meetkinect/features.aspx (date accessed 2015-08-24).

[41] G. Monaci and A. Pandharipande. Indoor user zoning and tracking in passive infrared sensing systems. In *Proceedings of the 20th European Signal Processing Conference (EUSIPCO)*, pages 1089–1093, 2012.

[42] S. Narayana, R.V. Prasad, V.S. Rao, T.V. Prabhakar, S.S. Kowshik, and M.S. Iyer. PIR sensors: Characterization and novel localization technique. In *Proceedings of the 14th International Conference on Information Processing in Sensor Networks*, IPSN '15, pages 142–153, 2015.

[43] A. Pachi and T. Ji. Frequency and velocity of people walking. *The Structural Engineer*, 83(3):36–40, 2005.

[44] Plessey Semiconductors. EPIC sensor. http://www.plesseysemiconductors.com/epic-plessey-semiconductors.php (date accessed 2015-12-09).

[45] H. Prance, P. Watson, R.J. Prance, and S.T. Beardsmore-Rust. Position and movement sensing at metre standoff distances using ambient electric field. *Meas. Sci. Technol.*, 23, 2012.

[46] R. Prance and C. Harland. Electric potential sensor, July 2 2009. US Patent App. 12/374,359.

[47] Q. Pu, S. Gupta, S. Gollakota, and S. Patel. Whole-home gesture recognition using wireless signals. In *Proceedings of the 19th Annual International Conference on Mobile Computing & Networking*, MobiCom '13, pages 27–38, New York, NY, USA, 2013. ACM.

[48] T.S. Ralston, G.L. Charvat, and J.E. Peabody. Real-time through-wall imaging using an ultrawideband multiple-input multiple-output (mimo) phased array radar system. In *Phased Array Systems and Technology (ARRAY), 2010 IEEE International Symposium on*, pages 551–558, Oct 2010.

[49] J. Rekimoto and H. Wang. Sensing gamepad: Electrostatic potential sensing for enhancing entertainment oriented interactions. In *Extended Abstracts on Human Factors in Computing Systems*, pages 1457–1460, 2004.

[50] C.A. Rezende, R.F. Gouveia, M.A. da Silva, and F. Galembeck. Detection of charge distributions in insulator surfaces. *Journal of Physics: Condensed Matter*, 21(26), 2009.

[51] H. Rimminen. *Detection of human movement by near field imaging: development of a novel method and applications*. PhD thesis, Aalto University, School of Science and Technology, 2011.

[52] M. Shankar, J.B. Burchett, Q. Hao, B.D. Guenther, and D.J. Brady. Human-tracking systems using pyroelectric infrared detectors. *Optical Engineering*, 45(10):106401–106401, 2006.

[53] J.R. Smith. *Electric Field Imaging*. PhD thesis, Massachusetts Institute of Technology, 1999.

[54] R. Srinivasan, C. Chen, and D.J. Cook. Activity recognition using actigraph sensor. In *Proceedings of the Fourth Int. Workshop on Knowledge Discovery form Sensor Data (ACM SensorKDD'10), Washington, DC, July*, pages 25–28, 2010.

[55] Statistisches Bundesamt. Mikrozensus - Fragen zur Gesundheit - Körpermaße der Bevölkerung 2013 (in German), 2014.

[56] T. Teixeira, G. Dublon, and A. Savvides. A survey of human-sensing: Methods for detecting presence, count, location, track, and identity. Technical report, ENALAB, 2010.

[57] M. Valtonen, T. Vuorela, L. Kaila, and J. Vanhala. Capacitive indoor positioning and contact sensing for

activity recognition in smart homes. *J. Ambient Intell. Smart Environ.*, 4(4):305–334, 2012.

[58] G. Wang, Y. Zou, and K.and Ni L.M. Zhou, Z.and Wu. We can hear you with wi-fi! In *Proceedings of the 20th Annual International Conference on Mobile Computing and Networking*, MobiCom '14, pages 593–604, New York, NY, USA, 2014. ACM.

[59] Q. Wang. Dynamic time warping (dtw), 2014. http://mathworks.com/matlabcentral/fileexchange/43156 (date accessed: 2015/11/15).

[60] A. Williams, D. Ganesan, and A. Hanson. Aging in place: Fall detection and localization in a distributed smart camera network. In *Proceedings of the 15th ACM International Conference on Multimedia*, MM '07, pages 892–901, New York, NY, USA, 2007. ACM.

[61] J. Wilson and N. Patwari. See-through walls: Motion tracking using variance-based radio tomography networks. *Mobile Computing, IEEE Transactions on*, 10(5):612–621, May 2011.

[62] K. Woolford. Defining accuracy in the use of kinect v2 for exercise monitoring. In *Proceedings of the 2nd International Workshop on Movement and Computing*, pages 112–119. ACM, 2015.

[63] P. Wu and F. Li. The pyroelectric sensor based system: Human tracking and self-calibration scheme. In *2012 International Conference on Information Science and Technology (ICIST)*, pages 839–846, 2012.

[64] C. You, H. Kao, B. Ho, N. Chen, Y. Hsieh, P. Huang, and H. Chu. Thermalprobe: Exploring the use of thermal identification for per-user energy metering. In *Internet of Things (iThings), 2014 IEEE International Conference on*, pages 554–561, Sept 2014.

[65] X. Zhou, Q. Hao, and H. Fei. 1-bit walker recognition with distributed binary pyroelectric sensors. In *2010 IEEE Conference on Multisensor Fusion and Integration for Intelligent Systems (MFI)*, pages 168–173, 2010.

The Design and Implementation of a Mobile RFID Tag Sorting Robot

Longfei Shangguan[†] and Kyle Jamieson[†,‡]
[†]Princeton University, [‡]University College London
{longfeis, kylej}@cs.princeton.edu

ABSTRACT

Libraries, manufacturing lines, and offices of the future all stand to benefit from knowing the exact spatial order of RFID-tagged books, components, and folders, respectively. To this end, radio-based localization has demonstrated the potential for high accuracy. Key enabling ideas include motion-based synthetic aperture radar, multipath detection, and the use of different frequencies (channels). But indoors in real-world situations, current systems often fall short of the mark, mainly because of the prevalence and strength of "multipath" reflections of the radio signal off nearby objects. In this paper we describe the design and implementation of MobiTagbot, an autonomous wheeled robot reader that conducts a roving survey of the above such areas to achieve an exact spatial order of RFID-tagged objects in very close (1–6 cm) spacings. Our approach leverages a serendipitous correlation between the changes in multipath reflections that occur with motion and the effect of changing the carrier frequency (channel) of the RFID query. By carefully observing the relationship between channel and phase, MobiTagbot detects if multipath is likely prevalent at a given robot reader location. If so, MobiTagbot excludes phase readings from that reader location, and generates a final location estimate using phase readings from other locations as the robot reader moves in space. Experimentally, we demonstrate that cutting-edge localization algorithms including Tagoram are not accurate enough to exactly order items in very close proximity, but MobiTagbot is, achieving nearly 100% ordering accuracy for items at low (3–6 cm) spacings and 86% accuracy for items at very low (1–3 cm) spacings.

Keywords

Order tracking; RFID; Localization; Multipath propagation

1. INTRODUCTION

Radio-based positioning of objects equipped with RFID tags is poised to play a key role in the Internet of Things for libraries, retail business, and next-generation manufacturing:

1. A library patron is frustrated in her search for a misshelved book in her local library. The library has RFID-tagged its stock of books for inventory control and loan tracking and placed RFID readers at the circulation desk, but not in the stacks. Could a RFID-based autonomous robot help locate the misshelved book, or continuously roam the library looking for misshelved books, alerting shelving clerks to the location of any that are found?
2. Supermarkets need to rotate stock as new stock arrives in order to maintain freshness for the consumer. This is highly labor-intensive, requiring the worker to visually inspect the sell-by date of each piece of stock, manually rotate the stock, and then visually check for any old stock out of place. Could an RFID-based autonomous robot roam the supermarket, scan the shelves for stock that needs rotating, and generate a report for the worker to action, saving worker time and reducing labor costs?
3. Manufacturing lines and supply chains already rely on passive RFID tags to track inventory as it moves through the manufacturing and supply chains to the consumer, benefiting from its non-line-of-sight functionality. This allows manufacturers to determine which parts recently passed by an RFID reader, but manufacturers must fall back on other mechanisms such as optical barcodes or physical separation to physically order parts in an assembly line, even if RFID tagged. Could the same technology used above in the autonomous robot be leveraged for a stationary RFID reader to order parts moving by on the assembly line, without the need for physical separation or optical barcode scanning?

Inspired by these and other applications of precision tracking and location for the Internet of Things, recent research efforts have leveraged many different techniques to improve the accuracy of RFID tag localization. To date, the fundamental challenge for the accuracy of indoor localization has been multipath reflections from

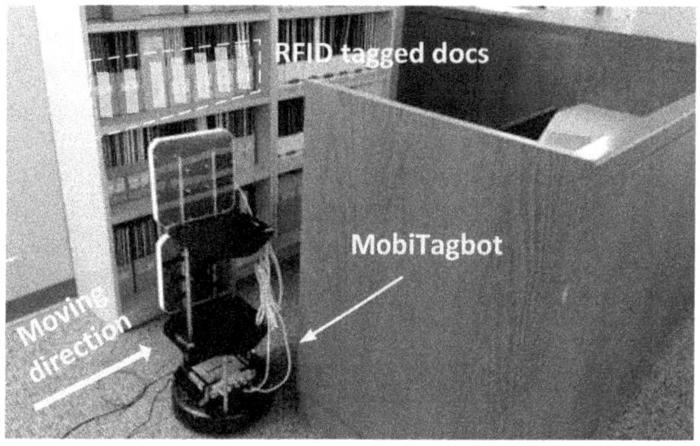

Figure 1— MobiTagbot roams a building floor, using its RFID antennas to scan objects such as these file folders on a bookshelf, checking that their spatial order is correct.

MobiSys'16 June 25–30, 2016, Singapore, Singapore

ACM ISBN 978-1-4503-4269-8/16/06.
DOI: http://dx.doi.org/10.1145/2906388.2906417

nearby objects: these reflections are especially strong and prevalent indoors. Pinit [34] addresses the multipath problem by deploying 200 manually-placed "reference tags," at *a priori*-known locations, to locate an RFID-tagged book in a $6 \times 5 \times 2.2$ m^3 space. RF-IDraw [35] uses grating lobes to very accurately trace the trajectory of an RFID tag over small distances (tens of centimeters) at short range (2–5 meters), skirting the problem of multipath. Tagoram [41] uses synthetic aperture radar techniques for a similar result, suffering in the presence of multipath reflections. Older approaches, such as LibBot [11], rely on a "radio map" as first proposed by the classical RADAR [8] system, with the associated difficulties of radio map construction and maintenance.

From the motivating applications mentioned above, we observe and articulate a subtly-new problem: to precisely ascertain the spatial order of closely-spaced RFID tags spread out over a large area (*e.g.*, an entire library floor filled with book stacks), rather than locate them in absolute space with precision, or trace their fine-grained motion. This motivates an approach where an autonomous robot, whose location is only imprecisely known (down to decimeters of precision), scans an area of interest with a mobile RFID reader.

In this paper we present the design and implementation of MobiTagbot, a robot-based RFID ordering system that roams a large area (*i.e.* an entire building floor), ascertaining the spatial order of nearby RFID-tagged objects such as the file folders shown in Figure 1 without the need for a tediously-constructed radio map. Like prior systems such as Tagoram [41], our robot moves its RFID reader over small distances in a straight lines, taking readings every few centimeters and forming a *synthetic aperture* radar system, essentially mimicking a radar system with multiple antennas separated by the distance between each reading. Through Wi-Fi, MobiTagbot maintains contact with a backend server cataloguing the expected order of RFID tags. When MobiTagbot detects a misordered pair of tags, it flags the location of the tags and their identities to the backend server, which alerts the user.

MobiTagbot's contributions are inter-related. First, we observe a problem endemic to phased array processing: the appearance of sidelobes in the generated *holograms* (location likelihood heatmaps) when a single frequency is used. Sidelobes appear because of ambiguities in the response of the antenna array to a tag at a certain distance. To address this problem, we leverage multiple carrier frequencies (§4.1) and combine them into a single hologram. In the absence or near-absence of strong multipath reflections, the differing wavelengths resulting from the use of multiple carrier frequencies reinforce at the true tag location and cancel the sidelobes as shown in Figure 5.

Next, we observe that Tagoram and similar systems run into practical problems indoors where multipath reflections are prevalent and strong: in these situations, their accuracy suffers. To mitigate this problem, MobiTagbot introduces a multipath suppression technique made possible by its use of multiple frequencies. At each location in the synthetic aperture, MobiTagbot sweeps through frequencies, measuring the RFID tag's phase response as it moves. This forms the basis of a technique described in §4.2 that tests for the presence of multipath reflections. If it detects the presence of multipath in a particular location, MobiTagbot eliminates that location from the synthetic aperture forming a location estimate of the tag using the remaining locations. Together these two techniques significantly improves tag localization: qualitative results are shown in Figure 2.

As a third, systems-building contribution, we implement MobiTagbot using a combination of off-the-shelf hardware: an ImpinJ RFID reader equipped with a UHF-band directional antenna sitting atop an iRobot Create 2 robot. Backend custom software written in Java collects phase readings from the RFID reader, location displacement estimates from the iRobot, and processes the data to yield our experimental results. Further details are available in §5.

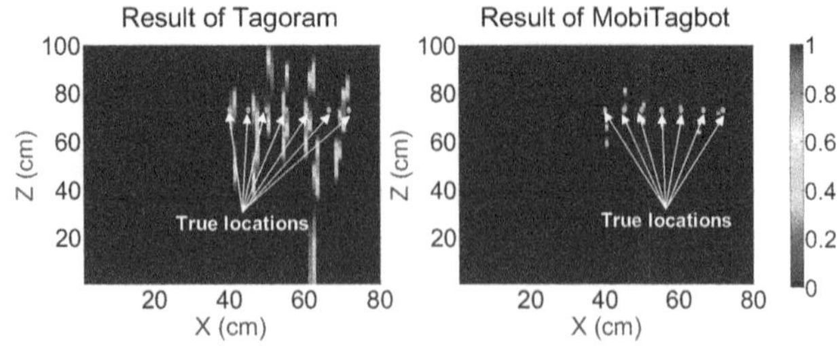

Figure 2— Qualitative comparison of holograms generated by Tagoram (*left*) and MobiTagbot (*right*).

Our experimental evaluation (§6) comprehensively measures MobiTagbot's end-to-end performance at ordering RFID tags in two different locations of a real-world office environment: one with significant nearby clutter, resulting in a multipath propagation environment (§6.2), and the other with less nearby clutter, resulting in less multipath (§6.3). Further experiments drill down into these results, measuring basic localization accuracy, the effect of varying the reader-to-tag distance and the tag read rate, and the effect of distance between MobiTagbot and the RFID tags. Microbenchmarks (§6.4) then further explain our performance improvements, measuring the effect of varying the number of frequencies at which MobiTagbot interrogates the RFID tags, the distance MobiTagbot moves, and the spacing between RFID tags. Results show that in multipath-prevalent environments, MobiTagbot achieves nearly 100% ordering accuracy for items at low (3–6 cm) spacings and 86% accuracy for items at very low (1–3 cm) spacings. Performance degrades only slightly up to 1.2 meters away from the tags. Our multipath suppression algorithm is responsible for much of the performance improvements over prior work, almost halving the uncertainty in simple localization.

We next (§2) present the related work and a holography primer (§3) to provide a context for our design (§4). Our implementation (§5) and experimental evaluation follow (§6). We discuss future work in §7, and conclude in §8.

2. RELATED WORK

MobiTagbot draws on prior works in multiple areas, chiefly indoor localization, robot navigation, and Simultaneous Localization and Mapping (SLAM).

2.1 RSSI-based localization

The received Signal Strength Indicator (RSSI) is an indication of the power level received by the radio receiver. Many RSSI-based localization techniques have been proposed during the past, which generally fall into two categories.

RF Fingerprinting. This idea, pioneered by Radar [8], employs RSSI based fingerprinting matching against a database to determine the location of interest indoors. Horus [44] introduces a probabilistic fingerprint matching scheme and achieves a much higher localization accuracy. LANDMARC [22] introduces this technique to RFID localization. SurroundSense [7] further extends this idea by introducing a multi-source (*e.g.*, ambient sound, light, color, *etc.*) based fingerprinting matching scheme for human localization.

Later on several other improvements over RSSI fingerprinting have been proposed, such as incorporating inertial sensor hints [24, 33], embracing fine-grained channel state information [26, 36], and extending to outdoor scenarios [21]. But RF fingerprinting based techniques suffer from ambient dynamics, hence failing to provide fine-grained location estimates.

Modeling instead of fingerprinting. An alternative to fingerprinting based method is to use RF propagation model to estimate the distance from the transmitter to multiple receivers, and estimating the target's location. In [18], the authors develop a zero-configuration localization system, where a Line-of-sight (LOS) path is assumed and a signal propagation model is used for ranging. More recent work makes an effort to use modeling with minimal assumptions. EZ [9] requires site surveys at only a few user locations. Whitehouse *et al.* [37] extend the RF propagation model to node localization in wireless sensor networks and achieve a localization error of 4.1 m in a 48-node network. But RF signal modeling based techniques suffer from prevalent multipath indoors due to the superposition of signals that propagate along all paths, making highly accurate localization difficult.

2.2 Phase-based localization

Phase reflects the distance that a wireless signal traverses in the physical world. There is a growing interest in using phase measurement for localization:

Distance ranging. The first category of works maps the distance between transmitter and receiver based on the received phase measurements. Liu *et al.* [19] introduces an RFID localization scheme by using multiple antennas to acquire phase measurements from tags. The hyperbolic positioning method is then employed to correlate the phase reading and the tag location. Li *et al.* [17] propose a multi-frequency based ranging method for passive RFID tag localization. Similarly, Zhou *et al.* [45] design a hybrid ranging system by leveraging dual-frequency continuous-wave (DFCW) and continuous-wave (CW) for passive RFID localization. It achieves cm-level localization accuracy using dedicated 5.8 GHz RFID tag. Using phase measurement for distance ranging, theoretically, could achieve high localization accuracy. However, due to the multipath, the phase measurement of an incoming signal is not corresponding to the direct path, and hence will lead to high ranging error.

Holography imaging. Holography is used for capturing the tomography of an object by the vision community. Later on it is introduced to both the radar and acoustic community for target localization [12, 31, 43]. Miesen *et al.* [20] employ holography to locate a moving tag on a transponder. It achieves an overall accuracy of 7 cm. Parr *et al.* [23] exploit tag mobility and adopt Inverse Synthetic Apertures Radar (ISAR) to generate hologram for tag localization and tracking. Tagoram [41] improves the hologram-based localization accuracy to around one centimeter by considering the impact of RFID hardware thermal noise on phase readings. However, it fails to address the multipath issue, hence will likely experience practical problems indoors where multipath reflections are prevalent and strong. MobiTagbot is inspired by above works in phase-based tag localization, but advances them in two ways. First, we propose a more robust holography method by leveraging multiple channels and combining them into a single hologram. Second, we design a novel multipath suppression algorithm, which can detect and find those multipath-prevalent reader locations, and exclude phase readings from these locations for hologram generation.

Angle-of-Arrival (AoA). Wong *et al.* [38] present measurements at high SNR and use AoA and channel impulse response measurements for localization. ArrayTrack [39] adds a novel multipath suppression algorithm, the first system to achieve sub-meter accuracy in a multipath-rich environment. PinPoint [15] introduces a novel AoA estimation algorithm to localize interfering radios and simultaneously identify the type of interference indoors. SpotFi [16] provides accurate indoor localization services using COTS WiFi NICs with three antennas. It achieves a median accuracy of 40 cm in multipath rich environment. Similarly, WiDraw [30] implements an AoA-based hand gesture recognition system using COTS WiFi NICs. These schemes, however, only provide decimeter localization accuracy for human localization, hence failing to correctly ordering tags to high precision.

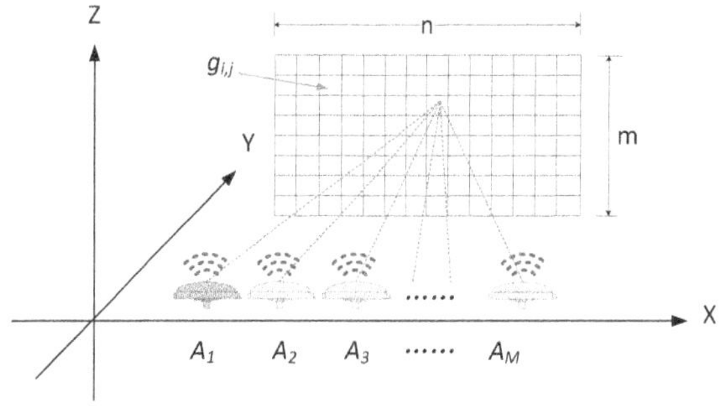

Figure 3— The geometry of synthetic-aperture array formed by the movement of MobiTagbot.

AoA information is also employed specifically for RFID localization. PinIt [34] uses a moving antenna to measure the multipath profile of the targeting tag, and compare this profile with reference tags for localization. The overall localization error of PinIt is above 10 cm, hence still not satisfying MobiTagbot's precise tracking and localization requirement. Rf-IDraw [35] uses grating lobes to very accurately trace the trajectory of an RFID tag over small distances (tens of centimeters) at short range, skirting the problem of multipath.

2.3 Simultaneous Localization and Mapping

Simultaneous Localization and Mapping (SLAM) jointly localizes a robot in an unknown environment, building a consistent map of the environment using sensors such as lidar and cameras [10, 14, 29]. With the proliferation of inertial sensors on smart phones, this problem is extended to human indoor localization. Walkie-Markie builds an indoor floorplan using multiple users' data [28]. WiFiSLAM [13] relates RSS fingerprints and human movement (*e.g.*, distance, direction) pattern by a Gaussian process latent variable model. When a small part of an indoor space is tagged with RSS measurements, WiFiSLAM performs a semi-supervised localization technique to estimate another user's location based on RSSI dissimilarity. LiFS [42] further extends SLAM to indoor radio map construction.

MobiTagbot differs from SLAM-related works in two aspects. First, MobiTagbot targets fine-grained object ordering by leveraging antenna mobility, whereas the above works focus on localizing the robot itself and drawing the indoor floorplan. Second, MobiTagbot's core technology is its multipath suppression algorithm, which allows it to achieve a localization accuracy of about 3 cm in a real indoor environment, whereas the above works significantly suffer in the presence of multipath indoors, achieving an overall localization accuracy of above one meter.

3. HOLOGRAPHY PRIMER

In this section, we review the basic mechanism of the *holography* technique [31, 32] in preparation for our discussion of MobiTagbot design in the next section.

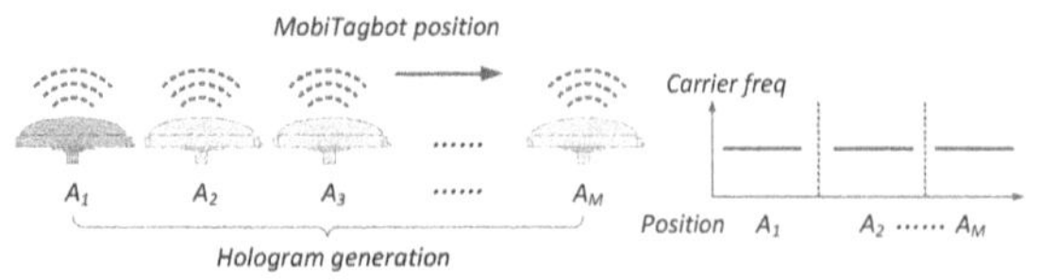

(a)— Traditional holography generation uses a large number of positions to interrogate tags on a single frequency.

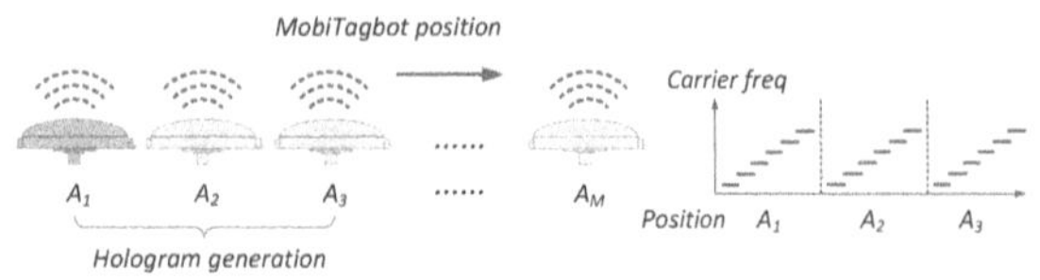

(b)— Multi-frequency based holography generation uses a smaller number of positions to interrogate tags on multiple frequencies.

Figure 4— Holography generation technique comparison.

The basic idea behind holography is to correlate an echo profile measured by multiple radar units with a reference echo profile generated at every possible location. The correlation reaches a maximum value if the target is actually located in the tested location. Conversely, the correlation will be low for a false assumption of the target position.

There are two steps involving in using holography for tag localization. The first step is to measure and store the backscattered signals at each possible location. The second step comprises hologram generation and tag localization. We derive the mathematical expression of the hologram by referring to the geometry shown in Figure 3. In this figure, a 2D image grid of points is used to characterize the possible location of a tag. The signal that bounces off grid location $g_{i,j}$ and then arrives at antenna location A_k can be written as:

$$s_r(A_k, g_{i,j}) = a_r(A_k, g_{i,j}) e^{j\theta_r(A_k, g_{i,j})} \tag{1}$$

where $a_r(A_k, g_{i,j})$ and $\theta_r(A_k, g_{i,j})$ are the amplitude and the phase of the backscatter signal, respectively. If the reader antenna moves to M known locations, we can compute M signals for grid location $g_{i,j}$. These M signals together comprise a *reference profile* for the grid location $g_{i,j}$ and are stored.

We use an *inverse correlation filter* to correlate two signals for hologram generation. Let $s_t(A_k)$ be the signal backscattered from the tag and received by the antenna A_k. The inverse correlation filter correlates $s_t(A_k)$ with the reference signal $s_r(A_k, g_{i,j})$ using the following formula:

$$C(s_t(A_k), s_r(A_k, g_{i,j})) = e^{j\theta_t(A_k)} \cdot e^{-j\theta_r(A_k, g_{i,j})} \tag{2}$$

In this equation,[1] $\theta_t(A_k)$ is the received phase reading by antenna A_k, which can be directly acquired from the COTS RFID reader. For each grid location, above correlation is then done for all M antennas and finally summed up. The pixel value $I(g_{i,j})$ of grid location $g_{i,j}$ in the hologram is then computed as follows:

$$I(g_{i,j}) = F \left| \sum_{k=1}^{M} C\left(s_t(A_k), s_r(A_k, g_{i,j})\right) \right| \tag{3}$$

[1]The amplitude of the signal $s_t(A_k)$ and $s_r(A_k, g_{i,j})$ is simply set to one, since the COTS RFID reader reports the amplitude as a superposition of radio signals off nearby objects, which fails to correctly reflect the amplitude changing of LOS path.

where F denotes an appropriate normalization factor. The interpretation of Equation 3 is straightforward. If the pixel position is the actual tag position and there is no multipath, the phase measurement of the received signals should equal to that of the reference signals and the resultant correlation coefficient (pixel value) is maximized. Conversely, if the tag is not located in grid $g_{i,j}$, the complex signals will be summed up with random phase, which causes destructive interference and, thus, results in a small value of $I(g_{i,j})$. To locate the tag, the hypothesis is tested for every grid on the hologram. In the absence of multipath (which we address in §4), the grid yielding highest $I(g_{i,j})$ should be the true location of the tag.

The advantage of holography lies in its probabilistic approach using signal correlation to compute the likelihood of each location to be the tag's true location. However, the granularity of the localization result is highly sensitive to the number of antennas used in hologram generation. The more signals captured at different antenna locations, the higher the accuracy of the hologram. Hence to capture the precise location of a tag, bulky antenna arrays would have to be used. This is due to the phase ambiguity problem: phase changes periodically from zero to 2π. As a result, a signal bouncing at two different grid locations may yield equivalent phase readings. To uniquely label each grid location with phase readings, it is thus necessary to collect readings from many spatially-separated antennas. Also, since holography is based on an assumption that multipath is weak, accuracy degrades significantly when multipath is prevalent.

4. DESIGN

In this section, we present the design of MobiTagbot's multi-frequency holography and multipath suppression techniques.

4.1 Multi-frequency based holography

In practice, it is difficult or even infeasible to deploy expensive antenna arrays for low-cost tag ordering. MobiTagbot moves, creating a number of spatially-separated *virtual antennas*, which potentially improves its localization accuracy. However, the challenge for a wheeled robot lies in knowing its precise antenna position as it moves. If these robot position estimations are inaccurate, adding up acquired signals will cause destructive interference at the true location, further degrading tag localization accuracy.

In order to minimize this adverse effect, we propose a multi-frequency based holography. The basic idea is to fully exploit the channel hopping capability of COTS RFID devices by changing the carrier frequency (channel) of the RFID query. Our new inverse correlation filter becomes:

$$I(g_{i,j}) = F' \left| \sum_{k=1}^{M} \sum_{l=1}^{N} C\left(s_t(A_k, f_l), s_r(A_k, f_l, g_{i,j})\right) \right| \tag{4}$$

where F' denotes an appropriate normalization factor. In this equation, N is the number of channels we use for RFID query; $s_t(A_k, f_l)$ represents the signal on l^{th} channel received by the antenna A_k. Figure 4 shows the basic principle of traditional holography and our multi-frequency based holography. Compared with traditional holography, the advantage of MobiTagbot's multi-frequency based holography is twofold. First, we reduce the large number of positions needed, hence minimizing the adverse effect of location uncertainty associated with a moving antenna. Second, we create many more virtual antennas via channel hopping, so the combined result of signals received from these virtual antennas reinforces at the true tag location and cancels the side lobes (shown qualitatively in Figure 5).

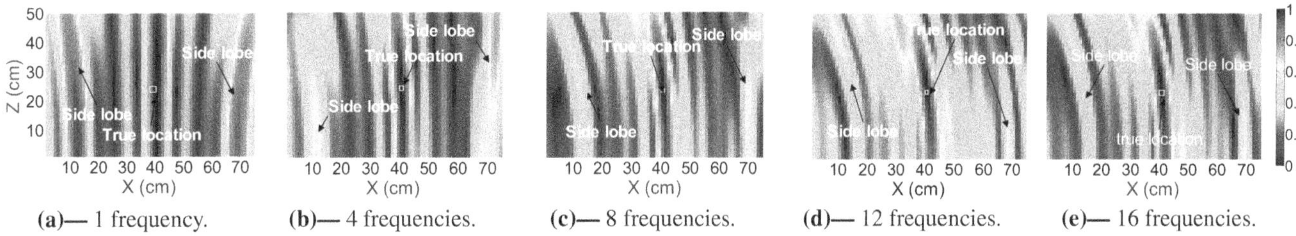

Figure 5— The hologram generated by using different numbers of carrier frequencies. The ground truth location of this tag is (25,40). Spurious side lobes are weakened when phase readings from multiple frequencies are incorporated into the hologram.

Figure 5 shows five pictures of holograms generated by using signals received on different numbers of carrier frequencies. As the figure shows, multiple side lobes appear in the hologram generated by the phase reading on a single carrier frequency, which renders the true location of the tag unclear. The likelihood of the tag being falsely located on these side lobes decreases significantly when using phase data from four, eight, and 12 frequencies. This is as expected since transmitting at a single location but over N different frequencies has a similar effect as transmitting a signal at N different locations but over a single frequency. The granularity improves as more channels are used. We also observe that the magnitude of the location accuracy improvement decreases as we further add channels.

4.2 Multipath suppression

A wireless signal returning from the tag emanates in all radial directions, reflecting off nearby walls, tables and other objects, leading to multipath propagation. The phase measurement reported by the RFID reader is the superposition of signals on all propagation paths, not necessarily just the direct path. Hence the localization accuracy achieved by holography will degrade significantly in prevalent multipath scenarios. While the multi-frequency based holography described above reduces moving antenna-induced distortion of phase measurements, it alone does not handle the adverse effect of multipath, hence multipath reflections are free to reduce system accuracy.

But the strength of multipath changes in space [25, 40], and so the basic idea of MobiTagbot's multipath suppression algorithm is to detect and find multipath-prevalent reader locations, excluding phase readings from these locations for hologram generation. This algorithm is based on the following observation—In a low-multipath reader location, the RFID reader's phase measurement corresponds to the signal that propagates along just the direct path. Hence the phase measurement change is constant when MobiTagbot changes the carrier frequency. In contrast, if the wireless signal suffers from severe multipath at a given reader location, the phase measurement should be the superposition of phase values corresponding to many propagation paths, and hence change irregularly (due to nonlinear superposition of phase values) when we change the carrier frequency.

We conduct a micro-benchmark to validate this observation. We program an RFID reader to hop over 16 carrier frequencies. The reader is placed one meter away from the tags. We conduct this micro-benchmark in both a low and prevalent multipath scenario (shown in Figure 8). We choose two tags and plot their phase series in Figure 6. In the low multipath scenario, for both these tags, the phase series stay around a stable value within each carrier frequency, and cha-nge linearly when hopping from one carrier frequency to another. In contrast, in prevalent multipath scenario, the phase series of these two tags change irregularly. Specifically, the phase value jumps abruptly due to human motion-induced dynamic

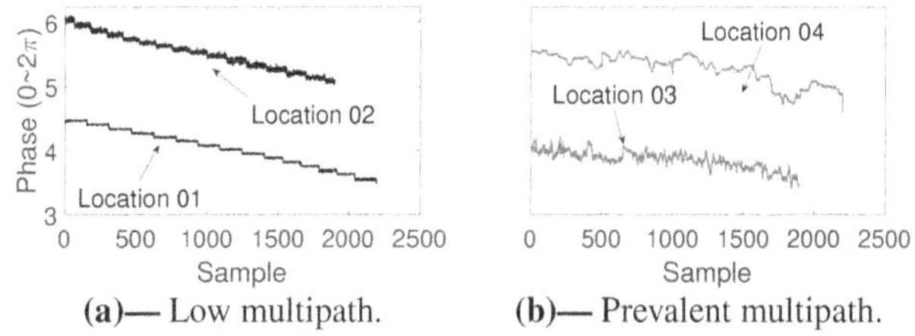

Figure 6— Comparison of phase profiles in low and prevalent multipath scenario.

multipath, and changes non-linearly during the channel hopping due to the superposition of phase from all paths.

Algorithm. Suppose MobiTagbot is programmed to hop over N channels. On each channel, the reader captures multiple phase measurements. Let $\bar{\theta}_l$ be the average phase measurement on l^{th} channel. The phase difference between two consecutive channels is: $\Delta\theta_l = \bar{\theta}_{l+1} - \bar{\theta}_l$ (there are $N-1$ phase difference values in total). We use entropy to measure the similarity of average phase differences across locations: we define $p_l = \frac{\Delta\theta_l}{\sum_{i=1}^{N-1}\Delta\theta_i}$, so we can write the entropy of $N-1$ phase differences at the kth reader location as:

$$e_k = -\frac{1}{\ln(N-1)} \cdot \sum_{l=1}^{N-1} p_l \lg p_l \tag{5}$$

In this equation, if all phase difference values are similar, e_k will be close to one. Otherwise, e_k will be close to zero. We further define the following weighting function and our new inverse correlation filter as follows:

$$\begin{aligned} w_k &= \frac{e_k}{M \quad \sum_{i=1}^{M} e_i} \\ I(g_{i,j}) &= F' \left| \sum_{k=1}^{M} w_k \sum_{l=1}^{N} C\left(s_t(A_k, f_l), s_r(A_k, f_l, g_{i,j})\right) \right| \end{aligned} \tag{6}$$

where M is the number of reader locations (motion-induced virtual antennas). The interpretation of this weighting function is straightforward: a higher entropy of phase differences at location k indicates a lower likelihood of prevalent multipath, and hence phase measurements reported at this location should have a higher weight for the final hologram generation. A lower entropy of phase differences at location k indicates a higher likelihood of prevalent multipath, hence phase measurements reported at this location should have a lower weight for final hologram generation.

Figure 7 shows the hologram generated without and with MobiTagbot's multipath suppression. The side lobes are weakened significantly when the multipath suppression algorithm is used. Also, the beam width of the main lobe is narrowed down to 3 cm after multipath suppression.

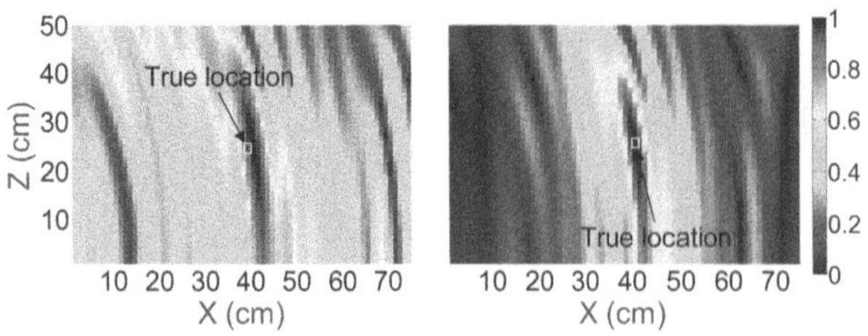

Figure 7— Hologram generated without (*left*) and with (*right*) multipath suppression.

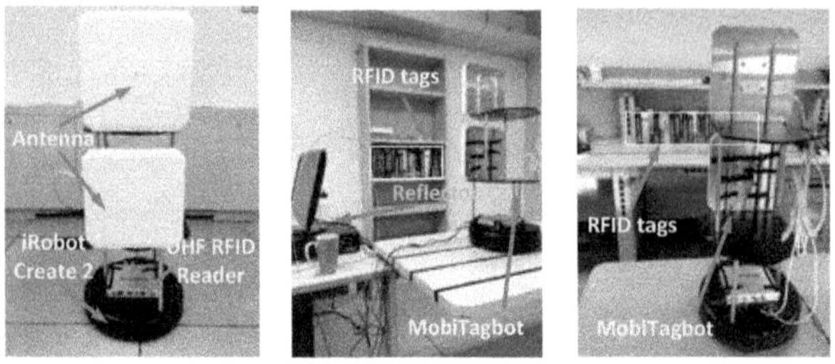

Figure 8— Experimental setups: MobiTagbot hardware (*left*); multipath-prevalent scenario (*center*); multipath-low scenario (*right*).

5. IMPLEMENTATION

So far we have provided the algorithmic basis of how MobiTagbot works. This section describes the specific implementation of MobiTagbot.

5.1 Frontend hardware

MobiTagbot's hardware consists of two parts: an RF communication module and a motion controller. All these hardware components are off-the-shelf devices.

An ImpinJ Speedway R420 RFID reader [2], two RFMAX S9028PCR directional antennas [5], and a set of Avery Dennison AD-227m5 UHF passive RFID tags [6] comprise the RF communication module. The R420 reader works at the UHF frequency band 920.625–924.375 MHz and is programed to hop over 16 channels. The S9028PCR antenna has a 9dBi gain, and 70° elevation and azimuth beam width.

The motion controller is based on an iRobot-Create 2 robot [3]. We hack it using the API provided by [1]. As Figure 8 shows, the robot serves as the chassis of MobiTagbot. The body of MobiTagbot is composed of lightweight support frames, which mount the RFID reader and antenna. In our experiment, we program MobiTagbot to move at the speed of 5 cm/s for tag ordering.

5.2 Backend Software

We now briefly discuss the back-end processing of MobiTagbot. The three main tasks of the back-end are to control the motion of MobiTagbot; manipulate the RFID reader to query tags; run the algorithms that are described in §4. The software of MobiTagbot is implemented in Java, and runs on a Lenovo ThinkCentre PC equipped with Intel(R) i5-4590 CPU and 4 GB RAM. It collects phase readings via the Low-level Reader Protocol (LLRP) [4].

Speed calibration. Figure 9 shows the CDF of the moving distance error when MobiTagbot moves on different kinds of floors. As the result indicates, error varies significantly when MobiTagbot moves on different kinds of floors, because the friction force of different material varies significantly. Hence the moving speed of MobiTagbot may deviate from its speed setting due to the change of floor

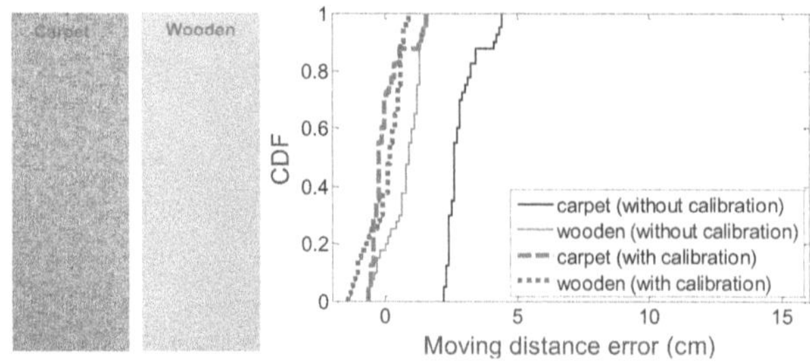

Figure 9— CDF of the moving distance error of MobiTagbot when it moves on two kinds of floors. The groundtruth distance is 100 cm.

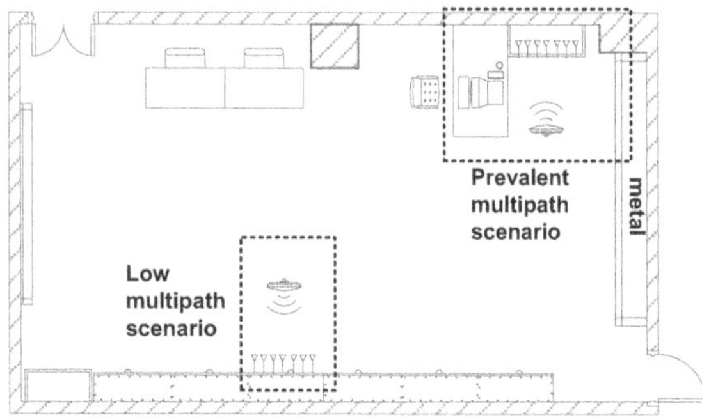

Figure 10— Floorplan of our experimental lab locations.

material. We also find that the span of each CDF is small, indicating a relatively stable distance error for each kind of floors. Based on this finding, we conduct a quick speed calibration before each experiment. Let v be the robot's speed set in program, and v' be the real speed of the robot. We have $v = v' + \Delta v$, where Δv is the speed drift caused by the friction force. Before the experiment, we let the robot move t s at the speed v. So the expected moving distance d is $t \cdot v$. We measure the robot's real moving distance (represent as d'), and compute the speed drift as: $\Delta v = \frac{d'-d}{t}$. The moving speed of MobiTagbot is finally calibrated by the equation $v - \frac{d'-d}{t}$.

6. EVALUATION

In this section, we first conduct field experiments to compare the ordering performance of MobiTagbot and other two state-of-the-arts. After that, we present micro-benchmark experiments to provide insights into MobiTagbot, particularly to explain which factors impact MobiTagbot's performance. Since the spacing between neighboring bookshelves is large, it can be more easily distinguished by prior efforts in time of arrival localization. Hence, in our experiments we focus on the more challenging part: ordering accuracy along one dimension where books closely stand by each other.

6.1 Experimental methodology

Unless the floor material is specified, experiments are conducted on wooden surface. We conduct field experiments to measure the end-to-end performance of MobiTagbot in two different locations of a real-world office environment. Figure 10 shows the floorplan of these two locations. In the first location, multiple objects are placed around RFID tagged objects, in order to generate a multipath-prevalent environment. In the second location, we move the RFID tagged objects to a relatively open space where only walls and tables generate a low amount of multipath. Figure 8 gives a snapshot of these two scenarios. In each scenario, we attach 20 passive RFID tags on the books' spines. The CDF of the spacing between adjacent tags is shown in Figure 11.

Table 1— Review of state-of-the-art RFID localization schemes.

Localization scheme	Antennas required	Method	Hardware	Applicability
PinIt [SIGICOMM'13]	One moving antenna	Proximity-based	SDR	Prevalent multipath
RF-compass [MobiCom'13]	One moving antenna	Geometry-based	SDR	Low multipath
RF-IDraw [SIGICOMM'14]	Eight antennas	Ranging-based	COTS RFID	Low multipath
Tagoram [MobiCom'14]	Four antennas	Hologram-based	COTS RFID	Low multipath
STPP [NSDI'15]	One moving antenna	Proximity-based	COTS RFID	Low multipath
MobiTagbot (our proposal)	Two moving antennas	Hologram-based	COTS RFID	Prevalent/low multipath

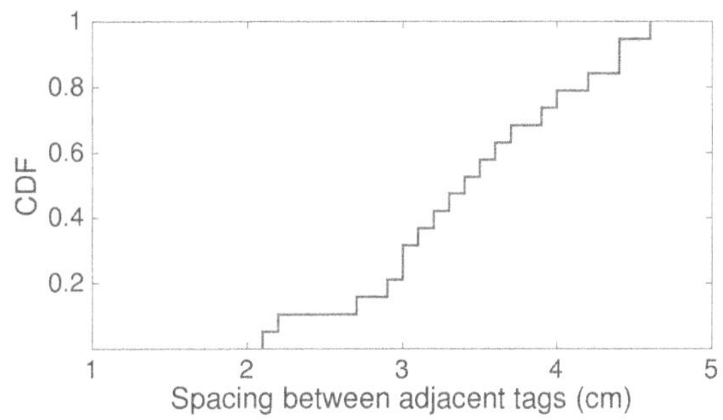

Figure 11— CDF of the distance between two adjacent tags attached on books in our experiment.

Table 2— Fraction of correct book order identification in a multipath-prevalent environment.

System	Group 1	Group 2	Group 3	Group 4
STPP	46%	52%	38%	40%
Tagoram	74	66	74	72
MobiTagbot	86	84	86	88

Metrics. In the evaluation of MobiTagbot, we mainly focus on the following two metrics: *ordering accuracy*, and *localization error*. The ordering accuracy is defined as the number of tags ordered correctly out of total tag number. The localization error is computed as the distance between the estimated location and the true location of this tag. In each experimental scenario, we first show how MobiTagbot performs tag ordering, and then we drill down into these results, measuring basic localization accuracy, the effect of varying the reader-to-tag distance and the tag read rate.

Comparisons. There are many notable research proposals in RFID based indoor localization. Table 1 summarizes the key features of several latest cutting-edge works. We highlight MobiTagbot in the last row of this table. As the table shows, PinIt and RF-Compass both rely on software defined radio for tag localization, while RF-IDraw, Tagoram, STPP and MobiTagbot are built upon COTS RFID devices. RF-IDraw is designed for tracking human finger movement in a fine-grained manner. It achieves cm-level accuracy based on eight spatially-separated antennas. Similarly, Tagoram achieves very high tracking accuracy by using multiple antennas and synthetic aperture radar techniques. STPP adopts a moving antenna to directly capture the tag order in 2D space, with an error margin of 8 cm. These three schemes, however, all require the antenna to communicate with tags over a short distance, so that the reported phase readings correspond to the signals propagate along the direct path.

We implement Tagoram [41] (DAH algorithm) and STPP [27], two state-of-the-art works that use the same hardware as MobiTagbot, for comparison. Tagoram employs multiple pre-calibrated antennas to generate a hologram for real-time tag tracking. It minimizes the impact of thermal noise on received phase readings and relaxes the computational overhead for hologram generation. STPP employs a moving antenna to generate a phase profile for each tag, exploring the spatial-temporal correlation of phase profiles to directly estimate the tag order.

Table 3— Fraction of correct book order identification (plus or minus one book) in a multipath-prevalent environment.

System	Group 1	Group 2	Group 3	Group 4
STPP	50%	56%	42%	44%
Tagoram	88	90	92	90
MobiTagbot	100	98	100	100

6.2 Field experiment: Prevalent multipath

This section presents results from the "multipath-prevalent" scenario in Figure 8.

6.2.1 Overall ordering accuracy

We first look at how each algorithm performs in book ordering. We put the reader antenna one meter away from the bookshelf and conduct four groups of experiments to measure the variance across experimental trials. In each group, we repeat the experiment five times and get 100 orders of books in total. The success rates are shown in Table 2. As we can see, MobiTagbot identified the right order of books with a minimum success rate of 84%. In contrast, STPP and Tagoram achieve a success rate of at most 52% and 74%, respectively. This clearly demonstrates that MobiTagbot achieves significantly higher ordering accuracy than these schemes.

We then look at how each algorithm works in ordering the books with an imprecision of up to one book. As Table 3 shows, there is no significant ordering accuracy improvement in STPP. Tagoram's performance increases a slightly from 72% on average to 90% on average, while MobiTagbot achieves almost 100% accuracy for all the four test groups.

6.2.2 Overall localization accuracy

To better understand why MobiTagbot outperforms other two algorithms in book ordering, we then analyze the localization accuracy of these three algorithms. Figure 12 shows the Cumulative Distributed Function (CDF) of the error distances in MobiTagbot, Tagoram and STPP. STPP achieves a median error distance of 8.6 cm and a 90th percentile of 11.2 cm. The maximum error margin of STPP reaches 14.2 cm. This large error margin comes from both thermal noise and severe multipath effect indoors. Tagoram outperforms STPP. It achieves a median error margin of 5.6 cm and a 90th percentile of 6.8 cm in a severe multipath environment. The maximum error distance is 7.6 cm. Tagoram achieves higher accuracy than STPP since it is based on a more robust localization scheme and it carefully handles the thermal noises introduced by both the reader antenna and the tag's hardware. However, due to

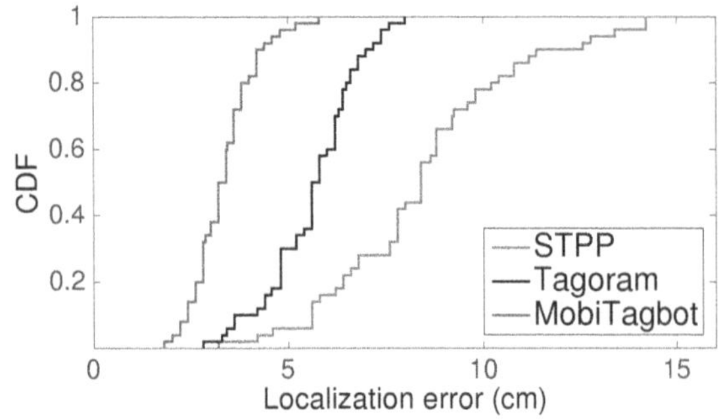

Figure 12— CDF of localization error margin achieved by three algorithms in a multipath-prevalent environment.

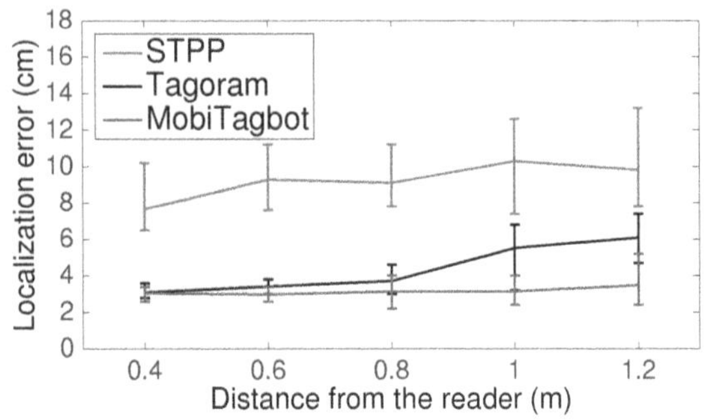

Figure 13— Impact of the distance from the reader. The error bar specifies the maximum, minimum and average localization error under different distance settings.

the following reason, it fails to achieve comparable accuracy as the previous result reported in [41]. Reflectors such as tables and books in the experimental environment create a complex multipath environment, undermining the correlation between location and phase readings. Tagoram did not explicitly handle the phase drifts introduced by the multipath effect. Hence it runs into practical problems indoors where multipath reflections are prevalent and strong.

MobiTagbot achieves a median error margin of 3.4 cm, outperforming both STPP and Tagoram by 2.5× and 1.6×, respectively. The 90th percentile and the maximum error margin is 4.8 cm and 5.6 cm, respectively. The improvement is due to MobiTagbot's ability to handle the distortion introduced by the multipath effect. Compared with Tagoram, MobiTagbot creates more virtual antennas by using multiple frequencies. The hologram combination of these virtual antennas reinforces the true location and removes false positive locations. Combined with the tag ordering accuracy result, we can see that 2.2 cm localization accuracy gain results in a significant ordering accuracy gain when applied to the application of book ordering.

6.2.3 *Varying the reader-to-tag distance*

We now show how the three localization algorithms perform under different tag-to-antenna distance settings. In these experiments, we vary the reader-to-tag distance from 0.4 m to 1.2 m, with a step of 0.2 m. In each distance setting, we collect phase readings at 10 locations. Figure 13 shows the error distance of each localization scheme. As the result indicates, the localization error of all these three schemes decreases steadily as we move the reader closer to the tags. This is because the short tag-to-reader distance results in relatively weaker reflections.

Although Tagoram shows similar error margin with MobiTagbot under short tag-to-reader distance setting (*e.g.*, 0.4 m), its performance degrades significantly when we gradually move the antenna away from tags. In contrast, MobiTagbot performs consistently robust under the five distance settings. This clearly demonstrates that MobiTagbot can successfully minimize the impact of multipath effect.

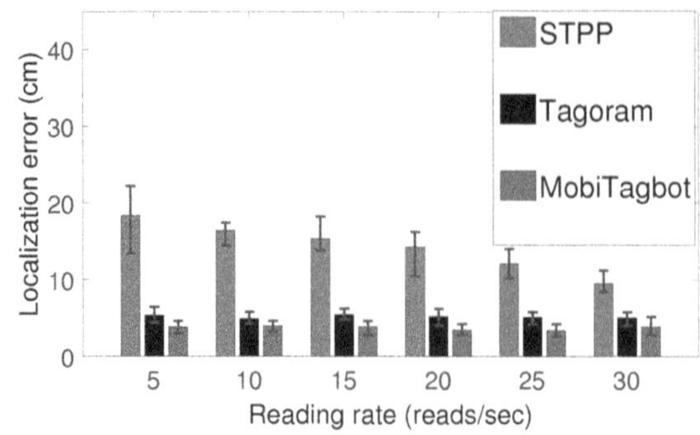

Figure 14— Impact of the tag reading rate. The error bar specifies the maximum, minimum and average localization error under different reading rate settings.

Table 4— Fraction of correct book order identification in a low-multipath environment.

System	Group 1	Group 2	Group 3	Group 4
STPP	52%	48%	54%	42%
Tagoram	82	84	84	86
MobiTagbot	88	88	90	86

6.2.4 *Varying tag reading rate*

We now show how these three schemes perform under different tag reading rate settings. In this series of experiments, we put the RFID reader 1 m away from tags. Since the reader uses the ALOHA protocol to interrogate the tag, each tag will be interrogated a similar number of times. We thus fix the reader's sampling rate, and manually increase or decrease the number of tags within the reader's interrogation range to change the tag reading rate. Figure 14 shows the error margin achieved by different algorithms with respect to different reading rates.

As the result indicates, MobiTagbot consistently outperforms other algorithms in all of the six reading rate settings. From this figure we can see that STPP's performance is highly sensitive to the tag's reading rate. Specifically, STPP achieves a localization error of 9.8 cm on average, when the tag reading rate is set to around 30 reading/second. It then increases significantly and reaches over 18 cm on average when we set the reading rate to 5 reading/second. Because the temporal phase profile becomes extremely sparse when the tag reading rate is low. Hence, it fails to correctly reflect the spatial relationship between tags.

6.3 Field experiment: Low multipath

This section presents results from the "Low multipath" scenario in Figure 8.

6.3.1 *Overall ordering accuracy*

We start by presenting the overall ordering accuracy of the three algorithms. Similar to the setup in multipath-prevalent scenario, we put the reader antenna 1 m away from books and conduct four groups of experiments. Table 4 summarizes the success rate of each algorithm in book ordering. As the result shows, STPP still achieves a success rate around 50%, much similar to the perfor-

Table 5— Fraction of correct book order identification (plus or minus one book) in a low-multipath environment.

System	Group 1	Group 2	Group 3	Group 4
STPP	54%	56%	60%	54%
Tagoram	94	94	90	92
MobiTagbot	100	100	100	100

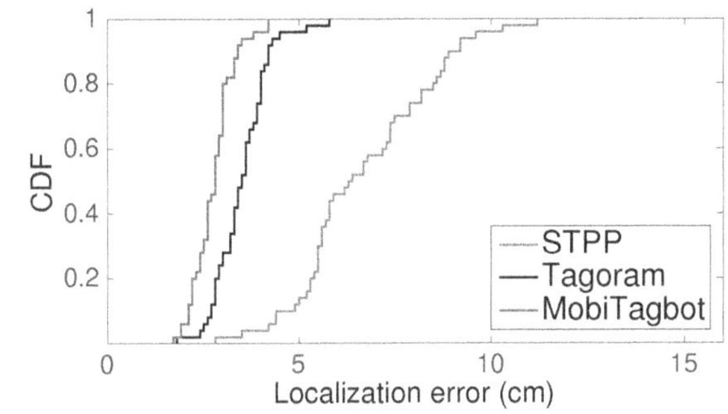

Figure 15— CDF of localization error margin achieved by three algorithms in a low-multipath environment.

mance in multipath-prevalent scenario. In contrast, Tagoram's performance increases remarkably and reaches to a level that is comparable to MobiTagbot. This is expected as the backscatter signal suffers from slight multipath effect in this scenario.

Similarly, we also look at how each algorithm works in ordering the books with one book in-between. As Table 5 shows, there is a small improvement of STPP. Tagoram's performance improves from 84% on average to above 92% on average, while MobiTagbot correctly identifies the order of all books in these four groups of experiments.

6.3.2 Overall localization accuracy

To understand why there is no significant ordering accuracy improvement in STPP, we present the overall localization results of these three localization schemes. The experiment setups are the same as the settings in prevalent multipath scenario. Figure 15 shows the CDF of the error distances in MobiTagbot, STPP and Tagoram.

STPP has a median error distance of 7.4 cm and a 90th percentile of 8.8 cm, much lower than it achieves in prevalent multipath environment. This is expected as the phase profile of each tag experiences light multipath effect. Hence it can reliably reflect the spatial-temporal correlation of tags. However, we can see that the median error margin achieved by STPP is still larger than the width of most books. Hence STPP fails to distinguish the correct order of most books. This explains why STPP fails to achieve a significant improvement in book ordering accuracy.

Tagoram outperforms STPP in a low-multipath environment. It achieves a median error distance of 3.8 cm and a 90th percentile of 4.2 cm. This error margin is mainly due to the small phase drift introduced by the multipath effect.

MobiTagbot achieves a median error margin of 2.8 cm, outperforming both STPP and Tagoram by 2.6× and 1.3×, respectively. The 90th percentile of MobiTagbot is 3.3cm, which outperforms STPP and Tagoram by 2.6× and 1.2×, respectively. These results clearly demonstrate that MobiTagbot can successfully detect and handle the multipath propagation.

6.3.3 Varying the reader-to-tag distance

We next show how these three localization algorithms perform

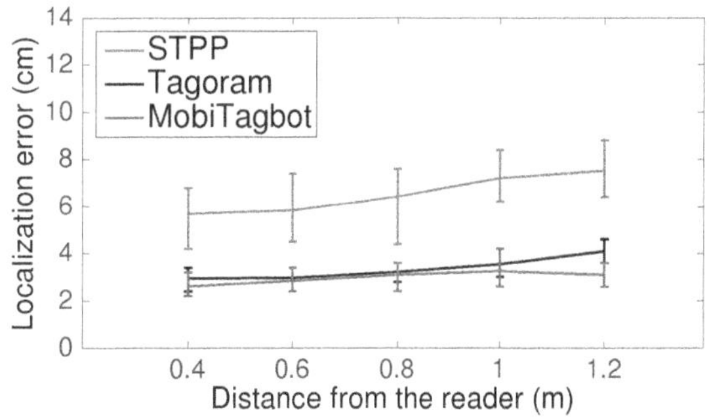

Figure 16— Impact of the distance from the reader. The error bar specifies the maximum, minimum and average localization error under each distance settings.

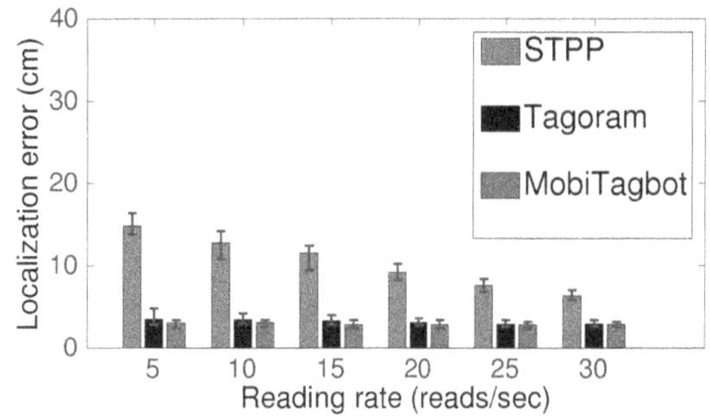

Figure 17— Impact of the tag reading rate. The error bar here specifies the maximum, minimum and average localization error achieved under different reading rate settings.

under different tag-to-antenna distance settings. As in prevalent multipath scenario, in this trail of experiments we also vary the tag-to-reader distance from 0.4 m to 1.2 m, with a step of 0.2 m. Figure 16 shows the localization error achieved by each localization scheme. We make the following three observations. First, similar to the variation of localization accuracy in prevalent multipath scenario, the localization error of all three schemes decreases steadily with the decrease of the distance between the reader and the tag. Second, for each localization scheme, its performance degradation is not as significant as in the prevalent multipath scenario. This is because the light multipath effect does not change so much on different tag-to-reader distances. Third, as expected, when there is low multipath, Tagoram achieves relatively similar performance to MobiTagbot. Nevertheless, the average localization error achieved by MobiTagbot is still below the performance achieved by Tagoram.

6.3.4 Varying the tag reading rate

We now show how these algorithms perform under different reading rate settings. Similarly to the experiment settings in multipath-prevalent scenario, we put the RFID reader 1 m away from tags in these experiments. Figure 17 shows the error margin achieved by different algorithms with respect to different reading rates. As the result indicates, STPP's performance degrades significantly when the reading rate drops. On the other hand, as expected, the multipath propagation of signals introduces faint distortion to phase readings in the low multipath scenario. Accordingly, Tagoram achieves a comparable performance to MobiTagbot in this setting.

6.4 Microbenchmarks

We conduct micro benchmarks to give further insight into MobiTagbot's performance. In particular, to understand which factors

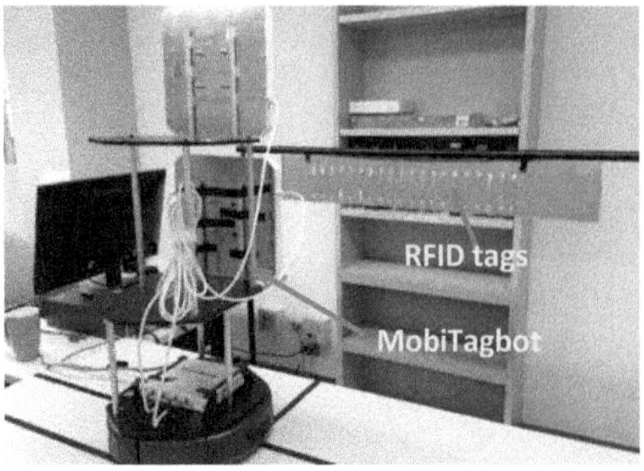

Figure 18— Illustration of micro benchmark scenario.

Table 6— Fraction of correct book order identification (plus or minus one book) with (Case 02) and without (Case 01) the multipath suppression algorithm.

Case	Group 1	Group 2	Group 3	Group 4
Case 01	92%	88%	90%	92%
Case 02	98	100	100	98

will most affect the localization performance of MobiTagbot. Figure 18 shows a view of the benchmark setup. In these experiments, we attach 20 UHF passive tags on the paperboard. The spacing between adjacent tags is 3 cm. The reader is placed 1 m away from the paperboard. Multiple reflectors are then put near the tag to generate a multipath-prevalent environment.

6.4.1 *Effect of multipath suppression*

We first look at how MobiTagbot works in ordering the books with an imprecision of up to one book. We put the reader antenna 1 m away from the books and conduct four groups of experiment. In each group, we repeat the experiment five times. Table 6 summarizes the ordering accuracy of MobiTagbot before and after multipath suppression. As the result shows, when MobiTagbot does not perform multipath suppression and blindly uses phase readings reported at all reader locations, the accuracy is at most 92%. In contrast, with multipath suppression, the accuracy boosts to almost 100%. This result clearly demonstrates the effectiveness of our multipath suppression algorithm.

We further explore the benefit of our multipath suppression algorithm on the tag localization accuracy. The result in shown in Figure 19. As this figure shows, when MobiTagbot does not execute the multipath suppression algorithm, the median and 90th percentile localization errors are 4.3 cm and 6.4 cm, respectively. With multipath suppression algorithm, the localization error decreases significantly. The median and 90th percentile localization errors are becoming 2.9 cm and 4.1 cm, respectively. These results clearly demonstrate the effectiveness of our multipath suppression algorithm.

6.4.2 *Varying the number of channels*

Next, we show how MobiTagbot works while using different number of channels. Specifically, we randomly choose 4, 6, 8, 10, 12, 14 channels out of 16 frequencies and use the phase readings on these channels for multipath suppression and hologram generation. The CDF of localization accuracy under each channel setting is shown in Figure 20. As this figure shows, the median accuracy increases significantly with the increased number of channels we use. The reason behind is two-fold. On one hand, MobiTagbot creates more virtual antennas when hopping in more channels. The hologram combination of these virtual antennas naturally reinforces the true location and removes false positive locations. On the other hand, it is more reliable to detect the multipath effect based on a larger amount of channels, which helps to minimize its impact on the localization result further. From the result we also find that when the number of channel we use is large enough (*i.e.*, n = 10), and it is unlikely to see further improvement on localization performance as the dominate factor will be correct alignment of moving antennas and even the ranging error for ground-truth.

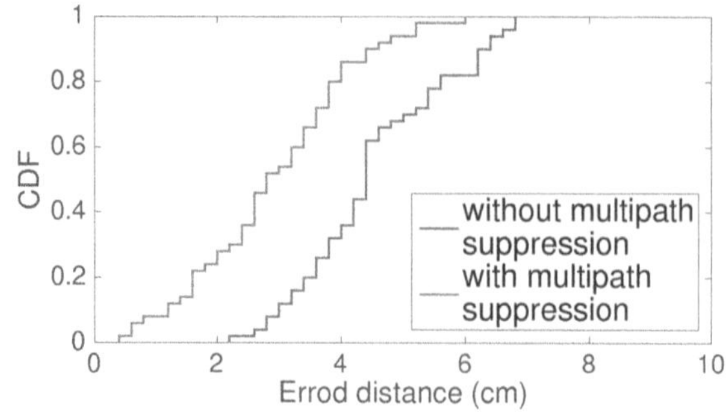

Figure 19— Localization accuracy with/without multipath suppression.

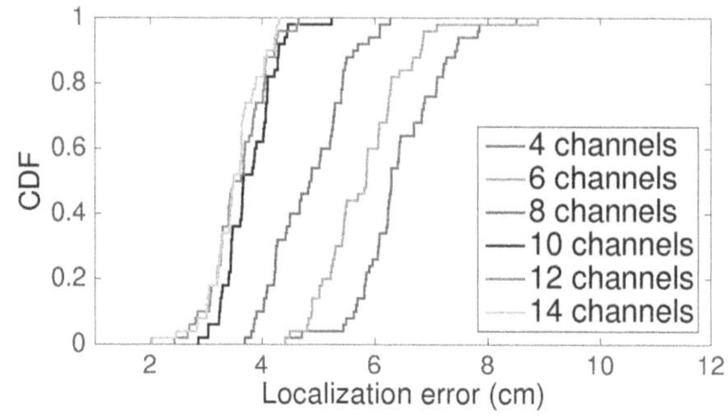

Figure 20— Impact of the number of channel hopping.

6.4.3 *Varying the number of robot read locations*

We then show how MobiTagbot works while using different number of virtual antennas (*i.e.*, number of positions MobiTagbot reads from). In these experiments, we make the reader hop over 16 channels and then capture the tag reading on each channel, respectively. Figure 21 shows the snapshot of the hologram generated by MobiTagbot under different number of virtual antenna settings. In this figure, we divide the X-Z plane into equal size blocks. The block size is set to 1 cm. The value on each block represents the likelihood of tag existing. The ground-truth of the tag is (100,100). As the result indicates, the localization accuracy improves significantly with the increasing number of virtual antennas we use. Specifically, when the number of virtual antennas is large such as five or six, the hologram combination inherently reinforces the true location and removes the false positives. In contrast, when the number of virtual antennas is small, *e.g.*, 2 or 3, the reinforcement is not strong hence MobiTagbot fails to distinguish the true location from a set of location candidates.

6.4.4 *Varying the spacing between adjacent tags*

We next examine how MobiTagbot performs with different adjacent tag spacings. In these experiments, we vary the tag spacing from 0.5 cm to 5 cm, and plot the localization accuracy in Figure 22. As this figure shows, when the spacing is large, *i.e.*, > 3 cm,

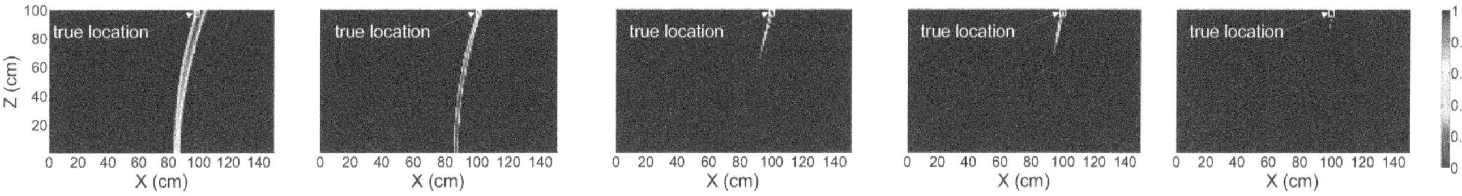

(a)— Two antennas. (b)— Three antennas. (c)— Four antennas. (d)— Five antennas. (e)— Six antennas.

Figure 21— Hologram showing the location likelihood of a tag with differing numbers of virtual antennas computing its location. The ground-truth location is (100,100).

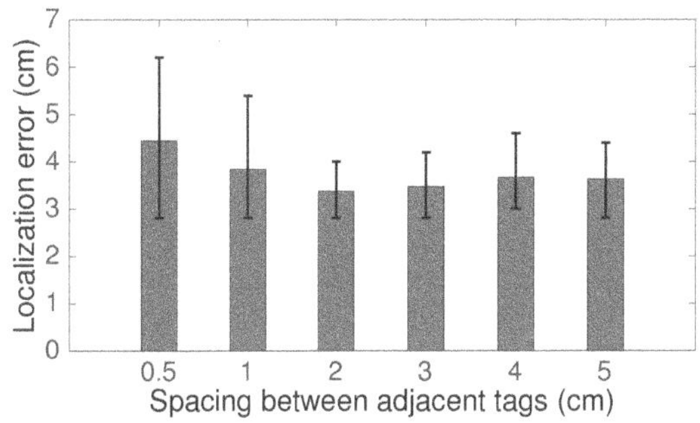

Figure 22— Impact of distance between adjacent tags. The error bar specifies the maximum, minimum and average localization error under different tag spacing settings.

there is no significant performance variation. Besides, the maximum and minimum localization errors retain in a relatively stable and small region. However, as we reduce the spacing between two tags from 2 cm to 1 cm and further to 0.5 cm, we can see a clear performance degradation. This is because when two tags are within extremely short distance, they form two identical circular loops, which will generate inductive coupling effect. Consequently, each tag will be shadowed by another, resulting in reduced signal power at the tag side.

7. DISCUSSION AND FUTURE WORK

We discuss practical deployment issues in this section.

Speed calibration. Calibration of the robot's speed is essential to ensure accuracy in environments with changing floor surfaces. We have obtained accurate results in our lab environment but plan next to investigate wireless, real-time wheel speed measurement using a small number of calibration tags with known spacings, placed near floor boundaries.

Dynamic multipath suppression. Although our experiments are conducted in the presence of moving humans and are robust to nearby motion, we believe schemes that actively reject dynamic multipath may lead to even better performance. This would involve examining the variance and other statistics of multiple phase readings from a tag taken at the same location and on the same channel.

NLOS tag readings. MobiTagbot requires a clear LOS between the tagged-book and the reader antenna. However, in libraries the RFID reader may interrogate the tagged-book behind the current bookshelf, leading to NLOS tag readings. In future work. we plan to address this issue by measuring the time-of-flight (ToF) of each incoming signal, filtering out tags with significantly different response delays in order to isolate a particular bookshelf.

Impact of tag orientation. The readability of a tag is affected by the relative orientation of this tag and the reader antenna. An orientation mismatch will result in a lower tag reading rate, hence degrading system performance. We plan to put antennas in different angles such that tags with diverse orientations will be covered.

Extending to tag moving case. MobiTagbot conducts a roving survey of the interested area to achieve an exact spatial order of RFID-tagged objects. Its core technique can be applied to other applications such as robot manipulation, assembly line construction, and baggage sorting in an airport.

8. CONCLUSION

In this paper, we present the design, implementation and evaluation of MobiTagbot, an autonomous wheeled robot reader that conducts a roving survey of libraries, manufacturing lines and offices to achieve an exact spatial order of RFID-tagged objects in very close (1–6 cm) spacings. MobiTagbot advances the cutting-edge RFID localization systems in its ability to detect and minimize the adversary effect of multipath. MobiTagbot is purely built upon COTS RFID devices and manipulated on backend custom software. The real-world based experiments demonstrate that MobiTagbot could achieve nearly 100% ordering accuracy for items at low (3–6 cm) spacings and 86% accuracy for items at very low (1–3 cm) spacings in multipath-prevalent scenario.

Acknowledgements

We sincerely thank our shepherd Prof. Marco Gruteser and the anonymous reviewers for their insightful comments. The research leading to these results has received funding from the European Research Council under the European Union's Seventh Framework Programme (FP/2007–2013) / ERC Grant Agreement No. 279976.

References

[1] Hacking Roomba. Web page.

[2] ImpinJ Speedway R420 reader. Web page.

[3] iRobot Create 2. Web page.

[4] LLRP Toolkit. Web page.

[5] RFMAX S9028PCR antenna. Web page.

[6] UHF RFID Inlays AD-227m5. Web page.

[7] M. Azizyan, I. Constandache, and R. Roy Choudhury. SurroundSense: Mobile phone localization via ambience fingerprinting. In *MobiCom*, 2009.

[8] P. Bahl and V. N. Padmanabhan. RADAR: An in-building RF-based user location and tracking system. In *Infocom*, 2000.

[9] K. Chintalapudi, A. Padmanabha Iyer, and V. N. Padmanabhan. Indoor localization without the pain. In *MobiCom*, 2010.

[10] E. Eade and T. Drummond. Scalable monocular SLAM. In *CVPR*, 2006.

[11] I. Ehrenberg, C. Floerkemeier, and S. Sarma. Inventory management with an RFID-equipped mobile robot. In *CASE*, 2007.

[12] H. Ermert and R. Karg. Multi-frequency acoustical holography. *TOSU*, 1979.

[13] B. Ferris, D. Fox, and N. D. Lawrence. WiFi-SLAM using Gaussian Process latent variable models. In *IJCAI*, 2007.

[14] A. Flint, C. Mei, I. Reid, and D. Murray. Growing semantically meaningful models for visual SLAM. In *CVPR*, 2010.

[15] K. R. Joshi, S. S. Hong, and S. Katti. PinPoint: Localizing interfering radios. In *NSDI*, 2013.

[16] M. Kotaru, K. Joshi, D. Bharadia, and S. Katti. SpotFi: Decimeter level localization using WiFi. In *SIGCOMM*, 2015.

[17] X. Li, Y. Zhang, and M. G. Amin. Multifrequency-based range estimation of RFID tags. In *RFID*, 2009.

[18] H. Lim, L.-C. Kung, J. C. Hou, and H. Luo. Zero-configuration, robust indoor localization: Theory and experimentation. In *Infocom*, 2005.

[19] T. Liu, L. Yang, Q. Lin, Y. Guo, and Y. Liu. Anchor-free backscatter positioning for RFID tags with high accuracy. In *infocom*, 2014.

[20] R. Miesen, F. Kirsch, and M. Vossiek. Holographic localization of passive UHF RFID transponders. In *RFID*, 2011.

[21] A. Musa and J. Eriksson. Tracking unmodified smartphones using Wi-Fi monitors. In *SenSys*, 2012.

[22] L. M. Ni, Y. Liu, Y. C. Lau, and A. P. Patil. LANDMARC: indoor location sensing using active RFID. *Wireless networks*, 2004.

[23] A. Parr, R. Miesen, and M. Vossiek. Inverse SAR approach for localization of moving RFID tags. In *RFID*, 2013.

[24] A. Rai, K. K. Chintalapudi, V. N. Padmanabhan, and R. Sen. Zee: zero-effort crowdsourcing for indoor localization. In *MobiCom*, 2012.

[25] S. Sen, J. Lee, K.-H. Kim, and P. Congdon. Avoiding multipath to revive inbuilding WiFi localization. In *MobiSys*, 2013.

[26] S. Sen, B. Radunovic, R. R. Choudhury, and T. Minka. You are facing the Mona Lisa: Spot localization using PHY layer information. In *MobiSys*, 2012.

[27] L. Shangguan, Z. Yang, A. X. Liu, Z. Zhou, and Y. Liu. Relative localization of RFID tags using spatial-temporal phase profiling. In *NSDI*, 2015.

[28] G. Shen, Z. Chen, P. Zhang, T. Moscibroda, and Y. Zhang. Walkie-Markie: Indoor pathway mapping made easy. In *NSDI*, 2013.

[29] H. Strasdat, A. J. Davison, J. Montiel, and K. Konolig. Double window optimisation for constant time visual SLAM. In *ICCV*, 2011.

[30] L. Sun, S. Sen, D. Koutsonikolas, and K.-H. Kim. WiDraw: Enabling hands-free drawing in the air on commodity WiFi devices. In *MobiCom*, 2015.

[31] M. Vossiek, V. Magori, and H. Ermert. An ultrasonic multi-element sensor system for position invariant object identification. In *US*, 1994.

[32] M. Vossiek, A. Urban, S. Max, and P. Gulden. Inverse synthetic aperture secondary radar concept for precise wireless positioning. *TMTT*, 2007.

[33] H. Wang, S. Sen, A. Elgohary, M. Farid, M. Youssef, and R. R. Choudhury. No need to war-drive: unsupervised indoor localization. In *MobiSys*, 2012.

[34] J. Wang and D. Katabi. Dude, where's my card?: RFID positioning that works with multipath and non-line of sight. In *SIGCOMM*, 2013.

[35] J. Wang, D. Vasisht, and D. Katabi. RF-IDraw: Virtual touch screen in the air using RF signals. In *SIGCOMM*, 2014.

[36] Y. Wang, J. Liu, Y. Chen, M. Gruteser, J. Yang, and H. Liu. E-eyes: device-free location-oriented activity identification using fine-grained WiFi signatures. In *MobiCom*, 2014.

[37] K. Whitehouse, C. Karlof, and D. Culler. A practical evaluation of radio signal strength for ranging-based localization. *MCCR*, 2007.

[38] C. Wong, R. Klukas, and G. Messier. Using WLAN infrastructure for Angle-of-Arrival indoor user location. In *VTC*, 2008.

[39] J. Xiong and K. Jamieson. ArrayTrack: A fine-grained indoor location system. In *NSDI*, 2013.

[40] J. Xiong, K. Sundaresan, and K. Jamieson. ToneTrack: Leveraging frequency-agile radios for time-based indoor wireless localization. In *MobiCom*, 2015.

[41] L. Yang, Y. Chen, X.-Y. Li, C. Xiao, M. Li, and Y. Liu. Tagoram: Real-time tracking of mobile RFID tags to high precision using COTS devices. In *MobiCom*, 2014.

[42] Z. Yang, C. Wu, and Y. Liu. Locating in fingerprint space: wireless indoor localization with little human intervention. In *MobiCom*, 2012.

[43] M. Younis, C. Fischer, and W. Wiesbeck. Digital beamforming in SAR systems. *TOGRS*, 2003.

[44] M. Youssef and A. Agrawala. The Horus WLAN location determination system. In *MobiSys*, 2005.

[45] C. Zhou and J. D. Griffin. Accurate phase-based ranging measurements for backscatter RFID tags. *Antennas and Wireless Propagation Letters*, 2012.

Idea: A System for Efficient Failure Management in Smart IoT Environments*

Palanivel Kodeswaran
IBM Research
Bangalore, KA, India
Email: palankod@in.ibm.com

Ravi Kokku
IBM Research
Yorktown Heights, NY, USA
Email: rkokku@us.ibm.com

Sayandeep Sen
IBM Research
Bangalore, KA, India
Email: sayandes@in.ibm.com

Mudhakar Srivatsa
IBM Research
Yorktown Heights, NY, USA
Email: msrivats@us.ibm.com

ABSTRACT

IoT enabled smart environments are expected to proliferate significantly in the near future, particularly in the context of monitoring services for wellness living, patient healthcare and elderly care. Timely maintenance of failed sensors is of critical importance in such deployments to ensure minimal disruption to monitoring services. However, maintenance of large and geographically spread deployments can be a significant challenge. We present Idea that significantly increases the *time-before-repair* for a smart home deployment, thereby reducing the maintenance overhead. Specifically, our approach leverages the facts that (a) there is inherent sensor redundancy when combinations of sensors monitor *activities of daily living* (ADLs) in smart environments, and (b) the *impact* of each sensor failure depends on the activities being monitored and the functional redundancy afforded by rest of the heterogeneous sensors available for detecting the activities. Consequently, Idea identifies homes that need to be fixed based on expected degradation in ADL detection performance, and optimizes maintenance scheduling accordingly. We demonstrate that our approach leads to 3–40 times fewer maintenance personnel than a scheme in which failed sensors are fixed without considering their impact.

1. INTRODUCTION

There is a significant proliferation of *IoT* enabled smart home products ranging from home security, environmental controls such as temperature, light, humidity etc, to voice activated device controls. Of particular interest, are applications in the health care domain that enable remote monitoring of patients, particularly the elderly. Industry projections [1] show that elderly-care products are expected to grow to $10.3 billion in 2020 globally, with $2 billion for elderly safety monitoring in the US and European markets. A number of medical studies [2–6] show that continuously monitoring *Activities of Daily Living* or ADLs such as `Cooking`, `Eating`, `Showering`, `Taking Pills` etc. is of prime importance in geriatric care as they allow for the early detection of the onset of diseases such as Alzheimer's, Dementia, Mild Cognitive Impairment, etc. For instance, caregivers of patients with Alzheimer's disease rank tracking and identifying activities of daily living of the patient at the top of their list of needs for health assistance [2].

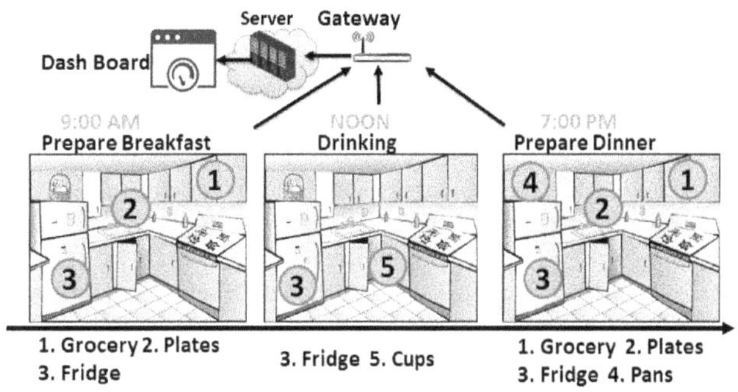

Figure 1: Sensors triggered for various activities.

Automated detection of an ADL is achieved by *learning patterns of sensors* that are *triggered in the smart home* when specific ADLs are performed. For example, in Figure 1, we depict the kitchen of a smart home that is instrumented with sensors to monitor the opening and closing of appliances such as microwave, fridge and multiple cabinets, etc. In the above home a `Drinking` ADL will be detected by monitoring the {`Cups_Cupboard`, `Fridge`} sensor events. For such residents, it is envisioned that a service provider will instrument a smart home and assist care givers by offering a service to remotely monitor the health of its residents by accurately detecting the ADLs being undertaken in the home.

Given the importance of health monitoring applications, it is critical to *continuously monitor and maintain functionality* of the IoT deployment [1]. Maintaining sensors by elderly residents is infeasible due to the miniature sizes as well as placement of these sen-

*Authors are listed in alphabetical order.

[1]In this paper we consider activity detection for remote health/wellness monitoring as the motivating use case. However, the designed system can be used for other remote monitoring applications such as home security, home activity monitoring with baby-sitters, etc.

MobiSys'16, June 25-30, 2016, Singapore, Singapore

DOI: http://dx.doi.org/10.1145/2906388.2906406

Label	Name	# User	Dur. (days)	# ADL (# Activity)	# Sensor (# Event)
kA	KasterenA [16]	1	25	16 (283)	14 (2006)
kB	KasterenB [16]	1	15	25 (172)	27 (22595)
kC	KasterenC [16]	1	19	27 (254)	23 (39861)
Ar	Aruba [17]	1	219	11 (6477)	39 (805268)
T1	Twor9-10 [17]	2	249	25 (3745)	100 (711421)
T3	Twor2009 [17]	2	57	14 (499)	100 (136504)
T2	TworSmr [17]	2	63	8 (1016)	100 (366075)
Mul	AdlNorm [17]	24	84	5 (120)	39 (6425)

Table 1: Datasets from IoT enabled Homes

sors [7]. Hence, we expect that the responsibility of maintaining the sensors, i.e. detecting and repairing failed sensors at the earliest to ensure that the monitoring applications continue to be effective will rest upon the service provider.

On the other hand, from a service provider's perspective, the maintenance of large scale sensor deployments becomes a significant challenge due to the high labor costs involved in monitoring and repairing sensors that have a non-zero probability of failing across reasonably large number of geographically spread homes. Thus there is an inherent tradeoff between maintaining acceptable application QoS and minimizing operational costs for the service provider.

We note that the standard approach of deploying redundant sensors to minimize maintenance load explored in the context of homogeneous sensors [8–15] is not directly applicable in the setting described above. This is because smart home deployments combine information from multiple heterogeneous sensors such as contact, motion and temperature sensors to detect ADLs. Similarly, as explained in Section 2, deploying multiple redundant sensors is not sufficient as it only improves failure time logarithmically and faces operational challenges in smart home environments.

Our approach for mitigating the maintenance load leverages the observation that *a number of sensors are triggered when an ADL is performed by a given user, implying some sensors could be functionally redundant for the purpose of detecting the activity from sensor firings.* To elucidate, in Figure 1, and ADL detector will detect `Prepare_Dinner` ADL when at 7PM, events of {`Fridge`, `Freezer`, `Grocery`, `Plates`, `Pans`} sensors are observed.

Note that even if the `Grocery_Cupboard` sensor fails to trigger, the triggering of other sensors can still detect the occurrence of `Prepare_Dinner` with reasonable accuracy. Thus, one of the key aspects of this work is to quantify the functional redundancies present among heterogeneous sensors for the task of ADL detection.

To this end, we build a system for **Integrated ADL detection, estimation of functional redundancy** and **alerting for maintenance visit** (Idea). The Idea system tolerates a number of sensor failures by leveraging the functional redundancy among heterogeneous sensors, and minimizes the degradation in ADL detection performance in the presence of smart home sensor failures. The desired consequence of our design is the significant reduction in maintenance effort as no maintenance visits are required as long as the ADL detection accuracy is maintained above a certain (user specified) threshold.

Contributions

Idea builds on prior work on accurate ADL detection [3–6, 18–26] by explicitly quantifying the functional redundancies available among sensors in smart homes to enable robust detection in the presence of sensor failures. It also advances the nascent area of IoT deployment maintenance [27, 28] by presenting the first joint technique for achieving systematic quantification of functional redundancy among heterogeneous sensors and assessment of impact of sensor failure on ADL detection performance.

In summary, we make the following contributions.

- We present Idea– the first integrated ADL detector that extracts functional redundancy among sensors to provide robust ADL detection in the presence of sensor failures.
- We propose a novel method based on *rarity estimation* to leverage the extracted functional redundancies to identify sensor failures (Section 3.4).
- We propose a method that leverages Idea's rule based design to estimate the impact of sensor failures on ADL detection (Section 3.3).
- We design and implement a cloud based maintenance scheduling technique that significantly reduces (3-40 times) maintenance cost by increasing the time before repair for homes with failures.
- We thoroughly evaluate Idea using publicly available datasets and realistic sensor failure models, and show that Idea's ADL detection method is more robust to failures than other approaches to ADL detection, in turn, leading to significant increase in the time to send repair mechanics to individual homes. Specifically, based on a representative home distribution in and around Manhattan, New York region, we show that Idea reduces the maintenance personnel overhead by a factor of 3-40 times, and increases average per-home inter-visit times from 18 to 211 days, minimizing user annoyance (Section 4).

Road map

The rest of the paper is organized as follows. In Section 2 we benchmark the magnitude of sensor failures for large sensor deployments, thus motivating the need for Idea. We also describe the intuition leveraged by Idea to reduce maintenance overhead. In Section 3, we describe the various components of Idea. We evaluate Idea's performance in Section 4, describe related work in Section 5 and finally conclude in Section 6.

2. MOTIVATION

Our goal in this work is to design a solution for the efficient maintenance of IoT sensors in smart homes to ensure disruption free continuous remote monitoring of ADLs. We begin with a brief description of the eight ADL datasets analyzed as part of our work. The datasets listed in Table 1 consist of time stamped sensor events that are generated when the variety of contact, temperature and motion sensors are triggered when the user undertakes various ADLs such as sleeping, eating, preparing meals, taking medicines, personal hygiene etc. [2]. The eight datasets together capture the heterogeneity typically seen across different smart home deployments in terms of the type of sensors deployed as well as the number of sensors, ranging between 14 and 99.

To motivate the need for designing efficient solutions for the *IoT sensor maintenance problem*, we carry out a modeling study for a representative deployment of 1000 homes, with topology shown in Figure 2 with a sensor configuration similar to the smart home from *KasterenA* dataset mentioned in Table 1 over a period of two years. We model the failure of each sensor using a Weibull distribution (a

[2]Refer papers cited in Table 1 for more detailed description of ADLs monitored in each home.

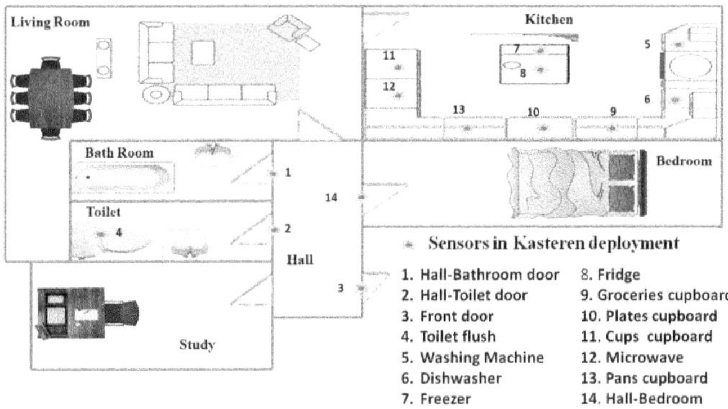

Figure 2: Sensor Layout in *KasterenA* dataset

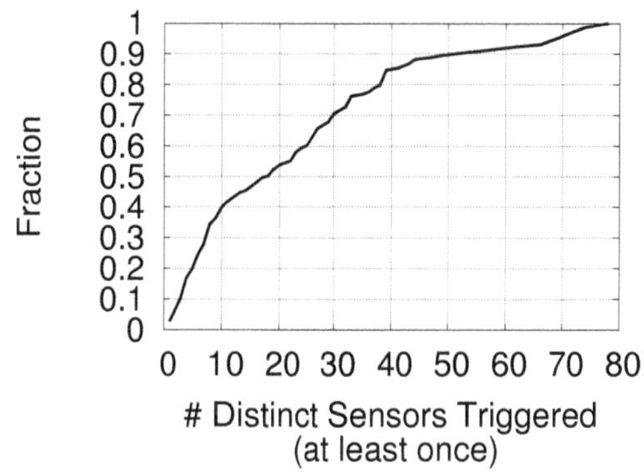

Figure 3: CDF of count of distinct sensors which triggered at least once for an ADL across all datasets in Table 1.

common choice of modeling failure of sensors) [29–31] with mean time to failure (MTTF) set to 1.0 *years*. Analytical calculations show that increasing the number of homes and sensors leads to an exponential increase in the number of sensor failures (results omitted for the sake of brevity). This exponential increase results in significantly high maintenance costs (operational expenditure) for the provider as they now need to devote a significant amount of manpower simply to monitor and service the deployment.

As mentioned in Section 1, our approach for mitigating the maintenance load leverages the key observation that a number of sensors are triggered when an ADL is performed by a given user, which would make a few sensors redundant for detecting the activity. To validate the above observation, in Figure 3 we plot the CDF of the number of sensors that are triggered by each ADL across all datasets in Table 1. From the figure, we see that fewer than 5% of ADLs trigger only one sensor; while for 50% of the ADLs, up to ten sensors are triggered per ADL. Intuitively, we can exploit the above *functional redundancy* amongst heterogeneous sensors, to delay the time to repair sensor failures in a home. As mentioned in Section 1, the task of ADL detection involves learning the sensor (and their temporal) activation patterns corresponding to the ADLs and then *detecting* the underlying activity based on the set of sensor events seen. However, note that ADL detection is not straightforward. For instance, a similar set of sensors are triggered by different ADLs as seen in the case of `Prepare_Breakfast` and `Prepare_Dinner` ADLs. Further, humans exhibit significant variability while performing the same ADL across different days, in terms of the set of sensors used as well as their sequence. Additionally, based on the user's behavioral patterns, the sensors co-relate differently for different ADLs, thereby implying that the set of redundant sensors must be learnt separately on a per ADL basis.

Hence, in this work we design a system called Idea, which (a) learns and leverages the functional redundancies among sensors leading to robust ADL detection in the presence of sensor failures (b) identifies when a sensor has failed, and (c) determines the impact of a failed sensor on the detection performance of all ADLs. Using these steps, Idea can significantly delay the Time-before-repair for a home resulting in significant savings in deployment maintenance costs.

Note that the alternate approach to reducing maintenance costs by deploying duplicate sensors beforehand as a way to achieve redundancy will not work due to the following reasons. First, adding 'n' sensors will improve redundancy by only log(n). We validated this observation using a tool available at [32]. Second, based on observations made by authors in [7], operational problems in smart homes such as limited number of power sockets and aesthetics also restrict the number of sensors that can be deployed in any home.

3. Idea SYSTEM DESIGN

In this section, we describe the design of Idea. At a high level, the functionality of Idea is divided into four key components (Figure 4): First, Idea includes an ADL Signature Generation phase to bootstrap the system with sensor events that are annotated with ADL labels, such that all possible ways of performing ADLs in the given home are captured at a central *IoT* gateway. The annotations can be done either generically for common human activities or on an application-domain basis by subject matter experts from the IoT service enterprise, or by competent residents of smart homes. Second, Idea assesses the impact of different sensor failures on the accuracy of detecting ADLs needed by the activity monitoring applications that run in the home. Third, as the system continues to run, Idea performs continuous ADL detection, and sensor failure detection, and raises an alert to the cloud when a sensor fails. Finally, on receiving sensor failure alerts, and determining the impact of the corresponding failure on ADL detection performance in the home, the maintenance scheduler on the cloud schedules maintenance visits for homes where critical sensors have failed[3].

3.1 ADL Signature Generation

The goal of the ADL signature generation component is to learn the sensory-temporal signatures of the various ADLs from annotated sensor events collected during the training phase. During the training phase, whenever the user performs an ADL, the generated set of sensor events are collected and annotated in the form of time-stamped event streams at the local gateway.

Sensory Signature Extraction

The key intuition behind sensory signature extraction is to identify frequently occurring subsets of sensor events across activi-

[3]For simplicity of description of Idea, we assume that the behavior of the resident exhibited in the learning phase does not change after learning. Since users' activity patterns change in reality, we note that the system can locally re-learn the ADLs when the system detects that significant behavioral change might have happened. We do not discuss this extension in the paper.

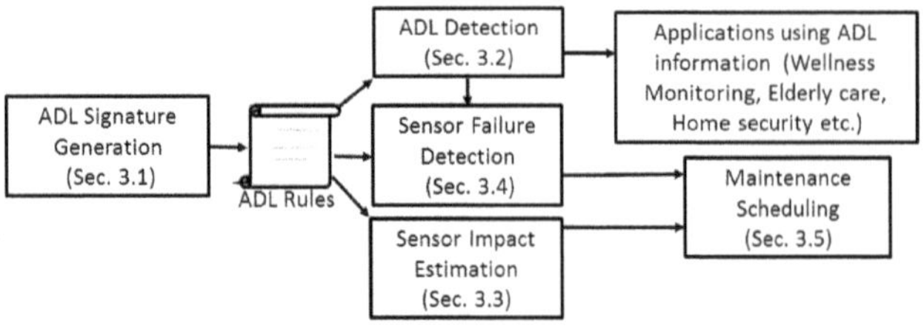

Figure 4: Solution Architecture of Idea

ties that are indicative of an underlying ADL. For example, in the home shown in Figure 2, when an elderly resident uses the toilet, the `Toilet Door`, `Bathroom Door` and `Flush` sensors are mostly triggered. Due to the inherent variability exhibited by humans regarding the set of sensors used and their corresponding sequences while performing ADLs, we focus on extracting frequent sensor *subsets* rather than sensor *sequences*. We employ a Frequent itemset mining (FIM) approach [33] for identifying frequently occurring subsets of sensors that are indicative of an ADL. The FIM algorithm takes as input a set of activities and the corresponding set of sensors that were triggered during the activity, and outputs frequently occurring subsets of sensors in the form of rules for each ADL. For example, we obtain the following rule for the `Prepare_Breakfast` ADL

`(R1)Fridge,Groceries_Cbrd,Plates_Cbrd ⇒ Prepare_Breakfast<support:0.05,confidence:0.7>`

The rule attributes of R1 provide various measures of the frequency and predictive power of the rule. In particular, the support of a sensor subset X, $Supp(X)$ is defined as the proportion of activities in the training dataset that contain the sensor subset X. The predictive power of a rule is reflected in its *confidence* value, which for a given association rule of the form $A \Rightarrow O$, is defined as $Conf(A \Rightarrow O) = Supp(A \cup O)/Supp(A)$.

Note that FIM generates, not one, but a *set* of rules for a given ADL based on the number of sensors that are typically triggered by the ADL. For example, the following rules are obtained for *Prepare_Breakfast* ADL in the KasterenA home as shown in Figure 2,

`(R2) Groceries_Cbrd, Plates_Cbrd ⇒ Prepare_Breakfast`

`(R3) Fridge, Groceries_Cbrd ⇒ Prepare_Breakfast`

`(R4) Groceries_Cbrd ⇒ Prepare_Breakfast`

In general, the number of rules generated for an ADL is a function of the redundancy exhibited by the triggered sensors. For example, in the *KasterenA* dataset, there is a single rule for the `leave_house` ADL which triggers a single sensor while the `Prepare_Dinner` ADL which triggers six sensors includes eighteen rules. By generating multiple association rules for each ADL, Idea is able to identify (heterogeneous) sensor subsets that are strongly co-related with each other on a per ADL basis, thus providing the provide functional redundancy for the task of detecting the ADL. For example, the sensor pair `[Freezer, Plates_Cbrd]` is strongly co-related with each other when occurring as part of `Prepare_Dinner` ADL, where as the sensor pair shows lower co-relation while occurring as part of `Prepare_Breakfast` ADL. This implies that the `Freezer` and `Plates_Cbrd` sensor pair are redundant with respect to `Prepare_Dinner` and a single sensor may be sufficient for ADL detection even if the other sensor fails. The above property holds for all rules for a given ADL that have the same support, but the set of sensors in one rule is a proper subset of the other. Thus Idea is able to systematically discover redundancies among sensors in ADL detection, using multiple association rules which in turn helps in estimating the importance of a sensor and in detecting sensor failures as described later.

Temporal Signature Extraction

We observe in the datasets that several ADLs (especially the related ones) trigger the same set of sensors and differ only in their temporal features such as time(hour) of day of occurrence and duration. For example, `Prepare_Breakfast` and `Prepare_Dinner` use a similar set of sensors as shown in Figure 2 while differing only in their time of day occurrence, peaking at 11 am and 8 pm respectively. Similarly, both `Brushing` and `Sleeping` use the Toilet door at roughly the same time of day around 10 PM, but significantly differ in the activity durations ranging from one minute for `Brushing` to about six hours for `Sleeping`. This indicates that temporal features such as time-of-day of occurrence as well as activity duration play a significant role in disambiguating ADLs when the sensory signatures alone are not discriminative enough, either due to sensor overlap among ADLs or due to the failure of sensors. Consequently, for each rule, Idea identifies the set of activities in the training set that match the rule, and determine the time of day of occurrence as well as duration of the activity. Based on the collected samples across days, Idea then estimates the *most probable* time of day of occurrence as well as duration based on the modal value and standard deviations of the samples.

At the end of this step, Idea generates for each ADL a set of sensory-temporal signatures of the form $< S_i, S_j ... S_n,$ $Mean\_Time\_of\_Day, Mean\_Duration \Rightarrow ADL >$.

3.2 ADL Detection

Once the ADL signatures are generated, Idea processes the sensor streams collected at the IoT gateway at run-time to detect ADLs based on matching the incoming sensor stream against the sensory temporal signatures learnt in the previous step. We assume that the incoming sensor event stream is cut into activities using an event segmentation model [22, 34, 35] such that each activity, T, potentially corresponds to an underlying ADL undertaken by a single user. The detection process consists of several scorer modules, each extracting specific features from the activity T and scoring the various ADLs that the activity could potentially map to. For each ADL_k, we denote the set of rules that are used to detect the ADL_k as R_k . Idea computes a closeness of match for the incoming activity with each rule in the rule base to obtain the following set of scores.

Sensor Scoring: We define that an activity T matches a rule if the set of sensors in the rule is a subset of the sensors in the activity. Let $R(T)$ denote the set of rules matching activity T. For each $ADL_k \in R_k(T)$, Idea computes the sensory score of T as the sum of the confidences of the matching rules multiplied by the prior probability of occurrence of the ADL_k that is estimated from the training dataset. Note that the above formulation handles the case where the same sensor set is used in multiple ADLs. In these cases, the confidence would be higher for the more frequently occurring ADL such as `Drinking` compared to the less frequent one such as `Prepare_Breakfast`, and consequently, the sensory score for the more frequent ADL would be higher compared to the less frequent ADL.

Temporal Scoring: Idea next computes the temporal scores by matching the activity T against the temporal features viz. time of day and duration of the rule set. We say that an activity temporally matches a temporal feature of a rule if it lies within a threshold k number of standard deviations from the modal value of the rule's feature. By experimenting with multiple datasets, we determine that $k = 1.5$ yields the best accuracy. For each rule R_i, we extract temporal features and denote the modal hour of day as $Tod(R_i)$ and average duration of the ADL as $Dur(R_i)$. For example, in KasterenA dataset, the modal ToD and duration for `Brushing` ADL are 10 PM and one minute respectively. For a given input activity T, we compute the hour of day (ToD), by extracting the hour from the timestamp of the first event in T, and duration as the time elapsed between the first and last sensor events. After identifying the set of temporally matching rules, Idea computes the time of day score as the sum of the confidences of the matching rules. Similarly, the duration score is computed as the sum of the confidences of the rules matching the duration.

Idea computes the composite scores for each ADL_k as weighted sum of the individual scores. Empirically, we observe that temporal features possess a stronger discriminating power in detecting ADLs compared to sensor usage, and consequently we set higher weights for the temporal scores compared to the sensor score weight (ratio of 1000:1). Finally, Idea assigns the ADL label corresponding to the highest composite score to the input activity.

3.3 Impact Estimation

The goal of impact estimation is to identify critical sensors for each ADL. We define a sensor as critical for a given ADL if the sensor is necessary to maintain the detection accuracy above a configured threshold. When a critical sensor for an ADL fails, there are two possibilities that arise for the corresponding input activities: (1) no ADL is detected, and (2) the ADL is misclassified as another ADL. The goal of Idea is to minimize both possibilities.

The impact estimation component takes as input the annotated event stream collected during the training phase along with the sensory temporal signatures learnt in Section 3.1. From the annotated data, Idea estimates the functional redundancy, for ADL detection, among sensor patterns that are triggered by the ADL as well as their corresponding proportions. For example, in the KasterenA dataset, the following subset of sensor patterns are triggered by the `Prepare_Breakfast` ADL in the corresponding proportions
$\{Fridge, Groceries\_Cbrd, Plates\_Cbrd\} = 0.05$,
$\{Groceries\_Cbrd, Plates\_Cbrd\} = 0.05$,
$\{Fridge, Plates\_Cbrd\} = 0.06$.

For a given [sensor, ADL] pair, Idea estimates the impact of sensor failure as follows. In the first step, Idea determines if the sensor is applicable for the ADL by checking if any of the sensory signatures for the ADL include the sensor. If no such signature exists, the impact is determined to be zero, as the sensor is not used for recognition of the given ADL; Idea also classifies the sensor as non-critical. In the above example, a `Toilet Flush` sensor is non-critical for `Prepare_Breakfast` as it is not part of any sensory signature for `Prepare_Breakfast`. In the second step, Idea determines if there are other sensors that can be used to detect the ADL. This is achieved by scanning the rule base to check if there are any sensory signatures for the ADL that do no include the given sensor. If no such signature exists, the ADL can no longer be detected in the absence of the sensor, and Idea classifies the sensor as critical for the ADL. For example, in KasterenA, only the `Front Door` that is used for detecting the `Leave_House` ADL, and in its absence, no `Leave_House` instance can be detected.

In the third step, Idea determines if the remaining set of sensors alone can detect the ADL and estimates the resulting detection accuracy. In this case, Idea estimates the *detection accuracy* with and without the sensor and returns the change in the estimated detection accuracy as the impact of losing the sensor on the ADL.

Estimating Detection Accuracy: Given an ADL, Idea estimates its detection accuracy by choosing each distinct sensor pattern of the ADL and estimating its accuracy individually as follows. For a

Algorithm 1: Compute Impact of Sensor loss on an ADL

ComputeImpact{ADL,S_{id}}
$impact \leftarrow 0$
for *SensorPattern* $P \in Adl$ **do**
  if $S_{id} \in P$ **then** $proportion \leftarrow \|P\| \div \|ADL\|$
  $noLoss \leftarrow EstAccuracy(P, ADL)$
  $wLoss \leftarrow EstAccuracy(P - \{S_{id}\}, ADL)$
  $\delta \leftarrow (noLoss - wLoss)/noLoss$
  $impact \leftarrow impact + proportion \times \delta$
  ;
end
Return $impact$

given sensor pattern and ADL, Idea determines if the rules matching the sensor pattern can accurately detect the ADL. If the sensor pattern matches only the single given ADL, then Idea assumes all these instances can be correctly detected. On the other hand, if the sensor pattern matches multiple ADLs, Idea determines if any of the other matching ADLs overlaps with the given ADL in the temporal domain. We define two ADLs to overlap in the temporal domain if any of their rules have temporal features (time of day or duration) that are within a threshold number of standard deviations of each other. In the case of overlapping ADLs, Idea chooses to be conservative, in estimation of functional redundancy and assumes all these instances of the ADL will be misclassified, and returns a detection accuracy of zero. This conservative design enables Idea to proactively maintain failed sensors, and prevent the application QoS from falling below the required threshold. Finally, Idea estimates the overall detection accuracy for the ADL by summing the individual estimates of each sensor pattern multiplied by their corresponding proportion. Algorithm 1 summarizes the impact estimation approach. At the end of this step, Idea computes the aggregate impact of a sensor as the sum of the impacts of the sensor for each individual ADL, and returns critical sensors both on a per ADL as well as aggregate basis.

Note that for ease of explanation we described impact estimation for a single sensor failure. However, the same calculation is easily extendable to estimating the impact of multiple sensor failures by carrying out the calculations for a set of failed sensors instead of a single one. We evaluate performance of Idea under multiple sensor failures in Section 4.

3.4 Sensor Failure Detection

We now describe how Idea detects sensor failures, while continuously monitoring ADLs in a smart home. Algorithm 2, shows the three techniques employed by Idea to generate failure alerts for both periodic and event-driven sensors. The first technique is for detecting the failure of sensors that send events (of their state) periodically. For such sensors, Idea raises a failure alert if a threshold amount of time has elapsed since last state report by the sensor. The second and third techniques are for event-driven sensors, which generate events only when certain activity is performed. For e.g., a working Toilet-door contact sensor reports an `"open"` (or `close`) event only when the door is opened (closed). Idea's task for such sensors that fail to report data over a period of time, is to differentiate between whether the corresponding ADL did not actually happen, or the sensor has failed. In our current design, we consider only fail-stop failures. Note that our approach, *in principle*, can be adapted to sensors giving inconsistent values when they fail, but we did not have sufficient datasets to explore this extension. The second technique focuses on sensors that are identified

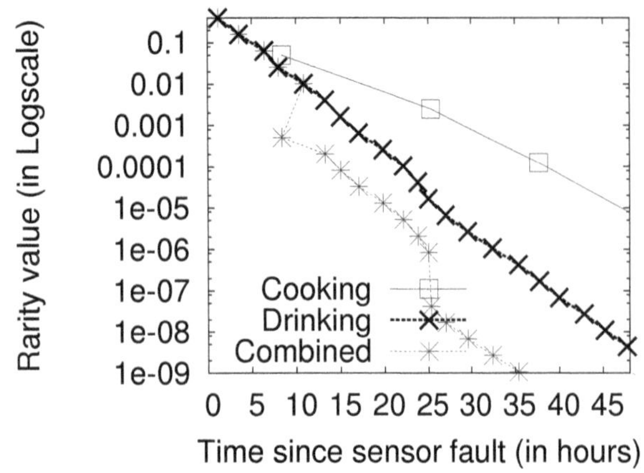

Figure 5: Detection of missing Fridge sensor in *KasterenA* dataset using three ADLs.

Algorithm 2: Missing Sensor alert generation

Data: S : Set of all sensors, t_{max} :, Maximum time allowed since last firing, τ : Rarity threshold

Phase 1 - Detect Stoppage of Periodic Sensors
forall the $\mathtt{s_{periodic}} \in$ S **do**
  if *Time since last* $\mathtt{s_{periodic}}$ *event* $> t_{max}$ **then**
   generateAlert($\mathtt{s_{periodic}}$) ;
end
Phase 2 - Detect Stoppage for Grave Sensors
forall the $\mathtt{s_{critical}} \in$ S **do**
  Data: $\mathtt{ADL_K}$ for which $\mathtt{s_{critical}}$ is critical
  if *Time since last* $\mathtt{ADL_K} > t_{max}$ **then**
   generateAlert($\mathtt{s_{critical}}$) ;
end
Phase 3 - Detect Stoppage using Rarity Score (ρ)
forall the $\mathtt{s_i} \in \mathtt{S} - \mathtt{S_{critical}} - \mathtt{S_{periodic}}$ **do**
  Data: Seq $= ADL_1, ADL2, \ldots$, sequence of ADLs detected since last s_i event
  $\rho = Pr(\overline{s_i}|Seq) \times Acc_{Seq}$
  if $\rho < \tau$ **then** generateAlert($\mathtt{s_i}$) ;
end

as critical by the impact estimation component in the previous step. In particular, the second technique focuses on those critical sensors that have a 100% impact on detection accuracy, i.e. the ADL can no longer be detected in the absence of the sensor. We call these sensors *grave* sensors. For example, the *Front Door* sensor is a *grave* sensor for `Leave House` ADL in *KasterenA* dataset. For such sensors, Idea raises a failure alert if the time elapsed since the last detection of the *ADL* exceeds a threshold that is based on previously observed ADL occurrence data.

The third technique is for the rest of the sensors that do not satisfy the criteria of the previous two techniques. The approach for such sensors, involves computing a *rarity score* (ρ). The ρ essentially, is the probability that the sensor has not triggered, while certain related activities (ADLs) that the sensor participates in have been detected by the detector using a combination of other sensors. If the ρ value falls below a *rarity threshold* (τ) we raise a sensor failure alert. We now explain alert generation in the context of an example. In Figure 5, we show the amount of time it will take to generate an alert for missing `Fridge` sensor in *KasterenA* dataset using occurrence traces of two activities `Drinking` and `Cooking` from *KasterenA* dataset. On X-axis, we plot the time since the Fridge sensor stopped generating events. On Y-axis, we plot ρ values. The points on each line represent the time when an ADL was detected since the `Fridge` failed.

First, for every tuple <$\mathtt{s_i}$, $\mathtt{ADL_k}$> we calculate the $Pr(\overline{\mathtt{s_i}}|\mathtt{ADL_k})$, probability of *non-occurrence* of $\mathtt{s_i}$ given $\mathtt{ADL_k}$ has occurred. Specifically, in *KasterenA* dataset,
$Pr(\overline{\mathtt{Fridge}}|\mathtt{Cooking}) = 0.05$ and $Pr(\overline{\mathtt{Fridge}}|\mathtt{Drinking}) = 0.4$ respectively. Assuming, that τ is set to 0.1, we observe that the sequence `[Drinking, Cooking]` was detected over last 6 hours without a single `Fridge` event. The ρ for the above sequence is defined as $Pr(\overline{\mathtt{Fridge}}|\mathtt{Sequence})$. We observe that the sensor trigger for a given activity are independent of other activities and hence,
$Pr(\overline{Fridge}|Sequence)$
$= Pr(\overline{\mathtt{Fridge}}|\mathtt{Drinking}) \times Pr(\overline{\mathtt{Fridge}}|\mathtt{Cooking})$. Note that, for each detected activity in which an expected (based on prior history) sensor has not triggered, besides sensor failure, two other possibilities could have happened:

- Idea could had misclassified the activity itself. We counter this by weighting the probability of non-occurrence of the sensor for a given activity with the detection accuracy of the ADL ($\mathtt{Acc_k}$). This introduces a slack in alert generation times. Based on experimentation, ADL detection accuracy, $Acc_{\mathtt{Drinking}} = 0.93$ and $Acc_{\mathtt{Cooking}} = 0.89$.
Hence, $\rho = \{Pr(\overline{Fridge}|Drink) \times Acc_{Drink}\} \times \{Pr(\overline{\mathtt{Fridge}}|\mathtt{Cook}) \times Acc_{Cook}\} = 0.02$.
- Or (2), The user behavior has changed and she has stopped using the specific sensor for conducting an activity. In this case, we assume that the behavior of the user will not change for all activities at the same time, and the presence of sensor triggers caused by other activities will inform us that the sensor has not failed.

Further, we periodically re-learn all the rules to account for behavioral changes [4] We raise a sensor failure alert when $\rho < \tau$. Note that, we track ρ across multiple activities as it leads to a faster alert generation than considering a single activity. For example, from Figure 5, when τ is set to 0.01 or lower, tracking only `Drinking` ADL will generate an alert around the 18 hour mark while tracking only `Cooking` will generate an alert after 24 hours.

We define that a false failure alert for a sensor occurs when a sensor signal is received sometime after Idea raises a failure alert for the sensor. We note that a high value of τ will lead to larger number of false alerts since a a smaller number of ADLs with non-occurrence of a specific sensor will cause the ρ to quickly fall below τ. On the other hand a lower τ reduces false alerts but increases the alert generation times. We evaluate this tradeoff and present results in later sections(Section 4.4).

3.5 Maintenance scheduling

The maintenance scheduling component in the cloud collects all sensor failure alerts across the various homes, and periodically determines the homes that need to be visited by maintenance personnel, and the order in which the visits should occur. To build the maintenance schedule, the system expects for each candidate home,

[4] In a deployment setting, we could also ask the user/maintenance personnel to provide feedback when false alerts occur to trigger re-learning of rules.

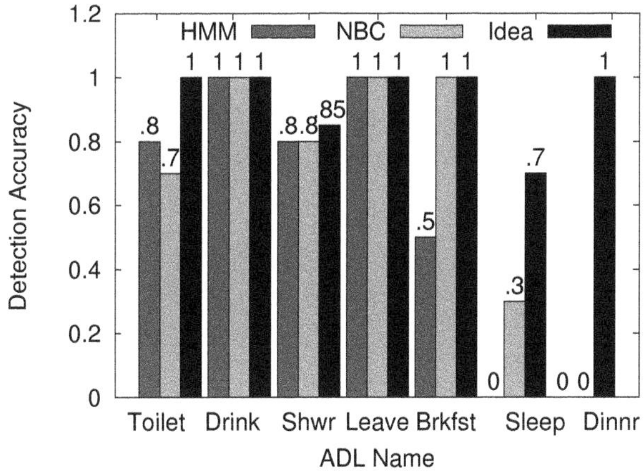

Figure 6: ADL Detection accuracy of Idea, NBC and HMM for the *KasterenA* dataset with no failed sensors.

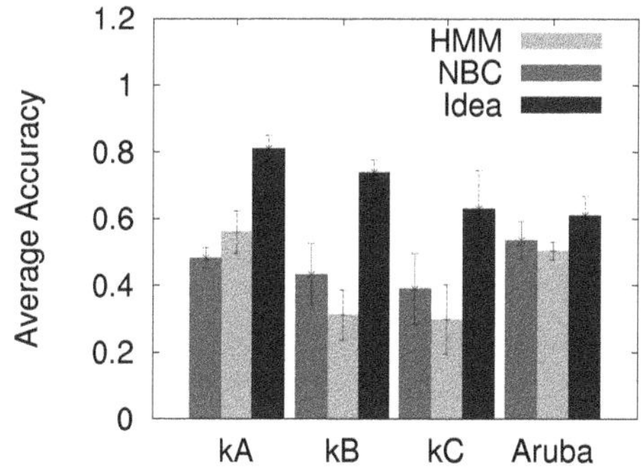

Figure 7: ADL Detection accuracy of NBC, HMM and Idea across multiple datasets described in table 1 with no sensor failures.

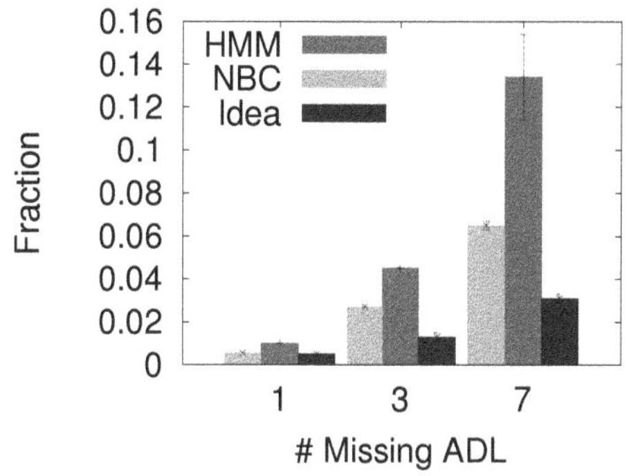

Figure 8: Reduction in Detection accuracy of NBC, HMM and Idea across all datasets in the presence of sensor failures

information on (a) impact of sensor failure, (b) location of the candidate home, and c) the maximum allowable reduction in accuracy for each ADL (or aggregated across all ADLs). The maintenance operation itself is simple and involves replacing *all* failed sensors in the home. Note that the main cost in maintenance involves the mechanic's hourly billing rate, and hence Idea optimizes for labor cost in the optimization formulation. Assuming that each mechanic's billing rate is same, Idea adds additional constraints on the maximum distance that can be traversed by each mechanic and then attempts to minimize the number of mechanics required to fix all the *critical* sensor failures. Thus minimizing the overall cost of maintenance while ensuring that the reduction in ADL detecting accuracy does not degrade below the required threshold.

We model the problem of finding optimal routes for maintenance personnel as a mixed integer program for Traveling Sales Man (TSP) problem. The solution to the problem is used for scheduling maintenance jobs periodically.

3.6 Prototype

Idea adopts a hybrid-deployment architecture wherein the service provider deploys an IoT gateway at the home to collect and process sensor data locally for enabling resident-centered functions like ADL monitoring, while sensor maintenance scheduling are centralized and run on the enterprise cloud. The centralized operation of maintenance scheduling allows the maintenance service provider to leverage failure information from all homes in the deployment to plan maintenance dispatches optimally. In our current implementation, the IoT gateway is emulated by an application that collects sensor data, performs ADL detection and sensor failure detection, and sends alerts to the cloud server that runs the maintenance scheduling component. We have implemented the components in Java, with the frequent itemset mining for ADL signature generation carried out using R packages. We use a CPLEX [36] solver for solving the mixed integer programming solution. The cloud server is a node hosted on a commercial cloud platform [37].

4. EVALUATION

In this section, we evaluate the performance of Idea. We begin by evaluating the constituent components of Idea to show the efficacy of our design choices. We then demonstrate the overall performance of Idea in increasing the time-before repair, and consequently the significant reduction in maintenance overhead across a variety of data sets. We begin by describing our methodology.

4.1 Methodology

We run experiments using the datasets listed in Table 1. For bench marking ADL detection performance, we use 80% of the dataset for training, and the remaining 20% for testing. In case we need to run an experiment for a much longer time than the available trace length, we re-create a longer trace by replaying the same trace of the home in a loop (e.g. for reliable detection of failed sensors in Section 4.4).

For statistical confidence, we randomly choose a different starting point in the trace for each run of the experiment; For example, the trace may start on the morning of Monday for one run, while starting at Thursday afternoon for the next run. Unless otherwise stated, we run each experiment 20 times and present the aggregate results. To evaluate the effects of sensor failure on ADL detection, we emulate a sensor failure by creating a trace with the failed sensor removed, and running the detector on this trace. To emulate sensor failures over large deployments in Section 4.5, we generate traces with failed sensors using the data sets as follows. We iterate over the trace, select a sensor at random and determine whether the sensor will fail at a specific time using a Weibull distribution, with mean time to failure of 1 year. Once sensor failure is determined, we remove its future instances from the trace. We present our evaluation results next.

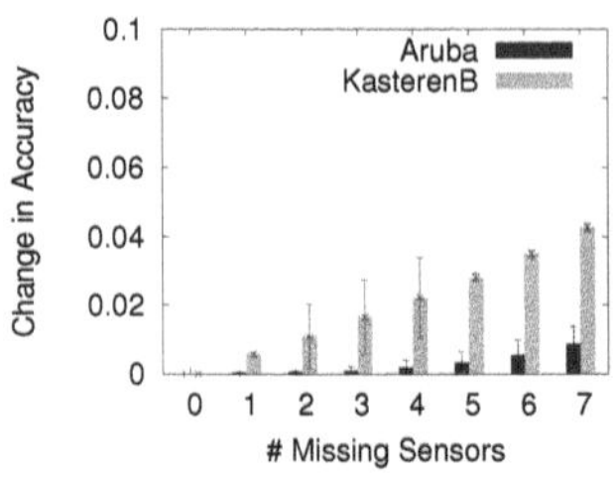

Figure 9: Reduction in ADL detection accuracy of Idea for *Aruba* and *KasterenB* datasets with increasing number of sensor failures.

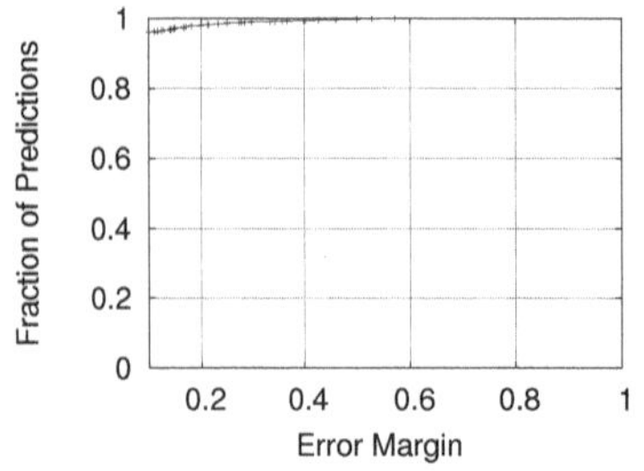

(a) CDF of estimation error in estimating sensor failure impact on detection accuracy for all sensors and ADLs across all datasets.

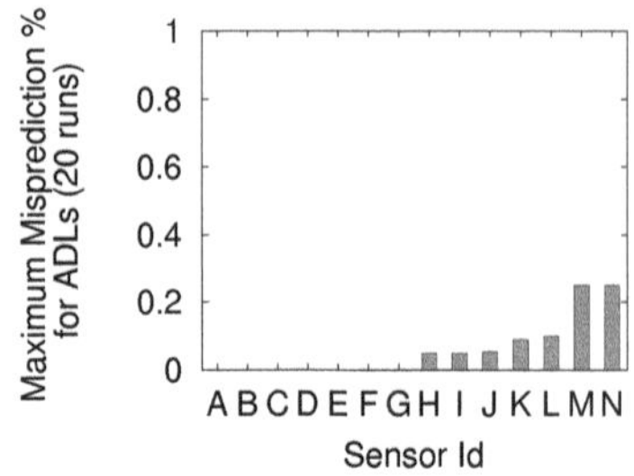

(b) Maximum estimation error for prepare_breakfast across all sensors for *KasterenA* dataset.

Figure 10: Benchmarking impact estimation

4.2 ADL Detection

We first demonstrate the efficacy of the ADL detection component in Idea. We compare the performance of Idea with two other detectors (NBC [25] and HMM [22]) that have been used in the past for ADL detection. Briefly, NBC learns a probabilistic model of the ADL from the underlying sensor event data, while HMM learns a sequential model for each ADL based on the sequence of sensor events that constitute the ADL. In particular, we evaluate the detection accuracy of the three schemes, both in the presence and absence of sensor failures. Figure 6 shows the detection accuracy of Idea, HMM and NBC for each individual ADL in *KasterenA* dataset when there are no sensor failures. As can be seen from the plot, Idea provides the highest detection accuracy across all ADLs. We observe similar results for other datasets.

In Figure 7, we present the average accuracy of the three schemes across all ADLs for several representative datasets with no sensor failures. We find that Idea performs better than NBC and HMM schemes in each data set. NBC performs worse compared to Idea since the NBC model assumes independence among the sensor events, while Idea is designed to extract the dependencies among sensors on a per ADL basis. Similarly, HMM performs worse, since it is based on *sequences* of human activities, whereas human activities are inherently variable and can happen out of sequence several times. On the other hand, Idea is designed to seamlessly handle human induced variabilities and achieves higher detection performance.

We next evaluate detection performance in the presence of sensor failures. Figure 8 depicts the aggregate drop in detection accuracy (compared to the baseline case of no sensor failures) for all possible combinations of 1, 3 and 7 failed sensors across all datasets. We observe that the drop in aggregate accuracy is the least for Idea compared to NBC and HMM, and Idea performs significantly better compared to the other schemes with increasing number of sensor failures. This lower deterioration in performance can be explained in terms of Idea's ability to effectively extract redundancy among sensors and leverage it for better detection.

To further explain, in Figure 9, we plot the aggregate change in detection accuracy of Idea with increasing number of sensor failures for *Aruba* and *KasterenB* respectively . We find that the deterioration in performance with sensor failures is lower for *Aruba* than *KasterenB* datasets. On deeper investigation, we found that *Aruba* has higher redundancy compared to *KasterenB*, thus, demonstrating that Idea effectively leverages sensor redundancies for ADL detection.

4.3 Impact Estimation

The impact estimation component enables identifying *critical* sensors for each ADL by computing the severity of the sensor failures in terms of deterioration in ADL detection accuracy. We benchmark the performance of impact estimation in terms of the estimation error. For this, we compare the impact estimated by the model on the training data against the actual change in ADL detection accuracy obtained by running the detector twice on the test data, once with all sensors included, and again with the failed sensor removed from the trace. In Figure 10(a), we plot the CDF of error between the estimated impact and the actual impact obtained by running the detector. As can be seen from the plot, for more than 95% of the activities the error in estimation is zero. This result shows that impact estimation is able to accurately predict the change in recognition accuracy, thereby allowing us to identify critical sensors, and reduce scheduling of "avoidable" maintenance visits. Figure 10(b), depicts the maximum estimation errors (over all sensors in 20 runs) for a specific ADL in *KasterenA* dataset. We have obtained similar performance on other datasets as well and present *KasterenA* as an exemplar. Seven out of fourteen sensors (50%) have zero error in the impact estimate. The `Groceries_Cbrd` and `Plates_Cbrd` sensors have a maximum error of 25% for `Prepare_Breakfast`. This is due to the fact that the remaining `Prepare_Breakfast` sensors such as fridge are shared with other ADLs such as `Drinking` and `Snacking` whose sensors overlap with `Prepare_Breakfast` in the absence of an critical sensor like `Groceries_Cbrd` or `Plates_Cbrd`. In this case, Idea assumes all these instances will be misdetected and overestimates the impact.

4.4 Sensor Failure Detection

We next evaluate the responsiveness and tradeoffs involved in sensor failure detection and alert generation in Idea. Figure 11 shows the time taken by the failure detection module to detect the failure of the *Fridge* sensor in *KasterenB* dataset, by analyzing the *(non-)*occurrence of *Fridge* events during the performance of four ADLs: `Eating`, `Cooking`, `Storing Groceries` in isolation. As can be seen from the plot, the alert for the failed Fridge sensor is generated the earliest (12 hours) by monitoring `Eating` activity. This is due to the combined effects of high triggering probability(0.95) for the $[sensor, ADL]$ pair and high frequency of the ADL (every 11.2 hrs). We also observe that `Cooking` provides the next best detection time of 13 hours, which is 4 hours less than that of `Drinking` ADL although the `Drinking` ADL (once every 0.81 hours) is more frequent than `Eating` event (once every

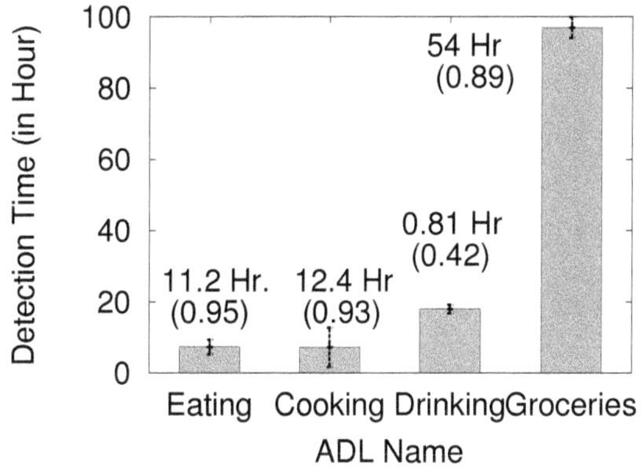

Figure 11: Time taken to detect failure of fridge sensor using a single ADL in *KasterenB* dataset. The numbers denote the occurrence frequency of each ADL and occurrence probability of the Fridge sensor(in brackets) for that ADL

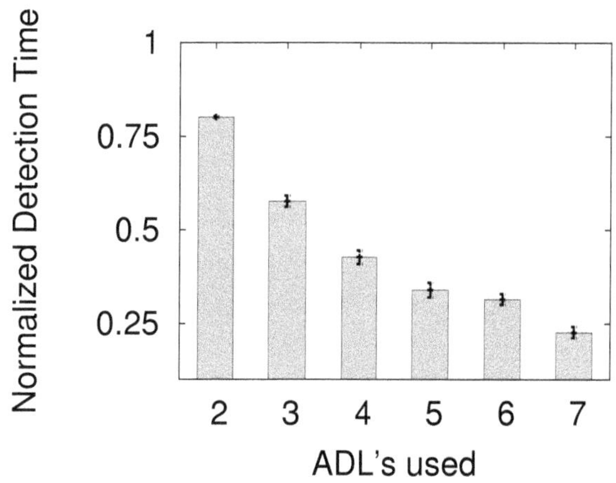

Figure 12: Time taken to detect failed sensors using multiple ADLs, with best ADL combination time normalized to single best ADL time.

12.4 hours). This is due to the fact that the probability of triggering fridge to Drinking is only 0.43, compared to 0.93 probability of triggering fridge for Cooking.

We next evaluate the improvements in failure detection times when multiple ADLs are combined and used together to detect a sensor failure. In Figure 12, we present the time taken to raise an alert from the time of occurrence of a failure, as a function of the maximum number of ADLs that are collectively monitored over all datasets, normalized to the time taken by the single best ADL to raise an alert. Particularly, we present the best possible time for alert generation by an ADL combination of specific size. As expected, the figure shows that the alert generation time decreases with an increasing number of ADL combinations. More interestingly, even having just combinations of three ADLs instead of one leads to halving of the time to detect a failure and raise an alert, showing the benefits of the collective monitoring scheme of Idea.

False positive trade-offs: Next we evaluate the effect of the rarity threshold on the sensor failure false (positive) alert rate. In Figure 13, we present the effect of the rarity threshold on the time taken to detect a sensor failure across all datasets. For the median case, compared to a baseline rarity threshold of 0.01, it takes 17× more time to detect sensor failures when the rarity threshold is set to 0.001. The detection time increase to 123× for the same failure when the rarity metric is set to 0.0001 (compared to baseline of 0.01). We next present the effect of the rarity threshold on false alert rates.

In our experiments, we found that with a rarity threshold of 0.001 we had 23× fewer false positive alerts compared to a threshold of 0.01, while the number of false alerts decreased 318× when the threshold was changed to 0.0001. The above results are expected, as a low value for rarity threshold implies that more instances of non firing events (when a ADL occurs) will have to be observed before the alert can be raised. Thus, a lower rarity threshold, will lead to a delay in raising a failure alert (false positive) while minimizing the number of false alerts (false positive).

4.5 End-to-end: Maintenance Scheduling

We now benchmark the performance of Idea on maintenance efficacy in terms of the number of maintenance visits and per-home maintenance inter-arrival times.

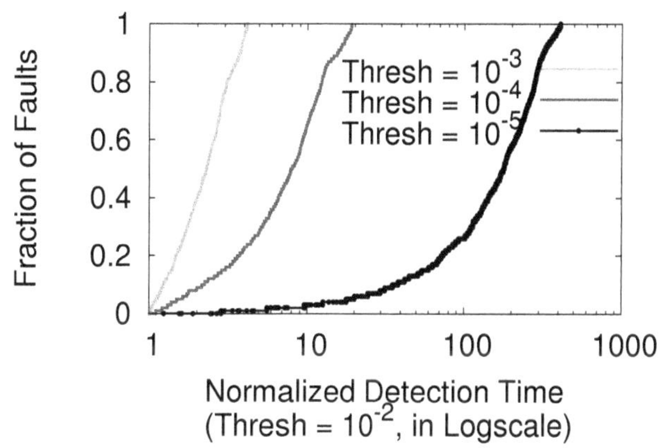

Figure 13: Normalized (to rarity threshold = 0.01) increase in time taken to detect sensor failures for different values of rarity threshold

Methodology

To quantify the maintenance benefits, we begin by emulating the geo-graphical distribution of homes over a large city, in our case, the Manhattan region of NY city. We generate home locations (latitude, longitude) of ten thousand homes over a 400 sq miles region of Manhattan as shown in Figure 14 using the City and Network Generator(CING) [38] that generates representative traces of the population distribution, mobility patterns as well as spatial distribution of homes and offices. We then randomly assign to each home a set of sensors identical to one of the testbed homes listed in Table 1. We emulate error probabilities of individual sensors in each home using the well accepted Weibull distribution [29, 30] with mean time to failure (MTTF) of 1 year for a period of 2 years. Once a sensor is determined as failed, it remains failed till a maintenance person visits the home and fixes the sensor. Finally, we collate the failures across the ten thousand homes and determine the maintenance visit schedules for each day based on the alerts received the previous day. We consider and alert as critical if the

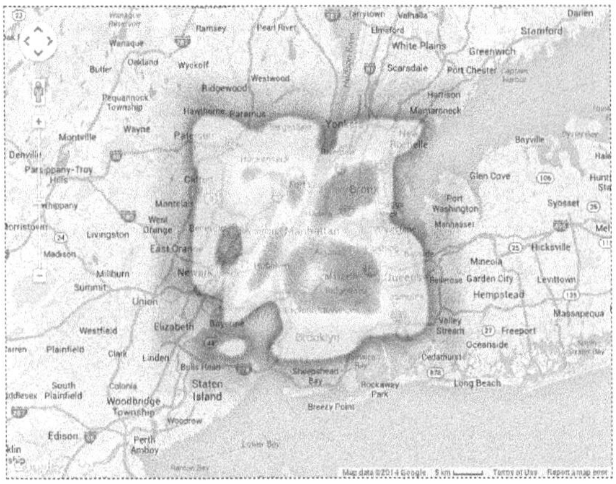

Figure 14: Home Location Distribution in NY

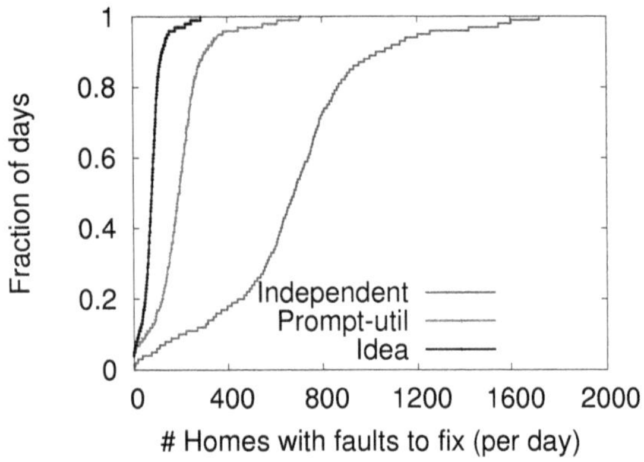

Figure 15: Number of homes with critical faults over 10K homes

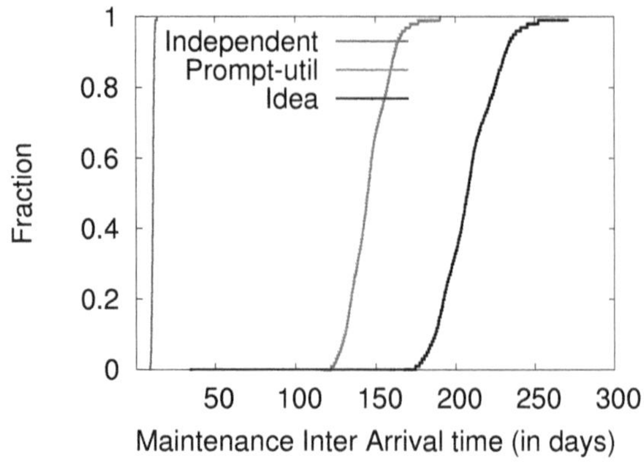

Figure 16: Inter maintenance visit time distribution for 10K homes

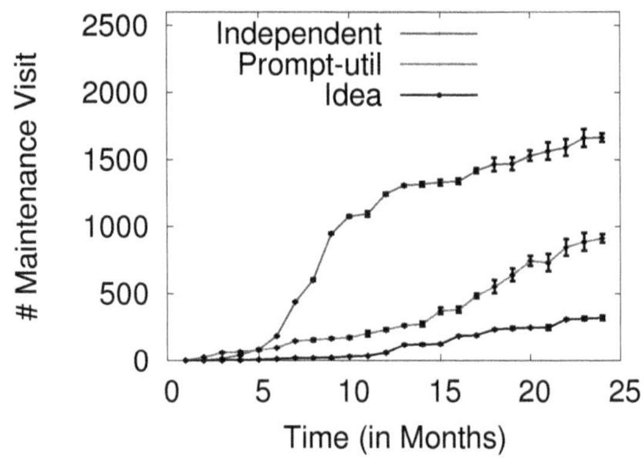

Figure 17: Maintenance visits with *Aruba* type deployments for 10K homes

impact of new sensor failures, along with potential prior failures is greater than 5%. We investigate the performance of Idea against three other schemes for scheduling maintenance visits:

- **Independent:** Any failed sensor in each home has to be fixed the next day.
- **Prompt-Util:** Maintenance is done only for sensors that are necessary for detecting one or more ADLs in the home. Any sensor that is part of at least one ADL signature (in Idea) is considered eligible for maintenance.
- **Periodic:** A maintenance person will periodically visit each home, and fix all the failed sensors on the day of visit.

We present the performance comparison results next.

Reactive Maintenance

In Figure 15, we present the CDF of the number of unique homes that need to be visited daily over the entire duration of the experiment. Observe that the number of homes is significantly fewer for Idea compared to other schemes. Specifically, we find that for more than 50% of the days Idea needs only 68 visits (less than 1% of the number of homes), while the independent scheme will require around 750 visits (11×) , and Prompt-Util needs around 134 visits (2×). Note that, Prompt-Util (a simplified version of Idea) itself leads to a significant reduction in the number of visits. In Figure 16, we plot the CDF of the inter-maintenance visit times (in days) to individual homes. We find that for the average case, Idea needs to visit a home every 211 days, whereas Independent and Prompt-Util need maintenance visits every 18 and 128 days respectively.

We illustrate the effects of passing time on the maintenance workload in Figure 17 and Figure 18, the figure shows the per month average number of maintenance visits for the three schemes for homes with sensor configurations similar to *Aruba* and *KasterenB* respectively. The figure shows that the number of maintenance visits will increase with time, as expected, since more sensors will fail with increasing time. However, the overall visits for Idea are fewer than the other schemes. We also note that for *Aruba* the improvement in performance of Prompt-Util scheme over Independent is higher than that of *KasterenB* homes; this is due to the fact that *Aruba* homes have around 21% sensors not useful for ADL detection, while *KasterenB* has only 8% such sensors.

Periodic Maintenance

The benefit of a periodic visit scheme is the fixed number of maintenance visits; however, the scheme suffers from the possibility of critical sensor failures (leading to reduced detection accuracy of important ADLs) in the home till the next maintenance visit. In Figure 19(a) we depict the average number of sensor failures (both

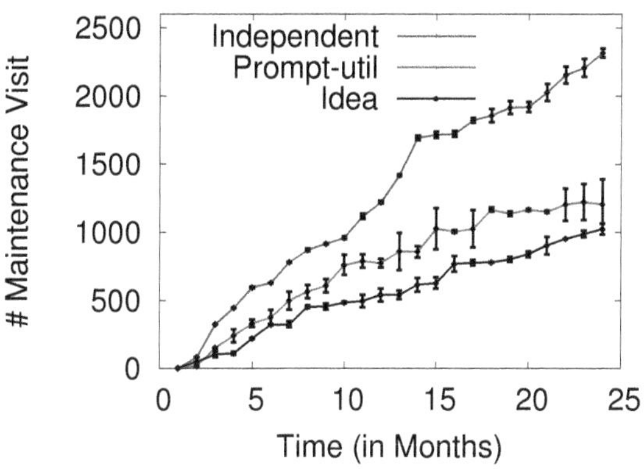

Figure 18: Maintenance visits with *KasterenB* type deployments

overall and critical) per home that will be present as a function of periodic maintenance times. As can be seen from the plot, with increased inter-visit time gap from 50 days to 250 days, the number of failed sensors also increases from 0.04 to 0.31. Figure 19(b) shows the number of days from the first critical failure till the arrival of maintenance operation. We find that on an average a home will have 19 days with failed critical sensors for a periodic visit of 50 days. The number goes up to 87 days for a visit gap of 250 days. Such under-performance of monitoring applications is clearly undesirable in a number of scenarios, esp. patient care and elderly care.

Effect of redundancy aware detector design on Maintenance load

We next benchmark the impact of Idea's redundancy aware detector design against other schemes such as NBC and HMM. In Figure 20, we plot the average inter-maintenance visit time (Time-before-repair) for the four schemes on a 1000 home *KasterenA* deployment. HMM and NBC improve Time-before-repair more than twice over the independent scheme having a Time-before-repair of 47 days. On the other hand, Idea has a approximately 2× longer Time-before repair of 207 days compared to 101 and 117 days for NBC and HMM schemes respectively. This is expected as detection performance of Idea degrades more gradually compared to NBC, HMM as shown in Figure 8. We note that techniques such as SMART [27] that also attempt to reduce maintenance visits by relying on off-the-shelf NBC and HMM detectors will also generate lesser number of maintenance visits by using Idea instead.

Such significant reductions in maintenance overhead have a direct implication on resource provisioning for an IoT enterprise. In practice, the total distance that can be covered by a maintenance person on any given day is limited. We consider this constraint in our MIP formulation and allow the use of multiple people to cover the tasks at hand. We conduct two sets of experiments - one that limits the total distance traveled per day to 40 Km and the other that limits it to 20 Km (Figure 21). Under each of these settings we compute the number of maintenance people needed to complete "‘X%"' of the tasks on any given day. In Figure 21(b), we find that under a 40 Km distance limit per day on the KasterenB dataset, we observe that our approach requires about 2.5x fewer maintenance personnel to cover 10% of the tasks and about 3.3x fewer personnel to cover all the tasks. In FigureFigure 21(a), we show similar results for 20 KM distance limit. These results demonstrate that our

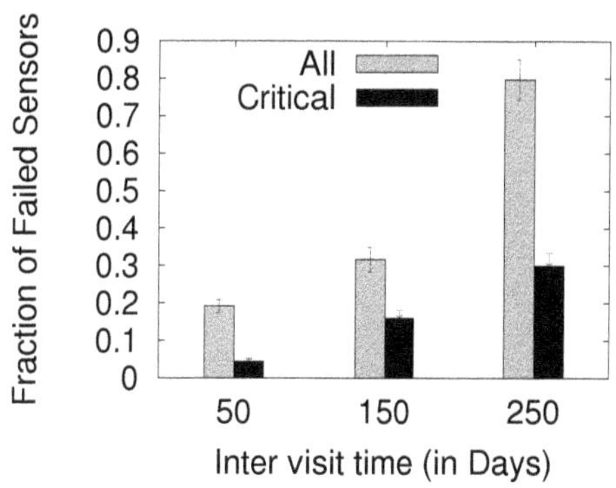

(a) % failed sensors to be fixed

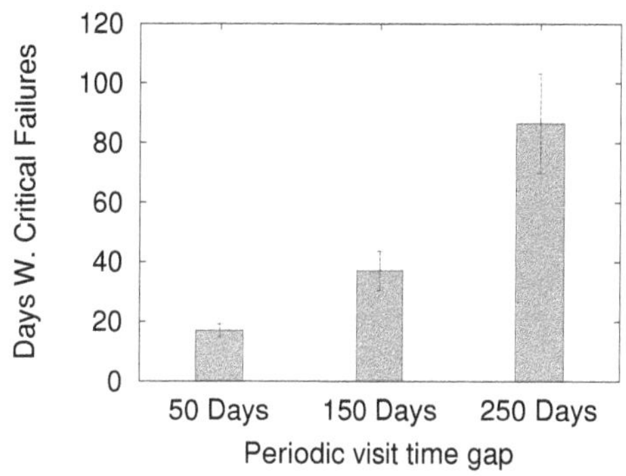

(b) Days with critical failures

Figure 19: Periodic maintenance scheme performance.

approach translates into significant (over one order of magnitude in dense deployments) savings in maintenance resources (costs), thereby making IoT enterprises more profitable.

5. RELATED WORK

We compare and contrast Idea with prior literature in the areas of diagnostics in smart homes, large scale asset management tools, robust sensor network deployment, fault detection in homogeneous sensor networks and ADL detection in smart homes.

Smart home fault diagnostics

The closest work to ours is SMART [27] that leverages application level semantics to identify *non-fail stop* failures. In the training phase, SMART learns multiple classifiers for recognizing the same set of activities based on different subsets of sensors. At run time, SMART analyzes the relative change in recognition accuracy of the different classifier instances, and uses this information to identify the failed sensors. We believe we make the following distinctions from SMART 1) SMART retrofits failure detection on state of the art detectors such as NBC and HMM by viewing the classifiers as black boxes and using relative changes in accuracy between the different classifiers for detecting a failure. On the other hand, Idea is a white box integrated approach that combines ADL detection with sensor failure detection and functional redundancy estimation for determining maintenance scheduling 2) SMART trains and simultaneously runs O(Number of Sensors) classifiers just for failure detection, with this ensemble of classifiers having no impact on the ADL detection accuracy. On the other hand, Idea runs a single classifier, that improves both ADL detection accuracy as well as sensor failure detection. 3) SMART cannot detect failures of sen-

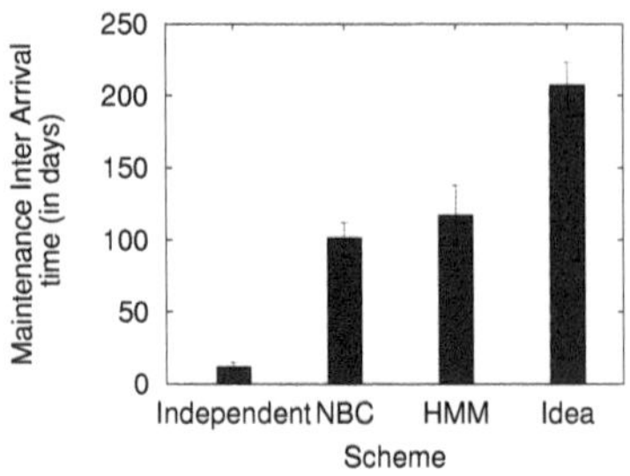

Figure 20: Average inter-maintenance visit times for a deployment of 1000 *KasterenA* homes across four schemes viz. Independent, HMM, NBC and Idea.

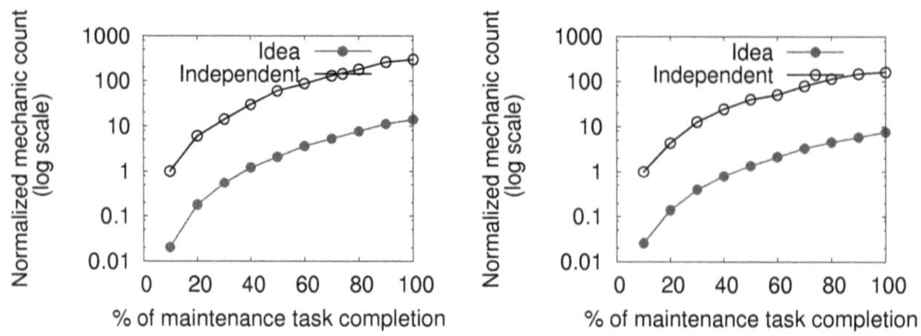

(a) 20 Km

(b) 40 Km

Figure 21: Distribution of number of mechanics necessary to repair "'X%"' of faults in a day, normalized to number of mechanics necessary to fix 10% faults, with a constraint of (a) 20 Km and (b) 40 Km travel radius

sors that are not frequently used in any of the activities. On the other hand, Idea will detect the failures of these sensors as well.

The authors in [28] present a complementary technique to detect failures by learning the regular patterns of sensor firings with respect to electrical appliance usage, and raising an alert when there is significant deviation from the regular firing interval distribution. This is an example of approaches that require extra electrical sensing infrastructure, and can be leveraged in Idea as well.

Commercial asset management software

Existing enterprise asset management products such as [39,40] automate the maintenance of large scale device deployments. Akin to Idea such software allows (automatic as well as manual) logging of fault tickets about various assets being maintained, and provides sophisticated algorithms for scheduling of maintenance operations. Idea enables complementary functionality by learning the inherent redundancies in capabilities of various sensors, which allows for significantly extending the time-before-repair.

Robust homogeneous sensor network deployments

There has been considerable research [8–15] in understanding and enhancing redundancy in *homogeneous* sensor deployments to enhance the lifetime of deployments, from both an energy efficiency and fault tolerance perspective. [41] and [42] enable applications to specify at a high level the relevant contexts and context changes, while the system optimizes and manages the sensing based on the available resource state. Similarly, [43] proposes an energy efficient sensing framework by exploiting the relationship among contexts, for example between driving and being at home, as well as the relationship between the cost of sensing and inferring a context. The key distinction of Idea from such prior art, lies in the fact that it focuses on systematically understanding the functional redundancies amongst *heterogeneous* sensors resulting from resident behavior. Furthermore, home deployments involve heterogeneous event-driven sensors that are triggered by human action as opposed to continuous sensing systems for which the prior approaches were developed.

Fault detection in homogeneous sensor networks

A number of works [44–46] address the problem of fault detection in sensor networks. The authors in [47] provide a survey of fault management approaches in sensor networks. Akin to Idea, authors in [48, 49] a) identify sensor faults by identifying outliers among neighboring sensors to build a community of trust among nodes to provide high data integrity and detect faulty sensors and b) prompt for human assistance to improve fault detection. However, in contrast to Idea prior work does not deal with finding outliers in heterogeneous sensor deployments.

Smart home ADL detection

A number of recent works [20,21,23,24] have addressed the problem of detecting ADLs from sensor firings in smart homes using machine learning based approaches Hidden Markov Models, Naive Bayes Classifier, Conditional Random Fields etc.. Specifically, the authors in [23] propose using hidden semi-Markov models for activity recognition while incorporating duration of activities as a feature for classification. Similarly, Roy et al. [50] address the problem of ADL recognition in multi-inhabitant environments by combining smart phone and infrastructure sensors and learning spatio-temporal constraints to infer the attributes such as location of the user.

However, the above body of work does not customize the design of their classifiers to address the unique problems and opportunities associated with sensor faults in smart home deployments.

6. CONCLUSION

In this paper, we design Idea a novel sensor failure management system for IoT-enabled smart environments. Our approach is based on learning and leveraging the functional redundancy available among sensors for robust ADL detection in the presence of sensor failures. Specifically, our approach leverages the fact that there is inherent redundancy when combinations of sensors monitor *activities of daily living* (ADLs) in smart environments, and the utility or impact of each sensor depends on the activity being monitored and the rest of the sensors available for detecting the activities. Based on estimated impact of sensor failures, the system schedules necessary maintenance visits. Results show that Idea significantly increases the *time-before-repair* of homes, thereby reducing the maintenance overhead of keeping such IoT deployments functioning as expected.

7. ACKNOWLEDGMENT

We thank our shepherd Aruna Balasubramanian and other anonymous reviewers whose feedback helped bring the paper to its final form.

8. REFERENCES

[1] Telehealth and self-monitoring in the elder-care markets: A global analysis. http://blog.bccresearch.com/telehealth-and-self-monitoring-in-the-elder-care-markets-a-global-analysis-0.

[2] V Rialle, C Ollivet, C Guigui, and C Hervï£¡. What do family caregivers of alzheimer's disease patients desire in smart home technologies? *Methods of information in medicine*, 47:63–69, 2008.

[3] G et. al. Acampora. A survey on ambient intelligence in healthcare. *Proceedings of the IEEE*, 101(12):2470–2494, 2013.

[4] S Robben, M Pol, and B Krose. Longitudinal ambient sensor monitoring for functional health assessments: a case study. In *UbiComp*, 2014.

[5] G. LeBellego, N. Noury, G. Virone, M. Mousseau, and J. Demongeot. A model for the measurement of patient activity in a hospital suite. *Information Technology in Biomedicine, IEEE*, 10:92–99, 2006.

[6] Basma M. Mohammad El-Basioni, Sherine Mohamed Abd El-Kader, and Hussein S. Eissa. Independent living for persons with disabilities and elderly people using smart home technology. *International Journal of Application or Innovation in Engineering & Management*, 2014.

[7] Timothy W. Hnat, Vijay Srinivasan, Jiakang Lu, Tamim I. Sookoor, Raymond Dawson, John Stankovic, and Kamin Whitehouse. The hitchhiker's guide to successful residential sensing deployments. In *Proceedings of the 9th ACM Conference on Embedded Networked Sensor Systems*, SenSys '11, pages 232–245, New York, NY, USA, 2011. ACM.

[8] Shouzhi Huang and Xuezeng Zhao. Redundant nodes elimination in wireless sensor networks. In *Information Computing and Applications*, pages 48–58. Springer, 2013.

[9] Chi-Fu Huang and Yu-Chee Tseng. The coverage problem in a wireless sensor network. In *Proceedings of the 2Nd ACM International Conference on Wireless Sensor Networks and Applications*, WSNA '03, pages 115–121, New York, NY, USA, 2003. ACM.

[10] Di Tian and Nicolas D. Georganas. A coverage-preserving node scheduling scheme for large wireless sensor networks. In *Proceedings of the 1st ACM international workshop on Wireless sensor networks and applications*, pages 32–41. ACM Press, 2002.

[11] Mihaela Cardei, My T Thai, Yingshu Li, and Weili Wu. Energy-efficient target coverage in wireless sensor networks. In *INFOCOM 2005. 24th Annual Joint Conference of the IEEE Computer and Communications Societies. Proceedings IEEE*, volume 3, pages 1976–1984. IEEE, 2005.

[12] Habib M. Ammari and Sajal K. Das. Fast track article: Scheduling protocols for homogeneous and heterogeneous k-covered wireless sensor networks. *Pervasive Mob. Comput.*, 7(1):79–97, February 2011.

[13] Honghai Zhang and Jennifer C Hou. Maintaining sensing coverage and connectivity in large sensor networks. *Ad Hoc & Sensor Wireless Networks*, 1(1-2):89–124, 2005.

[14] Yong Gao, Kui Wu, and Fulu Li. Analysis on the redundancy of wireless sensor networks. In *IN PROC. 2ND ACM INTL. WORKSHOP ON WIRELESS SENSOR NETWORKS AND APPLICATIONS (WSNA*, pages 108–114. ACM Press, 2003.

[15] Rajagopal Iyengar. Low-coordination topologies for redundancy in sensor networks. In *In ACM MobiHoc*, pages 332–342, 2005.

[16] Benchmark datasets; datasets for activity recognitions. https://sites.google.com/site/tim0306/datasets.

[17] Wsu casas dataset. http://ailab.wsu.edu/casas/datasets/.

[18] K.D. Feuz, D.J. Cook, C. Rosasco, K. Robertson, and M. Schmitter-Edgecombe. Automated detection of activity transitions for prompting. *Human-Machine Systems, IEEE Transactions*, 2014.

[19] Prafulla Nath Dawadi, Diane Joyce Cook, and Maureen Schmitter-Edgecombe. Automated clinical assessment from smart home-based behavior data. *IEEE Journal of Biomedical and Health Informatics*, 2015.

[20] Tim van Kasteren, Athanasios Noulas, Gwenn Englebienne, and Ben Kröse. Accurate activity recognition in a home setting. In *Proceedings of the 10th International Conference on Ubiquitous Computing*, UbiComp '08, pages 1–9, New York, NY, USA, 2008. ACM.

[21] Parisa Rashidi, Diane J. Cook, Lawrence B. Holder, and Maureen Schmitter-Edgecombe. Discovering activities to recognize and track in a smart environment. *IEEE Trans. Knowl. Data Eng.*, 23(4):527–539, 2011.

[22] Aaron S. Crandall and Diane J. Cook. Using a hidden markov model for resident identification. In *Sixth International Conference on Intelligent Environments, IE 2010, Kuala Lumpur, Malaysia, July 19-21, 2010*, pages 74–79, 2010.

[23] TLM Van Kasteren, Gwenn Englebienne, and Ben JA Kröse. Activity recognition using semi-markov models on real world smart home datasets. *Journal of ambient intelligence and smart environments*, 2(3):311–325, 2010.

[24] Emmanuel Munguia Tapia, Stephen S Intille, and Kent Larson. *Activity recognition in the home using simple and ubiquitous sensors*. Springer, 2004.

[25] T. van Kasteren and B. Krose. Bayesian activity recognition in residence for elders. In *3rd IET International Conference on Intelligent Environments (IE 07)*, pages 209–212, 2010.

[26] L Liao, D Fox, and H Kautz. Location-based activity recognition using relational markov networks. In *Proc. Int. Joint Conf. Artif. Intell.*, 2005.

[27] Krasimira Kapitanova, Enamul Hoque, John A. Stankovic, Kamin Whitehouse, and Sang H. Son. Being smart about failures: Assessing repairs in smart homes. In *Proceedings of the 2012 ACM Conference on Ubiquitous Computing*, UbiComp '12, pages 51–60, New York, NY, USA, 2012. ACM.

[28] Sirajum Munir, John Stankovic, et al. Failuresense: Detecting sensor failure using electrical appliances in the home. In *Mobile Ad Hoc and Sensor Systems (MASS), 2014 IEEE 11th International Conference on*, pages 73–81. IEEE, 2014.

[29] Hazewinkel Michiel ed. Weibull distribution. *Encyclopedia of Mathematics*, 2001.

[30] Curt Ronniger. Reliability analyses with weibull. http://www.crgraph.com/Weibull.pdf, 2012.

[31] Department of Defense USA. Electronic reliability design handbook. "http://reliabilityanalytics.com/reliability_engineering_library/MIL-HDBK-338-V1_Electronic_Reliability_Design_Handbook_15_Oct_1984/MIL-HDBK-338-V1_Electronic_Reliability_Design_Handbook_15_Oct_1984_pp_2.htm", 1984.

[32] Seymour Morris. Online redundancy calculator for effective failure rate of n active redundant units, with m required for success (with repair), assuming either exponential or Weibull failure distributions. http://reliabilityanalyticstoolkit.appspot.com/active_redundancy_integrate, 2010.

[33] Ehsan Nazerfard, Parisa Rashidi, and Diane J. Cook. Using association rule mining to discover temporal relations of daily activities. In *Proceedings of the 9th International Conference on Toward Useful Services for Elderly and People with Disabilities: Smart Homes and Health Telematics*, ICOST'11, pages 49–56, Berlin, Heidelberg, 2011. Springer-Verlag.

[34] P. Kodeswaran, R. Kokku, M. Mallick, and S. Sen. Demultiplexing Activities of Daily Living in IoT enabled Smarthomes (to appear). In *IEEE Infocom*, 2016.

[35] Nirmalya Roy, Archan Misra, and Diane J. Cook. Infrastructure-assisted smartphone-based ADL recognition in multi-inhabitant smart environments. In *2013 IEEE International Conference on Pervasive Computing and Communications, PerCom 2013, San Diego, CA, USA, March 18-22, 2013*, pages 38–46, 2013.

[36] Cplex optimizer. http://www-01.ibm.com/software/commerce/optimization/cplex-optimizer/.

[37] P Kodeswaran and S Sen. Intellihome: Activity detection in smart homes on IBM BlueMix. http://intellihome.eu-gb.mybluemix.net/.

[38] S. Mitra, S. Ranu, V. Kolar, A. Telang, A. Bhattacharya, R. Kokku, and S. Raghavan. Trajectory aware macro-cell planning for mobile users. In *Computer Communications (INFOCOM), 2015 IEEE Conference on*, pages 792–800, April 2015.

[39] Maximo:ibm enterprise asset management. http://www-03.ibm.com/software/products/en/maximoassetmanagement.

[40] Sap–enterprise asset management. http://go.sap.com/solution/lob/asset-management.html.

[41] Seungwoo Kang, Jinwon Lee, Hyukjae Jang, Hyonik Lee, Youngki Lee, Souneil Park, Taiwoo Park, and Junehwa Song. Seemon: Scalable and energy-efficient context monitoring framework for sensor-rich mobile environments. In *Proceedings of the 6th International Conference on Mobile Systems, Applications, and Services*, MobiSys '08, pages 267–280, New York, NY, USA, 2008. ACM.

[42] Seungwoo Kang, Youngki Lee, Chulhong Min, Younghyun Ju, Taiwoo Park, Jinwon Lee, Yunseok Rhee, and Junehwa Song. Orchestrator: An active resource orchestration framework for mobile context monitoring in sensor-rich mobile environments. In *PerCom*, 2010.

[43] Suman Nath. Ace: Exploiting correlation for energy-efficient and continuous context sensing. In *Proceedings of the 10th International Conference on Mobile Systems, Applications, and Services*, MobiSys '12, pages 29–42, New York, NY, USA, 2012. ACM.

[44] Jessica Staddon, Dirk Balfanz, and Glenn Durfee. Efficient tracing of failed nodes in sensor networks. In *Proceedings of the 1st ACM International Workshop on Wireless Sensor Networks and Applications*, WSNA '02, pages 122–130, New York, NY, USA, 2002. ACM.

[45] Sapon Tanachaiwiwat, Pinalkumar Dave, Rohan Bhindwale, and Ahmed Helmy. Secure locations: routing on trust and isolating compromised sensors in location-aware sensor networks. In Ian F. Akyildiz, Deborah Estrin, David E. Culler, and Mani B. Srivastava, editors, *SenSys*, pages 324–325. ACM, 2003.

[46] S. Rost and H. Balakrishnan. Memento: A health monitoring system for wireless sensor networks. In *Sensor and Ad Hoc Communications and Networks, 2006. SECON '06. 2006 3rd Annual IEEE Communications Society on*, volume 2, pages 575–584, Sept 2006.

[47] Lilia Paradis and Qi Han. A survey of fault management in wireless sensor networks. *Journal of Network and Systems Management*, 15(2):171–190, 2007.

[48] Nithya Ramanathan, Thomas Schoellhammer, Eddie Kohler, Kamin Whitehouse, Thomas Harmon, and Deborah Estrin. Suelo: Human-assisted sensing for exploratory soil monitoring studies. In *Proceedings of the 7th ACM Conference on Embedded Networked Sensor Systems*, SenSys '09, pages 197–210, New York, NY, USA, 2009. ACM.

[49] Saurabh Ganeriwal, Laura K. Balzano, and Mani B. Srivastava. Reputation-based framework for high integrity sensor networks. *ACM Trans. Sen. Netw.*, 4(3):15:1–15:37, June 2008.

[50] N. Roy, A. Misra, and D. Cook. Infrastructure-assisted smartphone-based adl recognition in multi-inhabitant smart environments. In *Pervasive Computing and Communications (PerCom), 2013 IEEE International Conference on*, pages 38–46, March 2013.

Listening through a Vibration Motor

Nirupam Roy, Romit Roy Choudhury
University of Illinois at Urbana-Champaign

ABSTRACT

This paper demonstrates the feasibility of using the vibration motor in mobile devices as a sound sensor, almost like a microphone. We show that the vibrating mass inside the motor – designed to oscillate to changing magnetic fields – also responds to air vibrations from nearby sounds. With appropriate processing, the responses become intelligible, to the extent that humans can understand the vibra-motor recorded words with greater than 80% average accuracy. Even off-the-shelf speech recognition softwares are able to decode at 60% accuracy, without any training or machine learning. While these findings are not fundamentally surprising (given that any vibrating object should respond to air vibrations), the fidelity to which this is possible has been somewhat unexpected. We present our overall techniques and results through a system called *VibraPhone*, and discuss implications to both sensing and security.

1. INTRODUCTION

Vibration motors, also called "vibra-motors", are small actuators embedded in all types of phones and wearables. These actuators have been classically used to provide tactile alerts to human users. This paper identifies the possibility of using vibra-motors as a sound sensor, based on the observation that the same movable mass that causes the pulsation, should also respond to changes in air pressure. Even though the vibra-motor is likely to be far less sensitive compared to the (much lighter) diaphragm of an actual microphone, the question we ask is: *to what fidelity can the sound be reproduced?*

Even modest reproduction could prompt new applications and threats. On one hand, wearable devices like fitbits, that otherwise do not have a microphone, could now respond to voice commands. Further, in devices that already have microphones, perhaps better SNR could be achieved by combining the uncorrelated (noise) properties of the vibra-motor and microphone. On the other hand, leaking sound through vibra-motors opens new side channels – a malware that has default access to a phone's vibra-motor may now be able to eavesdrop into every phone conversation. Toys that have vibra-motors embedded could potentially listen into the ambience. This paper is an investigation into the vibra-motor's efficacy as a sound sensor, speech in particular.

MobiSys'16, June 25 - 30, 2016, Singapore, Singapore

ISBN 978-1-4503-4269-8/16/06...$15.00
DOI: http://dx.doi.org/10.1145/2906388.2906415

Our work follows a recent line of work in which motion sensors in smartphones have been shown to detect sound. Authors of Gyrophone [30] first demonstrated the feasibility of detecting sound signals from the rotational motions of smartphone gyroscopes. A recent work [47] reported how accelerometers may also be able to detect sound, in fact, classify spoken keywords such as "OK Google" or "Hello Siri". Authors rightly identified the applicability to continuous sound sensing – the energy-efficient accelerometer could always stay active, and turn on the energy-hungry microphone only upon detecting a keyword. While certainly useful, we observe that these systems run pattern recognition algorithms on the features of the signals. The vocabulary is naturally limited to less than 3 keywords, trained by a specific speaker. VibraPhone is attempting a different problem altogether – instead of learning a motion signature, it attempts to reconstruct the inherent speech content from the low bandwidth, highly distorted output of the vibra-motor. Hence, there are no vocabulary restrictions, and the output of VibraPhone should be decodable by speech-to-text softwares.

As a first step towards converting a vibra-motor into a sound sensor, VibraPhone exploits the notion of *reverse electromotive force* (back-EMF) in electronic circuits. Briefly, the A/C current in the vibra-motor creates a changing magnetic field around a coil, which in turn causes the vibra-motor mass to vibrate. However, when an external force impinges on the same mass – say due to the pressure of ambient sound – it causes additional motion, translating into a current in the opposite direction. This current, called back-EMF, can be detected through an ADC after sufficient amplification. Of course, the signal extracted from the back-EMF is noisy and at a lower bandwidth than human speech. However, given that human speech obeys an "acoustic grammar", we find an opportunity to recover the spoken words even from the back-EMF's signal traces. VibraPhone focuses on exactly this problem, and develops a sequence of techniques, including *spectral subtraction, energy localization, formant extrapolation, and harmonic reconstruction*, to ultimately distill out legible speech.

Our experimentation platform is both a Samsung smartphone and a custom circuit that uses vibra-motor chips purchased online (these chips are exactly the ones used in today's phones and wearables). We characterize the extent of signal reconstruction as a function of the loudness of the sound source. Performance metrics are defined by the accuracy with which the reconstructed signals are intelligible to humans and to (open-source) automatic speech recognition softwares. We use the smartphone microphone as an upper bound, and for fairness, record the speech at the same sound pressure level (SPL) [24, 4, 42] across all the devices. We experiment across a range of scenarios within our university building, and observe that results are robust/useful when the speaker is less than 2 meters from the vibra-motor.

Finally, we emphasize that smartphone vibra-motors cannot be used as microphones today, primarily because the actuator is simply not connected to an ADC. To this end, launching side-channel attacks is not immediate. However, as discussed later, we find that enabling the listening capability requires almost trivial rewiring (just soldering at 4 clearly visible junctions). This paper sidesteps these immediacy questions and concentrates on the core nature of the information leakage. At the least, we hope this work will draw attention to the permission policies on vibra-motors, which today are open to all apps by default. We have made various audio demos of VibraPhone available on our website [5] – we request the readers to listen to them to better experience the audio effects and reconstructions. In closing, the main contributions in this paper may be summarized as:

- *Recognizing that ambient sound manifests itself as back-EMF inside vibra-motor chips.* This leads to an actuator becoming a sound sensor with minimal changes to the current mobile device hardware.
- *Designing techniques that exploit constraints and structure of human speech to decode words from a noisy, low bandwidth signal.* Building the system on a smartphone and custom hardware platform, and demonstrating decoding accuracy of up to 88% when a male user is speaking in normal voice near his phone.

The rest of the paper expands on these contributions. We begin with a brief introduction to vibra-motors and our hardware platform.

2. UNDERSTANDING VIBRA-MOTORS

A vibra-motor is an electro-mechanical device that moves a magnetic mass rhythmically around a neutral position to generate vibrations [36]. While there are various kinds of vibra-motors, a popular one is called *Linear Resonant Actuators (LRA)* shown in Figure 1. With LRA, vibration is generated by the linear movement of the magnetic mass suspended near a coil, called the "voice coil". Upon applying AC current to the motor, the coil also behaves like a magnet (due to the generated electromagnetic field) and causes the mass to be attracted or repelled, depending on the direction of the current. This generates vibration at the same frequency as the input AC signal, while the amplitude of vibration is dictated by the signal's peak-to-peak voltage. Thus LRAs offer control on both the magnitude and frequency of vibration. Most smartphones today use LRA based vibra-motors.

2.1 Sound Sensing through back-EMF

Back-EMF is an electro-magnetic effect observed in magnet-based motors when relative motion occurs between the current carrying armature/coil and the magnetic mass's own

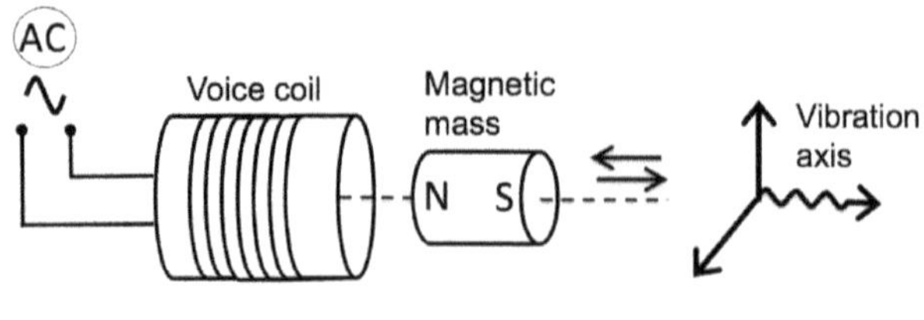

Figure 1: Basic sketch of an LRA vibra-motor.

field. According to Faraday's law of electromagnetic induction [16], this changing magnetic flux induces an electromotive force in the coil. Lenz's law [41] says this electromotive force acts in the reverse direction of the driving voltage, called *back-EMF of the motor.* As the rate of change of the magnetic flux is proportional to the speed of the magnetic mass, the back-EMF serves as an indicator of the extraneous vibration experienced by the mass.

Since sound is a source of external vibration, the movable mass in the vibra-motor is expected to exhibit a (subtle) response to it. Our experiments show that, when the vibra-motor is connected to an ADC, the back-EMF generated by the ambient sound can be recorded. This is possible even when the vibra-motor is passive (i.e., not pulsating to produce tactile alerts). We call this ADC output *vibra-signal* to distinguish it from the microphone signal that we will later use as a baseline for comparison. We now describe our platform to record and process the vibra-signal.

2.2 Experiment Platform

Custom hardware setup: Today's smartphones offer limited exposure/API to vibra-motor capabilities and other hardware components (e.g., amplifiers). To bypass these restrictions, we have designed a custom hardware setup using off-the-shelf LRA vibra-motor chips connected to our own ADC and amplifier. Figure 2 shows our setup – we mount this vibration motor adjacent to a standard microphone that serves as a comparative baseline. The vibra-signal is amplified and sampled at 16KHz. Test sounds include live speech from humans at varying distances, as well as sound playbacks through speakers at varying loudness levels.

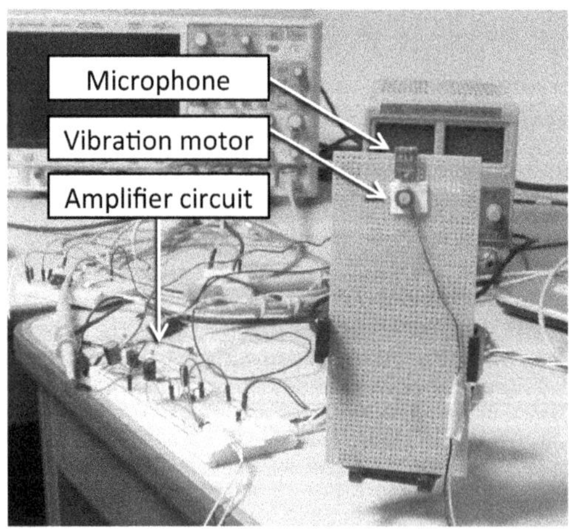

Figure 2: The custom hardware setup with collocated vibration motor and microphone.

Smartphones: While the custom hardware offers better programmability, we also use a smartphone setup to understand the possibilities with today's systems. Figure 3 shows our prototype – terminals of the built-in vibra-motor of a Samsung Galaxy S-III smartphone is connected to the audio line-in input port with a simple wire. The rewiring is trivial – for someone familiar with the process, it can be completed in less than 10 minutes. Once rewired, we collect the samples of the vibra-signal from the output channels of the earphone jack, using our custom Android application.

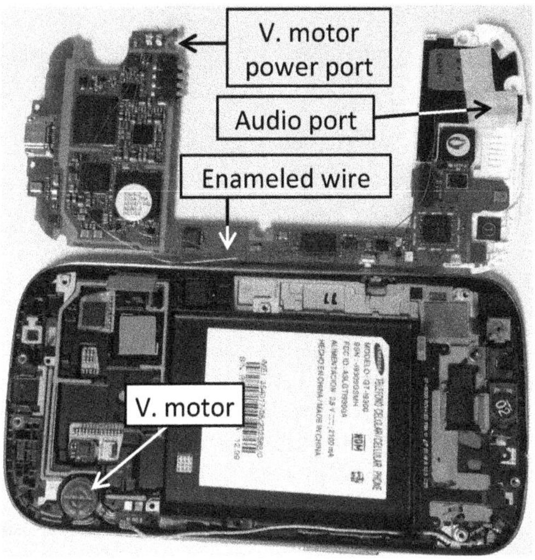

Figure 3: The smartphone setup with a simple wire connected between the vibra-motor's output to the audio line-in port.

Electromagnetic Coupling: We conduct a microbenchmark test to verify that the vibration motor signal is not influenced by the Electromagnetic coupling from the nearby microphone or speakers in our test setup. We remove the speakers and microphones from the test environment and directly record human speech with a vibration motor (find sample clips at project website [5]). Later we compare them with the recordings of the standard test setup to find no noticeable difference in signal quality.

3. SOUNDS AND HUMAN SPEECH

This section is a high level introduction to speech production in humans, followed by a discussion on the structure of speech signals.

3.1 Human Speech Production

Human speech can be viewed as periodic air waves produced by the lungs, modulated through a sequence of steps in the throat, nose, and mouth. More specifically, the air from the lungs first passes through the *vocal cords* – a pair of membranous tissue – that constricts or dilates to block or allow the air flow (Figure 4). When the vocal cords are constricted, the vibrations induced in the air-flow are called *voiced* signals. The voiced signals generate high energy pulses – in the frequency domain, the signal contains a fundamental frequency and its harmonics. All vowels and some consonants like "b" and "g" are sourced in voiced signals.

On the other hand, when the vocal cords dilate and allow the air to flow through without heavy vibrations, the outcome is called *unvoiced* signals. This generates sounds similar to noise, and is the origin of certain consonants, such as "s", "f", "p", "k", "t". Both voiced and unvoiced signals then pass through a flap of tissue, called *glottis*, which further pulsates to add power to the signal as well as distinctiveness to an individual's voice. These *glottal pulses* travel further and are finally modulated by the oral/nasal cavities to produce fine-tuned speech [11]. The overall speech production process is often modeled as a "source-filter" in literature, essentially implying that the human trachea/mouth applies a series of filters to the source sound signal. This source-filter model will later prove useful, when VibraPhone attempts to reconstruct the original speech signal.

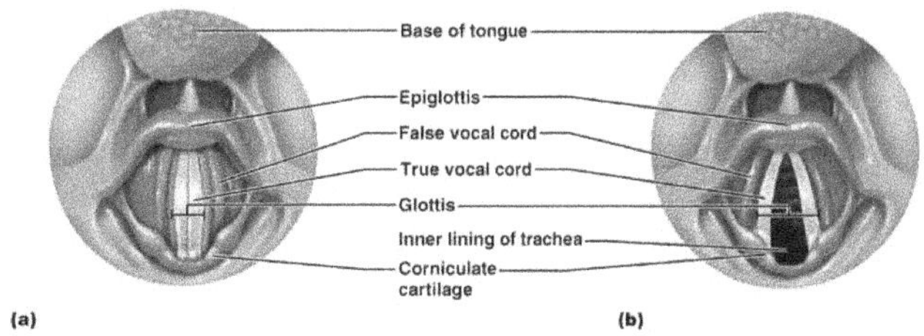

Figure 4: The vocal cords constricted in (a) and dilated in (b), creating *voiced* and *unvoiced* air vibrations, that are then shaped by the glottis and epiglottis.

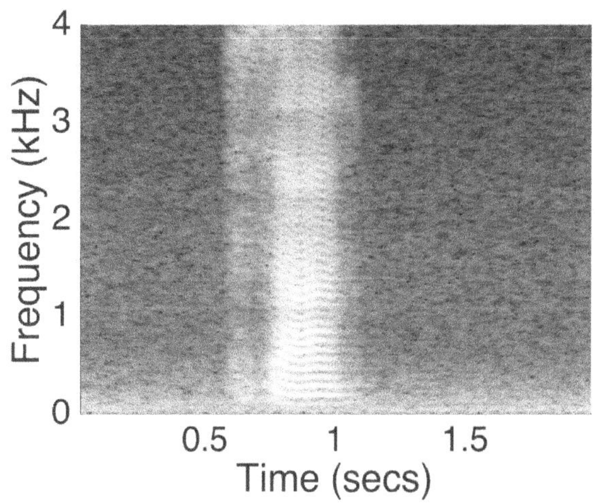

Figure 5: The spectrogram of the spoken consonant 's' followed by the vowel 'a' recorded with microphone.

3.2 Structure in Speech Signals

While the above discussions present a biological/linguistics point of view, we now discuss how they relate to the recorded speech signals and their structures. Figure 5 shows the spectrogram when a human user pronounces the alphabets "sa" – the signal was recorded through a smartphone microphone (not a vibra-motor)[1]. Although a toy case, the spectrogram captures the key building blocks of speech structure. We make a few observations that will underpin the challenges and the designs in the rest of the paper.

- The first visible signal (between 0.6 and 0.75 seconds) corresponds to the *unvoiced* component, the consonant "s". This signal is similar to noise with energy spread out rather uniformly across the frequency band. The energy content in this signal is low to moderate.

[1]The Y axis shows up to 4KHz, since normal human conversation in non-tonal languages like English is dominantly confined to this band.

- The second visible signal corresponds to the vowel "a" and is an example of the *voiced* component. The signal shows a low fundamental frequency and many harmonics all the way to 4KHz. Fundamental frequencies are around 85–180Hz for males and 165–255Hz for females [43]. The energy content of this signal is far stronger than the *unvoiced* counterpart.
- Within the *voiced* signal, the energy content is higher in the lower frequencies. These strong low frequency components determine the intelligibility of the spoken phonemes (i.e. the perceptually distinct units of sound [44]), and are referred to as *formants* [28]. The first two formants (say, $F1$, $F2$) remain between 300–2500Hz and completely forms the sound of the vowels, while some consonants have another significant formant, $F3$, at a higher frequency. Figure 6 shows examples of 2 vowel formants – "i" and "a" – recorded by the microphone.

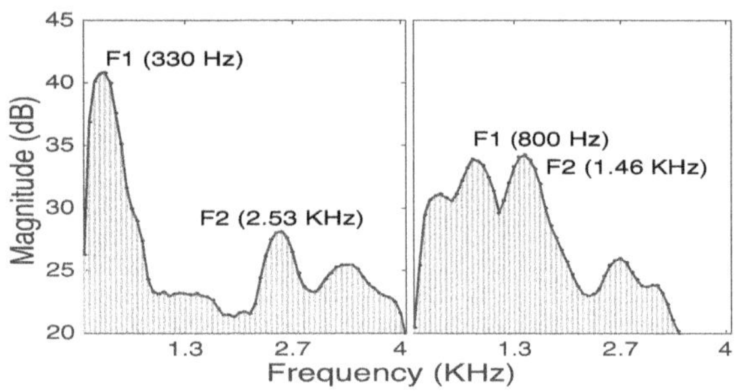

Figure 6: The locations of the first two formants (F1 and F2) for (a) the vowel sound *'i'* and (b) the vowel sound *'a'*, both recorded with microphone.

In extracting human speech from the vibra-motor's back-EMF signal, VibraPhone will need to identify, construct, and bolster these formants through signal processing.

4. CHALLENGES

Figure 7(a,b) compares the spectrogram of the microphone and the vibra-motor for the same spoken phoneme, "sa". Figure 7(c,d) shows the same comparison for a full word, namely, "entertainment". The reader is encouraged to listen to these sound clips at our project website [5]. Evidently, the vibra-motor's response is weak and incomplete, and on careful analysis, exhibits various kinds of distortions even where the signal is apparently strong. The goal in this paper is to reconstruct, to the extent possible, the left columns of Figure 7 from the right columns. We face 4 key challenges discussed next.

(1) Over-Sensitivity at Resonance Frequency

All rigid objects tend to oscillate at a fixed natural frequency when struck by an external force. When the force is periodically repeated at a frequency close to the object's natural frequency, the object shows exaggerated amplitude of oscillation – called *resonance* [34]. Resonance is often an undesirable phenomenon, destabilizing the operation of an electro-mechanical device. Microphones, for example, carefully avoid resonance by designing its diaphragm at a specific material, tension, and stiffness – that way, the resonance frequencies lie outside the operating region [19, 10]. In some cases, additional hardware is embedded to damp the vibration at the resonant frequencies [10].

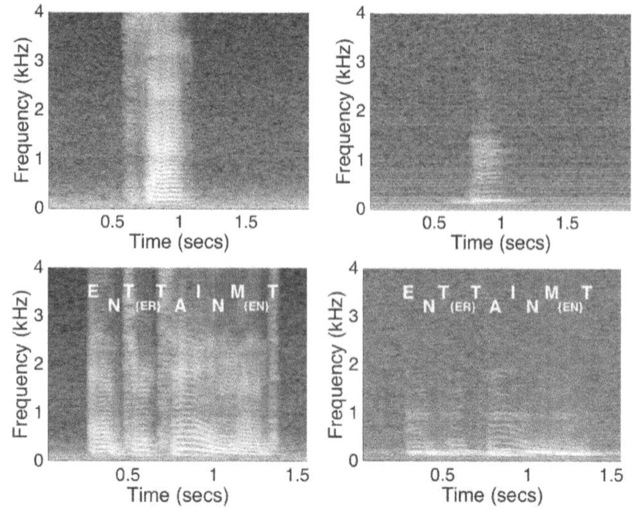

Figure 7: The spectrogram for "sa" as recorded by: (a) the microphone and (b) the vibra-motor. The spectrogram for the full word "entertainment" as recorded by: (c) the microphone and (d) the vibra-motor. The vibra-motor's response is weak and partially missing.

Unfortunately, vibra-motors used in today's smartphones exhibit sharp resonance between 216 to 232Hz, depending on the mounting structure. Some weak components of *speech formants* are often present in these bands – these components get amplified, appearing as a *pseudo-formant*. The *pseudo-formants* manifest as unexpected sounds within uttered words, affecting intelligibility. The impact is exacerbated when the fundamental frequency of the voiced signal is itself close to the resonant band – in such cases, the sound itself gets garbled. Figure 8 shows the effect of resonance when the vibration motor is sounded with different frequency tones in succession (called a *Sine Sweep* [13, 12]. Observe that for all tones in the *Sine Sweep*, the vibra-motor exhibited appreciable response in the resonance band. This is because the tones have some frequency tail around the 225Hz, and this always gets magnified. The microphone exhibits no such phenomenon. VibraPhone will certainly need to cope with resonance.

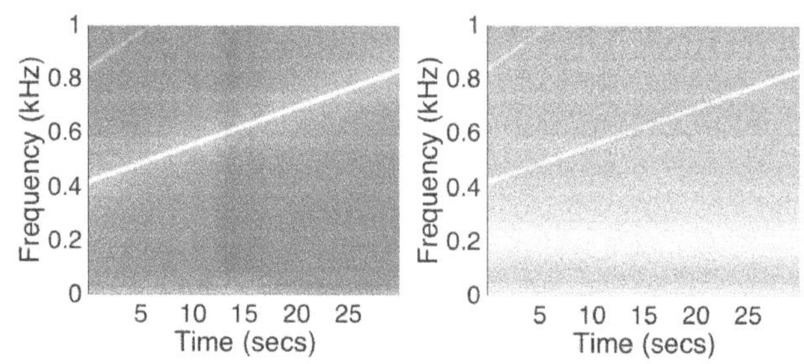

Figure 8: The spectrogram of (a) the microphone and (b) the vibra-motor, in response to a *Sine Sweep* (i.e., tones played at increasing narrow band frequencies). The vibration motor signal shows an over-sensitive resonance frequency band near 220Hz.

(2) High Frequency Deafness

The vibra-motor's effective diaphragm – the area amenable to the impinging sound – is around 10mm, almost 20x larger than that of a typical MEMS microphone (0.5mm). This makes the vibration motor directional for the high frequency sounds, i.e., the high frequencies arriving from other directions are suppressed, somewhat like a directional antenna. Unfortunately, human voices contain lesser energy at frequencies higher than 2KHz, thereby making the vibra-motor even less effective in "picking up" these sounds. Some consonants and some vowels – such as "i" and "e" – have formants close to or higher than 2KHz, and are severely affected. Figure 9 compares the spectrogram when just the vowel "*a*" was spoken – evidently, the vibra-motor is almost "deaf" to higher frequencies.

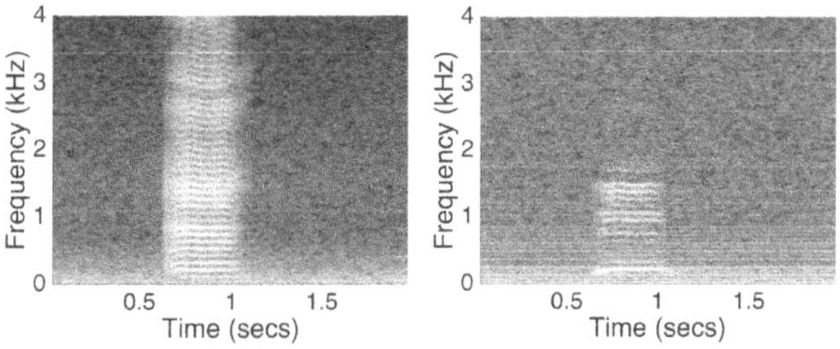

Figure 9: The spectrogram of the spoken vowel '*a*' recorded with (a) microphone and (b)vibration motor. The vibra-motor exhibits near-deafness for frequencies > 2KHz.

(3) Higher Energy Threshold

A microphone's sensitivity, i.e., the voltage produced for a given sound pressure level, heavily depends on the weight and stiffness of its diaphragm. The spring-mass arrangement of the vibra-motor is considerably more stiff, mainly due to the heavier mass and high spring constant. While this is desirable for a vibration actuator, it is unfavorable to sound sensing. Thus, using the actuator as a sensor yields low sensitivity in general, and particularly to certain kinds of low-energy consonants (like *f, s, v, z*), called *fricatives* [18]. The effect is visible in Figure 7 (a,b) – the *fricative* consonant "*s*" goes almost undetected with vibra-motors.

(4) Low Signal-to-Noise Ratio (SNR)

In any electrical circuit, *thermal noise* is an unavoidable phenomena arising from the Brownian motion of electrons in resistive components. Fortunately, the low 26 Ohm terminal resistance in vibra-motors leads to 10dB lower thermal noise than the reference MEMS microphone. However, due to low sensitivity, the strength of the vibra-signal is significantly lower, resulting in poor SNR across most of the spectrum. Figure 10 compares the SNR at different sound pressure levels – except around the resonance frequencies, the SNR of the vibra-signal is significantly less compared to the microphone.

Sound Pressure Level (SPL) is a metric to measure the effective pressure caused by sound waves with respect to a reference value, and is typically expressed in dBSPL [4]. This gives a standard estimate of the sound field at the receiver, irrespective of the location of the sound source.

5. SYSTEM DESIGN

Our system design is modeled as a *source-filter*, i.e., we treat the final output of the vibra-motor as a result of many filters applied serially to the original air-flow from the lungs.

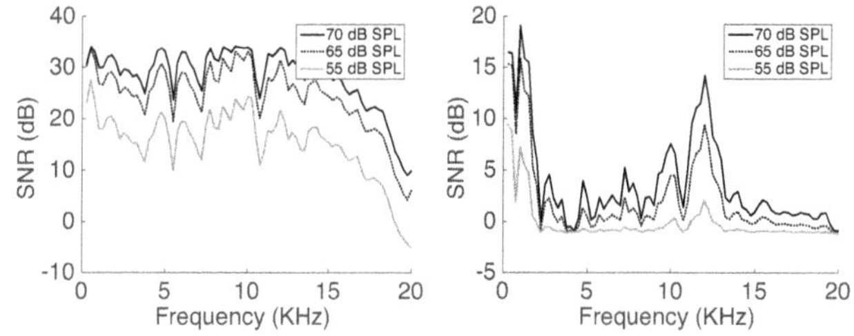

Figure 10: The SNR of (a) the microphone and (b) the vibra-motor at various frequencies for varying sound pressure levels (dB SPL). Note the unequal Y axis range.

Figure 11 illustrates this view, suggesting that an ideal solution should perform two broad tasks: (1) "undo" the vibra-motor's distortions for signal components that have been detected, and (2) reconstruct the undetected signals by leveraging the predictable speech structure in conjunction with the slight "signal hints" picked up by the vibra-motor. VibraPhone realizes these tasks through two corresponding modules, namely, *signal pre-processing* and *partial speech synthesis*. We describe them next.

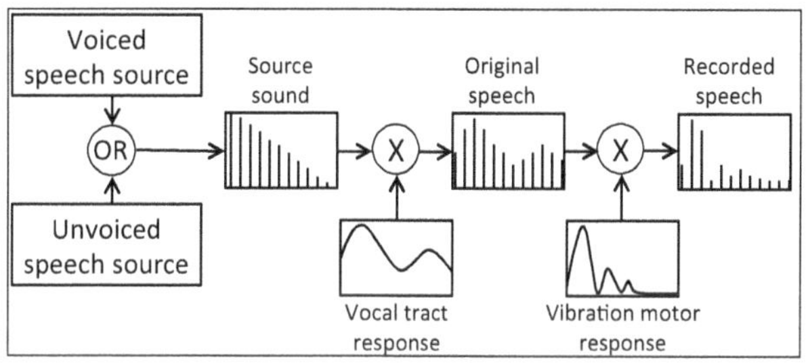

Figure 11: The source-filter model of the speech generation and recording.

5.1 Signal Pre-processing

All of our algorithms operate on the frequency domain representation of the signal. Therefore, we first convert the amplified signal to the time-frequency domain using the *Short Time Fourier Transform* (STFT), which basically computes the complex FFT coefficients from 100 millisecond segments (80% overlapped, Hanning windowed) of the input time signal. The result is a 2D matrix that we call time-frequency signal and illustrated in Figure 12 – each column is a time slice and each row is a positive frequency bin. We will refer to this matrix for various explanations.

Frequency Domain Equalization

When a microphone is subject to a *Sine Sweep* test, the frequency response is typically flat, meaning that the microphone responds almost uniformly to each frequency component. The vibra-motor's response, on the other hand, is considerably jagged, and thereby induces distortions into the arriving signal. Figure 13 shows a case where the vowel "u" is recorded by both the microphone and vibra-motor. The vibra-motor distortions on "u" are quite dramatic, altering the original formants at 266 and 600Hz to new formants at 300Hz and 1.06KHz. In fact, the altered formants bear resemblance to the vowel "aa" (as in "father"), and in reality, do sound like it. More generally, the vibra-motor's frequency

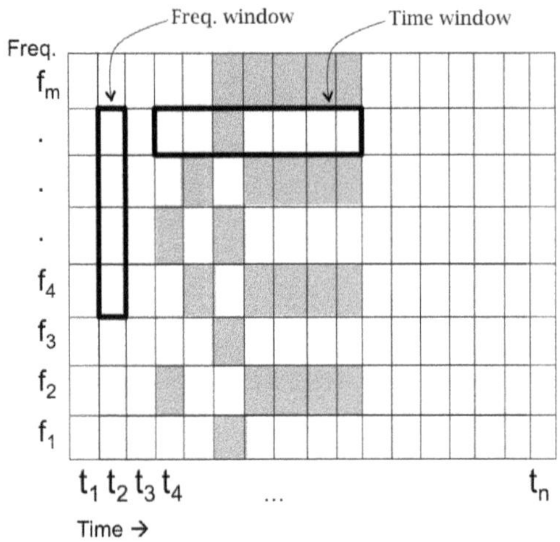

Figure 12: 2D time-frequency matrix

response exhibits this rough shape, thereby biasing all the vowels to the sound of "aa" or "o".

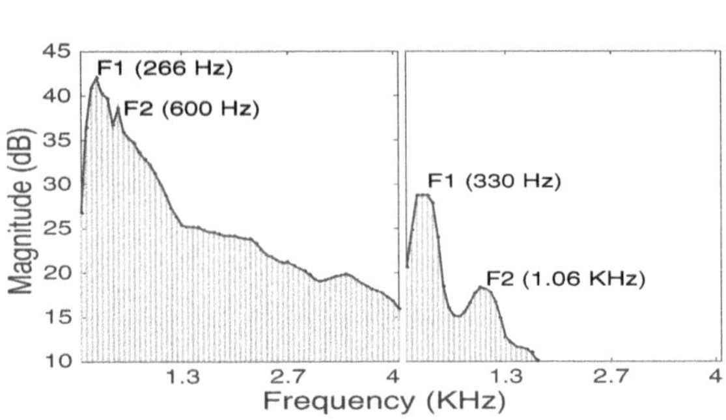

Figure 13: Formants of vowel *'u'* recorded through (a) microphone and (b) vibra-motor. The vibra-motor introduces a spurious formant near 1KHz.

Fortunately, the frequency response of the vibra-motor is only a function of the device and does not change with time (at least until there is wear and tear of the device). We tested this by computing the correlation of the *Sine Sweep* frequency response at various sound pressure levels – the correlation proved strong, except for a slight dip at the resonant frequencies due to the non-linearities. Knowing the frequency response, we apply an equalization technique, similar to channel equalization in communication. We estimate the inverse gain by computing the ratio of the coefficients from the microphone and the vibra-motor, and multiply the inverse gain with the frequency coefficients of the output signal.

Background Noise Removal

Deafness in vibra-motors implies that the motor's response to high frequency signals (i.e., > 2KHz) is indistinguishable from noise. If this noise exhibits a statistical structure, a family of *spectral subtraction* algorithms can be employed to improve SNR. However, two issues need attention. (1) The pure noise segments in the signal needs to be recognized, so that its statistical properties are modeled accurately. This means that noise segments must be discriminated from speech. (2) Within the speech segments, *voiced* and *unvoiced* segments must also be separated so that spectral subtraction is only applied on the *voiced* components. This is because *unvoiced* signals bear noise-like properties and spectral subtraction can be detrimental.

To reliably discriminate the presence of speech segments, we exploit the exaggerated behavior in the resonance frequency band. We consistently observed that speech brings out heavy resonance behavior in vibra-motors, while noise elicits a muted response. Thus, resonance proved to be an opportunity. Once speech is segregated from noise, the next step is to isolate the *voiced* components in speech. For this, we leverage its well-defined harmonic structure. Recall the 2D matrix in Figure 12. We consider a time window and slide it up/down to compute an autocorrelation coefficient across different frequencies. Due to the repetition of the harmonics, the autocorrelation spikes periodically, yielding robust detection accuracy. When autocorrelation does not detect such periodic spikes, they are deemed as the *unvoiced* segments.

The final task of spectral subtraction is performed on the *voiced* signal alone. For a given *voiced* signal (i.e., a set of columns in the matrix), the closest noise segments in time are selected – these noise segments are averaged over a modest time window. Put differently, for every frequency bin, the mean noise floor is computed, and then subtracted from the corresponding bin in the *voiced* signal. For zero mean Gaussian noise, this does not offer any benefit, however, the noise is often not zero mean. In such cases, the SNR improves and alleviates the deafness. Figure 14 shows the beneficial effect of spectral subtraction when "yes" is spoken.

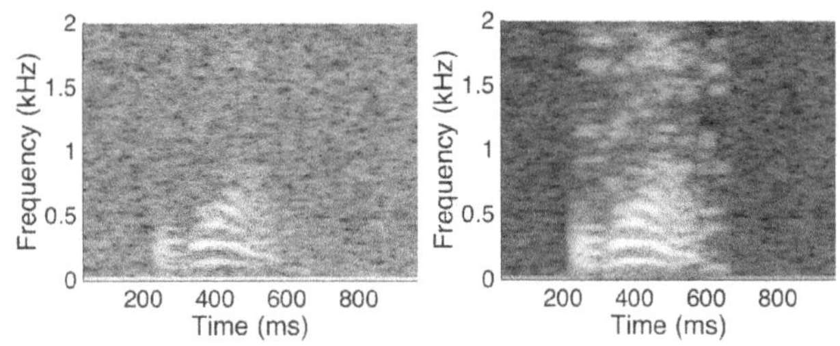

Figure 14: The spectrogram of the spoken word "yes" (a) before and (b) after the spectral subtraction.

Speech Energy Localization

Observe that noise removal described above brings the *mean noise* to zero, however, noise still exists and the SNR is still not adequate. In other words, deafness is still a problem. However, now that noise is zero mean and Gaussian, there is an opportunity to exploit its diversity to further suppress it. Even localizing the speech signal energy in the spectrogram would be valuable, even if the exact signal is not recovered in this step.

Our core idea is to average the signals from within a frequency window, and slide the frequency window all the way to 10KHz. Referring to the 2D matrix, we compute the average of W elements in each column (W being the window size), and slide the window vertically; the same operation is performed for each column. Each element is a complex frequency coefficient, containing both the signal and the noise. With sufficiently large W, the average converges to the average of the signal content in these elements since the (average) noise sum up to zero. Mathematically, if C_i denotes the signal at frequency f_i, and $C_i = S_i + N_i$, where S_i is the speech signal and N_i the noise, then the averaged C_i^* is computed as:

$$C_i^* = \frac{1}{W} \sum_{f=i-\frac{W}{2}}^{i+\frac{W}{2}} C_i = \frac{1}{W} \sum_{f=i-\frac{W}{2}}^{i+\frac{W}{2}} S_i + \frac{1}{W} \sum_{f=i-\frac{W}{2}}^{i+\frac{W}{2}} N_i \quad (1)$$

Since the term $\sum N_i$ is zero mean Gaussian, it approaches zero for larger W, while the $\frac{1}{W} \sum S_i$ term is simple smoothing. For every frequency bin, we normalize the C_i^* values over a time window so that they range between $[0, 1]$. The result is a 3D contour map, where the locations of higher elevations, i.e., hills, indicate the presence of speech signals. We identify the dominant hills and *zero force* all areas outside them. This is because speech signals always exhibit a large time-frequency footprint, since human voice is not capable of producing sounds that are narrow in frequency and time. Figure 15 illustrates the effect of this scheme – the dominant hills are demarcated as the location of speech energy. Evidently, the improvement is conspicuous after this energy localization step.

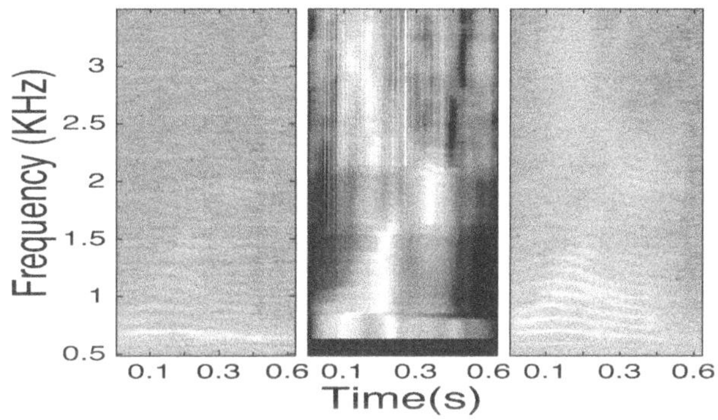

Figure 15: Readers are requested to view this figure in color: (a) Raw vibra-motor signal, (b) The output of the *speech energy localization* makes the signal energy visible through a heat-map like contour. (c) The corresponding microphone signal bearing good resemblance to the energy locations.

5.2 Partial Speech Synthesis

Once the vibra-motor output has been pre-processed, the structure of speech can now be leveraged for signal recovery – we describe our approach next.

Voice Source Expansion

After the localization step above, we know the location of speech energy (in time-frequency domain), but we do not know the speech signal. In attempting to recover this signal, we exploit the opportunity that the fundamental frequencies in speech actually manifest in higher frequency harmonics [35, 14]. Therefore, knowledge of the lower fundamental frequencies can be *expanded* to reconstruct the higher frequencies. Unfortunately, the actual fundamental frequency often gets distorted by the resonant bands.

As a workaround, we use the relatively high SNR signals in the range [250, 2000Hz] to synthesize the voice source signal at higher frequencies. Synthesis is essentially achieved through careful replication. Specifically, the algorithm copies the coefficient $C_{t,f}$, where t is the time segment and f is the frequency bin of the time-frequency signal, and adds it to $C_{t,kf}$ for all integer k, such that kf is less than the Nyquist frequency. Here integer k indicates the harmonic number for the frequency f. Intuitively, we are copying the harmonics from the reliable range, and replicating them at the higher frequencies. As shown in Figure 16, this only synthesizes the *voiced* components (recall the harmonics are only present in the *voiced* signals). For *unvoiced* signals, we blindly fill in the deaf frequencies with copies of the lower frequency signals.

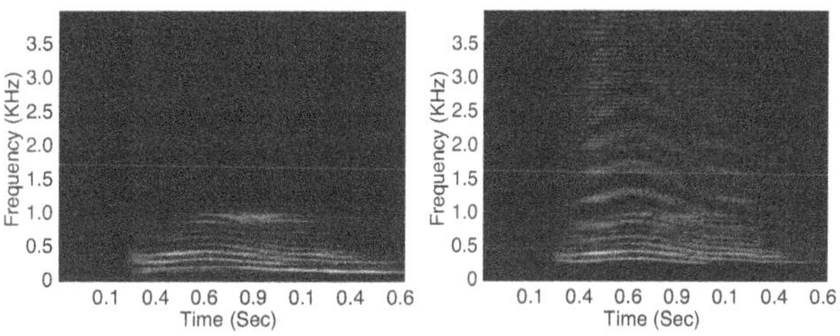

Figure 16: Result of source expansion for the *voiced* signal components. (a) Raw vibra-signal, and (b) after harmonic replication. Readers are requested to view this figure in color.

Speech Reconstruction

Recall that the mouth and nasal cavities finally modulate the air vibrations – this can be modeled as weights multiplied to the fundamental frequencies and their harmonics. While we do not know the values of these weights, the location of the energies – computed from the 3D contour hills – is indeed an estimate. We now utilize this location estimate as an *energy mask*. As a first step, we apply an exponential decay function along the frequency axis to model the low intensity of natural speech at the higher frequencies. Then the energy mask is multiplied with this modified signal, emulating an adaptive gain filter. As this also improves the SNR of the unvoiced section of the speech, we apply a deferred spectral subtraction method on these segments to further remove the background noise. Finally, we convert this resultant time-frequency signal to time domain using inverse short time Fourier transform (ISTFT). Figure 17 compares the output against the microphone and the raw vibra-motor signal.

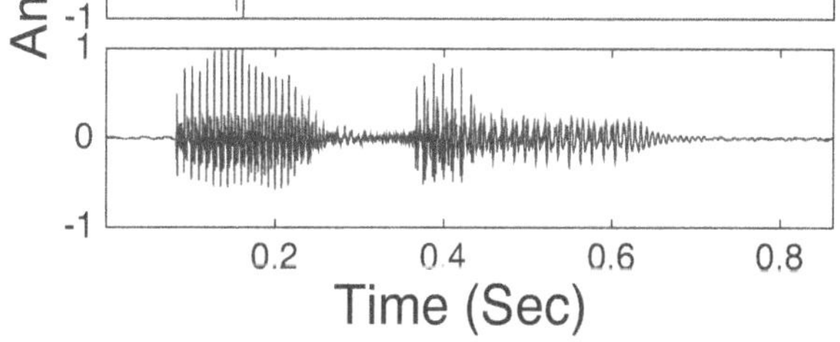

Figure 17: Word "often" as manifested in the (a) raw vibra-motor signal, (b) after VibraPhone's processing, and (c) microphone signal.

6. EVALUATION

Section 2.2 described the two experimentation platforms for our system, namely the custom hardware and the Samsung Galaxy smartphone. In both cases, we evaluate VibraPhone's speech intelligibility against the performance of the corresponding microphone. In the custom hardware, the microphone is positioned right next to the vibra-motor, while in the smartphone, their locations are modestly separated. We generate the speech signals using a text-to-speech (TTS) utility available in OS X 10.9, and play them at different volumes through a loudspeaker. The position/volume of the loudspeaker is adjusted such that the sound pressure levels at the vibra-motor and the microphone are equal. The accent and intonation of the TTS utility also does not affect the experiment since both VibraPhone and the microphone hear the same TTS speech. The content of the speech is drawn from Google's Trillion Word Corpus [3] – we pick 2000 most frequent words, which is prescribed as a good benchmark [33].

6.1 Methodology and Metrics

We perform automatic and manual speech recognition experiments as follows.

(1) Automatic Speech Recognition (ASR)

In ASR, a software programmatically converts the time domain speech signal to text. ASR tools typically have 3 distinct components: (a) an acoustic model, (b) a pronunciation dictionary, and (c) a language model. The *acoustic model* is a trained statistical model (e.g., HMM, Neural Networks, etc. [15, 20]) that maps segments of the input waveform to a sequence of phonemes. These phonemes are then looked up in the *pronunciation dictionary*, which lists the candidate words (along with their possible pronunciations) based on the matching phoneme sequence. Among these candidates, the most likely output is selected using a grammar or a *language model.*

Our ASR tools is the open-source *Sphinx4* (pre-alpha version) library published by CMU [1, 21]. The acoustic model is sensitive to the recording parameters, including the bandwidth and the features of the microphone. Such parameters do not apply to vibra-motors, so we used a generic acoustic model trained with standard microphone data. This is not ideal for VibraPhone, and hence, the reported results are perhaps a slight under-estimate of VibraPhone's capabilities.

(2) Manual Speech Recognition (MSR)

We recruited a group of 6 volunteers from our department building – 1 native English speaker, 1 Indian faculty with English as first language, 2 Indian PhD students, and 2 Chinese PhD students. We played the vibra-motor and microphone outputs to all the participants simultaneously and collected their responses. In some experiments, volunteers were asked to *guess the word or phrase from the playback*; in other experiments, the volunteers were given a list of phrases and asked to pick the most likely one, including the option of "none of the above". All human responses were accompanied by a subjective clarity score – every volunteer expressed how intelligible the word was, even when he/she could not guess with confidence. Finally, in some experiments, volunteers were asked to guess first, and then guess again based on a group discussion. Such discussions served as a "prior" for speech recognition, and often the group consensus was different from the first individual guess.

Metrics

Across all experiments, 9 hours of sound was recorded and a total of 20,000 words were tested with ASR at various sound pressure levels (measured in $dBSPL$). For MSR, a total of 300 words and 40 phrases were played, resulting in more than 2000 total human responses. We report "Accuracy" as the percentage of words/phrases that were correctly guessed, and show its variation across different loudness levels (measured in dBSPL). We report "Perceived Clarity" as a subjective score reported by individuals, even when they did not decode the word with confidence. Finally, we report "Precision", "Recall", and "Fallout" for experiments in which the users were asked to select from a list. Recall that *precision* intuitively refers to "*what fraction of your guesses were correct*", and *recall* intuitively means "*what fraction of the correct answers did you guess*". We now present the graphs, beginning with ASR.

6.2 Performance Results with ASR

Accuracy v/s Loudness

Custom Hardware: Figure 18(a) reports the accuracy with ASR as a function of the sound pressure level (dbSPL), a standard metric proportionally related to the loudness of the sound. VibraPhone's accuracy is around 88% at 80 dbSPL, which is equivalent to the sound pressure experienced by the smartphone's microphone during typical (against the ear) phone call. The microphone's accuracy is obviously better at 95%, while the raw vibra-motor signal performs poorly at 43% (almost half of VibraPhone). Importantly, the preprocessing and the synthesis gains are individually small, but since intelligibility is defined as binary metric here, the improvement jumps up when applied together.

Once the loudness decreases at 60 dbSPL – comparable to a normal conversation 1 meter away from the microphone [2] – VibraPhone's accuracy drops to ≈ 60%. At lower sound pressure level, the accuracy drops faster since the vibra-motor's sensitivity is inadequate for "picking up" the air vibrations. However, the accuracy can be improved with training the acoustic model with vibra-motors (recall that with ASR, the training is performed through microphones, which is unfavorable to VibraPhone).

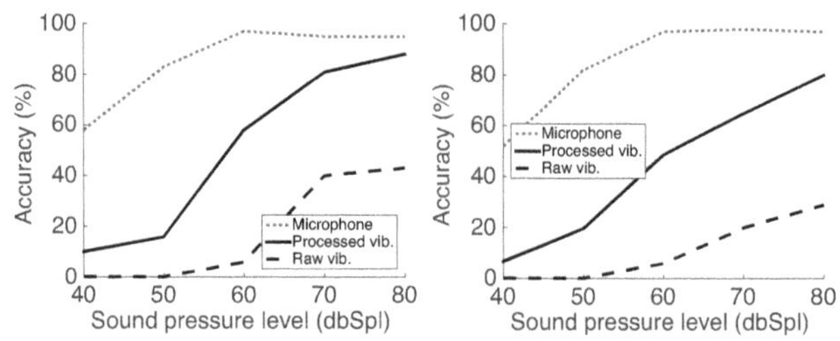

Figure 18: Automatic recognition accuracy as a function of loudness for (a) the custom hardware, (b) the Samsung smartphone.

Samsung Smartphone: Figure 18(b) plots the accuracy with ASR for the smartphone based platform. VibraPhone's performance is weaker compared to the custom hardware setup, although the difference is marginal – ASR output is still at 80% at 80 dbSPL. Admittedly, we are not exactly sure of the reason for this difference – we conjecture that the smartphone signal processing pipeline may not be exactly tuned to the vibra-motor like we have done in the custom case.

Rank of the Words

The accuracy results above counts only perfect matches between ASR's output and the actual spoken word. In certain applications, a list of possible words may also be useful, particularly when the quality of the speech is poor. We record the list of all predictions from ASR for each spoken word, played at 50 dbSPL. Figure 19 plots the CDF of the rank of the correct word in this list. At this relatively softer 50 dbSPL experiment, only $\approx$ 20% of the words are ranked at 1, implying exact match. In 41% of the cases, the words were within *top-5* of the list, and *top-10* presents a 58% accuracy.

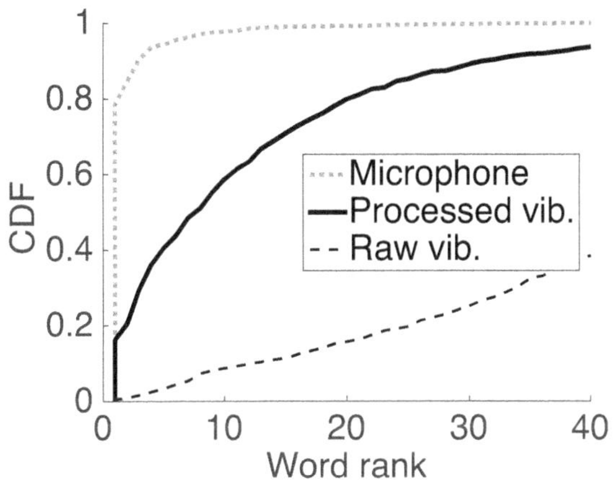

Figure 19: The CDF of word rank from ASR's prediction at 50 dbSPL for custom hardware.

Phoneme Similarity

The acoustic model we used with ASR is not ideal for VibraPhone – the impact is pronounced for distorted phonemes. Training ASR's acoustic model with the vibra-motor response is expected to offer improvements, but in the absence of that, we report a subjective overview of the entropy in different phonemes recorded by VibraPhone. In other words, we ask whether *autocorrelation* between the same phonemes is high and *cross correlation* across phonemes are low. We extract the STFT coefficients of the 100 phonemes (28 vowels and 72 consonants) from the International Phoneme Alphabet [6, 7] and use these coefficients as the features. We then calculate correlation coefficient of all pairs of phonemes in the list – Figure 20 presents the heat map. In case of raw vibra-signal in Figure 20(a), the (distorted) phonemes bear substantial similarity between each other, indicated by the multiple dark off-diagonal blocks. The two large darker squares in the figure represents the pulmonic (58 phonemes) and non-pulmonic (14 phonemes) consonant groups [27, 18]. However, with VibraPhone, Figure 20(b) shows substantial improvements. The autocorrelation is strong across the diagonal of the matrix, while the off-diagonal elements are much less correlated. This extends hope that a vibra-motor trained acoustic model could appreciably boost VibraPhone's performance.

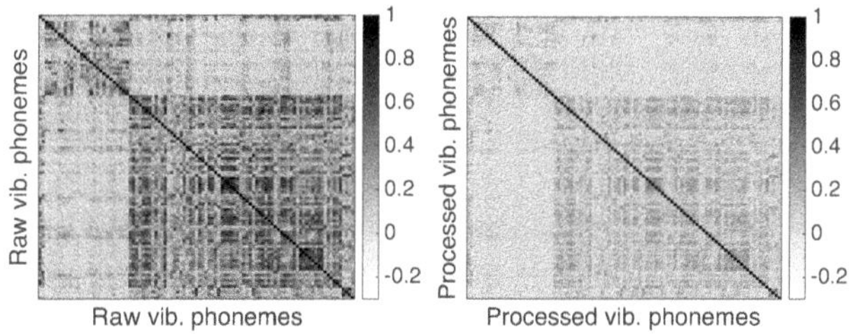

Figure 20: The heat-map shows the correlation of the frequency domain features of the phoneme sounds, recorded with custom vibration motor: (a) before processing and (b) after processing.

6.3 Performance Results with MSR

Accuracy v/s Loudness

Figure 21 shows the accuracy with manual speech recognition (MSR) in comparison to automatic (ASR). Unsurprisingly, the accuracy is around 20% more than ASR at higher loudness regimes (60 dbSPL or more) – the individuals guessed the words individually in these experiments. Using consensus from group discussion, the accuracy increases to 88% at 60 dbSPL. When the loudness is stronger, VibraPhone is comparable to microphones, both for custom hardware and smartphones.

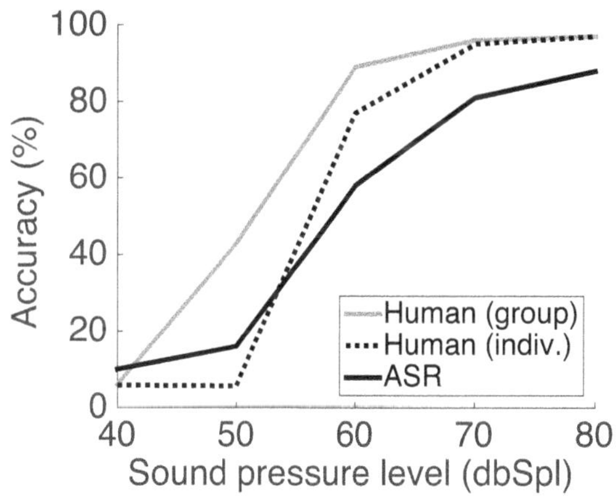

Figure 21: This plot compares the accuracy of human decoding with ASR. It shows the performance of the human decoders while working individually and as a collaborative team.

Hot-phrase Detection

Figure 22 shows manual performance with "hot phrases", i.e., where the volunteer was asked to pick a phrase from the list that best matched the spoken phrase (the volunteer could also select none of the phrases). We provided a list of 10 written phrases before playing the positive and negative samples in arbitrary sequence. Example phrases were "turn left", "happy birthday", "start the computer", etc., and the negative samples were chosen with comparable number of words and characters.

Figure 22(a) reports results from the custom hardware – volunteers almost perfectly identified the phrases and rejected the negative samples.
However, when using the smartphone vibra-motor, VibraPhone failed to identify some positive samples – Figure 22(b) shows the outcome in relatively higher false negative values. Of course, the degradation is relative – the absolute detection performance is still quite high, with accuracy and precision at 0.83 and 0.90, respectively, for the processed vibra-signal.

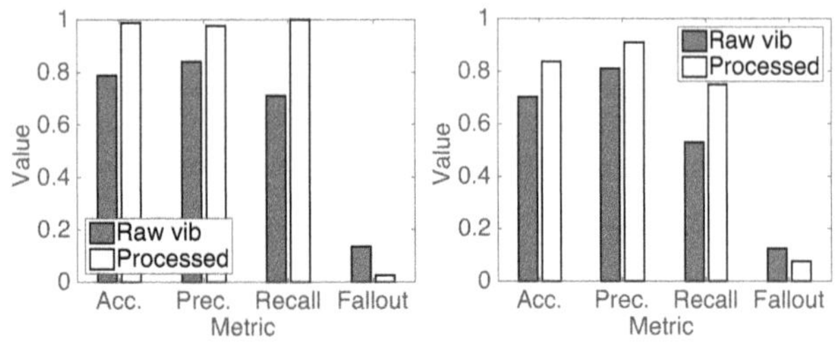

Figure 22: The accuracy, precision, recall, and fallout values for manual hot-phrase detection. The recording device is (a) the custom hardware and (b) the smartphone.

Perceived Clarity

Human volunteers also assigned a "clarity score" on a range of [0, 10] to every word/phrase he/she listened to (a score of 10 indicated a perfectly intelligible word). Figure 23 plots the average clarity score of the correctly decoded samples and compares it between the vibration motor and the microphone. The subjective perception of clarity does not change for the microphone for sound pressure levels 50 dbSPL and above. While VibraPhone's clarity is lower than microphone in general, the gap reduces at higher loudness levels. At 80 dbSPL, the perceived clarity scores for microphones and VibraPhone are 9.1 and 7.6, respectively.

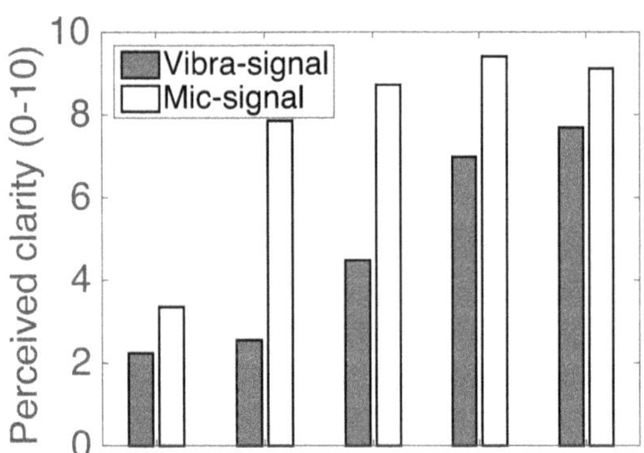

Figure 23: The perceived clarity of the correctly decoded speech recorded with microphone and vibration motor.

Kinds of Words

Figure 24 shows the top-10 and bottom-10 intelligible words from the ASR experiments. The font size is proportional to the decoding accuracy, indicating that "international" was decoded correctly most frequently, while prepositions like "a", "and", "or" were consistently missed. Unsurprisingly, longer words are decoded with higher accuracy because of better interpolation between the partially decoded phonemes. Figure 25 quantifies this with ASR and MSR, respectively – words with 5+ characters are mostly multi-syllable, yielding improved recognition.

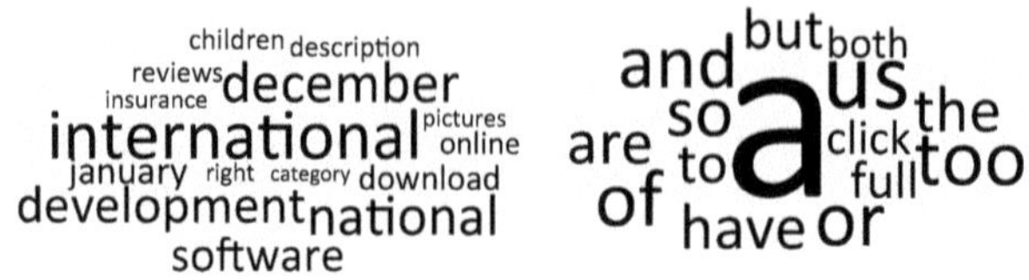

Figure 24: Top 10 words that are (a)correctly and (b)incorrectly decoded by ASR.

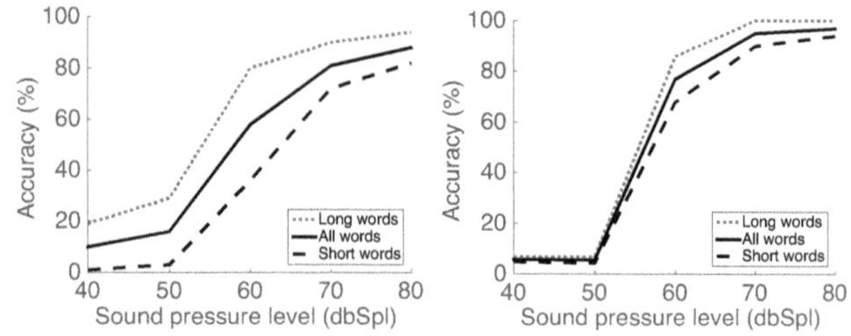

Figure 25: (a) ASR and (b) MSR accuracy for long (> 6 chars) and short (≤ 6 chars) words, as a function of loudness.

Electromagnetic Coupling:

Table 1 summarizes the manual speech recognition performance for the electromagnetic coupling test mentioned in section 2.2. In this microbenchmark we remove the equipment (microphone, speaker etc.) from the test environment that can potentially create electromagnetic coupling with the vibration motor. The signal recorded in this microbenchmark does not show any quantitative difference from that of our standard test environment. However, we run a manual speech recognition test on these recordings to identify possible perceptual differences in manual speech recognition. Here the volunteers transcribe the voice of a male non-native speaker recorded with a vibration motor during the microbenchmark test. In this test the volunteers individually listen to the recordings at sound levels according to their personal preferences. The percentage of the incorrect words in the transcription and the perceived quality score given by each user are shown in the table. The perceived sound quality is consistent with our previous results at 60dbSPL, the natural loudness of the speaker's voice at $3ft$ from the recording device.

Table 1: Coupling sensitivity data

User	A	B	C	D	E	F	G	H
Error(%)	8	0	0	8	0	0	17	25
Score	8	8	6	6	4	3	3	3

7. POINTS OF DISCUSSION

We discuss a few limitations of this paper, and a few other kinds of applications using VibraPhone.

What is the Best Possible? We have not been able to comment on the best possible performance possible with VibraPhone. Such an analysis will certainly need a deeper signal processing treatment, as well as detailed domain knowledge from speech recognition. This work is more of a lower bound on feasibility, drawing on a diverse set of established techniques from literature, and modifying them to suit the needs of this specific problem. We have initiated collaboration with signal processing researchers to push the envelope of this side channel leak.

Energy: We have sidestepped energy considerations in this paper. However, we intuitively believe that VibraPhone is not likely to be energy hungry (even though the vibra-motor consumes considerable energy while pulsating). This is because VibraPhone picks up the ambient sounds while it is in the inactive/passive mode, i.e., when it is not serving as an actuator. We plan to characterize the sensitivity and energy profile in future.

Applications: We observed that when vibra-motors are pasted to walls and floors, and music is being played in the adjacent rooms, VibraPhone is able to detect these sounds better than the microphone. We also observed that by placing the vibra-motor on the throat, various speech components can be detected, and in some cases, compliments the response of the microphone. Finally, we find that noise properties of vibra-motors and microphones are uncorrelated, enabling the possibility of diversity combining (i.e., they could together behave like a MIMO system, improving the capacity of acoustic channels). All these observations are preliminary, and hence, not reported in this paper – we plan to investigate them further as a continuation of VibraPhone.

8. RELATED WORK

Past work on acoustic side channels and speech recovery are most relevant to this paper. Given both are reasonably mature areas, we sample a subset of them.

Passive Speech Recording

Gyrophone and AccelWord [30, 47] are perhaps the closest to our work. In Gyrophone [30], authors identify the MEMS sensors' capability to capture sound. The paper presents a range of signal processing and machine learning techniques to recover traces of ambient sounds from the gyroscope data [37]. AccelWord [47] takes a step forward and uses speech information from the accelerometer [23] to implemented a low energy voice control application for a limited vocabulary of commands. However, these techniques recover only a low bandwidth of the spectrum (< 200Hz), which does not even cover the full range of fundamental frequencies in female speech (165 – 255 Hz). Therefore, these techniques mainly focus on extracting the reliable features of sound for consistent pattern classification. In contrast, VibraPhone concentrates on recovering a telephone-quality speech (bandwidth 4KHz [22, 31]) from the vibration motor signal, making the output amenable to manual or automatic decoding. Both Gyrophone and AccelWord are unable to produce (actually not designed for) machine understandable speech.

A family of techniques [32, 39, 45, 40] targets a light/LASER beam on an object exposed to the speech signal and records its vibration by measuring the fluctuation of the reflected beam. Visual microphone [9] is also a similar technique that uses high speed video of the target object to recover the vibration proportional to the speech signal. Camera based techniques are devoid of the noisy data that pollute motion sensors/actuators, while they must tackle other difficult challenges in computer vision. A number of solutions have monitored the change in received signal strength (RSS) and phase of the wireless radio signal reflected off the loudspeaker to capture the traces of sound. The projects [46] and [29] demonstrate successful sound recovery using reflected radio signal even when the receiver is not in the line-of-sight of the vibrating object.

Speech Recovery

We borrowed building blocks from the vast literature of speech processing. A body of research [8, 26, 25] explores artificial bandwidth expansion problems primarily to aid high quality voice transfer over band-limited telephonic channel. Some solutions attempt to identify the phonemes from the low bandwidth signal and then replace them with high bandwidth phonemes from a library. These solutions do not solve VibraPhone's problems as majority of them consider 4KHz signal as the input providing enough diversity for correct phoneme identification. VibraPhone attempts to extend the effective bandwidth from 2KHz to 4Khz – a challenge because the features up to 2KHz provide limited exposure to phonemes.

Data imputation techniques [38, 17] attempt to predict erasures in audio signals. When these signals exhibit a consistent statistical model, the erasures can be predicted well, enabling successful imputation. However, vibra-signals often lack such properties, and moreover, the location of erasures cannot be confidently demarcated.

9. CONCLUSION

This paper demonstrates that the vibration motor, present in almost all mobile devices today, can be used as a listening sensor, similar to a microphone. While this is not fundamentally surprising (since vibrating objects should respond to ambient air vibrations), the ease and extent to which the actuator has "picked up" sounds has been somewhat unexpected for us. Importantly, the decoded sounds are not merely vibration patterns that correlates to some spoken words. Rather, they actually contain the phonemes and structure of human voice, thereby requiring no machine learning or pattern recognition to extract them. We show that with basic signal processing techniques, combined with the structure of human speech, the vibra-motor's output can be quite intelligible to most human listeners. Even automatic speech recognizers were able to decode the majority of the detected words and phrases, especially at higher loudness. The application space of such systems remains open, and could range from malware eavesdropping into human phone conversation, to voice controlled wearables, to better microphones that use the vibra-motor as a second MIMO-antenna. Our ongoing work is in pursuit of a few such applications.

Acknowledgement

We sincerely thank our shepherd Dr. Xia Zhou and the anonymous reviewers for their valuable feedback. We are grateful to Qualcomm, Huawei, HP, and NSF (grant CNS-1430033 and 1423455) for partially funding this research.

10. REFERENCES

[1] Cmu sphinx. http://cmusphinx.sourceforge.net. Last accessed 6 December 2015.

[2] Sound pressure level chart. http://www.sengpielaudio.com/TableOfSoundPressureLevels.htm. Last accessed 6 December 2015.

[3] Top 10000 words from google's trillion word corpus. https://github.com/first20hours/google-10000-english. Last accessed 6 December 2015.

[4] Unit of sound pressure level. http://trace.wisc.edu/docs/2004-About-dB/. Last accessed 9 December 2015.

[5] Vibraphone project webpage. http://synrg.csl.illinois.edu/vibraphone/. Last accessed 9 December 2015.

[6] Association, I. P. *Handbook of the International Phonetic Association: A guide to the use of the International Phonetic Alphabet.* Cambridge University Press, 1999.

[7] Brown, A. International phonetic alphabet. *The Encyclopedia of Applied Linguistics* (2013).

[8] Chennoukh, S., Gerrits, A., Miet, G., and Sluijter, R. Speech enhancement via frequency bandwidth extension using line spectral frequencies. In *Acoustics, Speech, and Signal Processing, 2001. Proceedings.(ICASSP'01). 2001 IEEE International Conference on* (2001), vol. 1, IEEE, pp. 665–668.

[9] Davis, A., Rubinstein, M., Wadhwa, N., Mysore, G. J., Durand, F., and Freeman, W. T. The visual microphone: Passive recovery of sound from video. *ACM Trans. Graph 33*, 4 (2014), 79.

[10] Eargle, J. *The Microphone Book: From mono to stereo to surround-a guide to microphone design and application.* CRC Press, 2012.

[11] Fant, G. *Acoustic theory of speech production: with calculations based on X-ray studies of Russian articulations*, vol. 2. Walter de Gruyter, 1971.

[12] Farina, A. Simultaneous measurement of impulse response and distortion with a swept-sine technique. In *Audio Engineering Society Convention 108* (2000), Audio Engineering Society.

[13] Fausti, P., and Farina, A. Acoustic measurements in opera houses: comparison between different techniques and equipment. *Journal of Sound and Vibration 232*, 1 (2000), 213–229.

[14] Feinberg, D. R., Jones, B. C., Little, A. C., Burt, D. M., and Perrett, D. I. Manipulations of fundamental and formant frequencies influence the attractiveness of human male voices. *Animal Behaviour 69*, 3 (2005), 561–568.

[15] Gales, M. J. Maximum likelihood linear transformations for hmm-based speech recognition. *Computer speech & language 12*, 2 (1998), 75–98.

[16] Galili, I., Kaplan, D., and Lehavi, Y. Teaching faradayâĂŹs law of electromagnetic induction in an introductory physics course. *American journal of physics 74*, 4 (2006), 337–343.

[17] Gemmeke, J. F., Virtanen, T., and Hurmalainen, A. Exemplar-based sparse representations for noise robust automatic speech recognition. *Audio, Speech, and Language Processing, IEEE Transactions on 19*, 7 (2011), 2067–2080.

[18] Hayes, B. *Introductory phonology*, vol. 32. John Wiley & Sons, 2011.

[19] Hillenbrand, J., and Sessler, G. M. High-sensitivity piezoelectric microphones based on stacked cellular polymer films (l). *The Journal of the Acoustical Society of America 116*, 6 (2004), 3267–3270.

[20] Hinton, G., Deng, L., Yu, D., Dahl, G. E., Mohamed, A.-r., Jaitly, N., Senior, A., Vanhoucke, V., Nguyen, P., Sainath, T. N., et al. Deep neural networks for acoustic modeling in speech recognition: The shared views of four research groups. *Signal Processing Magazine, IEEE 29*, 6 (2012), 82–97.

[21] Huggins-daines, D., Kumar, M., Chan, A., Black, A. W., Ravishankar, M., and Rudnicky, A. I. Pocketsphinx: A free, real-time continuous speech recognition system for hand-held devices. In *in Proceedings of ICASSP* (2006).

[22] Jax, P., and Vary, P. On artificial bandwidth extension of telephone speech. *Signal Processing 83*, 8 (2003), 1707–1719.

[23] Johnson, C. D. Accelerometer principles. *Process Control Instrumentation Technology* (2009).

[24] Keele Jr, D. Low-frequency loudspeaker assessment by nearfield sound-pressure measurement. *Journal of the audio engineering society 22*, 3 (1974), 154–162.

[25] Kontio, J., Laaksonen, L., and Alku, P. Neural network-based artificial bandwidth expansion of speech. *Audio, Speech, and Language Processing, IEEE Transactions on 15*, 3 (2007), 873–881.

[26] Laaksonen, L., Kontio, J., and Alku, P. Artificial bandwidth expansion method to improve intelligibility and quality of amr-coded narrowband speech. In *ICASSP (1)* (2005), pp. 809–812.

[27] Ladefoged, P. The revised international phonetic alphabet. *Language* (1990), 550–552.

[28] Lapteva, O. *Speaker Perception and Recognition: An Integrative Framework for Computational Speech Processing.* kassel university press GmbH, 2011.

[29] McGrath, W. Technique and device for through-the-wall audio surveillance, Mar. 30 2005. US Patent App. 11/095,122.

[30] Michalevsky, Y., Boneh, D., and Nakibly, G. Gyrophone: Recognizing speech from gyroscope signals. In *Proc. 23rd USENIX Security Symposium (SEC?14), USENIX Association* (2014).

[31] Moreno, P. J., and Stern, R. M. Sources of degradation of speech recognition in the telephone network. In *Acoustics, Speech, and Signal Processing, 1994. ICASSP-94., 1994 IEEE International Conference on* (1994), vol. 1, IEEE, pp. I–109.

[32] Muscatell, R. P. Laser microphone, Oct. 23 1984. US Patent 4,479,265.

[33] Nation, P., and Waring, R. Vocabulary size, text coverage and word lists. *Vocabulary: Description, acquisition and pedagogy 14* (1997), 6–19.

[34] Ogata, K. *System dynamics*, vol. 3. Prentice Hall New Jersey, 1998.

[35] Qi, Y., and Hillman, R. E. Temporal and spectral estimations of harmonics-to-noise ratio in human voice

signals. *The Journal of the Acoustical Society of America 102*, 1 (1997), 537–543.

[36] ROY, N., GOWDA, M., AND CHOUDHURY, R. R. Ripple: Communicating through physical vibration.

[37] SCARBOROUGH, J. B. *The Gyroscope: Theory and Application.* Interscience Pub., 1958.

[38] SMARAGDIS, P., RAJ, B., AND SHASHANKA, M. Missing data imputation for spectral audio signals. In *Machine Learning for Signal Processing, 2009. MLSP 2009. IEEE International Workshop on* (2009), IEEE, pp. 1–6.

[39] SMEETS, G. Laser interference microphone for ultrasonics and nonlinear acoustics. *The Journal of the Acoustical Society of America 61*, 3 (1977), 872–875.

[40] SPECIALE, J. R. Pulsed laser microphone, Oct. 9 2001. US Patent 6,301,034.

[41] TANNER, P., LOEBACH, J., COOK, J., AND HALLEN, H. A pulsed jumping ring apparatus for demonstration of lenzâĂŹs law. *American Journal of Physics 69*, 8 (2001), 911–916.

[42] TAYLOR, B. *Guide for the Use of the International System of Units (SI): The Metric System.* DIANE Publishing, 1995.

[43] TITZE, I. R. *Principles of voice production.* National Center for Voice and Speech, 2000.

[44] WAIBEL, A., HANAZAWA, T., HINTON, G., SHIKANO, K., AND LANG, K. J. Phoneme recognition using time-delay neural networks. *Acoustics, Speech and Signal Processing, IEEE Transactions on 37*, 3 (1989), 328–339.

[45] WANG, C.-C., TRIVEDI, S., JIN, F., SWAMINATHAN, V., RODRIGUEZ, P., AND PRASAD, N. S. High sensitivity pulsed laser vibrometer and its application as a laser microphone. *Applied Physics Letters 94*, 5 (2009), 051112.

[46] WEI, T., WANG, S., ZHOU, A., AND ZHANG, X. Acoustic eavesdropping through wireless vibrometry. In *Proceedings of the 21st Annual International Conference on Mobile Computing and Networking* (2015), ACM, pp. 130–141.

[47] ZHANG, L., PATHAK, P. H., WU, M., ZHAO, Y., AND MOHAPATRA, P. Accelword: Energy efficient hotword detection through accelerometer. In *Proceedings of the 13th Annual International Conference on Mobile Systems, Applications, and Services* (2015), ACM, pp. 301–315.

Practical Human Sensing in the Light

Tianxing Li, Qiang Liu, and Xia Zhou
Department of Computer Science, Dartmouth College, Hanover, NH
{tianxing, qliu, xia}@cs.dartmouth.edu

ABSTRACT

We present StarLight, an infrastructure-based sensing system that reuses light emitted from ceiling LED panels to reconstruct fine-grained user skeleton postures continuously in real time. It relies on only a few (e.g., 20) photodiodes placed at optimized locations to passively capture low-level visual clues (light blockage information), with neither cameras capturing sensitive images, nor on-body devices, nor electromagnetic interference. It then aggregates the blockage information of a large number of light rays from LED panels and identifies best-fit 3D skeleton postures. StarLight greatly advances the prior light-based sensing design by dramatically reducing the number of intrusive sensors, overcoming furniture blockage, and supporting user mobility. We build and deploy StarLight in a 3.6 m × 4.8 m office room, with customized 20 LED panels and 20 photodiodes. Experiments show that StarLight achieves 13.6° mean angular error for five body joints and reconstructs a mobile skeleton at a high frame rate (40 FPS). StarLight enables a new unobtrusive sensing paradigm to augment today's mobile sensing for continuous and accurate behavioral monitoring.

Keywords

Visible light communication; skeleton tracking; localization; sensing

1. INTRODUCTION

Accurate, continuous behavioral sensing is crucial to our health and daily life. It helps detect early symptoms of health issues and disorders [17, 38] and foster behavioral changes to cultivate healthy lifestyles [12, 14, 29, 34, 38, 45, 49]. The technology shift is arriving with the advent of wearable and wellness sensors (e.g., Fitbit, Apple Watch). These sensing devices monitor our activities and health status at an unprecedented level of details (e.g., footsteps, heart beats).

However, these mobile sensing devices alone are still fundamentally limited. Not only do we have to constantly wear or carry and regularly charge them, but also they fall far short on gaining an accurate and complete view of our behaviors. Devices like Fitbit and Apple Watch can only infer physical movement using crude accelerometers. Similarly, not only are heartbeat sensors error-prone (especially during movement), but also they say nothing about the causes that trigger an increase in heart rate, which can be due to exercising, or potential health issues (e.g., stress) that need immediate intervention. This lack of the semantic context prevents these wearable sensors from bridging the gap between local measurements and a holistic view of our behaviors.

Figure 1: StarLight reuses ceiling LED panels together with a few photodiodes to reconstruct a mobile user's skeleton in a normal office setting with furniture.

To bring human sensing to the next level, we have to augment per-user, local sensors with environmental sensing data. Current methods all have significant drawbacks. They either require capturing raw images and video [11, 19, 21, 23, 42, 54] that present severe privacy risks involving the leaking of sensitive images [1] [52, 66], or reuse ambient radio frequency (RF) signals that are vulnerable to electromagnetic interference and offer only coarse sensing granularity (e.g., classifying pre-defined gestures and activities, tracking a single body part) [6, 7, 8, 18, 48, 58, 63, 65].

In this paper, we pursue the sensing paradigm that exploits the ubiquitous light as a passive sensing medium that accurately senses what we do at the infrastructure level, with neither on-body sensors, nor cameras capturing sensitive images/videos, nor electromagnetic interference. A light-based sensing system consists of Light-Emitting-Diodes (LEDs) on the ceiling and low-cost (<$3) light sensors (photodiodes, 3 mm in radius) in the environment (e.g., embedded in the carpet using smart textile [47]). These light sensors passively collect the shadow information created by our body blocking the lights and recover our behaviors continuously. By collecting such low-level visual clues (see examples in Figure 7(b)) and removing the need of high-fidelity sensors such as cameras, light-based sensing much better protects user privacy. It

[1]Although one can store only features of interests extracted from camera images to alleviate the privacy concern, such process is regularly conducted in software and thus still allows potential attacks for the adversary.

MobiSys'16, June 25-30, 2016, Singapore, Singapore

DOI: http://dx.doi.org/10.1145/2906388.2906401

also entails a low cost – it reuses the ubiquitous lighting infrastructure without the need to replace LEDs but only connecting LEDs to low-cost micro-controllers (e.g., FPGAs, Arduino boards).

Initial efforts [36] have demonstrated the feasibility of light-based sensing, however, several key limitations remain. *First*, prior design needs hundreds of photodiodes to acquire shadow information even for a 3 m $\times$ 3 m area. The overhead of photodiode deployment prevents its immediate adoption. *Second*, it assumes an open space with the user as the only light-blocking object, whereas in practice, other objects (e.g., furniture) in the environment can either block the shadow or create overlapping shadows, making it much more challenging to recover user behaviors. *Finally*, prior system works only for a single static user with known location and orientation, dictating rather limited working scenarios without user mobility.

The focus of this paper is to overcome the above limitations and further unleash the practical potential of light-based sensing in typical indoor settings. To this end, we present *StarLight, the first light-based sensing system that uses only a few (e.g., 20) photodiodes to reconstruct moving human skeletons in real time, even in the presence of furniture and other blocking objects*. The underlying principle of StarLight is a new sensing architecture that reuses ubiquitous LED panels on the ceiling. Designed to generate homogeneous and natural light, each LED panel contains arrays of LED chips inside.[2] Each LED chip functions as a point light source. These LEDs together provide a large number of light paths for analysis. Since the blockage of each light path is independent of which end of the path is LED and which end is the photodiode, by separating light rays from different LED chips, each photodiode can recover a *virtual shadow map*, which would have been projected on the ceiling if this photodiode were an LED and LED chips on the ceiling were photodiodes. By sprinkling a small number of photodiodes in the environment, we can collect virtual shadow maps from these photodiodes' viewing points. These virtual shadow maps allow the system to reconstruct a user's moving skeleton. Compared to the prior design [36] with a few LEDs and many photodiodes, this new sensing architecture drastically reduces the number of photodiodes to deploy, making the sensing system much easier to be integrated into existing and future lighting infrastructure.[3]

The new sensing architecture, on the other hand, also brings unique design challenges not present before. *First*, it is non-trivial to separate light rays from a large number of LEDs on the ceiling using low-cost photodiodes and micro-controllers. Prior design [36] requires each LED to flash at a unique frequency and thus cannot directly scale up to dense LEDs. *Second*, given the small number of photodiodes and their limited viewing angles, optimizing their placements is crucial to the sensing performance. Our experiments show that simple placement strategies (e.g., uniform) degrades the sensing accuracy. The placement optimization problem faces an exponential search space and needs to take into account practical factors such as the non-uniform placement of LED panels, furniture blockage, and user mobility. *Third*, the reconstruction algorithm deals with the unknown user location, as well as virtual shadows that can be incomplete due to the LED panel placement and furniture blockage. Additionally, it has to entail low complexity to realize real-time skeleton reconstruction.

StarLight addresses these challenges as follows. *First*, it reuses light beacons over time and thus reduces the number of concurrent light beacon frequencies that need to be separated. It also includes synchronization schemes and judicious light frequency assignment to facilitate light beacon identification at the photodiodes. *Second*, it turns the problem of optimizing photodiode placement into a submodular maximization and designs an efficient greedy solution with $(1 - 1/e)$ approximation ratio. It considers the practical layout of main furniture and LED panels as input and seeks the optimized sensor placement to minimize the impact of furniture blockage on the sensing performance. *Finally*, to support user mobility and orientation change, StarLight tracks user's location and orientation based on coarse-grained body features extracted from binary virtual shadow maps. It aggregates the virtual shadow maps from all photodiode sensors to overcome the incompleteness and the extremely low resolution of individual maps. It also leverages user's movement continuity to reduce the search space and identify the best-fit 3D skeleton posture.

StarLight Testbed. We implement and deploy StarLight in a 3.6 m $\times$ 4.8 m office room with normal furniture layout (Figure 8(a)). The testbed consists of 20 customized LED panels (Figure 8(b)) and 20 low-cost photodiodes [4] placed on the floor based on the greedy placement strategy. We design and fabricate the LED panels, each containing 16 off-the-shelf LEDs modulated by an FPGA independently (Figure 10). The photodiodes connect to Arduino Due micro-controllers, which sample light intensity data, separate light rays from different LEDs, and transfer results to a server. The server detects the blockage of each light ray, recovers virtual shadow maps, runs the skeleton reconstruction algorithm, and visualizes the reconstructed skeleton on a monitor in real time. Figure 1 is a snapshot of StarLight in action.

We evaluate StarLight under diverse settings and obtain the following key findings:

- StarLight achieves 13.6° mean angular error for 3D reconstructing five key body joint, comparable to the prior design while addressing several practical concerns (sensor deployment overhead, furniture blockage, user mobility);
- StarLight tracks a mobile skeleton with 2D localization error of 4 cm on average and 9.7 cm at the 95%-percentile;
- StarLight produces a reconstructed 3D skeleton within 25 ms and visualizes the human skeleton at 40 FPS, higher than that of Kinect (30 FPS);
- StarLight maintains a stable performance under different ambient light and furniture layout conditions.

2. LIGHT-BASED SENSING: CONCEPT AND CHALLENGES

The goal of light-based sensing is to turn everyday lighting into a powerful, accurate sensing medium that can reconstruct our whole-body gestures and infer our detailed activities. In this section, we start with the background of light-based sensing and the limitations of prior design. We then describe a new sensing architecture that helps overcome these limitations, followed by the practical challenges that we face to realize the new architecture.

2.1 Background of Light-Based Sensing

Concept. Light-based sensing is driven by a simple observation: shadows. Because the wavelength of visible light is measured in nanometers, any opaque macroscopic object (e.g., a user body) can block the light and cast a silhouette behind the object. The resulting shadow is essentially a 2D projection of the 3D object. Take the human body as an example, as the body moves and gestures, it blocks different light rays and its shadow shape changes at the light speed. Thus, by continuously collecting and analyzing the stream

[2] As an example, an off-the-shelf direct-lit LED panel [1] contains 132 LED chips in a 61 cm $\times$ 61 cm area.

[3] LED panels are envisioned to be the future of indoor lighting because of their efficiency and seamless ceiling integration [3].

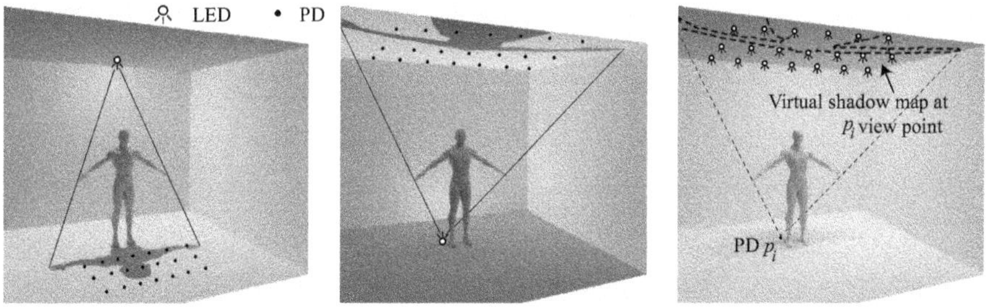

(a) Shadow on the floor (b) Shadow on the ceiling (c) Virtual shadow on the ceiling

Figure 2: Comparison of the sensing architecture. Prior design relies on few LEDs and many photodiodes (PDs) to collect shadow information on the floor (a). To minimize the photodiode deployment overhead, the new sensing architecture aims to recover the shadow projected on the ceiling (b), by reusing arrays of LED chips realized as LED panels on the ceiling (c).

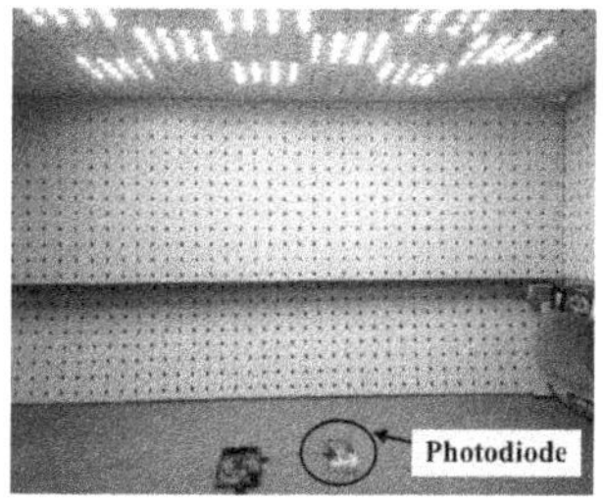

Figure 3: A table-top testbed measured 30 cm × 60 cm × 50 cm in size, with 9 customized LED mini-panels on the ceiling. Each LED mini-panel contains 16 CREE XML LED chips controlled by an FPGA board.

of shadows cast on the floor, we can infer user's 3D postures over time and recover the activities.

Prior design LiSense [36] has demonstrated the feasibility of light-based sensing. As illustrated in Figure 2(a), the system architecture of LiSense consists of dense (e.g., 36 photodiodes per m^2) photodiodes on the floor to capture the shadow information and a small (e.g., 5) number of LED lights on the ceiling. LiSense comprises two systems pieces: shadow acquisition and posture reconstruction. Shadow acquisition disambiguates the diluted and complex shadow patterns under multiple lights and acquires the shadow component corresponding to each light. Empowered by Visible Light Communication (VLC), LiSense leverages light beacons implemented with VLC to separate light rays from different LEDs and ambient light. Each LED emits light beacons by flashing at a unique high frequency imperceptible to human eyes. Each photodiode transforms the perceived light intensity values over time to the frequency domain and detects the blockage of the light path to each LED. Aggregating the blockage results of all photodiodes recovers the shadow maps cast by all LEDs. Based on these shadow maps, posture reconstruction infers a human 3D skeleton best matching the observed shadow maps cast in different directions.

Current Limitations. Although prior design provides promising sensing accuracy, its main practical concern is the deployment of dense photodiodes on the floor. Even if the use of smart textile allows integrating these tiny photodiodes with the environment (e.g., rugs, carpet) in an unobtrusive manner, other objects such as furniture can easily block user's shadows and severely interfere with the acquisition of shadow information. Furthermore, the prior posture reconstruction algorithm assumes a single static user with known location and orientation, unable to support user movement and orientation change.

2.2 Rethinking the Sensing Architecture

The need to greatly drive down the overhead of photodiode deployment motivates us to rethink the architecture of the sensing system. Instead of focusing on the shadow cast on the floor, we turn our attention to the shadow projected on the ceiling if LEDs are deployed on the floor. Consider a single LED on the floor (Figure 2(b)), the ceiling shadow created by the human body blocking this LED reflects how the body blocks each light ray emitting from the floor LED to the ceiling. Since the blockage of a light path is independent of which end of the path is the LED, we can switch the two ends of each light path, i.e., placing the LED as the ceiling end of each light path and the photodiode as the floor end, while still being able to infer the blockage of each light path. This switch leads us to a new sensing architecture with dense LEDs on the ceiling and a small number (e.g., dozens) of photodiodes sprinkled in the environment. Each photodiode separates the light rays from all ceiling LEDs, infers the blockage of each light path, and recovers a *virtual shadow map* that would have been projected on the ceiling if the photodiode were an LED and ceiling LEDs were photodiodes (Figure 2(c)). By aggregating the virtual shadow maps from all photodiodes' viewing points, we can infer the user's 3D posture, similarly to the prior design.

Benefit. This new sensing architecture allows more seamless integration with the existing indoor infrastructure. Leveraging the dense array of LEDs on the ceiling, it significantly reduces the number of photodiodes to deploy on the floor. More importantly, LED arrays can be realized as LED panels on the ceiling, which is envisioned to be the future of indoor lighting because of its efficiency and ability of generating natural light [3]. We can reuse these LED panels without the need to replace the LED chips but only attach to them a modulation unit (e.g., FPGA control board) that controls the input current to each LED.

2.3 Practical Challenges

To build a practical light-based sensing system based on the new sensing architecture, we face three main challenges. They arise from dealing with the *large* number of LED chips on the ceiling, optimizing the placement of the *small* number of photodiodes in the environment, and supporting user mobility while maintaining accurate posture sensing.

Dense LEDs. With multiple LED panels on the ceiling, adjacent LED chips can be only a few centimeters away. Commercial LED typically has a Field-of-View (FoV) of 90° – 120° to maximize the illumination region. Thus, a photodiode on the floor perceives light rays from a large number (e.g., ∼300) of LEDs. These many LEDs present new challenges when it comes to separating light rays. Prior light beacon design (see § 2.1) falls short.

To examine the impact of the number of LEDs, we build a scaled-down table-top testbed resembling a miniaturized room (Figure 3). It is made of wooden frames and plastic plates as walls and the ceiling. We attach 9 LED mini-panels to the ceiling, where each panel is 10 cm × 10 cm in size and contains 16 LED chips (CREE XML). Each panel is connected to an FPGA board (Digilent Basys 3), which modulates the input current to each LED independently. We build other electrical components (e.g., MOSFET, resistor) into a Printed Circuit Board (PCB) (Figure 10(c)) to minimize the electrical noise. We implement the prior light beacon design in the FPGA board. Each LED is assigned with a different light beacon frequency, ranging from 20.8 KHz to 41.5 KHz. We place a photodiode (OPT101 [4]) on the table center and fetch the light signals

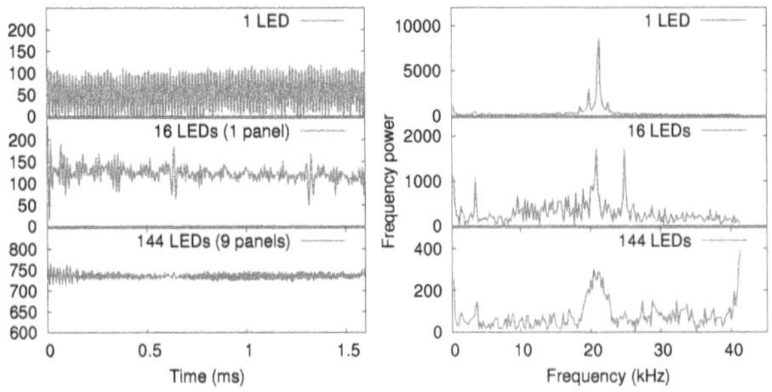

(a) Time domain (b) Frequency domain

Figure 4: The impact of the number of LEDs on separating light rays using the prior light beacon design [36].

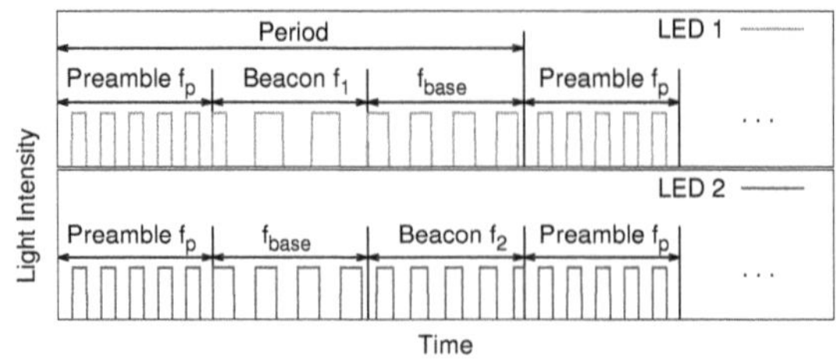

Figure 5: The light beacon design in StarLight. All LEDs first flash at the preamble frequency f_p for synchronization and then enter the beacon slots. Each LED i flashes at its light beacon frequency f_i only in its assigned beacon slot b_i, and at the based frequency f_{base} in other beacon slots. f_i and b_i together uniquely identify LED i.

using an Arduino DUE micro-controller, with the same setup as the previous study [36]. The Arduino reading (an integer within [0, 1023]) reflects the light intensity perceived by the photodiode.

Figure 4 plots the time series of Arduino's readings when we switch on different number of LED chips, as well as the results of transforming these values to the frequency domain after applying Fast Fourier Transform (FFT). Our key observation is that as the number of LEDs increases, the light intensity values perceived by the photodiode exhibit smaller variations, resulting into much lower frequency powers at light beacon frequencies. Therefore, the detection of light beacons is less reliable. Our further analysis shows that the variation decrease is due to the photodiode's response time, which measures the speed of the photodiode to change the output current upon light intensity change. When combining many asynchronous light rays flashing at different frequencies (i.e., different frequency of rising and falling edges), the minimal time interval T_{min} between adjacent rising or falling edges is small. Additionally, the asynchronous flashing of LEDs further shrinks T_{min} in practice.[4] For example, with all LEDs switched on in our table-top testbed, T_{min} is only 46 ns, much shorter than the response time (9 μs) of common low-cost photodiodes. As a result, the photodiode is unable to reach its final output current, leading to a lower Arduino reading and smaller variation. We can mitigate the problem using photodiodes with shorter response time, which, however, requires a smaller sensitivity area inside the photodiode, lowering the sensing gain and distance. As an example, the high-end photodiode [2] we have measured achieves 10-ns response time, whereas its sensing distance is only 30 cm, not applicable in our sensing scenario.

Sparse Photodiodes. Another challenge is to realize accurate gesture reconstruction using only a few photodiodes. The small quantity of photodiodes emphasizes the importance of their placement for the sensing performance. Ideally, photodiodes should be placed to maximally capture the light ray blockage information created by the user body. Their placement, however, is complicated by the following practical factors. *First*, other blocking objects (e.g., furniture) in the environment can block a photodiode, preventing it from capturing light rays from ceiling LEDs and recovering the virtual shadow map. *Second*, ceiling LED panels are commonly placed with intervals, not only for the cost, but also to circumvent other ceiling infrastructures like pipes, vents, and temperature sensors. The resulting layout of LED panels can be non-uniform and irregular. It presents a non-trivial constraint for the photodiode placement strategy to maximize the light rays captured by each photodiode. *Third*, photodiodes have their own limit on the viewing angle, i.e., Field of Vision (FoV). They cannot accurately perceive light rays coming near or outside its FoV. Thus, the photodiode's FoV is one additional constraint that the placement strategy has to consider given the layout of LED panels and the furniture.

User Mobility. Last but not least, user mobility brings additional challenges not only to the photodiode placement, but also to the reconstruction of the user skeleton. To the photodiode placement, user mobility means that the placement cannot be simply optimized towards a fixed user location, rather, it needs to ensure that photodiodes can capture sufficient light ray information to reconstruct user skeleton regardless of the user's current location and orientation. To the skeleton reconstruction, the uncertainty of user's location and orientation significantly increases the search space to identify the best-fit skeleton posture. As a result, it can lead to higher reconstruction latency and potentially higher reconstruction errors. We need efficient algorithms to guarantee real-time skeleton reconstruction while maintaining the reconstruction reliability.

We next present StarLight that is built atop the new sensing architecture (LED panels and few photodiodes) and addresses the above challenges. StarLight leverages a new light beacon design (§ 3) to deal with dense LEDs, a greedy algorithm to optimize the photodiode placement (§ 4) given the 3D layout of furniture and LED panels, and an efficient algorithm to track and reconstruct a moving user skeleton (§ 5).

3. RECOVERING VIRTUAL SHADOWS

We first describe how StarLight enables each photodiode to separate light rays from dense LEDs and recover the virtual shadow map that would have been projected on the ceiling if the photodiode were an LED. To support a large number of LEDs with a limited number of light beacon frequencies, StarLight reuses light beacon frequencies in the time domain while ensuring accurate and reliable separation of all light rays at each photodiode. We next present the new light beacon design for the LEDs, followed by the light ray separation and blockage detection schemes at photodiodes.

3.1 Time-Based Light Beacon

In the presence of dense LEDs, directly applying the prior light beacon design is no longer effective, mainly because it requires a large number of light beacon frequencies. As shown in the prior study [36], the highest light beacon frequency is limited by the sampling rate of the micro-controller fetching data from the photodiode, and the lowest has to be above 1 KHz to avoid the flickering effect [33, 35]. Thus, the more light beacon frequencies selected in this range, the smaller interval between adjacent frequencies. It results into faster transition between rising or falling edges in the light intensity perceived by the photodiode, which can outpace the photodiode's response time and lead to detection errors.

[4]Given the set F of light beacon frequencies, we have $T_{min} \leq (1/\max(F \setminus \{\max(F)\}) - 1/\max(F))/2$.

We address the problem by adding the time domain information to separate LEDs. The key idea is to reuse light beacon frequencies over time, so that it reduces the number of frequencies required to support a given number of LEDs. In particular, given N LEDs within a photodiode's viewing angle and the set F_b of available light beacon frequencies, we divide LEDs into groups, where each group contains no more than M (i.e., $|F_b|$) LEDs. Each LED i in the same group is assigned with a different light beacon frequency $f_i \in F_b$, and the same set F_b of frequencies are reused across groups. LED groups transmit light beacons in turns following a fixed order. When a group of LEDs are transmitting light beacons in the assigned beacon slot, LEDs in other groups flash at the *base frequency* $f_{base} \notin F_b$. This avoids two LEDs flashing at the same frequency simultaneously. Therefore, each LED i is identified by its light beacon frequency f_i and its beacon slot order b_i. This design echoes the principle of Pulse Position Modulation [13], where the time position of a pulse encodes bits. Similarly, here the time (beacon slot) when the light beacon occurs conveys additional information for the photodiode to identify light rays from an LED. The minimal number of beacon slots is $\lceil \frac{N}{M} \rceil$, where N is the number of LEDs within each photodiode sensor's FoV, and M is the maximal number of light frequencies that a photodiode can differentiate.[5] Thus, only the higher LED density needs more beacon slots. For a given LED density, we can scale the system to a large area without increasing beacon slots. We next describe two design enhancements to facilitate the light ray separation.

Synchronization. Adding the time domain information naturally requires tight synchronization among LEDs, as well as between LEDs and photodiodes, so that each LED transmits light beacons accurately in its assigned beacon slot and photodiodes correctly identify the start of each beacon slot. The synchronization among LEDs is straightforward, as LEDs are centrally controlled by a micro-controller[6]. The synchronization between LEDs and photodiodes is trickier. To that end, we add a *preamble slot* right before every set of beacon slots. In the preamble slot, all LEDs flash at the preamble frequency f_p (different from f_{base} and all light beacon frequencies F_b). The preamble creates a unique pattern for photodiodes to identify the start of following beacon slots. Figure 5 illustrates an example with two LEDs and two beacon slots, where these two LEDs are in different LED groups and thus transmit light beacons in different beacon slots.

Frequency Assignment. To further enhance the reliability of light beacon detection at photodiodes, we judiciously assign the light beacon frequencies F_b to LEDs based on their locations. The rationale is originated by our experimental finding: when light rays flashing at different frequencies arrive at a photodiode, the photodiode better extracts frequency powers of light rays with lower flashing frequencies. The reason is that the photodiode's response time results into a gradual rise or fall during light intensity changes. For light rays with lower flashing frequencies, more light signals are sampled, leading to higher frequency powers in the frequency domain and more robust blockage detection. Hence we assign lower frequencies to LEDs that are further from photodiodes, since their light rays arrive close to the photodiodes' FoV and their detections are less reliable. Specifically, we rank LEDs in a descend order based on their average distances to photodiodes that can perceive their light rays. We then assign to each LED a light beacon frequency from the lowest to the highest.

[5] M depends on the speed of the photodiode's rise/fall time and the ADC sampling speed of the mirco-controller it connects to.

[6] The FPGA board (Digilent Basys 3 FPGA board) used in our testbed (see § 6) introduces less than 1-ns clock shift.

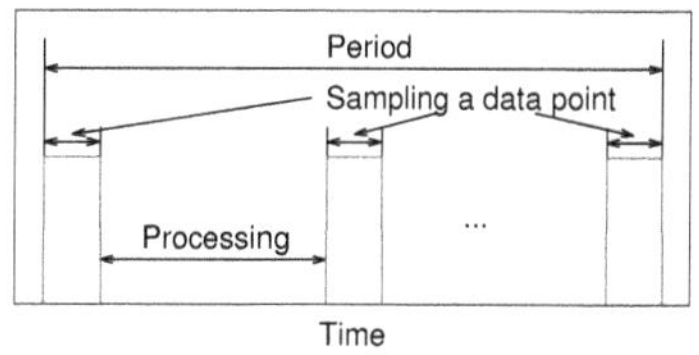

Figure 6: StarLight's processing pipeline. StarLight divides the whole data processing into small pieces and process these pieces during the intervals between adjacent samplings.

3.2 Blockage Detection

Given the light beacons from the LEDs, the micro-controller connecting to each photodiode performs two tasks: 1) *Sampling*: it periodically samples the light intensity data; and 2) *Processing*: it locates the preamble slot and thus the following beacon slots, fetches the light intensity values within each beacon slot, computes the frequency powers at the light beacon frequencies via FFT. The micro-controller transfers the results to a server. The server detects the blockage of a light ray based on its light beacon frequency power and its beacon slot number. It then recovers the virtual shadow map for this photodiode. We next discuss each step in detail.

Interleaving Sampling and Processing. To speed up the data sampling and processing at the micro-controller, we interleave the sampling and processing tasks, rather than executing them sequentially. As illustrated in Figure 6, during the intervals between adjacent data samplings, the micro-controller processes the data sampled in the last period. The interleaving is feasible because the maximal sampling rate (250 kHz) of the micro-controller's Analog-to-Digital Converter (ADC) is six times higher than the highest light beacon frequency (41.5 KHz, see § 6). Thus, the micro-controller can slightly space out its neighboring samplings and insert the processing task in between. The interleaving minimizes the idle duration of the micro-controller and fully utilizes its computation power. It is key for the system to later recover virtual shadow maps at a high frame rate.

Locating Preamble. Given the set of sampled data points D from one period, the micro-controller first locates the start of the preamble slot, which enables it to identify the subsequent beacon slots and compute frequency powers for each beacon slot. A strawman method is to slide a window with the preamble length L_p, perform FFT over the points in this window, and identify the window with the highest frequency power[7] at preamble frequency f_p. This method, however, requires performing FFT operations $|D|$ times, leading to a high processing delay.

To speed up the search, we locate the preamble in two steps. We first coarsely identify the region where the preamble potentially resides, and then narrow down to this region to conduct finer-grained search. Specifically, for the coarse-grain search, we divide D into disjoint subsets each with a length L_p of the preamble slot. Given the resulting $\frac{|D|}{L_p}$ subsets, we perform FFT over the points of each subset, extract the frequency power at f_p, and identify the subset $D_{i^\star}$ with the highest frequency power at f_p. Then the start of the actual preamble slot should lie in proximity of $i^\star$. In the second step, we fine-tune the $i^\star$ value using a binary search algorithm. The idea is to examine two candidate points within a range L of the current $i^\star$. We compute the frequency power at f_p using the

[7] One can also compute cross-correlation [46] over the series of frequency powers of f_p to locate the start of the preamble. We find that locating the peak suffices and entails less computation.

Algorithm 1: Locating the preamble slot.

input : 1) L_p, preamble slot length; 2) f_p, preamble frequency, i.e., LED's flashing frequency in the preamble slot; 3) $D = \{d_i\}$, sampled light intensity data
output: $i^\star$, the start time of the preamble slot.

for $i \leftarrow 1$ **to** $\frac{|D|}{L_p}$ **do**
  $D_i = \{d_k | (i-1)L_p < k \leq i \cdot L_p\}$
  $p_i = \texttt{FFT}(D_i, f_p)$
end
$p^\star = \max(\{p_i | i \in [1, \frac{|D|}{L_p}]\})$
$i^\star = \text{argmax}_{i \in [1, \frac{|D|}{L_p}]}\, p_i$
// Binary search to refine $i^\star$
$L = L_p$
while $\frac{L}{2} \geq 0$ **do**
  $L = \frac{L}{2}$
  $D_l = \{d_i | i \in [i^\star - L, i^\star - L + L_p)\}$
  $D_r = \{d_i | i \in [i^\star + L, i^\star + L + L_p)\}$
  $p_l = \texttt{FFT}(D_l, f_p)$
  $p_r = \texttt{FFT}(D_r, f_p)$
  if $p_l > p^\star$ **then**
    $p^\star = p_l$
    $i^\star = i^\star - L$
  end
  else if $p_r > p^\star$ **then**
    $p^\star = p_r$
    $i^\star = i^\star + L$
  end
end

L_p points starting from each candidate point, and determine the next search direction. We gradually shrink the search range L and the algorithm converges to the final output $i^\star$. Algorithm 1 lists the specific steps, where $FFT(D_i, f)$ applies FFT over the data points in D_i and extracts the frequency power at f. The total number of FFT operations in Algorithm 1 is $(\frac{|D|}{L_p} + 2 \cdot \log_2 L_p)$.

Adaptive Blockage Detection. The micro-controller sends to the server the extracted frequency powers at light beacon frequencies of all beacon slots. The server then associates each frequency power with an LED based on the light beacon frequency and its beacon slot. Since the frequency power is directly proportional to the light intensity, we can detect the blockage of an LED by examining its frequency power change. Given the heterogeneous light intensity from different LEDs, we compute the normalized, rather than the absolute, frequency power change as $\Delta P_{ij}(t) = |\frac{P_{ij}^{\text{nonBlock}} - P_{ij}(t)}{P_{ij}^{\text{nonBlock}}}|$, where P_{ij}^{nonBlock} and $P_{ij}(t)$ are the average non-blocking frequency power, and the frequency power at time t, from LED i at photodiode j, respectively. The light ray is considered to be blocked only if $\Delta P_{ij}(t)$ is above a threshold δ_{ij}. Our experiments show that light rays with higher intensity values experience larger normalized frequency power change caused by blockage. Therefore, unlike the prior design [36] that uses a uniform threshold for all light rays, StarLight sets δ_{ij} based on the light intensity I_{ij} normalized to the maximal light intensity I_{max} among all light rays. The light propagation model [30] indicates $I_{ij} \propto \frac{\cos\theta_{ij}}{d_{ij}^2}$, where θ_{ij} is the incidence angle, and d_{ij} is the distance between LED i and photodiode j. Thus, we compute δ_{ij} as:

$$\delta_{ij} = P_{min} + (P_{max} - P_{min}) \cdot \frac{\cos\theta_{ij}}{d_{ij}^2} \cdot \frac{d_{min}^2}{\cos\theta_{min}}, \quad (1)$$

where P_{min} and P_{max} are the minimal and maximal normalized

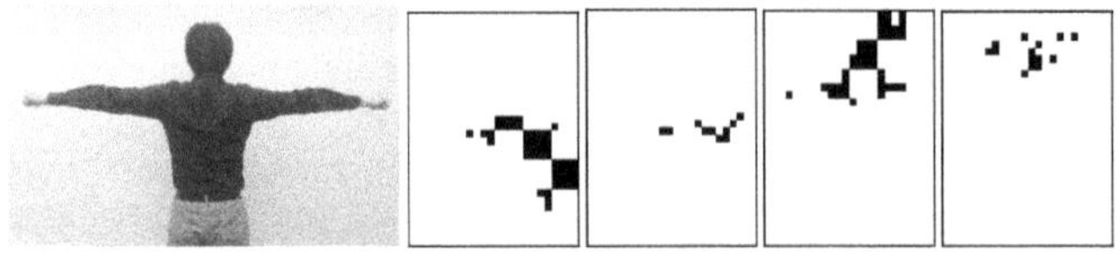

(a) User posture (b)Virtual shadow maps at 4 photodiodes

Figure 7: Four example virtual shadow maps recovered from our StarLight testbed, under a simple user posture.

frequency power changes, respectively, d_{min} and θ_{min} are related to I_{max} and are the minimal distance and incidence angle across all LED-photodiode pairs. We set P_{max} as 0.7 and P_{min} as 0.4 based on experiment results.

After detecting the blockage between each LED and a photodiode j, we recover the virtual shadow map $\widetilde{S}_j(t)$ at this photodiode's view point. With N LEDs, we have $\widetilde{S}_j(t) = \{\widetilde{s}_{ij}(t) | i \in [1, N]\}$, where $\widetilde{s}_{ij}(t) = 1$ if $\Delta P_{ij}(t) \geq \delta_{ij}$, and $\widetilde{s}_{ij}(t) = 0$ otherwise. Figure 7(b) shows examples of the virtual shadow maps at five photodiodes, given the user posture in Figure 7(a). The gaps in the virtual shadow maps are due to the non-uniform layout of the LED panels (Figure 8(b)). Clearly, the information conveyed by a virtual shadow map largely depends on the photodiode's location. Next we discuss how StarLight optimizes the photodiode placement to facilitate the user skeleton reconstruction.

4. OPTIMIZING SENSOR PLACEMENT

StarLight judiciously places photodiodes given a 3D environmental setup (e.g., layout of furniture and LED panels, room size and height). We aim to ensure that the virtual shadow maps at these photodiodes best facilitate the later skeleton reconstruction, considering furniture blockage, photodiode's limited FoV, and user mobility. A simple brute-force method is to exhaustively examine each possible combination of photodiode locations, estimate the resulting reconstruction errors, and identify the optimal photodiode placement that leads to the minimal reconstruction error. Clearly this method is not scalable given the exponential search space.

To boost the efficiency, StarLight defines an effective metric to evaluate the efficacy of a placement instance, without the need to repeatedly run the reconstruction algorithm. A key advantage of using this metric is that it turns the placement optimization problem into a *submodular maximization subject to a cardinality constraint* while retaining its direct link to the reconstruction performance. Thus a greedy algorithm to place photodiodes is highly effective. The algorithm entails polynomial-time complexity and achieves a proven $(1 - 1/e)$ approximation [44] to the optimal. Next, we first formally define the problem and analyze its property. We then present the greedy placement strategy in detail.

Problem Statement. While rich literature [10, 71] has studied the optimization of sensor placement in sensor networks, prior techniques have focused on information theoretic metrics [31]. However, in our context, the optimization goal is minimizing the 3D skeleton reconstruction error, which requires a new objective function. To eliminate the need to involve the skeleton reconstruction algorithm, we define an intermediate metric to evaluate the efficacy of a placement instance in minimizing reconstruction errors. The metric is based on a basic principle of the skeleton reconstruction, which leverages the information on which light rays intersect the user body to infer the 3D skeleton. Thus, to facilitate skeleton reconstruction and support user mobility, light rays arriving at the photodiodes should be diversely spread out, maximizing the likelihood that photodiodes capture light rays intersecting the user body.

Algorithm 2: Greedy placement of photodiodes.

input : 1) $U = \{u_1, ..., u_N\}$, N LEDs' locations; 2) Ω, feasible locations to place photodiodes; 3) Z, cube's edge length; 4) E, environmental setup (furniture layout, room size and height);

output: $w_1^\star, ..., w_K^\star$, locations of all K photodiodes.

$C = \texttt{genCubes}(E, Z)$ `// divide space into cubes`
for $m \leftarrow 1$ **to** $|C|$ **do**
  $cross[c_m] = 0$ `// clear cube status`
end
for $i \leftarrow 1$ **to** K **do**
  $new\_cubes = \emptyset$
  for $w_j \in \Omega$ **do**
    $tmp = \emptyset$
    for $k \leftarrow 1$ **to** N **do**
      if $\texttt{furBlock}(E, \overrightarrow{u_k w_j})$ **or** $\texttt{outFoV}(u_k, w_j)$ **then**
        continue
      end
      for $m \leftarrow 1$ **to** $|C|$ **do**
        if $cross[c_m] = 1$ **then continue**
        if $\texttt{dist}(\overrightarrow{u_k w_j}, c_m) < \frac{Z}{2}$ **then**
          $tmp = tmp \cup \{c_m\}$
        end
      end
    end
    if $|new\_cubes| < |tmp|$ **then**
      $new\_cubes = tmp$
      $w_i^\star = w_j$
    end
  end
  for $c_m \in new\_cubes$ **do**
    $cross[c_m] = 1$ `// mark newly-crossed cubes`
  end
  $\Omega = \Omega \setminus \{w_i^\star\}$
end

Based on this rationale, for a given placement instance $W = \{w_1, ..., w_K\}$ of K photodiodes, we evaluate its efficacy using the volume of the 3D space intersected by the light rays arriving at these photodiode locations. To simplify the calculation, we discretize the 3D space into small uniform cubes[8]. We define the metric $A(W)$ as the number of cubes crossed by light rays arriving at locations in W, ruling out light rays blocked by furniture or outside the photodiode's FoV. The placement optimization problem is to identify the placement $W^\star$ that maximizes this metric. Let Ω denote all the feasible locations to place photodiodes avoiding furniture, and $Q(w)$ is the set of cubes crossed by light rays arriving at location w. The problem can be formalized as a maximum coverage problem with a cardinality constraint:

$$\text{Maximize} \quad A(W) = |\bigcup_{w \in W} Q(w)| \tag{2a}$$

$$\text{subj. to:} \quad W \subset \Omega \tag{2b}$$

$$|W| \leq K \tag{2c}$$

The maximum coverage problem is NP-hard, but its objective function is known to be monotonic and submodular [20]. In our context, $A(W)$ increases monotonically with more photodiodes, and the contribution of the subsequent photodiodide diminishes. A greedy solution hence yields a $(1 - 1/e)$ approximation ratio, essentially the best approximation ratio one can achieve [16].

[8]For accurate tracking, each cube needs to be no larger than the smallest body part to be tracked. In our current implementation, we set the cube's edge length to 10 cm to allow the system to track user hands.

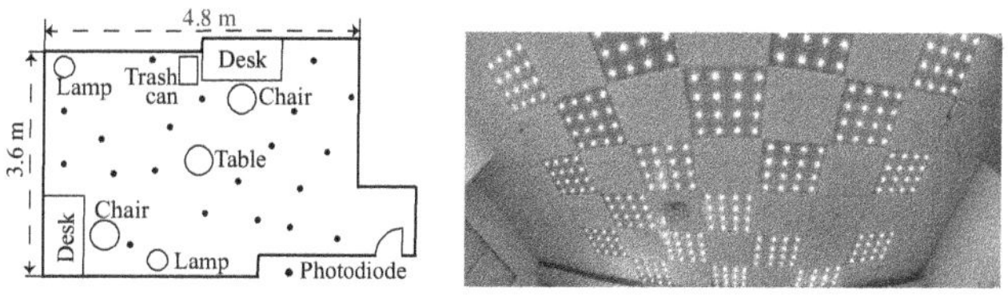

(a) Photodiode placement (b) LED panel layout

Figure 8: Placement of 20 photodiodes and 16 LED panels in StarLight testbed (§ 6).

Greedy Placement Strategy. Our greedy placement strategy works as follows. Given an environmental setup (e.g., furniture layout, room size and height), we can derive the free space E that user's body interacts with. We divide E into a set of cubes C ($\texttt{genCubes}(\cdot)$), where the edge length of each cube $c_m \in C$ is Z. We place K photodiodes sequentially. To determine the location of the i-th photodiode, we examine each candidate location $w_j \in \Omega$ and mark the cubes crossed by light rays from all LEDs to w_j. We exclude the light rays already blocked by the furniture ($\texttt{furBlock}(\cdot)$) or outside the photodiode's FoV ($\texttt{outFoV}(\cdot)$). We then count the number of newly-crossed cubes that have not been crossed by light rays arriving at the previous $(i-1)$ photodiodes. We identify the location $w_i^\star$ that brings the most newly-crossed cubes and place the i-th photodiode there. Algorithm 2 lists the details, where $\texttt{dist}(\overrightarrow{u_i w_j}, c_m)$ computes the distance between a vector $\overrightarrow{u_i w_j}$ and the center of cube c_m. Figure 8(a) marks the photodiode locations output by our algorithm for a given furniture setup and the LED panel layout in our testbed (Figure 8(b)).

The greedy algorithm runs in polynomial-time complexity. It outputs the optimized photodiode locations within 1 minute for our current setting. It implies that upon any environment changes (e.g., furniture removal or addition), we can quickly update the photodiode locations by running the placement algorithm again. In the future, to further speed up the calculation, we plan to examine algorithms that update the locations of photodiodes only within the areas affected by the environment change, rather than computing the locations of all photodiode sensors.

5. TRACKING A MOVING SKELETON

Armed with continuous streams of virtual shadow maps from different points of view (photodiodes), finally StarLight localizes and infers the user 3D skeleton over time. Unlike the prior work [36] that reconstructs the body skeleton of a static user with known orientation, StarLight seeks to reconstruct the skeleton of a moving user with unknown location and orientation while maintaining a similar reconstruction accuracy. Next, we begin with an overview of the inference algorithm design and then describe the key components in detail.

Overview. Reconstructing a moving skeleton is much more challenging because the search space of user's body segments expands exponentially given the uncertainty of user location and orientation. To address this challenge, we aggregate the virtual shadow maps from all photodiode sensors and extract coarse body features from the aggregated shadow map. These body features roughly indicate the user's location and possible orientation. Thus, they can be leveraged to reduce the search space greatly. We also leverage user's movement continuity to further reduce the search space and fine-tune the reconstruction results. Since the stream of virtual shadow maps are generated at a high frame rate (40 Hz, see § 7.2), the location and orientation offset between two adjacent inferences is very small. Hence the inference algorithm can start from the

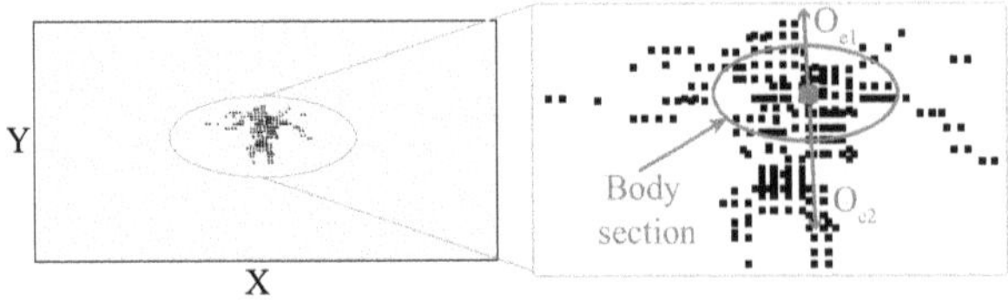

Figure 9: An example aggregated shadow map for the user posture in Figure 7(a). The ellipse maps to the user body and the ellipse minor axis (two arrows O_{e_1} and O_{e_2}) is the potential user orientation.

previous reconstruction results, search only within their small local range, and identify the optimal skeleton posture.

In particular, the inference is an iterative procedure with the following steps: 1) it refines the current set of virtual shadow maps by fixing apparent erroneous pixels; 2) it aggregates the shadow maps from all photodiodes and extracts coarse body features; 3) it then estimates the user's 2D location based on the extracted body feature and the last inferred skeleton posture; 4) next it computes user's current orientation based on the extracted body feature and user's moving trajectory; 5) using the inferred 2D user location and user orientation, it searches for the skeleton posture that best matches observed virtual shadows; 6) it repeats the above steps and iteratively refines the inference; and 7) finally it applies a Kalman Filter to smooth the inference results. Step 5) - 7) are based on the inference algorithm in the prior work [36]. Thus, we omit their details and focus on introducing the other steps.

Refining Virtual Shadow Maps. We start with correcting the apparent pixel errors in the collected virtual shadow maps. These erroneous pixels are caused by blockage detection errors on certain pairs of LED and photodiode (e.g., LED's light ray coming close to the photodiode's FoV). We spot these errors based on simple principles as follows: our body consists of connected body parts, thus the resulting shadow silhouette cannot have disconnected components; within a short time span between two consecutive set of virtual shadows, the offset generated by body movement is very small given the movement continuity. Applying these principles, we first pre-process each single virtual shadow map by filtering out black pixels disconnected from user's main body and far away from the previous user location. Next we leverage the past k (20 in our implementation) virtual shadow maps from the same photodiode and smooth pixels in the current virtual shadow map based on movement continuity. Such preprocessing prevents the propagation of shadow map errors to the later skeleton reconstruction.

Extracting Coarse Body Features. Based on the refined virtual shadow maps, we now extract coarse-grained body features from these maps. To support diverse users, we seek common body features independent of user's postures and body details. Specifically, we choose the cross section of a user's main body as the main body feature, as it is universally an ellipse regardless of user's postures. However, even for such a simple body feature, its extraction is still challenging in our context, because these virtual shadow maps (see Figure 7(b)) can be incomplete (limited by the photodiode's viewing angle) and they contain extremely low number (320) of pixels compared to typical photos or images. We overcome this challenge by aggregating the blockage information collected by all photodiodes. For all the blocked light rays observed by these photodiodes, we consider the intersection of these light rays with a flat horizontal plane at the height of the user's waist. Aggregating these intersection points leads to an aggregated shadow map projected on this horizontal plane. It reveals the cross section of the user's main body as an ellipse. To localize the ellipse, we exhaustively search the 2D area near the centroid of the aggregated shadow map and identify the ellipse that covers the most intersection points. The ellipse center approximates user's location and the direction of its minor axis indicates user's potential orientation. Figure 9 shows an example of the aggregated shadow map for the user posture in Figure 7(a), where we mark the identified ellipse representing user's main body and its minor axis indicating user orientation.

Locating A Moving Skeleton. Next, we locate the center of the user's main body in the 2D plane at time t. Although the center of the extracted ellipse provides an estimate of the user's location, its location error can be up to 10 cm, too high for inferring the skeleton posture accurately later. To lower the location error, we leverage user's movement continuity to refine the location estimate. Because of the short time interval (< 25 ms) between adjacent posture inferences, the skeleton posture at time t shares a high similarity with the last inferred posture at time $(t-1)$. Therefore, we can leverage the last inferred body segments B_{t-1} to estimate the most likely location offset at time t. In particular, we define a fitness function $F(\Delta x_t)$ to evaluate the likelihood of a candidate offset Δx_t. Based on current virtual shadow maps, $F(\Delta x_t)$ calculates the summation of the minimal distances from the blocked light rays to the body segments after applying the offset Δx_t to the last inferred posture B_{t-1}. We then estimate the user's current offset $\Delta x_t^\star$ as the one with the minimal $F(\Delta x_t)$ value. With N LEDs and K photodiodes, $\Delta x_t^\star$ is written as:

$$\Delta x_t^\star = \underset{\Delta x_t}{\operatorname{argmin}}\, F(\Delta x_t), \text{ where}$$

$$F(\Delta x_t) = \sum_{\substack{\tilde{s}_{ij}(t)=1 \\ i\in[1,N], j\in[1,K]}} \min_{b_m \in B_{t-1}} (\texttt{dist}(l_{ij}, b_m + \Delta x_t) - r_m), \quad (3)$$

$\texttt{dist}(l_1, l_2)$ calculates the perpendicular distance between two line segments l_1 and l_2, l_{ij} is the line segment between LED i and PD j, b_m is the 3D vector of body segment m, r_m is the radius of body segment m. Guided by the extracted ellipse, we search for $\Delta x_t^\star$ only within the 10-cm circle centered on the ellipse center, which greatly shortens the search duration. The user's current location x_t then is $(x_{t-1} + \Delta x_t^\star)$.

Determining User's Orientation. Given the direction of the ellipse's minor axis, user's orientation O_t at time t is within $\mathbb{O} = [O_{e1} - 30°, O_{e1} + 30°] \cup [O_{e2} - 30°, O_{e2} + 30°]$. We further reduce the search space by leveraging the movement continuity. Specifically we set O_t as follows. If the user moves in the 2D plane during $[t-1, t]$, i.e., $\Delta x_t^\star \neq 0$, we set O_t as $\overrightarrow{x_{t-1}x_t}$, where x_{t-1} and x_t denote the 2D location of the center of user's main body at time $t-1$ and t, respectively. Otherwise, if the user stays at the same 2D location within $[t-1, t]$, i.e., $\Delta x_t^\star = 0$, we analyze the mean O' of the previous k (5 in our implementation) orientation vectors. O_t is then within the intersection of $\mathbb{O}$ and $[O' - 30°, O' + 30°]$. We then rotate the user's 3D skeleton within the search space, compute a fitness value (similar to Eq. (3)) to evaluate how well it matches current virtual shadow maps, and search for the best-fit user orientation.

6. SYSTEM IMPLEMENTATION

We build and deploy StarLight in an office room (3.6 m× 4.8 m) with 2.6-m ceiling height. We mount 20 customized LED panels in 15-cm interval on the ceiling (Figure 8(b)). We distribute 20 low-cost photodiodes (OPT101 [4]) on the floor based on the greedy placement strategy (§ 4). Each photodiode connects to an Arduino Due micro-controller. A server collects data from all Arduino boards, runs our skeleton reconstruction algorithm (§ 5), and visualizes the reconstructed skeleton on the monitor (Figure 1).

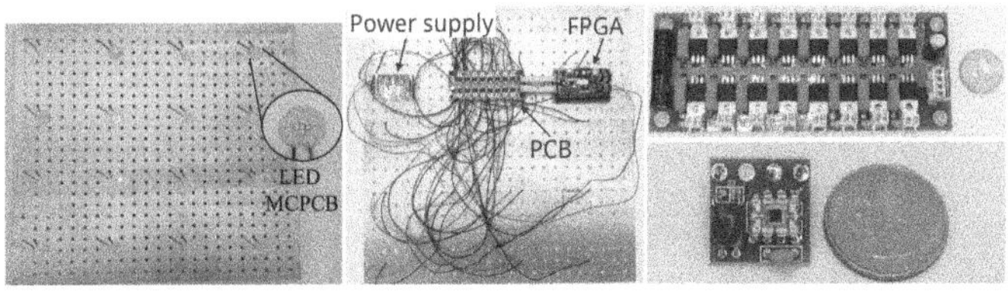

(a) Panel front (b) Panel back (c) PCBs

Figure 10: (a)(b) A customized LED panel and (c) the PCBs for the LED panel (top, 16 cm × 6.4 cm in size) and for the photodiode (bottom, 2 cm × 2 cm in size)).

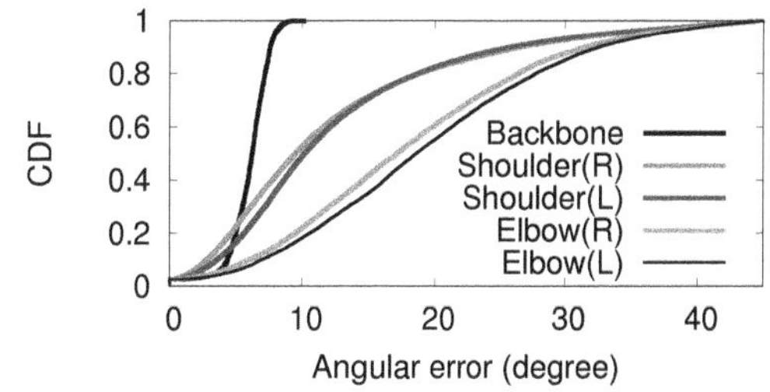

Figure 11: The overall reconstruction accuracy of StarLight, aggregating 195304 skeleton reconstruction results.

LED Panels. We design and fabricate 20 LED panels (61 cm × 61 cm in size), powered by independent 15-V DC supply. We do not directly use off-the-shelf LED panels because they commonly connect all LED chips in series. Thus, they do not allow independent control of each LED, which, however, is required for implementing StarLight's light beacons. Each panel contains 16 off-the-shelf LED Metal-Core PCBs (MCPCB) connected in parallel. Each MCPCB functions as a point light source with 5 LED chips (CREE XPG2) clustered in the center (Figure 10(a)). To control each LED MCPCB independently, we fabricate the electrical components as a PCB (Figure 10(c) top) connecting to each panel. We then connect the PCB to an FPGA board (Digilent Basys3), where we implement our light beacon design and synchronization scheme (§ 3.1). We leverage two 8-pin connectors on the FPGA to control LED's flashing frequency. To synchronize the FPGAs of all panels, a separate FPGA board sends a pulse to all 20 FPGAs every 20.8 ms.

We implement light beacons with 3 beacon slots and 108 flashing frequencies (107 for light beacons and 1 for f_{base}), ranging from 20.8 kHz to 41.5 kHz. Three beacon slots last 19.3 ms and the synchronization slot lasts 1.5 ms. The resulting illuminance in the room center is 400 lx on average and 500 lx at maximum, meeting the indoor lighting standard [51]. Figure 10(b) shows circuit boards, power supply, and wires on the back of the panel.

Photodiodes. For a miniaturized look, we design and fabricate a PCB (Figure 10(c) bottom) to include the photodiode and electrical components (e.g., resistors, capacitor). We then connect the PCB to an Arduino Due that samples the light signals from a photodiode. We select OPT101 as the photodiode for three reasons. First, it has a high responsivity (0.45 A/W for visible light wavelength of 650 nm), which helps detect multiple concurrent flashing frequencies. Second, it supports a wide FoV (140° on x-axis and 100° on y-axis based on our measurements), which enables the photodiode to perceive almost all LEDs in our testbed. Third, we can adjust its bandwidth of the frequency response to 56 kHz[9], which is much higher than the highest flashing frequency (41.5 kHz).

Micro-controllers. We implement our processing pipeline and blockage detection scheme (§ 3.2) on Arduino Due boards. The ADC sampling rate is set to 83.3 kHz and the number of sample points for a virtual shadow map is 1736. Due to the electrical noise on the PCB and control boards, the mean synchronization offset is 3 frames on average and 12 frame at the maximum. Thus, we set the beacon slot longer than the preamble slot to minimize the impact of the synchronization offset. We apply a 128-point FFT to detect the preamble slot and a 512-point FFT to extract light beacon frequency powers in the beacon slots. We implement our processing pipeline by adding interrupts in the main thread.

Arduino boards compute light beacon frequency powers of the beacon slots and send them to the server using RS232 ports, whose buad rate is limited to 115.2 Kbps. To improve the transmission efficiency, we increase the RingBuffer on the Arduino board to 4 KB and compress the data packet by rescaling the frequency power to 16. Thus, the packet length for a virtual shadow map is 72 bytes.

Server. The server aggregates data packets from all Arduino boards, recovers the virtual shadow maps, and reconstructs the user skeleton in the 3D space. To speed up the whole process, we implement virtual shadow recovering and skeleton reconstruction in C++ as two separate threads. Due to the RS232 transmission constraint, we place the server less than 3 m away from all Arduino boards.

7. StarLight EVALUATION

We now examine StarLight's practical performance using our testbed. We aim to evaluate its reconstruction accuracy and latency, the efficacy of each design component, and the impact of the environmental setting such as ambient light.

Experimental Setup. We evaluate StarLight in a typical indoor setting with furniture (e.g., tables, chairs, floor lamps, see Figure 8(a)). The only calibration required by StarLight is for each photodiode to measure the light intensity value without any users present, which helps configure the $P_{ij}^{nonBlock}$ for blockage detection (§ 3.2). Since $P_{ij}^{nonBlock}$ is the frequency power and StarLight's light beacon frequency (20 KHz – 40 KHz) is much higher than that of the ambient light fluctuation, we do not need to repeat the calibration under different ambient light conditions (see § 7.4 that examines the impact of ambient light). For a given furniture layout, the calibration only needs to be performed once. In each experiment, the user walks around in the room and freely performs consecutive upper-body gestures as he/she wishes, rather than performing specified gestures. The example gestures we have collected include pointing, waving, circling, stretching and more. Each experiment lasts 14 - 35 minutes and we repeat the experiment by 5 rounds. By default, we place 20 photodiodes at locations calculated by the greedy strategy (§ 4).

Ground Truth. In parallel to operating StarLight, we use a Kinect sensor (Version 2) to collect the 3D coordinates of user's key body joints continuously and treat Kinect data as the reference to evaluate StarLight's accuracy. We choose Kinect for two reasons. *First*, except Kinect, the only other existing system with the comparable ability is VICON. However, the room size requirement of installing VICON makes it infeasible in our experiment room. *Second*, compared to human labeling, which is the standard technique to obtain ground truth in computer vision [25, 42], the latest Kinect provides real-time, fine-grained, continuous (30 FPS) reconstruction results of all body joints, greatly facilitating the comparison to StarLight's reconstruction results. We do recognize, however, Kinect's imperfection, i.e., the limited viewing angle and support-

[9]We change the photodiode's bandwidth by connecting two 100-$k\Omega$ resistors and one 56-pF capacitor to the photodiode.

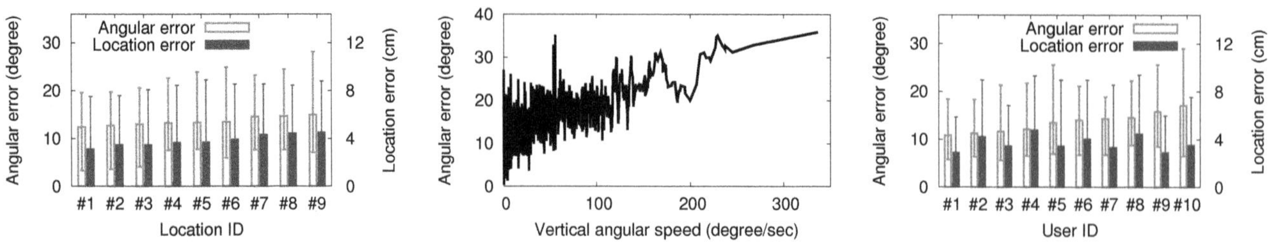

(a) Impact of location error (b) Impact of gesture speed (c) Impact of user diversity

Figure 12: Analyzing how StarLight's reconstruction accuracy is affected by the 2D localization error, gesture characteristics, and user diversity.

ing distance. Thus, we thoroughly test Kinect tracking users located in varying angles and distances, compare its results to human labeling results, and identify Kinect's best working condition. To acquire the human labeling results, we mount three DSLR cameras on the sides of the testbed. We build a MATLAB-based tool to label the key body joints in the captured videos and acquire the body skeleton data in the 3D space. We observe that as long as users are within 45° and 2 m - 6 m to the center of Kinect, the mean angular offset between Kinect and the human labeling method is negligible ($< 3°$). Given that Kinect can acquire body postures in real time while human labeling can take days to finish, we leverage Kinect data collected within its working range as the ground truth.

7.1 Reconstruction Accuracy

We begin with examining StarLight's overall reconstruction accuracy with ten users (see Table 1)[10]. We evaluate the reconstruction accuracy by calculating the absolute angular difference between the body segment vectors inferred by StarLight and that by Kinect. We focus on five key body joints including the backbone, left and right shoulder joints, left and right elbow joints. This angular metric has been widely used by prior studies [6, 9, 32, 36, 43] to examine skeleton tracking and reconstruction performance.

Figure 11 plots the CDFs of angular errors for the five body joints. Overall, StarLight achieves 5° mean angular error for the backbone joint and 14° mean angular error for all joints of the participants. The error is slightly higher than the prior design LiSense (10° [36]), however, StarLight addresses multiple practical constraints (e.g., furniture blockage, user mobility) while maintaining a similar accuracy. In comparison, LiSense assumes a static user with known location and orientation, which simplifies the reconstruction problem and eliminates the impact of user location tracking error on the reconstruction performance. Next we dive into specific factors that can affect StarLight's accuracy.

User Mobility. While the support of user mobility is one of the key features differentiating StarLight from LiSense, any slight inaccuracy in localization also contributes to the reconstruction error. Here we take the center of a user's main body projected on the floor as the user's location. To gather user's location data accurately during experiments, each participant wears a laser pen on the chest such that the laser pen points to the floor and forms a laster dot representing user's body center projected on the floor. We record the laser dot position to acquire the precise ground truth of the user location. To examine how the localization error is correlated with the reconstruction accuracy, we plot both errors (mean reconstruction errors for all body joints, and localization error) for 9 marked locations in Figure 12(a). We also include error bars to cover the minimal and maximal errors. As expected, we observe a positive

[10]Our study is conducted under the IRB approval at the local institution.

Table 1: The body parameters of 10 participants.

User ID	1	2	3	4	5	6	7	8	9	10
Height (cm)	190	190	183	173	170	170	176	170	169	158
Weight (kg)	84	80	64	67	65	68	66	63	60	50

correlation between these two errors. In particular, compared with the minimal localization error (3.14 cm Euclidean offset at Location 1), the highest location error (4.55 cm at Location 9) leads to 2.5 ° higher angular error. The reason is that StarLight relies on the inferred user location and orientation to identify the best-fit 3D skeleton posture. 2D localization error not only enlarges the search space for the reconstruction algorithm, but also misleads the algorithm to a wrong local minimum.

Gesture Characteristics. To examine the impact of user's gesture characteristics on StarLight's reconstruction accuracy, we aggregate the stream of body segment coordinates from Kinect, calculate the horizon and vertical offsets between adjacent body segment coordinates, and examine their correlation with reconstruction accuracy. Our key finding is that the speed of vertical movement has a noticeable impact on the accuracy (Figure 12(b)), while the impact of horizon movement speed does not exhibit noticeable patterns. The reason is that in the current StarLight testbed, all light rays are emitted from the ceiling to the floor and vertical movement affects fewer light rays than horizontal movements. To better deal with fast vertical movements, one solution is to consider light sources such as floor lamps or wall lights, which emit light rays from the sides.

User Diversity. We also compare StarLight's performance across users, seeking to examine the impact of user diversity on the reconstruction accuracy. Figure 12(c) shows the the mean angular errors of all body joints for each individual participant, as well as the 5% and 95%-percentiles. Overall, the mean angular errors across users differ within 5°. Interestingly, the system achieves higher reconstruction accuracy for users with larger bodies. As an example, the mean angular error is only 10° for the user 1.9 m in height and 84 kg in weight. This is because larger bodies block more light rays and generate richer blockage information for analysis. As a result, the fitting function (Eq. (3)) can converge more quickly to identify the local minimum and lead to higher reconstruction accuracy.

7.2 Reconstruction Latency

We next examine StarLight's reconstruction latency. We focus on the latency of its two real-time components: the acquisition of virtual shadow maps (§ 3) and the skeleton reconstruction (§ 5), which determine the frames per second for displaying the reconstructed skeleton. The photodiode placement strategy runs offline.

Acquisition of Virtual Shadow Maps. Recovering the virtual shadow maps comprises four steps: 1) each Arduino Due samples signals from the photodiode; 2) it detects the preamble slot within the samples and locate the subsequent beacon slots; 3) then it fetches the sampled data of each beacon slots and extracts the

Table 2: **Processing time of generating virtual shadow maps.**

Step	ADC sampling	Preamble detection	Blockage detection	Transmission
Time (ms)	6.7	8.2	4.5	0.5

Table 3: **Processing time of reconstructing a mobile skeleton.**

Step	Localization	Orientation detection	Inference
Time (ms)	6.4 – 8.2	0.4 – 1.1	4 – 15.6

frequency power at light beacon frequencies; and 4) finally it sends the frequency powers to the server. The server detects the blockage of each light ray and recovers the binary virtual shadow maps.

Table 2 lists the latency of each step running at the Arduino Due board. Given the 83.3 kHz ADC sampling rate and 1736 samples for each shadow map frame, the total sampling duration is 20 ms. To speed up the ADC processing time, we modify the ADC register on the Arduino board to shrink the ADC processing time to 4 μs/sample. The processing time for 1736 points is 6.6 ms. To detect the preamble (Algorithm 1), we need to compute 128-points FFT 27 times and each FFT takes 300 μs. For blockage detection, we need to compute 512-points FFT 3 times and each FFT takes 1.3 ms, generating 324 bits to represent a single virtual shadow map. We enlarge the ring buffer on the Arduino board to 8 Kb in order to continuous transit data without further latency. Overall, StarLight generates concurrent virtual shadow maps within 20 ms.

Reconstruction of Mobile Skeletons. Inferring a user gesture is an iterative process, where the algorithm iteratively updates the user's location, orientation, and gestures to fit the captured virtual shadow maps. Table 3 lists the latency of the three key components in the reconstruction algorithm. In terms of the size of the shadow on the virtual shadow maps, the reconstruction duration varies from 10.8 ms to 24.9 ms. Figure 13 shows the reconstruction latency as the number of photodiodes varies. The reconstruction latency increases almost linearly as the number of photodiodes increases, since the algorithm processes more virtual shadow maps.

Overall, since the above two components run in parallel, StarLight can produce a reconstructed human skeleton within 25 ms. Thus, it can produce at least 40 user skeleton postures per second on the fly, faster than the frame rate (30 FPS) of the latest Kinect.

7.3 Microbenchmarks

We now move on to examining the efficacy of StarLight's key components. In particular, photodiode placement strategy and indoor localization play crucial roles for StarLight to reconstruct the 3D skeleton accurately. We conduct two additional experiments to evaluate these two key components.

Efficacy of Photodiode Placement Strategy. To evaluate the greedy placement strategy, we consider the uniform placement strategy as a baseline. In particular, to deal with the irregular shape of the space available for placing photodiodes, we use the Lloyd's algorithm [37], a well-known sensor placement algorithm, to uniformly place photodiodes in areas not covered by furniture. Figure 14(a) compares these two strategies in terms of reconstruction angular errors. Overall, the greedy placement achieves moderate improvements, with a shorter tail and 3° lower mean angular error. The main reason is that the uniform strategy considers only the 2D plane (i.e, the floor) information. Thus, it fails to take into account the furniture 3D structure and LED panel layout in the 3rd dimension. As a result, placing photodiodes at its calculated locations leads to lower reconstruction accuracy.

Localization Accuracy. To evaluate the 2D localization accuracy of StarLight, we conduct experiments with the participant standing

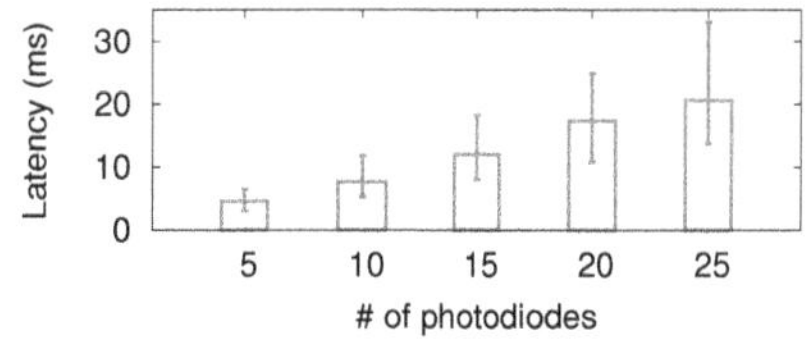

Figure 13: The impact of the number of photodiodes on StarLight's reconstruction latency.

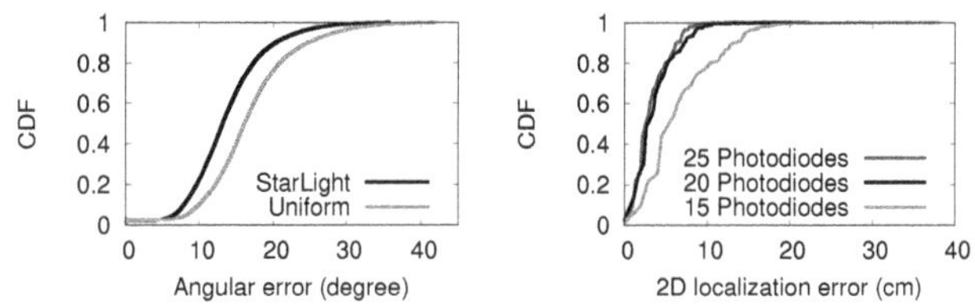

(a) Photodiode placement (b) 2D localization accuracy

Figure 14: Evaluating StarLight's photodiode placement and 2D skeleton localization.

at 30 marked spots. As described in § 7.1, the participant wears a laser pen on the chest and the laster pen points to floor. At each marked spot, the participant adjusts his/her location to ensure that the resulting laser point aligns with the marked spot. We then compare the actual locations of these marked spots and the locations inferred by StarLight to examine StarLight's localization accuracy. We repeat the experiment under different number of photodiodes and plot the CDF of localization errors in Figure 14(b). We observe that in the default setting (20 photodiodes) the median location error is 4 cm and the 95%-percentile tail is 9 cm. The error slightly increases with fewer photodiodes since less blockage information is available. Increasing the photodiodes to 25 brings diminishing returns. Given the possible offset introduced by the use of laser pen, we also compare the inferred user movement trajectory to that from Kinect. We observe that the mean trajectory deviation against Kinect is 2 cm and the 95%-percentile is 6 cm. Overall, StarLight's 2D location accuracy outperforms the latest localization techniques [33, 35, 50, 70] using VLC. StarLight fundamentally differs in that it does not require users to carry or wear any devices. The high 2D localization accuracy in StarLight is essential for its 3D skeleton reconstruction.

7.4 Environmental Factors

Impact of Ambient Light. First, we evaluate StarLight's reconstruction performance under natural ambient light varying from 300 lx at daytime, 70 lx at night with lamps, to 0 lx at night. We repeat the experiments in § 7.1 under the three ambient light conditions and plot the angular errors in Figure 15(a). Overall StarLight's performance is stable in all ambient light conditions. The difference in mean angular errors among the ambient light conditions is less than 1°. This is because StarLight's light beacon frequencies range from 20 KHz to 40 KHz, much higher than the blinking frequencies of other potential light sources, such as fluorescent light (60/120 Hz) and sun light (close to 0 Hz). The light from these interfering light sources can be easily filtered out in the frequency domain. Thus StarLight is robust against other interfering light sources. The reconstruction accuracy under bright ambient light (300 lx) is slightly lower than that without ambient light because high ambient light intensity pushes the photodiode into its saturation region and reduces its responsiveness. As the user blocks the LED, the corresponding frequency power change is smaller, leading to higher errors in virtual shadow maps and reconstruction results.

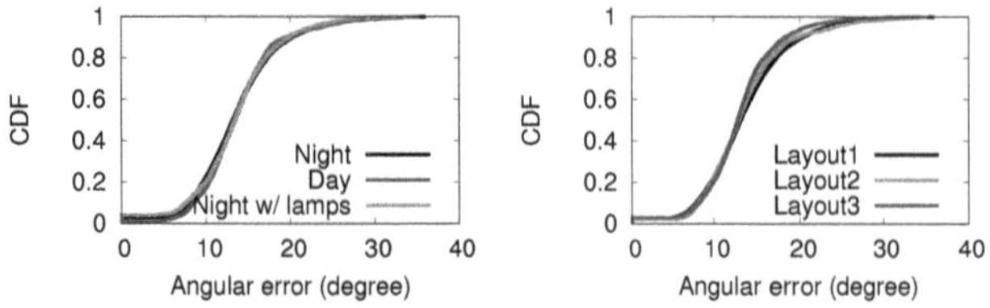

(a) Ambient light (b) Furniture layout

Figure 15: The impact of environmental factors such as ambient light (a) and furniture layout (b). In (b), layout1 is the default shown in Figure 8(a), while layout2 and layout3 are shown in Figure 16.

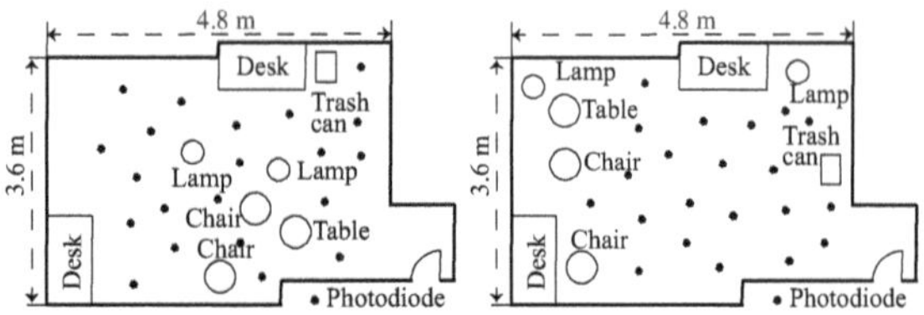

(a) Furniture layout2 (b) Furniture layout3

Figure 16: Two additional furniture layouts tested in Figure 15(b) as well as the optimized sensor placement.

Impact of Furniture Layout. Finally, we evaluate StarLight's reconstruction performance under different furniture layouts. We test two additional layouts (Figure 16) and plot the reconstruction accuracy in Figure 15(b). Overall the furniture rearrangement has negligible impact on StarLight. StarLight performs slightly better in layout3 because most furniture in this layout are clustered, leading to a larger sensing area and thus more candidate locations to place the photodiodes. As a result, the sensor placement strategy identifies better locations for the photodiodes to collect the light blockage information and improves the reconstruction accuracy.

8. RELATED WORK

We categorize related work into two classes:

Sensing with On-Body Devices. The first category of work relies on on-body devices (e.g., smartphones, wrist bands) to sense our behaviors and activities. In particular, prior studies in [34, 39, 38] have examined the use of smartphone sensing data to infer user's social events, activities, wellness, or even the psychological states. In [59, 60], Wang *et al* further focus on the student population and analyze the correlation between the smartphone sensing data and student's mental states and academic performance. In addition to smartphones, other wearable devices such as wrist bands (e.g., Fitbit, Apple Watch) are also actively used for sensing our biometrics (e.g., heart rates) and activities (e.g., footsteps). Existing research has further extended its use to identify smoking behaviors [45], or authenticate users [12], or capture our body sounds [49], or sense pedestrian walking [24]. Our work differs in that our system does not require users to wear any on-body devices.

Sensing at Infrastructure Level. Another sensing paradigm is to set up sensing devices in the environment or reuse ambient signals to track user behaviors. There are three types of methodologies:

1) camera-based methods [15, 27, 28, 53, 55, 56, 57, 61, 62, 67, 68] including Kinect, which leverage RGB cameras or depth cameras to capture high-resolution images and depth information to track user motion. With images containing millions of pixels, these methods commonly entail expensive computational overhead to process images. Furthermore, the raw images can be leaked to the adversary [52, 66] and bring privacy and security concerns. StarLight relies on low-level, low-resolution visual clues to track user motion. Thus it entails much lower computational overhead and better protects user privacy.

2) RF-based methods [7, 8, 26, 40, 48, 58, 64, 73], which reuses wireless signals in the radio frequency (RF) to sense our gestures. They leverage either the multi-path effect [7, 8], or Doppler effect of radio signals [48], or the fine-grained channel state information [64], or directional antennas [40] to classify pre-defined gestures. Recent works [58, 26] have further studied tracking users in the 3D space. However, they are limited to tracking a single body part. In comparison, StarLight is not limited to pre-defined gestures and enables full-body tracking in real time.

3) light-based methods [33, 35, 36, 41, 69, 70, 72], which leverage the infrared or visible light to sense users. However, the majority of existing work tracks the 2D location of either the user body [33, 35, 69, 70] or the user finger [41, 72]. While [36] enables the reconstruction of the user skeleton in the 3D space, it requires a large number of sensors, is vulnerable to furniture blockage, and assumes a static user. StarLight addresses these practical issues to reconstruct a mobile user's 3D postures in real time, further pushing light-based human sensing closer to practice.

9. CONCLUSION

We presented StarLight, a light-based sensing system that exploits LED panels on the ceiling and a few photodiodes in the environment to recover fine-grained human skeleton gestures on the fly (40 FPS). StarLight greatly advances the prior design [36] by significantly reducing the number of intrusive sensors, overcoming furniture blockage, and supporting user mobility. We built StarLight using 20 LED panels and 20 photodiodes in a 3.6 m $\times$ 4.8 m office. Our results demonstrated its efficacy in practice.

We conclude by discussing the limitations of our current study and plans for future work. *First*, our current experiments focus on a single user. When multiple users move around, their shadows intersect and depart, which introduces not only significant computational overhead but also a slower convergence. We plan to leverage the power of GPU and consider inferring user's body parameters to help associate shadows with individual users. *Second*, our current study is under a fixed LED panel setting. We will vary the number and layout (e.g., placing panels at ceiling edges) of LED panels. We will also include LEDs inside floor lamps and wall lamps. They emit light rays in more diverse directions, facilitating the movement detection. *Third*, upon environmental changes (e.g., furniture removal or addition), we currently need to re-calibrate the system. To lower the recalibration overhead, we will consider only updating the placement of affected sensors. *Finally*, we are interested in features other than the flashing rate to differentiate LEDs. Inspired by recent works [5, 22] that exploit RFID's physical features to separate RFIDs, we will examine whether an LED exhibits unique physical features (e.g., rise time). It will remove the need of modulating LED lights and further lower the deployment overhead.

10. ACKNOWLEDGMENTS

We sincerely thank our shepherd Marco Gruteser and the reviewers for their insightful comments. We thank Ronald Peterson for his helpful suggestions on fabricating PCB boards. We also thank Zhao Tian, Chuankai An, Weichen Wang and Linfeng Wang for their support on our study. This work is supported in part by the National Science Foundation under grants CNS-1421528 and CNS-1552924. Any opinions, findings, and conclusions or recommendations expressed in this material are those of the authors and do not necessarily reflect those of the funding agencies or others.

11. REFERENCES

[1] MaxLite Direct Lit LED Flat Panels. http://www.maxlite.com/item/instruction-manual?=MLFP22DS4035.

[2] PDA10A photodetector. https://www.thorlabs.com/thorproduct.cfm?partnumber=PDA10A.

[3] Philips OneSpace luminous ceiling. http://www.lighting.philips.com/content/B2B_LI/en_AA/products/onespace.html.

[4] Texas Instrument OPT101. http://www.ti.com/product/opt101?qgpn=opt101.

[5] ABARI, O., VASISHT, D., KATABI, D., AND CHANDRAKASAN, A. Caraoke: An E-Toll Transponder Network for Smart Cities. In *Proc. of SIGCOMM* (2015).

[6] ADIB, F., KABELAC, Z., AND KATABI, D. Multi-Person Motion Tracking via RF Body Reflections. In *Proc. of NSDI* (2015).

[7] ADIB, F., KABELAC, Z., KATABI, D., AND MILLER, R. C. 3D Tracking via Body Radio Reflections. In *Proc. of NSDI* (2014).

[8] ADIB, F., AND KATABI, D. See through walls with WiFi! In *Proc. of SIGCOMM* (2013).

[9] BEAUDOIN, P., POULIN, P., AND VAN DE PANNE, M. Adapting wavelet compression to human motion capture clips. In *Proc. of GI* (2007).

[10] CHENG, X., DU, D.-Z., WANG, L., AND XU, B. Relay sensor placement in wireless sensor networks. *Wireless Networks 14*, 3 (2008), 347–355.

[11] CHEUNG, G. K., KANADE, T., BOUGUET, J.-Y., AND HOLLER, M. A real time system for robust 3D voxel reconstruction of human motions. In *Proc. of CVPR* (2000).

[12] CORNELIUS, C., PETERSON, R., SKINNER, J., HALTER, R., AND KOTZ, D. A Wearable System That Knows Who Wears It. In *Proc. of MobiSys* (2014).

[13] DIMITROV, S., AND HAAS, H. *Principles of LED Light Communications: Towards Networked Li-Fi*. Cambridge University Press, 2015.

[14] DONG, Y., HOOVER, A., MUTH, E., AND SCISCO, J. A new method for measuring meal intake in humans via automated wrist motion tracking. *Applied Psychophysiology and Biofeedback 37*, 3 (2012), 205–215.

[15] FANELLO, S. R., KESKIN, C., IZADI, S., KOHLI, P., KIM, D., SWEENEY, D., CRIMINISI, A., SHOTTON, J., KANG, S. B., AND PAEK, T. Learning to Be a Depth Camera for Close-range Human Capture and Interaction. *ACM Trans. Graph. 33*, 4 (July 2014).

[16] FEIGE, U. A threshold of ln n for approximating set cover. *Journal of the ACM (JACM) 45*, 4 (1998), 634–652.

[17] FERNANDEZ-BAENA, A., SUSÍN, A., AND LLIGADAS, X. Biomechanical validation of upper-body and lower-body joint movements of kinect motion capture data for rehabilitation treatments. In *Proc. of INCoS* (2012).

[18] GUPTA, S., MORRIS, D., PATEL, S., AND TAN, D. SoundWave: Using the Doppler Effect to Sense Gestures. In *Proc. of CHI* (2012).

[19] HERDA, L., FUA, P., PLANKERS, R., BOULIC, R., AND THALMANN, D. Skeleton-based motion capture for robust reconstruction of human motion. In *Proc. of International Conference on Computer Animation* (2000).

[20] HOCHBAUM, D. S. *Approximation algorithms for NP-hard problems*. PWS Publishing Co., 1996.

[21] HOWE, N. R., LEVENTON, M. E., AND FREEMAN, W. T. Bayesian Reconstruction of 3D Human Motion from Single-Camera Video. In *Proc. of NIPS* (1999).

[22] HU, P., ZHANG, P., AND GANESAN, D. Laissez-Faire: Fully Asymmetric Backscatter Communication. In *Proc. of SIGCOMM* (2015).

[23] IZADI, S., KIM, D., HILLIGES, O., MOLYNEAUX, D., NEWCOMBE, R., KOHLI, P., SHOTTON, J., HODGES, S., FREEMAN, D., DAVISON, A., ET AL. KinectFusion: real-time 3D reconstruction and interaction using a moving depth camera. In *Proc. of UIST* (2011).

[24] JAIN, S., BORGIATTINO, C., REN, Y., GRUTESER, M., CHEN, Y., AND CHIASSERINI, C. F. LookUp: Enabling Pedestrian Safety Services via Shoe Sensing. In *Proc. of MobiSys* (2015).

[25] JHUANG, H., GALL, J., ZUFFI, S., SCHMID, C., AND BLACK, M. J. Towards understanding action recognition. In *Proc. of ICCV* (2013).

[26] JOSHI, K., BHARADIA, D., KOTARU, M., AND KATTI, S. Wideo: Fine-grained device-free motion tracing using rf backscatter. In *Proc. of NSDI* (2015).

[27] KIM, D., HILLIGES, O., IZADI, S., BUTLER, A. D., CHEN, J., OIKONOMIDIS, I., AND OLIVIER, P. Digits: Freehand 3D Interactions Anywhere Using a Wrist-worn Gloveless Sensor. In *Proc. of UIST* (2012).

[28] KIM, D., IZADI, S., DOSTAL, J., RHEMANN, C., KESKIN, C., ZACH, C., SHOTTON, J., LARGE, T., BATHICHE, S., NIESSNER, M., BUTLER, D. A., FANELLO, S., AND PRADEEP, V. RetroDepth: 3D Silhouette Sensing for High-precision Input on and Above Physical Surfaces. In *Proc. of CHI* (2014).

[29] KLASNJA, P. V., CONSOLVO, S., MCDONALD, D. W., LANDAY, J. A., AND PRATT, W. Using Mobile & Personal Sensing Technologies to Support Health Behavior Change in Everyday Life: Lessons Learned. In *Proc. of American Medical Informatics Association Annual Symposium* (2009).

[30] KOMINE, T., AND NAKAGAWA, M. Fundamental analysis for visible-light communication system using LED lights. *IEEE Transactions on Consumer Electronics 50*, 1 (2004), 100–107.

[31] KRAUSE, A., AND GUESTRIN, C. Near-optimal observation selection using submodular functions. In *AAAI* (2007).

[32] KROSSHAUG, T., AND BAHR, R. A model-based image-matching technique for three-dimensional reconstruction of human motion from uncalibrated video sequences. *Journal of biomechanics 38*, 4 (2005), 919–929.

[33] KUO, Y.-S., PANNUTO, P., HSIAO, K.-J., AND DUTTA, P. Luxapose: Indoor positioning with mobile phones and visible light. In *Proc. of MobiCom* (2014).

[34] LANE, N. D., LIN, M., MOHAMMOD, M., YANG, X., LU, H., CARDONE, G., ALI, S., DORYAB, A., BERKE, E., CAMPBELL, A. T., AND CHOUDHURY, T. BeWell: Sensing Sleep, Physical Activities and Social Interactions to Promote Wellbeing. *Mobile Networks and Applications* (2014).

[35] LI, L., HU, P., PENG, C., SHEN, G., AND ZHAO, F. Epsilon: A visible light based positioning system. In *Proc. of NSDI* (2014).

[36] LI, T., AN, C., TIAN, Z., CAMPBELL, A. T., AND ZHOU, X. Human sensing using visible light communication. In *Proc. of MobiCom* (2015).

[37] LLOYD, S. P. Least squares quantization in pcm. *Information Theory, IEEE Transactions on 28*, 2 (1982), 129–137.

[38] Lu, H., Frauendorfer, D., Rabbi, M., Mast, M. S., Chittaranjan, G. T., Campbell, A. T., Gatica-Perez, D., and Choudhury, T. StressSense: Detecting Stress in Unconstrained Acoustic Environments Using Smartphones. In *Proc. of UbiComp* (2012).

[39] Lu, H., Pan, W., Lane, N. D., Choudhury, T., and Campbell, A. T. SoundSense: Scalable Sound Sensing for People-centric Applications on Mobile Phones. In *Proc. of MobiSys* (2009).

[40] Melgarejo, P., Zhang, X., Ramanathan, P., and Chu, D. Leveraging Directional Antenna Capabilities for Fine-grained Gesture Recognition. In *Proc. of UbiComp* (2014).

[41] Moeller, J., and Kerne, A. ZeroTouch: An Optical Multi-touch and Free-air Interaction Architecture. In *Proc. of CHI* (2012).

[42] Moeslund, T. B., Hilton, A., and Krüger, V. A survey of advances in vision-based human motion capture and analysis. *Computer vision and image understanding 104*, 2 (2006), 90–126.

[43] Moschini, D., and Fusiello, A. Tracking human motion with multiple cameras using an articulated model. In *Computer Vision/Computer Graphics Collaboration Techniques*. Springer, 2009, pp. 1–12.

[44] Nemhauser, G. L., Wolsey, L. A., and Fisher, M. L. An analysis of approximations for maximizing submodular set functions. *Mathematical Programming* (1978).

[45] Parate, A., Chiu, M.-C., Chadowitz, C., Ganesan, D., and Kalogerakis, E. RisQ: Recognizing Smoking Gestures with Inertial Sensors on a Wristband. In *Proc. of MobiSys* (2014).

[46] Pearson, K. Mathematical contributions to the theory of evolution. iii. regression, heredity, and panmixia. *Philosophical Transactions of the Royal Society of London. Series. A 187* (1896), 253–318.

[47] Post, E. R., Orth, M., Russo, P. R., and Gershenfeld, N. E-broidery: Design and fabrication of textile-based computing. *IBM Systems Journal* (2000).

[48] Pu, Q., Gupta, S., Gollakota, S., and Patel, S. Whole-home gesture recognition using wireless signals. In *Proc. of MobiCom* (2013).

[49] Rahman, T., Adams, A. T., Zhang, M., Cherry, E., Zhou, B., Peng, H., and Choudhury, T. BodyBeat: A Mobile System for Sensing Non-speech Body Sounds. In *Proc. of MobiSys* (2014).

[50] Rajagopal, N., Lazik, P., and Rowe, A. Visual light landmarks for mobile devices. In *Proc. of IPSN* (2014).

[51] Richman, E. E. Requirements for lighting levels, 2012.

[52] Sbîrlea, D., Burke, M. G., Guarnieri, S., Pistoia, M., and Sarkar, V. Automatic detection of inter-application permission leaks in android applications. *IBM Journal of Research and Development* (2013).

[53] Sharp, T., Keskin, C., Robertson, D., Taylor, J., Shotton, J., Kim, D., Rhemann, C., Leichter, I., Vinnikov, A., Wei, Y., Freedman, D., Kohli, P., Krupka, E., Fitzgibbon, A., and Izadi, S. Accurate, Robust, and Flexible Real-time Hand Tracking. In *Proc. of CHI* (2015).

[54] Shotton, J., et al. Real-time human pose recognition in parts from single depth images. In *Proc. of CVPR* (2011).

[55] Shotton, J., Sharp, T., Kipman, A., Fitzgibbon, A., Finocchio, M., Blake, A., Cook, M., and Moore, R. Real-time human pose recognition in parts from single depth images. *Communications of the ACM 56*, 1 (2013), 116–124.

[56] Song, J., Pece, F., Sörös, G., Koelle, M., and Hilliges, O. Joint Estimation of 3D Hand Position and Gestures from Monocular Video for Mobile Interaction. In *Proc. of CHI* (2015).

[57] Song, J., Sörös, G., Pece, F., Fanello, S. R., Izadi, S., Keskin, C., and Hilliges, O. In-air Gestures Around Unmodified Mobile Devices. In *Proc. of UIST* (2014).

[58] Sun, L., Sen, S., Koutsonikolas, D., and Kim, K.-H. WiDraw: Enabling Hands-free Drawing in the Air on Commodity WiFi Devices. In *Proc. of MobiCom* (2015).

[59] Wang, R., Chen, F., Chen, Z., Li, T., Harari, G., Tignor, S., Zhou, X., Ben-Zeev, D., and Campbell, A. T. StudentLife: Assessing Mental Health, Academic Performance and Behavioral Trends of College Students Using Smartphones. In *Proc. of UbiComp* (2014).

[60] Wang, R., Harari, G., Hao, P., Zhou, X., and Campbell, A. T. SmartGPA: How Smartphones Can Assess and Predict Academic Performance of College Students. In *Proc. of UbiComp* (2015).

[61] Wang, R., Paris, S., and Popović, J. 6D Hands: Markerless Hand-tracking for Computer Aided Design. In *Proc. of UIST* (2011).

[62] Wang, R. Y., and Popović, J. Real-time hand-tracking with a color glove. *ACM Transactions on Graphics* (2009).

[63] Wang, W., Liu, A. X., Shahzad, M., Ling, K., and Lu, S. Understanding and Modeling of WiFi Signal Based Human Activity Recognition. In *Proc. of MobiCom* (2015).

[64] Wang, W., Liu, A. X., Shahzad, M., Ling, K., and Lu, S. Understanding and modeling of wifi signal based human activity recognition. In *Proc. of MobiCom* (2015).

[65] Wang, Y., Liu, J., Chen, Y., Gruteser, M., Yang, J., and Liu, H. E-eyes: Device-free Location-oriented Activity Identification Using Fine-grained WiFi Signatures. In *Proc. of MobiCom* (2014).

[66] Weinberg, Z., Chen, E. Y., Jayaraman, P. R., and Jackson, C. I still know what you visited last summer: Leaking browsing history via user interaction and side channel attacks. In *Security and Privacy (SP), 2011 IEEE Symposium on* (2011), IEEE, pp. 147–161.

[67] Wu, Y., and Huang, T. S. View-independent recognition of hand postures. In *Proc. of CVPR* (2000).

[68] Wu, Y., Lin, J. Y., and Huang, T. S. Capturing natural hand articulation. In *Proc. of ICCV* (2001).

[69] Xie, B., Tan, G., and He, T. Spinlight: A high accuracy and robust light positioning system for indoor applications. In *Proc. of SenSys* (2015).

[70] Yang, Z., Wang, Z., Zhang, J., Huang, C., and Zhang, Q. Wearables Can Afford: Light-weight Indoor Positioning with Visible Light. In *Proc. of MobiSys* (2015).

[71] Younis, M., and Akkaya, K. Strategies and techniques for node placement in wireless sensor networks: A survey. *Ad Hoc Networks 6*, 4 (2008), 621 – 655.

[72] Zhang, C., Tabor, J., Zhang, J., and Zhang, X. Extending Mobile Interaction Through Near-Field Visible Light Sensing. In *Proc. of MobiCom* (2015).

[73] Zhao, C., Chen, K.-Y., Aumi, M. T. I., Patel, S., and Reynolds, M. S. SideSwipe: Detecting In-air Gestures Around Mobile Devices Using Actual GSM Signal. In *Proc. of UIST* (2014).

I am a Smartwatch and I can Track my User's Arm

Sheng Shen, He Wang, Romit Roy Choudhury
University of Illinois at Urbana-Champaign
{sshen19, hewang5, croy}@illinois.edu

ABSTRACT

This paper aims to track the 3D *posture* of the entire arm – both wrist and elbow – using the motion and magnetic sensors on smartwatches. We do not intend to employ machine learning to train the system on a specific set of gestures. Instead, we aim to trace the geometric motion of the arm, which can then be used as a generic platform for gesture-based applications. The problem is challenging because the arm posture is a function of both elbow and shoulder motions, whereas the watch is only a single point of (noisy) measurement from the wrist. Moreover, while other tracking systems (like indoor/outdoor localization) often benefit from maps or landmarks to occasionally reset their estimates, such opportunities are almost absent here.

While this appears to be an under-constrained problem, we find that the pointing direction of the forearm is strongly coupled to the arm's posture. If the gyroscope and compass on the watch can be made to estimate this direction, the 3D search space can become smaller; the IMU sensors can then be applied to mitigate the remaining uncertainty. We leverage this observation to design *ArmTrak*, a system that fuses the IMU sensors and the anatomy of arm joints into a modified hidden Markov model (HMM) to continuously estimate state variables. Using Kinect 2.0 as ground truth, we achieve around 9.2 cm of median error for *free-form* postures; the errors increase to 13.3 cm for a real time version. We believe this is a step forward in posture tracking, and with some additional work, could become a generic underlay to various practical applications.

Keywords

Gesture, arm posture, kinematics, anatomy, tracking, smartwatch, hidden Markov model, accelerometer

1. INTRODUCTION

Analytics on human leg motion has fueled an industry on mobile health and well being. Nowadays, walking, running, biking and various other activities can be recognized from motion sensors embedded in smartphones and wearable devices. Understanding upper limb motion seems like the logical next step, and various research groups/start-ups have already made progress. Authors in [11, 21, 33, 35], for example, have employed various machine learning algorithms to detect meaningful arm and hand gestures – smoking, eating, typing, writing – on wearable wrist bands. Rithmio [4], perhaps the most advanced start-up in this space, is eliminating the need for training, so long as the user performs repetitive tasks, such as bouncing a basketball or exercises in the gym. Finally, for applications requiring full arm posture reconstruction (e.g., golf swing analysis, animation movie characters), today's solutions paste multiple sensors on the arm, or adopt computer vision based analytics [3, 5, 6, 8, 12, 13, 15–17, 20, 23, 28–31, 36, 38, 39]. This paper aims to construct the 3D arm posture using smartwatch sensors alone, and track the posture continuously over time, without any training. In addition, we desire the tracking techniques to be light-weight so they can be amenable to real time applications.

Before further discussion, we briefly clarify the notion of "postures" from "gestures". By posture, we mean the 3D geometric model of the arm. For a fixed shoulder location, arm posture is uniquely defined by 3 parameters – *elbow location, wrist location,* and *wrist rotation.* The wrist rotation captures the rotation of the wrist around the axis of the forearm[1]. A gesture, on the other hand, is a specific sequence of arm postures that carry semantic meaning (somewhat analogous to how words are meaningful sequences of alphabets). Hand gestures typically refer to gestures of the wrist, not necessarily the arm. This paper tracks the entire arm posture in 3D space over time (similar to a Kinect), and is expected to serve as building blocks to any application-defined gesture.

Designing *ArmTrak* entails 3 key research questions:

(1) The state space of the entire arm is large, meaning that the elbow and wrist could take up many configurations around the body. Without any pre-defined patterns to search for, the arm posture tracking problem translates to a Bayesian tracking problem in continuous space. While tracking is a mature area in signal processing, most of the problems are either guided by good motion models or able to obtain measurements directly from the object of interest. In our case, smartwatch sensors do not offer direct measurements from the elbow, are noisy, and lack models of how the arm is expected to move. To the best of our knowledge (based on literature survey in signal processing, robotics, and mobile computing), this still remains an unaddressed problem.

[1] For a fixed elbow and wrist location, the wrist rotation changes the palm's facing direction.

MobiSys'16, June 25-30, 2016, Singapore, Singapore
© 2016 ACM. ISBN 978-1-4503-4269-8/16/06...$15.00
DOI: http://dx.doi.org/10.1145/2906388.2906407

(2) It is possible that continuous space techniques, such as Particle Filters or an appropriate variant, map to posture tracking. However, such techniques incur high complexity and latency – when considering scalability to many users, or the real-time requirements of certain applications, the approaches prove prohibitively expensive. Low complexity and fast run-time are important factors for a practical end to end system.

(3) The final problem pertains to expressing the arm posture in different coordinate systems. For applications where a user is pointing to a TV to turn it on, it is important to understand the direction of pointing in the global reference frame. For other applications, like golf-swing analysis, hand posture needs to be tracked in the torso's coordinate system. The core problem is rooted in detecting the human's facing direction from the watch sensors. *ArmTrak* must resolve this problem to cater to various application needs.

The perspective we bring to the problem pertains to a synthesis of anatomy, sensor fusion, and Bayesian inference. From the anatomical models of shoulder and elbow joints, we observe that for a given 3D orientation of the wrist (which is estimated via sensor fusion using accelerometer, compass and gyroscope), the space of possible elbow locations is quite constrained. Given that the elbow is also constrained on a sphere around the shoulder point, we can further reduce the search space for the elbow – called a *point cloud*. Now, using the (rotation polluted) accelerometer data, we estimate the translational motion of the elbow through a hidden Markov model (HMM) framework, but apply the point cloud as a prior. Once the elbow location is known, the wrist location is computed as a simple shift along the (forearm pointing) direction prescribed by the wrist orientation. To cater to applications, we make a series of optimizations, resulting in an option to prioritize either accuracy or latency. On one extreme, Viterbi Decoding yields the best results but after offline processing; on the other extreme, we compute an averaging on the point cloud to operate in real-time. Finally, we use a combination of the watch orientation and the compass to opportunistically estimate the user's facing direction, ultimately yielding the arm posture in the desired coordinate system.

We evaluate *ArmTrak* using Samsung Gear Live smartwatches, with the sensor data processed on the watch (in real time) as well as on the cloud (running MATLAB). Recruited volunteers stand in front of a Kinect 2.0 sensor and perform various kinds of gestures, starting from simple wrist movements all the way to random, free-form arm gestures. The skeletal models from the Kinect serve as ground truth, and we report *ArmTrak*'s accuracy as a function of both the wrist location and elbow location errors. We also report the degradation in our accuracy in exchange for the improvement in latency. On average, our $\langle elbow,\ wrist\rangle$ posture tracking results are $\langle 7.9cm,\ 9.2cm\rangle$ respectively in the offline setting, and drop to $\langle 12.0cm,\ 13.3cm\rangle$ when performed in the "fast" mode. More importantly, the tracking errors remain bounded over time, allowing for continuous gesture recognition We encourage our readers to watch the video demonstration of our system here: http://synrg.csl.illinois.edu/posture/.

Besides what is achievable, we must also discuss the shortcomings of the current system. (1) We believe that ferromagnetic materials in indoor environments can present important ramifications on accuracy; our experiments were performed in our lab with stable magnetic ambience. (2) Our techniques falter when the user performs gestures while on the move – the sensor data from the motion pollutes both posture tracking and facing-direction estimation. (3) Finally, gyroscopes are known to consume energy – we have ignored the energy considerations in developing *ArmTrak*. In view of these capabilities and deficiencies, we summarize the contribution in this paper as follows.

- *Using sensor data from smartwatches to track the posture of the entire arm.* Using observations from anatomical models to constrain the search space for the elbow, a key enabler for 3D posture tracking.
- *Using the accelerometer data as an input to a (modified) hidden Markov model, ultimately tracking the motion of the elbow (and the wrist).* Parameterizing the system to achieve different tradeoffs between accuracy and latency, and offering them as a single knob to application developers.

2. PROBLEM SETUP

This section discusses the basics of smartwatch motion and posture tracking, and the deliberations that led us to the proposed ideas.

2.1 Torso Coordinate System

We will define the posture of the arm, and its motion, in the *torso coordinate system*. In this system, the left shoulder will serve as the origin, and the plane of the user's torso (i.e., the chest) will serve as the XY plane. The Z axis will be the line emanating from the left shoulder in the frontward direction, perpendicular to the torso. The Kinect also models its skeleton tracking data in a similar coordinate system – since we use the Kinect as ground truth, aligning our coordinate system with Kinect simplifies our evaluation process.

The torso coordinate system (TCS) is desirable to most applications, although some need the arm posture to be expressed in a global (North-East) coordinate system (GCS). For instance, analysis of gym exercises, golf swing analysis, smoking recognition, etc., can all be performed in the TCS framework. However, when controlling devices in a room (e.g., pointing to a TV to turn it on), the posture of the arm needs to be modeled in global coordinates. The compass on the watch offers the necessary information to estimate postures in GCS, however, its translation to TCS requires knowledge of the user's facing direction. We will develop the overall *ArmTrak* system assuming knowledge of the facing direction, and then relax the assumption through a facing-direction estimator.

2.2 Wrist/Elbow Orientation and Location

Figure 1 shows the X, Y, and Z axes of a smartwatch when a user wears it on her left wrist. These axes, that are local to the watch's coordinate system, can easily be expressed as vectors in the torso coordinate system, denoted as $\vec{X}_t$, $\vec{Y}_t$, and $\vec{Z}_t$ (the subscript means the vector changes over time as arm moves). We define the "orientation" of the watch (same as the orientation of the wrist) as this tuple: $\langle\vec{X}_t, \vec{Y}_t, \vec{Z}_t\rangle$. $\vec{X}_t$ always aligns with the pointing direction of the forearm in 3D space, and for a fixed forearm pointing direction, both $\vec{Y}_t$ and $\vec{Z}_t$ change along with the rotation of the forearm around the X axis.

Similarly, location of the elbow or the wrist (same as the location of the watch) can also be expressed as a separate 3D tuple, $\langle x_t, y_t, z_t\rangle$, in the torso coordinate system (TCS). Once the wrist orientation is known, the elbow location and the wrist location

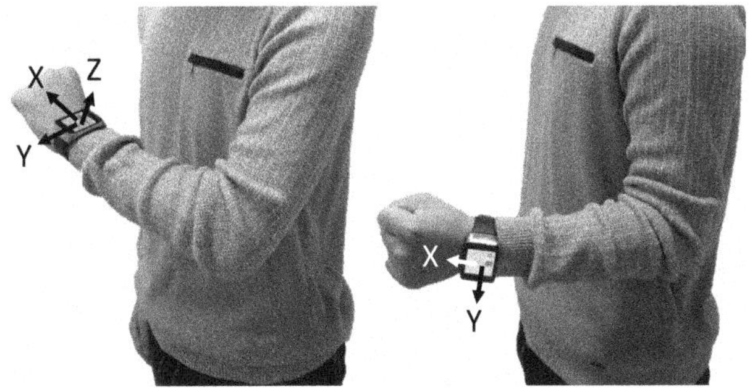

Figure 1: Smartwatch orientation changes with the pointing direction of the hand – the orientation is measured in the torso's reference frame.

are simply a *static shift* of each other, along the positive or negative forearm pointing direction (wrist's $\vec{X}_t$ orientation). The static shift is the length of the forearm, and thus needs to be known only once. With this, the posture of the entire arm can be determined in the torso coordinate system. The natural question is: how can the arm posture be tracked over time? Actually, we can ask a simpler sub-question: can the wrist location even be tracked over time? We make a few relevant observations next.

2.3 Noise: The Fundamental Problem

From basic physics, any motion of a body can be decomposed into translational and rotational motion. Thus, when a wrist moves from point A to a very close point, B, one can model this as a translational motion of the watch from A to B, followed by a change in orientation to reflect the orientation at B. Now, assume that the initial location and orientation are known at point A, and the accelerometer and gyroscope are super accurate. Then, the gyroscope can measure the angular velocity around each of the $\vec{X}_t$, $\vec{Y}_t$, and $\vec{Z}_t$ directions, and precisely estimate the orientation at point B. The accelerometer, on the other hand, measures a combination of translational and rotational motion (hence, plain double integration will not work). Instead, the double integration can be performed at infinitesimally small time steps, and after each step, the orientation of the device can be updated based on the corresponding gyroscope data. In other words, the system will be able to compute the linear displacements and rotations at extremely fine granularity, and concatenating them should result in perfect tracking.

Of course, the above is true under the assumption of perfect IMU sensors. With noisy sensors, we implemented the same algorithm (and appropriately subtracted gravity) to quantify the extent of divergence. Figure 2 shows the results – the orientation divergence is somewhat reasonable[2], but the translation error is excessive, more than 100 meters within 1 minute. In other words, deterministic techniques will always be affected by the randomness of noise; stochastic inference techniques are likely to be the appropriate approach.

2.4 An Estimation Problem: Particle Filter

The problem we are facing is obviously not new – robotics and signal processing researchers routinely face and solve these kinds of estimation problems (also called filtering). Briefly, the *state* of the object is modeled as variables and the range of these

[2]We cannot measure all 3 dimensions of orientation using Kinect, hence plot the error from 2 dimensions, calculated as the angular difference between the forearm's pointing direction and the ground truth.

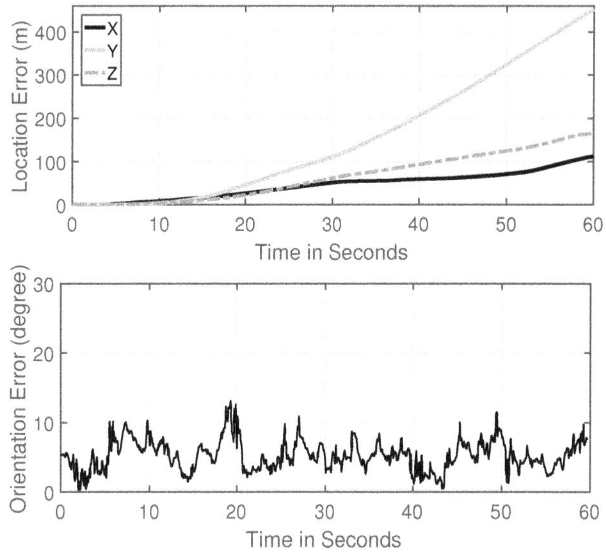

Figure 2: (a) Wrist location error diverges with double integral. (b) Wrist orientation error remains small over time.

variables together describe the *space* in which the object can exist. Then, based on some model of how the object is expected to move, and what the data reveals about its actual motion, these estimation algorithms compute the most likely state of the object. We implemented a particle filter, one of the popular state estimation algorithms in continuous space. However, given that the accelerometer and gyroscope data are differentials of location and orientation, the state of particles had to be defined with many variables to capture the entire arm posture. This resulted in a high-dimensional system and the estimator could hardly converge. We aborted the effort and focused on reducing the state space of the system for good tracking accuracy.

3. OPPORTUNITY AND VALIDATION

Following the failure of the particle filter, we focused on opportunities to reduce the state space of the system, i.e., constraining the possible postures of the arm. This seemed intuitive, i.e., since the arm joints have limits in their *range of motion* (RoM) [7, 14], they should constrain the arm postures as well. In exploring the arm joints and measurement data, we made the following empirical observation. Assume the shoulder location is fixed. *It appeared that for a fixed wrist orientation, the possible space of wrist locations is quite limited.* In other words, if one moves her wrist around without changing the wrist orientation, there are not many locations to which she can take her wrist.

To understand this intuition, let's first assume that we keep the elbow location fixed. Consider how the motion of the forearm will influence the wrist location and orientation. Since the elbow does not move, any forearm motion will change the wrist's orientation, no matter it is the twist of the wrist/forearm (which will change $\vec{Y}_t$ and $\vec{Z}_t$ of orientation) or the rotational motion around the elbow (which will change $\vec{X}_t$ of orientation and also change the wrist's location). Conversely, for a given wrist orientation, only one wrist location is possible (as it has to be along the $\vec{X}_t$ direction emanating from the elbow), under these artificial assumptions.

Of course, once the elbow starts moving, the wrist can move to multiple locations while preserving the same orientation. However, the elbow can only move on a sphere around the shoul-

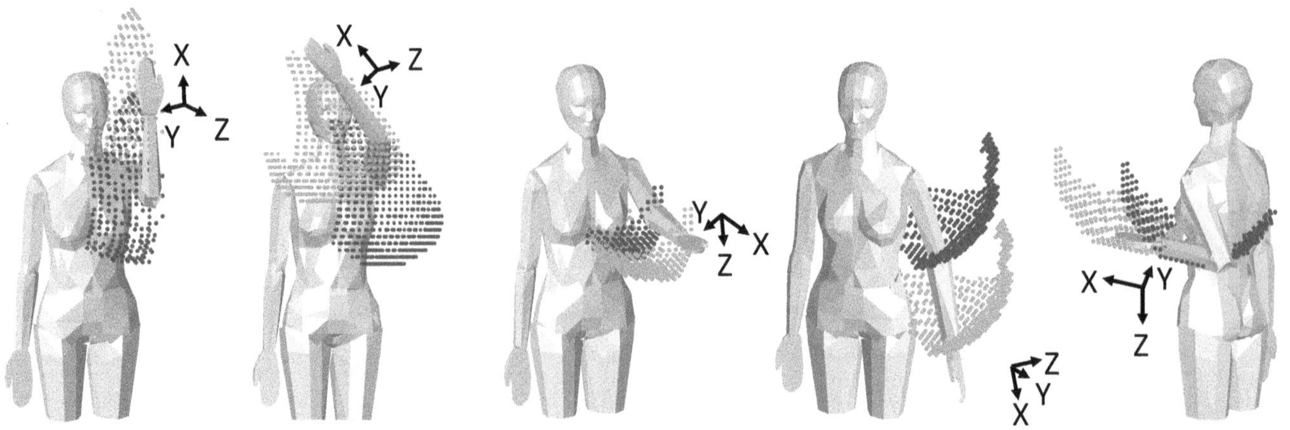

Figure 3: 5 different watch orientations and the corresponding wrist and elbow point clouds (shown in light green and dark red, respectively). The point clouds (essentially the space of feasible wrist and elbow locations for the given orientation) are relatively small and narrow down the uncertainty of the user's arm posture.

der, and the forearm's ability to twist is relatively limited. This suggests that for a given wrist orientation, the possible space of wrist locations may be reasonably restricted. The space will also vary across orientations, i.e., some wrist orientations will allow the wrist to move to more locations than others.

3.1 Preliminary Validation

As preliminary validation, we visualized the space of wrist locations for some wrist orientations. Figure 3 shows 5 example wrist orientations, along with the corresponding wrist and elbow location point clouds, marked in (light) green and (dark) red, respectively. The findings exhibit promise – the wrist location space is indeed a small fraction of the entire 3D space around the shoulder. Also, the elbow and wrist point clouds exhibit a 1:1 mapping, since they are simply a static shift of one another.

3.2 Formalizing through Arm Models

Figure 3 indicates the opportunity, but we need to generalize our observation. Therefore, we derived models from human arm kinematics, and reorganized them to formally express the relationship of wrist orientation, wrist location and elbow location. We describe the models here, followed by a quantification of state space reduction.

In robotics, a human arm is often modeled using 7 rotational degrees of freedom (DoF) [22] – 3 for the shoulder, 2 for the elbow, and 2 for the wrist. Since the watch is worn on the forearm near the wrist, the DoFs of the wrist are not manifested in the watch's sensor data. The remaining 5 DoFs define the state of the watch, as shown in Figure 4. When these 5 values are combined with the *known* lengths of the upper arm and forearm, the watch's location and orientation can be estimated uniquely.

Modeling this mathematically, let θ_1, θ_2, θ_3, θ_4 and θ_5 denote the 5 DoFs; let l_u and l_f denote the lengths of the upper arm and forearm. Using these, the Denavit-Hartenberg transformation [9] actually outputs the posture of the entire arm. For example, the elbow location is a function of θ_1 and θ_2, and can be expressed as:

$$loc_{elbow} = f(\theta_1,\theta_2) = l_u \begin{pmatrix} \cos(\theta_2)\sin(\theta_1) \\ \sin(\theta_2) \\ -\cos(\theta_1)\cos(\theta_2) \end{pmatrix} \tag{1}$$

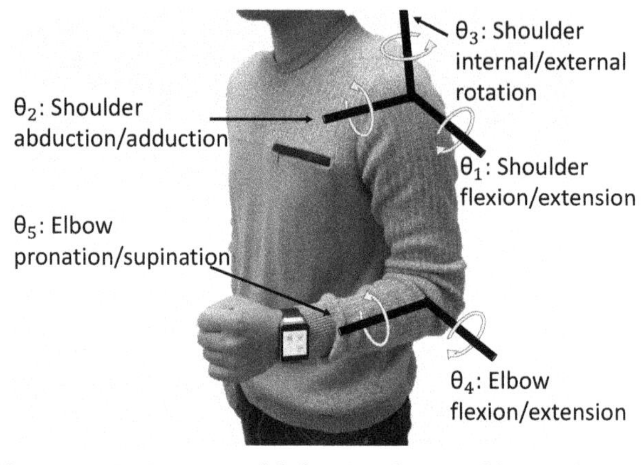

Figure 4: 5-DoF Arm Model showing the possible angular rotations.

and it satisfies

$$\parallel loc_{elbow} \parallel = l_u \tag{2}$$

Similarly, the wrist's relative location to the elbow can also be computed as

$$loc_{wrist-to-elbow} = g(\theta_1,\theta_2,\theta_3,\theta_4) \tag{3}$$

where the function $g()$ is a long equation omitted in the interest of space, but it of course satisfies

$$\parallel loc_{wrist-to-elbow} \parallel = l_f \tag{4}$$

Thus, the wrist's absolute location can be written as the vectorial addition of the elbow location and the wrist's relative location (to the elbow).

$$loc_{wrist} = loc_{elbow} + loc_{wrist-to-elbow} \tag{5}$$

Like location, the orientation of the wrist, expressed in the form of rotation matrix, can also be computed through a rotational function on the 5 θs (the function $h()$ omitted in the interest of space).

$$Rot_{watch} = h(\theta_1,\theta_2,\theta_3,\theta_4,\theta_5) \tag{6}$$

In summary, knowing these 5 θs can solve the entire state of the arm posture, i.e., wrist orientation, wrist location and elbow location.

3.3 Mapping Orientation to Point Cloud

For a given watch orientation, we intend to map it to the elbow and wrist's location point clouds. We derive the mapping to the elbow first, because it lies on a sphere around the shoulder which will later make the model mathematically easier. The translation from the elbow to the wrist will be a static shift.

Now, to derive the elbow's point cloud, we first referred to some medical papers [7, 14, 24] and summarized the average range of motion (ROM) for each joint angle in Table 1. Here $\theta_1 = \theta_2 = \theta_3 = \theta_4 = \theta_5 = 0°$ refers to the posture where the left arm is in free-fall on the left side of the torso, with the palm facing front. Then, for each watch orientation, we find all combination of $\{\theta_1, \theta_2, \theta_3, \theta_4, \theta_5\}$'s within the ROM that can generate that orientation according to (6). Each combination will map to one elbow location according to equation (1). Thus, we obtain a mapping from $\text{Rot}_{\text{watch}}$ to possible $\text{loc}_{\text{elbow}}$'s. We can also derive the mapping from $\text{Rot}_{\text{watch}}$ to possible $\text{loc}_{\text{wrist}}$'s easily, because for each $\text{Rot}_{\text{watch}}$, possible wrist locations are simply a shift of possible elbow locations, along the forearm's pointing direction – the equation described below.

$$\text{loc}_{\text{wrist-to-elbow}} = \text{Rot}_{\text{watch}} \begin{pmatrix} l_f \\ 0 \\ 0 \end{pmatrix} \tag{7}$$

Algorithm 1 presents the pseudo code.

Joint Angle	Min. Value	Max. Value
θ_1	-60°	180°
θ_2	-40°	120°
θ_3	-30°	120°
θ_4	0°	150°
θ_5	0°	180°

Table 1: Range of motions for each joint angle

Algorithm 1 Watch Orientation to Point Cloud Mapping

ElbowPointCloud = Empty Dictionary
WristPointCloud = Empty Dictionary
for all $\{\theta_1, \theta_2, \theta_3, \theta_4, \theta_5\} \in$ ROM **do**
  $\text{loc}_{\text{elbow}} = f(\theta_1, \theta_2)$
  $\text{Rot}_{\text{watch}} = h(\theta_1, \theta_2, \theta_3, \theta_4, \theta_5)$
  $\text{loc}_{\text{wrist-to-elbow}} = \text{Rot}_{\text{watch}}(t) \begin{pmatrix} l_f \\ 0 \\ 0 \end{pmatrix}$
  $\text{loc}_{\text{wrist}} = \text{loc}_{\text{elbow}} + \text{loc}_{\text{wrist-to-elbow}}$
  ElbowPointCloud[$\text{Rot}_{\text{watch}}$].Add($\text{loc}_{\text{elbow}}$)
  WristPointCloud[$\text{Rot}_{\text{watch}}$].Add($\text{loc}_{\text{wrist}}$)
end for

To quantify the reduction in uncertainty due to this mapping, Figure 5 plots the CDF of the elbow's point cloud, as a fraction of the surface area of the sphere around the shoulder. In 90% cases, the elbow can only reach $\frac{1}{4}$ of whole sphere area, and the median fraction is 8.3%. Of course, the fraction can be further reduced if we utilize the fact that these 5 DoFs are not entirely independent and thus model their RoMs jointly (instead of setting an upper/lower bound for each of the joint angle). We leave this optimization to future work.

If the mapped point cloud is moderately accurate (assuming that the orientation estimation is reasonably error-free), the next step is to leverage the point cloud in a state estimation framework. This motivates a discrete space hidden Markov model, with the elbow's point cloud as the prior. We describe these techniques next, as a part of a full posture recognition system.

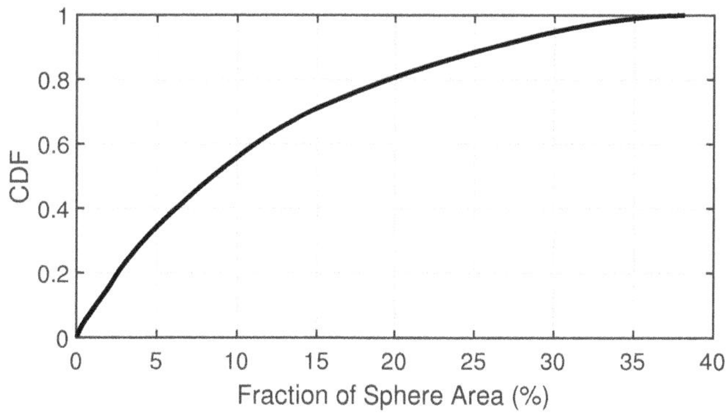

Figure 5: Elbow location subspace as a fraction of the sphere area (around the shoulder) – the state space is certainly smaller.

4. ARCHITECTURE

Figure 6 illustrates *ArmTrak*'s overall architecture. The raw sensor data from the smartwatch – composed of the accelerometer, gyroscope, and compass samples – are passed through an *Orientation Estimation Module* (OEM). This module computes the watch's orientation in the earth's coordinate system (ECS), using a borrowed technique called A^3 from MobiCom 2014 [40]. Since the user's facing direction is unknown, the transformation between ECS to TCS is still unknown. The *Facing Direction Module* (FDM) scans the sensor data stream and opportunistically recognizes samples that reveal the facing direction. The orientation is now transformed to TCS and forwarded to the *Orientation to Point Cloud Module* (OPM).

OPM consists of a pre-loaded mapping between orientation and point clouds (the mapping derived from our arm-joint models described earlier). Using the incoming orientation as an index, OPM outputs the corresponding point cloud. Not all candidates may be equally likely, therefore, a separate *Posture Priors Module* (PPM) analyzes general human arm motions and extracts priors. This information is used to bias the posture estimation process towards the sequences that are more likely in humans.

For applications that require high accuracy in arm posture estimation, the outputs of both OPM and PPM are forwarded to a Hidden Markov Model (HMM), along with the raw sensor data. The HMM observes sequences of data and estimates the most likely arm posture sequence. The outputs are favorable to applications that need higher accuracy and can tolerate latency in several seconds (even though the HMM has been carefully optimized for lower complexity). However, if some applications require a real-time arm posture, the outputs of OPM and PPM are sent together into an Averaging Filter. This filter computes a weighted average of all candidate arm postures for the current orientation, where the weights are guided by the priors. This serves as a faster but less accurate arm posture tracker.

4.1 Design for Higher Accuracy Postures

We first design for accuracy without latency considerations. As described earlier, once the orientation of the watch is known, posture estimation boils down to an elbow tracking problem. If

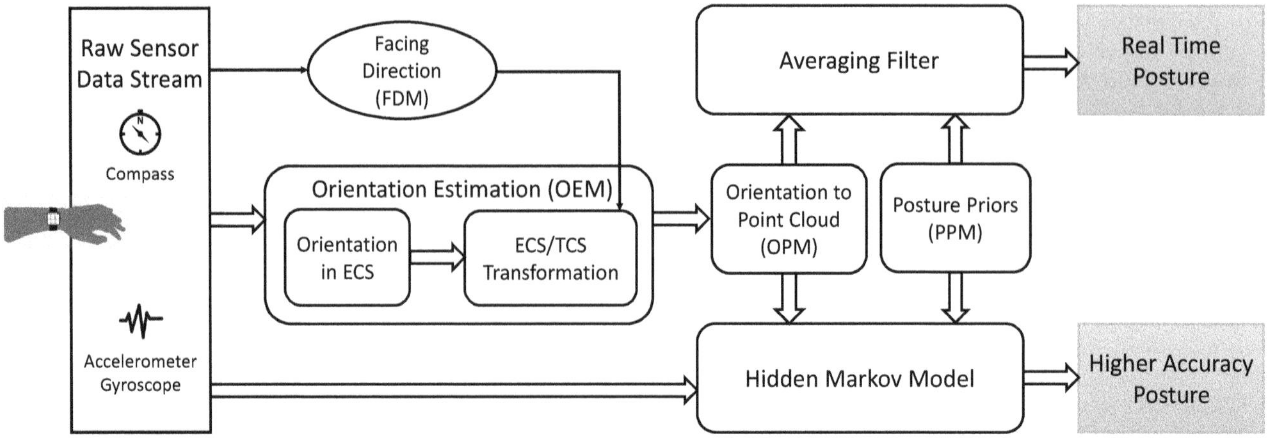

Figure 6: System Architecture. The raw sensor data is processed to obtain watch orientation and possible arm postures, and together with posture priors, they are sent to two different filters to obtain different posture estimations.

the elbow can be tracked, the wrist location can be computed as a static shift, yielding the complete arm posture. The resources we have (in addition to sensor data) are two-fold: (1) reasonable estimates of orientation, even though not precise, and (2) point cloud of all possible elbow locations, for a given orientation. The question then is: *at any given time, where is the elbow in the point cloud?*

Recall that the point cloud is often quite small – on average, it covers less than 10% of the sphere around the shoulder (Figure 5). Simply using the average location of the point cloud could result in a reasonably good estimate of the elbow location. However, in testing this simple averaging method with various kinds of gestures, we found much room for improvement. For instance, consider the punching gesture in Figure 7 – the forearm moves forward and backward while the orientation remains the same. The averaging scheme always shows the center of the point cloud (see Figure 8) since the point cloud remains almost the same for the entire gesture.

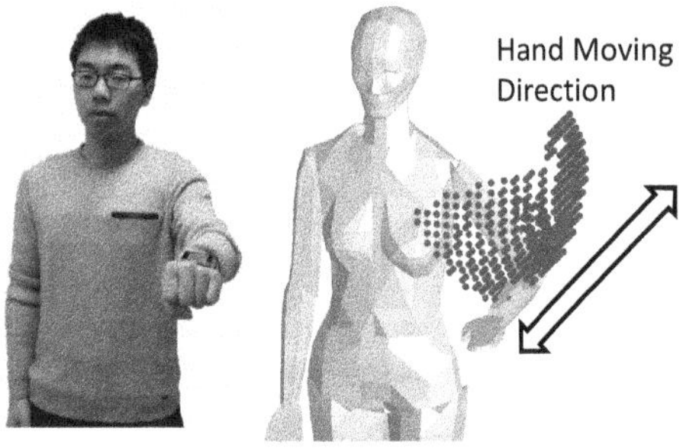

Figure 7: Punching: (a) video frame; (b) point cloud remains almost the same during punching.

The room for improvement (over simple averaging) arrives from using the smartwatch sensors as an estimate of the elbow's motion. In this specific punching case, the accelerometer data from the watch can be used to estimate the elbow's acceleration (in a straight line), which in turn can be converted to the wrist. In general, however, this is more complicated since the elbow will also experience rotational motion – in such cases, its acceleration has to be computed through a fusion of the gyroscope and accelerometer. To this end, we first introduce techniques to estimate acceleration, and then combine this elbow acceleration with the point cloud constraints to estimate elbow location.

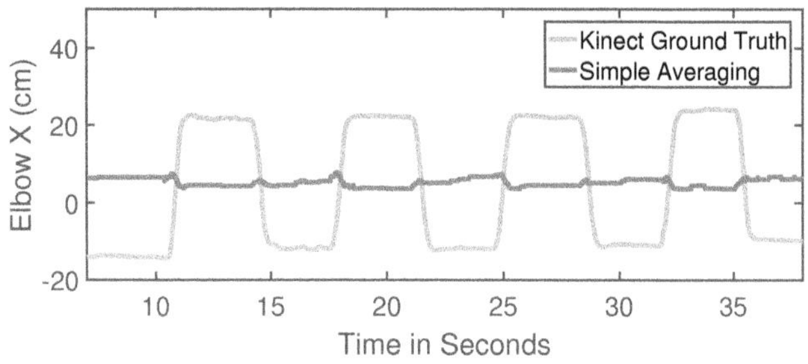

Figure 8: X coordinate of elbow location. During punching gesture, the orientation of the watch remains almost the same; therefore the point cloud doesn't change much over time. As a result, averaging the point cloud cannot follow the location of the elbow.

Estimate Elbow Acceleration

For any physical object, the acceleration is simply the second derivative of the location time series. For the elbow, we have

$$\mathrm{accel_e}(t) = \frac{\mathrm{d}^2}{\mathrm{d}t^2}\mathrm{loc_e}(t) \tag{8}$$

Applying Equation 5, we have:

$$\mathrm{accel_e}(t) = \frac{\mathrm{d}^2}{\mathrm{d}t^2}\left[\mathrm{loc_w}(t) - \mathrm{loc_{we}}(t)\right] \tag{9}$$

$$= \frac{\mathrm{d}^2}{\mathrm{d}t^2}\mathrm{loc_w}(t) - \frac{\mathrm{d}^2}{\mathrm{d}t^2}\mathrm{loc_{we}}(t) \tag{10}$$

The first term in Equation 10, $\frac{\mathrm{d}^2}{\mathrm{d}t^2}\mathrm{loc_w}(t)$, is simply wrist's acceleration in torso coordinate system, which we can get by projecting watch's accelerometer readings into torso coordinate system using estimated watch's orientation, $\mathrm{Rot_{watch}}$:

$$\frac{\mathrm{d}^2}{\mathrm{d}t^2}\mathrm{loc_w}(t) = \mathrm{Rot_{watch}}(t)\ \mathrm{accel_{watch}}(t) \tag{11}$$

The second term in Equation 10, $\frac{\mathrm{d}^2}{\mathrm{d}t^2}\mathrm{loc_{we}}(t)$, is the acceleration caused by wrist's relative motion to the elbow. According to equation 7, we can express this as:

$$\frac{d^2}{dt^2}\text{loc}_{\text{we}}(t) = \frac{d^2}{dt^2}\left[\text{Rot}_{\text{watch}}(t)\begin{pmatrix} l_f \\ 0 \\ 0 \end{pmatrix}\right] \tag{12}$$

Now, combining Equation 11 and Equation 12, we can re-write Equation 10 as

$$\begin{aligned}\text{accel}_{\text{e}}(t) = {} & \text{Rot}_{\text{watch}}(t)\,\text{accel}_{\text{watch}}(t) \\ & - \frac{d^2}{dt^2}\left[\text{Rot}_{\text{watch}}(t)\begin{pmatrix} l_f \\ 0 \\ 0 \end{pmatrix}\right]\end{aligned} \tag{13}$$

Equation 13 shows that given watch's accelerometer data and our estimation on the watch's orientation, the elbow acceleration can be inferred.

Estimate Elbow Location

Given the measured elbow acceleration, as well as the point clouds (on the sphere) on which the elbow must be located, we now ask the following question: *which sequence of elbow locations best matches the measured elbow acceleration?* To intuitively understand this problem, let's assume there are N locations that the elbow can possibly reach – this can be viewed as the union of all point clouds for the elbow. Assume the motion sequence contains T time steps. Since the elbow can be at any of the N locations at a given step, the possible number of sequences is N^T, which is the search space for tracking the elbow. One of the sequences is optimal and our goal is to find this sequence. Hidden Markov Models (HMM) are well suited to solve this problem due to its dynamic programming construction for efficiently searching the state space.

Modified HMM for Elbow Tracking

If we group 3 locations (at 3 consecutive time steps) as the state of the elbow, then elbow acceleration can be encoded in one state. By using the estimated acceleration as observation and properly designing transition probabilities, finding the best elbow location sequence reduces to the Viterbi algorithms (solvable in polynomial time). Viterbi Decoding has a time complexity of $O(|S|^2T)$, where $|S|$ is the state space size and T is the total number of time steps. In the above HMM formulation, the state space size is N^3, since each state is a location triple. As a result, the time complexity is $O(N^6T)$. In trying to reduce the running time, we reorganized the state definitions. Specifically, we apply the continuity constraint, move the emission probability into the transition probability, and $|S|$ can be greatly reduced by allowing each state to contain only two locations. The time complexity is reduced to $O(N^3T)$. The details are below.

For the ease of the description, let's assign each possible elbow location on the sphere a location ID, ranging from 1 to N. Let's also denote the T time steps of the motion sequence as $t_1, t_2, ..., t_T$, and the time step length as ΔT.

• **State definition**: Each state is defined as a pair of elbow locations:

$$\text{state}_i = <\text{loc}_{\text{e}}{}^{(i_1)}, \text{loc}_{\text{e}}{}^{(i_2)}> \tag{14}$$

where $loc_e^{(i_1)}$ and $loc_e^{(i_2)}$ are the locations with location IDs i_1 and i_2, which together uniquely define the i-th state.

In our HMM formulation, we use a state to represent the elbow's previous location and current location. In this representation, if the state at time t_k is state_i, it means that the elbow location is $loc_e^{(i_1)}$ at t_{k-1} and $loc_e^{(i_2)}$ at t_k.

At first glance, the size of state space is N^2. However, observe that the human's elbow movement is limited to a maximum speed, thus given a small time step, the elbow can only move within a small range. We can actually eliminate those states whose location pairs are separated by larger than this range. In this way, the size of state space is reduced to αN^2, where α is much smaller than 1.

• **Prior probability**: Since we do not know the initial elbow location, we set the prior probability to be uniform:

$$\Pi(\text{state}_i) = \frac{1}{\alpha N^2} \qquad \text{for any } i \tag{15}$$

• **Transition probability**: From current time t_k to next time t_{k+1}, the transition probability from state_i to state_j, denoted as $Pr(\text{state}_j \mid \text{state}_i; t_k, t_{k+1})$, contains three terms.

First, since the elbow trajectory is continuous, state_i and state_j must share the same location at the common time step t_k. This continuity constraint actually helps reduce the time complexity from $O(N^4T)$ to $O(N^3T)$.

$$\begin{aligned}\text{state}_i &= <\text{loc}_{\text{e}}{}^{(i_1)}, \text{loc}_{\text{e}}{}^{(i_2)}> \\ \text{state}_j &= <\text{loc}_{\text{e}}{}^{(j_1)}, \text{loc}_{\text{e}}{}^{(j_2)}> \\ \text{loc}_{\text{e}}{}^{(i_2)} &= \text{loc}_{\text{e}}{}^{(j_1)}\end{aligned} \tag{16}$$

We can express this limitation as an indicator function:

$$Pr_1 = I_{\text{loc}_{\text{e}}{}^{(i_2)} = \text{loc}_{\text{e}}{}^{(j_1)}} \tag{17}$$

Second, instead of using measured elbow acceleration as an observation in the location triple, here we directly model that probability into the transition probability between two location tuples. To be more specific, we can calculate the speed encoded in each state and derive acceleration using the speed of the two states:

$$\begin{aligned}\text{velocity}_j &= \frac{\text{loc}_{\text{e}}{}^{(j_2)} - \text{loc}_{\text{e}}{}^{(j_1)}}{\Delta T} \\ \text{velocity}_i &= \frac{\text{loc}_{\text{e}}{}^{(i_2)} - \text{loc}_{\text{e}}{}^{(i_1)}}{\Delta T} \\ \text{accel}_{i,j} &= \frac{\text{velocity}_j - \text{velocity}_i}{\Delta T}\end{aligned} \tag{18}$$

This acceleration, $\text{accel}_{i,j}$, is expected to be close to our observed acceleration $\text{accel}_{\text{observe}}(t_k)$. We assume that the error distribution of the observed acceleration is a zero mean Gaussian distribution with a standard deviation of σ_{accel}. Therefore, we have:

$$Pr_2 = \frac{1}{\sqrt{2\pi}\sigma_{\text{accel}}} e^{(\text{accel}_{i,j} - \text{accel}_{\text{observe}}(t_k))^2/(2\sigma^2_{\text{accel}})} \tag{19}$$

Third, in the new state_j, the elbow location $\text{loc}_{\text{e}}{}^{(j_2)}$ must be inside the point cloud inferred at time t_{k+1}.

$$Pr_3 = I_{\text{loc}_{\text{e}}{}^{(j_2)} \in \text{PointCloud}_{t_{k+1}}} \tag{20}$$

In sum, the transition probability is the product of these three probabilities:

$$Pr(\text{state}_j \mid \text{state}_i; t_k, t_{k+1}) = Pr_1 Pr_2 Pr_3 \tag{21}$$

• **Emission probability**: Since we have already integrated the observed acceleration into transition probability, emission probability is simply set as 1. Thus, we only use the output of Viterbi decoding – it is a sequence of states and the second element of each state is the estimated elbow location. Figure 9 shows the improved elbow tracking results (in this toy punching case) using HMM.

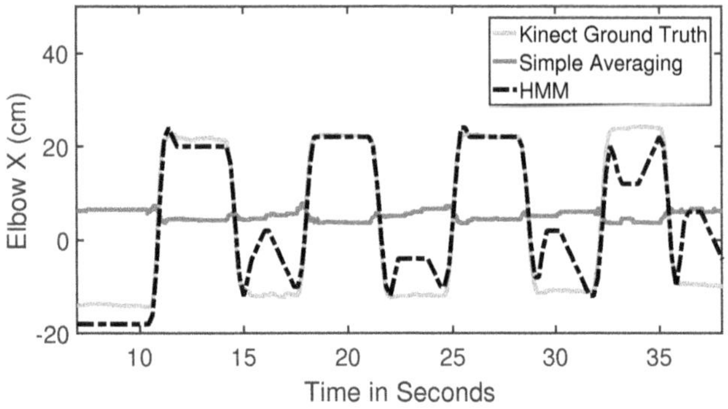

Figure 9: X coordinate of elbow location. Results from HMM better capture the location of the elbow.

• **Facing Direction**: We opportunistically sense the facing direction when the user's hand is in the vertical free-fall posture, or swinging through this position perhaps while walking. At this point, the X axis of the gyroscope is exactly pointed in gravity's direction, implying that the negative Y is the facing direction. We also observe that the hand swings to a small degree in this position and we utilize this to gain confidence.

4.2 Designing for Fast Posture Tracking

For the applications on smartwatches that require instantaneous posture information, the tracking algorithm must be light-weight in order to fit into the watch's limited computing power. As hinted earlier, we adopt a simple weighted averaging filter. This filter accepts (1) the point cloud of arm postures and (2) the corresponding prior from past measurements, and then outputs a weighted average of all the points in the cloud. The weights are determined by the probability density of each location – the more common postures will naturally bias the estimates. The weighted average is expressed as:

$$\mathrm{loc_e} = \sum_i \mathrm{loc_e^i} \frac{Pr(\mathrm{loc_e^i})}{\sum Pr(\mathrm{loc_e^i})} \quad (22)$$

$$\mathrm{loc_w} = \mathrm{loc_e} + \mathrm{Rot_{watch}}(t) \begin{pmatrix} l_f \\ 0 \\ 0 \end{pmatrix} \quad (23)$$

As an outcome of averaging, the results are naturally quite smooth. Also, the averaged 3D location (for each point cloud) can be stored in a lookup table, indexed by the orientation corresponding to the point cloud. For a given orientation from the *Orientation Estimation Module*, the smartwatch simply looks up the elbow location from this table, computes the corresponding wrist location, and outputs the posture. Both memory and CPU footprint is marginal.

5. EVALUATION

This section discusses the experiment methodology and performance results of *ArmTrak*.

5.1 Implementation

ArmTrak is implemented on the Samsung Gear Live smartwatch using JAVA as the programming platform. The accelerometer and gyroscope are both sampled at $200Hz$ and the magnetic field sensor is sampled at $100Hz$. The smartwatch runs the light-weight real-time version of *ArmTrak* to report instantaneous arm posture. The sensor data and light-weight arm posture estimates are stored locally and transferred to the *ArmTrak* server for analysis. The server side code is written in MATLAB and implements the full version of *ArmTrak* to provide offline, higher accuracy, posture estimates.

5.2 Methodology

We recruited 8 volunteers, including 6 males and 2 females, for our experimentation – the volunteers are all students in CS/ECE. The volunteers were asked to wear a Gear Live smartwatch during our experiment. Their upper arm and forearm lengths, $\mathrm{l_u}$ and $\mathrm{l_f}$, were measured beforehand.

Experiments with each volunteer were executed in 3 sessions. In the first session, volunteers were asked to move their arms totally freely for 3 minutes. Users performed random, meaningless, arm gestures – we requested them to not move their hands behind their backs to avoid losing ground truth from the Kinect. In the second session, we deliberately asked the volunteers not to put their elbows above the shoulder. The goal is to mimic real-world scenarios where most of the gestures need the elbow to be at lower heights. Under this constraint, the volunteers again moved their arms freely for 3 minutes. In the third session, volunteers were asked to repeat a set of pre-defined gestures for 10 times. The gesture set contains eating, drinking, boxing, bouncing a basketball, weight lifting, drawing a circle, drawing a triangle, drawing a square, and writing numeric digits in the air. During the whole experiment, a Kinect 2.0 was placed in front the volunteer to record ground truth. We prevent any movement in the background since that affects Kinect's ground truth calculations.

5.3 Performance Results

The following questions are of our interest in this section:

1. How well can *ArmTrak* track arm postures in general?
2. How does *ArmTrak*'s performance vary among different users and with pre-defined gestures? Are certain gestures better than others?
3. Will error accumulate and *ArmTrak*'s tracking diverge over time?
4. Accuracy and latency tradeoffs with the real-time version and the offline cloud version.
5. 2D shapes of different objects and digits drawn by users – a subjective measure.

In all these results, we measure error for every time step (i.e., output of HMM) and draw the CDF over all measurements.

(1) How well can *ArmTrak* track arm postures?

Figure 10 (a) and (b) show the CDF of tracking errors for the elbow and wrist, respectively. The results are for the higher accuracy HMM version. For free-form motion (where users performed completely random gestures), the median errors for the elbow and wrist are around 7.9cm and 9.2cm. Once the elbow was restricted to remain below the shoulder, the error reduced further to 6.6cm and 8.3cm for the elbow and wrist, respectively. Finally, for pre-defined gestures like "eating", "weight lifting", etc., we use the ground truth information from the 7 other users as priors for the 8th user, and perform cross-validation. Observe that the median error drops even further to 4.5cm and 5.7cm for elbow and wrist on average. Compared to the volunteers' average arm length of 50.2cm, we believe *ArmTrak*'s accuracy, with minimal prior information, makes it amenable to most gesture recognition applications, including gaming control, TV control, and daily activity patterns such as eating or exercising. Of course, the results can improve appreciably with more application-specific prior information.

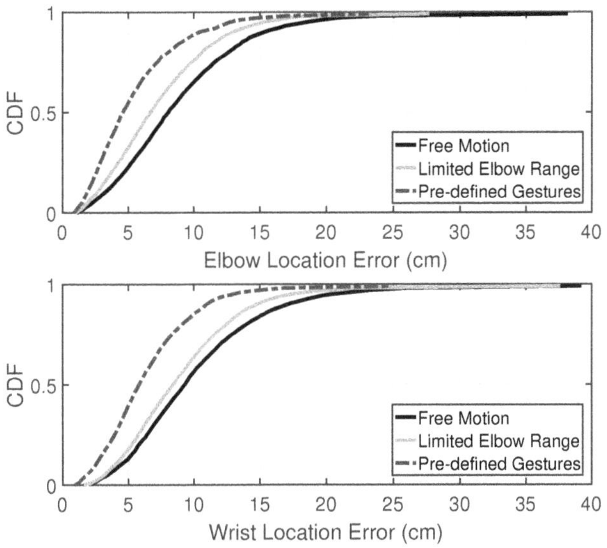

Figure 10: (a) *ArmTrak*'s performance on elbow tracking. (b) *ArmTrak*'s performance on wrist tracking.

(2) How does *ArmTrak*'s performance vary across different users and pre-defined gestures?

Figure 11 plots the performance across different users. We observe that performance is consistently high across all users, across all the 3 categories – pre-defined gestures, limited elbow range, and free motion. Also, the trend that pre-defined gestures are generally better than limited elbow range cases, and limited elbow range better than free-motion cases, holds across the users. The performance is worst for user 7. On examining the Kinect video, we find that user 7 moved that hand extremely fast. Still, the errors were around 10cm.

Figure 12 plots *ArmTrak*'s performance across all types of 8 gestures. Evidently, the performance did not show major variations across gestures, suggesting that the system is not biased to any patterns. Considering the fact that the prior is only obtained from 7 other users, we gained confidence that by improving the prior, *ArmTrak* can be generalized to and work well on other pre-defined gestures.

Upon comparing the performance among these gestures, we find that "Eating" has the best performance and "Drawing a triangle" is the worst. We again look into the Kinect video data and find that when volunteers were performing "Eating" gestures, their elbow only moved in a smaller region, while with "Drawing a triangle", the shape, size and position where they drew the triangle are all different, incurring a far greater elbow range.

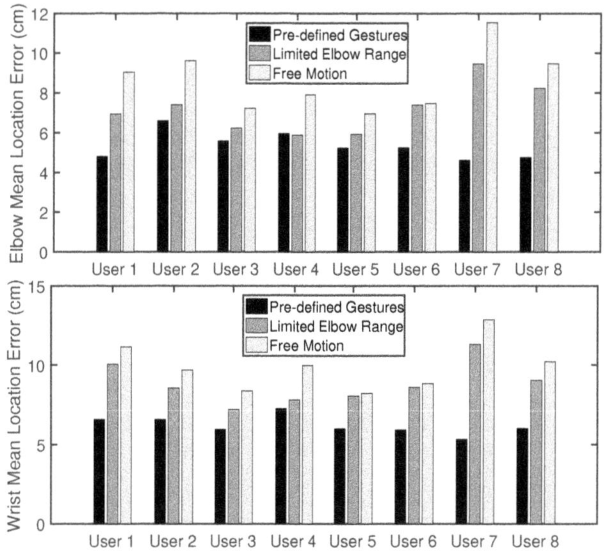

Figure 11: *ArmTrak*'s performance on (a) elbow and (b) wrist tracking, for different users.

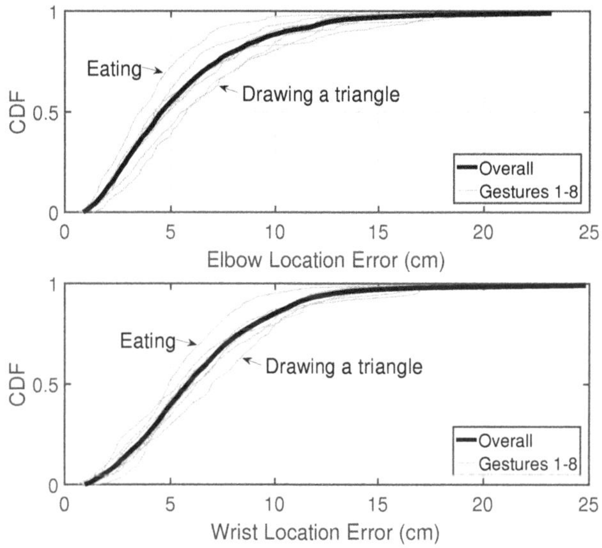

Figure 12: *ArmTrak*'s performance on (a) elbow and (b) wrist tracking, for different activities.

(3) Will error accumulate and *ArmTrak*'s performance degrade over time?

ArmTrak attempts to find a sequence of smartwatch locations (from the changing point clouds) that best matches with the observed acceleration data. This global optimization within point clouds ensures that the error will not accumulate over time, as it does with unconstrained double integration. One may argue that this optimization is performed offline over the whole motion sequence, thus intermediate states also benefit from future data. Therefore, characterizing the errors at every intermediate state, with no look-ahead into the future, is also of interest.

To understand the impact, we performed another experiment in which we ask the HMM to traceback to each timestamp and report the instantaneous location estimate at that point. Figure 13 shows the general wrist tracking error trend for 3 volunteers. Although this error is higher than applying the global Viterbi Decoding over the whole sequence, the error still does not accumulate. We believe this is perhaps the most important property of *ArmTrak*.

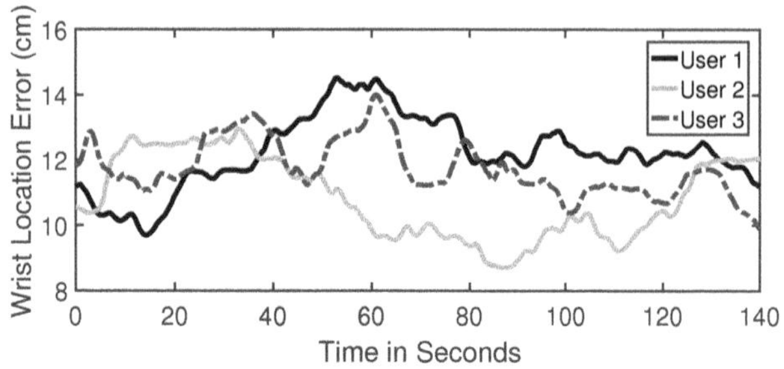

Figure 13: The general (smoothed) trend for wrist location error over time.

(4) Performance and latency tradeoffs between real-time version and offline version

Figure 14 shows the comparison of tracking accuracy for both elbow and wrist, using real-time and offline algorithms. Recall that the real-time algorithm computes a weighted average of the point cloud and stores a lookup table in the watch, indexed by 3D watch orientation. Compared with the offline algorithm, the median error of the real-time version increases to 12.0cm for the elbow and 13.3 cm for the wrist. Although high, the real-time version also remains stable over time. The reader is requested to visit the project website – http://synrg.csl.illinois.edu/posture/ – for a number of real-time and offline video demonstrations.

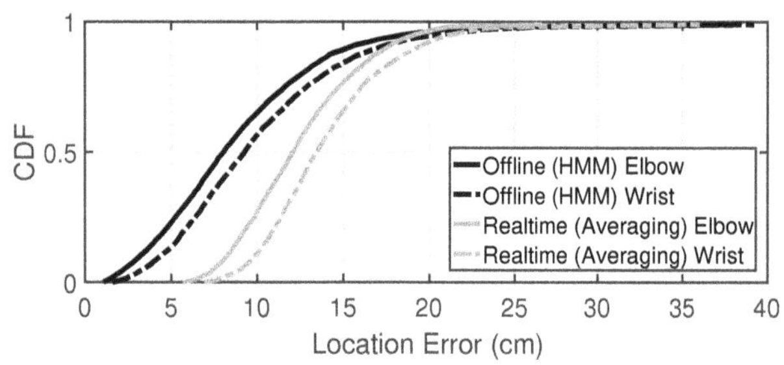

Figure 14: Performance comparison between offline (HMM) and real-time(simple averaging).

We computed the delay of both offline and real-time versions of *ArmTrak*. The real-time version running on the watch is essentially a look-up with orientation as index - even for very high update rate the lookup time is negligible. The delay of offline-version contains both the network upload/download delay of the sensor data, plus the computation time at the cloud (i.e., running MATLAB on a quad core graduate student desktop). The results are reported in Table 2 for 5Hz update frequency (i.e., HMM updates 5 times per second). Evidently, longer gesture data incurs almost a 10x increase in computation.

(5) What shapes have been inferred by *ArmTrak*?

Figure 15 shows some sample trajectories of the wrist, when users were asked to draw shapes and digits in the air. Although

Trajectory Time	10s	30s	1min	3min
Delay	98.2s	289.3s	9.1min	26.9min

Table 2: Latency of offline version increases with increase in the trace length. This is because Viterbi Decoding computes the globally optimal sequence of states, and incurs $O(N^3T)$ complexity.

the reproduction is not perfect, *ArmTrak* tracks the trend of the trajectory quite well. All users expressed satisfaction when they were shown the shapes that they drew in the air. For more complex situations, we asked the user to draw complicated shapes like a "star" or an "Olympic ring". Figure 15(c) shows one such case where the user drew for almost 1 minute – *ArmTrak* was consistently able to track the 3D shape.

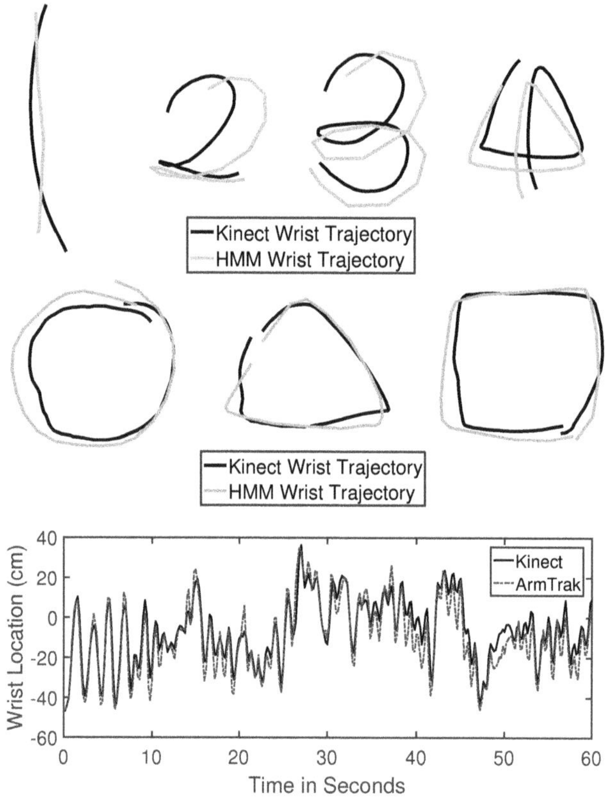

Figure 15: *ArmTrak*'s tracking result for (a) writing four digits, (b) drawing simple shapes, (c) a complicated 3D trajectory (only Z axis is shown).

6. LIMITATIONS AND NEXT STEPS

A few more technical pieces will need to come together before *ArmTrak* can be viewed as a usable technology – we discuss these below.

(1) Facing Direction and Tracking on the Move: We opportunistically estimate the user's facing direction when her hand is in the vertical free-fall posture, or swinging through this position perhaps while walking. Admittedly, we have not stress-tested this and are not confident this would scale in completely uncontrolled situations. For instance, if a user is sitting for a long duration, the free-fall opportunity may not arise, but the user may change her facing direction (perhaps by swiveling her chair). A deeper treatment of facing direction is necessary to better ground the initial state of the watch. On related lines, *ArmTrak* will falter when the user is on the move – we have sidestepped this case, but plan to evaluate the extent of degradation in future.

(2) Need for More Speed: The Viterbi Decoding is running on a quad-core student desktop and is roughly producing results at 10x rate. This means that tracking the arm motion for τ seconds requires 10τ seconds of processing time. Of course, more hardware on a cloud can certainly bring down this latency, but the more important question pertains to whether more speedup is possible. We believe some degree of optimization (such as beam search) and parallelism would be possible inside the dynamic programming; we also believe a marginal sacrifice in accuracy can offer considerable speedup. The latency-accuracy tradeoff proved far richer than we anticipated and we intend to investigate this thoroughly in future.

(3) Energy Consumption: We have ignored the energy implications of our technique. For the real time system, we expect the weighted averaging technique to impose minimal energy burden. For the HMM/Viterbi model, we expect the system to run on the cloud – thus the energy consumption mainly emerges from network uploads. We have not characterized this overhead, however, it appears that many offloading applications are viable under this model. This is perhaps because most applications are likely to be on-demand (e.g., the user turns on the app during her visit to the gym and turns off thereafter). Further, some apps can tolerate latency and can delay the uploads until the watch is connected to power.

7. RELATED WORK

Gesture/posture recognition has been studied from various perspectives. The literature is vast, but we sample the most relevant ones, mainly from computer vision and wearable motion sensors.

Computer vision: Camera data has been used to track and analyze human motion across different granularities [19]. At a lower granularity, humans can be automatically detected [10] and tracked with bounding boxes [34], using the video feeds from cameras. Beyond bounding boxes, human activity can also be recognized from camera data via machine learning [26,27]. At a higher granularity, pose estimation is a classical problem in human motion analysis, where the common approach is applying probabilistic models on the static RGB image or video sequence [6,13,15–17,20,23,28,29,31,36]. More recently, depth information has also been leveraged in the pose estimation solution landscape [3,30]. For instance, Microsoft Kinect [3] fuses RGB and depth image to track the locations of the human's joints for video gaming. One of the key differentiators between vision and sensing based approaches is that vision must estimate 3D motion from the 2D views – a challenging task. However, vision benefits from knowing the pixel locations far more precisely compared to the noise from sensor hardware.

Wearable motion sensors: Previous research has shown that embedded motion sensors on wearable devices can be used for human activity recognition [18]. Industry on mobile health and well being uses these sensors to recognize a user's leg motion such as walking, running, etc [1,2]. To measure meal intake, Bite Counter [11] uses a watch-like device with a gyroscope to detect and record when an individual has taken a bite of food. RisQ [21] leverages motion sensors on wristband to recognize smoking gestures. MoLe [33] analyzes motion data of smartwatches from typing activity to infer what the user has typed. Xu et al. [35] classified hand/finger gestures and written characters from smartwatch motion sensor data. However, all these motion analysis systems are designed for recognizing specific pre-defined motion patterns, as opposed to blind estimation of free-form postures. Similarly, authors in [25,32] tried to reconstruct full body motion from multiple wearable devices by comparing accelerometer data with those generated from motion capture databases. However, the reconstruction relies heavily on the similarity of training and testing accelerometer data and the disparity between different motion classes inside training databases, and as a result, neither can they track free-form arm motion.

Zhou et al. [38,39], Cutti et al. [8], and El-Gohary et al. [12] studied general upper limb movement tracking using motion sensors. However, they require users to be instrumented with multiple sensors on the arm. Perhaps the closest to our work is [37], where authors claimed to be able to track the upper limb by only mounting motion sensors on the wrist. However, the system is only evaluated on 1 subject, moving his arm up-to-down in a plane perpendicular to the ground. The same gesture is repeated constantly and lasted less than 15s. As a follow up to this work, the authors published a subsequent paper with multiple sensors on the arm to scale to a larger vocabulary of gestures [38,39]. In contrast, our system is tested with free-form motion, has been tested up to 3mins without signs of divergence, and has demonstrated robustness to all 8 test users. We believe this is an improvement over the state of the art.

8. CONCLUSION

This paper is an attempt to estimate/track the geometric motion of the human arm, using only the inertial sensors on the smartwatch. The problem is challenging primarily because the smartwatch is a single point of measurement on this otherwise large space of possibilities. Moreover, the measurements are noisy, making continuous tracking over longer time scales even more difficult. We develop *ArmTrak*, a system that distills observations from human kinematics, and uses them carefully inside a (modified) HMM framework. Our results are encouraging, and with some more effort, could become a useful underlay to a broad class of gesture-based applications.

9. ACKNOWLEDGMENTS

We sincerely thank our shepherd, Dr. Vishnu Navda, and the anonymous reviewers for their insightful comments and suggestions. We are also grateful to Intel, Google, Qualcomm, HP and NSF (grant NSF 1430064) for partially funding this research.

10. REFERENCES

[1] Apple watch. http://www.apple.com/watch/.

[2] Fitbit. https://www.fitbit.com/.

[3] Microsoft kinect. https://dev.windows.com/en-us/kinect.

[4] Rithmio. http://rithmio.com/.

[5] Xsens. https://www.xsens.com/.

[6] M. Andriluka, S. Roth, and B. Schiele. Pictorial structures revisited: People detection and articulated pose estimation. In *Computer Vision and Pattern Recognition, 2009. CVPR 2009. IEEE Conference on*, pages 1014–1021. IEEE, 2009.

[7] D. C. Boone and S. P. Azen. Normal range of motion of joints in male subjects. *J Bone Joint Surg Am*, 61(5):756–759, 1979.

[8] A. G. Cutti, A. Giovanardi, L. Rocchi, A. Davalli, and R. Sacchetti. Ambulatory measurement of shoulder and elbow kinematics through inertial and magnetic sensors. *Medical & biological engineering & computing*, 46(2):169–178, 2008.

[9] J. Denavit. A kinematic notation for lower-pair mechanisms based on matrices. *Trans. of the ASME. Journal of Applied Mechanics*, 22:215–221, 1955.

[10] P. Dollar, C. Wojek, B. Schiele, and P. Perona. Pedestrian detection: An evaluation of the state of the art. *Pattern Analysis and Machine Intelligence, IEEE Transactions on*, 34(4):743–761, 2012.

[11] Y. Dong, A. Hoover, J. Scisco, and E. Muth. A new method for measuring meal intake in humans via automated wrist motion tracking. *Applied psychophysiology and biofeedback*, 37(3):205–215, 2012.

[12] M. El-Gohary and J. McNames. Shoulder and elbow joint angle tracking with inertial sensors. *Biomedical Engineering, IEEE Transactions on*, 59(9):2635–2641, 2012.

[13] P. F. Felzenszwalb and D. P. Huttenlocher. Pictorial structures for object recognition. *International Journal of Computer Vision*, 61(1):55–79, 2005.

[14] R. L. Gajdosik and R. W. Bohannon. Clinical measurement of range of motion review of goniometry emphasizing reliability and validity. *Physical Therapy*, 67(12):1867–1872, 1987.

[15] D. Hogg. Model-based vision: a program to see a walking person. *Image and Vision computing*, 1(1):5–20, 1983.

[16] M. P. Kumar, A. Zisserman, and P. H. Torr. Efficient discriminative learning of parts-based models. In *Computer Vision, 2009 IEEE 12th International Conference on*, pages 552–559. IEEE, 2009.

[17] X. Lan and D. P. Huttenlocher. Beyond trees: Common-factor models for 2d human pose recovery. In *Computer Vision, 2005. ICCV 2005. Tenth IEEE International Conference on*, volume 1, pages 470–477. IEEE, 2005.

[18] O. D. Lara and M. A. Labrador. A survey on human activity recognition using wearable sensors. *Communications Surveys & Tutorials, IEEE*, 15(3):1192–1209, 2013.

[19] T. B. Moeslund, A. Hilton, and V. Krüger. A survey of advances in vision-based human motion capture and analysis. *Computer vision and image understanding*, 104(2):90–126, 2006.

[20] J. O'Rourke and N. I. Badler. Model-based image analysis of human motion using constraint propagation. *Pattern Analysis and Machine Intelligence, IEEE Transactions on*, (6):522–536, 1980.

[21] A. Parate, M.-C. Chiu, C. Chadowitz, D. Ganesan, and E. Kalogerakis. Risq: Recognizing smoking gestures with inertial sensors on a wristband. In *Proceedings of the 12th annual international conference on Mobile systems, applications, and services*, pages 149–161. ACM, 2014.

[22] J. C. Perry and J. Rosen. Design of a 7 degree-of-freedom upper-limb powered exoskeleton. In *Biomedical Robotics and Biomechatronics, 2006. BioRob 2006. The First IEEE/RAS-EMBS International Conference on*, pages 805–810. IEEE, 2006.

[23] D. Ramanan and C. Sminchisescu. Training deformable models for localization. In *Computer Vision and Pattern Recognition, 2006 IEEE Computer Society Conference on*, volume 1, pages 206–213. IEEE, 2006.

[24] N. B. Reese and W. D. Bandy. *Joint range of motion and muscle length testing*. Elsevier Health Sciences, 2013.

[25] Q. Riaz, G. Tao, B. Krüger, and A. Weber. Motion reconstruction using very few accelerometers and ground contacts. *Graphical Models*, 79:23–38, 2015.

[26] P. C. Ribeiro and J. Santos-Victor. Human activity recognition from video: modeling, feature selection and classification architecture. In *Proceedings of International Workshop on Human Activity Recognition and Modelling*, pages 61–78. Citeseer, 2005.

[27] N. Robertson and I. Reid. A general method for human activity recognition in video. *Computer Vision and Image Understanding*, 104(2):232–248, 2006.

[28] K. Rohr. Towards model-based recognition of human movements in image sequences. *CVGIP: Image understanding*, 59(1):94–115, 1994.

[29] B. Sapp, A. Toshev, and B. Taskar. Cascaded models for articulated pose estimation. *Computer Vision–ECCV 2010*, pages 406–420, 2010.

[30] J. Shotton, T. Sharp, A. Kipman, A. Fitzgibbon, M. Finocchio, A. Blake, M. Cook, and R. Moore. Real-time human pose recognition in parts from single depth images. *Communications of the ACM*, 56(1):116–124, 2013.

[31] V. K. Singh, R. Nevatia, and C. Huang. Efficient inference with multiple heterogeneous part detectors for human pose estimation. In *Computer Vision–ECCV 2010*, pages 314–327. Springer, 2010.

[32] J. Tautges, A. Zinke, B. Krüger, J. Baumann, A. Weber, T. Helten, M. Müller, H.-P. Seidel, and B. Eberhardt. Motion reconstruction using sparse accelerometer data. *ACM Transactions on Graphics (TOG)*, 30(3):18, 2011.

[33] H. Wang, T. T.-T. Lai, and R. Roy Choudhury. Mole: Motion leaks through smartwatch sensors. In *Proceedings of the 21st Annual International Conference on Mobile Computing and Networking*, pages 155–166. ACM, 2015.

[34] L. Wang, W. Hu, and T. Tan. Recent developments in human motion analysis. *Pattern recognition*, 36(3):585–601, 2003.

[35] C. Xu, P. H. Pathak, and P. Mohapatra. Finger-writing with smartwatch: A case for finger and hand gesture recognition using smartwatch. In *Proceedings of the 16th International Workshop on Mobile Computing Systems and Applications*, pages 9–14. ACM, 2015.

[36] Y. Yang and D. Ramanan. Articulated pose estimation with flexible mixtures-of-parts. In *Computer Vision and Pattern Recognition (CVPR), 2011 IEEE Conference on*, pages 1385–1392. IEEE, 2011.

[37] H. Zhou and H. Hu. Inertial motion tracking of human arm movements in stroke rehabilitation. In *Mechatronics and Automation, 2005 IEEE International Conference*, volume 3, pages 1306–1311. IEEE, 2005.

[38] H. Zhou and H. Hu. Upper limb motion estimation from inertial measurements. *International Journal of Information Technology*, 13(1):1–14, 2007.

[39] H. Zhou, H. Hu, and Y. Tao. Inertial measurements of upper limb motion. *Medical and Biological Engineering and Computing*, 44(6):479–487, 2006.

[40] P. Zhou, M. Li, and G. Shen. Use it free: Instantly knowing your phone attitude. In *Proceedings of the 20th annual international conference on Mobile computing and networking*, pages 605–616. ACM, 2014.

BodyScan: Enabling Radio-based Sensing on Wearable Devices for Contactless Activity and Vital Sign Monitoring

Biyi Fang‡, Nicholas D. Lane†*, Mi Zhang‡
Aidan Boran†, Fahim Kawsar†
‡Michigan State University, †Bell Labs, *University College London

ABSTRACT

Wearable devices are increasingly becoming mainstream consumer products carried by millions of consumers. However, the potential impact of these devices is currently constrained by fundamental limitations of their built-in sensors. In this paper, we introduce radio as a new powerful sensing modality for wearable devices and propose to transform radio into a mobile sensor of human activities and vital signs. We present *BodyScan*, a wearable system that enables radio to act as a single modality capable of providing whole-body continuous sensing of the user. BodyScan overcomes key limitations of existing wearable devices by providing a contactless and privacy-preserving approach to capturing a rich variety of human activities and vital sign information. Our prototype design of BodyScan is comprised of two components: one worn on the hip and the other worn on the wrist, and is inspired by the increasingly prevalent scenario where a user carries a smartphone while also wearing a wristband/smartwatch. This prototype can support daily usage with one single charge per day. Experimental results show that in controlled settings, BodyScan can recognize a diverse set of human activities while also estimating the user's breathing rate with high accuracy. Even in very challenging real-world settings, BodyScan can still infer activities with an average accuracy above 60% and monitor breathing rate information a reasonable amount of time during each day.

Keywords

Wearables; Radio-based Sensing; Channel State Information (CSI); Activity Recognition; Vital Signs

1. INTRODUCTION

Wearable devices are growing in popularity at a tremendous rate. The global market of wearable devices is expected to reach a value of 19 billion U.S. dollars in 2018, which is more than ten times its value five years prior [11]. Today, millions of people wear fitness trackers such as Fitbit on a daily basis to track steps, calories burned and sleep [5]. Apple, Google, and Samsung release smartwatches which provide an alternative interface for people to get notifications, respond to text messages, and make phone calls while keeping their smartphones inside pockets [3, 1, 10].

We envision that wearable devices could have a much broader impact on our daily lives beyond tracking steps and sleep as well as being an alternative interface of smartphones. Unfortunately, a key bottleneck that limits their impact is the constraints of the built-in sensors in existing wearable devices. Specifically, IMUs (i.e., accelerometers and gyroscopes) can only sense motions and rotations of body parts to which they are attached. As such, it requires users to wear multiple IMUs to capture whole-body movements. Microphones and image sensors can sense rich information but at the same time they also capture privacy-sensitive data that may cause severe privacy concerns. Physiological sensors such as respiration and ECG sensors are intrusive in that they must be placed at certain body locations and require tight skin contact to function. Motivated by those limitations, *this work is aimed at pushing the boundaries of wearable devices by exploring new sensing modalities that are contactless and privacy-preserving while still being able to provide rich information about users and their context.*

In recent years, radio-based sensing systems have drawn considerable attention because they provide a contactless and privacy-preserving approach to monitor a variety of human activities such as walking [50], cooking [49] and falling [19] as well as vital signs such as breathing and heartbeats [14, 31, 51]. These systems utilize radio transmitters and receivers that are deployed in the ambient environment. However, due to their dependence on the ambient wireless infrastructure, these infrastructure-based systems have three key limitations. First, they can only capture activities and vital signs when people are in the area covered by the ambient wireless infrastructure. Second, their sensing performance degrades when ambient environment changes (e.g., new or moved furniture) or the distance between radio transmitters/receivers and the person being monitored increases. Third, when there is more than one person in the monitored area, activities performed by different individuals interfere with each other, making robust activity recognition extremely challenging.

In this paper, we introduce *BodyScan*, a novel wearable sensing system that uses radio as a single sensing modality for continuous human activity and vital sign monitoring. BodyScan overcomes the aforementioned limitations of infrastructure-based systems. Specifically, BodyScan utilizes radio transmitter and receiver in the form of wearables. As such, it does not require the support of ambient wireless infrastructure and thus enables continuous and ambulatory human activity and vital sign monitoring in all indoor, in-vehicle, and outdoor scenarios. In addition, the wearable radio transmitter and receiver are always within close proximity to the user. As a result, the interference caused by the ambient environment as well as activities performed by surrounding people are

MobiSys'16, June 25-30, 2016, Singapore, Singapore

DOI: http://dx.doi.org/10.1145/2906388.2906411

dwarfed by the activity performed by the user, making BodyScan robust to various extraneous interference.

BodyScan is designed to emulate an increasingly prevalent scenario where a user carries a smartphone while wearing a wristband or a smartwatch at the same time. Figure 1 illustrates BodyScan being worn by a user in such scenario. As shown, BodyScan consists of two custom-made wearable devices. One device is a wristband containing a radio transmitter that continuously transmits radio signals. The other device is a wearable unit emulating a smartphone, which is worn on the hip containing a radio receiver that continuously receives radio signals. With the prevalence of smartphones and the increasing popularity of wristbands and smartwatches, we envision that this scenario will become more and more common in the near future. As such, we believe our design has the potential to be widely accepted by the general public.

Based on the design, BodyScan uses radio as a single sensing modality to provide a unified human activity and vital sign sensing solution in the wearable setting. The basic idea of BodyScan is that movements of different parts of the human body caused by different human activities generate different changes on radio signals that are observable at the radio receiver. By analyzing the changes on the received radio signals, the activity that causes the changes can be recognized. To capture the movements of different parts of the human body by just using the wristband and wearable unit, BodyScan uses two custom-designed directional antennas at the radio receiver to track upper body and lower body movements respectively. To analyze the received radio signals, BodyScan exploits the fine-grained Channel State Information (CSI) extracted from the received radio signals, and adopts a tree-structured radio signal processing pipeline that combines upper body and lower body movement information for activity recognition as well as breathing rate estimation. The algorithms involved in the signal processing pipeline are energy-efficient and lightweight to run on resource-constrained wearable platforms in real time.

Summary of Experimental Results: We built a lightweight small form-factor prototype of BodyScan and evaluated its performance by conducting experiments in both controlled and uncontrolled settings. With more than 40 hours of data collected from seven subjects, the results of our experiments show that:

- In controlled settings, BodyScan achieves an average classification accuracy of 72.3% for recognizing five most common activities of daily living (ADLs). When the subjects are stationary, it achieves an average accuracy of 97.4% for estimating subjects' breathing rates.
- BodyScan is capable of achieving real-time activity recognition and breathing rate estimation. It can continuously run more than 15 hours, which is sufficient for daily usage with one single charge per day.
- When deployed in the real world, BodyScan achieves an activity recognition accuracy of 60.2% and can opportunistically sense a user's breathing information a reasonable amount of time each day.

Summary of Contributions: We introduce the first wearable sensing system that uses only a single pair of on-body radio transmitter and receiver to monitor a wide range of human activities and vital sign in a unified framework. BodyScan takes an *audacious* step towards enabling radio-based sensing on wearable devices. It demonstrates the benefits over existing wearable devices including improved privacy protection by reducing the need for the use of cameras and microphones as well as enhanced comfort and usability by providing a contactless sensing solution and lowering the number of on-body sensors necessary. It also demonstrates the practicality of real-world usage including real-time signal processing as well as long-lasting battery life. Taken together, we believe radio-based wearable sensing systems have tremendous potential to be widely adopted in real world and open up new applications in areas such as mobile health, human-computer interaction, and social computing.

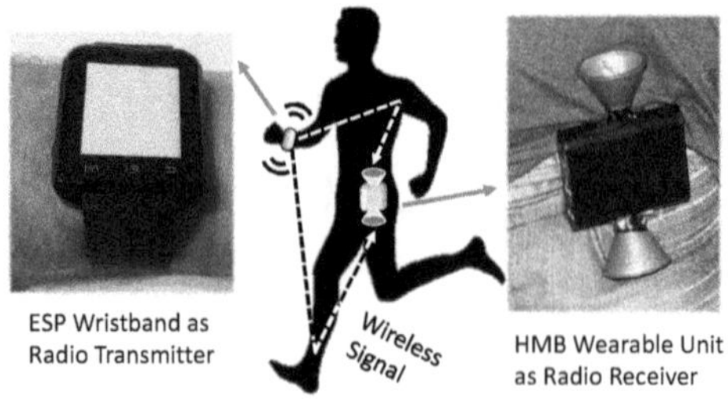

Figure 1: The user model of BodyScan. BodyScan consists of two devices: one worn at the wrist and the other worn on the hip. This design choice emulates an increasingly prevalent scenario where a user carries a smartphone while wearing a wristband or a smartwatch at the same time.

2. DESIGN CONSIDERATIONS

In this section, we first describe the design goals that BodyScan aims to achieve. To achieve these goals, BodyScan needs to address a number of challenges. We discuss these challenges and then explain how we tackle these challenges in the design of BodyScan. Based on the design goals, we list the taxonomy of human activities and vital signs which BodyScan aims to capture and recognize.

2.1 Design Goals

The following goals are central to the design of BodyScan:

- **Sensing Human Activities and Vital Signs using a Single Sensing Modality:** BodyScan is designed to sense and recognize a wide range of human activities and track vital signs using radio as a *single sensing modality*. Existing wearable sensing systems typically adopt a multimodal sensing approach where more than one sensing modality is employed to capture human activity and vital sign information. For example, physical activities can be sensed by accelerometers while vital signs such as heartbeat can be tracked by a separate pulse oximeter. However, the multimodal sensing approach requires users to wear more than one sensor on different parts of the body, which is a significant burden to users. In contrast, BodyScan aims to capture both human activity and vital sign information using radio only. BodyScan addresses this single sensing modality challenge by noting that both human activity and vital sign information are embedded in the radio signals but they exhibit their unique patterns. Hence, BodyScan utilizes a tree-structured signal processing pipeline that uses different schemes to extract the embedded human activity and vital sign information, respectively.
- **Enabling Whole-Body Sensing with One Pair of Wearable Radio Transmitter/Receiver:** BodyScan is designed to capture *whole-body movements* by using a *single* pair of on-body radio transmitter and receiver. Human activities involve movements from different parts of the body. To capture those movements by using a single pair of on-body radio transmitter and receiver, one straightforward approach is to use omnidirectional antenna at both transmitter and receiver. However, this approach is limited when movements from different parts of the body have similar influences on radio signals. To address this challenge, BodyScan adopts a design that incorporates two directional antennas at the receiver end, with one directional an-

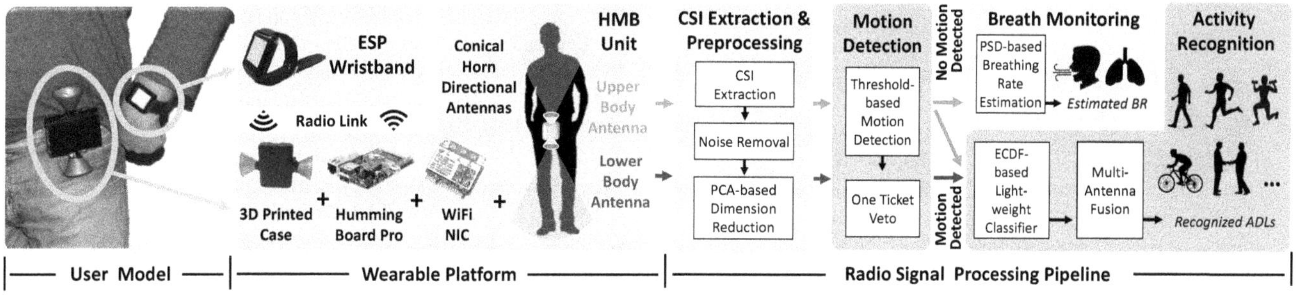

Figure 2: The system architecture of BodyScan.

tenna pointing upward to detect upper body movements while the other directional antenna pointing downward to detect lower body movements. BodyScan then combines the upper body and lower body movement information to obtain a complete picture of the whole-body movements. Based on this design, BodyScan achieves a higher resolution so that activities which involve movements from different parts of the body can be better differentiated.

- **Resilient to Noises from Environment and Nearby People:** BodyScan is designed to be *resilient to noises* from ambient environment as well as nearby people. This requires BodyScan to be able to filter out radio signals reflected back from the environment and nearby people. To address this challenge, BodyScan uses conical horn antennas as its directional antennas. Compared to the most commonly used patch antenna, conical horn antenna has a narrower beamwidth, making it more focused on the body areas of the user. As a result, radio reflections caused by ambient environment and nearby people are less likely to be captured by the conical horn antennas, making BodyScan more robust to noises.
- **Operating on Resource-Constrained Platform:** BodyScan is designed to be able to perform *real-time* and *energy-efficient* human activity recognition and vital sign monitoring on resource-constrained wearable platforms. To address this challenge, the tradeoff between computational complexity and real-time/power consumption performance is taken into serious considerations in the design of BodyScan. Specifically, BodyScan adopts a lightweight radio signal processing pipeline to reduce the computational complexity. The pipeline uses Principal Component Analysis (PCA) to reduce the dimensionality of the raw multi-subcarrier CSI measurements; it avoids computationally expensive features and extracts activity information directly from the empirical cumulative distribution function (ECDF) of the radio signals; finally, it utilizes a low computational cost fusion technique that combines movement information from both upper body and lower body to infer the performed activity.

To the best of our knowledge, no existing wearable sensing systems can meet all of the above design goals. This motivates us to design and develop BodyScan to fill this critical gap.

2.2 Target Human Activity and Vital Sign

To fully examine the feasibility and explore the potential of our BodyScan system, we have compiled a rich and diverse set of human activities and vital sign based on our design goals. We group them into six different categories which are listed in Table 1. We select these six categories for three main reasons. First, many activities included in the six categories such as *walk*, *brush teeth*, and *type on a keyboard* represent the most common activities performed in our everyday life. Second, the breadth of the considered activities enables us to explore the potential and to have a better understanding of the limitations of radio-based activity recognition in the wearable setting. Specifically, we include activities that involve lower body movements only such as *ride a bike*; upper body movements only such as *shake hands*; whole-body movements such as *run*; as well as isolated body part movements such as *shake head*. Finally, we only include *breathe* in the category of vital sign because we could not reliably detect heart beats and provide accurate heartbeat rate estimation due to the low signal-to-noise ratio (SNR) of the current version of BodyScan.

Category	Class
Physical Activities (P)	*walk, run*
Transportation Mode (T)	*ride a bike, drive a car*
Hand-related Activities (H)	*brush teeth, type on a phone, type on a keyboard, shake hands*
Free-weight Exercises (E)	*tricep press, front raise, bent-over row, bicep curl, chest fly*
Isolated Body (I) Part Movements	*curl left/right arm, swing left/right leg, shake head, bend over*
Vital Sign (V)	*breathe*

Table 1: The taxonomy of the target human activity and vital sign.

3. BodyScan OVERVIEW

The system architecture of BodyScan is illustrated in Figure 2. As shown, BodyScan consists of a wearable platform as well as a radio signal processing pipeline that runs inside the platform.

The *Wearable Platform* consists of two lightweight small form-factor hardware devices worn on the human body: (1) an ESP wristband (44 x 40 x 8 mm; 35 g) that is designed to be worn on the wrist; and (2) a Hummingboard Pro (HMB) wearable unit (50 x 90 x 140 mm; 200 g) that is designed to be worn on the hip. The ESP wristband acts as the radio transmitter that continuously transmits radio signals while the HMB wearable unit acts as the radio receiver that continuously receives radio signals. In particular, the HMB wearable unit incorporates two conical horn directional antennas, with one detecting the upper body movements (i.e., upper body antenna) and the other detecting the lower body movements (i.e., lower body antenna). Based on this design, BodyScan is able to capture whole-body movements by just using the wristband and the wearable unit.

The *Radio Signal Processing Pipeline* adopts a tree-structured architecture to provide a unified framework for human activity recognition and breath monitoring. At the input, BodyScan extracts multi-subcarrier CSI amplitude measurements from the received packets at both upper and lower body antennas and uses a sliding window to continuously partition the streaming CSI measurements into fixed-length segments. The segment is set to be five seconds

(a) ESP wristband.

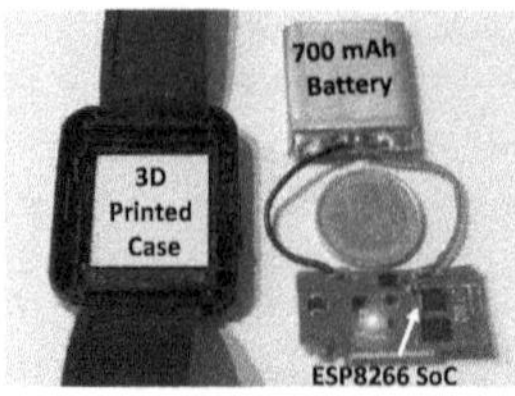

(b) Wristband components.

(c) HMB wearable unit.

(d) HMB device connected with an Intel 5300 NIC via a micro PCIe socket.

Figure 3: The ESP wristband and HMB wearable unit prototype.

long with 50% overlap. The segmented CSI measurements are processed by the *Preprocessing* module to filter out noises that are not caused by the body movements as well as to extract the most dominant changes that are caused by the body movements. The preprocessed segments from both upper and lower body antennas are then fed into the *Motion Detection* module to identify whether the segments contain upper body or lower body movements caused by human activities. If no movements from both upper and lower body are identified over 15 seconds, the user is determined to be stationary and a power spectral density (PSD)-based scheme is used in the *Breath Monitoring* module to extract the breathing rate information from the 15 seconds CSI measurements of the upper body antenna. Otherwise, the preprocessed segments are fed into the *Activity Recognition* module to be further classified into specific type of the target human activity by fusing upper body and lower body movement information.

In §4 and §5, we describe the design of wearable platform and the radio signal processing pipeline in details.

4. WEARABLE PLATFORM

4.1 ESP Wristband as Radio Transmitter

Figure 3(a) and 3(b) illustrate the assembled ESP wristband and its individual components respectively. The core component of the ESP wristband is the Espressif ESP8266, a low-power wireless SoC engineered for mobile applications [4]. We connect the ESP8266 to a custom-made small form-factor PCB (35 x 15 mm; 3 g) powered by an external 700 mAH battery. Both the PCB and the battery are housed inside an 3D printed case in the form of a wristband.

The ESP wristband acts as the radio transmitter in our BodyScan system. Radio connection with the HMB wearable unit is established based on the 802.11n protocol over 2.4 GHz band. We program the ESP wristband to operate in WiFi AP host mode and accept wireless connections only from the HMB wearable unit. Once a connection is established, the ESP wristband begins transmitting standard ping packets to the HMB wearable unit continuously. The transmission rate of the ping packets is set to 200 Hz by default.

4.2 HMB Wearable Unit as Radio Receiver

Figure 3(c) illustrates the assembled HMB wearable unit. As an overview, the HMB wearable unit consists of two custom-designed directional antennas attached at the top and bottom of the wearable unit respectively, a Hummingboard Pro (HMB) device [6], and a 5000 mAH battery. The HMB device is a lightweight small form-factor (85 x 56 mm; 78 g) ARM-based mini-computer that contains an on-board 1.2 GHz ARM Cortex-A9 processor. Both the HMB device and the battery are housed inside an 3D printed case that is designed to be attached to the hip of the user.

The HMB wearable unit acts as the radio receiver in our BodyScan system. We connect the HMB device with an Intel WiFi Link 5300 network interface card (NIC) [7] via a micro PCIe socket to collect CSI measurements (see Figure 3(d)). Once the radio connection with the ESP wristband is established, the HMB wearable unit begins receiving wireless packets continuously.

In the following, we describe the details of our custom-designed directional antennas as well as the antenna switching scheme that enables whole-body sensing with one pair of radio transmitter/receiver.

4.2.1 *Directional Antenna Design*

Design Rationale: Different human activities involve movements from different parts of the body. For example, *type on a keyboard* involves hand and finger movements from the upper body; *ride a bike* involves intense leg movements from the lower body; and *run* involves intense arm swings and leg movements from both the upper and lower body. To capture those movements, we adopt a *dual-directional antenna design* by using two conical horn directional antennas and mounting them on the top and bottom of the HMB wearable unit respectively (see Figure 3(c)). When the HMB wearable unit is worn on the hip of the user horizontally, one directional antenna is pointing toward the upper body and the other directional antenna is pointing toward the lower body. As such, the movements of both upper and lower parts of the body can be captured by our HMB wearable unit.

One important design consideration based on our dual-directional antenna design is the radiation angle of the directional antenna. Optimally, our dual-directional antennas should be able to capture all the movements involved in the performed activity from both the upper and lower body. At the same time, they should also be robust to interferences by not capturing radio reflections from ambient environment and nearby people. Figure 4 illustrates this design consideration by showing three scenarios where directional antennas have different radiation angles. Specifically, Figure 4(a) illustrates the scenario where the antenna has a narrow radiation angle. Although a narrow radiation angle is favored in terms of not covering the person spaced with social distance (i.e., 1.2 meters to 2.1 meters [24]), it fails to cover some parts of human body such as shoulders and arms. On the other hand, Figure 4(b) illustrates the scenario where the antenna has a wide radiation angle. Although the wide radiation angle has a full coverage of the whole body, it also covers the nearby people, making the antenna susceptible to interferences. Therefore, a dual-directional antenna design with a radiation angle neither too narrow nor too wide (Figure 4(c)) is desired.

Design Choice and Implementation: In antenna design, the half-

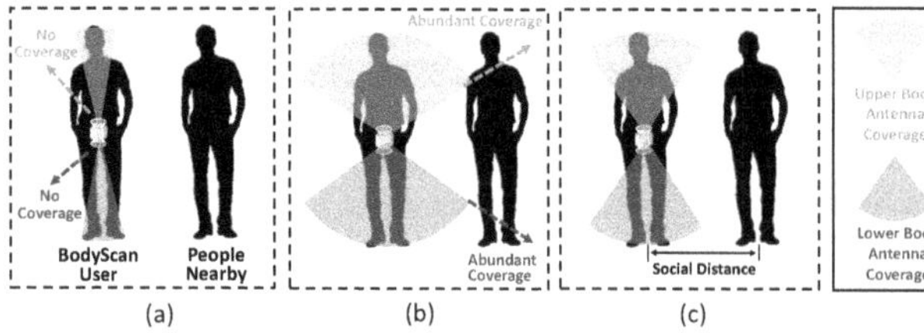

Figure 4: Illustration of three scenarios where directional antennas have different radiation angles.

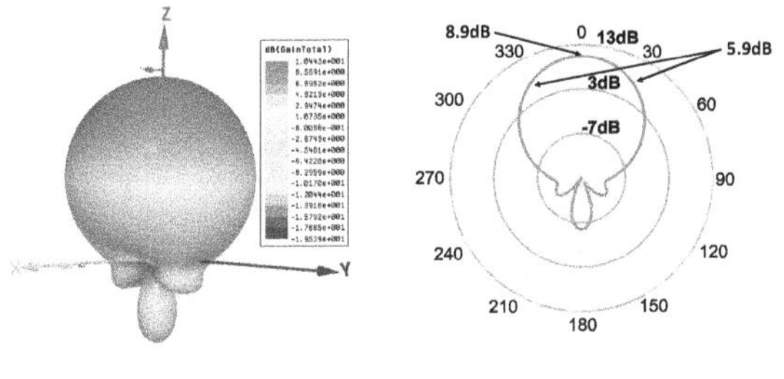

Figure 5: Illustration of the simulated radiation patterns of the designed conical horn directional antenna in both 3D space (left) and 2D plane (right). The 3D radiation pattern is characterized by a single main lobe radiated out from the front of the antenna and three back lobes. The 2D plane pattern depicts the elevation plane pattern obtained by slicing through the y-z plane of the 3D radiation pattern. The maximum gain of the designed conical horn directional antenna is 8.9 dB and the HPBW is 60 degrees.

power beamwidth (HPBW) is the metric used to define the radiation angle of an antenna. HPBW is defined as the the angular separation in which the magnitude of the radiation pattern decreases by 50% (i.e., -3.0 dB) from the peak of the main lobe. In our design, the HPBW of our two conical horn directional antennas is set to 60 degrees. As such, when the HMB wearable unit is worn on the hip of the user, the scenario illustrated in Figure 4(c) is achieved.

Based on our design choice, we used the commercial antenna design tool ANSYS HFSS to design and simulate our conical horn directional antenna [2]. Figure 5 illustrates the simulated radiation patterns of our conical horn directional antenna in both 3D space (left) and 2D plane (right). The 3D radiation pattern shown on the left is characterized by a single main lobe radiated out from the front of the antenna and three back lobes. The beamwidths of the main lobe in the azimuth and elevation planes are similar which results in a fairly circular beam. The 2D plane pattern plotted in polar coordinates is shown on the right. It depicts the elevation plane pattern which is obtained by slicing through the y-z plane of the 3D radiation pattern. As shown, the maximum gain of our conical horn directional antenna is 8.9 dB and the HPBW is 60 degrees. Finally, we 3D printed our design to implement our conical horn antennas.

4.2.2 Antenna Switching Scheme

Our HMB wearable unit is equipped with two conical horn directional antennas as receiving antennas, with one mounted at the top and the other mounted at the bottom. However, although the Hummingboard Pro device has three on-board antenna interfaces, to reliably receive radio packets, only one antenna interface can be used at one time. To support our dual-directional antenna design, we connect two conical horn directional antennas to two antenna interfaces on the Hummingboard Pro device, and adopt an antenna switching scheme by alternating the access to the two receiving antennas. As such, radio packets can be reliably received at both receiving antennas using one Hummingboard Pro device.

5. RADIO SIGNAL PROCESSING PIPELINE

5.1 Channel State Information Extraction

Today's wireless devices that support IEEE 802.11a/g/n/ac standards use the Orthogonal Frequency Division Multiplexing (OFDM) as their modulation scheme [21]. An OFDM modulated wireless channel consists of multiple closely spaced narrowband subcarriers at different frequencies. The Channel State Information (CSI) are measurements that describe both the amplitude frequency response as well as the phase frequency response of the wireless channel at the subcarrier level [29]. Compared to the conventionally used Received Signal Strength Indicator (RSSI) that provides a single measurement of the received signal power averaged over the entire channel, the CSI measurements contain more fine-grained information of the wireless channel.

BodyScan leverages the fine-grained CSI measurements provided by modern wireless devices to capture whole-body movements caused by different activities as well as specific chest movements caused by inhaling and exhaling due to breathing. We installed the modified firmware released by the CSI measurement tool [17] through the Debian Cubox-i Linux OS running on the Hummingboard Pro device at the receiver end, enabling the Intel WiFi Link 5300 NIC to extract CSI measurements from the received packets. Because the CSI phase measurements are reported to be unreliable due to the low-cost hardware components of the commodity wireless devices [37], BodyScan only uses the CSI amplitude measurements for signal processing.

5.2 Preprocessing

5.2.1 Noise Removal

The extracted CSI measurements are very noisy in the raw form. It is necessary to filter out the noises before meaningful body movement information can be extracted from the CSI measurements. We observe that the changes of CSI measurements caused by body movements lie at the lower end of the frequency spectrum. Therefore, BodyScan uses a Butterworth low-pass filter on the raw CSI measurements from all the subcarriers to remove high frequency noises that are unlikely to be caused by human body movements. The cut-off frequency of the low-pass filter is set to 20 Hz.

5.2.2 Dimension Reduction

Body movements cause changes on the CSI measurements across all the subcarriers in the wireless channel. As an example, Figure 6 illustrates the CSI amplitude measurements of four different subcarriers from a sample of five-second *walk* activity. There are two key observations that we could obtain from the figure. First, the CSI amplitude measurements across the four subcarriers are highly correlated. Second, different subcarriers have different sensitivity to body movements. Based on these observations, BodyScan utilizes the Principle Component Analysis (PCA) to extract principal components (PCs) from the filtered CSI amplitude measurements across all the subcarriers. The PCs capture the most dominant changes caused by the body movements while removing the redundant information due to the high correlation across subcarriers.

As one of the design goals, BodyScan is designed to be able to operate on resource-constrained wearable platforms. To reduce the computational complexity, only the first PC with the largest

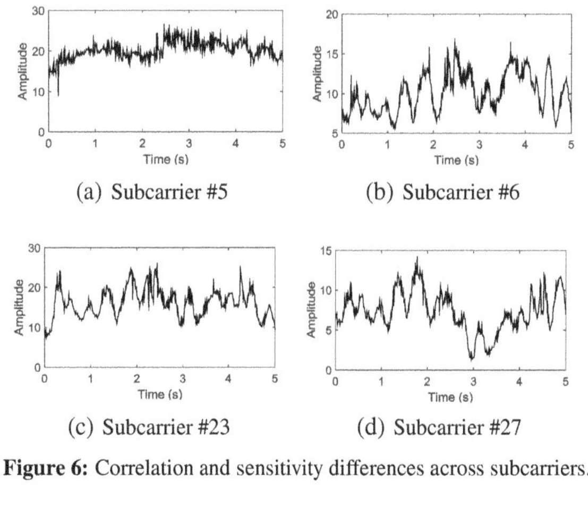

(a) Subcarrier #5 (b) Subcarrier #6

(c) Subcarrier #23 (d) Subcarrier #27

Figure 6: Correlation and sensitivity differences across subcarriers.

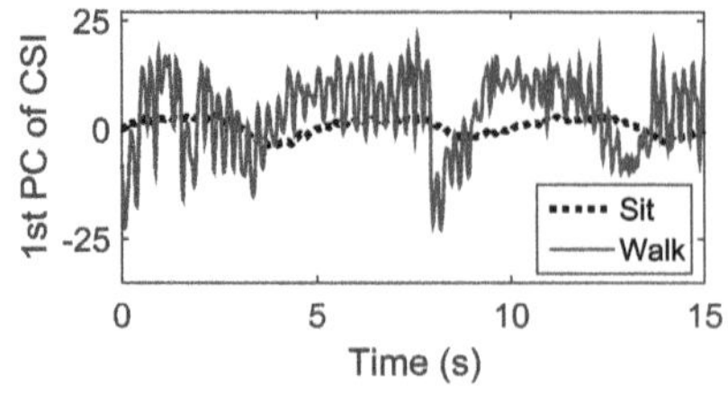

Figure 7: First PC of the CSI measurements between *walk* (blue) and *sit on a sofa* (black).

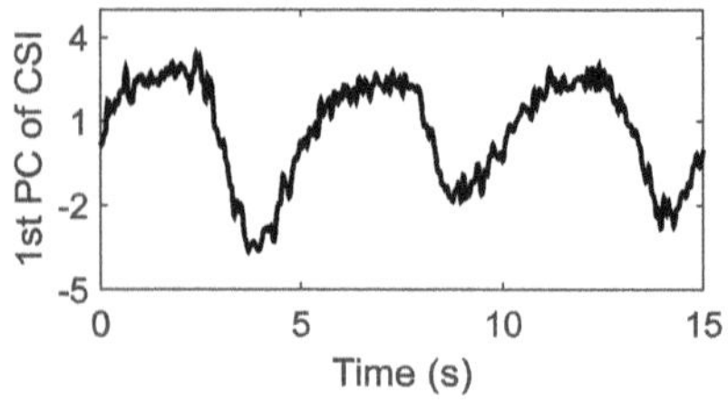

Figure 8: Illustration of the first PC of the CSI measurements when the user is stationary.

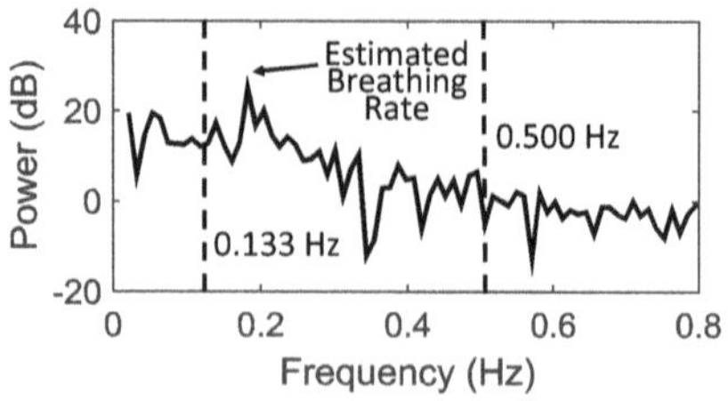

Figure 9: The power spectral density (PSD) of breathing.

magnitude of variation is retained in the signal processing pipeline. As such, the high-dimensionality multi-subcarrier CSI amplitude measurements are transformed into a univariate time series.

5.3 Motion Detection

The role of the *Motion Detection* module is to detect whether a segment of CSI measurements contains body movements caused by human activities or not. Figure 7 illustrates the first PC of the CSI measurements from *walk* activity and from *sit on a sofa.* Both segments of the CSI measurements are collected from the upper body antenna. We observe that body movements caused by *walk* activity generate much more significant changes on the CSI measurements than *sit on a sofa.* Based on this observation, we define *motion indicator* as the variance of the first PC of the CSI measurements and employ a threshold-based method based on *motion indicator* to determine whether a user is performing some activity or is stationary. Figure 10 shows the values of *motion indicator* of four target human activities (i.e., *walk, shake head, type on a phone*, and *bent-over row*) as well as being stationary from both upper body antenna (Figure 10(a)) and lower body antenna (Figure 10(b)). As shown, although the values of *motion indicator* of four target human activities vary across a wide range, they are much higher than those of being stationary. Given the data we have collected in this work, we empirically determine the threshold value of *motion indicator* to be 4.3 for upper body antenna and 3.8 for lower body antenna, respectively. Based on these two threshold values, we adopt an *One Ticket Veto* protocol for motion detection. Therefore, a human activity is detected if the *motion indicator* value of either upper or lower body antenna is higher than its corresponding threshold.

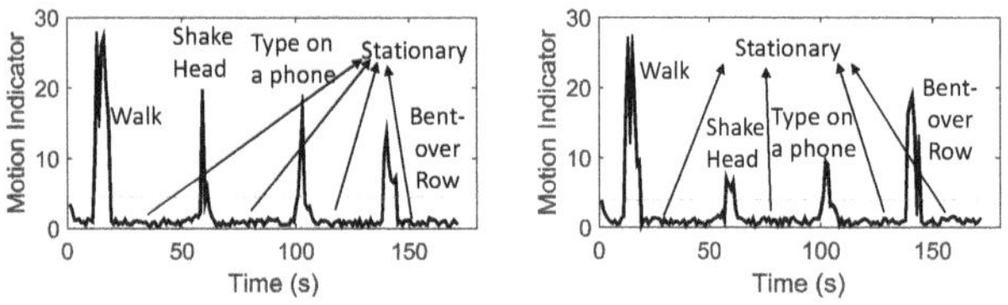

(a) Motion indicator values from upper body antenna.

(b) Motion indicator values from lower body antenna.

Figure 10: Illustration of the *motion indicator* values of four human activities and being stationary from upper and lower body antenna, respectively.

5.4 Breath Monitoring

To build our *Breath Monitoring* module, we leverage the fact that humans, when stationary (e.g., standing still, watching TV on a sofa), are exhibiting minute and periodic chest movements caused by inhaling and exhaling due to breathing [14, 31, 51]. Figure 8 illustrates the first PC of the CSI measurements collected from the upper body antenna when the user is stationary. As shown, the curve of the first PC presents an evident periodic up-and-down changing pattern over time. This observation indicates that the periodic chest movements caused by breathing, though minute, can be captured by the first PC of the CSI measurements. Therefore, we harness this fine granularity provided by the CSI measurements to capture those minute and periodic chest movements to estimate a user's breathing rate.

In particular, we use power spectral density (PSD) to extract the breathing rate information from the CSI measurements in the frequency domain [31, 51]. The PSD of the CSI measurements illustrates how power is distributed at each frequency component of the CSI measurements [46]. The rationale behind our PSD-based breathing rate estimation scheme is that the dominant frequency of the chest movements contains the most power across the frequency domain, and the dominant frequency can be used as an estimation of the user's breathing rate. Figure 9 depicts the PSD of the time domain signal illustrated in Figure 8. As shown, there is a strong peak representing the dominant frequency with the power of 26.9 dB at 0.19 Hz, which corresponds to an estimated breathing rate of 11.4 breaths per minute (bpm). This estimated breathing rate is within the range of breathing rates of children, adults and elderly from 8 bpm (0.133 Hz) to 30 bpm (0.5 Hz) [44, 30]. Therefore, when the user is stationary, our breathing rate estimation scheme calculates the PSD of the first PC of CSI measurements over 15 seconds, and determines the user's breathing rate by identifying the highest peak in the PSD within the considered breathing rate range.

5.5 Activity Recognition

Our *Activity Recognition* module consists of two components: a lightweight classification scheme based on empirical cumulative distribution function (ECDF) representation and a low computational cost multi-antenna fusion scheme that combines classification results from the upper and lower body antennas.

5.5.1 Classification Scheme

One of the design goals of BodyScan is to perform real-time and energy-efficient activity recognition on resource-constrained wearable platforms. To achieve this goal, we purposely avoid computationally expensive features and extract activity information directly from the ECDF of the preprocessed CSI measurements from both upper and lower body antennas. ECDF is able to capture the detailed information of CSI measurement distribution that simple statistical features such as mean or standard deviation can not capture. In addition, because of its low computational cost, ECDF is particularly suitable for resource-constrained wearable platforms [18].

Specifically, the ECDF of activity class i is defined as

$$P_c^{(i)}(x) = P^{(i)}(X \leq x) \tag{1}$$

where x covers the whole range of CSI measurement values observed in activity class i and $P_c^{(i)}(x)$ represents the left integral of the distribution of activity class i with value ranging from 0 to 1 [47]. In our ECDF-based classification scheme, we capture the shape of the ECDF curve of activity class i by selecting d points equally spaced between 0 and 1. For each of those points p_j, we derive the value x_j for which $P_c^{(i)}(x_j) = p_j$. Finally, we use these d derived values to construct a d-dimension feature vector, and utilize Support Vector Machine (SVM) with probabilistic outputs as the classifier for classification [40].

5.5.2 Multi-Antenna Fusion

As the last stage of our signal processing pipeline, given the separate classification results derived from upper and lower body movements respectively, we design a fusion scheme that combines the classification results together to infer the performed activity.

Specifically, let $P_u^{(i)}$ denote the probability of the performed activity classified as class i based on the upper body movements; and $P_l^{(i)}$ denote the probability of the performed activity classified as class i based on the lower body movements. Assuming upper and lower body movements are independent from each other, the probability of the performed activity classified as class i is

$$P_{wholebody}^{(i)} = (P_u^{(i)})^{\frac{var_u}{var_u+var_l}} \cdot (P_l^{(i)})^{\frac{var_l}{var_u+var_l}} \quad (2)$$

where var_u is the variance of CSI measurements collected by upper body antenna and var_l is the variance of CSI measurements collected by lower body antenna. The rationale behind our fusion scheme is that since radio signal variation indicates the occurrence of body movements, higher radio signal variation indicates more movements are involved from a particular body part. As such, the weights assigned to classification probability based on upper and lower body movements are determined by their corresponding radio signal variation ratio. Therefore, the performed activity is classified to the activity class which has the highest $P_{wholebody}$.

6. EXPERIMENTAL EVALUATION

We have conducted a set of experiments to evaluate the performance of BodyScan. We break down the whole evaluation into three parts. The first part focuses on benchmarking the performance of BodyScan on activity recognition and breathing rate estimation in controlled settings. We also conduct another four experiments to examine the impact of various factors on the activity recognition performance. These factors include radio frequency interference, interference from nearby people, radio signal transmission rate, and antenna configuration. The second part examines the system performance of BodyScan prototype in terms of runtime performance, power consumption, and battery lifetime. Finally, the third part involves a five-day deployment study that examines the efficacy of BodyScan in real-world settings.

6.1 Benchmark Evaluation

6.1.1 Experimental Setup

Subjects: We recruited seven subjects (two females) who volunteered to help collect data and conduct evaluation experiments. The subjects are university students and researchers between 25 to 37 (μ = 29.2) years old, weighted between 49 kg to 82 kg (μ = 74 kg) and were between 158 cm to 182 cm tall (μ = 172 cm).

Experimental Environment: All the experiments were conducted in controlled settings in both laboratory and outdoor environment. During the experiments, we used WireShark [12] configured in the promiscuous mode to sniff the transmitted packets to monitor the radio frequency interference (RFI) in the environment. To create a clean environment for the subjects to collect radio data using BodyScan, all the wireless devices in the laboratory were turned off. When collecting data in outdoor environment, locations where RFI was limited were selected. On average, the RFI in the environment during our experiments was 3.3 packets per second (p/s).

Data and Ground Truth Collection: Throughout the experiments, the subjects were requested to wear the ESP wristband on the left wrist and the HMB wearable unit on the right hip. To collect activity data, the subjects were instructed to perform the activities listed in Table 1 sequentially. Specifically, the data of *ride a bike*, *drive a car* and *run* was collected in outdoor environment while the data of all other target activities was collected in the laboratory. In the meantime, one researcher acted as an observer to record the ground truth. To collect breathing data, the subjects were instructed to sit still on a chair in the laboratory and breathe naturally. At the same time, the subjects were also asked to wear the NeuLog Respiration Monitor Belt Logger Sensor [9] around the lower ribs to obtain the ground truth measurements of their breathing rates. Figure 14 illustrates this setup. In total, 269 mins of data was collected from all seven subjects and was manually labeled. Table 2 breaks down the amount of data for each of the six categories.

	Benchmark Evaluation						Deployment Study	
Type	P	T	H	E	I	V	Labeled	Unlabeled
Time	63m	43m	70m	25m	36m	32m	86m	2413m
Total	269m						2499m	

Table 2: The breakdown of the amount of data collected for benchmark evaluation and deployment study (see Table 1 for data type abbreviations).

6.1.2 Performance of Motion Detection

First, we evaluate the performance of motion detection scheme. As our ground truth, all the data from the categories of P, T, H, E, and I are regarded as *moving* while the data from the category V is regarded as *stationary*. The confusion matrix of motion detection is presented in Table 3. We observe that the true positive rates of both *moving* and *stationary* are very high, indicating that our motion detection scheme can accurately determine whether users are stationary or performing activities in most cases. We also observe that the false positive rate of *moving* is relatively higher than the false positive rate of *stationary*. This is because some target activities such as *type on a keyboard* involve intermediate pauses.

Ground Truth/Predicted (G/P)	**Stationary**	**Moving**
Stationary	98.2%	1.8%
Moving	7.1%	92.9%

Table 3: Confusion matrix of motion detection.

6.1.3 Performance of Breathing Rate Estimation

Second, we evaluate the performance of our breathing rate estimation scheme. We collected approximately 32 mins of data in total from all seven subjects. Each subject performs 18 trials of breathing, each lasting for 15 seconds. Figure 11 illustrates the accuracies of estimated breathing rates of all seven subjects. As

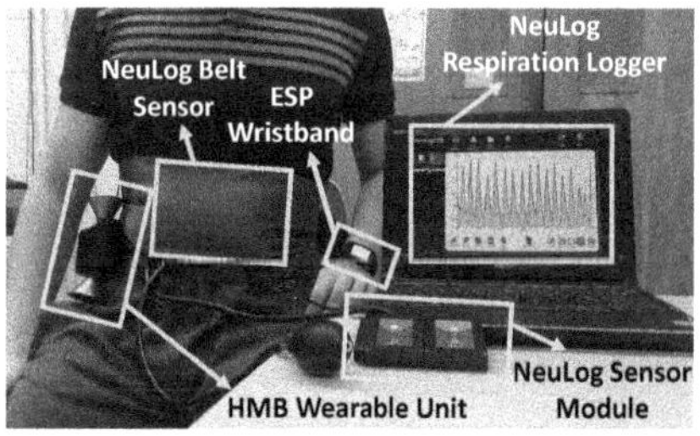

Figure 14: Data and ground truth collection for breathing rate estimation.

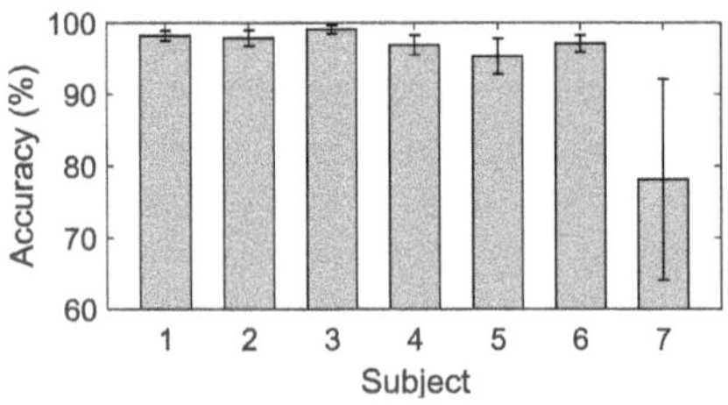

Figure 11: Breathing rate estimation accuracy.

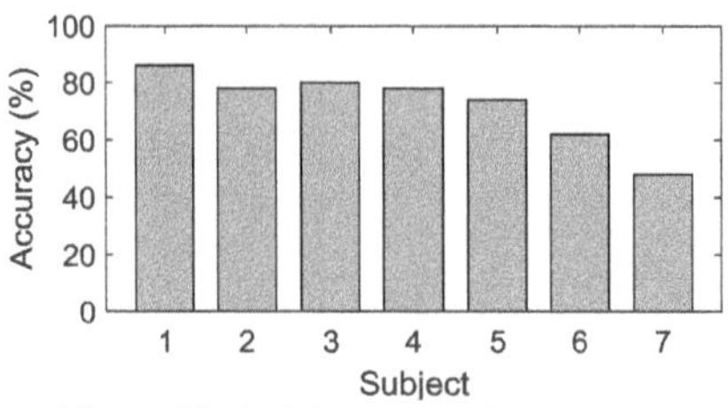

Figure 12: Activity recognition accuracy.

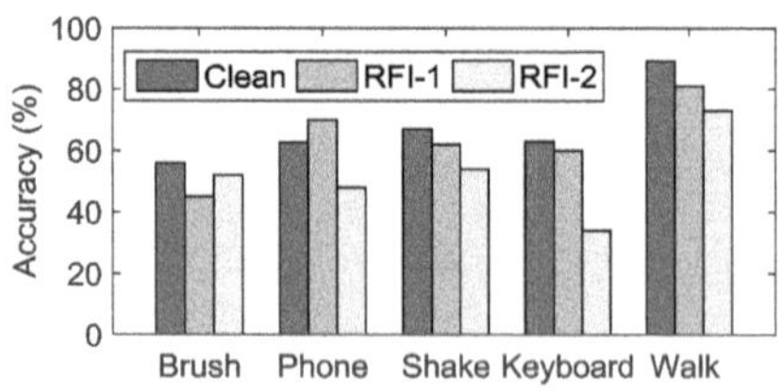

Figure 13: Impact of RFI.

shown, except Subject 7, the average accuracy of the estimated breathing rates over the other six subjects is 97.4%. This indicates that when the user is stationary, BodyScan is capable of estimating the breathing rate of the user at a very high accuracy despite the differences in gender, age, weight, and height. For Subject 7, the average accuracy drops to 78.1%. This is because during testing, the directional antenna did not point at the upper body of Subject 7 by accident. As such, the directional antenna failed to capture the minute chest movements of Subject 7.

6.1.4 *Performance of Activity Recognition*

Most Common Activities of Daily Living (ADLs): As the first experiment for our activity recognition evaluation, we evaluate the performance of our activity recognition scheme for recognizing five most common activities of daily living (ADLs). These ADLs include *walk*, *brush teeth*, *type on a phone*, *shake hands*, and *type on a keyboard*. We collected a total of 70 mins of data of five most common ADLs from seven subjects. The performance is evaluated using leave-one-subject-out validation.

Figure 12 illustrates the average activity recognition accuracies across five ADLs for all seven subjects. Overall, BodyScan achieves an average recognition accuracy of 72.3% across seven subjects. This result is very promising considering the result is achieved based on the user-independent model. At the same time, we observe that there is a significant difference between the highest (Subject 1) and the lowest (Subject 7) accuracies. This indicates that subjects perform these five ADLs very differently and a personalized model is needed for performance enhancement.

To provide a more detailed view of the result, Table 4 shows the confusion matrix for the five ADLs across seven subjects. We observe that *walk* achieves the best performance in terms of both precision and recall while the other four ADLs have some confusion between each other. This is because *walk* involves intense upper and lower body movements while the other four ADLs only involve hand movements.

G/P	Brush	Phone	Shake	Keyboard	Walk
Brush	60.0%	7.1%	12.9%	20.0%	0.0%
Phone	14.3%	67.1%	7.1%	11.4%	0.0%
Shake	15.7%	8.6%	71.4%	4.3%	0.0%
Keyboard	20.0%	5.7%	7.1%	67.1%	0.0%
Walk	1.4%	0.0%	1.4%	1.4%	95.1%

Table 4: Confusion matrix of Most Common Activities of Daily Living.

Physical (P) & Transportation (T) & Hand-related (H) Activities: We then evaluate the performance of our activity recognition scheme for recognizing physical (P), transportation (T) and hand-related (H) activities. These include the aforementioned five most common ADLs and another three activities including *drive a car*, *run* and *ride a bike*. We collected a total of 112 mins of data of the eight activities from seven subjects. The performance is evaluated using leave-one-subject-out validation.

Table 5 shows the confusion matrix for the activities in the P, T, and H categories across seven subjects. Overall, BodyScan achieves an average recognition accuracy of 62.5% across seven subjects. The performance drops compared to the previous ADLs experiment. An important reason accounts for the performance drop is the confusion between *walk* and *run*. As shown in the confusion matrix, almost one third of the *walk* trials are misclassified into *run*. This is because both activities involve intense movements of arms and legs.

G/P	Brush	Phone	Shake	Keyboard	Walk	Car	Run	Bike
Brush	63.2%	0.0%	10.5%	15.8%	10.5%	0.0%	0.0%	0.0%
Phone	0.0%	47.4%	5.8%	10.5%	0.0%	15.8%	0.0%	10.5%
Shake	10.5%	5.3%	42.1%	5.3%	10.5%	0.0%	0.0%	26.3%
Keyboard	10.5%	10.5%	15.7%	52.6%	0.0 %	10.5%	0.0%	0.0%
Walk	0.0%	0.0%	0.0%	0.0%	68.4%	0.0%	31.6%	0.0%
Car	5.3%	0.0%	5.3%	0.0%	10.5%	73.7%	5.3%	0.0%
Run	0.0%	0.0%	0.0%	0.0%	21.1%	0.0%	78.9%	0.0%
Bike	5.3%	5.3%	10.5%	0.0%	0.0%	0.0%	5.3%	73.7%

Table 5: Confusion matrix of Physical (P) & Transportation (T) & Hand-related Activities (H).

Free-Weight Exercises (E): Next, we evaluate the performance of our activity recognition scheme for recognizing free-weight exercises (E). We collected a total of 25 mins of data of five free-weight exercises from one subject. The performance is evaluated using leave-one-subject-out validation.

Table 6 shows the confusion matrix for the five free-weight exercises across seven subjects. As shown, BodyScan performs well in classifying these five exercises. Overall, it achieves an average recognition accuracy of 81.2% across these five activities. This result indicates that BodyScan has the potential of becoming a personal exercise tracking platform that identifies and records free-weight exercises.

G/P	Bicep	Raise	Bent-over	Tricep	Chest
Bicep	87.0%	0.0%	2.9%	0.0%	10.2%
Raise	13.3%	78.3%	11.6%	10.7%	0.0%
Bent-over	0.0%	8.7%	84.1%	4.0%	2.9%
Tricep	0.0%	17.4%	6.7%	73.9%	0.0%
Chest	15.9%	0.0%	1.4%	0.0%	82.6%

Table 6: Confusion matrix of Free-Weight Exercises (E).

Isolated Body Part Movements (I): Finally, we evaluate the performance of our activity recognition scheme for recognizing isolated body part movements (I). We collected a total of 36 mins of data from one subject. The performance is evaluated using leave-one-subject-out validation.

Table7 shows the confusion matrix for the six isolated body part movements. Overall, BodyScan achieves an average recognition accuracy of 84.5%, indicating that BodyScan is capable of capturing and differentiating the six considered isolated body movements. When taking a closer look, we observe that *curl right arm* achieves the highest recall and the lowest precision among all the six body parts. In contrast, *curl left arm* achieves the lowest recall and the

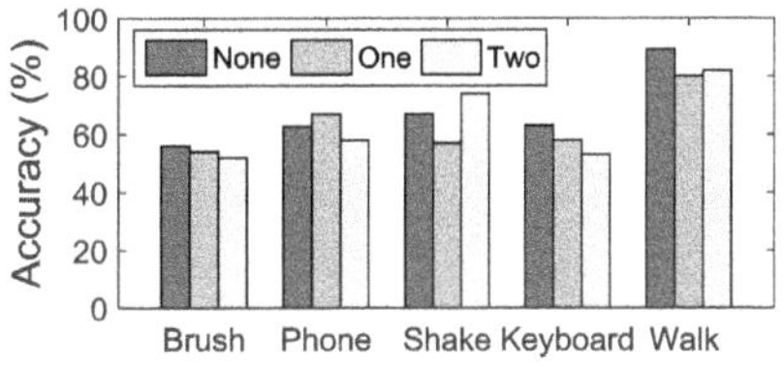

Figure 15: Impact of interference of nearby people.

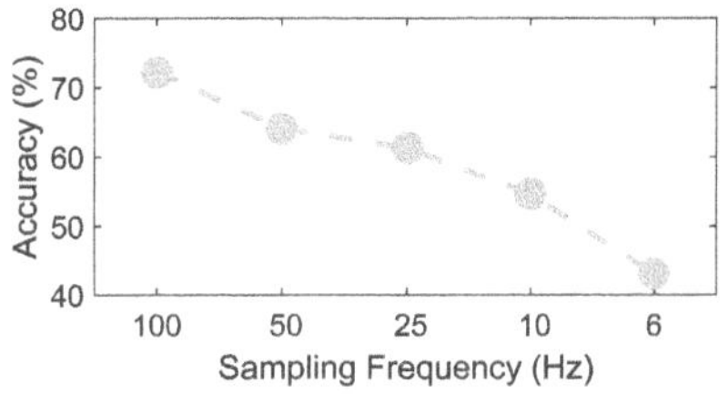

Figure 16: Impact of radio transmission rate.

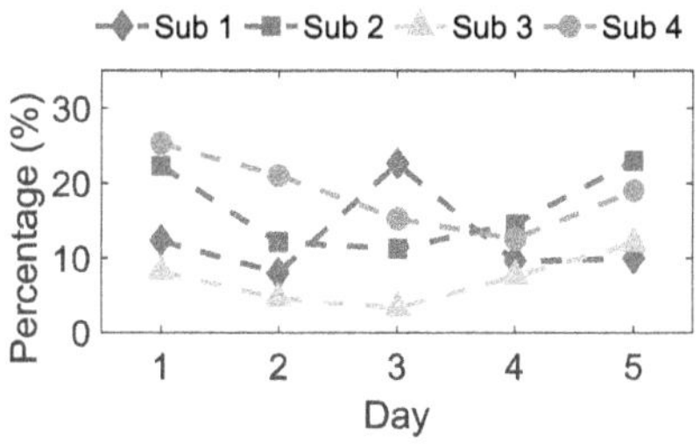

Figure 17: Vital sign sensing opportunity in the field.

G/P	CL	CR	SL	SR	SH	BO
CL	64.3%	28.6%	7.1%	0.0%	0.0%	0.0%
CR	0.0%	100%	0.0%	0.0%	0.0%	0.0%
SL	0.0%	0.0%	78.6%	7.1%	0.0%	14.3%
SR	0.0%	14.3%	0.0%	85.7%	0.0%	0.0%
SH	0.0%	7.1%	0.0%	0.0%	92.7%	0.0%
BO	0.0%	0.0%	14.3%	0.0%	0.0%	85.7%

Table 7: Confusion matrix of Isolated Body Part Movements (I). CL: *curl left arm*; CR: *curl right arm*; SL: *swing left leg*; SR: *swing right leg*; SH: *shake head*; BO: *bend over*.

highest precision. Recalling that the ESP wristband is worn on the left wrist and the HMB wearable unit is worn at the right hip, our observation implies that the performance of the isolated body movements are related to how close the body part is to the receiving antennas. This is because if the body part is closer to the receiving antennas, its intra-class variation can be more easily captured, resulting in a wider activity class boundary.

6.1.5 *Impact of Radio Frequency Interference*

In this experiment, we examine the impact of radio frequency interference (RFI) on the performance of activity recognition. Specifically, we used the clean environment with an average RFI value of 3.2 p/s as the baseline. In addition, we introduced extra RFI to create a noisy environment by setting up another radio transmission link at the same wireless channel using a TP-Link AC750 router and a laptop. Two RFI levels at 101.4 p/s and 214.3 p/s were created for our experiment. For both RFI levels and the baseline, we collected a total of 30 mins of data of five most common ADLs from one subject. The performance of BodyScan is evaluated using leave-one-trial-out validation.

Figure 13 illustrates the performance comparison between the clean and noisy environment. We observe that the activity recognition performance in general is jeopardized with the existence of RFI in the ambient environment. When taking a closer look, we find that RFI affects activities differently. Specifically, RFI has a more significant influence on the performance of activities that involve low-intensity body movements (i.e., *type on a phone*, *shake hands*, *type on a keyboard*) than those that involve high-intensity body movements (i.e., *walk*, *brush teeth*). This is because radio signals of activities with low-intensity body movements are more easily overshadowed by RFI.

6.1.6 *Impact of Interference from Nearby People*

Besides RFI, we also examine the impact of interference caused by nearby people on the performance of activity recognition. We examine three scenarios where we have zero, one, and two people staying within 1.2 to 2.1 meter range to the subject wearing BodyScan. During the experiment, one subject performs a total of 30 mins of data of five most common ADLs, while the people nearby performing some common activities such as speaking, typing on the keyboard, and walking around. The performance of BodyScan is evaluated using leave-one-trial-out validation.

Figure 15 illustrates the performance comparison when zero, one, and two people are nearby. As shown, the recognition accuracies for different activities do not decrease in general when there are one or two people moving nearby. This result indicates that BodyScan is resilient to the interference caused by nearby people, validating the design choice of our conical horn directional antennas.

6.1.7 *Impact of Radio Signal Transmission Rate*

Next, we examine the impact of radio signal transmission rate on the performance of activity recognition. Specifically, we examine five transmission rates including 100 Hz, 50 Hz, 25 Hz, 10 Hz and 6 Hz. For the five transmission rates, we collected a total of 70 mins of data of the five most common ADLs from seven subjects. The performance of BodyScan at each transmission rate is evaluated using leave-one-subject-out validation.

Figure 16 illustrates the average recognition accuracies at all five transmission rates. The average recognition accuracies across all five activities and seven subjects are 72.3%, 64.1%, 61.3%, 54.6% and 43.0% at transmission rate of 100 Hz, 50 Hz, 25 Hz, 10 Hz and 6 Hz, respectively. The figure shows a clear trend that as the radio signal transmission rate decreases, the recognition accuracy drops. This result indicates that with the higher resolution provided by the higher transmission rate, our ECDF-based classification scheme can capture the shape of the distribution of each activity class more accurately. As such, the recognition performance is improved.

6.1.8 *Impact of Antenna Configuration*

Finally, we examine the impact of antenna configuration on the performance of activity recognition. Specifically, we examine five different antenna configurations: (1) dual upper-lower body directional antennas (UL) (our BodyScan design); (2) single upper body directional antenna (SU); (3) single lower body directional antenna (SL); (4) dual left-right body directional antennas (LR) (i.e., the dual directional antennas pointing to the left and right side of the human body); and (5) single omnidirectional antenna (SO). For five antenna configurations, we collected a total of 45 mins of data of the five most common ADLs from one subject. The performance of BodyScan is evaluated using leave-one-trial-out validation.

Table 8 lists the performance of all five antenna configurations. As shown, among all the five antenna configurations, UL achieves

Antenna Configuration	Accuracy	Comment
UL	78.9%	Both upper and lower body antennas are considered
SU	69.8%	Only upper body antenna is considered
SL	56.0%	Only lower body antenna is considered
LR	23.6%	Dual antennas point to left & right side of the body
SO	50.3%	One antenna worn at the same body location as UL

Table 8: Impact of antenna configuration.

Processing Pipeline	100 Hz	50 Hz	25 Hz	10 Hz	6 Hz
CSI Extraction	0.702	0.596	0.354	0.278	0.134
Preprocessing	0.084	0.075	0.068	0.063	0.057
Motion Detection	0.083	0.064	0.046	0.035	0.028
Breathing Rate Estimation	0.182	0.167	0.146	0.138	0.122
Activity Classification	0.123	0.101	0.098	0.089	0.060
Sensor Fusion	0.001	0.001	0.001	0.001	0.001
Total (Breath Monitoring)	1.051	0.900	0.614	0.514	0.341
Total (Activity Recognition)	0.993	0.837	0.567	0.466	0.280

Table 9: Runtime performance of the radio signal processing pipeline at each stage measured on the HMB wearable unit. The processing time is measured in seconds.

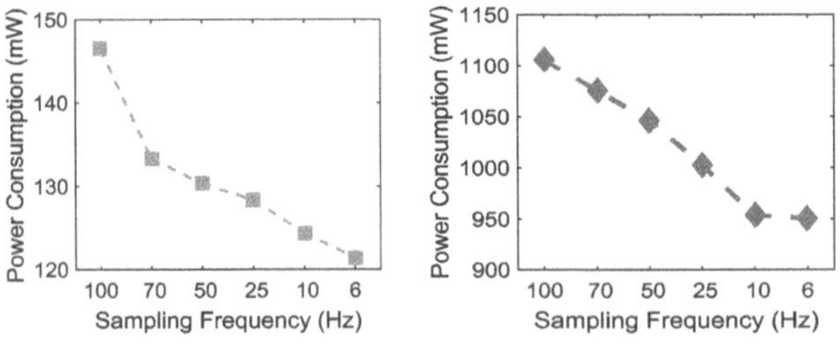

(a) Power consumption of ESP. (b) Power consumption of HMB.

Figure 18: Power consumption at different sampling frequencies.

Device	100 Hz	70 Hz	50 Hz	25 Hz	10 Hz	6 Hz
ESP	16.0	17.5	17.7	18.0	18.6	19.0
HMB	15.0	15.3	15.7	16.4	17.4	17.4

Table 10: Estimated battery lifetime of ESP wristband and HMB wearable unit under different sampling frequencies with the battery capacity of 700 mAh and 5000 mAh, respectively. The lifetime is measured in hours.

the best performance. This result is important because it validates the rationale behind the dual directional antenna design of BodyScan. In comparison, LR achieves the worst performance, with an average accuracy of only 23.6%. This is expected because with the dual directional antennas pointing toward the left and right side of the body, movements of upper and lower body caused by human activities can not be fully captured. We also observe that UL achieves better performance than SU and SL. This indicates that the activity recognition performance is improved if information from upper body and lower body movements are combined.

6.2 System Performance

6.2.1 Experimental Setup

We examine the system performance of our BodyScan prototype in terms of runtime performance as well as power consumption and battery lifetime. To perform the evaluation, we set up the ESP wristband to continuously send radio signals and let the HMB wearable unit continuously receive radio signals. In addition, we implement the radio signal processing pipeline in the HMB wearable unit and run the pipeline on its 1.2 GHz ARM Cortex-A9 processor.

6.2.2 Runtime Performance

To examine the runtime performance of our BodyScan prototype, we measure the average processing time consumed at each stage of the radio signal processing pipeline at different CSI sampling frequencies. Specifically, we examine the runtime performance at the sampling frequency of 100 Hz, 50 Hz, 25 Hz, 10 Hz and 6 Hz, respectively. At each sampling frequency, we run 20 trials of a mix of different types of the targeted human activities from different subjects, with each trial containing five seconds of CSI data. We also run another 20 trials of breathing events from different subjects, with each trial containing 15 seconds of CSI data. We report the average processing time over 20 trials at each stage for human activity recognition and breath monitoring respectively in Table 9. The table shows that among all the processing stages, CSI extraction takes the most amount of time. It also shows that the processing time increases as the sampling frequency increases due to the increased number of CSI samples in each trial. More importantly, the table shows that even at the sampling frequency of 100 Hz, the total processing time for both activity recognition and breath monitoring is around one second. This indicates that with our lightweight radio signal processing pipeline design, our BodyScan prototype can achieve real-time performance.

6.2.3 Power Consumption and Battery Lifetime

To examine the power consumption of our BodyScan prototype, we use the Monsoon Power Monitor [8] to measure the power consumption of both the ESP wristband and the HMB wearable unit at the CSI sampling frequency of 100 Hz, 70 Hz, 50 Hz, 25 Hz, 12 Hz and 6 Hz, respectively. In order to save energy, we configure both ESP wristband and HMB wearable unit to be at 50% duty cycle. At each sampling frequency, we measure the power consumption for 15 mins and report the average value in Figure 18. We also estimate the battery lifetimes of both ESP wristband and HMB wearable unit with the battery capacity of 700 mAh and 5000 mAh, respectively, assuming an ideal discharge curve of their batteries. Table 10 shows the estimated battery lifetimes at each sampling frequency. As shown, even at the sampling frequency of 100 Hz, our BodyScan prototype has an estimated battery lifetime of 15 hours. As users would not wear BodyScan continuously throughout the day (especially during sleep), the battery lifetime of our BodyScan prototype is sufficient for a daily usage with one single charge per day.

6.3 Deployment Study

6.3.1 Experimental Setup

Subjects: Four males out of the seven subjects we recruited volunteered to participate in the five-day deployment study.

Experimental Environment: The deployment study was conducted in real-world settings at subjects' homes and working places as well as in outdoor environment. The real-world environment is by no means clean from interference. Therefore, in our deployment study, we take into consideration both RFI and the interference caused by nearby people (i.e., people interference). In terms of RFI, we used WireShark to measure the RFI at places where target activities often occur. These include bedroom and bathroom at home, meeting room and corridor at working places as well as parking lot in outdoor environment. In terms of people interference, since it is impractical to accurately track the number of nearby people in the field, we used low, medium and high to provide a rough estimation of the level of people interference at different places.

Data and Ground Truth Collection: Throughout the five-day deployment study, the subjects were requested to wear the ESP wristband on the left wrist and the HMB wearable unit on the right hip and were encouraged to perform the target activities as much as they could. At the same time, they reserved the rights to take off BodyScan at any time when they did not feel comfortable of being monitored. To collect the ground truth, the subjects were asked to label the activities as well as to record the timestamps and places when the activities were performed. In total, 2499 mins of data

Location	RFI	People Interference	Duration	Activity Recognition Performance
Meeting room 1	6.3 p/s	Medium	12m	54.1%
Meeting room 2	8.6 p/s	Medium	14m	59.1%
Bedroom	14.0 p/s	Low	10m	67.5%
Bathroom	8.3 p/s	Low	2m	78.3%
Parking Lot	0.6 p/s	Low	19m	52.3%
Corridor	7.5 p/s	High	9m	74.1%
Street	N/A	Low	20m	60.4%

Table 11: Performance of activity recognition in the field (RFI of street is not available due to impracticality).

was collected from all four subjects during five days. However, a big portion of the collected data was either unlabeled or not belonging to the target activity categories. As such, only 86 mins of data was labeled.

6.3.2 *Performance of Activity Recognition in the Field*

Table 11 lists the activity recognition accuracies at different locations along with the corresponding average RFI values and people interference levels. The overall accuracy across all the seven locations is 60.2%. Given the challenging conditions in real-world settings, our result shows great promise of BodyScan as a practical solution for tracking a variety of human activities in the field. On the other hand, we also observe that the performance achieved in deployment study is worse than that achieved in controlled settings. One possible reason is that the orientation of the dual directional antennas was changed during data collection. As such, the antennas failed to capture the movements from both upper and lower body. Another possible reason that accounts for the worse performance is that more than one activity can be performed by the user simultaneously in the uncontrolled settings. For example, the user could type on the phone while walking. In such scenario, the collected radio signals contain mixed information from both activities, which is not covered by the activity model of BodyScan.

6.3.3 *Vital Sign Sensing Opportunity in the Field*

We are also interested in the feasibility of BodyScan for opportunistically sensing a user's vital sign information in real-world settings. Figure 17 shows the percentage of time in each day when the subjects' breathing rate information was captured by BodyScan during the deployment study. As shown, the average percentage of time over five days is 15.7%, 20.8%, 8.9% and 23.3% for each of the four subjects. This result indicates that BodyScan is capable of capturing breathing information for a reasonable amount of time in the uncontrolled real-world environment. It also demonstrates the great potential of BodyScan as a mobile health tool for monitoring an individual's breathing information in a non-intrusive manner.

6.3.4 *Usability Study*

Finally, at the end of the deployment study, we conduct a usability study on all four subjects by asking them to fill in a survey. The questions included in the survey are related to the comfortability, privacy, and safety of wearing BodyScan in real-world settings. We use the Likert Scale to code the answers of the subjects [33]. The Likert Scale adopts a five-point scale with points of -2 (strongly disagree), -1 (disagree), 0 (neutral), 1 (agree), and 2 (strongly agree).

Table 12 lists all the questions as well as the average and the standard deviation of the points calculated from the answers of all four subjects. In terms of comfortability, subjects in general feel comfortable when wearing BodyScan although their opinions vary significantly. In terms of privacy, subjects have a consensus that privacy is an issue they concern about in general. However, most subjects agree that they do not have a privacy concern about BodyScan. Finally, in terms of safety, subjects in general do not worry about the radio exposure from BodyScan. Taken together, the results of the usability study show great potential of BodyScan to be adopted by users.

Survey Questions	Mean	Standard Deviation
1. User feels comfortable wearing BodyScan	0.25	0.96
2. User concerns about privacy issues in general	1.00	0.82
3. Radio sensing is not privacy-intrusive	1.25	0.95
4. User does not worry about radio exposure	0.50	0.58
-2: Strongly Disagree, -1: Disagree, 0: Neutral, 1: Agree, 2: Strongly Agree		

Table 12: List of survey questions and survey results.

7. DISCUSSION AND FUTURE WORK

The experience of design and evaluation of BodyScan provides us with insights on both the promises and limitations of using radio as a sensor on wearable devices for human activity and vital sign monitoring. In this section, we elaborate on those insights in brief.

Impact on Mobile and Wearable Sensing Systems: BodyScan represents one of the pioneer explorations of transforming radio into an activity and vital sign sensor on wearable devices. In addition, one important element of the design of BodyScan is the correspondence of the form factor and the on-body locations with the smartphones and smartwatches/wristbands. With further research and optimization on both hardware platform and signal processing algorithms, we envision that the functionality of each component of BodyScan could be integrated into future generations of smartphones and wearables in the form of smartwatches, wristbands, or even eye glasses and cloth buttons. Given the prevalence of smartphones and the increasing popularity of wearables, as well as the new capabilities provided by radio-based sensing, we hope that this work could act as an enabler of inspiring new applications of smartphones and wearables in the areas such as mobile health, human-computer interaction, and social computing.

Limitations on Activity Recognition: BodyScan has made key strides in showing its feasibility in recognizing a rich and diverse set of human activities. However, it does not deliver perfect activity recognition performance mainly due to three limitations. First, it is possible that more than one activity can be performed by the user at the same time. In such case, the received radio signals contain mixed information from multiple activities, which is not covered by the activity model of BodyScan. Second, the activity recognition performance can be jeopardized if the dual directional antennas do not point to upper and lower body respectively. Since the wearable unit of our BodyScan prototype is still bulky, the orientation of the wearable unit is prone to be changed during usage. As such, the dual directional antennas may fail to capture the upper and lower body movements. We will work on miniaturizing the wearable unit to decrease its vulnerability to orientation change caused by its user. The third limitation is related to the tradeoff between computational complexity and real-time/power consumption performance. The resources of the current version of our BodyScan prototype are limited. To achieve real-time performance and to reduce power consumption, BodyScan sacrifices activity recognition performance by adopting computationally lightweight signal processing algorithms. We will work on improving the activity recognition performance by developing a new prototype with onboard dedicated low-power computational units (e.g., DSP) that can run complex algorithms efficiently.

Limitations on Vital Sign Monitoring: BodyScan is not able to provide accurate breathing rate estimation when the user is moving or performing activities that involve high-intensity body movements. This is because the intense body movements overshadow the minute chest movements caused by inhaling and exhaling when breathing. Another limitation in the direction of vital sign monitoring is that BodyScan could not provide accurate heartbeat rate estimation even when the user is static or quasi-static (e.g., watching TV). This is due to the reason that movements caused by diastole and systole of heart beating are even more subtle compared to breathing. The signal-to-noise ratio (SNR) of the current version of our BodyScan system is not high enough to extract meaningful heartbeat information from the noise. We will work on improving the SNR of BodyScan from both hardware platform and signal processing algorithms perspectives with the objective to extract heartbeat information in the next version of BodyScan.

8. RELATED WORK

Our work is closely related to two research areas: (1) wearable and mobile sensing systems and (2) radio-based sensing systems.

Mobile and Wearable Sensing Systems: The past many years have witnessed the surge of smartphones and wearable devices. Powered by a variety of onboard sensors, these devices are capable of continuously monitoring users' behaviors as well as physiological signals in an ambulatory manner. Accelerometer, GPS, microphone and camera are the most popular sensors that have been extensively explored in the past. For example, accelerometer-based systems have been developed for hand gesture recognition [32], free weight exercise tracking [35], fall detection [28] and energy expenditure estimation [48]. GPS-based systems have been developed for transportation mode recognition [22, 39], social network identification [53] and personal environmental impact and exposure estimation [36]. Microphone-based systems have been developed for sleep quality monitoring [20], social interaction detection [26], vital sign sensing [38, 42], as well as eating and drinking behavior monitoring [27, 52, 23]. Finally, camera-based systems in the form of eye glasses or wearables worn around the neck have been developed for eye gaze tracking [34], shopping behavior monitoring [43] and lifelogging [45]. Different from all these existing systems, BodyScan explores using radio as a new sensing modality on wearable devices. It complements the existing sensing modalities of current wearable and mobile sensing systems by providing a contactless and privacy-preserving scheme to continuously monitor users' behavioral and physiological information.

Radio-based Sensing Systems: BodyScan is also related to radio-based sensing systems. Existing radio-based sensing systems can be primarily classified into software-defined radio (SDR) based and commercial off-the-shelf wireless device based systems. Pioneer work in radio-based sensing systems used high-cost SDRs combined with special hardware such as interference-nulling hardware and ultra-wideband radar transceivers to track human activities and vital signs. For example, WiSee uses Universal Software Radio Peripheral (USRP) SDR to enable whole-home sensing and recognition of human gestures [41]. WiTrack leverages Frequency Modulated Carrier Wave (FMCW) radar to track the 3D motion of a user [13]. Vital-Radio also uses FMCW but is designed to track the changes of radio signals caused by chest movements and skin vibrations to monitor breathing and heart rates [14].

To lower the costs incurred from SDRs and special hardware, systems based on commercial off-the-shelf wireless devices such as Wi-Fi routers and laptop computers with Wi-Fi cards have been developed. Many of these systems leveraged the fine-grained CSI measurements extracted from the radio signals to recognize activities that involve intense full body movements as well as activities that involve minute movements. For example, E-eyes uses CSI measurements to detect and recognize daily household activities such as cooking and washing dishes [49]. WiFall leverages the time variability of the CSI measurements to detect accidental falls [19]. WiKey utilizes the unique patterns in the time-series of CSI measurements embedded in the minute movements of fingers and hands to recognize keystrokes [15].

BodyScan builds on the off-the-shelf wireless devices and the CSI-based scheme. However, the fundamental difference between the existing radio-based sensing systems and BodyScan is that existing systems use radio transmitters and receivers deployed in the ambient environment to sense human activities and physiological signals. In contrast, BodyScan utilizes radio transmitters and receivers in the form of wearables to achieve the same objective. In our recent work, we have developed a radio-based wearable sensing system called *HeadScan*, which uses a single pair of omnidirectional antennas worn on the shoulder and the collar respectively to capture head and mouth related activities including eating, drinking, speaking, and coughing [16]. In comparison, BodyScan adopts a different design by incorporating a pair of directional antennas with one pointing upward to detect upper body movements and the other pointing downward to detect lower body movements. Although the use of multiple antennas is a common practice in applications such as wireless localization [25], it is the first time this approach has been used for wearable radio-based sensing. Moreover, HeadScan employs a computationally expensive scheme based on sparse representation to process radio signals. In contrast, BodyScan utilizes lightweight schemes to realize on-device real-time radio signal processing.

9. CONCLUSION

In this paper, we presented the design, implementation and evaluation of BodyScan, a novel wearable system that uses radio alone to enable whole-body continuous sensing for human activity tracking and vital sign monitoring. Our prototype design of BodyScan comprises a pair of worn devices (wrist and hip placed); a design that corresponds to an increasingly common scenario where a user carries a smartphone while also wearing a wristband/smartwatch. Under controlled conditions, we find BodyScan – from just these two body positions – is able to recognize a wide range of activities (e.g., walk, ride a bike, shake hands, free-weight exercises) with promising accuracies and is able to estimate breathing rate with an average accuracy of 97.4%. Experiments under more realistic conditions show BodyScan can still achieve an average activity recognition accuracy above 60% and capture breathing information a reasonable amount of time each day. Through such results, BodyScan demonstrates the feasibility of radio-based wearable sensing. This is important because of the intrinsic benefits radio has over conventional mobile sensor modalities including more privacy preserving than a microphone or camera as well as requiring fewer body positions than an accelerometer for broad activity monitoring. For these reasons, we expect radio-based sensing to play an important role in the future evolution of wearable devices, and hope the design and techniques of BodyScan can act as a useful foundation for the subsequent investigations.

10. ACKNOWLEDGEMENT

We thank our shepherd Dr. Deepak Ganesan and the anonymous MobiSys reviewers for their valuable reviews and insightful comments. We are also grateful to Dr. Cecilia Mascolo for her considerable support on this work. Finally, we thank Dr. Andres Arcia-Moret, Chris Oakley, Mingquan Yuan, Tao Feng, Zhe Wang, Alessandro Montanari and Petko Georgiev for their suggestions that helped improve this work significantly.

11. REFERENCES

[1] Android Wear. https://www.android.com/wear/.

[2] Ansys HFSS. http://www.ansys.com/Products/Electronics/ANSYS-HFSS.

[3] Apple Watch. http://www.apple.com/watch/.

[4] Espressif ESP8266. http://www.espruino.com/EspruinoESP8266.

[5] Fitbit Activity Tracker. https://www.fitbit.com/.

[6] HummingBoard Pro. http://wiki.solid-run.com/doku.php?id=products:imx6:hummingboard.

[7] Intel 5300. http://www.intel.com/content/www/us/en/wireless-products/ultimate-n-wifi-link-5300-brief.html.

[8] Monsoon Power Monitor. http://www.msoon.com/LabEquipment/PowerMonitor/.

[9] NeuLog Respiration Monitor Belt Logger Sensor. https://neulog.com/.

[10] Samsung Wearables. http://www.samsung.com/us/mobile/wearable-tech.

[11] Wearable device market value from 2010 to 2018. http://www.statista.com/statistics/259372/wearable-device-market-value/.

[12] WireShark. https://www.wireshark.org/.

[13] F. Adib, Z. Kabelac, D. Katabi, and R. Miller. 3d tracking via body radio reflections. In *Usenix NSDI*, volume 14, 2014.

[14] F. Adib, H. Mao, Z. Kabelac, D. Katabi, and R. Miller. Smart homes that monitor breathing and heart rate. In *Proceedings of the 33rd Annual ACM Conference on Human Factors in Computing Systems*, pages 837–846. ACM, 2015.

[15] K. Ali, A. X. Liu, W. Wang, and M. Shahzad. Keystroke recognition using wifi signals. In *Proceedings of the 21st Annual International Conference on Mobile Computing and Networking*, pages 90–102. ACM, 2015.

[16] B. Fang, N. D. Lane, M. Zhang, and F. Kawsar. Headscan: A wearable system for radio-based sensing of head and mouth-related activities. In *Proceedings of the 15th ACM/IEEE International Conference on Information Processing in Sensor Networks (IPSN)*, 2016.

[17] D. Halperin, W. Hu, A. Sheth, and D. Wetherall. Tool release: Gathering 802.11n traces with channel state information. *ACM SIGCOMM CCR*, 41(1):53, Jan. 2011.

[18] N. Y. Hammerla, R. Kirkham, P. Andras, and T. Ploetz. On preserving statistical characteristics of accelerometry data using their empirical cumulative distribution. In *Proceedings of the 2013 International Symposium on Wearable Computers*, pages 65–68. ACM, 2013.

[19] C. Han, K. Wu, Y. Wang, and L. M. Ni. Wifall: Device-free fall detection by wireless networks. In *INFOCOM, 2014 Proceedings IEEE*, pages 271–279. IEEE, 2014.

[20] T. Hao, G. Xing, and G. Zhou. isleep: unobtrusive sleep quality monitoring using smartphones. In *Proceedings of the 11th ACM Conference on Embedded Networked Sensor Systems*, page 4. ACM, 2013.

[21] J. Heiskala and J. Terry. *OFDM wireless LANs: A theoretical and practical guide*. Sams, 2001.

[22] S. Hemminki, P. Nurmi, and S. Tarkoma. Accelerometer-based transportation mode detection on smartphones. In *Proceedings of the 11th ACM Conference on Embedded Networked Sensor Systems*, SenSys '13, pages 13:1–13:14, New York, NY, USA, 2013. ACM.

[23] Y. Ju, Y. Lee, J. Yu, C. Min, I. Shin, and J. Song. Symphoney: A coordinated sensing flow execution engine for concurrent mobile sensing applications. In *Proceedings of the 10th ACM Conference on Embedded Network Sensor Systems*, SenSys '12, pages 211–224, New York, NY, USA, 2012. ACM.

[24] N. Karakayali. Social distance and affective orientations. In *Sociological Forum*, volume 23, 2009.

[25] K. Kleisouris, Y. Chen, J. Yang, and R. P. Martin. The impact of using multiple antennas on wireless localization. In *Sensor, Mesh and Ad Hoc Communications and Networks, 2008. SECON'08. 5th Annual IEEE Communications Society Conference on*, pages 55–63. IEEE, 2008.

[26] Y. Lee, C. Min, C. Hwang, J. Lee, I. Hwang, Y. Ju, C. Yoo, M. Moon, U. Lee, and J. Song. Sociophone: Everyday face-to-face interaction monitoring platform using multi-phone sensor fusion. In *Proceeding of the 11th annual international conference on Mobile systems, applications, and services*, pages 375–388. ACM, 2013.

[27] Y. Lee, C. Min, C. Hwang, J. Lee, I. Hwang, Y. Ju, C. Yoo, M. Moon, U. Lee, and J. Song. Sociophone: Everyday face-to-face interaction monitoring platform using multi-phone sensor fusion. In *Proceeding of the 11th Annual International Conference on Mobile Systems, Applications, and Services*, MobiSys '13, pages 375–388, New York, NY, USA, 2013. ACM.

[28] Q. Li, J. A. Stankovic, M. A. Hanson, A. T. Barth, J. Lach, and G. Zhou. Accurate, fast fall detection using gyroscopes and accelerometer-derived posture information. In *Wearable and Implantable Body Sensor Networks, 2009. BSN 2009. Sixth International Workshop on*, pages 138–143. IEEE, 2009.

[29] Y. Li, L. J. Cimini Jr, and N. R. Sollenberger. Robust channel estimation for ofdm systems with rapid dispersive fading channels. *Communications, IEEE Transactions on*, 46(7):902–915, 1998.

[30] W. Lindh, M. Pooler, C. Tamparo, B. Dahl, and J. Morris. *Delmarqŕs comprehensive medical assisting: administrative and clinical competencies*. Cengage Learning, 2013.

[31] J. Liu, Y. Wang, Y. Chen, J. Yang, X. Chen, and J. Cheng. Tracking vital signs during sleep leveraging off-the-shelf wifi. In *Proceedings of the 16th ACM International Symposium on Mobile Ad Hoc Networking and Computing*, pages 267–276. ACM, 2015.

[32] J. Liu, L. Zhong, J. Wickramasuriya, and V. Vasudevan. uwave: Accelerometer-based personalized gesture recognition and its applications. *Pervasive and Mobile Computing*, 5(6):657–675, 2009.

[33] T. J. Maurer and H. R. Pierce. A comparison of likert scale and traditional measures of self-efficacy. *Journal of applied psychology*, 83(2):324, 1998.

[34] A. Mayberry, P. Hu, B. Marlin, C. Salthouse, and D. Ganesan. ishadow: Design of a wearable, real-time mobile gaze tracker. In *Proceedings of the 12th Annual International Conference on Mobile Systems, Applications, and Services*, MobiSys '14, pages 82–94, New York, NY, USA, 2014. ACM.

[35] D. Morris, T. S. Saponas, A. Guillory, and I. Kelner. Recofit: using a wearable sensor to find, recognize, and count repetitive exercises. In *Proceedings of the SIGCHI Conference on Human Factors in Computing Systems*, pages 3225–3234. ACM, 2014.

[36] M. Mun, S. Reddy, K. Shilton, N. Yau, J. Burke, D. Estrin, M. Hansen, E. Howard, R. West, and P. Boda. Peir, the personal environmental impact report, as a platform for participatory sensing systems research. In *Proceedings of the 7th international conference on Mobile systems, applications, and services*, pages 55–68. ACM, 2009.

[37] R. Nandakumar, B. Kellogg, and S. Gollakota. Wi-fi gesture recognition on existing devices. *arXiv preprint arXiv:1411.5394*, 2014.

[38] S. Nirjon, R. F. Dickerson, Q. Li, P. Asare, J. A. Stankovic, D. Hong, B. Zhang, X. Jiang, G. Shen, and F. Zhao. Musicalheart: A hearty way of listening to music. In *Proceedings of the 10th ACM Conference on Embedded Network Sensor Systems*, pages 43–56. ACM, 2012.

[39] D. Patterson, L. Liao, D. Fox, and H. Kautz. Inferring high-level behavior from low-level sensors. In *UbiComp 2003: Ubiquitous Computing*, pages 73–89. Springer, 2003.

[40] J. Platt et al. Probabilistic outputs for support vector machines and comparisons to regularized likelihood methods. *Advances in large margin classifiers*, 10(3):61–74, 1999.

[41] Q. Pu, S. Gupta, S. Gollakota, and S. Patel. Whole-home gesture recognition using wireless signals. In *Proceedings of the 19th annual international conference on Mobile computing & networking*, pages 27–38. ACM, 2013.

[42] T. Rahman, A. T. Adams, M. Zhang, E. Cherry, B. Zhou, H. Peng, and T. Choudhury. Bodybeat: A mobile system for sensing non-speech body sounds. In *Proceedings of the 12th Annual International Conference on Mobile Systems, Applications, and Services*, MobiSys '14, pages 2–13, New York, NY, USA, 2014. ACM.

[43] S. Rallapalli, A. Ganesan, K. Chintalapudi, V. Padmanabhan, and L. Qiu. Enabling physical analytics in retail stores using smart glasses. In *Proceedings of the 20th annual international conference on Mobile computing and networking*, pages 115–126. ACM, 2014.

[44] A. Rodríguez-Molinero, L. Narvaiza, J. Ruiz, and C. Gálvez-Barrón. Normal respiratory rate and peripheral blood oxygen saturation in the elderly population. *Journal of the American Geriatrics Society*, 61(12):2238–2240, 2013.

[45] A. Sellen, A. Fogg, M. Aitken, S. Hodges, C. Rother, and K. Wood. Do life-logging technologies support memory for the past?: an experimental study using sensecam. In *Proceedings of the SIGCHI conference on Human factors in computing systems*, pages 81–90. ACM, 2007.

[46] P. Stoica and R. Moses. *Introduction to spectral analysis*, volume 1. Prentice hall Upper Saddle River, 1997.

[47] A. W. Van der Vaart. *Asymptotic statistics*, volume 3. Cambridge university press, 2000.

[48] H. Vathsangam, M. Zhang, A. Tarashansky, A. A. Sawchuk, and G. Sukhatme. Towards practical energy expenditure estimation with mobile phones. In *Signals, Systems and Computers, 2013 Asilomar Conference on*, pages 74–79. IEEE, 2013.

[49] Y. Wang, J. Liu, Y. Chen, M. Gruteser, J. Yang, and H. Liu. E-eyes: device-free location-oriented activity identification using fine-grained wifi signatures. In *Proceedings of the 20th annual international conference on Mobile computing and networking*, pages 617–628. ACM, 2014.

[50] B. Wei, W. Hu, M. Yang, and C. T. Chou. Radio-based device-free activity recognition with radio frequency interference. In *Proceedings of the 14th International Conference on Information Processing in Sensor Networks*, IPSN '15, pages 154–165, New York, NY, USA, 2015. ACM.

[51] C. Wu, Z. Yang, Z. Zhou, X. Liu, Y. Liu, and J. Cao. Non-invasive detection of moving and stationary human with wifi. *Selected Areas in Communications, IEEE Journal on*, 33(11):2329–2342, 2015.

[52] K. Yatani and K. N. Truong. Bodyscope: A wearable acoustic sensor for activity recognition. In *Proceedings of the 2012 ACM Conference on Ubiquitous Computing*, UbiComp '12, pages 341–350, New York, NY, USA, 2012. ACM.

[53] Y. Zheng, Y. Chen, X. Xie, and W.-Y. Ma. Geolife2. 0: a location-based social networking service. In *Mobile Data Management: Systems, Services and Middleware, 2009. MDM'09. Tenth International Conference on*, pages 357–358. IEEE, 2009.

Beetle: Flexible Communication for Bluetooth Low Energy

Amit Levy, James Hong, Laurynas Riliskis, Philip Levis, Keith Winstein
Computer Science Department, Stanford University
Stanford, CA, U.S.A.
levya,jhong16,lauril,pal,keithw@cs.stanford.edu

ABSTRACT

The next generation of computing peripherals will be low-power ubiquitous computing devices such as door locks, smart watches, and heart rate monitors. Bluetooth Low Energy is a primary protocol for connecting such peripherals to mobile and gateway devices. Current operating system support for Bluetooth Low Energy forces peripherals into vertical application silos. As a result, simple, intuitive applications such as opening a door with a smart watch or simultaneously logging and viewing heart rate data are impossible. We present Beetle, a new hardware interface that virtualizes peripherals at the application layer, allowing safe access by multiple programs without requiring the operating system to understand hardware functionality, fine-grained access control to peripheral device resources, and transparent access to peripherals connected over the network. We describe a series of novel applications that are impossible with existing abstractions but simple to implement with Beetle.

1. INTRODUCTION

As a mobile device moves through the world, it encounters hundreds or thousands of different peripherals it might interact with. In the space of wireless peripherals, personal area networks such as Bluetooth Low Energy have become increasingly common due to low hardware costs and support for ultra-low power operation: an integrated 32-bit processor and Bluetooth Low Energy radio can last a year on a coin cell battery and costs ≈\$1. [19] Bluetooth Low Energy is particularly attractive due to a highly structured application-level protocol which enables interoperability between peripherals and applications. Today, there are Bluetooth Low Energy health trackers [2], medical devices [13], basketballs [24], door locks [11], fishing lures [17], light bulbs [16], and smart watches [15].

Current operating system abstractions are not designed to handle this peripheral proliferation. Traditionally, OS support for peripherals has come through standard, well-defined interfaces. For instance, frame buffers for displays, USB human interface devices (HIDs) for keyboards and mice, and LPD for printers. When a peripheral performs a function not anticipated by the OS (e.g., a logic analyzer), the operating system exposes the peripheral to an application as a raw hardware channel. As it has no knowledge of the underlying operations or semantics of the interface, the OS cannot safely multiplex access to the peripheral or enforce a security policy.

MobiSys'16, June 25 - 30, 2016, Singapore, Singapore

ISBN 978-1-4503-4269-8/16/06...\$15.00
DOI: http://dx.doi.org/10.1145/2906388.2906414

The diversity of available Bluetooth Low Energy peripherals makes it impractical for operating systems to anticipate the function of each new device. Instead, today's operating systems impose frustrating constraints on how applications may access Bluetooth Low Energy peripherals:

- Only a single application (process) can access a peripheral. This forces vertical software stacks (application, cloud, etc.) despite many Bluetooth Low Energy peripherals ability to interoperate with many applications. For example, many applications understand how to read data from a cycling cadence meter, but only one can do so at a time.

- The operating system does not impose any restrictions on how an application may use a peripheral. Once the an application connects to a peripheral, the application has complete control it. Allowing an application to check the battery charge of a glucose monitor *also* allows it to read a patient's blood sugar level.

- Only directly connected Bluetooth Low Energy peers may communicate with each other. As a result, applications on different computers cannot communicate with the same peripheral, and peripherals have no way of communicating with each other. For example, in order for a wireless switch to control a wireless light, a gateway they are both directly connected to must have an application that mediates that particular interaction.

This paper presents Beetle, an operating system service that mediates access between applications and mobile peripherals using GATT (Generic Attribute Profile), the application-level protocol of Bluetooth Low Energy. While GATT was designed for low-power personal area networks, its connection-oriented interface, naming hierarchy, and transactional semantics give sufficient structure for an OS to manage and understand application behavior and properly manage access.

A Beetle enabled operating system can support a peripheral's function without understanding it or knowing what it is. Beetle leverages the transactional nature of Bluetooth Low Energy to provide isolation to multiple applications concurrently accessing the device. Beetle takes advantage of Bluetooth Low Energy's structured protocol to enforce fine-grained security policies. Beetle is agnostic to the link used to connect to a peripheral: the peripheral may be connected directly over Bluetooth, remotely over TCP/IP or even emulated by a local process. Beetle includes a simple policy language that allows the operating system, the community or device manufacturers to provide sane default access and security policies.

We have implemented Beetle for Linux and Android (Section 4) and built three end-to-end applications that demonstrate Beetle's capabilities (Section 5). Each of these three applications is impossible with existing operating systems today:

- A battery monitoring application that collects battery levels from all nearby peripherals, The monitoring application is restricted to reading only battery levels but other applications can simultaneously have more permissive access.
- Two applications concurrently read the current heart rate from a heart-rate monitor. Both applications can make configuration changes (such as turning notifications on or off) without impacting the other.
- A door-lock that can be accessed by different types of users—*residents* can lock and unlock the door while *observers* can only see whether the door is currently locked. The door-lock connects through a generic home gateway, rather than one built specifically for the lock.

Our evaluation (Section 5) shows that Beetle's performance is comparable to or better than that of existing operating system Bluetooth Low Energy interfaces, even when peripherals are accessed from multiple apps concurrently.

Finally, we discuss some of the limitations of Beetle and how changes to the operating system or extensions to the Bluetooth Low Energy protocol might help resolve some of these limitations.

2. BACKGROUND & MOTIVATION

This section provides relevant details on the Bluetooth Low Energy protocol stack and how operating systems such as Linux and Android present the stack to applications. The limitations and restrictions in these APIs motivate requirements for a new abstraction.

2.1 Bluetooth Low Energy

Bluetooth Low Energy is an ultra-low power wireless protocol for single-hop networks at ranges of 1-10 meters. A Bluetooth Low Energy peripheral's average power draw can be low enough ($< 10\mu A$) to run for weeks, months or even years on a small, coin-cell battery.

Every Bluetooth Low Energy device has one of two roles. A *peripheral* (such as a heart-rate monitor, door lock or smart watch) can only connect to a single *central*[1] (such as a mobile phone or laptop) but many peripherals can connect to the same central. Bluetooth Low Energy networks therefore form star topologies, with peripherals at the spokes and a central as the hub. Bluetooth Low Energy's energy efficiency comes from tight time synchronization between a central and its peripherals, with the central deciding the communication schedule.

[1]Version 4.2 of the Bluetooth specification allows Peripherals to maintain an active connection with more than one Central at a time. However, it is very rare for actual devices to do so.

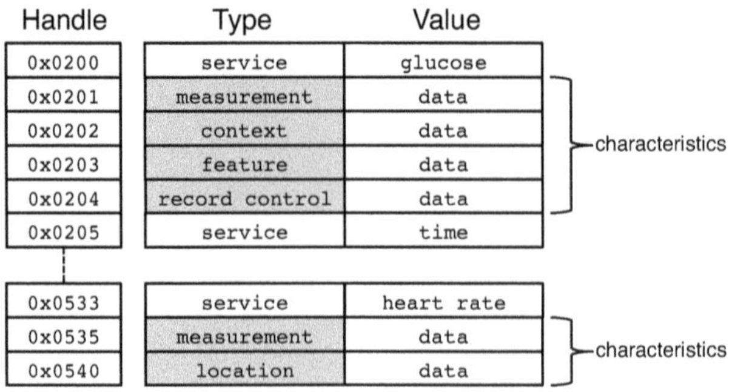

Figure 1: Bluetooth Low Energy attributes, services, characteristics, and handles.

Bluetooth Low Energy provides an application-level protocol called GATT (Generic Attribute Profile) on top of a link-layer connection (called L2CAP). Each side of a GATT connection exposes data objects through key-type-value tuples called *attributes*. An attribute's key, called a *handle*, is 16 bits long and is local to a connection (like OS-assigned ports for TCP and UDP connections). The type field is a 128-bit UUID. Using GATT, a central or peripheral can access attributes on the other using atomic commands like `READ`, `WRITE`, and `NOTIFY`.

GATT attributes provides a structured, fixed-depth hierarchical namespace, as shown in Figure 1. A device has zero or more *service* attributes. Each service attribute specifies a collection of related data values called *characteristics*. For example a heart rate monitor service provides characteristics on heart rate, location of the monitor, and battery level, while a lock service has a characteristic for whether the door is locked or unlocked. Characteristics can be read-only, write-only, or read-write.

The Bluetooth SIG defines common services and characteristics. For example, the battery service [4] defines a service and characteristics that battery powered devices can expose their battery level through, allowing a battery monitoring application to interoperate with any such device. In addition, developers can define their own services and characteristics. For example, the Angel Sensor (an activity monitor) [20] defines services for activity monitoring (e.g. step count, fall detection, etc.) allowing third-party client applications to interact with features not yet standardized by the Bluetooth SIG.

2.2 Existing OS support for BLE

As Figure 2 shows, operating systems expose the connection-oriented nature of GATT directly to applications. Linux and Windows, for example, provide a socket over which an application sends and receives binary GATT messages. Android, following its general object-oriented architecture, has an API of remote procedure calls and Java classes.

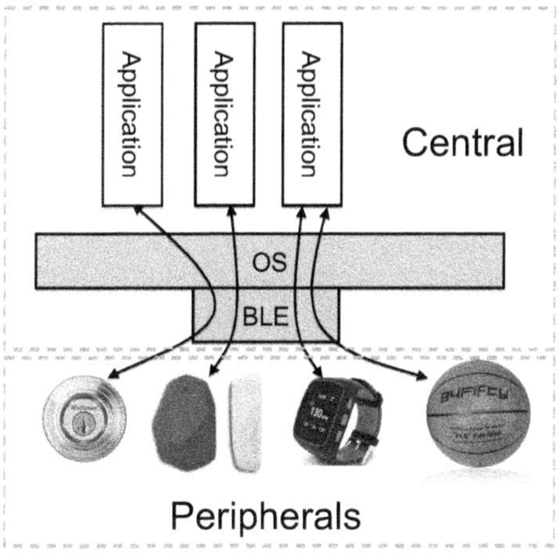

Figure 2: Bluetooth Low Energy communication pattern. Peripherals can only communicate with a central, and each peripheral has at most one open connection.

Existing operating system interfaces expose that a peripheral can have at most one connection. In Windows, OS X and Linux, only one application may open a socket to a peripheral, because in order to open a new socket the operating system always tries to establish a new connection to the peripheral. Android and OS X applications first scan for a peripheral device and connect when a callback from the system provides them an opaque handle to an object representing the device. Because scanning is the only way to get such a handle, applications cannot obtain one once the peripheral is connected to another application.

It is sometimes, none-the-less, possible to share a peripheral between applications. On OS X and Linux, for example, a process can explicitly pass a socket to child processes. On Android, if two applications happen to be scanning for peripherals simultaneously, they *may* be able to both obtain a handle to the same connection. However, in these cases, existing operating systems do nothing to help isolate applications' use of the connection from one another. For example, on Linux, each packet sent from the peripheral will go to one or the other application, but not both.

Moreover, existing operating systems provide all or nothing access to a peripheral. It is not possible, for example, to allow an application to access some services on a device but not others or to allow an application to read from but not write to characteristics. On both Android and iOS, applications can specify particular services to look for when scanning for peripherals – e.g. an application may only care about peripherals that have the Heart Rate service. However, this is merely used to filter which peripherals an application sees while scanning. Once the application establishes a connection to the peripheral it has full access to all of the peripherals services and characteristics.

2.3 Application Needs

Bluetooth Low Energy's communication restrictions and operating system APIs to peripherals prevent many applications and use cases that would seem natural and simple. We present three examples: a heart rate monitor used by multiple applications, monitoring the battery level of all of your peripherals, and managing a smart lock as well as opening it with a smart watch.

2.3.1 Battery Monitoring

The battery monitoring application reads the battery state of all of the peripherals paired with your phone and displays this information on a single screen. It provides warnings when peripheral batteries are low. This application can only access battery state information: it can tell that a scale is low on power, for example, but not read the user's weight.

This application needs to be able to read the battery status of many peripherals without preventing other applications from using those peripherals. It also needs to be restricted to only be able to read battery state.

2.3.2 Shared Heart Tracker

Wireless heart rate trackers are a common tool for professional as well as recreational athletes [23]. There is a wide range of software applications, with different features and interfaces. Strava [21], for example, has excellent recording capabilities, storing data in the cloud for later analysis. Other applications, such as Pear [14], provide excellent active interfaces that show the current workout.

Today, it is impossible to run both apps at the same time. A person must choose between logging data for later analysis or having a good real-time interface. Applications should be able to share data and peripherals, such that a user can gain the benefits of using multiple applications.

2.3.3 Generic Gateways

It is common for Bluetooth Low Energy enabled home peripherals (door-locks, lights, etc) to use a wall-powered gateway device to provide cloud connectivity. For example, the August Connect is a gateway allowing users to monitor their door lock over the Internet. The Lively smart-watch ships with a gateway that supports the emergency response features of the watch with a 3G modem that is too power consumptive to integrate into the battery powered watch.

Today, external connectivity depends on an application specific gateway for the particular device. For example, the August lock cannot connect to the Internet through the Lively gateway, and vice-versa. An increasing number of home-automation devices in the home means a similar increase in the number of gateways. Instead, a single gateway with generic ways of exporting Bluetooth Low Energy services of the network and specifying policies could serve all such devices.

2.4 Requirements

These three example applications motivate three requirements for how an operating system should provide access to peripherals:

1. **Sharing**: Multiple applications should be able to read, write and receive notifications from a peripheral. These applications should be isolated from one another, such that each one can behave as though it were the only one connected to the peripheral.
2. **Access control**: A person should be able to specify fine-grained policies about which applications can access which services and with what permissions.
3. **Many-to-many communication**: Multiple peripherals should be able to interact with one another. A

peripheral should be able to read, write and receive notifications from other peripherals.

3. DESIGN

Beetle reflects the insight that an operating system can effectively multiplex and control access to an *arbitrary* Bluetooth Low Energy peripheral—and to each of its individual attributes—by interposing itself at the layer of GATT transactions between an application and the device. These transactions include `GET`, `WRITE`, and `NOTIFY` commands.

By contrast, today's operating systems expose Bluetooth peripherals simply by routing a serialized byte-stream of GATT transactions between the device and a single application at a time. The OS doesn't try to interpret the byte-stream, even to know where one command stops and another starts. This prevents multiplexing and per-attribute access control (or even "read-only" access control).

Traditionally, an OS would provide special-case support for multiplexing certain kinds of devices at a more semantically-appropriate layer (e.g., printers via a print-specific API, or keyboards through an input bus). The assumption underlying this work is that it will not be practical to build a special-case multiplexing facility for every new type of Bluetooth Low Energy device—hence the benefit from Beetle's more general-purpose mechanism.

Beetle represents every Bluetooth Low Energy resource as a *Virtual Device*. A virtual device may be backed by a physical peripheral device, a user-level process running locally, or a network service. Virtual devices allow Beetle to enforce fine-grained access control policies, provide many-to-many communication between devices, and enhance peripheral functionality in user-space drivers.

3.1 Transaction Layer Interposition

As we described in Section 2, Bluetooth Low Energy devices use the GATT protocol to communicate with applications. GATT has a well-defined set of commands for reading, modifying, and discovering attributes. Beetle interposes at this layer, which provides enough semantic information to share a device between multiple applications while being generic across *all* Bluetooth Low Energy devices. Specifically, there are three command types that Beetle must handle: service discovery, notifications and read/write.

Read/Write.

The most common GATT commands are to read or write the value of an attribute. Typically these attributes contain a characteristic value (e.g. the current battery level) or represent an action (e.g. lock or unlock a door). For these types of attributes, Beetle simply forwards the read or write command from the application if authorized, changing only routing information in the request, and forwards back the reply (Section 3.2).

Notifications.

For some attributes, multiplexing access among applications calls for a different approach. When a GATT client wants to receive notifications of changes to a characteristic from a Bluetooth Low Energy peripheral, it subscribes to notifications by writing a "1" to the *Client Characteristic Descriptor*—a type of metadata attribute of a characteristic—and a "0" to unsubscribe. If one application subscribes while another unsubscribes for the same notifications, Beetle must handle the situation appropriately.

```
var device1 = find_heart_rate_band();
var device2 = find_cadence_meter();

var hrm = device1.find_services(HRM_SRVC)[0];
var cad = device2.find_services(CADENCE_SRVC)[0];

var my_server = beetle.create_server();

my_server.register_service(hrm);
my_server.register_service(cad);
```

Figure 3: Beetle lets users "mix and match" BLE peripherals. Above, example code to combine a heart-rate monitor and a bicycle cadence meter into one merged virtual device. The result has all the services and characteristics of the original devices, but appears like a single device across the Bluetooth bus—which allows unmodified Bluetooth peripherals to behave as if they were speaking with multiple peer devices at a time, by reading and writing with the merged virtual device. Beetle automatically renumbers the attributes in the constituent devices if necessary to avoid collisions and obey the consecutiveness requirements of the Bluetooth spec. In this example, the user is including all characteristics from the constituent devices in the combined device, but it is also possible to combine devices more selectively.

Beetle identifies writes to Client Characteristic Descriptor attributes, and maintains an associated subscription list. Beetle only writes to the Client Characteristic Descriptor when the first client subscribes or when the list becomes empty. Similarly, when the value of the underlying attribute changes and the device sends a `NOTIFY` command, Beetle consults the subscription list and forwards the command only to currently subscribed applications.

Service discovery.

GATT is a self-describing protocol. Connected devices perform discovery on each other to learn which services and characteristics each provides and with which handles they are associated. Beetle performs discovery once for each device, caches the result, and responds to discovery requests on behalf of the device. This is important for two reasons. First, when multiple applications might perform discovery for the same peripheral, it conserves peripheral device energy as only the first discovery process is performed. Second, properly dealing with notifications as described above requires Beetle to know the type of each attribute.

3.2 Virtual Devices

Interposing on the transaction layer (Section 3.1) allows multiple applications to communicate with the same device. However, it is not sufficient for controlling access to particular services and characteristics or for enabling many-to-many communication between peripherals.

Each connection between Bluetooth Low Energy devices has a GATT server and GATT client on each side of the connection. When a peripheral device is multiplexed across multiple applications, there are, logically, multiple GATT servers—one for each application. Beetle represents logical GATT servers as *Virtual Devices*. Each GATT client (be it an application, network service, or device) has a corresponding virtual device.

A virtual device may be backed by a single peripheral device, an application, a network service, or a combination of services from all of the above. It encapsulates state like notification subscriptions, applicable access control rules and attribute mappings.

Virtual devices enable many-to-many peripheral communication by re-exporting multiple device services over the same connection. For example, a virtual device might export GATT services from a connected glucose monitor as well as from a simultaneously connected heart rate monitor. An insulin pump, connected to that virtual device will see services from both devices.

Virtual devices also allow Beetle to enforce fine-grained access control by hiding services or characteristics or blocking commands from certain clients. For example, instead of an application connecting directly to a peripheral that has both the heart rate service and battery service, Beetle allows the user to connect the application to a virtual device that hides the heart rate service, so that only the battery service is exposed.

A key challenge for enabling these features is to honor GATT semantics regarding handle ordering and continuity. For example, all attributes in a GATT service (e.g. characteristics and included sub-services) must be consecutively numbered. Simply removing a characteristic from the middle of a service would create a "hole" in the service, violating the protocol.

Fortunately, the GATT protocol ensures that handles are constant for a particular connection, but does not require that handles are preserved between subsequent connections to the GATT client, or between concurrent connections to other clients. This allows Beetle to fill "holes" in the handle space by changing the handles visible to GATT clients.

Beetle keeps a mapping, for each virtual device, between virtual handles—the handles the client of that virtual device uses—and real handles on the peripheral or application. In the common case, handles do not change. However, there are two important cases where virtual handles are used.

Most Bluetooth Low Energy peripherals only support a single connection. Therefore, if a peripheral wants to consume services from multiple applications or other peripherals, those services must appear to come from the same GATT server. To support this, Beetle can combine attributes from multiple GATT servers into a single virtual device. As a result, services will likely appear at handles in the virtual device that are different from the handles in the backing peripheral or application.

To implement some access control policies (Section 3.3), Beetle may hide certain characteristics from a service. To compensate, Beetle shifts the virtual handles of the remaining attributes in the services to eliminate holes.

In Bluetooth Low Energy, if a device adds, removes or changes a service, it notifies connected GATT clients through the "Service Changed Characteristic" with a range of affected handle identifiers. A device must handle such notifications and adjust to the new settings. Beetle leverages this feature to model a change in connection status of a GATT server as a service change to the GATT client. This is important if a virtual device combines services from multiple GATT servers and one of them becomes disconnected, becomes available again, or if the access policy changes to hide or reveal an attribute in a virtual device.

```
{
  "ServerControler": "this-controller",
  "DeviceUUID": "5C:31:3E:42:BF:57",
  "ServiceUUID": "*",
  "CharacteristicUUID": "*",
  "LogicalResourceName": "my-heart-rate-monitor",
  "GatewayController": "this-controller",
  "AppGroup": "heart-rate-apps",
  "AccessMode": "rw",
  "TimeRestrictions" : "none",
  "Expiration": "never"
}
```

Figure 4: On Linux, users specify access policies in a JSON configuration file. Above, an example policy to allows read and write access to all services and characteristics on a device with a given UUID connected to this controller from any app running with effective group **heart-rate-apps** and also connected to this controller. The same rule can also be viewed or specified in the Beetle controller's web interface.

3.3 Access Control

Beetle exposes an interface to control a client's access to devices at a fine grain—allowing no access, read-only access, or read-write access to each individual attribute.

In some cases, access to a set of attributes, a whole service, or a whole device may need to be exclusive—only a single GATT client should be allowed access at a time. Although it is not common, writing to one attribute may affect the behavior of other attributes, for example, by changing the units or sampling rate of a sensor measurement.[2]

Future devices with these semantics would represent an exception to Beetle's assumption that access to a Bluetooth Low Energy peripheral may safely be multiplexed by merging read/write commands to each attribute separately. In these cases, an application should only be able to write to the attribute in question as long as no other GATT client can do so. That application may, in turn, re-expose those services in a device-specific manner.

To support these access control semantics, Beetle determines the set of rules to apply to a virtual device upon connection. Exclusivity can be enforced for an actual GATT server (an actual peripheral or application). The restriction will be carried through even to virtual devices that include services from the peripheral or application in question. More generally, Beetle can enforce exclusive access permissions across any arbitrary grouping of devices, services, and attributes under its control through the use of logical resource names. This can be useful for management purposes, for instance to enforce that one application uniformly controls all of the Bluetooth Low Energy light bulbs in a room.

The Beetle design is agnostic to exactly how access control policies are specified. The Linux implementation of Beetle uses configuration files (Figure 4), while the Android implementation prompts the user to specify a policy interactively when a connection is established (Figure 7). We also built a web interface to configure access policies on Linux for use in gateway devices. In both cases, the user specifies policy rules in terms of four columns: a service or characteristic

[2]We can't give an example of such a "problematic" device yet, because in currently standardized GATT profiles, measurement units are fixed: temperature is in Celsius, power in watts, etc. But we don't doubt that such devices may emerge in the future.

```
class HeartRateCallback extends BluetoothGattCallback
      {
  void onServicesDiscovered(BluetoothGatt gatt) {
    BluetoothGattCharacteristics hrmChar = gatt.
         getService(HRM_SRVC).getCharacteristic(
         HRM_CHAR);
    gatt.setCharacteristicNotification(hrmChar, true)
         ;
    BluetoothGattDescriptor desc = hrmChar.
         getDescriptor(CLIENT_CHAR_CONFIG_UUID);
    desc.setValue(BluetoothGattDescriptor.
         ENABLE_NOTIFICATION_VALUE);
    gatt.writeDescriptor(desc);
  }

  void onCharacteristicChanged(
       BluetoothGattCharacteristic c) {
    bpm = c.getIntValue(FORMAT_UINT8, 1);
    textBox.setText(Integer.toString(bpm, 10));
  }
}

bleScanner.startScan(new ScanCallback() {
  void onScanResult(ScanResult result) {
    BluetoothDevice hrm = result.getDevice();
    hrmGatt = hrm.connectGatt(this, false, new
         HeartRateCallback(heartRate));
  };
});
```

Figure 5: Example Android code, demonstrating the Beetle API for finding a device with a heart-rate-monitor service and subscribing to its stream of measurements. Some unused parameters and details omitted for brevity.

type, a device address, read and write flags and an exclusive flag. Both the service/characteristic and the device columns can be a wild-card, allowing the user to specify rules that apply for a particular service on all devices (e.g. the battery service on all devices that expose it) as well as all services on a particular device. Beetle has a base policy exposing the GAP service (which includes the device name and other metadata) as read-only. Additional rules are applied on top of the base policy and may override it.

4. IMPLEMENTATION

We implemented Beetle for Linux as a user-level process and for Android as a privileged system app. Linux and Android expose significantly different interfaces to applications for interacting with Bluetooth Low Energy peripherals. As a result, our Beetle implementation on each system differs significantly as well. This section describes and compares the two implementations, providing intuition on how difficult it is to incorporate Beetle into an existing operating system.

4.1 Android

Android applications interact with peripherals through an Android-specific IPC mechanism called Binder. For each peripheral type—GPS, camera, and Bluetooth Low Energy—there is a specially privileged system service that issues commands to the hardware through a C API provided by the device manufacturer.

In the case of Bluetooth Low Energy, the existing service is called `GattService`. The GattService exposes relatively high level API calls such as `startScan`, `connectGatt` and `readCharacteristic`. Figure 5 shows an example of an Android app using this API to connect to a heart rate monitor and subscribe to notifications from the heart rate characteristic.

There are a large number of existing Android apps that connect to Bluetooth Low Energy peripherals. Most of them are closed source and we could not easily modify or recompile them. In order to support unmodified existing applications our implementation of Beetle for Android is an API compatible replacement for the `GattService`.

4.1.1 Scanning for Peripherals

To scan for connectable peripherals, an Android application calls `startScan` passing in scan parameters (e.g. whether the scan should be low-power or low-latency), filters (e.g. a device name or services exposed) and a callback that accepts one scanned device per invocation.

When invoked, Beetle asks the user to approve the scan. Beetle interprets the passed in filter as a signal that the app may only require those services. Therefore, the confirmation prompt to the user allows her the option to pre-approve access to those services by the application for all connected devices.

If there are already connected devices matching the filter Beetle immediately returns them to through the app-provided callback. In addition, Beetle begins a scan for new devices. Beetle continues to return matching peripherals through the callback, both if they are found through subsequent scans or if other apps connect to those peripherals. This process continues until the app stops the scan explicitly. Most apps call `stopScan` immediately prior to connecting to their device of interest. However, this is not always the case. The battery monitor application in Section 5.1, for example, never stops scanning, as it is interested in any peripherals with the battery service that the phone may connect to in the future.

4.1.2 Establishing Connections

Once an application has discovered a device it would like to connect to, it calls `connectGatt`. Beetle establishes a connection, but does not give the application access to the connection until the user approves that the application may use that device. This approval can either be implicit or explicit. Implicit approval occurs when the user had pre-approved access to services in a scan. In this case, Beetle creates a virtual device containing only those pre-approved services and gives the application access to it. Explicit approval occurs when Beetle prompts the user asking to approve the connection and allows the user to restrict access to specific services.

4.1.3 Accessing Characteristics

Once a connection is established, Beetle generates a unique connection identifier that the application uses for all commands that access a characteristic. Beetle uses the connection identifier to store access control rules derived from user prompts during the connection phase.

The Android Bluetooth Low Energy interface does not expose GATT handles directly to applications, but instead uses characteristic and service "instance identifiers" generated by the mobile device manufacturers proprietary drivers [3]. As a result, Beetle on Android does not need to translate the handle specified in an application request to the real handle on a GATT server.

[3]In fact, on the Android devices we tested, these seem to correspond to the underlying handle. However, ordering of these identifiers is not guaranteed to be meaningful, so applications must treat them as opaque anyway.

```
beetle.scan([HRM_SRVC], function(scan_record) {
  if (scan_record.device_name == "MyHRM") {
    beetle.connect(scan_record.address, on_connect);
    return false;
  }
  return true;
});

function on_connect(device) {
  var srvc = device.find_services(HRM_SRVC)[0];
  var hrm = srvc.find_characteristics(HRM_CHAR)[0];
  hrm.subscribe(function(val) {
    console.log("Heart rate: ", val);
  });
}
```

Figure 6: Example code, demonstrating the same use-case as Figure 5 – finding and streaming heart-rate service data – in a Node.js app on Linux.

However, instance identifiers are forgeable (they are simply 32 bit integers and are generally sequential). Therefore, when an application requests to, e.g., write a characteristic, Beetle must consult the rules-set to decide whether the command is permissible.

4.2 Linux

The Linux Bluetooth subsystem [3] manages connections to Bluetooth Low Energy peripherals inside the kernel and exports a socket interface to user-level applications. To connect to a particular peripheral, an application creates an `L2CAP` socket and connects to the peripherals L2CAP address. The kernel handles connection establishment and when the `connect` system call returns, the application can communicate with the peripheral over the socket using GATT directly.

In our implementation of Beetle for Linux, on the other hand, all `L2CAP` sockets are owned by a Beetle daemon. Applications do not directly initiate connections with peripherals, but instead, the user uses a shell interface to the Beetle daemon to establish connections which applications can then access over UNIX domain sockets. However, once a connection is established, applications interact with peripherals the same—by sending and receiving GATT commands over a socket. This design differs from the current Linux Bluetooth Low Energy interface but more closely resembles the interface for basic rate Bluetooth.

An application finds peripherals to communicate with by navigating the filesystem depicted in Figure 8. Each directory represents a connected peripheral or virtual device. The contents of each directory includes the peripherals original advertising data and a a UNIX domain socket for each exposed service, named by the GATT UUID of the service. Applications access individual services by connecting to the respective UNIX domain sockets.

Once connected to a particular service, Linux applications issue GATT commands to the socket just as though they were connected over an L2CAP socket. Importantly, because GATT does not have a length field, applications must open sockets with the `SEQ_PACKET` option so only complete packets are ever returned from the `read` system call. The Beetle daemon intercepts GATT commands written to the socket and forwards them to the appropriate peripheral or virtual device.

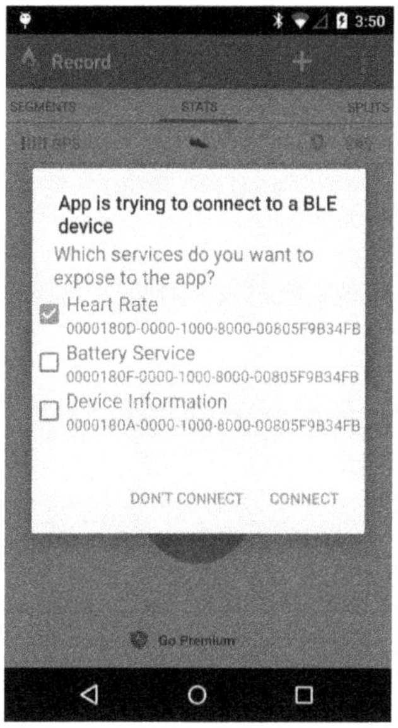

Figure 7: On Android, Beetle asks the user at runtime which services an app should be able to access if the app is not covered under any existing policy rules.

```
MyHRM/          ──► 00:12:55:3D:2C:FF/

00:12:55:3D:2C:FF/
   ├── 00001800-0000-1000-8000-00805F9B34FB=  # GAP Service
   ├── 0000180D-0000-1000-8000-00805F9B34FB=  # Heart Rate
   ├── 0000180F-0000-1000-8000-00805F9B34FB=  # Battery Service
   └── advertising_data

MyBike/         ──► E6:1D:1E:D0:16:0B/

E6:1D:1E:D0:16:0B/
   ├── 00001800-0000-1000-8000-00805F9B34FB=  # GAP Service
   ├── 00001816-0000-1000-8000-00805F9B34FB=  # Cadence Meter
   ├── 0000180F-0000-1000-8000-00805F9B34FB=  # Battery Service
   └── advertising_data

VirtualFit/     ──► DF:19:D5:77:44:9B/

DF:19:D5:77:44:9B/
   ├── 0000180D-0000-1000-8000-00805F9B34FB=   ──► ../MyHRM/00001800...
   ├── 00001816-0000-1000-8000-00805F9B34FB=   ──► ../MyBike/00001800...
   └── advertising_data
```

Figure 8: On Linux, Beetle represents Bluetooth Low Energy connected devices as a directory tree. Each device is a subdirectory, with each service as a Unix-domain socket inside. A user can create a merged virtual device by making a new directory with symbolic links to existing services.

4.3 GATT over TCP

Both the Linux and Android implementations of Beetle allow users to connect to GATT services over the LAN or even the Internet. Beetle on Linux exposes peripherals or virtual devices by giving each one a particular TCP port and listening for incoming connections over that port. To expose a device, the user uses the `export_tcp` command in the Beetle shell passing in the local device address and a TCP port to listen on.

Similarly, to connect to a remote service, the user specifies the IP and port of the Beetle server. On Linux, the user uses the `connect_tcp` command in the shell. Our Android implementation has a settings activity where users can enter the remote address.

Once a connection is established, endpoints communicate using a slight extension to the GATT protocol. First, each side exchanges its device address with the other by sending it as the first six bytes. Second, all GATT commands are prefixed with their length.

Just like with L2CAP sockets, in both implementations Beetle immediately performs a service discovery for a new TCP connection. Beetle uses this step to get the same information obtained during the advertising phase, allowing it to populate the directory tree and respond to filtered scan requests, on Linux and Android, respectively.

5. EVALUATION

We evaluated the Beetle design by implementing three applications: two heart rate apps on an Android phone simultaneously accessing the same heart rate monitor, a battery monitoring app on Android that tracks the battery usage of all connected Bluetooth Low Energy peripherals, and a generic gateway device for the home that provides access control and Internet tunneling to a keyless door-lock. We also evaluated the performance of Beetle on latency and throughput metrics.

5.1 Applications

5.1.1 Multi-app Heart Rate Monitor

Fitness applications, such as the Strava Android app [21], often connect to a user's Bluetooth Low Energy heart-rate monitor and record the heart-rate over the course of a workout for later analysis. Unfortunately, during the workout itself, the heart-rate is not displayed prominently, and might be difficult for the user to see while, e.g., running. There are several apps that only display the heart rate or some that display it on an smart-watch like the Pebble. However, it is not possible to use Strava to record the heart rate while simultaneously using another app to view it.

In order to support this functionality on existing operating systems, one of the two applications would get exclusive access to the heart-rate monitor and expose the heart-rate data through a separate interface (on Android this would most likely be a Binder IPC service). For example, Strava could would serve heart-rate data through a specially crafted IPC service. The Pebble app would have to be designed specifically to use that interface and, importantly, would have a dependency on the Strava app or else implement a path for accessing the heart-rate monitor over both interfaces. Moreover, there is no dependency management in the Android Play store; the user must install the Strava app manually for the Pebble app to work.

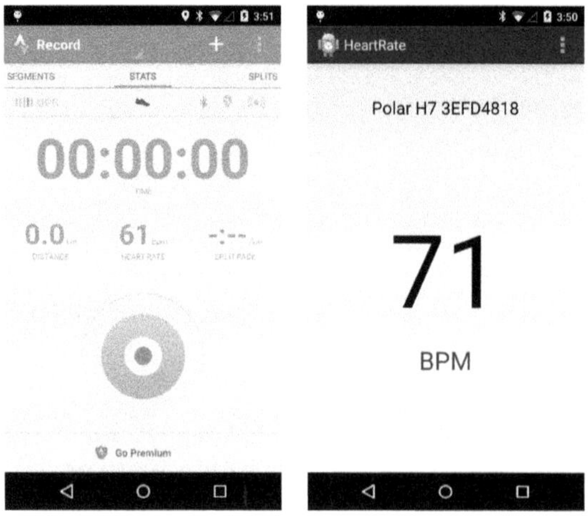

Figure 9: The Strava app (left) records the user's heart rate over time for later analysis, while our heart rate app (right) displays the current heart-rate more prominently. Both apps shown are running concurrently, connected to the same heart rate strap on the same phone.

Using Beetle, on the other hand, the desired functionality—accessing the heart-rate service from both apps—just works. We were able to run Strava, unmodified, alongside a simple app we built that just displays the current heart rate at the same time. Because Beetle keeps a subscription list for the heart-rate service data instead of issuing all subscription and unsubscription commands on behalf of applications, each app will continue to receive notifications regardless of whether the other has unsubscribed.

5.1.2 Battery Monitor

Many battery powered Bluetooth Low Energy devices implement the Bluetooth SIG standardized *Battery Service*. The battery service notifies a subscribing GATT client of changes in the battery level. One useful application is a dashboard that monitors the battery levels of all connected Bluetooth Low Energy devices. This dashboard could, for example, notify the user when one of her devices drops below a certain threshold.

Unfortunately, using the interfaces exposed by Linux and Android today, it is impossible to build such a dashboard without preventing other applications from using those peripherals. Since the dashboard would have to *own* the connection to all connected peripherals, the OS cannot allow other applications to safely access them at the same time. Moreover, even if the OS allowed multiple apps to access the peripheral (after all, it is unlikely for a battery monitoring dashboard and fitness application to interfere with each other in practice), the battery dashboard would be given access to *all services on all peripherals.*

Using our implementation of Beetle for Android, we were able to easily build such an app. Our dashboard, shown in Figure 10 monitors the battery level of each connected peripheral device connected to a phone. If the battery level drops below 10%, the app alerts the user.

The dashboard is a regular Android app. When launched, it makes a request to Beetle to scan for available Bluetooth Low Energy peripherals with the battery service. Beetle in-

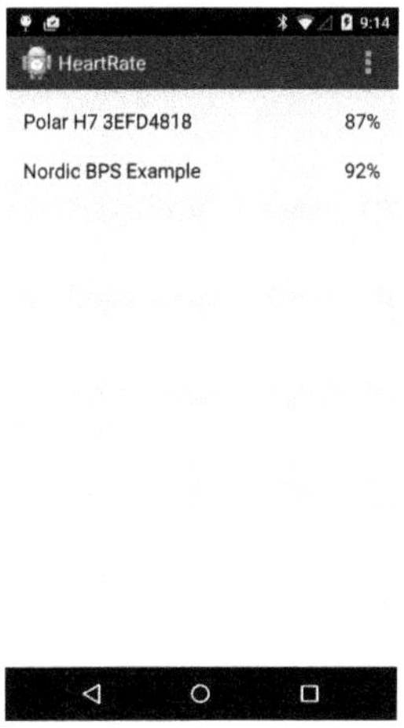

Figure 10: The battery monitor app can read the battery state of all connected Bluetooth Low Energy peripherals. It does not interfere with other applications accessing the same peripherals and it does not have access to other services.

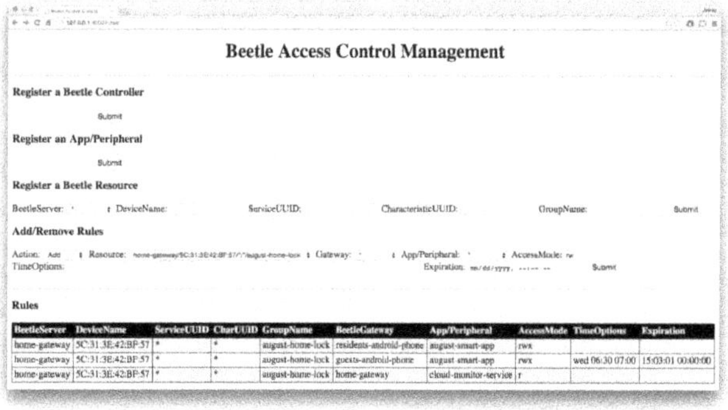

Figure 11: The access control policy web interface, with separate rules specified regarding residents, guests, and cloud-monitor for the August door lock.

fers from the scan request that the app might want access to the battery service across all devices. It prompts the user to approve the scan and provides the option to pre-approve restricted access to the battery service for any peripheral rather than have to approve each peripheral separately.

Once the user approves the scan request, Beetle first returns currently connected peripherals to the app. It also initiates an actual Bluetooth Low Energy scan, and continues to return unconnected peripherals to the app. Our dashboard app wants to be notified of all peripherals, even those that might connect in the future, so it does not explicitly stop the scan. Beetle automatically times out the scan on the radio after ten seconds, but if new matching peripherals are connected (e.g. by other apps) Beetle will return them to the dashboard app as well.

As soon as the dashboard app begins receiving peripherals in response to its scan request, it requests access to them from Beetle. If the user pre-approved access to the battery-service on all peripherals, Beetle does not need to prompt the user for each one and automatically exposes the battery service for each requested peripheral to the app. Otherwise, the user is prompted to approve access for each peripheral. Once the app gets access to a peripheral it subscribes to the battery level notification and updates an entry in the UI for the peripheral appropriately.

5.1.3 *Generic Home Gateway*

Many Bluetooth Low Energy enabled devices in the home require a proprietary gateway to make them accessible, e.g., over the Internet. Usually this is done to enable connectivity through a more power intensive link, such as WiFi or LTE. For example, the August smart lock uses the August Connect (a wall plug with WiFi and Bluetooth) to allow users to monitor the lock remotely. Similarly, the Lively watch (a medical alert smart-watch) comes with a dedicated gateway that bridges the Bluetooth Low Energy watch to Lively servers over the mobile phone network. One of the primary goals of Beetle is to remove reliance on different gateways for each device by directly forwarding GATT over non-Bluetooth links, like TCP, and providing a generic access control interface.

To evaluate our design we used Beetle to bridge an August lock with Android phones over a wireless network. We deploy a Beetle enabled Linux-based gateway machine near the lock that connects to the lock over Bluetooth Low Energy as well as to the local WiFi network. Users can connect their Beetle enabled Android phones to the door lock over TCP using the Android Beetle interface. The gateway exports the lock's GATT services over each TCP connection and Beetle running on the user's phone, in turn, re-exports the device to apps running locally—in this case, the August lock app.

Administrators grant access to different users through a general interface on the gateway. In our gateway, we use a browser based administrative interface, similar to most home WiFi routers. However, other common administrative interfaces, such as configuration files, are possible.

In the case of a door lock, there are three kinds of relevant access control rules, all of which are supported by Beetle.

1. *Residents* are people who should have full access to the lock at any time.

2. *Guests* should get full access to the lock, but only for a limited period of time.

3. *Monitors* are remote services that can monitor the state of the lock, but should not be able to lock or unlock it. For example, a cloud service might alert users via SMS when a door is unlocked at certain times during the day.

5.2 Performance

Performance is not a main goal of Beetle. However, it is nonetheless important that Beetle does not hurt performance in legacy applications and that performance for new applications is acceptable. In some cases, Beetle presents opportunities for better performance over alternative designs. We evaluated Beetle experimentally and present the results along with a discussion of ways in which to improve performance. In particular, we were concerned with round-trip latency in a multi-hop Bluetooth Low Energy network in addition to throughput and tail latency when multiple applications access the same peripheral concurrently.

We used three kinds of hardware for all of our experiments:

1. The `nrf8001` [18] Bluetooth Low Energy IC connected to an Arduino Uno [8] application controller. The `nrf8001` is a peripheral-only Bluetooth Low Energy radio. It communicates with the Arduino over an SPI bus using a high-level, proprietary protocol.

2. The `nrf51822` [19] is a Bluetooth Low Energy enabled, ARM Cortex-M0 [1] SoC. The `nrf51822` can act as both a peripheral and controller and exposes a relatively low-level Bluetooth Low Energy interface to the application controller. The ARM Cortex-M0 allowed us to perform high-resolution timing measurements on peripheral hardware.

3. A desktop with an Intel i7 quad-core CPU, 16GB of RAM and on-motherboard Bluetooth Low Energy hardware which served as our controller.

Bluetooth Low Energy performance is dominated by the connection interval—the frequency at which two connected Bluetooth Low Energy devices exchange data. Since the minimum connection interval is relatively high ($7.5ms$) the overhead of Beetle is negligible. We measured the latency between a Linux gateway application and a peripheral using connection intervals between $7.5ms$ and $960ms$, with random delays between requests. We sampled 30 requests for each interval with and without Beetle.

The average latencies were within one standard deviation of each other. For the lowest connection interval, $7.5ms$, request latency averaged $14.25ms$ ($\pm 3.52ms$) with Beetle and $13.35ms$ ($\pm 2.63ms$) without. For a $120ms$ interval, Beetle averaged $199.2ms$ ($\pm 43ms$) versus $206.4ms$ ($\pm 44.4ms$). Overall, latency averaged 1.7 times the connection interval, both with and without Beetle, with a slightly higher variance for Beetle (0.45 versus 0.37). We believe most of the variance is due to the timing of requests relative to the next connection event.

5.3 Round-trip Latency

An exception is when Beetle is used to bridge two peripheral devices. Each peripheral device's connection events with the central Beetle node occur independently. As a result, Beetle must queue a request from one peripheral to the other for the time between the two connection events.

We measured the round-trip latencies for different connection intervals in two scenarios, in both cases using the Arduino with `nrf8001` to service requests. First, we used the desktop as a client connected directly to the `nrf8001`, simulating two end-devices connected directly to each other. We also measured the round-trip latency of sending requests from a second peripheral, the `nrf51822`, with both peripherals connected to Beetle on the desktop. In both cases we performed read requests since the `nrf8001` serves those directly rather than pass them up to the Arduino. Thus we avoided measuring the cost of the SPI bus communication – which would have minimized the impact of Beetle.

We found in a single hop connection, it takes between one and two connection intervals to serve a request. This is probably due to a combination of the time spent queuing the request on the client until the next connection event and processing time on the server to serve the request.

Conversely, the overhead of adding a hop through a Beetle node is twice the round-trip latency of a single hop when the connection interval is short, and up to three times when the connection interval is long. For example, with a connection interval of 15 ms, the average round-trip time on a single hop was 26.1 ms, while with Beetle it was 58 ms. With a connection interval of 960 ms the round trip time with Beetle was 3.7 seconds versus 1.4 seconds without Beetle. Of course, peripheral-to-peripheral communication is not currently possible in Bluetooth Low Energy without an intermediate Beetle node.

We believe that most of the increase in latency is due to poor coordination of each peripheral's connection events. Currently, Beetle does nothing to manage connection timings. However, if the server's connection events were timed to occur just before and just after the client's connection events, Beetle Beetle could pass the request and response along immediately, reducing the time spent queuing. Unfortunately, this would require changes to the Bluetooth hardware on the central device to expose timing decisions to Beetle. We believe this is an interesting avenue for further research and are working on custom Bluetooth Low Energy firmware for the `nrf51822` that would enable such functionality.

5.4 Multi-application Throughput

Bluetooth Low Energy supports a limited number of data exchanges per connection event (typically 1 to 6). As a result, multiple apps accessing the same peripheral device will be unable to, naively, achieve linear increases in throughput. We evaluated the impact on throughput in the worst case (where each request from an app *must* be forwarded to the peripheral) as well as in cases like cacheable read requests or notifications, where Beetle can achieve linear throughput despite hardware restrictions.

In our experiments, we used one `nrf8001` as the GATT server with a connection interval of 25 ms connected to a desktop running Beetle and between one and 180 client applications issuing requests in a closed loop. For uncacheable commands (`WRITE` commands), overall throughput is constant at 39 queries per second (just under one command per connection event). Conversely, cacheable reads scaled linearly with the number of clients, reaching 7092 queries per second for 180 clients (just under one request per client per connection event).

6. RELATED WORK

The Bluetooth Low Energy protocol specification is large and complex, almost 3000 pages long. We have explained only a small number of pertinent details on how the protocol works. For example, we did not discuss its security model and the implications for Beetle. Curious readers can read more in several good overviews [10, 7] or the specification itself [5].

There has been extensive prior work on flexible network architectures for IP networks and some for Bluetooth Low Energy. In addition, existing operating systems have added some provisions to allow more flexibile communication with Bluetooth Low Energy peripherals in particular classes of applications. We summarize some of the work in both cases.

REST [9] describes the architectural principals underpinning the World Wide Web. Bluetooth Low Energy adheres to some of REST's principals, such the client-server model. Beetle shares a philosophical motivation with REST but differs in technical details. Beetle draws on principals of REST, specifically statelesness and cachable resources, to extend

Bluetooth Low Energy support in the operating system. Most notably, Beetle adds a layered system on top of Bluetooth Low Energy, where clients do not necessarily know if they are directly connected to the server or through a virtual device. Unlike REST, Beetle does not allow servers to extend the functionality of clients through code extensions.

Zachariah et al. [25] point out the need to use gateway devices to connect Bluetooth Low Energy peripherals to the broader internet. Beetle focuses on compatibility with existing peripherals as well as on communication between peripherals. Moreover, their security and access control model focuses on protecting the gateway while Beetle's protects peripheral devices.

Discovery systems like multicast DNS (mDNS) [6] and Universal Plug and Play (UPnP) [22] allow peers on an IP network to advertise and discover services (e.g. a printer) in a decentralized fashion. Clients reach discovered services directly over IP and use out-of-band means for authentication or access control (e.g. Kerberos, SSL). Bluetooth Low Energy peripherals cannot communicate directly and have no means of multi-client authentication or access control of. Beetle addresses all three problems (service discovery, many-to-many communication and access control) by allowing the controller to act as a mediator.

Android's Google Fit and iOS's HealthKit allow applications to access health and fitness related data, including from Bluetooth Low Energy connected heart rate monitors and pedometers. While these systems enable sharing of these devices in a safe manner, they are restricted to a narrow use case and they do not allow access to other services on of the peripherals like the battery level or unsupported sensors (e.g. body temperature).

Early research in sensor networks and ultra-low power wireless networks concluded that the connection-oriented nature of Bluetooth was a poor fit [12]. These networks, however, focused on multi-hop wireless meshes, which forced nodes to simultaneously be centrals and peripherals. Personal area networks, in contrast, fit well with Bluetooth's single-hop communication model. The emergence of proximity networks and Bluetooth Low Energy's dominance of them suggests that it is worth revisiting this decade-old conclusion.

7. LIMITATIONS & FUTURE WORK

While our results our encouraging there are several important limitations and avenues for future work. First, as noted in Section 3, Beetle cannot currently handle peripherals that do not conform to GATT's transactional semantics. In particular a GATT server where the ordering of writes to one attribute would affect the value read from another could not be exposed directly to multiple applications. For such devices, users can give one application exclusive access to that attribute and that application could re-expose the peripheral as a virtual device in an device-specific, safe manner.

Beetle's access control design assumes that users can easily name both peripherals and applications. All peripherals have addresses which are (statistically) unique but not human-readable and human readable names that are likely to collide. For example, all August locks are named "August 57". Furthermore, both addresses and names are forgeable, so it is up to the user to verify that the device they are connecting to is in fact the one named in their policy. On the other side of the connection, while Android has a notion of an application (each application gets a unique user ID), Linux does not. As a result, our implementation of Beetle on Linux can enforce access control policies on users running particular processes, but not on applications.

8. CONCLUSION

Beetle allows the operating system to provide a generic interface to Bluetooth Low Energy peripherals while satisfying our three goals:

1. **sharing** access to peripherals between multiple applications
2. fined grained **access control**, and
3. **many-to-many communication** between Bluetooth Low Energy peripherals.

Beetle is able to achieve these goals by leveraging three important properties of the GATT protocol. First, the GATT protocol is used by all Bluetooth Low Energy peripherals, regardless of their particular function, allowing Beetle to interpose on the communication between apps and peripherals without understanding the content of the communication. Second, the transactional nature of GATT means that retaining atomicity of individual commands is sufficient to provide isolation for the majority of peripherals. Finally, the GATT naming hierarchy of devices, services and characteristics allow peripherals to describe their functionality directly to applications.

We demonstrated the feasibility of Beetle by building prototype implementations for Android and Linux. Using these prototypes, we built three applications that are simple, but nonetheless impossible today. We also evaluated the performance of Beetle and demonstrated that virtualizing Bluetooth Low Energy connections at the application layer does not significantly limit performance.

By transforming Bluetooth Low Energy from a star topology to one in which peripherals can communicate, Beetle elevates it from a link-layer to a network-layer abstraction, with controllers routing data at the application level. This forwarding model resembles virtual circuits, giving a router explicit knowledge of each flow that might pass through it. This is a good thing: the security implications of Internet-style default-on connectivity could have disastrous implications to personal devices that are continually coming into range of potential new attackers. Beetle's properties suggest some ways in which the constraints and technologies of "Internet of Things" may lead it to differ from the Internet of today.

Acknowledgments

We would like to thank Jason Flinn, David Mazières, David Terei and the anonymous reviewers for their thoughtful comments. This work was supported by Intel/NSF CPS Security grant #1505728, the Secure Internet of Things Project, and gifts from VMware and Analog Devices International.

9. REFERENCES

[1] ARM. Arm cortex-m0 product specification, 2014.

[2] BASIS SCIENCE INC. Basis health tracker. http://www.mybasis.com/, Sept. 2014.

[3] Beutel, J., and Krasnyanskiy, M. Linux bluez howto, 2014.

[4] Bluetooth SIG. Battery service specification, Dec. 2011.

[5] Bluetooth SIG. Bluetooth core specification 4.1, December 2013.

[6] Cheshire, S., and Krochmal, M. Multicast dns. RFC 6762, IEFT, Feb. 2013.

[7] Decuir, J. Introducing bluetooth smart: Part ii: Applications and updates. *Consumer Electronics Magazine, IEEE 3*, 2 (April 2014), 25–29.

[8] DÂĂŹAusilio, A. Arduino: A low-cost multipurpose lab equipment. *Behavior research methods 44*, 2 (2012), 305–313.

[9] Fielding, R. T. *Architectural Styles and the Design of Network-based Software Architectures*. PhD thesis, University of California, Irvine, 2000. AAI9980887.

[10] Gomez, C., Oller, J., and Paradells, J. Overview and evaluation of bluetooth low energy: An emerging low-power wireless technology. *Sensors 12*, 9 (2012), 11734–11753.

[11] Kwikset. Door locks. http://www.kwikset.com/kevo/default.aspx, Sept. 2014.

[12] Leopold, M., Dydensborg, M. B., and Bonnet, P. Bluetooth and sensor networks: A reality check. In *Proceedings of the 1st International Conference on Embedded Networked Sensor Systems* (New York, NY, USA, 2003), SenSys '03, ACM, pp. 103–113.

[13] OneTouch. Veriosync blood glucose meter. http://www.onetouch.com/veriosync, Mar. 2015.

[14] Pear. Pear mobile bluetooth heart rate monitor. http://pearsports.com/shop/pear-bluetooth-heart-rate-strap.html, Mar. 2015.

[15] Pebble, I. Pebble Smartwatch. https://getpebble.com, Mar. 2015.

[16] Phillips. HUE: Personal Wireless Lighting. http://www2.meethue.com/en-us/, Mar. 2015.

[17] ReelSonar. Fish finders. http://reelsonar.com/, Sept. 2014.

[18] Semi, N. nrf8001 single-chip bluetooth bluetooth low energy product specification 1.2, 2013.

[19] Semi, N. nrf51822 product specification, 2014.

[20] Seraphim Sense Ltd. Angel Sensor - Open Mobile Health Wearable. http://angelsensor.com, Apr. 2016.

[21] Strava. Running and cycling gps tracker, performance analytics, maps, clubs and competition. https://www.strava.com, Mar. 2015.

[22] UPnP Forum Technical Committee. Upnp device architecture v1.0, Sept. 2014.

[23] USA, P. H7 heart rate sensor. http://www.polar.com/us-en/products/accessories/H7_heart_rate_sensor, Mar. 2015.

[24] Wilson Basketball. Smart basketballs. http://www.wilson.com/smart/, Sept. 2014.

[25] Zachariah, T., Klugman, N., Campbell, B., Adkins, J., Jackson, N., and Dutta, P. The internet of things has a gateway problem. In *Proceedings of the 16th International Workshop on Mobile Computing Systems and Applications* (New York, NY, USA, 2015), HotMobile '15, ACM, pp. 27–32.

MCDNN: An Approximation-Based Execution Framework for Deep Stream Processing Under Resource Constraints

Seungyeop Han* University of Washington

Haichen Shen* University of Washington

Matthai Philipose Microsoft Research

Sharad Agarwal Microsoft Research

Alec Wolman Microsoft Research

Arvind Krishnamurthy University of Washington

ABSTRACT

We consider applying computer vision to video on cloud-backed mobile devices using Deep Neural Networks (DNNs). The computational demands of DNNs are high enough that, without careful resource management, such applications strain device battery, wireless data, and cloud cost budgets. We pose the corresponding resource management problem, which we call *Approximate Model Scheduling*, as one of serving a stream of heterogeneous (i.e., solving multiple classification problems) requests under resource constraints. We present the design and implementation of an optimizing compiler and runtime scheduler to address this problem. Going beyond traditional resource allocators, we allow each request to be served *approximately*, by systematically trading off DNN classification accuracy for resource use, and *remotely*, by reasoning about on-device/cloud execution trade-offs. To inform the resource allocator, we characterize how several common DNNs, when subjected to state-of-the art optimizations, trade off accuracy for resource use such as memory, computation, and energy. The heterogeneous streaming setting is a novel one for DNN execution, and we introduce two new and powerful DNN optimizations that exploit it. Using the challenging continuous mobile vision domain as a case study, we show that our techniques yield significant reductions in resource usage and perform effectively over a broad range of operating conditions.

1. INTRODUCTION

Over the past three years, Deep Neural Networks (DNNs) have become the dominant approach to solving a variety of computing problems such as speech recognition, machine translation, handwriting recognition, and computer vision problems such as face, object and scene recognition. Although they are renowned for their excellent recognition performance, DNNs are also known to be computationally intensive: networks commonly used for speech, visual and language understanding tasks routinely consume hundreds of MB of memory and GFLOPS of computing power [30, 46], typically the province of servers (Table 1). However, given the relevance of such applications to the mobile setting, there is a strong case for executing DNNs on mobile devices. In this paper, we present a framework for executing *multiple* applications that use large DNNs on (intermittently) cloud-connected mobile devices to process *streams* of data such as video and speech. We target high-end mobile-GPU-accelerated devices, but our techniques are useful broadly. We require little specialized knowledge of DNNs from the developer.

	face [46]	scene [52]	object [44]
training time (days)	3	6	14-28
memory (floats)	103M	76M	138M
compute (FLOPs)	1.00G	2.54G	30.9G
accuracy (%)	97	51	94

Table 1: Although DNNs deliver state-of-the art classification accuracy on many recognition tasks, this functionality comes at very high memory (space shown is to store an active model) and computational cost (to execute a model on a *single* image window).

Recent work has attacked the overhead of DNNs from several directions. For high-value scenarios such as speech and object recognition, researchers have crafted efficient DNNs by hand [32, 42, 45] or structured them for execution on efficient co-processors such as DSPs (for smaller DNNs) [31]. In the somewhat longer term, work from the hardware community on custom accelerators seems very promising [11]. An intermediate approach that is both automatic and effective is what we term *model optimization*, which are techniques that apply automatically to any DNN and reduce memory [13, 22, 50, 51] and processing demands [25, 42] of DNNs, typically at the cost of some classification accuracy. These efforts have yielded promising results: it is possible to generate models that sacrifice a modest amount of classification accuracy (e.g., 1-3%) that are small enough to fit comfortably in mobile memories (e.g., 10× reduction in space used) and can be executed in real time (e.g., 3× reduction processing demands) on a mobile GPU.

MCDNN considers applying model optimization to the multi-programmed, streaming setting. We anticipate that in the near future, multiple applications will seek to run multiple DNNs on incoming high-datarate sensor streams such as video, audio, depth and thermal video. The large number of simultaneous DNNs in operation and the high frequency of their use will strain available resources, even when optimized models are used. We use two insights to address this problem. First, model optimization typically allows a graceful tradeoff between accuracy and resource use. Thus, a system could adapt to high workloads by using less accurate variants of optimized models. Second, both streaming and multi programming themselves provide additional structure that enable powerful new model optimizations. For instance, streams often have strong temporal locality (e.g., a few classes dominate output for stretches of time), and queries from

*Both authors contributed equally to this work.

MobiSys'16, June 25-30, 2016, Singapore, Singapore

© 2016 ACM. ISBN 978-1-4503-4269-8/16/06... $15.00

DOI: http://dx.doi.org/10.1145/2906388.2906396

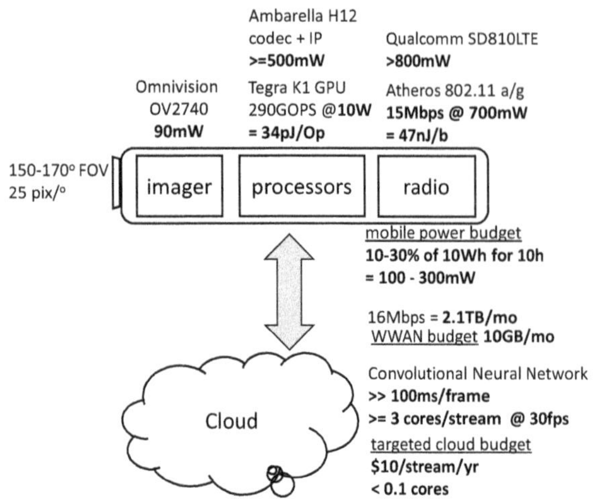

Figure 1: Basic components of a continuous mobile vision system.

multiple programs on the same stream may have semantic similarity that allows sharing of computation.

We formulate the problem of adaptively selecting model variants of differing accuracy in order to remain within per-request resource constraints (e.g., memory) and long-term constraints (e.g., energy) while maximizing average classification accuracy as a constrained optimization problem we call *Approximate Model Scheduling (AMS)*. To solve AMS, MCDNN contains three innovations. First, we generate optimized variants of models by automatically applying a variety of model optimization techniques with different settings. We record accuracy, memory use, execution energy, and execution latency of each variant to form a *catalog* for each model. Second, we introduce two new model optimizations, specialization and sharing, that are designed to take advantage of streaming and multi-programming respectively. Finally, we provide a heuristic scheduling algorithm for solving AMS that allocates resources proportionally to their frequency of use and uses the catalog to select the most accurate corresponding model variant.

As a running case study, and for purposes of evaluation, we target the continuous mobile vision setting: in particular, we look at enabling a large suite of DNN-based face, scene and object processing algorithms based on applying DNNs to video streams from (potentially wearable) devices. We consider continuous vision one of the most challenging settings for mobile DNNs, and therefore regard it as an adequate evaluation target. We evaluate MCDNN on very large standard datasets available from the computer vision community. Our results show that MCDNN can make effective trade-offs between resource utilization and accuracy (e.g., transform models to use 4× fewer FLOPs and roughly 5× less memory at 1-4% loss in accuracy), share models across DNNs with significant savings (e.g., 1-4 orders of magnitude less memory use and 1.2-100× less compute/energy), effectively specialize models to various contexts (e.g., specialize models with 5-25× less compute, two orders of magnitude less storage, and still achieve accuracy gains), and schedule computations across both mobile and cloud devices for diverse operating conditions (e.g., disconnected operation, low resource availability, and varying number of applications). To the best of our knowledge, MCDNN is the first system to examine how to apply DNNs efficiently to streams.

2. CONTINUOUS MOBILE VISION

Continuous mobile vision (CMV) refers to the setting in which a user wears a device that includes a continuously-on (we target ten hours of continuous operation) camera that covers their field of view [6, 19, 37, 39, 47]. The device is often a custom wearable such as Google Glass, but possibly just a mobile phone in a pocket. Video footage from the camera is analyzed, typically in real time, using computer vision techniques to infer information relevant to the user. While current systems are research efforts aimed at key niche applications such as cognitive assistance for the elderly and navigational assistance for the blind, in the near future we anticipate a *multi-programming* setting aimed at the general consumer, where multiple applications issue distinct queries simultaneously on the incoming stream. For example, various applications may need to recognize what the wearer eats, who they interact with, what objects they are handling as part of a task, the affect of the people they interact with and the attributes of the place they are in. In this section, we introduce the resources involved in such a system and motivate careful resource management via controlling the overhead of Deep Neural Network (DNN) execution.

Video processing itself usually involves some combination of *detecting* regions of interest in each frame (e.g., faces, pedestrians or objects), *tracking* the trajectory of detected regions across time and *recognizing* the detailed identities and attributes of these regions (e.g., recognizing the identity of people and objects interacted with). Although traditionally detection and tracking have been performed with relatively lightweight algorithms, state-of-the-art variants of these are switching to Deep Neural Networks (DNNs) [29, 33]. More recent work has begun to integrate detection and recognition using DNNs [41]. Since detection and tracking computations are expected to be performed frequently (e.g., a few times a second), we expect DNNs to be applied several times to many of the video frames. We therefore view DNN execution as the bulk of modern vision computation.

Figure 1 sketches the architecture of a state-of-the-art mobile/cloud Continuous Mobile Vision (CMV) system. The two main physical components are a battery-powered mobile device (typically some combination of a phone and a wearable) and powered computing infrastructure (some combination of a cloudlet and the deep cloud). The camera on the wearable device must usually capture a large field of view at high resolution and moderate frame rate. A resolution of 4k (4096×2160 pixels) at 15 frames per second is not unreasonable[1], drawing 90mW from a modern imager.

Consider performing all vision in the cloud, a "pure off-loading" architecture. For high-resolution video, spending 0.5W on compression and 0.7-1W on wireless offload is conservative, yielding a total average power draw of 1.3 to 1.6W for imaging, compression and communication. A realistic 100× compression yields a 16Mbps stream (= 4096×2160×15×1.5×8, using the 1.5 byte-per-pixel YUV representation), or roughly 2.1TB per month at 10 hours usage per day. Finally, we assume a conservative 1 DNN application per frame (we expect that, in practice, applications may run multiple DNNs on incoming frames). Additionally assuming a conservative 100ms execution latency (we have measured 300-2000ms latencies for models commonly in use) for a DNN on a single CPU, keeping up with 15-30fps will require *at least* 1.5-3 cores, and often many times more.

In comparison, a large 3Ah mobile phone battery of today yields roughly 1.2W over 10 hours. Further, today's consumer mobile plans cap data use at 10GB per month. Finally, continuous use of the required cores will cost roughly $150-300 per year[2]; more realistic workloads could easily be 10 times as costly. Offloading *all* data for cloud-processing using maximally accurate DNNs would thus probably only be practical in usages with a large dedicated wearable battery, lightly subscribed WiFi connection (thus limiting mobility) and substantial cloud budget. One path to reducing these resource

[1]Better vertical coverage (e.g., 4096×4096 pixels total) would be preferable, perhaps from *two* standard high-resolution imagers.

[2]Assuming a 3-year upfront lease on a C4.large machine from Amazon EC2. GPU-based costs are at least as high.

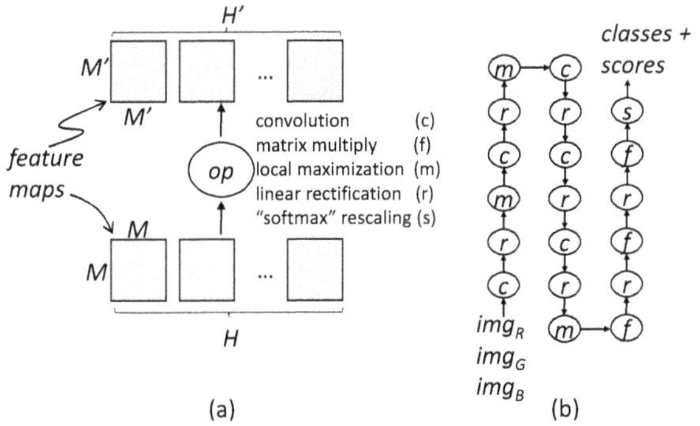

Figure 2: (a) DNN "layers" are array operations on lists of arrays called feature maps. (b) A state-of-the-art network for scene recognition, formed by connecting layers.

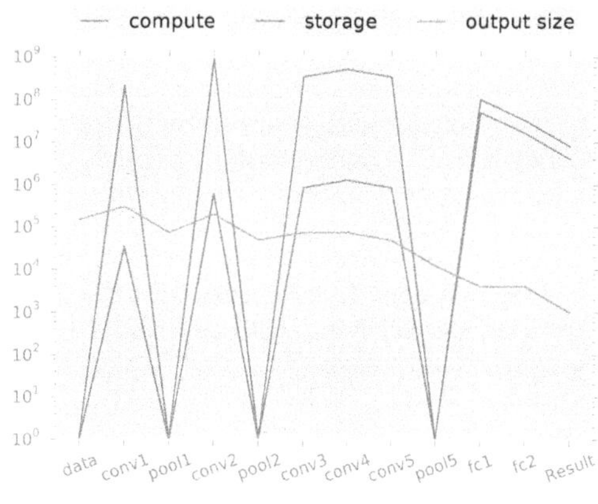

Figure 3: Resource usage of AlexNet across layers (note log scale).

demands is to reduce the amount of data transmitted by executing "more lightweight" DNN calculations (e.g. detection and tracking) on the device and only transmitting heavier calculations (e.g., recognition) to the cloud. Once at the cloud, reducing the overhead of (DNN) computations can support more modest cloud budgets.

Now consider performing vision computations on the device. Such local computation may be *necessary* during the inevitable disconnections from the cloud, or just *preferable* in order to reduce data transmission power and compute overhead. For simplicity, let us focus on the former ("purely local") case. Video encoding and communication overhead would now be replaced (at least partially) by computational overhead. Given mobile CPU execution speeds (several seconds of execution latency for standard DNNs), we focus on using mobile GPUs such as the NVIDIA Tegra K1 [3], which supports 300GFLOPS peak at a 10W *whole-system-wide* power draw. We time DNN execution on the K1 to take 100ms (for the "AlexNet" object recognition model) to 900ms (for "VGGNet"). Handling the aforementioned conservative processing rate of 1 DNN computation per frame at 15-30fps would require 1.5-30 mobile GPUs, which amounts to 15-300W of mobile power draw on the Jetson board for the K1 GPU. Even assuming a separate battery, a roughly 1-1.2W continuous power draw is at the high end of what is reasonable. Thus, it is important to substantially reduce the execution overhead of DNNs on mobile GPUs.

To summarize, significantly reducing the execution costs of DNNs can enable CMV in several ways. Allowing detection and tracking to run on the mobile devices while infrequently shipping to cloud can make transmission power and data rates manageable. Reducing the cost of execution in the cloud can make dollar costs more attractive. Allowing economical purely local execution maintains CMV service when back-end connectivity is unavailable. Finally, if execution costs are lowered far enough, pure local execution may become the default.

3. DEEP NEURAL NETWORKS

We now examine Deep Neural Networks, specifically the most commonly used variant called Convolutional Neural Networks (CNNs) in some detail. Our goal is to convey the basic structure of CNNs, their resource consumption patterns, the main current proposals for optimizing their resource consumption and further opportunities opened by streaming, multi-programmed settings.

3.1 Model structure

A CNN can be viewed as a dataflow graph where the nodes, or *layers*, are array-processing operations (see Figure 2(a)). Each layer takes as input a set of arrays (called *feature maps*), performs an array operation on them, and outputs a set of feature maps that will in turn be processed by downstream layers. The array operations belong to a small set, including matrix multiplication (that multiplies feature maps by a weight matrix), convolution (that convolves inputs by a convolution kernel, typically of size 3×3 or 5×5), max-pooling (that replaces each input array value by the maximum of its neighbors), non-linearizing (that replaces each array value by a non-linear function of itself) and re-scaling (that re-scales inputs to sum to 1). Figure 2(b) shows how layers are connected in a typical CNN: groups of convolution, pooling and non-linearizing layers are repeated several times before 1-2 matrix-multiplication (or *fully connected*) layers are applied, ended by re-scaling.

The matrix multiplication and convolution layers are parameterized by weight arrays that are estimated from training data. The network description before training is called a *model architecture*, and the trained network with weights instantiated is a *model*. Training DNNs takes several days to weeks. Unlike recent systems work in CNNs [15, 17], we are not concerned here with the efficient *learning* of CNNs, but rather, their efficient *execution*. Most CNNs today tend to be linear [30, 44], but DAGs [45] and loopy graphs, known as Recurrent Neural Networks (RNNs) [27], which are fully unrolled over incoming data before execution, have also been considered. We focus on linear networks below, but our techniques are applicable to others.

Figure 3 shows resource usage per layer for AlexNet, a representative architecture originally proposed for object recognition, but now used as the basis for other tasks such a scene recognition as well. For each layer on the x-axis, the y-axis (note the log scale) reports the number of operations to execute the layer (labeled "compute"), the number of floats to represent the layer ("storage") and the number of intermediate floats generated by the layer ("output size"). Two points are key to optimizing resource usage:

1. Memory use is dominated by the weight matrix of the matrix multiplication layers (labeled "fc" for fully connected). Convolutional kernels and even intermediate data size are small in comparison.
2. Computational overhead is dominated by convolution operations, exceeding matrix multiplication overhead by an order of magnitude, with negligible overheads for pooling and non-linearization.

3.2 Model optimization

Recent *model optimization* techniques for reducing resource use in DNNs have targeted these opportunities in three main ways:

1. *Matrix factorization* replaces the weight matrices and convolution kernels by their low-rank approximations[3] [25, 28, 42, 50]. Replacing a size-$M \times M$ weight matrix $W_{M\times M}$ with its singular value decomposition $U_{M\times k}V_{k\times M}$ reduces storage overhead from M^2 to $2Mk$ and computational overhead from M^3 to $2M^2k$. The

[3]Convolution is implemented as matrix multiplication [10].

most recent results [28] have reported reductions of 5.5× in memory use and 2.7× in FLOPs at a loss of 1.7% accuracy for the "AlexNet" model we use for scene recognition and 1.2×, 4.9× and 0.5% for the "VGG16" model we use for object recognition.

2. *Matrix pruning* [13, 22] sparsifies matrices by zeroing very small values, use low-bitwidth representations for remaining non-zero values and use compressed (e.g., Huffman coded) representations for these values. The most recent results [22] report 11/8× reduction in model size and 3/5× reduction on FLOPs for AlexNet/VGGNet, while sacrificing essentially no accuracy. However, for instance, sacrificing 2% points of accuracy can improve memory size reduction to 20×.
3. *Architectural changes* [44] explore the space of model architectures, including varying the number of layers, size of weight matrices including kernels, etc. For instance, reducing the number of layers from 19 to 11 results in a drop in accuracy of 4.1% points.

A common theme across these techniques is the trading off of resource use for accuracy. When applied to the distributed, streaming, multi-programmed setting of MCDNN, several related questions present themselves. What is the "best" level of approximation for any model, at any given time, given that many other models must also execute at limited energy and dollar budgets? Where (device or cloud) should this model execute? Do the streaming and multi-programming settings present opportunities for new kinds of optimizations? To clarify the issues involved, we first capture these questions in a formal problem definition below and then describe MCDNN's solution.

4. APPROXIMATE MODEL SCHEDULING

Given a stream of requests to execute models of various types, MCDNN needs to pick (and possibly generate), at each timestep, an approximate variant of these models and a location (device or cloud) to execute it in. These choices must satisfy both long-term (e.g., day-long) budget constraints regarding total energy and dollar budgets over many requests, and short-term capacity constraints (e.g., memory and processing-cycle availability). We call this problem the *approximate model scheduling (AMS)* problem and formalize it below.

4.1 Fractional packing and paging

In formalizing AMS, we are guided by the literature on online paging and packing. Our problem may be viewed as a distributed combination of online fractional packing and paging problems.

The standard fractional packing problem [8] seeks to *maximize* a linear sum of variables while allowing upper bounds on other linear sums of the same variables. In AMS, the assumption is that when some model is requested to be executed at a time step, we have the option of choosing to execute an arbitrary "fraction" of that model. In practice, this fraction is a variant of the model that has accuracy and resource use that are fractional with respect to the "best" model. These fractions x_t at each time step t are our variables. Assuming for the moment a linear relation between model fraction and accuracy, we have average accuracy over all time steps proportional to $\sum_t a_t x_t$, where a_t is the accuracy of the best model for request t. Finally, suppose one-time resource-use cost (e.g. energy, cloud cost) is proportional to the fraction of the model used, with e_t the resource use of the best variant of the model requested at t. A resource budget E over all time steps gives the upper-bound constraint $\sum_t e_t x_t \leq E$. Maximizing average accuracy under budget constraints of this form gives a packing problem.

The weighted paging problem [7] addresses a sequence of t requests, each for one of M pages. Let $x_{mj} \in [0,1]$ indicate what fraction of page m was evicted in between its ith and $i+1$th requests. The goal is to *minimize* over t requests the total number of (weighted) paging events $\sum_{mj} c_t x_{mj}$. At the same time, we must ensure *at every time step* that cache capacity is not exceeded: if k is cache size and R_{mt} is the number of requests for model m up to time t and N_t is the total number of requests in this time, we require $\forall_t N_t - \sum_m x_{mR_{mt}} \leq k$. If x's are once again interpreted as fractional models and c_i represent energy costs, this formulation minimizes day-long energy costs of paging while respecting cache capacity.

Finally, new to the AMS setting, the model may be executed either on the local device or in the cloud. The two settings have different constraints (e.g., devices have serious power and memory constraints), whereas cloud execution is typically constrained by dollars and device-to-cloud communication energy.

The *online* variant of the above problems requires that optimization be performed incrementally at each time step. For instance, which model is requested at time t, and therefore the identity of coefficient e_t is only revealed in timestep t. Fraction x_t must then be computed before $t+1$ (and similarly for c_{mj}, j and x_{mj}). On the other hand the upper bound values (e.g., E) are assumed known before the first step. Recent work based on primal-dual methods has yielded algorithms for these problems that have good behavior in theory and practice.

Below, we use these packing and paging problems as the basis for precise *specification* of AMS. However, the resulting problem does not fall purely into a packing or paging category. Our solution to the problem, described in later sections, is heuristic, albeit based on insights from the theory.

Note that we do not model several possibly relevant effects. The "cache size" may vary across timesteps because, e.g., the machine is being shared with other programs. The cost/accuracy tradeoff may change with context, since models are specializable in some contexts. Sharing across models may mean that some groups of models may cost much less together than as separately. Since different apps may register different models to handle the same input type (e.g., face ID, race and gender models may all be registered to process faces), we have a "multi-paging" scenario where models are loaded in small batches. Although we do not model these effects formally, our heuristic scheduling algorithm is flexible enough to handle them.

4.2 AMS problem definition

Our goal in this section is to provide a precise specification of AMS. We seek a form that maximizes (or minimizes) an objective function under inequalities that restrict the feasible region of optimization.

Assume a device memory of size S, device energy budget E and cloud cost budget of D. Assume a set $\{M_1,...,M_n\}$ of models, where each model M_i has a set V_i of *variants* $\{M_{ij} | n \geq i \geq 1, n_i \geq j \geq 1\}$, typically generated by model optimization. For instance, M_1 may be a model for face recognition, M_2 for object recognition, and so on. Say each variant M_{ij} has size s_{ij}, device paging energy cost e_{ij}, device execution energy cost c_{ij}, device execution latency l_{ij}, cloud execution cost cost d_{ij}, and accuracy a_{ij}. We assume accuracy and paging cost vary monotonically with size. Below, we also consider a continuous version $V_i' = \{M_{ix} | n \geq i \geq 1, x \in [0,1]\}$ of variants, with corresponding costs s_{ix}, e_{ix}, c_{ix}, l_{ix}, d_{ix} and accuracy a_{ix}.

Assume an input request sequence $m_{t_1}, m_{t_2}, ..., m_{t_T}$. Subscripts $t_\tau \in \mathbb{R}$ are timestamps. We call the indexes τ's "timesteps" below. Each m_{t_τ} is a request for model M_i (for some i) at time t_τ. For each request m_{t_τ}, the system must decide *where* (device or cloud) to execute this model. If on-device, it must decide *which variant* M_{ij}, if any, of M_i to load into the cache and execute at timestep t, while also deciding which, if any, models must be evicted from the cache to make space for M_{ij}. Similarly, if on-cloud, it must decide which variant to execute. We use the variables x, y and x' to represent these actions (paging, eviction and cloud execution) as detailed below.

Let $x_{ik} \in [0,1]$ represent the variant of model M_i executed on-device when it is requested for the kth time. Note $x_{ik} = 0$ implies no on-device execution; presumably execution will be in the cloud (see below). Although in practice $x_{ik} \in V_i$, and is therefore a discrete variable, we use a continuous relaxation $x_{ik} \in [0,1]$. In this setting, we interpret x_{ik} as representing the variant $M_{ix_{ik}}$. For model M_i, let τ_{ik} be the timestep it is requested for the kth time, and $n_{i\tau}$ be the number of times it is requested up to (and including) timestep τ. For any timestep τ, let $R(\tau) = \{M_i | n_{i\tau} \geq 1\}$ be the set of models requested up to and including timestep τ.

Let $y_{i\tau} \in [0,1]$ be the fraction of the largest variant M_i^* of M_i evicted in the τ'th timestep. Let $y_i^k = \sum_{\tau=\tau_{ik}}^{\tau_{ik+1}-1} y_{i\tau}$ be the total fraction of M_i^* evicted between its kth and $k+1$th request. Note that a fraction of several models may be evicted at each timestep.

Finally, let $x'_{ik} \in [0,1]$ represent the variant of model M_i executed on the cloud when it is requested for the k-th time. We require that a given request for a model be executed either on device or on cloud, but not both, i.e., that $x'_{ik}x_{ik} = 0$ for all i,k.

Now suppose $x_{i(k-1)}$ and x_{ik} are variants selected to serve the $k-1$th and kth requests for M_i. The energy cost for paging request k is $e_{ix_{ik}}$ if $x_{i(k-1)} \neq x_{ik}$, i.e., a different variant is served than previously, or if M_i was evicted since the last request, i.e., $y_i^{k-1} > 0$. Otherwise, we hit in the cache and the serving cost is zero. Writing $\delta(x) = 0$ if $x = 0$ and 1 otherwise, the energy cost for paging is therefore $e_{ix_{ik}}\delta(|x_{i(k-1)} - x_{ik}| + y_i^{k-1})$. Adding on execution cost c, total on-device energy cost of serving a request is therefore $e_{ix_{ik}}\delta(|x_{i(k-1)} - x_{ik}| + y_i^{k-1}) + c_{ix_{ik}}$.

We can now list the constraints on an acceptable policy (i.e., assignment to x_{ik}'s and $y_{i\tau}$'s). Across all model requests, maximize aggregate accuracy of model variants served,

$$\max_x \sum_{i=1}^{n} \sum_{k=1}^{n_{iT}} a_{ix_{ik}} + a_{ix'_{ik}}, \tag{1}$$

while keeping total on-device energy use within budget:

$$\sum_{i=1}^{n} \sum_{k=1}^{n_{iT}} e_{ix_{ik}}\delta(|x_{i(k-1)} - x_{ik}| + y_i^{k-1}) + c_{ix_{ik}} \leq E, \tag{2}$$

keeping within the cloud cost budget:

$$\sum_{i=1}^{n} \sum_{k=1}^{n_{iT}} d_{ix'_{ik}} \leq D, \tag{3}$$

and at each timestep, not exceeding cache capacity:

$$\forall_{1 \leq \tau \leq T} \sum_{\substack{M_i \in R(\tau) \\ 1 \leq k \leq n_{i\tau}}} s_{ix_{ik}} - \sum_{\substack{M_i \in R(\tau) \\ 1 \leq \tau' \leq \tau}} s_{iy_{i\tau'}} \leq S, \tag{4}$$

ensuring that the selected model variant executes fast enough:

$$\forall_{\substack{1 \leq i \leq n \\ 1 \leq k \leq n_{iT}}} l_{ix_{ik}} \leq t_{\tau_{ik}+1} - t_{\tau_{ik}}, \tag{5}$$

and ensuring various consistency conditions mentioned above:

$$\forall_{\substack{1 \leq i \leq n \\ 1 \leq k \leq n_{iT}}} 0 \leq x_{ik}, x'_{ik}, y_{ik} \leq 1 \text{ and } x_{ik}x'_{ik} = 0 \tag{6}$$

4.3 Discussion

We seek to solve the above optimization problem online. On the surface, AMS looks similar to fractional packing: we seek to maximize the weighted sum of the variables that are introduced in an online fashion, while upper-bounding various weighted combinations of these variables. If we could reduce AMS to packing, we could use the relevant primal-dual scheme [8] to solve the online variant. However, the AMS problem as stated has several key differences from the standard packing setting:

- Most fundamentally, the paging constraint (Equation 4) seeks to impose a cache capacity constraint *for every timestep*. The fractional packing problem strongly requires the number of constraints to be fixed before streaming, and therefore independent of the number of streaming elements.
- The mappings from the fractional size of the model x_{ik} to accuracy ($a_{x_{ik}}$), energy cost ($e_{x_{ik}}$), etc., are left unspecified in AMS. The standard formulation requires these to be linear, e.g, $a_{x_{ik}} = a_i x_{ik}$.
- The standard formulation requires the upper bounds to be independent of timestep. By requiring execution latency at timestep τ_{ik} to be less than the interval $t_{\tau_{ik}+1} - t_{\tau_{ik}}$, AMS introduces a time dependency on the upper bound.
- The mutual exclusion criterion (Equation 6) introduces a non-linearity over the variables.

Given the above wrinkles, it is unclear how to solve AMS with theoretical guarantees. MCDNN instead uses heuristic algorithms motivated by ideas from solutions to packing/paging problems.

Task	Description (# training images, # test images, # class)
V	VGGNet [44] on ImageNet data
A	AlexNet on ImageNet data [18] for object recognition (1.28M, 50K, 1000)
S	AlexNet on MITPlaces205 data [52] for scene recognition (2.45M, 20K, 205)
M	re-labeled S for inferring manmade/natural scenes
L	re-labeled S for inferring natural/aritificially lighting scenes
H	re-labeled S with Sun405 [49] for detecting horizons
D	DeepFaceNet replicating [46] with web-crawled face data (50K, 5K, 200)
Y	re-labeled D for age: 0-30, 30-60, 60+
G	re-labeled D for gender: M, F
R	re-labeled D for race: African American, White, Hispanic, East Asian, South Asian, Other

Table 2: Description of classification tasks.

5. SYSTEM DESIGN

Solving the AMS problem requires two main components. First, the entire notion of approximate model scheduling is predicated on the claim that the models involved allow a useful tradeoff between resource usage and accuracy. Instead of using a single hand-picked approximate variant of a model, MCDNN dynamically picks the most appropriate variant from its *model catalog*. The model catalog characterizes precisely how model optimization techniques of Section 3.2 affect the tradeoffs between accuracy and model-loading energy on device (e_{ix}; Equation 2), model-execution energy on device (c_{ix}; Equation 2), model-execution dollar cost on cloud ($d_{ix'_{ik}}$; Equation 3), model size ($s_{ix_{ik}}$; Equation 4) and model execution latency (l_{ix}; Equation 5). Below, we provide a detailed measurement-based characterization of these tradeoffs. Also, we introduce two new model optimization techniques that exploit the streaming and multi-programming setting introduced by MCDNN. The second component for solving AMS is of course an online algorithm for processing model request streams. We present a heuristically motivated scheduling algorithm below. Finally, we describe briefly the end-to-end system architecture and implementation that incorporates these components.

5.1 Model catalogs

MCDNN generates model catalogs, which are maps from versions of models to their accuracy and resource use, by applying model optimizations to DNNs at varying degrees of optimization. In this section, we focus on applying the popular factorization, pruning and architectural-change approaches described in Section 3.2. MCDNN applies the following traditional techniques:

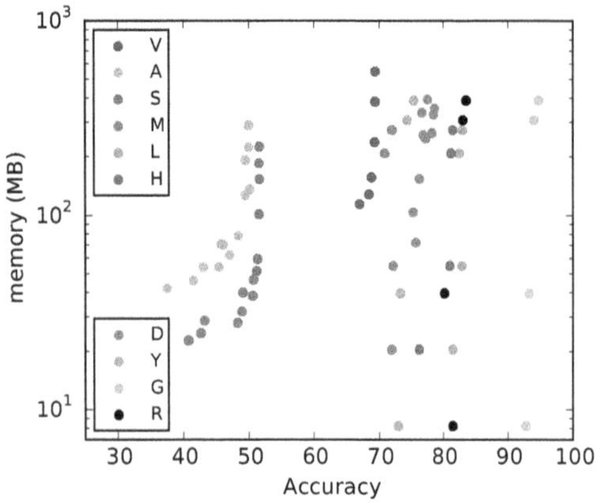

Figure 4: Memory/accuracy tradeoffs in MCDNN catalogs.

Factorization: It replaces size-$m \times n$ weight matrices with their factored variants of sizes $m \times k$ and $k \times n$ for progressively smaller values of k. It typically investigates $k = \frac{n}{2} \ldots \frac{n}{8}$. We factor both matrix multiplication and convolutional layers.
Pruning: It restricts itself to reducing the bit-widths used to represent weights in our models. We consider 32, 16 and 8-bit representations.
Architectural change: There is a wide variety of architectural transformations possible. It concentrates on the following: (1) For convolutional and locally connected layers, increase kernel/stride size or decrease number of kernels, to yield quadratic or linear reduction in computation. (2) For fully connected layers, reduce the size of the output layer to yield a linear reduction in size of the layer. (3) Eliminate convolutional layers entirely.

The individual impact of these optimizations have been reported elsewhere [22, 28, 44]. We focus here on understanding broad features of the tradeoff. For instance, does the accuracy plunge with lowering of resources or does it ramp down gently? Do various gains and trends persist across a large variety of models? How does resource use compare to key mobile budget parameters such as wireless transmission energy and commercial cloud compute costs? How do various options compare with each other: for instance, how does the energy use of model loading compare with that of execution (thus informing on the importance of caching)? Such system-level, cross-technique questions are not typically answered by the model-optimization literature.

To study these questions, we have generated catalogs for ten distinct classification *tasks* (a combination of model architecture and training data, the information a developer would input to MCDNN). We use state-of-the art architectures and standard large datasets when possible, or use similar variants if necessary. The wide variety of tasks hints at the broad utility of DNNs, and partially motivates systems like MCDNN for managing DNNs. Table 2 summarizes the classification tasks we use. For each model in the catalog, we measure average accuracy by executing it on its validation dataset, and resource use via the appropriate tool. We summarize key aspects of these catalogs below.

Figure 4 illustrates the memory/accuracy tradeoff in the MCDNN catalogs corresponding to the above classification tasks. For each classification task, we plot the set of variants produced by the model above optimization techniques in a single color. MCDNN generated 10 to 68 variants of models for various tasks. We show here points along the "Pareto curves" of the catalog i.e. the highest accuracy/lowest memory frontier. Each point in the graph illustrates the average accuracy and memory requirement of a single model variant. Note that the y-axis uses a log scale. Three points are worth noting. First, as observed elsewhere, optimization can significantly reduce resource demands at very modest accuracy loss. For instance, the VGGNet model loses roughly 4% average accuracy while using almost 10× less memory. Second, and perhaps most critically for

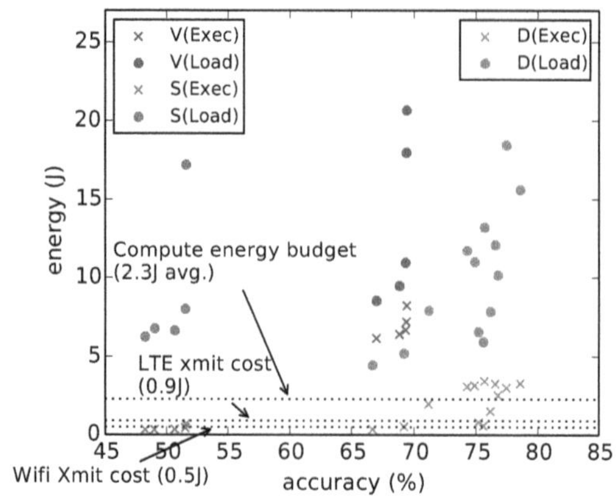

Figure 5: Energy/accuracy tradeoffs in MCDNN catalogs.

MCDNN, accuracy loss falls off gently with resource use. If small reductions in memory use required large sacrifices in accuracy, the resource/quality tradeoff at the heart of MCDNN would be unusable. Third, these trends hold across a variety of tasks.

Figure 5 illustrates energy/accuracy tradeoffs for the face, object and scene recognition tasks. Energy numbers are measured for an NVIDIA Tegra K1 GPU on a Jetson board using an attached DC power analyzer [1]. The figure shows both execution (crosses) and load (dots) energies for each model variant. Once again, across tasks, model optimizations yield significantly better resource use and modest loss of classification accuracy. Further, the falloff is gentle, but not as favorable as for memory use. In scene recognition, for instance, accuracy falls of relatively rapidly with energy use, albeit from a very low baseline. The horizontal dotted lines indicate the energy budget (2.3J) to support 5 events/minute with 25% of a 2Ah battery, to transmit a 10kB packet over LTE (0.9J), and over WiFi (0.5J) [12]. Note the packet transmit numbers are representative numbers based on measurements by us and others, but for instance LTE packet transmit overhead may be as high as 12J for a single packet [24], and a 100ms round trip over a 700mW WiFi link could take as little as 0.07J. For the most part, standard model optimizations do not tip the balance between local execution and transmission. If execution must happen locally due to disconnection, the mobile device could support at most a few queries per minute. Finally, as the colored dots in the figure show, the energy to load models is higher by 2-5× than to execute them: reducing model loading is thus likely a key to power efficiency.

Figure 6 illustrates latency/accuracy tradeoffs for the face, object and scene recognition tasks. The figure shows time taken to execute/load models on devices (crosses) and on the cloud (dots). The measurements shown are for GPUs on-device (a Tegra K1) and on-cloud (an NVIDIA k20), and for cloud-based CPUs. The dotted lines again indicate some illuminating thresholds. For instance, a

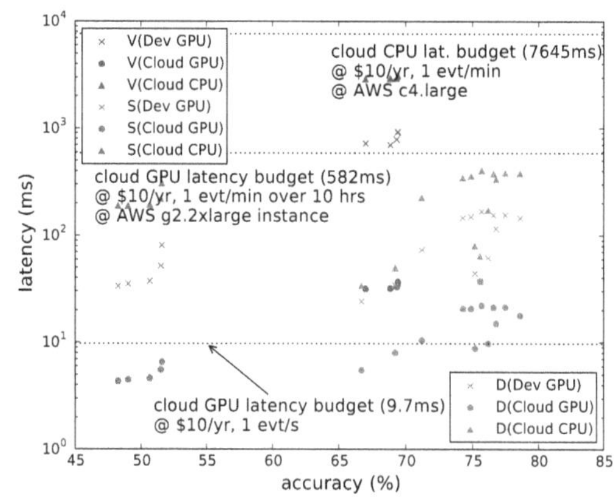

Figure 6: Latency/accuracy tradeoffs in MCDNN catalogs.

cloud-based GPU can already process one event per second on a \$10/year budget on a cloud GPU (which translates to 9.7ms per event) for scene recognition and some variants of face recognition, but not object recognition. A cloud-based CPU, however, can process one event per minute but not one per second (roughly 130ms budget, not shown) at this budget. The efficacy of model optimization carries over to execution and loading speed.

5.2 Novel model optimizations

The streaming, multi-programmed setting is a relatively uncommon one for model optimization. We therefore introduce two optimizations, one each to exploit streaming and multi-programming.

5.2.1 *Specialization*

One impressive ability of DNNs is their ability to classify accurately across large numbers of classes. For instance, DeepFace achieves roughly 93% accuracy over 4000 people [46]. When data flow from devices embedded in the real world, however, it is well-known that classes are heavily clustered by *context*. For instance you may tend to see the same 10 people 90% of the time you are at work, with a long tail of possible others seen infrequently; the objects you use in the living room are a small fraction of all those you use in your life; the places you visit while shopping at the mall are likewise a tiny fraction of all the places you may visit in daily life. With model specialization, MCDNN seeks to exploit class-clustering in contexts to derive more efficient DNN-based classifiers for those contexts.

We adopt a cascaded approach (Figure 7(a)) to exploit this opportunity. Intuitively, we seek to train a resource-light "specialized" variant of the developer-provided model for the few classes that dominate each context. Crucially, this model must also recognize well when an input *does not* belong to one of the classes; we refer to this class as "other" below. We chain this specialized model in series with the original "generic" variant of the model, which makes no assumptions about context, so that if the specialized model reports that an input is of class "other", the generic model can attempt to further classify it.

Figure 7(b) shows the machinery in MCDNN to support model specialization. The *profiler* maintains a cumulative distribution function (CDF) of the classes resulting from classifying inputs so far to each model. The *specializer*, which runs in the background in the cloud, determines if a small fraction of possible classes "dominate" the CDF for a given model. If so, it adds to the catalog specialized versions of the generic variants (stored in the catalog) of the model by "re-training" them on a subset of the original data dominated by these classes. If a few classes do indeed dominate strongly, we expect even smaller models, that are not particularly accurate on the general inputs, to be quite accurate on inputs drawn from the restricted context. **We seek to minimize the overhead of specialization to 10s or less, so we can exploit class skews lasting as little as five minutes, a key to making specialization broadly useful.**

Implementing the above raises three main questions. What is the criterion for whether a set of classes dominates the CDF? How can models be re-trained efficiently? How do we avoid re-training too many variants of models and focus our efforts on profitable ones? We describe how MCDNN addresses these.

The specializer determines that a CDF C is n,p*-dominated* if n of its most frequent classes account for at least fraction p of its weight. For instance, if 10 of 4000 possible people account for 90% of faces recognized, the corresponding CDF would be (10,0.9)-dominated. The specializer checks for n,p-dominance in incoming CDFs. MCDNN currently takes the simple approach of picking $n \in \{7,14,21\}$ and $p \in \{0.6,0.7,0.8,0.9,0.95\}$. Thus, for instance, if the top 7 people constitute over 60% of faces recognized, the specializer would add model variants to the catalog that are specialized to these seven faces.

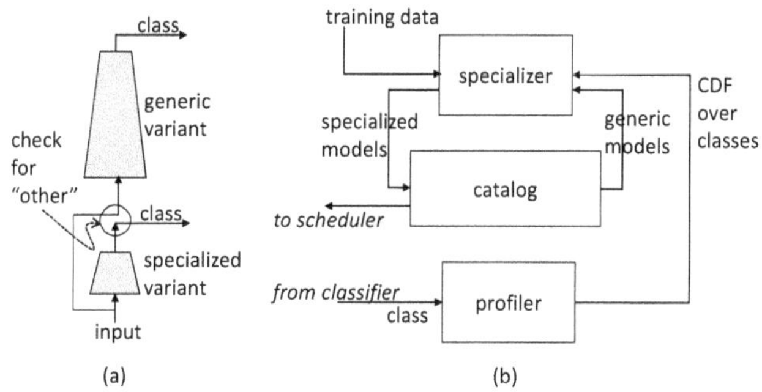

Figure 7: Model specialization: (a) Cascading specialized models. (b) MCDNN infrastructure for specialization.

The straightforward way to specialize a model in the catalog to a restricted context would be to re-train the schema for that model on the corresponding restricted dataset. Full retraining of DNNs is often expensive, as we discussed in the previous section. Further, the restricted datasets are often much smaller than the original ones; the reduction in data results in poorly trained models. The MCDNN specializer therefore uses a variant of the in-place transformation discussed in the previous section to retrain *just the output layer*, i.e., the last fully-connected layer and softmax layers, of the catalog model on the restricted data. We say that we *re-target* the original model. When re-training the output layer, the input values are the output of the penultimate layer, not the original training data, i.e., the input to the whole model. To obtain the output of the penultimate layer, we need flow the whole-model input through all lower layers. In an optimization we call *pre-forwarding*, we flow all training inputs through lower layers at *compile time* in order to avoid doing so at *specialization time*, an important optimization since executing lower layers cost hundreds of MFLOPs as mentioned before.

Finally, even with relatively fast re-training cost, applying it to every variant of a model and for up to $n \times p$ contexts is potentially expensive at run time. In fact, typically many of the specialized variants are strictly worse than others: they use more resources and are less accurate. To avoid this run-time expense, we use support from the MCDNN compiler. Note that the compiler cannot perform relevant specialization because the dominant classes are not known at compile time. However, for each model variant and (n,p) pair, the compiler can produce a *representative* dataset with randomly selected subsets of classes consistent with the (n,p) statistics, retarget the variant to the dataset and winnow out models that are strictly worse than others. At run time, the specializer can restrict itself to the (hopefully many fewer) remaining variant/context pairs.

5.2.2 *Sharing*

Until now, we have considered optimizing individual models for resource consumption. In practice, however, multiple applications could each have multiple models executing at any given time, further straining resource budgets. The *model sharing* optimization is aimed at addressing this challenge.

Figure 8(a) illustrates model sharing. Consider the case where (possibly different) applications wish to infer the identity (ID), race, age or gender of incoming faces. One option is to train one DNN for each task, thus incurring the cost of running all four simultaneously. However, recall that layers of a DNN can be viewed as increasingly less abstract layers of visual representation. It is conceivable therefore that representations captured by lower levels are shareable across many high-level tasks. If this were so, we would save the cost of

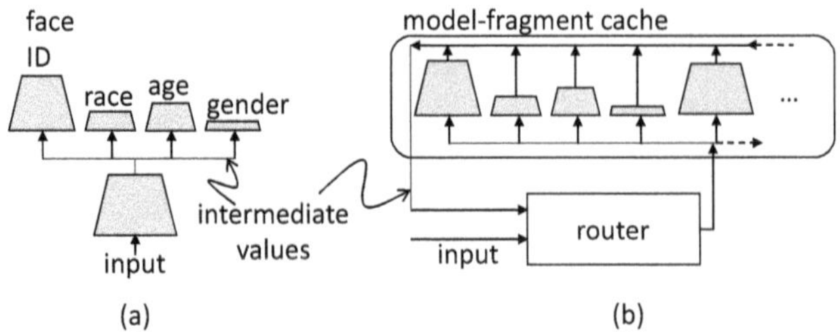

Figure 8: Model sharing: (a) Sharing model fragments for facial analysis. (b) MCDNN infrastructure for sharing, replicated in the client and cloud.

re-executing the shared bottom layers. Given that the lower (convolutional) layers of a DNN dominate its computational cost, the savings could be considerable. Indeed, we will show in the results section that re-targeting, where the shared fragment is close to the *whole* model in size is commonly applicable.

Implementing sharing requires cooperation between the MCDNN compiler and runtime. When defining input model schema, the compiler allows programmers to pick model schemas or prefixes of model schemas from a library appropriate for each domain. We currently simply use prefixes of AlexNet, VGGNet and DeepFace and their variants. Suppose the model schema s input to the MCDNN compiler has the form $s = s_l + s_u$, and t/v is the training/validation data, where layers s_l are from the library and intended for sharing. Let m_l be the trained version of s_l, also available pre-trained from the library. The compiler assembles a trained model $m_l + m_u$ consisting of two *fragments*. The lower fragment is m_l. The upper fragment, m_u, is a *freshly trained* variant of s_u, trained on $t' = m_l(t), v' = m_l(v)$, i.e., the training "input" to the upper fragment is the result of running the original training input through the lower fragment. The compiler records the fragments and their dependence in the catalog passed to the runtime. **Note that since the upper shared fragment needs to be re-trained sharing is not simply common-subexpression elimination on DNNs.**

Figure 8(b) illustrates the runtime infrastructure to support sharing. The scheduler loads complete models and model-fragments into memory for execution, notifying the router of dependencies between fragments. Given an input for classification the *router* sends it to all registered models (or their fragments). In the cases of fragments without output layers, the router collects their intermediate results and sends them on to all dependent fragments. The results of output layers are the classification results of their respective models. The router returns classification results as they become available.

5.3 MCDNN's approximate model scheduler

When applications are installed, they register with the *scheduler* a map from input types to a catalog of model fragments to be used to process those inputs, and handlers to be invoked with the result from each model. The catalog is stored on disk. When a new input appears, the scheduler (with help from the router and profiler) is responsible for identifying the model variants that need to be executed in response, paging if needed the appropriate model variants in from disk to the in-memory *model-fragment cache* in the appropriate location (i.e., on-device or on-cloud) for execution, executing the models on the input and dispatching the results to the registered handlers.

This online scheduling problem is challenging because it combines several elements considered separately in the scheduling literature. First, it has an "online paging" element [7], in that *every time an input is processed*, it must reckon with the limited capacity of the model cache. If no space is available for a model that needs to be loaded, it must evict existing models and page in new ones. Second, it has

Algorithm 1 The MCDNN scheduler.

```
function PROCESS(i,n)                                   ▷ i: input, n: model name
    if l,m ← CACHELOOKUP(n) ≠ null then                 ▷ Cache hit
        r ← EXEC(m,i)                                   ▷ Classify input i using model m
        async CACHEUPDATE(n,(l,m))                      ▷ Update cache in background
    else                                                ▷ Cache miss
        m ← CACHEUPDATE(n)
        r ← EXEC(m,i)
    end if
    return r
end function

▷ Update the cache by inserting the variant of n most suited to current resource
  availability in the right location.
function CACHEUPDATE(n,(l,m) = nil)      ▷ Insert n; variant m is already in
    e_d,ec_s,c_c ← CALCPERREQUESTBUDGETS(n)
    a_d,a_s,a_c ← CATALOGLOOKUPRES(n,e_d,ec_s,c_c,m)
    a*,l* ← max_l a_l, argmax_l a_l      ▷ Find optimal location and its accuracy
    v* ← CATALOGLOOKUPACC(n,a*)          ▷ Look up variant with accuracy a*
    m ← CACHEINSERT(l*,v*) if m.v ≠ v* or l ≠ l* else m
    return m
end function

▷ Calculate energy, energy/dollar and dollar budgets for executing model n on
  the mobile device, split between device/cloud and cloud only.
function CALCPERREQUESTBUDGETS(n)
    e,c ← REMAININGENERGY(),REMAININGCASH()
    ▷ Allocate remaining resource r so more frequent requests get more resources.
  f_i is the profiled frequency of model m_i, measured since it was last paged into
  the cache. T and r are the remaining time and resource budgets. Δr_n is the cost
  to load n. Δt_n is the time since n was loaded, set to ∞ if n is not in any cache.
    def RESPERREQ(r,l) = (r − Δr_n T/Δt_n) f_n / (T Σ_{i∈Cache_l} f_i^2)
    e_d,c_d ← RESPERREQ(e,"dev"),RESPERREQ(c,"cloud")
    ▷ Account for split models. t_n is the fraction of time spent executing the
  initial fragment of model n relative to executing the whole.
    e_s,c_s ← e_d t_n, c_d (1 − t_n)
    return e_d,(e_s,c_s),c_d
end function

▷ Find the accuracies of the model variants for model n in the catalog that best
  match energy budget e, dollar budget c and split budget s. If the catalog lookup is
  due to a miss in the cache (i.e., m is nil, revert to a model that loads fast enough.
function CATALOGLOOKUPRES(n,e,s,c,m)
    ▷ CLX2A(n,r) returns accuracy of model n in location X using resources r
    a_e,a_s,a_c ← CLD2A(n,e),CLS2A(n,s),CLC2A(n,c)
    ▷ On a miss, bound load latency. a*_l is the accuracy of the most accurate
  model that can be loaded to location l at acceptable miss latency.
    if m = nil then
        a_e,a_s,a_c ← min(a*_e,a_e),min(a*_s,a_s),min(a*_c,a_c)
    end if
    return a_e,a_s,a_c
end function

▷ Insert variant v in location l, where l ∈ "dev","split","cloud"
function CACHEINSERT(l,v)
    s ← SIZE(v)
    if (a = CACHEAVAILABLESPACE(l)) < s then
        CACHEEVICT(l,s − a)              ▷ Reclaim space by evicting LRU models.
    end if
    m ← CACHELOAD(l,v)                   ▷ Load variant v to location l
    return m
end function
```

an "online packing" [8] element: *over a long period of use* (we target 10 hrs), the total energy consumed on device and the total cash spent on the cloud must not exceed battery budgets and daily cloud cost budgets. Third, it must consider processing a request either on-device, on-cloud or split across the two, introducing a *multiple-knapsack* element [9]. Finally, it must exploit the tradeoff between model accuracy and resource usage, introducing a *fractional* aspect.

It is possible to show that even a single-knapsack variant of this problem has a competitive ratio lower-bounded proportional to $\log T$, where T is the number of incoming requests. The dependency on T indicates that no very efficient solution exists. We are unaware of a formal algorithm that approaches even this ratio in the simplified setting. We present a heuristic solution here. The goal of the scheduler is to maximize the average accuracy over all requests subject to paging

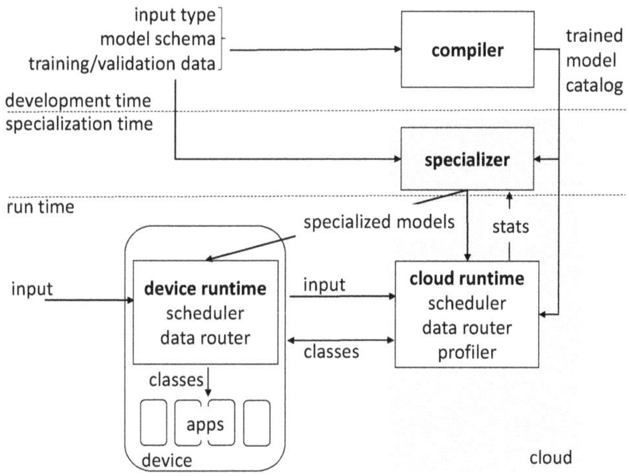

Figure 9: Architecture of the MCDNN system.

and packing constraints. The overall intuition behind our solution is to back in/out the size (or equivalently, accuracy) of a model as its use increases/decreases; the *amount* of change and the location (i.e., device/cloud/split) changed to are based on constraints imposed by the long-term budget.

Algorithm 1 provides details when processing input i on model n. On a cache miss, the key issues to be decided are *where* (device, cloud or split) to execute the model (Line 16) and *which* variant to execute (Line 17). The variant and location selected are the ones with the maximum accuracy (Line 17) under estimated future resource (energy on the device, and cash on the cloud) use (Lines 14,15).

To estimate future resource use, for model n (Lines 22-33), we maintain its frequency of use f_n, the number of times it has been requested per unit time since loading. Let us focus on how this estimation works for the on-device energy budget (Line 27) (cloud cash budgets are identical, and device/cloud split budgets (Line 29) follow easily). If e is the current *total* remaining energy budget on the device, and T the remaining runtime of the device (currently initialized to 10 hours), we allocate to n a *per-request energy budget* of $e_n = ef_n/T\Sigma_i f_i^2$, where the summation is over all models in the on-device cache. This expression ensures that *every future request* for model n is allocated energy proportional to f_n and, keeping in mind that each model i will be used Tf_i times, that the energy allocations sum to e in total (i.e., $\Sigma_i e_i f_i T = e$). To dampen oscillations in loading, we attribute a cost Δe_n to loading n. We further track the time Δt_n since the model was loaded, and estimate that if the model were reloaded at this time, and it is reloaded at this frequency in the future, it would be re-loaded $T/\Delta t_n$ times, with total re-loading cost $\Delta e_n T/\Delta t_n$. Discounting this cost from total available energy gives a refined per-request energy budget of $e_n = (e - \Delta e_n T/\Delta t_n) f_n/T\Sigma_i f_i^2$ (Line 26).

Given the estimated per-request resource budget for each location, we can consult the catalog to identify the variant providing the maximum accuracy for each location (Line 36) and update the cache at that location with that variant (Line 18). Note that even if a request hits in the cache, we consider (in the background) updating the cache for that model if a different location or variant is recommended. This has the effect of "backing in"/"backing out" models by accuracy and dynamically re-locating them: models that are used a lot (and therefore have high frequencies f_n) are replaced with more accurate variants (and vice-versa) over time at their next use.

5.4 End-to-end architecture

Figure 9 illustrates the architecture of the MCDNN system. An application developer interested in using a DNN in resource-constrained settings provides the *compiler* with the type of input to which the model should be applied (e.g., faces), a model schema, and training data. The compiler derives a *catalog* of trained models from this data, mapping each trained variant of a model to its resource costs, accuracy, and information relevant to executing them (e.g., the runtime context in which they apply). When a user installs the associated application, the catalog is stored on disk on the device and cloud and registered with the MCDNN *runtime* as handling input of a certain type for a certain app.

At run time, inputs for classification stream to the device. For each input, the *scheduler* selects the appropriate variant of all registered models from their catalogs, selects a location for executing them, pages them into memory if necessary, and executes them. Executing models may require *routing* data between fragments of models that are shared. After executing the model, the classification results (*classes*) are dispatched to the applications that registered to receive them. Finally, a *profiler* continuously collects *context statistics* on input data. The statistics are used occasionally by a *specializer* running in the background to specialize models to detected context, or to select model variants specialized for the context.

6. EVALUATION

We have implemented the MCDNN system end-to-end. We adapt the open source Caffe [26] DNN library for our DNN infrastructure. As our mobile device, we target the NVIDIA Jetson board TK1 board [3], which includes the NVIDIA Tegra K1 mobile GPU (with roughly 300 gflops nominal peak performance), a quad-core ARM Cortex C15 CPU, and 2GB of shared memory between CPU and GPU. The Jetson is a developer-board variant of the NVIDIA Shield tablet [4], running Ubuntu 14.04 instead of Android as the latter does. For cloud server, we use a Dell PowerEdge T620 with an NVIDIA K20c GPU (with 5GB dedicated memory and a nominal peak of 3.52 tflops), a 24-core Intel Xeon E5-2670 processors with 32 GB of memory running Ubuntu 14.04. Where cloud costs are mentioned, we use Amazon AWS G2.2xlarge single-core GPU instances and c4.large CPU instances, with pricing data obtained in early September 2015. All energy measurements mentioned are directly measured unless otherwise specified, using a Jetson board and Shield tablet instrumented with a DC power analyzer [1].

Our main results are:

- Stand-alone optimizations yield 4-10× relative improvements in memory use of models with little loss of accuracy. In absolute terms, this allows multiple DNNs to fit within mobile/embedded device memory. However, the energy used by these models, though often lower by 2× or more, is high enough that it is almost always more energy-efficient to offload execution when the device is connected to the cloud. Execution latencies on cloud CPU and GPU are also improved by a similar 2× factor, adequate to apply all but the largest models at 1 frame/minute at an annual budget of $10, but not enough to support a realistic 1 frame/second.
- Collective optimizations (specialization and sharing), when applicable, can yield 10× to 4 orders of magnitude reductions in memory consumption and 1.2× to over 100× reductions in execution speed and energy use. These improvements have significant qualitative implications. These models can fit in a fraction of a modern phone's memory making them suitable for both consumer mobile devices and for memory-constrained embedded devices such as smart cameras. It is often less expensive to execute them locally than to offload over LTE (or sometimes even WiFi). Finally, it is feasible to process 1 frame/second on a cloud-based CPU at $10/year.
- Both selecting which model to execute and where to run dynamically, as MCDNN does, can result in significant improvement in

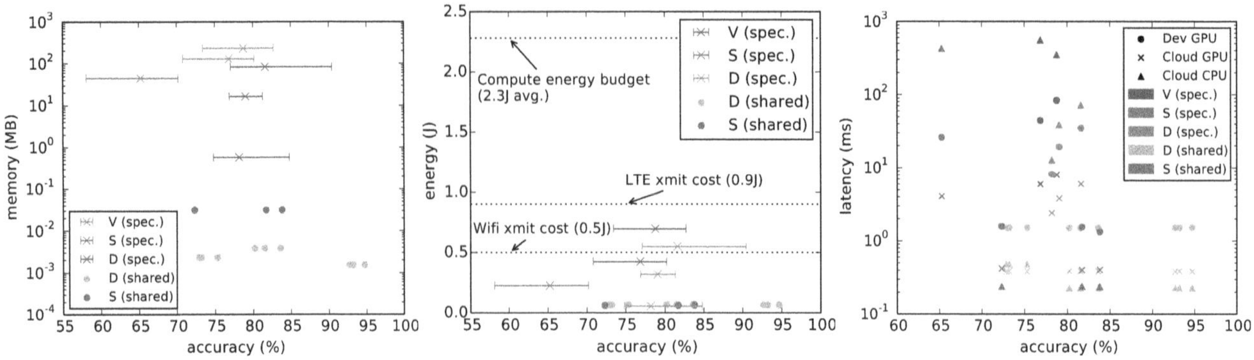

(a) Memory consumption (b) Energy consumption (c) Execution latency

Figure 10: Impact of collective optimization (best viewed in color).

Task (variant)	**Time to specialize (s)**		
	Full re-train	**+ Retarget**	**+ Pre-forward**
Face (C0)	2.6e4	30.4	4.3
Face (C4)	1.4e4	24.0	4.2
Object (A0)	4.8e5	152.4	14.2
Object (A9)	9.1e4	123.0	14.1

Table 3: Runtime overhead of specialization.

the number of requests served at fixed energy and dollar budget with little loss in accuracy. Essentially, common variations in classification task mix, optimization opportunities (such a specialization and sharing) and cloud-connectivity latencies defeat static model selection and placement schemes.

- MCDNN seems well-matched with emerging applications such as virtual assistants based on wearable video and query-able personal live video streams such as Meerkat[2] or Periscope[5]. We show promising early measurements supporting these two applications.

6.1 Evaluating optimizations

Figure 10 shows the impact of *collective* optimizations, specialization and sharing. For specialization, we train and re-target progressively simpler models under increasingly favorable assumption of data skew, starting from assuming that 60% of all classes drawn belong to a group of at most size 21 (e.g., 60% of person sightings during a period all come from at most the same 21 people) to 90%/7 classes. We test these models on datasets with the same skew (e.g., 60% of faces selected from 21 people, remaining selected randomly from 1000 people). The size, execution energy consumed, and latency of the model executed under these assumptions remains fixed, only the accuracy of using the model changes, resulting in horizontal line segments in the figure. We show mean, min and max under these assumptions. Two observations are key. First, **resource usage is dramatically lower** than even the statically optimized case. For instance (Figure 10a; compare with Figure 5), specialized object recognition consumes 0.4-0.7mJ versus the stand-alone-optimized 7-16mJ. Second, **accuracy is significantly higher** than in the unspecialized setting. For instance the 0.4mJ-model has recognition rates of 70-82%, compared to the baseline 69% for the original VGGNet. Latency wins are similar. These models take less energy to run on the device than to transmit to the cloud, and easily support 1 event *per second* on a $10/year GPU budget, and *often on a CPU budget as well.*

There is no free lunch here: specialization only works when the incoming data has class skew, i.e, when a few classes dominate over the period of use of the model. Class skew may seem an onerous restriction if the skew needs to last for hours or days. Table 3 details the time required to specialize a few representative variants of models including two models for face recognition and two for object recognition (C4 is a smaller variant of C0 and A9 of A0; A0 is the standard AlexNet model for object recognition). Re-training these models from scratch takes hours to days. However, MCDNN's optimizations cut this overhead dramatically. If we only seek to re-target the model (i.e., only retrain the top layer), overhead falls to tens of seconds and pre-forwarding (see Section 5.2.1) training data through lower layers yields roughly 10-second specialization times. **MCDNN is thus well positioned to exploit data skew that lasts for as little as tens of seconds to minutes**, a capability that we believe dramatically broadens the applicability of specialization.

The benefits of sharing, when applicable, are even more striking. For scene recognition, assuming that the baseline scene recognition model (dataset S in Table 2) is running, we share all but its last layer to infer three attributes: we check if the scene is man-made or not (dataset M), whether lighting is natural or artificial (L), and whether the horizon is visible (H). Similarly, for face identification (D), we consider inferring three related attributes: age (Y), gender (G) and race (R). When sharing is feasible, the resources consumed by shared models are remarkably low: tens of kilobytes per model (cyan and purple dots in Figure 10a), roughly 100mJ of energy consumption (Figure 10b) and under 1ms of execution latency (Figure 10c), representing over 100× savings in these parameters over standard models. Shared models can very easily run on mobile devices. Put another way, inferring attributes is "almost free" given the sharing optimization.

6.2 Evaluating the runtime

Given an incoming request to execute a particular model, MCDNN decides *which variant* of the model to execute and *where* to execute it.

Selecting the right variant is especially important when executing on-device because the device has a finite-sized memory and paging models into and out of memory can be quite expensive in terms of power and latency as discussed in the previous section. MCDNN essentially pages in small variants of models and increases their size over time as their relative execution frequency increases. To gauge the benefit of this scheme, in Figure 11, we use trace-driven evaluation to compare this dynamic scheme to two schemes that page *fixed-sized* models in LRU-fashion in and out of a 600MB-sized cache. In the "Original" scheme, the models used are the unoptimized models. In the "Best" scheme, we pick models from the knees of the curves in Figure 4, so as to get the best possible accuracy-to-size tradeoff. In the "All Models" scheme, the MCDNN model picks an appropriate model variant from a catalog of model sizes.

We generate traces of model requests that result in increasing *cache load rates* with respect to the original model: the load rate is the miss-rate weighted by the size of the missed model. We generate 10 traces per load rate. Each trace has roughly 36000 requests (one

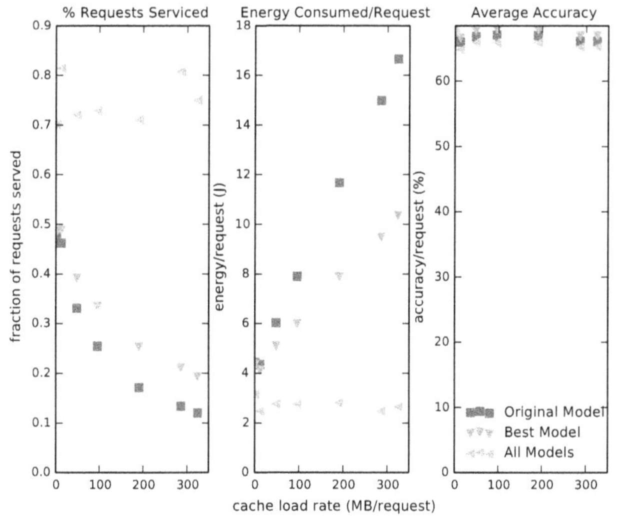

Figure 11: Impact of MCDNN's dynamically-sized caching scheme.

per second over 10 hours). Due to the energy required to service each request, none of the schemes is able to service all requests. The figure shows the number of requests served, the average energy expended per request, and the average accuracy per served request. The summary is that MCDNN constantly reduced the size of models in the cache so that even when the cache is increasingly oversubscribed with respect to fixed-size models, it still fits all the reduced-size models. As a result, MCDNN incurs minimal paging cost. **This results in a significantly higher percentage of requests served, lower average energy per request (in fact, the average energy remains fixed at execution cost for models rather than increasing amounts of paging costs), at a modest drop in accuracy**. Note that although the original and best models have higher accuracy *for requests that were served*, they serve far fewer requests.

We now move to the decision of where to execute. For each request, MCDNN uses dynamically estimated resource availability and system costs to decide where to execute. Given the relatively low cost of transmitting frames, a good strawman is a "server first" scheme that always executes on the cloud if cloud-budget and connectivity are available and on the device otherwise. This scheme if often quite good, but fails when transmission costs exceed local execution costs, which may happen due to the availability of inexpensive specialized or shared models (Figure 10b), an unexpectedly large client execution budget and/or high transmission energy costs (e.g., moving to a location far from the cloud and using a less energy-friendly transmission modality such as LTE). We examine this tradeoff in Figure 12.

Assuming full connectivity, day-long traces, and for three different transmission costs (0.1J, 0.3J and 0.5J), we examine the fraction of total requests served as increasing numbers of specialization and sharing opportunities materialize through the day. In server-first case, all requests are sent to the server, so that the number of requests served depends purely on transmission cost. **MCDNN, however, executes locally when it is less expensive to do so, thus handling a greater fraction of requests than the server-first configuration, and an increasing fraction of all requests, as specialization and sharing opportunities increase**. When transmit costs fall to 100mJ per transmit (blue line), however, remote execution is unconditionally better so that the two policies coincide.

6.3 MCDNN in applications

To understand the utility of MCDNN in practice, we built rough prototypes of two applications using it. The first, Glimpse, is a system for

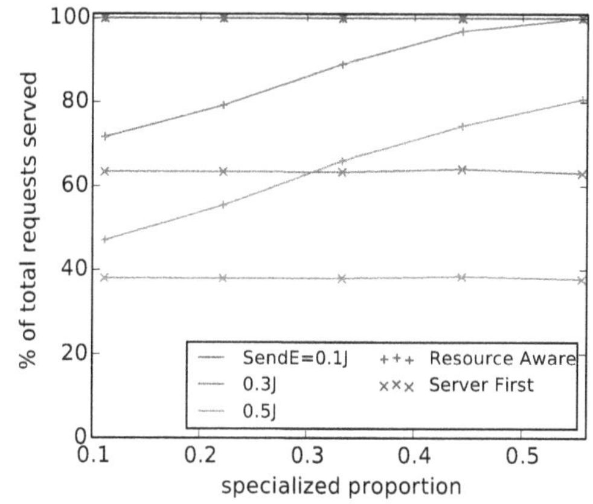

Figure 12: Impact of MCDNN's dynamic execution-location selection.

analyzing wearable camera input so as to provide personal assistance, essentially the scenario in Section 2. We connect the camera to an NVIDIA Shield tablet and thence to the cloud. In a production system, we assume a subsystem other than MCDNN (e.g., face detection hardware, or more generally a *gating* system [21]) that detects interesting frames and passes them on to MCDNN for classification. MCDNN then analyses these frames on the wearable and cloud. We currently use software detectors (which are themselves expensive) as a proxy for this detection sub-system. Figure 13 shows a trace reflecting MCDNN's behavior on face analysis (identification, age/race/gender recognition) and scene recognition tasks over a day[4]. The bottom panel shows the connectivity during the day. The straw man of always running on client has good accuracy but exhausts the battery. Always sending to cloud suffers during disconnected periods. MCDNN makes the trade-offs necessary to keep running through the day.

Our second application, Panorama, is a system that allows text querying of personal live video streams [2, 5] in real time. In this case, potentially millions of streams are sent to the cloud, and users can type textual queries (e.g., "man dog play") to discover streams of interest. The central challenge is to run VGGNet at 1-3 frames per second at minimal dollar cost. The key observation is that these streams have high class skew just as with wearable camera streams. We therefore aimed to apply specialized versions of VGGNet to a sample of ten 1-to-5-minute long personal video streams downloaded from YouTube; we labeled 1439 of 39012 frames with ground truth on objects present. VGGNet by itself takes an average of 364ms per frame to run on a K20 GPU at an average accuracy of 75%. MCDNN produces specialized variants of VGGNet for each video and reduces processing overhead to 42ms at an accuracy of 83%. Panorama does not run on the end-user device: MCDNN is also useful in cloud-only execution scenarios.

7. RELATED WORK

MCDNN provides shared, efficient infrastructure for mobile-cloud applications that need to process streaming data (especially video) using Deep Neural Networks (DNNs). MCDNN's main innovation is exploiting the systematic approximation of DNNs toward this goal, both revisiting scheduling to accommodate approximation, and revisiting DNN approximation techniques to exploit stream and application locality.

Recent work in the machine learning community has focused on

[4]The data fed to MCDNN in this experiment are synthesized based on statistics collected from the real world; at the time of writing we did not have Human Subjects Board permissions to capture and analyze facial data from the wild.

such as running another virtual machine. TaskFolder does so in a dynamic and fine-grained manner, allowing it to gradually and precisely respond to new task behavior.

In order to demonstrate the power of TaskFolder, in Section 4 we include a case study to exhibit how it regulates multi-core execution based on CC, and how it results in power savings. TaskFolder allows the system to take advantage of the mobile CPU's power management feature. It allows the active cores to run more efficiently with higher performance; the inactive cores and the associated "uncore" [13] can enter a deeper idle state and remain there longer.

This paper makes the following contributions:

1. We identified that most current systems simply engage all the cores regardless of the running workload as a problem for mobile devices. We argue that instead the system should understand how many cores the workload needs and then manage for it. With that understanding prior to multi-core scheduling, a better user experience can be promised.
2. We introduce Core Concurrency, a new system metric that dynamically measures the number of cores required to run a workload. The CC is used to make multi-core execution fast and efficient.
3. We introduce TaskFolder on top of the task scheduler. TaskFolder proposes a practical approach to calculating CC which takes into account the number of runnable tasks across the cores, balances the benefit versus the overhead of multi-core scheduling, and evaluates the system's temporal dynamics to allow it to quickly sense and react to workload changes. Based on CC, TaskFolder folds the tasks to the CC number of cores.
4. We present a case study to demonstrate the use of TaskFolder to save CPU energy. TaskFolder has been shipped on tens of millions of units of Intel's mobile platforms.

The rest of the paper is organized as follows: Section 2 is a brief background; Section 3 discusses the motivation, the CC, and the implementation; Section 4 presents a case study to show the benefits of applying TaskFolder to our mobile platform; Section 5 describes the origin of TaskFolder and its limitations; Section 6 discusses related work; Section 7 introduces future work and Section 8 concludes this paper.

2. BACKGROUND

This section briefly introduces the task scheduler from the perspective of multi-core management. We discuss some basics of CPU power management relevant to the case study in Section 4.

2.1 Task scheduler on multi-core CPUs

The task scheduler's basic job is to allow multiple tasks to run simultaneously. In a multi-core system, the scheduler can be imagined as a two-level scheme: (a) picking the next task to run from a queue of runnable tasks, and (b) load balancing among the cores by moving tasks between the cores. Figure 1 illustrates the two-level scheduling scheme.

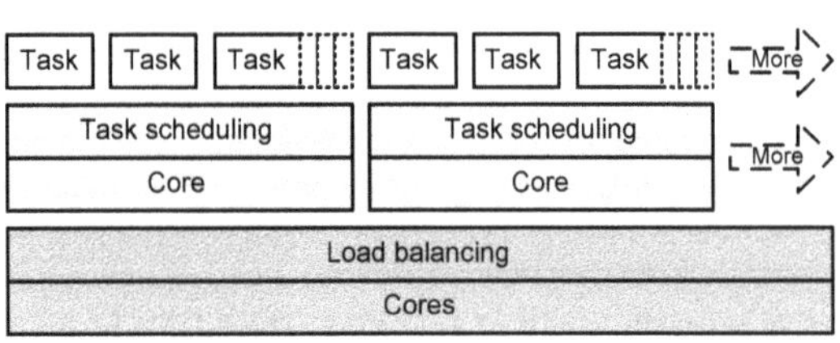

Figure 1 Task scheduling and load balancing

For best multitasking performance on multi-core CPUs, it is ideal if the number of cores is equal to the number of runnable tasks. Unfortunately, most of the time this is not the case since the core count is fixed. Moreover, as tasks come and go very frequently and quickly, load balancing becomes an important and challenging job.

2.2 CPU power management

The CPU power management (PM) subsystem can be roughly divided into active and idle components. The active PM adjusts CPU frequency and voltage depending on the workload's activity. The idle PM triggers when a core has no runnable task in queue, and then may choose to send the core into a low-power idle state. If later a wakeup event (such as an interrupt) occurs, the core exits the idle state to handle the event. There may be a number of idle states. Typically, deeper idle states consume less power but have longer entry and exit time than shallower idle states.

3. TASKFOLDER

This section introduces a multi-core management scheme named TaskFolder. TaskFolder assigns (folds) runnable tasks to the cores that are sufficient to run those tasks efficiently, and does so in a dynamic and fine-grained manner. We first reason about the need for such a management scheme. Then we discuss how we understand a workload with respect to multi-core execution. Based on this understanding, we propose Core Concurrency, a system metric to reflect the required number of cores. After that, we present the implementation of TaskFolder.

3.1 Motivation

Increased core count leads to an increased number of ways in which the cores can be efficiently managed. Existing schedulers (e.g., the Linux Completely Fair Scheduler (CFS) [34]) are inherited from PC and server environments, and are primarily designed and tuned for good performance rather than maximum efficiency. They try to engage as many cores as they can to allow tasks to run as fast as possible. They assume that (a) the CPU is free, and (b) the workload is heavy and critical. However, these assumptions are not true on a mobile device.

First, using all cores is not free on battery-powered devices. More running cores consume more power, even more so on mobile CPUs capable of fine-grained and aggressive idle PM because lower power states won't be reached [45].

Second, the workload may be neither heavy nor critical, and raw performance may matter only if the end user can perceive the difference it makes [46].

Third, engaging a core requires non-trivial overhead. Examples include software and hardware processing incurred by the frequent task migrations needed to evenly spread the workload, the negative impact on performance and power consumption due to hardware state transitions, and memory access overhead caused by lack of a shared cache among the cores in some mobile CPUs.

Last, the workload tends to change very quickly, most of the time much faster than the scheduler's response speed. Without reconciliation, this speed discrepancy will most likely lead to suboptimal scheduling.

To verify the above claims, we profiled the length of the run queues in a real-world workload – video playback on a tablet. The results are shown in Figure 2. Here we see the task dynamics of this workload, which is typically one of the most stable workloads on a mobile device. Out of the runnable task count distribution in Figure 2(a), one or two tasks occupy most of the time, with one task taking the majority – 66.3% in Figure 2(b). Figure 2(c) shows the real-time runnable task count over a small time frame of about

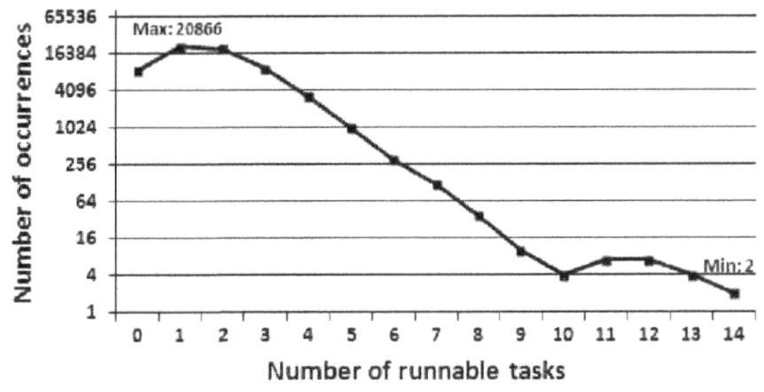

(a) Occurrences

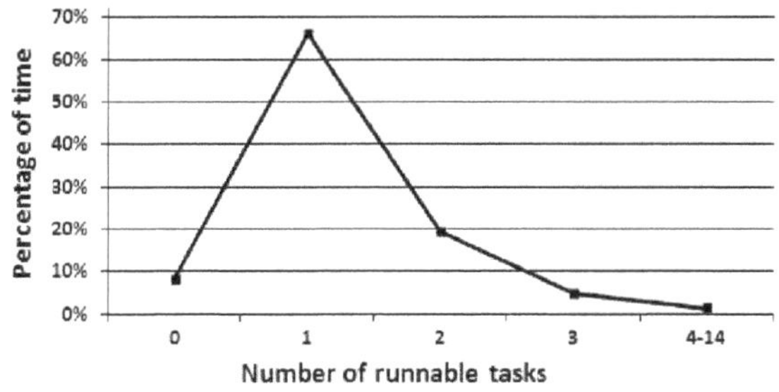

(b) Time distribution

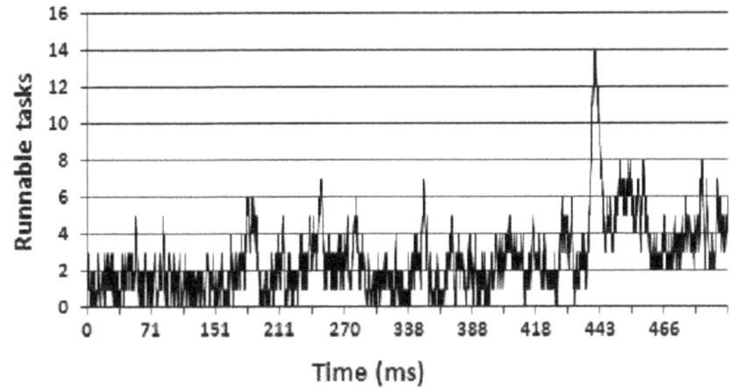

(c) Real-time length

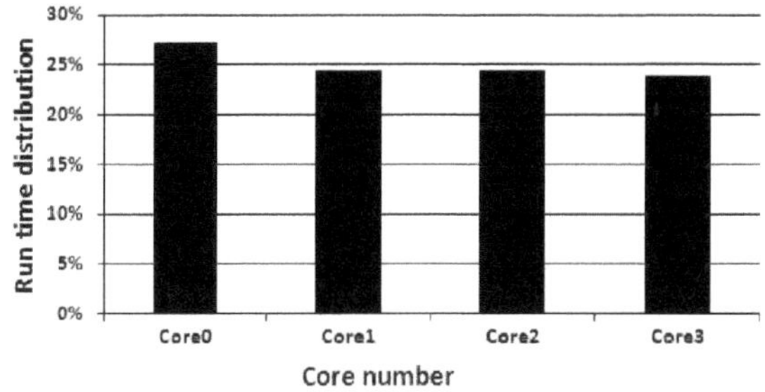

(d) Core run time

Figure 2 Run queue length statistics. The video playback workload runs for 20 seconds on a quad-core CPU.

500ms. The run queue length changes about 3114 times per second.

These tasks are simultaneously running for only a minor portion of time. Figure 2(b) shows that two cores run simultaneously less than 3% of the time, and that all four cores run simultaneously only 0.24% of the time. However, the tasks are still spread evenly across the cores (see Figure 2(d)). This is because the scheduler made unproductive task movements for this workload as follows:

1. A task that runs for a relatively long time regularly bounces among the cores, instead of staying on one core. Similarly if one core has a low load and can execute an additional task, there is no sense to activating another core. In the same workload as Figure 2, the top two tasks (see Figure 5(c)) migrate on average 178 times per second.
2. Small tasks migrate too early and frequently. Typically, a task migrates to another core but starts to run after the core from which it came has already gone idle.

We conclude that simply engaging all cores is not necessary, and more than likely the overhead exceeds the benefit. Therefore, we argue that the mobile system should decide how many cores to dedicate to running the workload. This is contrary to existing practice, which simply engages as many cores as possible, frequently moves tasks among cores to spread the load, but fails to match the workload's actual needs and state changes.

The system must assess how many cores the running workload needs. This is the number of cores dynamically demanded by the workload and may change over time. We call this number the Core Concurrency (CC). From the system's perspective, the CC describes the point at which multi-core execution is sufficient, in the sense that an additional core won't benefit the workload, and the point at which multi-core execution is so efficient that engaging an additional core adversely affects system performance due to increased overhead.

To compute the CC, the system must precisely track workload dynamics. This is described in the next section.

3.2 Understanding the workload

A workload can be decomposed into tasks – the basic units that a single core can execute. The number of simultaneously runnable tasks directly contributes to computing the CC, since ideally one task wants to run on one core. However, frequent changes to tasks' states make it difficult to determine this number.

A task can be in several states over its lifetime. A state transition diagram is shown in Figure 3. When in the runnable state, the task is inserted into the run queue associated with the core on which it is running. If there is more than one task in the queue, one of them is picked by the scheduler to execute. When blocked, the task is moved out of the run queue.

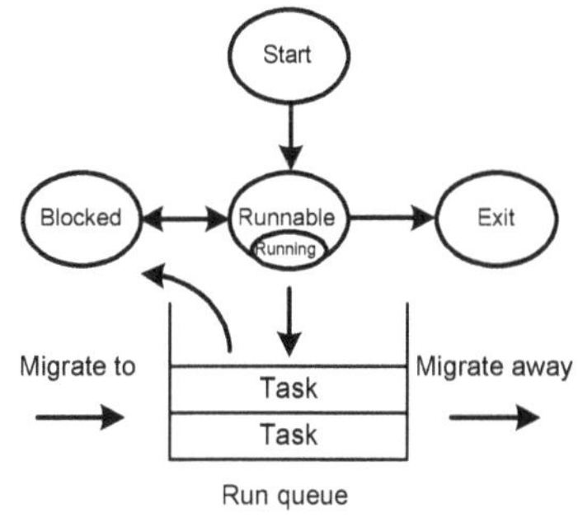

Figure 3 Task states and CPU run queue

The length of the run queue should finely correlate with how many cores are needed, so in principle the CC can be generalized as a function such as the following:

$$CC = F(R(t)) \tag{1}$$

where $R(t)$ is the number of runnable tasks at time t, and F takes $R(t)$ as input and outputs CC – the required number of cores for the workload. To take the tasks' temporal dynamics into account, we elaborate F to the form:

$$F(t) = \int_0^t f(R(t))dt \qquad (2)$$

where the function f represents how past run queue lengths serve as a component of the CC. In the current Linux CFS scheduler, the function F has the simplest general form:

$$CC = F(R(t)) = R(t) \qquad (3)$$

This is certainly suboptimal because, as mentioned in Section 3.1, (a) $R(t)$ can change much faster than any scheduling scheme can follow; (b) more importantly, multi-core scheduling induces nontrivial overhead from both software and hardware, such as core idle/active state transitions, task migration overhead, etc; and (c) this overhead is generally proportional to the rate of $R(t)$.

Consequently, what we are looking for should be a sweet-spot function F, where CC is optimal with respect to the benefit provided, the overhead involved, and the system computing environment. It should satisfy the following requirements:

1. The approach must be general and practical. It is aimed at production use of mobile devices.
2. The CC should quickly sense the workload changes, to the point that it allows multi-core scheduling to respond equally quickly.
3. It should have low overhead. Performance must not be sacrificed, and it should provide a means to tune performance.

3.3 A Practical Core Concurrency

A notable trait of the run queue length is that it rapidly fluctuates (see Figure 2(c)). To smooth out this behavior, the typical and simple method is to use the arithmetic mean. Rather than having to determine the timeframe over which the mean should be calculated, we instead use a time-weighted arithmetic mean, which virtually speaking is the mean over the entire past. The practical CC is then formalized by the following two steps.

First, the past is divided into periods of length T. We define the arithmetic mean of the run queue length for each period as:

$$q = \frac{\sum_{i=1}^{n} R_i * t_i}{T} \qquad (4)$$

where R_i is the ith run queue length which lasts for time t_i, and n is such that $\sum_{i=1}^{n} t_i = T$.

Second, we exponentially decay the weight of the past period over time, to reduce the weight of periods further in the past. For this purpose, we use two parameters: f and h. The parameter f is the decay factor, allowing a period's weight to be halved after h periods, i.e., $f^h = \frac{1}{2}$. The parameter h allows us to control the decay speed.

Given that q_j is the average of the jth period and there are a total of m periods, the weighted arithmetic mean of the run queue length is:

$$Q = \frac{1}{C} \sum_{j=1}^{m} f^{m-j} * q_j \qquad (5)$$

where C is a constant used to scale Q into the same range as the run queue length (i.e., $C = \lim_{m\to\infty} \sum_{j=1}^{m} f^{m-j}$).

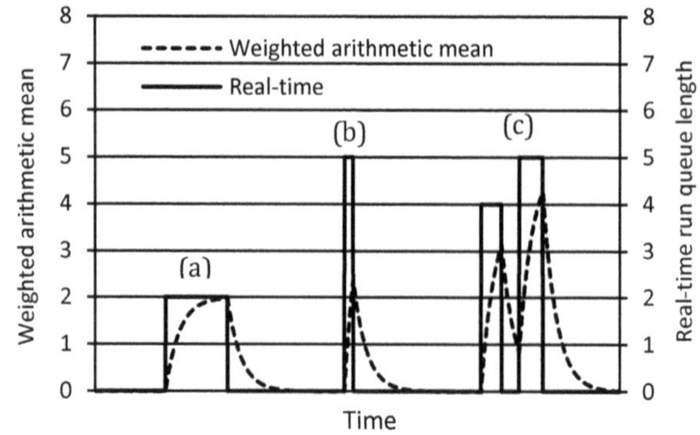

Figure 4 Q vs. real-time run queue length

In Figure 4, the interval marked (a) shows how Q accrues with time vs. the real-time run queue length. The interval marked (b) demonstrates Q's intended absorption of a transient task surge. The interval marked (c) shows the boosted ramp-up associated with consecutive duty cycles of the task's pulse wave to accelerate workload execution.

It only takes one multiplication to decay a series of averages, so the computing overhead for Q is very low. Generally, trade-offs must be made to parameter selection. We selected respectively 1 millisecond for the period T, and a value of 32 for the decay speed h. These values are selected for two reasons. (1) They are identical or comparable to the load tracking parameters in the load balancing level of the Linux scheduler [32][33]. Therefore, they have the same degree of sensitivity to workload change. (2) They are tuned to benefit the key performance and power indicators based on workload analysis during our mobile platform development.

We further compute the system-wide number of the runnable tasks based on Q, the per core average number of the runnable tasks. The sum of the Qs across the cores directly implies the value of the CC. Consider the following Equation (6), where the tasks across a total of N cores ideally make up CC tasks, each on one of the CC cores:

$$\sum_{k=1}^{N} Q_k = \sum_{k=1}^{CC} 1 = CC \qquad (6)$$

However, this equation may underestimate CC for the following reason. The relationship of tasks and cores follows a multi-producer-multi-consumer model, where tasks are producers and cores are consumers. With more cores, tasks can be executed and consumed faster, and thus there are fewer runnable tasks at any given time. We can formulate this fact by saying that the sum of the Qs across the cores is inversely proportional to the number of active cores n:

$$\sum_{k=1}^{n} Q_k \propto \frac{1}{n} \qquad (7)$$

In Equation (6), the left-hand side has N consumers, while the right-hand side has CC consumers, so the equation does not hold. Consequently, we multiply both sides of Equation (6) by the number of the cores (i.e., the consumers) respectively, which serves as

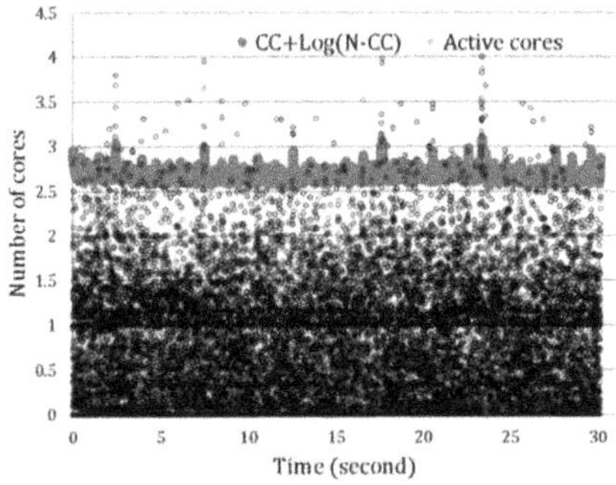

(a) Video playback: active cores

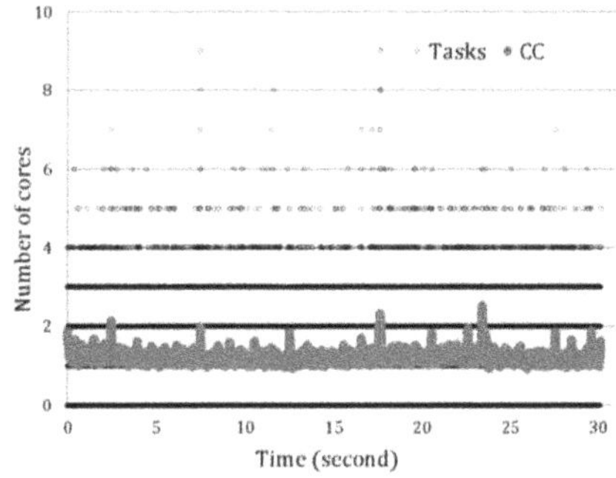

(b) Video playback: tasks vs. CC

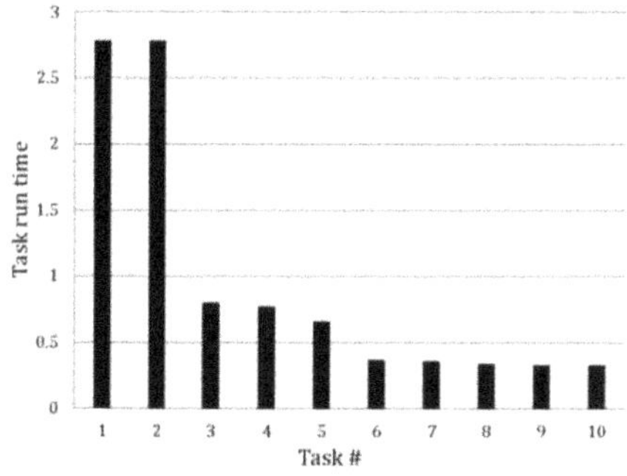

(c) Video playback: top 10 tasks

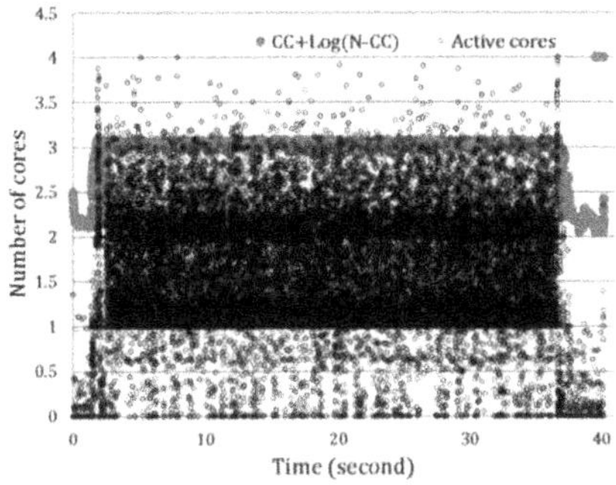

(d) SunSpider: active cores

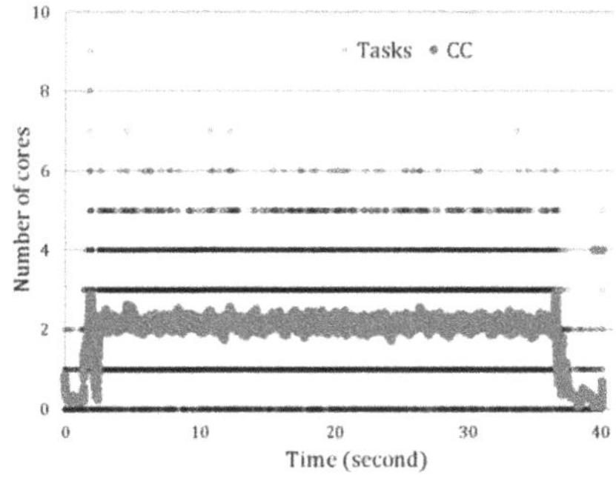

(e) SunSpider: tasks vs. CC

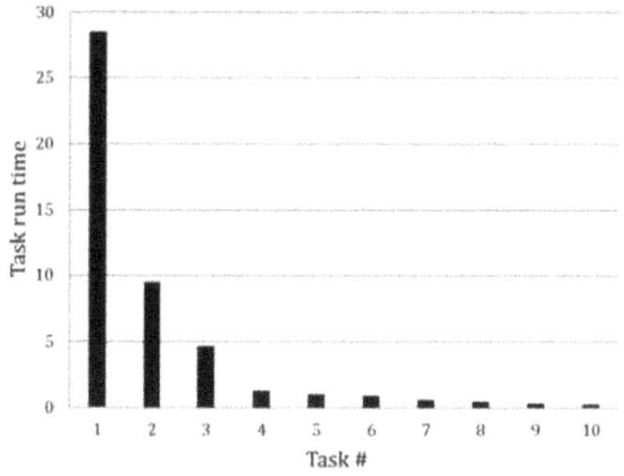

(f) SunSpider: top 10 tasks

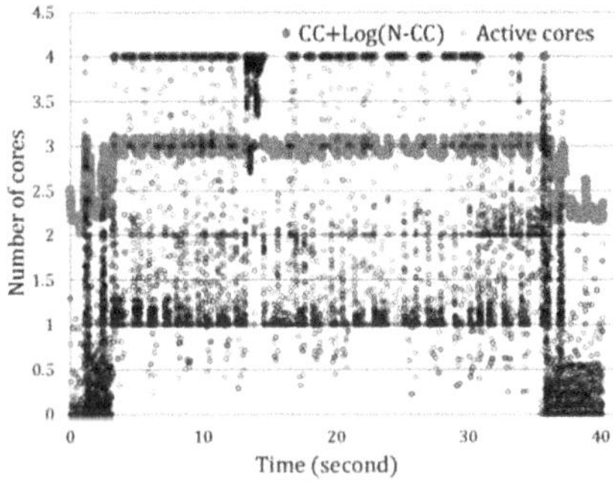

(g) Geekbench: active cores

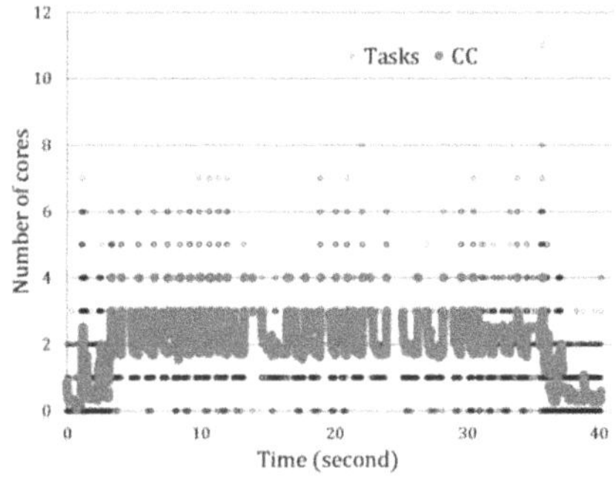

(h) Geekbench: tasks vs. CC

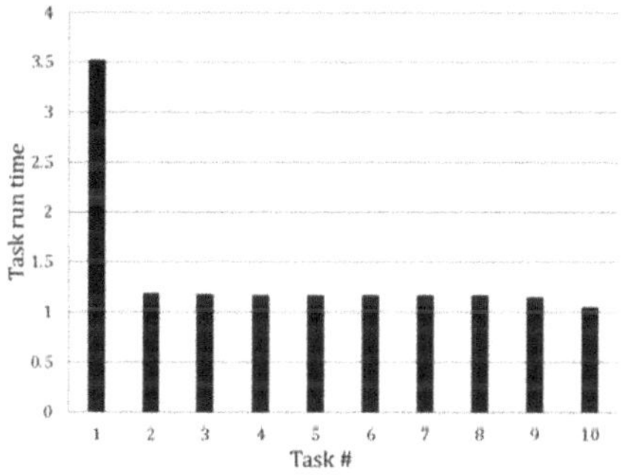

(i) Geekbench: top 10 tasks

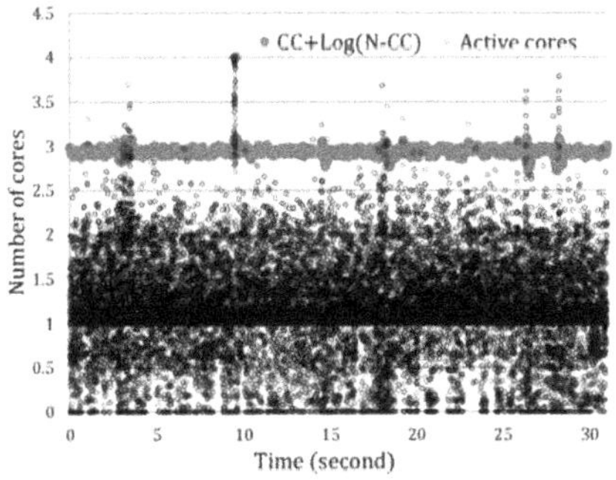

(j) AngryBirds: active cores

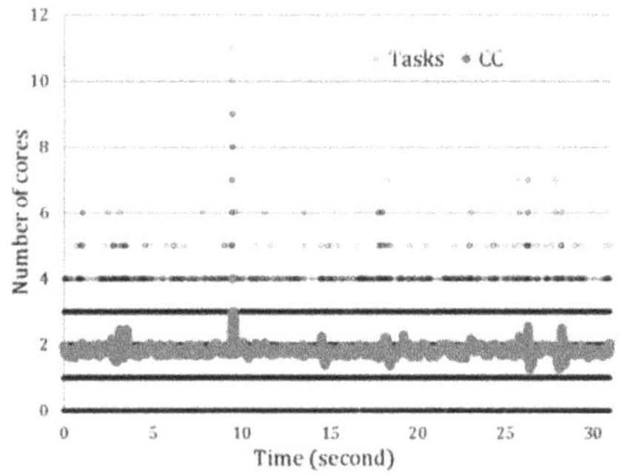

(k) AngryBirds: tasks vs. CC

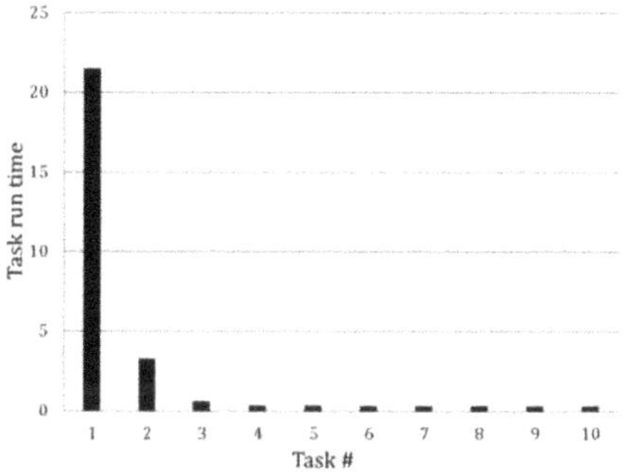

(l) AngryBirds: top 10 tasks

Figure 5 Run time CC and task profiles

a correction factor. As a result, Equation (6) is modified to take the producer-consumers relationship into account as follows:

$$N * \sum_{k=1}^{N} Q_k = CC * CC = CC^2 \quad (8)$$

But this time, unfortunately, the value of CC can be overestimated. This is because not all cores are simultaneously active, since the number of runnable tasks may be less than N, or the scheduler cannot follow task dynamics and spread them around. We can count the average number of active cores and replace N in Equation (8) with it, but the associated overhead is prohibitively high. On top of this, the average active core count changes too quickly to be used. Considering that the probability that runnable tasks can be made simultaneously running decreases when core count increases, we further modify the equation as follows:

$$(CC + log_2(N - CC)) * \sum_{k=1}^{N} Q_k = CC^2 \quad (9)$$

where $0 < CC \leq (N - 1)$. The term $(CC + log_2(N - CC))$ serves as an empirical estimate of the upper bound of the number of active cores.

Figure 5 gives a close look at the calculated CC when running four workloads respectively on a quad-core Atom CPU. Each workload exercises a different type of task dynamics. Among them, SunSpider [43] is a single-threaded benchmark, while Geekbench [44] is a benchmark composed of single-threaded and multi-threaded small sub-benchmarks. The figures in the first column of Figure 5 show the average number of simultaneously active cores vs. $(CC + log_2(N - CC))$. We can see that the real-time averages of active cores are well covered by our estimated upper bound except for only a few outliers (an average of 1.1% of the time across all four workloads and a maximum of 2.5% in Geekbench). The second column of Figure 5 compares the number of real-time runnable tasks with the CC. The CC correlates very well with the resulting top tasks in terms of the run time shown in the third column of Figure 5.

In addition, we further modify Equation (9) by adding a term tf as a tunable parameter on the equation's right side to adjust the degree of folding (the greater its value, the more aggressive the folding). This tunable, as is shown in Equation (10), will be discussed later in Section 4.

3.4 Implementation

This section presents the implementation of TaskFolder on Intel mobile platforms running Android. TaskFolder's architecture is illustrated in Figure 6. There are three components: the run queue monitor, the CC calculator, and the task migration manager. They are composed into a feedback loop where the effect of TaskFolder is available as an input to the run queue monitor, and the run queue monitor tracks workload dynamics and feeds information to the CC calculator.

3.4.1 Run queue monitor

The run queue monitor monitors the state of the run queue on each core. To capture all the changes, we modified the following five places in the Linux scheduler: (1) task enqueue, (2) task dequeue, (3) scheduler tick, (4) core entering/exiting idle state, and (5) load balancing time. The last three are there in case the run queue state has not changed for a long time. The run queue monitor updates all the Qs across the cores and then feeds them to the CC calculator.

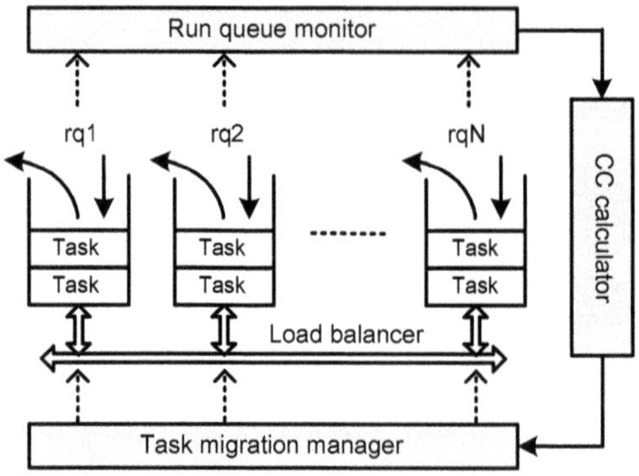

Figure 6 TaskFolder architecture

3.4.2 CC calculator

For speed and efficiency, TaskFolder does not directly solve Equation (9) to get CC. Instead, we enumerate the candidates in the set $\left\{\frac{N}{2}, \frac{N}{4}, \frac{N}{8}, \ldots, 1\right\}$ to find the smallest CC that satisfies the following equation:

$$(CC + log_2(N - CC)) * \sum_{k=1}^{N} Q_k \leq tf * CC^2 \quad (10)$$

where the term tf is discussed previously in Section 3.3. The value of tf is set to 1 by default, but can be adjusted dynamically in a running system to make task folding more aggressive (when greater than 1) or less aggressive (when smaller than 1).

When calculating CC, it is possible that no valid CC can be found. If so, it is set to the total number of cores, i.e., N. Theoretically, possible CC values range between 1 and N, but this range may be refined according to the CPU topology of the particular platform, which we will discuss in Section 3.4.4.

3.4.3 Task migration manager

TaskFolder will fold the runnable tasks to only the number of cores computed by the CC calculator. The remaining cores are allowed to go to the idle state. To determine which core to use, TaskFolder sorts the cores by their sequential numbers assigned at boot time. The lower-numbered CC cores are selected to run the workload with certain restrictions based on the CPU topology, as will be explained in section 3.4.4. We call this scheme *bias multicore usage* in the remainder of the paper.

The task migration manager modifies the load balancing level of the scheduler (see Section 2.1). It filters every task migration and only allows migration towards cores whose numbers are below the CC threshold. An alternate approach could be CPU hotplugging: turning on/off a CPU by software. While the CPU hot plug and unplug approach is easier, it cannot be performed fast enough to track the task change rate.

The task migration manager makes the following changes to the scheduler's behavior:

1. Wakeup/fork/exec core selection: when a task wakes up or a new task is created, the scheduler selects a core on which to run the task. At this point, TaskFolder ensures the scheduler only selects one of the lower-numbered CC cores.
2. Idle time work-stealing: if a core has no available task to run, before going to idle state the core will attempt to steal a waiting task from another core. TaskFolder skips work-stealing

toward the cores above the CC threshold, so those cores can be idle more often. Similarly, if a newly idle core is below the CC threshold, TaskFolder will try to actively steal tasks from the cores above the threshold.

3. Periodic idle balancing: during regular load balancing at each scheduler's tick time, the scheduler checks whether there is an imbalance among the cores. If this is the case, it will attempt to pull tasks from overloaded cores to lightly loaded cores. TaskFolder simply skips doing so on the cores above the CC threshold.
4. Real-time (RT) class task scheduling: we optionally intercept the task stealing/pushing/selecting of RT tasks to avoid placing them on the higher-numbered cores.

The effect of the above modifications is a "virtual" CPU mask imposed onto the system, which dictates which cores to use and which cores to leave aside, with CC drawing the line between the two. Using the task migration manager, the workload is gradually and precisely folded into the cores as specified by the mask.

3.4.4 CPU topology

As introduced in Section 2.2, when a core enters one of the idle states, power reduction varies depending on which and how many cores are in the idle state and the depth of the idle state. This relates to the CPU topology, which describes the relationship of the multiple cores on the CPU. Adjacent cores can be grouped together and share resources (e.g., cache, clock, etc). A bigger group can enter deeper idle states or lower power states because the shared resources can also be power gated.

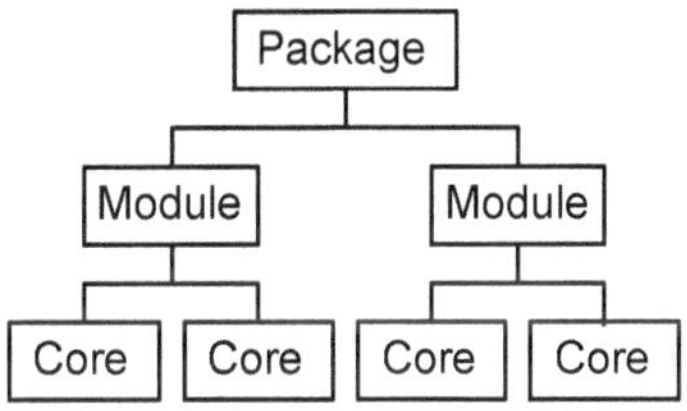

Figure 7 CPU topology of an Atom quad-core CPU

On our platforms, the Atom quad-core's CPU topology is a hierarchical structure, which has three levels: core, module, and package. A package contains two modules, each of which groups two cores together (see Figure 7).

In the Linux kernel, a CPU topology is described by schedule domain and schedule group structures. TaskFolder defines a flag in a schedule domain to specify whether this domain enables task folding or not. The above topology allows two levels of task consolidation: in-package and in-module, as illustrated in Figure 8. The dotted-line square marks the possible active cores after consolidation. These two levels are independent, so they can be either enabled as in Figure 8(a) and Figure 8(c), or both enabled as in Figure 8(b).

With in-package consolidation, the workload runs on either the first module or both modules, i.e., all of the four cores. This is the default configuration for the Atom quad-core processor. If in-package and in-module consolidation are both enabled, TaskFolder will first attempt to consolidate the workload into Module0. If the workload can further be consolidated, then tasks will be folded into Core0. With only in-module consolidation, TaskFolder will check within each module whether or not to consolidate to the first core.

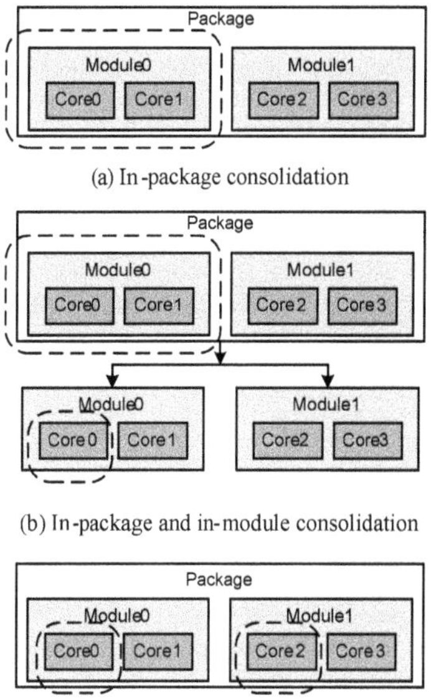

(a) In-package consolidation

(b) In-package and in-module consolidation

(c) In-module consolidation

Figure 8 In-package and in-module consolidation

3.5 Summary

TaskFolder attempts to fold the tasks into the number of cores sufficient to run the workload. To determine this number, we propose Core Concurrency, defined as the number of cores demanded by the current workload. TaskFolder proposes a practical approach to calculating CC. First, it averages each core's run queue length, taking into account the run queue's past evolution. Second, a heuristic is applied to approximate the optimal number of cores for low overhead. Based on CC, TaskFolder implements a bias multi-core usage scheme, which consolidates the workload to the lower-numbered CC cores. The implementation in the Linux kernel is viable and simple.

4. EXPERIMENTAL RESULTS

TaskFolder is applied in a case study to demonstrate its benefits. The study uses TaskFolder to save energy without sacrificing performance on an Intel's mobile platform. To make a full evaluation, in addition to power consumption, we also assess TaskFolder's impact on performance and user experience with a number of real-world use scenarios and benchmarks.

4.1 Saving energy on mobile devices

As introduced in Figure 7, the module level of the CPU topology on Intel mobile platforms allows an intermediate power management level between the core and the package. The idle PM is allowed a good opportunity to save power by putting a module into idle states, because although package idle states have the lowest power, they are the most difficult to get to. To take advantage of this PM feature, tasks must be assigned to cores in one single module, such that the other module can enter deep idle states for more time. The existing task scheduler, i.e., the Android's Linux kernel scheduler, does a poor job in this regard, because it unconditionally attempts to spread tasks onto all cores. In contrast, TaskFolder with the in-package consolidation enabled can do exactly what is required without compromising performance.

The following section shows our experiments and results. Industry benchmarks were used to measure performance, while power was assessed on workloads representative of typical mobile device uses, such as browsing a set of popular web sites, video playback, and gaming, etc.

4.2 Experimental settings

The data was collected on a system validation board with an Intel Atom x5 SoC, which features a low-power quad-core CPU clocked up to 2.24GHz. The four cores are organized in two modules, each containing two cores. This board has components similar to the Intel master reference design, but exposes voltage and current measurement points for all the power rails. Measurements were performed using a set of National Instruments data acquisition units. Tests were run in batches using a dedicated automation farm. The board runs Android Lollipop 5.1 on top of Linux kernel v3.14. We used the Android Interactive frequency governor in all our experiments.

The workloads analyzed are a mix of standard industry benchmarks and typical real-world workloads. TaskFolder is configured to run in in-package mode with $tf = 1.6$, selected empirically after balancing power, performance, and user experience across a broad range of workloads. This parameter is varied later to evaluate its effect on power. The results are compared with the baseline – the current scheduler in our Android platform, which has been tuned and optimized for years.

4.3 TaskFolder impact on power

Five workloads are used for power saving evaluation, representing casual games (AngryBirds and Temple Run with execution automated to avoid human interference), user interaction (web browsing and home screen swiping), and content consumption (video playback and web browsing).

We first look at how TaskFolder affects and shapes multi-core execution. Figure 9 compares the execution time on a per core basis between the baseline and TaskFolder. TaskFolder almost completely folds the tasks into the two cores in the first module except for the web browsing use case. The second module stays almost entirely in deep idle states.

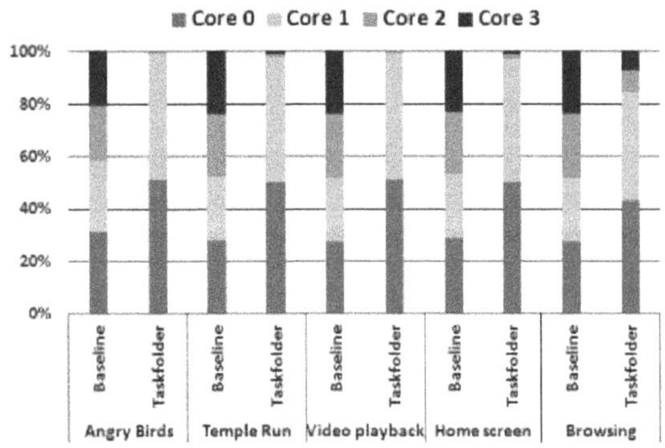

Figure 9 Core run time distribution

This redistribution is possible because the required number of cores for the workloads is usually less than two. It is worth noting that TaskFolder still attempts to spread tasks evenly across the two cores in the first module, since we use the in-package consolidation mode.

The primary means to save power is to reduce a core's active time. Figure 10 is an active time (a.k.a., C0 residency) comparison across the core, module, and package levels. The numbers are normalized to the baseline's results. At the core level (all cores combined), TaskFolder produces an up to 33% reduction. The most significant saving is from the modules (both modules combined), which is reduced by up to 47%. This is expected since the bias multi-core usage scheme allows the second module to stay idle almost the whole time. Although TaskFolder has unbalanced the load among the cores, it still noticeably reduces package active time. In other words, it prolongs the package idle state, in which all cores are idle. This demonstrates the effectiveness of CC at supplying sufficient number of cores demanded by the running workload – more than CC number of cores (or simply all cores) cannot contribute to reducing package run time.

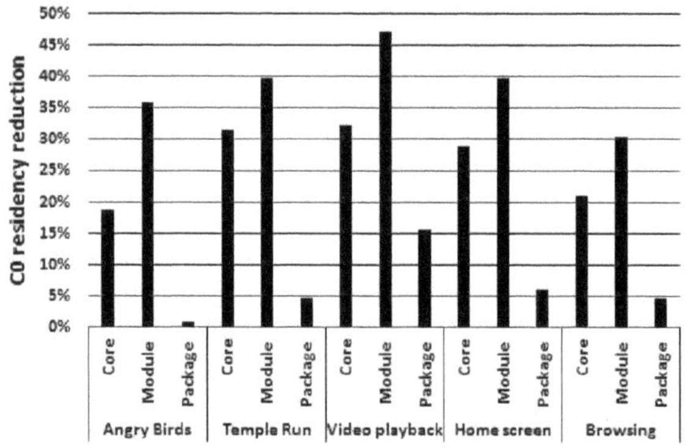

Figure 10 Sum of C0 residency reduction

To account for power savings at the core level, we dig deeper into the reduction in system overhead due to TaskFolder. We look at two system indicators, the number of task migrations and the number of power state transitions. Figure 11 shows that TaskFolder almost completely avoids migration between modules. This is quite beneficial on this platform since there is no shared cache between the modules.

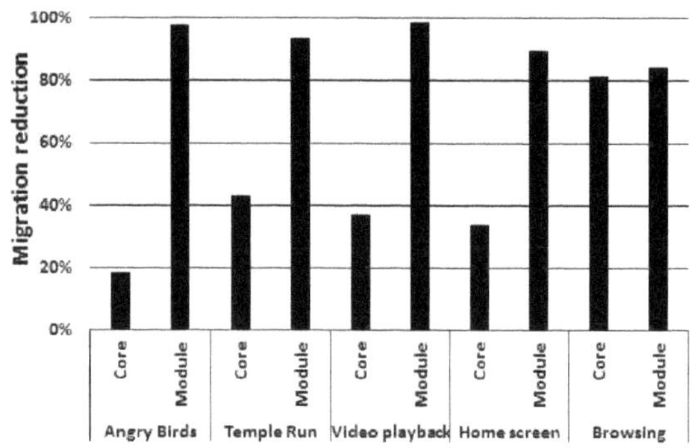

Figure 11 Task migrate reduction

In addition, TaskFolder dramatically decreases the number of power state transitions (between active and idle) at all hierarchy levels. Since power gating incurs both latency and energy consumption, this reduction is directly translated into power savings.

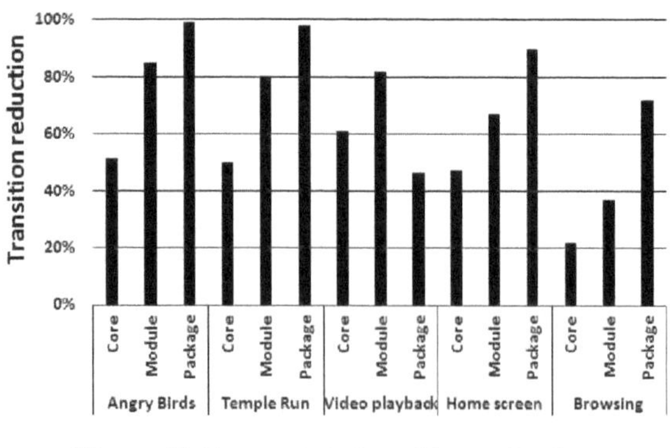

Figure 12 Power state transition reduction

The power results are shown in Figure 13. On average, TaskFolder saves about 19% of CPU power consumption, with the biggest saving at about 48% in the video playback use case. Although TaskFolder directly affects only the CPU, it also has a positive effect on the other components. We take a look at this from both the SoC and battery levels.

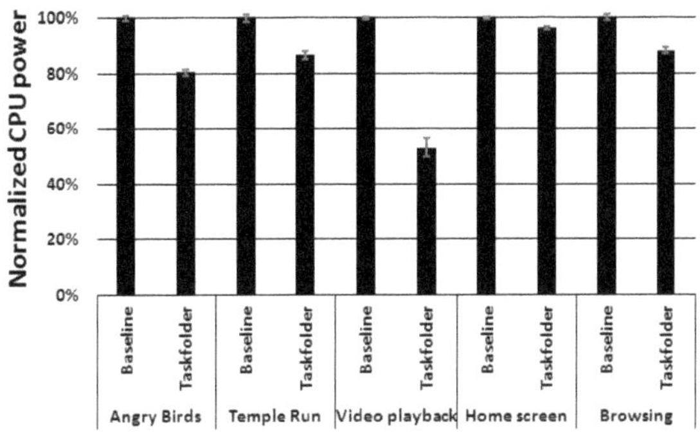

Figure 13 CPU power consumption

TaskFolder can put the whole CPU into idle state for longer than it otherwise would be. This allows deeper system power states to be reached, which allows more SoC power savings. Our results show that the absolute SoC savings are 3.4 times the CPU savings on average. At the SoC level, TaskFolder can reduce power consumption by up to 12%. Even when other components (such as GPU) dominate SoC power, TaskFolder saves 4% on average. For the same reason, it also has benefits on discrete components, such as memory (3% reduction).

But at the battery level, the display panel generally consumes a significant portion of power depending on its size. Our experimental board is for a tablet, so the savings are diluted further to 3% on average. However, for a smaller display, such as a smart watch or a smart phone, the battery savings can be much larger and more effective.

We argue, however, that TaskFolder's value is still significant. (1) It is a generic system solution irrespective of but effective on most mobile applications. (2) Our approach is orthogonal to other power saving approaches that reduce energy consumption of other components. More important, unlike others (such as dimmed displays) that degrade user experience or performance in one way or another, ours doesn't come with this tradeoff. (3) Power consumption is critical to user satisfaction and competitiveness, but it is very difficult to improve upon the state-of-the-art, and therefore every milliwatt matters.

We also studied the parameter tf's impact on task folding across the workloads. The same trend is observed: past a certain threshold, the power savings reach a plateau. We take the AngryBirds workload as an example in Figure 14. The power savings rise at 1.1, top out at 1.4, and are flat thereafter, suggesting that TaskFolder starts to further consolidate the workload at 1.1, does more up to 1.4, and then cannot do more because it already uses only the two cores in the first module (see Figure 14(a)).

Figure 14(b) shows power consumption by each module. The values are normalized to the baseline. With tf increasing, TaskFolder moves the workload from Module1 to Module0. At 1.4, Module1's power drops to almost zero, whereas Module0's power is increased by up to 50%. This explains the overall power gain for this workload.

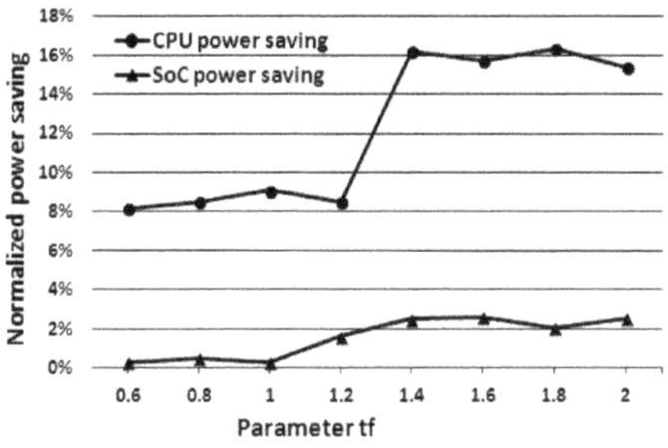

(a) Power savings

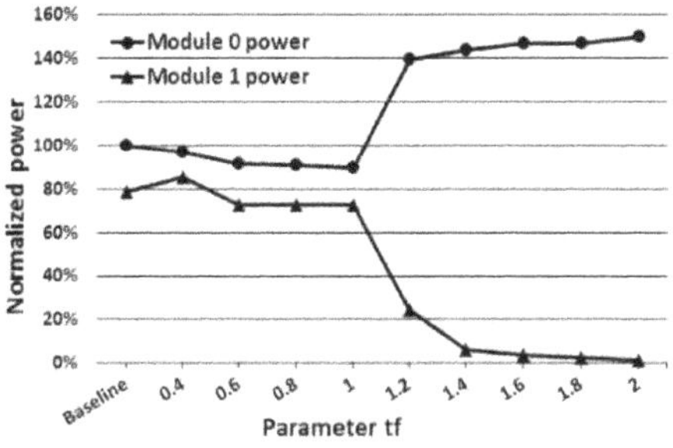

(b) Module power

Figure 14 Power savings when running AngryBirds

4.4 Effect on performance benchmarks

Similar task folding can be seen on the performance benchmarks, though the behavior differs between single-threaded and multi-threaded workloads. For benchmarks that are not heavily multi-threaded, e.g., GFXBench and JIO, task folding translates into an increase of activity in the first module, while the activity decreases in the second module. Multi-threaded benchmarks are less affected. The actual module C0 residency decrease is modest compared to the power cases, because the benchmark load is too high to fit in one module. However, the net activity in the two modules is always reduced by TaskFolder.

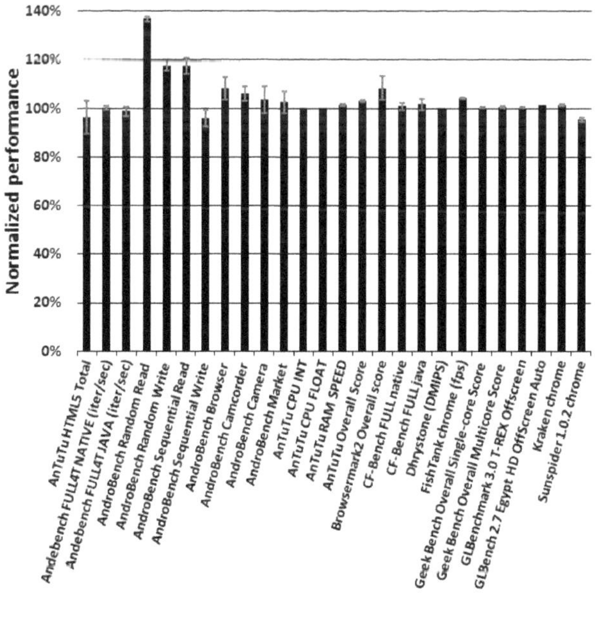

Figure 15 Performance benchmark scores

The power consumption for these benchmarks is negligibly relevant, because they are designed to overload the CPU. Nevertheless, the experiments show that even in these highly loaded cases, TaskFolder can still improve CPU execution efficiency by reducing CPU load balancing overhead.

One of the criteria for TaskFolder to be used for power reduction is that performance must be maintained. Figure 15 shows the results of a collection of industry benchmarks with tf set to 1.6. The performance is normalized to that of the baseline, which is 100%. Across those single-threaded, multi-threaded, CPU-intense, IO-intensive, and graphics workloads, TaskFolder's overall performance is on par with the baseline, and even shows improvement in a few cases.

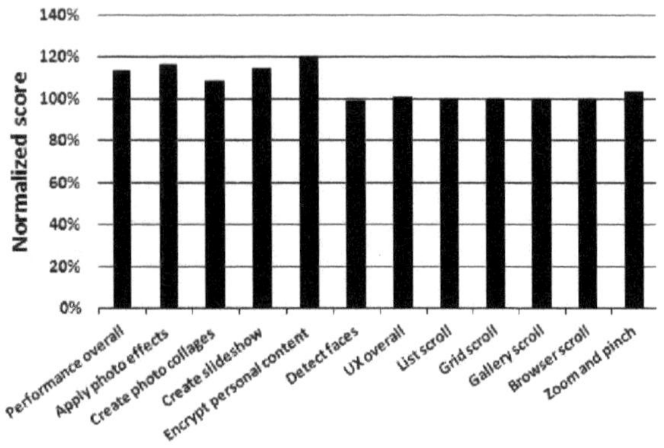

Figure 16 MobileXPRT user experience test scores

4.5 User experience benchmark

To evaluate the impact on synthetic workloads that measure both performance and user experience, we used MobileXPRT [30]. MobileXPRT is a benchmark composed of compute-intensive as well as user directed scenarios (e.g., photo editing, content scrolling and zooming). The user experience tests measure responsiveness, interactivity, jitter, and frames per second. TaskFolder does not sacrifice either performance or user experience and even improves almost half the cases, as shown in Figure 16 – the scores are normalized against the baseline, which is 100%.

5. LIMITATION

5.1 Applicability

TaskFolder originated from the analysis and optimization of our mobile platforms. Typically in such battery-powered computing environments, the heavy workloads are usually single-threaded, or use few threads: Android will heavily favor the foreground application, which might be multithreaded, but this will nevertheless limit the number of threads running concurrently on the platform. Other environments such as servers stand at the other end of the curve and usually run heavily multi-threaded workloads in parallel. This indicates that using TaskFolder would have little impact, if any, in those environments.

In fact, mobile workloads are evolving and starting to support multitasking, and the combination of productivity and content-consumption workloads on convertible devices. This is an interesting future study for us. Regardless of the workloads, the problem that TaskFolder addresses is general, but the work must evolve to accommodate changes in workload composition.

With regard to platform applicability, other architectures than x86 also have a hierarchical structure in CPU topology, and may also have a module level, such as ARM's multi-cluster CPUs. We believe TaskFolder, as a multi-core management scheme that addresses the general problem of determining how many cores are required for running a workload, can be applied to other mobile platforms including those from ARM.

5.2 Heterogeneous CPUs

Heterogeneous CPU designs advocate the combined advantage of power efficiency from small cores and good performance from large cores. A heterogeneous CPU aware task scheduler can place tasks on cores matching task characteristics [12][13] [14][15]. Yet, a homogenous CPU can offer both power efficiency and performance, if each core can offer good performance/power in a wide frequency range. In the context of heterogeneous CPUs, the CC idiom can be used as is in the scope of a small core cluster or a large core cluster. As we do not yet have a heterogeneous CPU platform, TaskFolder is implemented for homogeneous CPUs only. Extending TaskFolder to heterogeneous CPUs is possible and an interesting future study.

5.3 Frequency scaling

Since TaskFolder changes task scheduling, it will also have an indirect impact on frequency scaling. For most mobile workloads, however, we found that TaskFolder does not noticeably change core frequency. This is because the workloads usually have little computing demand, so the frequency is not increased even when the tasks are folded onto fewer active cores. For highly loaded CPU workloads, the situation may be different.

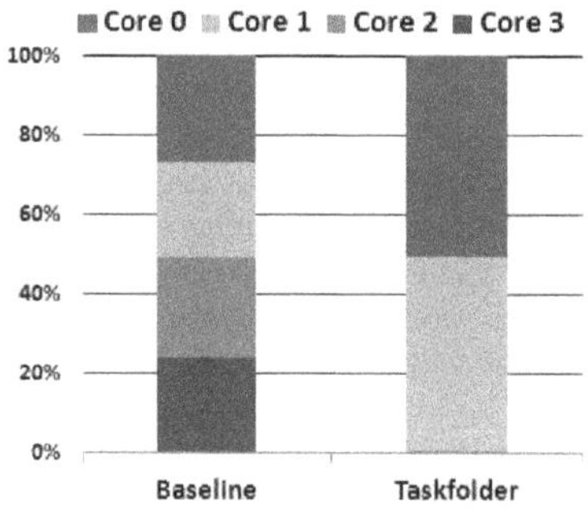

(a) Core run time distribution

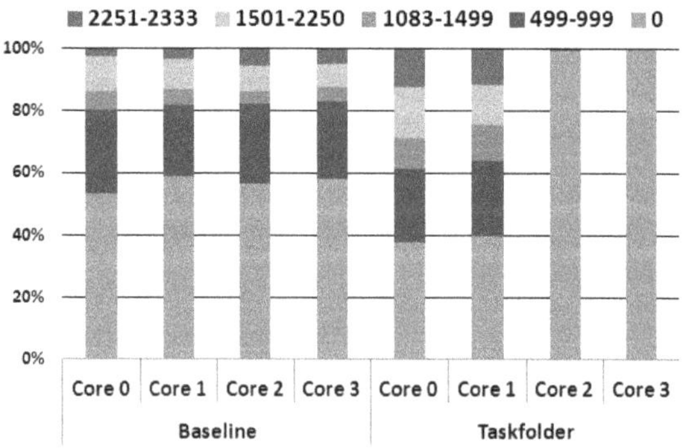

(b) Core frequency (MHz) distribution

Figure 17 Epic Citadel core power states

With TaskFolder, generally fewer cores will be active. This may cause the frequency controller to increase the frequency for those fewer cores. In the meantime, the saved power budget from the inactive cores allows the active ones to burst into a higher frequency in Turbo state. This is quite beneficial to performance, but

CPU power consumption may be increased as well. We observed this behavior on several of the heavier use cases, one of them being Epic Citadel (a 3D graphics benchmark). The CPU power increases by 12%, but it consistently has a better score by 2% (the score has reached the upper bound). Figure 17 shows the power states. Another reason for the baseline frequency being lower is that the heavy CPU consumption thread bounces across cores in such a way that the frequency controller fails to quickly ramp up the frequency.

This leads us to the proposal that TaskFolder should wisely manage the frequency as well. The topic has been discussed in the Linux kernel community with some proposals, such as energy-aware scheduling [41] and scheduler-based CPU frequency scaling [42]. However, these proposals are mostly effective on heterogeneous CPUs or incomplete. Frequency scaling is now under investigation for TaskFolder.

6. RELATED WORK

Mudge et al. [8][9][10] studied a variety of applications on desktop OSs, measuring thread level parallelism to analyze whether developers wrote applications to take advantage of multi-core. They compared the findings with their study done 10 years ago. The results showed that, 10 years later, 2-3 cores are still more than adequate for most applications. Similarly, Carroll et al. [11] made an analysis on a smart phone. They concluded that in realistic scenarios, the multiple cores are highly underutilized. On modeling a mobile device's activity to help understand how battery is used, there is significant work in the literature, including PowerScope [1], ARO [2], AppScope [3], WattsOn [4], eprof [5], Sesame [6], and V-edge [7]. Compared to these studies, TaskFolder focuses on multi-core scheduling and addresses how many cores the workload needs for optimal efficiency.

To save CPU power by active and idle power management, Pack & Cap [16] leverages DVFS and thread packing to maximize performance within a power budget for data centers by using input from performance counters, temperature, and power data. Ghasemazar [17] presented a framework to minimize energy consumption under a required throughput for CPU intensive benchmarks. Li et al. [18] proposed heuristics to reduce search space of active cores and DVFS. They targeted power consumption of a parallel application on many-core CPUs under given performance constraints. Their approach depends on online power measurement. PGCapping [19] claims better performance by power gating some cores and overclocking the rest. Thread Tailor [20] dynamically adjusts the number of threads in an application to optimize system efficiency. Cache capacity and memory bandwidth [21][22][23] or SMT [24] are used to bound the number of tasks for performance and power efficiency. These studies address heavy server workloads and are not directly applicable to mobile devices.

Closer to our first case, Medusa [25][26] is a frequency controller which also offlines cores. Medusa periodically examines the instantaneous number of runnable tasks and CPU utilization to either online cores before increasing frequency or to maximize frequency before onlining cores in a smart phone. In comparison, TaskFolder is a systematic solution to address the demanded number of cores driven by workload, and based on that influences task scheduling for efficient and sufficient multi-core execution.

7. FUTURE WORK

In addition to saving power, TaskFolder has the potential to be applied to many other cases that benefit from frugal use of multiple cores. For example, we are investigating a challenging problem that occurred on another mobile platform, which has a customized virtual machine monitor (VMM) running three virtual machines (VM), including a Modem VM (for cellular communication), an App VM (running the Android OS), and a Security VM (a trusted execution engine). The VMM statically maps each virtual CPU (VCPU) to a physical CPU (PCPU), and uses priority-based VCPU scheduling to meet the real-time requirements of the VMs.

This platform suffers from a starvation problem – after preemption, a victim VCPU must wait until a preempting VM is inactive. To make matters worse, the task scheduler in the App VM has no knowledge that it is running inside a VM. As on bare metal, it aggressively attempts to spread the workload evenly across all VCPUs, further aggravating the starvation problem.

We took advantage of TaskFolder's constrained and directed multi-core usage and applied it to the App VM, configuring it to favor VCPUs with a dedicated PCPU over VCPUs that share a PCPU. Preliminary results show that TaskFolder can significantly mitigate and often completely avoid contention between VMs. A video streaming workload via cellular network was evaluated. The results show that TaskFolder reduces the number of times the App VM is preempted by the Modem VM by 66.3% and VCPU preemption between the App VM and Security VM by 79.0%. The worst-case-scenario waiting time is reduced by 42.0% and 26.4% respectively.

Future work also includes investigating TaskFolder's impact on server workloads, better aligning TaskFolder with frequency scaling, and taking into account more factors that may affect CC, such as memory operations and I/O.

8. CONCLUSION

This paper tackles the problem of how many cores are needed for running mobile applications, and advocates that the system should understand that need prior to managing multi-core scheduling. To that end, this paper introduces TaskFolder. TaskFolder proposes a practical approach to computing Core Concurrency (CC) – a new system metric that dynamically reflects the required number of cores by the running workload. Based on CC, TaskFolder folds the tasks to the CC number of cores with a bias multi-core usage scheme. As such, the workload can be executed by the multi-core CPU more efficiently. We demonstrate the power of TaskFolder in a case study where it helps save energy without performance loss on mobile devices. The results show that TaskFolder saves an average of 19% and up to 48% of CPU power.

9. ACKNOWLEDGMENTS

We thank all the anonymous reviewers and our shepherd, Eduardo Cuervo, for their insightful comments and suggestions that improved this paper. We also thank Paul Hohensee, Thomas Baker, and Sharad Triphthi for their constructive feedback and careful proofreading. We appreciate the support from Kerry Jiang and Doug Sommer for this project.

The views and conclusions contained in this paper are those of the authors and should not be interpreted as representing the products or the official claims, either expressed or implied, of Intel Corporation.

10. REFERENCES

[1] J. Flinn and M. Satyanarayanan, PowerScope: A tool for profiling the energy usage of mobile applications. In IEEE WMCSA '99.

[2] F. Qian, Z. Wang, A. Gerber, Z. Mao, S. Sen, and O. Spatschech, Profiling resource usage for mobile applications: a cross-layer approach. In ACM Mobisys '11.

[3] W. Jung, C. Kang, C. Yoon, K. Dongwon, and H. Cha, AppScope: Application energy metering framework for Android smartphone using kernel activity monitoring. In USENIX Annual Technical Conference '12.
[4] R. Mittal, A. Kansal, R. Chandra, Empowering developers to estimate app energy consumption. In ACM MobiCom '12.
[5] A. Pathak, Y. Hu, M. Zhang, Fine grained energy accounting on smartphones with eprof. In EuroSys '12.
[6] M. Dong, L. Zhong, Self-constructive high-rate system energy modeling for battery-powered mobile systems. In the proceedings of ACM MobiSys '11.
[7] F. Xu, Y. Liu, Q. Li, and Y. Zhang, V-edge: Fast self-constructive power modeling of smartphones based on battery voltage dynamics. In USENIX NSDI '13.
[8] K. Flautner, R. Uhlig, S. Reinhardt, and T. Mudge. Thread-level parallelism and interactive performance of desktop applications. SIGARCH Comput. Archit. News, 28(5):129–138, 2000.
[9] K. Flautner, R. Uhlig, S. Reinhardt, and T. Mudge. Thread-level parallelism of desktop applications. Workshop on Multi-threaded Execution, Architecture and Compilation, 2000.
[10] G. Blake, R. G. Dreslinski, T. Mudge, et al. Evolution of thread-level parallelism in desktop applications, In ISCA'10, June 19–23, 2010, Saint-Malo, France.
[11] A. Carroll and G. Heiser. 2013. The systems hacker's guide to the galaxy energy usage in a modern smartphone. In the 4th APSys, 2013.
[12] Brian Jeff. big.LITTLE Technology Moves Towards Fully Heterogeneous Global Task Scheduling. ARM White Paper, 2013.
[13] V. Gupta, P. Brett, D. Koufaty, D. Reddy, S. Hahn, and K. Schwan. The forgotten 'uncore': On the energy-efficiency of heterogeneous cores. In 2012 USENIX ATC, Boston, MA, Jun 2012.
[14] J.C. Saez, A. Fedorova, D. Koufaty, and M. Prieto. Leveraging Core Specialization via OS Scheduling to Improve Performance on Asymmetric Multicore Systems. ACM Trans. Comput. Syst. 30, 2, April 2012.
[15] K. V. Craeynest, A. Jaleel, L. Eeckhout, P. Narvaez, and J. Emer, Scheduling heterogeneous multi-cores through performance impact estimation (PIE), in Proc. of the 39th Annual International Symposium on Computer Architecture, pp. 213-224, June 2012.
[16] R. Cochran, C. Hankendi, A. K Coskun, and S. Reda. Pack & cap: adaptive DVFS and thread packing under power caps. In MICRO, pages 175–185, 2011.
[17] M. Ghasemazar, E. Pakbaznia, and M. Pedram. Minimizing energy consumption of a chip multiprocessor through simultaneous core consolidation and DVFS. In ISCAS, pages 49–52. IEEE, 2010.
[18] J. Li and J.F. Martinez, Dynamic power-performance adaptation of parallel computation on chip multiprocessors, HPCA 2006, vol., no., pp.77-87, Feb. 2006.
[19] K. Ma and X. Wang. PGCapping: exploiting power gating for power capping and core lifetime balancing in CMPs. In Proceedings of the 21st PACT.
[20] J. Lee, H. Wu, M. Ravichandran, and N. Clark. Thread tailor: dynamically weaving threads together for efficient, adaptive parallel applications. In Proceedings of the 37th ISCA. ACM, New York, NY, USA, 270-279.
[21] W. Heirman, T. Carlson, K. Craeynest, I. Hur, A. Jaleel, and L. Eeckhout. Undersubscribed Threading on Clustered Cache Architectures. In 20th HPCA, pages 678–689. IEEE, 2014.
[22] M. A. Suleman, M. K. Qureshi, and Y. N. Patt. Feedback driven threading: power-efficient and high-performance execution of multi-threaded workloads on CMPs. In Proceedings of the ASPLOS, 2008.
[23] S. Chen, P. B. Gibbons, M. Kozuch, V. Liaskovitis, A. Ailamaki, G. E. Blelloch, B. Falsafi, L. Fix, N. Hardavellas, T. C. Mowry, and C. Wilkerson. Scheduling threads for constructive cache sharing on CMPs. In Proceedings of the ACM SPAA, June 2007.
[24] A. Fedorova, M. Seltzer, and M. D. Smith. A non-work-conserving operating system scheduler for SMT processors. In Proceedings of the Workshop on the Interaction between Operating Systems and Computer Architecture (WIOSCA), pages 10–17, June 2006.
[25] A. Carroll and G. Heiser. Mobile multicores: Use them or waste them. In HotPower'13, page 12, Farmington, PA, USA, Nov 2013.
[26] A. Carroll and G. Heiser. Unifying DVFS and Offlining in Mobile Multicores. In the 20th IEEE RTAS, Berlin, Germany, April 2014.
[27] K. Barr, P. Bungale, S. Deasy, V. Gyuris, P. Hung, C. Newell, H. Tuch, and B. Zoppis. The VMware Mobile Virtualization Platform: Is That a Hypervisor in Your Pocket? ACM SIGOPS Operating Systems in Review, 44(4):124–13.
[28] J. Andrus, C. Dall, A. Van't Hof, O. Laadan, and J. Nieh. Cells: A Virtual Mobile Smartphone Architecture. In SOSP '11, pages 173–187, Cascais, Portugal, Oct. 2011.
[29] Barham P, Dragovic B, Fraser K, et al. Xen and the art of virtualization. In SOSP '03, 37(5): 164-177.
[30] MobileXPRT. http://www.principledtechnologies.com/benchmarkxprt/mobilexprt/
[31] Antutu. http://www.antutu.com/en/index.shtml
[32] Paul Turner, sched: track the runnable average on a per-task entity basis, http://marc.info/?l=linux-kernel&m=134573145128188.
[33] Yuyang Du, sched: Rewrite runnable load and utilization average tracking, http://marc.info/?l=linux-kernel&m=143694701405109.
[34] Ingo Molnar, CFS Scheduler, https://www.kernel.org/doc/Documentation/scheduler/sched-design-CFS.txt.
[35] MediaTek Helio X10, http://www.mediatek.com/en/products/hero-products/helio-X10/.
[36] Qualcomm Snapdragon 810, https://www.qualcomm.com/products/snapdragon/processors/810.
[37] Andrei Frumusanu, The Mobile CPU Core-Count Debate: Analyzing The Real World, http://www.anandtech.com/show/9518/the-mobile-cpu-corecount-debate.
[38] A. Rahmati, A. Qian, L. Zhong, Understanding human-battery interaction on mobile phones, Proceedings of the 9th MobileHCI. ACM, 2007: 265-272.

[39] P. Ranganathan, Recipe for efficiency: principles of power-aware computing. Communications of the ACM, 2010, 53(4): 60-67.
[40] International Data Corporation (IDC), Market Analysis Perspective: Western Europe Mobile Phone and Tablet Markets, 2013. http://www.idc.com/getdoc.jsp?containerId =MS58W
[41] Morten Rasmussen, sched: Energy cost model for energy-aware scheduling, https://lkml.org/lkml/2015/2/4/537
[42] Steve Muckle, Scheduler-based cpu frequency scaling, http://thread.gmane.org/gmane.linux.power-management.g eneral/69176
[43] SunSpider JavaScript Benchmark 0.9.1, https://webkit.org/perf/sunspider-0.9.1/sunspider-0.9.1/driver.html
[44] Geekbench 3, https://play.google.com/store/apps/details?id=com.primatelabs.geekbench.
[45] Steven Tu, Intel Atom-X5/X7-8000 Series Processors (Codenamed Cherry Trail), http://www.hotchips.org/wpcontent/uploads/hc_archives/hc27/HC27.25-Tuesday-Epub/HC27.25.70-Processors-Epub/HC27.25.740-Atom-CherryTrail-Tu-Intel.pdf
[46] Ickin S, Wac K, Fiedler M, et al. Factors influencing quality of experience of commonly used mobile applications. Communications Magazine, IEEE, 2012, 50(4): 48-56

Understanding the Characteristics of Android Wear OS

Renju Liu
Purdue ECE
liu396@purdue.edu

Felix Xiaozhu Lin
Purdue ECE
xzl@purdue.edu

Abstract

Interactive wearable devices bring dramatic changes to apps and hardware, leaving operating system (OS) design in the mist. To this end, we thoroughly examine the execution efficiency of Android Wear, a popular wearable OS. By running a suite of fifteen benchmarks, we profile four system aspects: CPU usage, idle episodes, thread-level parallelism, and microarchitectural behaviors. We present the discovered inefficiencies and their root causes, together with a series of widespread, yet unknown OS design flaws. Towards designing future wearable OSes, our study has yielded a generic lesson, key insights, and specific action items.

1. INTRODUCTION

Interactive wearable, as exemplified by smart watches, is a newcomer to the spectrum of mobile computers. Being in close proximity to users, it further extends the boundary of mobile-cloud service, integrating computing even tighter with our daily lives.[1] In the year 2014, nearly three million of Android Wear and Apple watch devices have been shipped [7].

Wearable, as compared to existing mobile devices such as smartphones and tablets, exhibits unprecedented characteristics. On top of the software/hardware stack, the user frequently interacts with the wearable throughout daily life; each interaction is dedicated to a simple task and only lasts for a couple of seconds [2, 45, 10]. At the lowest level, a wearable device's small form factor diminishes the screen and battery, CPU runs slower, possesses fewer cores, and embraces simpler microarctechitures.

Operating systems (OS) for wearable, by contrast, evolve rather slowly. They often feature renovated, watch-friendly user interfaces (UI) while reusing most of the core components from hand-

[1]Recognizing the diversity of modern wearable devices, in this paper we use "wearable" to refer to commercially available, interactive devices that support third party apps and are intended for mass market.

MobiSys'16, June 25 - 30, 2016, Singapore, Singapore

ISBN 978-1-4503-4269-8/16/06...$15.00

DOI: http://dx.doi.org/10.1145/2906388.2906398

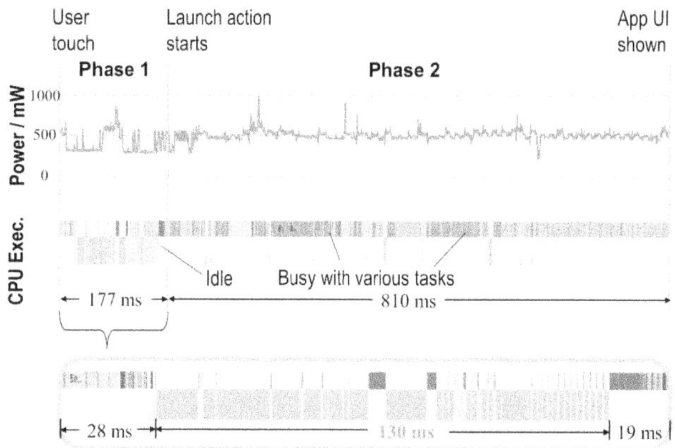

Figure 1: The timeline of launching the "Settings" app on Android Wear, showing both anomalous idle episodes (*not* due to I/O) and intensive CPU execution

held [10, 47] for compatibility and engineering ease. There was neither a clear understanding of how such a design choice impacts wearable efficiency nor a set of guidelines for wearable OS design.

Our pilot study [31] of Android Wear, one of the most popular wearable OSes, presented a framework for analyzing the OS behaviors and discovered preliminary evidences of design inadequacy: many simple scenarios were surprisingly CPU-intensive; numerous idle episodes slowed down system response and wasted energy. This pilot study, however, offered no thorough analysis. Beyond Android Wear, the Apple watch is also reported to show unsatisfactory battery life [50] and slow response [6], although little is known about its internals.

The high power and poor responsiveness are mostly due to *execution inefficiency*. Figure 1 shows a real case observed on an LG smart watch: while the device is awake, the user touches the screen to launch "Settings", a simple app that has already resided in memory. As shown in the Figure, the wearable device takes 987 ms before showing the UI of "Settings" to the user, which is unacceptably long, given that one interaction only lasts for seconds. In phase 1, i.e. from user touch until the launch action starts, the CPU exhibits anomalous idle spanning 130 ms, which we confirmed was not due to well-known reasons such as I/O; in phase 2, the OS performs the launch action and the CPU remains busy for about 810 ms. Note that the CPU, an ARM Cortex-A7 clocked at 780 MHz, is far from wimpy.

To demystify the execution inefficiency, this paper presents a systematic characterization of Android Wear. We focus on its major components – the OS shell and daemons – based on two rationales: these OS components dominate the overall CPU execution, as shown in our pilot study [31] and confirmed by the new evidence in this paper; these OS components are likely to remain as the core of future Android Wear systems.

Through running a suite of fifteen benchmarks on two cutting-edge wearable devices, we examine four key system aspects: CPU usage, idle episodes, thread-level parallelism (TLP), and microarchitectural behaviors. For each aspect, our examination covers the global statistics, their fine-grained breakdown, and the explanation of the observation. We have the following major findings:

Many costly OS services are likely software cruft. In the heavy OS execution, a significant fraction of CPU cycles are spent in the legacy code managing app life cycles, complex window layout, or animation. Given the simplicity of wearable apps, much of the code complexity is likely unwarranted.

Basic data structures are hot spots. Tens of hot functions, in particular those manipulating basic data structures, account for most CPU usage of the major OS services.

OS inadequacies and performance overprovision cause anomalous idle. OS flaws in managing voice UI and the power states of I/O peripherals lead to excessive idle time, slowing down system response and device's entry to deep sleep. In continuous interaction, the CPU and GPU performance provision exceeds the compute demand of simple animation, leaving plentiful (>50%) idle time.

System exhibits substantial TLP, showing the need for multicore. The concurrent execution of apps and OS daemons leads to TLP that is up to 2.2. This exceeds typical smartphone workloads and is even on a par with many desktop workloads. This disproves the common belief that wearables only need a single core and warrants the use of multicore.

Complex OS code mismatches the microarchitecture. The OS execution sees high rates of misses in the L1 icache, iTLB, and branch prediction. This mismatch roots in the large OS code base and the poor code locality; it is further exacerbated by the scaled-down microarchitecture of wearable CPUs.

In addition to these high-level findings, our investigation has yielded *i)* a large set of quantitative results such as CPU usage breakdown for individual OS services and the lists of hot functions, and *ii)* the discovery of multiple OS flaws that affect numerous commercial devices, have serious impact, but were unknown before. By presenting them, we clearly point out the targets of future software and hardware optimization.

Lesson & Insight. Our characterization shows a generic lesson regarding the origin of the discovered OS inefficiency: many existing designs that traded execution efficiency for engineering ease or flexibility now cause major bottlenecks on wearables. Towards evolving the wearable OS, we contribute a key insight: today, the inefficiency within individual OS components is the first-order concern. Accordingly, towards making the OS efficient, it is more rewarding to fix individual OS components in question rather than embracing a new OS structure.

We have made the following contributions:

- We present a comprehensive suite of benchmarks covering typical use of interactive wearable devices and a workflow for analyzing the benchmarks.
- For the first time, we thoroughly quantify a commodity wearable OS, present the outcome in detail, and report a series of OS inadequacies that had a wide impact but were unknown before.
- Through an in-depth analysis of the results, we reveal the root causes of the observed inefficiency, discuss their implications, and contribute a set of new guidelines for future wearable software system design.

All the code, data, and benchmark videos are at:

`http://xsel.rocks/p/wear`

2. BACKGROUND & MOTIVATION

Next, we highlight the wearable's unique usage that drives our benchmark design, discuss the hardware trends, and describe the Android Wear OS, the focus of our investigation.

2.1 Usage Patterns

Wearable introduces unprecedented usage patterns. According to the app design guidelines by major vendors [2, 17, 45], users interact with wearable devices frequently throughout daily use; each interaction is short, often less than 10 seconds, and is dedicated to a simple task, e.g., glancing over an email notification. Due to the limited content that can be displayed on one screen, users spend a short time on one screen before switching to the next. Accordingly, a wearable system should cater to such frequent, brief interactions with minimal latency and high efficiency.

2.2 Device Hardware

Compared to handheld, wearable is "leaner" on most hardware specifications, for which we identify three noteworthy trends.

First, the battery capacity is tiny. Ranging from 200 to 400mAh, it is almost one order of magnitude smaller than a typical smartphone battery which is around 2000 mAh. This calls for high energy efficiency.

Second, processing power dwarfs display power. On smartphones, display power dominates the system power. Compared to a smartphone display, a wearable display has 20 – 40× fewer pixels, fundamentally changing the proportion of display power. Our pilot study [31] shows that while a smart watch consumes up to 4 Watts during interaction, its display consumes no more than 150 mW. As a result, optimizing software activities becomes the first priority in quest of energy efficiency.

Third, the CPU is much simpler. To pursue high efficiency without losing software compatibility, wearable devices often embrace a scaled-down CPU that still remains architecturally identical to handheld's CPU. For instance, almost all commodity smart watches, from the Android devices [29] to the Apple Watch [1], use ARM Cortex-A7, a partial dual-issue, in-order core implementing the pervasive ARMv7 ISA. The core is often clocked at 500 – 800 MHz.

2.3 Android Wear OS

Android Wear is one of the most popular OSes for interactive wearables. Although not completely open-source (unlike Android for handheld), it is the wearable OS with the most public information. Targeting the common usage of smart watches, Android Wear supports third-party applications and features a resigned system UI, including Card for notifications, Context streams, and voice input. Assuming a companion smartphone is nearby, Android Wear wirelessly offloads to the smartphone heavy compute tasks, e.g., voice recognition.

The apps on Android Wear, despite their renovated UI, follow Android's conventional programming paradigm: they are written in Java, compiled ahead-of-time, and executed atop the managed Android Runtime.

Major OS components. Same as on handheld devices, most of Android Wear's *personality* is implemented as userspace processes. The most important ones are three:

- *System Server* is the key daemon hosting the core OS services, such as those managing app life cycles, display layout, and security policy. It is implemented with around 110K SLoC in over 100 files. It is managed, i.e., running atop the Android Runtime.
- *Surface Flinger*, the daemon controlling UI animation, periodically composites bitmaps rendered by multiple apps into the final framebuffer. It is implemented with around 11K SLoC in 81 files.
- *Clockwork* is the OS shell that implements the system UI such as app launcher and voice input. Its source code is unpublished at the time of writing (Dec. 2015). It runs atop the Android Runtime and is likely written in Java.

Underneath the userspace is a mostly vanilla Linux kernel enhanced by a handful of Android-specific facilities, e.g., WakeLocks [20] and Binder IPC [18]. Enforced by the kernel, all apps and OS processes are sealed in separate address spaces and may communicate through the Binder IPC. Within one given process, threads often communicate through shared message queues.

3. BENCHMARK SCENARIOS

The usage of wearables is dominated by a small set of scenarios [31, 25]. Accordingly, we conduct scenario-centric profiling, a proven approach to characterizing interactive systems [23, 27]. By augmenting the core scenarios identified in our pilot study [31], we design a suite of benchmarks with three goals: the benchmarks should cover common wearable usage as described in app design guidelines [2, 10]; they should exercise a variety of system aspects such as computing, IO, and power management; they should be simple and require minimal user inputs to ease reproducing.

As summarized in Table 1, our benchmark suite consists of fifteen benchmarks falling into the following four categories.

- *Wakeup.* Stimulated by internal or external events, a wearable device transits out of suspended mode and presents brief information. No user input follows the device wakeup. Since wakeup happens frequently throughout daily usage, energy efficiency is the most important metric.
- *Single input.* A waking wearable device responds to a single input from the user, e.g., touch or voice command, a common pattern of brief interactions. Because the user is waiting, the device needs sprinting to achieve low UI latency.
- *Continuous interaction.* Users are interacting with the device continuously, e.g. navigating among Cards [10]. The resultant UI animation requires the device to produce a steady stream of graphic frames, which often requires a synergy between CPU and GPU.
- *Sensing.* A set of minimalist programs sample and process sensor data periodically to collect context information, which is known to drive wearable app execution [10]. These programs keep their UI as a black screen with no updates.

Latency and power consumption. As the measurement in Table 1 shows, these conceptually simple scenarios often exhibit long user-perceivable latency and substantial power consumption. These two metrics, as exemplified by the case in Figure 1, are tightly coupled and are ultimately determined by the system's execution efficiency. This motivates our characterization as will be presented below.

4. METHODOLOGY

We next sketch our overall experiment setup and describe the four key aspects under profiling.

Experiment setup. We run all the benchmarks on two state-of-the-art Android Wear devices, the LG Watch R [29] and the Samsung Gear Live [46], both using Qualcomm's APQ8026 system-on-chip (SoC) and running the stock Android Wear 5.0 "Lollipop". Although the SoC is equipped with 4× Cortex-A7 cores, three are forced offline by both device vendors – a common practice among Android Wear watches. We will examine the CPU details in Section 5.3 and 5.4.

In the rest of this paper, we present the quantitative measurements from the LG Watch R; yet, all the discoveries, e.g., OS inefficiency, have been confirmed on both devices unless otherwise stated.

Power measurement. While it is common to measure a smartphone's power by interposing its battery interface, doing so for wearable is challenging: the latter's batteries have tiny contacts and are incompatible with commodity power monitors [38]. To this end, as shown in Figure 2, we carve out a compatible interface circuit from a smartphone battery by the same manufacturer and use the interface as an adapter between the smart watch and an external power monitor. This technique was unknown to the community before, to the best of our knowledge.

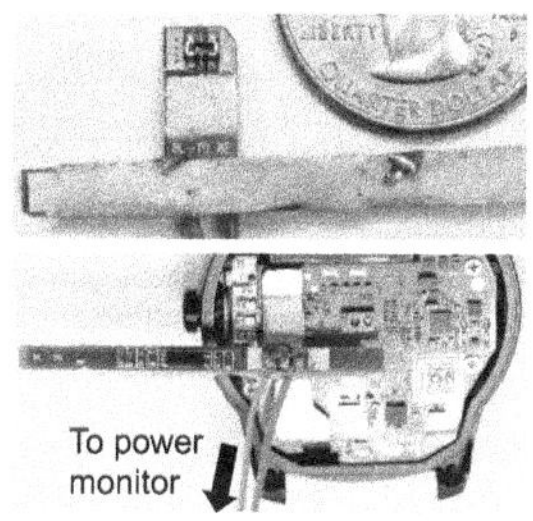

Figure 2: Top: the battery interface carved out from Nexus 5; bottom: the inter face (flipped) connected to the LG watch R.

Toolset. To examine system behaviors at different levels and granularities, we have employed a set of tools: systrace [19] for capturing global system events such as scheduling, I/O activities, and IPC; the Android Runtime's built-in function tracer for recording function call history in individual processes; the Linux perf for sampling CPU performance counters. We have further customized these tools for collecting additional information and overcoming the limitation of the current Android Wear [31]. All the customized tools are open for download as mentioned in Section 1.

Tackling profiling overhead. The major profiling overhead comes from event tracing: each tracepoint saves in memory a timestamp and a small amount of event information that is at most tens of bytes. While the overhead is negligible in tracing the relatively sparse system events, it can be overwhelming in tracing function invocations.

We tackle the overhead in two ways. First, in quantifying global system behaviors, we only rely on system events; in order to under-

Table 1: The benchmark suite. The power and energy are measured as described in Section 4; all time values are measured by systrace [19]. Some of the scenarios and their measurement were previously reported in our pilot study [31] and are included here for completeness. The slow-motion videos of the benchmarks are available as mentioned in Section 1.

	Scenario	Description	Duration (D) or Latency (P) /ms	Energy (E) /mJ Power (P) /mW	# of Tasks
Wakeup	update	A minimalist watch face is updated with a new minute value. Device gets suspended.	D: 364	E: 61	81
	notif	Receive a weather Card from the phone (over Bluetooth). Device gets suspended.	D: 4645	E: 539	135
	wrist	User's wrist motion wakes up the device.	D: 407	E: 155	113
	touch	Touch a sleeping watch to light up the watch face.	D: 184	E: 69	102
Single Input	lch.set	Screen is on; touch to launch "System Settings" (preloaded in memory).	P1:177 P2:810	E: 440	92
	lch.calc	Screen is on; touch to launch a calculator app (light).	P1:202 P2:520	E: 376	99
	lch.game	Screen is on; touch to launch "DeadlySpikes" (heavy).	P1:182 P2:1236	E: 775	107
	palming	Screen is on; cover the screen with palm so that the device is suspended.	D: 2343	E: 556	130
	voice	Screen is on; Bluetooth is off; speak "Ok Google" to activate the voice command UI.	D: 1671	E: 1675	65
Interact.	game	The interval between two adjacent touches in a busy game, "DeadlySpikes".	D: 409	E: 241	62
	notes	Speak the word "hello" for 3 times; user waits until the notes recognized and saved.	D: 3897	E: 2449	89
	navi	Screen is on; pop up a set of two "Weather" cards; navigate and dismiss.	D: 4119	E: 2400	67
Sensing	accel	A minimalist program sampling the accelerometer at the default rate (5Hz). Screen is blank.		P: 83	33
	heart	A minimalist program sampling the heart rate sensor at the default rate (5Hz). Screen is blank.		P: 105	21
	baro	A minimalist program sampling the barometer at the default rate (5Hz). Screen is blank.		P: 113	28

P1: from user touch to launch start; **P2**: from launch start to UI displayed

stand their causes, we collect function trace from extra runs. Second, in quantifying function-level activities, we deduct an overhead of 4 μs from each traced function invocation. The overhead is due to bookkeeping each function's entry and exit, and is measured and verified as constant regardless of the traced functions; specifically, we measured the overhead as the delay of tracing a no-op function.

CPU Usage

We collect and analyze CPU usage at two granularities.

Task-level breakdown. To identify the tasks[2] that are the major CPU consumers, we build an analyzer to scan all traced scheduling events and attribute the CPU busy episodes to individual tasks accordingly.

Function-level breakdown. To further locate the performance hot spots in *System Server*, the managed OS daemon where most services run, we tap into the function trace and attribute the CPU usage to distinct managed functions. More specifically, we employ the following two metrics, commonly used in Android app profiling, to characterize one invocation of a managed function:

- *Exclusive CPU cycles* are spent in the function's own code, i.e., excluding any of its subroutines. Intuitively, the total exclusive cycles of a given function imply the potential benefit from optimizing the function *per se*;
- *Inclusive CPU cycles* are spent in the function's code as well as in all subroutines being called. Intuitively, the total inclusive cycles of a given function imply the potential benefit from eliminating invocations to this function.

[2]Following Linux's lingo, we use *tasks* to refer to scheduling entities, regardless of whether they are in the same or separate address spaces.

Note that both metrics include the time spent in both user and kernel spaces; they do not cover the time when a task is off CPU due to being scheduled out.

Idle Time Analysis

In a pilot study of Android Wear [31] we have noticed excessive idle episodes. Although interactive systems are known for being intermittently idle, e.g. due to user think, the amount and duration of the observed idle episodes are unusual.

To reveal the root causes of all observed idle episodes, we first attempt to match them with system events known to cause idle, e.g. I/O and power management. Accounting for the remaining idle episodes, however, is more challenging: they often root in OS service's stalling in serving app's requests. To further obscure the true cause, as the service is stalled, the kernel will schedule in other unrelated tasks, making the CPU intermittently busy as exemplified by phase 1 of Figure 1.

To address this challenge, we build `IdleChecker`, an analyzer that helps mapping anomalous idle episodes to the responsible code regions, based on a simple rationale: the function calls and IPC transactions spanning an anomalous idle episode are suspicious. In a nutshell, `IdleChecker` runs the following steps for each idle episode.

First, it identifies suspicious app tasks that are blocked throughout the entire idle episode but run after the episode. Second, for each suspicious task, it identifies two suspicious CPU time quanta: the one right before the idle episode and the one right after it. Third, `IdleChecker` examines the suspicious quanta, looking for IPC transactions spanning across the idle episode. Finally, the analyzer identifies the function invocations that either coincide with the IPC or span across the idle episode. It maps the names of the identified functions, which are preserved in the trace, back to the source code.

`IdleChecker` effectively narrows down the investigating scope from tens of thousands of function invocations per benchmark down to a couple of functions, making our idle analysis tractable.

Thread-level Parallelism (TLP)

Despite the popular belief that one CPU core is enough for wearable workloads, we seek to experimentally test it by measuring thread-level parallelism (TLP), a metric widely used for gauging an interactive system's need for core count. Intuitively, TLP is the average number of busy CPU cores during the non-idle time. It is formally defined as follows [15]:

$$TLP = \sum_{i=1}^{n} i * c_i/(1 - c_0)$$

In the formula, c_0 is the total time when no threads are running; c_i stands for the time when exactly i threads are running simultaneously; n is the number of cores available.

To measure TLP, we override the device vendor's default configuration and force all four cores online, each running at their default clock rate. We repeat each scenario three times, identify the busy episodes of every core from the traced scheduling events, and calculate TLP based on the formula above.

Microarchitectural behaviors

Little work has been done on the microarchitectural behaviors of wearable workloads, making the microarchitecture design a mystery. To this end, we characterize the microarchitectural behaviors of the major OS components, due to their dominating CPU usage and importance in the current and future Android Wear systems. By using the Linux perf, we sample the performance counters of the Cortex-A7 CPU on our test devices. The full-fledged performance counters allow us to observe branch prediction, cache, and TLB in all benchmarks.

5. RESULTS

Next, we present the characterization results on the four aspects. For each aspect, we first highlight the key findings, explain them with evidence or case studies, and finally discuss their implications on future software or hardware design. Note that each experiment reported has been repeated at least 3 times.

5.1 CPU usage

Despite their conceptual simplicity, most benchmarks show substantial CPU utilization, as shown in Figure 3(a). In fact, the CPU often keeps spinning for tens to hundreds of ms without a break, as exemplified by the case shown in Figure 1. This observation raises one top profiling question: *where do these CPU cycles go?*

5.1.1 Global CPU Usage

- *Intensive OS execution often dominates the global CPU usage.*

As shown in Figure 3(a), the percentages of the OS-consumed CPU cycles in the total busy cycles range from 48% (*game*) to 93% (*wrist*). A further breakdown among the OS daemons, as shown in Figure 3(b), indicates that two daemons are in particular heavy: *System Server*, which hosts most OS services; *Surface Flinger*, which composites bitmaps for painting UI. It is worth noting that even for the *sensing* benchmarks where the app UI is blank, the OS seems to run *Surface Flinger* occasionally in order to update the entire system UI.

Overall, the observation confirms our intuition: since wearable apps are simple, the cost of OS execution becomes overwhelming. This observation also justifies our OS-focused investigation as stated in Section 1.

5.1.2 OS Services

- *Many costly OS services are likely software cruft.*

Due to the significance of *System Server*, we further examine how its enclosed OS services contribute to the CPU usage. We do this by studying each OS service's inclusive CPU cycles as defined in Section 4. As shown in Figure 3(c), among a variety of OS services, the most CPU-intensive ones are: activity manager, which manages the life cycles of apps; window manager, which manages the complex UI layout of multiple apps; power manager, which enables app to control device power state through WakeLock [20]; choreographer, which controls the timing of UI animation. These sophisticated OS mechanisms, despite being essential to smartphones, e.g. in managing app multitasking or handling screen rotation, become *cruft* in serving simple wearable apps that have minimalist UI.

5.1.3 Hot Functions in System Server

- *The distribution of hot functions is highly skewed.*
- *Manipulating basic data structures consumes substantial CPU cycles.*
- *Legacy OS functions may become serious performance bottlenecks.*

To gain further insights into *System Server*, we break down its CPU usage at the function level. We study the *exclusive* cycles of functions as defined in Section 4. As shown in Figure 4, the distribution of CPU time over all functions is heavily skewed. Although the total number of distinct functions per benchmark ranges from several hundreds to a few thousands, the top 5 "hot" functions constitute more than 20% of *System Server*'s CPU cycles in most benchmarks; the top 50 hot functions constitute more than 50%. This skewed distribution implies highly concentrated performance hot spots. The skewness is rare in commodity OS workloads: for instance, prior measurement shows that the Linux kernel often does not see a small set of functions dominating CPU usage [43].

In understanding the skewness, we have found a small set of functions – those manipulating basic data structures – are hot in almost all benchmarks. As shown in the Total column of Table 2, these functions collectively contribute a significant fraction to *System Server*'s CPU usage, up to 45%. In benchmarks such as *notes*, these functions are even more CPU-hungry than those implemented by the code of *System Server*.

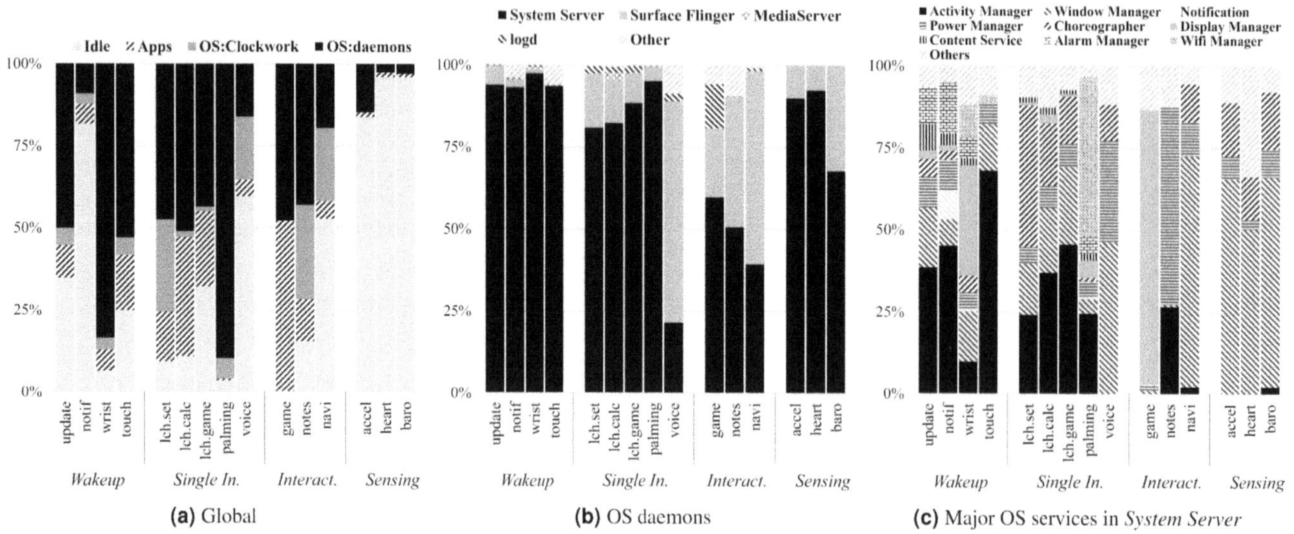

Figure 3: The CPU usage breakdown

A further breakdown shows that these functions concentrate on tens of basic data structures implemented in a couple of software packages, as summarized in Table 2:

- `java.core`: the utility data structures from Java's core API, such as arrays, collections, maps, and dictionaries;
- `java.string`, Java's string implementation;
- `android.util`, the utility data structures, such as SparseArray and ArraySet, from the Android framework libraries;
- `threadlocal`, thread-local variables and objects;
- `android.msgq`, message queues for inter-thread communication.

Although one single invocation of them is as short as a couple of μs, the large number of invocations per benchmark, sometimes multiple thousands, makes their CPU usage substantial as a whole. This can be observed in the full lists of top hot functions in Table 3.

5.1.4 *Discovered OS Execution Bottlenecks*

In addition to the operations on basic data structures, we found that multiple hot functions, among the top ones listed in Table 3, correspond to serious bottlenecks existing on various OS aspects.

Ad-hoc backlight effect. A mobile OS often varies the screen brightness as it sees fit. Yet, we have noticed `setLight..()`[3], the OS function setting the screen backlight, is expensive, taking more than 100 ms or 78M CPU cycles per affected benchmark. A deeper investigation holds a vendor library (`light.lenok.so`) responsible: in setting the backlight to a new level, the library emulates a transition effect by modulation, for which it repeatedly calls the kernel driver and thus increases the execution cost by 50×. This function is invoked by *System Server* every 35 ms to realize another level of light modulation. Together, they create an expensive anomaly we dubbed "modulating of modulation". This bottleneck, rooting in a device-specific library, affects the LG device but not the Samsung one.

UI layout. Due to the limited content that can be shown on a small display, a user often navigates among "Cards", or app windows, frequently. This new UI pattern, however, is poorly supported by the expensive OS mechanism for window switch. Every time a new window is brought to the foreground, *System Server* re-layouts the UI: it updates each app window's display properties, including size, location, and visibility, and runs transition animation. At the heart of this workflow is `perf..Layout()`, a giant function catering to the complex UI layout of multiple apps. On our test devices, each invocation takes 1 ms (780K CPU cycles); in one benchmark that lasts for a few seconds, this function alone may take up to 10 ms (7.8M cycles).

Maintaining low-memory killer. To reconcile app memory demand with the physical memory limit, the OS maintains a low-

[3]For all shortened function names mentioned in this section, see Table 3 for their full names.

Table 2: The percentages of *System Server*'s CPU cycles spent on manipulating basic data structures

	Benchmark	java.core	java.string	android.util	thread local	android.msgq	Misc	Total
Wakeup	update	2.6%	5.5%	4.5%	6.7%	6.1%	1.6%	**27.0%**
	notif	4.8%	8.5%	2.9%	8.5%	2.7%	3.3%	**30.7%**
	wrist	4.9%	5.2%	2.1%	3.6%	4.2%	2.0%	**22.0%**
	touch	2.8%	6.1%	8.7%	4.1%	10.9%	3.7%	**36.3%**
Single Input	lch.set	2.3%	3.8%	5.5%	6.0%	4.1%	2.5%	**24.2%**
	lch.calc	2.7%	4.2%	4.5%	7.0%	3.0%	3.0%	**24.4%**
	lch.game	2.3%	3.9%	5.1%	7.6%	2.9%	2.5%	**24.3%**
	palming	4.5%	2.1%	3.0%	3.2%	2.0%	2.9%	**17.7%**
	voice	1.4%	3.0%	3.7%	20.3%	1.2%	2.2%	**31.8%**
Interact.	game	0.0%	0.1%	1.8%	36.3%	0.9%	2.6%	**41.7%**
	notes	4.2%	4.1%	2.7%	18.7%	12.2%	3.2%	**45.1%**
	navi	1.0%	3.8%	5.3%	7.3%	3.1%	3.4%	**23.9%**
Sensing	accel	1.7%	4.0%	5.1%	5.9%	3.0%	1.5%	**21.2%**
	heart	1.6%	4.6%	5.5%	5.7%	4.3%	1.7%	**23.4%**
	baro	4.9%	6.1%	4.8%	5.1%	2.5%	5.9%	**29.3%**

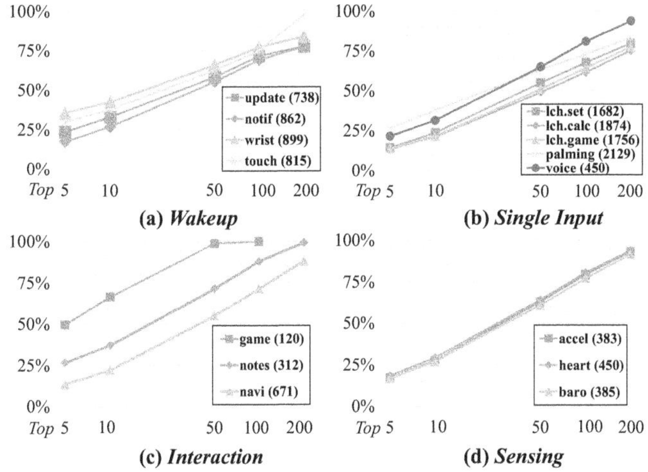

Figure 4: The percentages of CPU cycles spent by *System Server* on its top N hot functions (x-axis, logarithmic). Each subfigure is for one benchmark category. The legends contain the numbers of distinct functions invoked in each benchmark.

memory killer that works based on per-process threshold values. At run time, the OS may kill any process whose threshold is above the amount of available physical memory. By design, the per-process thresholds have to be adjusted in the event of significant changes to memory use, e.g., app startup, window switch, process termination, etc. To do the adjustment, *System Server* executes `computeOom..()` for each process, which turns out to be a heavy burden. For instance, in *update* or *wrist*, this function has been invoked for over 150 times; this function alone consumes around 15 ms or 11M CPU cycles.

Object reflection. A powerful mechanism, reflection enables program code to inspect its objects at run time [49]. However, its lazy behavior may incur significant overhead in wearable's brief use. In suspending a device, *System Server* stops the wireless networking service (among other OS services) by operating the service's state machine. For bookkeeping, *System Server* uses reflection to retrieve the name of a state object (`getSimpleName()`). The reflection leads to a flood of 33,000 function invocations, most spent on loading and parsing annotations from the object's class file (`getAnnotationReader()`). As a result, each reflection takes around 40 ms (3.1M cycles), deferring the device's entry to suspended mode in an expensive way. This accounts for the high CPU usage of WiFi manager in *palming* as shown in Figure 3(c).

5.1.5 Design Implications

Our findings clearly suggest that *i)* OS should be the primary target of system optimization and *ii)* optimizing the small set of hot functions is likely rewarding. In particular, the functions manipulating basic data structures should receive priority efforts, towards which we foresee a few promising approaches: hand-tuned implementation; exploiting SIMD hardware, e.g. ARM NEON [3], for vector operations; hardware-accelerating the most common data structures, an approach shown to benefit intensive mobile apps [55].

The discovered OS bottlenecks might already be known as non-cheap, but were still adopted by the current OS in favor of engineering ease, flexibility, visual appeal, etc. However, our results have shown that they now become unacceptably expensive for wearable devices. This observation urges a rethink of such OS design decisions. In order to do so, we contribute the following new guidelines: *i)* the software cruft for the complex runtime environment and UI layout should be aggressively trimmed down; *ii)* the OS should be frugal at spending CPU cycles on "add-on" user experience; *iii)* lazy or on-demand operations, despite their wide use for efficiency, may hurt system responsiveness when they come in the way of short user interactions.

5.2 Idle Episodes

- *The idle episodes are plentiful and of a variety of lengths.*
- *Idle anomalies are mainly contributed by improper OS implementations and performance overprovision during interaction.*

As shown in our pilot study [31] and discussed in Section 4, idle anomalies hurt both user experience and energy efficiency. Next, we present a quantification of them and describe our discovery of their root causes.

We select nine out of fifteen benchmarks whose idle time is larger than 5% of the benchmark duration. The statistics of idle time, as shown in Table 4, exhibit four unusual characteristics. First, over the duration of one benchmark, the accumulative idle time can take a significant fraction up to 87%. Second, the number of idle episodes is large, often multiple hundreds per benchmark. Third, many of the episodes are as short as a couple of ms, not enough for the device to enter low-power mode. Fourth, numerous idle episodes even emerge in CPU-bound benchmarks, e.g. launching an in-memory app (*lch.set*).

As summarized in Table 4, our investigation reveals a variety of causes, which, together, account for more than 91% of all the observed idle time. In addition to a couple of well-known causes such as user think, storage I/O or app policies, we have discovered two groups of causes originated in the OS design, as discussed below.

5.2.1 Improper OS Designs

Surprisingly, a large fraction of idle episodes are incurred by OS design flaws. We next describe the two most notable cases that have high impact on user experience and energy efficiency.

Interference from voice UI. *Clockwork*, the OS shell, hosts an always-on voice UI and thus is consuming a stream of audio input. Unfortunately, managing the voice UI incurs a long delay. When a user launches a new app through *Clockwork*, the foreground *Clockwork* releases its system resources and moves to the background. In doing so, *Clockwork* sends an IPC request to *MediaServer*, an OS daemon, asking to terminate the audio input stream. By design, this protocol is synchronous for security. On one hand, *Clockwork* stalls launching until the request is completed. On the other hand, *MediaServer* handles the request conservatively: its core function `setOutputDevice()` waits for the audio input pipeline to completely drain so that no leftover audio samples will enter the newly launched app. The draining holds the foreground app launch for around 120 ms, constituting up to 19% of the user-perceived latency in app launch benchmarks. Affecting both of our test devices, this flaw is responsible for the idle anomaly shown in phase 1 of Figure 1. Through experiments, we further confirmed that this flaw is introduced by Android Wear, i.e. not existing on smartphone: we

Table 3: Top 5 hot functions of System Server based on an average over three benchmark runs. Functions operating basic data structures are shaded. See Appendix for brief descriptions of these functions.

update	#Calls (mean/SD)		Total Time (mean/SD)	
computeOomAdjLocked	176	6.35	15.11	0.15
removeObserverLocked	152	0	9.74	0.52
MessageQueue.next	40	0.58	9.52	0.32
Values.cleanUp	98	2.08	6.68	0.22
updateOomAdjLocked	19	0	6.55	0.22

notif	#Calls (mean/SD)		Total Time (mean/SD)	
ProcessCpuTracker.collectStats	1	1	25.06	25.39
Values.cleanUp	220	48.39	15.06	3.45
computeOomAdjLocked	189	42.15	14.61	3.31
AlarmManager$Batch.remove	285	70.47	12.59	3.19
PendingIntent.equals	488	109.7	9.74	2.45

wrist	#Calls (mean/SD)		Total Time (mean/SD)	
LightImpl.setLightLocked	23	4.16	164.08	30.1
MessageQueue.next	130	7.57	15.53	1.12
parseProcWakelocks	1	0	14.4	0.08
computeOomAdjLocked	152	69	13.97	6.31
Values.cleanUp	121	11.36	8.36	0.62

touch	#Calls (mean/SD)		Total Time (mean/SD)	
LightImpl.setLightLocked	20	12	124.02	63.26
MessageQueue.next	124	51.62	15.67	8.35
Values.cleanUp	140	8.49	9.51	0.73
String.equals	525	78.49	8.74	1.10
setHalInteractiveModeLocked	6	2.12	7.34	0.96

lch.set	#Calls (mean/SD)		Total Time (mean/SD)	
SparseArray.get	2098	122.57	17.33	0.9
MessageQueue.next	70	3.46	13.21	0.66
Values.cleanUp	174	3.79	11.15	0.13
Parcel.writeLongArray	1	0	9.34	0.63
animateLocked	42	3.21	9.03	0.97

lch.calc	#Calls (mean/SD)		Total Time (mean/SD)	
Values.cleanUp	1	0	53.01	8.94
Parcel.writeLongArray	165	1.15	11.35	0.1
SparseArray.get	1	0	10.84	0.98
MessageQueue.next	1079	20.43	9.12	0.2
Parcel.writeLong	45	2.31	7.71	0.92

lch.game	#Calls (mean/SD)		Total Time (mean/SD)	
Values.cleanUp	220	22.11	14.96	1.27
SparseArray.get	1453	62.78	12.42	0.66
Parcel.writeLongArray	1	0	10.94	0.53
performLayoutAnd PlaceSurfacesLockedInner	9	0.58	9.41	0.48
MessageQueue.next	42	1	7.63	0.56

palming	#Calls (mean/SD)		Total Time (mean/SD)	
DirectByteBuffer.get	6040	1060.08	92.78	12.34
DirectByteBuffer. checkIsAccessible	6586	1155.05	85.94	11.25
computeOomAdjLocked	709	1.53	64.74	1.9
DirectByteBuffer. checkNotFreed	6933	1215.1	51.09	5.85
MemoryBlock.isAccessible	6586	1155.05	49.62	5.61

voice	#Calls (mean/SD)		Total Time (mean/SD)	
Values.cleanUp	41	5.03	2.81	0.35
Binder.execTransact	19	3.06	1.14	0.15
ThreadLocal.get	41	3.06	1.11	0.12
performLayoutAnd PlaceSurfacesLockedInner	1	0	0.85	0.01
ThreadLocal$Values.put	39	3.06	0.83	0.08

game	#Calls (mean/SD)		Total Time (mean/SD)	
Values.cleanUp	163	11.72	12.31	0.93
DisplayInfo.writeToParcel	54	3.21	10.83	0.64
Parcel.writeInt	1181	70.72	5.82	0.31
ThreadLocal.get	163	11.53	4.39	0.29
Values.put	163	11.72	3.84	0.28

notes	#Calls (mean/SD)		Total Time (mean/SD)	
ThreadLocal$Values. cleanUp	393	33.41	28.08	2.68
MessageQueue.next	67	6.03	27.76	2.41
MessageQueue. enqueueMessage	133	12.01	14.63	1.35
ThreadLocal.get	526	45.49	14.18	1.50
String.equals	292	38.08	10.26	0.99

navi	#Calls (mean/SD)		Total Time (mean/SD)	
performLayoutAnd PlaceSurfacesLockedInner	6	0	6.22	0.39
ThreadLocal$Values.clean Up	79	12.22	5.88	0.87
InputEventReceiver. finishInputEvent	60	5	5.02	0.44
SparseArray.get	533	58.29	4.9	0.59
consumeBatchedInputEvent s	51	4.51	4.57	0.34

accel	#Calls (mean/SD)		Total Time (mean/SD)	
performLayoutAnd PlaceSurfacesLockedInner	5	0	4.73	0.08
SparseArray.get	443	5.77	3.86	0.17
setInputWindows	10	0	2.69	0.12
MessageQueue.next	13	3.21	2.5	0.68
Values.cleanUp	31	4.04	2.22	0.28

heart	#Calls (mean/SD)		Total Time (mean/SD)	
performLayoutAnd PlaceSurfacesLockedInner	1	0	0.93	0.02
SparseArray.get	88	0	0.73	0.01
MessageQueue.next	3	0	0.6	0.04
setInputWindows	2	0	0.54	0.04
addInputWindowHandleLw	16	0	0.41	0

baro	#Calls (mean/SD)		Total Time (mean/SD)	
performLayoutAnd PlaceSurfacesLockedInner	5	0	4.58	0.23
SparseArray.get	440	0	3.78	0.19
setInputWindows	10	0	2.45	0.02
addInputWindowHandleLw	80	0	2.11	0.12
updateInputWindowsLw	10	0	1.96	0.1

have not observed similar idle anomalies on the Nexus 5 running Android Lollipop.

Legacy support for device suspending. The current kernel mechanism for device suspending is decades-old; initially designed for desktop and later adapted to handheld devices, the mechanism is now cumbersome for wearable's frequent, brief wakeups. Our measurement shows that one suspending action spends a continuous period of around 200 ms in kernel, a non-negligible overhead comparable to one interaction itself that often lasts for a couple of seconds (§2.1). Over the course of suspending, around 130 ms is in small idle episodes, each lasting for a couple of ms.

Our investigation shows power management for I/O peripherals as the deeper cause: in suspending a wearable device, the kernel checks all peripherals to ensure they are ready to enter low-power mode. Since a subset of peripherals take tens or even a couple of hundred ms to be ready, the CPU has to repeatedly poll them and sits idle in between. These peripherals include display controller, battery temperature monitor, and MMC host controller, based on our measurement. Note that this inefficiency roots in the Linux kernel and is not tied to specific wearable devices.

5.2.2 *Continuous Interaction*

Recall that continuous interaction and the resultant UI animation, e.g. scrolling a web page, used to be among the most intensive smartphone workloads [48]. In animating simple wearable UI, however, performance overprovision has produced numerous idle episodes.

As a user touches the device screen, the CPU processes a sequence of discrete input events, collaborates with the GPU to periodically render graphic frames, and sits idle between adjacent frames. In our benchmarks, almost all frames in continuous animation are rendered within 8 ms each, which is less than 50% of the 16 ms per-frame rendering budget (the displays of our test devices, as in most today's mobile devices, are refreshed at 60 Hz).

Table 4: Idle time in benchmarks. (Left) a breakdown based on their causes; (Right) the total idle time; its percentage over the benchmark duration; the number of episodes; the percentage of idle time that we provide explanations for. Note that the two bar graphs have different x-axis scales (time).

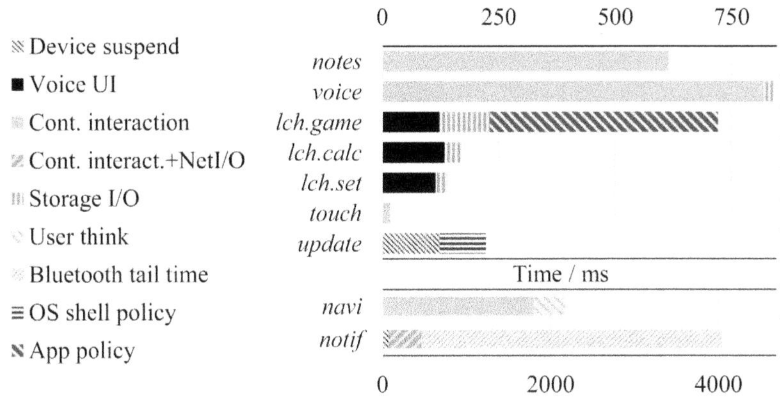

Time (ms)	Pct. Overall	Episodes	Pct. Explained	
614.1	17.1%	376	100.0%	*notes*
843.3	50.5%	352	100.0%	*voice*
722.6	50.9%	205	99.9%	*lch.game*
185.2	25.6%	110	92.9%	*lch.calc*
153.6	15.6%	120	91.4%	*lch.set*
16.8	10.6%	6	100.0%	*touch*
223.0	61.2%	44	100.0%	*update*
2173.0	52.80%	912	100.0%	*navi*
4035.6	86.80%	277	100.0%	*notif*

As a result, many short idle episodes come hand in hand with continuous interaction. For instance, in *navi* that lasts for 4119 ms, performance overprovision contributes 1805 ms idle time in about 630 episodes.

5.2.3 Design Implications

To cope with the excessive idle time, our findings suggest either eliminating their origins or utilizing them more efficiently.

Hunting OS inefficiencies. Fixing the *discovered* inefficiencies requires a rethink of the respective OS aspects, e.g. security policy and power management. What is even more challenging is to uncover the *unknown* inefficiencies: despite our success in identifying a few key cases, more subtle, non-deterministic ones are likely to exist. While the spirit of `IdleChecker` discussed in Section 4 is likely to apply, analyzing massive traces captured *in the wild* will be vital.

To this end, it is crucial to have a lightweight tracer that captures important software activities – from system events to function calls – related to anomalous idle episodes. Designing the tracer, despite a reminiscence of smartphone app tracking [44], raises two unique challenges: first, tracing should only be activated upon the manifest of anomalous idle, otherwise the amount of information will be overwhelming; second, tracing should span across multiple processes, most notably the OS daemons. Ultimately, we envision that the wearable OS, through integration with tools, can offer accountability of idle episodes, clearly pinpointing which software entity causes an idle episode and for what reason.

Filling idle time with useful work. As static power keeps increasing on future devices [13], it is compelling to fill the power-hungry idle episodes, e.g., those happened in continuous interaction, with useful work. We expect that two approaches are promising. First, compared to handheld, the wearable UI has fewer elements and much less variation in rendering time. These characteristics, together with the observed performance overprovision, suggest to lower the performance of CPU and GPU, e.g., by reducing their clock rates. This will shrink idle episodes and improve system energy efficiency.

Second, the idle episodes during interaction are ideal opportunities for predictive execution. Our rationales are twofold. First, since wearable usage is driven by user's daily routines, many tasks can be foreseen, e.g., retrieving calendar from the paired phone. Such prediction is already demonstrated as effective on smartphones [53, 33]. Second, due to the periodic rendering activity, the idle episodes show regular, predictable timing patterns. This simplifies scheduling predictive tasks and minimizing their contention with the foreground UI animation.

5.3 Thread-level parallelism

- *Short interactions exhibit substantial TLP, which is on a par with desktop workloads.*
- *While apps are mostly single-threaded, OS daemons contribute to TLP significantly.*
- *A wearable device needs at least two cores.*

As described in Section 4, we measure TLP by forcing all four CPU cores on at their default clock rate of 787 MHz. This is essentially a "what-if" study: *what core utilization can a wearable system achieve, if it has plentiful cores?*

Our experiments dispel the "one core is enough" myth mentioned in Section 4: despite that a wearable device is physically equipped with multiple cores, all but one are forced offline by the vendor. As shown in Figure 5(a), most benchmarks exhibit TLP higher than 1.5; for three *Wakeup* benchmarks the TLP rises to around 2. This TLP is unexpected to us, as it exceeds that of typical smartphone workloads (1.44 on average [16]), and is on a par with or even higher than many desktop workloads including Microsoft Office (1.2), 3D gaming (1.6), and web browsing (2) [4] . The concurrency values c2 – c4 shown in Figure 5(a) indicate that more than one core are in use for a significant amount of time.

Why is the TLP high? A closer examination reveals two causes of the high TLP. First, wearable's short span of interaction creates bursty TLP. Recall that compared to smartphones, user interaction periods on wearables are much shorter (§1). Although similar TLP peaks have been observed on smartphones [16], the peaks on wearable constitute a much larger fraction of the interaction span, leading to a higher TLP on average.

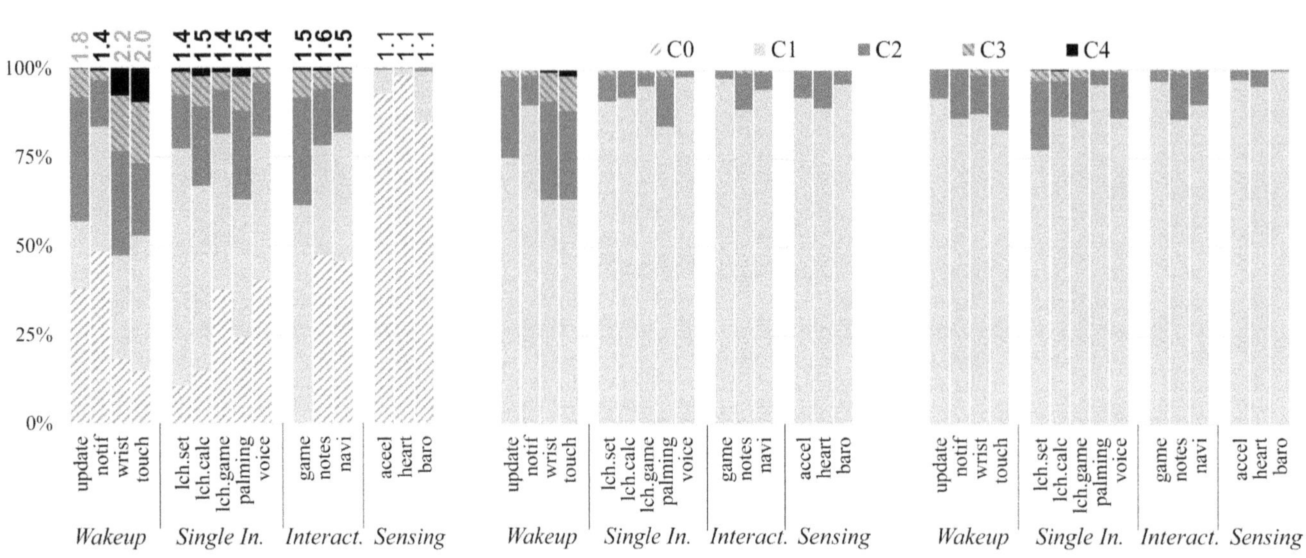

Figure 5: The system-wide TLP and the concurrency values. C_i indicates the time fraction when i threads are simultaneously running over (a) the whole benchmark duration or (b & c) the corresponding process execution duration.

Table 5: A comparison of popular mobile CPU cores

	Cortex-A7 *Current wearable*	***Cortex-A9*** *Smartphone*	***Cortex-A53*** *Next-gen wearable*
ISA	ARMv7A	ARMv7A	ARMv8A
Inst. Pipeline	8-stage in-order	8-stage out-of-order	8-stage in-order
Br. Predictor history buffer	256-entry	4096-entry	3072-entry
TLB entries	L1: 10I/10D L2: 256	L1: 32I/32D L2:128	L1: 10I/10D L2: 512
L1$ (I/D)	32KB/32KB	32KB/32KB	8-64KB/8-64KB
L2$	1024KB	512-1024KB	128-2048KB

Second, the OS daemons, which often dominate CPU usage (§5.1), contribute to the TLP substantially. As standalone processes, these daemons receive app requests over IPC and serve them in parallel with the app execution. In addition, an individual OS daemon is multi-threaded and moderately parallel, e.g., to run multiple service instances simultaneously. This can be seen from the concurrency values of two major OS daemons shown in Figure 5(b) and (c).

The two causes also account for the particularly high TLP in most *Wakeup* benchmarks: these benchmarks are OS-intensive as shown in Figure 3(a); in response to a wake up event, multiple OS services run in order to initialize the hardware or prepare themselves for the subsequent app execution, creating a surge of TLP.

The wearable apps, on the other hand, are mostly single-threaded. Even the most parallel app, "Deadly Spikes" in benchmark *game*, runs one thread for 93% of the time, i.e., its c1 value is as high as 93%.

Design Implications

OS structure. Our TLP measurement suggests the existing structure of Android Wear, i.e. realizing the OS personality as multi-process, multi-threaded daemons, is a viable design. By promoting TLP, the OS structure is capable of exploiting mobile multicores which have already demonstrated the advantage of energy efficiency [9]. Furthermore, the cost of app/daemon IPC is still a much lower-order concern as compared to the expensive hot functions shown in Section 5.1.

CPU core count. A wearable device needs to use at least two cores. The measured TLP already shows the need for a second core; eliminating the idle anomalies identified in Section 5.2 may further boost TLP for the affected benchmarks, e.g., in *Single Input*. To accommodate the lower, but still non-negligible, demand for more than two cores (c3 and c4 in Figure 5(a)), a wearable device may embrace even weaker cores to form 2+1 or 2+2 big.LITTLE clusters.

One may wonder the impact of multicore on device cost or energy efficiency. First, the use of extra cores will incur no extra cost: as mentioned in Section 4, the commodity Android wear devices already possess quad cores – three of them are just forced off. Second, previous study has already shown that catering to parallel workloads with extra cores will benefit, rather than hurting, energy efficiency [9], as the device can finish tasks sooner and fall into sleep. We expect the extra cores, when they become idle, can be aggressive power-gated in order to further reduce their static power.

5.4 Microarchitectural behaviors

- *A significant mismatch exists between the OS and CPU microarchitecture, particularly in L1 icache, iTLB, and branch predictor.*
- *The mismatch is largely due to the OS code complexity, and will not be eliminated by a unilateral enhancement of wearable CPU.*

We have listed three typical mobile CPUs in Table 5. Among them, Cortex-A9, a smartphone CPU, already showed microarchitectural inefficiency in running popular smartphone apps [21]. Cortex-

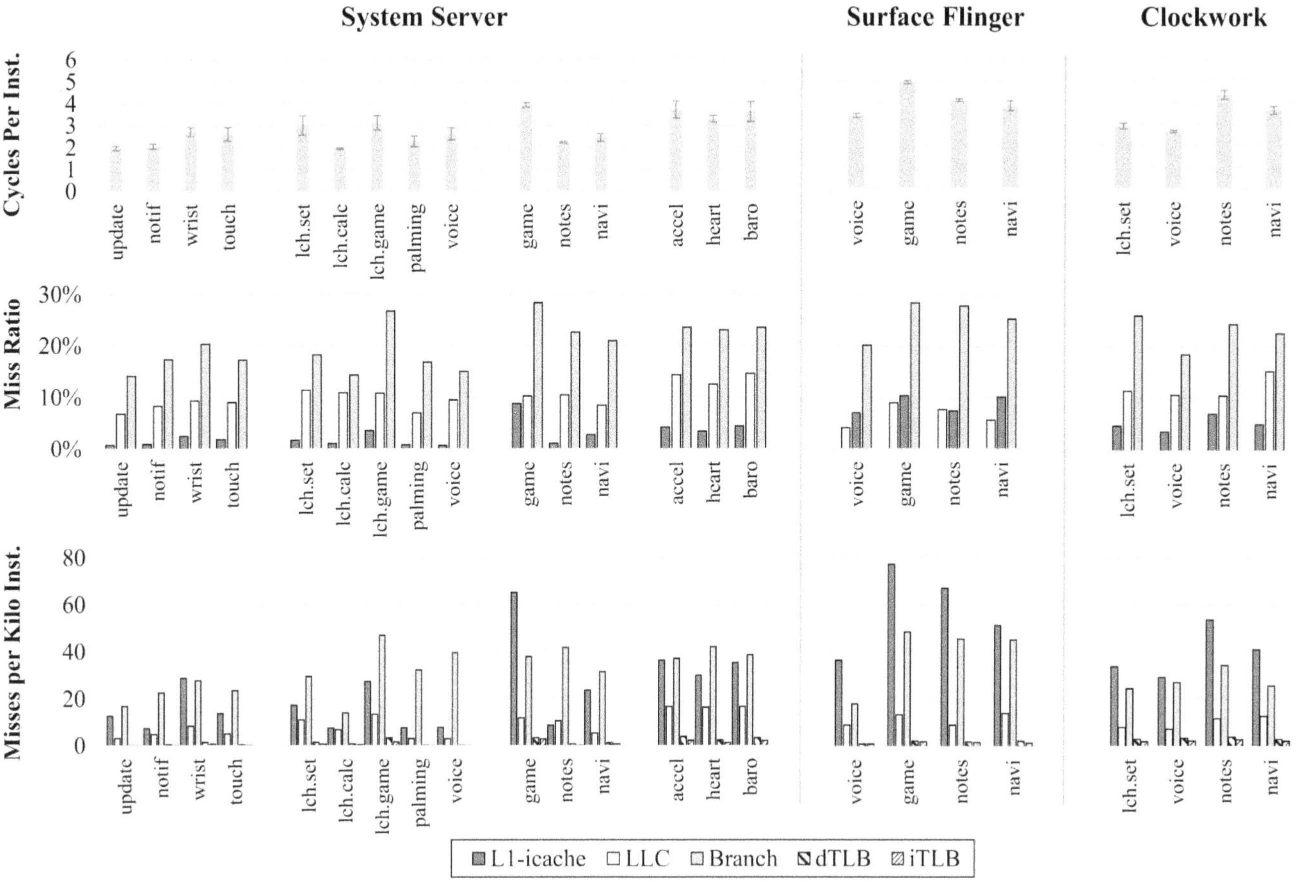

Figure 6: The measured microarchitectural behaviors of three major OS processes, covering their both user and kernel execution. Note that the LLC miss ratio is normalized to the total LLC references.

A7, a lighter version of smartphone CPU, is used as the *de facto* core for modern wearables. Cortex-A53 is a promising candidate for the next-generation wearables.

Atop our A7-based devices, we characterize the microarchitectural behaviors of the three major OS components, which collectively dominate the global CPU usage (§5.1). Note that for each OS component, we only show the benchmarks in which the component uses more than 10% of the system CPU cycles.

Perhaps contrary to common perception, the seemingly simple wearable workloads severely suffer from microarchitecture inefficiency. As shown in Figure 6, the cycles-per-instruction (CPI) ranges from 2 to 5, much higher than CPU-bound smartphone workloads such as web rendering (1.3 – 2.5) [21, 5]. The inefficiency also far exceeds that of desktop workloads: the CPI of SPEC INT on mobile CPUs rarely goes above 2 [5].

Through an analysis of the microarchitecture events, we have made three observations.

First, L1 icache and iTLB misses are high. As shown in Figure 6, *Surface Flinger* and *Clockwork* (and *System Server* in some benchmarks) exhibit a L1 icache misses-per-kilo-instructions (MPKI) ranging from 30 to 76. As reference points, the L1 icache MPKI in smartphone web rendering is around 28 [21, 26, 5] and in heavy smartphone gaming it is around 75 [21]; note that these misses were observed on A9, whose L1 cache is no larger than A7 as shown in Table 5. The fundamental reason lies in the complex OS codebase and its poor code locality, a nature likely inherited from the handheld OS [21]. In addition, the small iTLB of A7 may have worsened the situation.

Second, branch misprediction is substantial. Across all the benchmarks, the misprediction ratio is up to 28%, significantly higher than various smartphone workloads (all below 14% [26]) and SPEC INT (rarely above 17% [21]). The likely reasons are *i)* the complex OS execution paths and *ii)* the simple branch predictor in A7.

Last, the L1 dTLB and L2 cache are moderately effective. The misses are lower than data-intensive smartphone workloads, e.g., map or photo viewer [26], which have much larger working sets than wearable workloads.

Design Implications

The serious mismatch motivates two possible remedies. First, the CPU may evolve towards satisfying the demand of the OS. This is exemplified by an enhanced branch predictor of A53 shown in Table 5. However, one cannot satisfy all the microarchitectural demands, especially a larger L1 icache, due to the wearable's tight power and area constraints. Second, and more importantly, the observed inefficiencies – in icache, iTLB, and branch predictor – all root in the high complexity of the OS code. Our findings in Section 5.1 already suggest that the OS contains plentiful cruft. Should the OS be trimmed down to match the simplicity of its apps, the need for scaling up microarchitecture will significantly diminish.

6. RELATED WORK

Characterizing interactive workloads. Recognizing the significance of interactive systems, a large body of prior work has studied the key aspects including energy efficiency [8], latency [12, 54], thread-level parallelism [15, 4], and file I/O behaviors [23, 28]. Although none directly addressed wearables, their methodologies have been retrofit in our study.

Extensive study has been done towards understanding smartphone workloads. Power characterization has been a central topic [8], which highlights the importance of energy efficiency. Smartphone benchmarks, such as BBench [21], MobileBench [40], and Moby [26], often show non-traditional microarchitectural inefficiencies, including high TLB miss rate and icache miss rate. Our work shows that wearable workloads inherit many these behaviors due to the heavy OS execution. Gao *et al.* find that smartphone workloads show limited TLP, concluding that they need no more than two cores [16]. Our study shows that TLP in a wearable system can be even higher due to bursty OS workloads. ProfileDroid [52] contributes an approach for charactering smartphone apps at multiple layers; compared to it, our work addresses whole system efficiency with a focus on the OS components.

Little prior work has characterized wearable workloads. Among them, our prior work [30] studies the power and heat behaviors of Google glass. Our pilot study [31] on Android Wear reports power measurement, describes our custom toolset, and presents preliminary evidence of inefficiency. Our work [36] studies computational resource waste of the circular display commonly seen on wearables. Min *et al.* studies the battery usage of smart watches [37]; WearDrive [25] creates synthetic benchmarks to shed light on wearable storage. Compare to them, this work provides a holistic understanding of wearable systems.

Diagnosing mobile software anomalies. Various tools have been built to analyze smartphone software malfunctions, including quick battery drain [42, 34], sluggish GUI [32], and app crashes [24]. They enable systematic analysis of smartphone apps and inspire our work. Compared to them, we target a brand new platform – wearable; our diagnosis focuses on the anomalies originated in the OS, which have much wider impact than app anomalies.

While our `IdleChecker` (§4) may evoke user transaction trackers for smartphone such as AppInsight [44], it differs on three aspects: an offline diagnosis tool, `IdleChecker` does not instrument apps; targeting a system-level analysis, it takes all tasks into account instead of focusing on one single app; it identifies suspicious source code instead of just reporting delay numbers.

Quantifying microarchitectural behaviors. Much work has quantified microarchitectural behaviors of various workloads, including data-intensive workloads [51], scale-out servers [14], desktop apps [27], and smartphone apps [21, 26], We retrofit their methodologies and use their data as reference points for comparison.

Novel wearable apps. There is a large body of recent work on wearable, focusing on novel algorithms or app-specific systems. For instance, RisQ [41] and TypingRing [39] target gesture recognition; iShadow [35] tracks gaze in real time; Ha *et al.* build wearable for cognitive assistance [22]; Cornelius *et al.* focus on user identification [11]. While we recognize their importance, we focus on the OS internals of mass-market wearables.

7. CONCLUSIONS

We present an in-depth analysis of Android Wear, one of the most popular wearable OSes. Targeting OS design, we examine four key aspects – CPU usage, idle episodes, TLP, and microarchitectural behaviors – in fifteen benchmarks. We have reported detailed quantification, distilled a number of new findings, and discovered serious OS inefficiencies that were widespread but unknown before. Together, our results clearly point out the system bottlenecks for immediate optimization and have strong implications on future wearable system software and hardware design.

Acknowledgement

This work was supported in part by NSF Award #1464357 and by a Google Faculty Award. The authors thank the anonymous reviewers and the paper shepherd, Vishnu Navda, for their useful feedbacks.

8. REFERENCES

[1] ANANDTECH. The apple watch review. http://www.anandtech.com/show/9381/the-apple-watch-review, 2015.

[2] APPLE. Apple watch human interface guidelines. https://developer.apple.com/library/prerelease/ios/documentation/UserExperience/Conceptual/WatchHumanInterfaceGuidelines/, 2015.

[3] ARM. ARM architecture reference manual, armv7-a and armv7-r edition, 2014.

[4] BLAKE, G., DRESLINSKI, R. G., MUDGE, T., AND FLAUTNER, K. Evolution of thread-level parallelism in desktop applications. In *Proc. Int. Symp. Computer Architecture (ISCA)* (New York, NY, USA, 2010), ISCA '10, ACM, pp. 302–313.

[5] BLEM, E., MENON, J., AND SANKARALINGAM, K. Power struggles: Revisiting the risc vs. cisc debate on contemporary arm and x86 architectures. In *High Performance Computer Architecture (HPCA2013), 2013 IEEE 19th International Symposium on* (Feb 2013), pp. 1–12.

[6] BUSINESS INSIDER. The first round of apple watch apps weren't that great, but that's all about to change. http://www.businessinsider.com/why-the-first-apple-watch-apps-are-slow-2015-6, 2015.

[7] BUSINESSINSIDER. Apple just kneecapped google's smartwatch efforts, 2015.

[8] CARROLL, A., AND HEISER, G. The systems hacker's guide to the galaxy energy usage in a modern smartphone. In *Proceedings of the 4th Asia-Pacific Workshop on Systems* (New York, NY, USA, 2013), APSys '13, ACM, pp. 5:1–5:7.

[9] CARROLL, A., AND HEISER, G. Mobile multicores: Use them or waste them. *SIGOPS Oper. Syst. Rev. 48*, 1 (May 2014), 44–48.

[10] CONNOLLY, E., FAABORG, A., RAFFLE, H., AND RYSKAMP, B. Designing for wearables. Google I/O, 2014.

[11] CORNELIUS, C., PETERSON, R., SKINNER, J., HALTER, R., AND KOTZ, D. A wearable system that knows who wears it. In *Proceedings of the 12th Annual International Conference on Mobile Systems, Applications, and Services* (New York, NY, USA, 2014), MobiSys '14, ACM, pp. 55–67.

[12] ENDO, Y., WANG, Z., CHEN, J. B., AND SELTZER, M. Using latency to evaluate interactive system performance. In *Proc. USENIX Conf. Operating Systems Design and*

Implementation (OSDI) (New York, NY, USA, 1996), OSDI '96, ACM, pp. 185–199.

[13] ESMAEILZADEH, H., BLEM, E., ST. AMANT, R., SANKARALINGAM, K., AND BURGER, D. Dark silicon and the end of multicore scaling. In *Proc. Int. Symp. Computer Architecture (ISCA)* (New York, NY, USA, 2011), ISCA '11, ACM, pp. 365–376.

[14] FERDMAN, M., ADILEH, A., KOCBERBER, O., VOLOS, S., ALISAFAEE, M., JEVDJIC, D., KAYNAK, C., POPESCU, A. D., AILAMAKI, A., AND FALSAFI, B. Clearing the clouds: A study of emerging scale-out workloads on modern hardware. In *Proc. ACM Int. Conf. Architectural Support for Programming Languages & Operating Systems (ASPLOS)* (New York, NY, USA, 2012), ASPLOS XVII, ACM, pp. 37–48.

[15] FLAUTNER, K., UHLIG, R., REINHARDT, S., AND MUDGE, T. Thread-level parallelism and interactive performance of desktop applications. In *Proc. ACM Int. Conf. Architectural Support for Programming Languages & Operating Systems (ASPLOS)* (New York, NY, USA, 2000), ASPLOS IX, ACM, pp. 129–138.

[16] GAO, C., GUTIERREZ, A., RAJAN, M., DRESLINSKI, R., MUDGE, T., AND WU, C. A study of mobile device utilization. In *IEEE International Symposium on Performance Analysis of Systems and Software* (2015).

[17] GOOGLE. Ui patterns for android wear. https://developer.android.com/design/wear/patterns.html, 2014.

[18] GOOGLE INC. Binder. http://developer.android.com/reference/android/os/Binder.html.

[19] GOOGLE INC. Systrace. http://developer.android.com/tools/help/systrace.html.

[20] GOOGLE INC. Wakelock. http://developer.android.com/reference/android/os/PowerManager.WakeLock.html.

[21] GUTIERREZ, A., DRESLINSKI, R., WENISCH, T., MUDGE, T., SAIDI, A., EMMONS, C., AND PAVER, N. Full-system analysis and characterization of interactive smartphone applications. In *Workload Characterization (IISWC), 2011 IEEE International Symposium on* (Nov 2011), pp. 81–90.

[22] HA, K., CHEN, Z., HU, W., RICHTER, W., PILLAI, P., AND SATYANARAYANAN, M. Towards wearable cognitive assistance. In *Proc. ACM Int. Conf. Mobile Systems, Applications, & Services (MobiSys)* (New York, NY, USA, 2014), MobiSys '14, ACM, pp. 68–81.

[23] HARTER, T., DRAGGA, C., VAUGHN, M., ARPACI-DUSSEAU, A. C., AND ARPACI-DUSSEAU, R. H. A file is not a file: Understanding the i/o behavior of apple desktop applications. In *Proc. ACM Symp. Operating Systems Principles (SOSP)* (New York, NY, USA, 2011), SOSP '11, ACM, pp. 71–83.

[24] HU, G., YUAN, X., TANG, Y., AND YANG, J. Efficiently, effectively detecting mobile app bugs with appdoctor. In *Proceedings of the Ninth European Conference on Computer Systems* (New York, NY, USA, 2014), EuroSys '14, ACM, pp. 18:1–18:15.

[25] HUANG, J., BADAM, A., CHANDRA, R., AND NIGHTINGALE, E. B. Weardrive: Fast and energy-efficient storage for wearables. In *2015 USENIX Annual Technical Conference (USENIX ATC 15)* (Santa Clara, CA, July 2015), USENIX Association, pp. 613–625.

[26] HUANG, Y., ZHA, Z., CHEN, M., AND ZHANG, L. Moby: A mobile benchmark suite for architectural simulators. In *Performance Analysis of Systems and Software (ISPASS), 2014 IEEE International Symposium on* (March 2014), pp. 45–54.

[27] LEE, D. C., CROWLEY, P. J., BAER, J.-L., ANDERSON, T. E., AND BERSHAD, B. N. Execution characteristics of desktop applications on windows nt. In *Proceedings of the 25th Annual International Symposium on Computer Architecture* (Washington, DC, USA, 1998), ISCA '98, IEEE Computer Society, pp. 27–38.

[28] LEE, K., AND WON, Y. Smart layers and dumb result: Io characterization of an android-based smartphone. In *Proceedings of the Tenth ACM International Conference on Embedded Software* (New York, NY, USA, 2012), EMSOFT '12, ACM, pp. 23–32.

[29] LG USA. Design comes full circle. http://www.lg.com/us/smart-watches/lg-W110-g-watch-r, 2014.

[30] LIKAMWA, R., WANG, Z., CARROLL, A., LIN, F. X., AND ZHONG, L. Draining our glass: An energy and heat characterization of google glass. In *Proceedings of 5th Asia-Pacific Workshop on Systems* (New York, NY, USA, 2014), APSys '14, ACM, pp. 10:1–10:7.

[31] LIU, R., JIANG, L., JIANG, N., AND LIN, F. X. Anatomizing system activities on interactive wearable devices. In *Proceedings of the 6th Asia-Pacific Workshop on Systems* (New York, NY, USA, 2015), APSys '15, ACM, pp. 18:1–18:7.

[32] LIU, Y., XU, C., AND CHEUNG, S.-C. Characterizing and detecting performance bugs for smartphone applications. In *Proceedings of the 36th International Conference on Software Engineering* (New York, NY, USA, 2014), ICSE 2014, ACM, pp. 1013–1024.

[33] LYMBEROPOULOS, D., RIVA, O., STRAUSS, K., MITTAL, A., AND NTOULAS, A. Pocketweb: Instant web browsing for mobile devices. In *Proceedings of the Seventeenth International Conference on Architectural Support for Programming Languages and Operating Systems* (New York, NY, USA, 2012), ASPLOS XVII, ACM, pp. 1–12.

[34] MA, X., HUANG, P., JIN, X., WANG, P., PARK, S., SHEN, D., ZHOU, Y., SAUL, L. K., AND VOELKER, G. M. edoctor: Automatically diagnosing abnormal battery drain issues on smartphones. In *Presented as part of the 10th USENIX Symposium on Networked Systems Design and Implementation (NSDI 13)* (Lombard, IL, 2013), USENIX, pp. 57–70.

[35] MAYBERRY, A., HU, P., MARLIN, B., SALTHOUSE, C., AND GANESAN, D. ishadow: Design of a wearable, real-time mobile gaze tracker. In *Proceedings of the 12th Annual International Conference on Mobile Systems, Applications, and Services* (New York, NY, USA, 2014), MobiSys '14, ACM, pp. 82–94.

[36] MIAO, H., AND LIN, F. X. Tell your graphics stack that the display is circular. In *Proceedings of the 17th International Workshop on Mobile Computing Systems and Applications* (New York, NY, USA, 2016), HotMobile '16, ACM, pp. 57–62.

[37] MIN, C., KANG, S., YOO, C., CHA, J., CHOI, S., OH, Y., AND SONG, J. Exploring current practices for battery use and management of smartwatches. In *Proceedings of the 2015 ACM International Symposium on Wearable Computers* (New York, NY, USA, 2015), ISWC '15, ACM, pp. 11–18.

[38] MONSOON. Monsoon power monitor. http://msoon.com/LabEquipment/PowerMonitor.

[39] NIRJON, S., GUMMESON, J., GELB, D., AND KIM, K.-H. Typingring: A wearable ring platform for text input. In *Proceedings of the 13th Annual International Conference on Mobile Systems, Applications, and Services* (New York, NY, USA, 2015), MobiSys '15, ACM, pp. 227–239.

[40] PANDIYAN, D., LEE, S.-Y., AND WU, C.-J. Performance, energy characterizations and architectural implications of an emerging mobile platform benchmark suite - mobilebench. In *Workload Characterization (IISWC), 2013 IEEE International Symposium on* (Sept 2013), pp. 133–142.

[41] PARATE, A., CHIU, M.-C., CHADOWITZ, C., GANESAN, D., AND KALOGERAKIS, E. Risq: Recognizing smoking gestures with inertial sensors on a wristband. In *Proceedings of the 12th Annual International Conference on Mobile Systems, Applications, and Services* (New York, NY, USA, 2014), MobiSys '14, ACM, pp. 149–161.

[42] PATHAK, A., JINDAL, A., HU, Y. C., AND MIDKIFF, S. P. What is keeping my phone awake? Characterizing and

detecting no-sleep energy bugs in smartphone apps. In *Proc. of the 10th International Conference on Mobile Systems, Applications, and Services (MobiSys)* (2012), pp. 267–280.

[43] PESTEREV, A., ZELDOVICH, N., AND MORRIS, R. T. Locating cache performance bottlenecks using data profiling. In *Proceedings of the 5th European Conference on Computer Systems* (New York, NY, USA, 2010), EuroSys '10, ACM, pp. 335–348.

[44] RAVINDRANATH, L., PADHYE, J., AGARWAL, S., MAHAJAN, R., OBERMILLER, I., AND SHAYANDEH, S. Appinsight: Mobile app performance monitoring in the wild. In *Proceedings of the 10th USENIX Conference on Operating Systems Design and Implementation* (Berkeley, CA, USA, 2012), OSDI'12, USENIX Association, pp. 107–120.

[45] SAMSUNG. Samsun gear application programming guide. http://img-developer.samsung.com/contents/cmm/Samsung_Gear_Application_Programming_Guide_1.0.pdf, 2014.

[46] SAMSUNG. Samsung gear live. http://www.samsung.com/global/microsite/gear/gearlive_design.html, 2014.

[47] SAXENA, SUNIL. Tizen architecture overview. Linux Foundation Collaboration Summit, 2012.

[48] SIEVERS, D., AND DUCA, N. Chrome on mobile @ 60fps. GPU Technology Conference, 2014.

[49] SMITH, B. C. *Procedural reflection in programming languages*. PhD thesis, Massachusetts Institute of Technology, 1982.

[50] TECHRADAR. Apple watch battery life: How many hours does it last? http://www.techradar.com/us/news/wearables/apple-watch-battery-life-how-many-hours-does-it-last–1291435, 2015.

[51] WANG, L., ZHAN, J., LUO, C., ZHU, Y., YANG, Q., HE, Y., GAO, W., JIA, Z., SHI, Y., ZHANG, S., ZHENG, C., LU, G., ZHAN, K., LI, X., AND QIU, B. Bigdatabench: A big data benchmark suite from internet services. In *High Performance Computer Architecture (HPCA), 2014 IEEE 20th International Symposium on* (Feb 2014), pp. 488–499.

[52] WEI, X., GOMEZ, L., NEAMTIU, I., AND FALOUTSOS, M. Profiledroid: Multi-layer profiling of android applications. In *Proceedings of the 18th Annual International Conference on Mobile Computing and Networking* (New York, NY, USA, 2012), Mobicom '12, ACM, pp. 137–148.

[53] YAN, T., CHU, D., GANESAN, D., KANSAL, A., AND LIU, J. Fast app launching for mobile devices using predictive user context. In *Proc. ACM Int. Conf. Mobile Systems, Applications, & Services (MobiSys)* (New York, NY, USA, 2012), MobiSys '12, ACM, pp. 113–126.

[54] YANG, T., LIU, T., BERGER, E. D., KAPLAN, S. F., AND MOSS, J. E. B. Redline: First class support for interactivity in commodity operating systems. In *Proc. USENIX Conf. Operating Systems Design and Implementation (OSDI)* (Berkeley, CA, USA, 2008), OSDI'08, USENIX Association, pp. 73–86.

[55] ZHU, Y., AND REDDI, V. J. Webcore: Architectural support for mobileweb browsing. In *Proceeding of the 41st Annual International Symposium on Computer Architecuture* (Piscataway, NJ, USA, 2014), ISCA '14, IEEE Press, pp. 541–552.

Appendix: Brief descriptions of top hot functions listed in Table 3

computeOomAdjLocked Computing the Oom value for a given process.

consumeBatchedInputEvents Consuming a batch of input events.

DirectByteBuffer.get Reading one byte from a memory-mapped buffer.

InputEventReceiver.finishInputEvent Finishing the handling of an input event.

MessageQueue.next Retrieving an inter-thread message.

Parcel.writeLongArray Serializing an array of Long integers to an IPC parcel.

parseProcWakeLocks Parsing wakelock statistics in file `/proc/wakelocks`.

performLayoutAndPlaceSurfacesLockedInner Updating system UI and readjusting the look of each app window.

ProcessCpuTracker.collectStats Collecting CPU usage statistics.

removeObserverLocked Removing a given content observer.

setHalInteractiveModeLocked Informing the power HAL layer about the change of interactive mode.

setLightLocked Setting the screen backlight level.

SparseArray.get Get an element from a SparseArray.

updateOomAdjLocked The wrapper of computeOomAdjLocked(). It updates the OOM values for all the processes.

Values.cleanUp Cleaning up the garbage-collected thread-local variables.

Mobility Modeling and Prediction in Bike-Sharing Systems

Zidong Yang[†], Ji Hu[†], Yuanchao Shu[‡*], Peng Cheng[†], Jiming Chen[†], Thomas Moscibroda[‡]

[†] Zhejiang University, Hangzhou, China [‡] Microsoft Research Asia

ABSTRACT

As an innovative mobility strategy, public bike-sharing has grown dramatically worldwide. Though providing convenient, low-cost and environmental-friendly transportation, the unique features of bike-sharing systems give rise to problems to both users and operators. The primary issue among these problems is the uneven distribution of bicycles caused by the ever-changing usage and (available) supply. This bicycle imbalance issue necessitates efficient bike re-balancing strategies, which depends highly on bicycle mobility modeling and prediction. In this paper, for the first time, we propose a spatio-temporal bicycle mobility model based on historical bike-sharing data, and devise a traffic prediction mechanism on a per-station basis with sub-hour granularity. We extensively evaluated the performance of our design through a one-year dataset from the world's largest public bike-sharing system (BSS) with more than 2800 stations and over 103 million check in/out records. Evaluation results show an 85 percentile relative error of 0.6 for both check in and check out prediction. We believe this new mobility modeling and prediction approach can advance the bike re-balancing algorithm design and pave the way for the rapid deployment and adoption of bike-sharing systems across the globe.

Keywords

Sharing economy; Bike sharing; Mobility modeling; Flow prediction; Rebalancing

1. INTRODUCTION

Shared transportation has grown tremendously in recent years as a result of the rise of the sharing economy and growing environmental, energy and economic concerns. Among the various forms of shared-use mobility[1], public *bike-sharing systems* (BSS) have become increasingly popular with a significant growing presence over the past decade. Available figures indicate that there are more than 500 bike-sharing programs running in at least 49 countries with one million shared bikes in 2015 [1, 2].

In addition to its advantages of reducing traffic congestion and mitigating pollution, BSS feature unique characteristics compared with other forms of shared-use mobility. First, bike-sharing differs from classic ride-sharing (e.g., carpooling) and ride-sourcing (e.g., Uber and Lyft) in that bicycles are typically *unattended.* During vacant hours, bicycles are *concentrated* at a group of stations where operations of checking in or checking out are facilitated through a backbone network, i.e., an IT infrastructure that enables rent management and monitoring. Second, unlike conventional public transit (e.g., subways and buses) which follows a regular schedule and pre-determined routes, bike-sharing provides transportation on an *on-demand* basis with a *decentralized* structure. These two distinct features, however, pose characteristic challenges in BSS management and optimization. One common problem, for example, is that the system typically ends up with an uneven distribution of bikes across the different stations (due to the uncontrolled, uneven demand), often rendering the check in or check out service unavailable at some stations where bicycle docks are either fully occupied or empty.

This bicycle imbalance problem makes it necessary for bike-share cities to employ costly *bike redistribution*, which is typically performed by trucks or trailers driving around the city, moving bikes among stations. To increase service availability and minimize redistribution cost, studies have been conducted to improve these bike redistribution strategies based on bicycle mobility models and predictions. Yet, in spite of the researches on bike usage patterns and global rental volume forecasts (e.g., [3–7]), developing a fine-grained and localized prediction model for the number of bikes that should be optimally redistributed has proven to be elusive, and has remained a largely unstudied problem. The main technical challenge is that bike traffic is not only highly dynamic and inter-correlated in both the temporal and spatial domains, but also further influenced by complex issues such as timing and meteorology.

In this paper, we establish a spatio-temporal mobility model of bikes, and present a novel fine-grained traffic (i.e., check in and check out) prediction mechanism on a per-station basis by leveraging historical bike-sharing data as well as meteorological data. Our work differs fundamentally from previous approaches in that we model BSS as a dynamic network and predict the traffic by jointly considering the spatio-temporal correlations between stations and additional time factors and meteorology. To this end, we first decouple the bicycle transitions between stations from check out actions based on the counterbalance of bicycles and the mutual independence of user behaviors. Based on historical

*Yuanchao Shu is the corresponding author of this paper.

[1]Shared-use mobility–the shared use of transportation services–is an innovative transportation solution that enables users to have short-term access to transportation modes. It includes traditional public transit, bike-sharing, car-sharing, ride-sharing, ride-sourcing etc.

MobiSys'16, June 25-30, 2016, Singapore, Singapore

DOI: http://dx.doi.org/10.1145/2906388.2906408

data, we then use a probabilistic model to describe the spatio-temporal movements of bikes within the network, and estimate the number and time of check in at different stations. Combined with a random-forest-based check out prediction algorithm, we are able to estimate the number of docked bicycles at each station at any given time period in the future, which lays a foundation for efficient redistribution strategy design.

This paper makes the following three main contributions:

- We identify the mobility modeling problem and establish a spatio-temporal dynamic network model for BSS by taking into account the interactions among all stations;
- To our knowledge, we conduct the first work to devise a traffic prediction mechanism on a per-station basis with sub-hour granularity by using the mobility model and historical data;
- We evaluate the performance of mobility modeling and prediction through a one-year dataset from the city of Hangzhou, the world's largest public BSS with more than 2800 stations and over 103 million check in/out records [8, 9]. Compared with two benchmark methods, the proposed approach provides the best performance with an 85 percentile relative error of 0.6 for both check in and check out prediction.

The remainder of this paper is organized as follows. We first provide an overview of our design in Section 2. We then present the mobility model in Section 3, followed by detailed illustration of bicycle check out prediction in Section 4. Section 5 describes our datasets, and Section 6 presents an in-depth evaluation of mobility modeling and prediction. Several insights and related work are discussed in Section 7 and Section 8. We conclude the paper in Section 9.

2. DESIGN OVERVIEW

This section provides a design overview, including problem formulation in Section 2.1 and design methodology in Section 2.2.

2.1 Problem Formulation

Two types of entities constitute a BSS system (see Figure 1): *Active objects* (users) and *Reactive objects* (bikes), respectively. Users shift bikes from check in to check out operations, changing the status (i.e., the number of docked bicycles) of stations located at different places. Conversely, the spatial diversity of stations and bike availabilities also influence user behaviors. In this paper, we call a sequence of operations - bicycle check out, movement and check in - a *shift instance* (SI). As can be seen from Figure 1, *Active objects* and *Reactive objects* are coupled in both the temporal and spatial domain. However, it is worth noting that user activities in *Active objects* are *mutually independent*, though subject to the change of time factors and meteorology.

The objective of this paper is two-fold. First, we aim to model the mobility patterns of bikes in BSS. The mobility model characterizes the spatio-temporal transition of bikes among stations. Second, based on the mobility model, we aim to predict the number of docked bicycles at each station at a given time in the future. Due to the correlation between *Active objects* and *Reactive objects* as well as among stations, our design methodology proceeds from a decoupling operation, which disentangles these various correlations.

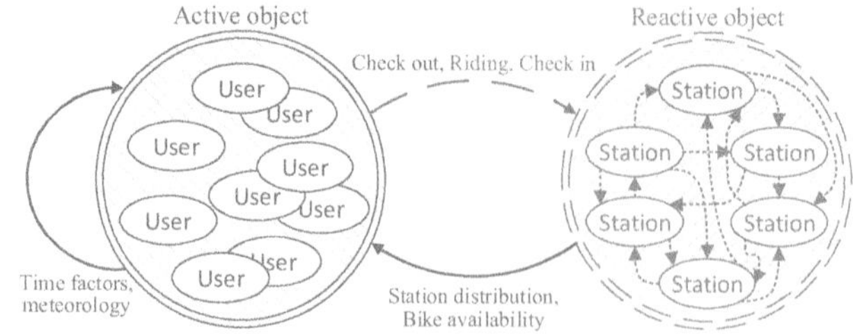

Figure 1: Components of a bike-sharing system.

2.2 Design Methodology

Despite the random bicycle check out time and location in each SI, bicycles are bound to be checked in at some station. Based on this simple observation, we decouple the system in Figure 1 into two parts (i.e., the left blue part and the right red part with dashed lines) by modeling the mobility of undocked bicycles and check out behaviors separately. Specifically, based on historical check out data, we first use a probabilistic model to describe the spatio-temporal movements of the undocked bikes, and then estimate the number and time of check in at different stations (see Section 3). We then apply the *random forest theory* to model and predict the users' check out behaviors with a joint consideration of time factors, meteorology and real-time bike availability (see Section 4). Both estimation and prediction results are updated in an online manner, and therefore can be integrated into any existing real-world BSS and used to infer and predict the number of docked bicycles at each station in real time.

3. BICYCLE MOBILITY MODELING

In this section, we develop a mobility model to capture the spatio-temporal transition of bikes. The model is established based on the uniqueness of bike flows between different pairs of stations at different times. For example, bicycles flow into stations in working areas in the morning on weekdays and flow out in the afternoon. Even for a random bicycle check out at a given station and a given time, the probabilities of the corresponding check in at different stations vary. Therefore, we propose a statistical model which uses historical check in/out data to describe the spatio-temporal shifts of bikes between pairs of stations, and estimate bicycle check in based on the online check out records. Compared with state-of-art approaches [10, 11] that treat each station independently, our model has the following two advantages:

- **Fine-grained Modeling.** A fine-grained mobility model with time-varying parameters is built based on the analysis of historical bicycle flows between stations. Check in estimations at each station can be obtained using this model.
- **Online Updating.** The estimation results are continuously updated based on recent check in and check out data, adapting to evolving user behaviors and network settings.

3.1 Theoretical Mobility Model

We first present a theoretical mobility model which estimates the check in numbers based on the analysis of historical SI data. Notations are defined in Table 1.

Without loss of generality, we consider the check in estimation of some station i. Given previous check out records (i.e., bikes checked out before t_{now}), we aim to quantify bikes that will be checked in at station i during a target period $[t, t + \Delta]$ in the future.

Table 1: Notations of the mobility model.

Notation	Description
$A_i(t, \Delta)$	Number of bikes check in to station i during $[t, t + \Delta]$
$D_i(t, \Delta)$	Number of bikes check out from station i during $[t, t + \Delta]$
$\gamma_{ji}(t)$	The probability of bikes that check out from station j at time t will check in to station i
$F_{ji}(\tau)$	The cumulative distribution function (CDF) of trip duration from station j to station i
N	The collection of stations

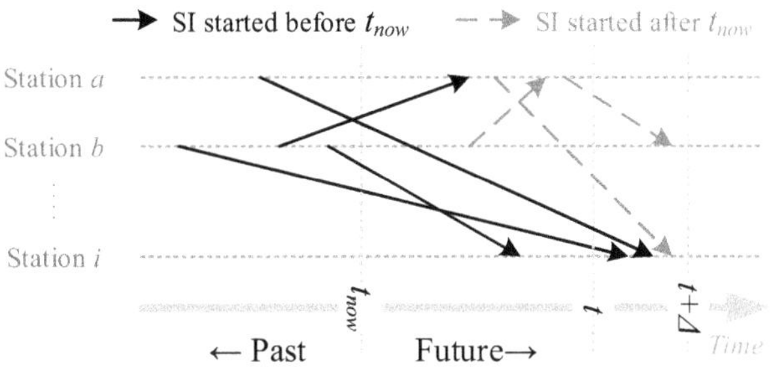

Figure 2: Basic idea of check in estimation.

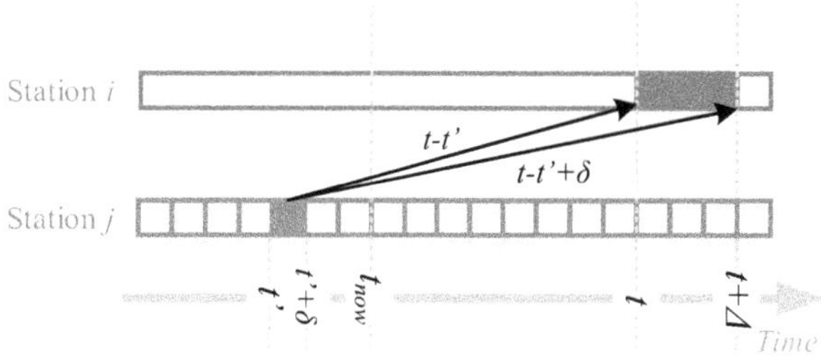

Figure 3: Traffic analysis between two stations.

To better illustrate the main idea of the estimation algorithm, we use an example shown in Figure 2. As can be seen in the figure, all bikes checked in at station i during $[t, t + \Delta]$ can be classified into two categories: bikes departed from all stations i) before t_{now} (i.e., black solid lines), and ii) after t_{now} (i.e, red dashed lines). In this section, we focus on the first category and illustrate how to quantify the bicycles arrived at station i during $[t, t + \Delta]$ from the entire group of bikes that are checked out before t_{now}. For those departed after t_{now}, the same approach can be applied once we perform the check out estimation for $[t_{now}, t + \Delta]$. The detailed algorithms of check out prediction will be presented in Section 4.

In general, the principal relationship between check in and check out can be written as

$$A_i = \sum_{j \in N} D_j \Gamma_{ji} P_t \tag{1}$$

where A_i is the number of bikes checking in to station i while D_j is the number of bikes checking out from station j. Since bikes from station j may have different destinations, Γ_{ji} is used to denote the transfer probability from station j to station i. Trip duration is another important factor in our model. The check in time may fall out of the target period if the trip duration is too short or too long. Thus, P_t is used to denote the probability that the bike will check in to station i within the target period.

Based on Equation 1, we derive a theoretical model for check in estimation. First consider SIs start from station j and end at station i. As discussed above, the value of P_t is determined by the trip duration. However, if a bicycle ends up in the destination station during the target period, the feasible range of the trip duration is subject to the check out time. For example, if the target period is $[10{:}\ 00a.m., 10{:}\ 30a.m.]$, the feasible trip duration for bikes checked out at 9:30 a.m. is 30~60 minutes while it is 45~75 minutes for bikes checked out at 9:15 a.m.

To cope with this problem, we perform *temporal discretization* and adopt a unified P_t for each time interval. Thus, we are able to enumerate SIs initiated in each time slot and add them up to obtain the aggregated bike flow between two stations.

As shown in Figure 3, if δ is sufficiently small, for bikes checked out from station j during $[t', t' + \delta]$, if they check in to station i within time window $[t, t + \Delta]$, the trip duration should be within $[t - t', t + \Delta - t']$. In addition, the transfer probability $\gamma_{ji}(\tau)$ can be viewed as a constant during $[t', t' + \delta]$. Then, the number of bikes from station j to station i which check in during $[t, t + \Delta]$ can be computed by adding up SIs in each time slot as

$$n_{ji} = \sum_{k=1}^{\infty} D_j(t_k, \delta)\gamma_{ji}(t_k)(F_{ji}(t+\Delta - t_k) - F_{ji}(t - t_k)) \tag{2}$$

where $[t_k, t_k + \delta]$ is the k-th interval before t_{now} and $t_k = t_{now} - k\delta$; n_{ji} is the number of SIs from station j to i. Both γ_{ji} and F_{ji} can be obtained probabilistically based on historical SI data.

So far, we are able to compute the SIs between two stations. Thus, by taking the summation of n_{ji} over all possible source stations, we can get the expression for $A_i(t, \Delta t)$ as

$$A_i(t, \Delta t) = \sum_{j \in N} n_{ji}. \tag{3}$$

Note that bikes checked out after t_{now} may end up at the destination station during the target period. One can simply ignore this part (i.e., treating it as 0) if $t \approx t_{now}$. However, omitting those SIs may cause a large error when $t \gg t_{now}$. To cope with this problem, we devise a check out prediction approach which is described in detail in Section 4. Once obtained the approximate numbers of check out bicycles (after t_{now}), we can feed them into the mobility model to compute the check in number (i.e., the red dashed lines in Figure 2).

3.2 Pruning

In Section 3.1, we derive a theoretical mobility model for check in estimation. Now we demonstrate how to compute the check in number of bicycles at each station in a practical way based on real check in/out data. Specifically, we adopt several pruning techniques by taking advantage of properties of BSS.

3.2.1 Temporal Pruning

In the theoretical mobility model, k ranges from 0 to ∞. Though it is infeasible to compute the sum of an infinite series, we find people usually use public bikes for the last miles of a commute for a short time. In other words, it is reasonable to set a cut off value on k to perform a temporal pruning.

Take the bike-sharing system in Hangzhou as an example. The distribution function of trip durations is depicted in Figure 4[2]. It demonstrates that 99.6% SIs are completed within 3 hours. Thus, instead of summing k from 0 to ∞, we can safely set a limit on k to 3 hours.

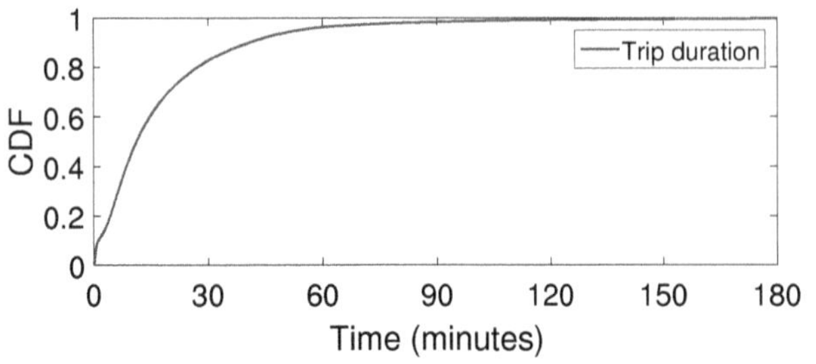

Figure 4: CDF of trip duration.

3.2.2 *Spatial Pruning*

In the theoretical model, SIs between any two stations are taken into consideration. However, we find it is not essential since the traffic between two far away stations is usually small and can be ignored. In other words, instead of taking all possible source stations into consideration, we use a subset of them to compute the potential check in bikes.

Let $M_i(n)$ denote the top-n source stations of station i in terms of the number of check in bicycles, and n_{ji} denote the number of bikes from station j to station i. We further define the top-n cumulative contribution rate $\lambda_i(n)$ as follows:

$$\lambda_i(n) = \frac{\sum_{j \in M_i(n)} n_{ji}}{\sum_{j \in N} n_{ji}}. \tag{4}$$

The average, minimal and maximal value of $\lambda_i(n)$ over all stations is depicted in Figure 5, which demonstrates that the majority of check in bikes of a specific station can be attributed to a small group of source stations. For example, the top 200 stations contribute more than 96.6% of bikes on average. Thus, we can perform a spatial pruning by limiting the number of source stations to a small value. Specially, we rank the numbers of SIs between each pair of source station and target station[3], and select the top 200 ones (at most) in check in estimation.

3.2.3 $\gamma_{ji}(t)$ *Discretization and Calculation*

It is also worth investigating how to efficiently update the parameter $\gamma_{ji}(t)$. By examining the SI data between stations, we find that γ_{ji} is highly volatile within a day whereas it remains relatively stable across days. Also, due to the sporadic check out of bicycles, we discretize $\gamma_{ji}(t)$ into a piece-wise function, and compute its value within each time slot (e.g., one hour) based on historical bicycle check in/out data. In the proposed mobility model, we set the length of each time slot to one hour to get a tradeoff between the computational overhead and accuracy.

By utilizing the above pruning techniques, it is computationally feasible to build a bicycle mobility model and perform check in estimations. In short, our model consists of two phases, namely a training phase and an estimation phase. In the training phase, model parameters (e.g, γ_{ji} and F_{ji}) are calculated from historical data while estimations are conducted by leveraging the model and online check out records during the estimation phase. The training and estimation algorithm for one station is presented in Algorithm 1 and Algorithm 2, respectively.

[2]The detailed dataset description is presented in Section 5.

[3]A time slot is set to 1 hour in our paper.

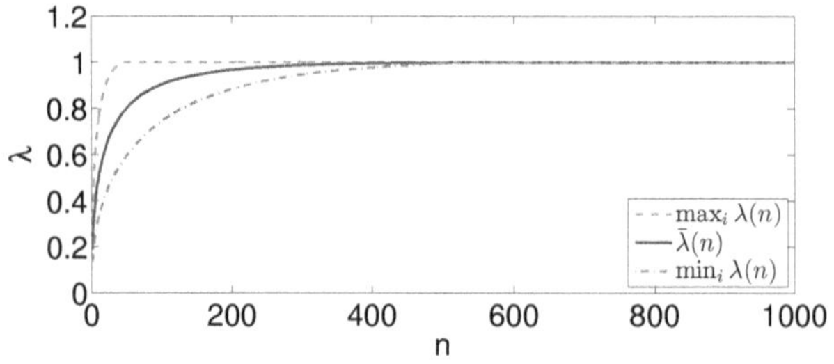

Figure 5: Cumulative contribution rate.

Input : Training dataset S, Number of source station considered m
Output: Mobility model of station i
$model_i = NULL$;
for *each time slot t* **do**
    $sources$ = TopSource (m);
    for *each station* $j \in sources$ **do**
        Compute γ_{ji} for time slot t;
        Estimate trip duration CDF F_{ji} from j to i;
        Add γ_{ji}, F_{ji} to $model_i$;
    end
end
return $model_i$

Algorithm 1: Mobility modeling training.

In the training phase, for each time slot, Algorithm 1 computes γ_{ji} and F_{ji} between top-m source stations and the target station. Thus, the computation complexity for each station is $O(nm)$ where n is the number of time slots and m is the number of considered source stations. In the estimation phase, for each time interval, Algorithm 2 estimates the traffic between each pair of source station and target station. Thus, the corresponding computation complexity is $O(pm)$ where p is the number of time intervals. Both algorithms can run in parallel, therefore being applied to all stations simultaneously in a large bike-sharing system. Due to the changes in BBS (e.g., new station deployment) and external conditions (e.g., road construction), we train the mobility model every one week by using all SI data from the past one year.

4. BICYCLE CHECK OUT PREDICTION

Section 3 presents a mobility model with check in analysis based on SIs started before t_{now}. In this part, we introduce how to predict the number of bicycle check out after t_{now}, thus completing the mobility model to obtain the total number of check in bicycles between $[t, t + \Delta]$.

Different from bicycle check in results which are correlated with stations, users' check out actions are mutually independent but subject to external factors such as time factors and meteorology. Therefore, we apply *random forest theory* [12] to model and forecast the check out behaviors based on historical SIs, corresponding time and meteorology data.

Input : Mobility model $model_i$, Estimation time period $[t, t+\Delta]$, k_{max}, δ

Output: Estimation result n

$n = 0, k = 1;$
$p = \frac{\Delta}{\delta};$
while $k < k_{max}$ **do**
  $sources$ = `GetSource` $(model_i, t + \Delta - k\delta)$;
  for *each station* j *in* $sources$ **do**
    Compute $D_j(t + \Delta - k\delta, \delta)$;
    Get γ_{ji} from $model_i$;
    Get $F_{ji}(k\delta)$ from $model_i$;
    if $k \geq p$ **then**
      // bikes depart before t
      Get $F_{ji}(k\delta - \Delta)$ from $model_i$;
      $n = n + D_j(t+\Delta-k\delta, \delta)\gamma_{ji}(F_{ji}(k\delta) - F_{ji}(k\delta-\Delta));$
    else
      // bikes depart after t
      $n = n + D_j(t + \Delta - k\delta, \delta)\gamma_{ji}F_{ji}(k\delta);$
    end
  end
  $k = k + 1$
end
return n

Algorithm 2: Check in estimation.

4.1 Feature Extraction

We first extract features from raw data and create feature vectors with fixed-size time window to build the random forest model. The features that affect the check out behaviors in a significant way can be categorized into two types: offline features and online features.

4.1.1 Offline Features

Time factors: Although characteristics of check out actions differ among stations, they are all closely related to time factors and show unique temporal patterns. We select the most significant four time factors: day of week, time of day, weekday and holiday.

Figure 6 shows the average check out number of a station in a tourist attraction area in different days of one week. We notice that the average check out number on weekdays is relatively smaller than that during weekends. Things are the opposite for the stations in residential areas or commercial areas. Therefore, day of week is informative for check out prediction.

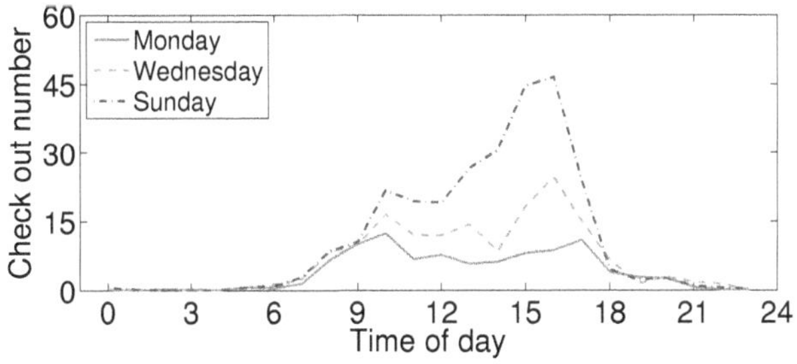

Figure 6: Check out number at one station in different days.

Figure 7 shows the check out number over time on a weekday which varies dramatically. There are two peaks at around 08:00 and 16:00. Since a significant portion of users rent bicycles for fixed purposes (e.g., commute), time of day is also considered as a feature in our model.

There are two additional features that are associated with date: weekday and holiday. These are binary indicators representing whether a particular day is a weekday or holiday.

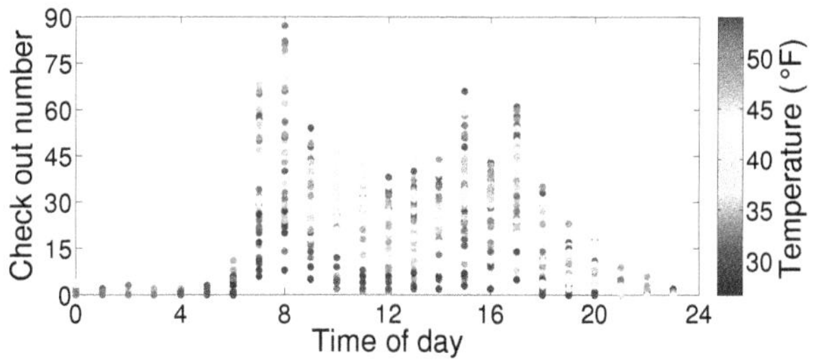

Figure 7: Check out number by time and temperature.

Meteorology: Meteorology condition has a huge influence on user behaviors in BSS [7, 10, 13]. As is shown in Figure 7, check out numbers grow when people feel more comfortable at higher temperatures. Similar patterns exist for other meteorological conditions such as humidity, visibility and wind speed. Nevertheless, these patterns vary with time and across stations. For example, users' check out behaviors are less influenced by weather conditions during peak hours.

4.1.2 Online Feature

Online check out number: Despite the tight correlations between users' check out behaviors and time factors as well as the meteorological data, there exist check out anomalies that differ significantly from the results observed at the same hours on other days. We notice that these anomalies are caused by sudden changes of bike availabilities at stations. For instance, bicycles in surrounding areas run out very quickly with large audiences coming from a stadium after a soccer game. Also, the bike-sharing service becomes unavailable when dock (or even station) failures happen. Since anomalies usually last for a short period of time, we adopt an online feature of check out number from the previous time window. By incorporating this feature, the model is capable of adapting to accidental events that dramatically change the bike availability at stations.

We combine all offline and online features mentioned above to generate a feature vector f_t for each time window t. Denote the ground truth of check out number for each time window as r_t, we combine feature f_t and r_t into a big vector $x_t = (f_t, r_t)$ to train the model.

4.2 Random Forest Model

Random forest is an ensemble learning method typically used for classification and regression. The general idea of random forest is to combine a large number of decision trees, each of which is individually built on bootstrapped samples of the data. The predictions are performed by taking the mean of outputs from each individual decision tree.

During the training, we first conduct the training set S_t by concatenating all the historical x_t mentioned above. Then we sample the training set randomly with replacement to create a subset. For each subset, a tree grows according to the following steps: at each node, it chooses some features randomly as split variables from all the predictor variables in the feature vector; it then finds the best split according to the criterion that maximizes the homogeneity of the two resulting groups. In our design, we use a mean square error function to measure the quality of a split; at the next node, the procedure is repeated and the training set is partitioned into smaller groups.

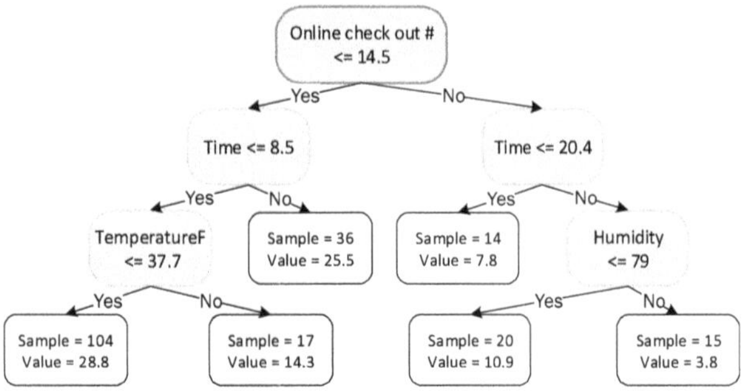

Figure 8: A decision tree in random forest.

Figure 8 shows an example decision tree with four layers. To predict the check out number of time $t+1$, the input feature vector f_{t+1} must contain the following fields: *day of week*, *hour of day*, *holiday*, *weekday*, the *meteorology forecast value* at time $t+1$ and *online check out number*. When f_{t+1} is entered into the tree, it needs to make a decision at each node based on the split variable and makes its way down till it reaches a leaf node. For example, in this figure, if the *online check out number* is smaller than or equal to 14.5, the next step is to decide whether *time* is larger than 8.5. If not, it will reach a leaf node where sample = 36 and value = 25.5. It means that there are 36 samples in the historical SIs that also meet the above conditions and the value 25.5 is the average check out number of those 36 samples. Let y_n be the prediction of the n_{th} single decision tree. Then $p = \frac{1}{N_{tree}} \sum_{n=1}^{N_{tree}} y_n$ is the final check out prediction.

For online check out prediction, the time window is set to 30 minutes. At time window t, we predict check out number for K steps to feed the mobility model, i.e., computing $\{p_{step}\}_{step=1}^{K}$. Under this situation, the input sequence depends on the ground truth of check out numbers from time window t to time window $t+K-1$, which is unknown by now. Hence we consider the check out prediction at time t as the ground truth and use it as an input feature for prediction in the next step. The detailed algorithm is shown in Algorithm 3. When it comes to the next time window, the preceding prediction sequence is discarded and we update prediction with new observations. Similar to the mobility model, we update the random forest model every one week.

Input : Training dataset S_t, prediction horizon length K
Output: Check out prediction $\{p_{step}\}_{step=1}^{K}$
Initialize *step* = 1;
for *each station j* **do**
  Use S_t to train the random forest model;
  Compute feature importance for station j;
  while *step < K* **do**
    predict the check out number p_{step} given observation f_{step} ;
    combine the perdition p_{step} and other offline features to f_{step+1};
    step = step + 1;
  end
end

Algorithm 3: Check out prediction for K steps.

Compared with other algorithms, the proposed random forest-based model has the following advantages:

- It can deal with both categorical and numerical variables without normalization. In our original data, some meteorology features such as temperature and wind speed are numerical variables while holiday and weekday are binary variables. We can just take these features as input without additional conversion.
- It provides importance of features based on the training dataset, which sheds light on the check out patterns. For example, meteorology features may have higher importance on stations near tourist attractions.
- It can deal with huge volumes of data and can be easily parallelized, and thus is very suitable for check out behavior modeling based on millions of SIs.

Denote the length of the training set S_t as N, the length of the test dataset as T. The complexity of feature extraction is $O(N+KT)$. With regard to the random forest building with N_{tree} number of trees, the complexity is $O(N_{tree} * Nlog(N))$. Hence, the total computation complexity is $O(Nlog(N))$.

4.3 Putting It All Together

In Section 3 and Section 4, we are able to predict SIs from two aspects: mobility modeling with check in estimation, and check out prediction. The combination of two parts presents a complete picture of the bike-sharing system. Specifically, for check out prediction in Section 4, we utilize a random forest model to capture the relationship between check out behaviors and key factors, including time/date, meteorology, and recent check out status. Then, given these features, we are able to predict check out instances in a future period.

In Section 3, we leverage the spatio-temporal relationships between pairs of stations and derive a probabilistic model to describe the bike mobility. By feeding both check out records in the past (i.e., the black lines in Figure 2) and the predicted results in the future (i.e., the red dashed lines in Figure 2) into the mobility model, we are able to estimate the check in numbers at each station at any given period in the future. In addition, the number of docked bicycles at each station can be inferred by integrating the check in and check out prediction results, which is of great value to both customers and system operators.

5. DATASET DESCRIPTION

Before presenting performance evaluations, in this section, we first describe the two datasets used in this paper: the *BSS Dataset* and the *Meteorology Dataset*. The BSS dataset is provided by Hangzhou Public Bicycle Transport Service Development Co., Ltd., and the meteorology dataset was collected from an online weather service provider Weather Underground[4].

5.1 BSS Dataset

The Chinese city of Hangzhou has the world's largest public BSS with more than 3300 stations and over 84,000 shared bicycles [8, 9]. The system adopts smart-card technology and automated check in and check out. Each check in and check out instance will be recorded in the back-end database with corresponding user ID, bicycle ID, time and etc.

The BSS dataset we use includes all bicycle sharing records in 2013. In summary, it contains 43705 bikes and 2806 stations,

[4]http://www.wunderground.com

Table 2: Primary fields in the BSS dataset.

user_id	rent_netid	tran_date	tran_time
6114381	4051	20130101	000152
return_netid	return_date	return_time	bike_id
4015	20130101	001547	913672

among which 103,661,080 trips are recorded. Each bike-sharing record has 47 fields, of which the primary fields are shown in Table 2. In 2013, the operational hour for check out service ranges from 6:00am to 9:00pm while the check in service is available until 11:00pm. In order to provide a better overview, we report statistical results of the dataset in terms of station distribution, station capacity and usage amount.

Station distribution: Bike stations in Hangzhou are located within the urban area spanning over 600 square kilometers; the average distance to the closest neighboring station being 300 meters [8]. The probability distribution function (PDF) of the number of stations within a certain range of one station is depicted in Figure 9. As we can see, half the stations have more than 3 neighbors within the range of 300 meters, and they typically have 20 neighbors within the range of 800 meters.

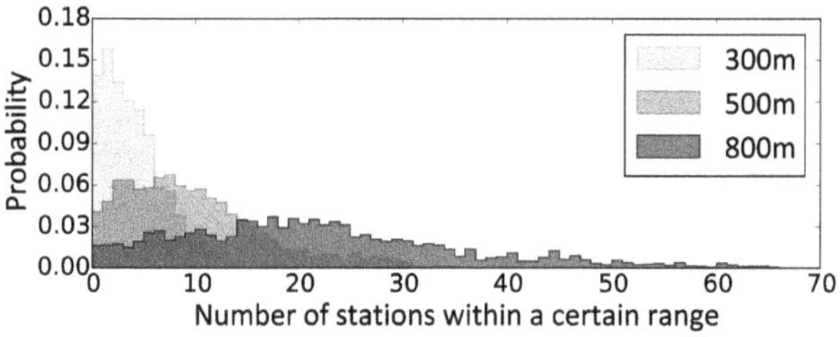

Figure 9: PDF of the number of stations within a certain range of one station.

Station capacity: Station capacity is measured as the number of stocks. As is shown in Figure 10, there are basically two types of stations in Hangzhou: normal stations with 21 docks and large station with around 33 docks.

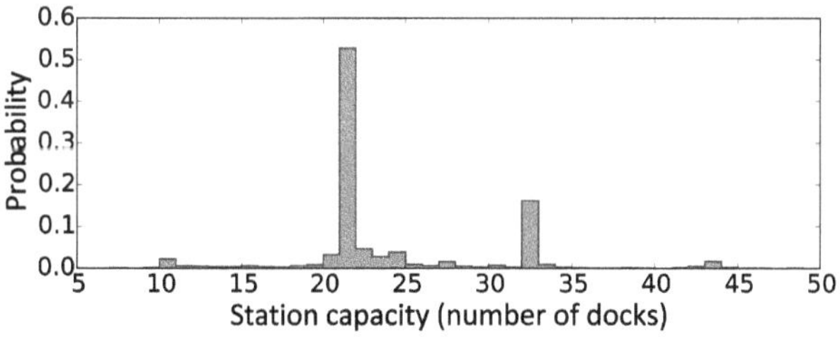

Figure 10: Distribution of station capacity.

Usage amount: Figure 11 presents the distribution of monthly usage amount (i.e., check in numbers) across all 2806 stations. We find that there are more than 100 busy stations with extremely high usage amount up to 30000 (check in/month). However, the median value of the usage amount is around 2000. The skewed distribution in Figure 11 indicates a high diversity of usage amount across different stations. We observe a similar pattern for check out numbers.

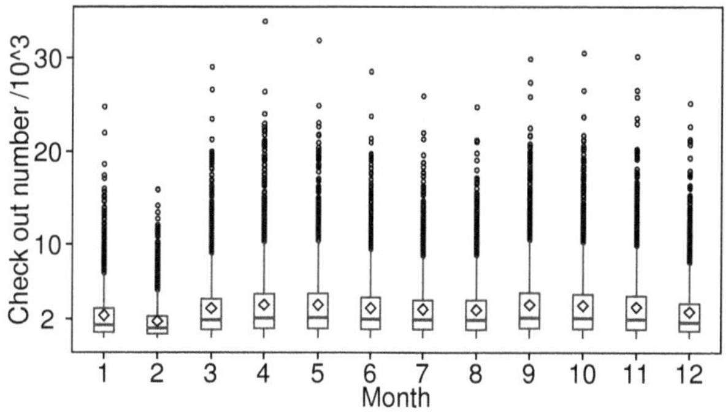

Figure 11: Distribution of monthly usage amount.

Table 3: Fields in the meteorology dataset.

Time (CST)	Temp (°F)	Dew Point (°F)
12:30 PM	100.4	69.8
Pressure (hPa)	Humidity (%)	Visibility (MPH)
29.65	37	6.2
Wind Dir	Wind Speed (MPH)	Conditions
WSW	8.9	Partly Cloudy

5.2 Meteorology Dataset

The meteorology dataset contains weather conditions of Hangzhou with totally $48 \times 365 = 17,520$ records. Meteorological observations were updated every half hour and the data format of each record is shown in Table 3.

6. EVALUATION

We conduct extensive data-driven simulations to evaluate the performance of our design. In the following, we first present the performance of check out prediction, and then show the check in estimation results based on the mobility model and check out prediction. Both case studies and overall performance are shown to provide a more comprehensive analysis.

6.1 Baseline Approaches

We first introduce three prediction techniques that comprise the baselines of our model.

- **Historical Average (HA)** uses the average of historical observations for the same time and location to forecast the future data [11]. Specially, when conducting prediction for a specific time period, we first find out historical days with same day/time values, and then average the check in/out results from these periods.
- **Auto-Regressive and Moving Average (ARMA)** is widely used for time series prediction and was adopted for BBS check in estimation [5]. It leverages check in/out information of the most recent p time windows for future prediction. Parameters are determined using historical data and the least squares method.
- **HP-MSI and P-TD** are the most recent studies of traffic prediction in bike-sharing system [7] where HP-MSI and P-TD are designed for check out and check in prediction, respectively. Since these two methods are applied to predict

traffic amount between clusters of stations, they cannot be directly compared with our station-basis design. As an approximation, we treat each station as an individual cluster in our evaluation.

For performance metrics, we adopt CDFs of both absolute and relative prediction error. In addition, we also use Root Mean Squared Logarithmic Error (RMLSE) [7] for evaluation. RMLSE is computed as

$$RMSLE = \sqrt{\frac{1}{n}\sum_{i=1}^{n}(log(\hat{y}+1) - log(y+1))^2} \quad (5)$$

where $\hat{y}$ and y are prediction and ground truth respectively while n is number of predictions.

6.2 Check Out Prediction

In this part, we evaluate the check out prediction model presented in Section 4, which serves as a component for check in estimation.

6.2.1 *Case Studies*

We first present a case study of station 3648 under different scenarios, and predict its check out number for 24 hours adopting HA, ARMA, HP-MSI and the proposed random-forest-based method (RF). The *ground truth* (GT) is also provided in Figure 12. Figure 12(a) presents the check out prediction results every 30 minutes in a rainy summer weekday while Figure 12(b) is generated in a sunny winter weekend.

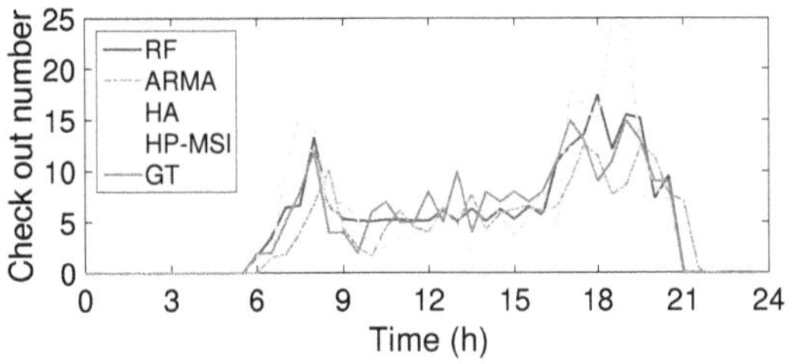

(a) A rainy summer weekday.

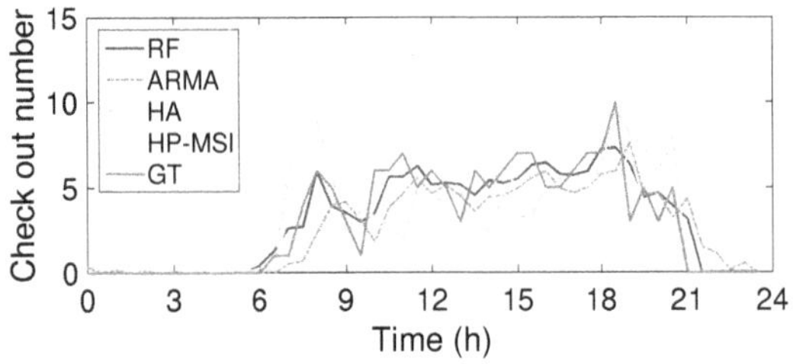

(b) A sunny winter weekend.

Figure 12: Check out prediction at station 3648.

From Figure 12 we find that check out number of station 3648 in summer are much larger than those in winter, especially during rush hours. It means that the feature "hour" is an influential factor to users' check out behaviors. We further record the importance of the features while growing trees in the random forest model in Table 4. For each internal node that splits on feature i, feature importance is computed by the impurity decrease from that feature. For regression trees, the impurity criterion that we use is variance. For station 3648, the importance of "hour" is as high as 0.1434. In addition, we find that the "online check out number" is the

Table 4: Feature importance.

Day of week	Hour	Temperature	Humidity
0.0288	0.1434	0.0846	0.0514
Visibility	Wind speed	Holiday	Workday
0.0332	0.0211	0.0030	0.0064
Online check out number			
0.6282			

most influential factor in this case. It represents the randomness of check out patterns at this station. Another evidence of that is the bad performance of HA which depends highly on previous observations. For example, the prediction error of HA at 19:00 in Figure 12(a) is as much as 24.14, 60.93% more than the ground truth. On the other hand, ARMA exhibits relatively large prediction delays in both figures. This is due to the sliding window technique used in the model. Among all three approaches, RF demonstrates the best performance both in terms of accuracy and delay.

6.2.2 *Overall Performance*

Figure 13 presents the overall prediction performance across all stations. We adopt the first 20 days of each month to train the random forest model, and predict check out numbers in remaining days. Compare the prediction results with ground truth, we can obtain the CDF of the errors. Figure 13(a) demonstrates the absolute error (i.e., numbers of bikes) while Figure 13(b) shows the relative error calculated by dividing the absolute error by the ground truth.

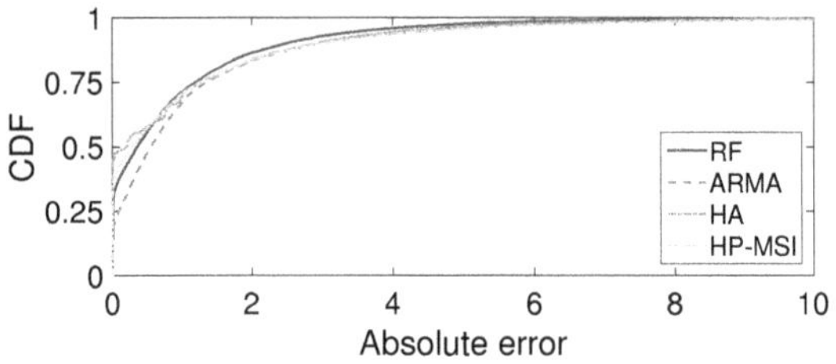

(a) CDF of absolute error.

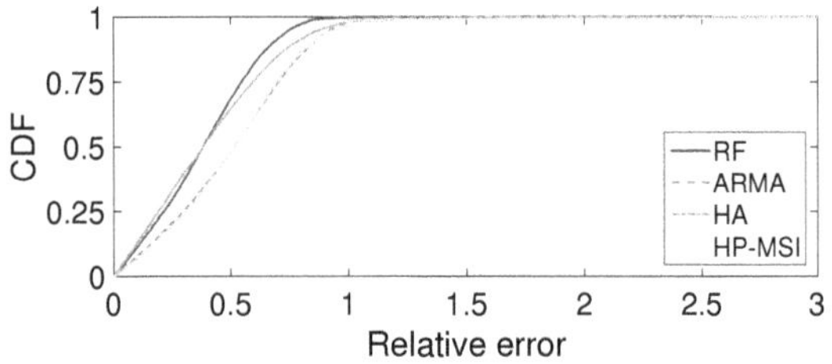

(b) CDF of relative error.

Figure 13: Overall check out prediction performance.

From Figure 13 we can see that 90% of the absolute error is less than 2.477 in our approach, outperforming three baselines. Table 5 also gives evidence of the advantages of our approach while the RMSLE of RF is as low as 0.4287. Similar patterns exist for relative error. For example, RF achieves an 85 percentile relative error of 0.62659 while the corresponding value for ARMA is 0.7039. It is even worse for HA and HP-MSI[5]. Both Table 5 and

[5]Note that the relative error is the ratio of absolute error to the

Table 5: **RMSLE of check out prediction.**

RF	ARMA	HA	HP-MSI
0.4287	0.4855	0.4600	0.4662

Figure 13 prove the effectiveness of the proposed random-forest-based model which takes both time factors, meteorology and real-time check out behaviors into consideration.

6.3 Check In Estimation

In this section, we evaluate the effectiveness of the proposed mobility model (MM) by demonstrating the results of check in estimations.

6.3.1 *Case Studies*

Similar to the previous section, we first present two case studies of a rainy summer weekend and a sunny winter weekday to provide intuitive feelings of performances of different approaches.

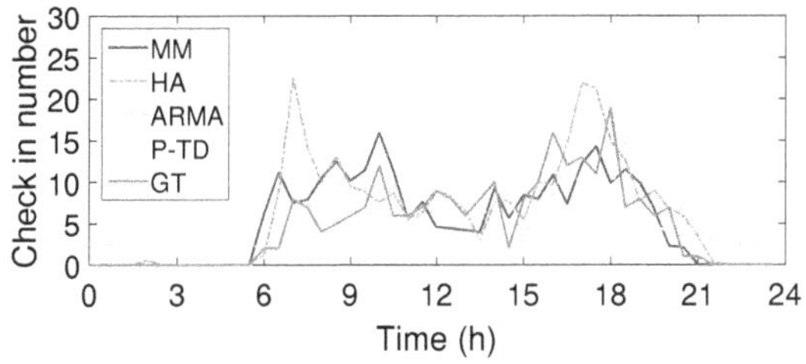

(a) A rainy summer weekend.

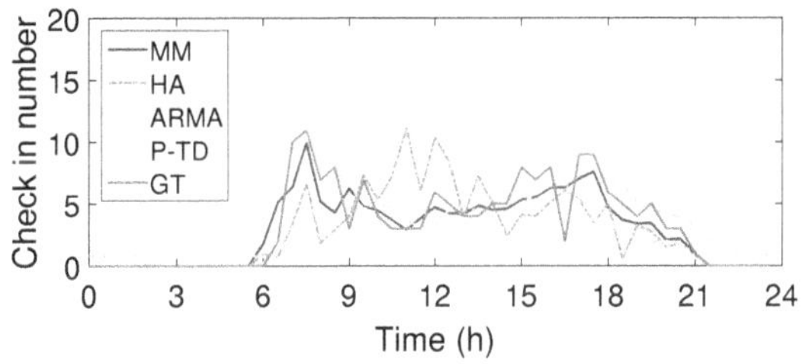

(b) A sunny winter weekday.

Figure 14: Check in prediction at station 3648.

As can be seen from Figure 14, MM is close to the ground truth. However, HA brings larger estimation error because it lacks online information. Similar to Figure 12, AR suffers from an estimation delay. As for P-TD, it tends to underestimate the result.

6.3.2 *Overall Performance*

We also evaluate the overall performance of check in estimation of all three approaches. Specifically, each approach is required to estimate check in number in the following 30 minutes (i.e., $\Delta = 30$). Similar to the random-forest-based model, we train each mobility model using SIs from the first 20 days of each month, and use the remaining days for testing. The CDF of absolute error and relative error is depicted in Figure 15, while RMSLE results are presented in Table 6.

As one can see from Figure 15(a), for absolute error, all approaches are quite close when absolute error is small. However,

ground truth, rather than the ratio of prediction result to the ground truth, therefore Figure 13(b) does not imply that the algorithm underestimates the check out number.

Table 6: RMSLE of check in prediction.

MM	ARMA	HA	P-TD
0.4736	0.5296	0.4865	0.5042

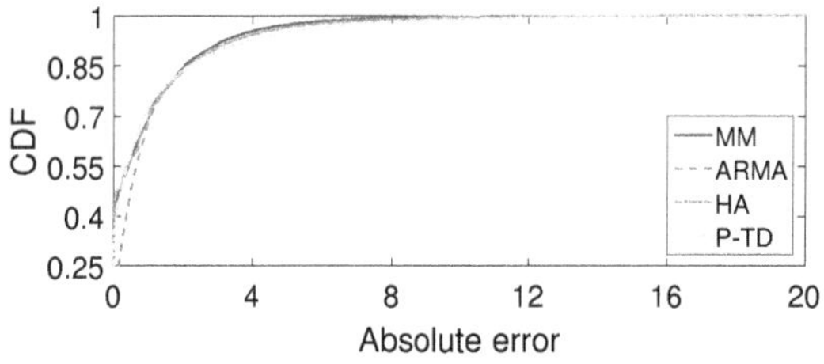

(a) CDF of absolute error.

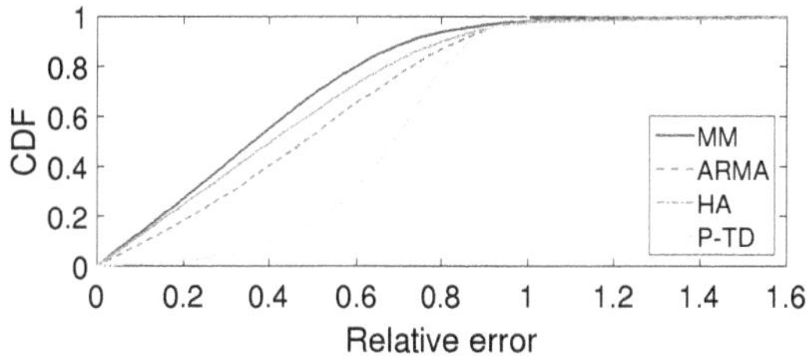

(b) CDF of relative error.

Figure 15: Overall Performance of check in Estimation.

as the error increases, MM outperforms other methods. This trend becomes more obvious in Figure 15(b). Recall that we only consider time slots with actual check in number larger than 5, which implies that MM performs well when the traffic increases. This is because when the total traffic rises, the expectation number calculated by MM suffers less from randomness and becomes more accurate.

Note that in Figure 15(b), we observe significant performance degradation of PT-D. This is caused by the approximation of single-station-clustering where relative errors will be amplified with smaller ground truth values. Also, PT-D has to fit the trip duration distribution function in log-normal form, and the lack of check in/check out records between certain stations results in larger fitting errors.

6.3.3 *Impact of Settings*

To better understand the performance of the proposed mobility model and the check in estimation approach under different settings, we further conduct three sets of evaluation by varying several key parameters in the mobility model. We present the results of both absolute error CDFs and RMSLE.

- **Check out prediction:** As mentioned in the Section 3, part of the check in bikes between $[t, t+\Delta]$ may depart later than t_{now}, which is unknown at the time of check in estimation. Thus, we utilize the check out prediction result. Figure 16 demonstrates the effectiveness of this approach. Specially, we compare three different strategies to estimate bikes depart after t_{now}: i) Check out prediction, which is the method used in this paper; ii) Ground truth, which uses the real number of bikes depart after t_{now}. It is infeasible to obtain this figure in practice hence the results are viewed as an upper bound; iii) Ignore this part, which simply treats the number as zero.

From Figure 16 and Table 7, we can see that the CDF

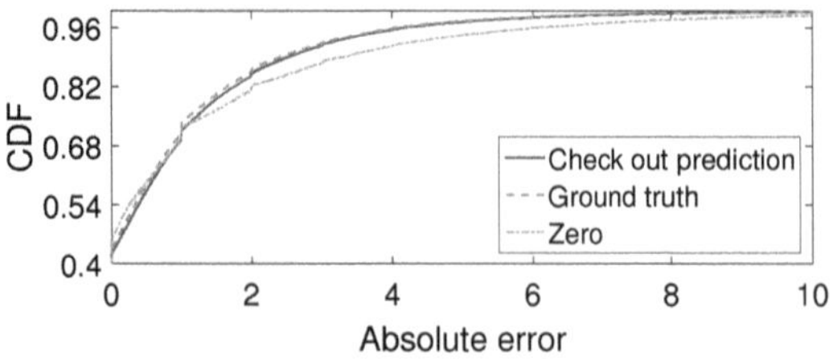

Figure 16: Impact of check out prediction.

Table 7: RMSLE of different strategies.

Ground truth	Check out prediction	Zero
0.4556	0.4736	0.5767

curves of the check out strategy and the Ground truth strategy are very close. In other words, the gap between our result and the theoretical upper bounding is quite small. In addition, we notice that ignoring this part degrades the system performance significantly, which justifies the necessity of adopting check out prediction result.

- **Granularity of time interval (δ):** In order to build a theoretical mobility model for BBS, we discretize time into intervals. Intuitively, shorter intervals will bring better estimation accuracy, but add to the cost of computational complexity. Therefore, we adopt three different time intervals 2, 5 and 10 minutes to compare their modeling and prediction results.

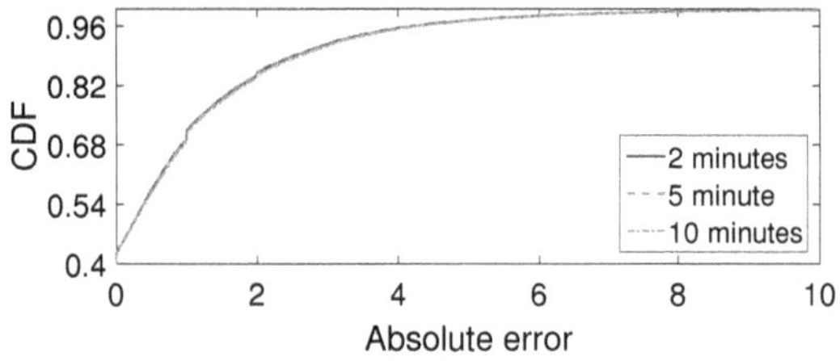

Figure 17: Impact of the granularity of time interval.

From Figure 17 and Table 8 we find that a smaller time interval results in a slightly better performance. However, gaps between each curve are all very small. Hence we use a larger time interval to reduce the computational overhead in current implementation.

- **Number of source stations:** In the mobility model, number of source stations is limited to a threshold to tradeoff between the accuracy and computational overhead. However, we are also curious to study the impacts of number of source stations on the estimation result. Figure 18 shows the CDF of absolute error of three different thresholds, 100, 200 and 400.

In Figure 18, it can be seen that algorithms perform better when more source stations are taken into consideration. However, one may also notice that the gap between 400 stations and 200 stations is smaller than that between 200 and 100. It is also verified in Table 9 where the RMSLE values

Table 8: RMSLE of different time intervals.

2 minutes	5 minutes	10 minutes
0.4736	0.4750	0.4844

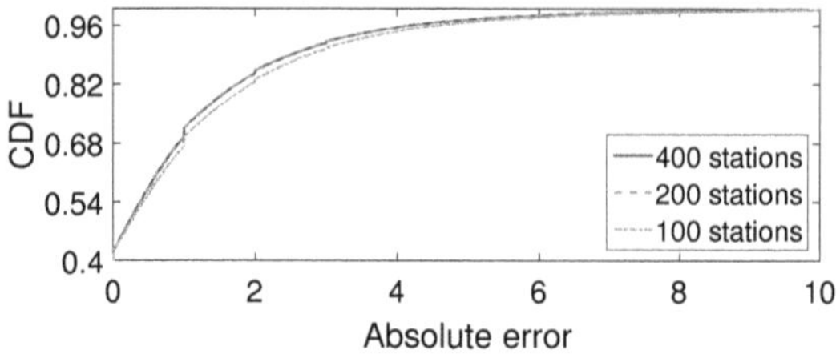

Figure 18: Impact of the number of source stations.

of 200 stations and 400 stations are identical. Thus, using a proper number of source stations (i.e., 200) achieves a good balance between estimation performance and computational overhead.

6.4 Evaluation on Other Datasets

To further demonstrate the effectiveness of proposed algorithms, we also perform small-scale evaluation on a bike-sharing dataset from New York City, U.S. [14]. We adopt same settings used in previous evaluation, and summarize the prediction error of check out and check in in Figure 19 and Figure 20, respectively.

As can be seen from both figures, all approaches demonstrate similar performance compared with the dataset from Hangzhou. The proposed algorithms still own the best prediction results, followed by HA, AMRA and P-TD. Taking check in prediction as an example, 80th percentile relative errors are 0.568, 0.5909, 0.6664, 0.8973 for MM, HA, AMRA and P-TD from the New York City dataset, while they are 0.598, 0.6667, 0.7276, 0.8061 from the Hangzhou dataset.

7. DISCUSSION AND FUTURE WORK

We provide several insights into the modeling and prediction results, and provide directions for future work in this part.

7.1 Insights

We first give some insights from both different scenarios and modeling approaches.

7.1.1 Variation Among Different Scenarios

We conduct studies in different scenarios to get a better understand of human mobility in BSS. CDFs of relative error of check in prediction are presented in Figure 21. The results of check out prediction are similar and omitted due to space limitation.

In Figure 21(a), we compare prediction results between stations in business area and tourist area. As we can see, stations in business area are more predictable due to users' regular mobility patterns (e.g., from home to office). Differences between rainy days and sunny days are shown in Figure 21(b). Consistent with our intuition, fewer people use public bikes in rainy days, which

Table 9: RMSLE of different numbers of source stations.

400 stations	200 stations	100 stations
0.4736	0.4736	0.5021

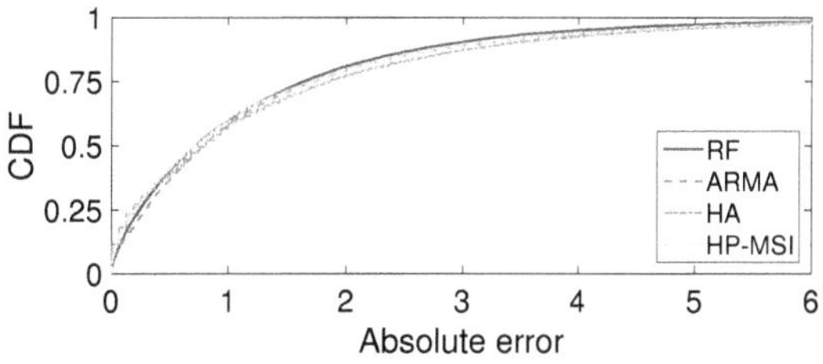

(a) CDF of absolute error.

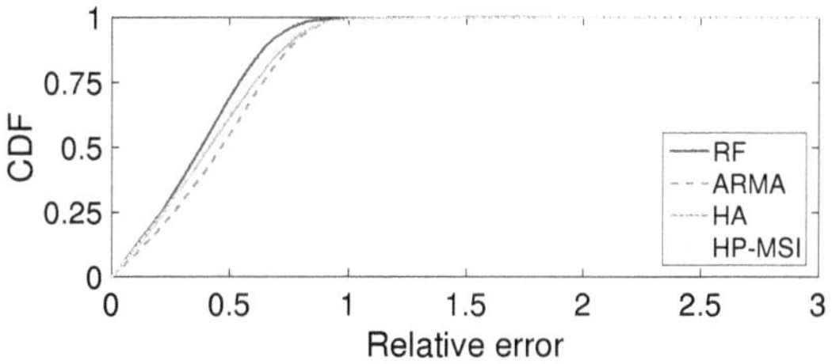

(b) CDF of relative error.

Figure 19: Overall check out prediction performance in NYC.

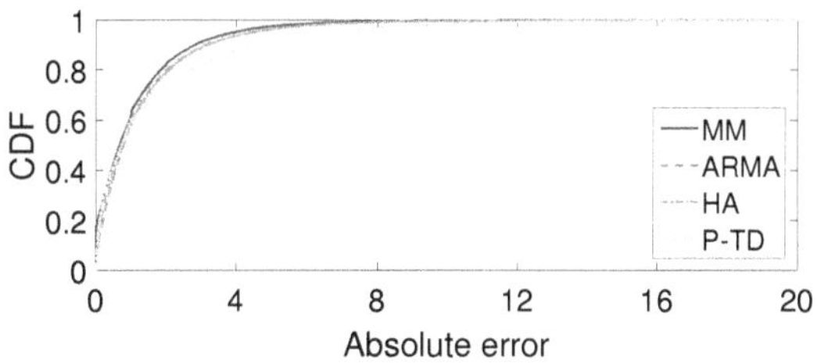

(a) CDF of absolute error.

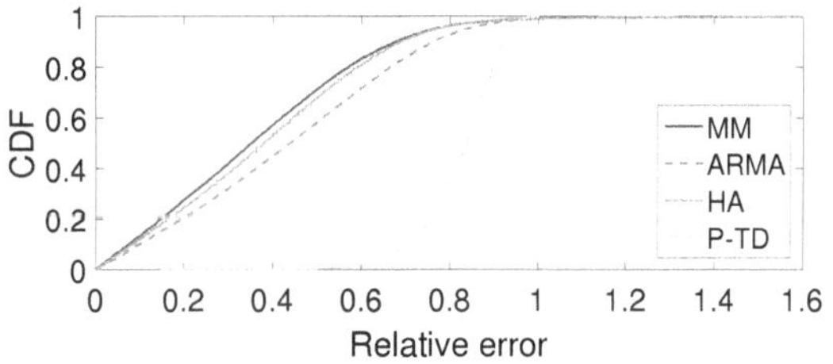

(b) CDF of relative error.

Figure 20: Overall check in prediction performance in NYC.

increases randomness and degrades prediction performance. As can be seen from Figure 21(c), workdays own better prediction results than holidays or weekends for similar reasons. Finally, stations with high utilization exhibit high predictability over stations with low throughputs in Figure 21(d).

In addition to the variations among days and stations, it is also interesting to see the impacts of special events. As can be seen from Figure 22, absolute error of check out prediction for one station near a stadium is 16.735 at 17:00, when an opening ceremony is over, which is around 4 times higher than that from the past half hour. When such special events happen, there tends to be a lot more people renting bikes than the historical average, inevitably causing bike usage anomalies and poor performance of prediction. Since these events happen less frequently and it is difficult to develop a

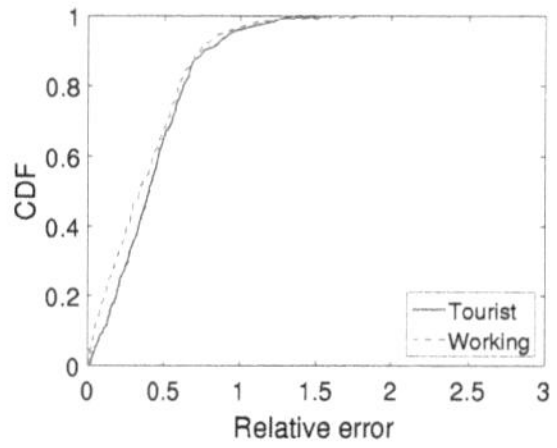

(a) Different areas.

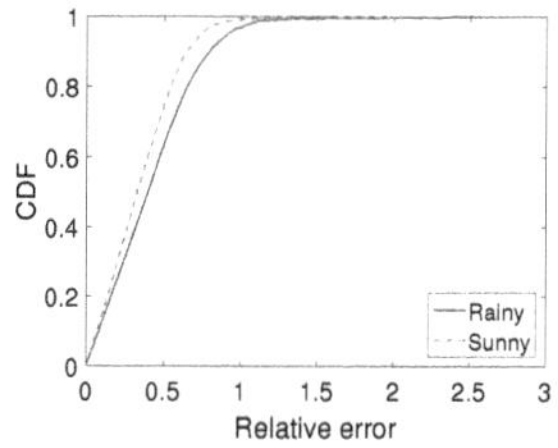

(b) Different weathers.

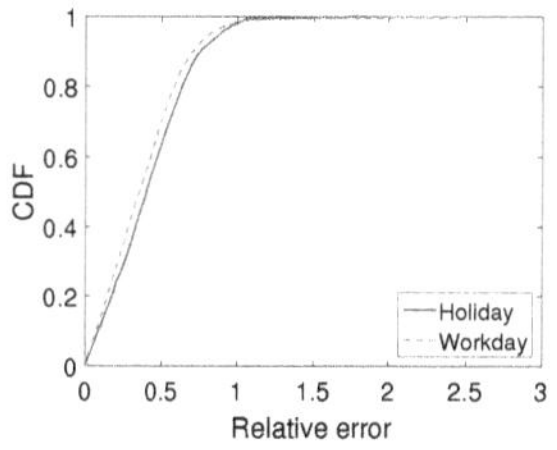

(c) Different days.

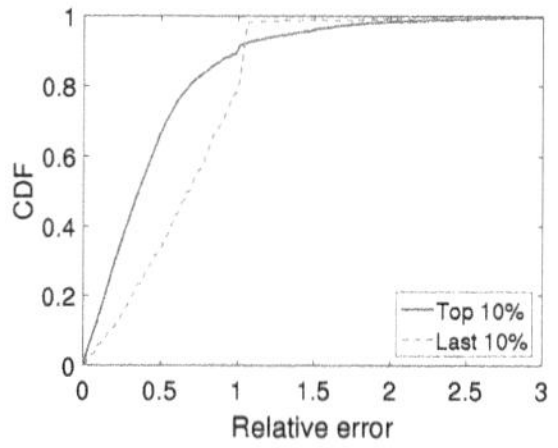

(d) Different stations.

Figure 21: Overall check in prediction performance (CDF of relative error).

static model to capture their impacts on BSS, we choose to leverage online features to compensate the impacts of special events in Section 4.

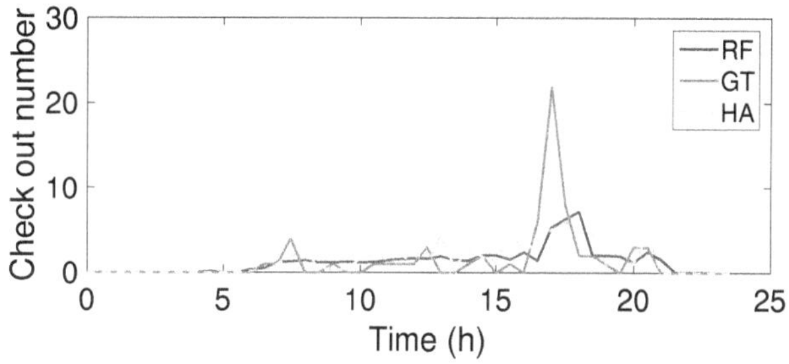

Figure 22: Check out prediction when the Games' opening ceremony are being held.

7.1.2 *User-centric Modeling and Prediction*

In this paper, we model and predict users' mobility in a station basis. However, one may also consider to do that in a user-centric way. We conduct some preliminary research in this direction and present the results here. Specifically, we aim to identify regular users who have fixed routes (e.g., from home to school), and exploit their profiles for modeling and prediction.

A user is categorized as a regular user if he or she has generated n routes of which the check out stations as well as check in stations fall into two small circles with 1km radius. In this study, we vary n and compute the percentage of regular users based on the data from January, 2013.

From Table 10, we can see that as n increases, the percentage of regular user decreases. However, even with a smaller n of 6, only 12.55% users can be classified as regular users. Therefore, the user-centric mobility modeling and prediction, while hopeful, left challenging problems due to the low percentages of regular users.

Table 10: Regular user percentage.

n	regular user(%)	n	regular user(%)
6	12.55%	14	3.85%
8	9.19%	16	2.87%
10	6.65%	18	2.02%
12	5.02%	20	1.23%

7.2 Open Research Issues

From a mobile system point of view, we summarize some open research issues related to the emerging bike-sharing systems.

7.2.1 Mobility Model Fusion with Multi-source Data

Study of human mobility has drawn significant attention in the mobile community. One intuitive idea is to improve the existing models by integrating bike-sharing data. In [15], authors have demonstrated the reduced bias of mobility modeling by exploiting the inherent diversities from multi-source data (i.e., taxi, bus, subway and smartphone CDR).

7.2.2 Bike Rebalancing

Rebalancing, a reality for pretty much every bike-sharing system, can benefit from the accurate mobility modeling and prediction. However, how to design an efficient and practical rebalancing algorithm is non-trivial. For example, one needs to calculate the number of shuffled bikes at each station and plan a route at the same time. Apart from operator's "passive" rebalancing, how to devise an incentive and price mechanism enabling user-based "proactive" rebalancing is also an interesting subject to pursue.

7.2.3 Service Optimizations

In addition to bike rebalancing, future work on service optimization includes station location optimization, service hour optimization, pricing strategy design, bicycle utilization balancing etc. From a customer perspective, prompt bike stock information delivery and user-friendly interaction design is also of great help. To achieve this goal, we have developed a demo application [16], which not only provides early stock warnings for operators, but also serves as a tour guide for bike users.

8. RELATED WORK

Extensive research has been done to describe the nature of bike-sharing systems, business models, how they have spread in time and space and why they have been adopted [8, 17–25]. For example, Shaheen *et al.* reviews the history, advantages and inadequacies of bike-sharing systems across the globe [17, 18, 24]. Martin *et al.* evaluates transit modal shift dynamics with the emergence of public bike-sharing [22]. Parkes *et al.* [19] uses diffusion theory to compare the adoption process of bike-sharing in Europe and North America. Comprehensive analysis and survey of city-scale bike-sharing systems in Paris [20], Hangzhou [8], New York [25], Washington D.C. [21] and Montreal [23] have also been conducted.

Adoption of bike-sharing systems have motivated studies on system design optimization. A first line of work focuses on the sensing of dynamics from bike-sharing system data [4–7, 10, 13, 20, 26–28], which broadly consider on two topics, namely clustering and prediction. Most clustering approaches identify mobility patterns in bike usage and partition the stations into clusters based on their usage profiles [3, 7, 10, 26, 27]. For instance, in [3], two clustering techniques using activity statistics derived either from the evolution of station occupancy or the number of available bicycles along the day. In [26], authors use graphs to describe the similarity of usage profiles between pairs of stations for weekdays and weekends, which is then analyzed using a community detection algorithm for clustering. In contrast to clustering, the aim of prediction is to forecast the occupancy of the stations or the network state over time by means of time series analysis [4–6, 28], Bayesian networks [3] and supervised regression model [13]. For instance, Borgnat *et al.* [6] forecasts the global rental volume, whereas Li *et al.* [7] infers the bike rental/return demand of a cluster of stations based on historical check in and check out data. To our knowledge, we are the first to generate a global spatio-temporal mobility model considering flows between stations, and to provide fine-grained prediction results on a per-station basis. Such a spatio-temporal mobility model is the key to any improvements of the bike redistribution strategy.

Based on insights into usage patterns and bike trip demand analysis, research has also been conducted to optimize the placement of stations in bike-sharing systems [10, 13, 29–31], and design strategies for bicycle re-balancing [32–35]. For example, Chen *et al.* [13] and García-Palomares *et al.* [29] solve the station placement problem by estimating the potential trip demand using a semi-supervised learning algorithm and a GIS-based method, respectively. Authors in [35] use a clustering-based heuristic for truck routing whereas in [32], Raviv *et al.* find truck routes by minimizing an objective function tied to both the operating cost of the vehicles as well as penalty functions relating to station imbalance. The mobility model and prediction mechanism derived in our work can be easily applied to other bike-sharing systems and lay a solid foundation for the upper layer design and optimization.

In addition to bike-sharing data, researchers analyzed human mobility based on other empirical data from taxicabs [36], buses [37], subways [38], private cars [39], WiFi APs [40, 41], cellular carriers [15, 42] and social networks [43]. Due to the unique intrinsic properties such as the decentralized structure, on-demand usage and unattended vehicles in BSS, our work provides a fundamentally different model from these designs.

9. CONCLUSION

This paper focuses on the mobility modeling and prediction in bike-sharing systems. Based on historical bicycle sharing data, we first use statistical methods to model the spatio-temporal shifts of bikes between stations, and then estimate bike check in results based on the model and online check out records. A random-forest-based prediction mechanism is further proposed to model and forecast the users' check out behaviors. The mobility modeling and prediction algorithms provide insights into the operations of bike-sharing systems, and have proved useful for the prediction of bike availability at each station, laying a foundation for further efficient re-balancing design in bike-sharing systems.

Acknowledgment

This work is supported in part by the National Basic Research Program (973 Program) under Grant 2015CB352500, and National Program for Special Support of Top Notch Young Professionals. We thank our partner BSS operator, Hangzhou Public Bicycle Transport Service Development Co., Ltd., and the anonymous reviewers and our shepherd Qin Lv for their constructive comments and support.

References

[1] LLC MetroBike. The Bike Sharing World - 2014 -Year End Data. http://bike-sharing.blogspot.com/2015/01/the-bike-sharing-world-2014-year-end.html.

[2] Wikipedia. List of Bicycle-sharing Systems. https://en.wikipedia.org/wiki/List_of_bicycle-sharing_systems.

[3] Jon Froehlich, Joachim Neumann, and Nuria Oliver. Sensing and Predicting the Pulse of the City through Shared Bicycling. In *IJCAI*, 2009.

[4] Andreas Kaltenbrunner, Rodrigo Meza, Jens Grivolla, Joan Codina, and Rafael Banchs. Urban Cycles and Mobility Patterns: Exploring and Predicting Trends in a Bicycle-based Public Transport System. *Pervasive and Mobile Computing*, 6(4):455–466, 2010.

[5] Patrick Vogel and Dirk C. Mattfeld. Strategic and Operational Planning of Bike-Sharing Systems by Data Mining - A Case Study. In *Computational Logistics*, pages 127–141. 2011.

[6] Pierre Borgnat, Eric Fleury, Céline Robardet, and Antoine Scherrer. Spatial Analysis of Dynamic Movements of Vélo'v, Lyon's Shared Bicycle Program. In *European Conference on Complex Systems (ECCS)*, 2009.

[7] Yexin Li, Yu Zheng, Huichu Zhang, and Lei Chen. Traffic Prediction in a Bike Sharing System. In *ACM SIGSPATIAL*, 2015.

[8] Susan a. Shaheen, Hua Zhang, Elliot Martin, and Stacey Guzman. China's Hangzhou Public Bicycle. *Transportation Research Record: Journal of the Transportation Research Board*, 2247(1):33–41, 2011.

[9] Wikipedia. Hangzhou Public Bicycle. https://en.wikipedia.org/wiki/Hangzhou_Public_Bicycle.

[10] Eoin O Mahony and David B Shmoys. Data Analysis and Optimization for (Citi) Bike Sharing. In *AAAI*, 2015.

[11] Nicolas Gast, Guillaume Massonnet, Daniël Reijsbergen, and Mirco Tribastone. Probabilistic forecasts of bike-sharing systems for journey planning. In *ACM CIKM*, 2015.

[12] Leo Breiman. Random Forests. *Machine Learning*, 45(1):5–32, 2001.

[13] Longbiao Chen, Daqing Zhang, Gang Pan, Xiaojuan Ma, Dingqi Yang, Kostadin Kushlev, Wangsheng Zhang, and Shijian Li. Bike Sharing Station Placement Leveraging Heterogeneous Urban Open Data. In *ACM Ubicomp*, 2015.

[14] Citi Bike. New York City Bike-sharing System Data. https://www.citibikenyc.com/system-data.

[15] Desheng Zhang, Jun Huang, Ye Li, Fan Zhang, Chengzhong Xu, and Tian He. Exploring Human Mobility with Multi-source Data at Extremely Large Metropolitan Scales. In *ACM MobiCom*, 2014.

[16] Lihuan Zhang, Siyuan Tang, Zidong Yang, Ji Hu, Yuanchao Shu, Peng Cheng, and Jiming Chen. Demo: Data Analysis and Visualization in Bike-Sharing Systems. http://www.sensornet.cn/bikevis/.

[17] Susan a. Shaheen, Stacey Guzman, and Hua Zhang. Bikesharing in Europe, the Americas, and Asia. *Transportation Research Record: Journal of the Transportation Research Board*, 2143:159–167, 2010.

[18] Susan a. Shaheen, Adam P. Cohen, and Elliot W. Martin. Public Bikesharing in North America: Early Operator Understanding and Emerging Trends. *Transportation Research Record: Journal of the Transportation Research Board*, 2387:83–92, 2013.

[19] Stephen D. Parkes, Greg Marsden, Susan A. Shaheen, and Adam P. Cohen. Understanding the Diffusion of Public Bikesharing Systems: Evidence from Europe and North America. *Journal of Transport Geography*, 31:94–103, 2013.

[20] Rahul Nair, Elise Miller-Hooks, Robert C. Hampshire, and Ana Bušić. Large-Scale Vehicle Sharing Systems: Analysis of Vélib'. *International Journal of Sustainable Transportation*, 7(1):85–106, 2013.

[21] LDA Consulting Washington. 2013 Capital Bikeshare Member Survey Report. Technical Report 202, 2013.

[22] Elliot W. Martin and Susan A. Shaheen. Evaluating Public Transit Modal Shift Dynamics in Response to Bikesharing: A Tale of Two U.S. Cities. *Journal of Transport Geography*, 41:315–324, 2014.

[23] Ahmadreza Faghih Imani, Naveen Eluru, Ahmed M. El-Geneidy, Michael Rabbat, and Usama Haq. How does Land-use and Urban Form Impact Bicycle Flows: Evidence from the Bicycle-sharing System (BIXI) in Montreal. *Transport Geography*, (February):1–20, 2014.

[24] Paul DeMaio. Bike-sharing: History, Impacts, Models of Provision, and Future. *Journal of Public Transportation*, 12(DeMaio 2004):41–56, 2009.

[25] Department for City Planning New York. Bike-Share. Opportunities in New York City. Technical report, 2009.

[26] P. Borgnat, C. Robardet, P. Abry, P. Flandrin, J. Rouquier, and N. Tremblay. A Dynamical Network View of Lyon's Vélo'v Shared Bicycle System. In *Dynamics On and Of Complex Networks*, volume 2, chapter A Dynamical, pages 267–284. Springer Berlin Heidelberg, 2013.

[27] C Ome and Oukhellou Latifa. Model-Based Count Series Clustering for Bike Sharing System Usage Mining : A Case Study with the Vélib System of Paris. *ACM Transactions on Intelligent Systems and Technology*, 5(3):1–21, 2014.

[28] Ji Won Yoon, Fabio Pinelli, and Francesco Calabrese. Cityride: A Predictive Bike Sharing Journey Advisor. In *IEEE ICMDM*, 2012.

[29] Juan Carlos García-Palomares, Javier Gutiénrrez, and Marta Latorre. Optimizing the Location of Stations in Bike-sharing Programs: A GIS Approach. *Applied Geography*, 35(1–2):235–246, 2012.

[30] Juan P. Romero, Angel Ibeas, Jose L. Moura, Juan Benavente, and Borja Alonso. A Simulation-optimization Approach to Design Efficient Systems of Bike-sharing. *Meeting of the EURO Working Group on Transportation*, 54:646–655, 2012.

[31] Jenn-Rong Lin and Ta-Hui Yang. Strategic Design of Public Bicycle Sharing Systems with Service Level Constraints. *Transportation Research Part E: Logistics and Transportation Review*, 47(2):284–294, 2011.

[32] Tal Raviv, Michal Tzur, and IrisA. Forma. Static Repositioning in a Bike-sharing System: Models and Solution Approaches. *EURO Journal on Transportation and Logistics*, 2(3):187–229, 2013.

[33] Jia Shu, Mabel C. Chou, Qizhang Liu, Chung-Piaw Teo, and I-Lin Wang. Models for Effective Deployment and Redistribution of Bicycles Within Public Bicycle-Sharing Systems. *Operations Research*, 61(6):1346–1359, 2013.

[34] Contardo, Claudio, Catherine Morency, and Louis-Martin Rousseau. Balancing a Dynamic Public Bike-sharing System. Technical report, 2012.

[35] Jasper Schuijbroek, Robert Hampshire, and Willem-Jan van Hoeve. Inventory Rebalancing and Vehicle Routing in Bike Sharing Systems. Technical report, 2013.

[36] Raghu Ganti, Mudhakar Srivatsa, Anand Ranganathan, and Jiawei Han. Inferring Human Mobility Patterns from Taxicab Location Traces. In *ACM UbiComp*, 2013.

[37] Sourav Bhattacharya, Santi Phithakkitnukoon, Petteri Nurmi, Arto Klami, Marco Veloso, and Carlos Bento. Gaussian Process-based Predictive Modeling for Bus Ridership. In *ACM UbiComp*, 2013.

[38] Neal Lathia and Licia Capra. How Smart is Your Smartcard?: Measuring Travel Behaviours, Perceptions, and Incentives. In *ACM UbiComp*, 2011.

[39] Fosca Giannotti, Mirco Nanni, Dino Pedreschi, Fabio Pinelli, Chiara Renso, Salvatore Rinzivillo, and Roberto Trasarti. Unveiling the Complexity of Human Mobility by Querying and Mining Massive Trajectory Data. *The VLDB Journal*, 20(5):695–719, October 2011.

[40] Jungkeun Yoon, Brian D. Noble, Mingyan Liu, and Minkyong Kim. Building Realistic Mobility Models from Coarse-grained Traces. In *ACM MobiSys*, 2006.

[41] Jennie Steshenko, Vasanta G. Chaganti, and James Kurose. Mobility in a Large-scale WiFi Network: From Syslog Events to Mobile User Sessions. In *ACM MSWiM*, 2014.

[42] Sibren Isaacman, Richard Becker, Ramón Cáceres, Margaret Martonosi, James Rowland, Alexander Varshavsky, and Walter Willinger. Human Mobility Modeling at Metropolitan Scales. In *ACM MobiSys*, 2012.

[43] Eunjoon Cho, Seth A. Myers, and Jure Leskovec. Friendship and mobility: User movement in location-based social networks. In *ACM KDD*, 2011.

Defending against Sybil Devices in Crowdsourced Mapping Services

Gang Wang[†], Bolun Wang[†], Tianyi Wang[†‡], Ana Nika[†], Haitao Zheng[†], Ben Y. Zhao[†]
[†]Department of Computer Science, UC Santa Barbara
[‡]Department of Electronic Engineering, Tsinghua University
{gangw, bolunwang, tianyi, anika, htzheng, ravenben}@cs.ucsb.edu

ABSTRACT

Real-time crowdsourced maps such as Waze provide timely updates on traffic, congestion, accidents and points of interest. In this paper, we demonstrate how lack of strong location authentication allows creation of software-based *Sybil devices* that expose crowdsourced map systems to a variety of security and privacy attacks. Our experiments show that a single Sybil device with limited resources can cause havoc on Waze, reporting false congestion and accidents and automatically rerouting user traffic. More importantly, we describe techniques to generate Sybil devices at scale, creating armies of virtual vehicles capable of remotely tracking precise movements for large user populations while avoiding detection. We propose a new approach to defend against Sybil devices based on *co-location edges*, authenticated records that attest to the one-time physical co-location of a pair of devices. Over time, co-location edges combine to form large *proximity graphs* that attest to physical interactions between devices, allowing scalable detection of virtual vehicles. We demonstrate the efficacy of this approach using large-scale simulations, and discuss how they can be used to dramatically reduce the impact of attacks against crowdsourced mapping services.

1. INTRODUCTION

Crowdsourcing is indispensable as a real-time data gathering tool for today's online services. Take for example map and navigation services. Both Google Maps and Waze use periodic GPS readings from mobile devices to infer traffic speed and congestion levels on streets and highways. Waze, the most popular crowdsourced map service, offers users more ways to actively share information on accidents, police cars, and even contribute content like editing roads, landmarks, and local fuel prices. This and the ability to interact with nearby users made Waze extremely popular, with an estimated 50 million users when it was acquired by Google for a reported $1.3 Billion USD in June 2013. Today, Google integrates selected crowdsourced data (*e.g.* accidents) from Waze into its own Maps application.

Unfortunately, systems that rely on crowdsourced data are inherently vulnerable to mischievous or malicious users seeking to disrupt or game the system [41]. For example, business owners can badmouth competitors by falsifying negative reviews on Yelp or TripAdvisor, and FourSquare users can forge their physical locations for discounts [11, 54]. For location-based services, these attacks are possible because there are no widely deployed tools to authenticate the location of mobile devices. In fact, there are few effective tools today to identify whether the origin of traffic requests are real mobile devices or software scripts.

The goal of our work is to explore the vulnerability of today's crowdsourced mobile apps against *Sybil devices*, software scripts that appear to application servers as "virtual mobile devices."[1] While a single Sybil device can damage mobile apps through misbehavior, larger groups of Sybil devices can overwhelm normal users and significantly disrupt any crowdsourced mobile app. In this paper, we identify techniques that allow malicious attackers to reliably create large populations of Sybil devices using software. Using the context of the Waze crowdsourced map service, we illustrate the powerful Sybil device attack, and then develop and evaluate robust defenses against them.

While our experiments and defenses are designed with Waze (and crowdsourced maps) in mind, our results generalize to a wide range of mobile apps. With minimal modifications, our techniques can be applied to services ranging from Foursquare and Yelp to Uber and YikYak, allowing attackers to cheaply emulate numerous virtual devices with forged locations to overwhelm these systems via misbehavior. Misbehavior can range from falsely obtaining coupons on FourSquare/Yelp, gaming the new user coupon system in Uber, to imposing censorship on YikYak. We believe our proposed defenses can be extended to these services as well. We discuss broader implications of our work in Section 8.

Sybil attacks in Waze. In the context of Waze, our experiments reveal a number of potential attacks by Sybil devices. First is simple *event forgery*, where devices can generate fake events to the Waze server, including congestion, accidents or police activity that might affect user routes. Second, we describe techniques to reverse engineer mobile app APIs, thus allowing attackers to create lightweight scripts that effectively emulate a large number of virtual vehicles that collude under the control of a single attacker. We call Sybil devices in Waze "ghost riders." These Sybils can effectively magnify the efficacy of any attack, and overwhelm contributions from any legitimate users. Finally, we discover a significant privacy attack where ghost riders can silently and invisibly "follow" and precisely track individual Waze users throughout their day, precisely mapping out their movement to work, stores, hotels, gas station, and home. We experimentally confirmed the accuracy

[1]We refer to these scripts as Sybil devices, since they are the manifestations of Sybil attacks [16] in the context of mobile networks.

MobiSys'16, June 25-30, 2016, Singapore, Singapore
 ISBN 978-1-4503-4269-8/16/06...$15.00
DOI: http://dx.doi.org/10.1145/2906388.2906420

of this attack against our own vehicles, quantifying the accuracy of the attack against GPS coordinates. Magnified by an army of ghost riders, an attacker can potentially track the constant whereabouts of millions of users, all without any risk of detection.

Defenses. Prior proposals to address the location authentication problem have limited appeal, because of reliance on widespread deployment of specialized hardware, either as part of physical infrastructure, *i.e.*, cellular base stations, or as modifications to mobile devices themselves. Instead, we propose a practical solution that limits the ability of Sybil devices to amplify the potential damage incurred by any single attacker. We introduce *collocation edges*, authenticated records that attest to the one-time physical proximity of a pair of mobile devices. The creation of collocation edges can be triggered opportunistically by the mapping service, *e.g.*, Waze. Over time, collocation edges combine to form large *proximity graphs*, network structures that attest to physical interactions between devices. Since ghost riders cannot physically interact with real devices, they cannot form direct edges with real devices, only indirectly through a small number of real devices operated by the attacker. Thus, the edges between an attacker and the rest of the network are limited by the number of real physical devices she has, regardless of how many ghost riders are under her control. This reduces the problem of detecting ghost riders to a community detection problem on the proximity graph (The graph is seeded by a small number of trusted infrastructure locations).

Our paper includes these key contributions:

- We explore limits and impacts of single device attacks on Waze, *e.g.*, artificial congestion and events.
- We describe techniques to create light-weight ghost riders, virtual vehicles emulated by client-side scripts, through reverse engineering of the Waze app's communication protocol with the server.
- We identify a new privacy attack that allows ghost riders to virtually follow and track individual Waze users in real-time, and describe techniques to produce precise, robust location updates.
- We propose and evaluate defenses against ghost riders, using *proximity graphs* constructed with edges representing authenticated collocation events between pairs of devices. Since collocation can only occur between pairs of physical devices, proximity graphs limit the number of edges between real devices and ghost riders, thus isolating groups of ghost riders and making them detectable using community detection algorithms.

2. WAZE BACKGROUND

Waze is the most popular crowdsourced navigation app on smartphones, with more than 50 million users when it was acquired by Google in June 2013 [19]. Waze collects GPS values of users' devices to estimate real-time traffic. It also allows users to report on-road events such as accidents, road closures and police vehicles, as well as curating points of interest, editing roads, and even updating local fuel prices. Some features, *e.g.*, user reported accidents, have been integrated into Google Maps [20]. Here, we briefly describe the key functionality in Waze as context for our work.

Trip Navigation. Waze's main feature is assist users to find the best route to their destination and turn-by-turn navigation. Waze generates aggregated real-time traffic updates using GPS data from its users, and optimizes user routes both during trip planning and during navigation. If and when traffic congestions is detected, Waze automatically re-routes users towards an alternative.

Figure 1: Before the attack (left), Waze shows the fastest route for the user. After the attack (right), the user gets automatically re-routed by the fake traffic jam.

Crowdsourced User Reports. Waze users can generate real-time *event reports* on their routes to inform others about ongoing incidents. Events range from accidents to road closures, hazards, and even police speed traps. Each report can include a short note with a photo. The event shows up on the map of users driving towards the reported location. As users get close, Waze pops up a window to let the user "say thanks," or report the event is "not there." If multiple users choose "not there", the event will be removed. Waze also merges multiple reports of the same event type at the same location into a single event.

Social Function. To increase user engagement, Waze supports simple social interactions. Users can see avatars and locations of nearby users. Clicking on a user's avatar shows more detailed user information, including nickname, ranking, and traveling speed. Also, users can send messages and chat with nearby users. This social function gives users the sense of a large community. Users can elevate their rankings in the community by contributing and receiving "thanks" from others.

3. ATTACKING CROWDSOURCED MAPS

In this section, we describe basic attacks to manipulate Waze by generating false road events and fake traffic congestion. Since Waze relies on real-time data for trip planning and route selection, these attacks can influence user's routing decisions. Attackers can attack specific users by forging congestion to force automatic rerouting on their trips. The attack is possible because Waze has no reliable authentication on user reported data, such as their device GPS.

We first discuss experimental ethics and steps we took to limit impact on real users. Then, we describe basic mechanisms and resources needed to launch attacks, and use controlled experiments on two attacks to understand their feasibility and limits. One attack creates fake road events at arbitrary locations, and the other seeks to generate artificial traffic hotspots to influence user routing.

3.1 Ethics

Our experiments seek to understand the feasibility and limits of practical attacks on crowdsourcing maps like Waze. We are very aware of the potential impact to real Waze users from any experiments. We consulted our local IRB and have taken all possible precautions to ensure that our experiments do not negatively impact real Waze users. In particular, we choose experiment locations

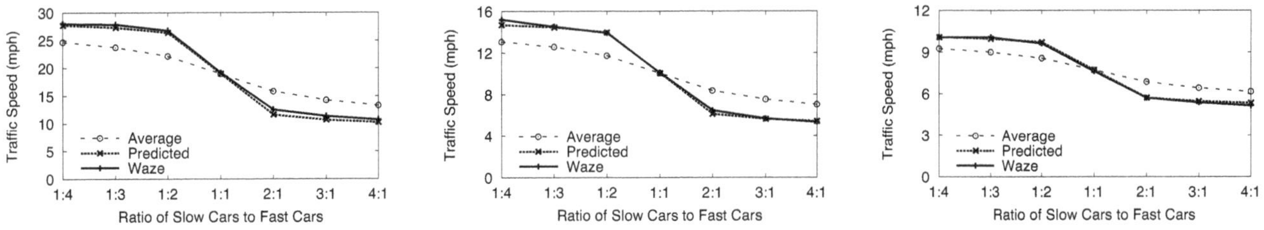

(a) Highway (b) Local Road (c) Residential

Figure 2: The traffic speed of the road with respect to different combinations of number of slow cars and fast cars. We show that Waze is not using the average speed of all cars, and our inferred function can correctly predict the traffic speed displayed on Waze.

where user population density is extremely low (unoccupied roads), and only perform experiments at low-traffic hours, *e.g.*, between 2am and 5am. During the experiments, we continuously scan the entire experiment region and neighboring areas, to ensure no other Waze users (except our own accounts) are within miles of the test area. If any Waze users are detected, we immediately terminate all running experiments. Our study received the IRB approval under protocol# COMS-ZH-YA-010-7N.

Our work is further motivated by our view of the risks of inaction versus risks posed to users by our study. On one hand, we can and have minimized risk to Waze users during our study, and we believe our experiments have not affected any Waze users. On the other hand, we believe the risk to millions of Waze users from pervasive location tracking (described in Section 5) is realistic and potentially very damaging. We feel that investigating these attacks and identifying these risks to the broad community at large was the ethically correct course of action. Furthermore, full understanding of the attacks was necessary to design an effective and *practical* defense. Please see Appendix A for more detailed information on our IRB approval and steps taken towards responsible disclosure.

3.2 Basic Attack: Generating Fake Events

Launching attacks against crowdsourced maps like Waze requires three steps: automate input to mobile devices that run the Waze app; control the device GPS and simulate device movements (*e.g.*, car driving); obtain access to *multiple* devices. All three are easily achieved using widely available mobile device emulators.

Most mobile emulators run a full OS (*e.g.*, Android, iOS) down to the kernel level, and simulate hardware features such as camera, SDCard and GPS. We choose the GenyMotion Android emulator [3] for its performance and reliability. Attackers can automatically control the GenyMotion emulator via Monkeyrunner scripts [4]. They can generate user actions such as clicking buttons and typing text, and feed pre-designed GPS sequences to the emulator (through a command line interface) to simulate location positioning and device movement. By controlling the timing of the GPS updates, they can simulate any "movement speed" of the simulated devices.

Using these tools, attackers can generate fake events (or alerts) at a given location by setting fake GPS on their virtual devices. This includes any events supported by Waze, including accidents, police, hazards, and road closures. We find that a single emulator can generate any event at arbitrary locations on the map. We validate this using experiments on a variety of unoccupied roads, including highways, local and rural roads (50+ locations, 3 repeated tests each). Note that our experiments only involve data in the Waze system, and do not affect real road vehicles not running the Waze app. Thus "unoccupied" means no vehicles on the road with mobile devices actively running the Waze app. After creation, the fake event stays on the map for about 30 minutes. Any Waze user can report that an event was "not there." We find it takes two consecutive "not theres" (without any "thanks" in between) to delete the event. Thus an attacker can ensure an event persists by occasionally "driving" other virtual devices to the region and "thanking" the original attacker for the event report.

3.3 Congestion and Traffic Routing

A more serious attack targets Waze's real-time trip routing function. Since route selection in Waze relies on predicted trip time, attackers can influence routes by creating "fake" traffic hotspots at specific locations. This can be done by configuring a group of virtual vehicles to travel slowly on a chosen road segment.

We use controlled experiments to answer two questions. First, under what conditions can attackers successfully create traffic hotspots? Second, how long can an artificial traffic hotspot last? We select three low-traffic roads in the state of Texas that are representative of three popular road types based on their speed limit—Highway (65 mph), Local (45 mph) and Residential (25 mph). To avoid real users, we choose roads in low population rural areas, and run tests at hours with the lowest traffic volumes (usually 3-5AM). We constantly scan for real users in or nearby the experimental region, and reset/terminate experiments if users come close to an area with ongoing experiments. Across all our experiments, only 2 tests were terminated due to detected presence of real users nearby. Finally, we have examined different road types and hours of the day to ensure they do not introduce bias into our results.

Creating Traffic Hotspots. Our experiment shows that it only takes one slow moving car to create a traffic congestion, when there are no real Waze users around. Waze displays a red overlay on the road to indicate traffic congestion (Figure 1, right). Different road types have different congestion thresholds, with thresholds strongly correlated to the speed limit. The congestion thresholds for Highway, Local and Residential roads are 40mph, 20mph and 15mph, respectively.

To understand if this is generalizable, we repeat our tests on other unoccupied roads in different states and countries. We picked 18 roads in five states in the US (CO, MO, NM, UT, MS) and British Columbia, Canada. In each region, we select three roads with different speed limits (highway, local and residential). We find consistent results: a single virtual vehicle can always generate a traffic hotspot; and the congestion thresholds were consistent across different roads of the same speed limit.

Outvoting Real Users. Generating traffic hotspot in practical scenarios faces a challenge from real Waze users who drive at normal (non-congested) speeds: attacker's virtual vehicles must "convince" the server there's a stream of slow speed traffic on the road

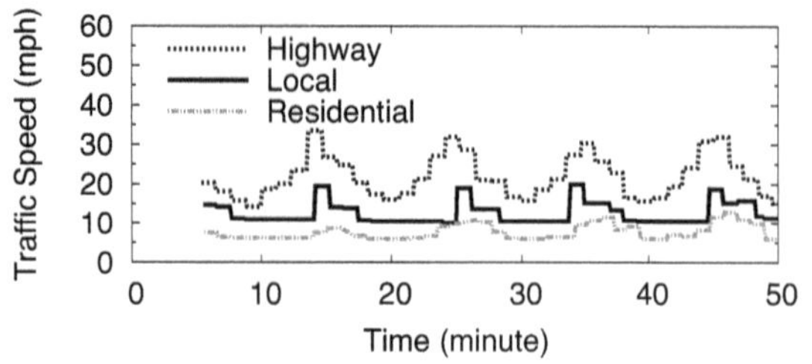

Figure 3: Long-last traffic jam created by slow cars driving-by.

even as real users tell the server otherwise. We need to understand how Waze aggregated multiple inputs to estimate traffic speed.

We perform an experiment to infer this aggregation function used by Waze. We create two groups of virtual vehicles: N_s slow-driving cars with speed S_s, and N_f fast-driving cars with speed S_f; and they all pass the target location at the same time. We study the congestion reported by Waze to infer the aggregation function. Note that the server-estimated traffic speed is visible on the map *only if* we formed a traffic hotspot. We achieve this by setting the speed tuple (S_s, S_f) to (10mph, 30mph) for Highway, (5, 15) for Local and (5, 10) for Residential.

As shown in Figure 2, when we vary the ratio of slow cars over fast cars (N_s:N_f), the Waze server produces different final traffic speeds. We observe that Waze does not simply compute an "average" speed over all the cars. Instead, it uses a weighted average with higher weight on the majority cars' speed. We infer an aggregation function as follows:

$$S_{waze} = \frac{S_{max} \cdot max(N_s, N_f) + S_{avg} \cdot min(N_s, N_f)}{N_s + N_f}$$

where $S_{avg} = \frac{S_s N_s + S_f N_f}{N_s + N_f}$, and S_{max} is the speed of the group with N_{max} cars. As shown in Figure 2, our function can predict Waze's aggregate traffic speed accurately, for all different types of roads in our test. For validation purposes, we run another set of experiments by raising S_f above the hotspot thresholds (65mph, 30mph and 20mph respectively for the three roads). We can still form traffic hotspots by using more slow-driving cars ($N_s > N_f$), and our function can still predict the traffic speed on Waze accurately.

Long-Lasting Traffic Congestion. A traffic hotspot will last for 25-30 minutes if no other cars drive by. Once aggregate speed normalizes, the congestion event is dismissed within 2-5 minutes. To create a long-lasting virtual traffic jam, attackers can simply keep sending slow-driving cars to the congestion area to resist the input from real users. We validate this using a simple, 50-minute long experiment where 3 virtual vehicles create a persistent congestion by driving slowly through an area, and then looping back every 10 minutes. Meanwhile, 2 other virtual cars emulate legitimate drivers that pass by at high speed every 10 minutes. As shown in Figure 3, the traffic hotspot persists for the entire experiment period.

Impact on End Users. Waze uses real-time traffic data to optimize routes during trip planning. Waze estimates the end-to-end trip time and recommends the fastest route. Once on the road, Waze continuously estimates the travel time, and automatically reroutes if the current route becomes congested. An attacker can launch physical attacks by placing fake traffic hotspots on the user's original route. While congestion alone does not trigger rerouting, Waze reroutes the user to a detour when the estimated travel time through the detour is shorter than the current congested route (see Figure 1).

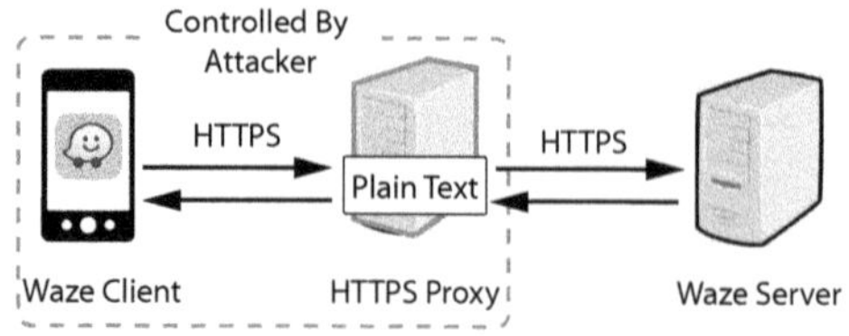

Figure 4: Using a HTTPS proxy as man-in-the-middle to intercept traffic between Waze client and server.

We also note that Waze data is used by Google Maps, and therefore can potentially impact their 1+ billion users [36]. Our experiment shows that artificial congestion do not appear on Google Maps, but fake events generated on Waze are displayed on Google Maps without verification, including "accidents", "construction" and "objects on road". Finally, event updates are synchronized on both services, with a 2-minute delay and persist for a similar period of time (*e.g.*, 30 minutes).

4. SYBIL ATTACKS

So far, we have shown that attackers using emulators can create "virtual vehicles" that manipulate the Waze map. An attacker can generate much higher impact using a large group of virtual vehicles (or *Sybils* [16]) under control. In this section, we describe techniques to produce light-weight virtual vehicles in Waze, and explore the scalability of the group-based attacks. We refer to large groups of virtual vehicles as "ghost riders" for two reasons. First, they are easy to create en masse, and can travel in packs to outvote real users to generate more complex events, *e.g.*, persistent traffic congestion. Second, as we show in §5, they can make themselves invisible to nearby vehicles.

Factors Limiting Sybil Creation. We start by looking at the limits of the large-scale Sybil attacks on Waze. First, we note user accounts do not pose a challenge to attackers, since account registration can be fully automated. We found that a single-threaded Monkeyrunner script could automatically register 1000 new accounts in a day. Even though the latest version of Waze app requires SMS verification to register accounts, attackers can use older versions of APIs to create accounts without verification. Alternatively, accounts can be verified through disposable phone/SMS services [44].

The limiting factor is the scalability of vehicle emulation. Even though emulators like GenyMotion are relatively lightweight, each instance still takes significant computational resources. For example, a MacBookPro with 8G of RAM supports only 10 simultaneous emulator instances. For this, we explore a more scalable approach to client emulation that can increase the number of supported virtual vehicles by orders of magnitude. Specifically, we reverse engineer the communication APIs used by the app, and replace emulators with simple Python scripts that mimic API calls.

Reverse Engineering Waze APIs. The Waze app uses HTTPS to communicate with the server, so API details cannot be directly observed by capturing network traffic (TLS/SSL encrypted). However, an attacker can still intercept HTTPS traffic, by setting up a proxy [2] between her phone and Waze server as a man-in-the-middle attack [40, 9]. As shown in Figure 4, an attacker needs to pre-install the proxy server's root Certificate Authorities (CA) to her own phone as a "trusted CA." This allows the proxy to present self-signed certificates to the phone claiming to be the Waze server. The Waze app on the phone will trust the proxy (since the certificate is signed by a "trusted CA"), and establish HTTPS connections with the proxy using proxy's public key. On the proxy side, the attacker can decrypt the traffic using proxy's private key, and then forward traffic from the phone to Waze server through a separate TLS/SSL channel. The proxy then observes traffic to the Waze servers and extracts the API calls from plain text traffic.

Hiding API calls using traffic encryption is fundamentally challenging, because the attacker has control over most of the components in the communication process, including phone, the app binary, and the proxy. A known countermeasure is certificate pinning [18], which embeds a copy of the server certificate within the app. When the app makes HTTPS requests, it validates the server-provided certificate with its known copy before establishing connections. However, dedicated attackers can extract and replace the embedded certificate by disassembling the app binary or attaching the app to a debugger [35, 17].

Scalability of Ghost Riders. With the knowledge of Waze APIs, we build extremely lightweight Waze clients using python scripts, allocating one thread for each client. Within each thread, we log in to the app using a separate account, and maintain a live session by sending periodic GPS coordinates to the Waze server. The Python client is a full Waze client, and can report fake events using the API. Scripted emulation is highly scalable. We run 1000 virtual vehicles on a single Linux Dell PowerEdge Server (Quad Core, 2GB RAM), and find that at steady state, 1000 virtual devices only introduces a small overhead: 11% of memory usage, 2% of CPU and 420 Kbps bandwidth. In practice, attackers can easily run tens of thousands of virtual devices on a commodity server.

Finally, we experimentally confirm the practical efficacy and scalability of ghost riders. We chose a secluded highway in rural Texas, and used 1000 virtual vehicles (hosted on a single server and single IP) to generate a highly congested traffic hotspot. We perform our experiment in the middle of the night after repeated scans showed no Waze users within miles of our test area. We positioned 1000 ghost riders one after another, and drove them slowly at 15 mph along the highway, looping them back every 15 minutes for an entire hour. The congestion shows up on Waze 5 minutes after our test began, and stayed on the map during the entire test period. No problems were observed during our test, and tests to generate fake events (accidents etc.) also succeeded.

5. USER TRACKING ATTACK

Next, we describe a powerful new attack on user privacy, where virtual vehicles can track Waze users continuously without risking detection themselves. By exploiting a key social functionality in Waze, attackers can remotely follow (or stalk) any individual user in real time. This is possible with single device emulation, but greatly amplified with the help of large groups of ghost riders, possibly tracking large user populations simultaneously and putting user (location) privacy at great risk. We start by examining the feasibility (and key enablers) of this attack. We then present a simple but highly effective tracking algorithm that follows individual users in real time, which we have validated using real life experiments (with ourselves as the targets).

The only way for Waze users to avoid tracking is to go "invisible" in Waze. However, doing so forfeits the ability to generate reports or message other users. Users are also reset to "visible" each time the Waze app opens.

5.1 Feasibility of User Tracking

A key feature in Waze allows users to socialize with others on the road. Each user sees on her screen icons representing the loca-

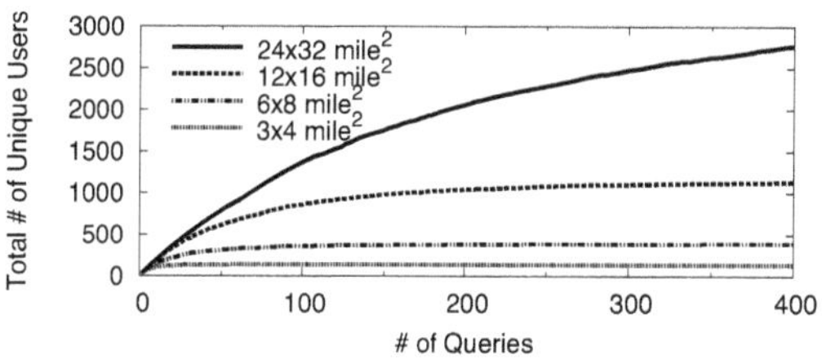

Figure 5: # of queries vs. unique returned users in the area.

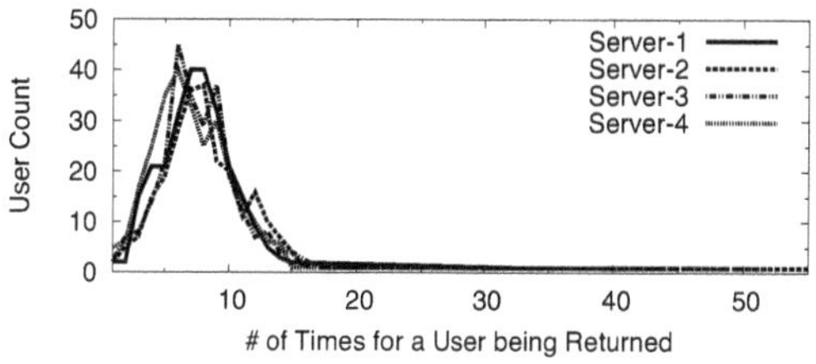

Figure 6: User's number of appearances in the returned results (6×8 mile^2 area).

tions of nearby users, and can chat or message with them through the app. Leveraging this feature, an attacker can pinpoint any target who has the Waze app running on her phone. By constantly "refreshing" the app screen (issuing an update query to the server), an attacker can query the victim's GPS location from Waze in real time. To understand this capability, we perform detailed measurements on Waze to evaluate the efficiency and precision of user tracking.

Tracking via User Queries. A Waze client periodically requests updates in her nearby area, by issuing an update query with its GPS coordinates and a rectangular "search area." This search area can be set to any location on the map, and does not depend on the requester's own location. The server returns a list of users located in the area, including userID, nickname, account creation time, GPS coordinates and the GPS timestamp. Thus an attacker can find and "follow" a target user by first locating them at any given location (work, home) and then continuously following them by issuing update queries centered on the target vehicle location, all automated by scripts.

Overcoming Downsampling. The user query approach faces a downsampling challenge, because Waze responds to each query with an "incomplete" set of users, *i.e.*, up to 20 users per query regardless of the search area size. This downsampled result is necessary to prevent flooding the app screen with too many user icons, but it also limits an attacker's ability to follow a moving target.

This downsampling can be overcome by simply repeatedly querying the system until the target is found. We perform query measurements on four test areas (of different sizes between 3×4 mile^2 and 24×32 mile^2) in the downtown area of Los Angeles (City A, with 10 million residents as of 2015). For each area, we issue 400 queries within 10 seconds, and examine the number of unique users returned by all the queries. Results in Figure 5 show that the number of unique users reported converges after 150-250 queries for the three small search areas ($\lesssim 12 \times 16$ mile^2). For the area of size 24×32 mile^2, more than 400 queries are required to reach convergence.

We confirm this "downsampling" is uniformly random, by comparing our measurement results to a mathematical model that projects the statistics of query results assuming uniform-random sampling.

Location	Route Length (Mile)	Travel Time (Minute)	GPS Sent By Victim	GPS Captured by Attacker	Followed to Destination?	Avg. Track Delay (Second)	Waze User Density (# of Users / mile^2)
City A	12.8	35	18	16	Yes	43.79	56.6
Highway B	36.6	40	20	19	Yes	9.24	2.8

Table 1: Tracking Experiment Results.

Consider total M users in the search area. The probability of a user x getting sampled in a single round of query (20 users per query) is $P(x) = \frac{20}{M}$. Over N queries, the number of appearances per user should follow a Binomial Distribution [25] with mean $N \cdot \frac{20}{M}$. Figure 6 plots the measured user appearances for the four servers on the 6×8 mile^2 area with $N = 100$. The measured statistics follow the projected Binomial Distribution (the measured mean values closely match the theoretical expectation). This confirms that the downsampling is indeed random, and thus an attacker can recover a (near) complete set of Waze users with repeated queries. While the number of queries required increases superlinearly with area size, a complementary technique is to divide an area into smaller, fixed size partitions and query each partition's users in parallel.

We also observe that user lists returned by different Waze servers had only a partial overlap (roughly 20% of users from each server were unique to that server). This "inconsistency" across servers is caused by synchronization delay among the servers. Each user only sends its GPS coordinates to a single server which takes 2-5 minutes to propagate to other servers. Therefore, a complete user set requires queries to cover all Waze servers. At the time of our experiments, the number of Waze servers could be traced through app traffic and could be covered by a moderate number of querying accounts.

Tracking Users over Time. Our analysis found that each active Waze app updates its GPS coordinates to the server every 2 minutes, regardless of whether the user is mobile or stationary. Even when running in the background, the Waze app reports GPS values every 5 minutes. As long as the Waze app is open (even running in the background), the user's location is continuously reported to Waze and potential attackers. Clearly, a more conservative approach to managing location data would be extremely helpful here.

We note that attackers can perform long-term tracking on a target user (*e.g.*, over months). The attacker needs a persistent ID associated to the target. The "userID" field in the metadata is insufficient, because it is a random "session" ID assigned upon user login and is released when the user kills the app. However, the "account creation time" can serve as a persistent ID, because a) it remains the same across the user's different login sessions, and b) it is precise down to the second, and is sufficiently to uniquely identify single users in the same geographic area. While Waze can remove the "account creation time" field from metadata, a persistent attacker can overcome this by analyzing the victim's mobility pattern. For example, the attacker can identify a set of locations where the victim has visited frequently or stayed during the past session, mapping to home or workplace. Then the attacker can assign a ghost rider to constantly monitor those areas, and re-identify the target once her icon shows up in a monitored location, *e.g.*, home.

Stealth Mode. We note that attackers remain invisible to their targets, because queries on any specific geographic area can be done by Sybils operating "remotely," i.e. claiming to be in a different city, state or country. Attackers can enable their "invisible" option to hide from other nearby users. Finally, disabling these features still does not make the attacker visible. Waze only updates each user's "nearby" screen every 2 minutes (while sending its own

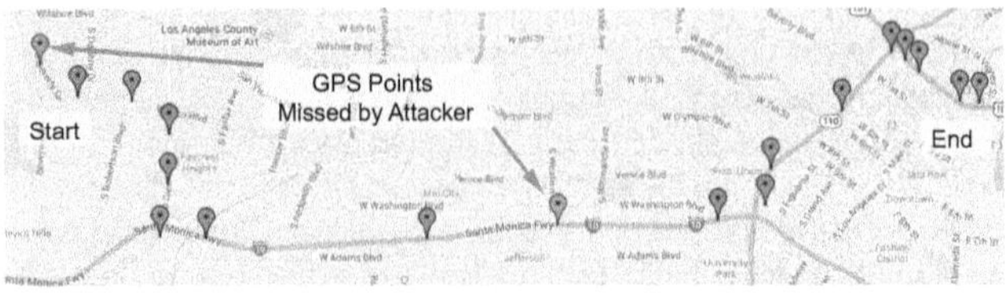

Figure 7: A graphical view of the tracking result in Los Angeles downtown (City A). Blue dots are GPS points captured by the attacker and the red dots are those missed by the attacker.

GPS update to the servers). Thus a tracker can "pop into" the target's region, query for the target, and then move out of the target's observable range, all before the target can update and detect it.

5.2 Real-time Individual User Tracking

To build a detailed trace of a target user's movements, an attacker first bootstraps by identifying the target's icon on the map. This can be done by identifying the target's icon while confirming her physical presence at a time and location. The attacker centers its search area on the victim's location, and issues a large number of queries (using Sybil accounts) until it captures the next GPS report from the target. If the target is moving, the attacker moves the search area along the target's direction of movement and repeats the process to get updates.

Experiments. To evaluate its effectiveness, we performed experiments by tracking one of our own Android smartphones and one of our virtual devices. Tracking was effective in both cases, but we experimented more with tracking our virtual device, since we could have it travel to any location. Using the OSRM tool [5], we generate detailed GPS traces of two driving trips, one in downtown area of Los Angeles (City A), and one along the interstate highway-101 (Highway B). The target device uses a realistic driving speed based on average traffic speeds estimated by Google Maps during the experiment. The attacker used 20 virtual devices to query Waze simultaneously in a rectangular search area of size 6×8 mile^2. This should be sufficient to track the GPS update of a fast-driving car (up to 160 mph). Both experiments were during morning hours, and we logged both the network traffic of the target phone and query data retrieved by the attacker. Note that we did not generate any "events" or otherwise affect the Waze system in this experiment.

Results. Table 1 lists the results of tracking our virtual device, and Figure 7 presents a graphical view of the City A result. For both routes, the attacker can consistently follow the victim to her destination, though the attacker fails to capture 1-2 GPS points out of the 18-20 reported. For City A, the tracking delay, *i.e.*, the time spent to capture the subsequent GPS of the victim, is larger (averaging 43s rather than 9s). This is because the downtown area has a higher Waze user density, and required more rounds of queries to locate the target.

Our experiments represent two highly challenging (*i.e.*, worst case) scenarios for the attacker. The high density of Waze users in City A downtown is makes it challenging to locate a target in real time with downsampling. On Highway B, the target travels at a high speed (~60mph), putting a stringent time limit on the tracking latency, *i.e.*, the attacker must capture the target before he leaves the search area. The success of both experiments confirms the effectiveness and practicality of the proposed attack.

6. DEFENSES

In this section, we propose defense mechanisms to significantly limit the magnitude and impact of these attacks. While individual devices can inflict limited damage, an attacker's ability to control a large number of virtual vehicles at low cost elevates the severity of the attack in both quantity and quality. Our priority, then, is to restrict the number of ghost riders available to each attacker, thus increasing the cost per "vehicle" and reducing potential damage.

The most intuitive approach is perform strong location authentication, so that attackers must use real devices physically located at the actual locations reported. This would make ghost riders as expensive to operate as real devices. Unfortunately, existing methods for location authentication do not extend well to our context. Some proposals solely rely on trusted infrastructures (*e.g.*, wireless access points) to verify the physical presence of devices in close proximity [30, 37]. However, this requires large scale retrofitting of cellular celltowers or installation of new hardware, neither of which is practical at large geographic scales. Others propose to embed tamperproof location hardware on mobile devices [32, 38], which incurs high cost per user, and is only effective if enforced across all devices. For our purposes, we need a scalable approach that works with current hardware, without incurring costs on mobile users or the map service (Waze).

6.1 Sybil Detection via Proximity Graph

Instead of optimizing per-device location authentication, our proposed defense is a Sybil detection mechanism based on the novel concept of *proximity graph*. Specifically, we leverage physical proximity between real devices to create *collocation edges*, which act as secure attestations of shared physical presence. In a proximity graph, nodes are Waze devices (uniquely identified by an account username and password on the server side). They perform secure peer-to-peer location authentication with the Waze app running in the background. An edge is established if the proximity authentication is successful.

Because Sybil devices are scripted software, they are highly unlikely to come into physical proximity with real devices. A Sybil device can only form collocation edges with other Sybil devices (with coordination by the attacker) or the attacker's own physical devices. The resulting graph should have only very few (or no) edges between virtual devices and real users (other than the attacker). Leveraging prior work on Sybil detection in social networks, groups of Sybils can be characterized by the few "attack edges" connecting them to the rest of the graph, making them identifiable through community-detection algorithms [47].

We use *a very small number* of trusted nodes only to bootstrap trust in the graph. We assume a small number of infrastructure access points are known to Waze servers, *e.g.*, hotels and public WiFi networks associated with physical locations stored in IP-location databases (used for geolocation by Apple and Google). Waze also can work with merchants that own public WiFi access points (*e.g.*, Starbucks). These infrastructures are trusted nodes (we assume trusted nodes don't collude with attackers). Any Waze device that communicates with the Waze server under their IPs (and reports a GPS location consistent with the IP) automatically creates a new collocation edge to the trusted node.

Our Sybil defense contains two key steps. First, we build a proximity graph based on the "encounters" between Waze users (§6.2). Second, we detect Sybils based on the trust propagation in proximity graph (§6.3).

6.2 Peer-based Proximity Authentication

To build the proximity graph, we first need a reliable method to verify the *physical* collocation of mobile devices. We cannot rely on GPS reports since attackers can forge arbitrary GPS coordinates, or Bluetooth based device ranging [55] because the coverage is too short (<10 meters) for vehicles. Instead, we consider a challenge-based proximity authentication method, which leverages the limited transmission range of WiFi radios.

WiFi Tethering Challenge. We use the smartphone's WiFi radio to implement a proximity challenge between two Waze devices. Because WiFi radios have limited ranges (<250 meters for 802.11n [45])), two Waze devices must be in physical proximity to complete the challenge. Specifically, we (or the Waze server) instruct one device to enable WiFi tethering and broadcast beacons with an SSID provided by the Waze server, *i.e.*, a randomly generated, time-varying bit string. This bit string cannot be forged by other users or used to re-identify a particular user. The second device proves its proximity to the first device by returning the SSID value heard over the air to the Waze server.

The key concerns of this approach are whether the WiFi link between two vehicles is stable/strong enough to complete the challenge, and whether the separation distance is long enough for our needs. This concern is valid given the high moving speed, potential signal blockage from vehicles' metal components, and the low transmit power of smartphones. We explore these issues with detailed measurements on real mobile devices.

First, we perform measurements on stationary vehicles to study the joint effect of blockage and limited mobile transmit power. We put two Android phones into two cars (with windows and doors closed), one running WiFi tethering to broadcast beacons and the other scanning for beacons. Figure 8 plots the WiFi beacon strength at different separation distances. We see that the above artifacts make the signal strength drop to -100 dBm before the distance reaches 250 meters. In the same figure, we also plot the probability of successful beacon decoding (thus challenge completion) across 400 attempts within 2 minutes. It remains 100% when the two cars are separated by <80 meters, and drops to zero at 160 meters.

Next, we perform driving experiments on a highway at normal traffic hours in the presence of other vehicles. The vehicles travel at speeds averaging 65 mph. During driving, we are able to vary the distance between the two cars, and use recorded GPS logs to calculate the separation distance. Figure 9 shows that while WiFi signal strength fluctuates during our experiments, the probability of beacon decoding remains very high at 98% when the separation is less than 80 meters but drops to <10% once the two cars are more than 140 meters apart.

Overall, the results suggest the proposed WiFi tethering challenge is a reliable method for proximity authentication for our system. In practice, Waze can start the challenge when detecting the two vehicles are within the effective range, *e.g.*, 80 meters. Since the WiFi channel scan is fast, *e.g.*, 1-2 seconds to do a full channel scan in our experiments, this challenge can be accomplished quickly with minimum energy cost on mobile devices. It is easy to implement this scheme using existing APIs to control WiFi radio to open tethering (`setWifiApEnabled` API in Android).

Constructing Proximity Graphs. In a proximity graph, each node is a Waze device, and an edge indicates the two users come

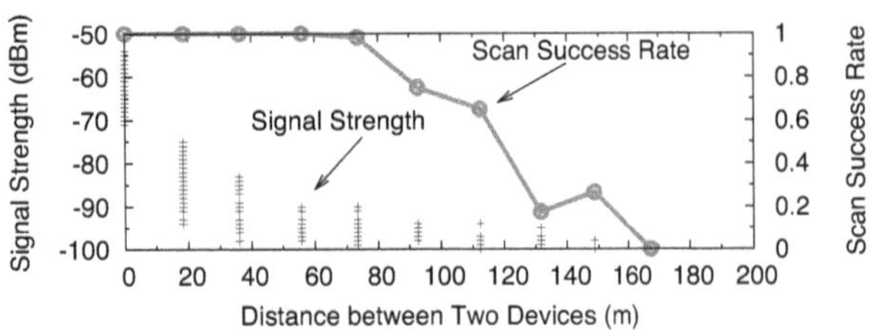

Figure 8: WiFi signal strength and scan success rate with respect to car distance in static scenarios.

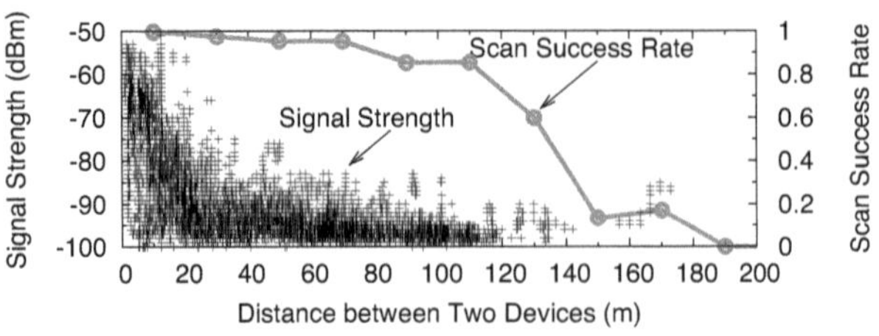

Figure 9: WiFi signal strength and scan success rate with respect to car distance in driving scenarios.

into physical proximity, *e.g.*, 80 meters, within a predefined time window. The resulting graph is undirected but weighted based on the number of times the two users have encountered. Using weighted graph makes it harder for Sybils to blend into the normal user region. Intuitively, real users will get more weights on their edges as they use Waze over time. For attackers, in order to blend in the graph, they need to build more weighted attack edges to real users (higher costs).

This approach should not introduce much energy consumption to users' phones. First, Waze server does not need to trigger collocation authentication every time two users are in close proximity. Instead, the proximity graph will be built up over time. A user only need to authenticate with other users occasionally, since we can require that device authentication expires after a moderate time period (*e.g.,* months) to reduce the net impact on wireless performance and energy usage. Second, since the process is triggered by the Waze server, Waze can can use WiFi sensing from devices to find "opportunistic" authentication times that minimize impact on performance and energy. Waze can also use one tether to simultaneously authenticate multiple colocated devices within an area. This further reduces authentication overhead, and avoids performance issues like wireless interference in areas with high user density.

6.3 Graph-based Sybil Detection

We apply graph-based Sybil detection algorithms to detect Sybils in Waze proximity graph. Graph-based Sybil detectors [53, 52, 47, 14, 10] were originally proposed in social networks. They all rely on the key assumption that Sybils have difficulty to form edges with real users, which results in a sparse cut between the Sybil and non-Sybil regions in the social graph. Because of the limited number of "attack edges" between Sybils and non-Sybils, a random walk from non-Sybil region has a higher landing probability to land on a non-Sybil node than a Sybil node. Our proximity graph holds the same assumption that these algorithms require—with the WiFi proximity authentication, it's difficult for Sybil devices (ghost riders) to build attack edges to real Waze users.

SybilRank. Among available algorithms, we use SybilRank [10]. Compared to its counterparts (SybilGuard [53], SybilLimit [52] and SybilInfer [14]), SybilRank achieves higher accuracy at a lower computational cost. At the high-level, its counterparts need to perform *actual random walks*, which is very costly and yet often gives incomplete views of the graph. Instead, SybilRank uses *power iteration* [28] to compute the random walk landing probability for all nodes. This significantly boosts the algorithm accuracy and speed. Furthermore, SybilRank has a better tolerance on community structures in the non-Sybil region (for using multiple trusted nodes), making it more suitable for real-world graphs.

As context, we briefly describe how SybilRank works and refer readers to [10] for more details. SybilRank ranks the nodes based on how likely they are Sybils. The algorithm starts with multiple trusted nodes in the graph. It iteratively computes the landing probability for short random walks (originated from trusted nodes) to land on all other nodes. The landing probability is normalized by the node's degree, which acts as the trust score for ranking. Intuitively, short random walks from trusted nodes are very unlikely to traverse the few attack edges to reach Sybil nodes, thus the ranking scores of Sybils should be lower. For Sybil detection, Waze can set a cutoff threshold on the trust score, and label the tail of the ranked list as Sybils.

The original SybilRank works on unweighted social graphs. We modified it to work on our weighted proximity graph: when a node propagates trust (or performs random walks) to its neighbors, instead of splitting the trust equally, it distributes proportionally based on the edge weights. This actually makes it harder for Sybils to evade SybilRank—they will need to build more high-weight attack edges to real users to receive trust.

7. COUNTERMEASURE EVALUATION

We use simulations to evaluate the effectiveness of our proposed defense. We focus on evaluating the feasibility and cost for attackers to maintain a large number of Sybils after the Sybil detection is in place. We quantify the cost by the number of attack edges a Sybil must establish with real users. In practice, this translates into the effort taken to physically drive around and use physical devices (with WiFi radios) per Sybil to complete proximity authentication. In the following, we first describe our simulation setup, and then present the key findings and their implications on Waze.

7.1 Evaluation Setup

We first discuss how we construct a synthetic proximity graph for our evaluation, followed by the counter strategies taken by attackers to evade detection. Finally, we describe the evaluation metrics for Sybil detection.

Simulating Proximity Graphs. We use well-known models on human encountering to create synthetic proximity graphs. This is because, to the best of our knowledge, there is no public *per-user* mobility dataset with sufficient scale and temporal coverage to support our evaluation. Also, directly crawling large-scale, per-user mobility trace from Waze can lead to questionable privacy implications, and thus we exclude this option.

Existing literatures [33, 13, 43, 23, 29] all suggest that human (and vehicle) encounter patterns display strong scale-free and "small-world" properties [6]. Thus we follow the methodology of [33] to simulate a power-law based encounter process among Waze users. Given a user population N, we first assign each user an encounter probability following a power-law distribution (α =2 based on the empirical values [33, 12]). We then simulate user encounter over

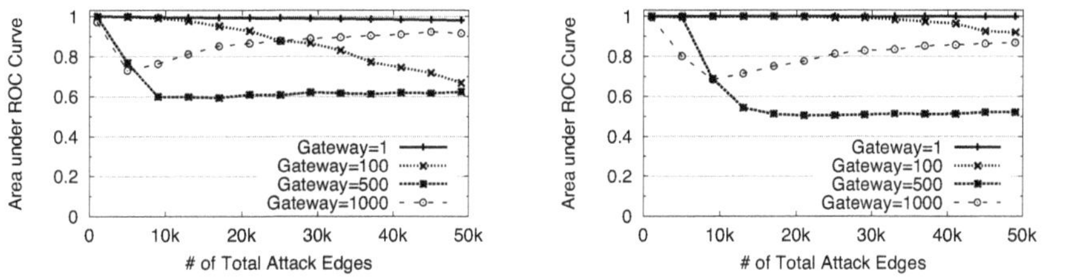

(a) Sybil inner connection avg. degree = 5 (b) Sybil inner connection avg. degree = 10

Figure 10: AUC with respect to number of attack edges, where Sybils form power-law inner connections.

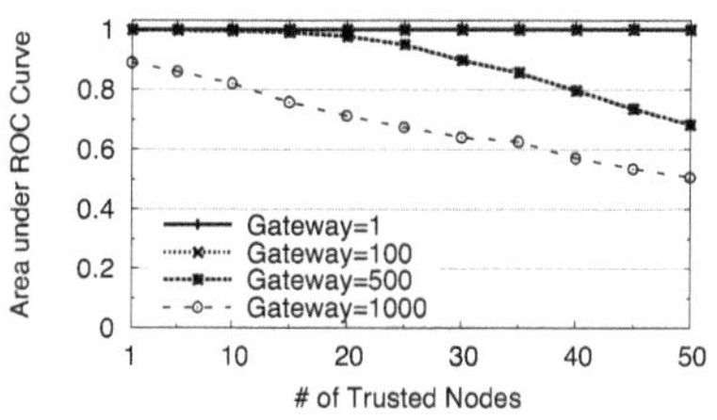

Figure 11: Impact of # of trusted nodes (average degree =10 for Sybil region; 5K attack edges).

time, by adding edges to the graph based on the joint probability of the two nodes.

For our evaluation, we produce a proximity graph for $N = 10000$ normal users and use the snapshot when 99.9% of nodes are connected. Note that as the graph gets denser over time, it is harder for Sybils to blend into normal user regions. We use this graph to simulate the lower-bound performance of Sybil detection.[2] As a potential limitation, the simulated graph parameters might be different for different cities of Waze. Thus we don't claim our reported numbers will exactly match what Waze produces. The idea is that Waze can follow our methodology to run the same experiments on their real graphs.

Attacker Models. In the presence of Sybil detection, an attacker will try mixing their Sybils into the proximity graph. We consider the following strategies:

1. **Single-Gateway** – An attacker first takes one Sybil account (as the gateway) to build attack edges to normal users. Then the attacker connects the remaining Sybils to this gateway. In practice, this means the attacker only needs to take one physical phone to go out and encounter normal users.
2. **Multi-Gateways** – An attacker distributes the attack edges to multiple gateways, and then evenly spreads the other Sybils across the gateways. This helps the Sybils to blend in with normal users. The attacker pays an extra cost in terms of using multiple real devices to build attack edges.

The attacker also builds edges among its own Sybils. This incurs no additional cost since Sybils can easily collude to pass proximity authentication, but introduces key benefits. *First*, it makes Sybils' degree distribution appear more legitimate. *Second*, it can potentially increase Sybils' trust score: when a random walk reaches one Sybil node, its edges to the fellow Sybils help to sustain the random walk within the Sybil region. In our simulation, we follow the scale-free distribution to add edges among Sybils mimicking normal user region (we did not use a fully connected network between Sybils since it is more easily detectable).

Evaluation Metrics. To evaluate Sybil detection efficacy, we use the standard false positive (negative) rate, and the Area under the Receiver Operating Characteristic curve (AUC) used by SybilRank [10]. AUC represents the probability that SybilRank ranks a random Sybil node lower than a random non-Sybil node. Its value ranges from 0 to 1, where 1 means the ranking is perfect (all Sybils are ranked lower than non-Sybils), 0 means the ranking is always flipped, and 0.5 matches the result of random guessing. Compared to false positive (negative) rates, AUC is independent of the cutoff threshold, and thus comparable across experiment settings.

[2]Validated by experiments: a denser, 99.99% connected graph can uniformly improve Sybil detection accuracy.

7.2 Results

Accuracy of Sybil Detection. We assume the attacker seeks to embed 1000 Sybils into the proximity graph. We use either single- or multi-gateway approaches to build attack edges on the proximity graph by connecting Sybils to randomly chosen normal users. We then add edges between Sybil nodes, following the power-law distribution and producing an average weighted degree of either 5 or 10 (to emulate different Sybil subgraph density). We randomly select 10 trusted nodes to bootstrap trust for SybilRank and run it on the proximity graph. We repeat each experiment 50 times.

Figure 10 shows that the Sybil detection mechanism is highly effective. For attackers of the single-gateway model, the AUC is very close to 1 (> 0.983), indicating Waze can identify almost all Sybils even after the attacker established a large number of attack edges, *e.g.*, 50000. Meanwhile, the multi-gateway method helps attackers add "undetected" Sybils, but the number of gateways required is significant. For example, to maintain 1000 Sybils, *i.e.*, by bringing down AUC to 0.5, the attacker needs at least 500 as gateways. In practice, this means wardriving with 500+ physical devices to meet real users, which is a significant overhead.

Interestingly, the 1000-gateway result (where every Sybil is a gateway) shows that, at certain point, adding more attack edges can actually hurt Sybils. This is potentially due to the fact that SybilRank uses node degree to normalize trust score. For gateways that connect to both normal users and other Sybils, the additional "trust" received by adding more attack edges cannot compensate the penalty of degree normalization.

For a better look at the *detection accuracy*, we convert the AUC in Figure 10(b) to false positives (classifying real users as Sybils) and false negatives (classifying Sybils as real users). For simplicity, we set a cutoff value to mark the bottom 10% of the ranked nodes as Sybils.[3] As shown in Figure 12, SybilRank is highly accurate to detect Sybils when the number of gateways is less than 100. Again 100 gateways incurs high cost in practice.

Next we quickly examine the impact of trusted nodes to Sybil detection. Figure 11 shows a small number of trusted node is enough to run SybilRank. Interestingly, adding more trusted nodes can slightly hurt Sybil detection, possibly because it gives the attacker (gateways) a higher chance to receive trust. In practice, multiple trusted nodes can help SybilRank overcome potential community structures in proximity graph (*e.g.*, users of the same city form a cluster). So Waze should place trusted nodes accordingly to cover geographic clusters.

Cost of Sybil Attacks. Next, we infer the rough cost of attackers on implementing successful Sybil attacks. For this we look at

[3]This cutoff value is only to convert the error rate. In practice, Waze can optimize this value based on the trust score or manual examination.

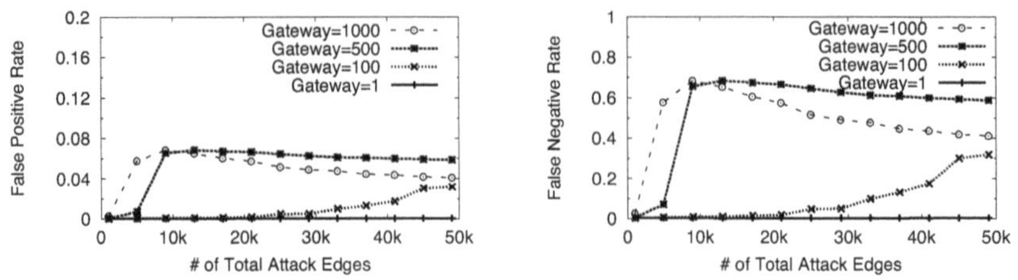

(a) False Positive Rate

(b) False Negative Rate

Figure 12: Detection error rates with respect to number of attack edges. We set average degree =10 for Sybils' power-law inner connections.

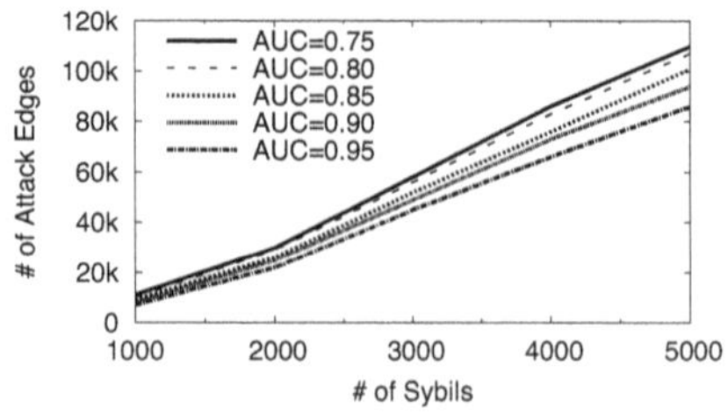

Figure 13: # of attack edges needed to maintain x Sybil devices with respect to different AUC level.

the number of attack edges required to successfully embed a given number of Sybils. Our experiment assumes the attacker uses 500 gateways and builds power-law distributed inner connections with average degree=10. Figure 13 shows the number of attack edges required to achieve a specific AUC under SybilRank as a function of the target number of Sybils. We see that the attack edge count increases linearly with the Sybil count. The cost of Sybil attack is high: to maintain 3000 Sybils, the attacker must make 60,000 attack edges to keep AUC below 0.75, and spread these attack edges across 500 high-cost gateways.

Smaller Sybil Groups. Finally, we examine how effective our system is in detecting much smaller Sybil groups. We test Sybil groups with size of 20, 50 and 100 using a single-gateway approach. We configure 50K attacking edges for Sybils with inner degree = 10. The resulting AUC of Sybil detection is 0.90, 0.95 and 0.99 respectively. This confirms our system can effectively identify small Sybil groups as well.

7.3 Implications on Waze

These results show that our Sybil detection method is highly effective. It significantly increases the cost (in purchasing physical devices and time spent actually driving on the road) to launch Sybil attacks. Also, SybilRank is scalable enough for large systems like Waze. A social network with tens of millions of users has been running SybilRank on Hadoop servers [10].

In addition to Sybil detection, Waze can incorporate other mechanisms to protect its users. We briefly describe a few key ideas, but leave the integration with our approach to future work. *First*, IP verification: when a user claims she is driving, Waze can examine whether her IP is a mobile IP that belongs to a valid cellular carrier or a suspicious web proxy. However, this approach is ineffective if dedicated attackers route the attack traffic through a cellular data plan. *Second*, strict rate limit: with that, attackers will need to run more Sybil devices to implement the same attack. *Third*, verifications on account registration: this needs to be handled carefully since email/SMS based verification can be bypassed using disposable email or phone numbers [44]. *Finally*, detecting extremely inconsistent GPS/event reports. The challenge, however, is to distinguish honest reports from the fake ones since attacker can easily outvote real users. If Waze chooses to ignore all the inconsistent reports, it will lead to DOS attack where attackers disable the service with inconsistent data.

8. BROADER IMPLICATIONS

While our experiments and defenses have focused strictly on Waze, our results are applicable to a wider range of mobile applications that rely on geolocation for user-contributed content and metadata. Examples include location based check-in and review services (Foursquare, Yelp), crowdsourced navigation systems (Waze, Moovit), crowdsourced taxi services (Uber, Lyft), mobile dating apps (Tinder, Bumble) and anonymous mobile communities (Yik Yak, Whisper).

These systems face two common challenges exposing them to potential attacks. First, our efforts show that it is difficult for app developers to build a truly secure channel between the app and the server. There are numerous avenues for an attacker to reverse-engineer and mimic an app's API calls, thereby creating "cheap" virtual devices and launching Sybil attack [16]. Second, there are no deployed mechanisms to authenticate location data (*e.g.*, GPS report). Without a secure channel to the server and authenticated location, these mobile apps are vulnerable to automated attacks ranging from nuisance (prank calls to Uber) to malicious content attacks (large-scale rating manipulation on Yelp).

To validate our point, we run a quick empirical analysis on a broad class of mobile apps to understand how easy it is to reverse-engineer their APIs and inject falsified data into the system. We pick one app from each category including Foursquare, Uber, Tinder and Yik Yak (an incomplete list). We find that, although all the listed apps use TLS/SSL to encrypt their network traffic, their APIs can be fully exposed by the method in §4. For each app, we were able to build a light-weight client using python script, and feed arbitrary GPS to their key function calls. For example, with forged GPS, a group of Foursquare clients can deliver large volumes of check-ins to a given venue without physically visiting it; On Uber, one can distribute many virtual devices as sensors, and passively monitor and track all drivers (and their passengers) within a large area (see §5). Similarly for Yik Yak and Tinder, the virtual devices make it possible to perform wardriving in a given location area to post and collect anonymous Yik Yak messages or Tinder profiles. In addition, apps like Tinder also display the geographical distance to a nearby user (*e.g.*, 1 mile). Attacker can use multiple virtual devices to measure the distance to the target user, and "triangulate" that user's exact location [50]. There are possible app-specific defenses, and we leave their design and evaluation to future work.

9. DISCLOSURE AND IMPACT

Before the first writeup of our work, we sought to inform the Google Waze team of our results. We first used multiple existing Google contacts on the security and Android teams. When that failed to reach the Waze team, we got in touch with Niels Provos, who then relayed information about our project to the Waze team.

Through our periodic tests of the Waze app, we noticed recent updates made significant changes to how the app reports user location data to the server (and other users). In the new Waze update (v4.4.0, released in April 2016), the app only reports user GPS values when the user is actively driving (moving at a moderate/fast rate of speed). GPS tracking stops when a user is walking or standing still. In addition, Waze automatically shuts down if the user puts it in the background, and has not driven for a while. To resume user tracking (GPS reporting), users must manually bring the app to the foreground. Finally, Waze now hide users' starting and destination locations of their trips.

While online documentation claims that these optimizations are to reduce energy usage for the Waze app, we are gratified by the dramatic steps taken to limit user tracking and improve user privacy. These changes dramatically reduce the amount of GPS data sent to the server (and made available to potential attackers through the API). By our estimates, the update reduces the amount of GPS tracking data for a typical user by nearly a factor of 10x. In addition, removing the first and last GPS values of a trip means that it is significantly harder to track a user through multiple trips. Previously, users could be tracked across new Waze sessions, despite new per-session identifiers, by matching the destination point of one trip with the starting point of the next.

We note that while Waze has taken significantly steps to improve user privacy, users can still be tracked while they are actively using the app. More importantly, the attack we identified here can still wreak havoc with a wide range of mobile apps, and Sybil devices are a real challenge still in need of practical solutions. We hope our work spurs future work to address this problem.

10. RELATED WORK

Security in Location-based Services. Location-based services face various threats, ranging from rogue users reporting fake GPS [11, 22], to malicious parties compromising user privacy [15, 26, 27]. A related study on Waze [39] demonstrated that small-scale attacks can create traffic jams or track user icons, with up to 15 mobile emulators. Our work differs in two key aspects. First, we show that it's possible to reverse engineer its APIs, enabling light-weight Sybil devices (simple scripts) to replace full-stack emulators. This increase the scale of potential attacks by orders of magnitude, to thousands of Waze clients per commodity laptop. The impact of thousands of virtual vehicles is qualitatively different from 10-15 mobile simulators. Second, as possible defenses, [39] cites known tools such as phone number/IP verification, or location authentication with cellular towers, which have limited applicability (see §6). In contrast, we propose a novel proximity graph approach to detect and constrain the impact of virtual devices.

Researchers have proposed to preserve user location privacy against map services such as Waze and Google. Earlier studies apply location cloaking by adding noise to the GPS reports [21]. Recent work use zero-knowledge [24] and differential privacy [8] to preserve the location privacy of individual users, while maintaining user accountability and the accuracy of aggregated statistics. Our work differs by focusing on the attacks against the map services.

Mobile Location Authentication. Defending against forged GPS is challenging. One direction is to authenticate user locations using wireless infrastructures: WiFi APs [30, 37], cellular base stations [30, 37] and femtocells [7]. Devices must come into physical proximity to these infrastructures to be authenticated. But it requires cooperation among a wide range of infrastructures (also modifications to their software/hardware), which is impractical for large-scale services like Waze. Our work only uses a small number of trusted infrastructures to bootstrap, and relies on peer-based trust propagation to achieve coverage. Other researchers have proposed "peer-based" methods to authenticate collocated mobile devices [42, 51, 55, 31, 34]. Different from existing work, we use peer-based collocation authentication to build proximity graphs for Sybil detection, instead of directly authenticating a device's physical location.

Sybil Detection. Sybil detection has been studied in P2P networks [16] and online social networks [47, 49, 48]. The most popular approach is graph-based where the key assumption is that Sybils have difficulty to connect to real users [10, 14, 46, 52, 53]. Thus Sybils would form a well-connected subgraph that has a small quotient-cut from the non-Sybil region. Our work constructs a proximity graph that holds the same assumption, and applies Sybil detection algorithm to locate ghost riders in Waze. We differ from [10] in the graph used and the attack models.

11. CONCLUSION

We describe our efforts to identify and study a range of attacks on crowdsourced map services. We identify a range of single and multi-user attacks, and describe techniques to build and control groups of virtual vehicles (ghost riders) to amplify these attacks. Our work shows that today's mapping services are highly vulnerable to software agents controlled by malicious users, and both the stability of these services and the privacy of millions of users are at stake. While our study and experiments focus on the Waze system, we believe the large majority of our results can be generalized to crowdsourced apps as a group. We propose and validate a suite of techniques that help services build proximity graphs and use them to effectively detect Sybil devices.

Throughout this work, we have taken active steps to isolate our experiments and prevent any negative consequence on real Waze users. We also used our existing Google/Waze contacts to inform Waze team of our results. More details on IRB, ethics and disclosure are contained in Appendix A.

Acknowledgments

We would like to thank our shepherd Z. Morley Mao and the anonymous reviewers for their comments. This project was supported by NSF grants CNS-1527939 and CNS-1224100. Any opinions, findings, and conclusions or recommendations expressed in this material are those of the authors and do not necessarily reflect the views of any funding agencies.

Appendix A— IRB, Ethics

Our study was reviewed and approved by our local IRB. Prior to doing any real measurements on the system, we submitted a human subject protocol for approval by our institutional IRB. The protocol was fully reviewed for ethics and privacy risks, and the response was our study can be exempt. We put the request into our IRB system and began our work. Then the confirmation of exemption arrived and our study received the IRB approval under protocol # COMS-ZH-YA-010-7N.

As described in the paper, we are very aware of the potential impact on real Waze users from any experiments. We took very careful precautions to ensure that our experiments will not negatively impact Waze servers or Waze users. In particular, we conducted numerous measurements of diverse traffic regions (read-only) to locate areas of extremely low traffic density. We chose experiment locations where user population density is extremely low (unoccupied roads), and only perform experiments at low-traffic hours, *e.g.* between 3am and 5am. During experiments, we continuously scan the entire region including our experimental area and neighboring regions, to ensure no other Waze users (except our own accounts) are within miles of the test area. If any Waze users are detected, we immediately terminate any running experiments. We took care to limit congestion tests to areas with lots of local route redundancy, thus we would not affect the routing of any long distance trips (e.g. taking highway 80 because the 101 was congested). Finally, while we cannot detect invisible users in our test area, we have taken every precaution to only test on roads and times that show very little traffic, e.g. low population areas at 4am local time. We believe in practice, invisible users make up a small subset of the Waze population, because they cannot send reports or message other users (effectively removing most/all of the social functionality in Waze), and Waze resets the invisible setting every time the app is opened [1].

12. REFERENCES

[1] About Waze: Privacy. https://support.google.com/waze/answer/6071193?hl=en.

[2] Charles Proxy. http://www.charlesproxy.com.

[3] GenyMotion Emulator. http://www.genymotion.com.

[4] Monkeyrunner. http://developer.android.com/tools/help/monkeyrunner_concepts.html.

[5] Open Source Routing Machine (OSRM). http://map.project-osrm.org.

[6] A.-L. Barabasi and R. Albert. Emergence of scaling in random networks. *Science*, 286, 1999.

[7] J. Brassil, P. K. Manadhata, and R. Netravali. Traffic signature-based mobile device location authentication. *IEEE Transactions on Mobile Computing*, 13(9):2156–2169, 2014.

[8] J. W. S. Brown, O. Ohrimenko, and R. Tamassia. Haze: Privacy-preserving real-time traffic statistics. In *Proc. of SIGSPATIAL*, 2013.

[9] C. Brubaker, S. Jana, B. Ray, S. Khurshid, and V. Shmatikov. Using frankencerts for automated adversarial testing of certificate validation in ssl/tls implementations. In *Proc. of IEEE S&P*, 2014.

[10] Q. Cao, M. Sirivianos, X. Yang, and T. Pregueiro. Aiding the detection of fake accounts in large scale social online services. In *Proc. of NSDI*, 2012.

[11] B. Carbunar and R. Potharaju. You unlocked the mt. everest badge on foursquare! countering location fraud in geosocial networks. In *Proc. of MASS*, 2012.

[12] A. Clauset, C. R. Shalizi, and M. E. Newman. Power-law distributions in empirical data. *SIAM review*, 51(4):661–703, 2009.

[13] F. Cunha, A. C. Viana, R. A. F. Mini, and A. A. F. Loureiro. Is it possible to find social properties in vehicular networks? In *Proc. of ISCC*, 2014.

[14] G. Danezis and P. Mittal. Sybilinfer: Detecting sybil nodes using social networks. In *Proc of NDSS*, 2009.

[15] Y.-A. de Montjoye, M. Verleysen, and V. D. Blondel. Unique in the crowd: The privacy bounds of human mobility. *Scientific Reports*, 3, 2013.

[16] J. R. Douceur. The Sybil attack. In *Proc. of IPTPS*, 2002.

[17] W. Enck, D. Octeau, P. McDaniel, and S. Chaudhuri. A study of android application security. In *Proc. of USENIX Security*, 2011.

[18] S. Fahl, M. Harbach, H. Perl, M. Koetter, and M. Smith. Rethinking ssl development in an appified world. In *Proc. of CCS*, 2013.

[19] V. Goel. Maps that live and breathe with data. The New York Times, June 2013.

[20] Google. Google maps and waze, outsmarting traffic together. Google Official Blog, June 2013.

[21] M. Gruteser and D. Grunwald. Anonymous usage of location-based services through spatial and temporal cloaking. In *Proc. of MobiSys*, 2003.

[22] W. He, X. Liu, and M. Ren. Location cheating: A security challenge to location-based social network services. In *Proc. of ICDCS*, 2011.

[23] T. Hossmann, T. Spyropoulos, and F. Legendre. Know thy neighbor: Towards optimal mapping of contacts to social graphs for dtn routing. In *Proc. of INFOCOM*, 2010.

[24] T. Jeske. Floating car data from smartphones: What google and waze know about you and how hackers can control traffic. *Black Hat*, 2013.

[25] V. Kachitvichyanukul and B. W. Schmeiser. Binomial random variate generation. *Commun. ACM*, 31(2):216–222, 1988.

[26] J. Krumm. Inference attacks on location tracks. In *Pervasive Computing*. 2007.

[27] J. Krumm. A survey of computational location privacy. *Personal and Ubiquitous Computing*, 2009.

[28] A. Langville and C. Meyer. Deeper inside pagerank. *Internet Mathematics*, 1(3):335–380, 2004.

[29] X. Liu, Z. Li, W. Li, S. Lu, X. Wang, and D. Chen. Exploring social properties in vehicular ad hoc networks. In *Proc. of Internetware*, 2012.

[30] W. Luo and U. Hengartner. Proving your location without giving up your privacy. In *Proc. of HotMobile*, 2010.

[31] J. Manweiler, R. Scudellari, and L. P. Cox. Smile: Encounter-based trust for mobile social services. In *Proc. of CCS*, 2009.

[32] C. Marforio, N. Karapanos, C. Soriente, and K. Capkun. Smartphones as practical and secure location verification tokens for payments. In *Proc. of NDSS*, 2014.

[33] A. G. Miklas, K. K. Gollu, K. K. W. Chan, S. Saroiu, K. P. Gummadi, and E. de Lara. Exploiting social interactions in mobile systems. In *Proc. of Ubicomp*, 2007.

[34] A. Narayanan, N. Thiagarajan, M. Lakhani, M. Hamburg, and D. Boneh. Location Privacy via Private Proximity Testing. In *Proc. of NDSS*, 2011.

[35] J. Osborne and A. Diquet. When security gets in the way: Pentesting mobile apps that use certificate pinning. *Black Hat*, 2012.

[36] B. Reed. Google maps becomes google's second 1 billion-download hit. Yahoo! News, June 2014.

[37] S. Saroiu and A. Wolman. Enabling new mobile applications with location proofs. In *Proc. of HotMobile*, 2009.

[38] S. Saroiu and A. Wolman. I am a sensor, and i approve this message. In *Proc. of HotMobile*, 2010.

[39] M. B. Sinai, N. Partush, S. Yadid, and E. Yahav. Exploiting social navigation. *Black Hat Asia*, CoRR:abs/1410.0151, 2015.

[40] D. Sounthiraraj, J. Sahs, G. Greenwood, Z. Lin, and L. Khan. Smv-hunter: Large scale, automated detection of ssl/tls man-in-the-middle vulnerabilities in android apps. In *Proc. of NDSS*, 2014.

[41] N. Stefanovitch, A. Alshamsi, M. Cebrian, and I. Rahwan. Error and attack tolerance of collective problem solving: The darpa shredder challenge. *EPJ Data Science*, 3(1):1–27, 2014.

[42] M. Talasila, R. Curtmola, and C. Borcea. LINK: location verification through immediate neighbors knowledge. In *Proc. of MobiQuitous*, 2010.

[43] F. Tan, Y. Borghol, and S. Ardon. Emo: A statistical encounter-based mobility model for simulating delay tolerant networks. In *Proc. of WOWMOM*, 2008.

[44] K. Thomas, D. Iatskiv, E. Bursztein, T. Pietraszek, C. Grier, and D. McCoy. Dialing back abuse on phone verified accounts. In *Proc. of CCS*, 2014.

[45] J. M. Tjensvold. Comparison of the IEEE 802.11, 802.15.1,802.15.4 and 802.15.6 wireless standards. http://janmagnet.files.wordpress.com/2008/07/comparison-ieee-802-standards.pdf, 2007.

[46] N. Tran, B. Min, J. Li, and L. Subramanian. Sybil-resilient online content voting. In *Proc. of NSDI*, 2009.

[47] B. Viswanath, A. Post, K. P. Gummadi, and A. Mislove. An analysis of social network-based sybil defenses. In *Proc. of SIGCOMM*, 2010.

[48] G. Wang, T. Konolige, C. Wilson, X. Wang, H. Zheng, and B. Y. Zhao. You are how you click: Clickstream analysis for sybil detection. In *Proc. of USENIX Security*, 2013.

[49] G. Wang, M. Mohanlal, C. Wilson, X. Wang, M. Metzger, H. Zheng, and B. Y. Zhao. Social turing tests: Crowdsourcing sybil detection. In *Proc. of NDSS*, 2013.

[50] G. Wang, B. Wang, T. Wang, A. Nika, H. Zheng, and B. Y. Zhao. Whispers in the dark: Analysis of an anonymous social network. In *Proc. of IMC*, 2014.

[51] X. Wang, J. Zhu, A. Pande, A. Raghuramu, P. Mohapatra, T. Abdelzaher, and R. Ganti. STAMP: Ad hoc spatial-temporal provenance assurance for mobile users. In *Proc. of ICNP*, 2013.

[52] H. Yu, P. B. Gibbons, M. Kaminsky, and F. Xiao. Sybillimit: A near-optimal social network defense against sybil attacks. In *Proc. of IEEE S&P*, 2008.

[53] H. Yu, M. Kaminsky, P. B. Gibbons, and A. Flaxman. Sybilguard: defending against sybil attacks via social networks. In *Proc. of SIGCOMM*, 2006.

[54] Z. Zhang, L. Zhou, X. Zhao, G. Wang, Y. Su, M. Metzger, H. Zheng, and B. Y. Zhao. On the validity of geosocial mobility traces. In *Proc. of HotNets*, 2013.

[55] Z. Zhu and G. Cao. Toward privacy preserving and collusion resistance in a location proof updating system. *IEEE Transactions on Mobile Computing*, 12(1):51–64, 2013.

TransitLabel: A Crowd-Sensing System for Automatic Labeling of Transit Stations Semantics

Moustafa Elhamshary[†‡], Moustafa Youssef[†], Akira Uchiyama[‡], Hirozumi Yamaguchi[‡], Teruo Higashino[‡]
† Wireless Research Center, Egypt-Japan University of Science and Technology (E-JUST), Alexandria, Egypt.
‡ Graduate School of Information Science and Technology, Osaka University, Suita, Osaka, Japan.
{mostafaelhamshary, moustafa.youssef}@ejust.edu.eg, {uchiyama, h-yamagu, higashino}@ist.osaka-u.ac.jp

ABSTRACT

We present *TransitLabel*, a crowd-sensing system for automatic enrichment of transit stations indoor floorplans with different semantics like ticket vending machines, entrance gates, drink vending machines, platforms, cars' waiting lines, restrooms, lockers, waiting (sitting) areas, among others. Our key observations show that certain passengers' activities (e.g., purchasing tickets, crossing entrance gates, etc) present identifiable signatures on one or more cell-phone sensors. *TransitLabel* leverages this fact to automatically and unobtrusively recognize different passengers' activities, which in turn are mined to infer their uniquely associated stations semantics. Furthermore, the locations of the discovered semantics are automatically estimated from the inaccurate passengers' positions when these semantics are identified.

We evaluate *TransitLabel* through a field experiment in eight different train stations in Japan. Our results show that *TransitLabel* can detect the fine-grained stations semantics accurately with 7.7% false positive rate and 7.5% false negative rate on average. In addition, it can consistently detect the location of discovered semantics accurately, achieving an error within 2.5m on average for all semantics. Finally, we show that *TransitLabel* has a small energy footprint on cell-phones, could be generalized to other stations, and is robust to different phone placements; highlighting its promise as a ubiquitous indoor maps enriching service.

1 Introduction

With the fact that people spend most of their time at indoor spaces, indoor Location Based Services (LBSs) are being developed at a phenomenal rate with a variety of applications including mapping and navigation services, point-of-interest finders, geo-social networks, and advertisements. With the fact that people spend most of their time at indoor spaces, indoor LBSs are being developed at a phenomenal rate. A key requirement to indoor LBSs is the availability of indoor maps to display the user location on. These LBSs have still a huge potential for enhancement if rich semantic information is attached to indoor maps to support a wide class of indoor mapping applications (especially large public buildings that are visited daily by many people like railway stations, airports, museums, shopping malls, etc). Realizing the economic value of this technology, a number of commercial navigation systems for indoor mapping have started to emerge. In late 2011, Google Maps started to expand its coverage by providing detailed floorplans for a few malls and airports in the U.S. and Japan as well as allowing buildings owners around the world to upload their indoor floorplans. Nevertheless, these maps are still limited in coverage to a small number of countries featuring only some major airports, shopping malls, etc. This limitation in coverage is due in part to the following reasons: (1) buildings owners may not allow sharing of their floorplans in public for privacy reason, (2) buildings internal structures often evolve over time, and/or (3) manual creation of these maps requires slow, labor-intensive tasks, and they are subject to intentional incorrect data entry by malicious users.

Railway stations, as an example of indoor places, are a key part of the day-to-day lives of people having millions of passengers every day (e.g., Shinjuku station in Japan has 3.64 million passengers/day on average[1]). In highly populated countries, major stations have large indoor spaces (e.g., Shinjuku station in Japan has 36 platforms and over 200 exits[1]). Therefore, a number of indoor navigation apps, e.g. the Tokyo station underground area navigation app[2], for stations have started to emerge. These applications, however, are built upon a manually created map of the building showing all important points of interest (e.g., fare collection gates, ticket vending machine, etc), which impedes their scalability to large scale deployments at different stations. For example, Google indoor maps covers less than 50 transit stations worldwide, which are a small fraction of the thousands of stations on Earth[3]. The lack of detailed digital floorplans for railway stations highlighting locations of various semantics limits passengers' experience, especially for foreigners or first-time visitors. Consequently, this sparks the need for the automatic construction of detailed indoor floorplans for transit stations.

To resolve this problem, the research community recently has embarked to address the problem of automatic construction of indoor floorplans by exploiting motion trajectories of mobile phone users [7, 21, 25]. These systems proved the feasibility of estimating the general layout of a building [7, 21, 25], identifying rooms shape and dimensions [7, 21], along with identifying other points of interest such as store entrances [7, 21]. Nevertheless, none of these approaches provide semantic-rich floorplans where various semantics are tagged on the floorplan that are necessary for many of today's map-based applications. For example, stations indoor navigation systems should rely on important semantics to better guide

MobiSys'16, June 25-30, 2016, Singapore, Singapore
© 2016 ACM. ISBN 978-1-4503-4269-8/16/06... $15.00
DOI: http://dx.doi.org/10.1145/2906388.2906395

[1]https://en.wikipedia.org/wiki/Shinjuku_Station
[2]http://en.rocketnews24.com/2016/02/17/tokyos-busiest-train-stations-have-a-new-free-english-compatible-navigation-app/
[3]https://support.google.com/gmm/answer/1685827?hl=en

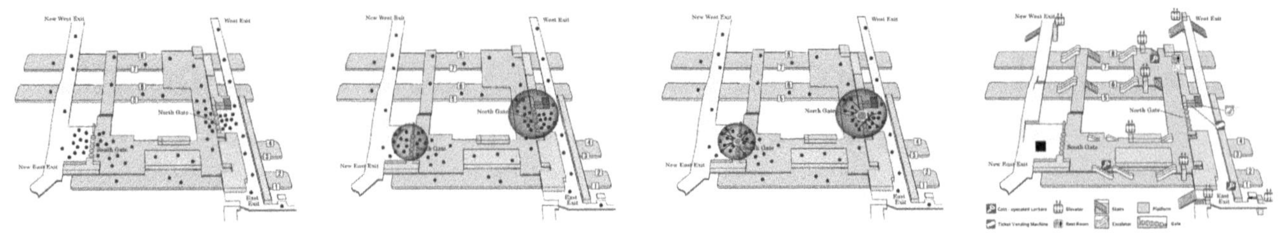

(a) The locations of passing through fare collection gate activity as estimated by pedestrian dead-reckoning (PDR) are highlighted on the floorplan.

(b) The output clusters from the DBSCAN based on crossing fare collection gates activity locations are highlighted on the floorplan.

(c) The semantics locations (e.g., fare collection gates) are estimated as the center of mass of all samples within the output clusters.

(d) The station indoor map with the discovered semantics locations, estimated by *TransitLabel*, are highlighted on the floorplan (*TransitLabel* output).

Figure 1: An example of *TransitLabel* in action to identify the location of ticket gates in a railway station.

passengers to their destinations; a station evacuation planning is ineffective if maps are not tagged with emergency exit stairs; a person with disability needs a map showing elevator-enabled routes; and an occasional passenger needs a map of important semantics that she must use to board the train (e.g., ticket gates, etc). Moreover, the discovered semantics can be leveraged to provide accurate calibration-free indoor localization, by providing opportunities for dead-reckoning error-resetting [3, 42]. Finally, fine-grained tracking of passengers' activities and interaction with the different detected semantics opens the door for indoor analytics, which is of great business value.

In this paper, we present *TransitLabel* as a crowdsensing system that leverages the ubiquitous sensors available in commodity cellphones to automatically enrich transit stations floorplans with different semantics. The core idea is that passengers perform many activities (e.g., crossing an entrance gate) that show identifiable signatures on the phone sensors. *TransitLabel* aims to recognize these high level activities and therefrom discover their uniquely associated semantics. Therefore, starting from an **unlabeled general** floorplan of a transit station, *TransitLabel* estimates the location of different semantics and tags their locations on the map accordingly to generate a detailed floorplan (Figure 1).

Translating this basic idea into a deployable system, however, involves addressing a number of challenges: First, identifying semantics signatures is based on the phone sensors during passengers' activities; which are prone to human behavior artifacts. Second, current indoor localization technologies may require infrastructure support or prior calibration; and all have an average localization error in the range of few meters [43]. This can place the passenger in a location on the floorplan that is far from the actual one, affecting the accuracy of semantics' location estimation. Finally, the system needs to be optimized for energy to avoid significant battery drainage.

To cope with these challenges, *TransitLabel* draws on a classifier-based approach based on the multi-modal sensors features to recognize passengers activities and thereby identify their associated semantics to address the first challenge. For the second challenge, *TransitLabel* relies on a DBSCAN clustering algorithm to cluster the correct crowdsensed samples of the same semantic to estimate its location and thus outlier locations are removed. To save energy, *TransitLabel* employs sensors with low energy footprint (i.e., inertial sensors) and the energy hungry sensor employed (i.e., sound) is turned on only when needed.

Implementation of *TransitLabel* over different Android phones shows that it can detect the fine-grained stations semantics accurately with 7.7% false positive rate and 7.5% false negative rate on average. In addition, it can estimate locations of the detected semantics accurately, achieving an error of 2.5m on average using as few as 40 samples of each semantic. This comes with low energy consumption of 41 Joule on average for typical traces. We believe this could be a promising and a potential candidate for the real-world.

In summary, our contributions are three-fold:

- We present the *TransitLabel* system to automatically and unobtrusively crowdsense and identify transit stations semantics (e.g., ticket and drink vending machines, entrance gates, lockers, waiting (sitting) areas, restrooms, platforms and cars' waiting lines, escalators, elevators and stairs) from the available sensors readings with minimal energy consumption.
- We provide a framework for extracting the features used to recognize high level user contexts (e.g., buying a ticket) from a sequence of temporal and spatial low level user states (e.g., walking, standing, etc) based on the phone sensors.
- We implement *TransitLabel* on Android phones, collect real data by 16 participants, and evaluate its accuracy, generalizability, robustness and energy-efficiency at eight different railway stations in Japan.

The rest of the paper is organized as follows: Section 2 presents the system overview. We give the details of identifying station's semantics from phone sensors in sections 3 and 4. Section 5 provides the evaluation of *TransitLabel*. Section 6 discusses the system limitations and possibilities for enhancement. Finally, sections 7 and 8 discuss related work and conclude the paper respectively.

2 The TransitLabel System

Figure 2 shows the *TransitLabel* system architecture. *TransitLabel* is based on a crowdsensing approach, where cell phones carried by users submit their data to the *TransitLabel* service running in the cloud. The data is first preprocessed to reduce the noise. Then, semantics are classified to separate the elevation change semantics (elevators, escalators, and stairs) from other railway stations exclusive semantics (ticket vending machines, entrance gates, etc). *TransitLabel* has two core components: one for extracting elevation change semantics and the other for extracting other stations exclusive semantics. *TransitLabel* takes a classifier approach to detect different semantics based on the extracted features from the collected sensor traces. In the rest of this section, we give an overview of the system architecture leaving the details for the semantics detection to sections 3 and 4.

2.1 Traces Collection

The system collects time-stamped sensor measurements including the available inertial sensors (accelerometer, gyroscope and mag-

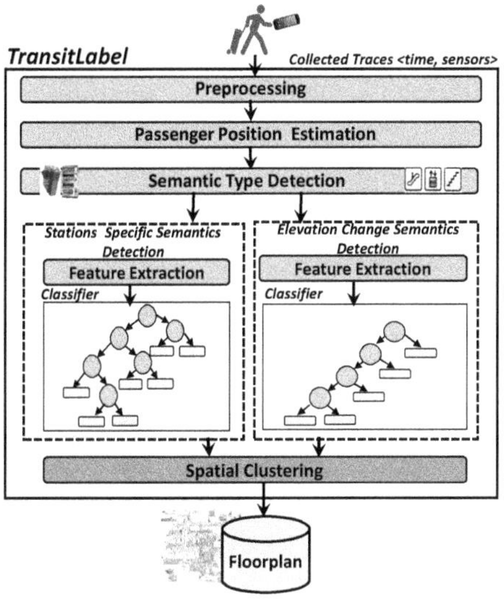

Figure 2: The *TransitLabel* system architecture.

netometer), barometer as well as the sound sensor (i.e., the microphone). Inertial sensors have a low-cost energy profile and they are already running all the time during the standard phone operation to detect phone orientation changes. Therefore, they consume zero extra energy. On the other hand, we use an adaptive sensor scheduling scheme called *triggered sensing* [31] to reduce the sound sensor energy consumption. The key idea is that sensors that are inexpensive in energy consumption (e.g., accelerometer) are used to trigger the operation of more expensive sensors (e.g., sound). Specifically, *TransitLabel* activates audio recordings only as soon as the passenger becomes stationary for a considerable time (4 seconds) and suspends it once she resumes walking. The intuition is that passengers traces inside railway stations are dominated by walking periods and they pause only to perform an activity (e.g., buying a ticket or a drink) which has a considerable stationarity time (more than 15 seconds). If the user does not resume walking after a certain time (60 seconds), the audio recordings will be suspended to save energy. The collected audio recordings during activities are used as a tie-breaker when other sensors (e.g., inertial sensor) fail to recognize certain activities.

Given the privacy implications of turning on the microphone, *TransitLabel* gives users full control over their own sensed data by means of a personalized privacy configuration. *TransitLabel* has different modes of operations (full sensor collection, privacy insensitive data only) that tailor the amount of data collected based on the user's preferences. In addition, according to a recent study [9], inertial sensors are enabled by most users and even the privacy-sensitive sensors (i.e., microphone) are enabled by about 78% of users. Finally, we **process audio data locally** on the user's device to further enhance the user privacy.

2.2 Preprocessing

This module is responsible for preprocessing the raw sensor measurements to reduce the effect of (a) phone orientation changes and (b) noise, e.g., small direction changes while moving. To handle the former, we transform the sensor readings from the mobile coordinate system to the world coordinate system leveraging the inertial sensors [32]. To address the latter, we apply a low-pass filter to raw sensors data using local weighted regression to smooth the data [10]. To filter out the noise in the employed frequency bands (350Hz and 3kHz) in audio recordings, the standard sliding window averaging technique, with a window of 32 samples, is used.

2.3 Passengers' Position Estimation

TransitLabel needs accurate passengers' locations during activities to estimate their uniquely associated semantics positions. To achieve this, *TransitLabel* employs the dead-reckoning technique to track the passenger's location starting from a reference point (e.g., the station entrance). We employ the step detection algorithm in [8] that takes into account the different users' profiles and gaits and apply them to the acceleration signal to detect the user steps. The user heading is estimated by incorporating the algorithm in [3,42] which leverages the correlation between compass and gyroscope to compensate gyroscope drift and compass interference errors to accurately estimate the user orientation. The estimated displacement and heading are fused to localize the user. However, the displacement error of dead reckoning is unbounded making it infeasible for indoor tracking. To alleviate this problem, *TransitLabel* incorporates the idea of SemanticSLAM [3,42] by leveraging **amble and unique** physical points in the stations (i.e., semantics) to reset the accumulated error. Since dead-reckoning provides a rough location to the phone, it is also possible to roughly localize the semantics based on when the phone senses them. Now, since the floorplan is known, we can estimate the locations of all semantics in a crowd-sensing approach (as discussed later) by combining the rough estimates (i.e., the dead-reckoned positions) from multiple passengers' phones. These semantics, once detected based on their unique sensor signatures, can then be used to improve dead-reckoning of subsequent passengers, which in turn can refine the semantic locations. This recursive dependence between estimating the semantic location and the user location is similar to the Simultaneous Localization And Mapping (SLAM) framework.

2.4 Semantic Type Detection

TransitLabel is designed to detect various stations semantics based on their unique usage patterns. This module separates between the two major types of semantics: elevation change semantics (elevators, stairs and escalators) and stations specific semantics (e.g., ticket vending machines, entrance gates, etc). The usage of elevation change semantics involves a noticeable change in the passenger's level (i.e., height) which is absent in other semantics (Figure 4). To separate them, we draw on the maximum difference among the relative barometer readings (i.e., pressure) in consecutive overlapping windows. The employed window size, 10 seconds, is small enough so that barometer readings are not affected by the environmental changes [33]. The intuition is that a change in pressure means a change in height which in turn means that the passenger is using one of the elevation change semantics. Moreover, the sign of the pressure difference indicates the direction of motion (up or down) which is useful for other purposes (e.g., detecting escalators direction). Evaluation of over 250 traces shows that the semantic type detection can achieve 0% false positive and negative rates. Later, the major two classes of semantics are further classified to their more fine-grained semantics.

2.5 Feature Extraction

In this section, we present the basic features used to identify the different semantics based on the data collected from the passengers' phone sensors. For instance, magnetic peak is a key feature to recognize many activities that involve direct interaction with electronic machines (e.g., vending machines). To extract it, we first apply a stream-based event detection algorithm to identify significant changes in the **magnitude** of the magnetic field. Once a sig-

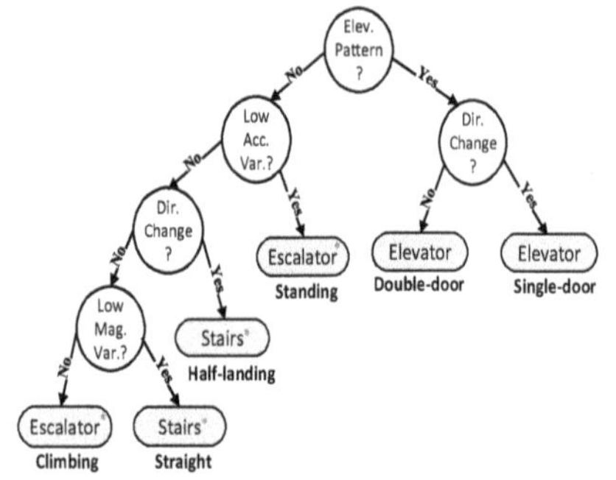

(a) Elevation change semantics. Star marked semantics are further classified as floor or level change semantics leading to different floors or different levels within the same floor respectively.

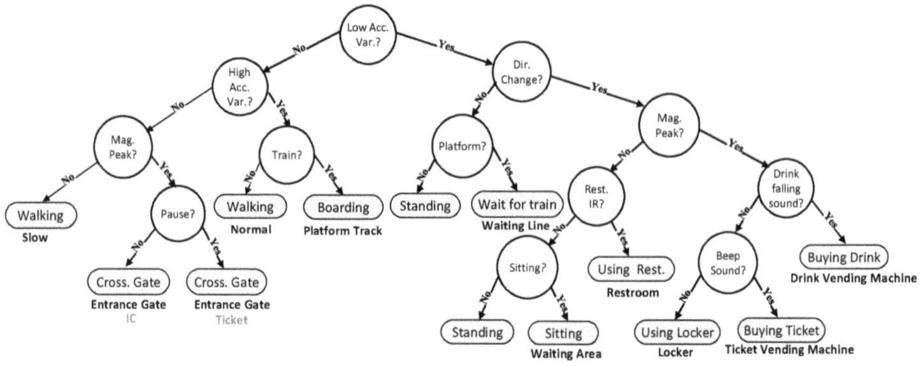

(b) Stations specific semantics.

Figure 3: A decision tree classifier for detecting different types of semantics.

nificant change (a *10uT* increase in a window of *50* samples[4]) has been observed, we mark the corresponding time instant as the starting boundary of the peak area. We buffer subsequent measurements until a significant decrease in the magnitude of the magnetic field is observed. Once the starting and ending boundaries have been identified, we extract two features that characterize the peak area: the peak duration and strength. Moreover, some activities (e.g., buying tickets) are characterized by a sudden change in the user direction (i.e., surge in gyroscope readings) during or directly after the activity period. To detect this sudden change, we used the *approximate derivative* method: The derivative of sensor values within a time window are compared against a predetermined threshold (*75°* in a window of *60* samples) to detect the surge in sensor values. Finally, the variance of the acceleration is used to discriminate various passenger motion types (stationary, slow walking and normal walking) which contributes to the identification of many higher level passenger activities (e.g, buying a ticket). The acceleration variance values of *1.8* and *7* for a window of *200* samples are used as thresholds to separate stationary, slow walking and normal walking motion patterns respectively.

2.6 Station Semantics Extraction

As many semantics share some sensors patterns while having different patterns on other sensors, the hierarchical classification is an intuitive solution. Therefor, to identify semantics, *TransitLabel* relies on a tree-based classifier as it is easy to understand and to generate its rules. This classifier decomposes the task hierarchically into subtasks, proceeding from a coarse-grained classification (shared patterns) towards the distinction of fine-grained semantics (distinctive patterns) as detailed in sections 3 and 4.

2.7 Semantic Location Estimation

Whenever a semantic is detected by the semantic detection modules discussed later, *TransitLabel* needs to determine whether it is a new instance of a station semantic (i.e., not discovered before) or not as well as determine its location.

To do this, *TransitLabel* applies spatial clustering for each type of the extracted semantics. It uses the density-based clustering algorithm (DBSCAN [19]) which has a number of advantages as the number of clusters is not required before carrying out clustering; the detected clusters can be represented in an arbitrary shape; and outliers can be detected. The DBSCAN is applied to all samples of each discovered semantic to cluster all samples that are adjacent to each other in the spatial space. The parameter *Eps* specifies the radius of each cluster controlling the maximum distance among samples on the same cluster. After clusters are formed, the locations of the newly discovered semantics are estimated as the weighted mean of the points inside their clusters. We weight the different locations based on their location accuracy reported by the localization approach. Specifically, in our position estimation approach, the longer the user trace from the last resetting point, the higher the error in the trace. Therefore, shorter traces have better accuracy. Based on the law of large numbers, the weighted average of independent noisy samples should converge to the actual location of the semantic. When a new semantic is identified, if there is an already discovered semantic within its neighborhood, we add it to the cluster and update its location. Otherwise, a new cluster is created to represent the new semantic. To reduce outliers, a semantic is not physically added to the floorplan until the cluster size reaches a certain threshold which is specified by the *Minpts* parameter (the minimum number of points that can form a cluster) of the DBSCAN algorithm. The DBSCAN parameters *Minpts* and *Eps* are selected empirically for each semantic type depending on its available number of samples, its physical dimension, and the average inter-distance among its physical instances in the real-world stations indoor maps. We do not state the DBSCAN parameters values for each semantic due to space constraints.

2.8 Practical Considerations

Sensor specifications are different from one phone manufacturer to another, which leads to different sensor readings for the same activity. To address this issue, *TransitLabel* applies a number of techniques including use of offset-independent features (e.g., variance), orientation independent features (e.g., magnitude of acceleration and magnetic field) and combining a number of features for detecting the same semantic. In addition, we experimented with various thresholds and select those leading to *high detection accuracy* with low false positive/negative rates while being robust to different users and stations. This is confirmed by experiment performed in the evaluation section.

TransitLabel does not also require real-time sensor data collection

[4]We experimented with different values of thresholds and selected values that are robust to changes in the platforms/stations as confirmed by our experiments.

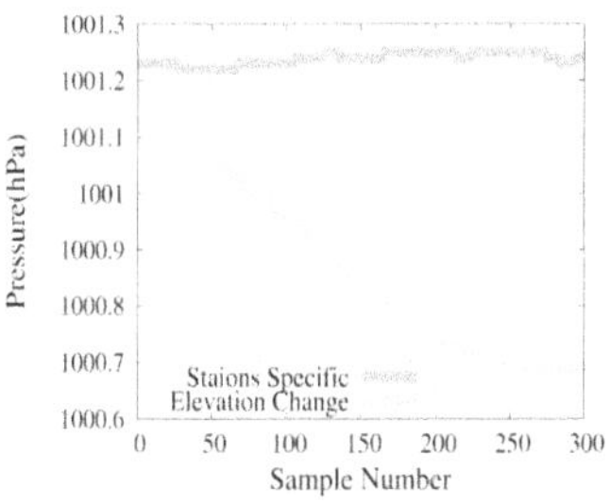

Figure 4: Comparing barometer readings of the usage of elevation change semantics (e.g., elevator) against station specific machines (e.g., ticket gate).

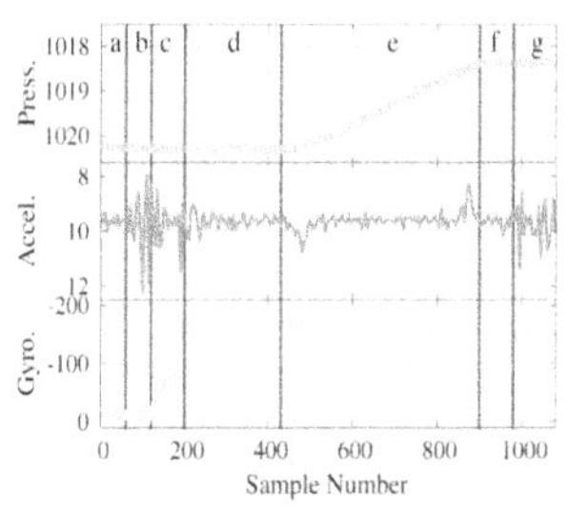

Figure 5: Elevator usage pattern: (a) waiting for it, (b) walking into it, (c) direction change, (d) stationary, (e) going **up**, (f) stopping, (g) walking out.

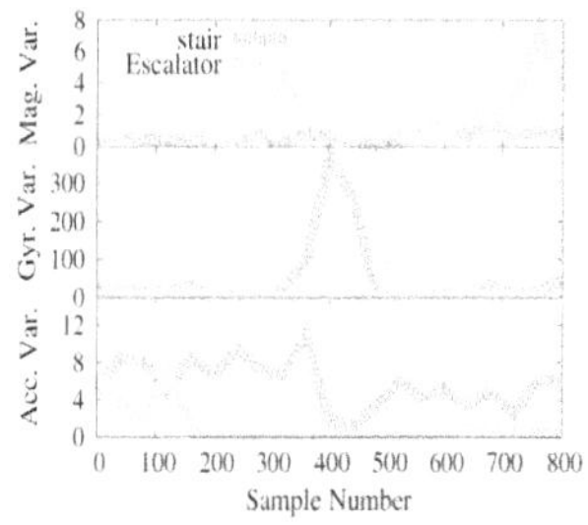

Figure 6: The sensor patterns that compare climbing up a half-landing stairs against standing on a moving up escalator.

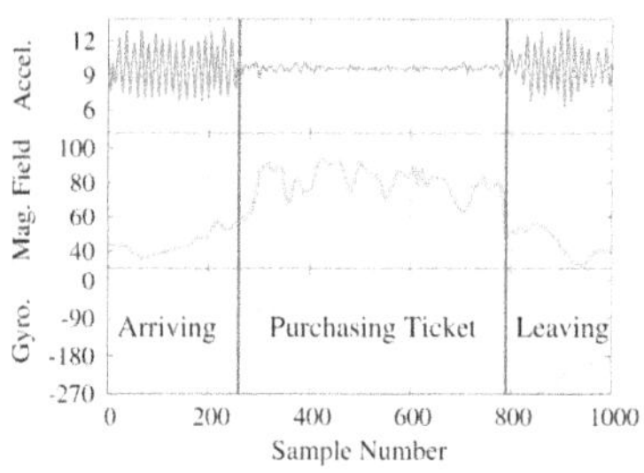

Figure 7: The acceleration, ambient magnetic field and gyroscope readings while using a coin operated machine.

(i.e., it works offline); it can store the different sensor measurements and opportunistically upload them to the cloud for processing; allowing it to save both communication energy and cost. This is outside the scope of this paper.

3 Elevation Change Semantics Detection

To classify elevation change semantics [5] into their fine-grained classes (elevators, escalators and staircases), we apply a decision tree classifier to the extracted features from passengers' phone sensors based on our observations of semantics usage scenarios and their physical structures (Figure 3a).

Elevators:
We begin by recognizing elevators as it is straightforward to distinguish their unique pattern. The typical usage scenario of an elevator consists of a normal working period, waiting for the elevator, walking into the elevator, changing direction to face the exit door, standing for a while, followed by a level change when it starts to move (Figure 5). This behavior is reflected to a unique pattern that consists of sequence of states: walking, stationary, stepping, direction change, level change, and Accelerate-Stationary-Decelerate emerging from the start and stop of the elevator. A set of features are extracted from accelerometer, gyroscope and barometer readings and fed to a Finite State Machine (FSM) to detect this multimodal pattern. Starting from the initial state which represent the user waiting for an elevator (state (a) in Figure 5), the transitions through all subsequent states (from (b) to (g)) have to occur to announce that a **single-door elevator** have been detected. However, for elevators having two doors, users do not need to turn around. Nevertheless, **two-doors elevators** can be recognized by the same FSM while skipping the direction change transition state.

Escalators (Standing):
The acceleration variance is used to decide whether a user is standing on an escalator or not. The intuition is that when a user keeps standing while carried by a moving staircase, the acceleration variance remains small compared to climbing stairs or escalators, which generates a high acceleration variance due to the vertical motion of the user. Conversely, if the acceleration variance is high, we cannot verify whether the user is climbing a stair or an escalator.

Half-landing Stairs (Climbing):
Half landing staircases have a turn in the middle forcing users to change their direction while straight stairs and escalators do not have any turns. Thus, if there is a surge in gyroscope readings (from the direction change) that took place in the middle of the elevation change period, it is affirmative that the user is climbing a half-landing stairs. Otherwise, if there is no direction change, we cannot verify whether a user is climbing a straight stair or climbing an escalator.

Escalators (Climbing):
The magnetic field variance, due to the escalator constant speed motors, can be used to reliably differentiate between climbing a straight stair and climbing an escalator (Figure 6). The value *100*, in a window of *200* samples, is used as the threshold of the variance of magnetic field.

Straight Stairs (Climbing):
After separating other elevation change semantics, the remaining samples are classified as straight stairs.

Level Change or Floor Change:
Many stations are multi-floor buildings with a typical floor height between 3.0 to 6.0 meters. The majority of elevation change semantics installed in railway stations move passengers from one floor to another (Floor change semantics). However, there exist some low height stairs and escalators which move passenger from level to another within the same floor (level change semantics). To classify the type of escalators and stairs (marked by red stars in Figure 3a), we rely on the magnitude of pressure difference during the elevation change period. Given that 1.0 meter height change corresponds to 0.12 hPa change in pressure, the pressure difference of *0.3* hPa is used as a threshold to separate level change escalators and stairs from floor change ones.

4 Station Specific Semantics Detection

Stations are rich with many exclusive semantics like ticket vending machines, entrance gates, drink vending machines, platforms, cars' waiting lines, lockers, restrooms, and waiting (sitting) areas. Based on our observations, these semantics force users to behave in predictable ways which are translated to unique sensor signatures that can be mined to identify them. For instance, a passenger crossing an entrance gate has to slow down her walking speed until she pauses to drop the ticket into the gate machine and then steps forward to grab it. Meanwhile her phone is experiencing a magnetic field distortion emanating from the gate machine electronics. *TransitLabel* draws on a decision tree classifier to recognize different passengers' activities (Figure 3b). The root of the decision tree separates activities into two main classes. The right branch of the tree comprises activities that require the passenger to be stationary during the service time (ticket and drink vending machines, lockers, restrooms, waiting (sitting) areas, etc). On contrast, the left

[5] We provide a thorough comparison with other related approaches in the related work section.

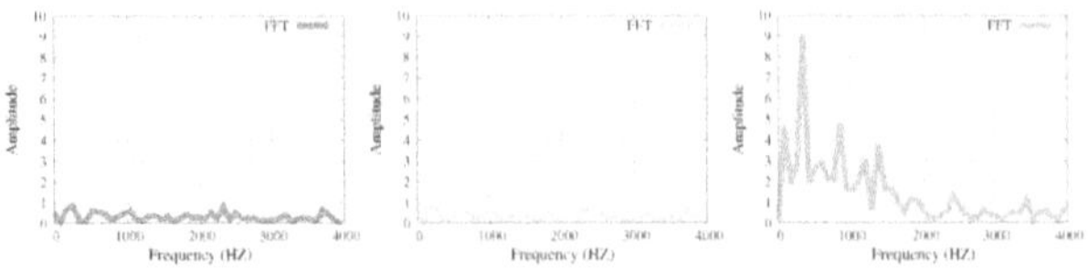

(a) Backgr. noise. (b) Coin insertion. (c) Drink falling.

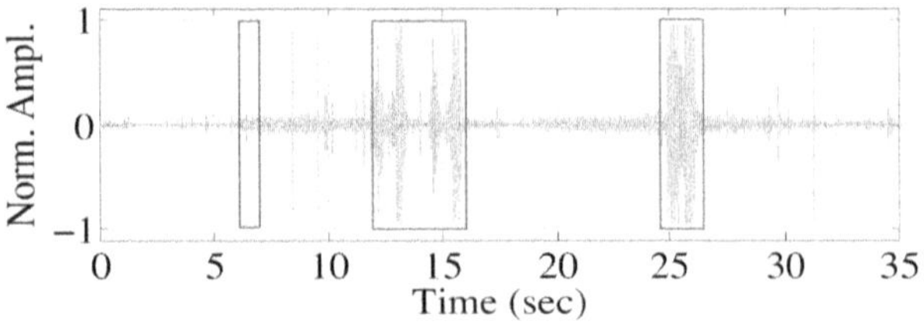

(d) The original audio signal in time domain

Figure 8: A time-domain sample of an audio signal depicting the usage of a drink vending machine is shown in (d) where three highlighted audio signal (bounded by blue boxes) corresponding to the background noise, the coin insertion sound, and the drink falling sound respectively. Figures (a), (b), (c) depict the frequency domain of these three audio signals respectively.

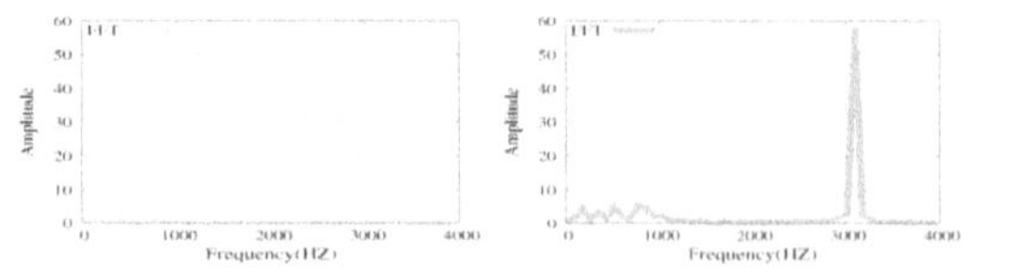

(a) Background noise. (b) Beep signal.

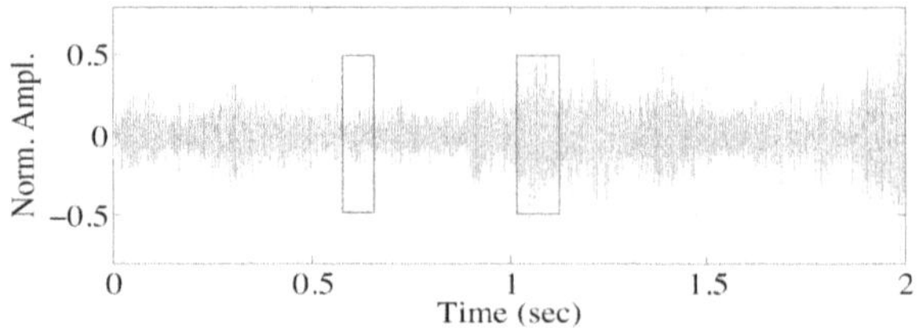

(c) The original audio signal in time domain

Figure 9: A sample of audio signal in the time domain depicting the usage of a ticket vending machine is shown in (c) where two different audio signal are highlighted (bounded by blue boxes) corresponding to the background noise and the beep audio signal respectively. Figures (a) and (b) depict the frequency domain of these two cropped signals respectively.

branch comprises activities that do not force passengers to pause (e.g., ticket gates, etc). In the balance of this section, we give the details of the classifier features that can differentiate the different station specifics semantics (coin operated machines, entrance gates, platforms track, sitting areas, restrooms).

4.1 Coin Operated Machines

Nowadays, ticket vending machines are found in every station and drink vending machines exist in many transits to dispense items (e.g. beverages, etc) to customers automatically. In addition, coin operated lockers are widely installed in railway stations to allow passengers to leave their baggages for several hours respectively to visit the surrounding area freely (especially in major stations in the downtown areas).

To identify these machines, we observed that their typical usage traces consist of normal walking to the machine, followed by standing in front of it, inserting currency, beginning the service (choosing a drink or the ticket type in case of drink and ticket vending machines respectively or opening the locker door in case of lockers), finishing the service (grabbing the ticket or the drink in case of ticket and drink vending machines respectively or putting luggage into the drawer and locking it), and finally walking away (Figure 7). This usage scenario is translated to the following unique patterns on the sensors. First, the user is stationary during the machine usage. Second, there is a fluctuation in the magnetic field readings as soon as the user interacts with the machine. This fluctuation is due to the distortion from metals and electronic chips installed in these machines forming a peak in the magnetic field readings (detected by the peak detector). Finally, as these machines are usually mounted to walls, the passenger is forced to change her direction to walk away as soon as she finishes the service. This instantaneous change in the user direction is reflected to a surge in the gyroscope readings when the user starts to resume walking (detected by the surge detector). This unique patterns are leveraged by *TransitLabel* to separate this type of machines from other semantics (Figure 3b). Now, we will give the detail of how to discriminate the three classes of coin operated machines.

4.1.1 Drink Vending Machines

Based on our observation, they have a unique loud sound emitted when they are dispensing drinks to the customer. This sound is emanated when the drink is pulled down from the machine storage into its outlet.

To verify that we can recognize the unique drink falling sound in the ambience, in our preliminary experiment, we recorded an audio clip during the usage of a drink vending machine (Figure 8). The time-domain audio signal contains coin insertion sound existing in all coin operated machines, the drink falling sound, and the background noise respectively (highlighted by the three consecutive blue boxes in Figure 8d). The Fast Fourier Transform (FFT) of the audio signal shows a clear peak at the 350Hz frequency band in the drink falling audio clip (Figure 8c) while no peaks are evident at the 350Hz frequency band neither in the coin insertion nor the background noise clips due to the absence of this distinct acoustic signal (Figs. 8a, 8b). We observed that this frequency is consistent across all drink vending machines we experienced in the eight different stations in our dataset. *During the system operation*, we use an empirical threshold of three standard deviations (i.e., 99.7% confidence level of noise) to detect the drink falling acoustic signal in the ambient sound recorded during the usage of coin operated machines. If the received audio signal strengths in the 350Hz frequency band exceeds the threshold, indicating that the sound level is significant at this frequency band (as signal strength is jumped significantly at this frequency band), the system confirms the detection of a drink vending machine.

4.1.2 Ticket Vending Machines

Similarly, they emit a unique beep sound many times during the user interaction (e.g., pressing a button, indicating the end of transaction, etc). We envision that this beep signal can be leveraged as a reliable discriminator as it is absent in lockers where users insert coin, put luggage and lock the drawer without any distinctive sound. We incorporate the same acoustic detection algorithm used to identify drink vending machines to separate ticket vending machines from lockers. Figure 9c shows a raw audio recording collected during buying a ticket from a vending machine. We crop two

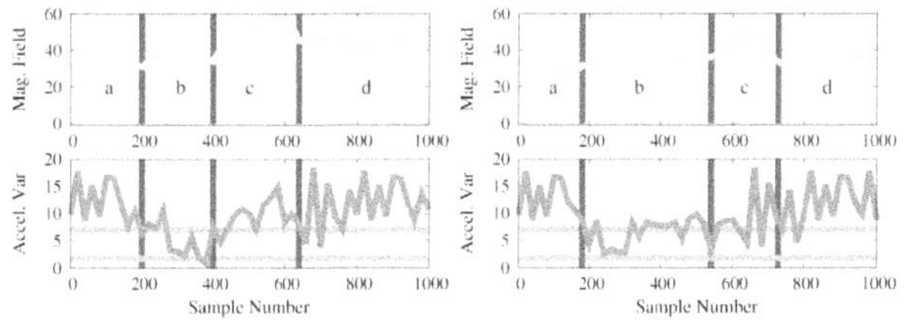

(a) Ticket (b) IC Card.

Figure 10: The sensor pattern of crossing a gate by a ticket and an IC card. Both consist of (a) normal walking, (b) deceleration near the gate, (c) acceleration accompanied by a peak on ambient magnetic field, and (d) normal walking.

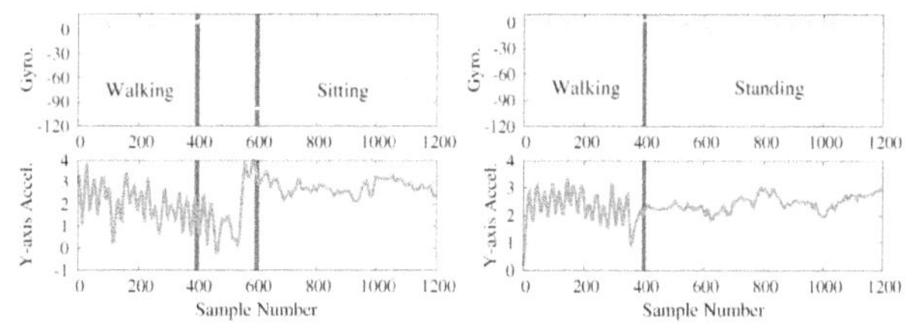

(a) Sitting. (b) Standing.

Figure 11: The effect of activity transition from walking to sitting against the effect of transition from walking to standing on the Y acceleration and gyroscope readings.

sections from the original audio signal comprising the background noise and the beep audio signal respectively and convert these signals into the frequency domain by using FFT (Figs. 9a, 9b). We observed a clear peak around the frequency of 3kHz in the beep audio signal whereas no peaks are observed at the frequency of 3kHz in the background noise (Figs. 9a, 9b). When the ticket vending machine starts beeping, the signal strength in the 3kHz frequency band jumps significantly and therefore the ticket vending machine can be detected.

4.1.3 Lockers

To recognize lockers, we first attempted to identify the coin insertion sound in the ambience to avoid classifying all unrecognized activities as using lockers (i.e., catching all). However, we observed that while some coin sound signatures were visible, in many cases it was difficult to separate them from other frequency components (e.g., background noise). In addition, we find that the number of traces, other than coin operated machines ones, having a stationary period accompanied with a significant magnetic distortion on the user's magnetometer followed by a direction change (i.e., surge in gyroscope readings) are small. So, once vending machines samples are separated, the remaining coin operated machines samples are classified as lockers.

4.2 Entrance Gates

Railway passengers have to pass through an automatic fare collection gate in their routes to the station's platform. To cross a gate, there are two ways:

With a Ticket:
Passengers mostly pass by a ticket vending machine to get a ticket. Thereafter, as a passenger approaches the gate, a noticeable slows down in her walking speed is observed till she pauses in front of the gate to drop the ticket into the machine, then she steps forward to grab it from the machine, and finally she resumes normal walking (Figure 10a). This scenario translates to a unique motion pattern consisting of the following sequence: normal walking, deceleration, accelerating and normal walking. This unique motion pattern is detected by using the variance of acceleration (Figure 10a) where the two horizontal lines correspond to the acceleration variance threshold values used to separate different motion patterns. Simultaneously, crossing the gate heavily distorts the magnetic field by the gate ferromagnetic metals forming a distinct peak on the magnetometer reading (detected by a simple peak detector).

With an IC Card:
IC cards are rechargeable cards that are recently used to conveniently pay fares on public transportation and to make payments at vending machines, shops by simply touching the card on a reader for about one second (e.g., Pasmo[6] in Japan, Ventra[7] in Chicago). This gate entrance method has two differences from the ticket based one. First, passengers using IC cards do not have to pause as the card reader can recognize the card while it is in close proximity in users' hand or wallet (acceleration variance still above the stationarity threshold (Figure 10b)). Second, mostly it is not preceded by the usage of a ticket vending machine activity (i.e., neither sequential nor dependent activities).

4.3 Waiting (Sitting) areas

Waiting areas are available in many stations platforms, especially those where trains inter-arrival time is long. Many people especially elderly people, pregnant women, people with disabilities and even normal passengers (e.g., in the winter) prefer to wait for trains in this area. We postulate that if there are many activities transitions from walking to sitting taking place within the premises of a certain area, then this area will be a waiting area with a high probability. To switch from walking to sitting, the passenger has to rotate first to be aligned with the seat and then sit down. The instantaneous surge in gyroscope reading (from the direction change) followed by a difference in relative magnitudes of Y acceleration values (from forward and backward motions while sitting) are used to characterize the transition from walking to sitting (Figure 11a). Conversely, the transition from walking to standing does not involve a noticeable difference on the readings of Y acceleration (Figure 11b). We leverage the change in direction as an affirmative feature to decrease the false positive rate in the sitting recognition given that the change in Y acceleration values may happen in other conditions (e.g., normal device bouncing while the user is walking).

4.4 Restrooms

Public restrooms are available in almost all stations. Normally, people must have stationary periods while they are at restrooms (e.g., hand washing). Moreover, due to the sensitive nature of public restrooms, their entry doors are faced by walls so users have to change their directions after crossing entry doors. However, the user stationarity and direction change patterns are not sufficient to efficiently separate the user being in a restroom from other contexts. To accurately identify restrooms, we incorporate the algorithm in [20] which detects restrooms by actively probing the acoustics of environment with the built-in speaker and microphone

[6]http://www.pasmo.co.jp/en/
[7]https://www.ventrachicago.com/

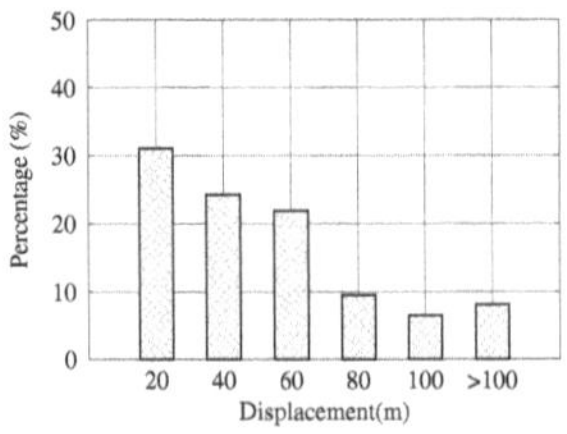

Figure 12: Passengers displacement distribution over the platform.

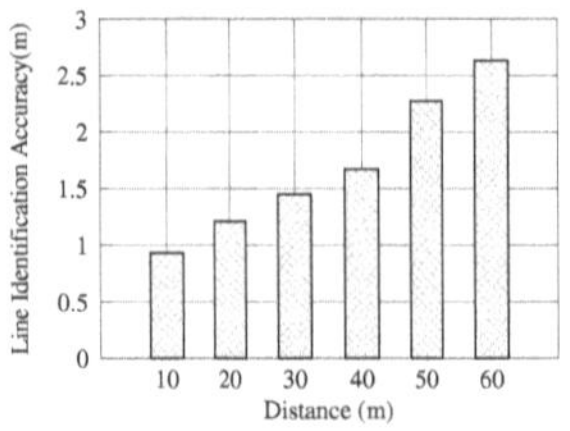

Figure 13: Lines location accuracy versus their distance from the platform access

on the mobile phone. A probing sound is emitted by the phone and the impulse response (IR) is analyzed to detect the type of space (restroom or not). The acoustic characteristics of an environment depend on its dimension and its ability to absorb sound. Since, public restrooms have similar affordances (e.g., water resistance floors and wall, toilets and sinks), they have a unique absorption coefficient of sound and thus they can be detected easily. Since the sweep volume level does not affect the accuracy of the model significantly [20], *TransitLabel* leverages sweeps with lower volumes to avoid being invasive. Additionally, the model prediction performance is robust against the restroom occupancy and sounds generated by the occupants (e.g., flushing or hand-washing) [20].

4.5 Platform and Waiting Lines

To further enrich the semantics of *TransitLabel*, we also identify the platform area and the location of waiting lines for train cars. The platform is the area where passengers board the train. Therefore, their transportation mode changes from standing (waiting for train) to walking (into the train car) to be in a motorized transport (when the train moves) during a short time period. Transportation mode detection has been thoroughly studied in literature, e.g. [1,23,28,36,41]. We follow the approach proposed in [23] that provides high accuracy of transportation mode detection (walking, stationary or in a motorized transport) based on the energy-efficient accelerometer sensor. The short temporal consequence of standing, walking shortly and being in a train activities is leveraged to detect the platform track and its position is estimated from passengers' positions during train boarding.

Once the platform area is identified, the waiting line positions can be estimated from the passengers' positions reported while they are waiting for the trains (i.e., switching from walking to standing activity on the platform (Figure 11b)). We videotaped a sample of 3000 passengers' traces starting for their access to the platform (escalator, elevators and stairs) until they join a waiting line. Figure 12 shows that about 76% of passengers walk a short distance (less than 60m) on the platform where they tend to join the nearest uncrowded waiting line. This is partially due to the fact that platforms are typically designed to have multi-accesses to disperse the passengers load. In addition, as passengers use elevation change semantics to access the platform, their dead-reckoned derailed position will be curbed and calibrated to the access locations of these semantics on the platform when this semantic surface on the user's trace. This verifies that *TransitLabel* can localize the user accurately on the platform. Thus, waiting lines positions can be estimated by the clustering approach from passengers' locations when they are waiting in a line for the train. Once lines are detected, every neighbored collection of n lines (where n is the number of doors per car, which is a known constant) are representing a queuing area for a train car.

5 Evaluation

TransitLabel is evaluated through a deployment at eight different stations of different sizes in two different cities (Osaka and Kobe) in Japan. Table 1 shows the detailed description of the collected dataset. The stations are managed by different companies; having different buildings designs and sizes; and semantics placement. This emphasizes the scalable nature of *TransitLabel*. The average length and width of platforms are 160m and 12m on average respectively. Train cars are of 20m length with 3 doors and the average inter-door distance is 5.2m.

5.1 Data Collection Methodology

A group of 16 volunteers, of different ages (11 in their 20's and 5 in their 30's) and gender (12 males and 4 females), collected the necessary data for evaluation. The collected data consists of two datasets-***scenario based and free***- differing in how the data is collected. In the scenario-based dataset, 10 participants were assigned specific trajectories starting from the station entrance to different platforms. The trajectories were selected carefully to cover all possible routes that were exhibited by daily passengers while covering all available semantics at the same time. While heading to a specific platform, some participants purchased tickets to cross entrance gates; others crossed gates directly using different types of IC cards; some participants used drink vending machines while others used lockers; and all participants passed through elevation change semantics to access the platform. On the other hand, the free dataset is collected by six individuals from their everyday train commutation in different stations.

We have deployed two Android applications: The first application is a data collection tool that runs in the background to sample all inertial sensors, the barometer at 50Hz as well as recording audio. The second application is designed for ground truth collection and runs in the foreground to allow participants to manually tag their activities. The data collection was conducted in different times, different days and using different Android phones including Samsung Galaxy S5 and LG Nexus 5. Participants carry smartphones in different placements (in hand or in the trouser pocket). When the participants carry the logger phones in the trouser pocket, they carry another phone in their hands to annotate their activities. This captures the time-variant nature of semantics signatures and stations congestion level; generalization of the system over different stations; as well as the heterogeneity of users and devices.

5.2 Performance Results

In this section, we evaluate the semantics identification accuracy, semantics location estimation accuracy, power consumption, impact of different phone placement and finally quantify the generalization performance of *TransitLabel*.

5.2.1 Semantics Detection Accuracy

We evaluate the semantics detection accuracy based on the scenario-based datasets. The detection accuracy is measured by false positive [8] and false negative [9] rates.

Table 2 shows the confusion matrix for detecting various elevation change semantics. It shows that some elevation change semantics are easy to detect due to their unique patterns. This leads to zero false positive and false negative rates for the elevators (the coarse-grained category), half-landing stairs, and escalator (when users are standing) cases. However, climbing straight stairs sometimes are misclassified as climbing escalators when the stairs are

[8] Samples of other semantics classified as the current semantic.

[9] Samples of the current semantic that are not detected.

Table 1: The description of collected data.

Station	Osaka	Umeda	Senrichuo	Juso	Higashi-Umeda	Nishinomaya	Kobe-Sanyomia	Shin-Kobe
No. of Traces	108	78	71	69	61	59	53	48
No. of Users	10	9	7	6	6	6	5	4
Type and City	JR- Osaka	Subway- Osaka	Subway- Osaka	Hankyu- Osaka	Hankyu- Osaka	Hankyu- Osaka	Subway- Kobe	Subway- Kobe

very close to escalators so they have a similar magnetic distortion signature. Moreover, separating the two types of elevators generates some misclassifications which is due to the different elevator usage patterns (e.g., some users of single-door elevators do not turn around completely in one step). Nevertheless, as standing in or climbing up escalators activities are translated to the same semantic (escalator), *TransitLabel* can still achieve a high detection accuracy for elevation change semantics with 3.3% false positive and 4.1% false negative rates on overage.

Table 3 shows the confusion matrix representing the detection accuracy of station specific semantics that force users to be stationary while using them (i.e., semantics in the right branch of the decision tree in Figure 3b). It shows that coin operated machines (the coarse-grained category) can be detected with near 100% accuracy using their unique inertial sensors pattern. To classify coin operated machines to their fine-grained categories (drink vending machines, ticket vending machines and lockers), the acoustic based detection scheme can achieve a good accuracy with 10.4% and 6.9% for false positive and false negative rates respectively on average. This is due to the responsive sound of vending machines that is universally used in many stations in Japan[10], making it an identifiable signature for classification. On the other hand, standing and waiting for train activities are sometimes interchangeably misclassified. For example, when a user is standing on the platform (to answer a phone call), this may be interpreted as waiting for train and oppositely the user may be waiting for train but it is misclassified as standing when the system failed to recognize that the user is on the platform. *TransitLabel* lessens this effect by using the transportation mode detection algorithm to detect when the train has moved, which comes after the waiting for train inactivity, as opposed to any other type of inactivity. The confusion matrix of classifying semantics from non stationary traces (i.e., semantics in the left branch of the decision tree in Figure 3b) is shown in Table 4. The table shows that *TransitLabel* can reliably detect crossing entrance gates using a ticket. The detection of crossing of entrance gates by IC cards is a bit challenging as some passengers either do not slow down their walking sufficiently or walk very slowly making their signature similar to ticket-based methods. Even worse, sometimes the card reader does not recognize the IC card and the passenger has to rollback and cross the gate again. However, since all gates have IC card readers and ticket slots integrated into the same machine, the two entrance methods (IC card and ticket) are aggregated into one semantic (entrance gate) that can be identified with 5.9% and 6% false positive and false negative rates, respectively. Moreover, the detection of train boarding is sometimes misclassified as crossing a gate by an IC card. The main reason is that train motors and electrical inverters emit large magnetic noise during the acceleration periods of the train which sometimes coincides with the pattern arising when the user crosses a gate using an IC card. To reduce this, *TransitLabel* leverages the sound emitted when the IC card touches the reader. Nevertheless, there is a trade-off between energy consumption and the semantic detection accuracy in this case.

[10]Vending machines around Japan are similar in their user interface and hardware to facilitate the Human-Machine interaction as well as to be able to recognize the same IC card types used to pay transit fees and drinks cost across the country.

Figure 13 reports the accuracy of detecting the waiting line locations, as computed by *TransitLabel*. Aligned with our intuition, the accuracy of waiting line locations detection relies on their placement with respect to the platform accesses. Due to the limited area of platform (average dimension is 160m$\times$12m), the short movement of a user on the platform (Figure 12), and the average inter-distance between waiting-line (5.2m); *TransitLabel* can estimate the line positions accurately, especially those near to the platform accesses where most user trails are short and thus the location accuracy is high [3,42].

Finally, *TransitLabel* can consistently detect the fine-grained classes of semantics accurately with 7.7% false positive rate and 7.5% false negative rates on average.

5.2.2 Discovered Semantics Location Accuracy

In this subsection, we study how much data is enough for *TransitLabel* to estimate semantics locations accurately as in crowdsensing-based systems the accumulation of more samples will enhance the system performance. Figure 14 quantifies the effect of the number of crowd-sensed samples on the accuracy of semantics (apart from waiting lines). The figure shows that even if some semantics have some outliers, the system can achieve a good accuracy in estimating their locations. This stems from the fact that independent correct samples of the same semantic are in adjacent locations and tend to cluster while erroneous samples are widely scattered in the spatial space and do not form a cluster. In addition, *TransitLabel* works offline so as a user encounters a semantic, *TransitLabel* learns her errors, and therefore can track back and partly correct her past trail thus the effect of the cold start problem is mitigated. Finally, as stations are rich with semantics, the localization error grows and sharply drops at semantics curbing the localization error and in its turn enhances the semantic location accuracy. Even though the instantaneous PDR error still has an effect on the semantics locations estimation, especially when the number of samples of semantics are small, it is evident from the figure that this error will drop quickly as the number of crowd-sensed samples increases. *TransitLabel* can consistently achieve the accuracy of 2.5m using as few as 40 samples for each discovered semantic type. Thus, *TransitLabel* converges reasonably quickly. However, we note that it needs to be periodically run to handle dynamic environment changes.

5.2.3 Energy Consumption

Figure 15 shows the energy consumption of *TransitLabel* averaged over typical traces from entering the station to boarding trains. For this, we run an application that samples the GPS every second to show the contrast in power consumption (*GPS is neither available in all locations in stations nor able to detect semantics but it is used as a baseline system*). The energy is calculated using the PowerTutor profiler [22] and the Android APIs using the HTC Nexus One cell phone. *TransitLabel* leverages the inertial sensors for passengers' activity recognition and position estimation. Since inertial sensors are indeed used during the normal phone operation, to detect the phone orientation change or estimate the user location for any indoor LBS, *TransitLabel* practically consumes little **extra** sensing power in addition to the standard phone operation. In addition, the sound sensor; which has a higher energy footprint; is

Table 2: Confusion Matrix for classifying different **elevation change** semantics.

	Elevator (Single)	Elevator (Double)	Stairs (Straight)	Stairs (Half-land.)	Escalator (Stand.)	Escalator (Climb.)	Escalator (Over.)	FP	FN	∑
Elevator (Single)	**100**	5	0	0	0	0	0	6.7%	4.8%	105
Elevator (Double)	7	**79**	0	0	0	0	0	5.8%	8.1%	86
Stairs (Straight)	0	0	**111**	0	0	9	9	0%	7.5%	120
Stairs (Half-land.)	0	0	0	**51**	0	0	0	0%	0%	51
Escalator (Stand.)	0	0	0	0	**114**	0	-	-	-	114
Escalator (Climb.)	0	0	0	0	0	**107**	-	-	-	107
Escalator (Over.)	0	0	0	0	-	-	**221**	4.1%	0%	221
Total								3.3%	4.1%	583

Table 3: Confusion Matrix for classifying different stations specific semantics discovered from **stationary** traces.

	Drink Vending Machine	Ticket Vending Machine	Locker	Restroom	Waiting (Sitting) Area	Standing	Cars' Waiting Lines	FP	FN	∑
Drink Vending Machine	**123**	1	6	0	0	0	1	7.6%	6.1%	131
Ticket Vending Machine	9	**260**	12	0	0	0	0	3.2%	7.5%	281
Locker	1	8	**119**	0	0	0	0	20.3%	7%	128
Restroom	0	0	4	**87**	2	4	0	7.2%	10.3%	97
Waiting (Sitting) Area	0	0	0	4	**88**	6	3	11.9%	12.9%	101
Standing	0	0	3	3	7	**140**	5	11.4%	11.4%	158
Cars' Waiting lines (waiting for a train)	0	0	1	0	3	8	**125**	6.6%	8.8%	137
Total								9.7%	9.1%	1033

Table 4: Confusion Matrix for classifying different stations specific semantics discovered from **non stationary** traces.

	Walking	Platform Track (Boarding)	Entrance Gate (Ticket)	Entrance gate (IC Card)	Entrance gate (Overall)	FP	FN	∑
Walking	**170**	7	5	9	14	10.5%	11%	191
Platform Track (Boarding)	3	**135**	2	11	13	15.2%	10.6%	151
Entrance Gate (Ticket)	9	2	**264**	6	-	-	-	281
Entrance gate (IC Card)	8	14	9	**234**	-	-	-	265
Entrance gate (Overall)	17	16	-	-	**513**	4.9%	6.0%	546
Total						10.2%	9.2%	888

Table 5: The semantics classification accuracy in a **one-station-out** cross validation.

	Elevator(S.)	**Elevator (D.)**	**Stairs (Str.)**	**Stairs (Half.)**	**Escalator**	**Drink Vd. Mch.**	**Ticket Vd. Mch.**	**Lock.**	**Restr.**	**Sit. Area**	**Wait. Lines**	**Plat. Tr.**	**Entr. gate**	∑
FP	8.6%	4.6%	0%	0%	5.4%	9.1%	3.9%	21%	8.2%	10.8%	8%	9.2%	5.3%	7.2%
FN	3.8%	10.4%	10%	0%	0%	7.6%	8.2%	8.6%	9.3%	15.8%	10.2%	11.9%	8.6%	8.0%

activated only shortly during the time of activities (average activity duration is short- 27 seconds- excluding the restroom). This also avoids the impact of false positive triggers of the sound sensor (e.g., sensor being activated while the user is standing doing a phone call). Finally, as soon as the user waits for the train on the platform, we suspend the activation of the sound sensor. All lead to a low energy consumption of *TransitLabel* that is significantly (44%) less than the GPS consumption.

5.2.4 *Impact of the Phone Placement*

To demonstrate that our approach is robust to different device placements, we carried out experiments on different phone placements (in a user hand or in a trouser pocket). Figure 16 shows the semantics detection accuracy as measured by the F-measure [11] in both phone placements. The results suggest that the semantic accuracy is not significantly dependent on device poses, with *TransitLabel* achieving a high accuracy of about 80% at least (in the case of non-stationary traces which is the most tricky case due to the effect of the legs movement on the phone in the pocket reading). *This robustness mainly comes from the transformation of sensor readings to the real world coordinates and the extraction of placement-independent features from phone sensors.* For example, the magnetometer readings features are not largely attenuated by human bodies (i.e., in pocket). While the acceleration can be affected by the motion noise to some extent, its impact is effectively mitigated by smoothing the raw acceleration and averaging the acceleration variance over a long time window. Finally, the collected audio data is not much derailed by the phone placement in pocket as passengers are forced to be close to semantics at the usage time. Note that *TransitLabel* uses different thresholds values to identify passenger's activities depending on the phone placement (pocket or hand). Nonetheless, the light proximity sensor can be used to detect the phone position and, accordingly, decide which thresholds value to be used. Other phone positions can be handled in a similar manner, which is a subject of future work for space constraints.

[11] F-measure is the harmonic mean of precision and recall and represents a single number for comparison.

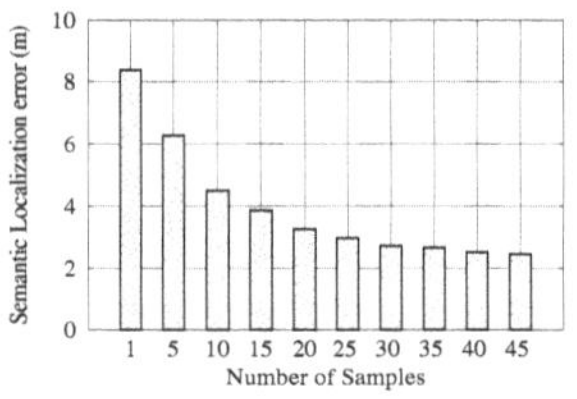

Figure 14: Effect of the number of samples on the accuracy of semantics location estimation.

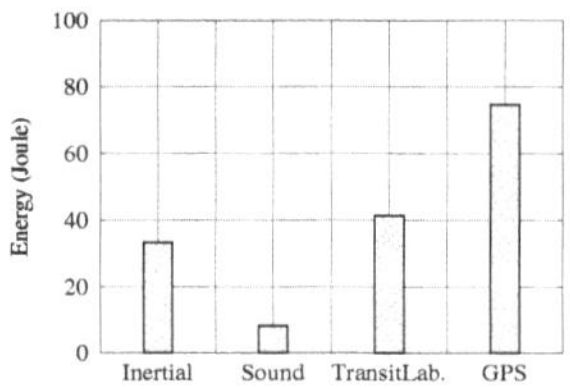

Figure 15: Energy footprint of *TransitLabel.*

5.2.5 *Generalization of TransitLabel*

We based our semantics identification on their typical usage pattern/signature by the majority of train commuters. However, some users may have different usage patterns (regular versus occasional travelers) and some stations have different building structures and different machines hardware (e.g., vending machines) that may lead

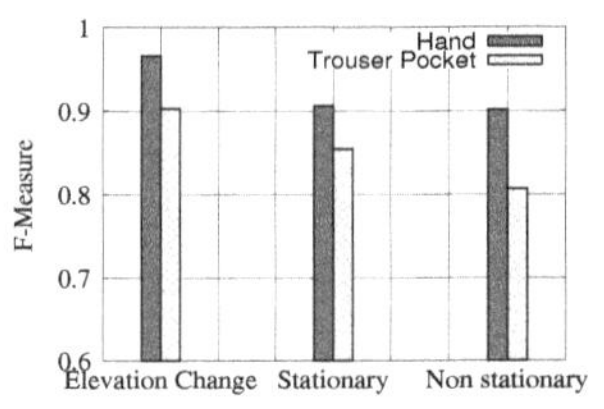

Figure 16: The Impact of phone placement on the semantics detection accuracy.

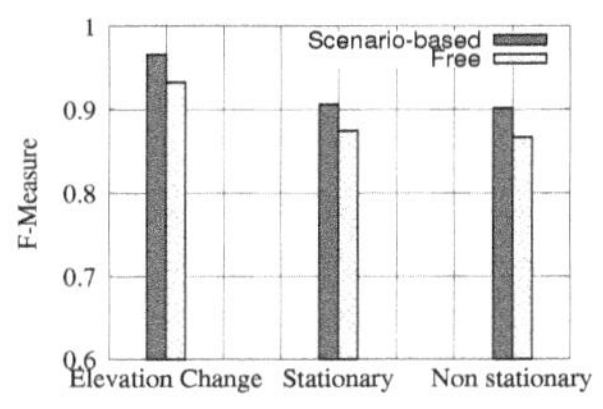

Figure 17: The generalization experiment of *TransitLabel* semantic detection.

to some semantics misclassifications. Thus, to demonstrate that *TransitLabel* could generalize over various users and stations, we consider an experiment where a group of daily train commuters are asked to collect data ***freely (without prescribed scenarios)*** in different stations in two different cities managed by different train companies in Japan. Figure 17 shows the accuracy of the semantic detection by *TransitLabel*. The results demonstrate that *TransitLabel* can still achieve a comparable semantic detection accuracy to the scenario-based experiments. This robustness is mainly due to the uniform nature of passengers' activities at railway station. Specifically, most passengers follow similar routes, exhibit uniform behavior as they have a common target (boarding the train) starting from getting a ticket to boarding the train. In addition, *TransitLabel* fuses multiple features (e.g., accelerometer, gyroscope and magnetometer based features are fused to identify the coin operated machines as shown in the classification tree in Figure 3b) to identify the same semantic, reducing the sensitivity to specific scenarios or machines.

Per-Station Accuracy: To understand the classification accuracy on a per-station basis, we show a one-station-out cross validation (one station data is selected as the validation data while all data collected at other stations is used as the database) results in Table 5. Evident from the table, the classification accuracy does not deviate much between different stations due to fusing many features and the uniform railway passengers' behaviors. This further emphasizes the generalization ability of *TransitLabel*.

6 Discussion and Limitations

We discuss some crowd-sensing challenges addressed by the current version of *TransitLabel* along with our ongoing work.

System Robustness

Our evaluation, quantified in Section 5, is carried out by different users using different phones in different placement through different data collection methodologies and spanned different stations and cities in Japan. These extensive experiments verified *TransitLabel* robustness under a wide range of scenarios. We believe that this robustness is based on a number of factors/design decisions including reorienting the phone sensors data, harnessing offset-invariant and orientation-invariant features, multi-modal sensor fusion, and combining a number of low level activities to identify the higher level passengers' activity. All allow *TransitLabel* to generalize to different stations run by different operators, users, devices, and operation scenarios.

Scalability

We have tested *TransitLabel* extensively in eight railway stations by 16 users under different scenarios. Scaling *TransitLabel* to a worldwide scale is directly based on location clustering and leveraging the cloud. In particular, the semantics of each station can be processed independently of other stations based on the location of the collected traces. This spatial clustering lends itself nicely to the processing in the cloud, further enhancing the system scalability.

Preserving User's Privacy

TransitLabel gives users full control over their sensed data and processes the audio data locally on the user's phone. Nonetheless, some users may opt to turn off the sound or other sensors for privacy concerns. However, since *TransitLabel* is a crowd-based system, it will still be able to identify these semantics from the samples submitted by other users.

Handling Dynamic Changes

The station internal structures may evolve over time and, accordingly, the state of the different semantics (location changed or removed). To address this, *TransitLabel* periodically rerun its clustering algorithm across time windows of different granularity to detect the removal of specific semantics. Specifically, the lack of a cluster with a specific size at the location of a previously detected semantic indicates the removal of this semantic. If clusters of correct samples of a semantic type formed in consecutive windows are being mapped to a location that vary substantially from old instances locations, this is indicative of a change in the environment. To classify the change type, we monitor newly uploaded samples of each instance of a semantic type. The change of location of a specific semantic is treated as a simple removal of this landmark and detecting it at a new location. We leave the evaluation of this aspect to future work due to space constraints.

Other Indoor Environments

Although *TransitLabel* is designed for railway stations, it can be customized to other indoor environments, e.g., airports, that have similar semantics (e.g., elevators, stairs, escalators, vending machines, lockers, security gates, and automated boarding-pass printing machine). Moreover, *TransitLabel* can be extended to use semi-unsupervised learning techniques [3,42] to extend to new environments without any prior knowledge about what activities are expected. Specifically, new automatically learned semantic classes can be presented to a human user to provide the label to them, significantly reducing the overhead of extending *TransitLabel* to new environments.

7 Related Work

The ideas in *TransitLabel* are built on three threads of research: mobile phone localization, human activity recognition and floorplan construction. We survey the most relevant work in each thread in the interest of space.

Mobile Phone Localization

Mobile phone localization has been well-studied with a variety of approaches so far [43]. As GPS signal is not available in many stations (e.g., subway stations), an indoor localization technique is needed to estimate the passenger's location. The most ubiquitous indoor localization techniques are either WiFi-based or dead-reckoning based. WiFi-based techniques, e.g., [12, 14, 24, 45–48], require calibration to create a prior wireless map for the building. However, the calibration process is time consuming, tedious, and requires periodic updates; leading to the emergence of new calibration-free techniques [13]. Dead-reckoning based localization techniques, e.g., [26, 42], leverage the inertial sensors on mobile phones to dead-reckon the user starting from a reference point [26]. However, dead-reckoning error quickly accumulates leading

to complete deviation from the actual path. Therefore, many techniques have been proposed to reset the dead-reckoning error including snapping to environment anchor points, such as elevators and stairs [3,42] and matching with the map information either indoor [34] or outdoor [4,5].
TransitLabel employs the basic concept in [3,42] as it provides accurate, energy-efficient localization, and does not require an infrastructure support. However, *TransitLabel* discovers novel, activity-based, fine-grained and richer set of semantics targeting railway stations (e.g., vending machines, lockers, entrance gates, platforms, waiting (sitting) areas, among others) to reset the accumulated localization error frequently.

Human Activity Recognition
Activity recognition literature has demonstrated the ability to recognize user behavior using phone equipped sensors. Accelerometer data was used to detect the user transportation mode (walking, stationary, being in motorized transport) [1, 23, 28, 36, 41] and it can classify more fine-grained activities and attributes like running, breathing rate, climbing up the stairs, biking, cleaning kitchen, vacuuming, and brushing teeth [2,6,18,29,35]. Moreover, accelerometer data is used to detect more complex human activities like biking, lying, cleaning kitchen, cooking, sweeping, washing hands, and medication [11]. Ambient sensors like temperature, humidity, pressure, and light have been used to label user's location directly as being in kitchen, bedroom, bathroom and living room [30]. Moreover, the AmbientSense system [37] can recognize 23 different contexts (e.g., coffee machine, raining, restaurant, dishwasher, toilet flush, etc) by analyzing ambient sounds sampled from phone. In addition, the RoomSense system in [38] uses active sound probing to classify the type of room (e.g., corridor, kitchen, lecture room, etc) where the user is located. Ref. [20] actively probes the environment and then analyzes the impulse response on the phone to separate restroom from other rooms. Recently, RF-based device-free activity tracking and recognition has been used to detect different activities and the location of the person using standard RF networks [27,39,44].
TransitLabel recognizes a higher level and novel set of passenger activities at railway stations. The crowd-sensed locations of these activities are then mined to discover their uniquely associated stations semantics.

Automatic Floorplan Construction
Recently, a number of systems have been proposed that employ pedestrian motion traces to automatically construct indoor floorplans [7, 15–17, 21, 25, 40]. For instance, CrowdInside [7] processes inertial motion traces using computational geometry techniques to extract the overall floorplan shape as well as corridors and room boundaries. It also identifies a variety of points of interest in the environment such as elevators and stairs. However, their semantic detection method neither targets stations specific semantics (e.g., entrance gate, etc) nor it provides fine-grained classes of elevation change semantics (e.g., stair types and elevator types). In addition, their elevator detection algorithm leverages only the motion pattern (Accelerate-Constant-Decelerate) which may coincide with normal human walking patterns. This cannot happen in our method as normal walking traces are separated beforehand using the semantic type detection module. Finally, different passengers' behaviors (e.g., climbing up or standing in escalators) makes the low acceleration variance, used in their method, is not a reliable discriminator between climbing stairs and escalators. Jigsaw [21] uses a computer vision approach to extract the position, size, and orientation of landmark objects from images taken by users. It then combines user mobility traces and locations where images are taken to produce the hallway connectivity and the room size. The system proposed in [25] leverages Wi-Fi fingerprints and user motion information to determine which rooms are adjacent in the building and estimating their sizes. It then orders them along each hallway and adjusts the room sizes to optimize the overall floorplan layout. *Nevertheless, all previous systems did not attach any semantic information to the floorplan layout.* Finally, Ref. [33] assumes that there is a difference in time to change floors using elevators, escalators, and stairs and thus relies on the rate of height change (i.e., pressure) to separate them. However, this hypothesis is neither robust to different users walking speeds nor to different elevators/ escalators motion speeds.
The closest work to ours is the automatic enrichment of indoor floorplans with semantic names technique in [17]. It exploits phone sensors data collected from users during their normal check-ins to location-based social networks (LBSNs) (e.g., Foursquare) and combines them with data extracted from the LBSNs databases to associate a place name with its location on an unlabeled floorplan. This system, however, can be applied only to indoor environments where the check-ins granularity level matches the semantic names needed to enrich the map. For example, in shopping malls, user check-ins with venues names which can by leveraged by Semsense [17] to attach a venue name to each room in the floorplan. However, users at railway stations usually do check-ins with stations names (they don't check-in using fine-grained station indoor semantics names) which is not sufficient to infer and locate the in-station semantics.
TransitLabel assumes in its operation the availability of an unlabeled station floorplan by using one of these approaches. It then enriches the input floorplan with different semantics based on data collected from users' phones.

8 Conclusion

We presented the *TransitLabel* system for automatically enriching transit indoor maps via a crowdsensing approach based on standard cell phones. For energy efficiency, *TransitLabel* leverages low-energy phone sensors and sensors that are already running for other purposes (e.g., inertial sensors). We presented the *TransitLabel* architecture as well as the features and classifiers that can accurately recognize different passenger's activities in railway stations which are mined to detect their uniquely associated semantics.
We implemented *TransitLabel* using commodity mobile phones running the Android operating system and evaluated it at different railway stations in Japan. Our results show that *TransitLabel* can detect stations fine-grained semantics accurately with 7.7% false positive and 7.5% false negative rates on average leading to high accuracy in semantics location estimation. Finally, *TransitLabel* can be generalized over various stations running by different operators and user groups; and is robust to different phone placements while having a significantly small energy profile.
Currently we are expanding *TransitLabel* in multiple directions including inferring more station semantics, handling dynamic changes in the environment, deployment of *TransitLabel* in other indoor environments, among others.

9 Acknowledgement

We sincerely thank the anonymous reviewers for their invaluable feedback which helped improve the paper.
This work is supported in part by JSPS KAKENHI grant numbers 26220001, 15H02690, and 26700006 to Osaka University and in part by a Google Research Award to E-JUST.

10 References

[1] A. M. AbdelAziz and M. Youssef. The diversity and scale matter: Ubiquitous transportation mode detection using single cell tower information. In *Proceedings of the 81st Vehicular Technology Conference (VTC Spring)*, pages 1–5. IEEE, 2015.

[2] H. Abdelnasser, K. A. Harras, and M. Youssef. UbiBreathe: A ubiquitous non-invasive WiFi-based breathing estimator. *Proceedings of the 16th ACM International Symposium on Mobile Ad Hoc Networking and Computing (MobiHoc)*, pages 277–286, 2015.

[3] H. Abdelnasser, R. Mohamed, A. Elgohary, M. Farid, H. Wang, S. Sen, R. Choudhury, and M. Youssef. SemanticSLAM: Using environment landmarks for unsupervised indoor localization. *IEEE Transactions on Mobile Computing*, (1):1–1.

[4] H. Aly, A. Basalamah, and M. Youssef. Map++: A crowd-sensing system for automatic map semantics identification. In *Proceedings of the Eleventh Annual IEEE International Conference on Sensing, Communication, and Networking (SECON)*, pages 546–554. IEEE, 2014.

[5] H. Aly and M. Youssef. Dejavu: An accurate energy-efficient outdoor localization system. In *Proceedings of the 21st ACM International Conference on Advances in Geographic Information Systems (SIGSPATIAL)*, pages 154–163. ACM, 2013.

[6] H. Aly and M. Youssef. Zephyr: Ubiquitous accurate multi-sensor fusion-based respiratory rate estimation using smartphones. In *Proceedings of IEEE Conference on Computer Communications (INFOCOM)*. IEEE, 2016.

[7] M. Alzantot and M. Youssef. CrowdInside: Automatic construction of indoor floorplans. In *Proceedings of the 20th International Conference on Advances in Geographic Information Systems (SIGSPATIAL)*, pages 99–108. ACM, 2012.

[8] M. Alzantot and M. Youssef. UPTIME: Ubiquitous pedestrian tracking using mobile phones. In *Proceedings of Wireless Communications and Networking Conference (WCNC)*, pages 3204–3209. IEEE, 2012.

[9] Y. Chon, N. D. Lane, Y. Kim, F. Zhao, and H. Cha. Understanding the coverage and scalability of place-centric crowdsensing. In *Proceedings of the 2013 ACM international joint conference on Pervasive and ubiquitous computing (UbiComp)*, pages 3–12. ACM, 2013.

[10] W. S. Cleveland and S. J. Devlin. Locally weighted regression: An approach to regression analysis by local fitting. *Journal of the American Statistical Association*, 83(403), 1988.

[11] S. Dernbach, B. Das, N. C. Krishnan, B. L. Thomas, and D. J. Cook. Simple and complex activity recognition through smart phones. In *Proceedings of 8th International Conference on Intelligent Environments (IE)*, pages 214–221. IEEE, 2012.

[12] K. El-Kafrawy, M. Youssef, A. El-Keyi, and A. Naguib. Propagation modeling for accurate indoor WLAN RSS-based localization. In *Proceedings of the 72nd Vehicular Technology Conference Fall (VTC -Fall)*, pages 1–5. IEEE, 2010.

[13] R. Elbakly and M. Youssef. A robust zero-calibration RF-based localization system for realistic environments. In *Proceedings of the Annual IEEE International Conference on Sensing, Communication, and Networking (SECON)*. IEEE, 2016.

[14] A. Eleryan, M. Elsabagh, and M. Youssef. Synthetic generation of radio maps for device-free passive localization. In *Proceedings of the Global Telecommunications Conference (GLOBECOM)*, pages 1–5. IEEE, 2011.

[15] M. Elhamshary, A. Uchiyama, H. Yamaguchi, and T. Higashino. LandmarkSense: A Mobile Sensing System for Automatic Detection of Railway Stations Landmarks. Technical report, IPSJ SIG, 12 2015.

[16] M. Elhamshary and M. Youssef. CheckInside: A fine-grained indoor location-based social network. In *Proceedings of the International Joint Conference on Pervasive and Ubiquitous Computing (UbiComp)*, pages 607–618. ACM, 2014.

[17] M. Elhamshary and M. Youssef. SemSense: Automatic construction of semantic indoor floorplans. In *Proceedings of the 6th International Conference on Indoor Positioning and Indoor Navigation (IPIN)*, pages 1–11. IEEE, 2015.

[18] M. Elhamshary, M. Youssef, A. Uchiyama, H. Yamaguchi, and T. Higashino. Activity recognition of railway passengers by fusion of low-power sensors in mobile phones. In *Proceedings of the 23rd International Conference on Advances in Geographic Information Systems (SIGSPATIAL)*, page 57. ACM, 2015.

[19] M. Ester, H.-P. Kriegel, J. Sander, and X. Xu. A density-based algorithm for discovering clusters in large spatial databases with noise. In *Kdd*, volume 96, pages 226–231, 1996.

[20] M. Fan, A. T. Adams, and K. N. Truong. Public restroom detection on mobile phone via active probing. In *Proceedings of the 2014 ACM International Symposium on Wearable Computers (ISWC)*, pages 27–34. ACM, 2014.

[21] R. Gao, M. Zhao, T. Ye, F. Ye, Y. Wang, K. Bian, T. Wang, and X. Li. Jigsaw: Indoor floor plan reconstruction via mobile crowdsensing. In *Proceedings of the 20th annual international conference on Mobile computing and networking (MobiCom)*, pages 249–260. ACM, 2014.

[22] M. Gordon et al. PowerTutor: a power monitor for android-based mobile platforms, 2013.

[23] S. Hemminki, P. Nurmi, and S. Tarkoma. Accelerometer-based transportation mode detection on smartphones. In *Proceedings of the 11th ACM Conference on Embedded Networked Sensor Systems (SenSys)*, page 13. ACM, 2013.

[24] M. Ibrahim and M. Youssef. A hidden markov model for localization using low-end GSM cell phones. In *Proceedings of IEEE International Conference on Communications (ICC)*, pages 1–5. IEEE, 2011.

[25] Y. Jiang, Y. Xiang, X. Pan, K. Li, Q. Lv, R. P. Dick, L. Shang, and M. Hannigan. Hallway based automatic indoor floorplan construction using room fingerprints. In *Proceedings of the 2013 ACM international joint conference on Pervasive and ubiquitous computing (UbiComp)*, pages 315–324. ACM, 2013.

[26] Y. Jin, H.-S. Toh, W.-S. Soh, and W.-C. Wong. A robust dead-reckoning pedestrian tracking system with low cost sensors. In *Proceedings of IEEE International Conference on Pervasive Computing and Communications (PerCom)*, pages 222–230. IEEE, 2011.

[27] A. E. Kosba, A. Abdelkader, and M. Youssef. Analysis of a device-free passive tracking system in typical wireless environments. In *Proceedings of the 3rd International*

Conference on New Technologies, Mobility and Security (NTMS), pages 1–5. IEEE, 2009.

[28] J. Krumm and E. Horvitz. LOCADIO: Inferring motion and location from Wi-Fi signal strengths. In *Proceedings of the Second Annual International Conference on Mobile and Ubiquitous Systems: Networking and Services (MobiQuitous)*, pages 4–13, 2004.

[29] J. R. Kwapisz, G. M. Weiss, and S. A. Moore. Activity recognition using cell phone accelerometers. *ACM SigKDD Explorations Newsletter*, 12(2):74–82, 2011.

[30] S. Mazilu and G. Troster. A study on using ambient sensors from smartphones for indoor location detection. In *Proceedings of 12th Workshop On positioning, navigation and communication (WPNC)*. IEEE, 2015.

[31] P. Mohan, V. N. Padmanabhan, and R. Ramjee. Nericell: Rich monitoring of road and traffic conditions using mobile smartphones. In *Proceedings of the 6th ACM conference on Embedded network sensor systems (SenSys)*, pages 323–336. ACM, 2008.

[32] N. Mohssen, R. Momtaz, H. Aly, and M. Youssef. It's the human that matters: Accurate user orientation estimation for mobile computing applications. In *Proceedings of the 11th International Conference on Mobile and Ubiquitous Systems: Computing, Networking and Services (MobiQuitous)*, pages 70–79. ICST, 2014.

[33] K. Muralidharan, A. J. Khan, A. Misra, R. K. Balan, and S. Agarwal. Barometric phone sensors: More hype than hope!. In *Proceedings of the 15th Workshop on Mobile Computing Systems and Applications (HotMobile)*, pages 12–18. ACM, 2014.

[34] A. Rai, K. K. Chintalapudi, V. N. Padmanabhan, and R. Sen. Zee: Zero-effort crowdsourcing for indoor localization. In *Proceedings of the 18th annual international conference on Mobile computing and networking (MobiCom)*, pages 293–304. ACM, 2012.

[35] N. Ravi, N. Dandekar, P. Mysore, and M. L. Littman. Activity recognition from accelerometer data. In *AAAI*, volume 5, pages 1541–1546, 2005.

[36] S. Reddy, M. Mun, J. Burke, D. Estrin, M. Hansen, and M. Srivastava. Using mobile phones to determine transportation modes. *ACM Transactions on Sensor Networks (TOSN)*, 6(2):13, 2010.

[37] M. Rossi, S. Feese, O. Amft, N. Braune, S. Martis, and G. Troster. AmbientSense: A real-time ambient sound recognition system for smartphones. In *Proceedings of IEEE International Conference on Pervasive Computing and Communications Workshops (PERCOM Workshops)*, pages 230–235. IEEE, 2013.

[38] M. Rossi, J. Seiter, O. Amft, S. Buchmeier, and G. Tröster. RoomSense: An indoor positioning system for smartphones using active sound probing. In *Proceedings of the 4th Augmented Human International Conference (AH)*, pages 89–95. ACM, 2013.

[39] M. Seifeldin and M. Youssef. A deterministic large-scale device-free passive localization system for wireless environments. In *Proceedings of the 3rd International Conference on PErvasive Technologies Related to Assistive Environments (PETRA)*, page 51. ACM, 2010.

[40] H. Shin, Y. Chon, and H. Cha. Unsupervised construction of an indoor floor plan using a smartphone. *IEEE Transactions on Systems, Man, and Cybernetics, Part C: Applications and Reviews*, 42(6):889–898, 2012.

[41] T. Sohn, A. Varshavsky, A. LaMarca, M. Y. Chen, T. Choudhury, I. Smith, S. Consolvo, J. Hightower, W. G. Griswold, and E. De Lara. Mobility detection using everyday GSM traces. In *Proceedings of international conference on Ubiquitous Computing (UbiComp)*, pages 212–224. Springer, 2006.

[42] H. Wang, S. Sen, A. Elgohary, M. Farid, M. Youssef, and R. R. Choudhury. No need to war-drive: unsupervised indoor localization. In *Proceedings of the 10th international conference on Mobile systems, applications, and services (MobiSys)*, pages 197–210. ACM, 2012.

[43] M. Youssef. Towards truly ubiquitous indoor localization on a worldwide scale. In *Proceedings of the 23rd International Conference on Advances in Geographic Information Systems (SIGSPATIAL)*, page 12. ACM, 2015.

[44] M. Youssef. A Decade Later - Challenges: Device-free passive localization for wireless environments. In *Proceedings of the Fifth IEEE COSDEO Workshop, IEEE PerCom*, 2016.

[45] M. Youssef, M. Abdallah, and A. Agrawala. Multivariate analysis for probabilistic WLAN location determination systems. In *Proceedings of the Second Annual International Conference on Mobile and Ubiquitous Systems: Networking and Services (MobiQuitous)*, pages 353–362. IEEE, 2005.

[46] M. Youssef and A. Agrawala. The Horus WLAN location determination system. In *Proceedings of the 3rd international conference on Mobile systems, applications, and services (MobiSys)*, pages 205–218. ACM, 2005.

[47] M. Youssef and A. Agrawala. Location-clustering techniques for WLAN location determination systems. *International Journal of Computers and Applications*, 28(3):278–284, 2006.

[48] M. Youssef and A. Agrawala. The Horus location determination system. *Wireless Networks*, 2008.

Reactive Control of Autonomous Drones

Endri Bregu[†], Nicola Casamassima[†], Daniel Cantoni[†],
Luca Mottola[†*], and Kamin Whitehouse[‡]
[†]Politecnico di Milano (Italy), [*]SICS Swedish ICT, [‡]University of Virginia (USA)
Contact author: luca.mottola@polimi.it

ABSTRACT

Aerial drones, ground robots, and aquatic rovers enable mobile applications that no other technology can realize with comparable flexibility and costs. In existing platforms, the low-level control enabling a drone's autonomous movement is currently realized in a time-triggered fashion, which simplifies implementations. In contrast, we conceive a notion of *reactive control* that supersedes the time-triggered approach by leveraging the characteristics of existing control logic and of the hardware it runs on. Using reactive control, control decisions are taken only upon recognizing the need to, based on observed changes in the navigation sensors. As a result, the rate of execution *dynamically adapts* to the circumstances. Compared to time-triggered control, this allows us to: *i)* attain more timely control decisions, *ii)* improve hardware utilization, *iii)* lessen the need to over-provision control rates. Based on 260+ hours of real-world experiments using three aerial drones, three different control logic, and three hardware platforms, we demonstrate, for example, up to 41% improvements in control accuracy and up to 22% improvements in flight time.

1. INTRODUCTION

Aerial drones, ground robots, and aquatic rovers enable novel mobile applications. Compared to mobile phones and connected cars that only opportunistically sense or communicate, these platforms offer *direct control* over their movements. They can thus implement functionality that were previously beyond reach, such as collecting high-resolution imagery of civil infrastructures [10, 38], exploring near-inaccessible areas [16], or inspecting the sea floor to gain fine-grained environmental data [19, 54].

Existing platforms. Most existing drone platforms are architected as in Fig. 1. Two components are involved. Specialized software runs at a ground-control station (GCS) to let users configure mission parameters, such as the coordinates to cover through waypoint navigation and the action to take at each waypoint. The GCS is typically a standard computer that communicates with the drone using a long-range low-bandwidth radio.

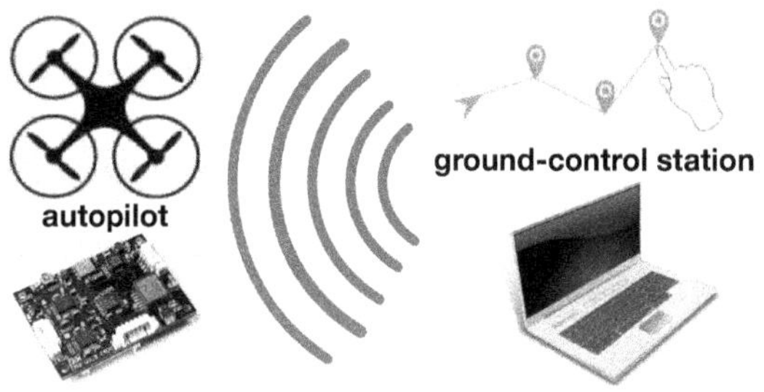

Figure 1: Software components in mainstream drone platforms. *The ground control station let users configure high-level mission parameters, the autopilot software implements the low-level motion control aboard the drone.*

Aboard the drone, the *autopilot* software implements the low-level control in charge of *autonomously* driving the drone to the next desired coordinate. The control loop processes various sensor inputs, such as accelerations and GPS coordinates, to operate actuators such as electrical motors that set the 3D orientation of the drone, also commonly termed as the drone's *attitude*. Because of size, cost, and energy concerns, autopilots run on resource-constrained embedded hardware. For example, ARM MCUs of the Cortex M series are often used as the main processing unit.

Together with the mechanical design, the low-level control determines the effectiveness of physical motion. For example, when using aerial drones in imagery applications, the low-level control directly influences the quality of the shots [37, 38]. Further, the low-level control is partly responsible for how the energy available from batteries is consumed. The drone's lifetime is often a result of how streamlined is its operation [11, 55].

Most existing autopilot implementations employ Proportional-Integral-Derivative (PID) [7] designs for low-level control. These controllers run in a time-triggered fashion: every T time units, sensors are probed, control decisions are computed, and commands are sent to the actuators. Such an approach enjoys the advantage of highly deterministic operation, which simplifies implementations.

Reactive control. Despite these advantages, current implementations overlook two essential aspects, as we further illustrate in Sec. 2:

1) Most PID controllers on the drones are tuned so that it is mostly the Proportional component to bear an influ-

MobiSys'16, June 25 - 30, 2016, Singapore, Singapore

ISBN 978-1-4503-4269-8/16/06...$15.00
DOI: http://dx.doi.org/10.1145/2906388.2906410

ence. As long as the weights are balanced, the Derivative component can be kept to a minimum [13, 26]. A proper calibration of navigation sensors may also reduce the Integral component [13, 26, 44]. This yields executions where: *i)* small variations in the sensor inputs tend to correspond to small variations in the actuator settings, and *ii)* as long as the sensor inputs do not change, the actuator settings remain almost unaltered. Therefore, *in principle*, one may spare control executions that starts from the same or similar sensor inputs as the previous iteration, by simply maintaining the earlier actuator settings. We quantitatively verify this intuition in Sec. 3 through real-world experiments.

2) Autopilot software typically runs on hardware that closely resembles mobile phones. This especially applies to the sensing equipment. Many argue that without the push to improve sensors due to the rise of mobile phones, drone technology would have not emerged [17]. These sensors are especially designed to enable energy-efficient high-frequency sensing; for example, for tracking human activity [20, 35]. Many of them can also be programmed to return a value only upon verifying certain conditions [27, 49]; for example, when a threshold is passed, which is useful to implement functionality such as fall detection [22].

Reactive control builds upon these observations. Rather than periodically triggering the control logic, we constantly monitor the navigation sensors and run the control logic only upon recognizing *the need to*. As a result, reactive control *dynamically adapts* the control rate. When sensor inputs change often, control runs repeatedly, possibly even more frequently than the fixed rate of a time-triggered implementation. When sensor inputs exhibit small or no variations, the rate of control execution reduces, freeing up resources that may be needed at different times. Unlike other emerging forms of asynchronous control [6], however, we require no changes to the underlying control logic. The design methodologies of traditional control still apply [7].

Reactive control yields several advantages, for example: *i)* it enables more timely and adaptive control decisions, *ii)* it spares unnecessary processing, improving the utilization of the hardware, and *iii)* it lessens the need to overprovision control rates to handle extreme situations. As it exclusively works in software, reactive control also requires no hardware modifications. Nevertheless, we demonstrate that reactive control is applicable beyond waypoint navigation. Further use cases include, for example, active sensing functionality [14, 36, 51] and advanced motion control [1].

Challenges and solutions. Realizing reactive control is, however, non-trivial. Three issues are to be solved:

1) What is a "significant" change in the sensor input depends on several factors, including the accuracy of sensor hardware, the physical characteristics of the drone, the control logic, and the granularity of actuator output. This notion is thus difficult to generalize. Sec. 4 illustrates our probabilistic approach to tackle this problem, which *abstracts* from all these aspects by employing a form of auto-tuning of the conditions leading to running the control logic.
2) An indication for running the control logic may originate from different sensors, at different rates, and asynchronously with respect to each other. One problem is thus how to handle the possible interleavings. Moreover, not running the control loop for too long may negatively affect the drone's stability, possibly preventing to reclaim the correct behavior. Sec. 5 illustrates how we tackle these issues by only changing the *execution* of the control logic over time, rather than the logic itself.
3) Reactive control must run on resource-constrained embedded hardware. When implementing reactive control, however, the code quickly turns into a "callback hell" [25] as the operation becomes inherently event-driven. We experimentally find that, using standard languages and compilers, this negatively affects the execution speed, thus limiting the gains. Sec. 6 describes our custom realization of reactive programming (RP) techniques [8] to tackle this problem.

Sec. 7 illustrates the effectiveness of reactive control compared to the time-triggered approach. We consider the challenging case of aerial drone control. These require continuous attitude adjustments because of the potentially severe environment influence, for example, due to wind gusts in unpredictable directions. We report on 260+ hours of test flights in three increasingly demanding environments, using a combination of three aerial drones, three autopilot software, and three embedded hardware platforms.

Our results indicate that reactive control obtains up to 41% improvements in the accuracy of motion, which results in up to 22% extension of flight times. We also demonstrate that our RP-based implementation is fundamental to obtain this performance, in that a traditional implementation would only obtain about half of the improvements. Finally, we report on the benefits reactive control provides in two end-user applications beyond waypoint navigation, including 3D reconstruction and active sensing in search-and-rescue scenarios.

2. BACKGROUND

First, we survey efforts in related areas, showing that the goal we pursue sets us apart from existing literature. Next, to better understand our context, we describe the Ardupilot [5] autopilot and supported hardware.

2.1 Related Work

The drones we target in this work can be regarded as a cruder form of modern robotics [17]. In this field, control operates at two levels. *High-level* control implements advanced navigation functionality, such as simultaneous localization and mapping [23], path planning [9], and obstacle avoidance [30]. In our context, this is the job of the GCS, even though it is certainly realized in a simplified form here.

The output of high-level control may be a waypoint or a trajectory, given as input to the *low-level* control that operates the robot actuators. In the majority of the cases, PID controllers are used for this [13]. The rate to run the controller is statically set to find a trade-off between accuracy and resource consumption, based on a few "rules of thumbs" [56]. In contrast, our goal is to run the PID controller in a reactive fashion, dynamically adapting to the circumstances dictated by, for example, the instantaneous environment influence.

In the field of aerial drones, demonstrations exist showing motion control in tasks such as throwing and catching balls [43] and poles [15], building architectural structures [32], flying in formation [50], and carrying large payloads [34]. In

Figure 2: Ardupilot's control loop. *The time for a single iteration of the loop is split between* fast loop, *which only includes critical motion control functionality, and an application-level* scheduler *that runs non-critical tasks.*

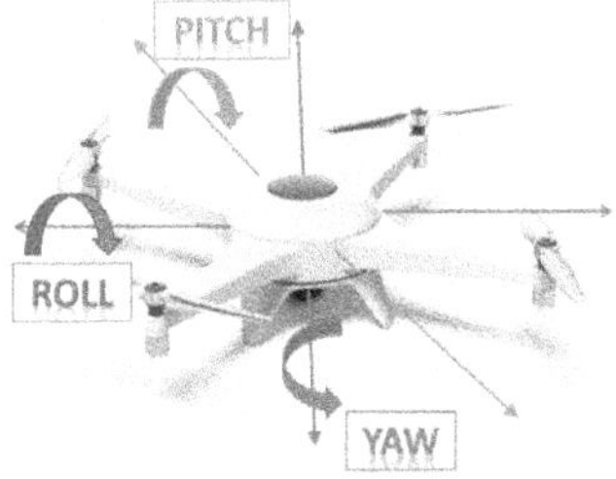

Figure 3: Attitude control with raw, pitch, and yaw.

these settings, the low-level control does not operate aboard the drone. At 100 Hz or more, a powerful computer receives accurate localization data [52], runs sophisticated control algorithms based on drone-specific mechanical models often expressed through differential equations, and sends actuator commands back to the drones. Differently, we aim at improving the performance of mainstream low-level control running on embedded hardware, targeting mobile sensing applications that operate in the wild.

On the surface, reactive control may resemble the notion of event-based control [6]. In the latter, however, the control logic is expressly redesigned for settings different than ours; for example, in distributed control systems to better cope with limited communication bandwidth. This requires an entirely different theoretical framework [6]. Our work aims at re-using existing control logic, whose properties are well understood. Different than event-based control, however, reactive control is mainly applicable only to PID-like controllers where the Proportional component dominates.

2.2 Autopilots

Autopilots provide critical functionality for the efficient and dependable operation of drone platforms. Their implementation is also often coupled with dedicated hardware.

Among available autopilot implementation, Ardupilot[1] is a mature open-source project that provides reliable autopilot functionality for aerial drones and ground robots [5]. The project is at the basis of many commercial products, including those of 3DRobotics [2] and many others, and boasts a large on-line community. Nonetheless, our evaluation in Sec. 7 demonstrates the applicability of reactive control with autopilots other than Ardupilot and dedicated hardware.

Software. Fig. 2 shows the execution of Ardupilot's control loop. Following the initial setup, the control loop is split in two parts. The *fast loop* only includes critical motion control functionality. The time left from the execution of *fast loop* is given to an application-level *scheduler* that distributes it among non-critical tasks that may not execute at every iteration, such as logging. The scheduler operates in a *best-effort* preemptable manner based on programmer-provided priorities. Many autopilots share similar designs [18, 39].

Initially, *fast loop* blocks waiting for a new value from the Inertial Measurement Unit (IMU), which provides an indication of the forces the drone is subject to in the three dimensions. This is obtained by combining the readings of accelerometers, gyroscopes, magnetometers, and barometers. Once a new value is available, IMU information is combined with GPS readings to determine updated attitude control by minimizing the error between the desired and actual pitch, roll, and yaw, shown in Fig. 3. Multiple PID controllers inside *fast loop* are used to this end. Their output is converted into commands sent to the motors to orient the drone.

Ardupilot well exemplifies the state of the art. Control is periodic and proceeds sequentially, which simplifies the implementation. Most importantly, the control rate is statically set as discussed in Sec. 2.1. For example, Ardupilot runs at a *fixed* 400 Hz on the hardware we describe next. This rate is not necessarily the maximum the hardware supports. The 400 Hz of Ardupilot, for example, are thought to leave enough room—on average—to the scheduler. In short bursts, control may run much faster than 400 Hz, as long as some resources are eventually allocated to the scheduler; for example, at times when control does not need to run that frequently. By recognizing the situations when control does need to run—or not—reactive control enables precisely this kind of dynamic adaptation of control rate.

Hardware. Ardupilot runs on various embedded hardware. A primary example is the Pixhawk board [41], which features a Cortex M4 core at 168 MHz and a full sensor array for navigation, including a 16-bit gyroscope, a 14-bit accelerometer/magnetometer, a 16-bit 3-axis accelerometer/gyroscope, and a 24-bit barometer. Most often, at least a sonar and a GPS are added to the built-in sensor array to provide positioning and altitude information, respectively.

The sensors on Pixhawk have similar capabilities as those on modern mobile phones. They support energy-efficient high-frequency sampling and often provide interrupt-driven modes to generate a value upon verifying certain conditions. The ST LSM303D [49] on the Pixhawk, for example, can be programmed to generate an SPI interrupt based on three thresholds. While useful, for example, in crowdsensing applications for specific functionality such as fall detection [35], these features are rarely exploited in autopilots.

The commands sent from the autopilot to the actuators are encoded in Pulse-Width Modulation (PWM). These are converted to a current flowing into the motors through dedicated Electronic Speed Controllers (ESC): tiny embedded boards that govern the current flow to the motors according to some analog input. Typically, ESCs hold the output value as long as the input does not change. Because of size and cost, ESCs are extremely primitive; most of them employing 8-bit Atmel ATMega MCUs. The granularity of their inputs/outputs is also often quite coarse. This further limits the degrees of changes to the actual motor operation.

3. MOTIVATION

Experimentally verifying that some iterations of the control loop are, in fact, unnecessary is a challenge per se. One issue is that of *visibility*: the most un-biased measure we may get is the current flowing into the motors, namely, the output of the ESC. Next is a problem of *realism*: one would

[1]At the start of the project, Ardupilot ran on Arduino hardware. However, developers eventually moved to more capable hardware while retaining the name.

(a) Quadcopter. (b) Hexacopter.

Figure 4: Custom aerial drones used to gain evidence of the opportunities for reactive control.

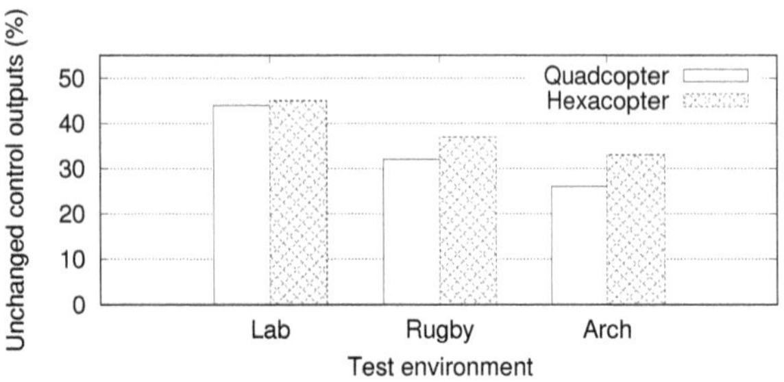

Figure 5: Preliminary experiments: fraction of time the control outputs do not change. *The less influence the environment plays, the more the control decisions tend to remain the same. The hexacopter shows higher values as it is more resilient to the environment.*

need to gather the measurements during actual operation. Finally, high-frequency logging is *expensive* on embedded hardware, and may affect the processing of the control loop.

Setup. To address the issues above, we instrument two custom-built aerial drones, shown in Fig. 4, with Hall-effect current sensors [47] placed between the ESC and the motors. We choose aerial drones because they represent a challenging case for autopilots, as they require continuous attitude adjustment. By contrast, for example, a ground robot may simply not run any control loop once it reaches the destination, as in most cases it naturally maintains the position. The Hall-effect sensors are sampled at the same rate of the control loop from an independently-powered Waspmote [31] aboard the drones. Data is dumped on an SD card. The measurement subsystem is thus completely decoupled from the drone, and does not affect its operation but for the minimal added weight.

We test several flight paths at a maximum speed of 3 m/s and 5 m altitude, each with 8 random waypoints in a loop and lasting at least 20 min, in three environments: *i)* a 20x20 m lab where drones localize themselves using on-drone visual techniques [42], termed LAB; *ii)* a rugby field in front of our department termed RUGBY, using GPS; and *iii)* an archaeological site in Aquileia (Italy) termed ARCH, the size of almost four soccer fields [36], stll using GPS. The sites exhibit increasing environment influence. LAB only suffers from air conditioning from the ceiling. RUGBY is protected on two sides by trees. ARCH lies in an area with average wind speeds of 8+ knots. We record a total of 10 flight hours for each drone in every site.

Results. Fig. 5 shows the fraction of samples from the Hall-effect sensor within the sensor accuracy of the previous sample. This quantity can be understood as the fraction of time the control decisions at one iteration are the same as the previous one. This figure is highest for LAB, because of the little environment influence. By contrast, the values are smallest for ARCH: sudden wind gusts may require unanticipated attitude corrections. The physical design also plays a role: the hexacopter, which is heavier and mounts more powerful motors, is more resilient. Thus, the control logic outputs the same decisions more often than the quadcopter.

Fig. 5 shows that there would be ample margin to spare a fraction of control executions, even in the most challenging environment, *if only one were able to recognize these unnecessary iterations beforehand.* By freeing resources when they are not needed, we may make them available when there is a need to promptly *react*, thus overcoming the limitations of a fixed control rate. Sparing unnecessary executions of the control logic may also create room for running additional functionality on the same hardware, or yield an opportunity for downsizing the hardware itself.

The rest of the paper describes how reactive control provides these benefits by changing the temporal execution of *existing* control logic. Three issues are to be addressed. Sec. 4 describes how to recognize, based only on sensor inputs and with minimal overhead, when there is a need for running the control logic. Next, Sec. 5 describes how to regulate the executions in a setting where different sensors may require running the control logic asynchronously with respect to each other. Sec. 6 describes how to implement these functionality efficiently on resource-constrained hardware.

4. CONDITIONS FOR REACTING

In principle, one may simply assume that control decisions do not change whenever the inputs do not change.

Problem. Although correct, such a reasoning is, in fact, quite naive. The control logic used to govern the drones is not at all trivial. It involves combining several readings from diverse sensors with varying precision and generated at different rates across multiple steps of processing. Moreover, the control logic runs on embedded resource-constrained hardware and using simplified numerical libraries, which affects the precision of processing. Thus, it is often the case that control decisions remain the same even when the sensor inputs *do change.*

The issue is thus to distinguish those changes in the sensor inputs that would alter the control decisions from those that would not. Whenever a sensor input changes in a way that—all other sensor inputs staying the same—the control decisions change as well, we say we record a *trigger* on that sensor. It is difficult to determine beforehand the conditions to search in the sensor readings to identify a trigger. Factors such as the accuracy and calibration of sensors, the physical characteristics of the drone, the control logic, and the granularity of actuator outputs all concur to determine these conditions.

Approach. We opt for a lightweight on-line approach that *self-adapts* to different instances of the aspects above *without* assuming any specific knowledge on any of them, including the control logic. This makes our approach applicable to different implementations, as we demonstrate in Sec. 7.

Despite the control logic is deterministic, we abstract away the underlying complexity by considering *a change in the control output* as a random phenomena. The input to this phenomena is the difference between consecutive samples of the same sensor; the output is a binary value indicating whether the control decisions change. An accurate statisti-

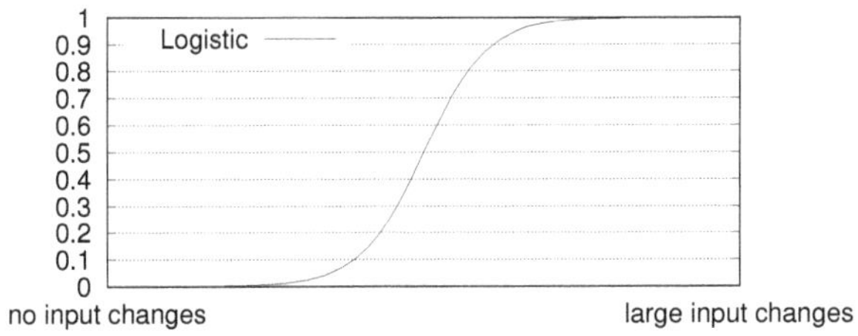

Figure 6: Example logistic function.

cal estimator of such phenomena would allow us to take an informed decision on whether to run the control logic.

Among statistical estimators with a *binary* dependent variable, *logistic regression* [28] is both simple and closely matches the intuition on when one would need to execute the control logic. Fig. 6 shows its probability distribution. For small changes in the sensor inputs, the probability of changes in the control outputs is small. When changes in sensor inputs are large, a change in the control decisions becomes (almost) certain. The logistic function we employ is expressed as:

$$L(x) = \frac{1}{1 + e^{-(\beta_1 + \beta_2 x)}} \quad (1)$$

where $L(x)$ is the probability of new control decisions compared to the previous iteration, given a change of x in the inputs of a navigation sensor. The problem thus becomes how to estimate parameters β_1 and β_2 at run-time. Existing results indicate that, for $0 < L(x) < 1$, eq. (1) can be re-written in *generalized linear form* [28]. Barring the cases $L(x) = 0$ and $L(x) = 1$, this allows us to employ simple estimation models to determine β_1 and β_2, such as ordinary least squares [28].

Detecting triggers. We employ one logistic regression model per navigation sensor. Given a change x in the sensor readings from one iteration to the next, we compute the probability $L(x)$ that the change corresponds to new control decisions. If this is greater than a threshold P_{run}, we detect a trigger on that sensor and execute the control logic, with all other inputs set to the most recent value; otherwise, we maintain the earlier output to the actuators.

This approach assumes that changes in a sensor's inputs at different times are statistically independent. This is justified because the time-dependent I, D components of the PID controllers bear little influence in our setting, as discussed earlier. Moreover, maintaining the earlier output to the actuators is possible only as long as the control setpoint does not change in the mean time. This is most often the case when drones hover or perform waypoint navigation, but rarely happens in applications such as aerial acrobatics, where this approach would probably be inefficient.

Parameter P_{run} offers a knob to trade computational resources against the tightness of control. Large values of P_{run} spare a significant fraction of control executions. However, the drone may require drastic corrections whenever the control loop does run; in a sense, motion becomes more "nervous". Small values of P_{run} limit the processing gains. However, control runs more often, ensuring the drone smoothly maintains the right attitude. Sec. 7 illustrates that gains over time-triggered control are seen for many different settings of P_{run}. Also, P_{run} is no threat to dependable operation, in that we make sure there is a minimum frequency the control loop runs anyways, as described in Sec. 5.

Run-time operation. The least square estimation has two operating modes. At start-up, control runs in a time-triggered fashion for T_{boot}. For each execution of the control logic within T_{boot}, we record whether that run was necessary. This provides an initial data set for the least square estimation to compute preliminary values for β_1 and β_2. The value of T_{boot} can be small; for the experiments of Sec. 7, we use $T_{boot} = 30$ sec.

After T_{boot}, we start identifying the triggers by comparing $L(x)$ with P_{run}. Upon occurrence of a false positive, that is, a value of x recognized as a trigger that does *not* change the control decisions, we feed back the value of x to the estimation of β_1 and β_2. This occurs by adding x to the data set for least square estimation and by periodically re-evaluating β_1 and β_2. The parameter estimation runs with medium priority in the scheduler part of the control loop, shown in Fig. 2.

This design considers the execution up to T_{boot} as representative of the rest of the flight. Should this not be the case, for example, whenever after T_{boot} a drone would enter an area with significantly different environment conditions, the initial parameter estimation would need to be recomputed. Moreover, Sec. 5 shows there may also be cases when we recognize false negatives. From the perspective of parameter estimation, we treat these occurrences in the same way as false positives. Overall, this processing implements a simplified form of *auto-tuning* [56] that improves the accuracy of logistic regression as the system runs.

5. TRIGGERS OVER TIME

Existing control logic, such as the various PID controllers used in autopilots, is designed under the assumption that sensors are sampled simultaneously according to a known frequency [7]. Removing such assumptions changes the control problem and requires a different conceptual framework [6]. In contrast, we aim at re-using existing control logic, and thus intend to approximate its timing assumptions.

Problems. Because of the above, how to process triggers deserves some thoughts:

1) We should be careful when multiple sensors record triggers close in time. It is unclear if these triggers deserve separate executions of the control logic as they are "too far" in time, or rather a single iteration of the control logic suffices because the triggers are "sufficiently close" to approximate simultaneity.
2) The way we recognize triggers is essentially probabilistic, as described in Sec. 4. Therefore, to ensure dependable operation we must consider the unlucky case when we miss a large number of consecutive triggers, and avoid running the control logic for too long. Otherwise, when we finally recognize a trigger, it may be too late to reclaim the drone's stability.

Several aspects are to be taken into account to find appropriate solutions to these problems.

Sampling frequency. Ideally, one would aim at continuously sampling the environment waiting for triggers. This way, they would be promptly recognized. In reality, such a sampling only occurs at discrete times.

To recognize triggers as early as possible, we sample every sensor at the highest frequency allowed by the hardware. Using sensors like those of Pixhawk boards, this is usually not a problem. They are expressly designed for energy-efficient high-frequency sampling, while the major energy drain aboard the drones is anyways due to the motors. Moreover, whenever the sensors permit, as in the case of the ST LSM303D [49], we compute the inverse of eq. (1) and program the sensor to return an interrupt only when a change x would return $L(x) > P_{run}$.

Hyperperiod triggers. To match the assumptions of existing control logic, we must approximate the simultaneous sampling of all input sensors. However, the time of sampling, and therefore of possibly recognizing a trigger, is not necessarily aligned across sensors. Drastic changes in the sensor inputs may also be correlated. For example, when the accelerometers record a sudden increase, it may be because environmental factors such as wind gusts; in these cases, a gyroscope also likely records changes. A time-triggered implementation would likely process these inputs together.

We take a conservative approach to address these issues. Based on the sampling frequency of every sensor in the system, we compute the system's *hyperperiod* as the smallest interval of time after which the sampling of all sensors repeats. Upon recognizing a trigger, we wait until the current hyperperiod completes before running the control logic. This allows us to "accumulate" all triggers possibly recognized on different sensors, giving the most up-to-date inputs to the execution of the control logic at once.

Note that all such executions are not taken into account as feedback to the regression models described in Sec. 4. With multiple triggers from different sensors, it is difficult to determine which sensors are responsible for the change of control decisions. This would require an understanding of the underlying control laws, which we wish avoid to foster general applicability of reactive control.

Failsafe. There may be unlucky cases when false negatives in the trigger conditions happen in a row. This may hurt dependability: it may be too late to reclaim the drone's stability when a trigger is recognized.

To cater for these extreme cases, we run the control logic anyhow every $T_{failsafe}$. Whenever this happens after a row of false negatives, the drone most likely applies some significant corrections that make sensor inputs change drastically. In turn, this triggers reactive control already at the immediately following iteration. In other words, $T_{failsafe}$ prompts reactive control to execute as soon as possible whenever there is a need to. In the experiments of Sec. 7, including those in ARCH with winds blowing at 8+ knots, we use $T_{failsafe} = .1$ sec. This is negligible compared to a control logic that normally runs at 400 Hz.

For all executions due to $T_{failsafe}$ resulting in a change of actuator settings, if the logistic regression models of Sec. 4 return a false negative for every sensors, the last changes to the sensor inputs are fed back for the next round of least square estimation of β_1 and β_2. We do this to reduce false negatives. We also demonstrate that the setting of $T_{failsafe}$ bears little influence on the final performance. $T_{failsafe}$ should be set to ensure the drone's stability in worst-case conditions. Determining this value analytically would require an accurate model of the environment to identify these worst-case conditions. In this work, we take a practical approach—as in the vast majority of operational control systems [4]—and employ a setting of $T_{failsafe}$ that is most likely overprovisioned, but safely ensures the dependable system operation without appreciably impacting the performance.

6. IMPLEMENTATION

For simplicity, Sec. 4 and Sec. 5 describe the control logic as a single processing unit. In reality, things are more complex. As a matter of fact, the control logic is composed of multiple processing steps arranged in a complex multi-branch pipeline. Depending on what trigger occurs, different slices of the control logic may need to run while other parts may not. Moreover, each such processing step may—in addition to producing an output *immediately* useful—update global state used *at a different iteration* elsewhere in the control pipeline.

In this setting, using triggers makes the processing event-driven not just because of the triggers themselves, but also because of asynchronous updates to global state. Thus, *every* processing step—not just those that directly process the sensors' inputs—might potentially need to execute upon recognizing a change in the inputs. Employing standard programming techniques to this end quickly turns implementations into a "callback hell" [25]. This fragments the program's control flow across numerous syntactically-independent fragments of code, hampering compile-time optimizations. As shown in Sec. 7, this causes a processing overhead that limits the benefits of reactive control.

We tackle this issue using a technique called *reactive programming* (RP) [8], illustrated in Sec. 6.1. This technique is rarely employed in embedded computing, because of resource constraints. We thus create an RP implementation tailored to the hardware we target, described in Sec. 6.2, with additional custom semantics to better support reactive control. Next, Sec. 6.3 describes the use of our realization of RP to implement reactive control.

6.1 Reactive Programming

RP is increasingly employed to realize applications that maintain a continuous interaction with the environment [8]. In these settings, it is generally impossible to predict the time of arrival of interesting events. Programmers thus implement the required processing through asynchronous callbacks and by manually propagating the relevant updates throughout the application's global state. Besides being error-prone, this is usually also inefficient. The control flow is hidden in the interactions across callbacks, which typically happens through side-effects and updates to global state variables. Thus, compilers and linkers have little control-flow information to optimize the execution.

RP provides abstractions to automatically manage data dependencies in programs where updates to variables happen unpredictably. Consider the example:

```
a= 2;
b= 3;
c= a + b;
```

In sequential programming, variable `c` retains the value 5 regardless of any future update to variable `a` or `b`. Updating `c` requires an explicit assignment following the changes in `a` or `b`. It becomes an issue to determine *where* to place such an assignment without knowing when `a` or `b` might change.

Using RP, one declaratively describes the data dependencies between variables `a`, `b`, and `c`. As variables `a` and `b` change, the value of `c` is constantly kept up-to-date. Then, variable `c` may be input to the computation of further state variables. Conceptually, the data dependencies take the form of an (acylic) graph, where the nodes represent individual values, and edges represent input/output relations.

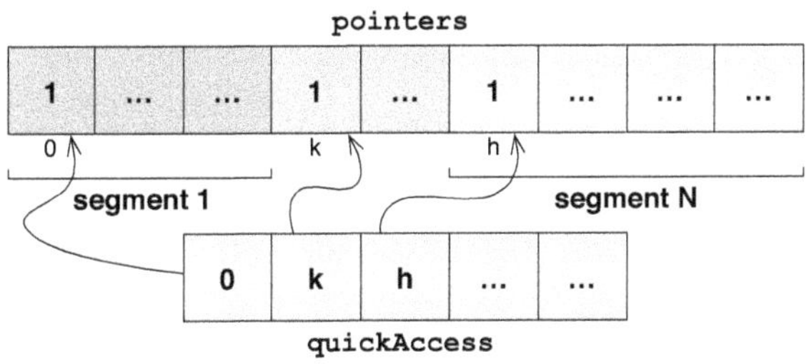

Figure 7: Data structures used in RP-Embedded to store the data dependency graph. *Using statically dimensioned vectors helps reduce memory consumption at the price of reduced flexibility.*

Together with the value, every node is also associated to a processing function that determines the value based on the inputs, executed whenever any of the input nodes changes. This resembles synchronous programming [12], yet with the fundamental difference that the arrival of events remains generally unknown.

The RP run-time support traverses the data dependency graph every time a data change occurs, stopping whenever a variable does not change its value as a result of changes in its inputs. Any further processing would be unnecessary because the other values in the graph would remain the same.

6.2 RP-Embedded

Run-time support for RP is provided through specialized libraries embedded in mainstream languages. Autopilots are generally written in C/C++, so we focus primarily on these.

Motivation. Existing C++ RP libraries [21, 46, 48] implement the propagation of changes in the data dependency graph using complex functionality to speed up the operation. One example is the use of Intel's Threading Building Blocks (TBB) [29]: a C++ library to handle concurrent events in a multi-core system. These functionality are not applicable to resource-constrained MCUs. Existing RP libraries also pay little attention to memory consumption, employing dynamic and even redundant data structures. These provide flexibility at run-time and reduce execution times with a large number of inputs.

Our setting is different. First, the data dependency graph encodes the control logic; therefore, its layout is known at compile-time. Further, memory consumption must be limited, as we use resource-constrained hardware. The sensors we wish to map to behaviors are also only a handful. Finally, the highest frequency of data changes is known; for each input sensors, we are aware or can safely approximate the highest sampling frequency. Based on these considerations, we design and implement RP-EMBEDDED: a C++ library to support RP on embedded resource-constrained hardware.

Data structures. Unlike existing libraries, we employ two statically allocated vectors to encode the graph, as shown in Fig. 8. The `pointers` vector is split in as many segments as the maximum number N of nodes in the dependency graph. Each segment stores a sequence of object pointers that indicate what other nodes in the dependency graph use the value of that node as input. The `quickAccess` vector serves to speed up random accesses to the `pointers` vector. Using these structures, memory occupation is greatly reduced, especially compared to the container classes of the STD library used in many C++ RP libraries. For the same reason, the traversal of the graph requires fewer pointer dereferences and indirection operations, which tend to be costly on embedded hardware.

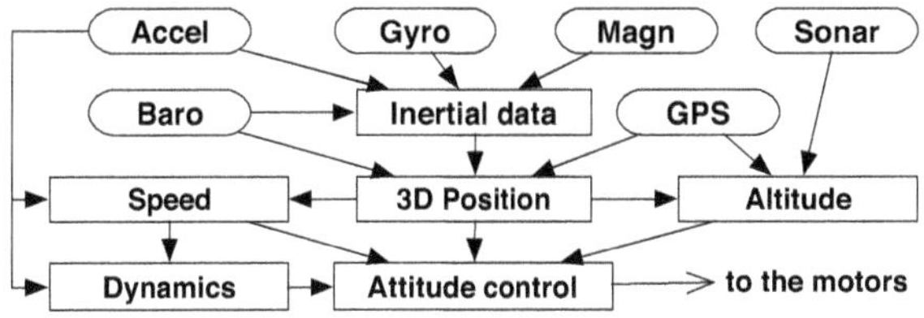

Figure 8: Ardupilot's control loop for copters after refactoring to use RP-Embedded. *Squashed rectangles indicate triggers possibly signalled by sensors, squared rectangles indicate global state information.*

These features come at the cost of limited flexibility. Programmers must place an upper bound on the number of nodes N and on their fan-out. At run-time, the data dependency graph can only change within these bounds, yet these needs should be rare in autopilots.

Hyperperiods. From the discussion in Sec. 5, we know it makes sense to await the possible signaling of all triggers within the same hyperperiod.

Besides having an effect on control decisions, this may impact the processing overhead. Say we implement a classical RP semantics and propagate any data change independent of any other. The propagation caused by triggers from a high-frequency sensor may simply be immediately superseded by another trigger caused by another sensor within the same hyperperiod. The control decisions that become effective, however, are only those of the second propagation.

To avoid this unnecessary processing, RP-EMBEDDED allows the initial input values to be classified based on their maximum rate of change. Based on this information, RP-EMBEDDED computes the system's hyperperiod and, for all downstream nodes in the dependency graph, it recursively determines their maximum rate of update. Every time a value is updated in the graph, RP-EMBEDDED knows the maximum time to wait before propagating the change, as further updates in other inputs may occur. As far as we know, such a semantics is not available in any RP implementation, regardless of the language.

6.3 Using RP-Embedded

Employing RP-EMBEDDED for reactive control requires to reformulate the *implementation* of the control logic—not the logic itself—in the form of a data dependency graph. The sensor inputs, as well as the outputs to the motors, remain the same as in the original time-triggered implementation. Triggers generated by sensors when applying reactive control become the initial inputs to the dependency graph, whereas global state variables are explicitly associated to the functions that compute their values. The implementation of trigger functionality is straightforward, as it boils down to computing $L(x)$ and comparing the output against P_{run}. The run-time estimation of β_1 and β_2 simply consists in running an ordinary least square estimation [28].

The problem above is, in essence, a problem of code refactoring. We currently perform this transformation manually, using code inspection tools such as Understand [45]. Software engineering, however, offers a wide literature on code refactoring that can be leveraged to further ease this transformation [33]. Even in the absence of dedicated support, our experience indicates that the needed transformations can be implemented with very little effort. Fig. 8 shows the data dependency graph of the Ardupilot control loop for copters, which a single person on our team realized and tested in *three* days of work. Ardupilot is one of the most complex autopilot implementations. The other autopilots we test in Sec. 7 are simpler. It took from one to two work days to refactor them. We plan to perform a complete study to better quantify the efforts and benefits due to implementing control logic in a reactive fashion as opposed to a time-triggered approach.

7. EVALUATION

We assess the effectiveness of reactive control along several dimensions, using aerial drones as a challenging use case. We compare the performance of implementations using reactive control against the original time-triggered versions.

In the following, Sec. 7.2 reports on the improvements in navigation and flight time. Sec. 7.3 discusses a series of micro-benchmarks investigating the influence of RP and parameter settings. Sec. 7.4 illustrates the impact of reactive control in two end-user applications, demonstrating the benefits beyond waypoint navigation. The next section illustrates the experimental setup common to all experiments.

7.1 Setup

Drones. We use the two drones of Fig. 4 plus a Y6 drone from 3D Robotics [2]. The latter is peculiar; it is composed of three arms with two co-axial motor-propeller assemblies at each end. One propeller faces up and "pulls"; the other propeller faces down and "pushes". This configuration obtains almost the same thrust of a hexacopter, but with fewer components and a lighter frame, which allows it to carry larger payloads.

Using a Y6 configuration, however, control is more complex. The autopilot needs to set the desired attitude by carefully tuning the motor settings on the same arm while counteracting the gyro effect. Due to this, not all autopilots support this configuration.

Autopilots. Besides Ardupilot and Pixhawk, we consider two other autopilots and corresponding hardware. We implement reactive control on both as described in Sec. 6, even though the results of the refactoring generally differ from that of Ardupilot, shown earlier in Fig. 8.

OpenPilot [39] is an open-source community-driven autopilot tightly co-designed with the underlying hardware. It generally offers fewer navigation features than Ardupilot. The corresponding CC3D board mounts a Cortex M3 MCU clocked at 72 MHz, coupled to a 16-bit 3-axis accelerometer/gyroscope, a 24-bit barometer, and a 12-bit magnetometer. *Cleanflight* [18] is the youngest of the three and is expressly designed for Cortex M MCUs. It focuses on the robustness of the implementation at the cost of only supporting copter drones . We use the SP Racing F3 (SPRF3) board for Cleanflight. It features a 32-bit Cortex M4 core running at 72 MHz, together with a 16-bit 3-axis accelerometer/gyroscope, a 24-bit barometer, and a 12-bit magnetometer.

The implementations of OpenPilot and Cleanflight resemble the design of Ardupilot shown in Fig. 2, but the control logic differs substantially in both sophistication and tuning. This aspect is likely to bear an impact on the effectiveness of reactive control. Further, the boards we employ differ in processing capabilities and sensor equipment, which is instrumental to understand the general applicability of reactive control. We test OpenPilot and Cleanflight by replacing Ardupilot and the Pixhawk board on either the quadcopter or the hexacopter of Fig. 4; however, only Ardupilot supports the Y6. Besides the sensors mounted directly on the boards themselves, the remainder of the equipment on the drones remains the same.

Metrics and setting. To study the accuracy of flight control, we measure the *attitude error*, that is, the difference between the desired and actual attitude. The former is determined by the autopilot to reach the next waypoint and changes seldomly, for example, when reaching a waypoint and turning to the next one The actual attitude is recorded through the on-board sensors. Their difference is the figure the control logic aims at minimizing. If the error was constantly zero, the control would attain perfect performance; the larger this figure, the less effective is the autopilot.

The attitude error is measured along the tree axis as the error between desired and actual raw, pitch, and yaw, shown in Fig. 3. When navigating from one waypoint to the next, all three are subject to the environment influence. To measure the error in a minimally invasive way, we connect a separately-powered RaspberryPI board to the I2C or GPIO interfaces of the boards we test. The modifications to the autopilot to output these information are minimal; the impact of this processing and the added weight of the RaspberryPI and its battery are negligible and equally affect time-triggered and reactive control.

To understand how the accuracy of flight control impacts the drone lifetime, we also record the *flight time* as the time between the start of an experiment and the time when the battery falls below a 20% threshold. For safety, most GCS implementations instruct the drone to return to the launch point upon reaching this threshold. In general, the lifetime of aerial drones is currently extremely limited. State of the art technology usually provides at most half an hour of operation [24]. As a result, this aspect is widely perceived as a major hampering factor.

We test 18 different flight paths in the three environments of Sec. 3. Each path is composed of 8 random waypoints covered at a maximum speed of 3 m/s and 5 m altitude. We repeat every run at least 3 times with every drone. The path loops as long as the battery stays above 20%. Note that it is extremely difficult for RUGBY and ARCH to ensure that the comparisons are performed in the exact same conditions. We use a 5 m tall digital anemometer in the middle of the fields to record the wind speed during an experiment, and consider the conditions comparable within ± 1 knot. The results we present next are based on more than 260 flight hours, and exhibit a variance constantly within 5% of the average value given comparable environment conditions. Running these experiments took almost 8 months, as we often had to wait for the right conditions to run the tests in comparable conditions.

7.2 Navigation

Based on empirical tests and our own experience in developing reactive control, we set $P_{run} = 0.6$ and $T_{failsafe} = .1$ sec. We study the impact of different settings for these parameters in Sec. 7.3.

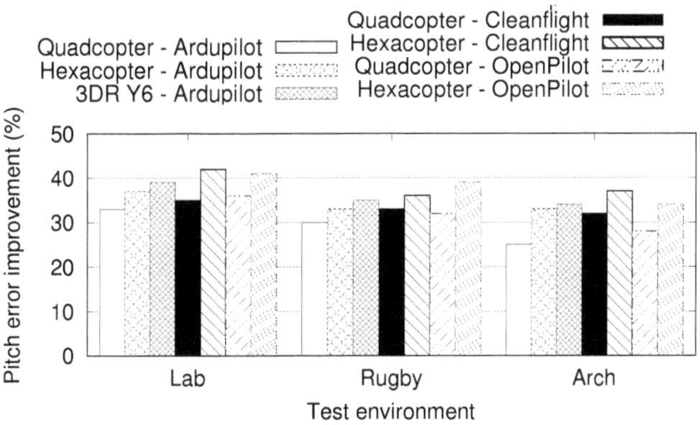

Figure 9: Average improvement in pitch error. *The absolute values range from a 41% improvement with Cleanflight in* LAB *to a 27% improvement with Ardupilot in* ARCH. *The improvements for the latter are proportional to the time control outputs the same decisions, shown in Fig. 5; it is the opportunity to spare iterations of the control loop that enables more accurate control decisions.*

Test environment	Yaw improvement (min/max)	Roll improvement (min/max)
LAB	29%/41%	31%/41%
RUGBY	31%/37%	30%/39%
ARCH	22%/35%	24%/37%

Figure 10: Improvements for yaw and roll across all autopilots and drone types.

Results: attitude error. Fig. 9 shows the average improvements in pitch error enabled by reactive control. The improvements are significant, ranging from a 41% reduction with Cleanflight in LAB to a 27% reduction with Ardupilot in the challenging ARCH. We obtain very similar results, sometimes better, for yaw and roll, summarized in Fig. 10.

The improvements for Ardupilot are proportional to the time the control logic outputs the same decisions, shown in Fig. 5. This confirms that it is the opportunity to spare iterations of the control loop that enables more accurate control decisions. Not running the control loop unnecessarily frees resources, increasing their availability whenever there is actually the need to use them. In these circumstances, reactive control dynamically increases the rate of control, possibly beyond the pre-set rate of time-triggered control. This means reactive control does not necessarily decreases the utilization of resources, but rather moves that utilization at times where the demands are more crucial to satisfy.

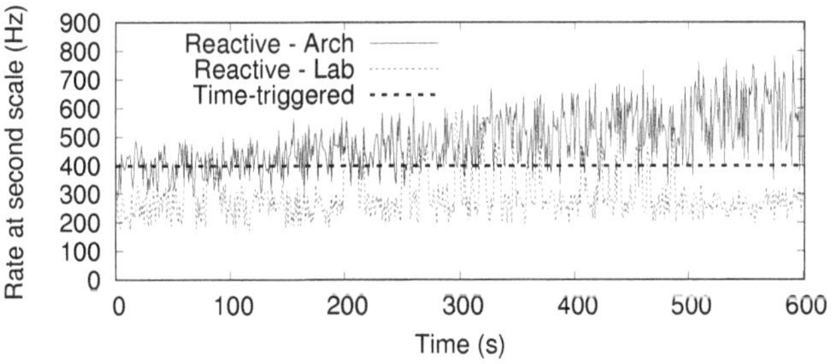

Figure 11: Average rate of control at second scale in two example Ardupilot runs. *Reactive control adapts the rate of control executions both in the short and long term, and according to the perceived environment influence.*

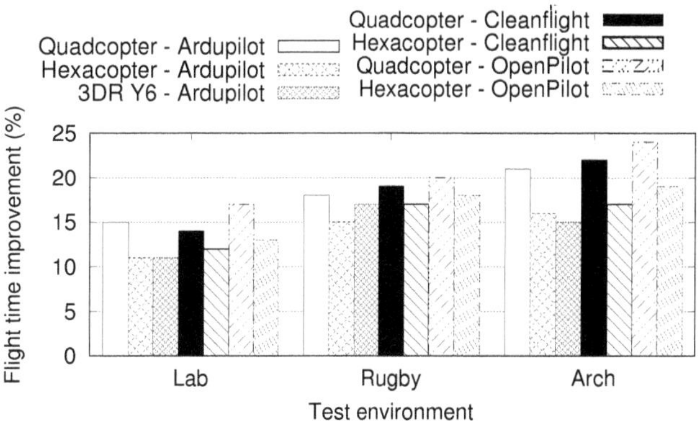

Figure 12: Improvement in flight time. *More accurate motion control reduces the energy overhead in attitude corrections. As a result, battery utilization improves and flight times increase. The improvements are higher in the more demanding settings.*

Evidence of this is shown in Fig. 11, showing an example trace that indicates the average control rate at second scale using Ardupilot and the hexacopter. In ARCH, reactive control results in rapid adaptations of the control rate in response to the environment influence. On average, the control rate starts slightly below the 400 Hz used in time-triggered control and slowly increases. Our anemometer confirms that the average wind speed is growing during this experiment.

In contrast, Fig. 11 shows reactive control in LAB exhibiting more limited short-term adaptations. The average control rate stays below the rate of time-triggered control, with occasional bursts above the rate of time-triggered control whenever corrections are needed to respond to environmental events, for example, when passing close to a ventilation duct. The trends in Fig. 11 demonstrate reactive control's adaptation abilities both in the short and long term.

Still in Fig. 9, the improvements of reactive control apply to the Y6 as well; in fact, these are highest in a given environment. This cannot be attributed to its structural robustness; the Y6 is definitely the least "sturdy" of the three. We conjecture that the different control logic of the Y6 offers additional opportunities to reactive control. This provides evidence of the general applicability of reactive control independent of the control logic. This is also demonstrated by the results for Cleanflight, still shown in Fig. 9. Being the youngest of the autopilot we test, it is fair to expect the control logic to be the least refined. Reactive control is still able to drastically improve the pitch error, by a 32% (37%) factor with the quadcopter (hexacopter) in ARCH.

The results for OpenPilot in Fig. 9 also show how reactive control leads to better hardware utilization. All other settings being equal, the improvements for OpenPilot are higher than with Ardupilot, yet the OpenPilot hardware is the least powerful we test. Sparing unnecessary iterations of the control loop is thus increasingly important, and the effect of reactive control amplifies. This testifies the opportunity for downsizing the hardware, as reactive control can utilize it better and, most importantly, at the right times.

Results: flight time. The improvements in attitude error translate into more accurate motion control. This reduces the energy overhead in attitude corrections, for example, due to operating the motors at higher rates to adjust the trajectory. As a result, battery utilization improves and flight times increase.

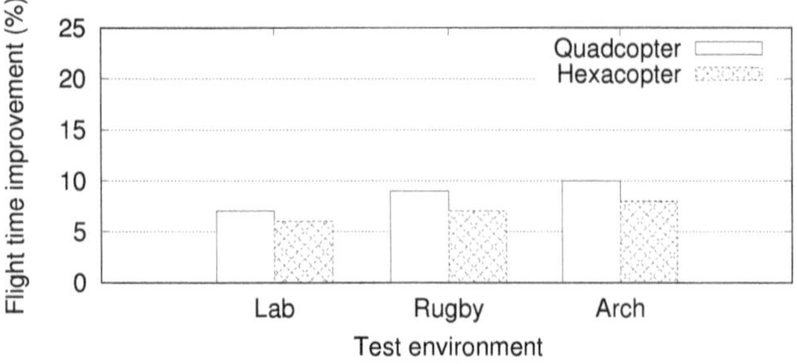

Figure 13: Improvement in flight time without using RP-Embedded, with Cleanflight. *The improvements are still appreciable, but almost halved. Part of the resources freed by reactive control are eaten up by an inefficient implementation.*

Fig. 12 shows the results we obtain in this respect. Reactive control reaches up to a 24% improvement compared to time-triggered control, with a worst-case improvement of 11%. This means flying more than 27 min instead of 22 min with OpenPilot in ARCH, that is, covering 6 to 8 additional waypoints: almost an entire additional lap. This figure is crucial for aerial drones, as discussed earlier. The improvements reactive control enables in this respect are thus extremely valuable.

Perhaps most importantly, these improvements are higher in the more demanding settings. Compared to the results of Fig. 9, the trends are indeed opposite. The better resource utilization enabled by reactive control becomes more important as it is more urgent to react. Similarly, the quadcopter shows higher improvements than the hexacopter. The mechanical design of the latter already makes it physically resilient. Differently, the quadcopter offers more ample margin to cope with the environment influence in software.

7.3 Micro-benchmarks

Based on the results of the previous section, we study the impact of employing RP-EMBEDDED for implementing reactive control and the influence of P_{run} and $T_{failsafe}$.

Impact of RP-Embedded. Conceptually, reactive control is not necessarily tied to any specific implementation technique. The question then arises as to what is the role of RP-EMBEDDED in the performance of Sec. 7.2. To answer this, we run 20 hours of experiments with an implementation of reactive control that exclusively employs standard C/C++ and mainstream libraries. Code is always compiled using the GNU GCC toolchain.

Fig. 13 exemplifies the performance in flight time improvements with this implementation, using Cleanflight running on SPRF3. Compared to Fig. 12, the improvements are still appreciable, but are almost halved now. Basically, at least part of the resources freed by reactive control are eaten up by an inefficient implementation. These results demonstrate that provisioning an efficient implementation is essential to fully harvest the advantages of reactive control, and our RP-EMBEDDED implementation of RP is effective to this end.

Parameter setting. We run another 20 hours of test flights to understand the influence of P_{run} and $T_{failsafe}$ on the performance of Sec. 7.2.

Initially, we vary the setting of P_{run} from 0.2 to 0.8 and keep a fixed $T_{failsafe} = .1$ sec. As example, Fig. 14 depicts the pitch error improvement we observe using Ardupilot. Worth noticing is that for all values and settings we test, the results

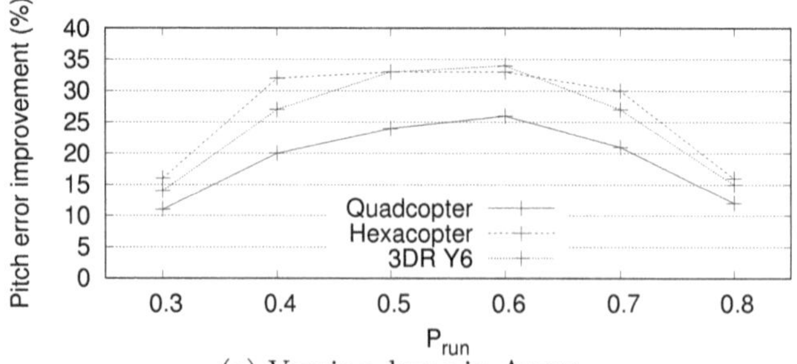

(a) Varying drone in ARCH.

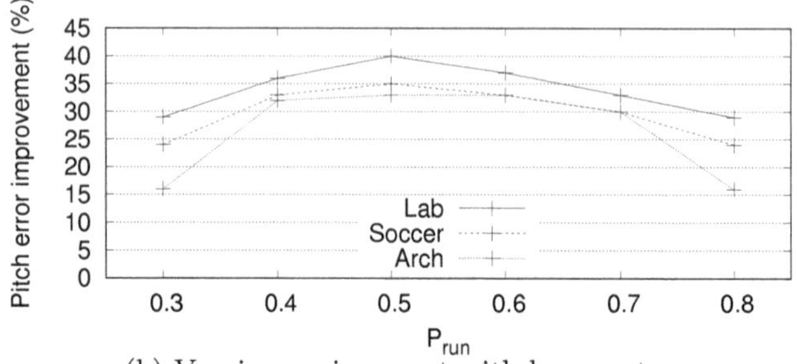

(b) Varying environment with hexacopter.

Figure 14: Improvement in pitch error with different P_{run}, using Ardupilot. *Some improvements are obtained for* all *values and settings we test.*

are positive, that is, some improvements are *always* obtained regardless of the parameters' values.

The performance shown in Fig. 14(a) demonstrates the robustness of reactive control against different settings for P_{run} in the most challenging environment. A setting in the $[0.4, 0.7]$ range offers a performance close to the best attainable. Within this range, the probability of false positives in logistic regression as described in Sec. 4 is also very small: it is about 7% right after T_{boot}, and quickly reaches a steady 2%[2]. In Fig. 14(a), the performance only degrades when P_{run} takes extreme values. When P_{run} is too large, control happens too seldom so corrections tend to be abrupt. When P_{run} is too small, the execution approximates time-triggered control, which sub-optimally uses resources. Again, the structural robustness of the hexacopter yields the least sensitivity to different P_{run}: its curve is almost flat in the $[0.4, 0.7]$ interval.

We show the performance with varying P_{run} across the three environments in Fig. 14(b), using the hexacopter. We obtain similar results with the quadcopter and the Y6. We observe how the range of robust values for P_{run} tends to become larger as the environment plays less influence. The curve for ARCH is the most concave, the curve for LAB tends to flatten, and the one for RUGBY lies in the middle.

Based on these results, and without relying on any knowledge on the environment, values in a $[0.5, 0.6]$ range should be preferred. The more the drone can sustain the environment influence, the more it is safe to increase P_{run}, as observed in Fig. 14(a). Similarly, if the environment is ex-

[2]Note that computing the general probability of false negatives would, in principle, require to run the control loop anyways and on the same hardware of reactive control. This would affect the timing of the following iterations and thus the whole execution. We offer next some insights into the probability of false negatives for failsafe executions, which do occur anyways.

pected not to play any strong influence, it makes sense to increase P_{run}, as the range of robust values is probably large as observed in Fig. 14(b).

In a different set of experiments, we fix $P_{run} = 0.6$ and test $T_{failsafe} \in \{.01, .05, .1, .2, .3\}$ sec, again using Ardupilot with all three drones across all environments. The performance in attitude error turns out largely insensitive of the value of $T_{failsafe}$, demonstrating how this is in fact only a safety measure. Moreover, for all failsafe executions, the probability of a false negative compared to the output of logistic regression turns out negligible. The only exception is for $T_{failsafe} = .01$ sec, which yields a slight performance degradation. With this setting, the frequency of failsafe executions starts interfering with reactive control.

7.4 End-user Applications

We demonstrate the benefits of reactive control in end-user applications beyond waypoint navigation.

7.4.1 3D Reconstruction

We perform 3D reconstruction of static objects using aerial pictures [38]. This is a paradigmatic aerial drone application of great societal interest [53]. The procedure requires gathering a predetermined set of aerial pictures, followed by a post-processing step with 3D reconstruction software, such as Photoscan [3].

Setup. In LAB, we attempt the 3D reconstruction of a puppet on a table in the middle of the area. In RUGBY, our target is a car kindly provided by one of the authors[3]. We are interested in the *quality* of the 3D reconstructions. The more stable is the drone while hovering for taking a picture, the less blurred or distorted is the picture. In turn, the better are the input pictures, the higher quality is the resulting 3D reconstruction. The latter is usually measured based on the *density of the point cloud* [38], that is, the number of image points the reconstruction software found to be the same across pictures. This is the information that enables the transition from a 2D plane to a 3D surface.

We use Ardupilot and the hexacopter equipped with a Nikon D5500+ camera. We refactor the PID controllers for Ardupilot's *Hovering* mode, which are different than those for waypoint navigation, to use reactive control. We determine a total of 30 target coordinates where to take a picture, and repeat the experiment 3 times using either reactive or time-triggered control at 400 Hz. Because the number of pictures input to Photoscan is the same in both cases, any improvement due to reactive control is only due to the quality of individual pictures.

Results. Photoscan returns that the point cloud is 23% or 29% more dense when using reactive control in LAB or RUGBY, respectively. Reactive control thus translates into tangible benefits also in a challenging end-user application. Coherently with the earlier observations, these advantages are greater in the more challenging environment. The higher environment influence in RUGBY amplifies the improvements of reactive control compared to LAB.

7.4.2 Search-and-rescue

We demonstrate how reactive control is amenable to implement active sensing functionality.

[3]It was not possible to obtain the needed authorization to place an object of proper size in ARCH; thus, we could not perform any 3D reconstruction experiment there.

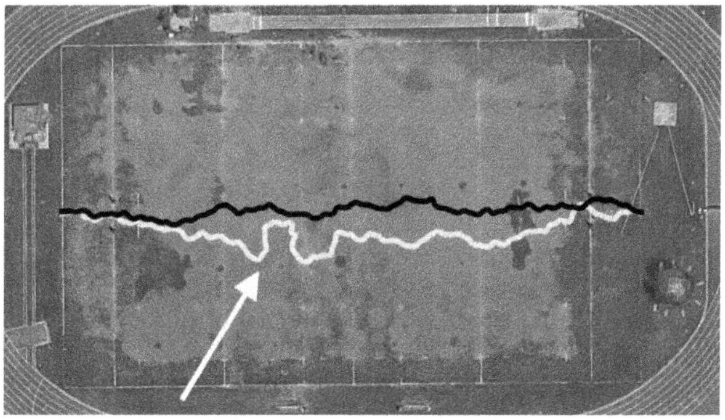

Figure 15: Example of ARVA-driven navigation when using reactive control (black) and time-triggered processing (yellow). *Time-triggered control occasionally produces highly inefficient paths, whereas we never observe similar behaviors with reactive control.*

Setup. Professional skiers are recommended to carry a device called "Appareil de Recherche de Victimes en Avalanche" (ARVA) [40], that is, a radio transceiver operating at 457 KHz and specialized for the purpose of finding people under snow. Normally, the device emits a low-power beacon. Following an avalanche, a rescue team can use another ARVA device as a direction finding device, searching for signals from trapped persons. The searching device generates a "U-turn" signal whenever it detects the owner starts moving away from the victim. Modern ARVA devices reach a 5 m accuracy in locating a transmitter under 10 m of snow [40].

We integrate a Pieps DSP PRO [40] ARVA transceiver with the Pixhawk board through the UART port. A custom PID controller drives the drone's yaw to align it with the direction pointed by the ARVA. Roll and pitch, instead, are determined to fly at constant 1 m/s along the direction indicated by the ARVA. The resulting control does not make any use of GPS information; navigation is entirely determined by the ARVA inputs. We implement this controller both using reactive control by probing the ARVA device as fast as possible, and with time-triggered control at 400 Hz.

We place an ARVA transmitter at one end of RUGBY, and set up the quadcopter at 100 m distance facing opposite to it. Even though GPS does not provide any inputs for navigation, we use it to track the path until the first time the ARVA device generates the "U-turn" signal. We compare the duration and length of the flight when using reactive or time-triggered control. The results are obtained from 20 repetitions in comparable conditions.

Results. On average, reactive control results in a 21% (11%) reduction in the duration (length) of the flight. Besides the averages, time-triggered control shows higher variance in the results, occasionally producing highly inefficient paths. Fig. 15 reports a visual example. The path followed by reactive control appears fairly smooth. In contrast, time-triggered control shows a convoluted trajectory at about one-third of the distance, where the drone's yaw is basically $\pm 90°$ compared to the target.

By looking at the logs, we find the reason to be in the inability of time-triggered control to promptly react. Probably because of sudden wind gusts, at some point the drone gains a lateral momentum. Time-triggered control is unable to react fast enough; a higher than 400 Hz rate would probably be needed in this case, so the drone turns almost 90°. At this point, time-triggered control takes some seconds to remedy the situation. We never observe this behavior with reactive control, which better manages available resources against environment influences.

8. CONCLUSION

Reactive control replaces time-triggered control by governing the execution of the low-level control logic based on changes in the navigation sensors, rather than time. This allows the system to dynamically adapt the control rate to varying environment dynamics. We described how we enable reactive control by conceiving a probabilistic approach to trigger the execution of the control logic, by carefully regulating the control executions over time, and by provisioning an efficient implementation on resource-constrained hardware. We then extensively demonstrated the benefits reactive control provides, including higher accuracy in motion control, longer operational times, and better performance in two diverse end-user applications.

Acknowledgments. We thank Marco Zimmerling for his feedback on earlier versions of this paper. The work was partly supported by the Projects "Zero-energy Buildings in Smart Urban Districts" (EEB), "ICT Solutions to Support Logistics and Transport Processes" (ITS), and "Smart Living Technologies" (SHELL) of the Italian Ministry for University and Research.

9. REFERENCES

[1] 3D Robotics. Advanced flight modes. goo.gl/CeGp6Y.

[2] 3D Robotics. UAV Technology. goo.gl/sBoH6.

[3] Agisoft. Photoscan. goo.gl/1gcwbs.

[4] K. H. Ang, G. Chong, and Y. Li. PID control system analysis, design, and technology. *IEEE Transactions on Control Systems Technology*, 13(4), 2005.

[5] Ardupilot. Home. goo.gl/x2CHyM.

[6] K. J. Åström. Event based control. In *Analysis and Design of Nonlinear Control Systems*. Springer Verlag, 2007.

[7] K. J. Åström and T. Hägglund. *Advanced PID control*. ISA - The Instrumentation, Systems, and Automation Society, 2006.

[8] E. Bainomugisha et al. A survey on reactive programming. *ACM Comput. Surv.*, 45(4), 2013.

[9] J. Barraquand, et al. B. Langlois, and J. C. Latombe. Numerical potential field techniques for robot path planning. *IEEE Transactions on Systems, Man and Cybernetics*, 22(2), 1992.

[10] BBC News. Disaster drones: How robot teams can help in a crisis. goo.gl/6efliV.

[11] G. A. Bekey. *Autonomous robots: From biological inspiration to implementation and control.* The MIT Press, 2005.

[12] A. Benveniste et al. The synchronous languages 12 years later. *Proceedings of the IEEE*, 91(1), 2003.

[13] S. Bouabdallah, A. Noth, and R. Siegwart. PID vs LQ control techniques applied to an indoor micro quadrotor. In *Proceedings of IROS*, 2004.

[14] M. Brambilla et al. Swarm robotics: A review from the swarm engineering perspective. *Swarm Intelligence*, 2013.

[15] D. Brescianini, M. Hehn, and R. D'Andrea. Quadrocopter pole acrobatics. In *Proceedings of IROS*, 2013.

[16] W. Burgard et al. Collaborative multi-robot exploration. In *Proceedings of ICRA*, 2000.

[17] C. Anderson. How I accidentally kickstarted the domestic drone boom. goo.gl/SPOIR.

[18] Cleanflight. Home. goo.gl/uCGmr4.

[19] CNN.com. Your personal $849 underwater drone. goo.gl/m1JRuD.

[20] S. Consolvo et al. Activity sensing in the wild: A field trial of Ubifit garden. In *Proceedings of ACM CHI*, 2008.

[21] CPPReact. A reactive programming library for C++11. goo.gl/Q78cRK.

[22] J. Dai, X. Bai, Z. Yang, Z. Shen, and D. Xuan. PerFallD: A pervasive fall detection system using mobile phones. In *Proceedings of IEEE PERCOM*, 2010.

[23] A. Davison. Real-time simultaneous localisation and mapping with a single camera. In *Proceedings of the IEEE International Conference on Computer Vision*, 2003.

[24] DJI. Phantom Drone. goo.gl/wLbVic.

[25] J. Edwards. Coherent reaction. In *Proceedings of the ACM Conference on Object Oriented Programming Systems Languages and Applications (OOPSLA)*, 2009.

[26] R. M. Faragher et al. Captain Buzz: An all-smartphone autonomous delta-wing drone. In *Workshop on Micro Aerial Vehicle Networks, Systems, and Applications (with ACM MOBISYS)*, 2015.

[27] Good-ARK Semiconductors. eCompass modules with 3D accelerometer and 3D magnetometer. goo.gl/D0CH6y.

[28] D. W. Hosmer Jr, S. Lemeshow, and R. X. Sturdivant. *Applied logistic regression*, volume 398. John Wiley & Sons, 2013.

[29] Intel. Threading building blocks. goo.gl/Wlvp44.

[30] O. Khatib. Real-time obstacle avoidance for manipulators and mobile robots. *International Journal of Robotics Research*, 5(1), 1986.

[31] Libelium Inc. WaspMote. www.libelium.com.

[32] Q. Lindsey, D. Mellinger, and V. Kumar. Construction with quadrotor teams. *Autonomous Robots*, 33(3), 2012.

[33] T. Mens and T. Tourwé. A survey of software refactoring. *IEEE Transactions on Software Engineering*, 30(2), 2004.

[34] N. Michael et al. Cooperative manipulation and transportation with aerial robots. *Autonomous Robots*, 30(1), 2011.

[35] E. Miluzzo et al. Sensing meets mobile social networks: The design, implementation and evaluation of the CenceMe application. In *Proceedings of ACM SENSYS*, 2008.

[36] L. Mottola, M. Moretta, C. Ghezzi, and K. Whitehouse. Team-level programming of drone sensor networks. In *Proceedings of ACM SENSYS*, 2014.

[37] E. Natalizio et al. Filming sport events with mobile

camera drones: Mathematical modeling and algorithms. goo.gl/v7Qo80, 2012. Technical report.
[38] F. Nex and F. Remondino. UAV for 3D mapping applications: A review. *Applied Geomatics*, 2003.
[39] OpenPilot. Home. goo.gl/D89lkb.
[40] Pieps. ARVA Transceivers. goo.gl/tPywra.
[41] PixHawk.org. PX4 autopilot. goo.gl/wU4fmk.
[42] K. Pulli, A. Baksheev, K. Kornyakov, and V. Eruhimov. Real-time computer vision with OpenCV. *Communications of the ACM*, 55(6), 2012.
[43] R. Ritz et al. Cooperative quadrocopter ball throwing and catching. In *Proceedings of IROS*, 2012.
[44] I. Sadeghzadeh and Y. Zhang. Actuator fault-tolerant control based on gain-scheduled PID with application to fixed-wing unmanned aerial vehicles. In *IEEE International Conference on Control and Fault-Tolerant Systems*, 2013.
[45] SciTools. Code analysis with Understand. goo.gl/0VZGAc.
[46] Sodium. Functional reactive programming (FRP) for C++. goo.gl/vwJH1P.
[47] SparkFun. Low current sensor breakout - ACS712. goo.gl/VPV3HW.
[48] SpiraFRP. Yet another C++ reactive programming library. goo.gl/HfDQsT.
[49] ST Microelectronics. Ultra compact high performance e-compasses. goo.gl/TLrdy5.
[50] M. Turpin, N. Michael, and V. Kumar. Decentralized formation control with variable shapes for aerial robots. In *Proceedings of ICRA*, 2012.
[51] U.S. Environmental Protection Agency. Air Pollutants. goo.gl/stvh8.
[52] Vicom. Motion capture systems. goo.gl/Vh5Q4c.
[53] J. Villasenor. Observations from above: Unmanned Aircraft Systems. *Harvard Journal of Law and Public Policy*, 2012.
[54] P. Wardle. Personal submersible drone for aquatic exploration. goo.gl/XTVgQF, 2015. US Patent App. 14/143,713.
[55] M. Yim et al. Modular self-reconfigurable robot systems. *IEEE Robotics Automation Magazine*, 14(1), 2007.
[56] M. Zhuang and D. Atherton. Automatic tuning of optimum PID controllers. *IEEE Proceedings on Control Theory and Applications*, 140(3), 1993.

DefDroid: Towards a More Defensive Mobile OS Against Disruptive App Behavior

Peng Huang, Tianyin Xu, Xinxin Jin, and Yuanyuan Zhou
University of California, San Diego

ABSTRACT

The mobile app market is enjoying an explosive growth. Many people, including teenagers, set about developing mobile apps. Unfortunately, due to developers' inexperience and the unique mobile programming paradigms, a growing number of immature apps are released to users. Despite having useful functionalities, these apps exhibit *disruptive* behaviors that are inconsiderate to the mobile system as a whole, *e.g.*, retrying network connections too aggressively, waking up the device too frequently, or holding resources for unnecessarily long. These behaviors adversely affect other apps running on the same device and frustrate users with battery drain, excessive cellular data consumption, storage overuse, *etc.*

In this paper, we investigate *Disruptive App Behavior (DAB)* with a study on 287 real-world DAB issues. Guided by the study, we present DefDroid, a mobile OS designed to protect users from the negative impact of DAB at runtime. DefDroid monitors important app activities and tries to adjust app behaviors using fine-grained actions (*e.g.*, enforce back-off to continuous retries, decrease aggressive timer frequency) without breaking app main functionality. Our experiments show that DefDroid effectively curbs 125 real-world DAB cases with small overhead and marginal impact to the usability of both the misbehaving apps and normal apps. During a small-scale user trial, DefDroid also found 6 new DAB issues. We further deployed DefDroid to 185 real users through the PhoneLab testbed for 43 days and found DAB issues from at least 57 apps.

CCS Concepts

•**Computer systems organization** → **Reliability;** •**Software and its engineering** → **Operating systems;** •**Human-centered computing** → *Mobile computing;*

Keywords

Mobile apps; Operating system; Defensive actions

MobiSys'16, June 25-30, 2016, Singapore, Singapore
© 2016 ACM. ISBN 978-1-4503-4269-8/16/06...$15.00
DOI: http://dx.doi.org/10.1145/2906388.2906419

```
<?xml version="1.0" encoding="utf-8"?>
<appwidget-provider
  android:minHeight="146dp"
  android:minWidth="146dp"
  android:updatePeriodMillis="2500"/>
```

Figure 1: Anki-Droid sets an aggressive widget update interval (2.5s) that causes severe battery drain [17].

1. INTRODUCTION

The booming of mobile users and device shipments [46] has driven a surge of mobile app developers. According to a recent report [37], the mobile developer population has doubled since 2010. In tandem with these growths, abundant mobile apps are released, *e.g.*, up to 60,000 apps are added to App Store monthly [27].

Unfortunately, due to inexperienced app developers and the lack of development resources, many mobile apps are weaker in terms of quality compared to traditional desktop and server applications, especially in dealing with system-level issues such as resource management, exception handling, and network programming. Consequently, many mobile users encounter immature app behaviors (dubbed "naughty apps") once in a while.

1.1 Disruptive App Behavior

In this work, we attempt to understand and address an emerging class of issues in mobile apps – **Disruptive App Behavior** (*DAB*). DAB refers to apps acting immaturely to its hosting ecosystem and adversely affecting other apps running on the same device.[1] For example, an app may keep the device awake for too long, forget to unregister GPS after use, retry network too aggressively, download large cellular data without user consent, or flood the device screen with noisy notifications. These disruptive behaviors waste or overuse resources without considering other apps, and cause significant battery drain, excessive consumption of bandwidth or storage, *etc.*

DAB issues are mainly caused by programming mistakes and/or aggressive configurations. For example, mobile platform typically provides APIs for apps to schedule periodical task. Some app developers can configure the update frequency to be very aggressive like in Figure 1. As another example, Android provides wakelock APIs [5] to allow apps to prevent hardware components like CPU from entering low-power state. Inexperienced developers often leak an acquired wakelock [52] or hold a wakelock for unnecessarily long [7]. Another common cause for DAB is that developers fail to thoroughly consider and handle changing environment.

[1] We exclude malicious apps that cause security or privacy issues from this definition and our scope of interest

App	Version	Disruptive behavior
F-Droid	0.72	Create "infinite" copies of XML files due to a bug, eating up storage
ownCloud	1.5.4	Sync with server too often and request too much info, consuming large cellular data
Chrome	28.0	Overuse Gyroscope sensor in background, draining battery
AntennaPod	1.2	Display notification for every background podcast download, flooding notification area
Facebook	40.0	CPU spin in network handling, leaking audio session, draining battery
WHERE	3.2.1	Continuously use GPS on standby, draining battery
DAVdroid	0.6	Sync lots of high resolution contact pictures, consuming large cellular data

Table 1: Real-world examples of disruptive app behavior.

```
private requestLocation(LocationManager lm) {
  lm.requestUpdate(provider, mlistener);
+ gpsFixHandler.postDelayed(new Runnable(){
+   public void run(){
+     disableLocationListener();
+   }}, 30 * 1000); // give up after 30s
}
private LocationListener mlistener =
  new LocationListener() {
    public void onLocationChanged() {
+     gpsFixHandler.removeCallbacks(null);
  }
}
```

Figure 2: BetterWeather keeps searching GPS signals and drains battery quickly when users are in a poor-signal environment [6]. Developers fix it by giving up search after 30s.

Figure 2 shows a DAB in a popular weather app that will keep searching for GPS non-stop when its users are in an environment with poor GPS signal. Table 1 further lists several real-world DAB reports.

From app development perspective, the rise of pervasive DAB issues is mainly due to the following reasons:

(1) *Mobile apps are in general "young"*. We examined the top 1,000 apps in two platforms and found that the average age of these apps is 2.5 years for App Store, and 1.5 years for Google Play (Table 2), even though both app stores started in 2008. Therefore, many popular apps have not aged enough to be stable and well-engineered. In comparison, popular desktop/server applications are much more mature: *e.g.*, Firefox is 12 years old and MySQL is 19 years old.

(2) *Mobile app developers also tend to be less experienced and take less rigorous software development training* [64, 63, 57]. Inexperienced app developers often make mistakes in using APIs properly (*e.g.*, calling `release` inside `onStop` instead of `onPause`, forgetting to check network type before transferring data) or inproperly handle various external conditions (*e.g.*, Figure 2). They also tend to uncousiouly assume that their apps will be frequently used by users for a long session, resulting in writing aggressive code or configurations without considering the overall user experiences.

(3) *Many mobile apps are built by a small development team, sometimes individuals.* We find that in App Store, at least 12% of the developers for the top 1,000 apps are individuals (Table 2). Small teams often do not have sufficient resources to conduct comprehensive testing to catch DAB issues before releasing to users, which is especially pressing given that mobile testing faces unique challenges [56].

Platform	Avg. app age	Indie developers
iOS	2.5 years	$> 12\%$
Android	1.5 years	$> 5\%$

Table 2: The average age (time since first release) of the top 1,000 apps in two platforms, and the percent. of independent developers for these apps.

1.2 Diagnosis and Bug Detection Tools

Users who have poor experiences due to DAB often have no clues of why it is happening and how to fix it. Some tech-proficient users leverage advanced tools to diagnose the issues. For example, Android and iOS provide built-in tools to display the battery and data usage by apps. Third-party tools like PowerTutor [68], Wakelock Detector [22], eDoctor [44], and Carat [48] offer more details for troubleshooting.

While these tools can help users find some issues, they suffer from several drawbacks. First, many ordinary users lack the expertise needed to use these tools effectively. Second, these tools are at user level and thus have limited knowledge about app activities. Even when a symptom is successfully diagnosed, the tools need to constantly involve users to take privileged actions for resolution. Most importantly, when these tools are invoked, app misbehaviors usually already cause significant negative impact, *e.g.*, overuse of cellular data. It is desirable to prevent such issues from happening in the first place, or to at least limit their impact to the overall system health.

A number of research work has been proposed to eliminate certain type of app misbehavior using scalable app testing [56, 42], energy bug detection [41, 67, 52, 65], accurate energy profiling [61, 32, 68, 51, 50], and advanced mobile prefetching [39, 55]. Unfortunately, the defects can still escape these tools and be released. Additionally, DAB issues due to aggressive configurations (*cf.*, Figure 1) or complex environment (*cf.*, Figure 2) are not addressed by these tools.

1.3 System-level Support to Prevent DAB

Given that many DAB issues still exist in the field despite fruitful existing tools, it is important to think from mobile system perspective to prevent DAB. One way towards this direction is to re-desining existing framework APIs to be less prone to mistakes, which requires developers to rewrite existing apps. This paper focuses on a complementary system-level solution to protect users from DAB without the burden of rewriting apps – runtime mitigation. We argue that mobile system designers should anticipate the common occurrence of DAB during users' daily use of mobile devices, and enhance the OS to deal with DAB at runtime. This not only provides a last defense to DAB for end users but also can reduce some burden for app developers because the mitigation resembles a hotfix.

Interestingly, we have observed several recent changes in mainstream mobile OSes to address certain DAB issues. For example, after Android OS 2.3, the OS may kill apps for excessive wakelock usage [38]; iOS used to allow apps to run background tasks according to apps' own schedules, but iOS 7 and later versions restrict the actual scheduling to be mainly determined by the OS [23].

Nevertheless, these changes are insufficient and sacrifice usability (*e.g.*, directly killing apps). The OS lacks a comprehensive solution for DAB. As an evidence, users running the latest mobile OS still encounter a significant number of DAB cases, as we will show in §2.

The challenges for designing a comprehensive OS-level solution to tackle DAB are in three folds. First, DAB issues have diverse manifestations, which requires understanding the common patterns to address the issues. Second, the solution needs to target a suspicious app misbehavior without breaking app main functionality. Third, the solution should not get in the way of normal user interactions with apps, and should not incur significant overhead.

1.4 Our Contribution

In this work, we first conduct a study of 287 real-world DAB issues to understand the characteristics of the problem; we then present DefDroid, an Android-based mobile OS designed to restrict the impact of DAB at runtime.

DefDroid modifies Android to monitor important app activities for potential DAB patterns, and, if necessary, dynamically adjust app behavior using *fine-grained defensive actions*. The defensive actions may adjust frequencies, trade off accuracies, change priorities, delay executions, release resources, or warn users. For example, when an app wakes up the device too frequently, DefDroid may adjust the app's alarm intervals; when an app retries network connection too aggressively, DefDroid may enforce a back-off; when an app requests fine locations too frequently in background, DefDroid may start returning coarse locations to that app.

We implement DefDroid based on Android 4.4.3, and evaluate it using 128 real-world DAB cases. The defensive mechanisms in DefDroid successfully limit the negative impact of 125 cases. Compared to unmodified Android, DefDroid reduces the resource consumption impact of the 125 cases in terms of power, mobile data, and storage by up to 481mW, 183MB, and 145MB, respectively, over 30-minute experiment periods.

Our evaluation also shows that the defensive mechanisms in DefDroid cause marginal negative impact to the overall app usability. To be specific, in 40 cases, DefDroid does not induce any side effects to the affected apps. In 80 cases, the defensive actions defer request execution or fail aggressive requests but without causing noticeable impact from users' perspective. For the remaining 5 cases, DefDroid's defensive actions cause checked exceptions that the compilers already enforce developers to handle. There is no crash or abnormal behavior of the test apps caused by defensive actions in our experiments.

During user trials, DefDroid also found and addressed 6 new DAB cases in the field. We have released DefDroid to the PhoneLab testbed [47] and deployed to 185 *real users* for 43 days. Based on logs collected from the deployment, we found DAB issues from 81 apps, 57 of which can be reproduced. We did not receive user complaint about DefDroid breaking app functionality or causing unexpected behavior for any of these apps that DefDroid applied actions to.

Category	# of apps	Downloads	Ratings
Productivity	18	1K–5M	3.2–4.5
Tools	38	10K–50M	3.4–4.8
Social	10	1K–5B	3.5–4.7
Communication	26	5K–5B	3.7–4.6
News	10	1K–5M	3.8–4.6
Media	13	1K–500M	3.5–4.7
Navigation	20	1K–500K	3.6–4.9
Other	46	1K–50M	2.7–4.7

Table 3: Apps in the studied DAB cases.

2. UNDERSTANDING DISRUPTIVE APP BEHAVIORS

To understand the characteristics of DAB, we conduct a study on 287 real-world DAB issues. The purpose of the study is to provide us with insights on solutions to address common DAB. While there are prior studies on certain aspect of DAB (*e.g.*, no-sleep energy bug [52], abnormal battery drain [44]), there is a lack of study on the generic DAB problems as a whole.

2.1 Methodology

We collect the study cases from two sources. First, we manually inspect popular user forums [4, 3, 25] to find posts where users complained about app misbehavior; Second, we examine the issue trackers of open-source mobile apps that have user-reported issues. We obtain an initial set of around 1,000 potential issues from the first source, and 9,200 cases from the second source. We go through each case and filter duplicates. We also ignore misbehavior that only hurts the apps themselves (*i.e.*, crashes, feature bugs).

After filtering, there are **287** cases of DAB from 181 unique apps. Table 3 shows the category and popularity of the apps in the dataset. The majority (265) of studied cases are from open-source apps. This is due to the limitation in our data sources instead of intentional preference. For cases from open-source apps, we know the exact defect causing the DAB. For the remaining 22 cases from closed-source apps, we understand their symptoms and high-level causes.

We also try to reproduce the collected cases on our smartphones running the latest Android OS to further confirm these issues. In total, we successfully reproduced 96 cases. The cases that we failed to reproduce are mainly because of compilation issues, incompatibility, or complex external requirements (*e.g.*, server setup).

2.2 Common Disruptive App Behavior

A first step to understand DAB is to study, both qualitatively and quantitatively, what user-frustrating app misbehaviors affect the ecosystem. Our collected cases are all real user reports/complaints and thus provide a data point to understand this question.

Based on the collected cases, we summarize the common types of disruptive behavior and present the finding in Table 4. We can see that, as a generic class of problems, DAB has diverse patterns. While a few aspect of DAB is studied in literature, *e.g.*, wakelock leak [52], improper prefetching [67, 55], others are under-explored, *e.g.*, aggressive network retry, excessive storage use, and noisy notifications. The summarized patterns provide us with clues about the changes in mobile OS we need to make in order to restrict common DAB. The reproduced DAB issues will be used as evaluation subjects later.

Disruptive behavior	Cases*
Too frequent connection, aggressive retry	44 (10)
Excessive data transfer over cellular network	42 (10)
Excessive storage, cache	33 (5)
Excessive or stuck notifications	33 (9)
Very high CPU usage	31 (8)
Wakelock leak or overuse	25 (13)
GPS leak or overuse	19 (11)
Too aggressive sensor/GPS updates	15 (6)
Misc. resource leak or overuse	15 (3)
Too frequent wake-up alarms	12 (8)
Sensors leak or overuse	12 (8)
Too frequent broadcasts, receivers	6 (5)
Total	287 (96)

Table 4: Common DAB summarized from our study of 287 real-world cases. *: parenthesized numbers are the cases we successfully reproduced.

2.3 Observations

In addition to the common disruptive behavior patterns, we also make the following observations:

(1). Even expert developers can make mistakes. The misbehaving apps we study include apps written by novice developers or developers who write apps as a hobby (*e.g.* at night after work), as well as apps written by professional teams (*e.g.*, Facebook, Google, Spotify).

Implication 1: *Only relying on developers to always ensure app quality is challenging. The OS needs to anticipate common disruptive app behavior at runtime.*

(2). The root causes of DAB are diverse, including bugs (*e.g.*, duplicate downloads [12]), correct but unfriendly implementation (*e.g.*, fetch all messages from all friends at once [1]), and improper settings (*e.g.*, aggressive update frequency [17]). This is the case even for the same DAB. Take "excessive cellular data transfer" as an example. It could occur *a).* because the app does not support WiFi-only feature; *b).* because the app implements this feature but the default configuration is incorrect: *e.g.*, *"I just installed Podax on my new phone and I forgot to change the setting and it used up nearly my entire month of bandwidth in an hour"* [13]; *c).* because of a complex bug that causes a loop of network activities [21].

This poses challenges for existing tools to statically detect DAB before app release. For example, unfriendly implementation and improper settings that lead to DAB are under-explored in existing literature. In our study, 34% of the cases are caused by improper settings.

Implication 2: *Enhancing OS to deal with DAB dynamically from app execution has the advantage that the resolution does not depend on the root causes of DAB.*

(3). Some DAB is triggered under complex conditions. In 57 cases, the DAB is only manifested under certain external conditions such as when GPS signal is poor, network is unstable, contact-list is large, or remote host does not support password authentication. These defects can escape testing and occur on users' mobile devices when the apps are deployed.

Implication 3: *To protect users from being affected by these complex DAB requires dynamic solutions that run continuously at users' side.*

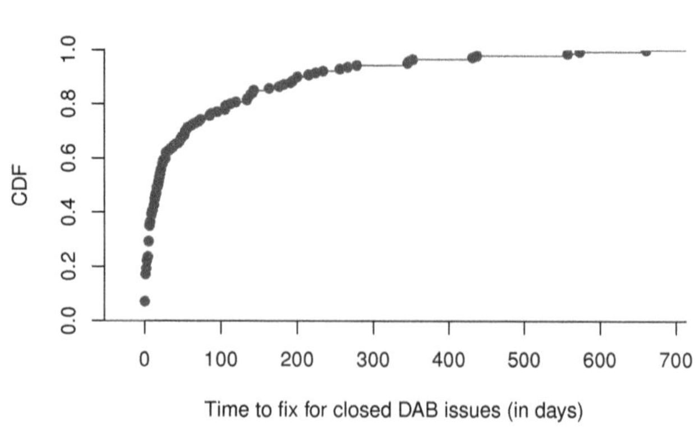

Figure 3: CDF of time from DAB being reported to issue being fixed.

(4). While frustrated by the DAB, users often still need to use the apps for functionalities. For example, a user comments on a battery drain issue caused by excessive wakelock in CSipSimple [10]: *"this issue makes this program less acceptable to me than Sipdroid. Otherwise, I am happy with the UI and satisfied with stability."* Quantitatively, despite having defects, the studied apps on average have overall rating (across all versions) of 4.1 out of 5.

Implication 4: *In dealing with DAB, simple coarse-grained solutions like killing or uninstalling the app are undesirable; the solution should restrict disruptive behavior without sacrificing app main functionality.*

(5). Fixing DAB takes time and/or is not easy. In some cases, it took a long time for developers to fix the defect because developers could not find the defect easily [14] or because the developers do not have enough time to implement the fix [20]. Figure 3 shows the CDF of time from a DAB is reported to it is fixed. The median fix time is 17.5 days and the mean is 70 days. Moreover, 18% of our studied cases still do not have a fix to date (not shown in Figure 3).

Implication 5.1: *While developers are working on fixing DAB, it is desirable for OS to limit the impact of DAB at user side.*

A few apps implement advanced fix such as adding a dynamic mechanism to decide whether to perform an expensive operation or not based on the system health. For example, an app adds a mode in which it will not perform lookups or show pop-ups if the battery is low [18]. However, such dynamic optimization is not easy to implement correctly for many app developers.

Implication 5.2: *Having OS provide runtime mitigation to DAB may help reduce efforts of complex optimization for inexperienced developers.*

3. DefDroid DESIGN

DefDroid aims to restrain DAB without breaking app main functionality or introducing much overhead. The key idea of DefDroid is to execute various fine-grained defensive[2] operations to mitigate app misbehavior, and optionally revert these operations after misbehavior subsides.

3.1 Overview

We make several design decisions guided by our study (§2). First, DefDroid only applies coarse-grained actions such as killing

[2]In the sense that the OS is vigilant about potential DAB and protects the ecosystem/users from the negative impact of DAB.

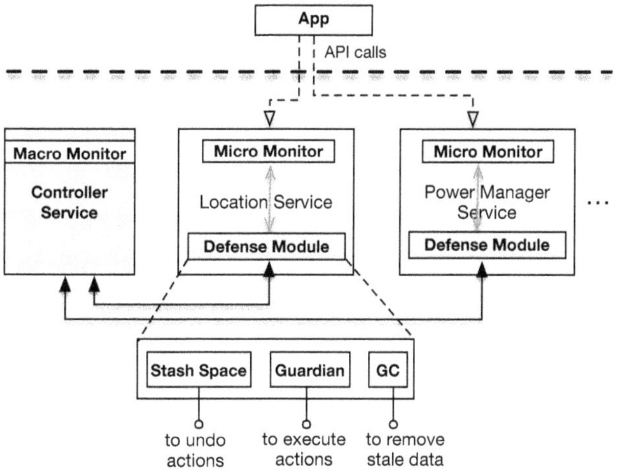

Figure 4: Overview of DefDroid

apps as a last resort. This is because the app misbehaviors we address are mainly due to programming mistakes instead of malice, and users need to use the app's main functionalities. Second, DefDroid only corrects specific apps instead of the whole system. It avoids employing actions that have global impact such as stopping sensors, underclocking CPU or adjusting global timer. Third, to avoid hurting user experience, DefDroid currently does *not* execute defensive actions to system apps or foreground apps that users are interacting with because aggressive behavior during user interaction is often expected by users.

There are several challenges in designing DefDroid: *a).* handle a diverse and growing set of app misbehaviors; *b).* collect fine-grained app activity information to monitor misbehavior without significant overhead; *c).* execute actions precisely to misbehaving app and responsible requests; *d).* determine appropriate policies for the defensive mechanisms, and *e).* revoke the imposed adjustments when the misbehavior subsides.

Figure 4 shows the architecture of DefDroid. DefDroid adopts a modular design. It uses a *controller service* to monitor macro-level system conditions (*e.g.*, battery, storage), and to manage an extensible set of *defense modules* to address different DAB. A defense module resides in an OS subsystem together with a *micro monitor* who records important app activities. Within a defense module are: 1). a *guardian* that analyzes monitor information and executes defensive actions to potential DAB; 2). a *stash space* to store information necessary for undoing defensive actions; and 3) a *garbage collector* to remove stale monitor and stash data to control overhead.

DefDroid has a notion of *permissive* and *defensive* modes. In the permissive mode, DefDroid provides services faithfully to apps like what its base OS does. When there are signs of unhealthy system conditions and suspicious app activities (*e.g.*, frequent wake-ups, lingering wakelock), DefDroid may transit into the defensive mode. In the defensive mode, DefDroid executes fine-grained defensive actions to misbehaving apps, *e.g.*, decreasing an app's timer frequency temporarily, releasing long-held wakelock.

3.2 Controller Service

DefDroid adds a controller service to its base OS to record macro-level system conditions such as battery level and data usage at a regular interval. But the macro information alone is not enough to infer whether an app is misbehaving. Nor is the information sufficient to devise a fine-grained action.

```
protected class AlarmMonitor extends DefenseMonitor {
  private AlarmTable<PendingIntent> mTable;
  public void alarmSet(Alarm alarm) {
    mTable.setDescriptor(alarm.operation, alarm);
    mTable.updateAlloc(alarm.operation);
  }
  public void alarmCancelled(PendingIntent operation) {
    mTable.updateRelease(operation);
  }
  public void alarmTriggered(PendingIntent operation,
      long duration) {
    mTable.incrementUsage(operation, duration);
  }
}
```

Figure 5: A micro monitor inserted in `AlarmManagerService`. We modify implementations of the `AlarmManagerService` API methods such as `set` and `cancel` to invoke the micro monitor.

To identify potential disruptive behavior (caller, stats) — For use by defensive actions (token, params)

caller	stats	token	params
uid/pid/ package	time of API call, frequency,...	PendingIntent, IBinder,...	flags,tag,...

Figure 6: Typical data entries in a micro monitor to record app API request information.

Therefore, DefDroid delegates the main mechanisms of addressing DAB to a set of specific defense modules that live inside various important subsystems. The controller is lightweight to facilitate these modules. For example, the controller propagates macro-level system conditions to the defense modules and manages the life cycle of these modules. The controller also exposes the configurations, such as the policies of defensive actions, and a whitelist of apps, to end users.

3.3 Micro Monitors

To enable fine-grained defensive mechanisms, DefDroid monitors not only system-level conditions but also app-level activities. This is accomplished by inserting a set of micro monitors in major OS subsystems that apps interact with, *e.g.*, the power service and the location service. Figure 5 shows a snippet of the micro monitor class for the `AlarmManagerService`.

The exact information recorded by a micro monitor is component-dependant. But it usually covers app API requests information, including four parts (Figure 6): the caller (UID or package name), request stats (*e.g.*, first time a type of request is made, request rate), tokens that uniquely identify requests (*e.g.*, `IBinder` object in Android) and request parameters.

We need to track and aggregate app request stats because judging from an individual API request alone usually cannot distinguish between legitimate requests and disruptive requests at the time of the API call. For example, a timer request with a small interval may not adversely impact the system if it is used only for a brief period. To identify frequent wake-up misbehavior, DefDroid needs to track the timer triggering counters (Figure 5). As another example, a wakelock `acquire` call by an misbehaving app is no different than the calls from other apps. It is only after some time, well-behaved apps call `release` while the misbehaving apps forget to call `release`. Therefore, DefDroid needs to track the wakelock holding time to identify potential wakelock leaks.

Recording tokens and request parameters in micro monitor is

Action type	Example
Release	release long-held wakelock, GPS
Slowdown	enlarge alarm interval, reduce sensor frequency
Delay	delay excessive cellular network requests
Approximate	use coarse-grained location
Downgrade	switch to passive GPS provider
Deprioritize	decrease scheduling priority
Block	reject frequent alarm requests for a while
Warn	warn users about large data consumption
Kill	kill naughty app processes or services (last resort)

Table 5: Types of defensive actions

needed because DefDroid may take defensive actions such as decreasing frequency of aggressive alarms. These defensive actions need to know the details of the original request. Tokens like `IBinder` objects or resource descriptors are the unique keys to identify the original requests. Together with the original request parameters, DefDroid can tweak an app's behavior.

Some of the OS subsystems that micro monitors reside in already store some request information internally as part of API implementations (*e.g.*, the alarm object in Figure 5). In such situation, the micro monitor simply keeps references in its data structures and only needs to update request statistics. For information not stored originally, the micro monitor creates data structures to track the information.

To control the monitoring overhead, micro monitors do not track all app activities. Only the kinds of requests that may cause adverse impact to the systems will be monitored. Moreover, most data in micro monitors will be removed when apps make requests like `release` and `cancel`. Each defense module also has a garbage collector that periodically cleans up old monitor data to control the memory overhead (Figure 4).

3.4 Guardians

Guardians in DefDroid are the main components to take fine-grained actions to reduce various disruptive behaviors. They periodically check the monitor data for potential DAB patterns and carry out actions. A guardian will register with the controller service when its residing subsystem starts. The guardian gets commands from controller, *e.g.*, to start/stop. It also obtains updates on system-level conditions and policies from the controller.

3.4.1 Defensive Action

Defensive actions are the key operations to tackle DAB at a fine granularity. We design the defensive actions by devising a counter-action for each DAB pattern summarized from our study (Table 4). In executing the defensive actions, DefDroid leverages the caller, requests and token information from micro monitors to precisely target the responsible app and requests.

Table 5 shows the types of defensive actions used in DefDroid. These actions may release resources, adjust frequencies, trade off accuracies, change priorities, delay/deny requests, or warn users. For example, a guardian may release an expensive resource if the requesting app has not been active for a while to prevent the resource-leak disruptive behavior. For the aggressive alarm behavior pattern, a guardian may increase the timer interval. For overly frequent wakelock acquisitions, a guardian may block future wakelock acquire requests from that app for a while. For aggressive GPS requests, a guardian may opt to return coarse-grained location information, switch to passive location providers (*i.e.*, receiving location updates only when there are other apps requesting them) or unregister the app's listener.

```
public class RequestDelayerBase<T> {
  public DelayResult delayTime(String owner, T request,
      IRequestReviver<T> reviver, long time, ...) {
    DelayData data = mDelayMap.get(owner);
    if (data == null || !data.active)
      return DelayResult.NOT_IN_LIST;
    if (data.requestQueue.size() > MAX_BUFFER)
      return DelayResult.BUFFER_FULL;
    data.requestQueue.add(request);
    handler.postDelayed(new Runnable() {
        public void run() {
          reviver.reviveRequest(request);
          ...
        }
      }, time);
    return DelayResult.DELAYED;
  }
}
```

Figure 7: Outline of a basic `delay` by time action.

Like micro monitors, implementing these defensive actions depends on the detailed internals of the specific subsystem: *e.g.* to implement *release* action for wakelock, we periodically check a table of request information such as start time for all wakelocks, and remove the corresponding lock object from an internal array of wakelocks when the duration exceeds a pre-defined threshold[3]; to implement *slowdown* for alarm, we adjust the `repeatInterval` field of an internal data structure; to implement *delay* by time action, we put the request in a buffer and process the request after certain time (Figure 7).

The defensive actions are mainly designed based on what a well-behaved app would do for the benefit of the ecosystem. For example, a well-behaved app would do exponential back-offs when it fails to connect to network, similar to our *slowdown* action; a well-behaved app would only use high-accuracy location when needed and would otherwise switch to lower-accuracy or lower-update-frequency location [11], similar to our *approximate* or *slowdown* action.

When multiple defensive actions are applicable for a DAB, DefDroid tries the actions with least perturbation first before executing more strict actions. For example, when an app uses sensor aggressively in background for a while, DefDroid may first adjust the sampling period or max report latency in the app's sensor request if possible; if it is ineffective, DefDroid may decrease the thread priority or release the listener. A defensive action may also be applied multiple times. For example, for frequent wake-up behavior, the guardian in alarm service will increase the alarm request interval. If it is ineffective, it will keep increasing the interval for multiple times.

3.4.2 Policy

The guardians in DefDroid are controlled by a number of settings. These settings define the thresholds of disruptive behavior listed in Table 4, *e.g.*, wakelock session duration that is considered "too long", number of updates in a period that is considered "too aggressive".

In studying real-world DAB issues (§2), we find disruptive behaviors often clearly distinguish from normal behaviors in terms of request patterns. This makes choosing the settings relatively easy and less sensitive to tuning. For example, Figure 8 shows the CDF

[3]Wakelock object is different from traditional locks: it is only a kernel reference counter to hardware components.

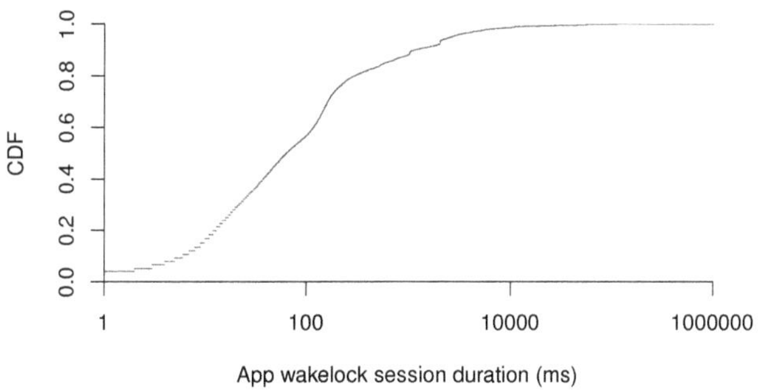

Figure 8: CDF of 46,875 wakelock request sessions (from `acquire` to `release`) from 36 popular apps over a one-week period on a Samsung Galaxy S4 device.

Parameter	Setting
Rate limit minimum window	3 min.
Wakelock duration throttle	5 min.
Wakelock alloc. rate limit	3 per min.
GPS duration throttle	10 min.
Sensor alloc. rate limit	20 per sec
Network checker frequency	3 min.
Data threshold per time slice	5 MB
Max consecutive overused slices	4
Back-off multiplier	1.5

Table 6: Some default settings for DefDroid.

of wakelock request sessions gathered from 36 popular apps that use wakelock over a one-week period in a Samsung Galaxy S4 device. We can see the majority of wakelock request session is very short (the 99th percentile is 12 secs) with a few clear outliers (the long tail).

To set the thresholds for disruptive behavior, we empirically profile many popular apps for a long period offline to obtain the distribution of some interested metrics. Then we choose an empirical setting that significantly deviates from the majority distribution.

For some metrics such as mobile data consumption, simply using a single threshold may falsely alarm some legitimate bursty app activities. To avoid this problem, we divide the app behavior monitoring into time slices (*e.g.*, 3-minute slice), and mark a time slice as bad when a threshold is crossed (*e.g.*, used 5+ MB data). Then we only consider that app is misbehaving when a number of *consecutive* time slices are all bad. Table 6 shows some default settings in DefDroid.

The defense policies also specify the intervals to check DAB patterns, the order to try different actions, and parameters related to a specific defensive action (*e.g.*, the extent to increase a timer interval). By default, system apps are exempt from the defensive mechanisms to protect the most important functionalities like phone call and messaging. Additionally, in a given checking interval, guardians currently will not apply defensive actions on apps that are in the foreground to avoid affecting user experiences. But the monitors still record important requests in case defensive actions need them later. When the device is being charged and connected to WiFi, DefDroid does not enter defensive mode because many apps are designed to perform heavy and aggressive work in this scenario and the impact usually does not bother users.

DefDroid also provides user interfaces to show apps being penalized by defensive actions, and to allow users to configure a white-

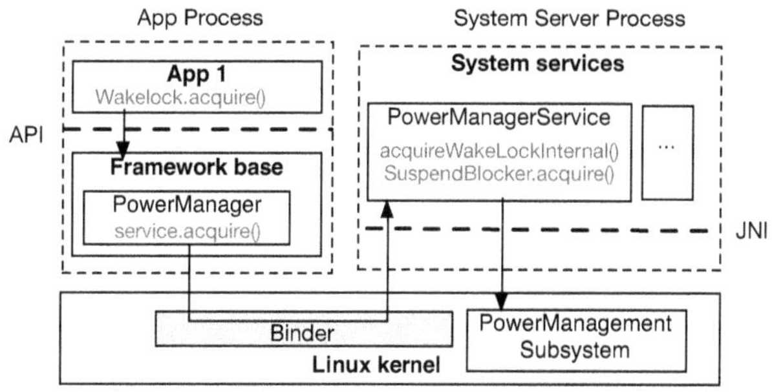

Figure 9: Several layers that a typical Android API call goes through.

list of apps to be immune from penalty. For potentially intrusive action such as releasing lingering GPS listener, DefDroid asks users to confirm before executing the action.

3.4.3 Reverting Defensive Actions

The defensive actions executed by DefDroid are usually temporary. After an observation period, if the actions are effective or healthy external conditions occur (*e.g.*, battery recharged, connected to Wi-Fi), the actions might be reverted. For example, if the guardian adjusted the timer frequency for an app, it may later restore timer frequency for that app. Reversion gives chances for misbehaving apps to behave normally again.

To implement reversions, the defense module reserves a stash area to bookkeep recently applied defensive actions (Figure 4). The stash area also keeps important tokens and parameters for reversions. The data in the stash area is removed when apps explicitly revoke the recorded requests, *e.g.*, canceling timer, terminating unexpectedly. The garbage collector in a defense module will also clean the data in stash area after it expires.

4. IMPLEMENTATION

We have built DefDroid in Android AOSP 4.4.3, AOSP 5.1.1 and Cyanogenmod 11. We implemented 10 defense modules (namely Wakelock, Location, Sensor, Alarm, Network, Notification, CPU, Storage, Bluetooth, and Light). These modules are managed by a controller service added to the Android system server [66].

Layers to implement the defense modules. There are several layers in the Android stack (*cf.* Figure 9) a defense module could reside in: the Android framework base layer in app address space (*e.g.*, `PowerManager` class), the system service in system server (*e.g.*, `PowerManagerService` class), and native Linux kernel (*e.g.*, power management subsystem).

While placing the defense modules at the framework base layer allows direct access to app objects, doing so can incur significant overhead (*e.g.*, monitoring data structures) because the modules live in *every* app's address space. This is a lesson we learned during our initial prototype of DefDroid in this way with the Xposed framework [26]. Moreover, directly manipulating app objects can cause side effects to app state. Our initial Xposed-based prototype occasionally causes apps to crash.

Therefore, we move away from this approach and implement the defense modules mainly at the system service layer. One challenge of doing so is that DefDroid is unable to directly access app objects to implement defensive actions. We solve this issue by leveraging the IPC tokens (mainly `IBinder`) that app uses to communicate with system services. With the token, the defensive actions can uniquely identify a request, and invoke the IPC methods for an API call within the system service as if the request comes from the app. In this way, the defensive actions will not mutate an app's state.

The sensor and camera defensive modules currently reside in the framework layer because there are no corresponding system services in the original Android. We also modify the native code layer, *e.g.*, the scheduler and network daemon, to support low-level defensive actions.

Avoid breaking invariants in OS subsystems. Since defensive guardians live inside subsystems, some defensive actions may alter the system internal states. Incautious modifications can break the original invariants in the subsystem. For example, releasing an app's wakelock in Android is essentially removing the `IBinder` object from an internal array in the power management subsystem. But if the guardian only does the removal, the internal state of the subsystem may be incorrect, because when an app calls `release`, the subsystem will also update other internal data (*e.g.*, battery statistics). To address this issue, instead of directly manipulating system states, the defensive guardians in DefDroid often implements an action by making API calls as if the call is from an app. For example, when a guardian alters a timer frequency, it does so by calling `cancel` API and then `set` API with the updated parameters.

Orders of starting defensive modules. Some defensive modules reside in the first few core subsystems but they have dependencies on subsystems that are started later. Running these modules immediately when their residing subsystems start may cause exceptions. We address this issue by starting the defensive service as the last system component. Since defensive modules will register with the defensive service and can only be started by the defensive service, when a defensive module is started, its dependent subsystems will be running.

5. EVALUATION

We first evaluate DefDroid on the 96 real-world DAB cases that we reproduced in §2. We measure the effectiveness of DefDroid in curbing DAB, as well as quantitative benefits (e.g., savings of battery and cellular data).

In addition, we evaluate DefDroid on 32 *newly* collected real-world cases that cover all DAB symptoms listed in Table 4. As some of the new cases are caused by different programming mistakes than the studied ones, the evaluation tells whether DefDroid, as a dynamic solution, is effective in handling *new* DAB cases.

Another critical aspect of a defensive OS like DefDroid is its impact on the usability of apps. To understand this, we first quantitatively measure DefDroid's usability impact on the evaluated apps. Second, we conduct a small-scale user trial to observe how DefDroid performs in a user's daily use of smartphone. Third, we deploy DefDroid to 185 *real users* through the PhoneLab [47]. Lastly, we measure the performance overhead of DefDroid compared to vanilla Android.

5.1 Experimental Setup

The experiments are conducted on two Motorola G devices and one Nexus 4 device running DefDroid that is modified from Android 4.4.3. We use the Qualcomm Trepn Profiler 5.1 [19] to profile system and app performance values. Experiments that involve performance values are all run on the Nexus 4 device for consistency. The default defense policies used in the experiments are set empirically as described in §3.4.2, and we evaluate how different policies affect the results in §5.5.

When evaluating the 128 DAB cases, we run each case in turn on DefDroid and compare the effect with running these cases on unmodified Android. For the sake of comparability, we toggle a knob in DefDroid to control the changes that are added to Android. When turned off, the defensive service and all modules will be completely disabled so that the system behaves the same as unmodified Android. In this way, the experiments are conducted within the same ecosystems.

Studied cases		New cases	
Total	**Handled**	**Total**	**Handled**
96	94	32	31

Table 7: The number of real-world DAB cases DefDroid succesfully handles among all the evaluated DAB cases.

Resource	Reduction		
	Min	**Median**	**Max**
Power	72mW, 6%	189mW, 21%	481mW, 87%
Mobile data	17MB, 15%	54MB, 34%	183MB, 86%
Storage	30MB, 25%	48MB, 37%	145MB, 90%

Table 8: Resource consumption reduction value and percentage for running the real-world DAB cases on DefDroid compared to Android.

For each case, we first interact with the app for 5 minutes and perform user actions to trigger the misbehavior. Then we return to the Home screen and wait for 25 minutes to observe the effect of disruptive behavior. For fair comparison, we interact with the app in similar way when switching from DefDroid to unmodified Android.

5.2 Curbing Disruptive App Behavior

5.2.1 *Overall Result*

We first show how effective is DefDroid in handling the 128 real-world DAB cases. A case is considered to be successfully handled when DefDroid took actions on the misbehaviors during the experiments. As shown in Table 7, DefDroid successfully handled 125 out of 128 cases in total (94 studied cases and 31 new cases).

DefDroid misses 3 cases due to the defensive policy settings. In our default policies, we define an app as potentially over-consuming mobile data if it crosses a threshold for 4 *consecutive* monitoring intervals. This policy can tolerate legitimate spike in data usage. But in two of the missed cases, the apps did not cross the threshold for one interval. To catch them requires adjusting the default policy settings. The third missed case is related to storage over-use. The consumption did not exceed the empirical thresholds that we set via profiling popular apps. But the user considered the consumption abnormally high given that the app is text-based. We plan to improve defensive policies by considering app categories and usage history.

5.2.2 *Resource Consumption Reduction*

From a user's perspective, the impact of DAB is mainly perceived as excessive usage of resources like battery and cellular data. A primary benefit of using a defensive mobile OS like DefDroid is to restrict such negative impact. Therefore, for the 125 cases that are handled by DefDroid, we further measure the reduction in resource consumption compared with unmodified Android.

Table 8 shows the reduction results (both absolute amount and percentage-wise) for power, mobile data and storage. For each resource, we measure cases that have impact on that resource. The re-

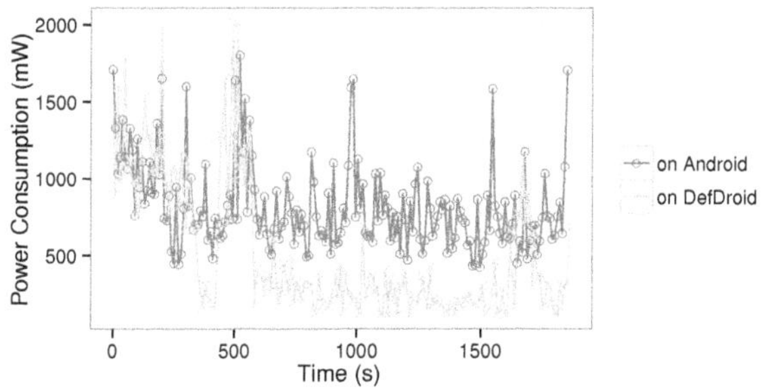

Figure 10: Power consumption comparison for a DAB case running on Android versus running on DefDroid.

Metric	Android	DefDroid
Wakelock held time	26–30min	7–10min
GPS held time	30min	10–13min
Sensor held time	30min	6–8min
Other resource held time	30min	6–9min
Number of wake-ups	61–203	26–49
Number of broadcasts	64–80	28–31
Number of notifications	43–110	13–41
Number of connections	180–1173	64–477
CPU load	70–100%	43–67%

Table 9: Micro metrics comparison of running the DAB cases on Android and running them on DefDroid.

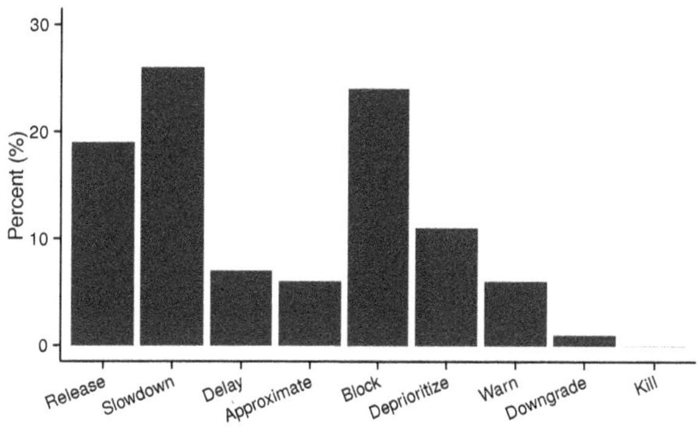

Figure 11: The distribution of defensive actions that DefDroid took during experiment. Refer to Table 5 for examples of a defensive action.

Impact	Cases
No side effect	40 (32%)
Deferred executions	49 (39%)
Failed requests	31 (25%)
Checked exceptions*	5 (4%)
Termination	0 (0%)

Table 10: Impact of DefDroid defensive mechanisms to evaluated disruptive apps. *: exceptions that compilers enforce developers to handle, *e.g.* IOException.

sults show that, the defensive mechanisms in DefDroid drastically limit the impact of DAB and achieve significant resource consumption reduction.

Figure 10 shows an example that illustrates the power consumption of running an evaluated DAB case (OSMTracker GPS leak) on DefDroid versus on unmodified Android. Since we interact with the app on DefDroid similarly as on unmodified Android in the first 5 minutes, the app power consumptions on the two systems are similar in the initial phase. But at around the 10th minute, DefDroid unregistered the leaked listener which still persisted on the unmodified Android. Therefore the power consumptions on the two systems start to diverge.

5.2.3 Micro Analysis

In addition to the resource consumption reductions, we also analyze key system micro metrics that reflect the symptoms of a given DAB pattern, *e.g.* wakelock held time for the wakelock leak/overuse pattern. For each evaluated case, we compare the micro metrics on DefDroid with the metrics on unmodified Android.

Table 9 shows the result. Since there are multiple relevant cases for a particular metric, we show the values in a range form. The comparison results are in line with macro resource consumption analysis: the defensive mechanisms in DefDroid successfully restrained the effect of evaluated misbehaviors at the micro level.

Moreover, we analyze the defense actions that DefDroid took when handling the evaluated DAB cases. In total, 258 actions were executed during the experiments. In dealing with 89 cases, DefDroid applied multiple actions (*e.g.*, *approximate* then *release*) or one action multiple times (*e.g.*, *slowdown*).

Figure 11 shows the distribution of the defensive actions applied by DefDroid. The most applied actions are *slowdown*, *block* and *release*. Interestingly, we observe that having a diverse set of defensive modules in DefDroid helps catch some misbehaviors more quickly. For instance, in dealing with some "endless connection" misbehavior, the CPU and alarm defensive module took actions (as they used CPU or alarms too aggressively) to limit the disruptive behavior before the network defensive module took actions. Figure 11 also shows that the *kill* actions were not invoked during the experiments.

5.3 Usability Impact

Being effective in curbing DAB is not enough. Another important requirement of DefDroid is to still preserve the main functionalities of the misbehaving apps.

To meet this requirement, when DefDroid detects a potential misbehavior, it tries defensive actions with least perturbation to app usability, before executing more strict actions. Moreover, when executing an action such as adjusting an app's frequent alarms, DefDroid makes gradual adjustments instead of abrupt changes. DefDroid also exempts foreground apps from defensive actions to allow legitimate heavy usage (*e.g.*, using Google Maps for a long time will not be affected by DefDroid).

We analyze the usability impact of our defensive actions to the misbehaving apps used in the experiments from both execution logs and theory of related OS mechanism. Take the wakelock as an example. A wakelock is essentially a kernel reference counter to certain hardware components (typically CPU). As long as *any* app has an active wakelock, the hardware components will not go into low-power state. Apps use wakelock to ensure the hardware component stays on to finish tasks that are deemed important. When an app holds a wakelock for too long, DefDroid may force a *release* on that wakelock. From app perspective, the effects of the *release* action depend on several situations:

a). The app leaks the wakelock and the tasks have already finished. Then the *release* action curbs the misbehavior and causes no side effect to the app at all.

b). The app leaks the wakelock and the tasks have not finished yet. The *release* action may also induce no side effect. This is because as long as there are some other apps holding an active wakelock at that moment, the hardware component will keep on, giving chance for the affected app to finish the tasks as usual. If the released wakelock is the last reference, the CPU will be put into low-power state soon after *release*. The system will freeze the app state before suspending. When important interrupts wake up the system later, the app state will be resumed. Therefore, the *release* action causes delay in app execution. In certain scenarios, when the app resumes execution, it might cause exceptions (*e.g.*, `IOException`). These exceptions are usually enforced to be handled by the developers, *i.e.*, the corresponding exception handling code in the app will be triggered.

c). The app does not leak the wakelock but holds it for unusually long. The *release* action does not affect the app to later refer to and release the lock object. This is because the defensive action is executed inside system services; Therefore, depending on whether the tasks have finished or not, the impact is similar to *a)* or *b)*, respectively.

The analysis result for usability impact to all the evaluated apps is presented in Table 10. It shows that the executed defensive actions cause only marginal usability impact for most of the evaluated apps. For a significant percentage of the cases, the defensive actions do not cause any side effects to the misbehaving apps. Moreover, DefDroid does not cause crashes for the evaluated apps.

The significant percentage (32%) of no-side-effect cases is mainly attributable to our designs. Additionally, some defensive action (*e.g.*, *release*) is in fact a "hot fix" for certain DAB cases like resource leak. Moreover, our choice to implement the defensive modules in system server rather than app address space also ensures that the action does not tamper with app internal state. Lastly, from the app's perspective, the effect of some defensive actions is the same as an environment condition that the app has to cope with, *e.g.*, network disconnection and losing GPS signal.

In 80 cases, the defensive actions cause deferred execution or failed requests. Such impact may be undesirable for well-behaved apps. But note that the evaluated subjects are apps that are behaving aggressively, *e.g.*, a weather app updating locations every minute, a chat app entering infinite connection loops due to a bug. DefDroid makes these behaviors less aggressive but still maintains the main functionalities of these apps, *e.g.*, reduce the weather location update frequency to be every three minutes. Such impact is usually not noticeable to users as validated in §5.4.

In the remaining 5 cases, the defensive actions caused checked exceptions – exceptions that the compilers enforce developers to handle, *e.g.*, `SSLException` due to connection time out when the app resumes. Therefore, the defensive actions triggered the error handling code to be executed as if external conditions (*e.g.*, network disconnection) occurred. These exceptions did not cause the apps to crash or enter unexpected states.

5.4 Real User Deployment

Except for evaluating DefDroid on existing real-world DAB cases, we further understand how DefDroid performs in a real user's daily usage scenario.

5.4.1 Small-scale User Trial

We first conduct a trial with 4 volunteer users for 10 days. We flash the DefDroid system image to these users' smartphones and ask the users to report any suspicious problems encountered during their daily use. At the end of the trial, we collect the DefDroid logs from their devices and interview the users for their experiences.

App	Disruptive behavior
cClock	Constrant GPS search
The Economist	Wakelock leak or overuse
Sina News	Long-held GPS
Xiami	Excessive wakelock requests
Kik	Too frequent wake-ups
Zillow	Excessive toasts (notifications)

Table 11: Newly found DAB issues that DefDroid identified and handled in user trials.

In total, we received two reports of DefDroid falsely warning the users about potential large mobile data usage. Both users think the data usage is acceptable, and they simply chose the default ignore action provided by DefDroid. Beside these two, we did not receive any other reports during the trial; nor are any other noticeable anomalies/slowdowns reported in the final interview.

Interestingly, when we analyze the collected logs, we find DefDroid took a number of actions to several apps in the user trials. We further confirmed these misbehaviors DefDroid identified by reproducing them in our smartphones. Table 11 shows these new DAB issues. Some users are surprised about these findings. One user said, *"I installed the Xiami app but found it did not support the U.S. users, so I did not use it at all afterwards."* But DefDroid discovered the app was requesting wakelock excessively in the background and denied its requests for certain time. We reproduced the misbehavior and found it could drain battery quickly. With DefDroid, the users did not experience negative impact such as fast battery drain for these new DAB issues during the trial. Some of the new DAB issues are also confirmed by other users or developers, *e.g.* the issue of cClock constantly searching GPS and draining battery [9, 8] and the issue of Kik battery drain due to excessive wake-ups.

5.4.2 Large-scale Deployment

In addition to the small-scale user trial, we have also deployed DefDroid via the PhoneLab testbed [47] to 185 real users. The deployment follows PhoneLab release policy: the platform change is first rolled out to a small group of PhoneLab developers to be used for at least one week to make sure the change does not cause significant user experience disruption; then the change will be pushed to all users.

The DefDroid experiment on PhoneLab lasted for 43 days from 2015/09/21 to 2015/11/3. During this period, DefDroid applied actions on 81 unique apps in 105 of the 185 participants. We recreated the logged disruptive behavior for 57 apps such as Viber, TWC WiFi Finder, Bejeweled Blitz, GPS Odometer. Some cases were initially puzzling to us based on the collected logs. For example, we found DefDroid applied actions on the NY Times app in several devices because the app used sensor aggressively even when users were not using it. We decompiled the app binary to make sense of the behavior. Even though the source code is obfuscated, based on the path name of the source file that made the sensor requests, we suspect the aggressive behavior came from an advertisement module that the app is using. There are 6 *potential* false alarms (from sleep tracking apps and fitness apps). These aggressive behaviors are likely expected by users. For those logged disruptive behavior that we could not reproduce, we suspect it is be-

	CPU Load	Memory	Power
Android	37.5%	1721.9MB	1688.4mW
DefDroid	39.2%	1749.8MB	1719.8mW
Overhead	1.7±0.3%	27.9±0.9MB	31.4±7.4mW

Table 12: Performance overhead of DefDroid with 95% confidence interval.

cause the latest version fixed the issue or the user conducted some special interactions.

Through the PhoneLab experiment, we also learned some lessons: *1).* Our primary goal of the PhoneLab deployment is to get an assessment on whether DefDroid may break app functionality in real world. In this regard, the experiment shows positive result: for all the apps that DefDroid applied actions during the experiment, we did not receive any user complaint that the functionality of these apps became broken or eccentric. But we got some user complaints about overall battery drains. Before the deployment, the authors had already used phones running DefDroid based on Android 4.4 for more than one month without encountering major issues. When we were requesting to deploy DefDroid on PhoneLab, the PhoneLab codebase was in the middle of migrating to Android 5.1. Due to release time constraint, we ported DefDroid from Android 4.4 to 5.1 in about 10 days. As a result, even though we preliminarily tested the new DefDroid, we did not expose the inefficiency under Android 5.1 that caused battery drain for some users. We later found and fixed the issue; *2).* When we started to analyze the logs after deployment, we realized the deployment is also a good opportunity to collaboratively tune the defense policies (*e.g.*, sensor rate limit). The log statements we added in DefDroid for the experiment missed some important details that could have been benefitial to understand about DAB in the wild.

5.5 Different Defense Policies

The effectiveness of DefDroid depends on both the defensive actions and policies. We set the default policies by profiling the behaviors of many popular apps and empirically choose the settings. Besides the default policies, DefDroid provides users with two additional policy templates, a "conservative" policy template and a more "aggressive" one, to trade-off the defense and the impact. Under the conservative policies (*e.g.*, GPS duration throttle increased to 20 min), DefDroid may miss some DAB but the usability side effects tend to be reduced. Under the aggressive policies, DefDroid may catch more DAB but at the cost of more side effects.

We experiment DefDroid with both the conservative policies and aggressive policies on the 128 DAB cases. Compared to the default policy, the conservative policies would miss 6 more cases while increasing the no-impact cases in Table 10 by 11; the aggressive policy would catch all 3 missed cases in default policy while decreasing the no-impact cases in Table 10 by 8.

5.6 Performance Overhead

We evaluate the performance overhead of DefDroid during normal usage scenario. We repeatedly interact with 10 popular apps such as Facebook, Angry Birds, and Gmail in turns for a total session of 30 minutes. During the interaction session, these apps will switch between background and foreground. The experiments are first conducted three times on our Nexus 4 device running DefDroid, and then conducted three times on our Nexus 4 device running unmodified Android. In all the experiments, we try to interact with the apps in the same way for fair comparison. Even if DefDroid does not execute defensive action during the experiment session, DefDroid still needs to actively monitor app activities, which is the main component of DefDroid's overhead.

We measure the CPU load, memory usage and power consumption of DefDroid and unmodified Android when running the above workloads. Table 12 shows the averaged results and overhead with 95% confidence intervals. The results indicate that DefDroid incurs little overhead compared with unmodified Android.

6. DISCUSSION AND LIMITATIONS

API semantics guarantees to apps: A design trade-off that needs to be considered in making mobile OS more defensive is the API guarantees to apps. Some defensive actions may relax the original API contract under aggressive condition. For example, in DefDroid, an app's wake-up requests may be suppressed by the OS if they are too frequent. In contrast, vanilla Android always satisfies the app requests. We believe that the pervasive DAB issues and the rise of novice app developers make such trade-off necessary to prevent DAB from impacting users. As mentioned in §1.3, this trade-off is echoed by some recent changes in mainstream mobile OSes. For example, all repeating alarms are inexact starting from Android 4.4. DefDroid leverages fine-grained action and reversion to minimize the compromise on API contract. To app developers, such nondeterminism might provide incentive for more cautious usage of APIs (since nondeterminism only arises when the request pattern is potentially aggressive). In the future, we plan to explore exposing some callbacks to developers when a contract is going to be broken to give apps some grace period to react.

Other mobile OSes: Many of the DAB issues we study such as aggressive sensor usage, frequent wake-ups, and excessive mobile data usage are not specific to Android but widely exist in other platforms including iOS and Windows Phone as well [49, 42, 48]. We choose to implement DefDroid on Android because it is open-sourced. We leave studying and addressing the DAB issues in the other platforms for future work.

Using DefDroid as a developer tool: The main goal of DefDroid is to provide a last level of runtime defense to prevent DAB issues from affecting users. But it is also possible to use DefDroid as a developer tool to help developers catch their apps' disruptive behavior that is hard to be exposed with testing or static code analysis. For example, developers can run their apps in DefDroid for a while before a release, and then use the action logs from DefDroid to determine if potential DAB defects exist in the new version.

Limitations of DefDroid: While our evaluation shows DefDroid is effective on real-world DAB, there are several limitations that we plan to address as our future work. First, each defensive module and action in DefDroid is implemented separately because different resources are managed differently in the base OS. We are looking into whether designing a more generic approach of managing different resources would allow the techniques in DefDroid to be more systematic. Second, since DefDroid does not understand the semantics of app configurations for users, the defensive actions may overrule user configurations. For example, a news app may aggressively refresh content because users configure it so. Users currently can white-list the app to preserve the behavior. Third, the policies for defensive actions in DefDroid are statically set based on offline profiling. We plan to adjust the policies dynamically based on app usage history. Fourth, there may be new DAB patterns that cannot be addressed by the current defensive mechanisms in DefDroid. But DefDroid makes it easy to add new defense modules.

7. RELATED WORK

A few aspects of DAB have been explored individually in literature, *e.g.*, energy bugs [49, 41, 67, 52, 65], inefficient network activity [59, 55, 33, 39, 40, 53, 30], abnormal battery drain [35, 44, 48, 50, 34]. Our work builds upon these prior work but uniquely investigates the generic DAB problem as a whole, and proposes solution from mobile system perspective to address DAB. DefDroid enhances mobile OS to react to a wide range of DAB issues at runtime.

Mobile OSes allow apps to run in background to perform certain task. But background task is often responsible for abnormal battery drain [36]. Many task managers exist to allow users to kill heavy background tasks. ZapDroid [62] automatically disables infrequently used apps. These coarse-grained solutions break app usability and suffer from well-known issues [24, 15]. Amplify [2] and TAMER [45] uses Xposed framework [26] to dynamically hook app method calls in app address space and release/throttle wakelock and GPS requests in background tasks to save battery. While our work takes similar runtime mitigation approach for the two issues, we study a wide range of DAB issues that are not addressed by these tools. Our solution lies natively in the OS to systematically address DAB. Additionally, we comprehensively evaluate the app usability impact of runtime mitigation, which is not investigated in the prior work.

Compared to work that optimizes mobile operating systems such as Ghost hint [29], Cinder [60], Rio [28], K2 [43], and Android Doze mode [16], we focus on improving mobile OS to consider inexperienced app developers who can make various programming mistakes, and proactively protect users from DAB.

The idea of defensive actions in DefDroid is inspired by failure-oblivious computing [58, 54, 31]. But rather than trying to tolerate failures like memory errors of server applications to enhance availability, DefDroid aims to limit the negative impact of DAB at runtime.

8. CONCLUSION

As the mobile developer population and app market continue to soar, disruptive app behavior is an emerging class of issues that calls for more system-level solutions. In this paper, we study a large number of real-world DAB issues and present DefDroid, an Android-based OS that is designed to be more defensive and use fine-grained defensive mechanisms to curb DAB dynamically.

Our evaluation of DefDroid on 128 real-world DAB cases shows that, with careful designs and implementation, a more defensive mobile OS can not only curb DAB effectively but also achieve the effectiveness with little performance overhead and marginal negative usability impact to apps.

DefDroid found and addressed 6 new DAB cases in the field during user trials. We have deployed DefDroid to 185 *real users* via the PhoneLab testbed for 43 days and found DAB issues from at least 57 apps. DefDroid is available at http://defdroid.org.

9. ACKNOWLEDGEMENTS

We thank the MobiSys reviewers and our shepherd, Lenin Ravindranath, for their valuable feedback that improved the paper. We appreciate the great help from the PhoneLab team, especially Jinghao Shi and Geoffrey Challen, on deploying DefDroid on PhoneLab. We are very grateful to the volunteer users and the PhoneLab participants for using DefDroid, and providing useful feedback for us to improve DefDroid. This work was supported by NSF CNS-1017784 and CNS-1321006.

10. REFERENCES

[1] Aggressive behavior in AndStatus - massive requests of "users/show". https://github.com/owncloud/android/issues/554.

[2] Amplify. http://forum.xda-developers.com/xposed/modules/mod-nlpunbounce-reduce-nlp-wakelocks-t2853874.

[3] Android Central. www.androidcentral.com.

[4] Android Forums. http://androidforums.com.

[5] Android WakeLock. http://developer.android.com/reference/android/os/PowerManager.WakeLock.html.

[6] App BetterWeather high battery drain in environment with poor GPS signal. https://github.com/MarcDufresne/BetterWeather/issues/6.

[7] Battery drain because of long-lived wakelock in Kontalk. https://github.com/kontalk/androidclient/issues/143.

[8] cClock app bug report. https://jira.cyanogenmod.org/browse/CYAN-2742.

[9] Clock is draining battery due to constant GPS search. http://forum.cyanogenmod.org/topic/80799-clock-is-draining-battery-due-to-constant-gps-search/.

[10] CSipSimple battery consumption issue discussion. https://code.google.com/p/csipsimple/issues/detail?id=81.

[11] Discussion about proper rules of using GPS. https://github.com/SecUpwN/Android-IMSI-Catcher-Detector/issues/87.

[12] Instantupload bug in ownCloud - continuous retry but file exists on server. https://github.com/owncloud/android/issues/554.

[13] Issue in podax: Default to wifi only download. https://github.com/thasmin/Podax/issues/13.

[14] Location provider drains battery. https://github.com/rtreffer/LocalGSMLocationProvider/issues/8.

[15] Multitasking the Android way. http://android-developers.blogspot.com/2010/04/multitasking-android-way.html.

[16] Optimizing for Doze and app standby in Android. http://developer.android.com/training/monitoring-device-state/doze-standby.html.

[17] Patch to fix aggressive widget update period configuration in anki-droid. https://github.com/nicolas-raoul/Anki-Android/commit/9193806eb0546bf8d7c040ad40272d632b4d3e99.

[18] Power saving mode optimization in AnySoftKeyboard. https://github.com/AnySoftKeyboard/AnySoftKeyboard/issues/463.

[19] Qualcomm Trepn profiler. https://developer.qualcomm.com/mobile-development/increase-app-performance/trepn-profiler.

[20] Request: Auto sync over WiFi only. https://github.com/AndlyticsProject/andlytics/issues/678.

[21] Seadroid downloads files in loop. https://github.com/thasmin/Podax/issues/13.

[22] Wakelock detector app. https://play.google.com/store/apps/details?id=com.uzumapps.wakelockdetector.

[23] What's new in iOS 7 background multitasking. https://www.captechconsulting.com/blogs/ios-7-tutorial-series-whats-new-in-background-multitasking.

[24] Why you shouldn't use a task killer on Android. http://www.howtogeek.com/127388/htg-explains-why-you-shouldnt-use-a-task-killer-on-android.

[25] XDA developers. http://www.xda-developers.com.

[26] Xposed framework. http://repo.xposed.info.

[27] Adjust. Birth, life and death of an app - A look at the Apple App Store. 2014.

[28] A. Amiri Sani, K. Boos, M. H. Yun, and L. Zhong. Rio: A system solution for sharing i/o between mobile systems. In *Proceedings of the 12th Annual International Conference on Mobile Systems, Applications, and Services*, MobiSys '14, pages 259–272, Bretton Woods, New Hampshire, USA, 2014. ACM.

[29] M. Anand, E. B. Nightingale, and J. Flinn. Ghosts in the machine: interfaces for better power management. In *Proc. of the 2nd international conference on Mobile systems, applications, and services*, MobiSys '04, pages 23–35, Boston, Massachusetts, 2004. ACM.

[30] N. Balasubramanian, A. Balasubramanian, and A. Venkataramani. Energy consumption in mobile phones: A measurement study and implications for network applications. In *Proceedings of the 9th ACM SIGCOMM Conference on Internet Measurement Conference*, IMC '09, pages 280–293, Chicago, Illinois, USA, 2009. ACM.

[31] E. D. Berger and B. G. Zorn. DieHard: Probabilistic memory safety for unsafe languages. In *Proceedings of the 2006 ACM SIGPLAN Conference on Programming Language Design and Implementation*, PLDI '06, pages 158–168, Ottawa, Ontario, Canada, 2006. ACM.

[32] A. Carroll and G. Heiser. An analysis of power consumption in a smartphone. In *Proc. of the 2010 USENIX conference on USENIX annual technical conference*, USENIXATC'10, pages 21–21. USENIX Association, 2010.

[33] A. Chakraborty, V. Navda, V. N. Padmanabhan, and R. Ramjee. Coordinating cellular background transfers using loadsense. In *Proceedings of the 19th Annual International Conference on Mobile Computing & Networking*, MobiCom '13, pages 63–74, Miami, Florida, USA, 2013. ACM.

[34] R. Chandra, O. Fatemieh, P. Moinzadeh, C. A. Thekkath, and Y. Xie. End-to-end energy management of mobile devices. Technical Report MSR-TR-2013-69, July 2013.

[35] X. Chen, N. Ding, A. Jindal, Y. C. Hu, M. Gupta, and R. Vannithamby. Smartphone energy drain in the wild: Analysis and implications. In *Proceedings of the 2015 ACM SIGMETRICS International Conference on Measurement and Modeling of Computer Systems*, SIGMETRICS '15, pages 151–164, Portland, Oregon, USA, 2015. ACM.

[36] X. Chen, A. Jindal, N. Ding, Y. C. Hu, M. Gupta, and R. Vannithamby. Smartphone background activities in the wild: Origin, energy drain, and optimization. In *Proceedings of the 21st Annual International Conference on Mobile Computing and Networking*, MobiCom '15, pages 40–52, Paris, France, 2015. ACM.

[37] Evans Data. Global developer population and demographic study. 2014.

[38] D. Hackborn. Comments on Android OS check for excessive wake lock usage. https://groups.google.com/forum/#!topic/android-developers/Tg7_sUL8Ec4.

[39] B. D. Higgins, J. Flinn, T. J. Giuli, B. Noble, C. Peplin, and D. Watson. Informed mobile prefetching. In *Proceedings of the 10th International Conference on Mobile Systems, Applications, and Services*, MobiSys '12, pages 155–168, Low Wood Bay, Lake District, UK, 2012. ACM.

[40] J. Huang, F. Qian, Z. M. Mao, S. Sen, and O. Spatscheck. Screen-off traffic characterization and optimization in 3g/4g networks. In *Proceedings of the 2012 ACM Conference on Internet Measurement Conference*, IMC '12, pages 357–364, Boston, Massachusetts, USA, 2012. ACM.

[41] A. Jindal, A. Pathak, Y. C. Hu, and S. Midkiff. Hypnos: Understanding and treating sleep conflicts in smartphones. In *Proceedings of the 8th ACM European Conference on Computer Systems*, EuroSys '13, pages 253–266, Prague, Czech Republic, 2013. ACM.

[42] C.-J. M. Liang, N. D. Lane, N. Brouwers, L. Zhang, B. F. Karlsson, H. Liu, Y. Liu, J. Tang, X. Shan, R. Chandra, and F. Zhao. Caiipa: Automated large-scale mobile app testing through contextual fuzzing. In *Proceedings of the 20th Annual International Conference on Mobile Computing and Networking*, MobiCom '14, pages 519–530, Maui, Hawaii, USA, 2014. ACM.

[43] F. X. Lin, Z. Wang, and L. Zhong. K2: A mobile operating system for heterogeneous coherence domains. In *Proceedings of the 19th International Conference on Architectural Support for Programming Languages and Operating Systems*, ASPLOS '14, pages 285–300, Salt Lake City, Utah, USA, 2014. ACM.

[44] X. Ma, P. Huang, X. Jin, P. Wang, S. Park, D. Shen, Y. Zhou, L. K. Saul, and G. M. Voelker. eDoctor: Automatically diagnosing abnormal battery drain issues on smartphones. In *Proceedings of the 10th USENIX Conference on Networked Systems Design and Implementation*, NSDI'13, pages 57–70, Lombard, IL, 2013. USENIX Association.

[45] M. Martins, J. Cappos, and R. Fonseca. Selectively taming background Android apps to improve battery lifetime. In *Proceedings of the 2015 USENIX Conference on Usenix Annual Technical Conference*, USENIX ATC '15, pages 563–575, Santa Clara, CA, 2015. USENIX Association.

[46] M. Meeker. KPCB Internet trends. 2014.

[47] A. Nandugudi, A. Maiti, T. Ki, F. Bulut, M. Demirbas, T. Kosar, C. Qiao, S. Y. Ko, and G. Challen. PhoneLab: A large programmable smartphone testbed. In *Proceedings of First International Workshop on Sensing and Big Data Mining*, SENSEMINE'13, pages 4:1–4:6, Roma, Italy, 2013. ACM.

[48] A. J. Oliner, A. P. Iyer, I. Stoica, E. Lagerspetz, and S. Tarkoma. Carat: Collaborative energy diagnosis for mobile devices. In *Proceedings of the 11th ACM Conference on Embedded Networked Sensor Systems*, SenSys '13, pages 10:1–10:14, Roma, Italy, 2013. ACM.

[49] A. Pathak, Y. C. Hu, and M. Zhang. Bootstrapping energy debugging on smartphones: A first look at energy bugs in mobile devices. In *Proceedings of the 10th ACM Workshop on Hot Topics in Networks*, HotNets-X, pages 5:1–5:6, Cambridge, Massachusetts, 2011. ACM.

[50] A. Pathak, Y. C. Hu, and M. Zhang. Where is the energy spent inside my app?: Fine grained energy accounting on smartphones with Eprof. In *Proceedings of the 7th ACM European Conference on Computer Systems*, EuroSys '12, pages 29–42, Bern, Switzerland, 2012. ACM.

[51] A. Pathak, Y. C. Hu, M. Zhang, P. Bahl, and Y.-M. Wang. Fine-grained power modeling for smartphones using system call tracing. In *Proc. of the sixth conference on Computer systems*, EuroSys '11, pages 153–168. ACM, 2011.

[52] A. Pathak, A. Jindal, Y. C. Hu, and S. P. Midkiff. What is keeping my phone awake?: Characterizing and detecting no-sleep energy bugs in smartphone apps. In *Proceedings of the 10th International Conference on Mobile Systems, Applications, and Services*, MobiSys '12, pages 267–280, Low Wood Bay, Lake District, UK, 2012. ACM.

[53] F. Qian, Z. Wang, Y. Gao, J. Huang, A. Gerber, Z. Mao,

S. Sen, and O. Spatscheck. Periodic transfers in mobile applications: Network-wide origin, impact, and optimization. In *Proceedings of the 21st International Conference on World Wide Web*, WWW '12, pages 51–60, Lyon, France, 2012. ACM.

[54] F. Qin, J. Tucek, J. Sundaresan, and Y. Zhou. Rx: Treating bugs as allergies—a safe method to survive software failures. In *Proceedings of the Twentieth ACM Symposium on Operating Systems Principles*, SOSP '05, pages 235–248, Brighton, United Kingdom, 2005. ACM.

[55] L. Ravindranath, S. Agarwal, J. Padhye, and C. Riederer. Procrastinator: Pacing mobile apps' usage of the network. In *Proceedings of the 12th Annual International Conference on Mobile Systems, Applications, and Services*, MobiSys '14, pages 232–244, Bretton Woods, New Hampshire, USA, 2014. ACM.

[56] L. Ravindranath, S. Nath, J. Padhye, and H. Balakrishnan. Automatic and scalable fault detection for mobile applications. In *Proceedings of the 12th Annual International Conference on Mobile Systems, Applications, and Services*, MobiSys '14, pages 190–203, Bretton Woods, New Hampshire, USA, 2014. ACM.

[57] M. Richtel. The youngest technorati. http://www.nytimes.com/2014/03/09/technology/the-youngest-technorati.html.

[58] M. Rinard, C. Cadar, D. Dumitran, D. M. Roy, T. Leu, and W. S. Beebee, Jr. Enhancing server availability and security through failure-oblivious computing. In *Proceedings of the 6th Conference on Symposium on Opearting Systems Design & Implementation - Volume 6*, OSDI'04, pages 21–21, San Francisco, CA, 2004. USENIX Association.

[59] S. Rosen, A. Nikravesh, Y. Guo, Z. M. Mao, F. Qian, and S. Sen. Revisiting network energy efficiency of mobile apps: Performance in the wild. In *Proceedings of the 2015 ACM Conference on Internet Measurement Conference*, IMC '15, pages 339–345, Tokyo, Japan, 2015. ACM.

[60] A. Roy, S. M. Rumble, R. Stutsman, P. Levis, D. Mazières, and N. Zeldovich. Energy management in mobile devices with the Cinder operating system. In *Proc. of the sixth conference on Computer systems*, EuroSys '11, pages 139–152. ACM, 2011.

[61] A. Shye, B. Scholbrock, and G. Memik. Into the wild: studying real user activity patterns to guide power optimizations for mobile architectures. In *Proc. of the 42nd Annual IEEE/ACM International Symposium on Microarchitecture*, MICRO 42, pages 168–178. ACM, 2009.

[62] I. Singh, S. V. Krishnamurthy, H. V. Madhyastha, and I. Neamtiu. Zapdroid: Managing infrequently used applications on smartphones. In *Proceedings of the 2015 ACM International Joint Conference on Pervasive and Ubiquitous Computing*, UbiComp '15, pages 1185–1196, Osaka, Japan, 2015. ACM.

[63] T. W. Staff. The rise of the teenage app-developer. http://theweek.com/article/index/229474/the-rise-of-the-teenage-app-developer.

[64] J. E. Vascellaro. App developers who are too young to drive. http://online.wsj.com/articles/SB10001424052702303410404577468670147772802.

[65] P. Vekris, R. Jhala, S. Lerner, and Y. Agarwal. Towards verifying android apps for the absence of no-sleep energy bugs. In *Proceedings of the 2012 USENIX Conference on Power-Aware Computing and Systems*, HotPower'12, pages 3–3, Hollywood, CA, 2012. USENIX Association.

[66] K. Yaghmour. *Embedded Android: Porting, Extending, and Customizing*. O'Reilly Media, Inc., 1st edition, 2013.

[67] L. Zhang, M. S. Gordon, R. P. Dick, Z. M. Mao, P. Dinda, and L. Yang. Adel: An automatic detector of energy leaks for smartphone applications. In *Proceedings of the Eighth IEEE/ACM/IFIP International Conference on Hardware/Software Codesign and System Synthesis*, CODES+ISSS '12, pages 363–372, Tampere, Finland, 2012. ACM.

[68] L. Zhang, B. Tiwana, Z. Qian, Z. Wang, R. P. Dick, Z. M. Mao, and L. Yang. Accurate online power estimation and automatic battery behavior based power model generation for smartphones. In *Proc. of the eighth IEEE/ACM/IFIP international conference on Hardware/software codesign and system synthesis*, CODES/ISSS '10, pages 105–114. ACM, 2010.

I-Pic: A Platform for Privacy-Compliant Image Capture

Paarijaat Aditya, Rijurekha Sen and Peter Druschel
Max Planck Institute for Software Systems (MPI-SWS)

Seong Joon Oh, Rodrigo Benenson, Mario Fritz and Bernt Schiele
Max Planck Institute for Informatics

Bobby Bhattacharjee
University of Maryland

Tong Tong Wu
University of Rochester

Abstract

The ubiquity of portable mobile devices equipped with built-in cameras have led to a transformation in how and when digital images are captured, shared, and archived. Photographs and videos from social gatherings, public events, and even crime scenes are commonplace online. While the spontaneity afforded by these devices have led to new personal and creative outlets, privacy concerns of bystanders (and indeed, in some cases, unwilling subjects) have remained largely unaddressed.

We present I-Pic, a trusted software platform that integrates digital capture with user-defined privacy. In I-Pic, users choose a level of privacy (e.g., image capture allowed or not) based upon social context (e.g., out in public vs. with friends vs. at workplace). Privacy choices of nearby users are advertised via short-range radio, and I-Pic-compliant capture platforms generate edited media to conform to privacy choices of image subjects.

I-Pic uses secure multiparty computation to ensure that users' visual features and privacy choices are not revealed publicly, regardless of whether they are the subjects of an image capture. Just as importantly, I-Pic preserves the ease-of-use and spontaneous nature of capture and sharing between trusted users. Our evaluation of I-Pic shows that a practical, energy-efficient system that conforms to the privacy choices of many users within a scene can be built and deployed using current hardware.

1. INTRODUCTION

The spontaneity afforded by mobile devices with cameras have led to new creative outlets that continue to have broad and lasting social impact. As every facet of event reporting, ranging from personal journals to war correspondence, is transformed, however, there is a growing unease about the dilution of privacy that inevitably accompanies digital capture in public, and in some cases, private fora. This paper describes I-Pic, a platform for *policy-compliant* image capture, whereby captured images are automatically edited according to the privacy choices of individuals photographed. I-Pic's design was motivated by a user-study, described in Section 2, which found that:

MobiSys'16 June 25-30, 2016, Singapore, Singapore
ACM 978-1-4503-4269-8/16/06.
http://dx.doi.org/10.1145/2906388.2906412.

Capture policies should be individualized: Privacy concerns vary between individuals. Even in the same situation, different subjects have different preferences. This finding motivated I-Pic to preclude options that impose blanket or venue specific policies [1, 2, 3].

Policies should be situational: Study subjects stated consent to be photographed at certain times, places, events, or by certain photographers, but would make different choices in other circumstances. This motivated I-Pic to not impose a static policy per individual [4], and to avoid solutions that require prior arrangements between specific subjects and photographers (whitelisting or blacklisting).

Compliance by courtesy is sufficient: An overwhelming majority of our subjects stated that they would choose to comply with the privacy preferences of friends and strangers, especially if doing so didn't interfere with the spontaneity of image capture. I-Pic provides such a platform but is not meant to stop determined users from taking pictures against the wishes of others; indeed, these users could simply use a non-I-Pic compliant device.

Consider a strawman system where mobile devices broadcast their owner's privacy preferences via Bluetooth. Without additional information, a camera would have to edit the image according to the most restrictive policy received, even if the corresponding person does not appear in the image at all! To be practical, polices must be accompanied by a visual signature so that a camera can associate a person captured in an image with a policy.

However, Bluetooth transmissions can cross walls, which would create a serious privacy problem if visual signatures were broadcast in the clear: Next-door neighbors could identify persons whom they have never seen or photographed! To avoid this problem, I-Pic relies on secure multiparty computation (MPC) to ensure that a capture device learns only a person's privacy choice, and only if that person was captured; otherwise, neither side learns anything.

User studies and privacy requirements inform the architectural components of I-Pic: Users advertise their presence over BLE (Bluetooth Low Energy): these broadcasts are received by I-Pic-compliant capture platforms. When an image is taken, the platform determines if any of the captured people match the visual signatures of nearby users using MPC. If there is a match, the platform learns the policy and edits the image accordingly, e.g., by occluding the person's face. To maintain the responsiveness of image capture, unedited images are shown to the photographer immediately, but cannot be shared until the image is processed in the background.

After presenting the results of our online survey in Section 2, we describe the main technical design of I-Pic in Section 4, along with prior work in face recognition and cryptography we build on. Next,

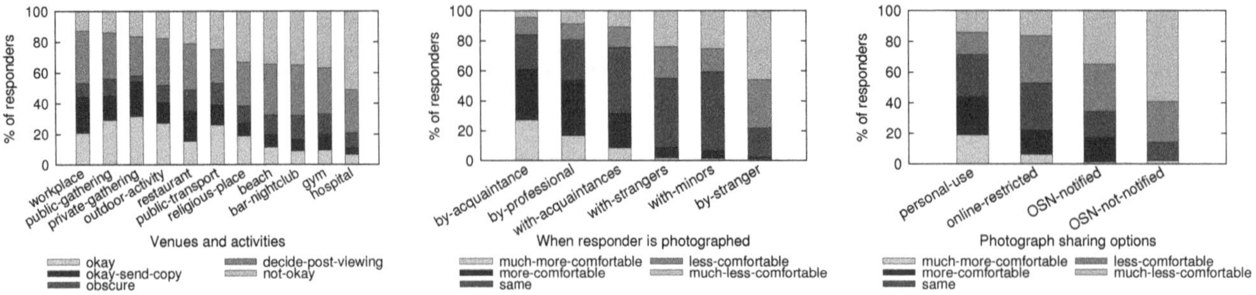

(a) Choices based on physical situations (b) Choices based on social situations (c) Choices based on use of images

Figure 1. Variety in privacy preferences under similar physical, social and image usage scenarios

we presents results of an experimental evaluation in Section 5. We discuss related work in Section 6 and conclude in Section 7.

2. ONLINE SURVEY

I-Pic's design was informed by an online survey designed to provide a broader perspective on personal expectations and desires for privacy. The survey, and experiments with I-Pic, were conducted with user consent under an IRB approval from the University of Maryland. The survey included an optional section on user demographic, including gender, age, and ethnicity.

We publicized the survey on mailing lists and online social networks on November 10th, 2015. The survey is available online at `http://goo.gl/forms/6tGG0YmFFG`, and the results here present a snapshot of all responses collected on December 4th, 2015. As of this date, there were 227 responses, with 208 responders also answering the demographic questions. Respondents represented 32 countries. The age distribution is shown in Table 1.

Age group	Fraction of participants
less than 20 years	9.2%
20 - 30 years	56.6%
30 - 40 years	25.1%
40 - 50	4.8%
more than 50 years	3.9%
Unspecified	0.4%

Table 1. Age groups of survey participants

Questions in the survey envisioned different venues and activities and presented participants with different privacy options: (a) agree to be captured in any photograph, (b) agree, but would like a copy of the image, (c) please obscure my appearance in any image, (d) can decide my preference only after viewing the photo, or (e) do not wish to be captured in any photograph. Participants were asked to choose the privacy action they considered most appropriate for each scenario (Figure 1(a)). To help visualize a common scenario and to provide perspective for others, participants were shown an image of people on a platform waiting to board a train, some with faces clearly visible. The survey also gauged individual's level of comfort depending on their relationship to the photographer or the other subjects in the photograph (Figure 1(b)). Finally, we asked how potential uses of an image influence responders' level of comfort with being captured (Figure 1(c)).

In Figure 1(a), the x-axis is sorted by the percentage of responders who chose the most private action of "do not wish to be captured", increasing from left to right. Our results show a mix of privacy concerns for different scenarios. In Figures 1(b) and 1(c), the x-axis is sorted by the percentage of responders who were much less comfortable with photography, increasing from left to right. Once again, for these social situations or image usage scenarios, the privacy concerns of responders is not uniform. *These results demonstrate the necessity of diversity in privacy policy, and argue against venue based policies that cannot be customized for individuals [2, 5].*

Unsurprisingly, privacy preferences are not unanimous for any scenario; there are, however, trends. Responders tend to be more restrictive in venues such as beaches, gyms and hospitals (in Figure 1(a)); with strangers in a social situation (in Figure 1(b)); and when images can potentially be shared online (in Figure 1(c)). These trends can be useful as they suggest default policies appropriate for different situations.

Number of privacy preferences	Fraction of participants
1	12.7%
2	27.8%
3	32.2%
4	19.4%
5	7.9%

Table 2. Variety in privacy preferences for same person

Table 2 shows the percentage of responders versus the number of different privacy choices for each responder. The table shows that individuals prefer different privacy choices depending on the given situation. *This finding illustrates the utility of context-specific policies, and demonstrates the shortcomings of individualized hard-coded policies, e.g., bar-codes on clothing [4].*

The survey asked whether responders cared about *by-stander* privacy when respondents themselves capture images. An overwhelming majority (96.47%) answered in the affirmative, motivating a system such as I-Pic. About a quarter (28%) agreed if the overhead of the solution was low; another quarter (26%) agreed if the aesthetics of images remain good.

Respondent Selection Bias The survey was voluntary and anonymous. The URL for the survey was advertised on mailing lists and social networks used by the authors and their friends, leading to a bias in how respondents learned about the survey. However, we believe that the results presented here still have merit as they represent views across different age groups and ethnicities. The results overwhelmingly support the thesis that users often desire privacy from digital capture in social situations, and further that "one-size-fits-all" solutions to image privacy are not effective. Moreover, as photographers, the responders overwhelmingly consider bystander privacy to be important. These observations inform I-Pic's design, described next.

3. I-PIC ARCHITECTURE

3.1 I-Pic overview

Figure 2 shows I-Pic's major components and their interaction. The two types of principals in the system are *bystanders* or users who may be photographed, and *photographers* who capture images. Both are assumed to operate an I-Pic-compliant *platform*. Associated with each principal is a cloud-based *agent* to which the principals offload compute-intensive tasks. The photographer is associated with a *Capture Agent*; each bystander is associated with a *Bystander Agent*. We note that agents are logical constructs; functions provided by the agent can be implemented within mobile devices should I-Pic be used without wide-area connectivity.

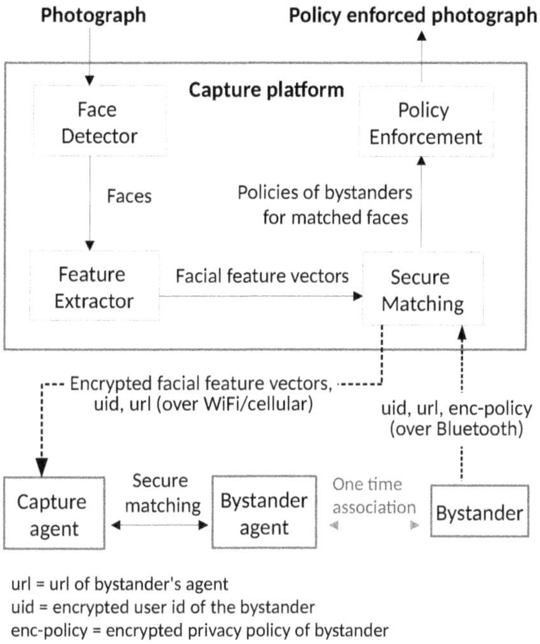

Figure 2. I-Pic major components

I-Pic requires a one-time *Association* protocol between users and their agent. Users *periodically broadcast* their presence using BLE. Once an image is captured, the *Face Detection*, *Feature Extraction*, and *Secure Matching* protocols are executed. If a user is identified, the capture platform uses the *Policy Enforcement* protocol to modify the photograph as requested. We describe these sub-protocols next.

Association: Users select an agent as a proxy and provide it with photographs, which are used to train an SVM classifier for face recognition. A user trusts her agent not to leak her visual signature. The association protocol also exchanges a master key between agent and user's device, which is used to generate session keys in the future.

Next, users initialize their privacy profile, which is locally stored on their device, by choosing relevant contexts based on location (e.g. office, home, gym, bar/restaurant, public spaces) and time (work hours, off-work hours), and by choosing an appropriate action for each context (agree to appear with face, blur face).

Periodic Broadcast: Users periodically broadcast a encrypted policy that specifies how to treat the user's picture if she appears in a photograph. This broadcast also includes sufficient information to identify the user's agent. The policy is encrypted with a session key generated using the current time (divided into 15-minutes epochs) and the master key exchanged with the user's agent.

Capture platforms receive and cache policies. Once a photograph is captured, if a user is identified, then the associated policy can be decrypted.

Secure Matching: Upon image capture, the platform detects and tries to recognize faces. These components leverage our prior work in face detection [6] and facial feature extraction [7], as detailed in Section 4.1.

The capture platform encrypts the extracted features and uploads them to its agent, along with the network identifiers of all bystander agents that it has received as broadcast recently. The *Capture Agent* and the *Bystander Agent* compare extracted features and a bystander's classifier weight vector by implementing a secure dot-product protocol [8] followed by a secure threshold comparison protocol based on garbled circuits [9]. If the threshold passes, then the session key used to encrypt user's policy is revealed to the capture platform.

Policy Enforcement: When granted a session key for a user, the capture platform decrypts the corresponding user's privacy policy and performs the action requested. Our current implementation only supports face obfuscation, which we implement using the OpenCV library. More sophisticated techniques exist. For instance, it is possible to morph a face into another face [10] instead of blurring it. Furthermore, it is also possible to remove an entire body from an image and extrapolate the background so that the removal is not obvious [11]. While such advanced image processing techniques are not the subject of this paper, I-Pic can take advantage of them.

If a captured face cannot be matched against any bystander, but all advertised policies have been evaluated, I-Pic defaults to blurring the face. This protects the privacy of bystanders who either do not own a smart device or are not I-Pic users.

Similarly, all unmatched faces are blurred if the identification protocol does not complete for some policies, likely due to lack of network connectivity. The platform maintains an encrypted copy of the original image, which can be used to release an unblurred face in the original image as the protocol completes in the future.

3.2 Threat model

I-Pic's cryptographic protocols ensure that a non-compliant capture device cannot learn the feature vectors of a bystander who does not appear in a captured image. For privacy policies of bystanders to be correctly applied, the capture platform on users' devices is assumed to implement the I-Pic protocol correctly. Third-party applications installed on users' devices are untrusted.

Users of capture devices may be able to bypass I-Pic by "rooting" their device; a different implementation could integrate I-Pic into the device firmware or implement the protocol on a trusted hardware platform, thus raising the bar for bypassing I-Pic's privacy protection. We dismissed this approach, because uncooperative photographers could in any case use a non-I-Pic compliant camera. Our goal instead is to enable cooperative photographers to respect bystander's privacy wishes in an unobtrusive manner, without introducing new attack vectors. We believe that most users welcome the ability to automatically comply with bystander's wishes, as it enables them to take pictures freely, without worrying whether they might offend others. This was also observed in our online survey (Section 2), where 96% of the participants indicated that they cared about bystanders' privacy.

The *Bystander Agent* must be trusted by the bystander not to leak her visual signature. The *Capture Agent*, on the other hand, does not have access to either the users' visual signature stored on the *Bystander Agent* or the features vectors extracted by the capture device. However, *Bystander Agent* and *Capture Agent* are assumed not to collude, else they could joinly extract the feature vectors of people captured in an image. *Capture Agent* is additionally expected to construct the garbled circuit used for secure threshold comparison (described in Section 4.2) accurately.

Cloud agents learn when an I-Pic compliant device captures an image, and the *Capture Agent* learns the IP address of that camera device (Technically, both could be spoofed since the request may use an identifier without capturing an image, and the source IP address in a request could be that of a forwarding relay). I-Pic protocols are designed to ensure that the cloud agents do not learn if a user appears in an image, or the user's current context or policy. The following Section 4 describes the I-Pic protocols in detail.

4. I-PIC DESIGN

Next, we describe the design of I-Pic in more detail. Figure 3 shows the I-Pic workflow in normal operation.

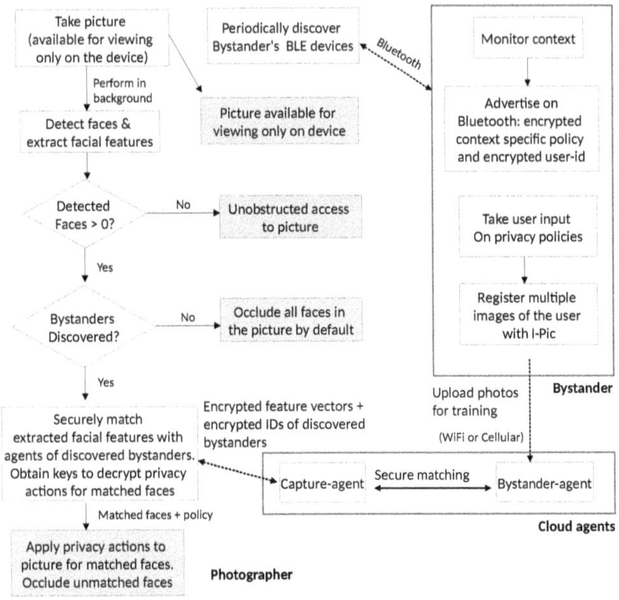

Figure 3. I-Pic workflow

I-Pic compliant devices broadcast their encrypted $(userid, policy)$ pairs periodically. I-Pic compliant capture devices additionally discover other Bluetooth devices periodically and add any received pairs to a local cache of nearby users. The entries are flushed from the cache when a device's broadcast has not been received for 10 minutes.

When an image is captured, I-Pic intercepts the raw image data. The captured image is available for viewing immediately but cannot be shared until the image is processed. A background task runs the vision pipeline described below in Section 4.1 to detect faces and extract feature vectors for each. Next, for each feature vector extracted from the image, the background task performs the secure matching protocol described below in Section 4.3 to determine if it matches with the registered classifiers of any of the bystanders in the cache, and decrypts the policies of any matching bystanders.

Finally, the I-Pic background task edits the image according to the policies of the users captured in the image. By default, any face detected in the image that did not match the signature of a bystander is occluded. This conservative choice errs on the side of privacy in case of a bystanders who does not carry a mobile device or does not use I-Pic, whose BLE broadcast was not received, or whose visual signature did not match due to a false negative of the face recognition.

4.1 Image processing

The goal of I-Pic's image processing is to identify people captured in the image, extract visual signatures for each person, and match these signatures with those advertised by nearby bystanders.

Detecting and recognizing people in images is an active area of research in computer vision. The current I-Pic prototype relies on face recognition as a well-understood and natural technique for detecting and recognizing people. More general techniques for people detection and recognition based on full-body visual signatures can be integrated into I-Pic in the future.

In the following, we briefly describe I-Pic's face detection, feature extraction, and face recognition pipeline.

Face detection: I-Pic must detect faces with high recall, ensuring that bystanders' faces are detected with high probability regardless of size, focus, pose, angle, lighting, or partial occlusion. Unlike the primary subjects of an image, bystanders are not posing for the camera, may be in the background, poorly lit, or out of focus, which makes their detection challenging.

We use the open source HeadHunter [6] prototype developed as part of our prior work on face detection. HeadHunter achieves face detection recall of $\sim$95% on standard image datasets like the Annotated Faces in the Wild (AFW) [12]. For I-Pic, we ported HeadHunter to a mobile tablet with a GPU, as described in Section 5. As we will show in Section 5.4.3, HeadHunter is superior to other face detectors available for mobile platforms.

Feature extraction: We use the state of the art person recognition method from our prior work [7]. Unlike typical face recognition systems that can recognize only the frontal faces, our person recognition system has been trained to generalize across head pose by utilizing hairstyle and context information. Due to this generalization, it outperforms other cutting-edge face recognition systems in a social media photo setting [13], where individuals often do not pose for the camera. Since I-Pic aims at identifying bystanders, this person recognition system is highly relevant.

Our person recognition system is based on a convolutional neural network (AlexNet [14]) pretrained on the ImageNet [15] classification task, and fine-tuned for the person identification task on People In Photo Albums (PIPA [13]), a large database of people in social media photos. While our prior work [7] uses five different body regions (face, head, upper/full body, and scene) to maximize the performance, we only extract features from the face region, and denote this cue as FNet.

Given a face, the original FNet extracts a 4096-dimensional feature vector. To ensure the efficiency of the secure matching algorithm, which is inversely proportional to the number of dimensions, we reduce this feature vector to 128 dimensions. We found that using the neural network itself for dimensionality reduction results in a smaller drop in overall recognition accuracy than using Principal Component Analysis. Specifically, we insert a 128-dimensional fully connected layer before the last layer in the AlexNet, randomly initialize the weights, and tune it using Stochastic Gradient Descent. Our FNet features are extracted from this 128-dimensional layer after forward passing Headhunter face detections through the network. All the training and feature extraction in neural networks are done using the open source deep learning framework Caffe [16].

Face recognition: When a user registers, I-Pic extracts FNet features from the set of portraits he or she provides. Per-user SVM classifiers are then trained on the FNet features, where positive examples consist of the portraits provided by the corresponding user, and negative examples from the other users and $\sim$12K celebrity faces in the Labeled Faces in the Wild dataset (LFW) [17]. On average, there are $\sim$15 positive examples per user, captured with different viewpoints and facial expressions. Users may subsequently provide additional images for training, for instance, if they start to wear glasses or grow a beard. The liblinear [18] package has been used to train the SVMs.

In normal operation, HeadHunter detects faces in captured images, and the corresponding FNet features are extracted. I-Pic compares the feature vector of each detected face against the trained SVM classifiers of each bystander using a dot product computation. If the dot product is above a certain threshold, the classifier indicates a match. To ensure privacy, I-Pic computes the dot product and threshold comparison as part of a secure multiparty computation between the photographer's capture agent and each bystander's agent.

Before we describe the secure matching protocol, we briefly review the underlying crypto protocols.

4.2 Cryptographic Protocols

I-Pic composes two standard protocols to achieve secure matching: secure dot product and garbled circuits.

Secure dot product: The secure dot product protocol allows two parties, each with a private vector, to compute the vector dot product without divulging the vectors. We use the protocol described in [8], which is based on the Paillier homomorphic encryption scheme [19]. We use the notation $[\![a]\!]_{pk}$ to represent the encryption of a number a using a public key pk. The Paillier encryption scheme is additively homomorphic, i.e., given $[\![a]\!]_{pk}$ and $[\![b]\!]_{pk}$, it is possible to compute $[\![a+b]\!]_{pk} = [\![a]\!]_{pk}[\![b]\!]_{pk}$. It follows that given $[\![a]\!]_{pk}$ and an integer c, one can compute $[\![ca]\!]_{pk} = ([\![a]\!]_{pk})^c$. These two primitives can be combined to compute the dot product securely. More detail can be found in [20, 8].

A straightforward application of this protocol in I-Pic, however, faces two problems: First, the capture device learns the dot products, which would enable a 'rogue' capture device to learn the classifier weight vector of each bystander. By computing dot products using a series of standard basis vectors (vectors that have a value of one in one dimension and zero in all others), the dot product values reveal the dimensions of a bystander's weight vector. To prevent this attack, we use garbled circuits [9], described below, to compute whether the dot product exceeds a threshold $\mathcal{E}$ without revealing the dot product itself.

Second, a capture device typically needs to compare several feature vectors, corresponding to multiple faces that appear in a photo, to the classifier weight vector of a bystander. For n feature vectors with m dimensions, the secure dot product computations require nm encryptions (and n decryptions). We can optimize this computation as follows.

Optimized n x 1 secure dot product: I-Pic reduces the number of encryptions from nm to m using ideas from [21]. Consider a matrix V of n vectors with m dimensions each, corresponding to n faces in a photograph, where $V_{i,j}$ is the jth element in the ith vector. Let $c_j = [V_{1,j}, V_{2,j}, ..., V_{n,j}]$ be the jth column of V. The photographer computes an encryption of c_j as $[\![c_j]\!]_{pk} = [\![(V_{1,j}) \parallel (V_{2,j}) \parallel ... \parallel (V_{n,j})]\!]_{pk}$, where $\parallel$ denotes concatenation. This involves only one encryption to produce the ciphertext for n values. The photographer sends $[\![\mathbf{c}_1]\!]_{pk}, ..., [\![\mathbf{c}_m]\!]_{pk}$, the encrypted user ids (*uid*) of the discovered bystanders, and pk to the *Bystander Agent*. For each bystander, the *Bystander Agent* computes $[\![v_{b_j}\mathbf{c}_j]\!]_{pk} = ([\![\mathbf{c}_j]\!]_{pk})^{v_{b_j}}$ for $1 \le j \le m$, where v_b is the classifier weight vector of a bystander. Multiplying these encrypted values, the *Bystander Agent* obtains a packed encryption of the dot products, $[\![P_1 \parallel ... \parallel P_n]\!]_{pk} = [\![V_1 \cdot v_b \parallel V_2 \cdot v_b \parallel ... \parallel V_n \cdot v_b]\!]_{pk} = [\![v_{b_1}\mathbf{c}_1]\!]_{pk}[\![v_{b_2}\mathbf{c}_2]\!]_{pk}...[\![v_{b_m}\mathbf{c}_m]\!]_{pk}$ and sends it back to the photographer, who decrypts (using sk) and unpacks the values to recover the individual dot products.

Garbled circuits for secure threshold computation: Garbled circuits allow two parties holding inputs x and y, respectively, to evaluate an arbitrary function *f(x,y)* without disclosing their inputs. The basic idea is that one party (the garbled circuit generator—the *Capture Agent* in our setting), prepares an "encrypted" version of a boolean circuit computing *f*; the second party (the circuit evaluator—the *Bystander Agent* in our case) then obliviously computes the output of the circuit. The combination of *secure dot product* and *garbled circuits* can provide the property that the bystander's session key is revealed to the capture device if, and only if, there is a match between an extracted feature vector and the classifier weight vector of a bystander. The capture device can then decrypt the bystander's policy.

4.3 Secure matching protocol

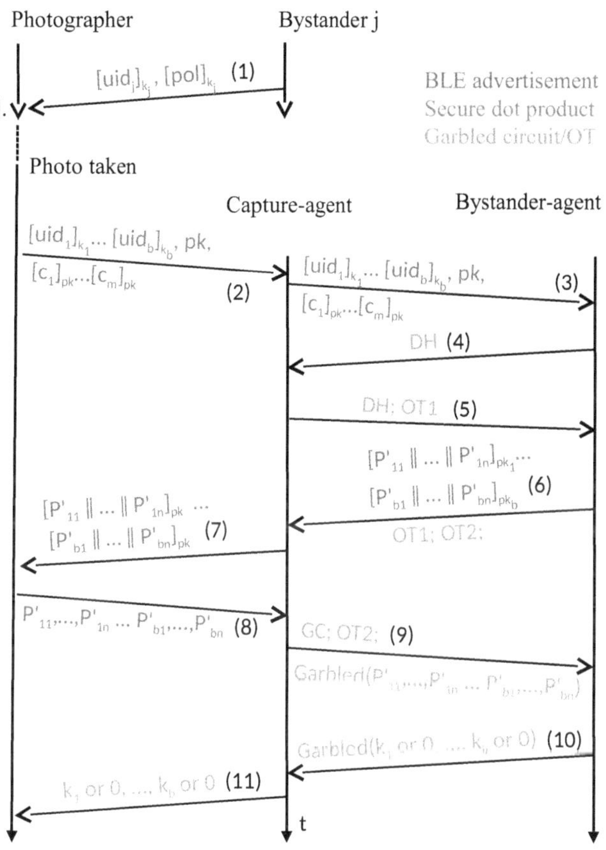

Figure 4. I-Pic secure matching protocol for one image with n faces (each facial feature vector has m dimensions). The photographer receives an advertisement from one of b bystanders (blue). The secure dot product computation requires one round trip (red). The garbled circuit (GC) requires a DH key exchange and two rounds of oblivious transfers (OT) (green).

An example message exchange of the secure matching protocol for one image with n detected faces and b bystanders is shown in Figure 4. The photographer's device computes the m encrypted column vectors according to the "optimized n x 1" secure dot product protocol, which requires m encryptions. The device sends these vectors to the *Bystander Agent* (via the *Capture Agent*) along with the encrypted user ids of the b bystanders (Message 2 and 3 in Figure 4).

The I-Pic *Bystander Agent*[1] now looks up the classifier weight vectors of the b bystanders. For each bystander, it computes the encrypted packed dot products, $[\![P_{i,1} \parallel P_{i,2} \parallel ... \parallel P_{i,n}]\!]_{pk}, 1 \leq i \leq b$, of the bystander feature vector and the n image feature vectors.

Secure thresholding The *Bystander Agent* computes *obscured* encrypted packed dot products, $[\![P'_{i,1} \parallel P'_{i,2} \parallel ... \parallel P'_{i,n}]\!], 1 \leq i \leq b$, by adding a different random value $R_{i,j}$ to each dot product $P_{i,j}$, for $1 \leq i \leq b, 1 \leq j \leq n$. This is performed by multiplying each of the b packed encrypted values containing n dot products each, $[\![P_{i,1} \parallel P_{i,2} \parallel ... \parallel P_{i,n}]\!]_{pk}$, with $[\![R_{i,1} \parallel R_{i,2} \parallel ... \parallel R_{i,n}]\!]_{pk}$ for $1 \leq i \leq b$. These *obscured* encrypted packed dot products are sent to the photographer's device via the *Capture Agent* (Message 6 and 7).

The photographer's device decrypts the b packed encrypted values containing n *obscured* dot products each, which requires b decryption operations. The device forwards these obscured dot products to the *Capture Agent* (Message 8), which then constructs a garbled circuit that takes as input n obscured dot products $P'_{i,j} = P_{i,j} + R_{i,j}$, n random values $R_{i,j}$, a session key K_i, and the threshold $\mathcal{E}$ (all provided by the *Bystander Agent*), for $1 \leq i \leq b, 1 \leq j \leq n$. The circuit computes

$$f(P'_{i,j}, \mathcal{E}, R_{i,j}, K_i) = \begin{cases} K_i & \text{if } P'_{i,j} > \mathcal{E} + R_{i,j} \\ 0 & \text{Otherwise} \end{cases}$$

that is, the circuit reveals a bystander's session key iff the dot product of the bystander's classifier weight vector and an image feature vector exceed the threshold.

Delivering the *Bystander Agent*'s inputs to the garbled circuit requires a Diffie-Hellman key exchange (DH) and two rounds of oblivious transfers (NPOT [22] and OTEXT [23]), which are partly piggy-backed on the secure dot product protocol messages, and shown in Figure 4 (Messages 4, 5, 6 and 9). The *Capture Agent* now sends the circuit to the *Bystander Agent*, along with the garbled values of the obfuscated inputs $P'_{i,j}$, and the garbled values of *Bystander Agent*'s inputs as part of the OTEXT oblivious transfer (Message 9). The *Bystander Agent* executes the circuit b times with the appropriate inputs, and returns the garbled results to the *Capture Agent* (Message 10). After ungarbling the results, the *Capture Agent* returns the session keys for the matched bystanders to the photographer's device (Message 11).

As composed, the matching protocol has the desired property that a photographer learns a bystander's current session key if and only if a feature vector in the image matches that bystander's classifier weight vector. Garbled circuits also ensure that the *Bystander Agent* does not learn whether there was a match between the encrypted facial feature vectors and a bystander. Additionally, no principal learns the vectors held by the other principals nor the magnitude of the dot products.

Note that the *Capture Agent* is trusted to construct the garbled circuit correctly. This requirement could be relaxed if one is willing to run additional checks [24] at some additional computational and runtime overhead.

5. EVALUATION

We have prototyped I-Pic on Android version 4.4.2. In our deployment, we used a Google Project Tango Tablet [25] as the photographer's capture device and Galaxy Nexus[2] phones as bystander devices. The Nexus phones advertised their presence once every 640ms over BLE.

We ported HeadHunter [6] to Android for face detection. HeadHunter is optimized for execution on CUDA-enabled GPUs [26]; the Tango Tablet allows us to access CUDA cores. The camera output on the tablet (available as a JPEG file) is first histogram equalized [27] and then resized to 640x360 before being input to HeadHunter. HeadHunter outputs bounding boxes corresponding to detected faces.

To extract feature vectors from facial images, we used an Android port of the Caffe framework [28] and ran it with our FNet neural network. The extracted vectors were normalised such that each feature value was in the range $[0, 1]$. We ported existing Java secure dot product and garbled circuit implementations [29] to C++ on Android to optimize for runtime and energy consumption. The various agents were implemented as HTTP servers.

We begin with a description of I-Pic deployments in various settings; these deployments were also approved by the University of Maryland IRB. While we gained intuition about our vision pipeline using standard face recognition datasets (and the pipeline's performance compares well with the state-of-the-art on them), all results presented here evaluate I-Pic on images captured "in the wild", reflecting spontaneous image capture in different social situations with a range of lighting conditions, camera angles, distances, and poses.

5.1 Deployments

To evaluate I-Pic, we registered fifteen volunteers from our institutions using the registration procedure detailed in Section 4.1. Each volunteer received a Galaxy Nexus device for BLE advertisement, which they carried on their person. Registered users could choose to either *show* or *blur* their face when photographed; this setting could be changed at their discretion.

The photographs in our results were captured over three days (see Table 3), and were taken using the Tango tablet and a DSLR camera. We used the DSLR setup (Sony A7, 35mm f/2.8 lens, 1/80 fixed exposure time with Sony HVL-F32M flash) to simulate better tablet cameras with higher resolution and faster apertures expected in future tablets. The photographs captured by the DSLR were manually fed into the I-Pic processing pipeline.

We annotated all photographs manually with ground truth face rectangles using the open source annotation tool Sloth [30]. For each face, we manually added other information, such as the identity of registered users, pose, and lighting condition.

Date	Capture device	Number of photographs	Number of ground-truth faces
Nov 20	Tango tablet	81	277
Nov 27	Tango tablet	176	553
Dec 02	DSLR	130	843
	All	387	1673

Table 3. Experimental dataset

5.2 I-Pic decision tree

In I-Pic, faces in photographs end up being edited (e.g., blurred) or remain unchanged, correctly or incorrectly, depending on decisions made by different subsystems. Figure 5 shows the possible paths through I-Pic, culminating in leaf nodes colored green if I-Pic preserves user privacy and red if it does not. Note that it is possible

[1]To simplify exposition, the description here assumes a single *Bystander Agent* service. The capture device would have to execute the protocol for each *Bystander Agent* in case more than one is discovered.

[2]Galaxy Nexus has Bluetooth hardware capable of BLE advertising, but the functionality is not available via standard API calls. We patched the kernel to enable BLE advertising.

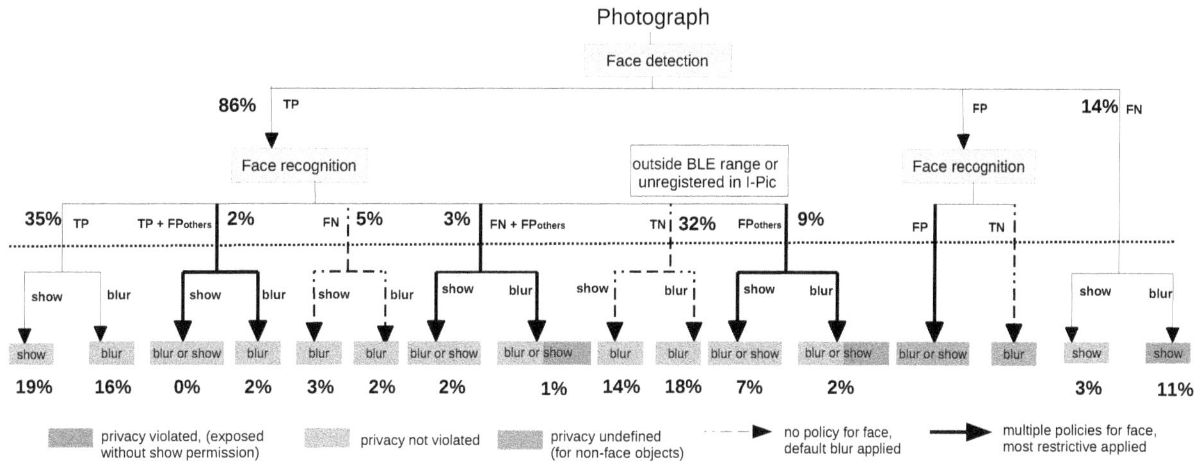

Figure 5. I-Pic decision tree

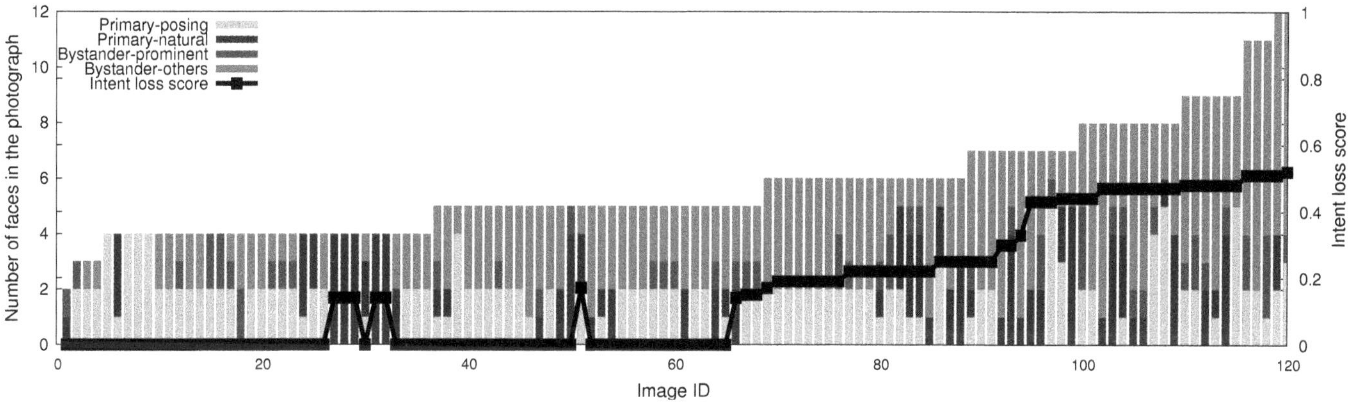

Figure 6. I-Pic Intent score of images

for I-Pic to make a mistake, e.g., not recognize a face, and for the corresponding path to still lead to a green leaf node, e.g., because the user policy stated not to obscure their face. Finally, some leaf nodes are grey, corresponding to privacy irrelevant mistakes where non-faces were detected as faces and possibly blurred.

Understanding this decision tree, and in particular, analyzing where privacy-relevant errors can accrue, will enable us to parameterize and evaluate our vision pipeline in the context of I-Pic's overall goal.

The decision tree has three stages: (1) face detection, (2) face recognition and (3) policy application. Stages 1 and 2 are computational and depend solely on the accuracy of the vision pipeline. The diagram separates these from Stage 3, which is contingent on user choices. For instance, if users choose more permissive policies, then errors from previous stages will less likely result in privacy violations, and vice-versa.

Face Detection: Stage 1 may result in three outcomes: True Positive (*TP*), where I-Pic detects a face marked in ground truth; False Positive (*FP*), where I-Pic detects a non-face object as a face; or False Negative (*FN*), where I-Pic does not detect a face marked by ground truth. All *TP* and *FP* detections are passed to the face recognition engine in the next stage.

The *FN* faces bypass the I-Pic pipeline and remain unchanged, and can potentially lead to a privacy violation (red leaf node). To minimize these cases, we bias the face detection engine towards higher recall (lower *FN*) at the expense of lower precision (higher *FP*). This means that a non-face object occasionally gets blurred in an image, in exchange for increased privacy.

Face Recognition: For a *TP* face detection output, there are six possible choices for recognition in the I-Pic pipeline: (1) True Positive (*TP*), where the detected face is matched only with the individual identified in ground truth; (2) True Positive along with False Positives (*TP**), where the face is matched with the ground truth individual, but also with others[3]; (3) False Negative (*FN*), where the face is not matched with the ground truth person; (4) False Negative along with False Positives (*FN**): I-Pic does not match with the ground truth, but instead matches with one or more other registered individuals; (5) True Negative (*TN*), where I-Pic correctly does not match the face to any registered individual; and (6) False Positive(s) (*FP**), where I-Pic incorrectly matches the face to one or more registered users.

Two leaf nodes have privacy violations for face recognition. *FP* is responsible for both paths, while one of them also requires a *FN*. Thus lower *FP* or high precision has higher priority for recognition, and adequate balance with low *FN* or high recall is also necessary. These requirements guide the parameterization of the I-Pic face recognition engine.

[3]We allow multiple matches; any registered face that exceeds a similarity threshold is considered a match.

Misdetected faces (*FP* in detection) are also fed into the recognition protocol, and may lead to (1) True Negatives (*TN*) whereby I-Pic does not recognize the "face" as a registered user, or (2) False Positives (*FP**) where I-Pic mistakenly matches the "face" to one or more registered users.

Policy: Each detected face leads to an action, as shown by the leaves of the tree. If the recognition engine outputs a single user, then the action corresponding to that users' policy is undertaken. However, in cases of multiple matches, e.g., due to *TP**, *FN** or *FP**, the most restrictive policy chosen by any "recognized" user is applied. For all unrecognized users, I-Pic blurs faces by default.

We will detail an experiment with 687 faces in 120 images to examine I-Pic's privacy violations in Section 5.3. The percentages below the leaves in Figure 5 show the fraction of faces that mapped to each path in the decision tree, in this experiment. As can be seen from the percentage values, the privacy preferences of 14% of 687 captured faces were violated, primarily due to errors early in the vision pipeline (face detection). In the next sections, we will present detailed evaluations of the vision pipeline, whose accuracy primarily determines I-Pic's performance.

5.3 I-Pic overall performance

We begin with an evaluation of I-Pic's overall performance in terms of its primary goals, which are to (i) respect bystanders' privacy, and to (ii) preserve the photographer's intent to the extent allowed by subjects' privacy choices.

Toward this end, we took a sample of 120 images with 687 faces marked in the ground-truth. We additionally marked each face according to its role in the image, as shown in Table 4, along with the frequency of faces with a given role.

Name	Role in photograph	Number of occurrences
PP	primary subject posing	185
PN	primary subject natural	115
BP	prominent bystander	56
BO	other bystanders	331

Table 4. Roles of faces captured in images

Many of the captured faces correspond to unregistered individuals. Since we don't know the privacy preferences of these individuals, we assigned them policies manually, so that we can process each image as if each captured person were registered with a policy. We assigned the *show-face* policy to the 185 PP faces, since it would be inconsistent for a person who poses for a photograph to refuse to have their face shown. For the remaining 502 faces, we randomly choose one of *show-face* or *blur-face* policies.

The percentage values given at the leaves in Figure 5 show what fraction of these 687 faces had what outcome when run through the I-Pic system. As we can see, privacy was violated in 14% of the cases, while the remaining 86% had no privacy violation.

We also assign a privacy loss score in each case of violation. These scores provide a subjective measure of the severity of the privacy violation depending on the role of the face in the image, with higher scores indicating a more severe violation. The privacy loss scores are given in Table 5, with the last column indicating how many of each type of violation occurred in the 687 faces.

About 2% of cases had the most severe privacy violation, which is to show a primary subject not posing for the camera against their wishes. Also about 2% of cases had a clearly visible bystander shown against their wishes, and around 10% were less severe cases, where a not prominently depicted bystander was not blurred. We conclude that, overall, I-Pic observes subjects' policies in most cases (86%). Moreover, violations that did occur were mostly in the moderate or mild category.

Privacy loss score	penalization scenario	occurrences
3	PN privacy violated	15 (2.18%)
2	BP privacy violated	12 (1.75%)
1	BO privacy violated	70 (10.19%)
0	no privacy violated	590 (85.88%)

Table 5. Privacy loss scores

The second aspect of I-Pic's overall performance is its ability to preserve the photographer's intent, to the extent allowed by the subject's policies. Similar to the privacy loss score, we can define a subjective intent loss score, which penalizes blurring a posing primary subject (score 3), blurring a non-posing primary subject with a *show-face* policy (score 2), and bystanders with *show-face* policies (score 1) in decreasing order of severity. The ordering is based on a subjective judgment of intent loss severity when a face is unnecessarily blurred, based on the face's role in the image. We note that our assignment of an intent penalty for the bystander case is conservative, as it is unclear whether a photographer should have expectations about capturing bystanders.

Figure 6 shows the intent loss scores for the 120 images, normalized by the maximum intent loss that could occur in a given image. The images are sorted by increasing number of faces from left to right. The bars represent the image composition in terms of roles of the faces depicted in it. I-Pic preserves the photographer's intent, as measured by our score, perfectly in 55 (45.8%) of the images, with the intent loss increasing for pictures with more faces. The vast majority of intent loss cases are caused by a failure to recognize the face of a bystander with a permissive policy, combined with I-Pic's default policy to blur.

Being focused on privacy, I-Pic biases its choices towards privacy, including the default policy and the rule to apply the most restrictive policy in case of multiple matches. As a result, losses in the vision pipeline come at the expense of intent rather than privacy. In the following subsections, we investigate circumstances that lead to imperfections in the vision pipeline, which are causal for the losses in privacy and intent reported here.

5.4 Vision pipeline analysis

The I-Pic decision tree demonstrates how (and how many) privacy violations occur as a result of errors in the vision pipeline. An obvious case is when a face is not detected, and thus not blurred in post-process. We have identified and manually labeled images with factors that affect detection and analysis, as we explain next. This analysis is done with our full image dataset of 387 images, where 1673 faces have been manually marked with ground truth (Table 3).

5.4.1 Factors affecting detection and recognition

The factors labeled in the ground truth (lighting, pose, and size) greatly affect whether a face is detected or not. We determine size based on the number of pixels in the image the face occupies; "small" faces (**s-Sm**) have a bounding box with at least one dimension less than 100 pixels[4]; all other faces are "large" (**s-Lg**). Pose is one of "frontal, profile, tilted head" (**p-Std**); "facing up, down" (**p-Avert**); "back turned, obstructed view" (**p-Occ**). Lighting is one of "Bright, even lighting" (**l-Good**); "Low even lighting" (**l-Low**); "Backlit, Shadow, Strong directional" (**l-Poor**).

Figure 7 decomposes face detection recall along these factors, for our image dataset (Table 3). The figure includes example images corresponding to different conditions for visual reference. The recall values for detection can be as high as 95% to as low as 32%,

[4]The Tango camera produces 2688 x 1520 pixels images and Sony A7 produces 4240 x 2832 pixels images

based on lighting, face size, and how occluded a face is in a photograph.

The leftmost bar with recall around 32% represents all combinations of factors combined with a partly occluded pose (**p-Occ**). 20% of the faces in our dataset are in this category. Together with the faces that suffer from low or poor illumination and an averted pose (four leftmost bars), they have recall below 50%. Faces in this category are probably not clearly recognizable even for humans without contextual information.

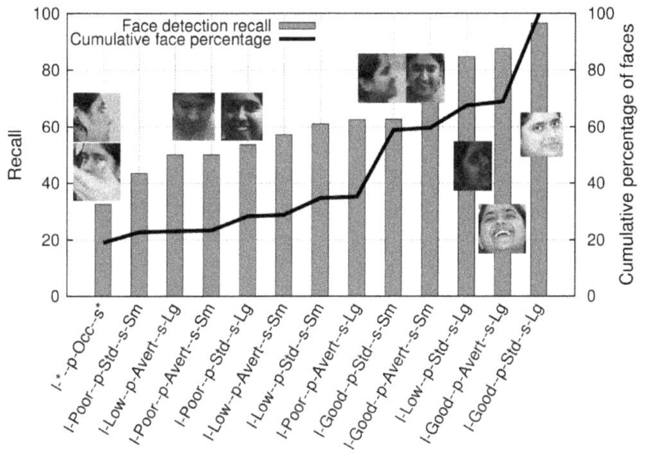

Figure 7. Face detection accuracy vs. illumination conditions, face poses and face sizes

Face characteristic	Recognition recall
l-Good–p-Std–s-Lg	85.22%
l-Good–p-Avert–s-Lg	82.79%
l-Low–p-Std–s-Lg	78.62%
l-Good–p-Avert–s-Sm	67.38%
l-Good–p-Std–s-Sm	66.29%
p-Occ or **l-Poor**	20.49%

Table 6. Face recognition recall vs. different illumination conditions, face poses and face sizes

Table 6 shows the face recognition recall for a subset of illumination, pose and size characteristics. Recognition recall is only meaningful for individuals who are registered in the I-Pic system. Our 15 registered individuals occured with the subset of conditions given in Table 6, while only unregistered individuals occured in other conditions.

p-Occ and **l-Poor** lead to poor recognition recall. This effect is intuitive, as occlusion or directional lighting distorts the facial features, making it harder to match with registered face models. Additionally, **s-Sm** performs worse than **s-Lg**. Our FNet neural network scales the input image to 227 x 227 pixels before feature extraction. Since **s-Sm** faces are less than 100 pixels in either width or height, this upscaling potentially affects the face recognition accuracy for small faces.

Precision for face detection or recognition do not show any marked correlation under different illumination, pose or size. In summary, good detection recall (>60%) and excellent recognition recall of nearly 80% occurs when pose is frontal or averted, illumination is good or low, or the size is large. This category includes about 65% of the faces in our images, and represents cases where subjects are clearly recognizable and privacy is most important.

5.4.2 Mapping back to events

The previous section identified different factors affecting I-Pic's face detection and recognition. But in what scenarios can one expect favorable conditions? In this section, we describe the scenarios in which we have evaluated I-Pic, and catalog photographs and faces from each scenario according to our factors. We note that photographers were *not* aware of these factors when the photographs were taken.

Table 7 lists four events where we obtained about 64% of our captured images. These images contain 970 manually annotated faces; the table lists the number of faces for each context. Figure 8 shows representative images from each event; Figures 9(a)-(c), show the illumination, poses and size distribution for these 970 faces.

Context name	characteristics	illumination
Campus (180 faces)	Individuals posing outdoors, with some bystanders present	Natural light
Social (237 faces)	Afternoon tea session with 40 people in an indoor atrium	Combination natural and fluorescent light
Office (129 faces)	Daily exchanges in offices and corridors	Fluorescent light
Party (424 faces)	Crowded party in small indoor venue	Back and directional lighting from lamps

Table 7. Four different social contexts

Figure 10 plots the recall ($\frac{TP}{TP+FN}$) and precision ($\frac{TP}{TP+FP}$) for both detection and recognition for the four events. The plot also includes data for *All*, corresponding to all 1673 faces in our evaluation, including those taken outside the four events.

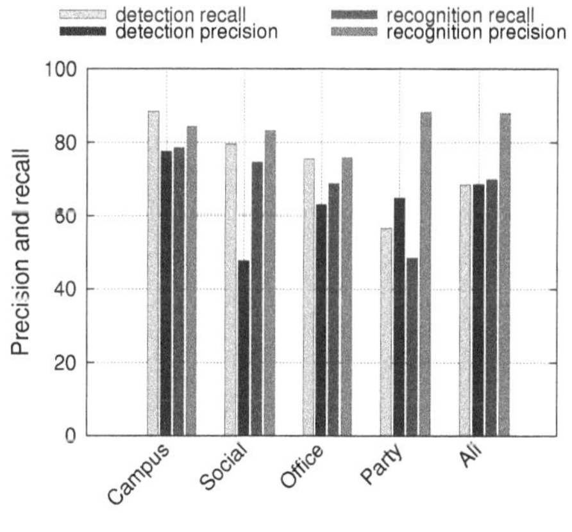

Figure 10. I-Pic vision pipeline performance

Both detection and recognition recalls depend on contexts: *Campus* photographs taken outdoors with favorable poses have high recall for both detection and recognition. In contrast, challenging lighting and occluded faces in the indoor *Party* context lead to low recall.

Face recognition precision is high, independent of the social context. However, face detection precision varies with context. Manual inspection of the images revealed that busy scenes with many people have more false positives in face detection. Here, body parts like ears or hands, or striped clothing, accidentally match the face detection template of HeadHunter. This shows up as lower precision in the *Social* context, which has crowded scenes.

As discussed in Section 5.2, I-Pic is biased towards higher recall for face detection and higher precision for face recognition, to

Figure 8. Examples images from four events used in evaluating I-Pic.

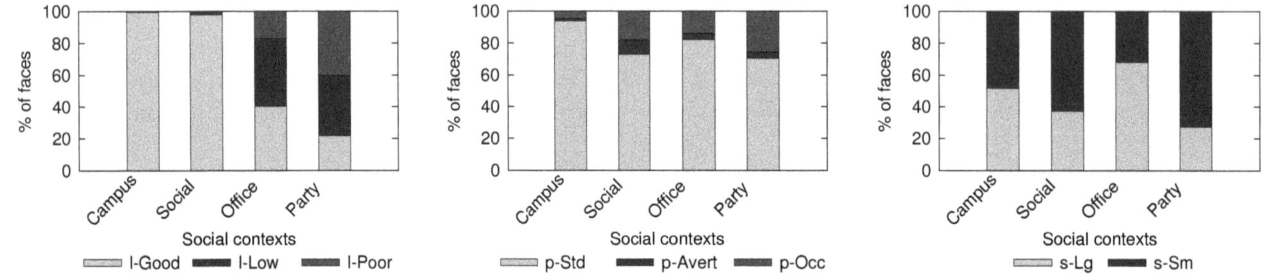

(a) Illumination (b) Face poses (c) Face sizes

Figure 9. Variety in illumination conditions, faces poses and face sizes in different contexts and resulting performance

maximize the privacy scores of the system. Figure 10 shows the effects of these choices on the vision pipeline performance.

In summary, the *Campus*, *Social*, and *Office* contexts have recall in the 70-80% range for both face detection and recognition. The challenging scenarios like *Party* provide an opportunity for future vision research. Our image dataset, captured with mobile cameras, will be very useful to design new vision algorithms, which I-Pic can incorporate in the future.

5.4.3 *Comparison to existing face detectors*

We have used our own research prototype, HeadHunter, for face detection. A natural question to consider is how well existing, widely used face detectors, such as those bundled with Android or OpenCV, compare. Table 8 shows the precision and recall for different face detection libraries on our dataset. HeadHunter vastly outperforms the competition, justifying its use within I-Pic. Note that low detection recall, in particular, leads to false negatives in I-Pic, which can lead to privacy violations.

Library	Precision	Recall
Android	38.65	5.49
Snapdragon	94.28	5.91
OpenCV	31.27	49.91
HeadHunter	68.47	68.55

Table 8. Comparison of face detection libraries

5.5 Secure Feature Comparison

Next, we present microbenchmarks evaluating the processing and bandwidth requirements of the secure vector matching protocol with varying numbers of faces and bystanders. During these experiments, both the cloud agents are running on the same machine and are on the same 802.11 WiFi network as the I-Pic devices. In each run of the experiment, we generated feature vectors randomly.

Consider Figures 11 and 12, which show the protocol's total runtime latency and its breakdown. Latency includes computations on the device, on the cloud agents, and the network transit time between the device and the *Capture Agent*.

The number of input vectors that have to be encrypted and transmitted increases with the number of faces in the photograph, resulting in an expected linear increase in runtime in Figure 11. Figure 12 shows that a major contribution to this runtime is the client side encryption of feature vectors for the secure dot product part of the protocol (Step 2 in Figure 4). Due to the "n x 1 dot product" optimization, described in Section 4.2, the client side runtime does not increase significantly with the number of faces.

From separate measurements (not shown in Figure 12) we know that these client side encryption operations show a 2x reduction in runtime on mobile platforms supporting a 64bit ARMv8-A instruction set. [5]

Increasing the number of bystanders for a fixed number of faces increases the runtime linearly, but importantly, it does not significantly increase the client-side runtime (Figure 12). This is a desirable property as the photographer's overhead does not signficantly depend on the number of bystanders in the vicinity.

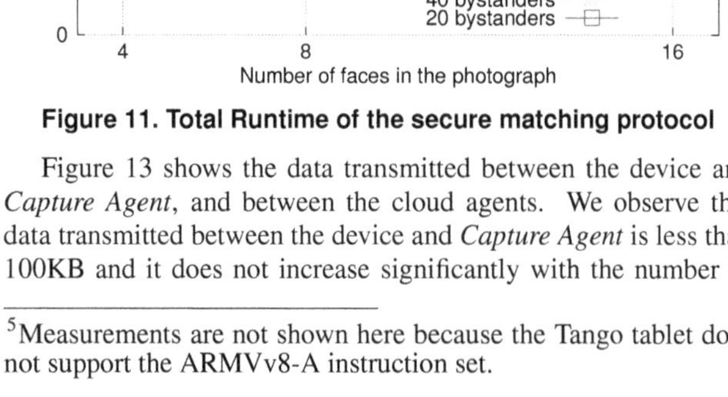

Figure 11. Total Runtime of the secure matching protocol

Figure 13 shows the data transmitted between the device and *Capture Agent*, and between the cloud agents. We observe that data transmitted between the device and *Capture Agent* is less than 100KB and it does not increase significantly with the number of

[5] Measurements are not shown here because the Tango tablet does not support the ARMVv8-A instruction set.

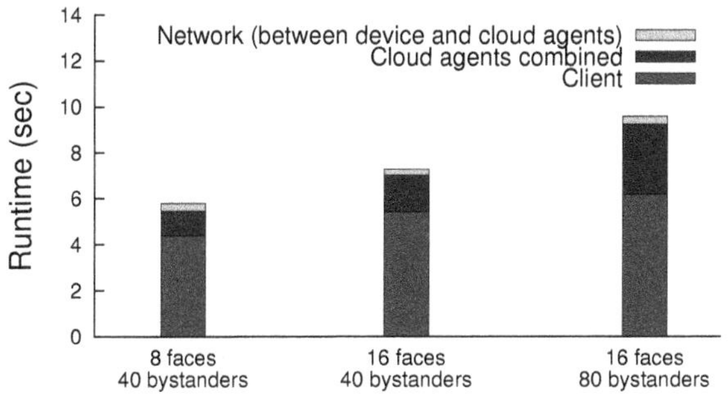

Figure 12. Runtime breakdown of secure matching protocol

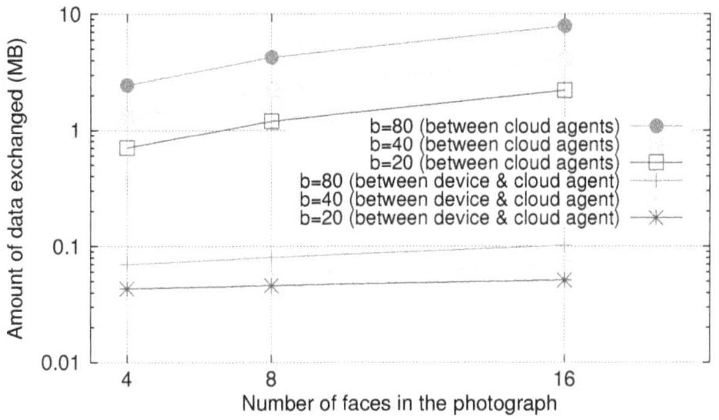

Figure 13. Total data exchanged for the secure matching protocol for different number of bystanders

faces or bystanders. This figure also shows the effects of adding the garbled circuit. The garbled circuit affects the data exchanged (and the latency) between the cloud agents, which increases both with the number of bystanders and the number of faces. Garbled circuits are evaluated by the *Bystander Agent* for each bystander and the number of inputs to each garbled circuit depends on the number of faces.

Overall the results show that the secure matching protocol can be efficiently executed. Moreover, computation can be offloaded to a significant extent from the client devices to the cloud agents.

5.6 Runtime and Energy Consumption

Figure 14 plots the overall time taken for I-Pic to process different photographs, along with times spent in different vision and secure matching tasks. In each case, the capture platform received and processed between 3 and 10 BLE advertisements, with varying number of faces in the photograph as plotted along the x-axis. The times for secure matching includes network communication and all cryptographic functions. Face detection dominates, often requiring 25 seconds per photograph. Recall that the processing takes place asynchronously in the background, and does not interfere with the users' experience while capturing and reviewing images.

While the face detection cost in particular is high in our prototype (70–80% of total processing time), we believe it is encouraging that best-of-breed face detection is feasible on mobile devices available today. Advances in mobile hardware capabilities, driven in part by emerging virtual reality applications, will benefit HeadHunter and other stages of the I-Pic pipeline in the near future. Moreover, face detection is already being offered as a standard feature on mobile platforms, and future implementations (possibly hardware supported) with better accuracy could directly benefit I-Pic.

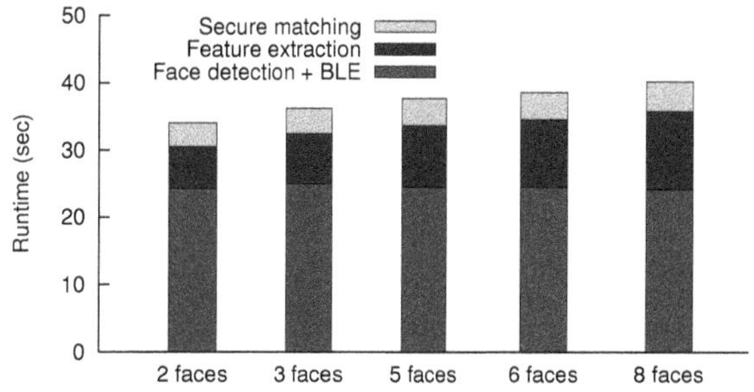

Figure 14. Overall and task level runtimes of I-Pic prototype. 10 bystanders were discovered in each case.

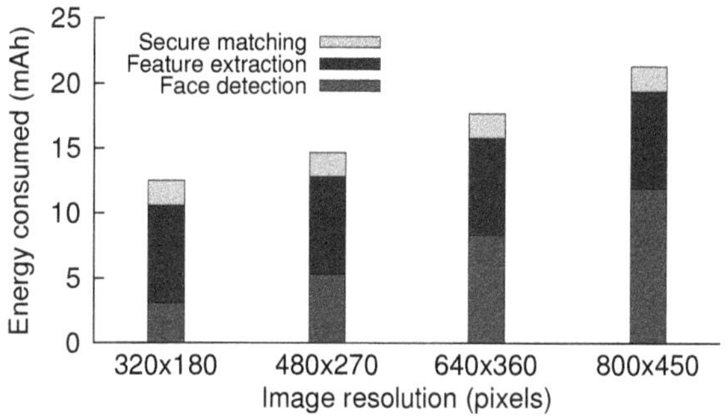

Figure 15. Energy consumption of I-Pic prototype for different image resolutions, 30 faces.

We measured the energy consumption of the various subcomponents of I-Pic using the Monsoon Power Monitor [31]. We attached the power monitor to a Nvidia Shield Tablet K1 [32][6] and processed an image with 30 faces in it. Figure 15 shows the energy consumption for different resolutions of the input image. The face detector uses the GPU, whereas the feature extraction is CPU bound. Energy consumption of face detection is independent of the number of faces in an image, whereas it is linear in the number of faces for feature extraction. The secure matching algorithm was run with the 30 faces extracted from the image along with 40 simulated bystanders[7].

Image resolution (pixels)	Number of images processed (containing 30 faces each)
320x180	408
480x270	347
640x360	288
800x450	239

Table 9. I-Pic's projected capacity on a 5100 mAh battery

Using these measurements, Table 9 shows I-Pic's projected capacity on the Nvidia Shield tablet, which has a 5100 mAh battery. More than 288 images and 8640 faces can be processed on a single charge. Figure 16 compares the face detection accuracy versus the resolution of input images, and serves to highlight the tradeoff between accuracy and energy consumption of the prototype. Reducing the resolution to 480x270 pixels enables the prototype

[6]We used the Shield tablet for the power measurements because the Monsoon power monitor is unable to power the Tango tablet. The latter requires a 7.5 volts power supply whereas the Monsoon power monitor can only supply a maximum of 4.5 volts.

[7]BLE scanning for 5 seconds consumes 0.12 mAh of energy, which is accounted for in Figure 15 but not shown separately.

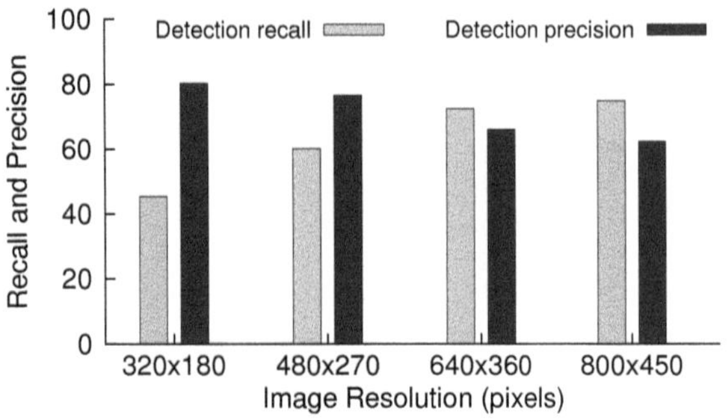

Figure 16. Face detection accuracy of I-Pic prototype for different image resolutions

to process 20% more images, but comes at a high (12%) drop in face detection recall. On the other hand increasing the resolution to 800x450 only gives diminishing returns for face detection recall when compared to the increased energy consumption that accompanies it.

6. RELATED WORK

Privacy in the presence of recording devices: Hoyle et al. [33] seek to understand users' concerns about continuous recording using wearable cameras, by studying a large user population of avid life-loggers. Denning et al. [34] conduct a large scale user survey to understand bystanders' privacy concerns in public places like coffee shops and possible ways to mitigate them. Our online survey additionally shows that privacy concerns are very personal and dependent on the situation.

Roesner et al. [2] present a system that shares a venue's privacy preferences with wearable devices in an unobtrusive way. The idea is to convey privacy expectations associated with places like gyms and washrooms with broadcast messages or visual signs. The wearable devices in the venue pick up these messages or visual cues and obey the specified privacy protocol. Unlike I-Pic, this system has no way to associate a privacy policy with an object or person that appears in an audiovisual recording.

Visual markers to convey privacy policies to nearby wearable recording devices are also used in [3]. [35] explores the expression of bystanders' privacy intent using gestures. Unlike I-Pic, these approaches require either physical tagging of objects and locations, or explicit user actions (i.e., gestures) to convey privacy choices. Moreover, I-Pic enables user-defined, personalized, context-dependent privacy choices.

In the work by Bo et al. [4], individuals wear clothes with a printed barcode, which encodes the wearer's public key. When an image of an individual showing face and barcode is uploaded to an image server, the server garbles the face pixels, using the public key encoded in the barcode. Only the individual who owns the associated private key can later extract the actual face image. I-Pic, on the other hand, does not require its users to wear any visual markers, it does not require users to trust an image server with their private images, and can support context-dependent privacy policies.

In [36, 37, 38], the authors address privacy concerns in untrusted perceptual and augmented reality applications, by partially processing media stream within the trusted platform, thus denying apps access to the raw media streams. An augmented reality app, for instance, might be provided only with the position of relevant objects within a video stream sufficient for the app to overlay its own information, but not the full video. I-Pic also relies on the trusted platform, but focuses on enforcing individual's privacy policies regarding image capture by nearby devices.

Zero-Effort Payments [39], similar to I-Pic, uses face recognition and proximate device detection using BLE to identify a user in an image, but their goal instead is to create a mobile payment system. Unlike I-Pic, which is tuned to identify even small faces in diverse range of photographic contexts, their system is meant to visually identify a user, with human assistance, when she is in close proximity to the cashier. Furthermore, they acknowledge concerns of user privacy in such a monitored environment and propose the use of signage indicating that a face recognition system is deployed in the area. Such a privacy solution is only viable in select scenarios, and lacks the flexibility provided by I-Pic.

Visual fingerprints: Performance on human identification and re-identification tasks has greatly improved over the last decade. Most notably, face recognition on large databases in realistic settings is even approaching human performance [40]. Besides the identity, a person can also be described and identified by a set of attributes [41, 42]. I-Pic uses a state of the art face recognition algorithm based on neural networks, but can benefit from using semantic attributes describing a face, including features from other body parts in addition to the face.

Cryptograhic primitives: There is complementary work to protect the privacy of biometric data [43, 44] by projecting or encrypting representations. It is possible that these approaches could be used in I-Pic to further reduce trust in the Cloud service by obscuring users' visual signatures.

InnerCircle [45] describes a secure multi-party protocol for location privacy, which computes in a single round whether the distance between two encrypted coordinates is within some radius r. This computation is similar to I-Pic's secure dot product and theshholding computation. However, the protocol's efficiency degrades exponentially with the number of bits of precision of the distance. Since our threshold comparison involves dot products of large feature vectors, we use garbled circuits for the threshold comparison instead.

7. CONCLUSIONS AND FUTURE WORK

I-Pic allows users to respect each others' individual and situational privacy preferences, without giving up the spontaneity, ubiquity, and flexibility of digital capture. The I-Pic design and prototype demonstrate that the technical impediments for privacy-compliant imaging can be reasonably overcome using current hardware platforms. I-Pic leverages cutting-edge face detection and recognition technology, which is often perceived as a threat to privacy, to instead increase user's privacy regarding digital capture. Future advances in mobile platform hardware and computer vision will directly benefit I-Pic and further improve the efficiency and accuracy of its I-Pic privacy enforcement.

8. ACKNOWLEDGMENTS

We would like to thank the participants in our online survey and the live photography sessions. Our special thanks to Aniket Kate and Michelle Mazurek for their advise on the crypto pipeline and online survey, respectively. We are grateful to Christian Klein and Aaron Schulman for their help with energy measurements. Finally, we would like to thank the anonymous reviewers and our shepherd Jeremy Gummeson for their helpful feedback. This research was supported by the European Research Council (ERC Synergy imPACT 610150) and the German Research Foundation (DFG CRC 1223). Rijurekha Sen was support by a Humboldt post-doctoral research fellowship.

9. REFERENCES

[1] Lost lake cafe, seattle restaurant, kicks out patron for wearing google glass. http://www.huffingtonpost.com/2013/11/27/lost-lake-cafe-google-glass_n_4350039.html.

[2] Franziska Roesner, David Molnar, Alexander Moshchuk, Tadayoshi Kohno, and Helen J. Wang. World-driven access control for continuous sensing. In *ACM Conference on Computer and Communications Security (CCS)*, 2014.

[3] Nisarg Raval, Animesh Srivastava, Ali Razeen, Kiron Lebeck, Ashwin Machanavajjhala, and Landon P. Cox. What you mark is what apps see. In *ACM International Conference on Mobile Systems, Applications, and Services (Mobisys)*, 2016.

[4] Cheng Bo, Guobin Shen, Jie Liu, Xiang-Yang Li, Yongguang Zhang, and Feng Zhao. Privacy.tag: Privacy concern expressed and respected. In *ACM Conference on Embedded Networked Sensor Systems (Sensys)*, 2014.

[5] Nisarg Raval, Animesh Srivastava, Kiron Lebeck, Landon P. Cox, and Ashwin Machanavajjhala. Markit: Privacy markers for protecting visual secrets. In *UPSIDE, Workshop at ACM International Joint Conference on Pervasive and Ubiquitous Computing (Ubicomp)*, 2014.

[6] M. Mathias, R. Benenson, M. Pedersoli, and L. Van Gool. Face detection without bells and whistles. In *European Conference on Computer Vision (ECCV)*, 2014.

[7] S. Joon Oh, R. Benenson, M. Fritz, and B. Schiele. Person recognition in personal photo collections. In *International Conference on Computer Vision (ICCV)*, 2015.

[8] Bart Goethals, Sven Laur, Helger Lipmaa, and Taneli Mielikainen. On private scalar product computation for privacy-preserving data mining. In *7th Annual International Conference in Information Security and Cryptology (ICISC)*, 2004.

[9] Andrew Chi-Chih Yao. How to generate and exchange secrets. In *27th Annual Symposium on Foundations of Computer Science (FOCS)*, 1986.

[10] Terence Sim and Li Zhang. Controllable face privacy. In *The 11th IEEE International Conference and Workshops on Automatic Face and Gesture Recognition (FG)*, 2015.

[11] Antonio Criminisi, Patrick Perez, , and Kentaro Toyama. Region filling and object removal by exemplar-based image inpainting. In *IEEE Transactions on image processing, vol. 13, no. 9, September*, 2004.

[12] X. Zhu and D. Ramanan. Face detection, pose estimation and landmark localization in the wild. In *Computer Vision and Pattern Recognition (CVPR)*, 2012.

[13] Ning Zhang, Manohar Paluri, Yaniv Taigman, Rob Fergus, and Lubomir Bourdev. Beyond frontal faces: Improving person recognition using multiple cues. In *Conference on Computer Vision and Pattern Recognition (CVPR)*, 2015.

[14] A. Krizhevsky, I. Sutskever, and G. E. Hinton. Imagenet classification with deep convolutional neural networks. In *Conference on Neural Information Processing Systems (NIPS)*. 2012.

[15] J. Deng, W. Dong, R. Socher, L.-J. Li, K. Li, and L. Fei-Fei. ImageNet: A Large-Scale Hierarchical Image Database. *Computer Vision and Pattern Recognition (CVPR)*, 2009.

[16] Yangqing Jia, Evan Shelhamer, Jeff Donahue, Sergey Karayev, Jonathan Long, Ross Girshick, Sergio Guadarrama, and Trevor Darrell. Caffe: Convolutional architecture for fast feature embedding. *arXiv preprint arXiv:1408.5093*, 2014.

[17] Gary B. Huang Erik Learned-Miller. Labeled faces in the wild: Updates and new reporting procedures. Technical Report UM-CS-2014-003, University of Massachusetts, Amherst, May 2014.

[18] Rong-En Fan, Kai-Wei Chang, Cho-Jui Hsieh, Xiang-Rui Wang, and Chih-Jen Lin. LIBLINEAR: A library for large linear classification. *Journal of Machine Learning Research*, 2008.

[19] Pascal Paillier. Public-key cryptosystems based on composite degree residuosity classes. In *Advances in Cryptology (EUROCRYPT)*, 1999.

[20] Paarijaat Aditya et al. Technical Report: I-Pic: A Platform for Privacy-Compliant Image Capture. http://www.mpi-sws.org/~paditya/papers/ipic-tr.pdf.

[21] Yan Huang, Lior Malka, David Evans, and Jonathan Katz. Efficient privacy-preserving biometric identification. In *18th Network and Distributed System Security Conference (NDSS)*, 2011.

[22] Moni Naor and Benny Pinkas. Computationally secure oblivious transfer. In *Journal of Cryptology*, 2005.

[23] Yuval Ishai, Joe Kilian, Kobbi Nissim, and Erez Petrank. Extending oblivious transfers efficiently. In *Advances in Cryptology (CRYPTO)*, 2003.

[24] Yehuda Lindell. Fast cut-and-choose based protocols for malicious and covert adversaries. In *Advances in Cryptology (CRYPTO)*, 2013.

[25] Project Tango Tablet Development Kit. https://store.google.com/product/project_tango_tablet_development_kit.

[26] CUDA. http://www.nvidia.com/object/cuda_home_new.html.

[27] Jose-Luis Lisani, Ana-Belen Petro, and Catalina Sbert. Color and Contrast Enhancement by Controlled Piecewise Affine Histogram Equalization. *Image Processing On Line*, 2:243–265, 2012. http://dx.doi.org/10.5201/ipol.2012.lps-pae.

[28] Caffe-Android-Lib. https://github.com/sh1r0/caffe-android-lib.

[29] Might Be Evil. http://mightbeevil.org/.

[30] A universal labeling tool: Sloth. https://cvhci.anthropomatik.kit.edu/~baeuml/projects/a-universal-labeling-tool-for-computer-vision-sloth/.

[31] Monsoon Power Monitor. https://www.msoon.com/LabEquipment/PowerMonitor.

[32] Nvidia. Nvidia Shield Tablet K1. https://shield.nvidia.com/tablet/k1.

[33] Roberto Hoyle, Robert Templeman, Steven Armes, Denise Anthony, David Crandall, and Apu Kapadia. Privacy behaviors of lifeloggers using wearable cameras. In *ACM International Joint Conference on Pervasive and Ubiquitous Computing (Ubicomp)*, 2014.

[34] Tamara Denning, Zakariya Dehlawi, and Tadayoshi Kohno. In situ with bystanders of augmented reality glasses: Perspectives on recording and privacy-mediating technologies. In *ACM Conference on Human Factors in Computing Systems (CHI)*, 2014.

[35] Jaeyeon Jung and Matthai Philipose. Courteous glass. In *UPSIDE, Workshop at ACM International Joint Conference on Pervasive and Ubiquitous Computing (Ubicomp)*, 2014.

[36] Loris D'Antoni, Alan Dunn, Suman Jana, Tadayoshi Kohno, Benjamin Livshits, David Molnar, Alexander Moshchuk, Eyal Ofek, Franziska Roesner, Scott Saponas, Margus Veanes, and Helen J. Wang. Operating system support for augmented reality applications. In *Workshop on Hot Topics in Operating Systems (HotOS)*, 2013.

[37] Suman Jana, Arvind Narayanan, and Vitaly Shmatikov. A scanner darkly: Protecting user privacy from perceptual applications. In *IEEE Symposium on Security and Privacy*, 2013.

[38] Suman Jana, David Molnar, Alexander Moshchuk, Alan Dunn, Benjamin Livshits, Helen J. Wang, and Eyal Ofek. Enabling fine-grained permissions for augmented reality applications with recognizers. In *Usenix Security Symposium (Usenix Security)*, 2013.

[39] Christopher Smowton, Jacob R. Lorch, David Molnar, Stefan Saroiu, and Alec Wolman. Zero-effort payments: Design, deployment, and lessons. In *Proceedings of the ACM International Joint Conference on Pervasive and UbiquitousComputing (UbiComp)*, 2014.

[40] Yaniv Taigman, Ming Yang, Marc'Aurelio Ranzato, and Lior Wolf. Deepface: Closing the gap to human-level performance in face verification. In *Conference on Computer Vision and Pattern Recognition (CVPR)*, 2014.

[41] Lubomir Bourdev, Subhransu Maji, and Jitendra Malik. Describing people: Poselet-based attribute classification. In *International Conference on Computer Vision (ICCV)*, 2011.

[42] Ning Zhang, Manohar Paluri, Marc'Aurelio Ranzato, Trevor Darrell, and Lubomir D. Bourdev. PANDA: pose aligned networks for deep attribute modeling. In *Conference on Computer Vision and Pattern Recognition (CVPR)*, 2014.

[43] Zhou Lingli and Lai Jianghuang. Security algorithm of face recognition based on local binary pattern and random projection. In *International Conference on Computational Intelligence (ICCI)*, 2010.

[44] Yongjin Wang and Konstantinos N. Plataniotis. An analysis of random projection for changeable and privacy-preserving biometric verification. *IEEE Transactions on Systems, Man, and, Cybernetics: part B: CYBERNETICS, Vol. 40, No. 5*, 2010.

[45] Per Hallgren, Martin Ochoa, and Andrei Sabelfeld. Innercircle: A parallelizable decentralized privacy-preserving location proximity protocol. In *Proceedings of the 13th Annual Conference on Privacy, Security and Trust (PST)*, 2015.

What You Mark is What Apps See

Nisarg Raval, Animesh Srivastava, Ali Razeen, Kiron Lebeck[†],
Ashwin Machanavajjhala, and Landon P. Cox
Duke University
[†] University of Washington

ABSTRACT

Users are increasingly vulnerable to inadvertently leaking sensitive information through cameras. In this paper, we investigate an approach to mitigating the risk of such inadvertent leaks called *privacy markers*. Privacy markers give users fine-grained control of what visual information an app can access through a device's camera. We present two examples of this approach: *PrivateEye*, which allows a user to mark regions of a two-dimensional surface as safe to release to an app, and *WaveOff*, which does the same for three-dimensional objects. We have integrated both systems with Android's camera subsystem. Experiments with our prototype show that a Nexus 5 smartphone can deliver near realtime frame rates while protecting secret information, and a 26-person user study elicited positive feedback on our prototype's speed and ease-of-use.

1. INTRODUCTION

Cameras are pervasive and multiplying. All modern PCs and smartphones have cameras, as do most gaming consoles and televisions. Furthermore, emerging wearable computers, household robots, and Internet-of-things devices provide a glimpse of the not-too-distant future: continuous recording by crowds of nearby devices. This proliferation of cameras has created a growing sense that the most confidential details of a person's life are perpetually at risk of leaking.

Our goal is to develop tools that give users fine-grained control over the information that apps can access through a camera. Preventing all leaks, particularly those by determined attackers, is likely impossible, but preventing inadvertent leaks by trusted cameras is much more feasible. Such inadvertent leaks will be problematic for all users, but enterprises are particularly vulnerable since workers are surrounded by secrets and opportunities to accidently leak information abound. For example, video chatting with an external collaborator could accidentally reveal sensitive information drawn on a background whiteboard, and a photo of a receipt on a desk could also capture portions of other nearby documents.

MobiSys'16, June 25-30, 2016, Singapore, Singapore

 ISBN 978-1-4503-4269-8/16/06. . . $15.00

DOI: http://dx.doi.org/10.1145/2906388.2906405

Prior work on protecting visual secrets has relied on computer vision to identify classes of objects within images. Vision algorithms can be used to transform images so that (1) they contain only objects that an app is allowed to view [9, 10, 20] (e.g., providing a gesture-recognition application with only an outline of a user's hands), or (2) they do not contain any sensitive objects [4, 6, 16] (e.g., blurring background faces).

Unfortunately, both approaches suffer from the same limitations. First, system designers are unlikely to anticipate all objects that users will want to hide or reveal. Absent classifiers will either lead to more leaks or hinder legitimate apps' functionality. However, even for object classes that a designer correctly anticipates, developing recognition algorithms that are accurate, precise, and efficient enough to handle realtime analysis is challenging. For example, it is unclear how one would develop practical recognizers for items as nuanced as sales figures, meeting notes, and receipts.

Due to these limitations, we have been investigating an alternative approach based on *privacy markers* [14]. Compared to prior work, privacy markers provide a natural way for users to express fine-grained access-control policies over visual information while also simplifying the system software responsible for enforcing restrictions. In this paper, we describe the design and implementation of two privacy-marker systems: *PrivateEye* and *WaveOff*.

PrivateEye allows users to mark a two-dimensional region by enclosing it with a special shape. The shape can be drawn by hand (e.g., on a whiteboard with standard markers) or embedded in a digital document (e.g., on a slide using presentation software). A PrivateEye-enabled device recognizes the shape in its camera stream at runtime and marks those portions of the data. WaveOff allows users to mark three-dimensional objects through a special user interface (UI). The WaveOff UI shows a live camera feed, on top of which users can specify a bounded region containing the object they wish to mark. WaveOff extracts visual features for the object from the region and stores them in a database so that objects can be identified in future images.

Alice is attending a client presentation in Shanghai. Since some of the text is in Mandarin, Alice would like to verify that she translated the text correctly using a third-party translation app on her mobile device. The app captures slides from the presentation, runs optical character recognition on each frame, and displays the translated text on her mobile device. However, the slides also contain sensitive corporate secrets (e.g., a table of earnings predictions) that the client does not want to leak. Both Alice and the client are uncomfortable that her translation app may forward the secret information to untrusted servers for processing.

(a) Scenario one: Presentation

Bob is video chatting on his laptop with collaborators. He would like to use his whiteboard to work out a problem, and hence would like his collaborators to see it. However, he has a confidential product roadmap on his whiteboard that his collaborators should not see. He also has a prototype model of a newly designed drone and a bottle of medication on his desk. Bob would like to show the prototype to his collaborators, but would be upset if his collaborators saw his medication.

(b) Scenario two: Video chat

Cathy relies on an augmented-reality app on her mobile device to superimpose indicators over her keyboard to help her input a complex password. While she is comfortable allowing the password app to view her keyboard, she does not want the app to capture her computer screen or anything else on her desk.

(c) Scenario three: Password entry

Figure 1: Hypothetical scenarios.

To prevent apps from accessing secret information, users put their device into a restricted privacy-mode. In privacy-mode, PrivateEye and WaveOff convert raw camera data into a stream of *public regions* defined by the privacy markers they detect. That is, when a user puts her device into privacy-mode, PrivateEye and WaveOff block all unmarked regions of the camera stream so that apps can only access regions that have been explicitly marked public. Using markers to define public regions was a key design decision. In our experience, computer-vision algorithms are not robust enough to handle practical considerations such as motion-induced blur and changing light conditions at usable framerates. Blocking unmarked regions provides strong assurances that apps cannot access sensitive information without unduly limiting app functionality.

We have integrated PrivateEye and WaveOff with a Nexus 5 smartphone running Android. In a 26-person user study with our prototype, participants successfully used PrivateEye and WaveOff to mark public regions containing QR codes, and reported that marking and scanning the QR code was easy and fast. Furthermore, using a benchmark of representative videos, our prototype blocked at least 99% of non-public regions while supporting at least 20 frames per second.

The rest of this paper is organized as follows. Section 2 motivates the problem of protecting visual secrets and our approach of using privacy markers. Section 3 provides a design overview. Section 4 describes our prototype implementations of PrivateEye and WaveOff. Section 5 describes the results of our user study as well as a comprehensive evaluation of our prototype's privacy-utility tradeoffs, and its performance. Related work is discussed in Section 6. Section 7 provides our conclusions.

2. USE CASES AND MOTIVATION

Figure 1 describes three scenarios that capture how camera-driven apps can put secret information at risk: a *presentation* containing sensitive material, a *video chat* with sensitive information visible in the background, and a *password-entry* app that should only view a small number of objects.

The simplest solution for protecting visual secrets is *coarse-grained blocking*. That is, users can turn off their cameras when sensitive information is in view. However, in all three of our scenarios, secret information and application-essential information are co-mingled. Alternatively, a system can take a more fine-grained approach to protect visual secrets. One fine-grained approach is to apply the principle of *least privilege* to visual content and give applications access to only the visual information required for their functionality [9, 10]. Under least privilege, applications must request access to classes of objects within a camera's view. If a request is granted, the system can use computer vision to ensure that only allowed objects of interest pass from a camera's view to an application.

Systems that take a least-privilege approach must anticipate the classes of objects that applications will want to access, and provide *recognizers* to accurately and efficiently detect these objects. For instance, a study of Kinect applications found that 87 only needed access to objects identified by four recognizers [9]. However, as illustrated by our use cases, one is unlikely to anticipate all classes of objects that mobile apps may need to access.

Thus, least-privilege systems that use predefined recognizers are likely to provide strong security, but support fewer applications. For example, in the "video chat" scenario, if the application can only access faces and hands, then it cannot capture more spontaneous moments, such as sharing an equation written on the whiteboard. Predefined recognizers will also fail when nuanced differentiation between objects is required, such as between the sensitive and non-sensitive slides in the "presentation" scenario.

A second fine-grained approach is to *block secrets* by defining sets of sensitive objects and using computer vision to remove those objects from an application's view [4, 6, 16]. As with least privilege, these systems require designers to anticipate a large universe of objects, which vision algorithms must detect and block. For example, to protect a confidential roadmap from a video-chat application, the system would have to construct a recognizer for product roadmaps.

In light of these challenges, this paper expands on our earlier proposal of *privacy markers* [14], which provide a promising new approach to mitigating camera-based leaks. At a high level, privacy markers consist of two parts: (1) a simple interface for marking objects in the physical environment, and (2) device software for efficiently recognizing marked objects. PrivateEye and WaveOff are privacy-marker systems that take a least-privilege approach. When a user puts her device into privacy-mode, apps can view only marked objects through the camera. This approach provides solutions to each scenario described in Figure 1.

In the "presentation" scenario, Alice's client would enclose most of her slides in a special rectangle. The client trusts that Alice is using a mobile device equipped with PrivateEye that will only reveal the marked slides to her translation app. Unmarked slides containing secret information will be blocked from the app's view. In the "password" scenario, Cathy can use WaveOff on her mobile device to mark any keyboard she uses to enter a password. Thereafter, Cathy can safely allow the password-manager app to view the camera input and be assured that everything except the marked keyboard will be blocked from its view. Finally, in the "video chat" scenario, Bob can mark his face, the part of the whiteboard that he would like to share via video, and his prototype drone model using PrivateEye and WaveOff before starting the chat session so that only those objects are visible to his collaborators.

3. APPROACH OVERVIEW

This section provides an overview of our two privacy-marker systems, PrivateEye and WaveOff, including the attacker model and principles underlying their designs. We also summarize the systems' limitations.

3.1 Trust and attacker model

We assume that recording devices run a combination of trusted and untrusted software. The computer-vision software needed to recognize and track marked regions must be part of the trusted computing base. This software must reside in the camera subsystem of the platform, either integrated with the camera driver or with a trusted camera service.

We are primarily concerned with inadvertent leaks by untrusted, third-party software, such as video-chat and receipt-scanning apps. We assume that untrusted software can only access camera data through well known APIs defined by the device platform, and that privacy-marker software is properly isolated from third-party software.

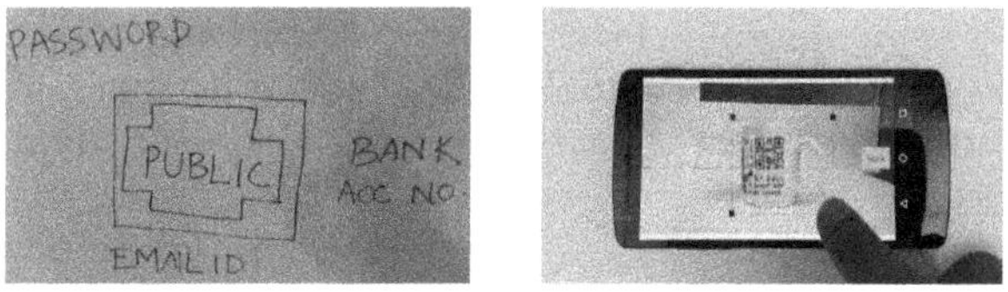

(a) (b)

Figure 2: (a) A region on a whiteboard marked as public using PrivateEye's marker. (b) A coffee mug marked as public using WaveOff.

Our trust model is based on settings such as an enterprise in which a company may purchase video-chat stations and employee equipment like laptops and smartphones. We cannot prevent a determined attacker from capturing secrets using a malicious recording device, such as an analog video recorder or a digital device that ignores users' markers.

3.2 Design principles

PrivateEye and WaveOff must be easy to use and efficiently block all non-public regions from a camera's view at runtime. The following design principles guided our work.

Avoid special equipment

Ease-of-use was a primary goal for PrivateEye and WaveOff. Before arriving at our current designs, we considered alternatives, such as affixing or projecting QR codes onto surfaces and objects. However, we rejected these approaches as being too inconvenient in practice. Ideally, a user should be able to mark an object or region without special equipment.

PrivateEye is used for marking content on two dimensional surfaces like whiteboards and presentations. Its marker is a pair of concentric rectangles delineating a public region as shown in Figure 2a. The inner rectangle has truncated corners to differentiate it from other unmarked objects with concentric rectangles (e.g., window frames). This marker is unusual and easy to draw, either by hand (e.g., using whiteboard markers) or using digital tools (e.g., in a presentation).

WaveOff is used for sharing objects that are difficult to physically mark, such as three-dimensional objects. To mark these objects, we take advantage of the recording device's screen by overlaying a bounding box on a live camera feed, as seen in Figure 2b. The marking UI is part of an app that is trusted to handle unmodified camera data.

Simplify recognition

A potential drawback of simplifying life for users is that it can create complexity for the vision algorithms needed to identify objects. Hence, we carefully designed markers for PrivateEye and WaveOff that play to computer vision's strengths.

The concentric rectangle marker in PrivateEye addresses the nearly impossible task of differentiating between public and private text.[1] Public text can be enclosed within a marked region, and all other text is private by default.

At the same time, PrivateEye markers can be easily detected by vision algorithms due to the strong contrast of straight, dark lines on a light two-dimensional surface. Such features are apparent under low resolution and regardless of the lines' colors. Moreover, by choosing inner rectangles with truncated corners, the marker is easier to detect since detecting corners is more robust and faster than detecting edges. Furthermore, this design distinguishes our marker from other parts of a camera's view that contain concentric rectangles (e.g., window frames).

PrivateEye detects privacy markers using a combination of computer-vision algorithms. For each frame, it first detects edges in a frame using the well-known Canny algorithm [2]. After edge detection, the system detects contours in the edge-based image using Suzuki's algorithm [18]. The contours are stored in a tree hierarchy structure. Each contour has information about four other contours: (a) parent - the contour that encompasses the current contour, (b) previous - the previous sibling contour, (c) next - the next sibling contour, and (d) child - the contour which is completely inside the current contour. Upon detecting a contour that can be approximated as rectangle [5] (i.e., a convex area polygon with four vertices), PrivateEye searches its children contours. If PrivateEye finds a contour that has 12 corners with area at least 50% of the parent rectangle contour, the system concludes that it is a marked region.

WaveOff recognizes objects by extracting features from the bounded area of a camera's view to build a model of the objects within and stores the model in a database. We would like to note that WaveOff recognizes a specific object (e.g., Cathy's Mac keyboard) rather than a class of objects (e.g., any Mac keyboard). This simplifies recognition since the model can use all distinctive keypoints (including those that might not be present in other objects of the same type) without worrying about over-fitting. In order to build the model, WaveOff computes descriptors at selective keypoints in the marked region of the camera's view.

The keypoints are the distinctive regions (e.g., corners and edges) of the object and descriptors are the features at those keypoints (e.g., gradient and orientation). We use BRISK [12], a set of binary features, to compute keypoints and the corresponding descriptors. Computing and matching BRISK features is efficient and is ideal for realtime performance on low-power mobile devices.

WaveOff uses feature matching to detect the presence of a marked object in a given frame. For each frame, it computes the BRISK features and matches them with the features of models in the database. Since matching is independent for every object, they can be identified in parallel. WaveOff unblocks a region when at least 20% of its features match a model in the database.

[1]We do not utilize optical character recognition due to poor accuracy and computational intensity.

Track to mitigate recognition failures

Recognizing privacy markers on every incoming camera frame is computationally intensive and can cause a low frame rate. Furthermore, recognizers can fail if the camera's viewpoint changes significantly. Building recognizers for multiple viewpoints is costly and inconvenient. We address both issues by tracking features since tracking is robust to minor changes in viewpoints and faster than object recognition.

Once PrivateEye detects a marked region, it extracts prominent corners in the region (using [17]) and tracks these features using the Lucas-Kanade optical-flow-in-pyramids technique [21]. WaveOff also tracks object features across consecutive frames using Lucas-Kanade. While recognition is essential when an object appears in a stream for the first time, it is less helpful when the object is fully visible, because tracking alone is sufficient to identify the object's location in subsequent frames. Hence, we skip recognition altogether when tracking finds enough features (at least 75% of the features stored in the model).

However, when there are not enough features, tracking alone can introduce localization errors that propagate across subsequent frames. Hence, we use both matching and tracking to find a larger set of features when tracking alone is insufficient. We estimate an object's location in the camera's view using CMT [13].

Block under uncertainty

For privacy-sensitive applications, blocking the entire camera view might be acceptable when the system is uncertain about the presence of public regions. In fact, in our user study, we found that initially blocking entire frames for several seconds while scanning a QR code did not impact the utility of the app. Based on this observation, we take a conservative approach and only reveal a region when we are confident that it has been marked. However, blocking the entire frame under uncertainty may create a poor user experience when an object is blocked frequently after it appears. This can happen when a frame becomes blurry due to motion. To address this issue, during times of uncertainty, the system displays the previous frame (in which the object was visible) instead of showing nothing. This approach does not harm security because it does not reveal any new information, but it can help usability. Note, that if the view changes significantly (i.e., the object disappears), we quickly detect the change and stop showing the old frame.

3.3 Limitations

Though PrivateEye and WaveOff are robust in many settings, their reliance on standard computer-vision algorithms limit their security guarantees and can impinge on apps' utility.

First, both systems require users to mark public regions with a rectangle. As a result, it is possible for sensitive information to inadvertently appear within a marked area and cause a leak. For example, consider a presentation with slides that have been marked public. If the speaker or anyone else steps in front of the slides, then their identity will be revealed regardless of whether this should be kept secret. Similarly, if a user marks an object with WaveOff as public, but a secret object is placed in front of it without completely occluding the public object, then an app may view the secret object. We believe that experience using privacy markers would reduce the likelihood of such incidents, but they could never be eliminated.

Second, a camera could zoom so far into a region marked by PrivateEye that the marker falls outside the camera's field of view. In this case, PrivateEye would block the content of the public region. While this would not be insecure, it would hurt the utility of an app that needs access to the blocked region. This could be particularly problematic for large, marked regions with very small details inside; the only way to take a picture would be from a far enough distance that the marker was visible, but at this distance little of the content may be legible.

Finally, while PrivateEye and WaveOff allow users to mark arbitrary objects, they only allow objects to be treated as public or private. Thus, when a device is in privacy-mode, an app can access *all* public regions. It is easy to imagine scenarios in which a user may want to restrict an app to a narrow subset of private objects, such as our hypothetical password-entry app. For WaveOff, one could provide a UI that allows users to specify which marked objects should be revealed to which apps. Unfortunately, it is much less clear how to support rich access-control policies for PrivateEye, such as making a document recordable for executives' smartphones but not engineers'. Increasing marker expressiveness would likely compromise usability and recognition performance (i.e., accuracy, precision, and efficiency), and understanding these tradeoffs is beyond the scope of this paper.

4. IMPLEMENTATION

We implemented PrivateEye and WaveOff by modifying the Android Open Source Project (AOSP) version of Android 5.1. Our prototype currently runs on a Nexus 5 smartphone. Before we describe the implementations of PrivateEye and WaveOff, we first provide some background on Android's camera subsystem. We then present the design of an initial implementation that recorded video at an unacceptable four frames-per-second (FPS). We then highlight the causes of this poor performance and describe techniques that allow us to record video at a median framerate of 20 FPS.

4.1 Android's camera subsystem

In Android 5, Google made significant changes to the camera subsystem to give apps more control over the camera feed. Figure 3 shows how the subsystem is split between hardware-dependent and hardware-independent software layers. The hardware-dependent layer consists of the camera device-driver that interacts directly with the physical camera, and a hardware abstraction layer (HAL) that implements a common interface for the camera service. Because the camera service is hardware independent, it is the ideal place to integrate PrivateEye and WaveOff.

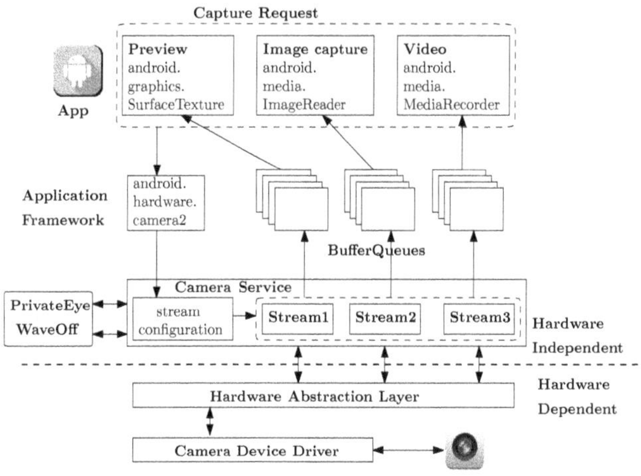

Figure 3: Android's camera subsystem. The colored box denotes PrivateEye and WaveOff, which intercept all incoming frames before they are passed to the application framework.

An app can submit a *capture request* to the camera service in one or more of the following modes: (a) preview, (b) image capture, and (c) video recording. In addition to a mode, each capture request describes a set of image attributes, such as resolution and pixel format. For instance, an app may request access to the camera in preview mode at a resolution of 1280 × 960, or in image-capture mode, with the image stored in a file at a resolution of 640 × 480.

The camera service creates one *stream* (an internal buffer) for each capture mode. The camera service and HAL can access all streams, and each stream is protected by its own lock. Multiple streams can be active at at time, e.g., a preview stream and a video-recording stream, and the active streams are configured according to their corresponding capture-request attributes. The application framework also creates a *BufferQueue* for each capture mode so that the camera service can send image data to an app. When the camera driver delivers a frame, HAL locks all active streams, copies image data to those streams according to their configuration parameters, and then releases the locks. To forward frames to an app, the camera service acquires all active streams' locks, copies image data from the streams to their corresponding BufferQueues, and releases all locks.

4.2 PrivateEye and WaveOff in Android

In this section, we present our Android implementations of PrivateEye and WaveOff. We start with a naive design that highlights the challenges of achieving realtime performance, and then describe how we overcame these challenges.

4.2.1 A simple implementation

Our initial implementation integrated PrivateEye and WaveOff into Android as follows: (1) the camera service locked each active stream and sequentially passed each stream's image data to PrivateEye or WaveOff; (2) PrivateEye or WaveOff detected any public regions and masked the rest of the image; (3) the camera service copied each modified image to its corresponding BufferQueue and released all locks.

This straightforward implementation resulted in unacceptable video-recording performance. In particular, on our Nexus 5 we could only record video at a median rate of four FPS. This was due to two factors. First, the camera service held all active-stream locks while waiting for PrivateEye and WaveOff to identify public regions within a frame. This blocked the HAL for long stretches, and caused it to drop frames. Second, streams with different resolution and pixel format still contain most of the same visual information. Our initial implementation ignored similarities across streams, e.g., between a preview and video-recording stream, and needlessly analyzed each frame independently. Our current implementation addresses both of these problems.

4.2.2 Improved implementation

PrivateEye and WaveOff are separate modules loaded by the camera service when the camera is turned on. We rely on OpenCV for all computer-vision algorithms. Each module exposes an API of six calls to the camera service, which is described in Table 1.

Both PrivateEye and WaveOff modules maintain one queue for incoming frames, $InQueue$, and a second queue for processed frames, $OutQueue$. The camera-service thread blocks until it receives a frame from HAL, and then passes the frame to PrivateEye and WaveOff via a `processFrame` call. We currently set InQueue's maximum depth to 15, and calls to `processFrame` will add a new frame to InQueue as long as there is enough room. If there are already 15 frames in the queue, `processFrame` drops the new frame. An alternative approach would have been to make room for the new frame by dropping the oldest frame in InQueue, but we found that this made tracking objects across frames more difficult. All calls to `processFrame` return as soon as the passed-in frame has been copied onto InQueue or dropped.

To process frames in InQueue, PrivateEye and WaveOff each have a dispatch thread that blocks waiting for frames to be added to InQueue. After dequeueing a frame from InQueue, the dispatch thread hands off the frame for further processing. Processed frames are eventually forwarded back to the camera service by placing them in OutQueue.

After calling `processFrame`, the camera-service checks for processed frames by calling `isFrameAvailable`. If a frame is available in OutQueue, `isFrameAvailable` dequeues the frame and returns it to the camera service. The camera service then copies the processed frame to the appropriate BufferQueues. Allowing the camera service to accept new frames from HAL before older ones have been processed prevents the HAL from dropping frames. However, if PrivateEye and WaveOff cannot analyze frames fast enough, InQueue will fill up and cause the camera service to drop frames.

To make frame processing faster, PrivateEye is implemented as a four-stage pipeline, with a separate thread for each stage. The four stages are: (1) downsize a frame and convert it to grayscale, (2) detect marker contours, (3) track previously detected markers and merge them with newly detected markers, and (4) mask all non-public regions and add the final image to OutQueue.

WaveOff's performance depends on the number of object models in its database, and for each model WaveOff spawns one thread. Each thread is responsible for matching and tracking a specific public object. However, before tasking the object threads, WaveOff's dispatch thread dequeues a frame from InQueue and makes a single pass over the data to compute all image features. It then passes these features to the object threads before they begin their work. The last object thread to complete its analysis aggregates the results of the others to render the final frame.

Video recording

When multiple streams are active, e.g., the preview and video-recording streams, our initial implementation sequentially and independently processed a frame from each source. This effectively doubled the work that PrivateEye and WaveOff had to perform even though the visual content of each stream was nearly identical. To eliminate redundant analysis, PrivateEye and WaveOff only process frames from the preview stream. After processing a preview frame, they add the modified frame to OutQueue and save the coordinates of all public regions so that they can be applied to other frames. In particular, for non-preview streams, the camera service uses the `getLastRects` method to retrieve the coordinates of any public regions that were identified in the preview stream. It then masks the non-preview frame after adjusting for the stream's settings, such as its resolution.

In addition, to re-using processing results across multiple streams, PrivateEye and WaveOff applied several other optimizations. First, analyzing frames in the Nexus 5's original resolution of 1280×960 takes several seconds. Therefore, PrivateEye and WaveOff resize each frame to 400×240 and 320×240, respectively, before performing any compute-intensive operations.

In addition, PrivateEye and WaveOff operate on grayscale frames to reduce processing times. The camera-preview stream delivers frame data in the full-color YUV format, and OpenCV converts a YUV frame with resolution 1280×960 to grayscale in about 30 ms. However, for a 1280×960 image, the YUV format uses the first 1280×960 bytes to store an image's luminance data, which encodes a grayscale version of the frame. We found that simply copying the luminance data of a YUV frame into a separate buffer creates a grayscale version of the frame in under one ms.

Finally, PrivateEye and WaveOff avoid allocating and de-allocating memory whenever possible. The camera service pre-allocates all circular buffers, queues, and other data structures when it loads our modules. We only allocate new memory when a stream's configuration, such as its resolution, changes, and we only de-allocate memory when the camera is turned off.

Image capture

Capturing an image with an active preview stream is slightly different than video recording. When a user takes a picture, the HAL returns a JPEG-compressed byte stream rather than

Method	Description
processFrame	sends a camera frame data for processing
isFrameAvailable	checks if a frame is available for the delivery to application
getLastRects	returns a list of regions marked public in the last frame
addObjectModel	builds and adds model of the marked public object in model database
removeObjectModel	removes a model of the marked public object from the model database

Table 1: PrivateEye and WaveOff API for interacting with the camera service.

a YUV frame. The coordinates returned by `getLastRects` correspond to raw pixels, and thus the JPEG image must first be converted before it can be masked. After masking any non-public regions, the camera service converts the result back to a JPEG and forwards it to the appropriate BufferQueue.

AOSP provides jpeglib (version 6b) for encoding and decoding JPEG data. However, this version of the library only decodes and encodes JPEG data through the file system. Thus, we avoided costly system calls by adding two support functions to perform in-memory encoding and decoding.

Finally, to read and write to the image-capture JPEG stream in the camera service, we modified the Nexus 5 HAL implementation provided by LG. Each stream has a usage flag that determines how the stream will be accessed by different components in the camera subsystem. We added two flags to the JPEG stream: `GRALLOC_USAGE_SW_READ_OFTEN` and `GRALLOC_USAGE_SW_WRITE_OFTEN`. These flags direct all JPEG data to the camera service for reading and writing. These small changes were the only modifications we made to a hardware-dependent component.

5. EVALUATION

To evaluate PrivateEye and WaveOff, we sought answers to the following questions:

- What is the perceived burden of using PrivateEye and WaveOff?
- Do PrivateEye and WaveOff interfere with app functionality?
- How well do PrivateEye and WaveOff detect public regions, and under what conditions?
- How well do PrivateEye and WaveOff perform when the number of objects increases?
- What are the energy and performance overheads of PrivateEye and WaveOff?

To answer the first two questions we conducted a user study with 26 participants. The study was approved by our university Internal Review Board (IRB), and involved marking and scanning QR codes on flat and curved surfaces. We answered the next question by developing a benchmark with videos of typical settings and camera movements. We used these videos to measure how precisely, accurately, and efficiently our prototype would handle these scenarios. We evaluated scalability using experiments with multiple marked regions and objects. Finally, we answered the last question by measuring our prototype's resource usage with the camera preview enabled.

As mentioned previously, our prototype is based on AOSP for Android 5.1 and runs on a Nexus 5 smartphone.

5.1 User Study

To better understand PrivateEye and WaveOff's impact on usability we conducted a user study in which participants marked public regions containing QR codes and then used a third-party app to scan the codes.

5.1.1 Study design

The aim of our user study was to understand how privacy markers affect the experience of using a camera-enabled app. We randomized participants into two groups. Members of the *control group* performed tasks on a Nexus 5 running unmodified AOSP, and members of the *case group* performed tasks on a Nexus 5 running AOSP augmented with PrivateEye or WaveOff.

Both groups performed simple tasks with a QR-code scanning app. Marking and scanning a QR code provided a limited but informative context for understanding PrivateEye and WaveOff's usability. First, QR-code scanning is a common smartphone task that requires realtime image processing. Second, input images must be clear enough for accurate and fast scanning. Third, scanning codes allowed us to measure usability quantitatively (e.g., time to scan and scanning accuracy) and qualitatively (e.g., user-perceived ease and speed). We used the *Barcode Scanner*[2] app for our tests. At the time of testing, this app was freely available on the Google Play Store, had been downloaded more than 100 million times, and had received an average rating of 4.1 out of 5.

We initially asked each participant to complete a short pre-study questionnaire about their familiarity with smartphone apps and, in particular, camera-enabled apps. Then we explained the purpose of the study and described the tasks they would perform. Each control session involved using AOSP to scan a QR code affixed to a whiteboard and scanning a QR code affixed to a coffee mug. Case sessions were similar, except that participants marked the QR codes before scanning them. After completing these tasks, we asked each participant to fill out a post-study questionnaire about their experience. If a participant could not scan a QR code within one minute, we asked them to repeat the experiment at most three times.

To ensure that volunteers were comfortable performing their tasks, we showed them how to scan a QR code. We told them to start the app and point the camera at the QR code so that it stayed in focus in the center of the viewfinder. We also showed them how to adjust the position of the camera (e.g., near or far from the code) while scanning.

For PrivateEye, we showed volunteers a marker and demonstrated how to draw it on a blank sheet of paper. We stressed

[2]https://play.google.com/store/apps/details?id=com.google.zxing.client.android&hl=en

that the marker lines needed to be thick and continuous. Because participants had not seen the PrivateEye marker before, we asked them to practice drawing a marker on paper and pointed out any mistakes they made.

We similarly explained how to mark an object using WaveOff. First, we showed them how to mark a cup using the WaveOff UI. We emphasized that the marked object should be clearly visible and fully enclosed by the UI's bounding box. Once participants understood how to mark an object, we asked them to mark the coffee mug and to scan its QR code.

To measure how quickly and accurately participants scanned QR codes, we created a testing app. The app allowed users to launch *Barcode Scanner* via an Android Intent. After a successful scan, our testing app received the captured image. Using this app, we recorded the time to scan each QR code and whether the scan was successful.

We also measured the time participants took to mark a public region. For PrivateEye, we manually measured marking time with a stopwatch. For WaveOff, the marking UI logged the time taken to capture an image of the target object, to adjust the marker bounding box, to extract the object's features, and to store the object's model.

Finally, we designed a short post-study questionnaire that asked participants to respond to two statements and provided an optional section for general feedback. The questionnaire statements were '*Completing the study tasks was fast*' and '*Completing the study tasks was easy*'. Users reported their level of agreement with each statement on a scale from one (strongly disagree) to seven (strongly agree).

5.1.2 Recruiting participants

We recruited participants by sending messages to university mailing lists and posting on Facebook. We asked potential participants to fill out a demographic questionnaire on a website, and based on the completeness of the responses, we selected 26 volunteers for our study.

Among the 26 participants, 19 were male and seven were female. The median age was 27, with the youngest 23 and the oldest 53. Due to soliciting participation through university mailing lists and Facebook, 20 of the 26 had some kind of computer-science degree.

Many of our participants frequently used their smartphone camera. Seven reported using their smartphone camera at least ten times per week; eight reported video chatting at least twice per week; 14 reported using at least three different camera-enabled apps each month. Finally, many participants had used a smartphone to scan documents, with 16 reporting that they had scanned a check and seven reporting that they had scanned a receipt.

We randomly divided our 26 volunteers between two equally sized control and case groups. As an incentive to participate, we gave each volunteer a $10 Amazon gift card once they had completed the study.

5.1.3 Results

Figure 4b shows how long participants took to mark the regions around the QR codes. The median time taken to draw a marker on the whiteboard was 20.64 seconds, whereas the median time for marking a coffee mug was 11.2 seconds. While most participants felt that the marking scheme for WaveOff was simple, 20% of participants reported that the PrivateEye marker was complex. Two participants needed two attempts to correctly draw the PrivateEye marker.

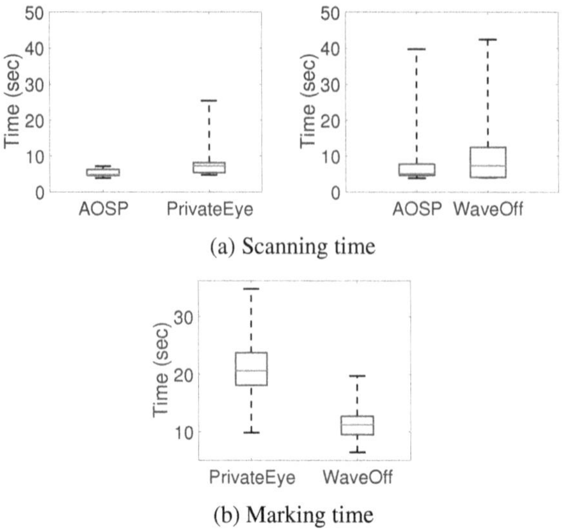

Figure 4: User-study results: (a) Time taken by users to scan a QR code with and without using our systems. (b) Time taken by users to mark a QR code with PrivateEye and WaveOff.

Each participant correctly scanned the QR codes and completed the study within 10 minutes. The 100% success rate indicates that PrivateEye and WaveOff preserve enough information in camera frames to support applications like QR-code scanning.

Figure 4a shows how long participants took to scan QR codes under PrivateEye and WaveOff compared to a baseline of unmodified AOSP. Our AOSP control group took a median of 4.9 seconds to scan a QR code on a whiteboard and a median of 5.5 seconds to scan a code on a mug. One member of the control group took nearly 40 seconds to scan the mug code because they initially held the camera too close.

Scan times for case-group members using PrivateEye and WaveOff were comparable to the baseline. For PrivateEye, the median scan time was 7.2 seconds, and for WaveOff the median scan time was 7.4 seconds. The main reason that case participants took longer is that PrivateEye and WaveOff block all camera input to an app until they have detected a marked region. As a result, users needed to guess the initial location of the QR codes before they became visible through the display.

Despite the additional time, participants rated the speed and ease of using PrivateEye and WaveOff on par with using AOSP. Figure 5 shows users' average levels of agreement with statements that scanning codes was fast and that scanning codes was easy. Users chose their level of agreement on a scale of one to seven, where one meant strong disagreement and seven meant strong agreement.

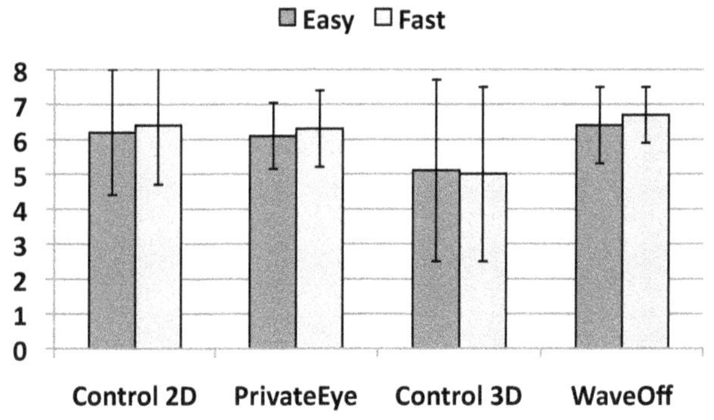

Figure 5: On a scale from one (strong disagreement) to seven (strong agreement), user-study participants' average levels of agreement that scanning QR codes was easy and fast. Error bars represent standard deviations.

When rating the speed of scanning the whiteboard code, the average levels of agreement were 6.4 (standard deviation 1.7) and 6.3 (standard deviation 1.2) for AOSP and PrivateEye, respectively. When rating the speed of scanning the mug code, the average levels of agreement were 5 (standard deviation 2.5) and 6.7 (standard deviation 0.8) for AOSP and WaveOff, respectively. When rating the ease of scanning the whiteboard code, the average levels of agreement were 6.2 (standard deviation 1.7) and 6.1 (standard deviation 0.9) for AOSP and PrivateEye, respectively. When rating the ease of scanning the mug code, the average levels of agreement were 5.1 (standard deviation 2.6) and 6.4 (standard deviation 1.1) for AOSP and WaveOff, respectively.

The high standard deviation in ratings for the control groups scanning under AOSP is due to two participants' requiring multiple attempts to scan the code. We found that in general, it is hard to scan a QR code on the curved surface if the camera is not positioned properly. This did not impact the WaveOff experiment because participants initially marked the object through the camera preview, and therefore were more careful when positioning the camera while scanning the code.

There were several notable results from our user ratings. First, PrivateEye's perceived ease-of-use and speed were statistically equivalent to unmodified AOSP. Second, for AOSP, users' felt that scanning a QR code on a flat surface was easier and faster than scanning a code on a curved surface. This makes sense since scanning a code on the mug using AOSP took longer, on average, than scanning a code on the whiteboard. Yet despite being quantitatively slower, WaveOff's perceived ease-of-use and speed were greater than PrivateEye's. Even more surprising, WaveOff's perceived ease-of-use and speed were greater than AOSP's!

We believe that these counter-intuitive results were due to users' mental model of the camera subsystem, and that WaveOff primed video streams for fast QR-code capture. Under WaveOff, the camera-preview screen was completely black until it recognized the coffee mug, and users likely attributed the blank screen to a camera delay rather than to WaveOff. Furthermore, the camera preview only appeared when a frame was clear enough for WaveOff to recognize the mug, which meant that the frame was also clear enough to scan the code. As a result, users likely scanned the QR code almost immediately after the camera preview appeared.

Note that PrivateEye also kept the screen blank until it recognized the whiteboard marker, but users rated PrivateEye the same as AOSP. This is because recognizing the PrivateEye marker was faster than recognizing either the mug or QR code, which caused a greater delay between the time the preview appeared and the time the QR code could be scanned than under WaveOff. As a result, WaveOff likely seemed faster and easier to use than either PrivateEye or AOSP.

5.2 Video benchmark

To characterize how well PrivateEye and WaveOff perform under a variety of settings and camera movements, we developed a simple video benchmark. Each video in the benchmark lasted 10 seconds, was shot with our Nexus 5 at a resolution of 1280×960 at 30 FPS, and captured public regions in controlled settings using predefined camera movements.

In particular, we shot videos of a public region on three two-dimensional surfaces and a three-dimensional object in three settings. To test two-dimensional surfaces we marked public regions on a whiteboard, a paper document, and in a presentation slide shown on a laptop screen. To test three-dimensional objects, we placed a white coffee mug alone in front of a white background, next to a soda can in front of a white background, and alone with a PC monitor and a keyboard in the near background.

We also designed three camera movements to understand how motion affected PrivateEye and WaveOff. Under the *still* movement, the camera was steady and remained focused on the marked region for the entire video. This movement approximated taking a picture. Under the *spin* movement, the camera rotated while keeping its view centered on the same region. This camera movement helped us understand orientation changes. Finally, under the *scan* movement, public regions moved in and out of the camera's view. For the first three seconds of these videos, a public region was centered. Then the camera panned to the right so that the public region disappeared from view. Lastly, the camera panned left so that the region returned to its original position, where it remained for final three seconds.

All together, our benchmark consisted of 18 videos: each two-dimensional surface captured under each camera movement, plus each three-dimensional setting captured under each camera movement. To test our PrivateEye and WaveOff implementations, we modified the Android camera subsystem to load pre-recorded videos from memory rather than from the HAL. After loading a video frame, we passed it along the same path that live frames pass, i.e., through our PrivateEye and WaveOff modules and ultimately to a video-recording app. Using this setup we evaluated PrivateEye and WaveOff's precision, recall, and performance.

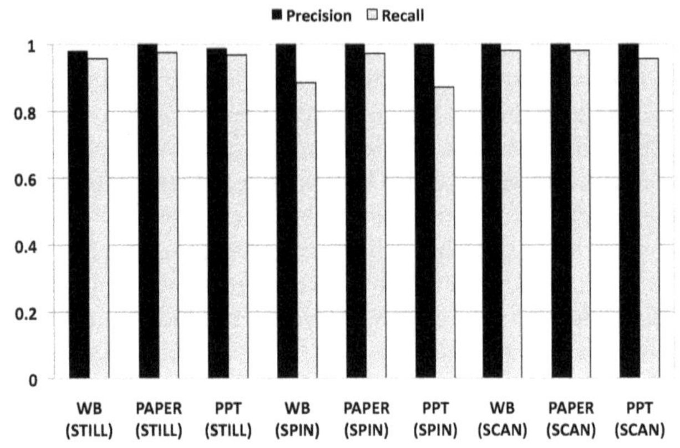

Figure 6: Median precision and recall for PrivateEye analyzing video frames of a public region on a whiteboard (WB), on a paper document (PAPER), and in a presentation slide on a laptop screen (PPT) under steady (STILL), rotating (SPIN), and panning (SCAN) camera movements.

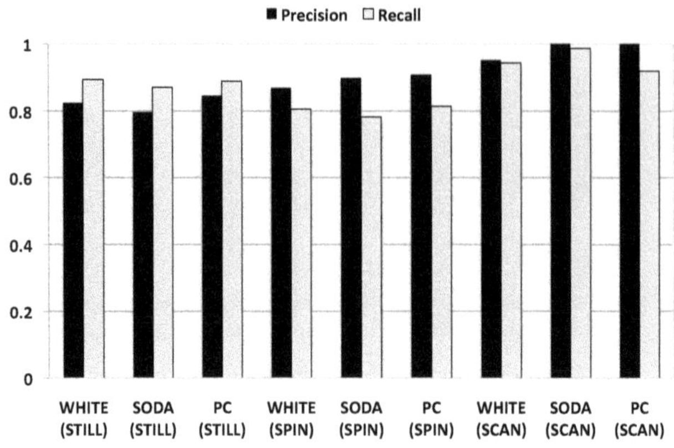

Figure 7: Median precision and recall for WaveOff analyzing video frames of a white coffee mug in front of a white background (WHITE), the mug next to a soda can in front of a white background (SODA), and the mug in front of a PC screen and keyboard (PC) under steady (STILL), rotating (SPIN), and panning (SCAN) camera movements.

5.2.1 Precision and recall

To calculate precision and recall, we partitioned each video frame into a grid of 5×5 pixel cells. Since we captured the original videos at a resolution of 1280×960 resolution, each frame contained 49,152 cells. We manually labeled all cells containing part of a marked region or object as *public*. We labeled all other cells *private*. Public cells should be revealed to applications, and private cells should be blocked from applications.

For each frame in the output videos, we analyzed which public cells PrivateEye and WaveOff revealed to compute precision and recall. We considered a cell blocked if *none* of it appeared in the frame; otherwise, we considered the cell to be revealed. More formally, let pb_t be the set of true public cells and pb_r be the set of cells revealed in a given frame. For all output videos, we calculated precision and recall for each frame as follows:

$$precision = \frac{|pb_t \cap pb_r|}{|pb_r|} \qquad recall = \frac{|pb_t \cap pb_r|}{|pb_t|}$$

Precision captures the percent of revealed cells that were truly public, and is a measure of a system's security. A perfectly secure system would reveal only true public cells, and thus have a precision of one. However, a system that blocked all cells would also be perfectly secure but would not support applications. Thus, precision must be considered in tandem with recall. Recall captures the percent of true public cells that a system revealed, and is a measure of how compatible the system is with applications. Similar to precision, if a system revealed all cells it would have perfect recall but provide no security. An ideal system would score highly on both precision and recall.

Figure 6 shows the median precision and recall under PrivateEye for frames in nine videos of two-dimensional surfaces. PrivateEye's lowest median precision was 0.98 for frames of a whiteboard with the camera still. In seven of the nine videos, PrivateEye exhibited a median precision of one. These results indicate that PrivateEye will provide strong security for many surfaces and under a variety camera movements.

It is worth noting that PrivateEye's median precision was greater than its median recall for all videos. This is a consequence of our design decision to prioritize security by revealing marked regions instead of blocking them. Our results show how blocking marked regions can compromise security. In particular, camera motion would cause systems that block marked regions to expose sensitive information, whereas PrivateEye exhibited a median precision of one for all spin and scan video frames.

It may seem counter-intuitive that PrivateEye's precision was lowest when the camera was still, i.e., 0.98 and 0.99 for the whiteboard and presentation slide, respectively. Across all videos, PrivateEye most often incorrectly revealed cells near the border of the marked region because marker lines were not perfectly straight, which led to slight differences between the marked region and PrivateEye's mask. In frames with motion blur, as in the spin and scan videos, border-cell features became fuzzy and did not register with our tracking algorithm. Still videos contained many more frames with clear marker boundaries, leading to lower median precision across the entire video.

PrivateEye's lowest median recall was 0.87 for the on-screen presentation slide with the camera rotating. In this case, the rotating camera created image blur that caused PrivateEye's tracking to incorrectly block cells just inside the public region. Nonetheless, in seven of the nine videos, PrivateEye exhibited a recall of 0.96 or greater. Overall, these results are highly encouraging and indicate that, despite providing strong security, PrivateEye is likely to reliably reveal public regions under most conditions.

Figure 7 shows the median precision and recall for frames under WaveOff. WaveOff's lowest median precision was

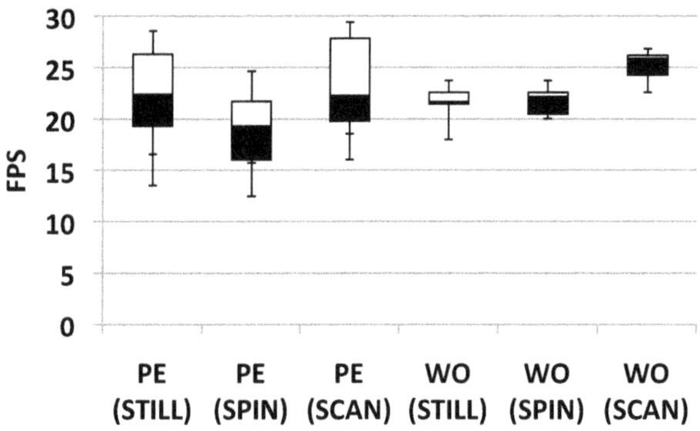

Figure 8: PrivateEye (PE) and WaveOff (WO) box plots for FPS under steady (STILL), rotating (SPIN), and panning (SCAN) camera movements.

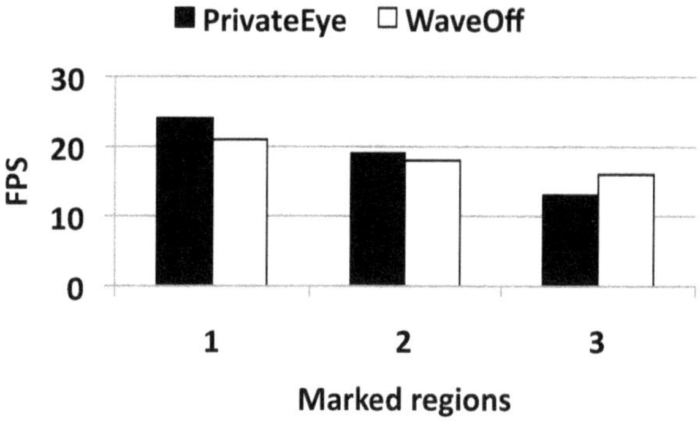

Figure 9: PrivateEye and WaveOff framerates with multiple marked regions.

0.79 for the still video when the coffee mug was next to a soda can. Precision scores for WaveOff in still videos with the mug front of a white background and in front of a PC were 0.82 and 0.84, respectively. As with PrivateEye, WaveOff's precision was lowest in still videos because they had no motion blur. However, mask mis-alignment was more acute with WaveOff than with PrivateEye because of the irregular shape of the coffee mug. WaveOff occasionally revealed cells close to the mug's handle when they should have been blocked. PrivateEye's rectangular marker was less prone to these errors.

WaveOff's lowest median recall scores were in spin videos. Its lowest median recall was 0.78 in the spin video with the mug next to a soda can. Recall was highest in scan videos because approximately 40% of the frames in these videos did not contain the mug. When the mug was absent, WaveOff correctly blocked all content and scored a perfect recall even though pb_t was empty. As with PrivateEye, median recall was lower in still videos because every frame contained the mug, and these frames provided more opportunities for WaveOff to incorrectly block cells near the border of the mug.

Overall, we were encouraged by WaveOff's benchmark results. Marking irregularly shaped three-dimensional objects is more challenging than marking two-dimensional regions with PrivateEye. In general, whenever WaveOff incorrectly blocked or revealed cells it was due to mask misalignment at the boundary of the coffee mug. Errors by PrivateEye and WaveOff were all localized to cells in the immediate vicinity of the marked regions. Consistent with our user-study, errors at the edge of an object seem unlikely to create major problems for applications or to leak sensitive information.

5.2.2 *Performance*

Supporting live camera feeds is critical for PrivateEye and WaveOff. Figure 8 shows box plots of PrivateEye and WaveOff's framerates on our video benchmark; the top whisker shows the max FPS achieved by a system for a collection of videos, the top of the white box shows the 75th percentile, the bottom of the white box shows the median, the bottom of the black box shows the 25th percentile, and the bottom whisker shows the minimum. The median framerate over all benchmark videos was 20 FPS and 22 FPS for PrivateEye and WaveOff, respectively. PrivateEye and WaveOff exhibited their highest median framerates on scan videos. The public regions and objects were absent for large portions of the scan videos, which eliminated the overhead of feature tracking on those frames. On the other hand, both systems exhibited their lowest median framerates on spin videos because camera rotation caused more tracking overhead. Finally, WaveOff achieved higher framerates than PrivateEye because WaveOff processes lower resolution images, i.e., 320×240 for WaveOff and 400×240 for PrivateEye. PrivateEye requires higher resolution images to reliably detect the concentric rectangle marker. Overall, these framerates are encouraging. Consistent with feedback from our user study, framerates between 20 and 25 FPS are acceptable for many camera-based applications.

5.3 Scalability

Our video benchmark evaluated PrivateEye and WaveOff using scenes with a single marked region or object. It is natural to ask how scenes with multiple marked regions and objects affect our systems' precision, recall, and performance. To answer this question, we recorded videos for PrivateEye with one, two, and three marked regions on a whiteboard, and a video for WaveOff with three objects (i.e., a soda can, green robot toy, and white coffee mug) in front of a white background. For WaveOff, we pre-computed models for all three objects, and loaded one, two, or three models at a time. The camera was still in all videos.

For both PrivateEye and WaveOff, the number of regions and objects did not have a significant impact on precision and recall. PrivateEye's average precision and recall were between 0.97 and 0.99 for all videos. WaveOff's recall declined from 0.95 to 0.90 after adding the toy model, but this was primarily due to its irregular shape. On the other hand, as Figure 9 shows, increasing the number of regions and objects decreased the framerates of both systems. The framerates for PrivateEye with one, two, and three public regions

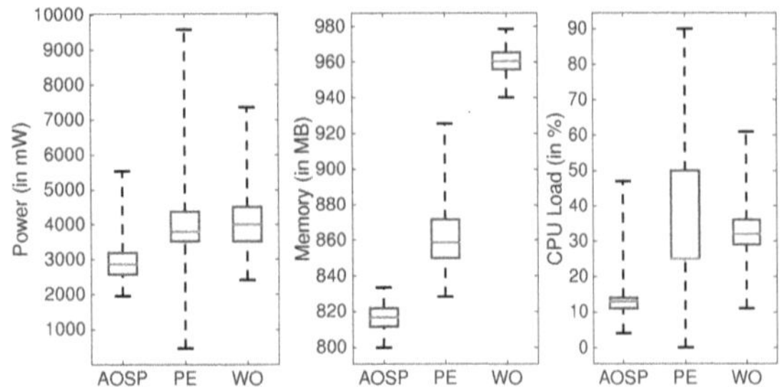

Figure 10: Power consumption, memory usage, and CPU load for AOSP, PrivateEye (PE), and WaveOff (WO) for a 60-second camera preview.

were 24, 19, and 13, respectively. The framerates for WaveOff with one, two, and three objects were 21 FPS, 18 FPS, and 16 FPS, respectively. These results suggest that PrivateEye and WaveOff are best suited to applications that require a small number of public regions per video frame.

5.4 Resource usage

Our final experiment was designed to measure the impact of PrivateEye and WaveOff on a mobile device's resource usage. We performed a simple experiment in which we turned on the camera and let it run for one minute in preview mode while measuring CPU load (in percentage), memory consumption (in MB) and power consumption (in mW). We took measurements every 100 ms using Trepn [8], a performance monitoring tool developed by Qualcomm. For this experiment, we set the smartphone on airplane mode to avoid measurement fluctuations due to network usage. We ran the experiment five times with unmodified AOSP, AOSP with PrivateEye, and AOSP with WaveOff, and rebooted our Nexus 5 between trials. For PrivateEye, the camera was focused on a public region, for WaveOff, the camera was focused on an object whose model was loaded in memory.

Figure 10 shows the power, memory, and CPU load results of our experiment. PrivateEye required a median of 40 MB more memory than AOSP. WaveOff's memory consumption was higher than PrivateEye's because it stores an object model in memory to perform matching. PrivateEye and WaveOff both increased the CPU load from a median of 11% to 26% and 31%, respectively. This CPU load was due to the detection and tracking algorithms applied on every frame during a camera session. As expected, power consumption exhibited a similar trend, with PrivateEye and WaveOff introducing median increases of 935 mW and 1150 mW, respectively. Overall, the additional resource usage of PrivateEye and WaveOff are reasonable, particularly since they only impose overhead when an app accesses the camera.

6. RELATED WORK

Several systems have applied the principle of least privilege to control fine-grained access to visual information [9, 20]. Recognizer [9] analyzes camera frames at runtime and limits third-party apps to accessing only the visual objects that they are authorized to view. SurroundWeb [20] limits 3D web browsers to skeleton views of rooms. An alternative but similar approach is to detect objects of interest and remove them [1, 4, 16]. Respectful Cameras use clothing such as special hats and vests to identify which users to remove from an image [16]. I-Pic uses a combination of short-range wireless signaling to disseminate policies and remote multiparty computation to transform captured images [1]. Privacy markers provide a more general way for users to specify what image data may be revealed to apps.

Another approach is to allow apps to manipulate transformed images through a high-level API rather than directly accessing them. Darkly [10] has some support for object-specific distortion (e.g., face morphing), but its primary means of restricting access to sensitive information are image-wide transformations (e.g., sketching) and limited access to the OpenCV API. However, because Darkly applies transformations to an entire image, it cannot support an arbitrary mix of high- and low-fidelity regions within an image as PrivateEye and WaveOff do.

Several projects [11, 19] protect visual content through sophisticated machine-learning tools. These systems require a great deal of training data and time, which limits their use to offline applications. PrivateEye and WaveOff both support realtime camera use.

Finally, many projects have tried to give users greater insight into and control over how apps use sensor data. Sensor-access widgets [7] graphically indicate when an app accesses sensor data, and SensorSift [6] automatically removes selected facial attributes, such as age, race, and expression, from images. ipShield [3] conveys privacy risks by listing inferences that could be drawn from sensor data. In world-driven access-control (WDAC) [15], real-world objects broadcast access-control policies to nearby recording devices. All of these projects are orthogonal to PrivateEye and WaveOff and could be easily integrated.

7. CONCLUSION

This paper made the case that *privacy markers* are a promising way to prevent third-party apps from inadvertently leaking visual information. We designed and implemented two privacy-marker systems, PrivateEye and WaveOff, that help users mark public regions in a camera's view and deliver only content within the public regions to apps. A user study with our prototype implementation revealed that users deemed camera operations with PrivateEye and WaveOff fast and easy-to-use. Other experiments with our prototype showed that PrivateEye and WaveOff provide strong security without compromising app functionality.

8. ACKNOWLEDGEMENTS

We would like to thank the anonymous reviewers and our shepherd Jakob Eriksson for their invaluable feedback. Our work was supported by Intel, Google, NSF award CNS-1253327, and DARPA and SPAWAR under contract N66001-15-C-4067.

References

[1] P. Aditya, R. Sen, S. J. Oh, R. Benenson, B. Bhattacharjee, P. Druschel, T. T. Wu, M. Fritz, and B. Schiele. I-pic: A platform for privacy-compliant image capture. MobiSys, 2016.

[2] J. Canny. A computational approach to edge detection. *TMAPI*, 1986.

[3] S. Chakraborty, C. Shen, K. R. Raghavan, Y. Shoukry, M. Millar, and M. Srivastava. ipshield: A framework for enforcing context-aware privacy. In *NSDI*, 2014.

[4] J. Chaudhari, S. Cheung, and M. Venkatesh. Privacy protection for life-log video. In *SAFE*, 2007.

[5] D. H. Douglas and T. K. Peucker. Algorithms for the reduction of the number of points required to represent a digitized line or its caricature. *Cartographica: The International Journal for Geographic Information and Geovisualization*, 1973.

[6] M. Enev, J. Jung, L. Bo, X. Ren, and T. Kohno. Sensorsift: Balancing sensor data privacy and utility in automated face understanding. ACSAC, 2012.

[7] J. Howell and S. Schechter. What you see is what they get: Protecting users from unwanted use of microphones, cameras, and other sensors. In *Web 2.0 Security and Privacy*. IEEE, May 2010.

[8] Q. T. Inc. Trepn Power Profiler. https://developer.qualcomm.com/software/trepn-power-profiler. [Online; accessed 7-Dec-2015].

[9] S. Jana, D. Molnar, A. Moshchuk, A. Dunn, B. Livshits, H. J. Wang, and E. Ofek. Enabling Fine-Grained Permissions for Augmented Reality Applications With Recognizers. In *USENIX Security*, 2013.

[10] S. Jana, A. Narayanan, and V. Shmatikov. A Scanner Darkly: Protecting User Privacy from Perceptual Applications. In *S & P*, 2013.

[11] M. Korayem, R. Templeman, D. Chen, D. J. Crandall, and A. Kapadia. Screenavoider: Protecting computer screens from ubiquitous cameras. *CoRR*, 2014.

[12] S. Leutenegger, M. Chli, and R. Siegwart. Brisk: Binary robust invariant scalable keypoints. In *ICCV*, 2011.

[13] G. Nebehay and R. Pflugfelder. Clustering of Static-Adaptive correspondences for deformable object tracking. In *CVPR*, 2015.

[14] N. Raval, A. Srivastava, K. Lebeck, L. Cox, and A. Machanavajjhala. Markit: Privacy markers for protecting visual secrets. UbiComp '14 Adjunct, 2014.

[15] F. Roesner, D. Molnar, A. Moshchuk, T. Kohno, and H. J. Wang. World-driven access control for continuous sensing. Technical Report MSR-TR-2014-67, 2014.

[16] J. Schiff, M. Meingast, D. Mulligan, S. Sastry, and K. Goldberg. Respectful cameras: detecting visual markers in real-time to address privacy concerns. In *IROS*, 2007.

[17] J. Shi and C. Tomasi. Good features to track. 1994.

[18] S. Suzuki and K. Abe. Topological structural analysis of digitized binary images by border following. *Computer Vision, Graphics, and Image Processing*, 1985.

[19] R. Templeman, M. Korayem, D. Crandall, and A. Kapadia. PlaceAvoider: Steering first-person cameras away from sensitive spaces. In *NDSS*, 2014.

[20] J. Vilk, D. Molnar, E. Ofek, C. Rossbach, B. Livshits, A. Moshchuk, H. J. Wang, and R. Gal. Surroundweb : Mitigating privacy concerns in a 3d web browser. In *IEEE Symposium on Security and Privacy*, May 2015.

[21] J. yves Bouguet. Pyramidal implementation of the lucas kanade feature tracker. *Intel Corporation, Microprocessor Research Labs*, 2000.

Viola: Trustworthy Sensor Notifications for Enhanced Privacy on Mobile Systems

Saeed Mirzamohammadi, Ardalan Amiri Sani

University of California, Irvine
saeed@uci.edu, ardalan@uci.edu

Abstract

Modern mobile systems such as smartphones, tablets, and wearables contain a plethora of sensors such as camera, microphone, GPS, and accelerometer. Moreover, being mobile, these systems are with the user all the time, e.g., in user's purse or pocket. Therefore, mobile sensors can capture extremely sensitive and private information about the user including daily conversations, photos, videos, and visited locations. Such a powerful sensing capability raises important privacy concerns.

To address these concerns, we believe that mobile systems must be equipped with *trustworthy sensor notifications*, which use indicators such as LED to inform the user unconditionally when the sensors are on. We present *Viola*, our design and implementation of trustworthy sensor notifications, in which we leverage two novel solutions. First, we deploy a runtime monitor in low-level system software, e.g., *in the operating system kernel or in the hypervisor*. The monitor intercepts writes to the registers of sensors and indicators, evaluates them against checks on sensor notification invariants, and rejects those that fail the checks. Second, we use *formal verification methods* to prove the functional correctness of the compilation of our invariant checks from a high-level language.

We demonstrate the effectiveness of Viola on different mobile systems, such as Nexus 5, Galaxy Nexus, and ODROID XU4, and for various sensors and indicators, such as camera, microphone, LED, and vibrator. We demonstrate that Viola incurs almost no overhead to the sensor's performance and incurs only small power consumption overhead.

Keywords

Mobile systems; Sensors; Notifications; Indicators; Invariants; Virtualization; Verification

1. INTRODUCTION

Modern mobile systems such as smartphones, tablets, and wearables have one important property in common: they contain a plethora of sensors. A smartphone today, for example, contains tens of sensors including camera, microphone, GPS, accelerometer, and fingerprint scanner. Moreover, being mobile, these systems are with the user at all times. Such a usage model exposes mobile sensors to extremely private information about the user, including daily conversations, photos, videos, and visited locations, all of which is considered to be sensitive by some or most users according to a study by Muslukhov et al. [46].

Such a powerful sensing capability raises important privacy concerns for users. These concerns are reinforced given the recent incidents where women were spied on through their webcams [7, 8] and where users were spied on through their smartphone microphones and cameras [6]. In fact, in Android, the camera and microphone were shown to be hacked and controlled remotely using a commercialized trojan [4].

We believe that an important and practical remedy to this problem is to provide *trustworthy sensor notifications* on mobile systems in order to provide *unconditional and immediate feedback* to the user when the sensors are being used. That is, we believe that mobile systems must use an *indicator*, such as LED or vibrator, to unexceptionally notify the user when a sensor is on. This way, even if the sensor is accessed maliciously, the user becomes aware and can take action, e.g., by turning the system off. The usefulness of trustworthy sensor notifications is due to the fundamental observation that the user is able to reason about the correct status of a sensor at a given time. For example, the user correctly expects the camera to be on only when she explicitly launches a camera application. Similarly, she expects the microphone to be recording only if she launches a voice recorder application or if she makes a voice call. With such knowledge, the user can leverage trustworthy sensor notifications to detect malicious access to sensors.

Unfortunately, sensor notifications are not systematically enforced in mobile systems today and existing notifications are ad hoc. First, some applications implement their own notifications. For example, the built-in microphone application on Samsung Galaxy Note 3 blinks a blue LED while recording if the display is turned off. It also adds an unremovable glyph to Android notification bar when the application is in the background. Or the built-in camera application in the same smartphone only records video if it is in the foreground with the display on (which can be considered as some form of notification). However, these notifications do not apply to other applications. For example, the Detective Video Recorder application [1] can record video and audio when

MobiSys'16, June 25 - 30, 2016, Singapore.

ISBN 978-1-4503-4269-8/16/06...$15.00

DOI: http://dx.doi.org/10.1145/2906388.2906391

Figure 1: LED notification for microphone using Viola. The LED blinks even if the application is in the background or if the display is off. Malicious attempts to break this notification will be blocked.

in the background and with the display off. Second, laptop webcams often notify the user with a built-in LED. These notifications are implemented by the webcams themselves and do not apply to other sensors. Moreover, as Brocker et al. [18] showed, these notifications can be circumvented in some MacBook laptops and iMac desktops by rewriting the webcam firmware, demonstrating the difficulty of implementing trustworthy sensor notifications.

We present *Viola*, a system solution for providing trustworthy sensor notifications in mobile systems. Our fundamental observation is that it is possible to formulate a sensor notification as a logical *invariant* on the hardware states of the sensor and indicator. For example, for an LED notification for microphone, the invariant is `microphone recording` → `LED blinks`, where → depicts logical implication. Viola employs runtime invariant checks in the system to guarantee that this invariant is never violated even if the system is compromised by an attacker. That is, the check does not allow the microphone to start recording unless the LED is blinking and does not allow the LED to be turned off while the microphone is recording. Figure 1 shows Viola in action. See a video demo of Viola in [12].

We answer two important questions about the design of the invariant checks.

Q1. Where should the runtime invariant checks be inserted? In Viola, we insert the checks in the low-level system software, e.g., in the operating system kernel or in the hypervisor. Since sensor notifications are mostly about constraints on the hardware states of the sensors and the indicators, it is possible to check the notification' invariant in the low-level system software irrespective of the state of higher level software. At these low-level layers, we intercept the writes to the registers of sensors and indicators and pass them to the invariant checks. We allow the successful execution of a register write only if it successfully passes all the checks.

Inserting the checks in the low-level system software enhances the trustworthiness of Viola as it reduces the size of the Trusted Computing Base (TCB). In this design, bugs in the device drivers and I/O services, which are very common [5,17,23,31,48], will not undermine the sensor notification invariants. Moreover, this design protects the integrity of the notification invariant against powerful malware including those with root or kernel privileges. The two layers mentioned above, i.e., kernel or hypervisor, provide a tradeoff between trustworthiness, support for different operating systems, support for legacy systems, and performance, as will be explained in §4.

Q2. How can system designers develop provably correct invariant checks? Writing error-free invariant checks that operate on the parameters of writes to registers is fairly complicated given the complex hardware interface of many I/O devices, their peripheral buses, and the components they rely on, such as power supplies and clock sources in the System-on-a-Chip (SoC).

We tackle this challenge using an invariant language and its verified compiler. Viola's invariant language enables the developer to mainly focus on the invariant logic using a high-level and intuitive syntax. A verified compiler, which we build and verify using the Coq language and its proof assistant [11], guarantees that the generated invariant checks preserve the semantics of Viola's invariant language. The compiler uses device specifications for inferring device state transitions as a result of register writes.

We present an implementation of Viola that supports different sensors and indicators, such as camera, microphone, LED, and vibrator, on two smartphones, Nexus 5 and Galaxy Nexus. While hardware support for virtualization is increasingly available on mobile systems [13], commercial mobile systems either do not leverage this hardware support or, if they do, they do not provide open access support for programming the hypervisor. Therefore, to demonstrate the feasibility of using the hypervisor layer, we implement Viola on the ODROID XU4 development board as well.

In the evaluation, we demonstrate that implementing sensor notifications using Viola does not require significant engineering effort. We also demonstrate that Viola adds significant latency to every monitored registered write (especially if Viola's monitor runs in the hypervisor) but that this latency incurs almost no overhead to the sensor's performance due to the infrequency of monitored register writes. Moreover, we show the added power consumption is small.

Note that trustworthy sensor notifications do not address all the privacy concerns that a user may have with respect to the sensitive information captured by mobile sensors, including unauthorized access to already-captured information. Moreover, Viola's notification do not tell the user which application is using a sensor. It just informs the user that the sensor is being used relying on the user to decide whether the access is malicious or not and, if yes, to detect the malicious application. Addressing these concerns is orthogonal to our work.

Also note that Viola requires modifications to various parts of the system software and hence is not easily deployable by ordinary users on their mobile systems, e.g., by simply installing an application. We mainly envision Viola to be adopted by mobile system vendors, such as Samsung and LG. However, we believe that expert users can also benefit from Viola especially since Viola's verified compiler makes it easy for them to develop the required invariant checks.

In summary, we make the following contributions.

- We present Viola, a system solution for enabling trustworthy sensor notifications on mobile systems that inserts invariant checks in the low-level system software, such as the kernel or the hypervisor.
- We use formal verification and provide machine-checked proofs to guarantee the functional correctness of the compilation of invariant checks used in Viola from a high-level language. To the best of our knowledge, this is the first work to provide formal guarantees on the behavior of I/O devices (e.g., the relationship between the states of sensors and indicators).

2. SENSOR NOTIFICATIONS

In this section, we provide background information for sensor notifications including different types of indicators that can be used and different notification guarantees.

2.1 Indicators

Various indicators including LED, vibrator, speaker, and display can be used on mobile systems today. Here, we discuss the pros and cons of these indicators.

LED. Today's mobile systems incorporate several LEDs on various locations on the system's exterior, e.g., on top or bottom of the display. LEDs come in different colors and can be used in different modes, e.g., constant illumination and blinking. LEDs provide the most lightweight indicators possible and we anticipate them to be the most dominant indicators for many sensors. However, LEDs have two important shortcomings. First, they are ineffective if the system is out of user's sight, e.g., in the user's purse or pocket. Second, they are often overloaded with informing the user of other events in the system as well (e.g., a missed call or text message), which might reduce their effectiveness in attracting the user's attention.

Vibrator and speaker. These two indicators are effective in capturing the user's attention even when the system is out of the user's sight. However, they can be intrusive and distracting especially if used for extended periods of time. Moreover, they pollute the data captured by some sensors, e.g., microphone and accelerometer.

Display. Display is an effective channel to convey notifications to the user. Indeed, in [49], authors demonstrate that showing a glyph on the display is more effective than an LED in capturing the user's attention. However, not only these notifications require the display to be in user's sight, they also require the display to be on, which is power hungry.

Note that the best notification might be achieved by leveraging several indicators. For example, for microphone, it might be best to play a short beeping sound on the speaker and illuminate an LED afterwards.

Also, note that our goal in this paper is to build a trustworthy framework for notifications. Determining the best indicator for each sensor requires a user study, similar to the study in [49], which is orthogonal to this work and is part of our future work.

2.2 Notification Guarantees

Causal guarantees. We envision two types of notifications in terms of causal guarantees provided to the user. *One-way* notifications guarantee that the indicator is on, e.g., the LED is illuminated, when the sensor is on. However, they do not provide any guarantees on the state of the indicator when the sensor is off. The logical invariant for one-way notifications can be expressed as **`sensor in target state`** $\rightarrow$ **`indicator in target state`**. For a simple uni-color LED, the target state can be as simple as LED being illuminated. Or for an RGB LED with built-in blinking capabilities and varying illumination levels [10], the target state may be that the LED blinks in a red color with a given frequency and illumination level. In the rest of the paper, we use the terms "in target state" and "on" interchangeably.

Two-way notifications provide both guarantees. That is, they guarantee that the indicator is on *if and only if* the sensor is on, or **`sensor on`** $\leftrightarrow$ **`indicator on`**. With one-way notifications, the indicator can be turned on while the sensor is off, which will result in false positives for the user. By triggering a large number of false positives, an attacker can reduce the effectiveness of the notification as the user will likely ignore the notifications thinking that they are broken. Two-way notifications eliminate the false positives and hence solve this problem.

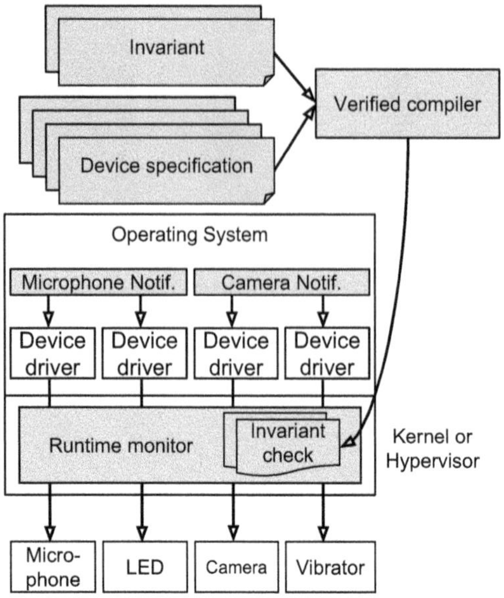

Figure 2: Viola's design. The darker components belong to Viola.

Temporal guarantees. We envision two types of notifications in terms of the duration in which the indicator is active. *Continuous* notifications guarantee the indicator to be on for as long as the sensor is recording and are best suited for LED and display indicators. *Temporary* notifications guarantee the indicator is turned on only for a short period of time when the sensor starts capturing and are best suited for speaker and vibrator indicators.

In this paper, we demonstrate the use of LED and vibrator as indicators while supporting one-way and continuous notifications. §8 discusses the challenges of providing formal guarantees for the use of speaker and display as indicators, and for two-way and temporary notifications. It further discusses our plans to overcome these challenges in the future.

3. OVERVIEW

Figure 2 illustrates the design of Viola. There are three main components. The first component is the implementation of sensor notification, which leverages the device driver (either directly or indirectly through user space I/O service API) to turn on the indicator before the sensor starts recording and to turn the indicator off after the sensor stops. This implementation is not trusted and hence errors in it will not break the notification invariant. Malfunction in this implementation, e.g., failure to turn on the indicator, will be detected and blocked by the invariant checks (the third component, explained below).

The second component is a trusted runtime monitor, which runs in the kernel or in the hypervisor. It intercepts the device drivers' attempts to write to the registers of sensors and indicators by removing the write permissions from the corresponding page table entries. It then consults with a set of deployed invariant checks, which inspect the parameters of the write and decide whether, if allowed, the write would break the invariants corresponding to the sensor notifications or not. The monitor allows for the successful execution of the write only if it passes all the checks, and rejects it otherwise. In case of a reject, it blocks the write and force-reboots the system. §4 elaborates on the monitor.

The third component of our design is a set of invariant checks deployed in the monitor. To enable developing provably correct invariant checks, we present a high-level language for writing the sensor notification invariants. We also develop a verified compiler for the language using Coq that guarantees that the generated invariant checks maintain the semantic of sensor notification invariant. The compiler uses device specifications for inferring the device state transitions as a result of register writes. In addition, for off-chip devices whose registers are only accessible through a peripheral bus, we design a verified bus interpreter module that can infer the device register writes from the bus adapter register writes. §5 discusses the details of the invariant language, its compiler, and the bus interpreter module.

3.1 Threat Model

We have designed Viola to enforce sensor notifications' invariants in the system and prevent buggy or malicious code from breaking them. We will assume attackers with varying capabilities. The first attacker can only use the application API in the operating system, e.g., Android API. This attacker can run native code as well but without root privileges. The second attacker runs native code with root privileges in the user space, however cannot run code with kernel privileges or secretly modify the system image (for future boots). More specifically, in this case, we assume that the attacker cannot leverage the kernel vulnerabilities to inject code and assume that the kernel is configured to prevent a root user from easily modifying the running kernel memory. The latter is achieved by configuring the kernel to disallow loading of kernel modules and to avoid exposing the `/dev/kmem` file, which would allow user space code to have access to the kernel memory. Moreover, we assume that the mobile system implements the verified boot feature [3], which checks and verifies the integrity of the loaded system images. As a result, the attacker's attempt to modify the system images (i.e., the kernel and hypervisor images), which will take effect in future boots, will be detected and then blocked or at least communicated to the user with a notification at boot time. The third attacker leverages the vulnerabilities of the kernel to compromise it and hence can run code with kernel privileges. The fourth attacker is a more advanced version of the third attacker that, after compromising the kernel, leverages the vulnerabilities of the hypervisor to compromise it and hence can run code with hypervisor privileges. The fifth attacker is a root user in a system without the verified boot feature, which would allow him to rewrite the kernel and hypervisor images (to be used after a reboot). Finally, the sixth attacker has physical access to the device and can manipulate the hardware.

As mentioned earlier, we run Viola's monitor either in the kernel or the hypervisor. In both cases, Viola enforces the integrity of the sensor notifications despite bugs in the I/O stack (including device drivers and user space I/O services), which would otherwise violate the notifications' invariants. Moreover, both types of monitor protect against the first two attackers. However, only the hypervisor-based monitor protects against the third attacker. This attacker can circumvent the kernel-based monitor in three ways: (*i*) it can manipulate the fault handler in the kernel in order to prevent the deployed invariant checks from evaluating a register write, (*ii*) it can access the registers through a different set of virtual addresses mapped to the same register pages, or (*iii*) it can manipulate the page tables to re-enable the write permissions on the page table entries removed by Viola's monitor. None of the solutions can protect against the fourth attacker either. This attacker is a super set of the third attacker and hence can circumvent the kernel-based monitor as explained above. Moreover, it can use very similar techniques to circumvent the checks implemented in the hypervisor after it manages to compromise the hypervisor. Similarly, none of the solutions can protect against the fifth attacker since it can simply remove Viola's monitor from the system image used for future system boots. Finally, none of the solutions can protect against the sixth attacker as it can modify the hardware, e.g., disconnect the LEDs.

4. RUNTIME MONITOR

Viola's runtime monitor runs in the low-level system software, e.g., in the operating system kernel or the hypervisor, in order to monitor the device drivers' interactions with sensors and indicators. The monitor intercepts any attempts to write to device registers and feeds the write parameters to the invariant checks (§5). It allows the successful execution of a write only if it passes all the checks. Note that we focus on register writes, and not register reads, since the former is typically used to alter the state of a device. However, all the discussions are easily extended to register reads if they need to be monitored as well.

Using the kernel or hypervisor to insert the invariant checks provides a trade-off between trustworthiness, support for different operating systems, support for legacy systems, and performance. On the one hand, a hypervisor-based solution isolates the monitor from the operating system, which enhances its trustworthiness even against malware with complete control over the kernel execution (i.e., the third attacker in §3.1). It also makes the monitor implementation agnostic to the operating system, e.g., Android or iOS, or to the operating system version. The use of the hypervisor is further motivated by the fact that ARM processors have recently added virtualization hardware support [13] allowing an efficient implementation of the monitor in the hypervisor.

On the other hand, a kernel-based solution can be used in many existing mobile systems. This is because commercial mobile systems either currently do not have hardware support for virtualization or do not provide open access for programming the hypervisor. Also, inserting the checks in the kernel incurs less overhead to a register write compared to a hypervisor-based solutions (§7.2).

Note that an alternative layer for adding the invariant checks is the hardware. Such a solution is the most trustworthy as it minimizes the Trusted Computing Base to only the hardware. However, a hardware-based solution is costly as it requires additional circuitry per invariant. Moreover, such a solution is often practically impossible since the invariants span multiple I/O devices, e.g., camera and LED, which are typically integrated on and off the System-on-a-Chip (SoC) from various vendors in the form of closed source IP modules. Furthermore, while we want the notifications to be unbreakable, it might be desirable to make them customizable by the user or the system designer, for example, if the user wants to intentionally turn off all notifications for a short period of time. Such customizations are not feasible with a hardware solution. In §8.1, we discuss how we can add support for secure customizations to Viola. Finally, note that, while we have not done so, if we employ our invariant checks in a verified kernel or hypervisor [20,34,36,38,44], we can reduce the TCB to only the hardware as well.

Viola's monitor intercepts device drivers' attempts to write to registers by removing the write permissions from the corresponding page table entries. This is feasible since in the ARM architecture all the registers are memory-mapped (i.e., Memory-Mapped I/O or MMIO). Depending on where the monitor is hosted, we use different page tables. First, for the hypervisor-based monitor, we leverage ARM's Stage-2 page tables [13,25]. In this case, a memory address is translated by two sets of page tables, one maintained by the operating system and one (i.e., Stage-2 page tables) maintained by the hypervisor. Removing the write permission from a Stage-2 page table entry forces writes to every register in the corresponding page to trap in the hypervisor, allowing the monitor to inspect them. Second, for the kernel-based monitor, we simply use the page tables used by the kernel. In this case, a write to protected register pages raises a page fault exception in the kernel.

When the monitor detects an unauthorized register write, it blocks the write and force-reboots the system. It does so by returning a permission violation error to the page fault handler in the kernel or hypervisor, which leads to a reboot.

Initially, we planned to identify and kill the responsible application upon detecting such page faults. However, doing so is challenging, as the violation might be triggered not by an application but by powerful malware with kernel or hypervisor privileges. Therefore, we believe that force-reboot is a safe approach to handle these attacks. Note that the force-reboot approach does not create an easily-exploitable and additional denial-of-service attack vector. This is because attackers with root, kernel, or hypervisor privileges can reboot the system using other methods anyway and the attacker without these privileges (i.e., the first attacker in §3.1) cannot trigger such page faults easily unless it circumvents the implementation of the sensor notification.

5. VERIFIED INVARIANT CHECKS

Viola's verified invariant checks receive the parameters of a register write as input from the monitor and decide whether the write, if executed, breaks any of the sensor notifications' invariants in the system. Unfortunately, manually developing checks that operate on the parameters of register writes is cumbersome and error-prone. An I/O device, i.e., a sensor or an indicator, might have several registers, each affecting the behavior of the device in some way. Moreover, a single register might contain a few device variables (i.e., the variable formed by a subset of bits in a register [45]), requiring bitwise operations in the invariant checks. Furthermore, the correct behavior of an I/O device might depend on other components as well, such as its power supply and clock source in the SoC, requiring Viola to monitor these components as well. Finally, Viola's monitor cannot directly monitor the writes to device registers for off-chip devices. It can only monitor the writes to registers of the peripheral bus adapters and must infer the device register writes.

```
Definition mic_rec :=
    State mic_spec [mic_bias_on; ...].
Definition led_blink :=
    State led_spec [led_blink_mode;
                    led_color_red; ...].
Definition mic_led_notif :=
    Binder mic_rec led_blink.
```

Figure 3: The implementation of a microphone LED notification in Viola. For brevity, we have not shown the complete array of device variable states and the device specifications used in the code.

In this section, we present our solution that enables the system designer to easily develop provably correct invariant checks. Our solution is an invariant language with a high-level and intuitive syntax, which enables developers to mainly focus on the invariant logic (which is quite simple), rather than the low-level implementation. We then present a verified compiler for this invariant language that generates provably correct assembly code that maintains the logical semantics of the invariant. Moreover, we present a verified bus interpreter module for off-chip devices.

5.1 Viola's Invariant Language Syntax

Viola's invariant language leverages two main programming constructs. (*i*) *State* is used to specify the target states of the sensor or indicator, e.g., microphone recording or LED blinking. A device target state is a list of device variable states, where each device variable state is a 2-tuple containing a device variable and a value. As mentioned earlier, a device variable is the variable formed by a subset of the bits in a register [45]. As a hypothetical example, the three least significant bits of a register could form the device variable for camera resolution. These device variables must be defined in the device specifications (§5.2.1). (*ii*) *Binder* is finally used to bind the target states of the sensor and indicator.

Figure 3 shows an example invariant written in Viola for the microphone LED notification (LED blinking). In this example, we have first defined the target states of the sensor and indicator, `mic_rec` and `led_blink`, respectively. Each of these target states is defined as an array of device variable states, e.g., `led_blink_mode`. Moreover, in defining these target states, we have used the device specifications, i.e., `mic_spec` and `led_spec`, which provide the definition of each of the device variable states. Finally, the sensor notification invariant is defined by binding the target states of the sensor and indicator together.

5.2 Verified Compiler

We build a verified compiler for Viola's invariant language. Given an invariant written in this language, the compiler generates provably correct invariant checks to be inserted in Viola's monitor.

Building and verifying a compiler is a cumbersome task. Our key idea to reduce this effort is to implement our compiler as a frontend for the formally verified CompCert C compiler [39], similar to the approach used by Wang et al. for Jitk [55]. The frontend compiles Viola's code to Cminor, an intermediate language in CompCert, which is then compiled to assembly by the CompCert backend. The assembly code is then translated to machine code using a commodity

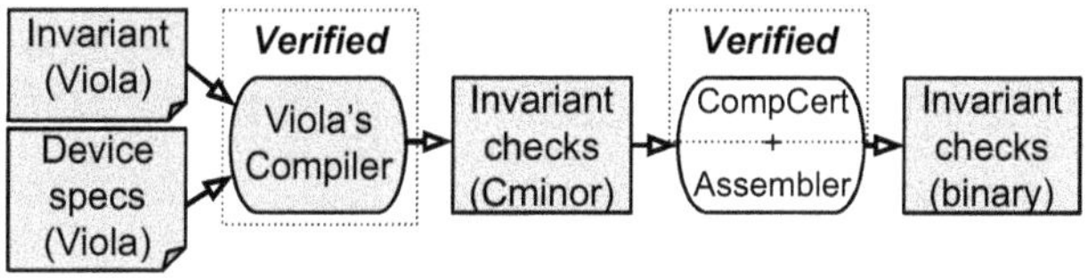

Figure 4: Compilation of Viola invariant code. Viola's compiler translates Viola code to Cminor code, which is then compiled to machine code using the verified CompCert compiler and an assembler. The darker components belong to Viola.

assembler since CompCert does not currently provide a verified assembler. Cminor is a simplified and typeless variant of a subset of C with support for integers, floats, pointers (but not the & operator), control constructs such as if/else (but not the goto statement), and functions (see [39] for more details).

Given that CompCert is a verified compiler, it preserves the semantics of the code in Cminor while generating the assembly code. Therefore, we only need to prove that our frontend maintains the semantics of Viola's code while generating the Cminor code. To achieve this, we implement the frontend in Coq and use Coq's interactive proof assistant [11] to prove the semantic preservation property. As will be explained, our compiler relies on device specifications to infer the device state transitions as a result of register writes. Figure 4 illustrates our approach.

We prove the semantic preservation property as follows. We formalize the I/O devices (i.e., sensors and indicators) as blocks of memory (MMIO) corresponding to their register spaces. We then prove, through forward simulation [41,42], that both programs (i.e., the one written in Viola and its compiled Cminor program) return the same decision (i.e., allowing or rejecting a register write) given the state of these MMIO blocks, the invariant logic, and the device specifications. Put formally, we prove the following theorem.

Theorem *Viola_compile_correct:* `forward_simulation (Viola.semantics Vprog) (Cminor.semantics Cprog).`

The heart and the majority of the proof for the aforementioned theorem is proving the following lemma (slightly simplified for clarify).

Lemma *compile_step:* `∀ S1 S2, Viola.step S1 S2 → ∀ R1, match_states S1 R1 → ∃ R2, plus Cminor.step R1 R2 ∧ match_states S2 R2.`

Both languages, Viola and Cminor, are modeled as a series of steps from some initial state to some final state. This lemma mentions that, for every two states in Viola code, for which there is a transition (i.e., a step) according to the semantics of the language, and for all Cminor states equivalent to the source state in Viola code, there exists a state in Cminor code that can be reached from this equivalent source state, possibly in multiple steps (as signified by `plus`), and that the reached target state in Cminor code is also equivalent to the target state in Viola code. The states and steps in Viola are part of the specification of the language semantics. Moreover, the definition of equivalence between the states of the two programs is part of the specification that we develop for the proof.

In Viola, each step is equivalent to the evaluation of one invariant check on the register write parameters. There are two main types of steps: reject and pass. In the former, the invariant check fails and Viola returns reject. In the latter, the invariant check passes and Viola continues to evaluate the next check. If all checks pass, Viola returns pass.

Reject or pass steps are determined based on *reject and pass conditions* that we have also defined as part of the language semantics. The reject condition is satisfied when either of its two sub-conditions are satisfied. The first sub-condition is when the register write causes the sensor to transition to its target state and the indicator is not in its target state. The second sub-condition is when the register write causes the indicator to go out of its target state and the sensor is in its target state. We specify transitioning to the target state as when all the device variables acquire the values defined in the device target state. We specify transitioning out of the target state as when at least one device variable acquires a value other than the one defined in the device target state. The pass condition is simply the negation of the reject condition.

In addition to this lemma, we also prove that for all initial states in Viola program, there is an equivalent initial state in the compiled Cminor program and that if the two programs reach equivalent final states, they both return the same value.

In proving the aforementioned theorem, we prove the soundness and completeness of the generated checks: that is, we prove that the generated checks always reject the register writes that violate the invariants (soundness) and that the checks never reject benign register writes (completeness).

5.2.1 Device Specifications

The compiler uses the device specifications to generate the invariant checks. The compiler needs these specifications for *device state transition inference* upon a register write. The specification must contain the following definitions: the list of registers (in the form of the register address offset from a base address), the list of device variables built on top of each registers, the list of device variable states, the list of register write events for the device variables, where an event is a write with a given value to a device variable, and the list of device variable transitions, where a transition is a 3-tuple consisting of a source state, an event, and a target state. Note that checking the source state of a transition in the invariant check is important in order to enforce the order of register writes. As a simple example, consider a device with a single 8 bit register, which consists of only one single-bit device variable. The list of register write events can be writes with values of 0 and 1. The list of device variable transitions are transitions from 0 to 1 (with a write with a value of 1) and from 1 to 0 (with a write with a value of 0). For brevity of writing the events, Viola supports two types of events representing a write to a device variable with a value equal to or different from a specified value. This significantly reduces the size of the specification as it alleviates the need to enumerate all the events one by one. Note that while Viola enforces the order of register writes, it currently does not support specifying and enforcing the maximum time interval between consecutive register writes. Adding this feature is part of our future work.

Currently, we manually develop these specifications for the devices that we support. Fortunately, as observed by

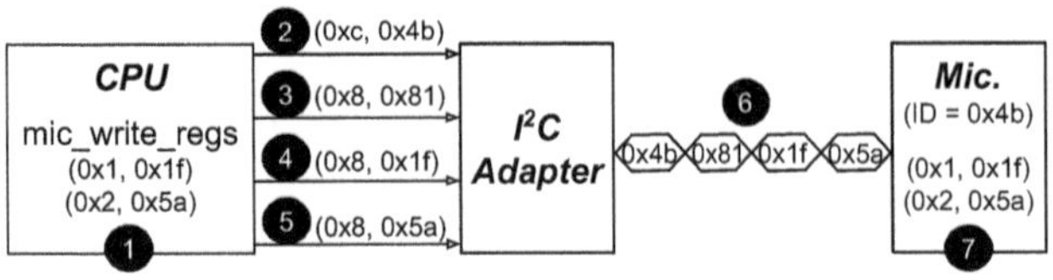

Figure 5: Simplified steps for writing to registers of a device over an I^{2}C bus. The numbers in parenthesis show register writes parameters (offset, value). The dark numbered circles represent the approximate progression of events.

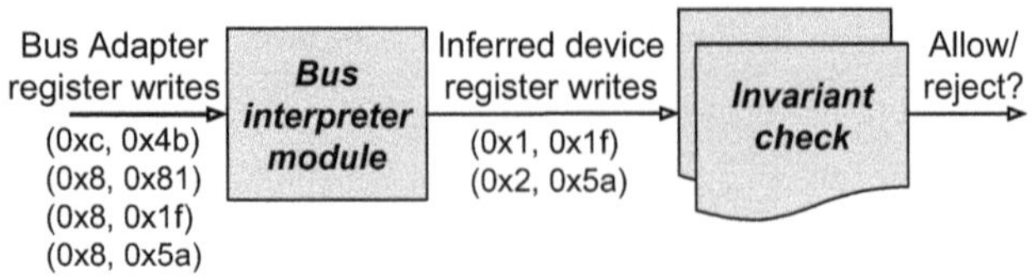

Figure 6: Bus interpreter module role. The bus register writes are intercepted in the monitor and passed to the bus interpreter module, which infers the register writes of the device and passes them to the sensor notification invariant checks.

Ryzhyk et al. [52], device specifications are increasingly available from hardware vendors as the same specifications are also used in the device design process. However, to leverage these specifications, a translator is needed to transform the existing specifications into the format supported by Viola.

Partial device specifications. Writing the complete device specifications can be a daunting task, especially for complex devices such as camera. However, in Viola, partial specifications suffice for two reasons. First, one does not need to develop the complete specification of the sensor; the specification of a few device variables used for turning on the sensor is adequate. As long as the invariant check guarantees that these device variables will take on their target value only when the indicator is on, the sensor notification invariant will not be violated. Second, while a more elaborate specification is often needed for the indicator (e.g., for its dependencies as explained next), still a complete specification might not be needed. For example, if an LED is required to illuminate constantly, and not blink, one does not need to write the specifications for the blinking functionality of the LED.

5.3 Checks on Dependencies

Viola's goal is to guarantee that the indicator is on when the sensor is on. However, the indicator's state often has dependencies on other hardware components including the power supply and the clock source on the SoC that provide power and clock for the indicator. Therefore, the invariant logic to enforce in the system should be refined to `sensor on` → `indicator on` → `(indicator) power supply on` → `(indicator) clock source on`. Note that Viola does not monitor the sensor's dependencies since the failure to turn on the sensor does not violate the notification invariant.

We enforce this logical relationship using a chain of invariant checks all developed by Viola's invariant language and its compiler. In the example above, we develop three checks, one for `power supply on` → `clock source on`, one for `indicator on` → `power supply on`, and one for `sensor on` → `indicator on`. Moreover, in the monitor, we evaluate these checks in the aforementioned order to properly capture the dependencies.

5.4 Bus Interpreter Module

Registers of off-chip devices on a mobile SoC are not directly mapped into the CPU address space and are accessed through a peripheral bus, e.g., I^{2}C. Viola's monitor can only intercept and monitor the writes to the bus adapter registers. It must then "infer" the writes to the device registers.

Figure 5 illustrates a simplified, yet realistic, example. In order to write to two microphone registers (step 1), the CPU writes four values to the registers of the I^{2}C bus adapter, including the microphone device ID, a command byte, and two data bytes (steps 2 to 5). The I^{2}C adapter sends out these values on the bus to the connected devices (step 6). The microphone interprets the command byte as the register offset and the data bytes as the values to be written to consecutive registers (step 7).

Each device's interpretation of the same signal can be different, although most adhere to the same interpretation. For example, many devices support a continuous write mode (as in Figure 5): if the second most significant bit of the command value is set (i.e., the auto increment bit), the device then writes the following data bytes to consecutive registers starting at the register offset specified in the command.

Manually writing code to infer the device register writes can be challenging and error-prone. Hence, we present a *verified bus interpreter module* that achieves this goal. Figure 6 illustrates this module's role. The bus interpreter module receives the parameters of the register writes to the bus adapter and returns the inferred parameters of register writes to the device. The bus interpreter module is built from one or more state machines (in a daisy-chain). Different state machines can be created by providing "rules". Each rule operates on the input parameters and make modifications to the output parameters or to an accumulator. The output parameters are fed back to the machine allowing the rules to gradually (i.e., across multiple bus adapter register writes) infer the device register write. Similar to the invariant checks, we provide a high-level language for writing the state machine rules and implement a verified compiler for it. In the paper, we mainly use the word compiler to refer to invariant check's compiler, and not the bus interpreter module compiler, unless otherwise stated.

6. IMPLEMENTATION

The implementation of Viola consists of four components: the sensor notifications, the monitor, the invariant checks, and the bus interpreter module. Table 1 breaks down Viola's code base. Below, we elaborate on these components (except for sensor notifications, which are simple).

6.1 Runtime Monitor

Viola's monitor intercepts writes to registers of sensors and indicators by removing the write permissions from their page table entries. Upon a page fault, it consults with the deployed invariant checks; if the checks pass, the monitor emulates the faulting instructions, and if they fail, the monitor reports an error to the fault handler.

Viola's monitor emulates the instructions as follows. It maps the register pages into a second set of virtual addresses,

Lang.	Total LoC	Component	LoC
Coq	6812	Invariant compiler	211
		Invariant language spec	251
		Invariant compiler proof	4812
		Device specs	282
		Bus interpr. compiler	126
		Bus interpr. language spec	203
		Bus interpr. compiler proof	879
		Bus specs (rules)	48
C	552	Monitor (Linux)	265
		Monitor (Xen)	223
		Cam. vib. notif.	10
		Mic. LED notif.	54

Table 1: Viola code breakdown.

which are used by the monitor only. Upon each page fault, it inspects the CPU registers to determine the value that was going to be written to the faulting address. It then issues an instruction to write this value to the same register using the second virtual address. Finally, it increases the program counter to point to the next instruction and returns.

It is important to note why the monitor must emulate the instruction rather than allowing it to execute natively. This is because the latter requires the monitor to – at least temporarily – enable the write permissions on the page table entry corresponding to the faulting address. However, doing this will create an attack vector given that modern mobile system hardware leverages multiple CPU cores, allowing the malware running on other cores to take advantage of this period of time to silently write to device registers. Emulation of the faulting instruction protects against such an attack as page table entries corresponding to the monitored register pages always remain read-only.

6.2 Verified components

We verify the functional correctness of the compilers for the invariant and bus interpreter languages. We implement and verify the compilers in Coq, which provides functional programming constructs in addition to logic constructs. The implementation of the invariant compiler translates the invariant logic to Cminor code and the implementation of the bus interpreter compiler translates the developer-provided rules to Cminor code. Figure 7 shows an example procedure from Viola's invariant compiler implementation. This procedure checks the input register offset against all the register offsets specified in the device specifications to find a match. It is implemented as a recursive procedure, which computes the inclusive disjunction (`Ebinop Oor`) of comparison (`Ebinop (Ocmp Ceq)`) of the input register offset (`reg_off`) with the list of registers in the specification (`regs`).

Once we develop and prove the functional correctness of the compilers, we generate their executable machine code. For this, we first use the code extraction facilities in Coq to generate equivalent OCaml code from the source code in Coq and then use the OCaml compiler to generate the machine code. Figure 8 illustrates these steps for our verified invariant language compiler. The same figure also shows that the implementation, the specification, and the proof are passed to the Coq proof checker for checking the correctness of the proof.

```
Fixpoint is_there_reg_match (regs : list register)
                (reg_off : ident) : Cminor.expr :=
  match regs with
  | nil => Econst (Ointconst Int.zero)
  | hd :: tl => let _reg_off := hd.(reg_off) in
    Ebinop Oor (Ebinop (Ocmp Ceq)
      (Evar reg_off)
      (Econst (Ointconst (Int.repr _reg_off))))
        (is_there_reg_match tl)
  end.
```

Figure 7: A sample procedure from the implementation of Viola's invariant compiler.

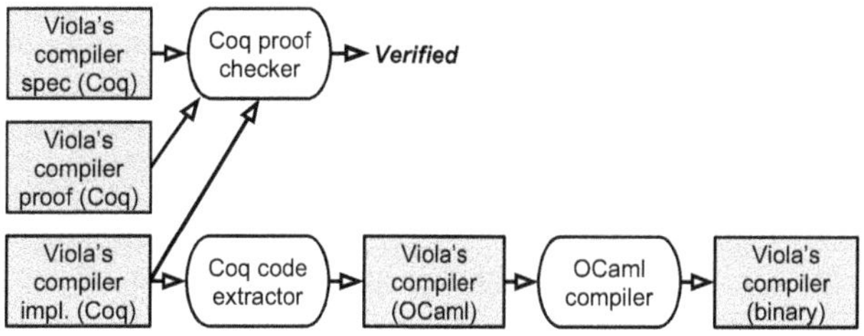

Figure 8: The compiler code is generated by first extracting the OCaml code from the Coq implementation and then compiling the OCaml code to machine code. The compiler's specification, implementation, and proof are also passed to Coq proof checker to verify the correctness of the proof. The darker components belong to Viola.

6.3 Supported Systems and Devices

We test Viola on two smartphones: LG Nexus 5 running Android 5.1.1 (CyanogenMod 12.1) and Samsung Galaxy Nexus running Android 4.2.2 (CyanogenMod 10.1). Since these smartphones do not support a hypervisor mode, we insert Viola's monitor in the Linux kernel. Moreover, to demonstrate the feasibility of a hypervisor-based monitor, we implement Viola on the ODROID XU4 development board as well, which incorporates an Exynos 5422 SoC with virtualization support in its ARM Cortex-A15 and Cortex-A7 processors. On this board, we use the Xen hypervisor (version 4.6.0) and Ubuntu operating system (version 14.04) running on Linux kernel (version 3.10.82). We currently run the operating system in Xen's control domain, i.e., dom0. In this case, we need to deprivilege the dom0 by disallowing the dom0-specific hypercalls in the hypervisor. We have not currently implemented this but we expect it to be trivial. Alternatively, we can run the operating system in a Xen's domU, which is deprivileged by default.

We test Viola with the microphone and LED on Galaxy Nexus, with the camera and vibrator on Nexus 5, and (as a proof of concept) with GPIO LEDs on ODROID XU4. The audio chip (TWL6040) and the LED [10] in Galaxy Nexus are accessed through the OMAP4 I^2C bus, for which, we leverage our bus interpreter module. The rest of the devices are memory-mapped. Moreover, as discussed earlier, we currently only support continuous notifications (§2.2), which are not ideal for the vibrator. Yet, we use the vibrator in our implementation to demonstrate the applicability of Viola to a diverse set of indicators. We also implement the checks on the clock source dependency (§5.3) for the vibrator in Nexus 5. We do not, however, currently support the power supply for the vibrator due to its use of a message passing interface (see §8.2 for more details).

The sensor notification implementation varies in each case. In Galaxy Nexus, we implemented the notification for the microphone in `tinyalsa`, a library used by the audio service in Android. In Nexus 5, we implement the notification for the camera in the camera device driver in the kernel.

6.4 Trusted Computing Base

Here, we explain the trusted components in Viola.

Trusted components for the monitor. The trusted components for the monitor differ for the kernel-based and hypervisor-based implementations. The hardware and the monitor itself are trusted in both implementations. However, in the hypervisor-based monitor, the hypervisor is trusted, but not the kernel (including all its device drivers), which is trusted in the kernel-based implementation. Given that a hypervisor is typically smaller than an operating system kernel, our hypervisor-based implementation provides a smaller TCB. Moreover, while we currently use a commodity hypervisor (i.e., Xen), it is possible to use a smaller hypervisor to reduce the TCB. This is because we do not use the features of the hypervisor needed to run multiple virtual machines in the system, such as scheduling the virtual CPUs between virtual machines. Furthermore, as discussed in §4, it is possible to use a verified kernel or hypervisor [20, 34, 36, 38, 44] in the implementation, which will then reduce the TCB to only the hardware. Finally, note that in the kernel-based monitor, only the kernel is trusted, but not the user space including all of Android services and applications.

Trusted components for the verified compilers. In our compilers' implementation, the specifications that we develop for the languages' semantics, for the proof, for the devices, and for the buses (i.e., rules), are assumed to be correct. Moreover, the Coq's simple proof checker that verifies the correctness of the proof is trusted but not the tactics used in the construction of the proof. Also, the Coq extraction facilities and the OCaml compiler are trusted. In addition, we leverage an existing assembler in the backend of our compiler and hence the assembler needs to be trusted. However, if a verified assembler is added to CompCert [39], we can simply leverage it in our solution without requiring any further engineering effort. We can also leverage other solutions for verifying assembly programs [28, 29, 54, 58].

While bugs in any of these trusted components can undermine the functional correctness of the compilers, we believe that Viola provides more reliable guarantees compared to the alternative of (*i*) not using invariant checks or (*ii*) developing the checks manually. In (*i*), the whole operating system and the applications will be trusted. In (*ii*), not only the implementation of the checks can have bugs and need to be trusted, the compiler for the language used, e.g., gcc, must be trusted as well.

7. EVALUATION

Next, we evaluate the engineering effort needed to use Viola and its performance and power consumption overheads.

7.1 Engineering Effort

For one to use Viola, one must develop the sensor notification, Viola code corresponding to the notification invariant (e.g., Figure 3), the specifications for the devices and, if needed, the rules for the peripheral buses. The first two are quite straightforward. However, the last two can be cumbersome depending on the devices and the buses. However, as mentioned in §5.2.1, often partial specifications are enough in Viola, which significantly reduces the required effort for device specifications. Moreover, device specifications are increasingly available from hardware vendors [52]. We plan to support these specifications in the future with a translator, which then reduces the effort needed by the developer. Finally, writing the specification for a device or the rules for a bus is a one-time engineering effort. The same device specification and especially the same bus rules can then be reused for various sensor notifications.

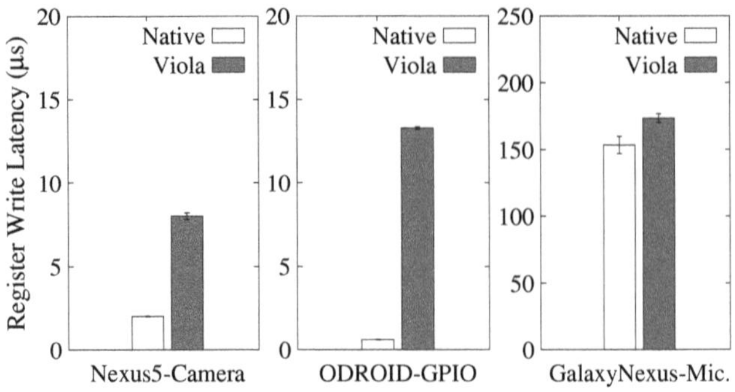

Figure 9: Register write latency. Note that the rightmost figure uses a different y-axis range. Also, the figure in the middle is based on a hypervisor-based monitor, whereas the other two figures are based on a kernel-based monitor.

7.2 Performance

Microbenchmarks. We measure the added latency of Viola to a single register write. We measure it for accessing camera registers in Nexus 5, the GPIO registers in ODROID XU4 (with a hypervisor-based monitor), and the microphone registers in Galaxy Nexus.

Figure 9 summarizes the results. It shows the average and standard deviation of monitored register write latency in these systems. It demonstrates that the added latency is significant. Part of this latency is due to the page fault exception and part is due to the code running in the fault handler including a large part of the runtime monitor's code (such as the code that inspects the CPU registers) and the invariant checks.

Moreover, the figure shows that the hypervisor-based monitor incurs higher overhead. This is mainly because a trap in the hypervisor incurs a virtualization mode switch (from the kernel mode to the hypervisor mode), whereas a page fault in the kernel does not incur a mode switch since both the faulting code and the fault handler are in the kernel mode.

Another observation is that the register write latency for microphone on Galaxy Nexus is much higher than the rest. This is because the microphone registers are accessed through the I^2C peripheral bus, which is not only slower than a memory-mapped access, it also requires multiple writes to the bus adapter registers.

Macrobenchmarks. We measure the overhead of Viola on the performance of sensors.

First, we measure the performance of the camera on the Nexus 5 in terms of the framerate. We measure the framerate for varying resolutions with and without Viola. For each

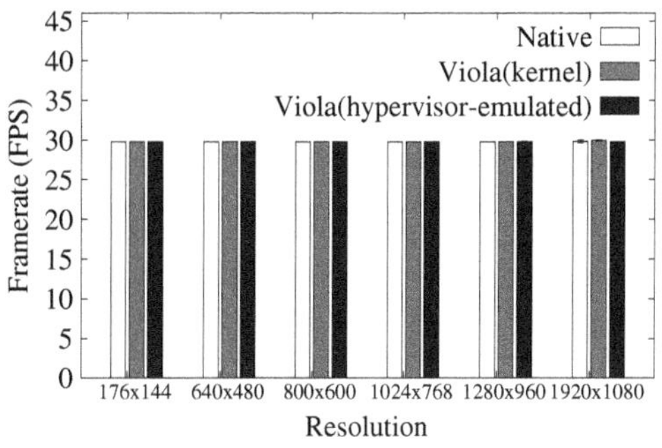

Figure 10: Camera's performance in Nexus 5 for both kernel-based and hypervisor-based monitors. Note that we emulate the overhead of the hypervisor-based monitor in Nexus 5 (§7.2).

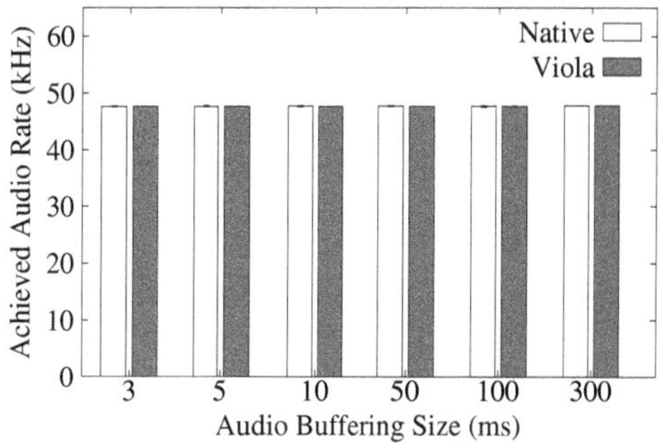

Figure 11: Microphone's performance in Galaxy Nexus based on a kernel-based monitor.

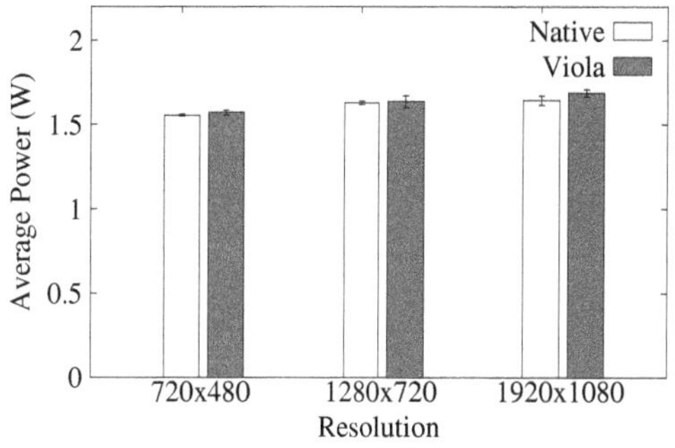

Figure 12: Power consumption of Nexus 5 when running a video recording application [1] in the background and with the display off. The results are based on a kernel-based monitor.

resolution, we measure the average framerate achieved over a 1000 frames. We discard the first 50 frames to avoid the camera initialization overhead and repeat each experiment three times. Figure 10 shows the results. It demonstrates that Viola's overhead on the camera performance is negligible irrespective of the resolution.

The reason for this negligible performance overhead is the infrequency of register writes. To demonstrate this, we measure the number of register writes that are intercepted by Viola when the camera is on. We find that there is one register write interception every 19.3 ms, which is significantly larger than the latency of a single register write (i.e., 2 and 8 μs for native and Viola). The number of register writes are relatively small since they are used mainly for sending control commands to the camera and not for exchanging data. Moreover, in the case of camera, Viola does not intercept writes to all the registers (see discussion on partial specifications (§5.2.1)). Only writes to the registers in the same register page as those monitored by Viola are intercepted. Our experiment shows that this constitute 4% of all register writes.

Moreover, we demonstrate that even the more significant register write latency incurred by a hypervisor-based monitor will not impact the performance of the camera. For this, we emulate the overhead of the hypervisor-based monitor in Nexus 5 by artificially adding a delay of about 6.7 μs to our fault handler since this is the additional latency incurred by the hypervisor as derived from the ODROID XU4 results in Figure 9. We then measure the camera framerate and show the results in Figure 10, which demonstrate almost no performance overhead. This is, similarly, due to the infrequency of register write interceptions.

Second, we measure the performance of the microphone on Galaxy Nexus in terms of the audio rate. We measure the audio rate for a one-minute recording experiment and with varying audio buffering sizes, which determines the audio latency. We repeat each experiment three times. Figure 11 shows the results. Similar to camera, we notice that Viola's overhead on the microphone performance is negligible. We also measure the number of intercepted register writes for the microphone and find them to be very small, i.e., only about 20 when starting the capture.

7.3 Power Consumption

Battery lifetime on mobile systems is one of the most important usability metrics. Therefore, it is important that Viola does not enhance user's privacy at the cost of reduced battery lifetime. We therefore measure the power consumption of the system with and without monitoring by Viola. We measure the power consumption using the Monsoon Power Monitor [9].

First, we measure the power consumption of Nexus 5 when recording a video. To magnify the relative overhead by Viola, we put the camera application [1] in the background and turn the display off. Figure 12 shows the results. It demonstrates that Viola incurs additional power consumption but that the overhead is small (less than 45 mW). Note that the high baseline power consumption of the smartphone is mainly due to the CPU and camera being on.

Second, we measure the power consumption of Galaxy Nexus when using an application [2] to record audio. Similarly, to magnify the relative overhead of Viola, we turn the display off. Our measurements show that, for audio buffering size of 300 ms, the power consumption of the smartphone is about 1.025 and 1.038 W for native and Viola, respectively. The additional overhead is about 13 mW, smaller than the video recording overhead, which might be partly due to different hardware in the two smartphones, and party due to fewer intercepted register writes. Moreover, note that the baseline power consumption is high because of the CPU.

8. LIMITATIONS AND FUTURE WORK

8.1 Sensor Notification Customizations

It is critical that the sensor notifications cannot be deactivated by attackers. This has motivated us to design a solution that enforces the notifications unconditionally. However, we envision scenarios that the user might need to disable the notifications temporarily, e.g., if light, vibration, or sound interferes with user's activities. Allowing customizations while protecting against malware raises new challenges that we plan to address in future work. One key idea is to provide an orthogonal channel (to the operating system) in order to deploy and update the invariant checks. One candidate channel is a minimal virtual machine, which can be interacted with only if the user presses a certain key combination, enforced by a few permanent invariants.

8.2 Message-Passing Hardware Interfaces

The control commands to most I/O devices and hardware components are programmed using a set of registers. However, some devices and components adopt a message-passing interface for control commands, where they exchange messages with the CPU using shared memory buffers. We have encountered two such devices: the image subsystem in Galaxy Nexus (which includes the camera) and the voltage regulators in Nexus 5 (one of the vibrator' dependencies (§5.3)). Viola does not currently support these devices. To overcome this limitation, we plan to extend our bus interpreter module to support message-passing interfaces.

8.3 Speaker and Display as Indicators

In this paper, we demonstrated the use of LED and vibrator as indicators. Other possible indicators are the speaker and display. However, the use of these indicators in Viola present important challenges that we plan to address in our future work. First, for both indicators, the *data passed to the device* must be inspected and verified, e.g., audio samples and display pixels. Doing so requires support in the monitor to intercept and inspect the Direct Memory Access (DMA) operations. It also requires support in Viola's language to allow the developer to concisely specify the intended data. Second, in the case of the speaker, the time that each audio sample is played must also be monitored and verified to be correct. This is because tampering with the timing of the samples can affect the effective sounds heard by the user.

8.4 Context-Sensitive Notifications

The best indicator to use might depend on the mobile system's context. For example, if the ambient noise level is high, vibration may be more effective than a beep. Viola can be extended to support context-sensitive notifications as well. For this, Viola needs to monitor various sensor readings and enforce the indicators accordingly.

8.5 Two-Way Notifications

Two-way notifications require the sensor and indicator to be in their target states only simultaneously (§2.2). This is challenging as the states of the sensor and indicator have to change atomically. We plan to solve this challenge by implementing *verified I/O transactions*, in which Viola's monitor buffers several register write parameters, and execute all of them atomically.

8.6 Temporary Notifications

While some types of indicators, such as LED, should stay on as long as the sensor is on, other indicators are best if temporary, e.g., a short vibration or a brief beeping sound (§2.2). Implementing temporary notifications requires the invariant checks to store timing information. Moreover, in case the indicator is not turned off after the specified period of time, the monitor must turn it off on its own. Implementing such behavior in the monitor requires code synthesis from the device specifications and is part of our future work.

9. RELATED WORK

9.1 Untrusted Operating Systems and Drivers

Applications rely heavily on the correctness of the operating systems. However, contemporary operating systems are large, complex, and full of bugs, allowing malicious applications to compromise them. This observation has fueled research into protecting the applications from a compromised operating system. Most solutions, such as Overshadow [22] and InkTag [35], do so with a trusted hypervisor, which mediates applications' interactions with the operating system. However, due to the wide and complex interface between an application and the underlying operating system, these solutions cannot protect the applications against all possible attacks, such as Iago attacks [19]. Similar to this line of work, we leverage the hypervisor in Viola in order to make the operating system untrusted. However, while the focus of this line of work is on protecting the application from the operating system, Viola's focus is on the correctness of sensor notifications.

Nexus [56] makes the device drivers untrusted by running them in user space and by vetting their interactions with the I/O devices. Similar to Viola, Nexus adopts a domain-specific language to write specifications for the devices, which are then compiled into reference monitors used in the kernel. Unlike Nexus, Viola's compiler is formally verified. Moreover, Viola's invariant checks monitor more than one I/O device (i.e., a sensor and an indicator) and enforce a relationship between their states. Unlike Nexus, which implements the monitor in the kernel, we have demonstrated an implementation of our monitor in the hypervisor as well. Finally, while Nexus is implemented for the x86 architecture and PCI devices, Viola is implemented for the ARM architecture and devices that are directly accessed by the CPU or through an I^2C bus. Despite these differences, Viola can benefit from the design of Nexus by moving the device drivers to user space. Such a design will enhance the security guarantees of Viola's kernel-based monitor as it removes the device drivers out of the TCB.

9.2 Virtual Machine Introspection

Virtual machine introspection (VMI) uses the hypervisor to monitor the operating system for intrusion detection [26, 30, 32]. It provides good visibility of the operating system internals while protecting the monitoring system from the attacks on the operating system. Similar to VMI, we leverage the hypervisor to enforce the I/O invariants eliminating the need to trust the operating system. Our work is, however, fundamentally different as, unlike VMI, we provide guarantees on the correct behavior of I/O devices.

9.3 Software Verification

An alternative approach to Viola for implementing trustworthy sensor notifications is to guarantee that there are no bugs in the whole mobile operating system. A large amount of work has tried to face such a challenge head-on by finding and eliminating bugs in existing software using static analysis [15] and model checking [24, 47]. These solutions have an important limitation: they do not scale to large software systems, e.g., the whole Android code base. Moreover, some of these solutions might not be practical as important parts of the I/O stack in mobile operating systems, including Android, are closed source.

Our key insight in Viola is that we can *enforce sensor notification invariants in low level system software* eliminating the need to verify the correctness of the whole operating system. However, it is important to note that existing solutions discussed above are more generic than ours. They can find various types of bugs in software systems or can be used to find violations of arbitrary invariants. Our solution is specific to sensor notifications.

More specifically, several existing solutions improve the quality of device drivers by finding or avoiding driver bugs either through static analysis [14,23,48], better interface language [45], synthesis [51,52], or symbolic execution [37,50]. We note that this line of work reduces the probability of the violation of sensor notification invariants, but on their own, these solutions are not adequate to guarantee the invariants for two reasons. First, the device driver is only part of the I/O stack, and the invariant can be violated as a result of bugs in other components of the stack, e.g., the I/O system services in Android. Second, existing solutions are often best efforts to eliminate bugs but cannot eliminate all the bugs nor provide formal guarantees about an invariant.

Finally, our verified compiler for Viola (§5.2) is related to existing work on verified compilers [39], verified kernels and hypervisors [20, 34, 36, 38, 44], and verified file systems [21]. Indeed, our compiler is built on top of a verified compiler (i.e., CompCert [39]). However, unlike Viola, none of these solutions provide formal guarantees about the behavior of I/O devices.

9.4 Information Flow Control

Systems such as TaintDroid [27] and Panorama [57] can track the flow of information from sources that produce sensitive information, e.g., camera and microphone, to sinks that can leak the information, e.g., network interface card. Such systems can therefore be used to notify the user when sensor data propagate to sensitive sinks. However, there are four important differences between such notifications and Viola. First, Viola is designed to reliably detect when sensors are turned on and off. To do this, Viola uses device specifications of sensors and monitors writes to registers of these devices. In contrast, information flow control systems cannot reliably detect the states of the sensors. Instead, given some sensor data stored in memory, even if the data were captured legitimately with the user's approval, information flow control systems can reliably track the propagation of data and potentially inform the user if the data leave the mobile system. In this sense, Viola and information flow control systems can provide complementary forms of notifications, i.e., notification about when the sensor is on vs. notification about when the sensor data are about to leave the mobile system. Second, information flow tracking systems incur noticeable performance overhead in the system as they need to instrument and track several processor or high-level language instructions. On the other hand, Viola's overhead is negligible since it only monitors infrequent writes to registers of I/O devices. Third, Viola supports a hypervisor-based implementation, which will make the operating system fully untrusted. While some information flow control systems are implemented in the hypervisor as well, e.g., Panorama [57], others are implemented at higher layers of the stack, e.g., Java Virtual Machine (JVM) in case of TaintDroid [27], resulting in a larger TCB. Finally, unlike some information flow control systems that have dependency on the JVM implementation (e.g., TaintDroid), Viola has dependency on the kernel or hypervisor.

9.5 Other Related Work

Operating systems have employed kernel interpreters for syscall monitoring, e.g., Linux Seccomp, or packet filtering [43]. Jitk [55] provides a trustworthy kernel interpreter using Coq. Our solution can also be considered as filtering the states and behavior of sensors and indicators in mobile systems. Indeed, our approach in how we use Coq to verify the functional correctness of our compilers has been influenced by Jitk. However, unlike Jitk that performs syscall and network filtering and socket monitoring, Viola monitors the operating system's interactions with I/O devices.

Bianchi et al. implement a notification on the Android system navigation bar to notify the user of the origin of the application she is interacting with [16]. Our work on Viola is in line with this work in terms of motivation. However, unlike our solution, their solution does not provide any guarantees on the correctness of the notification.

Trusted sensors provide mechanisms for maintaining the integrity of sensor readings in mobile systems for the user of the data [33, 40, 53]. This line of work is orthogonal to Viola, which is concerned with immediate and unconditional feedback to the user about the usage of sensors, and not with the integrity of the sensor data after capture.

10. CONCLUSIONS

We presented Viola, a system aimed at enhancing mobile systems users' privacy by providing trustworthy sensor notifications, which unconditionally inform the user when the sensors are on. Viola uses verified invariant checks to inspect the writes to sensors' and indicators' registers in the kernel or in the hypervisor, and rejects those that violate the sensor notifications' invariants. We reported an implementation of Viola on various mobile systems, including LG Nexus 5, Samsung Galaxy Nexus, and ODROID XU4, and for various sensors and indicators, such as camera, microphone, LED, and vibrator. We demonstrated that Viola's overheads to the sensor's performance and system's power consumption are negligible and small, respectively. We believe that trustworthy sensor notifications are critical for mobile systems, which are increasingly capable of recording private information about their users.

Acknowledgments

The authors thank their shepherd, Dr. Eduardo Cuervo, and the anonymous reviewers for their insightful comments. The authors also thank Justin A. Chen for his help in revising the paper.

11. REFERENCES

[1] Android Detective Video Recorder. https://play.google.com/store/apps/details?id=com.rivalogic.android.video&hl=en.

[2] Android Easy Voice Recorder. https://play.google.com/store/apps/details?id=com.coffeebeanventures.easyvoicerecorder&hl=en.

[3] Android Verified Boot. https://source.android.com/security/verifiedboot/verified-boot.html.

[4] Dendroid: Android Trojan Being Commercialized. http://blog.trustlook.com/2014/03/20/dendroid-android-trojan-commercialized/.

[5] Fuzzing Android System Services by Binder Call to Escalate Privilege. https://www.blackhat.com/docs/us-15/materials/us-15-Gong-Fuzzing-Android-System-Services-By-Binder-Call-To-Escalate-Privilege.pdf.

[6] How the NSA can 'turn on' your phone remotely. http://money.cnn.com/2014/06/06/technology/security/nsa-turn-on-phone/.

[7] Man spies on Miss Teen USA. http://www.reuters.com/article/2013/10/31/us-usa-missteen-extortion-idUSBRE99U1G520131031.

[8] Men spy on women through their webcams. http://arstechnica.com/tech-policy/2013/03/rat-breeders-meet-the-men-who-spy-on-women-through-their-webcams/.

[9] Monsoon Power Monitor. http://www.msoon.com/LabEquipment/PowerMonitor/.

[10] Panasonic AN30259A LED (used in Galaxy Nexus). http://www.semicon.panasonic.co.jp/ds4/AN30259A_AEB.pdf.

[11] The Coq Proof Assistant. https://coq.inria.fr/.

[12] Viola's video demo. http://www.ics.uci.edu/~ardalan/viola.html.

[13] ARM. ARM Cortex-A15 MPCore Processor Technical Reference Manual, Revision: r4p0. *ARM DDI*, 0438I (ID062913), 2013.

[14] T. Ball, E. Bounimova, B. Cook, V. Levin, J. Lichtenberg, C. McGarvey, B. Ondrusek, S. K. Rajamani, and A. Ustuner. Thorough Static Analysis of Device Drivers. In *Proc. ACM EuroSys*, 2006.

[15] T. Ball and S. K. Rajamani. The SLAM Project: Debugging System Software via Static Analysis. In *Proc. ACM Symposium on Principles of Programming Languages (POPL)*, 2002.

[16] A. Bianchi, J. Corbetta, L. Invernizzi, Y. Fratantonio, C. Kruegel, and G. Vigna. What the App is That? Deception and Countermeasures in the Android User Interface. In *Proc. IEEE Symposium on Security and Privacy (S&P)*, 2015.

[17] K. Boos, A. Amiri Sani, and L. Zhong. Eliminating State Entanglement with Checkpoint-based Virtualization of Mobile OS Services. In *Proc. ACM SIGOPS Asia-Pacific Workshop on Systems (APSys)*, 2015.

[18] M. Brocker and S. Checkoway. iSeeYou: Disabling the MacBook Webcam Indicator LED. In *Proc. USENIX Security Symposium*, 2014.

[19] S. Checkoway and H. Shacham. Iago Attacks: Why the System Call API is a Bad Untrusted RPC Interface. In *Proc. ACM ASPLOS*, 2013.

[20] H. Chen, X. Wu, Z. Shao, J. Lockerman, and R. Gu. Toward Compositional Verification of Interruptible OS Kernels and Device Drivers. In *Proc. ACM PLDI*, 2016.

[21] H. Chen, D. Ziegler, T. Chajed, A. Chlipala, M. F. Kaashoek, and N. Zeldovich. Using Crash Hoare Logic for Certifying the FSCQ File System. In *Proc. ACM SOSP*, 2015.

[22] X. Chen, T. Garfinkel, E. C. Lewis, P. Subrahmanyam, C. A. Waldspurger, D. Boneh, J. Dwoskin, and D. R. K. Ports. Overshadow: a Virtualization-Based Approach to Retrofitting Protection in Commodity Operating Systems. In *Proc. ACM ASPLOS*, 2008.

[23] A. Chou, J. Yang, B. Chelf, S. Hallem, and D. Engler. An Empirical Study of Operating Systems Errors. In *Proc. ACM SOSP*, 2001.

[24] J. Croft, R. Mahajan, M. Caesar, and M. Musuvathi. Systematically Exploring the Behavior of Control Programs. In *Proc. USENIX ATC*, 2015.

[25] C. Dall and J. Nieh. KVM/ARM: The Design and Implementation of the Linux ARM Hypervisor. In *Proc. ACM ASPLOS*, 2014.

[26] B. Dolan-Gavitt, T. Leek, M. Zhivich, J. Giffin, and W. Lee. Virtuoso: Narrowing the Semantic Gap in Virtual Machine Introspection. In *Proc. IEEE Security and Privacy (S&P)*, 2011.

[27] W. Enck, P. Gilbert, B. Chun, L. P. Cox, J. Jung, P. McDaniel, and A. N. Sheth. TaintDroid: An Information-Flow Tracking System for Realtime Privacy Monitoring on Smartphones. In *Proc. USENIX OSDI*, 2010.

[28] X. Feng and Z. Shao. Modular Verification of Concurrent Assembly Code with Dynamic Thread Creation and Termination. In *Proc. ACM International Conference on Functional Programming (ICFP)*, 2005.

[29] X. Feng, Z. Shao, A. Vaynberg, S. Xiang, and Z. Ni. Modular Verification of Assembly Code with Stack-Based Control Abstractions. In *Proc. ACM PLDI*, 2006.

[30] Y. Fu and Z. Lin. Space Traveling across VM: Automatically Bridging the Semantic Gap in Virtual Machine Introspection via Online Kernel Data Redirection. In *Proc. IEEE Security and Privacy (S&P)*, 2012.

[31] A. Ganapathi, V. Ganapathi, and D. Patterson. Windows XP Kernel Crash Analysis. In *Proc. USENIX LISA*, 2006.

[32] T. Garfinkel and M. Rosenblum. A Virtual Machine Introspection Based Architecture for Intrusion Detection. In *Proc. Network and Distributed Systems Security Symposium (NDSS)*, 2003.

[33] P. Gilbert, L. P. Cox, J. Jung, and D. Wetherall. Toward Trustworthy Mobile Sensing. In *Proc. ACM Workshop on Mobile Computing Systems & Applications (HotMobile)*, 2010.

[34] R. Gu, J. Koenig, T. Ramananandro, Z. Shao, X. Wu, S. Weng, H. Zhang, and Y. Guo. Deep Specifications

and Certified Abstraction Layers. In *Proc. ACM POPL*, 2015.

[35] O. S. Hofmann, S. Kim, A. M. Dunn, M. Z. Lee, and E. Witchel. InkTag: Secure Applications on an Untrusted Operating System. In *Proc. ACM ASPLOS*, 2013.

[36] G. Klein, K. Elphinstone, G. Heiser, J. Andronick, D. Cock, P. Derrin, D. Elkaduwe, K. Engelhardt, R. Kolanski, M. Norrish, T. Sewell, H. Tuch, and S. Winwood. seL4: Formal Verification of an OS Kernel. In *Proc. ACM SOSP*, 2009.

[37] V. Kuznetsov, V. Chipounov, and G. Candea. Testing Closed-Source Binary Device Drivers with DDT. In *Proc. USENIX Annual Technical Conference*, 2010.

[38] D. Leinenbach and T. Santen. Verifying the Microsoft Hyper-V hypervisor with VCC. In *Proc. International Symposium on Formal Methods (FM)*. Springer, 2009.

[39] X. Leroy. Formal Verification of a Realistic Compiler. *Communications of the ACM*, 2009.

[40] H. Liu, S. Saroiu, A. Wolman, and H. Raj. Software Abstractions for Trusted Sensors. In *Proc. ACM MobiSys*, 2012.

[41] N. Lynch and F. Vaandrager. Forward and Backward Simulations Part I: Untimed Systems. *Information and Computation*, 1995.

[42] N. Lynch and F. Vaandrager. Forward and Backward Simulations Part II: Timing-Based Systems. *Information and Computation*, 1996.

[43] S. McCanne and V. Jacobson. The BSD Packet Filter: A New Architecture for User-Level Packet Capture. In *Proc. Winter 1993 USENIX Technical Conference*, 1993.

[44] M. McCoyd, R. B. Krug, D. Goel, M. Dahlin, and W. Young. Building a Hypervisor on a Formally Verifiable Protection Layer. In *Proc. IEEE Hawaii International Conference on System Sciences (HICSS)*, 2013.

[45] F. Mérillon, L. Réveillère, C. Consel, R. Marlet, and G. Muller. Devil: An IDL for Hardware Programming. In *Proc. USENIX OSDI*, 2000.

[46] I. Muslukhov, Y. Boshmaf, C. Kuo, J. Lester, and K. Beznosov. Understanding Users' Requirements for Data Protection in Smartphones. In *Proc. IEEE Int. Conf. on Data Engineering Workshops (ICDEW)*, 2012.

[47] M. Musuvathi, D. Y. W. Park, A. Chou, D. R. Engler, and D. L. Dill. CMC: A Pragmatic Approach to Model Checking Real Code. In *Proc. USENIX OSDI*, 2002.

[48] N. Palix, G. Thomas, S. Saha, C. Calvès, J. Lawall, and G. Muller. Faults in Linux: Ten Years Later. In *Proc. ACM ASPLOS*, 2011.

[49] R. S. Portnoff, L. N. Lee, S. Egelman, P. Mishra, D. Leung, and D. Wagner. Somebody's Watching Me? Assessing the Effectiveness of Webcam Indicator Lights. In *Proc. ACM Conference on Human Factors in Computing Systems (CHI)*, 2015.

[50] M. J. Renzelmann, A. Kadav, and M. M. Swift. SymDrive: Testing Drivers without Devices. In *Proc. USENIX OSDI*, 2012.

[51] L. Ryzhyk, P. Chubb, I. Kuz, E. Le Sueur, and G. Heiser. Automatic Device Driver Synthesis with Termite. In *Proc. ACM SOSP*, 2009.

[52] L. Ryzhyk, A. Walker, J. Keys, A. Legg, A. Raghunath, M. Stumm, and M. Vij. User-Guided Device Driver Synthesis. In *Proc. USENIX OSDI*, 2014.

[53] S. Saroiu and A. Wolman. I Am a Sensor, and I Approve This Message. In *Proc. ACM Workshop on Mobile Computing Systems & Applications (HotMobile)*, 2010.

[54] W. Wang, Z. Shao, X. Jiang, and Y. Guo. A Simple Model for Certifying Assembly Programs with First-Class Function Pointers. In *Proc. IEEE International Symposium on Theoretical Aspects of Software Engineering (TASE)*, 2011.

[55] X. Wang, D. Lazar, N. Zeldovich, A. Chlipala, and Z. Tatlock. Jitk: a Trustworthy In-Kernel Interpreter Infrastructure. In *Proc. USENIX OSDI*, 2014.

[56] D. Williams, P. Reynolds, K. Walsh, E. G. Sirer, and F. B. Schneider. Device Driver Safety Through a Reference Validation Mechanism. In *Proc. USENIX OSDI*, 2008.

[57] H. Yin, D. Song, M. Egele, C. Kruegel, and E. Kirda. Panorama: Capturing System-wide Information Flow for Malware Detection and Analysis. In *Proc. ACM CCS*, 2007.

[58] D. Yu and Z. Shao. Verification of Safety Properties for Concurrent Assembly Code. In *Proc. ACM International Conference on Functional Programming (ICFP)*, 2004.

Expansion of Human–Phone Interface By Sensing Structure-Borne Sound Propagation

Yu-Chih Tung and Kang G. Shin
The University of Michigan
Email: {yctung,kgshin}@umich.edu

ABSTRACT

ForcePhone is a novel system that enables commodity phones to recognize the force applied to their touch screen and body. Researchers have shown the usefulness and importance of this expressive input interface (especially for the one-hand operation), but this advanced function has not yet been realized and deployed in most state-of-the-art smartphones. Instead of employing or augmenting specialized/proprietary sensors, ForcePhone uses only the phone's built-in sensors to measure the applied force via a physical property called *structure-borne sound propagation*. ForcePhone has been implemented and evaluated on both iOS and Android phones. Multiple demo applications, such as getting the option menu by hard-pressing a button or surfing the previous webpage by squeezing the phone, have been implemented and tested successfully. The estimated force is shown highly correlated to the real applied force and the estimation error is less than 54g when the phone is stationary. Users can easily control the applied force at two different levels with a 97% accuracy. Moreover, ForcePhone can detect the squeeze of the phone body with a higher than 90% accuracy. Most participants in our usability study were able to master the ForcePhone-based apps and find them very useful.

General Terms

Design, Measurement, Performance, Algorithms

Keywords

Force sensing, Sound, Structure-borne sound, Mobile Phones

1. INTRODUCTION

As smartphones become an essential part of our daily activities, human–phone interactions have become a norm. To enhance the input capability on the severely limited space of a phone's touch screen, researchers and practitioners have been seeking various ways to expand the input dimensions. For example, augmenting a force-sensitive, deformable, or squeezable input is shown to enrich the input vocabulary significantly, especially for the one-hand operations [13, 29, 36]. However, most of those extended input interfaces have not yet been fully developed nor deployed in commodity phones for two reasons. First, they usually require additional hardware, such as capacitive or contact piezoelectric sensors [14, 32, 34], which are usually unavailable in commodity phones, and the

MobiSys'16, June 25-30, 2016, Singapore, Singapore

 ISBN 978-1-4503-4269-8/16/06... $15.00
DOI: http://dx.doi.org/10.1145/2906388.2906394

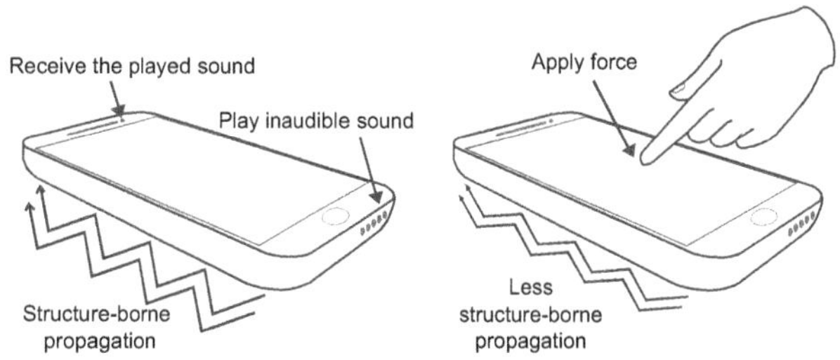

(a) No force (b) Force applied

Figure 1—Structure-borne propagation and the applied force. When no force is applied to the phone, the frame and internal components of the phone can vibrate freely, and hence the played inaudible sound can easily propagate through the phone's body.

requirement of additional cost and space make them less attractive to phone users and manufacturers [9]. Second, systems based only on built-in sensors usually impose unnatural/inconvenient usage restrictions because it is challenging to recognize those interactions without additional sensors. For example, users are required to touch the microphone reception hole or block the camera flash light source for sensing a touch interaction [22, 27], both of which limit the usability of this additional sensing. Other systems require continuous vibration of the phone with a vibration motor, causing significant annoyance to users [21]. To the best of our knowledge, the only commodity phone supporting a force-sensitive touch screen is the latest iPhone 6s, enabled by their proprietary sensors [3]. Unlike these systems, we propose a new, inexpensive solution, called ForcePhone, which provides a force-sensitive input interface to commodity phones without any addition/modification of hardware. Moreover, ForcePhone provides this force-sensing capability to the touch screen as well as the phone's body, called a *squeezable interface*.

ForcePhone estimates the user-applied force by utilizing the structure-borne sound propagation, i.e., the sound transmitted through subtle vibrations of the device body. In most designs, such as headphones or pipe-work, this type of propagation is usually considered as a mechanical noise, but ForcePhone uses it in a novel way to estimate the force applied to commodity phones. As shown in Fig. 1, when the phone is left free to vibrate (e.g., the user is not touching/squeezing the phone), the sound sent from the phone's speakers can easily travel through its body to its microphone. However, when force is applied to the phone, it restricts the phone body's vibration with the sound, thus degrading the sound traveling through this structure-borne pathway. ForcePhone estimates the amount of force applied to the phone by monitoring the degree of this degradation.

As mentioned earlier, it is challenging to provide extended input interfaces with only limited built-in phone sensors. For example, in ForcePhone, the recorded audio includes not only the sound

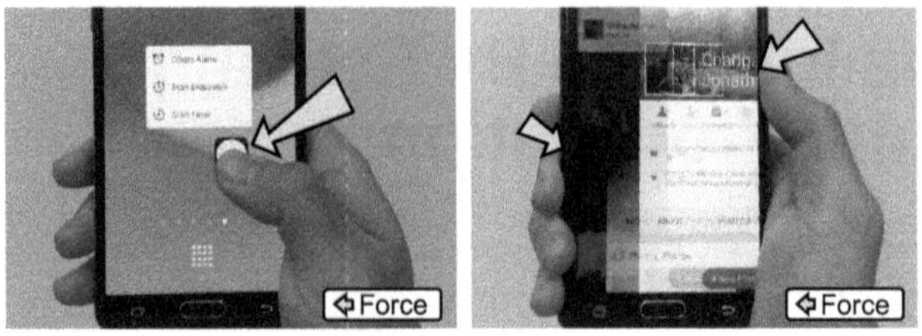

(a) Hard-pressed option (b) Squeezable back button

Figure 2—Demo apps of ForcePhone. Users can reach an option page when a button is pressed hard and can also surf the previous webpage by squeezing the phone.

signal transmitted through the phone's body but also that through air, and other reflections. To achieve reliable force estimation, ForcePhone exploits the feature of *active* acoustic sensing to get a proper reference point for fetching the signal traveling through the phone's body. ForcePhone also utilizes the information of other sensing materials to enhance sensing accuracy and reduce the false detection rate. For example, the location and the start time of a touch are inferred from the touch screen, and the phone's movement is inferred from accelerometer readings, which are then used to *filter* out unexpected audio signal changes caused by environment and human noises. By integrating readings of these sensors, ForcePhone can achieve high force-sensing accuracy while limiting the false positive rate.

To date, ForcePhone has been implemented on Android and iOS phones to provide a force-sensitive and squeezable interface. We have realized several apps based on ForcePhone. Fig. 2 presents two examples of those apps which have been shown useful: (1) the hard-pressed option, which is similar to the 3D Touch on iPhone 6s where varying options are given to users when applying different amounts of force to buttons, and (2) the squeezable back of a phone, which allows users to surf the previous webpage by just squeezing the phone. Note ForcePhone is not limited to these two use-cases, and can extend human–mobile interactions in many ways. For example, it has been shown useful to zoom in/out maps by squeezing phones or type upper-case letters by applying force to keyboards [13, 29, 36]. Other potential apps of ForcePhone are discussed in Section 7.

In our experiments, the estimated force is shown greater than 0.9 correlation to the real applied force with 54g errors in stationary environments. The participants in our controlled experiments were able to use ForcePhone for applying force at 2 different levels with a higher than 97% accuracy and squeezing the phone body correctly with a greater than 90% accuracy. After trying our demo apps of ForcePhone most participants think our current design comparable to state-of-the-art proprietary sensors in accomplishing simple tasks, such as hard-pressing of a button. A demo video of ForcePhone can be found from [4].

This paper makes the following four main contributions:

- Design of force-sensitive and squeezable interfaces via structure-borne sound propagation;
- Implementation of ForcePhone on both iOS and Android phones;
- Demonstration and evaluation of two popular apps; and
- Achieving a higher than 90% accuracy of using the demo apps in most scenarios.

The rest of this paper is organized as follows. Section 2 discusses the related work on expressive input interfaces. Section 3 describes the principle of structure-borne propagation, and Section 4 details the design of ForcePhone based on this principle. The implementation and evaluation of ForcePhone are presented in Sections 5 and 6, respectively. Limitations and potential use-cases are discussed in Section 7, and the paper concludes with Section 8.

2. RELATED WORK

Expanding the dimension of touch inputs has been a major research topic for many years owing to the limited-size touch screens of mobile phones. Users are shown to be able to easily and effectively control force-sensitive, deformable, or squeezable input interfaces as they are akin to many natural interfaces, such as applying force to a water knob [13, 29, 36]. A force-sensitive interface can be implemented by adding capacity sensors [36], adding contact piezoelectric sensors [32], checking the flash light source blocked by a human hand [27], monitoring the reduction of sound volume by covering the microphone reception hole [22], and estimating the damped motor vibration with accelerometers [21]. These systems either require additional sensors or impose stringent usage restrictions, such as blocking the flash light source by hand or continuously vibrating the phone.

There have also been systems that extend the user's input by recognizing the materials of tapping or the instantaneous tapping force. For example, TapSense [17] classifies the touch sound to recognize if the user touches the screen by a finger tip or a fist. ForceTap [19] utilizes the accelerometer to learn how hard the user taps or shakes the device. It is also possible to extend the touch surface by other accessible objects. SurfaceLink [14] allows users to perform gestures on a table where the phone is placed, while Skin-Input [18] uses the human body as an extension of input interface. Here we focus on how to provide a force-sensitive and squeezable input interface by utilizing the structure-borne sound propagation. Table 1 shows a comparative summary of ForcePhone and other related work. Note that instantaneous tapping force is different from the force sensing introduced in this paper; the former only represents the instantaneous force sensed at the time of the user contacting the touch screen, while the latter continuously monitors the force applied to the phone after the user touches the phone. Our system is parallel to these instantaneous-tapping-force systems and can be integrated with others to enrich the user experience further.

Sound has been a widely-used sensing method as it only requires microphones and speakers on commodity phones. For example, knowing the surrounding sounds and reflections can provide accurate indoor localization [28, 38] or tracking human living/sleeping behaviors [30, 31]. ForcePhone is also sound-based but designed for providing force-sensitive and squeezable interactions. The closest to ForcePhone are Touch & Active [33] and PseudoButton [22]. Touch & Active attaches external contact piezoelectric microphones and speakers to objects to learn how the user is touching the object, which is achieved by fingerprinting the object's resonants. A follow-on study [32] showed that the same fingerprinting technique can also be used to infer the force applied to objects, which aimed mainly to ease product prototyping. Using the built-in speakers and microphones on commodity phones was mentioned as a potential interface for Touch & Active, but no further details were provided. Moreover, ForcePhone directly models and interprets the signal changes caused by the applied force, rather than classifying the resonants by using machine learning. The latter usually requires a significantly more effort for periodic training and retraining. On the other hand, PseudoButton utilizes similar sound degradation to estimate the applied force. However,

System	Interaction	Sensing Methods	Additional Sensors	Working Areas
Apple 3D Touch [3]	Force	Proprietary sensors	Additional	Touch screen
Camera and Flash[27]	Force	Camera+Flash light	Existing	Camera lens
Touch & Active [33, 32]	Force	Sound	Additional	Any object (w/ sensors attached)
PseudoButton [22]	Force	Sound	Existing	Microphone reception hole
Expressive Touch [34]	Tapping material	Sound	Existing	Touch screen
ForceTap [19]	Instantaneous tapping force	Accelerometer	Existing	Touch screen+Phone body
VibPress [21]	Force+Squeeze	Actuator+Accelerometer	Existing	Vibrated phone body
Acoustruments [24]	Force+Squeeze	Sound	Additional	External connected objects
ForcePhone	**Force+Squeeze**	**Structure-Borne sound**	**Existing**	**Touch screen+Phone body**

Table 1—Existing touch interfaces to enrich input dimensions.

it focuses on the sound degradation of airborne propagation, so it can only estimate the force changes at the microphone reception hole, e.g., the recorded volume decreases when the user completely blocks the microphone reception hole. In contrast, ForcePhone utilizes the structure-borne sound propagation, which can provide this force-sensitive touch around the entire body of each phone.

3. STRUCTURE-BORNE PROPAGATION

Sound is a mechanical wave broadcasted by compressions and rarefactions. The most common material for sound to propagate is the air, which is known as *airborne propagation*. Besides the air path, as shown in Fig. 3, when the sound is generated and received by the same device, its body becomes another pathway for the sound to travel, which is called *structure-borne propagation*. Since the structure-borne propagation is usually unrelated to the intended application, it is generally considered as a noise [12, 26, 39]. However, ForcePhone utilizes it in a novel way to estimate the force applied to the phone by monitoring the degradation of structure-borne propagated sound.

As shown in Fig. 4, we model a vibrating phone as a forced, damped mass–spring system, where the phone vibrates up and down with the force F_v, which is caused by the sound played at the phone speaker. When there is no external force applied, the phone can vibrate freely with amplitude A_0, which is captured by the system's effective spring constant, K_0, and also the damping coefficient. Moreover, since the phone is considered as a rigid body, the equilibrium is located at A_0 above the table. Based on Hooke's law [20], when an external force F_h is applied to the screen, the system equilibrium moves downward by F_h/K_0. However, since the phone (a rigid body) is impossible to move downward "into" the table, the applied force also makes the system spring constant increase to K so as to meet this equilibrium change and rigid body constraint. In such a case, if the vibration energy is constant, the potential energy for both systems will be identical, thus leading to:

$$\frac{1}{2}K_0A_0^2 = \frac{1}{2}KA^2 = \frac{F_h}{A_0 - A}A^2 \qquad (1)$$

which defines the relation between the applied force and the reduced vibration amplitude. Note that this basic model is designed only for an illustrative purpose as it doesn't consider the horizontal vibration and the increased friction caused by the applied force. Moreover, since the hand and the table also slightly vibrate with the phone, the system's damping coefficient and effective mass will change accordingly, which are not accounted for, either. However, according to our vibration measurements, this simplified model suffices to describe the principle of ForcePhone's operation.

We used the Polytec OFV-303 laser vibrometer [7] to measure the nm-level vibration of a phone, capturing the change of

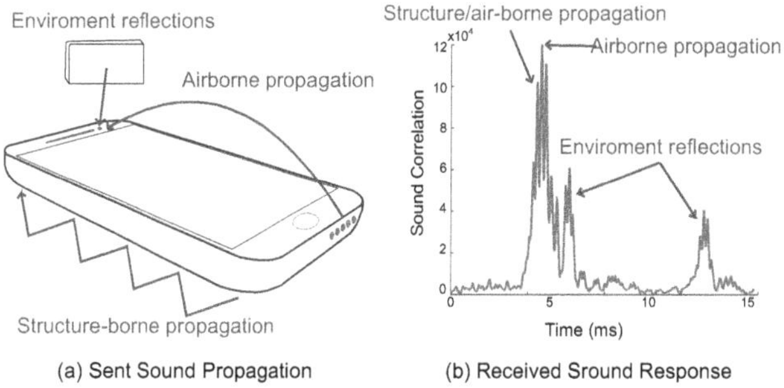

Figure 3—Structure-borne propagation in a phone. The sound received at a phone is a combination of structure- and air-borne propagations as well as the environments' reflections (echo). ForcePhone uses 20 samples before the strongest correlation peak as an indicator for a structure-borne propagation.

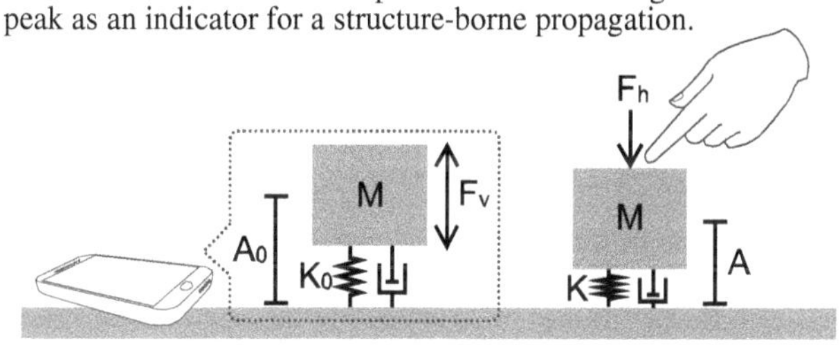

Figure 4—Phone vibration model. Phone vibration is modeled as a forced and damped mass–spring system where the phone vibrates with amplitude A_0 due to the force F_v from the phone speaker. The vibration amplitude is decreased to A and the effective system spring coefficient is increased to K due to the applied force F_h.

structure-borne propagation caused by touching the phone with hand. Compared to capturing the structure-borne propagation via microphones (which ForcePhone is using as described in the next section), this vibration measurement helps neglect the noises caused by the air-propagated sound and the imperfect microphone hardware. Fig. 5 shows our experimental setting where the phone is placed on a metal surface under the laser vibrometer. The laser's focus has been calibrated before the test to ensure that the laser beam will be reflected properly by the phone surface. The latest Apple iPhone 6s is used for these measurements owing to its capability of estimating the applied force. Thumb is used to apply force at the middle of the phone and the iPhone 3D Touch reading (ranging from 0 to 1) is used as a reference of the applied force. From our preliminary test, we found that the Apple 3D Touch sensors can only read the applied force up to about 380g. Hence, we also repeat the same measurements with the Interlink force sensor [5] which can measure force up to 10kg. Its current change caused by the applied force is recorded by the Monsoon power monitor [6].

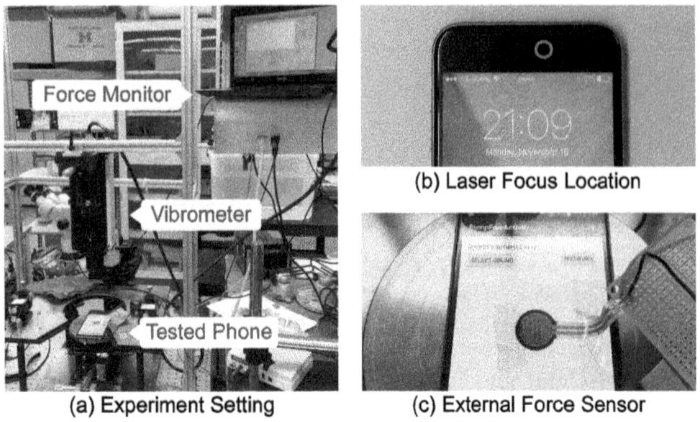

Figure 5—Vibration measurement setting. Vibration is measured by Polytec OFV-303 laser vibrometer when force is applied.

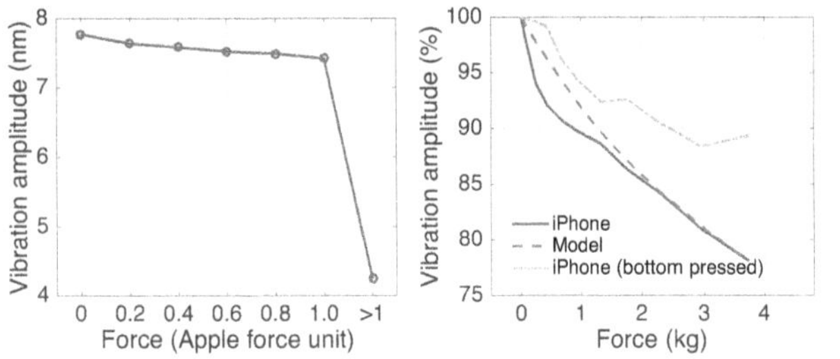

(a) By Apple Sensors (b) By External Sensors

Figure 6—Phone vibration damped by force. The correlation between the damped vibration and the applied force enables ForcePhone's force-sensitive and squeezable interfaces.

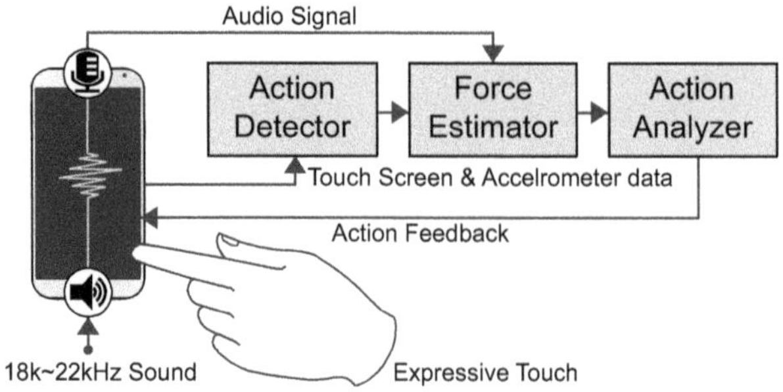

Figure 7—System overview. Force applied to the phone damps the inaudible sound sent from the phone's speaker to its microphone. Accelerometer and gyroscope readings are used to avoid other audio signal noises caused by movements.

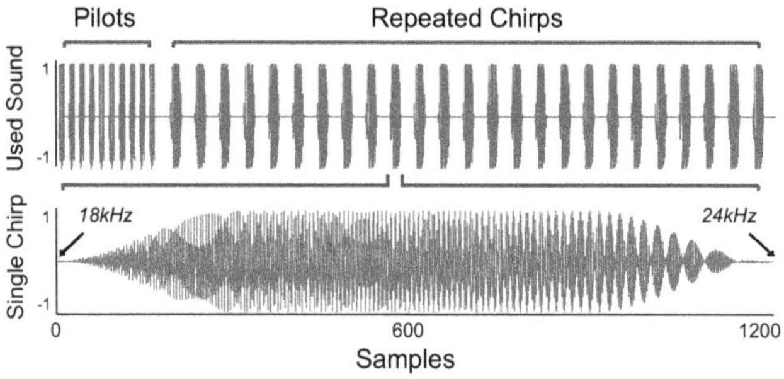

Figure 8—Example of transmitted inaudible sound. The pilots are used to synchronize the phone's microphone and speaker. The subsequent chirps stop for 25ms before playing the next chirp to avoid unexpected noises from environmental reflections. (This figure is rescaled for easy visualization)

Fig. 6 shows the results of phone vibration while applying different amounts of force. As shown in Fig. 6(a), when the Apple 3D Touch reaches its maximum sensitivity, the amplitude of phone vibration decreases about 5%. If more force is applied further (marked as > 1), near 50% of the vibration amplitude is damped by hand. Fig. 6(b) shows the results of measuring the force with external force sensors. The vibration amplitude also decreases about 5% when a 380g force is applied to the phone. Our system model is shown to be able to capture the main trend of vibration amplitude when the initial system spring constant $K_0 = 2.7$(kg/nm) is assumed. The most important property observed in this experiment is the high correlation between the applied force and the decreased vibration amplitude. Based on this property, ForcePhone can provide useful force-sensitive applications as introduced in the following sections.

As mentioned earlier, our model is not perfect. For example, as shown in Fig. 6(b), when the force is applied to the bottom of the phone, it incurs less vibration change since the measured location (i.e., the top of the phone) has less restriction when the phone's bottom is pressed. A similar phenomenon also occurs when different speakers are used to play sound. Thus, it is necessary for ForcePhone to make one-time calibration for unifying different estimations when force is applied at different locations on the screen. The calibration needs to be tuned to the phone models as they have varying vibration patterns depending on the phone material. For example, the vibration of Galaxy Note 4 is found to be 50% larger than the vibration of iPhone 6s, and more sensitive to the applied force since its plastic body is easier to compress. We also found, for some phone models, such as iPhone 6s, this vibration decays too fast when sound is played by the bottom speaker and received by the top microphone, making the force estimation less accurate. In such a case, we used the top speaker to get an adequate signal to noise ratio (SNR) of collected sound even though the collected sound will include a part of airborne propagation components.

4. SYSTEM DESIGN

As shown in Fig. 7, ForcePhone actively plays an *inaudible* sound with the phone speaker, and then picks up this sound with the phone microphone. The touch screen input (such as the location or the start time of a touch) and the data from the other motion sensors are also recorded. These sensor data are then used to improve the force estimation and reduce the number of false detections. When force is applied to the touch screen or the other parts of the phone body, the action analyzer triggers the pre-designed feedback/behavior based on the monitored (inaudible) sounds and user motions.

4.1 Sound Selection

The design of sound is critical to the system performance. While there are many other possible options, the current design of ForcePhone uses a 1200-sample linear chirp from 18kHz to 24kHz. A hamming window is multiplied to the first and last of 300 samples to eliminate the audible noise caused by spectral leakage [16]. The main frequency range of sound signals used to sense is about 20kHz–22kHz while the remaining signals close to 18kHz and 24kHz are played with minimal volume which are "stuffed" only to avoid signal loss due to the windowing. ForcePhone samples this chirp at 48kHz and replays it every 50ms. This sound is designed to achieve (i) minimal user annoyance, (ii) high SNR, and (iii) adequate force sensing delay.

According to the field study in [35], humans are shown to have a limited ability to hear sound above 20kHz. Since most modern smartphones only support the sampling rate up to 48kHz, the highest sound frequency to use is 24kHz. This setting is likely to be expanded in the near future; for example, Android 6.0 has announced a plan to support a higher sample rate. Our experiments have shown that playing a high frequency chirp directly is still audible to humans because an abrupt increase/decrease of energy in time domain incurs frequency leakages. To avoid this problem, ForcePhone uses a similar windowing process as in [25] to reduce the noise burst at the beginning and end of signals. This windowing process adds an envelope to the sent signal that controls the signal amplitude to 0 in the beginning and then gradually restores the signal amplitude to the normal range (the same principle is also applied to the end of the signal). This design choice will cause SNR degradation when we estimate the audio correlation of received/sent signals, but it is practically important to avoid any audible sound. Note that the chirp starts at 18kHz but is still inaudible because the beginning of the chirp is played only at the minimal volume (windowing). None of the participants in our user study noticed/heard the sound used in ForcePhone.

Ideally, less stop time between chirps will provide a smaller sensing delay, but the chirps in ForcePhone are designed to be played every 50ms. This parameter setting is chosen to prevent the inclusion of audio signals reflected by environments as an unexpected/unwanted noise. For example, as shown in Fig. 3(b), after the sound transmitted via airborne propagation (i.e., the highest correlation peak) is received, there are multiple following local peaks which indicate the reception of sound reflected by the environment. From our experiments, the received reflections are found to degrade 20dB after 25ms, which is small enough to let ForcePhone play and receive the next round of chirp correctly with only minimal noise due to environmental reflections. Thus, it is necessary for ForcePhone to have a 25ms (i.e., 1200-sample) stop time after playing each chirp.

ForcePhone uses the signal correlation (also known as the *matched filter*) to estimate the reception of the played sound. The SNR of this correlation in the chirp is proportional to the signal length and sweeping frequency [37]. We selected the sweeping frequency as above in order to not annoy users and cope with the hardware limitation while setting the signal length to 25ms. Even though a longer chirp can achieve a higher SNR, it also increases the sensing delay because ForcePhone needs to wait for the completion of the sound being played. To strike a balance between SNR and the sensing delay, ForcePhone sets the chirp length to 25ms, which makes the total delay in sensing each chirp equal to 50ms (i.e., 20 force estimations can be made every second). This setting is found to provide enough SNR for estimation of the applied force and an adequate sensing delay which meets most users' needs.

Besides the design of sound signal, there is another parameter that affects the received SNR: the phone's speaker volume. In the current setting, the audio volume is set to 50% of the maximum to avoid some audible noise due to the imperfect speaker hardware and deal with the coexistence of multiple phones that run

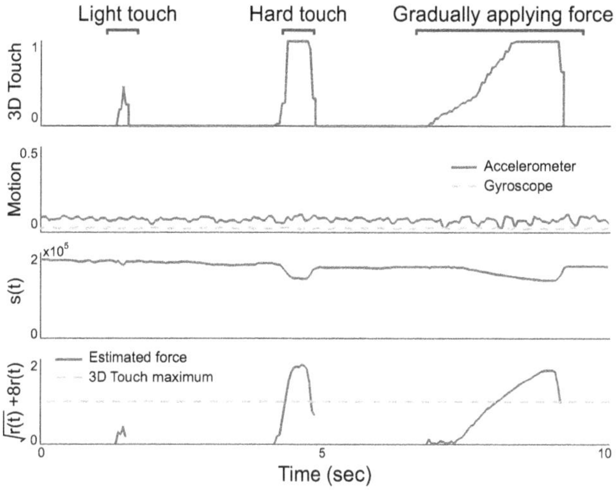

Figure 9—Responses of different amounts of applied force. Motion sensors only capture the initial response of a touch, but the sound response can monitor the subsequent applied force.

ForcePhone. An example of the sent sound is shown in Fig. 8. One thing to note is that there are 10 additional chirps sweeping from 24kHz to 10kHz played before the above-mentioned chirps, which are used as the pilot signal for synchronizing the timing of the phone's microphones and speakers. If the synchronization fails, ForcePhone will stop the sensing process and replay the pilot to achieve correct time synchronization. Detailed performance measurements are presented and discussed in Section 6.

4.2 Estimation of Applied Force

ForcePhone utilizes the structure-borne sound propagation to estimate the applied force. As mentioned in Section 3, when force is applied to the phone body, the hand in contact with the phone body damps/degrades the structure-borne sound propagation. Besides the structure-borne propagation, there are other factors that affect the received sound strength. For example, the airborne propagation might be blocked by hand, and the overall sound signal strength may be enhanced by reflections from the environment or the internal resonant. In ForcePhone, these noises are identified and removed by timestamping the received audio signal. For example, the reflection from an object 10cm away will be received 28 samples later than the airborne propagation since it travels a 10cm longer distance. Moreover, sound usually travels 100x faster in a solid phone [23]. Thus, the structure-borne propagation will be received 21 samples ahead of the airborne propagation when the microphone and the speaker are 15cm apart. Based on these observations, ForcePhone uses the signal which is 20 samples ahead of the airborne propagation as the indicator of the structure-borne propagation, thus removing the most undesirable noise.

Note that the reference of airborne propagation is assumed to be the strongest audio correlation because the sound energy decays faster through the solid phone body and absorbed more on the reflection objects than air. Ideally, the temporal -3dB width of audio correlation are 7 samples for our chirp selection, so it would be possible to find a clear peak ahead of the airborne propagation, indicating the reception of structure-borne propagation. However, as shown in Fig. 3(b), there is no such clear peak found before airborne propagation, and the temporal -3dB width of audio correla-

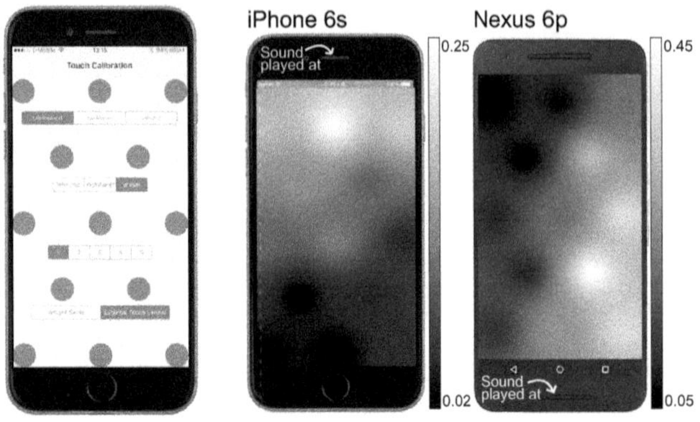

(a) Calibration UI (b) Signal change $\overline{r(t)}$ of 500g force

Figure 10—Touch calibration. The extent of signal changes caused by the applied force varies with the touch location. Thus, a one-time touch calibration is made at the 13 marked locations to compensate the estimated force at different locations.

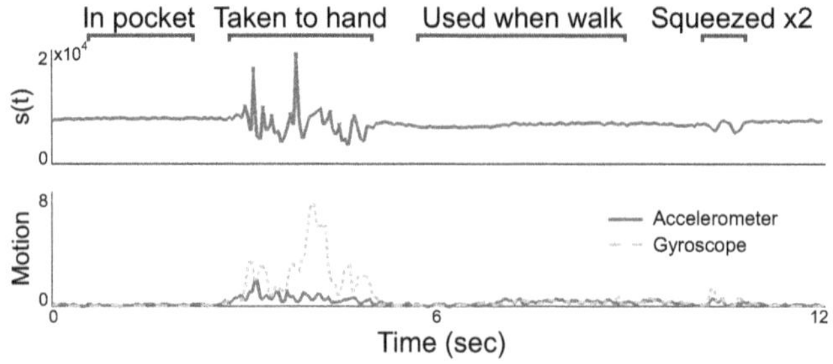

Figure 11—Response of movement and squeeze. Sound correlation changes when the environment changes, such as moving the phone from the pocket to hands, but it becomes stable quickly when people hold phones in their hands.

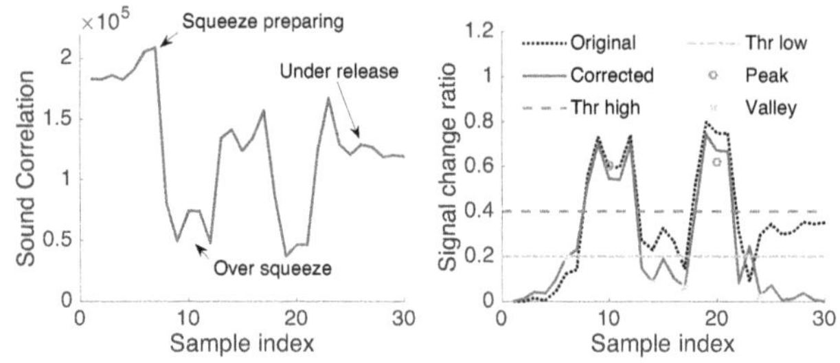

(a) Squeeze response (b) Squeeze detection

Figure 12—Squeeze detection example. Received signal is first normalized by the start and the end of signal amplitudes. Peak is identified when the corrected signal passing the high threshold and the signal above the low threshold is considered as part of the peak.

tion is about 40 samples in this measurement. This phenomenon is caused by the adoption of windowing, which suppresses the frequency-domain signal leakage but incurs the time-domain signal leakage. This 20-sample-ahead sampling heuristic will thus include both air- and structure-borne propagations. To get a reliable estimation of the applied force, `ForcePhone` utilizes the sound strength when the touch begins as a reference to estimate the subsequent change caused by the force applied later. In the rest of this paper, we will denote the sound correction at time t as signal $s(t)$ and the signal at the beginning of a touch as s_{start}. The subsequent force at time t is estimated based on a metric called the *signal changing ratio*, $r(t) = |(s(t) - s_{start})/s_{start}|$. The applied force $f(t)$ at time t is then determined by a linear regression model with $r(t)$. Fig. 9 shows a real-world example of applying force to an iPhone 6s placed on a wooden table. We simply visualize the estimated force as $\sqrt{r(t)} + 8r(t)$; the intuition behind this setting will be discussed later. In this measurement, there are 3 different types of touch, each with a different applied force: (1) light touch, (2) hard touch, and (3) touch with a gradually increasing force. The ground truth of the applied force can be read from the Apple 3D Touch sensors [3]. As shown in the figure, motion sensors can only detect the slight movement at the start/end of a touch but are unable to determine the applied force. Our heuristic based on $r(t)$ captures most of the force characteristics even when the applied force exceeds the maximum sensing range of Apple 3D Touch.

Note the calibration between $f(t)$ and $r(t)$ varies with the location of force applied on the phone as described in Section 3. Thus, a preparatory experiment is needed for each phone model before `ForcePhone` is activated. However, this calibration is just a one-time requirement, which is different from other sound-fingerprinting systems that need laborious training each time before using the application.

Our current implementation of `ForcePhone` is calibrated by using external force sensors. The calibration is done by applying different amounts of force (up to 1.5kg) at 13 selected locations as shown in Fig 10(a). The remaining parts of touch screen are calibrated by interpolating the estimated force at those 13 locations. Fig. 10(b) shows examples of average signal change ratio, $\overline{r(t)}$, when a 500g force is applied to the 13 calibrated locations and the estimated $\overline{r(t)}$ over the remaining parts of the phone. As shown in this figure, $\overline{r(t)}$ varies with location due to different distances from/to the speaker/microphone and also with the structure of the phone. In general, touching near the speaker used to play sounds generates more pronounced signal changes while touching locations far away from the speaker causes less pronounced changes. Note that our current calibration is done when the phone is placed on a static surface, thus ignoring the airborne signal changes due to the movement of the phone during the touch. However, as we will discuss later, the added estimation noise due to the phone movement can be tolerated with proper app design since users are also unaware of the actual amount of force being applied to the phone unless the response from the phone is sensed. Most participants of our usability study felt comfortable with the current setting. Improving this calibration process with more advanced sensors and algorithms is part of our future work.

4.3 Squeeze Detection

It is challenging to detect the squeeze of phone body. Fig. 11 shows an example of the observed signal change when a phone is taken out of the pocket with hand, used while walking, and then squeezed twice. As shown in this figure, even though the signal response of a squeeze is clearly observable, it is also possible to include lots of noise due to the phone's movements. To avoid this noise from large phone movements, we have built a motion detector based on both accelerometer and gyroscope readings, which turns off our squeeze detection when there is a large phone movement and the signal is noisy. We thus set a threshold to turn off the detection during large phone movements (such as taking the phone out of pocket and transferring it to a hand) but keep the squeeze function on during slow/small phone movements, such as walking and using the phone in hand.

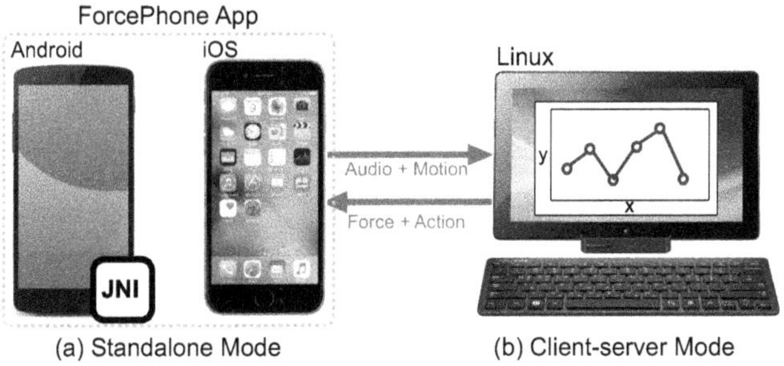

Figure 13—Implementation overview. `ForcePhone` has been implemented as a standalone app on Android via Java Native Interface (JNI). Our iOS implementation requires the force estimation done at a remote server.

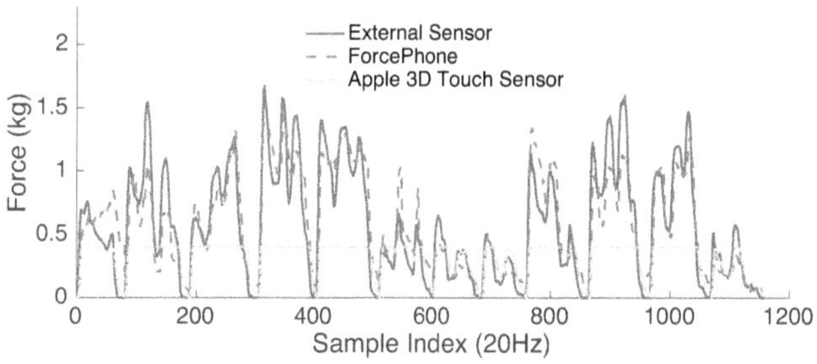

Figure 14—Accuracy of force estimation. 12 touch events with different amounts of applied force are plotted. The force estimated by `ForcePhone` provides high correlation with the ground truth estimated by using our external force sensors.

Even though the movement noise is removed by the motion detector, determining if the user squeezes the phone is still harder than estimating the force applied to the touch screen. Due to the lack of touch screen input, we don't know when the squeeze starts. Moreover, the location of squeeze is inaccessible, thus making it difficult to perform a proper calibration. To solve these issues, our squeezable back function is made to respond only to a predefined squeeze behavior, such as double squeezes applied to the phone's left and right body frame as shown in Fig. 2, and the entire squeeze process is assumed to complete in 1.5 seconds.

Fig. 12(a) shows an example of this predefined squeeze response, where the applied squeezes cause two significant signal drops at time 10 and 20. Besides the signal response to the squeeze operation, there are three characteristics of human squeezing behavior, which are critical to our design of squeeze detection. First, the the applied force might decrease slightly before a squeeze, probably because the users need to relax their hands before squeezing their phone. After the squeeze, the applied force may also decrease around the expected force peak. We call this phenomenon *over-squeeze*, and think it is caused by the fact that users actually release part of their fingers/palms from the phone body when they try to apply more force with the other part(s) of the hand. At the end of squeeze, the applied force may not return to its initial condition either, because the users may change their position of holding the phone during the squeeze.

Squeezes are also detected based on the signal change ratio $r(t)$. `ForcePhone` continuously checks each 30-sample received signal to see if the predefined squeeze pattern has occurred. As the hand position is likely to change during a squeeze, it is less accurate to estimate the applied force based only on s_{start}. For example, the larger drop of the second squeeze shown in Fig. 12(a) might be caused by a hand position change rather than a larger squeezing force. To account for this phenomenon, we heuristically set the reference signal based on both the start and end of this 30-sample signal. This new reference signal varies over time and is defined as $s(t)_{reference} = ((t_{end} - t)s_{start} + (t - t_{start})s_{end})/(t_{end} - t_{start})$. The signal change ratio $r(t)$ is calculated based on $s(t)_{reference}$ using the same process as described earlier. Basically, this method estimates $r(t)$ by weighting the reference signal proportional to the difference between t and t_{start}, t_{end}. Fig. 12(b) shows the result of this correction. After estimating $r(t)$, `ForcePhone` sets two thresholds to identify the force peaks caused by squeezes. A peak occurs when $r(t) > thr_{high}$. The following samples where $r(t) > thr_{low}$ are defined as parts of this identified peak. This setting is designed to avoid false identification due to the *over squeeze* and *squeeze preparation*. Thus, thr_{high} is set larger than the assumed squeeze preparation force change, and thr_{low} is set smaller than the over squeeze force change. A valid squeeze is identified when the number of detected peaks, the peak widths, and the peak-to-valley ratios fit a predefined criterion. The performance of our current setting will be evaluated in Section 6.

5. IMPLEMENTATION

We have implemented `ForcePhone` on both Android and iOS devices. As shown in Fig. 7, our Android implementation runs as a standalone app; the force estimation is implemented as a library in native code (C++) which we integrate into the app via Java Native Interface (JNI). On the other hand, the current iOS implementation requires the force estimation to be done at a remote server using Matlab. Both implementations provide real-time force estimations. The delay between recording each chirp and receiving a force estimation is 15ms and 61ms at our local and remote implementations, respectively. We are currently porting the force estimation library implemented in C++ to iOS.

One implementation challenge is that `ForcePhone` needs accurate time synchronization between the phone speaker and microphone to extract valid structure-borne propagations. However, both iOS and Android platforms don't meet this real-time requirement since both take 20–100ms to run the play/record audio command. To overcome this difficulty, `ForcePhone` adds 10 pilot sequences ahead of the used chirps. In this synchronization, `ForcePhone` checks if the received signal contains the identical sent pilots, such as having the same stop time among pilots. In our experiments, more than 95% of the received pilots have less than 5-sample jitters in their stop time, and 15% of trials on Android experience a special 960-sample delay before the 4-th pilots. The criterion for `ForcePhone` to finish this synchronization test is the existence of these 10 pilots, and 50% of received pilots have the exact same stop time, and the last three pilots have less than 5-sample jitters. Once the pilots are identified correctly, the timing of the last pilot is used as a reference to extract the structure-borne propagation from the subsequent chirps as described earlier.

6. EVALUATION

We first measure system performance, such as force estimation accuracy, overhead, and robustness to noise. We then measure the user's benefit of using `ForcePhone`, such as the probability of an assigned request being honored or whether the users think it useful.

6.1 Accuracy of Force Estimation

We evaluate the accuracy of force estimation by using the mean square errors and correlation coefficients where the former represents the ability to estimate exact force while the later indicates the capability to learn how force is changed. Fig. 14 shows an example of 12 different touches when the iPhone 6s is held in left hand and the center of the touch screen is pressed with left thumb. The applied force is estimated by the internal Apple 3D Touch sensors, external force sensors, and ForcePhone. Since Apple 3D Touch can only provide normalized results and no documented interpretation of the sensed values is available, we built our own post-hoc translation based on an external force scale. We found the sensed value is linear in the applied force, and the maximum value is reached when 380g is applied.

As shown in Fig. 14, the proprietary sensors used in Apple 3D Touch captures the force change below its maximum (380g in this case) with high accuracy. Even though ForcePhone estimates the force under 380g with less accuracy, it captures most force-change characteristics as shown in Fig. 14. Meanwhile, ForcePhone can estimate the force above 380g without using any additional sensors.

The mean square error of this in-hand example is 205g and the correlation coefficient to the force estimated by external sensors is 0.87. Compared to the maximum sensed force up to 1.5kg, this error is tolerable for most force-sensitive apps as shown later. When the phone is stationary on a wooden table, the mean square error falls to 54g and the correlation coefficient increases to 0.91. Note that the error in estimating the exact value of the applied force could change if the force is applied in a different way than our calibration (as we don't consider the damping coefficient change in our current model as introduced in Section 3.) For example, there might be an estimation drift, so applying a varying force from 500g to 1000g might be estimated wrongly as changing from 400g to 900g plus the previously-mentioned errors. However, this feature doesn't hurt the experience of using ForcePhone because users are not aware of the exact value of the force applied to a phone unless this value is shown in the user interface [36]. With a proper user interface design, even though the estimated force is 100g less than the real force applied to the phone, users can easily learn to adjust the applied force for getting a correct response. Actually, even the proprietary sensors used for 3D Touch have about 100g errors between the corners of touch screen, and it is suggested not to be used for estimating exact force [1]. In our current setting, when the force is applied to the middle area of the phone, the estimated force (in g) is calculated as $f(t) = 15 + 230\sqrt{(r(t))} + 2800r(t)$ in iPhone 6s and $f(t) = 1900r(t)$ on Galaxy Note 4. As shown in our usability study, this setting is adequate for building useful force-sensitive and squeezable apps. Calibration while considering how users touch the phone is part of our future work, which could be accomplished by other grip detection systems like GripSense [15].

6.2 Noise and Interference

The estimation of force based on sound propagation becomes erroneous if there is a strong audio noise with a similar structure as the chirps used in ForcePhone. For example, the mean square error of ForcePhone can increase from 50g to more than 500g when the same chirps are played by nearby computers's speakers. Even tough this is the natural limitation of any audio-based application, it is not the case in most real-life scenarios. In our measurements, ForcePhone is shown to be resistant to: (1) real-life background audio noise such as music being played in the testing room, (2) inter-device interference from ForcePhone running on another nearby device, and (3) self-interference from the audio played on the same device. To study the performance degradation caused only by the audio noise, rather than the force instability of human hands or other movement noises, we kept the test phone stationary on a wooden table and no force is applied. The standard deviation of force estimations is recorded and reported. This estimated force variation also represents errors when there is a force applied to the phone if the received noise is modeled as an additive noise.

Particularly, we use an Apple MAC Air or an iPhone 6s placed on the same surface as test devices. Multiple sets of noises were played, but no significant differences were observed, so we only report the results of music-playing noise, i.e., rock music "Jump – Van Halen" or gaming background music "Spot On". Since we place both the test device and the noise source on the same table, the results account for the vibration coupling and the noise transmitted through the surface.

We found ForcePhone to be resistant to most external real-life noises. As shown in Fig. 15, even when the rock music is played at full-volume by a laptop 20cm away from the test device, the sound correlation of the used chirps doesn't change much. This is because most human (singing or chatting) noises have limited signals in the 18kHz – 24kHz range. Moreover, this natural noise usually has only a limited correlation to our 1200-sample chirps. In this measurement, the increased estimation errors are less than 10g, which does not affect most of ForcePhone's functionality, even when the noise level is 20dB higher than the used chirps.

Compared to the uncorrelated noises, ForcePhone is more sensitive to the noise that has a similar structure as the chirp it uses. Solutions of this issue are critical in allowing multiple phones to run ForcePhone in the same environment. To measure this, we had another device playing the same chirps used by ForcePhone, but with random stop time between consecutive chirps. This is

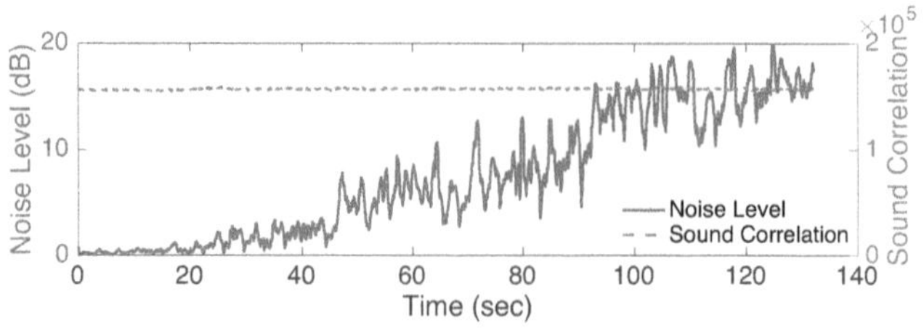

Figure 15—Resistance to background noise. Music (i.e., noise) played by a laptop 20cm away from the device under test has limited effect on the sound correlation even if the noise level is increased to 20dB higher than the used chirps.

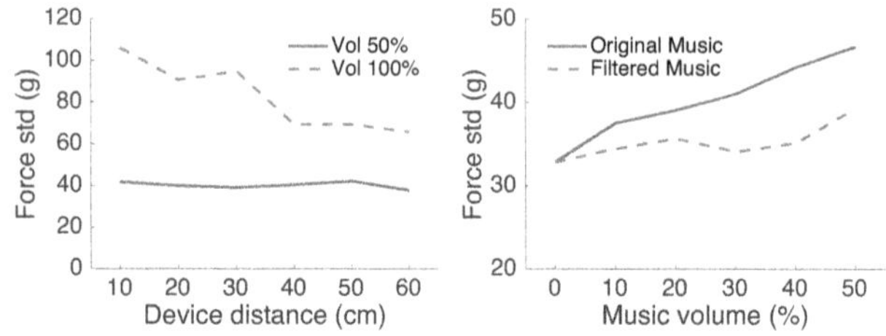

(a) Inter-device interference (b) Self interference

Figure 16—Resistance to inter-device and self interferences. The variation of sound correlation for each second is used to indicate the error when another device is running ForcePhone or a music is played on the same device.

Setting	Idle	Backlight	ForcePhone	Website	Game
Power (mean)	33	856	1160	2564	3692

Table 2—Power consumption (mW). The additional power consumption by `ForcePhone` is about 304mW, which is small relative to that of normal phone usage.

designed to learn the average performance when two devices run `ForcePhone` simultaneously. As shown in Fig. 16(a), the average estimated error increases to 110g when the correlated noise is played at full-volume by another device. This trend is mitigated when the noise volume is reduced. Since `ForcePhone` only requires the designed chirps to be played at 50% of full-volume, multiple devices can run `ForcePhone` if they are at least 10cm apart from each other.

In the last scenario, we evaluate whether other audio signals can be played on the same device when `ForcePhone` is running. This capability is critical to the user experience, especially when using `ForcePhone` for a game control. We play a game background music from the same device when `ForcePhone` is running, and record the increased estimation error. As shown in Fig. 16(b), when the music is played by the same speaker at 50% of full-volume, `ForcePhone` experiences about 46g of additional estimation error, which does not affect the core functionality of `ForcePhone`. Moreover, when the played music is processed further by using a 15kHz low-pass filter, the imposed error decreased further to 37g. Note that the current design of `ForcePhone` allows game music to be played at most 50% of full-volume, as the other 50% is dedicated for `ForcePhone`'s functionality. This limitation can be addressed when the phone development kit supports streaming music/chirps to different speakers (devices usually have 2 or more speakers, but only one of them can be used at a time).

6.3 Power Consumption

We measure the power consumption of `ForcePhone` with the Monsoon Power Monitor [6] on Galaxy Note 4. For the baseline measurements, we turn off the phone's radios and estimate the force through our JNI/C++ local implementation. We ran each scenario for 20 seconds in 6 different states: 1) idle, with the screen off, 2) backlight, with the screen displaying a white background, 3) `ForcePhone`, with the screen on, 4) website surfing, when networking is enabled, and 5) video game, "Puzzle&Dragon". These measurement results are summarized in Table 2.

Activating the naive implementation of `ForcePhone` consumes an additional power of 304mW compared to the case when nothing is executed and background is on. More than 90% of this power consumption comes from using the hardware of speaker, microphone, and accelerometer — this is consistent with the results in [10]. The computation cost of `ForcePhone` is minimal since it builds a model to estimate the applied force rather than fingerprinting the sound changes. Note that the ratio of `ForcePhone`'s power consumption is dependent on its usage. For example, though `ForcePhone` incurs 26% power overhead (compared to the blacklight case) when it is used to select app options at home screen, users won't press this option for a long time and `ForcePhone` can be turned off once the selection is done. If the proposed squeezable back function is used for web surfing, activating `ForcePhone` incurs only an 11% power-consumption overhead, which reduces the life of Note 4's 12 Wh battery by about 30min. The percentage overhead is reduced further if `ForcePhone` is used for game control or when microphones or speakers have been activated for other purposes.

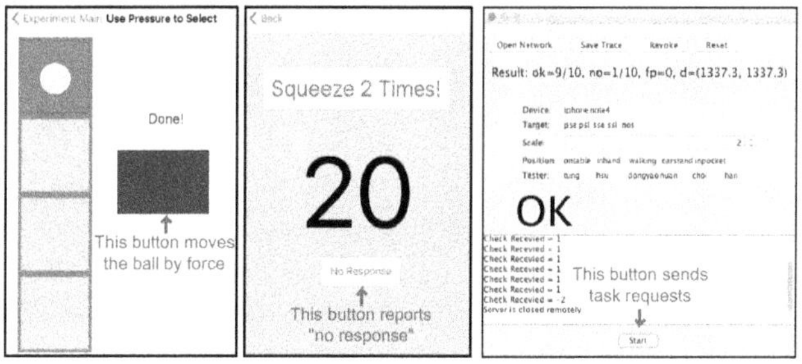

(a) Experiment App (b) Experiment Controller

Figure 17—User interface for experiments. Users are requested to move a ball to the marked red box by applying different amounts of force to the blue button and squeeze the phone twice for surfing the previous web page. Action requests are sent, and the results are recorded by the controller.

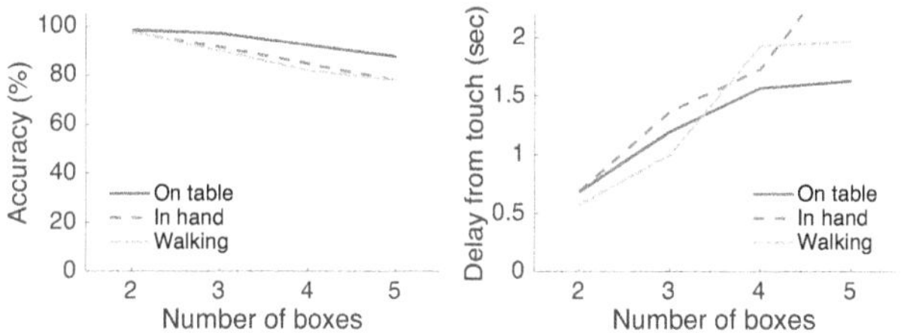

(a) Accuracy (b) Delay

Figure 18—Result of controlling a ball with `ForcePhone`. Results are averaged over 6 participants. Delay is estimated as the time between the user presses/releases the button.

6.4 Usability Test

We recruited 6 participants (4 males and 2 females) to test the usability of `ForcePhone` by asking them to perform a set of tasks as shown in Fig. 17(a). Since these 6 participants are students who are aware of this project, we only tested their ability to complete the assigned tasks. (The results of the other users' opinions on `ForcePhone` will be provided in the next subsection.) In the first task, users are asked to move a ball by applying force and stop it at a randomly-selected red box; the highest box is reached by applying a 500g force and the ball located at the bottom of boxes (0g) when the task starts. This experiment follows a similar design principle as that in [36] to test if the user can effectively control the force at different levels. Experiments start from stopping the ball at one of the two big boxes (i.e., only two levels) to one of the five small boxes. We asked users to perform these tasks at different positions, such as controlling the phone while it is on a table, while holding it in hand, or while walking and using it simultaneously. A remote controller sends requests and records the accuracy and delay of users' reaction as shown in Fig. 17(b).

Fig. 18 shows the accuracy (the success rate of moving the ball into the selected box) and the delay between the user touching the blue button and finishing the task. The plots show that most participants can effectively control ball movement with `ForcePhone` when there are only 2 – 3 boxes. This result supports our hard-pressed option app since the users can easily control the applied force at two levels with higher than 97% accuracy. When more than 3 boxes (levels) are provided, users can still achieve higher than 90% accuracy when the phone is stationary on the table. This is consistent with our earlier evaluation of estimation accuracy. Although different touch positions might incur additional errors, the

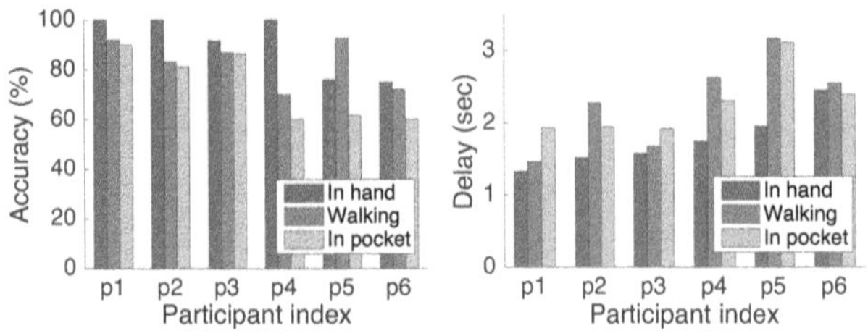

(a) Accuracy (b) Delay

Figure 19—Results of squeeze detection. The accuracy of the last three participants is increased to more than 90% when the detection criterion is adjusted after this test.

Questions	Strongly disagree /Disagree	No option	Strongly agree /Agree
Hard-pressed option is helpful	0	0	21
Hard-pressing(3D Touch) is responsive	1	1	19
Hard-pressing is responsive	0	1	20
Ball-moving game is interesting	0	3	18
Moving ball is responsive	2	4	15
Squeezable back is helpful	1	2	18
Squeezing is responsive	2	1	18
False detection is acceptable	4	7	10

Table 3—App study results.

high correlation between the force estimated by `ForcePhone` and the real force is sufficient for users to control the phone effectively. It is worth noting that moving the ball toward the top/bottom boxes is easier than the box in the middle; moving the ball to the bottom or top box has 13% higher accuracy than moving the ball into the middle box. A similar property was also reported in [36].

On average, users require only 0.7 second to stop the ball at the correct position when there are two boxes. This delay increases to 2 seconds when the users attempt moving the ball among 5 boxes while walking. Interestingly, controlling the ball when the phone is stationary is considered the easiest task, but the participants use a slightly less time to complete the 2-box task while walking. We conjecture this phenomenon is caused by the order of tests we perform, where the walking test is executed after testing the phone–table and in-hand cases. This property implies that performance can be improved further once the users become familiar with `ForcePhone`. The average accuracy of repeating the same task on the Galaxy Note 4 is increased by 3%. We think this minimal improvement is due to the users' familiarity with this task rather than the force estimation accuracy. In summary, users can effectively use `ForcePhone` to control different levels of applied force for various scenarios.

In the second experiment, we asked the participants to squeeze the phone's body. Once `ForcePhone` detects the squeeze, the testing app switches to the previous UI page with a different background and indicates the page number as shown in Fig. 17(a). Due to the lack of ground truth (no touch event exists), we asked the users to click the *no response* button once the user observes the applied squeeze not detected. We count the number of times the squeeze is detected without any instruction from the remote controller as a false positive.

Fig. 19 shows the accuracy and delay for each user. Participant 1 has the highest accuracy and the lowest delay because the detection setting is tuned according to his own preliminary test and since he practiced this task more than the other users. The average accuracy when the phone is held in hand is 90%. The accuracy drops to 82% when the participants use their phones while walking. Due to the lack of timing information on when the user applies and stops the squeeze, we only record the delay between the instruction and the squeeze feedback (either success or fail). As shown in Fig. 19(b), the average delay of each squeeze is about 2 seconds. Users experience low accuracy usually experience a long delay since they have to wait and then click the "no response" button if the squeeze is not detected. From the measurements of our previous moving-ball test, we found users usually need 0.8 second to react to the displayed instruction, and hence the delay of squeeze detection is expected no longer than 1.5 seconds.

It is possible to detect a squeeze in users' pocket, which can be used to turn off alarms or notifications when the phone is in pocket. However, our measurement shows that its performance depends not only on how the phone is squeezed but also on the clothing material. Tight jeans (e.g., worn by p1 to p3) generally have a better detection accuracy than loose pants. During this controlled experiment, only 4 false detections are observed. Users' feedback on the false positive rate will be presented in the next section.

Based on more than 600 squeeze profiles collected from the 6 participants, we tuned our final squeeze detection setting as follows. We set the high and low thresholds of squeeze detection to 310g and 175g, respectively. We identify signals as a peak only when the peak width lies between 2 and 8 samples and the peak-to-valley ratio is greater than 2.5. By applying these new criteria to the collected traces, the overall detection accuracies for the last three participants increase to higher than 90% for both in-hand and walking scenarios. We used the same setting in our subsequent application tests for other participants.

6.5 Users Study of Proposed Apps

For a users study of `ForcePhone`-based apps, we randomly chose 21 participants (7 females and 14 males) among a large student population at the University of Michigan. All of recruited participants own smartphones; only 3 of them have the latest iPhone 6s and knew how to use 3D Touch prior to this test. In contrast to our previous usability test, these participants were unaware of `ForcePhone` and our research group (so they have no initial bias). We first ask the participants to use the built-in hard-pressed option of iPhone 6s and then try the same function implemented by `ForcePhone` on Galaxy Note 4. We built a fake UI (as shown in Fig. 2(a)) to make them feel if they were triggering the real option on Android. We set the testing threshold for enabling options to 340g, which is similar to the iPhone's. We chose not to make a blind test by using our iPhone implementation because the current iOS disables the vibration service when audio is being recorded. According to our preliminary test, vibrating the phone when the hard-pressed option is being activated is critical to the user experience. After trying the hard-pressed option, the users were instructed to play a simple game with the moving-ball test app. This allows us to record the users' feedback on using `ForcePhone` as a continuous UI input. While playing the game, users have to move the ball into the red box, and the number of boxes was increased when the users completed the task. Last, we asked the participants to test our squeezable back app that automatically navigates the previous UI page when they squeeze the phone twice. The threshold is set based on the results of our previous usability study. It took about 15 minutes on average, to complete the entire test.

After testing our app, a survey form was filled out by the participants, and the results are summarized in Table 3. The question mark by "3D Touch" in Table 3 refers to the hard-pressed option implemented by Apple 3D Touch, while the others refer to ForcePhone. Most users are positive of the proposed apps and think them helpful. For the hard-press option, most users think ForcePhone has a comparable performance to Apple 3D Touch. One of them said ForcePhone is better than 3D Touch because the vibration in Android is much clearer (stronger) than iPhone's, which is not related to the force detection. Only 3 users think iPhone's performance is better, but still acknowledge ForcePhone is responsive enough for the hard-pressed option app. This indicates that ForcePhone can handle simple tasks with a comparable performance as adding proprietary sensors. Moreover, most users feel the squeezable back app is helpful, which is a unique capability of ForcePhone.

Most users regard that controlling the ball based on the applied force is relatively difficult, but still were able to control the ball. Two users think our test setting is too sensitive, making it difficult to move the ball. We also discovered some errors caused by applying a large initial force and releasing the button immediately, which was not the intended case for ForcePhone. After the users are instructed to move the ball by gradually applying force, they are able to control the ball with ForcePhone. The squeezable back app received a similar rating as the ball-moving game. In our other survey, 16 users indicated difficulty in clicking the app back button when operating the phone with one hand which supports the design of our squeezable back app. Most users think our current parameter setting tuned by previous 6 participants is responsive and acceptable. A half of users experienced false detections when they moved the phone from one hand to the other. During the test, none of users heard the sound used in ForcePhone, so no user annoyance. The test locations were close to a cafe crowded with students, but ForcePhone was robust to human noises. Most common comments from the users are "cool idea" and "useful'. We plan to have extensive and large-scale tests before releasing ForcePhone to public.

7. DISCUSSION

ForcePhone has been shown to be able to expand user input interfaces by using only built-in sensors. Several demonstrative apps have been developed and tested, but there are many other use-cases of ForcePhone. Discussed below are the limitations of current ForcePhone and some of possible directions of our future work.

7.1 Limitations

As our evaluation results show, ForcePhone's force estimation includes noise from object contacts and human movements, calling for an app design to eliminate this noise. An extreme example that breaks ForcePhone's functionality is to activate the force estimation by placing the phone on a table then quickly moving and holding it in hand. However, this limitation of ForcePhone can be avoided by a proper app design. For example, the hard-pressed option app only needs force measurements within a short period of time (e.g., 2 seconds) and is inactivated if the phone is being moved. Apps like drawing lines with different line styles/thickness by applying different amounts of force is not suitable for the current ForcePhone as it is more probable for the user to (unintentionally) change the environment during the line drawing. But selection of thickness by applying different amounts of force is possible since it is akin to our ball-moving test. In our measurement, to achieve accurate and long-lasting force sensing, ForcePhone needs the

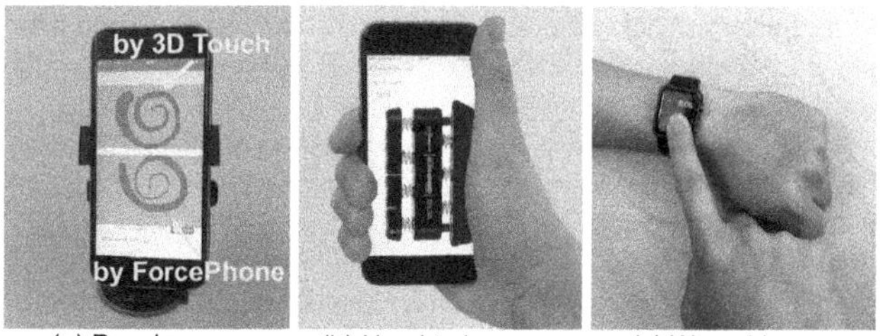

(a) Drawing app (b) Hand-trainer app (c) Wearable app

Figure 20—Potential usage of ForcePhone.

phone to be fixed at a certain location. For example, Fig. 20(a) demonstrates the above-mentioned force-sensitive drawing app by attaching the phone on a stand.

In our squeezable back app, missed detections occur when the detection is intentionally turned off upon identification of extensive movements, such as sudden turns or stops. This is a safety mechanism for ForcePhone to avoid false detections, but the users are not aware of this. One way to avoid this misunderstanding and improve the user experience is to provide a feedback when the squeeze detection is temporarily turned off. For example, the background of website or the title bar can be dimmed slightly when the squeezable back app is deactivated. Studying the users' reaction to this new UI design is part of our future work.

While the touch location near the speaker/microphone used to play/record sounds is found more sensitive to the applied force (i.e., making more pronounced signal changes), the middle area of touch screen usually provides more reliable force estimation. For example, when more than 1.2kg force is applied to the top area of iPhone 6s, the received signals jump quickly and the relation between $f(t)$ and $r(t)$ breaks down. We suspect this phenomenon is due to the pressuring of phone's microphone and other internal components. So, we suggest to limit the estimated force to 500g for consistent performance, even though certain locations can sense the force up to 3kg. This phenomenon also causes the estimated signal strength $s(t)$ at certain locations to rise when the force is applied. Most of these situations caused by pressing the phone can be compensated by our calibration of $r(t)$ and the estimation constraints caused by this problem will likely be addressed in the near future since commodity phones start to increase the number and fidelity of speakers/microphones. For example, when multiple speaker–microphone pairs are used to sense force interactively, the locations yielding erroneous estimations for a single microphone–speaker pair can be corrected by the other microphones and speakers. We should also note that, as shown in our measurements, these minor issues incur minimal annoyance to users when ForcePhone is properly applied.

7.2 Potential Applications of ForcePhone

The participants of our usability study suggested many potential uses of ForcePhone after trying the proposed apps. Of them, two most promising and interesting uses are mobile health apps and force-sensitive wearable devices.

Mobile phones or wearables are good candidate platforms for mobile health apps since people carry them all time. For example, systems of notifying/requesting users to walk or excise are now built in most commodity phones [2, 8]. Researchers have also shown the benefits of drinking more water via mobile apps [11]. ForcePhone can provide a new function/capability of these systems because it can determine how hard a user squeezes/touches the phone. As shown in Fig. 20(b), this functionality can be used as a replacement of force-finger-trainer that is helpful for the people with disability and those who use hands and fingers excessively for their work, e.g., computer programmers.

ForcePhone can also be implemented in wearable devices that have even less space for user inputs than smartphones. Unfortunately, current wearable devices usually have less sensing capabilities than smartphones, especially for the microphone sensitivity and sample rate. For example, Samsung Gear S (watch) can only support an audio sample rate up to 32kHz, which is inadequate for the current design of ForcePhone. Apple Watch hardware is found to be the best to implement ForcePhone, but its current API does not yet support data reading from the audio queue and process audio data in real time. In future, we expect the sensing capability of wearables to improve so that ForcePhone can be implemented and used for numerous apps.

8. CONCLUSION

We have proposed ForcePhone, an inexpensive solution that adds a force-sensitive and squeezable interface to commodity phones without any hardware modification/addition. ForcePhone has been implemented on iOS and Android platforms, and several apps based on its functionality have been developed and tested. Our evaluation has shown ForcePhone to provide comparable performance as augmented proprietary force sensors and to be robust to most real-life noises. The proposed apps are easy to use with higher than 90% accuracy and minimal overheads. In future, we plan to test ForcePhone on a wide range of devices and scenarios.

ACKNOWLEDGEMENTS

The authors would like to thank Karl Grosh, Chuming Zhao, Kassem Fawaz, Lung-Pan Cheng, Chuan-Che Huang, Ming-Yuan Yu, Chen-Ming Chang, Meng-Ting Chung and the anonymous reviewers and the shepherd for constructive comments on the earlier versions of this paper.

9. REFERENCES

[1] Apple doesn't want you weighing things with your iPhone just yet. http://www.theverge.com/2015/10/28/9625340/iphone-6s-gravity-app-digital-scales.

[2] Apple Health App. http://www.apple.com/ios/health/.

[3] Apple iPhone 6s 3D Touch. http://www.apple.com/iphone-6s/3d-touch/.

[4] ForcePhone Demo Video. https://youtu.be/cYxr2wnQVMU.

[5] Interlink 402 FSR. http://www.interlinkelectronics.com/FSR402.php.

[6] Monsoon Power Monitor. http://www.msoon.com/LabEquipment/PowerMonitor/.

[7] Polytec OFV-303 Laser Vibrometer. http://www.polytec.com/us/products/vibration-sensors/.

[8] Samsung S Health App. http://shealth.samsung.com/.

[9] Why Apple's iPhone SE lacks 3D Touch technology. http://appleinsider.com/articles/16/03/23/why-apples-iphone-se-lacks-3d-touch-technology.

[10] F. Ben Abdesslem, A. Phillips, and T. Henderson. Less is more: Energy-efficient mobile sensing with senseless. In *Proceedings of ACM MobiHeld '09*, pages 61–62.

[11] M.-C. Chiu, S.-P. Chang, Y.-C. Chang, H.-H. Chu, C. C.-H. Chen, F.-H. Hsiao, and J.-C. Ko. Playful bottle: A mobile social persuasion system to motivate healthy water intake. In *Proceedings of ACM UbiComp '09*, pages 185–194.

[12] S. Elliott. Active control of structure-borne noise. *Journal of Sound and Vibration*, 177(5):651 – 673, 1994.

[13] A. Girouard, J. Lo, M. Riyadh, F. Daliri, A. K. Eady, and J. Pasquero. One-handed bend interactions with deformable smartphones. In *Proceedings of ACM CHI '15*, pages 1509–1518, 2015.

[14] M. Goel, B. Lee, M. T. Islam Aumi, S. Patel, G. Borriello, S. Hibino, and B. Begole. Surfacelink: Using inertial and acoustic sensing to enable multi-device interaction on a surface. In *Proceedings of ACM CHI '14*, pages 1387–1396.

[15] M. Goel, J. Wobbrock, and S. Patel. Gripsense: Using built-in sensors to detect hand posture and pressure on commodity mobile phones. In *Proceedings of ACM UIST '12*, pages 545–554.

[16] F. Harris. On the use of windows for harmonic analysis with the discrete fourier transform. *Proceedings of the IEEE*, 66(1):51–83, 1978.

[17] C. Harrison, J. Schwarz, and S. E. Hudson. Tapsense: Enhancing finger interaction on touch surfaces. In *Proceedings of ACM UIST '11*, pages 627–636.

[18] C. Harrison, D. Tan, and D. Morris. Skinput: Appropriating the body as an input surface. In *Proceedings of ACM CHI '10*, pages 453–462.

[19] S. Heo and G. Lee. Forcetap: Extending the input vocabulary of mobile touch screens by adding tap gestures. In *Proceedings of ACM MobileHCI '11*, pages 113–122.

[20] R. Hooke and J. Yonge. *Lectures de Potentia Restitutiva, Or of Spring Explaining the Power of Springing Bodies...* John Martyn, 1931.

[21] S. Hwang, A. Bianchi, and K.-y. Wohn. Vibpress: Estimating pressure input using vibration absorption on mobile devices. In *Proceedings of ACM MobileHCI '13*, pages 31–34, 2013.

[22] S. Hwang and K.-y. Wohn. Pseudobutton: Enabling pressure-sensitive interaction by repurposing microphone on mobile device. In *ACM CHI '12 Extended Abstracts*, pages 1565–1570.

[23] Y.-H. Kim. Sound propagation: An impedance based approach. Wiley, 2010.

[24] G. Laput, E. Brockmeyer, M. Mahler, S. E. Hudson, and C. Harrison. Acoustruments: Passive, acoustically-driven, interactive controls for handheld devices. In *Proceedings ACM CHI '15*.

[25] P. Lazik and A. Rowe. Indoor pseudo-ranging of mobile devices using ultrasonic chirps. In *Proceedings of ACM SenSys '12*, pages 391–392.

[26] Q. Li, J. long Han, and D. jun Wu. Survey on predicting and controlling of structure-borne noise from rail transit bridges. In *Electric Technology and Civil Engineering (ICETCE), 2011 International Conference on*, pages 4559–4563.

[27] S. Low, Y. Sugiura, D. Lo, and M. Inami. Pressure detection on mobile phone by camera and flash. In *Proceedings of ACM AH '14*, pages 11:1–11:4.

[28] H. Lu, W. Pan, N. D. Lane, T. Choudhury, and A. T. Campbell. SoundSense: Scalable Sound Sensing for People-centric Applications on Mobile Phones. In *Proceedings of ACM MobiSys '09*, pages 165–178.

[29] P. Marti and I. Iacono. Evaluating the experience of use of a squeezable interface. In *Proceedings of CHItaly '15*, pages

42–49.

[30] R. Nandakumar, S. Gollakota, and N. Watson. Contactless sleep apnea detection on smartphones. In *Proceedings of ACM MobiSys '15*, pages 45–57.

[31] S. Nirjon, R. F. Dickerson, P. Asare, Q. Li, D. Hong, J. A. Stankovic, P. Hu, G. Shen, and X. Jiang. Auditeur: A mobile-cloud service platform for acoustic event detection on smartphones. In *Proceeding of ACM MobiSys '13*, pages 403–416.

[32] M. Ono, B. Shizuki, and J. Tanaka. Sensing touch force using active acoustic sensing. In *Proceedings of ACM TEI '15*, pages 355–358.

[33] M. Ono, B. Shizuki, and J. Tanaka. Touch & activate: Adding interactivity to existing objects using active acoustic sensing. In *Proceedings of ACM UIST '13*, pages 31–40.

[34] E. W. Pedersen and K. Hornbæk. Expressive touch: Studying tapping force on tabletops. In *Proceedings of ACM CHI '14*, pages 421–430.

[35] C. J. Plack. The sense of hearing. Lawrence Erlbaum Associates, Inc., 2005.

[36] G. Ramos, M. Boulos, and R. Balakrishnan. Pressure widgets. In *Proceedings of CHI '04*, pages 487–494.

[37] S. Salemian, M. Jamshihi, and A. Rafiee. Radar pulse compression techniques. In *Proceedings of WSEAS AEE'05*, pages 203–209.

[38] Y.-C. Tung and K. G. Shin. Echotag: Accurate infrastructure-free indoor location tagging with smartphones. In *Proceedings of ACM MobiCom '15*, pages 525–536.

[39] H. Zheng, J. Mou, W. Lin, and E. Ong. Modeling and prediction of structure-borne seek noise of hard disk drives. *Magnetics, IEEE Transactions on*, 45(11):4933–4936, 2009.

FlashBack: Immersive Virtual Reality on Mobile Devices via Rendering Memoization

Kevin Boos
Rice University
kevinaboos@rice.edu

David Chu
Microsoft Research
davidchu@microsoft.com

Eduardo Cuervo
Microsoft Research
cuervo@microsoft.com

ABSTRACT

Virtual reality head-mounted displays (VR HMDs) are attracting users with the promise of full sensory immersion in virtual environments. Creating the illusion of immersion for a near-eye display results in very heavy rendering workloads: low latency, high framerate, and high visual quality are all needed. Tethered VR setups in which the HMD is bound to a powerful gaming desktop limit mobility and exploration, and are difficult to deploy widely. Products such as Google Cardboard and Samsung Gear VR purport to offer any user a mobile VR experience, but their GPUs are too power-constrained to produce an acceptable framerate and latency, even for scenes of modest visual quality.

We present FLASHBACK, an unorthodox design point for HMD VR that eschews all real-time scene rendering. Instead, FLASHBACK aggressively precomputes and caches all possible images that a VR user might encounter. FLASHBACK memoizes costly rendering effort in an offline step to build a cache full of panoramic images. During runtime, FLASHBACK constructs and maintains a hierarchical storage cache index to quickly lookup images that the user should be seeing. On a cache miss, FLASHBACK uses fast approximations of the correct image while concurrently fetching more closely-matching entries from its cache for future requests. Moreover, FLASHBACK not only works for static scenes, but also for dynamic scenes with moving and animated objects.

We evaluate a prototype implementation of FLASHBACK and report up to a 8× improvement in framerate, 97× reduction in energy consumption per frame, and 15× latency reduction compared to a locally-rendered mobile VR setup. In some cases, FLASHBACK even delivers better framerates and responsiveness than a tethered HMD configuration on graphically complex scenes.

1. INTRODUCTION

Driven by recent advances in the mobile computing hardware ecosystem, wearable Virtual Reality (VR) is experiencing a boom in popularity, with many offerings becoming available. Wearable VR head-mounted displays (HMDs) fall into two device classes: *(i) Tethered HMDs:* HMDs tethered to powerful, expensive gaming desktops, such as the Oculus Rift, HTC Vive, and Sony Playstation VR; *(ii) Mobile-rendered HMDs:* Self-contained, untethered HMDs that run on mobile phones slotted into head mounts, e.g., Google Cardboard and Samsung Gear VR.

However, both device classes present significant drawbacks. Tethered HMDs are capable of rendering rich graphical scenes at high framerates and visual quality, but require significant GPU and compute resources in the form of a dedicated gaming desktop or console co-located with the user. Tethered HMDs obviously limit mobility and come with a high barrier to entry, but also suffer the risk of tethered cords wrapping around a user's neck.

Mobile-rendered HMDs are widely available but suffer from low graphical quality, poor battery life, and uncomfortable thermal radiation, all of which break the illusion of immersion. Mobile GPU rendering can consume up to 20W of peak power [20], making thermal output a safety concern for near-eye devices without active cooling. Limiting mobile GPU power (and thus, performance) is highly undesirable because *(i)* mobile GPUs are already over an order of magnitude slower than desktop GPUs, and *(ii)* a near-eye display exacerbates any performance degradations, often causing motion discomfort or simulator sickness.

In addition, we believe that affordability is vital to widespread VR adoption. Tethered HMDs are clearly cost-prohibitive, but even mobile-rendered HMDs require high-end phones with high-end GPUs. Providing immersive VR experiences on widely available, affordable devices will enable exciting new use cases: virtual field trips for low-income or remote classrooms, enhanced training simulations, medical education and examination, therapeutic rehabilitation, and many more beyond VR gaming [6].

The FLASHBACK Design

In this paper, we present FLASHBACK, a system that overcomes the limitations of both Tethered and Mobile-rendered HMDs to offer a full-quality VR experience on weak mobile devices. FLASHBACK does so by serving *all* of a VR application's high data rate rendering requests from a local cache of pre-rendered HD frames, effectively memoizing prior rendering efforts. We are agnostic as to what machine generates the cache — it could be a dedicated cloud rendering server, a nearby desktop, or the HMD device itself (given plenty of time) — as long as the cached contents can be downloaded to the HMD device before run time.

Precaching avoids the struggle of real-time rendering on a weak mobile GPU while leveraging a prevailing trend among mobile devices: *storage is low-power, increasingly abundant, cheap, and often underutilized*, while graphical processing remains restricted due to thermal and energy constraints. In fact, we show that storage is sufficient to fully cache entire VR scenes.

MobiSys'16, June 25-30, 2016, Singapore, Singapore
© 2016 ACM. ISBN 978-1-4503-4269-8/16/06... $15.00
DOI: http://dx.doi.org/10.1145/2906388.2906418

Moreover, FLASHBACK fundamentally changes how VR applications can be deployed and executed on mobile devices. Instead of running the application binary itself, one simply downloads the application's pre-rendered results (or generates them locally ahead of time) for future use during playback, similar to downloading a movie. However, unlike a movie, the VR experience is *highly* non-linear and interactive.

FLASHBACK builds a three-tier frame cache across GPU video memory (VRAM), system RAM, and secondary storage to store the set of frames needed for a given VR application. The cache is indexed by the player's current *pose*, its 3D position in the environment. As the player moves around, FLASHBACK retrieves and displays a new frame from the cache that matches the updated pose, using a nearest-neighbor algorithm to quickly search the 3D space. Based on R-trees, our index is optimized to quickly return results in GPU memory for immediate display while concurrently fetching better cache entries from deeper in the storage hierarchy for future requests. On a cache miss, FLASHBACK uses cheap and fast approximations of the correct image based on well-established mesh warping techniques from the computer graphics community [25]. We further introduce cache compression techniques to not only fit more cache entries in storage, but also to increase system throughput. Section 4 explains the layout, usage, creation, and compression of the frame cache in greater detail.

In addition to handling a static background scene, FLASHBACK even supports dynamically-moving, animated objects (e.g., a person walking, or *n* cars driving) using a per-object cache data structure. Dynamic object caches are indexed by the object's animation stage, orientation, and relative distance from the player pose for a given time- or movement-based trigger. Unlike the static scene cache, a dynamic object cache stores frames that contain a view of the dynamic object only, allowing FLASHBACK to combine the static frame with multiple dynamic frames using pixel depth metadata embedded in each frame. With support for both static scenes and dynamic objects, FLASHBACK can handle many types of VR applications. Section 5 provides a deeper exploration of dynamic animated objects.

We develop a prototype implementation of FLASHBACK on Windows 10 that supports rendering memoization of VR applications created with Unity, the most popular commercial game and virtual reality creation tool. Our implementation is in three parts: a Unity-side instrumentation suite that automates offline cache generation, a `CacheManager` library that controls local cache contents on the HMD, and a runtime based on DirectX 11 that issues cache queries, composites cache entries into final scenes, and displays rendered content onto the HMD. Our implementation does not require modifying the Unity VR application or the HMD's VR drivers, as described in Section 6.

Finally, we investigate the performance limits of FLASHBACK with a thorough evaluation of our prototype on an Oculus Rift VR headset powered by a weak HP Pavilion Mini device. FLASHBACK achieves up to a 15× reduction in end-to-end latency, an 8× increase in overall framerate, and a 97× reduction in per-frame energy consumption compared with a Mobile-rendered configuration running a complex, fully-fledged VR environment. The graphical quality, framerate, and latency of FLASHBACK are even on par with and sometimes better than that of a strong gaming desktop. We also show that FLASHBACK's cache can scale to large virtual environments and can handle a reasonable number of concurrently visible dynamic objects. Therefore, FLASHBACK is well-positioned to bring immersive VR experiences to mobile devices through its novel rendering memoization techniques.

As VR is a visceral experience better seen than described, we provide a video demonstration of FLASHBACK at [21].

2. BACKGROUND

Basic Operation of a VR System: A modern HMD, like the Oculus Rift, has a variety of internal sensors, e.g., IMUs, that track the player's *pose*, comprised of 3D *position* and 3D *orientation*. Some systems also have external sensors or cameras that track the position of the HMD on the user's face with respect to the surrounding physical room. The display of the HMD is often the same class as those used on smartphones and tablets. HMDs use the tracked position to render the corresponding virtual environment to the display.

Virtual Environment Creation Tools: The virtual environment can be rendered from any computer-generated scene. Commercial virtual environment creation tools are often the same as game creation IDEs, such as Unity and Unreal. These IDEs provide a convenient WYSIWYG way to rapidly construct and script scenes based on pre-existing game objects. We leverage two important properties of these tools. First, they clearly delineate *static objects* from *dynamic objects*. Static objects in the virtual environment do not change. Examples include buildings, terrain, landscape and other immutable objects. A *static scene* consists of all static objects rendered together. Dynamic object examples include vehicles, animals, people, and anything with motion animations. Second, the camera that generates the rendered result is conceptually abstracted from the scene. As a result, it is straightforward to replace a scene's camera with a custom camera, which we do to generate cache entries.

VR as a mobile workload: VR HMD systems place heavy rendering and power demands on computing systems. Modern VR systems target:

- *low latency:* total end-to-end (motion-to-photon) latency of under 25ms, half that of previous VR systems;
- *high framerate:* throughput of at least 60 frames per second (FPS) to ensure smooth playback;
- *scene complexity:* visually rich, photo-realistic scenes.

These requirements are among the most demanding for consumer mobile applications. In the temporal dimension, the latency and framerate requirements derive from the fact that we are physiologically very sensitive to lag in near-eye displays because the human visual and vestibular sensory systems are tightly coupled. Even minor motion-to-photon latency can induce oscilloscopia (the sensation that your view and vestibular signals are mismatched), and eventually motion sickness [7, 23, 4]. While classic studies found tolerance thresholds of 50ms (which coincided with measurement resolution) [3], more recent anecdotal evidence suggests that 10-20ms is a better target, depending upon the scene and user [26].

In the spatial domain, *scene complexity* refers to substantive detail in a graphical scene, such as rich geometry and texture detail. A near-eye display intensifies the importance of scene complexity because the HMD's pixels are mere centimeters from the eye and magnified on the retina; thus, graphical detail (or lack thereof) becomes immediately more noticeable. Delivering photo-realistic scenes requires substantial GPU processing capabilities.

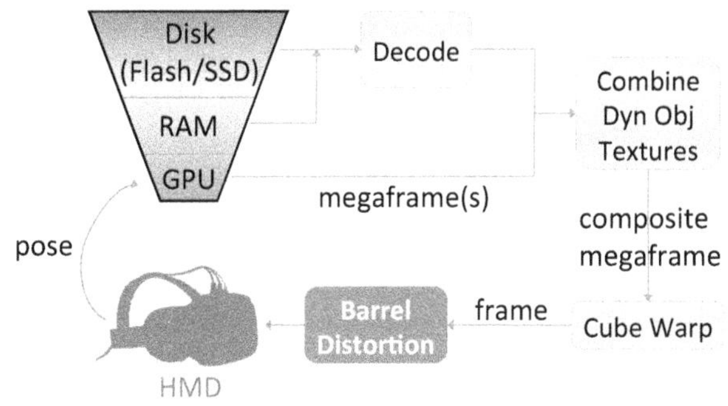

Figure 1: FLASHBACK runtime operation. FLASHBACK uses the HMD pose to query the cache and decode the retrieved megaframe if necessary, then it combines that static megaframe with any dynamic object megaframes, and finally warps the megaframe into a single final frame for the HMD.

The core challenge facing an untethered mobile HMD system such as FLASHBACK is to provide all of the above properties — low latency, high framerate and graphical quality — simultaneously at low power. Unfortunately, in Mobile-endered (and even Tethered) HMDs, latency and high framerate are at odds with resolution and scene complexity: striving for higher quality scenes impinges upon latency and framerate, and vice versa.

3. SYSTEM OVERVIEW

Figure 1 depicts the high-level operation of FLASHBACK, from sampled input to displayed output. First, the current player *pose* is read in from the HMD driver, comprising *position* and view *orientation*. The position is the location of the player in 3D world space; the view orientation is a rotation vector that represents where the player is looking.

FLASHBACK then finds and reads multiple cache entries that are needed for the user's view. One of these cache entries corresponds to the static scene and the other entries correspond to the dynamic objects in the scene. The cache lookup encompasses GPU memory, system memory, and non-volatile secondary storage, with varying levels of access speed. We optimize this lookup with cache indexing (Section 4.4) and cache compression (Section 4.3). When required, entries are pulled from higher to lower levels of the cache hierarchy, evicting older entries. The matched cache entries are then composited into a final view.

Upon a cache miss, instead of rendering the correct view in real time, we synthesize an approximation of the correct view from available cache entries with a computer graphics technique known as mesh warping (Section 4.5). Warping is two orders of magnitude faster than rendering. Most importantly, unlike rendering, warping speed is not dependent on scene complexity; it is only a fixed function of the screen resolution and runs efficiently even on mobile GPUs. As a result, the scene can have arbitrarily complex visual detail and effects, yet warping speed remains constant.

As a final step, the HMD device driver performs lens-offsetting barrel distortion and displays the final frame to the screen. The components of this entire process are the main contributors to the system's end-to-end motion-to-photon latency, so we strive to make them as efficient and performant as possible.

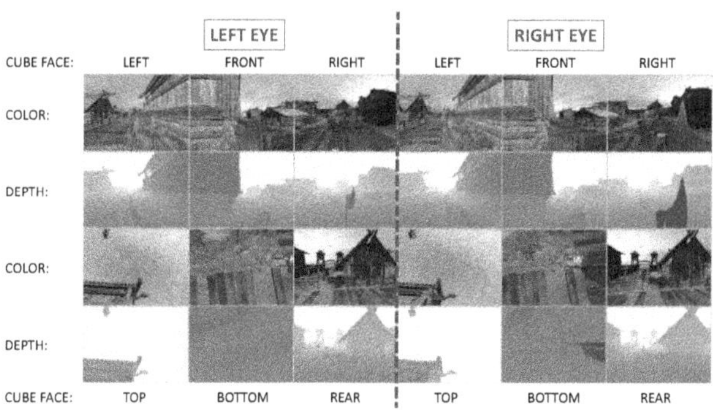

Figure 2: Each cache entry contains a megaframe. The twenty-four faces of the megaframe represent the left and right eye cube maps for RGB color and depth.

4. CACHE ORGANIZATION

In this section, we describe the overall design of FLASHBACK's rendering memoization mechanism, its cache structure and behavior, and optimizations for scalability and performance of static scenes.

4.1 A Single Cache Entry: The Megaframe

Each entry of the cache consists of a high resolution *megaframe* as shown in Figure 2. A megaframe is defined with respect to a pose $\mathbf{p} = ((x, y, z), (\theta, \phi, \psi))$. The parameters (x, y, z) represent the position in 3D world coordinates. The parameters (θ, ϕ, ψ) represent the orientation (sometimes referred to as rotation) as a Euler angle comprising yaw, pitch, and roll, respectively. With appropriate warping (Section 4.5), the megaframe allows us to reconstruct nearby views that are translated or rotated with respect to the megaframe's pose.

Internally, a megaframe is composed of four *cube maps*. A cube map is a classic computer graphics 360° representation of an environment [14]. The cube map draws a panoramic image on the six sides of a cube, with the centerpoint of the cube being the current pose. The four cube maps in a single megaframe include:

- Left eye color (RGB) cube map,
- Left eye depth cube map,
- Right eye color (RGB) cube map, and
- Right eye depth cube map.

The left and right eye cube maps exist separately in order to generate a proper stereo view. Their positions are each offset from the megaframe's pose by half the inter-pupillary distance (IPD), which is a user-specific anatomical property that represents the distance between human eyes. The depth cube maps are not necessary for representing the RGB pixel content of the scene, but are useful during the warping step. All four cube maps in every megaframe are stored consistently at a fixed, canonical orientation looking straight ahead, i.e., $(\theta, \phi, \psi) = (0, 0, 0)$. With four cube maps and six faces per cube, the megaframe consists of 24 faces, as illustrated in the megaframe layout of Figure 2.

4.2 Cache Layout and Hierarchy

Figure 3 provides a visualization of how the cache is laid out in logical 3D space. The megaframes conceptually occupy the 3D point matching the pose at which they were rendered; as a

Figure 3: Logical layout of megaframes. Each cube represents a megaframe's cache index visualized in 3D space. Arrows depict the distance from the closest few megaframes to the current pose query, represented by the camera icon.

player (camera icon) moves throughout the environment, it becomes closer to certain cubes and further from others. Distance is defined with respect to the position difference in Euclidean space. It is not necessary to consider orientation differences since megaframe cube maps are panoramic; in fact, cube maps inherently contain all possible orientations for a given position.

In terms of physical layout in memory or on storage, FLASHBACK builds a three-tier cache of megaframes, depicted in Figure 1 as an inverted triangle consisting of GPU VRAM as L1, system RAM as L2, and persistent secondary storage, like SSD or Flash, as L3. Although the size of each tier in Figure 1 is not to scale, GPU VRAM is the smallest, followed by a larger-sized RAM, and finally a massive secondary storage unit. Current mobile SoCs have GPU VRAMs statically allocated from system memory, typically a few hundred MBs on integrated chips. System RAM is usually 0.5–2GB (excluding GPU VRAM carve out). Secondary storage sizes of flash can be up to several hundred GBs. SSDs, a composition of multiple flash chips, can be thousands of GBs. While SSDs are not common on mobile devices today, they are worth consideration as they provide a point of extrapolation for future device storage trends. As such, a moderate number of megaframes are on the GPU VRAM, while all other megaframes are relegated to the other two layers.

We initially considered how the physical storage layout of cached frames would affect performance, believing that retrieving a cached frame from disk could incur a substantial and unpredictable latency penalty due to random reads with poor locality. However, as demonstrated in §7, decoder latency (explained below) dominates storage read latency by 2-3 orders of magnitude. Therefore, we find it unnecessary to optimize the cache's on-disk layout.

4.3 Cache Compression

Cache compression provides for better performance and spatial efficiency. Were we to store megaframes in a raw, uncompressed format, we would rapidly saturate the data transfer bandwidth between stages [9], as megaframes must be passed between GPU VRAM and system RAM. Saturation leads to low framerates and high latency. Note that even though GPU and system memory share the same physical memory banks in mobile SoCs, data transfer between the two still entails data copy because of format incompatibility and pointer swizzling. Therefore, we elect to store megaframes in a compressed format (equivalent to a single-frame H.264 video) when in system memory and stable storage. We only decompress frames in GPU memory when they are most likely to be displayed to the user. For efficiency, we leverage the dedicated hardware H.264 decoder available in all modern devices (typically used for video playback).

Another benefit of storing encoded frames on stable storage is that each cache entry is smaller in size. As an example, a decoded 4k texture consumes over 8MB of memory, but encoding that texture reduces it to under 100KB, allowing FLASHBACK to maintain vastly larger caches.

Even with frame compression at the L2 and L3 layer, the performance gap between L1 access and L2 or L3 access is large, as demonstrated in Section 7. This is because decoding frames still takes time, even with a dedicated hardware-accelerated decoder. On balance, trading data transfer time for decompression time and an increase in the maximum number of cache entries is an important part of the FLASHBACK design.

4.4 Cache Lookup and Indexing

FLASHBACK appoints a `CacheManager` to control the behavior of the cache and the flow or eviction of megaframes between different cache levels. The `CacheManager`'s primary function is to accept a request in the form of a `CacheKey` (`CK`) structure, containing player pose, and return a `CacheValue` (`CV`) structure containing a reference to a retrieved megaframe, decoding it if necessary. The arrows in Figure 3 show the Euclidean distance vectors used to locate the closest matching megaframe cube for a given requested `CK` pose.

We realize this querying semantic via a *nearest-neighbor search* using R-trees [17]. The R-tree algorithm constructs a set of minimally-overlapping bounding boxes that each contain subsets of points (in our case, the megaframe positions) in the 3D space, helping to rapidly eliminate large portions of the search space. When the correct box is located, the algorithm calculates the distance from each existing point to the target point (the desired pose's position) and selects the closest one. We choose R-trees because they support: *(i)* fast lookup; *(ii)* queries across storage hierarchies, better than other nearest-neighbor indexes like quad-trees and kd-trees, and *(iii)* good support for insertions and deletions.

We design our use of R-trees in such a way that whenever we receive a new pose request, we can always immediately return a megaframe result from the GPU cache for display. At the same time, if there is an even closer megaframe that exists in either L2 or L3 cache, it is fetched asynchronously to the GPU such that it is available to service future pose requests, taking advantage of temporal locality. As such, the notion of a cache miss refers to the requested megaframe not having an identical match in the GPU cache.

To support this goal, we use a dual R-tree data structure. Specifically, we maintain two distinct R-trees: a *GPU R-tree* and a *universal R-tree*. The GPU R-tree only indexes cache entries that are currently resident in the GPU cache, whereas the universal R-tree indexes all cache entries across all three storage levels. A pose request is issued to both the GPU R-tree and universal R-tree in parallel. The nearest neighbor megaframe in the GPU R-tree is returned immediately for display. The nearest neighbor megaframe in the universal R-tree is also looked up. If it is the same as the megaframe returned from the GPU R-tree, no further action is taken. If it differs, it is then transferred from secondary storage (if it was on L3, from RAM if L2) and then decoded to L1 asynchronously. When a new megaframe is decoded, it is inserted into the GPU R-tree and updated in the universal R-tree.

FLASHBACK's CV structure must be kept to a minimal size because there are potentially millions of instances, one for every cached megaframe. A CV holds a pointer to either a file location on persistent storage (L3), byte array in system memory (L2), or raw texture on GPU VRAM (L1), depending on which cache level it resides. In fact, a CV can exist in multiple cache levels simultaneously, offering redundancy if the CV must be evicted from VRAM or RAM cache to relieve memory pressure. Since our cache contents are read-only, we never need to write back cache entries into stable storage. Furthermore, cache eviction is simply a matter of removing a cache entry from the index, a fast operation for R-trees.

4.5 Cache Miss and Approximate Results

An embedded assumption in FLASHBACK is that every possible rendering request can be served by cached contents in one of the cache layers. Of course, even plentiful stable storage is finite. Therefore, in order to handle cache misses, we reuse nearby cached entries to approximate the desired result. This allows us to substantially increase FLASHBACK's effective cache hit rate.

However, naïvely substituting a view centered at pose $\mathbf{p}$ in lieu of a desired view at pose $\mathbf{p}'$ results in a poor experience with uncomfortable visual stuttering. Therefore, we apply a mesh warp to the megaframe at $\mathbf{p}$ in order to derive an appropriate view for $\mathbf{p}'$. Mesh warping is a classic technique from the family of computer graphics techniques known as Image-Based Rendering (IBR) [25]. We explain the mechanics, limitations, and advantages of mesh warp below.

Given an RGB cube map and matching depth cube map both at pose $\mathbf{p}$ (say, of the left eye), we can generate a novel view v' as if it had been taken from a new pose $\mathbf{p}'$. At a high level, each pixel of the original view is mapped to a 3D position (since $\mathbf{p}$ and the depth map are known), and then the 3D position is reprojected to a pixel in the new view (since $\mathbf{p}'$ is known). The final view v' resolution is proportional to the size of the megaframe. Assuming a typical HMD field of view (106° height, 94° width), a 4k megaframe (3840×2160) generates 720p final view frames (1280×720).

However, if translation is too great (i.e., the position of $\mathbf{p}$ and the position of $\mathbf{p}'$ are too far apart) then v' will suffer from *visual artifacts* such as disocclusions. Imagine looking at an open doorway and then stepping forward; from the original view, it is unclear what should appear in the disoccluded "holes" that are now visible. This suggests that we may desire additional cube maps to handle translations that are beyond a threshold, which is precisely what our additional megaframes provide. On the other hand, since our cube map covers a panoramic view, mesh warping is robust to arbitrary changes in rotation without introducing artifacts.

4.6 Populating the Cache

We now discuss how FLASHBACK actually generates the megaframes that will occupy the cache. These frames are generated offline, either on the mobile device itself (given enough time) or alternatively downloaded much like a video file from a desktop computer or powerful rendering server in the cloud. Deploying a dataset as large as the megaframe cache from a cloud server to the mobile device seems prohibitive at first, but is in actuality quite tractable due to the cache's extremely high compressability. The cache can be greatly compressed on the server due to adjacent megaframes having largely identical blocks, and then decompressed (decoded) on the mobile device in an ahead-of-time cache unpacking step.

Logically, FLASHBACK performs a 3D grid sweep across the virtual space constituting the static scene. At each grid point, FLASHBACK captures a panoramic stereo image of the world and writes this to a cube map. It does this again for depth, and then composites the corresponding megaframe. The megaframe is then encoded as an individual key frame (I-frame) using the H.264 codec. Finally, FLASHBACK writes the encoded megaframe to secondary storage with a unique identifier linking back to the pose from which it was generated. This fully-automated procedure repeats for every possible pose in the environment, which is potentially n^3 combinations due to the three dimensions of the pose's position value. The density of the grid, or *quantization*, impacts both the final cache size and the visual artifacts encountered during the warping approximation, as well as latency and framerate. We found that a virtual grid density between 0.02 and 0.05 virtual-world units offers a good trade-off between unnoticeable visual artifacts and cache size (§8).

Furthermore, we can aggressively cull the set of possible pose values based on the geometry and restricted movement paths of the environment. For example, for a virtual environment in which the player walks on the ground, we can limit the potential height values to a smaller range, e.g., five to seven feet above the ground. This technique significantly reduces the pose state space by eliminating impossible values, such as being underground or inside of a solid wall. Thus, while the worst case complexity of generating the megaframe cache is $O(n^3)$, the typical case is much less.

5. HANDLING DYNAMIC OBJECTS

In addition to caching the static environment's megaframes, FLASHBACK supports dynamic objects complete with freeform motion paths and animations. Dynamic object caching extends the base semantics of static caching with a more complex cache key structure and querying procedure.

5.1 Generating the Dynamic Object Cache

Rendering memoization for dynamic objects involves a procedure similar to that of static scenes. Offline, FLASHBACK iterates over the input space and renders megaframes. However, instead of only iterating over possible positions, dynamic objects have more dimensions: position, orientation, and animations. This results in a massive input space for each object, but fortunately it can be pruned along all three dimensions.

Capturing Dynamic Object Megaframes

We now describe the full procedure for populating a dynamic object's cache. As a preprocessing step, we extract and treat each dynamic object independently by placing it in an otherwise empty virtual world. This is important for megaframe composition free from side effects, described in Section 5.3 below.

Next, we iterate over all possible values along the position, orientation and animation dimensions in a set of nested loops. The outer loop is position. This position value consists of the same 3D point format but has a different semantic meaning from a static

Figure 4: FLASHBACK caches dynamic objects by rendering a megaframe from all possible relative player positions and viewing angles, depicted here as camera icons. This repeats for all object animations and rotations.

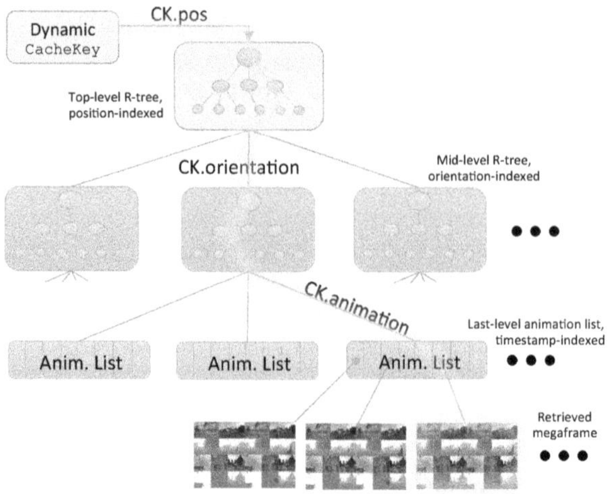

Figure 5: Nested R-Trees for Retrieval of Dynamic Objects. Dynamic objects are indexed by relative position (top-level R-tree), orientation (nested R-trees), and animation stages (simple lists).

megaframe's position: it is the position of the player *relative* to that of the object, which is calculated by the Euclidean distance between the object position and the player camera position. We prune the position dimension in the same way as for static frames: the dynamic object is only visible to the player from a limited geographical area (e.g., distance). It is important to understand that the position value used for dynamic objects is *not* the physical location of the dynamic object itself in world space, but rather the position of the player relative to the dynamic object. This vastly reduces the position-dimension state space. For example, when the player stands 5 meters north (in a bird's-eye view) of the dynamic object, this configuration results in the same player view of that object no matter the absolute position of the two bodies in the virtual environment.

The next inner loop iterates over all possible values along the orientation dimension. Just like the player, a dynamic object can have its own view orientation, commonly referred to as the object's rotation. We prune the orientation dimension according to both the potential player viewpoints as well as the possible rotations of the object itself. For example, if the object rotates along the vertical y-axis only, a very common behavior for animated objects, we only need to iterate over angles in the y direction.

The final inner loop iterates over all possible *animation stages* in the object's animation sequence. There are up to as many stages as there are frames in the animation sequence; stages can be a downsampling of the number of frames in the animation. For example, the horse-drawn cart in Figure 4, which is a professionally produced dynamic object with animations, has a detailed "trotting" animation sequence, but we were able to represent it as a periodically repeating set of 36 stages with no loss in animation fidelity. If an object has multiple animation sequences (e.g., walking, running, or standing), the procedure is repeated for every sequence.

Capturing Dynamic Object Pose Traces

In order to know which megaframe should be used for a dynamic object at a given point in time, FLASHBACK records a *pose trace* of the dynamic object during offline playback of the original VR application. This trace defines the object's motion path and stage in the animation sequence for a given timestamp. Note that this means dynamic objects appear deterministically based on the timeline. For example, a horse always trots along the same path in the virtual environment, independent of where the user is positioned or looking. Future work includes extending the cache index to support different dynamic object behavior based on the player's actions and pose.

5.2 Dynamic Object Index and Lookup

The query execution for dynamic object caches is a two-step process. First, the object's pose trace is queried using the current timestamp to determine at what view orientation and animation stage that object should appear.

Once the dynamic object pose descriptor is acquired, step two is to query the actual megaframe cache using a *dynamic cache key* (dynamic `CK`), consisting of the pose descriptor from the trace in step one (orientation and animation) and the relative player position. The dynamic `CK` consists of 7 values: a 3D position vector, 3D orientation vector, and scalar animation stage.

While it is possible to construct a 7 dimension R-tree, it would suffer because a high-dimension data structure is ill-suited for use with spatial indexing algorithms. Instead, we construct a *nested R-tree* as shown in Figure 5 that reduces the R-tree to 3 dimensions at most. It consists of a top-level R-tree indexed by position (similar to the universal R-tree for static scenes). However, instead of its leaf nodes pointing to megaframes, each leaf node points to a second-level R-tree indexed by orientation; there are n such orientation R-trees, one for each node in the position R-tree. Finally, each leaf node of the orientation R-tree points to a simple list that maps a timestamp to an animation stage pointer. Finally, the animation stage pointer points to a megaframe that was captured with the corresponding 7-tuple.

The logic behind the nesting ordering of position, orientation and animation stage is that it prioritizes position distance. Suddenly seeing a large translation jump in a dynamic object will throw off the player's inner balance more so than seeing that object at an unexpected rotation angle or a strange animation frame.

To execute a query, the `CacheManager` first queries the top-level (position-indexed) R-tree using the relative position value to obtain a reference to the mid-level R-tree of orientation indices.

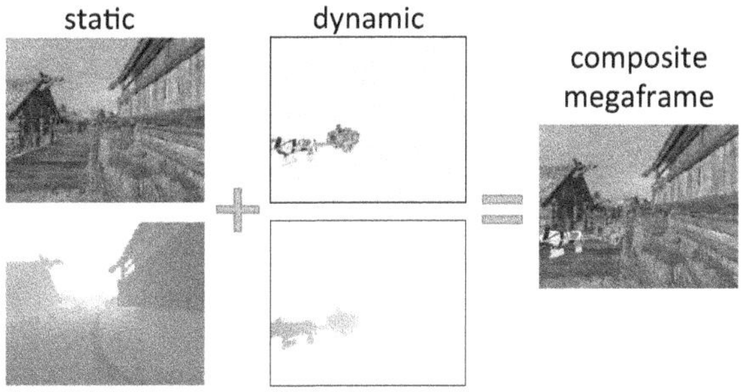

Figure 6: Compositing Dynamic Objects With Static Scenes. Croppings of the megaframes (a single cube face) for one static scene and one dynamic object are shown.

It then queries that mid-level R-tree using the dynamic object's current orientation to obtain a reference to the lowest level list of animation frame sequences, which is finally indexed using the animation stage timestamp to obtain the actual megaframe that best matches the dynamic CK's values.

5.3 Compositing Dynamic Objects

Once a megaframe has been retrieved for every visible dynamic object, all of their megaframes along with the static scene megaframe are overlaid into a single composite megaframe. Recall that each megaframe includes not only the cube faces representing the actual scene pixels, but also the depth values for each pixel (see Figure 2). We utilize these depth values in a pixel shader to determine which objects should occlude other objects and components of the static scene, and vice versa. Therefore, FLASHBACK can support a complex layering of both dynamic and static objects, e.g., placing a sprite in front of one building but behind another. An illustrative example is shown in Figure 6. After composition is complete, the composite megaframe is handed off to the cube map warp routine to construct the final view.

5.4 Look-ahead Decoding

When we have idle decode cycles (e.g., when many requests are hitting the GPU cache), it is worthwhile from an energy and performance perspective to speculate on which megaframes will be requested in the near future. That way, we can preemptively decode the chosen megaframes and have them ready on GPU VRAM by the time they are needed. We employ a relatively straightforward speculation mechanism that looks n frame periods into the future (e.g., 5 frames from now) by reading n future values of the dynamic object's pose trace. FLASHBACK then instructs the CacheManager to lookup those n future megaframes and decode as many as time permits.

Though this is particularly well-suited for dynamic objects due to their predictable motion pattern known ahead of time, we can also apply it to the static scene by speculating on the player's movement. This turns out to be less successful than for dynamic objects (§7) because it relies on accurately predicting the user's future pose, which has much more uncertainty than deterministic dynamic object poses [22].

5.5 Limitations of Dynamic Objects

As FLASHBACK composites the pixel representation of dynamic objects, it is more limited than general rendering.

Lighting Models: Our approach cannot support certain lighting models and special effects for dynamic objects: these include scene-dependent lighting and reflections. For example, if the appearance of a dynamic object depends on where it is relative to the scene's light sources, our caching mechanism will fail to capture the object's lighting variations. These limitations stem from the fact that we construct the cache entries for the dynamic object in isolation from the static scene. It is conceivable that the cache can also be augmented to include indexing by relative light source positions and orientations, much like it is already indexed by relative player pose. We leave this as future work.

Scalability: FLASHBACK's technique for handling dynamic objects has unique scalability properties; we quantify and explain its behavior in Section 8.2.

6. IMPLEMENTATION

Our prototype implementation of FLASHBACK runs on Windows 10 using the Oculus Rift DK2 HMD. It is powered by a weak HP Mini computer equivalent in compute and GPU power to a mid-range smartphone (§7). Our implementation is in three parts: the Unity cache generator that automates the rendering memoization process, the CacheManager on the HMD, and the lightweight playback client on the HMD.

Unity-side Cache Generation: We implement Unity-side cache generation by adding a special array of rendering cameras that automatically generate megaframes. A series of scripts coordinate the camera behavior with the automated pose enumeration (§5.1), which can be either manually bounded or automatically inferred based on the collision boxes and environment geometry of the Unity application. Every megaframe is encoded with an external ffmpeg toolchain and saved to cache storage. In total, we package 3900 lines of C# code into a Unity *prefab* that simplifies the incorporation of our caching scripts down to a simple drag-and-drop import operation. Thus, any Unity game or VR application can be quickly and easily transformed to work with FLASHBACK.

CacheManager: We implement the CacheManager, including all querying, organization, and handling of cached megaframes, with approximately 1200 lines of C++ code. In addition to the functions described in Sections 4 and 5, the CacheManager provides raw megaframes to the playback program for display, meaning that it must handle decoding. The CacheManager is also responsible for parsing the cache contents from storage. Because FLASHBACK's caches can scale to very large proportions, parsing them must also perform well at scale. Iterating through every cached file is prohibitively slow, so FLASHBACK creates a special index file for each cache instance once the cache is fully generated, enabling the playback program to bypass the parsing process altogether. Instead, it memory maps or reads each index file directly into a pre-allocated R-tree instance, using an *initial packing algorithm* to create the whole R-tree in one batch, offering better query performance as a side benefit.

Lightweight Playback Program: The cache population procedure effectively flattens a VR application's complex behavior into a collection of data structures on storage. As such, the program needed to "play" the application on the mobile device is relatively simple. We develop a reference implementation of the playback program atop a remote desktop client framework with skeleton

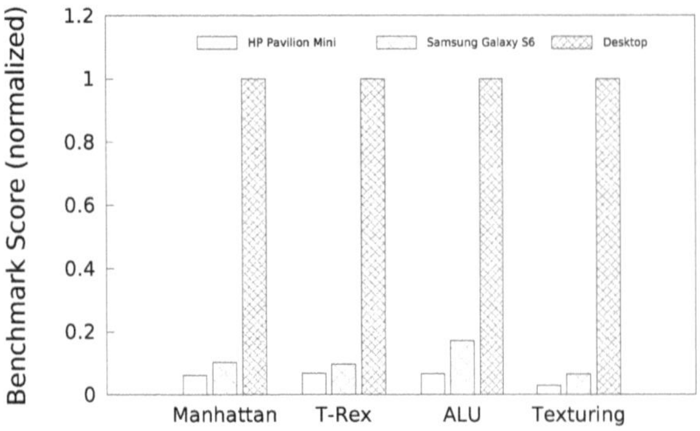

Figure 7: Four GFXBench benchmarks across three devices demonstrate that the HP Pavilion Mini is less capable than a Galaxy S6, and that both devices are an order of magnitude weaker than a VR-capable desktop [1].

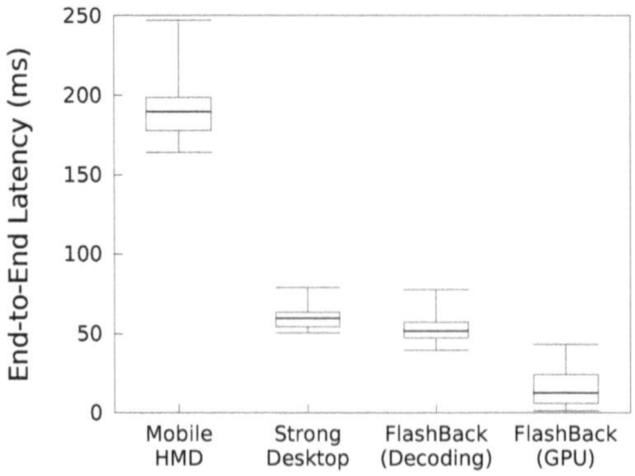

Figure 8: FLASHBACK achieves an end-to-end latency up to 15X shorter than a weak mobile device rendering locally, with worst-case latency no higher than that of a gaming desktop.

code for decoding and displaying VNC-like screenshots. The playback program is responsible for initializing and interfacing with the `CacheManager`, reading pose information from the HMD driver, and driving the display with frames obtained from the `CacheManager`.

Due to its simplicity, our playback program is wholly application agnostic; the single executable can play any memoized VR application without modification or recompilation. To switch between different VR applications, one simply redirects the program to a different set of data structures.

7. EVALUATION

We evaluate FLASHBACK's ability to improve the framerate and reduce the end-to-end latency and energy consumption of full-quality VR applications on mobile devices, using a combination of macrobenchmarks (§7.2) and microbenchmarks (§7.3).

7.1 Setup and Methodology

As mentioned in Section 6, we use the HP Pavilion 300-030 Mini as our mobile device that powers an Oculus Rift DK2 HMD. The HP Mini is a small, weak computer equipped with a mobile-class Intel HD 4400 GPU, an Intel i3 1.9GHz dual-core processor, 4GB of RAM, and a 240GB OCZ Arc 100 SSD. This setup is compatible with our existing Windows-based software stack, and as Figure 7 shows, is a suitable approximation for the state-of-the-art Samsung Galaxy S6 Gear VR mobile HMD, with HP Mini being outperformed by the Gear VR in all benchmarks. Similarly, the OCZ ARC SSD that we used presents sequential and random read speeds approximately equivalent to that of the Galaxy S6's secondary storage [33].

We evaluated FLASHBACK with Viking Village [2], a demanding virtual-world Unity application designed for high-end desktop PCs, with complex scenes that exceed the capabilities of current mobile devices. We augmented Viking Village to support virtual reality and generate megaframes; a 4K (3840x2160) megaframe allows our prototype to display 720p final frames on the HMD. We measured energy consumption on the mobile device using a P3 P4460 Kill-A-Watt Electricity Usage Monitor.

7.2 Macrobenchmarks

We evaluate FLASHBACK's real-world performance with assessments of four target objectives: *(i)* low end-to-end latency, *(ii)* high framerate, *(iii)* good visual quality, and *(iv)* low energy consumption. The following sections demonstrate that FLASHBACK compares favorably to locally rendering the VR application on both a strong desktop PC and a weak mobile device.

FLASHBACK achieves low end-to-end latency

Figure 8 demonstrates the low end-to-end latency of FLASHBACK compared to other systems. This represents the elapsed time from when the latest pose is received from the HMD until when the frame corresponding to that pose is sent to the display. It does not include the latency contributed by the input subsystem and the display hardware, as FLASHBACK has no impact on these difficult-to-measure components; those latencies are equally present when VR applications execute locally and therefore do not affect the contributions of our work.

As shown in Figure 8, FLASHBACK achieves a median end-to-end latency of 12.4ms for GPU cache hits. FLASHBACK can achieve such low latency on a GPU hit because the player pose can be sampled *right before* choosing a texture to display. Even when the requested megaframe is absent from the GPU cache and must be retrieved and decoded, FLASHBACK still incurs lower end-to-end latency than a strong desktop PC.

FLASHBACK delivers high framerates

Figure 9 presents a framerate comparison of three different VR configurations running Viking Village: local rendering on our mobile device (HP Mini), local rendering on a strong desktop PC, and FLASHBACK on the HP Mini. For a truly immersive experience, it is necessary for the system hardware running the VR application to deliver as high a framerate as the HMD supports. Figure 9 indicates that a mobile device's capabilities are insufficient to deliver a satisfactory framerate when locally rendering on a demanding VR application. In contrast, our unoptimized FLASHBACK prototype delivers a framerate 8× higher than a mobile device and even exceeds that of a desktop PC with a high-end GPU. On a GPU hit for a static scene, FLASHBACK's framerate is limited not by our system but by the hardware refresh rate limitations of the display on the Oculus Rift DK2. We note

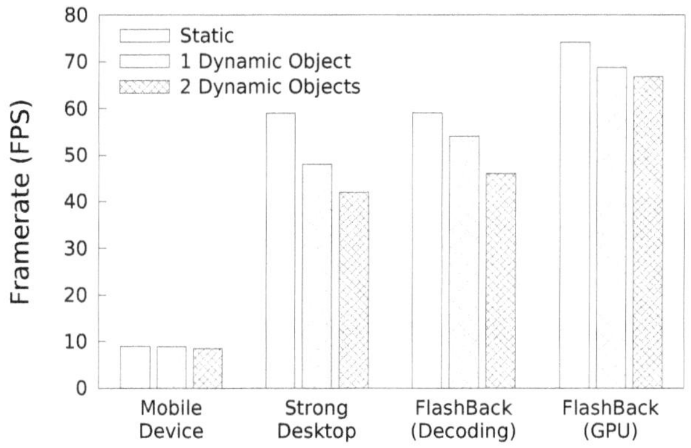

Figure 9: FLASHBACK delivers framerates up to 8X higher than a mobile HMD rendering locally.

VR implementation	Visual Quality
Standalone mobile device	0.81
FLASHBACK	0.932

Table 1: SSIM metrics showing that FLASHBACK does not negatively affect visual quality, delivering great image quality at much higher framerates. An SSIM of 1.0 indicates perfect image fidelity, and values above 0.9 are very good [12].

that the performance of FLASHBACK decreases with more visible dynamic objects, which we discuss and quantify in Section 8.2.

FLASHBACK offers higher visual quality

Thus far, we have used the term *visual quality* loosely; now we provide a more rigorous definition. *Structural Similarity (SSIM)* [34] score is a standard criterion from the video compression community used to quantify the perceived loss in video quality between a pristine image f^* and a distorted version of that image, f. For example, the images f^* and f might represent the same scene rendered with a High graphics setting and a Low graphics setting, respectively. The function $SSIM_{f^*}(f)$ outputs a real value in $[0, 1]$, where a lower values indicates lower fidelity to the pristine image. By definition, $SSIM_{f^*}(f^*) = 1$ and $SSIM_{f^*}(f) = 0$ when f is random noise. While SSIM is not perfect representation of human quality assessment, it is more accurate than alternative measures such as SNR and PSNR, and maps reasonably to the standard subjective measure for video quality based on user studies, Mean Opinion Score [34].

SSIM extends from still images to video in a straightforward way: a frame-by-frame comparison of a pristine video v^* against a distorted video v, with each frame's $SSIM$ scores averaged to obtain an overall score. In our case, v^* is the pristine video generated by our high-end desktop PC tethered to the HMD, and v is the video generated and displayed by FLASHBACK.

Table 1 shows FLASHBACK's effect on Viking Village's visual quality using SSIM. We recorded a trace of head movements and replayed it on our FLASHBACK prototype to obtain v^*, and again on a stock Viking Village implementation to obtain v. Figure 10 shows a side-by-side comparison of two sample frames as outputted by Viking Village and FLASHBACK. Due to an inalterable Oculus SDK difference between Viking Village and our implementation of FLASHBACK, the images are rendered with slightly different pose values, resulting in a minor translation-only pixel misalignment. This difference stems from a Unity-specific implementation of the Oculus library that is unavailable outside of Unity and is not unique to Viking Village. We correct this alignment issue with Hugin [27], a well-known panoramic stitching tool that we configure to crop each unaligned image to the same aligned bounds. We restrict Hugin to simply shift and crop the images by a few pixels, disabling stretching, re-projection, or warping of any kind. Configured as such, Hugin does not alter the quality of either image nor unfairly affects the SSIM test results.

Figure 10: Sample frames outputted at the same trace pose (post-alignment), used as SSIM inputs. The left frame is the pristine image (f^*) from stock Viking Village. The right frame (f) represents a worst-case GPU cache miss in FLASHBACK, demonstrating the quality of our graphical warp.

We found that FLASHBACK does not adversely affect visual quality, but rather achieves a higher SSIM score while delivering a much higher framerate; it also does not significantly degrade the quality as compared to stock Viking Village. Our prototype of FLASHBACK obtained a median SSIM score of 0.932 with a standard deviation of 0.015, which falls within the "great quality" threshold of the SSIM scale [34, 12]. In order to be as critical of FLASHBACK as possible, we chose to compare undistorted eye textures instead of the final frame displayed on the HMD. Eye textures are rendered at a much higher resolution than the final frame and thus represent the worst-case degradation due to FLASHBACK. On the other hand, the standalone mobile device rendering Viking Village locally obtained a poor SSIM score of 0.81, falling beneath the 0.86 threshold of "visually acceptable" [34, 12].

FLASHBACK significantly improves energy efficiency

We evaluate FLASHBACK to exemplify the energy-saving benefits of rendering memoization. Figure 11 shows that FLASHBACK consumes significantly less energy — under 250mJ per frame — than local execution on both a mobile device and desktop PC. As a frame of reference, the HP system has a minimum power consumption of 6.6W when idling with the screen on, and a maximum consumption of 28W under full utilization. Energy-efficient VR playback enables FLASHBACK to run longer on an untethered mobile HMD, providing a more immersive VR experience.

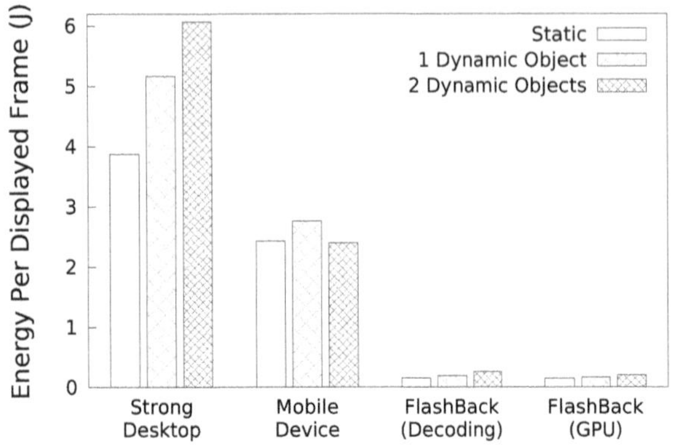

Figure 11: FLASHBACK significantly reduces the energy consumed per frame displayed even when a frame must be decoded first. Desktop measurements were conducted on a different, less energy-efficient machine.

7.3 Microbenchmarks

We now characterize the behavior of FLASHBACK with the following microbenchmarks that test query scalability to large-size caches and retrieval performance of the cache.

Cache Scalability and Performance

To determine whether the performance and scalability of FLASHBACK's frame cache satisfies the requirements of demanding VR applications like Viking Village, we designed several microbenchmarks with caches of different sizes. Figure 12a plots the median lookup time to query the cache using our universal R-tree, where all cache values are indexed at a single hierarchical level. Therefore, locating (not retrieving) a cached frame in RAM is equally as fast as locating one on disk or GPU. Figure 12a also shows that FLASHBACK's additional GPU R-tree lookup will always have a very low query time, because the on-GPU cache never exceeds a few hundred entries due to limited VRAM.

We present the cache retrieval performance from the three different sources in our current FLASHBACK implementation: the disk, system memory, and the GPU. Figure 12b shows the retrieval results for 4k megaframes. A GPU cache hit is very fast, taking less time than a vsync refresh interval. In fact, this is the reason that FLASHBACK's performance on a GPU hit is limited not by the cache itself but by the HMD's refresh rate. On the other hand, the cost of retrieving from memory and the disk is higher because the cache entry must first be decoded, the bottleneck in both cases.

Typical Cache Storage Requirements

We present in Figure 12c the cache storage size necessary to support a virtual environment of varying dimensions and complexities using our preferred quantization of 0.02 virtual-world units. As discussed in Section 4.6, the size of the static cache depends not only on the range of possible position values but also on the granularity with which we quantize the virtual environment. At this quantization granularity, while not modest, our requirements for a complex VR environment like Viking Village can fit well within the flash storage of a modern smartphone; this can be reduced significantly with selective post-deployment decompression (§4.6). In addition, while our preferred granularity is 0.02, for some users, the visual inconsistencies introduced by a granularity of up to 0.05 or 0.1 may be too small to distinguish, further reducing FLASHBACK storage requirements vastly.

8. DISCUSSION

In this sections, we discuss unique aspects of FLASHBACK's behavior and characterize its limitations with both quantitative and qualitative analyses.

8.1 Cache Hit Ratios

In FLASHBACK, latency is heavily determined by cache hit ratios. As our evaluation has shown, the performance of FLASHBACK on a GPU hit is much higher than on misses due to decoding. While it is difficult to provide hard numbers for cache hit ratios with VR being a novelty in the consumer market, we can provide estimates. The average effective latency L_{avg} is given by the following equation:

$$L_{avg} = (hit\%) \times (L_{hit}) + (1 - hit\%) \times (L_{miss})$$

For example, a 40% GPU cache hit ratio would produce an expected latency of 34ms. Energy savings are similarly proportional to this hit ratio. In our anecdotal experience, we play-tested both a simple, single-room VR application as well as the complex Viking Village application in an informal experiment, and experienced GPU cache hit ratios from 18-47% depending on motion path and player behavior.

8.2 Scalability to Multiple Dynamic Objects

Figure 13 demonstrates that FLASHBACK can scale to compositing a moderate number of concurrently visible dynamic objects. The performance degradation is due to our unoptimized pixel shader comparing every pixel of a dynamic object's megaframe with the static scene's megaframe in the backbuffer. The current FLASHBACK prototype drastically reduces the number of pixel comparisons by merging it with the graphical warp shader, such that only pixels appearing in the *final frame* are pairwise compared instead of all pixels in the megaframe. Future improvements are possible by comparing only pixels within the dynamic object's active region instead of the entire frame.

Though the number of visible dynamic objects can be a bottleneck, this limitation warrants clarification. FLASHBACK is performance-limited by the number of *currently-visible* dynamic objects with *independent motion paths or animation characteristics*. Thus, if there are 50 instances of a rotating sprite that all rotate together or in some deterministic pattern — a rather common scenario — all 50 of those object instances can be clustered into a single dynamic object for FLASHBACK's display purposes, and quickly rendered as such. When the visible dynamic objects are truly independent, as in Figure 13, our approach is scalable only to tens of simultaneously visible dynamic objects. Anecdotally, this is a reasonable number for many virtual environments.

In the case of Figure 13, our HP setup reaches 100% physical memory usage when rendering 8 or more independent dynamic objects. This causes a memory thrashing effect where decoded textures fill GPU memory, which subsequently causes system RAM pages to be rapidly swapped to/from disk. This phenomenon occurs because our HP setup has an integrated graphics card, meaning that GPU memory is physically shared with system RAM, so the HP's 4GB of RAM must be split between the

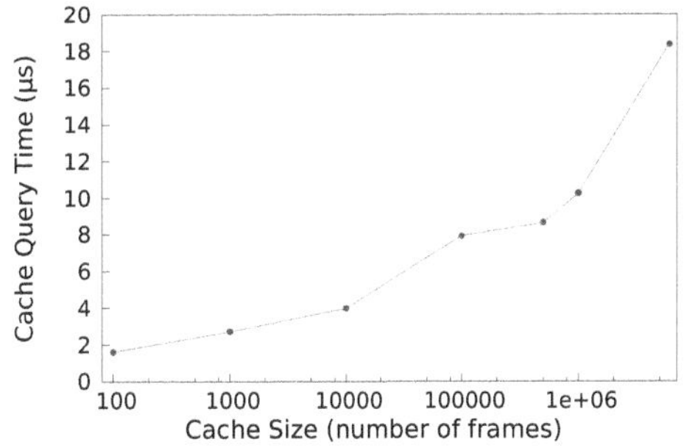

(a)

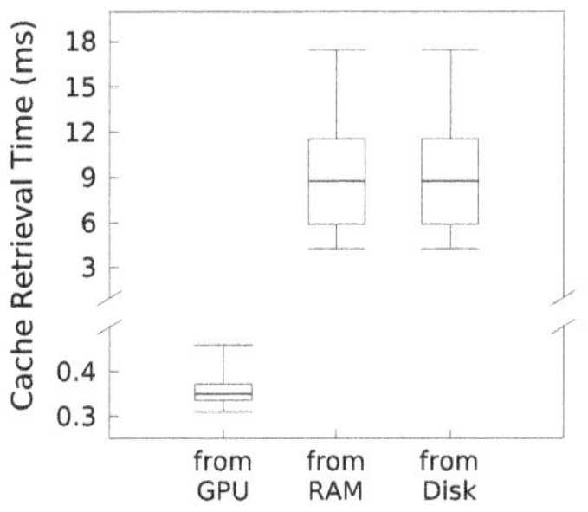

(b)

VR Environment	Cache Size
Car interior	115 MB
10x10 bedroom	730 MB
20x25 lounge	2.8 GB
2500 sqft. house	8.7 GB
Basketball arena	29 GB
Viking Village [2]	54 GB

(c)

Figure 12: (a) Cache query time scales well with the size of the cache, allowing FLASHBACK to performantly support very large caches. (b) Performance when retrieving 4k megaframes from all three cache levels. The y-axis break shows very small retrieval times from GPU. (c) Cache size on Flash storage (uncompressed) for various static virtual environments.

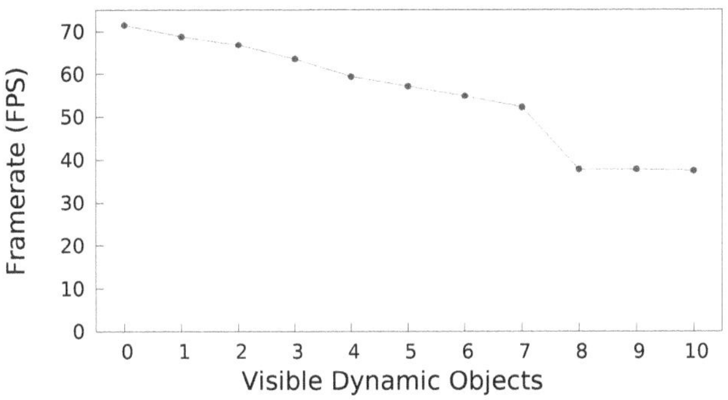

Figure 13: FLASHBACK scales well to a moderate number of visible dynamic objects, maintaining a high framerate until insufficient memory causes page thrashing.

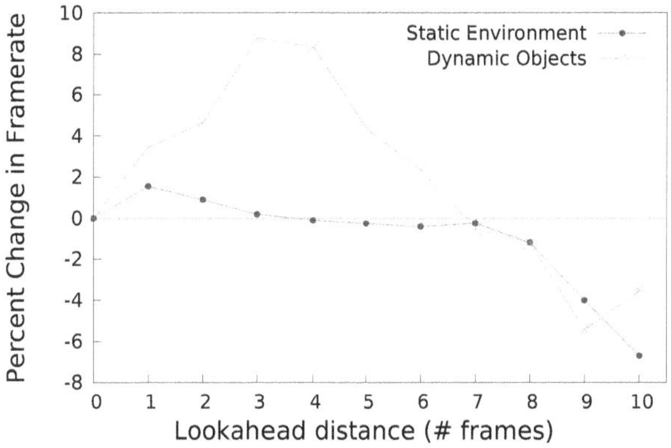

Figure 14: Speculative decoding offers some improvement for dynamic objects at moderate lookahead distances, but is ineffective when overly aggressive. All framerates are >50 FPS.

OS, other applications, our VR application, and FLASHBACK's cache. Even with poor memory management behavior, FLASHBACK is still able to maintain approximately 37 FPS for 10+ visible dynamic objects. Note that we did not observe this thrashing behavior on systems with dedicated graphics VRAM, as the contents of under-pressure GPU memory cannot force system RAM pages to be evicted to swap space.

8.3 Speculative Decoding Tradeoffs

As indicated in Figure 12b, decoding cached frames is among the most expensive operations on the critical display path. Fortunately, both low- and high-end mobile devices today feature an optimized hardware codec that outperforms our HP device's codec. Nevertheless, we evaluate the utility of speculative decoding to mask the decoder latency.

Figure 14 shows the effect of our simple speculative decoding method in terms of the percent framerate change for a given lookahead distance, as described in §5.4. As expected, dynamic objects are much more amenable to speculation because their poses can be easily predicted, at least when they do not interact with the player. Predicting a static frame pose is much more difficult because it depends on the player's movement, which requires a more advanced speculation algorithm to be truly effective. Our speculation turns out to be less accurate and even counterproductive when looking further ahead, as it causes frames with a higher likelihood of usage to be prematurely evicted from the GPU cache in favor of unused speculative frames.

8.4 Quantization Affects Performance

The choice of quantization granularity also has an impact on FLASHBACK's performance, as seen in Figure 15. Towards the left side, coarser quantizations increase cache hit ratios, maximizing framerate and minimizing latency, but reduce visual quality because the graphical warp must stretch the image to a further perspective. Towards the right, finer quantizations maintain excellent visual quality but reduce cache locality, causing performance to degrade.

The worst-case effect of superfine quantization is that every new pose results in a new megaframe, i.e., zero GPU cache hits. Thus, the theoretical lower bound on performance is equivalent to decoding every megaframe, shown in the third column of Figures 8 and 9. It is therefore important to select a quantization that represents the sweet spot between performance and visual quality. We have found that a quantization 0.05 virtual units (e.g., 5cm) offers playback free from noticeable visual artifacts, and that quantizations finer than 0.02 offer diminishing returns that are visually indistinguishable, hence why we chose a quantization of 0.02 when evaluating FLASHBACK.

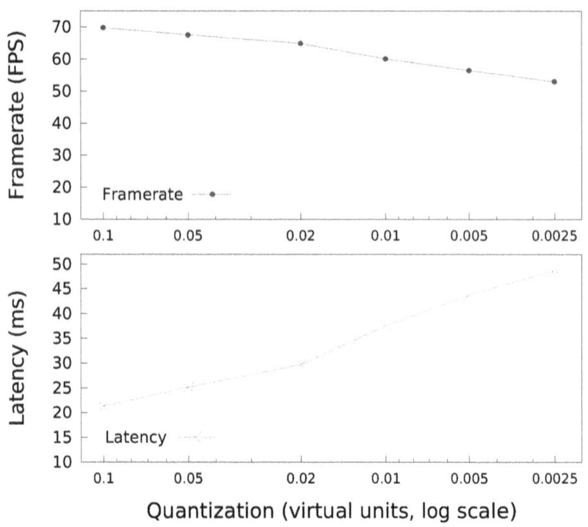

Figure 15: The effects of quantization (cache density) on FLASHBACK's performance: framerate and latency.

9. RELATED WORK

The general idea of precomputing or precaching results to service interactive requests on mobile devices has appeared in numerous forms [15]. For example, work has looked at precomputing statistical models for mobile appointment reminders [19], precaching web search results on mobile devices [24], and precaching database query results on mobile devices [5]. Our scenario is highly targeted at VR rendering, and therefore makes many domain-specific choices to improve graphical quality, latency, and framerate.

Instead of precomputation, an alternative way to enhance the capabilities of a mobile device is to offload computation to more powerful computers. The mobile computing community has a rich history of exploring computation offload to enhance the capabilities of resource-constrained devices. Among these, Maui, Clone Cloud, and Comet investigated the implications of general purpose compute offload [11, 10, 16]. In the domain of wearable visual augmented reality offload, the authors of [18] evaluated computation offload for visual and cognitive assistance tasks with Google Glass. The timing, compute, bandwidth, and quality requirements for full resolution, wide field of view, high-framerate HMDs are qualitatively much more strict than for text annotations on Google Glass, and therefore yield different points in the wearable design space. Such offloading techniques would be inappropriate for mobile VR, causing high latencies and poor visual quality.

In the space of offloading real-time rendering for mobile devices, recent work has demonstrated that it can be done with low latency [22] or high quality [12]. Specifically, Outatime [22] focuses on the case of synchronous client-server execution, in which a powerful rendering server speculates on future inputs and delivers predicted frames to the mobile client ahead of time, masking network latency. In contrast, FLASHBACK fully decouples client execution from the server — if a server is used at all — and relies instead on the mobile device's local storage hierarchy. FLASHBACK does indeed utilize a similar cube map and graphical warp IBR approximation as Outatime, albeit adapted for virtual reality. In the future, we are likely to merge these two complementary techniques into a hybrid system employing both speculation and caching to jointly improve latency and quality.

In summary, all offloading strategies, including some preliminary forays into the HMD space [13], require active, stable network connectivity to servers, ignoring the plentiful high-performance storage on the device itself.

The graphics community has examined the quality vs. performance trade-off of caching objects as rendered images. One such pioneering effort, Apple's QuickTime VR, allowed for free-viewpoint viewing of static virtual environments or objects from a desktop computer [8]. Later works helped develop algorithms to efficiently add dynamic objects into virtual environments [31, 30, 32]. However, these efforts were primarily focused on desktop environments and preceded mobile device architectures, such as: multi-level storage hierarchies, flash storage, video decoders and energy constraints. They were also less ambitious in terms of exploring the limits of memoizing dynamic object motion paths and animation sequences, standard elements of modern 3D scenes. Previous work has also proposed a cube map-like frame layout for warping pre-rendered images to the user's head pose at runtime [29, 28]. However, these latter solutions relied on specialized hardware support, termed virtual reality address recalculation pipelines, which is not present in modern GPUs. All of our work operates on commodity low end mobile GPUs.

10. CONCLUSION

We present FLASHBACK, an unorthodox solution for bringing full-quality VR experiences to weak mobile HMD devices. FLASHBACK avoids the expensive costs of a VR application's heavy rendering demands by aggressively pre-generating and caching all possible frames that a player might see. With support for caching of both static scenes and dynamic animated objects, FLASHBACK can support most VR applications in an application-agnostic fashion. We implement and evaluate a prototype of FLASHBACK to demonstrate improved energy efficiency per frame, higher overall framerates, and lower end-to-end latency compared to that of local rendering on a mobile device.

Acknowledgments

The authors thank Bernhard Reinert and Wei-ge Chen for their invaluable advice and implementation assistance. We also thank our shepherd, Youngki Lee, for his useful guidance and feedback. Kevin Boos was supported in part by NSF Award #1422312.

11. REFERENCES

[1] Minimum requirements for the Oculus DK2. https://support.oculus.com/hc/en-us/articles/201955653-Minimum-requirements-for-the-Oculus-Rift-Development-Kit-2. Accessed: 2015-11-30.

[2] Viking Village Unity Application. https://www.assetstore.unity3d.com/en/#!/content/29140. Accessed: 2015-11-30.

[3] R. Allison, L. Harris, M. Jenkin, U. Jasiobedzka, and J. Zacher. Tolerance of temporal delay in virtual environments. In *Virtual Reality, 2001. Proceedings. IEEE*, March 2001.

[4] M. Bajura, H. Fuchs, and R. Ohbuchi. Merging virtual objects with the real world: Seeing ultrasound imagery within the patient. In *Proceedings of the 19th Annual Conference on Computer Graphics and Interactive Techniques*, SIGGRAPH '92. ACM, 1992.

[5] D. Barbará and T. Imieliński. Sleepers and workaholics: Caching strategies in mobile environments. In *Proceedings of the 1994 ACM SIGMOD International Conference on Management of Data*, SIGMOD '94. ACM, 1994.

[6] D. Boman. International survey: virtual-environment research. *Computer*, Jun 1995.

[7] S. T. Bryson and S. S. Fisher. Defining, modeling, and measuring system lag in virtual environments. volume 1256, 1990.

[8] S. E. Chen. Quicktime vr: An image-based approach to virtual environment navigation. In *Proceedings of the 22nd Annual Conference on Computer Graphics and Interactive Techniques*, SIGGRAPH '95. ACM, 1995.

[9] D. Chu, Z. Zhang, A. Wolman, and N. D. Lane. Prime: a framework for co-located multi-device apps. In *Proceedings of the 2015 ACM International Joint Conference on Pervasive and Ubiquitous Computing, UbiComp 2015.*

[10] B.-G. Chun, S. Ihm, P. Maniatis, M. Naik, and A. Patti. Clonecloud: Elastic execution between mobile device and cloud. In *Proceedings of the Sixth Conference on Computer Systems*, EuroSys '11. ACM, 2011.

[11] E. Cuervo, A. Balasubramanian, D.-k. Cho, A. Wolman, S. Saroiu, R. Chandra, and P. Bahl. Maui: Making smartphones last longer with code offload. In *MobiSys 2010*, 2010.

[12] E. Cuervo, A. Wolman, L. P. Cox, K. Lebeck, A. Razeen, S. Saroiu, and M. Musuvathi. Kahawai: High-quality mobile gaming using gpu offload. In *MobiSys*, May 2015.

[13] Y. Degtyarev, E. Cuervo, and D. Chu. Demo: Irides: Attaining quality, responsiveness and mobility for virtual reality head-mounted displays. In *Proceedings of the 13th Annual International Conference on Mobile Systems, Applications, and Services, MobiSys 2015, Florence, Italy, May 19-22, 2015*, 2015.

[14] M. Deloura. *Game Programming Gems*. Charles River Media, Inc., Rockland, MA, USA, 2000.

[15] G. Forman and J. Zahorjan. The challenges of mobile computing. *Computer*, 27(4), April 1994.

[16] M. S. Gordon, D. A. Jamshidi, S. Mahlke, Z. M. Mao, and X. Chen. Comet: Code offload by migrating execution transparently. In *Proceedings of the 10th USENIX Conference on Operating Systems Design and Implementation*, OSDI'12, Berkeley, CA, USA, 2012. USENIX Association.

[17] A. Guttman. R-trees: A dynamic index structure for spatial searching. In *Proceedings of the 1984 ACM SIGMOD International Conference on Management of Data*, SIGMOD '84. ACM, 1984.

[18] K. Ha, Z. Chen, W. Hu, W. Richter, P. Pillai, and M. Satyanarayanan. Towards wearable cognitive assistance. In *Proceedings of the 12th Annual International Conference on Mobile Systems, Applications, and Services*, MobiSys '14. ACM, 2014.

[19] E. Horvitz, P. Koch, R. Sarin, J. Apacible, and M. Subramani. Bayesphone: Precomputation of context-sensitive policies for inquiry and action in mobile devices. *User Modeling 2005*, 2005.

[20] T. Jin, S. He, and Y. Liu. Towards accurate gpu power modeling for smartphones. In *Proceedings of the 2nd Workshop on Mobile Gaming*, MobiGames '15, 2015.

[21] Kevin Boos. FlashBack Website. http://kevinaboos.web.rice.edu/vr.html.

[22] K. Lee, D. Chu, E. Cuervo, J. Kopf, Y. Degtyarev, S. Grizan, A. Wolman, and J. Flinn. Outatime: Using speculation to enable low-latency continuous interaction for cloud gaming. MobiSys 2015, May 2015.

[23] J. Liang, C. Shaw, and M. Green. On temporal-spatial realism in the virtual reality environment. In *Proceedings of the 4th Annual ACM Symposium on User Interface Software and Technology*, UIST '91. ACM, 1991.

[24] D. Lymberopoulos, O. Riva, K. Strauss, A. Mittal, and A. Ntoulas. Pocketweb: Instant web browsing for mobile devices. In *ASPLOS 2012 (Architectural Support for Programming Languages and Operating Systems).* ACM, March 2012.

[25] W. R. Mark, L. McMillan, and G. Bishop. Post-rendering 3d warping. In *Proceedings of the 1997 Symposium on Interactive 3D Graphics*, I3D '97. ACM, 1997.

[26] Michael Abrash. What VR Could, Should, and almost certainly Will be within two years. http://media.steampowered.com/apps/abrashblog/Abrash%20Dev%20Days%202014.pdf. Accessed: 2015-11-30.

[27] Pablo d'Angelo. Hugin – Panorama photo stitcher. http://hugin.sourceforge.net/. Accessed: 2015-12-04.

[28] M. Regan and R. Pose. An interactive graphics display architecture. In *Virtual Reality Annual International Symposium, 1993., 1993 IEEE*, Sep 1993.

[29] M. Regan and R. Pose. Priority rendering with a virtual reality address recalculation pipeline. In *Proceedings of the 21st Annual Conference on Computer Graphics and Interactive Techniques*, SIGGRAPH '94. ACM, 1994.

[30] G. Schaufler. Exploiting frame-to-frame coherence in a virtual reality system. In *Virtual Reality Annual International Symposium, 1996., Proceedings of the IEEE 1996*, Mar 1996.

[31] G. Schaufler and W. Sturzlinger. A Three Dimensional Image Cache for Virtual Reality. *Computer Graphics Forum*, 1996.

[32] J. Shade, D. Lischinski, D. H. Salesin, T. DeRose, and J. Snyder. Hierarchical image caching for accelerated walkthroughs of complex environments. In *Proceedings of the 23rd Annual Conference on Computer Graphics and Interactive Techniques*, SIGGRAPH '96. ACM, 1996.

[33] K. Vättö. OCZ ARC 100 (240 GB) SSD Review. http://www.anandtech.com/show/8407/ocz-arc-100-240gb-review/5. Accessed: 2015-12-03.

[34] Z. Wang, A. C. Bovik, H. R. Sheikh, and E. P. Simoncelli. Image quality assessment: From error visibility to structural similarity. *Trans. Img. Proc.*, 13(4), Apr. 2004.

uLink: Enabling User-Defined Deep Linking to App Content

Tanzirul Azim*
University of California, Riverside

Oriana Riva
Microsoft Research

Suman Nath
Microsoft Research

ABSTRACT

Web deep links are instrumental to many fundamental user experiences such as navigating to one web page from another, bookmarking a page, or sharing it with others. Such experiences are not possible with individual pages inside mobile apps, since historically mobile apps did not have links equivalent to web deep links. Mobile deep links, introduced in recent years, still lack many important properties of web deep links. Unlike web links, mobile deep links need significant developer effort, cover a small number of predefined pages, and are defined statically to navigate to a page for a given link, but not to dynamically generate a link for a given page. We propose uLink, a novel deep linking mechanism that addresses these problems. uLink is implemented as an application library, which transparently tracks data- and UI-event-dependencies of app pages, and encodes the information in links to the pages; when a link is invoked, the information is utilized to recreate the target page quickly and accurately. uLink also employs techniques, based on static and dynamic analysis of the app, that can provide feedback to users about whether a link may break in the future due to, e.g., modifications of external resources such as a file the link depends on. We have implemented uLink on Android. Our evaluation with 34 (of 1000 most downloaded) Android apps shows that compared to existing mobile deep links, uLink requires minimal developer effort, achieves significantly higher coverage, and can provide accurate user feedback on a broken link.

1. INTRODUCTION

In the web, deep linking refers to the use of hyperlinks to a specific piece of web content (e.g., http://ulink.com/code/) on a website (e.g., http://ulink.com). Web deep links are instrumental to many fundamental user experiences: navigating to one web page from another, bookmarking it, and sharing it with others. They have also been crucial for many important services; for example, search engines use deep links to crawl web pages and to map search results to appropriate landing pages. Historically, mobile apps did not have any equivalent deep links, making the aforementioned tasks impossible for individual pages within the apps. As VentureBeat rightly put, "Imagine a web without URLs. That's what the mobile app world looks like now [July, 2014]" [42].

To address this, mobile deep links have been introduced in recent years [6,7,10,39]. Mobile deep links are URIs that point to specific locations within apps. A mobile deep link can launch an already installed app on a user's mobile device (similar to loading the home page of a website) or it can directly open a specific location within the app (similar to deep linking to an arbitrary web page). For example, the URI fandango://thelegomovie_159272/movieoverview directly navigates to the page with the details of the "The Lego Movie" in the Fandango app. Today, all major mobile platforms, including Android, iOS, and Windows, support mobile deep links.

Even though mobile deep linking is an important first step towards randomly accessing any arbitrary location within an app, it lacks many useful properties of web deep linking. First, unlike web deep links, mobile deep links require *nontrivial developer effort*–several lines of codes per deep link—resulting in a low adoption rate even within the top apps [40]. Second, unlike its web counterpart, mobile deep links have *poor coverage*—a small number of locations within an app, predefined by the developer, are directly accessible via deep links (details in §2.3). Finally, today's deep links are *defined statically* by developers to facilitate navigation to a target page given its link; the dual process of dynamically determining the link for a given page is not possible even if a deep link to that page exists.

In this paper we propose *uLink*, a lightweight approach that addresses the above problems. uLink is compatible with existing mobile deep links (i.e., the underlying mobile OS handles them in the same way); but it requires minimal developer effort, it supports dynamic link creation, and it achieves significantly higher coverage than existing mobile deep links. All this enables many novel user experiences that so far existed only in the web world.

One key challenge uLink addresses is improving coverage—creating links to any app location (referred to as *app view* or *view* hereafter), including to the ones that depend on previous views or on user interactions. uLink uses two key mechanisms. The first mechanism is *shortcut*. uLink continuously monitors for explicit data dependency between successive runtime views in an app. In Figure 1, view (a) launches view (b), by providing the location "New York, NY" selected by the user in (a). In some cases, e.g., if (a) and (b) are separate Android activities (i.e., pages), uLink can transparently capture the data transferred from (a) to (b) and encode it in the link to (b). This allows uLink to quickly invoke the link to go to (b), without first going to (a). More importantly, it improves coverage to views that depend on data from previous views (location in this example).

Shortcuts do not cover all app views. The view shown in Figure 1(c) is created when the user taps on the "POLLEN" tab, and

*Work done while at Microsoft Research.

MobiSys'16, June 25–30, 2016, Singapore.

DOI: http://dx.doi.org/10.1145/2906388.2906416

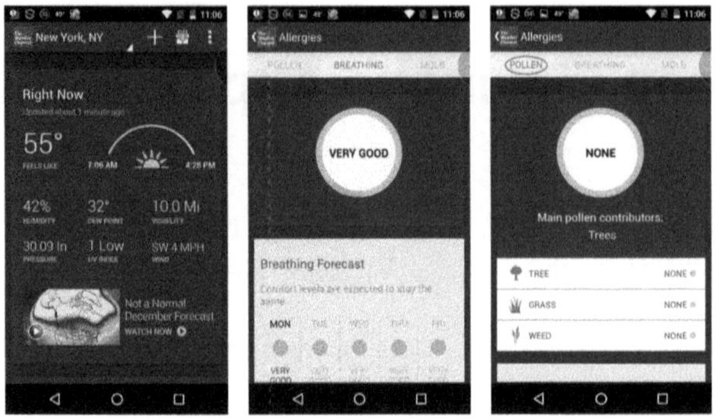

(a) An independent view (b) A view dependent on a previous view (c) A view dependent on a UI action (tap on "POLLEN" tab)

Figure 1. Examples of views uLink can support. Mobile deep links can support only (a).

there is no explicit data transfer between (b) and (c) for uLink to capture—both views are within the same Android activity. To create links to such views, uLink uses a limited form of record and replay. uLink continuously records UI actions in the current view, and encodes them in the link (we call this a *shortcut-and-replay link*). When the link is invoked, uLink first directly navigates to the most recent shortcut-reachable view (e.g., (b) in Figure 1), and then replays the UI actions to navigate to the target view.

uLink's record and replay mechanism is different from existing record and replay techniques that have been successfully used to repeatedly navigate to arbitrary locations of an application for desktop, server [14, 21, 31, 33, 36, 44], web [29, 34], and mobile platforms [19, 23]. Compared to traditional record and replay systems, uLink's record and replay is (1) lightweight and universally deployable—this is because it records and replays only UI events, which, as we show later, is often sufficient to recreate a target view with high fidelity; (2) fast—this is because uLink does not replay a whole session; rather it replays UI events only after reaching the most recent shortcut-reachable view; and (3) user-friendly—during link creation, a user does not have to specify the starting point of recording (it is implicitly given by the most recent shortcut-reachable view), and, during link invocation, replay happens in the background to give users a true click-and-go experience.

Another challenge uLink addresses is reducing developer effort. uLink is implemented as a library that developers include in their app. The library transparently interposes UI events and data dependency between views with minimal developer effort. For shortcut-only links, which are the only ones existing mobile deep links can support, uLink needs only one line of code *per page class* of the app (as opposed to tens of lines of code per deep link in existing mobile deep links). For shortcut-and-replay links, which existing mobile deep links do *not* support, developers need to write one line of code *per UI event handler*. Our evaluation with existing apps shows that the overall effort is minimal.

The final challenge uLink addresses is identifying links that may not open correctly at some later point in time. This is not surprising since even a full-featured record and replay tool may not guarantee reproducibility of the target view due to many nondeterministic factors. Broken links are common in the web as well. A link may not open correctly e.g., if the target view opens a file that is deleted after the link is saved, if a user is logged out from the app, or if some UI events cannot be captured or replayed (e.g., Android does not provide APIs for applying long taps on list items). However, it is important that the user gets a consistent experience—when she bookmarks a view, she should know whether she will be able to open the saved link in the future or not, and if not, why it might fail. A key contribution of this paper is to develop efficient techniques to provide such user feedback when a link is saved or opened.

We have implemented uLink as an Android library and evaluated it with 34 (of 1000 most downloaded) Android apps. While existing mobile deep links require in the order of 20–30 LoC *per deep link*, uLink can support shortcut-only links (a superset of deep links) to *all* views in an app with an average of 8 LoC *per app*. Overall, uLink achieved 70% links coverage and provided accurate user feedback (especially for links with file system dependencies). We also found that app links remain reasonably stable over time, with new app versions and updates in app contents.

In summary, we make the following contributions. (1) We develop uLink, a mobile app deep linking mechanism that requires much less developer effort, but provides significantly more coverage than existing mobile deep linking. (2) We develop techniques to predict if an app link may break in the future, and, if so, under what conditions. (3) We evaluate uLink with 34 real apps.

2. MOTIVATION AND GOALS

In this section, we motivate the need for uLink, set our goals, and review related work.

2.1 uLink in Action

We motivate uLink with a few concrete scenarios. Our goal here is to demonstrate some of what uLink can enable. We leave details of its design, challenges, solution, and implementation to next sections of the paper.

Developer experience. For ease of deployment, uLink is implemented as a user-level library, similar to existing analytics libraries, such as Localytics [30], Flurry [18], and Appsee [8]. The developer includes the uLink library in the app, and this alone readily makes the app uLink-enabled, with shortcut-only links (Figure 1(a) and 1(b)). To enable shortcut-and-replay links (Figure 1(c)), the developer adds one line of code in every UI event handler of the app.

uLink library and companion services. As the user uses a uLink-enabled app, the uLink library continuously tracks explicit data flow between app views (e.g., intents transferred between Android activities) and UI events. At any point in time, the user can request a link to the current app view, e.g., by shaking the device in our current implementation. An external companion service, typically a first-party service, can request to be notified each time a user requests a new link or it can request uLink to automatically create links to all views the user visits within specific types of apps (e.g., all third party apps). Two such companion services we implemented are: Bookmark, which stores all links the user wishes to save and invoke later; and Stuff-I've-Seen, which indexes contents and links to all app views the user visits and, like a web search engine, allows the user to search app content and directly navigate to content of interest using the associated link.

User experience. Here are few scenarios a user can experience with a uLink-enabled app and companion services.

(1) In a recipe app, the user can bookmark any page containing her favorite recipes. She can later invoke the saved links from the Bookmark service to directly open each recipe page.[1]

(2) She can create macro-like links for frequent tasks in an app. For example, in a library app, she can go to the "renew book" page,

[1] In theory, these bookmarks can also be shared with friends, in the same way we share web links.

System	Dynamic links	Convenience	Coverage	Dev effort	Ease of deployment
Web URLs	Yes	High	Good	None	Yes
Web macros	Yes	Low	High	None	Yes
Mobile deep links	No	-	Low	Some	Yes
App record&replay	Yes	Low	High	None	No
uLink	**Yes**	**High**	**Good**	**Little**	**Yes**

Table 1. uLink goals and comparison with the state-of-the-art.

select all books, extend the return date by one more month, and finally hit the "renew" button, and create a link to capture the whole sequence of actions. Later, she can invoke the saved link (from the Bookmark service) to renew all her books with one single click.

(3) The Stuff-I've-Seen service runs in the background to index contents of all app views the user visits (recipes, news articles, hotels, etc.) along with their links. She can use the service to search previously-seen content, such as a recipe she read in some app in the past, and click on the link of the result to directly open it in the app.

For implementations of these scenarios see §4.2.

2.2 uLink Goals

Our overall goal is to enable mobile deep links that are similar to web deep links in terms of functionality and convenience. To provide useful and user-friendly links, uLink should satisfy the following requirements: **(1)** A user should be able to create a link *dynamically*, like web links, by specifying only the target app view. **(2)** uLink should have *good coverage*—a user should be able to create links to most, if not all, views of an app. **(3)** Invoking a link should be *fast*, and it should produce a *consistent* app view, despite minor changes in the app or its contents.

To be practical and reach a large population of smartphone users, **(1)** uLink should require *minimal developer effort* to make an app uLink-enabled. **(2)** uLink should incur *minimal runtime overhead* and have no impact on the app experience. For *ease of deployment*, uLink should not require changing the mobile OS or rooting the device. **(3)** uLink should be *compatible with existing mobile deep links* so that the underlying OS can offer the same user experience. For example, if a user generates a link for an app and later uninstalls the app and invokes the link, the OS will notice that the target app is missing and will redirect the user to the app store to install the app (this procedure is currently in place for deep links).

Ideally, uLink must capture *correct* links. Our notion of correctness tries to be as close as possible to that of today's web links. To illustrate, we classify web links into three broad categories based on how they behave.

- Client-side **immutable** links navigate to contents that remain the same, across devices, users, time and location. For instance, http://www.dictionary.com/browse/uri?s=t *always* points to the definition of the word "uri".
- Client-side **mutable** links navigate to contents that may change depending on: (1) *user* (e.g., a link to amazon.com page showing personalized recommendation), (2) *time* (e.g., a link to a news web site showing current top stories), (3) *location* or other sensors (e.g., a link to a weather web site showing local weather), and (4) the *device* (e.g., a link to the html5 web site https://www.picozu.com/ editing an image from the local file system).
- **Broken** links fail to navigate to any useful web page. This can happen if the original web page has been removed or renamed. A mutable link can break too, e.g., due to unavailability of some resources it depends on. For instance, a Facebook URL, saved on a device where the user is logged in, may fail when opened on a device where the user is currently logged out.

In other words, web links are best effort—they may break or may lead to contents that are different than the original contents. uLink provides a similar best-effort experience for app links. Many app links generated by uLink will be immutable and will always navigate to the same content. At the same time, some app links will be mutable and may show different contents based on current location, time, user, and device. For instance, an app link to the "Daily Top Stories" view of a news app will show different news stories every day.

We also note that it may not always be obvious to a user whether a link is mutable or not, and whether she should expect the content to remain unchanged. Consider the link to the app view in Figure 1(b). Since the location information ("New York") used by the view is provided by the previous view and is captured by uLink, the link generated by uLink will always show forecast for New York, irrespective of the user's current location. In contrast, had the app been written such that the current location was acquired dynamically by view Figure 1(b), the content of the link would have been different at different locations. Such ambiguity, however, is also common for web links. For instance, both the links www.foreca.com/United_States/Washington/Seattle and https://www.wunderground.com/ show weather information; but the first link always shows the weather of Seattle, while the second one shows the weather of the current location. We expect users to adapt to mutable app links in the same way they adapt with their web counterparts. For more discussion, see §7.

Finally, as in the web, app links may also break. uLink promptly detects when a link cannot be safely saved or replayed, and provides detailed feedback to the user or to the application capturing such links on the user behalf. Fundamentally, uLink cannot guarantee 100% coverage of an app's views because of the deployment constraints (minimal development effort and ease of deployment) it must satisfy. In §3.3, we enumerate uLink's possible failure cases, and explain what the feedback contains.

2.3 Related Work

We compare uLink with other related approaches, and explain why they are not sufficient to achieve our goals. Table 1 summarizes the discussion below.

Mobile deep links. As mentioned in §1, existing mobile deep links require nontrivial developer effort, have poor coverage, and are statically defined; therefore they do not satisfy many of our goals. We now elaborate on these limitations.

Mobile deep links require *nontrivial developer effort*. As an example, the open source Wikipedia app for Android has one deep link, and it requires 23 LoC to handle the associated intent. As a consequence, a small number of mobile apps, even among the top ones, expose deep links. An estimate by URX from 2014 says that 19% of the top 100 Android apps expose deep links (and only 11% have deep links for Android, iOS and iPad [40]). To confirm, we analyzed 13,848 Android apps downloaded in the month of May 2015 and covering all app categories.[2] Figure 2 reports the CDF of the number of deep links across apps.[3] 75% of the tested apps

[2]We counted deep links by looking in app manifest files for declarations of intent filters complying with the Android specifications for deep links [3]. Our counts can be over-estimates, since we did not verify if the app actually supports the deep links.

[3]The CDF excludes 0.25% of the apps which have more than 20 deep links. The maximum was for a social forum app with 1503 deep links.

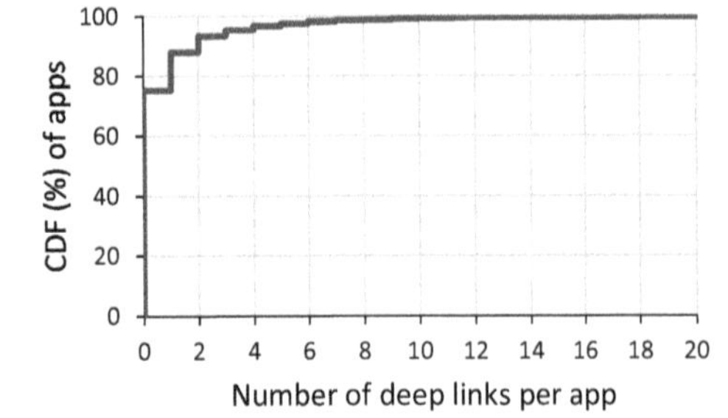

Figure 2. Number of deep links in top 14k Android apps.

do not expose any deep link; confirming the URX estimate of less than a quarter of apps having deep links.

Existing mobile deep links have *poor coverage*—a small number of locations, predefined by developers, within an app are directly accessible via deep links. As Figure 2 shows, 92% of the apps supporting deep links (23% of the total apps we analyzed) expose 5 or fewer deep links, indicating a small coverage. This is due to two key reasons. Developer's effort to support deep linking increases almost linearly with the number of unique deep links, and hence apps tend to expose very few deep links. It is unlikely that developers will open up all possible deep links in the app. Another more fundamental reason is that while deep links are stateless, mobile apps are stateful—an app's current view may depend on data from a previous view (e.g., location selected in a previous view) or as a result of specific user interactions (e.g., doing a search, selecting an item) on the current view. Thus, reaching the view may not be possible without transferring states from previous views or without applying the UI interactions. The stateful nature of apps also implies that even if deep links are free and a developer includes deep links to each and every page in an app and with a large number of supported input parameters, existing deep links, due to their statelessness, would not be able to capture and preserve user data generated in an app during interaction.

Finally, today's deep links are *defined statically* by developers, and must be known in advance to navigate to a target view; the dual process of dynamically determining the link for a given view is not possible even if a deep link to that view exists.

Record and replay. Record and replay techniques can record macros that can later be replayed to navigate to an arbitrary location of an application for desktop, server [14, 21, 31, 33, 36, 44], web [4, 24, 28, 29, 34], and mobile platforms [19, 23]. One might consider using such macros as links. A full blown record and replay mechanism can generate dynamic links and can have very good coverage, but it is not suitable to be augmented to support links for several reasons. First, these systems are too heavyweight to be used in the wild. Recording and replaying all sources of nondeterminism has prohibitive costs on mobile devices [17] (e.g., special hardware support or virtual machine instrumentation). There are tools that successfully record and replay smartphone apps by relying only on the sensor and UI event streams [19, 23], but they are still heavyweight and they require either a rooted phone or changes to the mobile OS, thus limiting their applicability to consumers' phones, at scale. Second, record and replay can be slow, especially when the user uses the app for a long period of time before arriving to the current view, and hence the replay phase needs to replay many user interactions. Finally, existing record and replay tools require the user to explicitly specify when a recording starts and ends—an unacceptable user experience when a user dynamically wants to generate a link to the current app view (e.g., for bookmarking it).

Figure 3. Examples of shortcut-only and shortcut-and-replay links.

2.4 uLink Approach

We now briefly describe how uLink achieves the goals listed above; the details will come in the next section. uLink is implemented as a library that a developer includes in the app with *minimal effort*. The library continuously monitors various data dependencies and UI events of the current view so that, anytime, it can *dynamically* create a link with the dependencies encoded in it. Figure 3 shows two examples of links: the first link points to page 598 in a Kindle book, and the second encodes the sequence of actions for requesting a lift in the Lyft app (the result is the dialog for entering payment). After being saved, a link can later be invoked to *quickly* access the view, by taking shortcuts to views that depend only on data encoded in the link (e.g., book page), and/or by replaying, in the background, the UI events encoded in the link (a clickable button in the second link in Figure 3). This approach gives uLink *high coverage* of dependent views, which are not supported by existing mobile deep links. The overhead of shortcut-and-replay links is reduced by recording and replaying only UI events (button clicks, checkbox selections, etc.), which, as we will show later, is sufficient to recreate the target view with high fidelity, in many cases.

3. SYSTEM DESIGN

This section describes how uLink was designed to meet the aforementioned goals: high coverage and speed (§3.2), while ensuring minimal developer effort (§3.4).

3.1 Overview

Mobile apps consist of a set of *pages*, where each page typically contains a set of *UI elements* such as buttons, checkboxes, lists, or menus. Each UI element can have an associated *event handler*, which is invoked when the element is interacted with. The whole of a page may not be viewable to the user at once; we call a part of the page shown in the current screen a *view*. A page may contain many views: the default view is what is shown on the screen when the user navigates to the page (Figure 1(b)), and the user can navigate to a different view within the same page by UI interactions such as selecting a tab (Figure 1(c)), choosing a date from a date picker control, filling out a search box, or clicking on a search button. A UI interaction can also lead from a view to the default view of a separate page.

Mobile apps are stateful and pages/views can have state dependencies. A page can use some data generated in a previous page. For example, the page containing the view in Figure 1(b) needs the location selected by the user in the previous page (in Figure 1(a)).

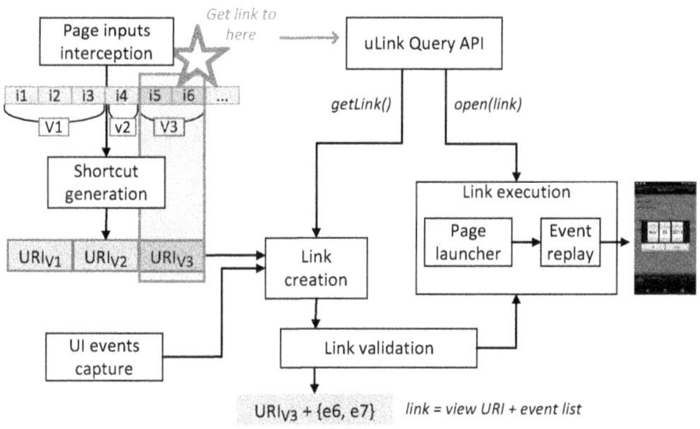

Figure 4. uLink system architecture.

A view can also depend on other views (e.g., one tab uses a flag set in another tab). Finally, a view can also depend on the sequence of UI actions starting from the default view. For example, the view in Figure 1(c) is obtained by tapping on the "POLLEN" tab in the default view.

Using this terminology, we identify three broad classes of links a user may capture in an app (listed in increasing order of complexity to support them). A user-defined link can link to the following states in an app:

1. *Stateless view*: A view whose state does *not* depend on states created in previous pages/views (e.g., a view showing weather, as in Figure 1(a)). It can be created without any input parameter, or with a set of statically-defined parameters that do not depend on previous pages/views.
2. *Stateful view*: A view whose state *depends* on app states created in previous pages (e.g., showing breathing forecast at a location *selected in the previous page*, as in Figure 1(b).
3. *UI-driven view*: A view created by UI events generated on the *same* page (e.g., Figure 1(c), created by tapping on the "POLLEN" tab in Figure 1(b)).

Existing mobile deep links support stateless views only. They can pass static parameters to target views, but cannot observe the internal state of the app (i.e., they live *outside* the app). This is precisely the reason why they cannot cover stateful or UI-driven views that depend on states (e.g., location selected by the user) and UI events (e.g., tapping on a particular tab) *inside* the app.

In contrast, uLink supports links to all the three types of views, and thus achieves its high coverage goal. Figure 4 shows the entire system architecture. In the following, we discuss the techniques we propose for creating, executing, and validating links.

3.2 Improving View Coverage

We first describe how uLink supports links for stateful and UI-driven views (not supported by deep links).

3.2.1 Links for stateful views

Stateful views depend on data from previous pages. By definition, a link to a stateful view points to the default view of its page.

uLink uses a novel technique called *shortcuts* to generate links to stateful views. We observe that a page in an app is usually instantiated through a launcher method responsible for rendering the page in the foreground (startActivity(intent,options) in Android and prepareForSegue:(uiStoryboardSegue) in iOS). This method usually expects as input a description of the page to render and possibly other parameters, which are not known to processes external to the app. This is equivalent to the query string in a web URL (e.g., in https://uLink.com/index.php?title=uLink_details&action=edit the query string is the part of the URI after '?').

Our key insight is that uLink can *program user-defined links by demonstration*: by observing how views are assembled during user interaction (V1, V2 and V3 in Figure 4), uLink can learn how to re-construct them. Specifically, uLink continuously intercepts all messages (i1, i2, etc.) sent to the page launcher method, so to infer message structures and input parameters necessary to render a view. uLink encodes the message structure and input parameters in a URI generated for the view (URI_{V3}). To open a saved link, the uLink library simply invokes the page launcher method with properly structured messages assembled using the parameters stored in the URI. In this way, uLink can *shortcut* to the default view of any page in the app. We call these shortcut-only links.

Assuming the link is opened under the *same conditions* (e.g., file system, sensors, and so forth) as when it was created, this approach guarantees accurate and safe, stateful links. They are accurate because this approach is goal-oriented. When a user requests capturing a link to the current view, the link is derived directly based on what app state was provided to *that* view. They are safe because this process does not risk breaking the program logic. We discuss later what happens if the link is opened under conditions different from those at creation time.

The above idea is simple and can be implemented by overloading the launcher method of the framework page classes (e.g., startActivity method of Android Activity classes).

3.2.2 Links for UI-driven views

The above technique of intercepting data passed between pages does not capture UI events within a page, and hence is not sufficient to recreate a UI-driven view. To support such views, uLink adopts a limited form of record and replay.

uLink continuously monitors UI events triggered during user interactions, and associated event handlers that are fired. To reduce overhead, uLink monitors UI events only in the current page; when the user moves to a different page, the UI events of the previous page are discarded. This approach does not compromise coverage since uLink can directly navigate to the default view of the current page by using a shortcut-only link to the (stateful) view. To create a link to a UI-driven view, uLink encodes two pieces of information in the link: (1) input parameters to launcher method of the current page (same as shortcut-only links), and (2) UI events that lead the user from the page's default view to the current view. When the link is invoked, uLink first launches the page's default view by using its input parameters, and then replays the UI events to navigate to the target view. The UI events are replayed in the background, and so the user sees the same click-and-go experience as shortcut-only links. We call such links shortcut-and-replay links.

Mobile app contents can be dynamic. For example, suppose a page's default view shows a list of restaurants. User clicks on the second item "Kabab Palace" to generate a view with the details and menu of the restaurant, and saves a link to the view. Now suppose, after a month, the app updates its contents, and the same restaurant "Kabab Palace" appears as the fifth item in the list. To deal with such changes, unlike traditional record and replay systems, uLink prioritizes content over UI structure during replay—it will search the list to find "Kabab Palace"; if it exists, uLink will click on it irrespective of its position in the list. Only if "Kabab Palace" does not appear in the list anymore, uLink will fall back to structural replay and click on the second item of the list. Such fallback is useful to deal with highly dynamic contents, such as a link to the top news story, which may change frequently.

We also observe that compared to record and replay tools, this approach does not require any recording start point, and it is much faster. Imagine a task where a user searches through old news by first entering some keywords and then specifying a date range, thus landing on the view with the news matching the specified criteria. The user wants to save a link to this view with the results. A standard record and replay tool (i) would require the user to specify the task's start point (i.e., the view where the keywords were entered), and (ii) would replay every single user action, i.e., entering the search string, clicking on the Start date button, pressing the search button, etc. Instead, uLink intercepts the inputs needed to generate the search result page and, through *a single* function call, loads the page. Then, only some, if any, UI events are replayed.

uLink does *not* need to record the time gaps between separate UI events. Instead uLink replays the sequence of recorded UI events such that each UI event is fired after the previous event has been dispatched, as notified by the device framework (e.g., on Android through the onUserInteraction callback). In this way, it is also possible to remove user-induced delays or idle periods.

On the other hand, uLink's record and replay is limited compared to existing record and replay systems: it captures only UI events (button clicks, checkbox selections, etc.), which, as we will show later, is sufficient in many cases. Capturing I/O and sensor access operations would bring us closer to the ideal world of deterministic replay, but monitoring these events would lead to unsupportable overheads in terms of annotations that developers would have to provide, in terms of OS modifications, or in terms of runtime overhead. By capturing only UI events, uLink hits a sweet spot between existing lightweight but low-coverage deep links and heavyweight but high coverage full-blown record and replay.

3.2.3 *Limitations*

Since uLink captures only data passed through page launcher methods and UI events within a page, there will be cases where uLink won't be able to correctly open a saved link at a later point in time. For example, consider an eReader app's link that opens a book (stored in the local device) at a specific page (saved in a configuration file). The link will fail if the book is removed from the device, or it may lead to a different page of the book if the page number in the configuration file is modified after the link is created. As mentioned before, taking a snapshot of all resources that a link might depend on can be prohibitively expensive.

To address this, uLink incorporates a feedback mechanism. Intuitively, uLink tracks all dependencies that it may fail to capture in the link. This gives users, or applications on their behalf, an idea about whether the link can be faithfully invoked in the future, and if not, why. Using the feedback, users can rely on their own judgment to decide how to use the link. Such feedback can also be useful to deal with link ambiguity (§2.2). For example, while bookmarking a link, uLink may notify the user that the current view depends on her location, which uLink is not capturing in the link. Knowing this, the user may or may not save the link in her favorites, depending on whether she expects to invoke the link from a different location.

3.3 Link Validation

uLink provides feedback to users (or applications on their behalf) at the time of link creation and of link execution. To be more concrete, suppose a user navigates from Page1 to Page2 of an app, and wishes to create a link to Page2. Can the link be correctly invoked later to see the same content? The answer depends on whether the pages access any external resource such as a file (outside the

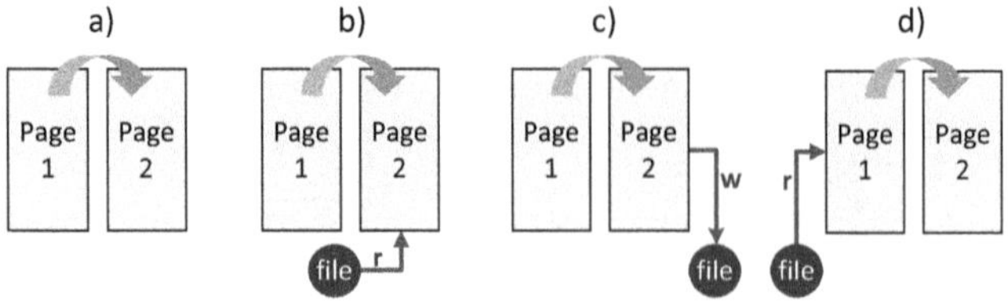

Figure 5. uLink can replay correctly a link to Page2 in case a), c) and d), and in case b) if the file doesn't change after link creation.

parameters explicitly transferred from Page1 to Page2's launcher method). Let us consider the four cases in Figure 5, with different dependencies from external resources.

Case (a) No external dependencies: uLink can correctly open Page2, by providing the parameters stored in the link to the launcher method of Page2.

Case (b) Page2 reads an external resource: (1) uLink may not be able to correctly open Page2, or (2) it may be able to open the page, but with potentially different content. This may happen if the content of the external resource is modified after the link is created. For example, if Page2 plays a specific music file from the local device, a link to the page will fail if the music file is deleted from the device. Similarly, if Page2 shows content of a local file, a link to the page will show different content if the file is modified after the link is created.

Case (c) Page2 writes an external resource: uLink can correctly open Page2, since the content of the external resource does not affect the content of Page2. So Page2 remains unaffected even if the external resource is modified after the link is created.

Case (d) Page1 reads an external resource: uLink can correctly open Page2. If the external resource somehow affects the content of Page2, its value must propagate through the data passed from Page1 to Page2, which uLink correctly captures. Note that, in order to capture possible changes to the external resource that Page 1 depends on (which may affect the value passed to Page2), the *reference* to the value (e.g., filename) and *not* the value itself should be passed from Page 1 to Page 2. Whether link arguments are passed by value or by reference is up to the application, and links behave accordingly.

Of all the cases above, Case (b) is the only case where uLink *may* not be able to correctly open a link to Page2. Ideally, preventing such behavior would require recording contents of all the external resources as well, which can be prohibitively expensive. uLink therefore does not try to prevent such behavior, and rather notifies users or the companion services at link creation or execution time that the link may not be replayed correctly, if a specific resource is modified. We call this process link validation.

Lightweight dependency tracking. The key challenge in supporting link validation is that it must happen during user interaction, at minimal overhead, and with minimal changes to the app. A possible approach, which requires no app changes, is to monitor I/O and sensors by instrumenting generic OS-provided APIs (e.g., system calls). However, this is not ideal because it needs instrumentation of the framework and incurs runtime processing and storage overhead. Another approach is to inject the monitoring logic in the app and track information flow in the app (similar to taint tracking [15]); however, this requires nontrivial development effort and incurs high runtime overhead. Our solution is to rely on an offline, automated analysis of the application to generate an app-specific *summary* of resource dependencies of relevant event handlers. Once the summary is built offline, it is installed on the device (by the uLink library downloading it from the cloud), and consulted each time a link is saved or opened. By design, this approach cannot be as accurate as heavyweight API instrumentation, taint tracking or other approaches requiring OS modifications, but it provides a first, practical approximation of the problem, while not compromising our goals of low overhead and minimal developer effort.

To frame the problem, we define the following terms. We collectively call *resources* entities external to the app that can change arbitrarily, after link creation. These include files, databases, and sensors. Our definition of "change" means any type of modification to the content or properties of the resource. For example, a file content can be "changed" by overwriting the file or by modifying one of the attributes such as read/write permissions. We call *source APIs* and *sink APIs*, the APIs the application framework provides to get or to put data, respectively, into such resources. In particular, we consider the following categories: file system read and write, database read and write, and sensor read operations. The list of such APIs can be obtained using tools such as SuSi [37]. Finally, we collectively call *callbacks* event handlers triggered, synchronously or asynchronously, by the app (e.g., in response to interacted UI elements) or by the framework (e.g., app lifecycle events).

Note that we do not include the network because, as with web URLs, we have no control on the app (or web site) backend, so we aim for link correctness under the assumption that the backend has not made the link's content unavailable (e.g., by removing the corresponding data objects nor by changing their identifiers, without providing a redirection).

Static analysis. Our first effort on generating offline app summaries is to rely on static analysis of the app. We generate the call graph of the app, and then recursively traverse it to find out a connected path from a callback to a source or a sink API. If we find any connecting path, we add the mapping <callback,source> or <callback,sink> to the summary. Online, each time a link is saved, the uLink library logs which callbacks have been invoked to generate the app state. In this way, uLink can use the summary to look up whether any of such link-required callbacks has dependencies on external resources, and report that in the feedback. Note that once the uLink library is added to the app, the developer effort required for the feedback generation is zero, because all link-required callbacks are logged directly by the library.

This approach proved relatively robust, meaning that we did not encounter any case in which a resource that was accessed by a link was not caught by the summary. However, we found it too conservative because of its coarse-granularity. For example, knowing that a specific callback reads *some* file is not sufficient to infer whether this operation may or may not compromise the link. If that file doesn't change after link creation, then the link will work correctly. If the file has changed, the link may or may not work. However, the problem is that online, with our restricted monitoring setup, we cannot capture the identifiers of the modified resources.

Static + dynamic analysis. To address this, we augment static analysis of the app with dynamic analysis. To exemplify, let us consider the file system resource. Our key insight is that while we do *not* know the file identifiers online, we can capture them offline and leverage them to establish *callback relationships*. We run each app using a Monkey (such as the Android [22] or Windows Phone [32] UI automation tools). We collect logs of all invoked callbacks as well as traces of file system accesses (using `strace` like utilities). We then intersect read and write operations that share files with the same identifiers. The obtained file-relationships are added to the summary. For example, the dynamic analysis may produce a trace where callback `c1` reads file `f`, and callback `c4` writes to file `f`, so a `c1` → `c4` file-relationship is added to the summary.

Note that a perfect dynamic analysis would deem static analysis unnecessary. However, existing Monkeys have less than ideal coverage; we therefore primarily rely on static analysis to generate summaries for *all* callbacks, and refine the summaries with more fine grained information whenever they are available from dynamic analysis (i.e., whenever the Monkey exercises the event handler).

Once we have generated the summaries, we use them online in the following way. As the user interacts with her apps, the uLink library continuously monitors all callbacks invoked due to user interaction, and keeps a log *only* of the callbacks that led to a file system or database write. When a link previously saved is opened, the link-required callbacks (recorded when the link was saved) are processed using the summary. Any link-required callbacks associated with file system (or database) writes can be safely ignored (as in Case (c) in Figure 5). Instead, any link-required callbacks associated with file system (or database) reads can be ignored only if they have no relationships with other write callbacks that were logged after the link was saved. In fact, this means that re-creating the link state requires reading a file (or a database) that was modified in the past, after the link was saved (as in Case (b)). If such file (or database) dependency is found, uLink generates a feedback report including details about the identified root cause, i.e., the callback information and the source/sink API. Using the example above, suppose that the link-required callbacks of the saved link include callback `c1`, and that the callback log contains `c4`. Because `c1` has a file dependency on `c4`, the link correctness may be compromised.

We cannot keep indefinite logs of all write callbacks, for all apps. We approximate by keeping a runtime log for a maximum period of time (currently an hour). Our intuition is that writes that are older than that period are likely to have been absorbed by the system (e.g., changes in preferences) so that they can be safely forgotten.

Our implementation currently provides fine-grained feedback only for the file system, while detects database changes only at the granularity of read/write (through static analysis). However, the same approach can be applied to databases by intercepting database APIs in the app framework (offline, during dynamic analysis). For sensors, fine-grained analysis of read/write operations is less critical because with the exception of a few sensors (e.g., microphone) sensor operations are always reads. This also means that links cannot break because of changes in sensor values. However, sensors can cause link ambiguity, which we discuss in §7. Finally, since it happens offline, the dynamic analysis could also be improved by adopting heavyweight tools such as taint tracking [15].

Other failure types. A captured link may fail also due to technical limitations of our system or of the app framework on which it runs. For instance, on Android, it is possible to track long tap UI events for items in a list, but the framework doesn't provide an API for replaying such events (while it does for single tap events). A link may also fail because of developer errors. Record and replay requires the developers to add one line of code per each UI event handler. If the developer forgets to instrument them all, a link may fail. Such kind of problems are captured by the uLink library when re-creating the link state, and feedback is provided.

3.4 Developer Effort

uLink is implemented as an application library. To make her app uLink-enabled, a developer includes the uLink library and extends the `uLinkPage` class provided by uLink, instead of the original `Page` class provided by the underlying framework (this is needed to overload the framework's page launcher method). Once the library is added, shortcut-only links are readily enabled.

To support shortcut-and-replay links, app developers must add one line of code in each UI event handler of the app. This effort

Change	Dev effort (LoC)	Enabled links
Add uLink library, extend from uLink-provided Activity	1 per main Activity class	shortcut-only links
Log UI event handlers	1 per UI event handler	shortcut-and-replay links

Table 2. Developer effort to add uLink in Android apps.

is larger, but still small (see §5.1). Moreover, since this process is rather mechanical, the logging statements could be injected automatically through a source-to-source transformation tool. Table 2 summarizes the developer effort for Android apps.

4. IMPLEMENTATION AND USE CASES

This section provides details on our Android implementation of uLink, and describes three companion services we have built.

4.1 uLink Library

We have implemented uLink on Android 5.1.1. On Android, pages, called *activities*, are started by taking a direct Android *intent*. Activity classes are created by extending one of 13 Activity classes provided by Android. An activity can be launched by supplying an Android intent, which is essentially a passive data structure containing an abstract description of an action to be performed. To transparently capture the intents, so that a target activity can be directly launched by supplying the necessary intent, uLink uses the following tricks: (1) It provides one *uLinkActivity* class for each of the framework-provided Activity classes, with the same external interfaces, so that developers can extend the uLinkActivity class, instead of the framework-provided Activity classes, to create a new Activity class. (2) The launcher methods of the uLinkActivity classes are instrumented to dynamically capture the intents provided to them, and to encode them in URIs to the app views.

The above tricks could be used also in other platforms. In iOS, Scene extends NsObject.UIResponder.UIViewController, and, in Windows, Page extends Systems.Windows.Controls.Page. So the uLink library for those platform could provide replacement classes to be extended by developers to create app pages.

Developer effort. To enable shortcut-only links, each *main* Activity must extend the corresponding uLink-provided Activity class. By main Activity, we mean any Activity that implements one of the 13 Android Activity classes. App developers often create one or a few customized main Activity classes that extend from the framework-provided classes, and use them to instantiate all other activities. Hence, the overhead is rather small (see §5.1).

To support shortcut-and-replay links, uLink requires app developers to invoke the trackEventHandler(view, view_type) method of the uLink library, each time a UI event handler is fired. Developers provide the corresponding View object (i.e., UI Element) that raised the event and its type, such as button, list item or textbox. Note that for some types of UI event handler, such as click event handlers, this information could be captured automatically through the framework by probing the View objects inside an Activity (effectively its UI tree), when it is first loaded and assigned trackers. Since click event handlers are the most common type of UI event handlers, this would be a significant reduction in the developer effort for shortcut-and-replay links. We are currently exploring this approach. Table 2 summaries the uLink developer effort.

To provide summaries for link validation, for the static and dynamic analysis of Android apps, we generated the call graphs using the Soot [35,41] analysis framework. Since Android applications do not have a traditional Main entry point, we created a dummy

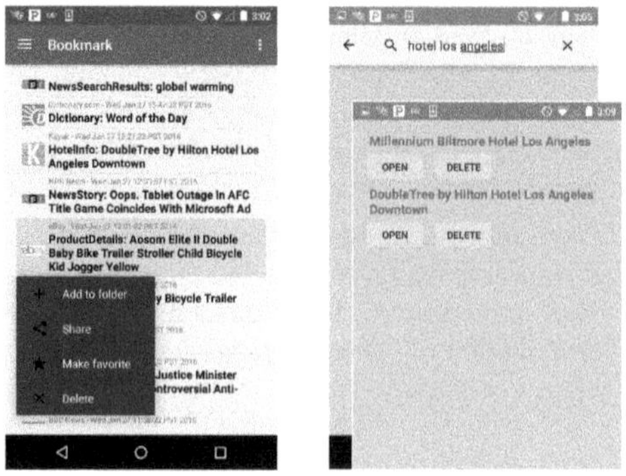

Figure 6. Bookmark (left) and Stuff-I've-Seen (right) services we have built using uLink.

entry point leveraging the approach of Flowdroid [9]. We used the Android source-sink APIs listed by SuSi [37]. This list includes 26,322 source and sink APIs available from Android 4.2. We selected 2280 sources and sinks, and grouped them into six classes: file system, database, resources, media, camera, and sensors.

Query API. uLink provides the following API that an application or companion service can use to programmatically generate or invoke links. (1) getLinkToCurrentView(): Returns a link to the current view. (2) getLinkOnCondition(condition, callback): Registers a callback, which will be invoked with a link and content of the current view, when the current view matches a condition. For example, for the Stuff-I've-Seen service described below, the condition can be "when the view belongs to a third party app and the user has spent more than 5 seconds on it". (3) openLink(link): Opens the specified link. If the app is not currently installed, it takes the user to the app store to install it. The object link (viewURI, events, callbacks) contains the view URI, the list of events for replay (possibly empty), and the list of link-required callbacks (i.e., callbacks that were invoked when the link was first saved).

4.2 Companion Services using uLink

The following three services demonstrate different usages of uLink.

Bookmark. Being able to bookmark links to an arbitrary state in an app is useful for various purposes. (i) When launched, mobile apps always start from the same entry page. Even if a user *always* only cares about the content appearing on a certain page, say the third, she must always go through the first and second page. A user that uses such app every day, perhaps multiple times, would benefit from being able to create a shortcut to the target page. (ii) When interacting with an app, a user may find some content she wants to save for later. (iii) Most users have tasks that repeat identical every day or every so often, such as monitoring the price of an item to purchase, ordering a pizza or checking whether new interesting houses are on the market. These tasks are likely to always take the same user inputs (e.g., number and type of pizzas). Users would benefit from being able to record such repetitive tasks and automate their execution. (iv) Filling forms in mobile apps is notoriously painful. Having the ability to record user inputs (e.g., login information, search parameters, etc.) for specific app pages can improve user productivity. We built Bookmark (left-hand side of Figure 6) that collects links to content, actions, tasks a user wishes to save. Each time a user shakes her phone, a link to the current view is saved into the Bookmark. Links are opened by clicking on them.

Stuff-I've-Seen. Users browse lots of content inside their apps (e.g., hotels to book, restaurants to visit, news article to read), and

App	Category	Description	Downloads	Total LoC	uLink LoC shortcut-only	uLink LoC shortcut-and-replay
NPR News	News & Magazines	News reader	1M-5M	13,114	2	18
AnkiDroid	Education	Flash card manager	1M-5M	45,959	7	66
Book Catalogue	Productivity	Book list manager	100K-500K	41,587	8	228
Vanilla Music	Music & Audio	Music player	500K-1M	15,518	4	79
K9-Mail	Communication	Email client	5M - 10M	67,721	4	75
eBay	Shopping	e-Commerce app	100M-500M	500,251	6	368
Lyft	Transportation	Taxi service	1M-5M	356,894	1	30
Spotify	Music & Audio	Streaming music service	100M-500M	523,999	12	430
Amazon	Shopping	e-Commerce app	10M-50M	418,503	10	235
Amazon Kindle	Books & Reference	e-Book reader	100M-500M	432,040	13	346
BBC News	News & Magazines	News reader	10M-50M	398,835	12	170
Watch ESPN	Sports	Live sports	10M-50M	452,437	5	125
AccuWeather	Weather	Weather update	50M-100M	392,707	20	132
Aldiko Book Reader	Books & Reference	e-Book reader	10M-50M	239,967	6	198
ASTRO File Manager	Productivity	File manager	50M-100M	393,712	10	231
Photo Editor by Aviary	Photography	Photo editor	50M-100M	340,653	3	181
Booking.com Hotel Reservations	Travel & Local	Hotel reservations	10M-50M	317,012	5	491
APUS Booster+	Productivity	System utility	10M-50M	29,923	7	75
Compass PRO	Tools	Utility	5M-10M	167,415	3	68
Dictionary.com	Books & Reference	Dictionary software	10M-50M	388,963	32	229
Duolingo	Education	Language tutorial	10M-50M	253,975	2	190
Hulu Plus	Entertainment	Live streaming	100K-500K	411,272	11	204
KAYAK Flights, Hotels & Cars	Travel & Local	Hotel, flight, & car manager	10M-50M	380,609	6	390
MakeMyTrip-Flights Hotel	Travel & Local	Hotel, & flight	5M-10M	421,598	15	345
Dictionary-Merriam-Webster	Books & Reference	Dictionary software	10M-50M	217,013	3	71
Music Player for Android	Music & Audio	Music player	10M-50M	89,411	5	79
Retrica	Photography	Camera & photoeditor	100M-500M	266,428	8	172
SPB TV	Media & Video	Streaming TV	10M-50M	318,170	5	163
the Weather	Weather	Weather update	10M-50M	273,724	7	167
TuneIn Radio	Music & Audio	Streaming radio	100M-500M	340,260	19	276
Advanced Task Killer	Productivity	System utility	50M-100M	12,843	6	50
WebMD for Android	Health & Fitness	Health app	5M-10M	319,537	7	170
Yahoo!	News & Magazines	News reader	10M-50M	395,316	10	260
Zillow	Lifestyle	Apartment finder	10M-50M	404,068	11	344
			Average	**283,572**	**8.4**	**195.8**

Table 3. The 34 Android apps to which we added the uLink library and the developer effort required. (First 5 apps are open source.)

sometimes would like to be able to search through "all the stuff they have seen", and *not* through all the content those apps (or the web) offer. We built Stuff-I've-Seen (right-hand side of Figure 6), reminiscent of similar work for the web [13], for desktop applications [27], and for entire computers [11]. This service transparently logs contents the user sees in her apps, it indexes them, and provides basic search capability. The app contents (i.e., texts appearing in the UI elements in the app page) are obtained by processing the app's UI tree. For indexing, the service uses the Apache Lucene library [5]. Semantics analysis (currently not implemented) could also be performed locally [16] or in the cloud (as in Google's Now on Tap [20] and Bing Snapp [43]). The app currently tracks eBay product details, Kayak searches, NPRNews news, Spotify's songs and artists, and Kindle's books.

360-IFTTT. IFTTT [25] is a popular app that allows users to "program" <if-do> recipes such as "If it rains, remind me to take an umbrella". Currently these recipes are built using open APIs and web sites. With uLink, recipes can tap into third party apps. We built 360-IFTTT. Users can specify simple "if" conditions based on location and time. "Do" actions are specified by executing the desired task with the app (once), saving the link by shaking the phone, and copying the link from Bookmark into 360-IFTTT.

5. EVALUATION

In this section, we evaluate uLink on five metrics: *developer effort*, *coverage*, *correctness of link validation*, *link consistency over time* (i.e., whether the links remain valid over time and across app versions), and *runtime overhead and performance*. We report the results for both shortcut-only and shortcut-and-replay links. Our evaluation is based on 34 Android apps, shown in Table 3. We first tested the library with three apps (NPRNews, Lyft, eBay) and later integrated it into 31 more apps, *without* any changes to the library, confirming the generality and applicability of our approach.

5.1 App Dataset and Developer Effort

The uLink library was integrated successfully in a total of 34 apps. Among the top 1000 Android apps, we selected apps based on popularity and compatibility with Android 5.0 from a variety of app categories, with the exclusion of games (they are not in scope of our uLink-based scenarios) and native code apps. Five of the selected apps are open source, and hence we could modify their source code to include uLink. For the other apps, we used Soot [35, 41] for Dalvik bytecode instrumentation. The limiting factor in integrating uLink into closed source apps was not the complexity of the logic for injecting our changes, but the recurrence of bytecode obfuscation in apps. Once instrumented, we verified that they worked with 5 random links to 5 different pages.

The fact that we were able to integrate uLink through an automated instrumentation process is a first proof of how easy and mechanical the required changes are. In addition, we counted the lines of code (LoC) that were changed or added to integrate the shortcut-only or shortcut-and-replay variants of uLink. Table 3 shows the results. For comparison the table also reports the size of each app's codebase. To obtain an estimate for closed source apps, we counted the LoC after decompiling the app to Java source code using the dex2jar [12] and jd-gui [26] tools.The numbers do not give an exact count for LOC, but they provide a good approximation.

On average, shortcut-only required to change only 8.4 LoC in the app code. The smallest effort was 1 LoC (Lyft), and the largest 32 LoC (Dictionary.com). Recall that today's deep links can support only stateless links. Shortcut-only provides a superset of deep

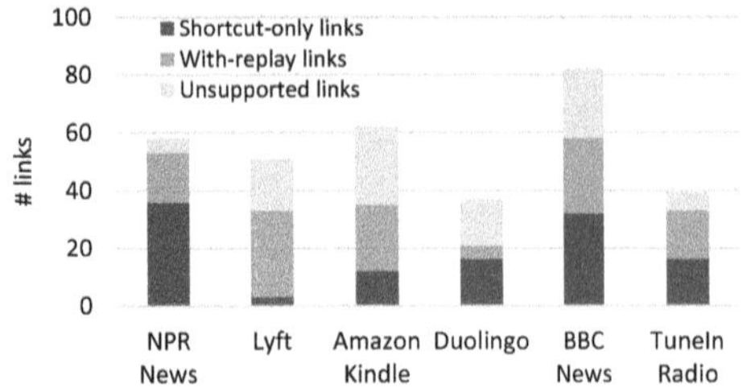

Figure 7. uLink link coverage in 6 apps (NPR News is open source, others are closed source).

links, with a much smaller developer effort. To give some comparison points, we inspected the code of two open source apps that support deep links. Ankidroid exposes one deep link which is handled in 35 LoC. Wikipedia also exposes one deep link coded in 23 LoC. With much less developer effort, uLink enables deep links to most app views (as we will show in the next experiment), and preserves application state.

The developer effort for shortcut-and-replay is higher (196 LoC on average) because it depends on the number of UI event handlers in the app, but the changes are still relatively few (on average 0.07% LoC of the entire codebase needed to be changed) and are rather mechanical. As discussed in §4, in the Android framework, at least the very popular click event handlers could be handled automatically.

Needless to say, if the uLink library could be added to the Android framework, it would require zero developer effort.

5.2 Coverage

We evaluate whether uLink can provide high coverage of an app views. We picked 6 apps, and manually enumerated all possible views in them. We were careful to report only unique views (e.g., if the same menu for adjusting screen zoom appeared in three different views, we counted it as one link rather than three). Then, we manually saved links to every such view, and opened them to verify whether the result was correct. In these tests we did not vary the operating conditions (e.g., same file system), so if links failed it was because of technical limitations of uLink or of the app framework.

Figure 7 reports the results. Across the 6 apps we found that on average there were 55 views one may save in a link. uLink provided coverage for 71% of them. Compared to the state-of-the-art, where if apps have deep links it is no more than a handful of links, this is a significant improvement. In particular, shortcut-only alone (which requires a tiny developer effort, see Table 3) provided an average of 19 links per app, and successfully enabled links to almost all pages' default views in the tested apps. Hence, with a much smaller developer effort, uLink provides much higher coverage.

The unsupported links were mainly due to failures in replaying UI events. Most failures were an artifact of binary instrumentation. In fact, for NPR News, the only open source app here, the coverage was 91%. In closed source apps, instrumentation failed to log custom UI event handlers (in the real world, the developer would provide the correct annotations), so some UI events (although captured) could not be replayed. Other reasons for link failures were the following: i) there were UI elements to which the developer did not assign a resource identifier so they could not be replayed (this was the reason for the 9% failed links in NPR News), ii) there were some special UI events (e.g., list long click) for which the Android framework does not provide a replay API, and iii) there were page views that were displayed in a browser (in Kindle) which could not be reached by uLink.

Overall, uLink provides good coverage. With the framework's support we are optimistic this coverage can be almost 100%.

5.3 Correctness of Link Validation

To evaluate whether uLink can discover external dependencies of a saved link and correctly report when a link may fail, we conducted a controlled experiment with 16 links in 11 apps, with dependencies on file system, sensors, and databases.[4] The links emulate what a real user would like to save in such apps, such as shortcuts to relevant pages (e.g., hourly news, product pages) or to recurrent actions with saved inputs (e.g., refill a prescription, locate nearest radio stations, etc.). To verify the dependencies reported by uLink, we changed the resources after the links were created, and examined whether each link could open the original app view. For instance, in the Vanilla Music app, we saved a link for playing a song stored in the SD card, deleted the song (from the app) and opened the link. Each link was opened twice: (1) in the same conditions: after creating the link, we interacted with the app for a while and then opened the saved link, and (ii) in altered conditions: after creating the link, we forced a change in the resource(s) that the link depended on and opened it.

Table 4 shows the results. In analyzing them, recall that uLink currently monitors file system dependencies at fine-granularity, but database dependencies at coarse granularity. The table reports the ground truth and the uLink's output for both conditions. "Yes" means that the link can be safely opened, "No" that the link won't work, and "Maybe" that the link may not work (if the resource it depends on is modified). For No and Maybe, uLink provided a feedback on the root cause. Overall, uLink was wrong in only 2 out of 26 cases (marked in bold in the table). In 75% of the cases it agreed with the ground truth, and in the remaining 19% of the cases it took a conservative decision, mainly due to the lack of details on database read/writes. For instance, the "open a Kindle book" link requires reading the database. As uLink cannot yet track whether those reads have been affected by previous writes, it fires a warning. For links requiring reading the file system, uLink was more accurate. For instance, the open photo link in Aviatar requires reading a file (the photo). In the same conditions, uLink correctly detected that the link would work. In the altered conditions, it captured that the photo had been deleted and that the link-required callbacks had a dependency on that operation, thus reaching the correct conclusion. The feedback provided in No/Maybe situations was generally accurate – it was complete in 88% of the tested cases.

Overall, uLink's feedback is relatively accurate. With the addition of fine-grained database analysis, we expect the accuracy to be close to 100%. The services consuming app links can further decide how to interpret this feedback, especially in Maybe situations. For instance, "Stuff-I've-Seen" may be less conservative, and treat Maybe verdicts as Yes. Another service for automating recurrent user tasks (e.g., refill prescriptions) may be more conservative, and treat them as No.

5.4 Consistency over Time

We now explore whether uLink generates links that are reliable over time, in the face of i) app updates and ii) app content changes. To evaluate consistency across different app versions, we downloaded several older versions of some of our apps and tested

[4]For clarity of analysis, we further distinguished between read and write operations on preferences and cache. These resources can be easily recognized as their names remain constant across apps.

App	Link description	Dependency	Same conditions			Altered conditions		
				Ground truth	uLink		Ground truth	uLink
Amazon Kindle	Open a book page	r db, r pref	same db & pref	Yes	Maybe (r db, r pref)	del db, w pref	**No** (r db, w pref)	**Maybe** (r db)
Amazon Kindle	Sync books with cloud	w db, w pref	same db & pref	Yes	Yes	del db, w pref	Yes	Yes
Photo Editor by Aviary	Open a photo	r file	same files	Yes	Yes	del files	No (r file)	No (r file)
Lyft	Share referral code	w pref	same pref	Yes	Yes	del pref	Yes	Yes
Lyft	Request a lift	loc	same loc	Maybe (loc)	Maybe (loc)	different loc	Maybe (loc)	Maybe (loc)
NPR News	Open a story	r/w cache in db	same cache	Yes	Yes	del cache	Yes	Yes
NPR News	Add news to playlist	r/w db	same db	Yes	Maybe (r/w db)	del db	Yes	Maybe (r/w db)
NPR News	Locate nearest station	loc	same loc	Maybe (loc)	Maybe (loc)	different loc	Maybe (loc)	Maybe (loc)
eBay	View product	r db	same DB	Yes	Maybe (r db)	del db	Yes	Maybe (r db)
WebMD	Refill a prescription through Wallgreens	camera, r pref loc	same loc same pref	Maybe (camera, r pref, loc)	Maybe (camera, r pref)	different loc, del pref	Maybe (camera, r pref, loc)	Maybe (camera, r pref)
Vanilla Music	Play a song	r file, w pref	same files & pref	Yes	Yes (r file)	del files, w pref	No (r file)	No (r file)
AnkiDroid	View a card	r db, r pref	same db & pref	Yes	Maybe (r db, r pref)	del db, w pref	**No** (r db, r pref)	**Maybe** (r db, r pref)
Book Catalogue	Reset hint	w db, w pref	same db & pref	Yes	Yes	del db, w pref	Yes	Yes
Book Catalogue	Manually add a book	w db	same db	Yes	Yes	del db	Yes	Yes
Dict. Merriam-Webster	View word of the day	w pref	same pref	Yes	Yes	del pref	Yes	Yes
Dictionary.com	Search a word	w pref	same pref	Yes	Yes	del pref	Yes	Yes
Summary	**Decision (Yes, No, Maybe):**		**Wrong: 2 (6%)**	**Same as ground truth: 24 (75%)**		**Conservative: 6 (19%)**		
	No/Maybe feedback accuracy:		**Complete: 23 (88%)**	**Incomplete: 3 (12%)**				

Table 4. uLink feedback for links with dependencies on sensors, file system, and database (r=read, w=write, db=database, pref=preferences).

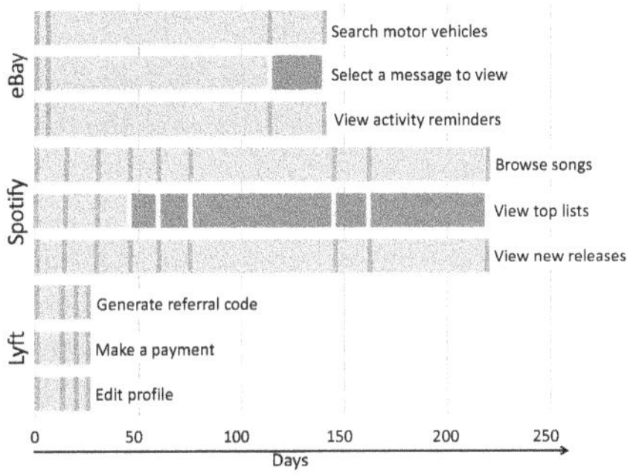

Figure 8. uLink across different app versions over time (green = link opened correctly, red = link failed).

whether links saved in the oldest version could be opened correctly in the newer versions. We tested 3 different links in Spotify (9 versions covering 7 months), in eBay (4 versions covering 4.5 months), and in Lyft (4 versions covering 1 month). Figure 8 reports our findings. For Spotify, 2 out of 3 links worked for the entire period; one link broke after the 3rd version update. Upon investigating further, we found that the cause was the removal of a UI element in the page layout. The second failure we noticed was for an eBay link which did not work for an intermediate version. In this case, uLink could not load the UI element and the app showed a dialog instead, but there was no crash. This study shows that links are relatively stable over a short period of time—there was no single failure for 50 days after link creation.

Then we investigated how uLink copes with updates to app contents. We created 10 links from 5 different apps (NPR News, Vanilla Music, Spotify, Book Catalogue and eBay). We selected common links such as viewing an eBay item, viewing the top NPR news, playing a song in Vanilla Music, or viewing the top releases in Spotify. Then for 4 weeks (8 weeks for NPR News), at least once a day, we ran a script that would open each of the links, and save a screenshot of the resulting view and debug logs. By inspecting the saved screenshots and logs, we observed that all 10 links, except 1, provided correct results for the entire duration of the experiment. Note that *some of the content were no longer available in the app itself; but the app backend still maintained the content and hence uLink could retrieve it*, highlighting the benefit of uLink. The failed link was for viewing a specific top news in NPR News. After 4 weeks, the link returned an empty page: the news item was not available anymore in the app backend with the same identifier.

5.5 System Overhead and Performance

The uLink library is 245 kB bytes big, so it adds a small storage overhead to existing apps. The computation overhead is also minimal, and processing occurs asynchronously to the app execution with no app slowdown. Generated app links are typically 100–150 bytes (e.g., the average size of the links used in Table 4 is 136 bytes).[5] For shortcut-and-replay links, uLink needs to log UI events. We executed AnkiDroid, a relatively I/O intensive app, for 10 minutes, and measured a callback log size of only 432 kB. With an hour time windows the cost is a few MBytes. We conclude uLink is a lightweight system.

uLink is also fast in opening saved links. When opening a link, if the app targeted by the link is already running (in foreground or background), the delay is the page rendering time. If the app is not running, uLink needs to first start the app and then render the page, so the total delay consists of the app loading time (typically 1–2 seconds depending on the app) and the page rendering time. We executed a simple experiment to verify that uLink's overhead on an app page's rendering time is negligible. We took 5 apps and created 3 links for each. We measured the uLink page rendering overhead as the difference between the 1) the average time necessary to open each link and achieve a stable page in the uLink-enabled app, and 2) the time the unmodified app takes to load the same page. As we were interested in comparing the page rendering times, we kept the app running in both conditions, but ensured the cache was cleared after each test. Moreover, when measuring the uLink rendering delay, we ensured the Activity targeted by the link was cleared on the stack (i.e., when the link is opened, we force a call to OnCreate). To measure the rendering time, we measured the time between the first call of OnCreate and the time when the root view of the Activity was inflated (i.e., all UI elements in the page are rendered). Across the 15 tests, the mean delay was 28 ms, so negligible.

In the previous test, we considered shortcut-only links. To evaluate the delay of shortcut-and-replay links we used RERAN [19], a record and replay tool for Android, as a baseline. Table 5 shows three example tasks with three different apps. We recorded the tasks (saved links) with both systems, stored the necessary logs, and then replayed each task (opened the link). We report execution time, number of replayed UI events, and logs size. Tasks are ordered by increasing number of clicks. uLink is from 5 up to 13

[5]The size of a link mainly depends on the size of the intent object captured by input interception. According to Android guidelines, this is maximum 1 MB. However, to keep links small, rather than saving large objects in the URI, the objects can be saved in storage and their reference be included.

App and link description	Replay time (ms) (& UI events)		Replay log size (bytes)	
	RERAN	uLink	RERAN	uLink
TuneInRadio: Stream a radio station	5,351 (4)	1,105 (1)	7,480	651
VanillaMusic: Go to a song and play it	7,762 (4)	982 (1)	6,880	693
NPRNews: Search news for some dates	17,345 (5)	1,392 (0)	11,296	984

Table 5. Comparison of uLink and the record and replay RERAN tool in terms of replay time, number of replayed UI events and log size.

times faster than RERAN. More importantly, while in RERAN the replay time increases as the task's complexity increases (number of visited pages and clicks), with uLink it remains fairly constant. The RERAN log sizes are also at least 10 times larger—for uLink, the replay log is essentially the link itself, which is quite small (last column). Finally, with uLink the average replay time is 1.2 seconds, which is close to what users expect for page loading times.

Overall, these experiments show that uLink is a lightweight system and provides an acceptable user experience.

6. OTHER RELATED WORK

We have discussed related work in §2.3. In addition to that, there are various companies offering mobile deep linking solutions with different corollary services (for a summary see [6]). AppLinks [7] comes with the Facebook Index API to check whether links are able to be deep-linked, and the possibility to code custom API. Deeplink.me [10] provides the AppWords Network for discovery and monetization of deep links across apps. URX [39] crawls web pages and constructs deep links metadata to be leveraged by app developers. Moreover, it dynamically extracts information from app pages to understand user intent, and provide deep links to content of interest. All these approaches contribute to building effective deep linking to app content, but all of them require significant developer effort and provide statically-defined deep links. Hence, compared to uLink, they suffer from the limitations we discussed earlier: low coverage and no support for stateful and UI-driven views.

7. LIMITATIONS

We discuss some key limitations of our work.

Technical limitations. uLink can currently capture only UI elements that have a unique resource identifier associated. Moreover, we rely on the Android framework APIs to programmatically replay UI events. For UI events for which Android provides only the screen coordinates (e.g., random screen touches), uLink can only mimic that action across devices with similar resolutions. uLink cannot handle certain gestures such as swipe, pinch or zoom, because they do not have replay APIs. These limitations have little impact on most apps and on our use cases. However, they can be a problem for use cases involving maps, games, etc.

uLink relies on the intents transferred between app pages. If the syntactic structure of the program changes, mostly due to a new app version (or to different versions across devices), uLink will be unable to reflect those changes. This means that old links may stop working. Changes in app versions could be tracked with cloud support, so to automatically detect/update broken links.

Fine-grained app summaries. uLink currently provides fine-grained summaries only for file system operations. For the file system we were able to leverage OS utilities (strace). For databases it is necessary to instrument the Android framework and app APIs to track the information flow. Taint-tracking [15] can also improve the precision of our approach.

Link ambiguity. It is not always possible to correctly understand a user's expectations when saving a link. For example, after saving a link to the "Nearby restaurants" view, when the user invokes this link later on, does she expect to see the restaurants near the current location or near the location the link was recorded at? In the NPR News app, when clicking on the *first* news item in the list of "Hot Daily News", a view showing the selected news story is displayed. If a user saves a link to this view, does she want to save a link to that specific news article or to the top daily news (i.e., the first item in the list)? As discussed in §2.2, link ambiguity is not unique to uLink, and, as for web links, practice will help users understand what app links can or cannot capture, on a per app basis. However, the system can help identify ambiguous situations, and prompt the user for clarification. Our system-generated feedback is a first step towards this goal. In addition, as in the web, link titles can also give hints on what the link is storing (e.g., uLink/NearbyRestaurants vs. uLink/NearbyRestaurants/NE+5th+St+Redmond+WA).

Unwanted replay. How can we prevent users from buying the same Amazon item twice by mistakenly clicking twice the same app link? This kind of problems are unlikely to be fully resolved without help from the app developer (e.g., in the form of annotations for pages or UI elements which should be excluded from link capture or that should request user confirmation) or without extracting app contents and action semantics so the system can reason about link purposes.

Link sharing: security and privacy. Users can share web links. From a technical point of view, users can share also app links. However, to make this viable, uLink needs to address at least two problems. First, it needs to handle cases in which a user may receive a link for an app that is not installed or that was saved in an app with a different version than the installed one. Second, security and privacy issues must be addressed: What if the shared link is malicious? What if the shared link makes changes to the app's preferences? What if the shared link contains personal information, such as login information or home address? Link encryption, cloud-aided link security analysis, and user/developer opt-out policies can help alleviate these issues.

App content revisitation. By default, uLink always provides the most updated content that a link references (which is also the case for web links). Revisiting app content is currently not supported, but it could be enabled by relying on a caching infrastructure and diffing tools similar to what proposed for the web [1,2,38].

8. CONCLUSIONS

uLink is a novel approach to enable deep links in mobile apps. uLink is distributed as a small library that developers include in their apps with tiny changes. Compared to mobile deep links, uLink provides higher coverage of an app views with less developer effort. uLink goes beyond the state-of-the-art: it provides links that are stateful and that can be specified by a user on demand, and it achieves these benefits without incurring large resource overheads nor modifying the OS. Although usability is not a goal of our system, uLink provides the first elements towards that goal: fast experience, no specification of a session start point, and feedback for links that may not work properly. We implemented uLink on Android and used it with 30+ apps with promising results.

9. ACKNOWLEDGEMENTS

We thank our shepherd, Landon Cox, and the anonymous reviewers for their thoughtful feedback. We also thank Earlence Fernandes for early discussion on the uLink design.

References

[1] E. Adar, J. Teevan, and S. T. Dumais. Large scale analysis of web revisitation patterns. In *Proc. of the SIGCHI Conference on Human Factors in Computing Systems*, CHI '08, pages 1197–1206. ACM, 2008.

[2] E. Adar, J. Teevan, S. T. Dumais, and J. L. Elsas. The web changes everything: Understanding the dynamics of web content. In *Proc. of the Second ACM International Conference on Web Search and Data Mining*, WSDM '09, pages 282–291. ACM, 2009.

[3] Android Developers. Enabling Deep Links for App Content. http://developer.android.com/training/app-indexing/deep-linking.html.

[4] V. Anupam, J. Freire, B. Kumar, and D. Lieuwen. Automating Web Navigation with the WebVCR. In *Proc. of the 9th International World Wide Web Conference on Computer Networks*, pages 503–517, 2000.

[5] Apache Lucene. http://lucene.apache.org/.

[6] AppIndex. App Deep Linking Guide. http://appindex.com/blog/app-deep-linking-guide/.

[7] Applinks. http://www.applinks.org.

[8] Appsee. https://www.appsee.com/.

[9] S. Arzt, S. Rasthofer, C. Fritz, E. Bodden, A. Bartel, J. Klein, Y. Le Traon, D. Octeau, and P. McDaniel. FlowDroid: Precise Context, Flow, Field, Object-sensitive and Lifecycle-aware Taint Analysis for Android Apps. In *Proc. of the 35th ACM SIGPLAN Conference on Programming Language Design and Implementation*, PLDI '14, pages 259–269, 2014.

[10] Deeplink. https://www.deeplink.me.

[11] D. Devecsery, M. Chow, X. Dou, J. Flinn, and P. M. Chen. Eidetic systems. In *Proc of. the 11th USENIX Symposium on Operating Systems Design and Implementation (OSDI 14)*, pages 525–540, 2014.

[12] dex2jar. https://github.com/pxb1988/dex2jar.

[13] S. Dumais, E. Cutrell, J. Cadiz, G. Jancke, R. Sarin, and D. C. Robbins. Stuff I'Ve Seen: A System for Personal Information Retrieval and Re-use. In *Proc. of the 26th Annual International ACM SIGIR Conference on Research and Development in Informaion Retrieval*, SIGIR '03, pages 72–79. ACM, 2003.

[14] G. W. Dunlap, S. T. King, S. Cinar, M. A. Basrai, and P. M. Chen. Revirt: Enabling intrusion analysis through virtual-machine logging and replay. *SIGOPS Oper. Syst. Rev.*, 36(SI):211–224, Dec. 2002.

[15] W. Enck, P. Gilbert, B. gon Chun, L. P. Cox, J. Jung, P. McDaniel, and A. Sheth. TaintDroid: An Information-Flow Tracking System for Realtime Privacy Monitoring on Smartphones. In *Proc. of the 9th USENIX Symposium on Operating Systems Design and Implementation (OSDI '10)*, pages 393–407. USENIX Association, 2010.

[16] E. Fernandes, O. Riva, and S. Nath. My OS ought to know me better: In-app behavioural analytics as an OS service. In *Proc. of HotOS XV*, 2015.

[17] J. Flinn and Z. M. Mao. Can deterministic replay be an enabling tool for mobile computing? In *Proc. of the 12th Workshop on Mobile Computing Systems and Applications*, HotMobile '11, pages 84–89. ACM, 2011.

[18] Flurry. http://www.flurry.com.

[19] L. Gomez, I. Neamtiu, T. Azim, and T. Millstein. RERAN: Timing- and Touch-sensitive Record and Replay for Android. In *Proc. of the 2013 International Conference on Software Engineering*, ICSE '13, pages 72–81. IEEE Press, 2013.

[20] Google. Now on Tap. https://support.google.com/websearch/answer/6304517?hl=en.

[21] Z. Guo, X. Wang, J. Tang, X. Liu, Z. Xu, M. Wu, M. F. Kaashoek, and Z. Zhang. R2: An Application-level Kernel for Record and Replay. In *Proc. of the 8th USENIX Conference on Operating Systems Design and Implementation*, OSDI'08, pages 193–208. USENIX Association, 2008.

[22] S. Hao, B. Liu, S. Nath, W. G. Halfond, and R. Govindan. PUMA: Programmable UI-Automation for Large Scale Dynamic Analysis of Mobile Apps. In *Proc. of MobiSys*, pages 204–217. ACM, June 2014.

[23] Y. Hu, T. Azim, and I. Neamtiu. Versatile yet lightweight record-and-replay for android. In *Proc. of the 2015 ACM SIGPLAN International Conference on Object-Oriented Programming, Systems, Languages, and Applications*, OOPSLA 2015, pages 349–366. ACM, 2015.

[24] D. Hupp and R. C. Miller. Smart Bookmarks: Automatic Retroactive Macro Recording on the Web. In *Proc. of the 20th Annual ACM Symposium on User Interface Software and Technology*, UIST '07, pages 81–90. ACM, 2007.

[25] IFTTT. https://ifttt.com/recipes.

[26] JD-GUI. http://jd.benow.ca/.

[27] O. Laadan, R. A. Baratto, D. B. Phung, S. Potter, and J. Nieh. DejaView: A Personal Virtual Computer Recorder. In *Proc. of the 21st ACM SIGOPS Symposium on Operating Systems Principles*, SOSP '07, pages 279–292, 2007.

[28] G. Leshed, E. M. Haber, T. Matthews, and T. Lau. Coscripter: Automating & sharing how-to knowledge in the enterprise. In *Proc. of the SIGCHI Conference on Human Factors in Computing Systems*, CHI '08, pages 1719–1728, New York, NY, USA, 2008. ACM.

[29] I. Li, J. Nichols, T. Lau, C. Drews, and A. Cypher. Here's What I Did: Sharing and Reusing Web Activity with ActionShot. In *Proc. of the SIGCHI Conference on Human Factors in Computing Systems*, CHI '10, pages 723–732, 2010.

[30] Localytics. http://www.localytics.com/.

[31] S. Narayanasamy, G. Pokam, and B. Calder. Bugnet: Continuously recording program execution for deterministic replay debugging. *SIGARCH Comput. Archit. News*, 33(2):284–295, May 2005.

[32] S. Nath, F. X. Lin, L. Ravindranath, and J. Padhye. SmartAds: bringing contextual ads to mobile apps. In *Proc. of MobiSys*, pages 111–124, 2013.

[33] E. B. Nightingale, D. Peek, P. M. Chen, and J. Flinn. Parallelizing security checks on commodity hardware. *SIGPLAN Not.*, 43(3):308–318, Mar. 2008.

[34] A. Safonov, J. A. Konstan, and J. V. Carlis. End-user web automation: Challenges, experiences, recommendations. In *Proc. of WebNet 2001*, pages 1077–1085, 2001.

[35] Soot. Soot: A Framework for Analyzing and transforming Java and Android applications. http://sable.github.io/soot/.

[36] S. M. Srinivasan, S. Kandula, C. R. Andrews, and Y. Zhou. Flashback: A lightweight extension for rollback and deterministic replay for software debugging. In *Proc. of the Annual Conference on USENIX Annual Technical Conference*, pages 3–3. USENIX Association, 2004.

[37] SuSi - Sources and Sinks. http://sseblog.ec-spride.de/tools/susi/.

[38] J. Teevan, E. Cutrell, D. Fisher, S. M. Drucker, G. Ramos, P. André, and C. Hu. Visual snippets: Summarizing web pages for search and revisitation. In *Proc. of the SIGCHI Conference on Human Factors in Computing Systems*, CHI '09, pages 2023–2032. ACM, 2009.

[39] URX. http://www.urx.com.

[40] URX Blog. How Many of the Top 200 Mobile Apps Use Deeplinks? http://blog.urx.com/urx-blog/how-many-of-the-top-200-mobile-apps-use-deeplinks.

[41] R. Vallée-Rai, P. Co, E. Gagnon, L. Hendren, P. Lam, and V. Sundaresan. Soot - a Java Bytecode Optimization Framework. In *Proc. of the 1999 Conference of the Centre for Advanced Studies on Collaborative Research*, CASCON '99, pages 13–. IBM Press, 1999.

[42] VentureBeat. Imagine a web without URLs. That's what the mobile app world looks like now. http://venturebeat.com/2014/07/08/imagine-a-web-without-urls-thats-what-the-mobile-app-world-looks-like-now/.

[43] VentureBeat. Microsoft beats Google to the punch: Bing for Android update does what Now on Tap will do. http://venturebeat.com/2015/08/20/microsoft-beats-google-to-the-punch-bing-for-android-update-does-what-now-on-tap-will-do/.

[44] M. Xu, R. Bodik, and M. D. Hill. A Flight Data Recorder for enabling full-system multiprocessor deterministic replay. *SIGARCH Comput. Archit. News*, 31(2):122–135, May 2003.

Focus: Robust Visual Codes for Everyone

Frederik Hermans*, Liam McNamara†, Gábor Sörös‡,
Christian Rohner*, Thiemo Voigt*†, Edith Ngai*
*Uppsala University †SICS Swedish ICT ‡ETH Zurich

ABSTRACT

Visual codes are used to embed digital data in physical objects, or they are shown in video sequences to transfer data over screen/camera links. Existing codes either carry limited data to make them robust against a range of channel conditions (e.g., low camera quality or long distances), or they support a high data capacity but only work over a narrow range of channel conditions. We present FOCUS, a new code design that does not require this explicit trade-off between code capacity and the reader's channel quality. Instead, FOCUS builds on concepts from OFDM to encode data at different levels of spatial detail. This enables each reader to decode as much data from a code as its channel quality allows. We build a prototype of FOCUS devices and evaluate it experimentally. Our results show that FOCUS gracefully adapts to the reader's channel, and that it provides a significant performance improvement over recently proposed designs, including Strata and PixNet.

1. INTRODUCTION

Codes that represent data through visual patterns provide a simple and proven means of wireless communication. For example, QR codes (Fig. 1a) are ubiquitously used to tag physical objects with digital data [8, 20] in applications including warehouse management, logistics, and supply chain management. Visual codes are also common in augmented reality scenarios, where they are used for relative positioning of the user [1] or to provide information to overlay on objects [18]. Recent work explored the use of streams of visual codes to transfer larger payloads from screens to hand-held devices over so-called screen/camera links [10, 13, 29, 39].

Although RFID is replacing visual codes in some applications, they remain attractive today. They are cheap and quick to produce, immune to radio interference, and do not end up as electronic waste. Furthermore, suitable readers are readily available almost everywhere: many people carry a camera-equipped smartphone with them.

MobiSys'16, June 25-30, 2016, Singapore, Singapore

DOI: http://dx.doi.org/10.1145/2906388.2906399

(a) (b) (c)

Figure 1: **Challenges of visual channels.** (a) Good channel: the QR code can be decoded. (b) Distance problem: the code is too blurred to decode. (c) Capture rate problem: a reader captures a stream of codes too slowly, resulting in an undecodable mix of two codes.

Challenge. Scanning visual codes, such as QR codes, can be a frustrating experience for consumers: the user may have to move very close to the code for scanning to succeed, only to find out that the code contains only a trivial amount of data. Short read distances, high error rates and low data capacity similarly hold back the usefulness of visual codes in industrial applications.

These issues are rooted in the high variance in quality of communication channels between readers and visual codes. In general, the quality of a visual channel is affected by the *distance* between the reader and the code (Fig. 1b) and by the reader's camera *resolution*. In the case of screen/camera links, the channel quality is also affected by the *rate* at which the reader captures frames [13]; too low capture rates cause readers to capture undecodable mixes of codes (Fig. 1c). These three factors—distance, resolution, and capture rate—vary widely between users and the devices they are using. Thus, a key challenge when designing visual codes is how to handle the wide range of channels over which users attempt to read them.

Existing codes handle this challenge in one of two ways. Either, they trade data capacity for increased robustness. For example, QR v1 codes can be read from long distances, but carry little data. Or, codes support high data rates, but make stringent requirements on the channel. For example, RDCode [39] requires the distance between code and reader to be within a few tens of centimeters, and PixNet [29] assumes capture rates of at least 60 FPS.

In this paper, we consider the design of high-capacity codes that can be fully decoded by readers with good channels, while at the same time readers with poor channels can extract essential data from them. Such codes would be uniquely useful. For example, a warehouse worker could get coarse-grained information about the items on a shelf even when reading the codes from a long distance, while he could obtain more detailed information when close-by. We discuss further application scenarios in §8.

Approach. We design FOCUS to address the stated challenge. A key idea of FOCUS codes is to partition a code's spectrum, i.e., its representation in the frequency domain, into many separate *sub-channels*. Each sub-channel encodes one part of the payload. By design, the sub-channels differ from each other in their robustness to the effects of distance and resolution. Furthermore, they can be decoded independently of each other. A reader who fails to decode one sub-channel may still decode other, more robust sub-channels.

Intuitively, each FOCUS sub-channel represents data with a different amount of *spatial detail.* Because distance and camera resolution affect a reader's ability to resolve detail (see Fig. 1b), the number of sub-channels that a reader can decode from a FOCUS code scales with its camera resolution and distance to the code. In particular, the sub-channels that use the least amount of detail can be decoded even by readers that are far away or that have poor cameras. Additionally, our design ensures that codes never contain more spatial detail than necessary to represent their payload, thereby improving the decodability over poor channels.

The use of independent sub-channels furthermore allows us to alleviate the *rate matching problem* on screen/camera links, which requires a transmitter's display rate to be matched to the readers' capture rates to avoid frame mixing (Fig. 1c). Instead of fixing the display rate, our *multi-rate streams* enable a transmitter to use different rates on different sub-channels. As a result, the transmitter can concurrently send data to readers with a variety of capture rates.

While FOCUS shares similarities with earlier work, namely Strata [14] and PixNet [29], it differs from them in important ways. FOCUS significantly improves on the performance of Strata by scaling more smoothly to the reader's channel and by ensuring that decoding errors cannot propagate between sub-channels. While PixNet targets high-quality DSLR cameras as readers, FOCUS is suited to a wide range of readers including smartphones, because it uses the spectrum more efficiently and has lower computational overhead.

Contributions. We make the following contributions:

- We present FOCUS, a new code design that is robust to common impairments of visual channels. Each reader can decode as much data from a code as its channel allows.
- We extend the design of our codes to support communication of large payloads over streams of codes on screen/camera links. We present *multi-rate* streams that enable a transmitter to concurrently support multiple readers with different frame capture rates.
- We experimentally evaluate a prototype implementation over a range of smart devices, display technologies, and channel conditions. The results show that FOCUS codes can be read at much longer distances and with significantly fewer errors than Strata [14] codes. On screen/camera links, FOCUS improves on the throughput of PixNet [29] by at least 3× for older smartphones and 2× for newer models; it improves on the communication range of RDCode [39] by 2× while providing superior goodput.

2. RELATED WORK

2D barcodes. There are many established 2D code designs, including QR [8], Data Matrix [16], and Aztec codes [17]. These codes are used in both professional [24] and consumer applications [20]. Recent designs like Microsoft's High Capacity Color Barcode [27] aim to improve the data capacity.

Of particular relevance for this work is Strata [14], a design that also represents data at different levels of spatial detail. Strata encodes payload in hierarchical, recursively-defined layers. The capacity and spatial detail in each layer grows exponentially, and thus requires an increasingly better channel for decoding. FOCUS differs from Strata in that it encodes data in the frequency domain; this enables FOCUS codes to contain less visual detail to represent the same amount of data. Furthermore, the level of spatial detail in a FOCUS code grows linearly between sub-channels, and their capacity is constant.

Visual OFDM. Encoding data in a code's spectrum rather than in blocks of pixels can be thought of as a visual variant of Orthogonal Frequency Division Multiplexing (OFDM). The concept of applying OFDM to visual codes was pioneered by Hranilovic et al. [12]. They provide a characterization of the link capacity of visual OFDM as well as an experimental validation of the idea.

PixNet [29] builds on visual OFDM to establish screen/camera links between LCDs and high-quality cameras, such as DSLR cameras with optical zoom, achieving throughputs of several MBit/s. A PixNet code consists of many small sub-codes, each of which is encoded with OFDM. A reader uses its knowledge about the spatial subdivision when correcting perspective distortion. The reader computes three Fourier transforms for each sub-code, which means that it computes hundreds of transforms for one captured code. In contrast, FOCUS codes are not spatially subdivided, but are exclusively partitioned in the frequency domain. They use less spatial detail and require a reader to only compute one Fourier transform for each captured code, thereby significantly reducing the computational overhead.

To the best of our knowledge, FOCUS is the first code design to bring the advantages of OFDM to smart devices with limited computational capacity and camera quality. Indeed, earlier work has claimed OFDM-based codes on smartphones to be infeasible [14], a claim that this paper refutes.

Barcode-based screen/camera links. Several 2D barcode designs have been proposed for screen/camera links [10, 22, 40]. RDCode [39] aims to improve the reliability of screen/camera links by designing custom error correction to handle device-specific limitations and impairments that arise from user behavior. In contrast, FOCUS builds on established Reed-Solomon and Fountain codes. LightSync [13] was designed to handle the rate mismatch problem, which leads to capturing a mix of two or more displayed codes. To that end, readers use per-line tracking to identify the constituent codes that make up a mixed code. In contrast, in FOCUS it is the transmitter that mitigates rate mismatch problems by using multi-rate streams (§4.3).

Recent efforts aim to embed data in video streams by using codes that cannot be noticed by human viewers [21, 34, 38]. They build on transmitters that support very high display rates (120 FPS), and currently require short distances between display and reader. The design of unnoticeable codes is out of the scope of this paper.

3. IMPAIRMENTS OF VISUAL CHANNELS

The quality of a visual channel depends on how accurately the reader's camera captures the displayed code. In this

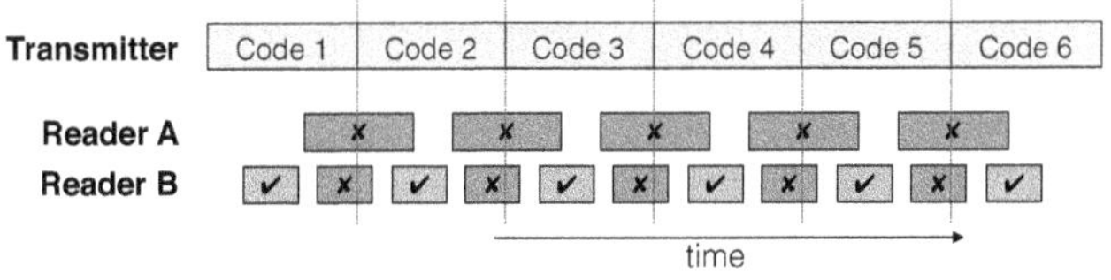

Figure 2: **Impact of frame capture rate.** Reader A captures mixes of two codes because its capture rate is too low. Reader B correctly captures each displayed code since its capture rate is twice the display rate.

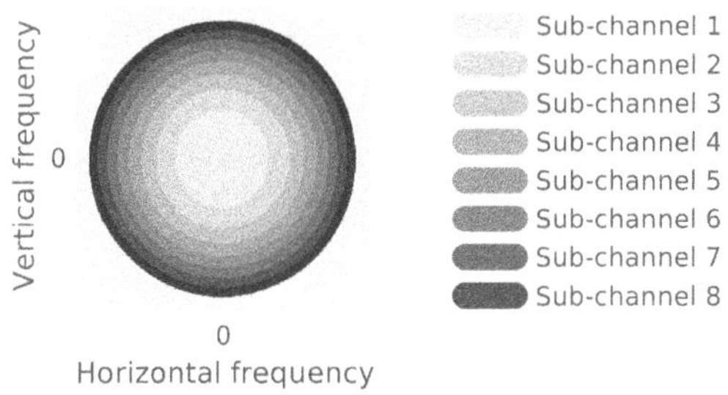

Figure 3: **Partitioning of a Focus code's spectrum into sub-channels.** Sub-channels with lower indices contain lower-frequency elements of the spectrum, which are more robust to undersampling.

section, we analyze three factors that have a strong impact on channel quality: the camera's *resolution*, the *distance* between camera and display, and the camera's *frame capture rate*. Our discussion of these impairments guides the design of Focus (§4, §5).

3.1 Impact of Camera Resolution & Distance

If a reader attempts to read a code from far away or with a very low resolution camera, the reader will *undersample* the displayed code. We now consider the impact of undersampling in the frequency domain.

Impact of too low resolution. Consider an idealized scenario where a camera is placed at a fixed distance from a display and is perfectly aligned with the display and focused on it. In this scenario, the camera's resolution effectively determines its spatial sampling rate Ω_c. Clearly, the camera's sampling rate has a crucial impact on whether a captured frame accurately represents the displayed code.

Let $\Omega_{\max}$ be the maximum frequency with a non-zero amplitude in the spectrum of the displayed code. Intuitively, $\Omega_{\max}$ corresponds to the size of the finest detail in the displayed code [36]. The Nyquist–Shannon sampling theorem states that if the camera's sampling rate Ω_c is $> 2\Omega_{\max}$, then the captured frame will accurately represent the displayed code. However, if $\Omega_c < 2\Omega_{\max}$, then the camera undersamples the displayed code and *foldback aliasing* occurs. In this case, the camera's sampling rate is too low to distinguish between the frequencies $\Omega_{\max}$ and $\Omega_f := \Omega_c - \Omega_{\max}$, the so-called foldback frequency [26]. Visually, the effect of undersampling is that crisp details in the displayed code are blurry in the captured code, as Fig. 1b illustrates.

A crucial observation that Focus builds on is that all frequencies below the foldback frequency remain unaffected by undersampling, i.e., the spectrum of the captured code matches the spectrum of the displayed code for frequencies $< \Omega_f$. This can also be seen in Fig. 1b, where the markers in the corners of the QR code—which are represented by relatively low frequencies—are better preserved than the small data-carrying blocks.

Impact of distance. The cameras in most smart devices do not have optical zoom. Therefore, increasing the distance to the displayed code implies shrinking the area of the code's projection onto the camera's image sensor. As a result, the effective spatial sampling rate decreases. However, as in the case of low camera resolution, the spectrum of the captured code will match the spectrum of the displayed code for all frequencies below the foldback frequency.

3.2 Impact of Frame Capture Rate

Frame mixing is a common issue when streams of codes are used to transfer data over screen/camera links [13, 22, 29]. The problem arises if the transmitter's display rate and a reader's capture rate are misaligned as illustrated in Fig. 2. In the shown scenario, Reader A captures frames at the same rate as the transmitter displays codes. Because the exposure time of each captured frame overlaps with the time at which the transmitter updates the displayed code, every frame that Reader A captures contains two codes overlaid on each other. An example of two mixed codes is shown in Fig. 1c. In general, mixed codes cannot be decoded.

The problem does not affect readers whose capture rate is at least twice as large as the display rate, such as Reader B in Fig. 2. In this case, at least every other captured frame will contain only one displayed code. However, setting the display rate to be half the slowest reader's capture rate is an unsatisfying solution, because frame capture rates vary widely between readers. For example, an Apple iPhone 6 can capture up to 240 frames per second (FPS), whereas we observe a capture rate of around 5 FPS for a 2010 Google Nexus One. Thus, a transmitter that displayed codes at a rate of 2.5 FPS would leave the channel of an Apple iPhone 6 vastly underutilized.

3.3 Other Impairments

In practical settings, there are additional factors that may affect the quality of a visual channel, such as unfavorable lighting, perspective distortion, lens distortion, or blur. Focus readers correct for perspective and lens distortion, but do not employ explicit measures against other channel impairments. However, we experimentally study the impact of lighting and perspective distortion in the evaluation.

4. FOCUS CODES

With the given background on channel impairments, we now present the core ideas behind Focus codes. We concentrate on the ideas in this section, and consider the complete design of a transmitter and a reader in §5.

4.1 Code Construction

Rather than encoding data directly into spatial blocks of pixels, as most visual codes do, Focus encodes data in a code's spectrum. This means that for a given payload we construct the complex spectrum S of the code, and then apply the inverse Fourier transform to produce a grayscale image, which is the actual code.

First, we conceptually partition the spectrum into *sub-channels*. Note that an element $S[u,v]$ of the spectrum describes a sinusoid with frequency $\sqrt{u^2+v^2}\cdot 2\pi$. Higher frequencies correspond to finer spatial detail. We define a set of sub-channels on the spectrum as follows. Let $s_1, s_2, s_3, \ldots$ be the sequence of elements of S ordered by increasing frequency. We define the first sub-channel to contain the first k elements of this sequence, the second sub-channel to contain the next k elements, and so on. The choice of k defines the data capacity of each sub-channel. Fig. 3 shows the spectrum partitioning of an example code with 8 sub-channels. By construction, the first sub-channel contains the elements with the lowest frequencies. Thus, it corresponds to gradual changes in light intensity in the spatial representation of the code, and it uses the least amount of spatial detail. Each subsequent sub-channel uses more spatial detail. The last sub-channel defines the code's finest details.

Next, we encode the payload in the sub-channels. The payload bytes are modulated using quadrature phase-shift keying (QPSK), yielding a sequence of complex symbols. Each symbol encodes two bits of payload data in its phase. We load the first k symbols into the first sub-channel, the next k symbols into the next sub-channel, and so on. Because each sub-channel describes a subset of elements of the spectrum, we are essentially populating the spectrum with our payload symbols. During this process, we ensure that the resulting spectrum observes Hermitian symmetry, so that its inverse Fourier transform is real-valued.

Finally, we compute the inverse Fourier transform of the spectrum. The result is a real-valued matrix, which we can interpret as a grayscale image. This grayscale image is the FOCUS code that corresponds to the given payload. A reader that captures the code can recover the payload by computing the code's Fourier transform and demodulating the symbols from the sub-channels.

4.2 Robustness to Undersampling

There are two reasons why FOCUS codes are particularly robust to undersampling caused by long distances or low camera resolution.

First, a FOCUS code uses only the lowest frequencies that are necessary to represent its payload. For example, if the entire payload fits into the first sub-channel, then the other sub-channels will not carry any data. Consequently, a FOCUS code never contains more spatial detail than necessary. This is important, as an image's finest details are most prone to undersampling. Therefore, FOCUS codes can be read over longer distances or with worse cameras than codes that encode data in higher frequencies, such as the high-contrast edges that are characteristic of most barcodes.

Second, if a FOCUS code is undersampled and aliasing occurs, the *later* sub-channels will be affected, since their symbols are represented by the highest frequencies. Crucially, due to the nature of aliasing, the sub-channels whose elements are represented by frequencies less than Ω_f are unaffected. A reader can still correctly decode the data from the unaffected sub-channels[1]. Furthermore, decoding errors in one sub-channel do not cause decoding errors in other sub-channels, because sub-channels are independent from each other. The independence follows from the fact that the symbols in the sub-channels correspond to elements in the spectrum, which in turn are coefficients of basis vectors. These are independent of each other by definition. The partitioning of the code's spectrum into sub-channels thus enables partial decoding, which in turn ensures that the amount of data a reader can decode from a FOCUS code scales with the amount of undersampling—the less a code is undersampled, the more data can be decoded.

[1]Note that the reader does not need to know the value of Ω_f. It is enough for the reader to verify if a sub-channel was decoded correctly, e.g. by using a checksum.

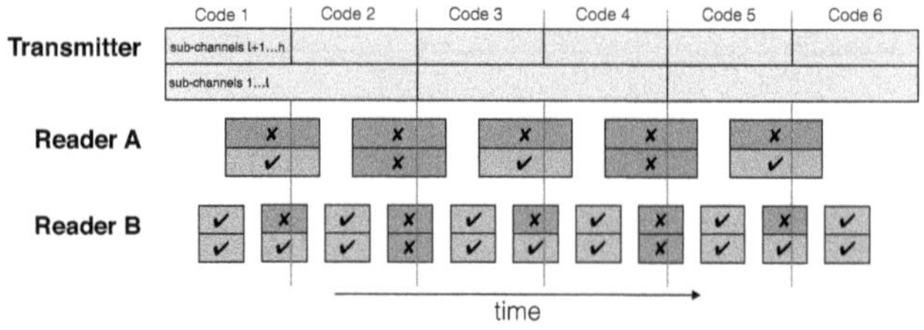

Figure 4: **Multi-rate streams alleviate the problem of mixed frames.** Reader A only captures mixed frames because its capture rate is too low, but it can nonetheless successfully decode data from the stream.

4.3 Robustness to Frame Mixing

FOCUS's independent sub-channels allow us to alleviate the frame mixing problem on screen/camera links. We design *multi-rate streams* that use different data rates across the sub-channels to enable a transmitter to simultaneously accommodate readers with different capture rates.

The concept is best explained by an example. If a transmitter wants to support readers with captures rate of 15 FPS and 30 FPS, it constructs a multi-rate stream with a total of $h + l$ sub-channels per code. The transmitter then updates the l sub-channels at 7.5 FPS, i.e., for every other code it displays. And it updates the h sub-channels at 15 FPS, i.e., for every code. Fig. 4 illustrates the situation.

The capture rate of a 30 FPS reader (Reader B) is twice the display rate. Thus, Reader B is guaranteed to correctly capture every code the transmitter displays, and can decode the data from all sub-channels. In contrast, every frame captured by a 15 FPS reader (Reader A) contains mixed codes. However, because the data in the first l sub-channels changes only in every other code, Reader A can nonetheless decode data from every second mixed frame it captures.

To see how this works, we can model a mixed frame c_{mix} as a linear combination $c_{\text{mix}} = ac_i + bc_{i+1}$ of two codes c_i, c_{i+1}, where a and b are attenuation factors. Assume that the data on the first l sub-channels did not change between c_i and c_{i+1}. This means that the spectra S_i, S_{i+1} of c_i and c_{i+1} are identical in the first l sub-channels. Now, for any symbol $S_{\text{mix}}[u, v]$ in the first l sub-channels of the mixed code:

$$\begin{aligned} S_{\text{mix}}[u, v] &= \mathcal{F}(c_{\text{mix}})[u, v] = \mathcal{F}(ac_i + bc_{i+1})[u, v] \\ &= aS_i[u, v] + bS_{i+1}[u, v] \\ &= (a + b)S_i[u, v] = (a + b)S_{i+1}[u, v]. \end{aligned}$$

The second line holds due to the linearity of the Fourier transform. The third line follows because the symbols in the first l sub-channels are identical. The above equation implies that frame mixing only scales the magnitude of identical symbols by $(a + b)$. Crucially, the phase is unaffected. Since FOCUS encodes data only in the phase, the 15 FPS reader can decode the data from the first l sub-channels, as illustrated in Fig. 4. This simple example can be readily extended to readers with a range of different capture rates. However, transmitting the same payload at different rates on different sub-channels would lead to an underutilization of

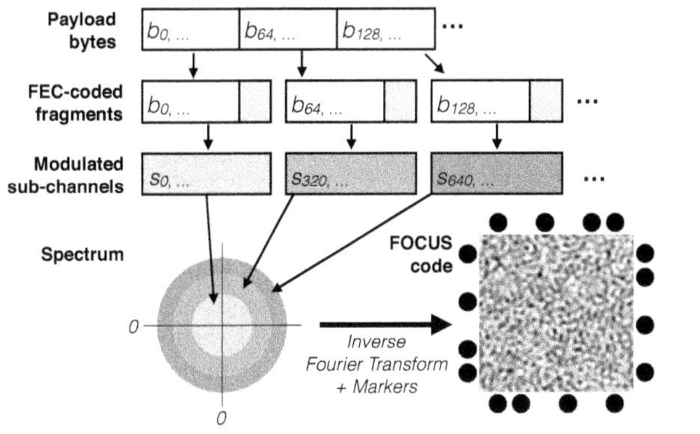

Figure 5: **Construction of a Focus code.** By design, a FOCUS code represents different parts of the payload by different amounts of spatial detail.

high-rate readers, since they would receive many data blocks multiple times in both the higher and the lower sub-channels. Therefore, FOCUS uses Fountain coding [35] across the sub-channels to make sure that high-rate readers can use the data from all sub-channels. We describe the use of Fountain codes in §5.3.

5. DESIGN

Based on the description of our core ideas, we now describe the complete encoding and decoding process, as well as the construction of streams of FOCUS codes.

5.1 Encoding

Fig. 5 provides an overview of how a FOCUS code is constructed. For simplicity, we refer to the entity that generates a code as the *transmitter*, even though the transmitter may actually simply print a code on paper.

Fragmentation and forward error correction. Transmitters split the payload bytes into *fragments* of 64 bytes each. Each of the payload fragments is later encoded in one sub-channel. Due to effects such as sensor noise, even a reader that samples a code at a sufficiently high rate may sporadically decode some bytes incorrectly. Therefore, the transmitter applies a Reed-Solomon error correcting code [32] to each fragment. Since we aim to support a wide range of channels, the transmitter conservatively adds 16 parity bytes to each fragment. Thus, a coded fragment is 80 bytes long, and readers can recover up to 8 byte errors per fragment. Note that error correction is applied to individual fragments rather than to the payload as a whole. This enables a reader to decode data from all fragments that have eight errors or fewer. Note also that redundancy in the code is effectively spread throughout the spatial representation of the code.

Modulation and spectrum construction. Because FOCUS represents data in the frequency domain, the coded fragments need to be modulated into complex symbols. To ensure the decodability of multi-rate streams, only the phase of a symbol is used to carry data. We use QPSK as the modulation scheme, so each symbol represents two payload bits. We empirically found QPSK to give a good trade-off between code capacity and robustness. Each modulated fragment is encoded in one sub-channel and consists of $k = 320$ symbols ($= 80$ bytes $\times$ 4 symbols/byte).

Next, the transmitter constructs the code's spectrum. The spectrum is a complex-valued matrix whose entries are initially all zero. The symbols of the first sub-channel are copied to the entries around the origin of the spectrum, as shown in Fig. 5. The symbols of the second sub-channel are arranged in the second ring around the center, and so on. During the construction process, the transmitter ensures that the resulting spectrum observes Hermitian symmetry through the origin [12]. This is necessary to ensure that the spectrum's inverse Fourier transform is real-valued, and thus can be displayed as a grayscale image. To ensure symmetry, the transmitter only populates the upper half of the spectrum, and sets the lower half to be a conjugate point reflection around the origin.

Inverse Fourier transform and clipping. Next, the transmitter computes the inverse Fourier transform of the constructed spectrum. The result is a real matrix that can be displayed as a grayscale image. However, the image may have a high peak-to-average ratio (PAR), a well-known issue in OFDM [31]. Due to finite levels of intensity in the output image, a high PAR in the real matrix causes quantization errors. To reduce the PAR, transmitters employ a standard technique of clipping the real matrix's maximum value [31].

Location markers. Finally, the transmitter adds markers around the code which help the reader to locate the code in a captured frame. We use a simple set of 16 filled circles as markers, as they enable a reader to locate a code with very high accuracy, as we describe in the next section. The robust localization of FOCUS codes without external markers is part of our ongoing research.

5.2 Decoding

We now describe how a reader decodes data from a code in a frame that it captured.

Correcting lens distortion and locating a code. As a first step, the reader corrects the captured frame for lens distortion. Radial lens distortion maps straight lines in a scene to bent lines in the captured frame, and is very common for the cheap lenses used in smart devices. We use standard techniques for undistortion [19]. Our experience shows that this correction step is crucial for good decoding performance at short distances.

Next, to locate a code in a captured frame, the reader looks for the 16 circular markers, which may appear as ellipses due to perspective distortion. The reader then computes the geometric center of each marker. We use circular markers because their centers are invariant to perspective distortion and can be computed with sub-pixel accuracy [4].

Correcting perspective distortion. Perspective distortion occurs if the reader views the code at an angle. As a result, a square code may appear as a more general quadrilateral in a captured frame. To compute the Fourier transform of a code, the reader must first undo the effect of perspective distortion. To this end, the reader determines the affine transform that describes the distortion. The transformation matrix can be constructed from the location of the markers in the captured frame, and knowledge about the location of markers in an undistorted frame. Then, the reader resamples the distorted code into its original form.

Locating and resampling a code in a captured frame can be viewed as achieving spatial synchronization with the transmitter. Just as in traditional OFDM systems, synchronization errors cause severe inter-symbol interference and poor decoding performance [2, 30, 33]. Therefore, the reader must

Model	Resolution		Capture rate
	Photo	Video	
Samsung Galaxy S6 (2015)	16 MP	2 MP	30 FPS
Samsung Galaxy S3 (2012)	8 MP	2 MP	30 FPS
Google Nexus One (2010)	5 MP	0.3 MP	5 FPS
Google Glass (2014)	5 MP	0.9 MP	30 FPS

Table 1: **Reader devices used in the evaluation.**

determine the projection matrix with high accuracy. This is why the sub-pixel localization accuracy of our markers is especially important.

Fourier transform, demodulation, and error correction. Finally, the reader computes the Fourier transform of the undistorted code. It unloads the code's spectrum, reversing the process described in §5.1. The reader then demodulates the symbols into bytes, and corrects errors using the Reed-Solomon code. All recovered and error-free fragments are passed to the application.

5.3 Streams of FOCUS Codes

Streams of FOCUS codes are used to communicate data of arbitrary size on screen/camera links. We briefly describe the construction of multi-rate streams and the use of Fountain codes in FOCUS.

Multi-rate streams. The construction of FOCUS's multi-rate streams is a simple generalization of the example from §4.3. Assume the transmitter would like to support readers with capture rates of $r_1, r_2, \ldots, r_n$, where n is at most as large as the number of sub-channels in the codes. Before the transmission starts, the transmitter chooses for each r_i a subset of sub-channels on which it transmits at a rate of $\frac{1}{2}r_i$. More specifically, if the transmitter's display rate is d, the data on the chosen sub-channels changes only on every $2\frac{d}{r_i}$-th code that the transmitter displays.

It is up to the system designer to decide which capture rates should be supported and how many sub-channels are assigned to each capture rate. The larger the number of sub-channels assigned to a capture rate, the higher the throughput for readers with that rate. In practice, we suggest that most sub-channels are assigned rates that are suitable for the most common capture rates (e.g., 30 FPS), a few are assigned higher rates (e.g., 60 FPS) to boost throughput for high-end smart devices, and few transmit at low rates (e.g., 2 FPS) to ensure that even legacy devices can receive data.

Fountain erasure coding. Screen/camera links are commonly uni-directional, and so a transmitter does not know which parts of the payload the readers have already successfully decoded. This makes it difficult to decide which parts of the payload should be re-sent, and on which sub-channels.

We avoid the issue by using Raptor erasure codes [35], a state-of-the-art Fountain code [6]. To transmit a payload consisting of n data blocks, the transmitter uses the Raptor code to produce a (infinite) sequence of fragments, which are then encoded in the sub-channels of the stream's codes. A crucial property of Raptor codes is that a reader only needs to receive *any* $n + \epsilon$ of the transmitted fragments to recover the full payload. Thus, it does not matter which fragment is encoded in which sub-channel, and there is no need for explicit synchronization between reader and transmitter. Furthermore, Raptor coding enables us to avoid sending the same payload in sub-channels that use different rates. Instead, every fragment that a reader decodes provides useful progress towards obtaining the full payload.

6. EVALUATION OF STATIC CODES

We now present our evaluation of a prototype implementation of FOCUS[2]. The prototype is written in Python and Java and runs on both Android devices and regular computers. We make heavy use of OpenCV [5] for image processing, and use FFTW [9] for computing Fourier transforms. We have further optimized critical code sections using ARM NEON instructions, and our implementation supports real-time decoding even on handheld Android devices.

We use four different reader devices in the evaluation that differ in their camera quality: a Samsung Galaxy S6, which is a state-of-the-art smartphone; a Samsung Galaxy S3, which is an older, yet popular model; a Google Nexus One, which represents a legacy smartphone released in 2010; and Google Glass as a representative for wearable technology. Key information about the devices is summarized in Tab. 1.

In this part of the evaluation, we study the decoding performance of static FOCUS codes. To capture static codes, readers take high-resolution photos of the codes, rather than videos. The readers are placed on a tripod except for our experiments on the impact of hand motion. The displayed codes are 20×20 cm^2 large. We vary the distance between readers and codes to assess the impact of code size.

6.1 Impact of Camera Quality

We begin by testing the claim that a reader's decoding performance scales with its camera quality. To get a detailed insight, we consider the bit error rates of different sub-channels as a measure of decoding performance. We expect an increase in error rates for later sub-channels, particularly on low-end cameras.

Experimental setup. We place the four readers at a distance of 3 m from an LCD at no angle. The LCD shows a FOCUS code carrying a payload of 1.6 KB. For each reader, we repeat the experiment 20 times with different code payloads.

Results. Fig. 6 shows the average bit error rates (BER) in the spectra of codes captured with the Galaxy S6, Galaxy S3, Nexus One, and Google Glass. A low bit error rate is denoted by white, a high error rate is denoted by red. The gray circles indicate the sub-channels (cf. Fig. 3). We observe only little variance in error rates between codes, and thus do not show variance in the plot.

The figure shows that bits encoded in lower frequencies generally have lower error rates than bits encoded in higher frequencies. The first sub-channel, closest to the origin, poses an exception that we address in the next paragraph. We can also see that there are more error-free channels for readers with better cameras. The plot for the Galaxy S6 is virtually error free (Fig. 6a) except for the first sub-channel. For the Galaxy S3 (Fig. 6b), we observe error rates of ca. 5% for very high frequencies. For the Google Nexus One (Fig. 6c), we see an increase in errors in later sub-channels, but there are still several sub-channels with error rates < 5%. Google Glass's camera does not support autofocus and is by far the worst camera in our experiment, but nonetheless a few sub-channels that use very low frequencies have only few errors (Fig. 6d).

[2]FOCUS is available as open source under `https://github.com/frederikhermans/focus`.

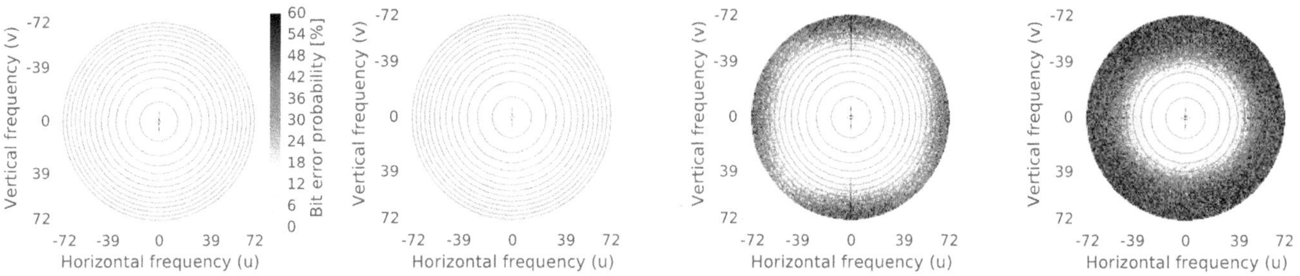

(a) Galaxy S6 (b) Galaxy S3 (c) Nexus One (d) Google Glass

Figure 6: **Location of bit errors in the frequency spectrum of static Focus codes for different readers.** Lower frequencies (closer to the center) are more robust to bit errors.

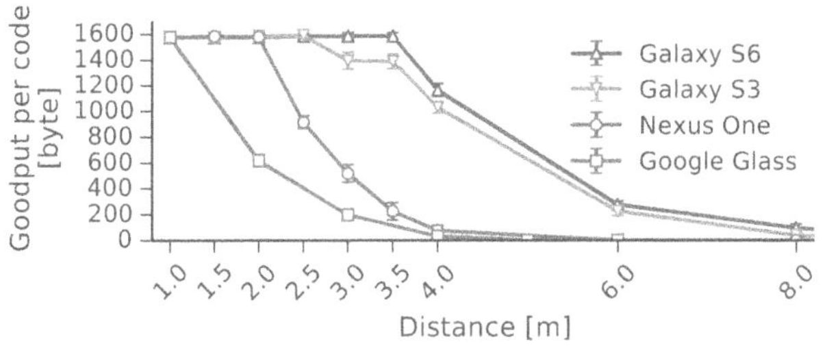

Figure 7: **Successfully decoded payload bytes as a function of distance to the code.** Each reader's goodput scales smoothly with its distance to the code.

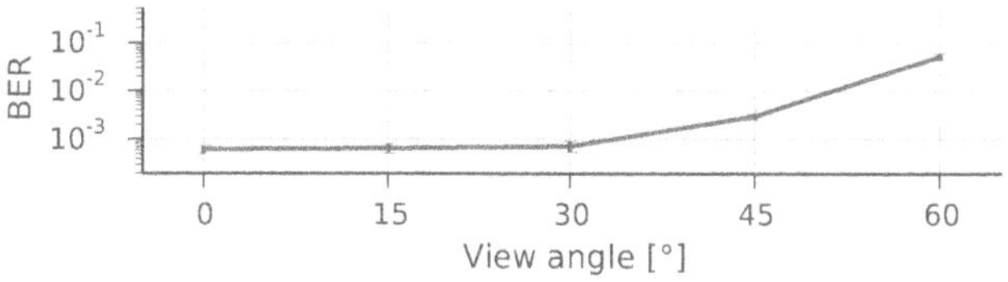

Figure 8: **Impact of view angle between camera and display on the bit error rate.** Perspective distortion has only little impact on decoding performance.

Some payload symbols in the first sub-channel, i.e., the one closest to the spectrum's origin, have high BER, as evidenced by the small cross in the origin. Our investigation showed that this is an effect of the LCD's refresh, which manifests as a dark bar across the captured frame. The effect can be observed for all LCDs, but disappears when codes are printed on a sheet of paper. Since few bits are affected, the errors can be recovered by error correction.

We conclude that FOCUS's basic premise is correct: lower frequencies provide a higher robustness to bit errors. By encoding data in sub-channels, even a reader with a poor camera, such as Google Glass, can at least partially decode a FOCUS code. The better the reader's channel in terms of camera quality, the more data it can decode from the very same code.

6.2 Impact of Distance

We now consider how decoding performance changes with the distance between reader and display. Distance has a major impact on channel quality, because the area of the captured code decreases as the distance between reader and display increases. The following experiment also allows us to gauge the impact of the (spatial) code size. The effect of increasing the distance to a code of fixed size is similar to the effect of reducing the code size while keeping the distance constant—both reduce the size of the code's projection on the reader's image sensor.

Experimental setup. An LCD screen shows a FOCUS code with a payload of 1.6 KB. We place the readers at distances ranging from 1 m to 10 m from the display and measure the goodput and the bit error rate. We define the goodput as the number of correctly decoded bytes (after error correction) excluding parity bytes. For each reader, we capture 20 codes with different payloads and present averages and their respective standard deviations.

Results. Fig. 7 shows the goodput for the different readers as a function of distance to the display. The distance at which a code can be completely decoded depends on the reader's camera quality. While the Galaxy S6 can decode all data at a distance of 3.5 m, Google Glass needs to be at a distance of 1 m from the display. For all readers, the goodput decreases smoothly (rather than abruptly) as the distance increases. This graceful degradation is an effect of the independence of sub-channels. These observations demonstrate how the decoding performance adapts to the reader's channel quality. We also note that the variance in goodput is very low. This suggests that the decoding performance is independent of the code's payload; i.e., there are no codes that are particularly difficult to decode. We conclude that the goodput scales smoothly with the reader's channel quality in terms of distance to the code.

6.3 View Angle, Lighting, Display Medium, and Hand Motion

Next, we briefly consider the impact of view angle, ambient lighting, display medium, and hand motion in terms of BER.

View angle. If the reader views a code at an angle, the captured code will be subject to perspective distortion. To understand the impact of perspective distortion on the decoding performance, we perform an experiment in which the Galaxy S6 is placed at a distance of 2 m from an LCD displaying FOCUS codes with a capacity of 1.6 KB. Between experiments, we vary the angle at which the reader views the display from 0° to 60°.

Fig. 8 shows the average BER we observe for different view angles. Even at a view angle of 60°, the BER is only 5%, so errors can be corrected by Reed-Solomon coding. For angles less than 45°, the impact of perspective distortion is barely noticeable. We conclude that FOCUS codes are robust to perspective distortion.

Lighting. We next consider the impact of ambient lighting. Variable lighting conditions cause reader cameras to perform various adaptations, such as with exposure time. We perform

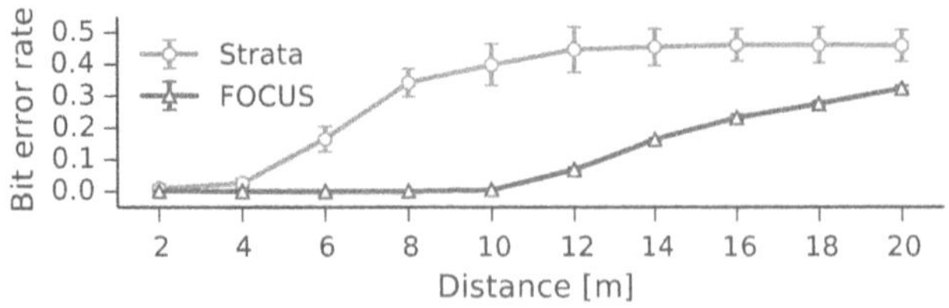

(a) Bit error rate

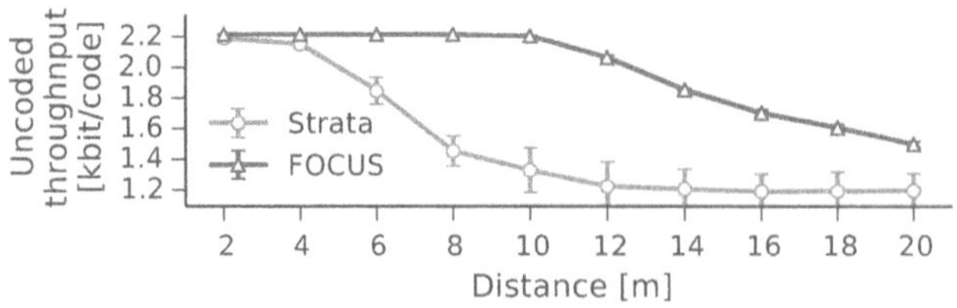

(b) Uncoded throughput

Figure 9: **Performance of Strata and Focus as the reading distance increases.** FOCUS codes have lower bit error rates (left) and deliver more data (right) than Strata codes across all distances in our experiment.

an experiment similar to the previous setup, but we fix the view angle at 0°, distance at 2 m, and vary the lighting conditions from darkness to full neon strip lights. We also perform the experiment outdoors. Our results showed BERs below 0.06%, so we conclude that ambient lighting does not have an appreciable impact.

Ambient lighting does not impair the decoding performance of FOCUS codes because it only affects the average light intensity of a captured code. As such, it changes only the DC component of the code's Fourier transform [29], which does not encode any data. Note that a shadow cast over a FOCUS code will also affect only the average light intensity of the captured code, and therefore is not expected to significantly impact bit error rates either.

Display medium. FOCUS codes can be displayed on a variety of media. We now consider the impact of the display medium on decoding performance. We display a low-capacity FOCUS code (384 bytes) on an LCD monitor, an LED monitor, a 3rd generation Apple iPad, and a sheet of paper. The printed code was printed with an office laser printer. We use the Galaxy S6 as the reader and place it at distances from 30 cm to 150 cm from the codes.

The receiver decoded the complete payload from all media and at all distances. Our inspection of the BER did not reveal any medium-specific characteristics. This is particularly encouraging when considering that laser printers produce grayscales by varying the number of black dots in an area (halftoning), since they can only produce monochrome output. Our result suggests that even codes reproduced with halftoning can be successfully decoded. We conclude that FOCUS codes are suitable for a range of display media.

Hand motion. In the experiments we have presented so far, the readers were placed on tripods to ensure repeatability and to simplify experimentation. In a real-world scenario a user may hold a reader in their hands instead. In this case, the reader will be subject to inevitable minor tremors and movements. These may cause motion blur in the captured image if there is movement during the exposure, and it may make it hard to align the reader's image plane center with the code's center, in particular at longer distances.

Our experience with the FOCUS prototype during a live demo [11] suggests that minor movements of the reader do not degrade decoding performance. To test this more systematically, we repeat a subset of the experiments described in §6.2. A user holds the Samsung Galaxy S6 in their hand and decodes ten codes at distances of 2 m, 4 m, 5 m, and 6 m from the display. We then compare the BER of codes captured with a handheld reader with the BER when the reader is placed on a tripod. We found that the difference in BER is very low (< 3%) across all distances. In particular, we did not find the BER for handheld readers to increase with the distance to the code. We conclude that minor movements, which are inevitable if a reader is handheld rather than statically positioned, do not have a significant impact on FOCUS's performance.

6.4 Comparing FOCUS and Strata

We now compare FOCUS to Strata [14], a recently proposed 2D code that shares FOCUS's goal of supporting different channel qualities. Strata codes are comprised of several spatial layers whose purpose is similar to that of sub-channels in FOCUS. In this experiment, we investigate which code can deliver more data on a given channel, and which code adapts more gracefully to a decrease in channel quality. Because Strata does not specify its error correction parameters, and in order to get a general view of the performance, we focus on the bit error rate (BER) as the primary metric for the experiment. We have been unable to obtain a copy of Strata. Therefore, we have implemented Strata ourselves based on the paper [14].

Experimental setup. We construct four-layer Strata codes with a capacity of 2267 bits and FOCUS codes with identical capacity and dimensions. The codes are displayed on an LCD and we use the Galaxy S6 as the reader. We vary the distance between reader and display from 1 m to 20 m. At each distance, we display 10 codes of each type and compute the average BER and the average uncoded throughput as well as the respective standard deviations.

Results. FOCUS codes have a lower bit error rate than Strata codes over all distances (Fig. 9a). Furthermore, FOCUS's bit error rate is close to zero for distances less than 12 m, and then grows slowly[3]; in comparison, Strata's bit error rate already exceeds 15% at a distance of 6 m, and then grows much more quickly. FOCUS provides a 3× longer read range than Strata (12 m vs. 4 m), if we assume the tolerable error rate to be 10%.

Fig. 9b shows the uncoded throughput per code for FOCUS and Strata, which we define as the number of bits in the decoded payload that match the transmitted payload, without any error correction. Note that the uncoded throughput has a lower bound of $\frac{1}{2}\times$ code capacity, as a reader that simply guessed each bit would be expected to guess half of the transmitted payload bits correctly. The plot shows that FOCUS delivers more bits correctly than Strata across all distances in our experiment.

One reason for Strata's larger BER (and hence its lower throughput) is that it uses more spatial detail to represent data than a FOCUS code of comparable capacity. Strata organizes payload into recursively-defined layers, and most of the payload is encoded in the deepest layer. This deepest

[3]We reach longer distances in this experiment compared to §6.2 because the code's payload is considerably smaller.

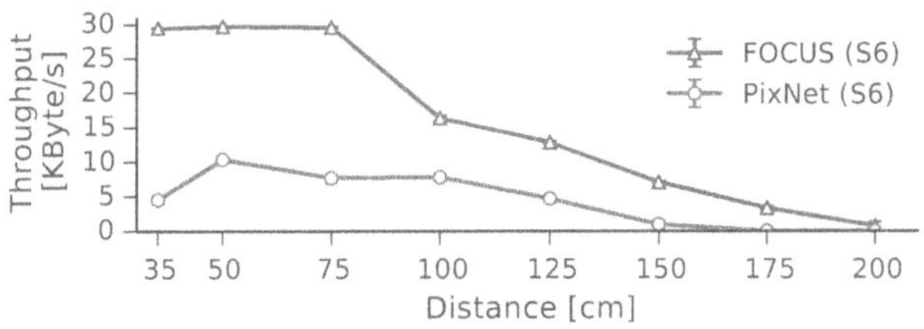

(a) Samsung Galaxy S6 reader

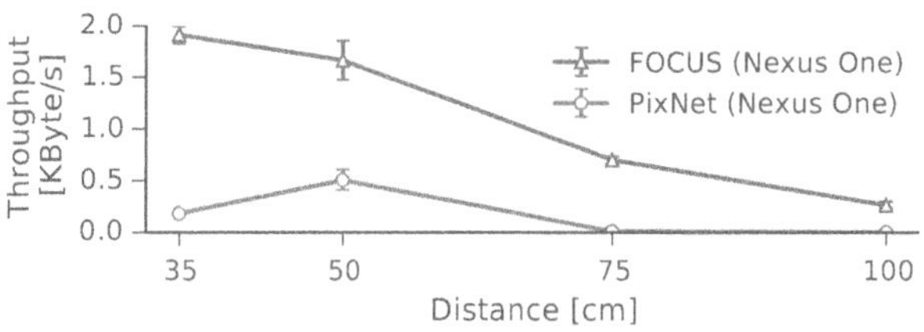

(b) Google Nexus One reader

Figure 10: **Throughput achieved by Focus and PixNet over distance for (a) a recent and (b) an old smartphone.** FOCUS improves the throughput by a factor of at least 2× for all distances and both devices.

Task	Duration (ms)	Relative
Correct lens distortion	7 ms	13%
Locate code	10 ms	19%
Perspective transform	4 ms	7%
Fourier transform	20 ms	37%
Demodulation	2 ms	4%
Error correction	2 ms	4%
Total	54 ms	100%

Table 2: **Decoding overhead breakdown for one frame on an S6.** By parallelizing the decoding of multiple frames, our prototype can decode at a rate of 56 FPS.

layer represents data in fine spatial details that are $\frac{1}{64}$th of the code's width. This explains the steep increase in BER as the distance to the display increases. In contrast, the finest detail that a FOCUS code uses to display a 2267 bit code is about $\frac{1}{26}$th of the code's width. This makes them more robust to undersampling.

Furthermore, decoding errors can propagate to deeper layers in Strata. This happens if the orientation of a block is incorrectly detected. We attribute the large performance variance of Strata to the propagation of decoding errors. In contrast, sub-channels in FOCUS codes can be decoded independently of each other, and we observe very little variance. We conclude that FOCUS codes enable a reader to make better use of their channel capacity, as they deliver data with lower bit error rates.

7. EVALUATION OF STREAMS OF CODES

We now evaluate streams of FOCUS codes that are used to transmit large payloads on screen/camera links. This scenario differs from the decoding of static codes because the displayed codes change rapidly. Furthermore, the reader's resolution of video frames is usually much lower than the resolution of photos (cf. Tab. 1).

7.1 Microbenchmarks

A reader on a screen/camera link must process its captured frames at a high speed to achieve a satisfying throughput. We briefly characterize the processing speed of our prototype reader on the Galaxy S6. We measure the time that it takes on the S6 to decode 900 captured frames, i.e., 30 seconds of video captured at 30 FPS. The multi-threaded prototype takes 15.9 s for this task, which corresponds to an effective processing rate of 56.7 FPS. This means that our prototype supports real-time decoding of frames that are captured at a rate of 56 FPS or less. A breakdown of a single thread's decoding overhead of one frame is provided in Tab. 2.

7.2 FOCUS and PixNet

We now consider FOCUS's throughput under different channel conditions. For reference, we also measure the throughput of PixNet [29], an earlier OFDM-based code for screen/camera links. We have been unable to obtain a copy of PixNet, and thus have implemented it based on a study of the relevant papers [28, 29].

We define the throughput as the number of correctly received bytes (*after* error correction) per second. Duplicate chunks of data (i.e., identical chunks that have already been received earlier) do not count towards the throughput: if a receiver captures the same code from a transmitter's stream twice, any data it decodes again from the second capture does not increase the throughput. While our definition of throughput is rather strict, we believe that it provides a better understanding of the rate at which a reader can obtain useful data. We also briefly consider the bit error rates of FOCUS and PixNet to obtain a better low-level characterization of the respective channels.

Experimental setup. An LCD shows a stream of either FOCUS or PixNet codes. The individual codes in both streams have the same size and capacity (2 KB). We use the Galaxy S6 and the Nexus One as readers to represent high- and low-end readers, respectively. The transmitter's display rate is set to half the reader's capture rate. We vary the distance between display and reader from 35 cm to 200 cm. Each experiment run is repeated six times, and we present averages and their respective standard deviations.

Throughput results. Fig. 10a shows the throughput for the Galaxy S6. PixNet's throughput peaks at 10 KB/s at a distance of 50 cm. It then gradually falls to zero at 175 cm. We attribute the poor throughput at 35 cm to the fact that PixNet does not correct lens distortion. FOCUS achieves the maximum achievable throughput (30 KB/s) for distances up to (including) 75 cm. At larger distances, its throughput gradually declines until it reaches 0.6 KB/s at a distance of 200 cm. Over all distances, FOCUS's throughput is at least twice as high as PixNet's. Fig. 10b shows the throughput for the Nexus One. In this experiment, the maximum achievable throughput is 4 KB/s due to the transmitter's reduced display rate. While both FOCUS and PixNet fall short of the maximum throughput, FOCUS provides an improvement of at least 3.3× over all distances.

There are several reasons for FOCUS's superior throughput. First, FOCUS uses lower frequencies to represent data than PixNet. PixNet divides its codes spatially into many smaller sub-codes, each of which then encodes part of the payload using OFDM. Note that the lowest frequency in an OFDM code is determined by the size of the code. As a result, most data in a PixNet code is represented by similar, relatively high frequencies. In contrast, FOCUS codes are only divided

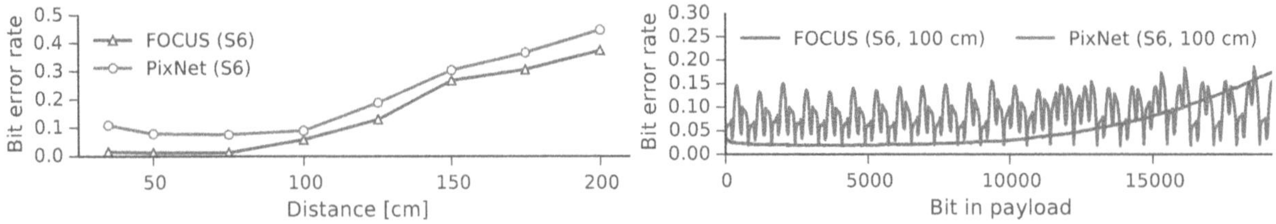

(a) Bit error rate over distance (b) Bit error rate within the payload at a distance of 100 cm

Figure 11: **Bit error rates for Focus and PixNet over distance and within the payload.** (a) FOCUS's average bit error rate per frame is consistently lower than PixNet's; (b) through its careful arrangement of the payload in the frequency domain, FOCUS ensures that errors are concentrated toward the end of the payload, enabling effective error correction.

in the frequency domain and so use lower frequencies with a wider frequency range to represent data. Second, unlike PixNet, FOCUS readers correct for lens distortions that are common on smart devices. Third, PixNet discards all mixed frames, whereas FOCUS readers are able to decode mixed frames. Finally, since PixNet targets good channels, it uses relatively weak error protection for some parts of the payloads. We believe that while PixNet is well-suited for the high-end cameras it targets, FOCUS provides superior performance on smart devices.

BER results. Throughput is an important metric for developers who want to understand which system delivers more useful bytes per second. To obtain a more fine-grained characterization of the communication channels provided by FOCUS and PixNet, we now consider the respective bit error rates.

Fig. 11a shows the average bit error rate over distance for the Samsung Galaxy S6. Across all distances, FOCUS achieves a lower bit error rate than PixNet. However, it may be surprising that the difference in bit error rate is not as large as the difference in throughput. This is because FOCUS readers try to decode mixed frames, rather than discard them as PixNet does. The advantage of decoding mixed frames is that it relaxes the need for tight temporal synchronization between the transmitter and the reader (§4.3). If the mixing is not too severe, or if the transmitter uses multi-rate streams, a FOCUS reader can partially decode mixed frames. However, a mixed frame will generally have a higher bit error rate than a clean frame. Thus, because FOCUS considers mixed frames whereas PixNet discards them, FOCUS's average bit error rate is relatively high in Fig. 11a.

It is instructive to consider how errors are distributed within the payload. Fig. 11b shows the bit error rate as a function of bit position in the payload for a distance of 100 cm between reader and transmitter. PixNet's bit error rate is similar across the whole payload. The pattern in its curve is an artifact of how PixNet arranges data in the frequency domain. In particular, the valleys correspond to parts of the payload that happen to be encoded at low frequencies. In contrast, FOCUS's bit error rate is much smoother across the whole payload. Most importantly, errors are concentrated towards the end of the payload, whereas the first half of the payload suffers relatively few errors that can be corrected with forward error correction. This is an effect of FOCUS's encoding of data in increasingly higher frequencies (§4.1), which ensures that error rates for adjacent bits in the payload are similar. This, in turn, enables effective error correction.

7.2.1 *High-end Cameras*

The original PixNet paper [29] reports much higher throughput (MBit/s rather than kBit/s) than what we have measured. However, the PixNet authors used high-end DSLR cameras with optical zoom, which provide a much better image quality than smartphone cameras. In contrast, FOCUS targets low-end to mid-range cameras and aims to be robust against their deficiencies, such as low resolution. We nonetheless carry out a simple experiment with a high-end camera as a reader. This experiment serves two purposes: it allows us to understand whether FOCUS is capable of delivering MBit/s throughput on the near-perfect links provided by high-end cameras; and it serves as a validation of our implementation of PixNet.

Experimental setup. We place a Nikon D7100 DSLR camera at a distance of 1.5 m from an LCD. The LCD displays either FOCUS codes or PixNet codes with a capacity of 66 kbit at a rate of 60 codes/s. We follow the methodology of the PixNet paper [29, see pg. 8] and set the camera's shutter speed to 1/60 s corresponding to an effective frame rate of 30 codes/s.

Results. Both FOCUS and our implementation of PixNet were able to fully decode the data encoded in the respective codes. The throughput for both systems was 2 MBit/s, which is the maximum possible throughput for the given code capacities. Decoding was virtually error free. The results serve as a validation of our PixNet implementation and allow us to conclude that FOCUS can deliver throughput in the order of MBit/s with high-end cameras.

7.3 Throughput under Rate Mismatch

In many scenarios, a transmitter wants to send data to several readers with different capture rates. Instead of adapting its display rate to the slowest reader, FOCUS's multi-rate streams allow a transmitter to concurrently transmit at different rates. We now evaluate how multi-rate streams alleviate the problems of rate mismatch and frame mixing. In particular, we study the throughput for different ratios of capture rate to display rate.

Experimental setup. To isolate the effects of rate mismatch from the effects of camera quality, we use only the Galaxy S6 with a capture rate of 30 FPS as a reader in this experiment. We vary the display rate from 15 FPS to 60 FPS to study the throughput under various capture/display rate ratios. The reader is placed 75 cm from the display. The transmitter shows a multi-rate stream of FOCUS codes. One third of the sub-channels of the stream is updated at a rate of 1/4 of the display rate, the next third of sub-channels is updated at a rate of 1/2 of the display rate, and the last third is updated at a rate equal to the display rate.

Results. Fig. 12 shows the experimental results. The x-axis denotes the ratio of capture rate to display rate, i.e., the

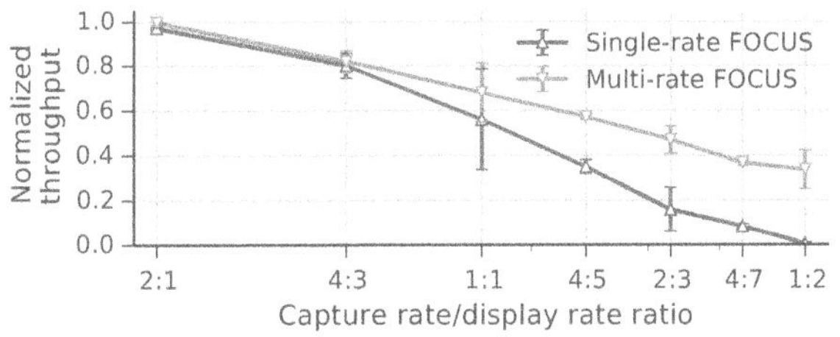

Figure 12: **Impact of mismatch between display and capture rate on the throughput.** FOCUS's multi-rate streams enable readers to receive data even if the display rate is larger than their capture rate.

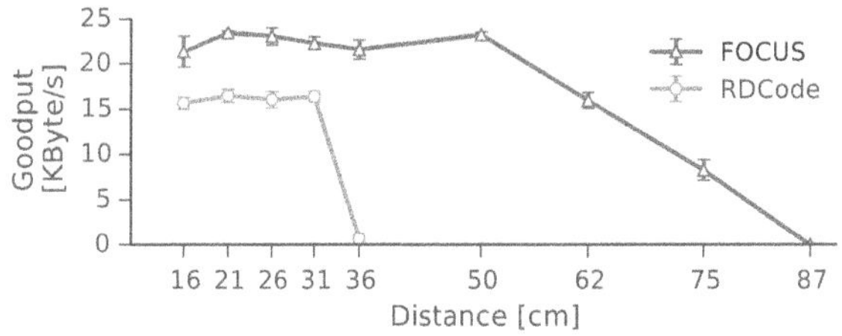

Figure 13: **Goodput of Focus and RDCode for varying distance between transmitter and reader.** FOCUS provides superior goodput and range.

number of captured frames per displayed code. The y-axis shows the reader's throughput normalized by the sender's data rate. Thus, the y-axis shows which fraction of the transmission could be decoded.

For single rate streams, the highest throughput is reached when the capture/display rate ratio is 2:1, because only then is the reader guaranteed to capture each displayed code at least once without mixing. As the ratio decreases, the throughput decreases, because the reader captures more and more mixed codes. When the ratio is 1:2, the reader cannot decode any data.

In contrast, multi-rate streams enable a transmitter to simultaneously support a wide range of capture/display rate ratios. Even though throughput decreases for readers that capture less than two frames for every displayed frame, the decrease is much smoother for multi-rate codes: if the capture rate is equal to the display rate, the reader can nonetheless decode 66% of the transmitted data; and even if the display rate is twice as high as the capture rate, the reader can decode 33% of the data, albeit every captured frame being mixed. The reader can partially decode the mixed codes because the data on some sub-channels stays constant over multiple frames, as described in §4.3. We conclude that FOCUS multi-rate streams enable a transmitter to concurrently support readers with a range of capture rates.

7.4 Goodput of FOCUS and RDCode

We now study the *goodput* of FOCUS code streams by continuously broadcasting a file and measuring the delay until complete file reception. Note that goodput may differ substantially from throughput on uni-directional screen/camera links if the reader repeatedly misses a specific part of the transmission without the means of explicitly requesting the missing part to be retransmitted. Therefore this section provides a necessary complement to the throughput evaluation. We compare the goodput of FOCUS to RDCode, a recently proposed barcode design for screen/camera links [39]. It is a useful comparison reference, because it is specifically designed for robustness—a goal we also share in the design of FOCUS. The authors of RDCode have provided us with a copy of the source code.

Experimental setup. We transmit from a 3rd generation Apple iPad and receive on the Galaxy S6. The transmitter displays an infinite stream of either RDCode codes or FOCUS codes, which contain a 50.3 KB file. We vary the distance of the S6 to the iPad. We repeat each experiment run five times and show the mean goodput and its standard deviation.

Results. Fig. 13 shows the goodput (file size divided by total transfer time) as a function of the distance between the transmitter and the reader. For distances below 31 cm, we observe a goodput of around 17 KB/s for RDCode, and around 23 KB/s for FOCUS; for larger distances, the goodput of RDCode sharply falls off and the reader is unable to retrieve the file completely. In contrast, FOCUS can maintain the goodput of 23 KB/s for distances up to 50 cm; only beyond this does the goodput gradually decline until it reaches zero at a distance of 87 cm.

FOCUS consistently outperforms RDCode over all distances in our experiment. While the increase in goodput is moderate (36%), FOCUS supports a significantly larger communication range: its goodput at 62 cm is similar to RDCode's goodput at 31 cm. Even at 75 cm, transferring a 50 KB file only takes 5 s. Examining the implementation internals it seems that RDCode's locator detection algorithm begins to fail at longer distances. We conclude that FOCUS provides improved goodput and communication range over RDCode.

7.5 Embedded FOCUS Streams

For demonstration purposes, we embedded a FOCUS stream into a music video. Fig. 14 shows a frame of the video. We play the music video on a laptop and measure the throughput at the reader, which a user holds in their hand. The embedded stream has a data rate of 30.7 KB/s. In our experiments, we measure the reader's throughput to be 28.6 KB/s. We draw two conclusions from this simple experiment: first, minor hand movements, which are inevitable when the reader is hand-held rather than placed on a tripod, do not significantly degrade throughput. Second, the frequent changes in lighting due to scene changes in the video do not significantly degrade throughput either.

8. APPLICATIONS

FOCUS codes are characterized by their robustness and high capacity. FOCUS codes can be read over long distances and their decoding performance scales with the reader's channel conditions. We now briefly discuss some applications which we expect to benefit most from FOCUS.

We see immediate benefits in scenarios such as logistics, warehouses, and supply chain management. FOCUS codes store more data than traditional visual codes. For example, a QR code can store up to 3 KB, whereas we have successfully used FOCUS codes encoding more than 8 KB. This improved capacity is especially useful to store information that needs to be shared across organizational boundaries. For example, hazardous materials in the supply chain may be labeled with detailed information about their origin and destination, instructions for handling and storing, etc. By embedding all this information in a code, rather than requiring network access and lookup in a cross-organizational database, the

Figure 14: **Music video with an embedded Focus stream.** A recent smartphone can decode data at a rate of 28.6 KB/s from the stream.

information is robustly self-contained and instantly available. Furthermore, extra capacity allows cryptographic signing of data. This enables a reader to verify the authenticity and integrity of a code's information, and renders attacks like code-based phishing ineffective [37, 41].

In processes that require automated identification, such as luggage routing, FOCUS's improved robustness can reduce the need for costly human intervention by ameliorating decoding failures. FOCUS codes can also be read over long distances, which is particularly beneficial for scenarios such as warehouse inventory management [24]. Today, long distance reading is only possible with laser-based scanners, which can scan only one code at a time. In contrast, a camera can read multiple FOCUS codes at once.

Visual codes and markers are also widely used in augmented reality scenarios for pose estimation or to attach digital data to physical objects [1, 18]. With FOCUS codes, these functions can be combined: data encoded in higher frequencies could, for example, describe different modes of interaction with an object or information to be displayed to users [23], whereas data encoded in the lower frequencies can be used for pose estimation and relative positioning.

Screen/camera links may be used to broadcast data to large audiences, e.g., at sports events, where WiFi and cell networks may be underprovisioned, for broadcasting to many users. Screen/camera links also have the salient security property that they require both nodes on a link to be physically present. In contrast, even short-range RF communication, such as NFC, can be tampered with at a distance using directional antennas [7, 25]. Furthermore, jamming screen/camera links requires the physical presence and visibility of the jammer, thereby raising the bar for such an attack. Alternatively, digital communication through visual codes embedded in a video stream (e.g., TV or web stream), can be used to provide enhancements to the media such as subtitles, without a separate file or data stream.

9. DISCUSSION AND FUTURE WORK

We briefly discuss some of the requirements that FOCUS makes on transmitters and readers and contrast them with the requirements of existing visual codes. We also describe related prospects for future work.

In contrast to codes that use spatial coding, such as Strata, QR, or DataMatrix, FOCUS codes represent data in the frequency domain. Therefore, encoding and decoding involve the computation of a Fourier transform. While 2D Fourier transforms can be computationally complex (the running time is $O(n^2 \log n)$), FOCUS usually operates on small images (e.g., 512×512 pixels), and an implementation can make use of highly optimized libraries for computing Fourier transforms. As such, we do not consider the Fourier transform's overhead to be impractical.

Some visual codes can be represented using black and white only, whereas FOCUS codes leverage grayscales. Our experience has shown though that FOCUS codes can be displayed and decoded from devices that support only a limited number of grayscales. For example, FOCUS codes printed with regular laser printers consist of very small black dots rather than actual grayscales, but can be decoded nonetheless (§6.3). Similarly, we confirmed that FOCUS codes can be decoded from eInk displays that support only sixteen grayscales; in simulations, we found that FOCUS codes can even be decoded from black-and-white displays that use dithering to approximate grayscales. In summary, FOCUS codes can be used over a wide range of display media (LCD, LED, paper, eInk), but a more detailed study of the impact of the characteristics of display media may be of interest in the future.

FOCUS requires high localization accuracy for codes in a captured photo. As explained in §5.2, low-accuracy localization would cause synchronization errors and lead to inter-symbol interference [29, 33]. However, there are well-established and computationally cheap techniques for sub-pixel localization [4] that we exploit. We are currently exploring alternative designs that use less space for markers while providing comparable localization accuracy.

Finally, modern smartphone cameras can capture several images of a scene in rapid succession. There is a large body of research on how such bursts of images may be used, e.g., to undo the effects of blur [3] or enhance the resolution of the captured images [15]. Understanding whether bursts of photos can improve the decoding performance and data capacity of FOCUS codes is another direction for future work.

10. CONCLUSION

We presented FOCUS, a visual code design that is robust to the most common impairments of visual channels. The amount of data that a reader can decode from a FOCUS code scales automatically with its channel conditions. Our experiments demonstrated the suitability of FOCUS for smart devices with poor cameras and limited computational capacity. We also showed that FOCUS significantly advances the state of the art: it improves on the read distance of Strata by a factor 3×, on the throughput of PixNet by at least 2×, and on the communication range of RDCode by 2×.

The key to FOCUS's performance lies in its encoding of data in many independent sub-channels in the frequency domain. The sub-channels differ from each other in their robustness to channel impairments, and even a reader with a poor channel can decode data from the more robust sub-channels of a code. We conclude that frequency-based visual codes need not be limited to readers with high-end cameras, and that they provide superior capacity and robustness over existing designs.

Acknowledgments

We would like to thank our shepherd Xia Zhou and the anonymous reviewers for their insightful comments. We thank Peter Nyström of IAR Systems for his help with the ARM NEON optimizations. We thank Anran Wang for providing us with a copy of RDCode.

11. REFERENCES

[1] F. Ababsa and M. Mallem. Robust Camera Pose Estimation Using 2D Fiducials Tracking for Real-time Augmented Reality Systems. In *Proc. of VRCAI '04*. ACM, 2004.

[2] A. Ashok, S. Jain, M. Gruteser, N. Mandayam, W. Yuan, and K. Dana. Capacity of Pervasive Camera Based Communication Under Perspective Distortions. In *Proc. of PerCom '14*. IEEE, March 2014.

[3] A. C. S. Atsushi Ito, A. Veeraraghavan, and R. G. Baraniuk. Blurburst: Removing blur due to camera shake using multiple images. *ACM Transactions on Graphics*, to appear.

[4] C. B. Bose and I. Amir. Design of Fiducials for Accurate Registration Using Machine Vision. *IEEE Transactions on Pattern Analysis and Machine Intelligence*, Dec. 1990.

[5] G. Bradski. The OpenCV Library. *Dr. Dobb's Journal of Software Tools*, 2000.

[6] J. W. Byers, M. Luby, M. Mitzenmacher, and A. Rege. A Digital Fountain Approach to Reliable Distribution of Bulk Data. *SIGCOMM Computer Communincation Review*, 28(4), Oct. 1998.

[7] T. P. Diakos, J. A. Briffa, T. W. C. Brown, and S. Wesemeyer. Eavesdropping Near-Field Contactless Payments: a Quantitative Analysis. *The Journal of Engineering*, January 2013.

[8] European Committee for Standardization. *Automatic Identification and Data Capture Techniques – QR Code 2005 Bar Code Symbology Specification: ISO/IEC 18004-2006*. 2006.

[9] M. Frigo. A Fast Fourier Transform Compiler. In *Proc. of PLDI '99*. ACM, 1999.

[10] T. Hao, R. Zhou, and G. Xing. Cobra: Color Barcode Streaming For Smartphone Systems. In *Proc. of MobiSys*. ACM, 2012.

[11] F. Hermans, L. McNamara, and T. Voigt. Demo: Scalable Visual Codes for Embedding Digital Data in the Physical World. In *Proc. of SenSys '15*. ACM, 2015.

[12] S. Hranilovic and F. Kschischang. A Pixelated MIMO Wireless Optical Communication System. *IEEE Journal of Selected Topics in Quantum Electronics*, 12(4), 2006.

[13] W. Hu, H. Gu, and Q. Pu. LightSync: Unsynchronized Visual Communication over Screen-camera Links. In *Proc. of MobiCom '13*. ACM, 2013.

[14] W. Hu, J. Mao, Z. Huang, Y. Xue, J. She, K. Bian, and G. Shen. Strata: Layered Coding for Scalable Visual Communication. In *Proc. of MobiCom '14*. ACM, 2014.

[15] Y. Huang, W. Wang, and L. Wang. Bidirectional recurrent convolutional networks for multi-frame super-resolution. In C. Cortes, N. D. Lawrence, D. D. Lee, M. Sugiyama, and R. Garnett, editors, *Advances in Neural Information Processing Systems 28*. Curran Associates, Inc., 2015.

[16] ISO. *Information technology—Automatic Identification and Data Capture Techniques—Data Matrix Bar Code Symbology Specification*. Number ISO/IEC 16022:2006. Geneva, Switzerland, 2006.

[17] ISO. *Information Technology – Automatic Identification and Data Capture Techniques – Aztec Code Bar Code Symbology Specification*. Number ISO/IEC 24778:2008. Geneva, Switzerland, 2008.

[18] T.-W. Kan, C.-H. Teng, and W.-S. Chou. Applying QR Code in Augmented Reality Applications. In *Proc. of VRCAI '09*. ACM, 2009.

[19] V. Lepetit and P. Fua. Monocular Model-based 3D Tracking of Rigid Objects. *Foundations and Trends in Computer Graphics and Vision*, 1(1), Jan. 2005.

[20] A. Lerner, A. Saxena, K. Ouimet, B. Turley, A. Vance, T. Kohno, and F. Roesner. Analyzing the Use of Quick Response Codes in the Wild. In *Proc. of MobiSys*. ACM, 2015.

[21] T. Li, C. An, X. Xiao, A. T. Campbell, and X. Zhou. Real-Time Screen-Camera Communication Behind Any Scene. In *Proc. of MobiSys '15*. ACM, 2015.

[22] R. LiKamWa, D. Ramirez, and J. Holloway. Styrofoam: A Tightly Packed Coding Scheme for Camera-based Visible Light Communication. In *Proc. of MobiCom Workshop on Visible Light Communication Systems*. ACM, 2014.

[23] S. Mayer and G. Soros. User Interface Beaming – Seamless Interaction with Smart Things Using Personal Wearable Computers. In *Proc of. Wearable and Implantable Body Sensor Networks Workshops (BSN Workshops)*, June 2014.

[24] Motorala Inc. The Next-Generation Warehouse — Long Range Scanning And Emergence of 2D Bar Codes. Technical report, 2011.

[25] C. Mulliner. Vulnerability Analysis and Attacks on NFC-Enabled Mobile Phones. In *Proc. of ARES '09*, pages 695–700, March 2009.

[26] A. V. Oppenheim, A. S. Willsky, and S. H. Nawab. *Signals and Systems*. Prentice-Hall, Inc., NJ, USA, 1996.

[27] D. Parikh and G. Jancke. Localization and Segmentation of a 2D High Capacity Color Barcode. In *Proc. of Workshop on Applications of Computer Vision*. IEEE, 2008.

[28] S. D. Perli. MIT Masters Thesis - PixNet: Designing Interference-free Wireless Links Using LCD-camera Pairs, 2010.

[29] S. D. Perli, N. Ahmed, and D. Katabi. PixNet: Interference-free Wireless Links Using LCD-camera Pairs. In *Proc. of MobiCom '10*. ACM, 2010.

[30] T. Pollet, M. Van Bladel, and M. Moeneclaey. BER Sensitivity of OFDM Systems to Carrier Frequency Offset and Wiener Phase Noise. *IEEE Transactions on Communications*, 43(2/3/4), Feb 1995.

[31] Y. Rahmatallah and S. Mohan. Peak-To-Average Power Ratio Reduction in OFDM Systems: A Survey And Taxonomy. *IEEE Communications Surveys Tutorials*, 15(4):1567–1592, April 2013.

[32] I. Reed and G. Solomon. Polynomial Codes Over Certain Finite Fields. *Journal of the Society of Industrial and Applied Mathematics*, 8(2), June 1960.

[33] T. Schmidl and D. Cox. Robust Frequency and Timing Synchronization for OFDM. *IEEE Transactions on Communications*, 45(12), Dec 1997.

[34] S. Shi, L. Chen, W. Hu, and M. Gruteser. Reading Between Lines: High-rate, Non-intrusive Visual Codes

Within Regular Videos via ImplicitCode. In *Proc. of UbiComp '15*. ACM, 2015.

[35] A. Shokrollahi. Raptor Codes. *IEEE/ACM Transactions on Networking*, 14(SI), June 2006.

[36] M. Sonka, V. Hlavac, and R. Boyle. *Image Processing, Analysis, and Machine Vision*. CL Engineering, 2007.

[37] T. Vidas, E. Owusu, S. Wang, C. Zeng, L. Cranor, and N. Christin. QRishing: The Susceptibility of Smartphone Users to QR Code Phishing Attacks. In *Financial Cryptography and Data Security*, Lecture Notes in Computer Science. Springer Berlin Heidelberg, 2013.

[38] A. Wang, Z. Li, C. Peng, G. Shen, G. Fang, and B. Zeng. InFrame++: Achieve Simultaneous Screen-Human Viewing and Hidden Screen-Camera Communication. In *Proc. of MobiSys '15*. ACM, 2015.

[39] A. Wang, S. Ma, C. Hu, J. Huai, C. Peng, and G. Shen. Enhancing Reliability to Boost the Throughput over Screen-Camera Links. In *Proc. of MobiCom '14*. ACM, 2014.

[40] Q. Wang, M. Zhou, K. Ren, T. Lei, J. Li, and Z. Wang. Rain Bar: Robust Application-Driven Visual Communication Using Color Barcodes. In *Proc. of ICDCS '15*, June 2015.

[41] H. Yao and D. Shin. Towards Preventing QR Code Based Attacks on Android Phone Using Security Warnings. In *Proc. of ASIA CCS '13*. ACM, 2013.

Practical Bluetooth Traffic Sniffing: Systems and Privacy Implications

Wahhab Albazrqaoe[†‡], Jun Huang[†], Guoliang Xing[†]
[†]Department of Computer Science and Enginnering, Michigan State University, USA.
[‡]University of Karbala, Karbala City, Iraq.
{albazrqa, huangjun, glxing}@cse.msu.edu

ABSTRACT

With the prevalence of personal Bluetooth devices, potential breach of user privacy has been an increasing concern. To date, sniffing Bluetooth traffic has been widely considered an extremely intricate task due to Bluetooth's indiscoverable mode, vendor-dependent adaptive hopping behavior, and the interference in the open 2.4 GHz band. In this paper, we present *BlueEar* – a practical Bluetooth traffic sniffer. BlueEar features a novel *dual-radio architecture* where two Bluetooth-compliant radios coordinate with each other on learning the hopping sequence of indiscoverable Bluetooth networks, predicting adaptive hopping behavior, and mitigating the impacts of RF interference. Experiment results show that BlueEar can maintain a packet capture rate higher than 90% consistently in real-world environments, where the target Bluetooth network exhibits diverse hopping behaviors in the presence of dynamic interference from coexisting 802.11 devices. In addition, we discuss the privacy implications of the BlueEar system, and present a practical countermeasure that effectively reduces the packet capture rate of the sniffer to 20%. The proposed countermeasure can be easily implemented on the Bluetooth master device while requiring no modification to slave devices like keyboards and headsets.

1. INTRODUCTION

In recent years, Bluetooth has enjoyed an unprecedented penetration rate in mobile devices. About three billions Bluetooth units will be shipped worldwide in 2017 [2]. In particular, Bluetooth has become the *de facto* connectivity interface for wireless accessories and smart devices including keyboard/mouse, headsets, wearables like fitness trackers and smart watches, smart appliances, and in-car telematic systems like Android Auto [1] and CarPlay [4]. Because the communication of these devices is privacy-sensitive in nature, Bluetooth employs a two-level stream cipher to encrypt packets at the link-layer [32]. Unfortunately, recent studies have revealed many critical flaws of this encryption scheme [17] [10] [24] [26] [25] [31] [9] [28]. In particular, it is shown that Bluetooth is subject to several practical attacks that can circumvent, compromise, or even crack the link-layer encryption, leading to potential user privacy breach [9] [31] [24].

MobiSys'16, June 25-30, 2016, Singapore, Singapore

DOI: http://dx.doi.org/10.1145/2906388.2906403

Despite the well-documented flaws of Bluetooth encryption, to date, sniffing Bluetooth traffic has been considered an extremely intricate task due to the following reasons. *(i)* Bluetooth employs frequency hopping spread spectrum, where carrier frequency is rapidly switched following a pseudo-random hopping sequence. The hopping sequence is hidden when Bluetooth is in indiscoverable mode, making it difficult for a sniffer to hop following the target. *(ii)* When coexisting with other wireless devices on overlapping frequencies, Bluetooth performs adaptive hopping, where the hopping sequence is frequently modified to adapt spectrum use. Such an adaptive hopping behavior is vendor-dependent, and may differ significantly across different devices. *(iii)* In the crowded 2.4 GHz band, the sniffer may experience intensive interference from coexisting wireless devices, especially the prevalent 802.11 based WLANs, resulting in poor sniffing performance.

There exist a few proprietary off-the-shelf Bluetooth sniffers [12] [13], which are primarily designed for protocol diagnosis in controlled wireless settings. In addition, to sniff the traffic of frequency hopping Bluetooth, they rely on specialized radio to monitor all Bluetooth subchannels in parallel, which makes them costly. As an example, off-the-shelf sniffers manufactured by Frontline Test Equipment [11] – the leading provider of Bluetooth protocol analyzer – cost $10K to $25K per unit. Recently, a few low-cost Bluetooth packet sniffers have been developed based on open-source wireless platforms [6] [5] [29] [33] [30] [7] [20] [3]. These systems are exclusively designed for sniffing Bluetooth traffic in basic hopping mode. In practice, they suffer prohibitively poor sniffing performance due to the misprediction of adaptive hopping behavior, as well as excessive packet corruptions caused by the interference in the open 2.4 GHz band.

As Bluetooth becomes increasingly popular worldwide, an in-depth study on its resistance to traffic sniffing becomes imperative. In this paper, we explore the feasibility and privacy implications of sniffing Bluetooth traffic in practical environments using general, inexpensive wireless platforms. Our major contribution is two-fold.

The BlueEar system. We present the design, implementation, and evaluation of *BlueEar* – the first practical Bluetooth traffic sniffer that consists of only inexpensive, Bluetooth-compliant radios. BlueEar features a novel *dual-*

radio architecture, where two radios – named as *scout* and *snooper* – coordinate with each other on learning the hopping sequence of indiscoverable Bluetooth, predicting adaptive hopping behavior, and handling complex interference conditions. Specifically, the scout hops over all Bluetooth subchannels to survey interference conditions and monitors the target's packet transmissions. By fusing these measurements, BlueEar uses a probabilistic clock matching algorithm to determine the basic hopping sequence, and then integrates statistical models and a lightweight machine learning algorithm to predict the adaptive hopping behavior, which allows the snooper to hop following the target. To maintain reliable sniffing performance in complex interference conditions, the scout runs a selective jamming algorithm, which manipulates the hopping of the target to mitigate the impacts of interference. We have implemented a prototype of BlueEar for sniffing the traffic of Bluetooth Classic, which offers enhanced data rates and a more complex hopping protocol than Bluetooth Low Energy (BLE). The prototype employs two Ubertooths [6] to implement the scout and the snooper, and interfaces them to a controller running on a Linux laptop. We identify critical issues in Ubertooth firmware that severely degrades its performance during frequency hopping, and present novel solutions to address these flaws. Extensive experiments results show that BlueEar can maintain a packet capture rate higher than 90% consistently in practical environments, where the target Bluetooth network exhibits diverse hopping behaviors in the presence of interference from coexisting 802.11 based WLANs.

Privacy implications. We discuss the implication of the BlueEar system on BLE privacy. Moreover, we evaluate the performance of BlueEar when eavesdropping on audio traffic, which is known to be extremely sensitive to packet loss. We show that the packet capture rate achieved by BlueEar translates to a high audio quality with a mean opinion score (MOS) of 3.5, which is translated into 'Fair' and 'Good' from the listener's perspective. Furthermore, we present a practical countermeasure, that can be easily implemented in the user-space driver of the Bluetooth master device, while requiring no modification to existing slave devices like keyboards and headsets. The countermeasure effectively reduces the packet capture rate of the sniffer to 20%, and degrades the MOS of eavesdropped audio to 1.5, which is between 'Bad' and 'Poor'.

The rest of the paper is organized as follows. Section 2 reviews related work. In section 3, we introduce the background on Bluetooth system in general. We present system overview and architecture in section 4. In section 5, we discuss BlueEar system design in detail. Evaluation of BlueEar system performance is presented in section 7. We discuss the impacts of BlueEar on privacy breach for Bluetooth system, including BLE, in section 8. Section 9 concludes the paper.

2. RELATED WORK

Bluetooth employs E_0 – a two-level stream cipher based on 128-bit link key – to encrypt packet payloads. The link key is established through *pairing*, where Bluetooth devices authenticate each other using a secret PIN. Recent studies have revealed many critical flaws of this encryption scheme [31] [17] [10] [24] [26] [25]. First, the security of E_0 relies on the strength of PIN – which is often too weak and can be easily cracked [31]. Moreover, recent cryptanalysis studies have shown that the 128-bit link key of E_0 is considerably weaker than what is originally intended [17]. It can be cracked in 2^{65} operations, instead of 2^{128} [10]. Furthermore, the effective security of the link key will further degrade when a packet sniffer is employed by the attacker [24] [26] [25]. In particular, after capturing 44.3 MB of data transferred by the target, the attacker can reverse the link key in 2^{38} operations, which makes fast key recovery possible in practice [24].

Recent studies have demonstrated the feasibility of circumventing Bluetooth encryption using expensive, proprietary packet sniffers. For instance, the traffic pattern of popular fitness trackers is found to be strongly correlated with the user's activity, making it possible to track user gait and identity. As a result, a passive traffic sniffer can uncover important private information about the user, even without decrypting packet payloads [9]. Moreover, due to computation and power constraints, many Bluetooth peripherals – including most Bluetooth mice manufactured by major vendors like Logitech [23] – do not support encryption, which may result in user privacy breach.

Despite the well-documented flaws of Bluetooth encryption, sniffing Bluetooth traffic has been widely considered an extremely intricate task. There exist several proprietary and open source systems for sniffing Bluetooth traffic. For example, the firmware of a few Bluetooth chipsets allow the radio to report packet-level diagnosis by working in sniffing mode [7] [20] [3]. However, the sniffing device must pair with the target, which makes it incapable of passive sniffing. The GNURadio/USRP [5] [29] platform can be programmed to decode Bluetooth packets [33]. Due to large signal processing overhead and frequency switching delay, they are limited to sniffing one subchannel at a time. There exist several proprietary Bluetooth packet sniffers designed for protocol diagnosis in controlled wireless settings [12] [13]. They rely on specialized radio to monitor all subchannels in parallel, which makes them extremely costly. For instance, off-the-shelf sniffers manufactured by Frontline Test Equipment [11] – the leading provider of Bluetooth protocol analyzer – cost \$10K to \$25K per unit.

Recently, several low-cost Bluetooth packet sniffers [6] [30] have been developed based on Ubertooth [6] – an open-source Bluetooth development platform. However, existing Ubertooth-based sniffers are exclusively designed for sniffing Bluetooth traffic in basic hopping mode. In the crowded 2.4 GHz band, Bluetooth rarely hops in basic hopping mode because of the interference from coexisting wireless devices, especially the prevalent 802.11 based WLANs [14] [22] [34] [19]. As a result, existing low-cost sniffers suffer prohibitively poor sniffing performance in practice due to the misprediction of adaptive hopping behavior, as well as excessive packet corruptions caused by interference.

Compared with existing Ubertooth-based systems, BlueEar is designed for sniffing Bluetooth traffic in practical environments where both the sniffer and the target may suffer from intensive interference from coexisting wireless devices. To achieve this goal, we address the key challenges posed by the indiscoverable mode of Bluetooth, the vendor-dependent adaptive hopping behavior, and the difficulties in maintaining consistent sniffing performance in the crowded 2.4 GHz band. In addition, we identify various critical issues in Ubertooth firmware that significantly degrade its performance during frequency hopping, and present solutions to address these flaws. We note that although our prototype is developed based on Ubertooth, the design of BlueEar is platform-independent and can be easily ported to other systems.

3. BLUETOOTH BACKGROUND

Piconet. Bluetooth networks employ a master-slave structure called *piconet*. The device that has the least computation and power constraints is usually selected as the master to manage communication. Other devices are slaves. Bluetooth piconets use the MAC address of the master device as the *piconet address*. All devices from the same piconet are synchronized to the *piconet clock* – a clock signal generated by the master.

The hopping protocol. We now introduce the hopping protocol of Bluetooth Classic, which is more complex than that of BLE. The hopping protocol of BLE is discussed in Section 8. In Bluetooth Classic, the hopping protocol is defined by a *physical channel*, which is characterized by pseudo-random hopping over 79 subchannels from 2.4 to 2.48 GHz. The carrier frequency is switched every 625 μs, resulting in a maximum hopping rate of 1600 hops/s. Specifically, there are two types of physical channel for data communication, including,

(i) Basic channel. In each hop of the basic channel, the subchannel index is calculated by $\mathcal{H}(A, c)$, where $\mathcal{H}(\cdot)$ denotes the basic hop selection kernel specified by the Bluetooth standard [32], A is the piconet address, and c is the piconet clock. In Bluetooth Classic, the piconet clock is a 27-bit logic counter that ticks every hop. Because piconet clock wraps around every 2^{27} ticks, the basic channel repeats itself every 134,217,728 hops, which take approximately 24 hours. In other words, the basic channel can be characterized by a *basic hopping sequence* and a *hopping phase*. The basic hopping sequence, which is determined by the piconet address, is composed of 2^{27} subchannel indices $\{i_0, ..., i_{2^{27}-1}\}$, where $i_n = \mathcal{H}(A, n)$. The hopping phase, which is determined by the piconet clock, is the index of the current hop.

(ii) Adapted channel. When coexisting with other wireless devices on overlapping frequencies, Bluetooth performs adaptive hopping where the basic channel is frequently modified to adapt spectrum use. The adaptation is guided by a *subchannel map*, which classifies subchannels as good and bad based on interference conditions. When the subchannel selected in a hop is bad, a *remap* function is called to compute a pseudo-random index i based on piconet address and clock. The bad subchannel is then replaced by the i-th good subchannel. Although adaptive hopping is the *de facto* scheme used by off-the-shelf Bluetooth devices, the Bluetooth standard does not specify the implementation of subchannel classification, resulting in different adaptive hopping behaviors across devices manufactured by different vendors.

Indiscoverable mode. When establishing the piconet, Bluetooth devices authenticate each other through a *pairing* process. To enhance privacy, Bluetooth piconets can be put in indiscoverable mode to hide key technical parameters from unpaired devices. These parameters – including piconet address, piconet clock, and subchannel map – determines hopping behavior. Although recent study has demonstrated the possibility of extracting piconet address from packet preambles [33], a Bluetooth packet sniffer cannot hop following the target unless it acquires all hidden parameters.

4. BLUEEAR OVERVIEW

4.1 Objectives and Challenges

We study Bluetooth privacy by exploring the feasibility of sniffing Bluetooth traffic in practical environments. To this end, BlueEar is designed as a *passive* traffic sniffer that leverages general, inexpensive wireless platform to capture Bluetooth packets without pairing with the target piconet. To achieve this goal, we tackle the following challenges.

(i) Secret hopping phase. In indiscoverable mode, the piconet clock that indicates the hopping phase is hidden from BlueEar. In adaptive hopping mode, determining the hopping phase is particularly challenging because the basic hopping sequence of the target is subject to frequent modifications.

(ii) Vendor-dependent adaptive hopping. The adaptive hopping of Bluetooth is guided by a subchannel map, which classifies subchannels as good and bad based on dynamic interference conditions. However, the Bluetooth standard does not specify the implementation of subchannel classification, resulting in vendor-dependent implementation, where Bluetooth chipsets manufactured by different vendors may hop over different subchannels even in the same spectrum context.

(iii) Interference in the crowded 2.4 GHz band. When coexisting with other wireless devices, BlueEar may experience hidden and exposed interference. When an RF signal that interferes with the target is too weak to be measured at BlueEar, the spectrum contexts observed by BlueEar and the target may differ, making it difficult to predict adaptive hopping behavior. When an RF source interferes with the target but BlueEar, significant degradation of sniffing performance may occur. While authorized devices can maintain packet reception performance by coordinating their hopping, designed as a passive sniffer, BlueEar cannot coordinate with the target, which may lead to substantial packet corruptions.

4.2 System Architecture

Instead of using specialized radio to monitor all subchannels in parallel, BlueEar tackles the above challenges based on a simple *dual-radio architecture* that consists of two inexpensive, Bluetooth-compliant radios. The two radios – named as *scout* and *snooper* – are interfaced to a controller, which employs a suite of novel algorithms to coordinate the two radios, gluing them as a powerful passive traffic sniffer. Fig. 1 illustrates the architecture of BlueEar. Specifically, the working flow of BlueEar can be divided into the following steps.

(i) Traffic filtering. When multiple piconets coexist in the same environment, BlueEar separates their traffics based on the piconet address of captured packets. Specifically, the preamble of each Bluetooth packet carries a synchronization word, which is derived from the piconet address using an encoding function specified by the standard [32]. BlueEar employs the brute force algorithm proposed in [33] to extract piconet address from the synchronization word, and then filters out the packets whose piconet address mismatches the target piconet address specified by the BlueEar user.

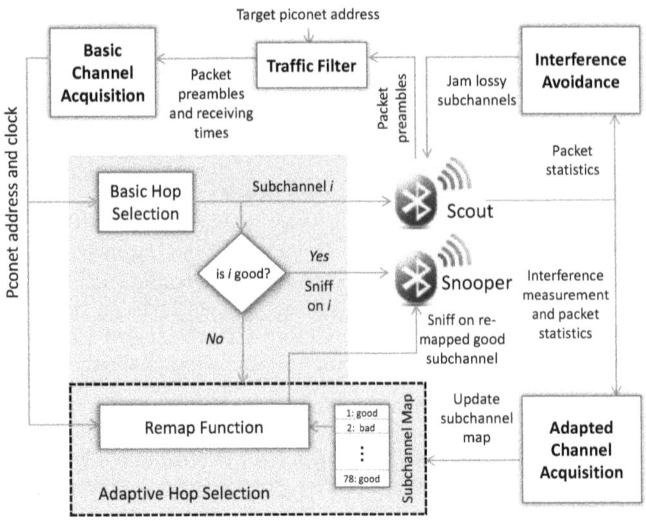

Figure 1: The dual-radio architecture of BlueEar. Components in the gray area comprise a standard-compliant hop selection kernel.

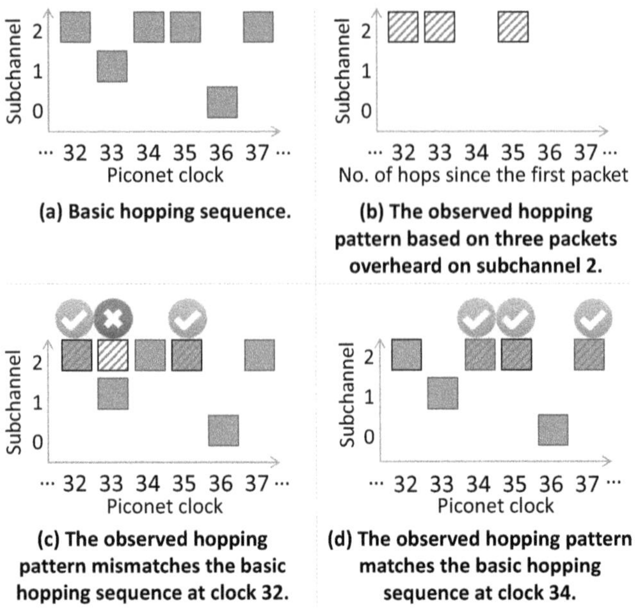

Figure 2: An illustrative example of brute force clock acquisition.

(ii) Basic channel acquisition. To acquire the basic channel of the target piconet, the scout listens on an arbitrary subchannel to monitor the target's packet transmissions. After extracting piconet address from packet preamble, BlueEar derives the entire basic hopping sequence, and then reverses the piconet clock using an interference resilient, probabilistic clock matching algorithm. Specifically, the receiving times of captured packets are compared with the basic hopping sequence at different hopping phases, until a correct phase is found. The acquired piconet address and clock are then fed to a standard-compliant basic hop selection kernel to compute the basic channel.

(iii) Adapted channel acquisition. To acquire the adapted channel, BlueEar needs to predict how the target reacts in dynamic spectrum context. To this end, the scout hops over all subchannels on the acquired basic channel to survey interference conditions, and monitors packet transmissions to infer the target's subchannel utilization. By fusing these measurements, BlueEar trains a subchannel classifier at run-time, which accurately derives the target's subchannel map despite vendor-dependent adaptive hopping behavior and the possible disparity between the spectrum contexts of the scout and the target. The subchannel map is then fed to a standard-compliant adaptive hop selection kernel for computing the adapted channel.

(iv) Interference avoidance. The snooper hops following the target on the adapted channel to sniff traffic. BlueEar handles complex interference in the crowded 2.4 GHz band using a selective jamming algorithm. Specifically, a loss detector is employed to monitor the sniffing performance of all subchannels. When substantial packet corruptions are detected on a subchannel i, the scout deliberately generates interference on i while the target visits i during hopping. Because of adaptive hopping, the target will be driven away from lossy subchannels where BlueEar observes poor sniffing performance. The objective is to manipulate the target's hopping to enforce implicit coordination.

5. DESIGN OF BLUEEAR

In this section, we present the design of key BlueEar components in detail.

5.1 Clock Acquisition

In the following, we first introduce an algorithm that can reverse the piconet clock when the target hops in the basic mode, and then augment it with probabilistic matching to determine the piconet clock in the presence of interference.

5.1.1 Brute Force Clock Acquisition

Because the entire hopping sequence is known after the piconet address is extracted from packet preamble [33], it is possible to reverse the piconet clock through a simple brute force search, which compares the observed hopping pattern with the entire hopping sequence at all phases to search for a match. Fig. 2 shows an illustrative example of brute force clock acquisition. At the beginning, the scout listens on a single subchannel to monitor the target's packet transmissions. As shown in the example given in Fig. 2, the scout listens on subchannel 2 where three packets are captured. The receiving times of these packets compose a hopping pattern that describes how the target visits the monitored subchannel. As shown in Fig. 2(c) and (d), BlueEar then compares the observed hopping pattern with the entire basic hopping sequence at all phases. A match is found at clock 34.

Before capturing a sufficient number of packets, the observed hopping pattern may happen to match the basic hopping sequence at multiple clock values, resulting in clock ambiguity. Because the basic hopping sequence is pseudo-random, probability that an observed hopping pattern that comprises n packets matches the basic hopping sequence at an arbitrary clock can be computed as $\frac{1}{79^n}$. Therefore, clock ambiguity decreases exponentially fast as the number of captured packets increases. As a result, the target piconet clock can be determined in a short time period, which we will evaluate in detail in Section 7.2.

5.1.2 Probabilistic Clock Matching

In the crowded 2.4 GHz band, Bluetooth devices rarely hop in the basic mode because of the impacts of interference from coexisting wireless devices [14] [22] [34] [19]. To adapt spectrum use, Bluetooth modifies the basic channel by remapping bad subchannels subjected to interference with pseudo-randomly selected good subchannels. Since the adapted channel may differ from the basic channel in various phases, the hopping pattern observed by the scout may mismatch the basic hopping sequence even at the correct clock. Fig. 3 illustrates the impact of subchannel remapping using the same example shown in Fig. 2. As illustrated in the figure, brute force search may fail to find a perfect match due to the packet transmitted on the remapped subchannel.

To acquire the piconet clock in the presence of interference, BlueEar leverages the following key observation. When comparing the observed hopping pattern with the basic hopping sequence at the correct clock, the ratio of mismatches should equal the ratio of remapped subchannels. As required by FCC, Bluetooth Classic must use at least 20 subchannels for frequency hopping [32]. Therefore, the ratio of remapped subchannels is at most $\frac{59}{79}$. Hence, if the ratio of mismatches at a clock c is significantly larger than $\frac{59}{79}$, then c is likely an incorrect clock.

Driven by the above observation, BlueEar employs a probabilistic clock matching algorithm for clock acquisition. Instead of seeking a perfectly matched clock, BlueEar determines the correct clock by eliminating incorrect clocks based on the number of mismatches. When a new packet is captured, BlueEar updates the mismatch ratios for remaining clock candidates. A clock is identified as incorrect if the 95% confidence interval of its mismatch ratio exceeds $\frac{59}{79}$. Specifically, let d_c be the number of mismatches when comparing the observed hopping pattern with the basic hopping sequence at clock c, and n be the total number of overheard packets. If c is the correct clock, the ratio of mismatches $\mu = \frac{d_c}{n}$ should be close to the ratio of unused subchannels. Based on the central limit theory, the distribution of $\sqrt{n}(\frac{d_c}{n} - \mu)$ should approach normality when n is reasonably large. The 95% confidence interval of μ can be estimated as $\frac{d_c}{n} \pm 2\frac{\sigma}{\sqrt{n}}$, where σ^2 is the variance. Therefore, clock c is determined as incorrect if

$$\frac{d_c}{n} - 2\frac{\sigma}{\sqrt{n}} \geq \frac{59}{79}.$$

5.2 Subchannel Classification

The adaptive hopping of Bluetooth is guided by a subchannel map that classifies subchannels as good and bad based on dynamic interference conditions. To acquire the adapted channel, BlueEar employs a subchannel classifier, which infers how the target classifies subchannels. The subchannel classifier must meet the following requirements.

- *Accuracy.* When a subchannel is misclassified, the snooper may hop to a wrong subchannel different from the one used by the target. Poor subchannel classification accuracy may result in substantial packet misses.
- *Responsiveness.* In dynamic spectrum contexts, the subchannel classifier must be responsive to the change of interference conditions.

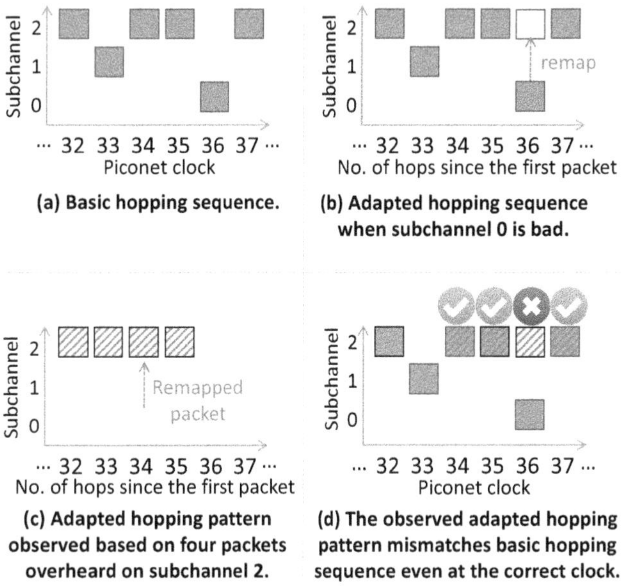

Figure 3: The effect of subchannel remapping on brute force search based on the same example shown in Fig. 2.

In the following, we present two complementary subchannel classification algorithms, and discuss their advantages and limitations in achieving the above goals. We then discuss how BlueEar integrates the two algorithms for subchannel classification.

5.2.1 Packet-based Classifier

Design. As Bluetooth only transmits on good subchannels, it is possible to infer the status of a subchannel based on its *packet rate*, which indicates how frequently the target transmits on a subchannel. To measure packet rates, the scout hops over all 79 subchannels on the acquired basic channel to monitor the target's packet transmissions. For each subchannel i, BlueEar computes its packet rate as $r_i = \frac{p_i}{v_i}$, where p_i is the number of packets received on i, and v_i is the number of times the scout visits i. When a subchannel is classified as bad by the target, the packet rate measured by the scout will be substantially lower than that of good subchannels.

A key challenge to achieve accurate packet-based classification is that packet rates differ significantly across different applications (*e.g.*, data transfer, audio, and keystroking, etc.), and may vary with time depending on the traffic dynamics in the target piconet. To address this challenge, we leverage the fact that, as required by FCC, Bluetooth Classic uses at least 20 subchannels for frequency hopping [32]. As a result, the 20 subchannels that have the highest packet rates can be used as a reference to estimate the current packet rate of the target piconet. Driven by this observation, the packet-based classifier identifies bad subchannels using the following algorithm.

- *Step 1*: Initially, the 20 subchannels that have the highest packet rates are classified as good. Let $\mathcal{R}_g = \{r_{i_1}, ..., r_{i_{20}}\}$ be the set of their packet rates.
- *Step 2*: In remaining unclassified subchannels, the classifier searches for the one with the highest packet rate. Denote this subchannel as i, and its packet rate as r_i.

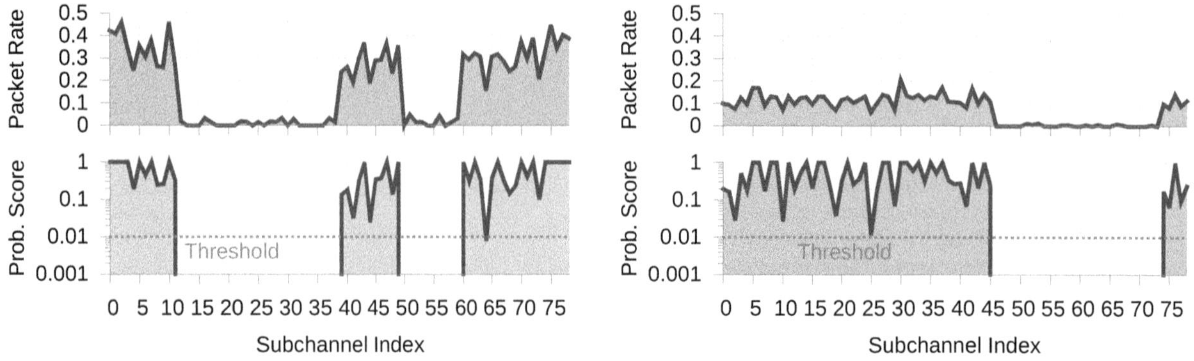

(a) Data. (b) Audio.

Figure 4: Running examples of packet-based subchannel classification for data and voice traffic under in different spectrum contexts. The packet-based classifier calculates a probability score based on Eq. (1) to determine subchannel status. A subchannel is classified as bad if the probability score is below the pre-defined threshold.

- *Step 3*: The packet-based classifier determines whether subchannel i is bad by checking if r_i is an outlier of $\mathcal{R}_g$. If r_i is an outlier, i and all remaining subchannels of even lower packet rates are classified as bad. Otherwise, i is classified as good and its packet rate r_i is inserted to $\mathcal{R}_g$. The algorithm then goes back to step 2 until a bad subchannel is identified.

We determine if $r_i = \frac{p_i}{n_i}$ is an outlier of $\mathcal{R}_g$ as follows. Let r_g be the average packet rate of $\mathcal{R}_g$. Assuming subchannel i is good, probability that the target transmits less than p_i packets after v_i visits can be computed as,

$$\rho_i = \sum_{n=0}^{p_i} \binom{v_i}{n} (1 - r_g)^{v_i - n} r_g^n \qquad (1)$$

We identify outliers under a given confidence level, denoted as θ. Subchannel i is classified as bad if $\rho_i \leq 1 - \theta$.

Fig. 4 gives two examples of packet-based subchannel classification for data and audio traffics in different spectrum contexts. The upper figure shows the packet rates measured on 79 subchannels. Low packet rates are observed on bad subchannels subjected to interference. The bottom figure shows the probability scores ρ_i for each subchannel i calculated using Eq. (1). As shown in the figure, the packet-based classifier reliably identifies bad subchannels despite the significant variation of packet rates across different applications.

Discussion. By classifying subchannels based on packet rates, packet-based classifier offers two advantages: *(i)* it works efficiently across different Bluetooth devices despite vendor-dependent subchannel classification methods, *(ii)* the classification is not affected by the disparity between the spectrum contexts of the target and BlueEar. However, packet-based classifier is less responsive in dynamic spectrum context because a subchannel cannot be classified as good or bad before overhearing a sufficient number of packets. As a result, packet-based classifier may perform poorly when subchannel status changes fast with time-varying interference.

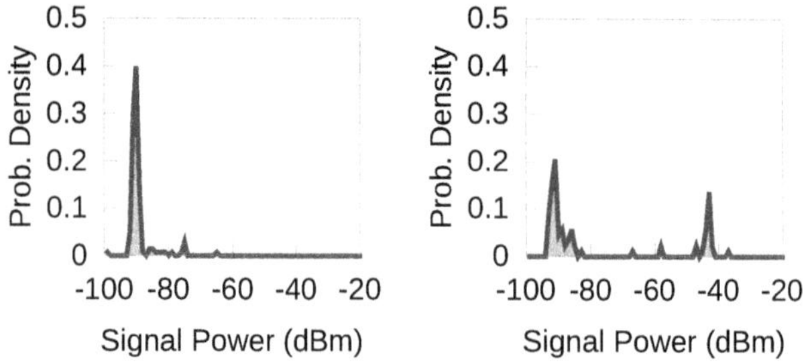

(a) Clean subchannel. (b) Dirty subchannel.

Figure 5: Probability densities of interference power measured on clean and dirty subchannels.

5.2.2 *Spectrum Sensing-based Classifier*

Design. Since Bluetooth piconet classifies subchannel based on interference conditions, subchannel i is likely bad if strong interference is measured on i. Driven by this observation, spectrum sensing-based classifier infers subchannel status based on interference measurements. When hopping on the basic channel, the scout measures interference power on each subchannel. The interference condition on a given subchannel is characterized using the probability density of interference power. Fig. 5 illustrates two examples measured by the scout on clean and dirty subchannels. On both subchannels, the environment noise floor is found at -95 dBm. An interference source whose signal power ranges from -45 dBm and -40 dBm can be observed in Fig. 5(b). The interference source is active in about 15% of time.

Based on interference measurement, the spectrum sensing based classifier employs an SVM to determine subchannel status. The SVM takes as input a feature vector obtained by discretizing the probability density of interference power based on $\mathcal{X}_i = \{x_{-100,i}, x_{-99,i} \ldots, x_{-20,i}\}$, where $x_{s,i}$ is the probability of observing an interfering signal power of s dBm on subchannel i. $\mathcal{X}_i$ characterizes interference condition between -100 dBm and -20 dBm, which is sufficient to capture the activities of all interfering sources in practice.

Discussion. Although spectrum sensing-based classifier is responsive to time-varying interference conditions, achiev-

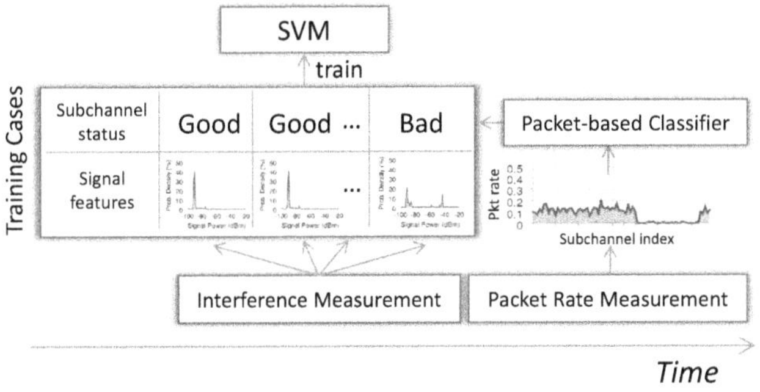

Figure 6: Time-domain illustration of run-time training of the spectrum sensing-based classifier.

Figure 7: A prototype of BlueEar that consists of two Ubertooths [6].

ing satisfactory accuracy is difficult because *(i)* depending on the location of interference source, the spectrum measured by the scout may differ from the one observed by the target; *(ii)* the subchannel classification method adopted by the target is vendor-dependent and may differ across different devices. To address these limitations, the spectrum sensing-based classifier must be trained at run-time.

5.2.3 Hybrid Classifier

For accurate and responsive classification of subchannel status, BlueEar employs a hybrid classifier that combines the complementary packet- and spectrum sensing-based classifiers. At run-time, the hybrid classifier uses packet-based classification results to train a spectrum sensing-based classifier, which learns the vendor-dependent subchannel classification method of the target. After training, BlueEar fuses the outputs of packet- and spectrum sensing-based classifiers to infer subchannel status.

To train the spectrum sensing-based classifier, BlueEar labels interference conditions measured by the scout using the outputs of packet-based classification. Note that packet-based classifier infers subchannel status based on packet rates derived from the history of overheard packets, therefore its result may lag behind the true subchannel status. To compensate this delay, BlueEar composes training cases by labeling $\mathcal{X}_f$ using packet-based classification results obtained at a later time point. Fig. 6 illustrates this training procedure in time-domain.

For subchannel classification, the hybrid classifier fuses the outputs of packet- and spectrum sensing-based classifier based on the responsiveness and confidence of results. The soft-output of SVM is utilized to characterize the confidence of classification. The soft-output of SVM is a log-likelihood ratio computed as $\lambda_i = \log \frac{\rho_i}{1-\rho_i}$, where ρ_i is the probability that i is good, and $|\lambda_i|$ indicates confidence. Because spectrum sensing-based classifier is more responsive to dynamic spectrum context, the hybrid classifier adopts the output of SVM as the final classification result if its confidence $|\lambda_i|$ is higher than a predefined threshold. Otherwise, the output of packet-based classifier is adopted.

5.3 Selective Jamming

In the crowded 2.4 GHz frequency band, BlueEar is subjected to the interference of coexisting wireless devices, especially the prevalent 802.11 based WLANs. Unlike authorized Bluetooth devices that can handle such interference by coordinating their hopping, designed as a passive packet sniffer, BlueEar cannot coordinate with the target, which may result in poor sniffing performance. BlueEar mitigates the impacts of such interference using a selective jamming algorithm. In the following, we present the algorithm design in detail, and then discuss the impact of jamming on 802.11 devices.

When the interference causes substantial packet corruptions on a subchannel i, the scout deliberately generates interference on i while the target visits i. Because of adaptive hopping, the target will be driven away from subchannels i, resulting in implicit coordination. To this end, BlueEar employs a loss detector to identify subchannels subjected to hidden interference. Whenever the scout overhears a packet, it checks packet integrity using CRC, and then sends the result to the loss detector. For each subchannel, the loss detector employs a moving window to compute the ratio of corrupted packets. The scout is commanded to jam a subchannel if the packet corruption ratio is higher than a predefined threshold. To effectively drive the target, a class one Bluetooth radio capable of high power transmission is employed to implement the scout.

Despite deliberately generating interference in the 2.4 GHz band, the impacts of selective jamming on 802.11 devices is very limited because of two reasons. *First*, BlueEar only jams a selected subchannel when the target is staying on that subchannel during hopping. *Second*, 802.11 is robust against narrow-band, short-period interference thanks to the design of OFDM and channel coding [8]. Moreover, previous study has shown that wireless devices are sensitive to strategically engineered interference patterns generated using the same communication technology [15]. By incorporating such patterns to generate low-power, narrow-band interference, the impact of selective jamming on 802.11 can be further reduced.

6. IMPLEMENTATION

In this section, we present the implementation of BlueEar in detail. As shown in Fig. 7, we employ two Ubertooths [6] to implement the scout and the snooper, and then interface them to a controller running on a Linux laptop. Computation intensive tasks like clock acquisition and subchannel classification are implemented on the laptop. Time-sensitive components like basic and adaptive hop selection are implemented by extending the firmware of Ubertooth. In addition, we identify critical issues in Ubertooth firmware that severely degrade its performance during frequency hopping, and present novel solutions to address these flaws. We note that although our current prototype is built based on Ubertooth, the design of BlueEar is platform-independent and can be easily ported to other systems.

6.1 Ubertooth-End Implementation

Ubertooth is an open source 2.4 GHz wireless development board that costs around $80 per unit [6]. Each Ubertooth is equipped with an LPC17xx microcontroller, and a low-power Bluetooth-compliant CC2400 transceiver connected to a 4-inch 2.2 dBi antenna. Ubertooth is capable of transmitting at 22 dBm, which assures the effectiveness of selective jamming.

The original firmware of Ubertooth is implemented in 823 lines of C code, which implements DMA management, basic hop selection, and carrier sense, etc. Data in DMA buffer is framed into USB packets and forwarded to the host. However, the original firmware lacks support for adaptive hop selection and run-time clock synchronization. In addition, we find that the firmware is poorly optimized for real-time frequency hopping. In particular, because of resource contention among multiple tasks, subchannel switching may be improperly delayed (e.g., by USB packet streaming, which typically takes around $50\mu s$ according to our measurements). Such delay will break the hop synchronization between BlueEar and the target.

We extend the firmware of Ubertooth using 400 lines of C code, which implement the following functions.

(i) Run-time clock synchronization. To hop following the basic and the adapted channel of the target, the scout and the snooper must synchronize their native clocks with the target's piconet clock, *i.e.* their clocks must have the same value and tick at the same time. Run-time clock synchronization is imperative because the clocks of the scout, the snooper, and the target may have clock skews [18], which make them run at different rates, accumulating a drift that breaks hop synchronization. The extended firmware accomplishes clock synchronization as follows. After clock acquisition, the firmware receives a piconet clock value from the clock acquisition component. The clock value is used as the initial value of a native clock, which is obtained by programming a 10MHz timer provided by LPC17xx into a 27-bit counter that ticks every hop. To assure that the native clock and the piconet clock tick at the same time, the extended firmware leverages the fact that Bluetooth packets are always transmitted immediately after clock ticks. Therefore, the receiving times of overheard packets can be utilized as a clock reference to correct clock drift. To avoid packet miss caused by remaining clock drift, the native clocks of the scout and the snooper are programmed to tick 1 μs earlier than the target.

(ii) Adaptive hop selection. The firmware of the snooper implements a standard-compliant adaptive hop selection kernel. The kernel takes three inputs, including the inferred subchannel map, the piconet address obtained from the controller, and the value of the native clock. The inferred subchannel map is updated every second.

(iii) Task scheduler. To assure real-time hopping performance, the extended firmware schedules tasks based on their time sensitivities. Hop selection and subchannel switching are given the highest priority to assure the right hop synchronization. USB packet streaming and carrier sense are given the second and lowest priority, respectively. Tasks are executed in the interval between subchannel switching in the order of their priorities.

6.2 Controller implementation

The controller implements compute intensive tasks, including packet decoding, clock acquisition, subchannel classification, and jamming subchannel selection. In addition, it interacts with the scout and the snooper via high-speed USB. These tasks are implemented as multiple processes, which share a 3 KB of memory for coordination and parameter exchange. For packet-based subchannel classification, the controller implements the algorithm described in Section 5.2.1 in 53 lines of C code. A confidence level of 99% is used to assure accurate identification of bad subchannels. The spectrum sensing-based classifier is implemented based on SVM^{light}, which is an open-source computation-efficient SVM library [21]. The spectrum sensing-based classifier takes about 51.2 KB of memory at run-time. To compensate the delay of packet-based classification when training the SVM (as explained in Section 5.2.2 and Fig. 6), the controller uses packet-based classification results obtained in $t+4s$ to label the signal features measured at t. This choice is motivated by our empirical measurements, which show that most Bluetooth devices update subchannel map every $4s$. The hybrid classifier chooses the result of SVM as output if the confidence of SVM is higher than 90%. Otherwise the output of packet-based classifier is adopted. The controller is responsible for decoding the raw bit stream received from Ubertooth. Packet integrity is examined by checking the received CRC. A subchannel is jammed if the ratio of corrupted packets is higher than 10%.

7. BLUEEAR PERFORMANCE

In this section, we present a thorough evaluation of BlueEar performance. In the following, we first introduce our experimental methodology, and then discuss experiment results in detail.

7.1 Experimental Methodology

We study BlueEar performance when sniffing data transfer and audio streaming, which are representative Bluetooth traffics that have distinct packet rates. Data traffic is generated by transferring data files between two laptops equipped with Broadcom dongles. Audio traffic is generated by playing an audio file on a laptop equipped with CSR dongle, and a Samsung Bluetooth headset is set as the audio sink. We conduct experiments in an office building under the interference of a large-scale 802.11 based WLAN, as well as in various controlled settings to benchmark BlueEar performance under specific interference patterns.

We evaluate the synchronization delay, the subchannel classification accuracy, and the packet capture rate of BlueEar. The synchronization delay is measured as the time needed to determine the correct piconet clock. To measure subchannel classification accuracy and packet capture rate, we log the groundtruth subchannel map and packet rates at the target master using a script written based on hcitool. The host of BlueEar is connected with the target master via an Ethernet link. The instantaneous readings of groundtruth subchannel map and packet rates are transferred to the BlueEar host using UDP.

We compare BlueEar with a set of baselines. First, we

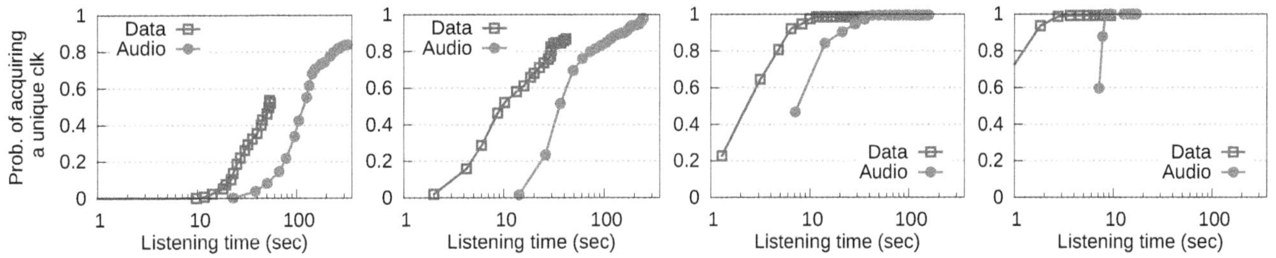

(a) No bad subchannels. (b) 25% bad subchannels. (c) 50% bad subchannels. (d) 75% bad subchannels.

Figure 8: Clock acquisition delay when sniffing data and audio traffics in different spectrum contexts (characterized by the percentage of bad subchannels at the target piconet).

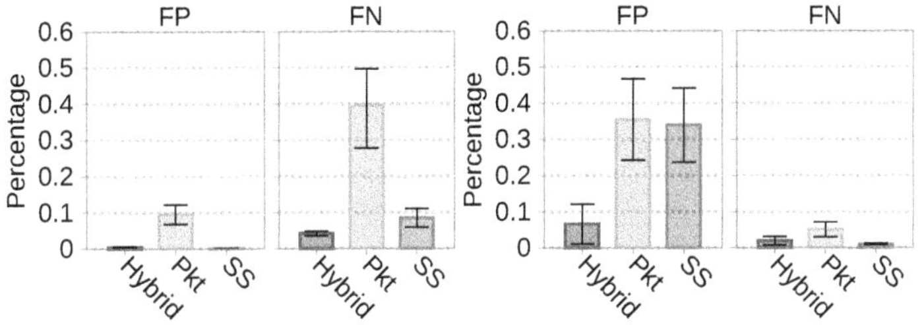

(a) Data. (b) Audio.

Figure 9: Subchannel classification accuracy in fast varying spectrum context.

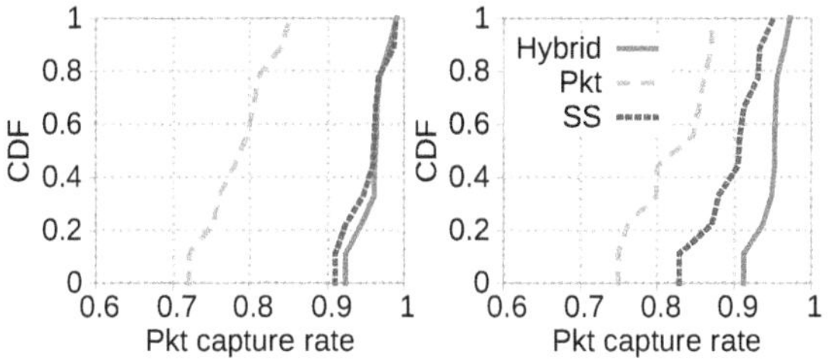

(a) Data. (b) Audio.

Figure 10: Packet capture rate in fast varying spectrum context.

compare the hybrid subchannel classifier proposed in Section 5.2.3 with pure packet-, and spectrum sensing-based classifiers (abbreviated as 'Pkt' and 'SS' in figures). The SVM of pure spectrum sensing-based classifier is trained offline in a controlled setting consisting of an 802.11 access point (AP) and a Broadcom piconet. During training, we tune the power and temporal pattern of 802.11 transmissions to introduce different interference conditions, which enables extensive profiling of the adaptive hopping behavior of the Broadcom device. We then use the trained classifier to predict the subchannel maps in data and audio tests, where the piconets are formed using different Bluetooth devices. Second, to evaluate the gain of selective jamming, we compare BlueEar with a baseline where the selective jamming is disabled. Third, we compare the packet capture rate of BlueEar with that of an existing Ubertooth-based sniffer [6], which operates in the basic hopping mode, and is oblivious to the adaptive hopping behavior and the impacts of interference.

7.2 Synchronization Delay

We first evaluate the delay incurred when synchronizing BlueEar with the target piconet. The dominant component of this delay is introduced by clock acquisition, during which the scout listens on a single subchannel until it captures enough packets to reverse the piconet clock. We benchmark clock acquisition delay in different spectrum contexts where the targets exhibits diverse hopping behaviors. Our experiments are conducted in a controlled setting where three 802.11 access points (APs) are deployed around the target. Each AP occupies one of the three non-overlapping 20 MHz channels. When all APs are active, they create a crowded spectrum where about 75% subchannels of the target piconet are bad.

Fig. 8 shows the probability of successfully determining the piconet clock as the listening time of the scout increases. We observe that clock acquisition delay when sniffing audio traffic is higher than that when sniffing data traffic. This is mainly because of the lower packet rate of audio traffic. Interestingly, the delay substantially reduces when the spectrum becomes more crowded. This is because, when more subchannels are occupied by 802.11 APs, the target piconet has to use fewer subchannels for packet transmissions, resulting in an increased packet rate on the subchannel monitored by the scout. Specifically, when 75% of subchannels are occupied by 802.11 APs, the clock acquisition delay is less than 10s in both data and audio tests. The result implies that Bluetooth traffic sniffers can substantially reduce its synchronization delay using deliberately planned interference.

7.3 Fast Varying Spectrum Context

We now evaluate BlueEar in dynamic spectrum contexts where the subchannel map of the target is modified frequently. The transmission of AP is turned on/off every a couple of seconds to create a fast varying spectrum context, which causes the target to modify its subchannel map every update period.

Fig. 9 evaluates subchannel classification accuracy based on false positive (FP) and false negative (FN) rates. As expected, the packet-based classifier performs the worst because of its poor responsiveness. In comparison, the spectrum sensing-based classifier offers better performance when sniffing data traffic, but fails to maintain its accuracy when sniffing audio. This is because the spectrum sensing-based classifier is trained offline against Broadcom devices, and it fails to predict the adaptive hopping of the CSR devices used in the audio test. We also observe that the hybrid classifier

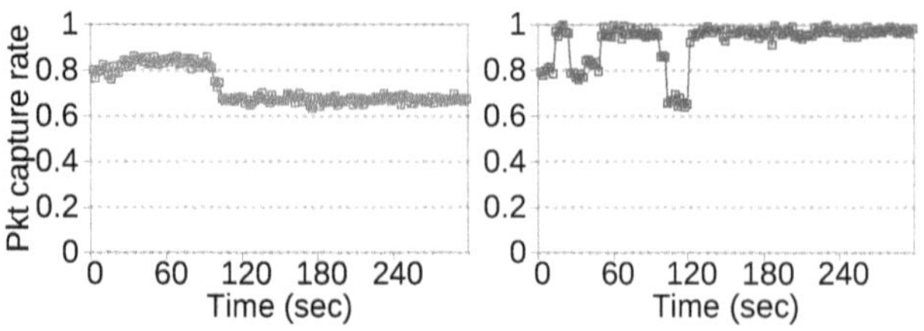

(a) Selective jam disabled. (b) Selective jam enabled.

Figure 11: The gain of selective jamming in the presence of hidden interference.

performs best among the three classifiers. In particular, the FP and FN rates are lower than 8% in both data and audio tests. Fig. 10 further compares the packet capture rates when BlueEar uses the three classifiers to predict adaptive hopping. Similar with the results shown in Fig. 9, the hybrid classifier is able to maintain the best packet capture rate, which is higher than 90% in both data and audio tests.

7.4 Hidden and Exposed Interference

We now evaluate the packet capture rate of BlueEar in the presence of hidden and exposed interference. Fig. 11 evaluates the gain of selective jamming in the presence of hidden interference, where an RF signal does not interfere with the target, but collide with captured packets at BlueEar. The experiments are conducted in a controlled setting where an 802.11 device generates hidden interference starting from the 100-th second. When selective jamming is enabled, BlueEar is able to maintain high packet capture rate, despite a short period of performance drop before the target piconet reacts to the generated interference. In comparison, when selective jamming is disabled, BlueEar suffers substantial performance degradation, where the packet capture rate is reduced to about 60% from higher than 95%.

We further evaluate BlueEar in the presence of exposed interference, where an RF signal interferes the target, but is too weak to be measurable at the scout. Exposed interference results in significant disparity between the spectrum contexts at BlueEar and the target. We conduct experiments in a controlled setting where an 802.11 device is deployed to generate exposed interference. During our experiment, the 802.11 device keeps active, and interferes with 20 of 79 subchannels of the target piconet. Fig. 12 compares the subchannel classification accuracy of the hybrid, the packet-based, and the spectrum sensing-based classifiers. Different from what we observed in Fig. 9, the spectrum sensing-based classifier suffers high FP in both tests. This is because spectrum sensing-based classifier relies on the interference measurements of the scout to identify bad subchannels, which works poorly when the interference signal cannot be detected by the scout. In comparison, hybrid and packet-based classifiers are able to maintain extremely low FP and FN rates and high packet sniffing performance, as shown in Fig. 13.

7.5 Crowded Spectrum

We then evaluate the misclassification rate of the hybrid classifier in spectrum contexts with different levels of crowdedness. The FPs, FNs, and overall misclassification rates are shown in Fig. 14. We observe that the hybrid classifier maintains high accuracy despite the increasingly crowded spectrum. In particular, when 50% of subchannels are bad, the overall misclassification rate is below 8% in both data and audio tests. Fig. 15 shows the packet capture rates measured in the same experiment. As shown in the figure, BlueEar captures more than 90% packets in both data and audio tests.

7.6 Ambient Interference

We further evaluates the performance of BlueEar in an office building under the ambient interference from a large-scale 802.11 based WLAN. Fig. 16(a) shows the packet capture rates measured at four randomly selected locations, where BlueEar is deployed at 10m away from the target piconet. In all of the four locations, the number of active 802.11 APs is higher than 20 during our experiments. We compare BlueEar with an existing Ubertooth-based sniffer [6] that hops following the basic channel of the target. Because the basic hopping sniffer is oblivious to the adaptive hopping behavior, it suffers 50% to 25% packet misses. In comparison, BlueEar is able to maintain a packet capture rate higher than 95% at all of the four locations.

Fig. 16(b) evaluates the packet capture rate at site D when BlueEar is deployed at different distances to the target. The disparity in spectrum contexts is expected to increase as BlueEar moves away from the target. However, thanks to the high-performance subchannel classifier, BlueEar is able to capture more than 85% packets even when it is 27m away from the target.

8. IMPLICATIONS OF BLUEEAR

In this section, we discuss the privacy implications of BlueEar in detail.

8.1 Implications on BLE privacy

In the following, we briefly introduce the hopping protocol of BLE, highlight the essential differences with the hopping protocol of Bluetooth Classic, and elaborate on the impacts of BlueEar on BLE privacy breach.

The hopping protocol of BLE defines the physical channel, which hops over 37 data subchannels in the open 2.4 GHz spectrum starting from 2.402 to 2.48 GHz. All subchannels are equally spaced with 2 MHz of bandwidth. The connection state of BLE can be characterized as a set of connection events. At initialization of a connection event, the master defines (i) connection interval, a multiple of $1.25ms$ ranging from $7.5ms$ to $4.0s$ that defines the event lifetime; (ii) transmission window size, a multiple of $1.25ms$ that defines the size of transmit window, i.e. packet size; and (iii) hop increment inc, a random value ranges from 5 to 16. The *basic channel* hopping is characterized by $\mathcal{K}(c, inc)$, where $\mathcal{K}(.)$ is the hop selection kernel, c is the index of current subchannel, and inc which is the hop increment. At the first connection event, the first subchannel is defined to be zero [32], and we note that the basic channel sequence repeats itself whenever subchannel zero is visited. On the other hand, BLE defines *adapted channel* hop mode just as Bluetooth Classic. BLE might modify the basic channel to adapt spectrum use in the presence of ambient interference. The adaptive channel is defined by a subchannel map, which classifies the data subchannels into good and bad. If the basic kernel $\mathcal{K}(c, inc)$ selects a bad subchannel, a remapping procedure is invoked to calculate a *remapped subchannel index*. The master maintains the subchannel map and it notifies slave(s) about any updates [32].

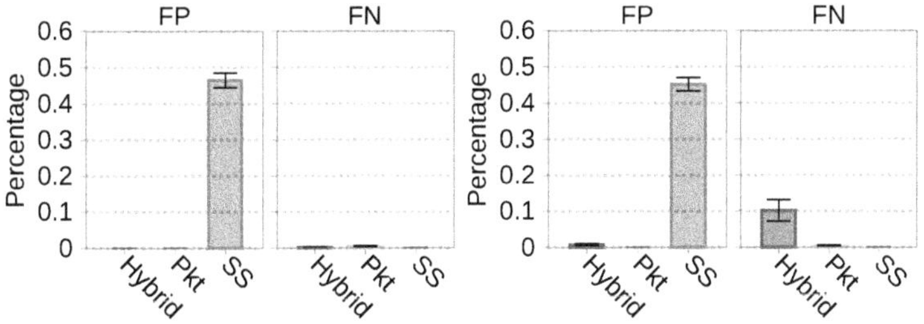

(a) Data. (b) Audio.

Figure 12: Subchannel classification accuracy under exposed interference.

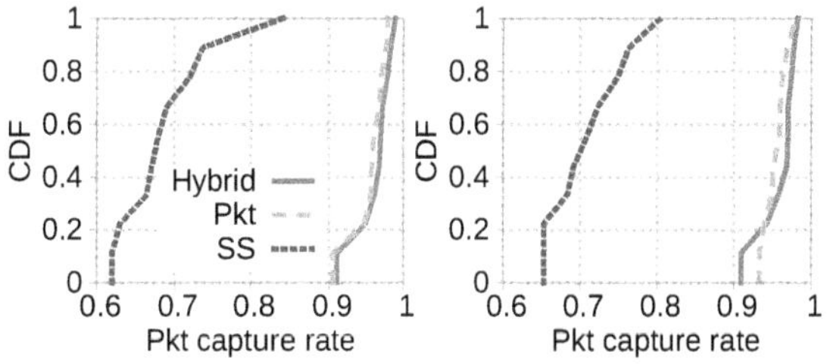

(a) Data. (b) Audio.

Figure 13: Packet capture rate under exposed interference.

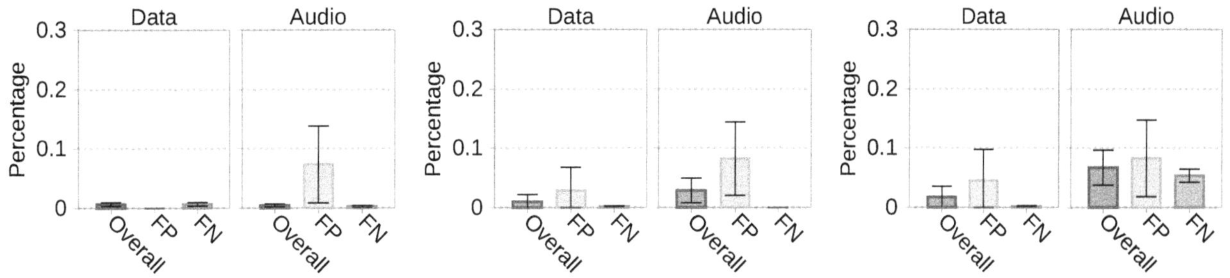

(a) No bad subchannels. (b) 25% basd subchannels. (c) 50% bad subchannels.

Figure 14: Subchannel classification accuracy in crowded spectrum (characterized by the percentage of bad subchannels at the target piconet).

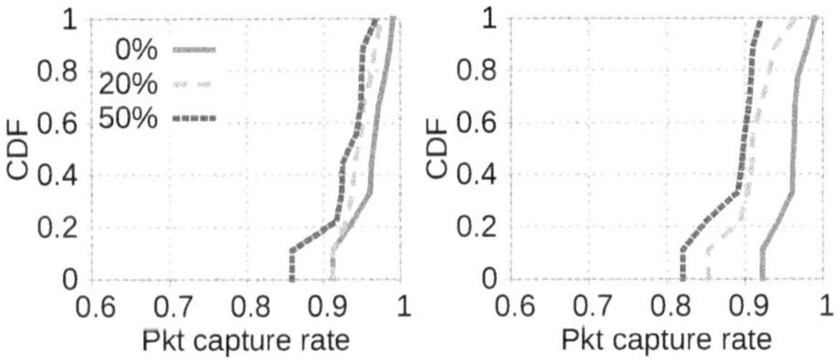

(a) Data. (b) Audio.

Figure 15: Packet capture rates in crowded spectrum (characterized by the perctange of bad subchannels at the target piconet)

The hopping protocol of BLE is different from the hopping protocol of Bluetooth Classic in the following ways. First, basic channel sequence of BLE is characterized by a random value of the hop increment *inc*. In contrast, basic channel sequence of Bluetooth Classic is characterized by the piconet address. The second difference between BLE and Bluetooth Classic, is hopping phase, which is not defined in BLE hopping protocol. Unlike Bluetooth Classic basic channel sequence, which repeats itself every about 23 hours, BLE basic sequence repeats itself whenever subchannel zero is visited. Due to power constraints, the hopping protocol of BLE is much simpler than that of Bluetooth Classic, making BLE basic sequence easier to compromise.

As BLE becomes pervasive, the privacy leakage of BLE devices has been an increasing concern. Although BlueEar is designed for Bluetooth Classic, it has significant impacts on the privacy leakage of BLE devices and this calls for research to further investigate and enhance the privacy of BLE. In particular, the key components of BlueEar system, including subchannel classification and selective jamming, are independent of the hopping protocol. These techniques can be directly ported to BLE as well as other adaptive hopping systems without modifications. Unfortunately, the clock acquisition component, the hop selection subsystem, and the packet decoder of our prototype are specifically engineered for Bluetooth classic, which make the current version of BlueEar incompatible with BLE.

8.2 Impacts on privacy breach

Previous research has shown the possibilities of cracking Bluetooth encryption and compromising user privacy [17] [10] [24] [26] [25] [28] [9]. A prerequisite of these attacks is to passively sniff Bluetooth traffic. Existing attacks [28] [9] employ prohibitively expensive commodity sniffers, which limits their widespread distribution. The BlueEar system we demonstrated in this paper may unleash such attacks, making them a real issue for off-the-shelf Bluetooth devices.

We conduct an experiment to further understand the impacts of BlueEar on privacy leakage. In particular, we study if the packet capture rate of BlueEar can result in successful eavesdropping on speech conversation, which is known to be challenging because audio streams are extremely sensitive to packet loss. This experiment precedes as follows: (1) We collect real traces of packet loss rates. Bluetooth piconet is first established to stream speech. BlueEar is then deployed to sniff the speech stream and we obtain a detailed packet loss trace, which logs the locations of all packets missed by BlueEar. (2) We write a computer script to simulate the

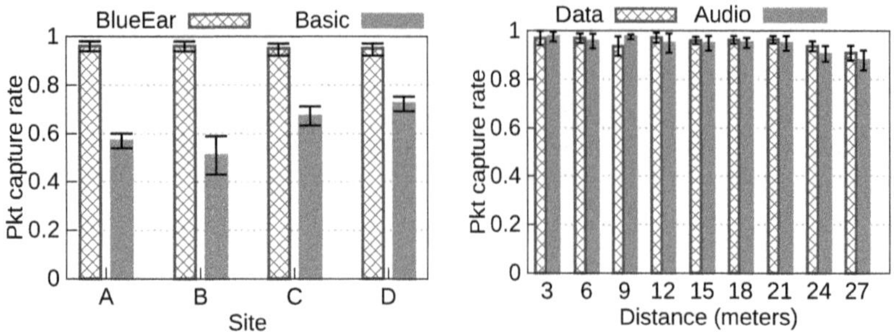

(a) Different locations in a building. (b) Different distances to the target.

Figure 16: Packet capture rate under the ambient interference at: (a) different locations in an office building under the interference of a large-scale 802.11 based WLAN; (b) different distances to the target.

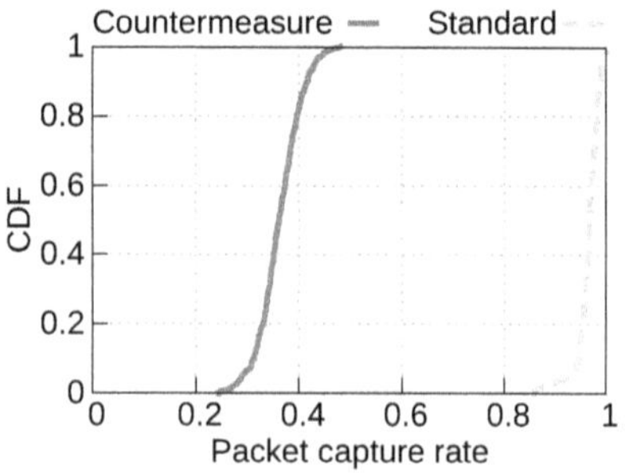

Figure 17: The packet capture rate of BlueEar with and without the countermeasure.

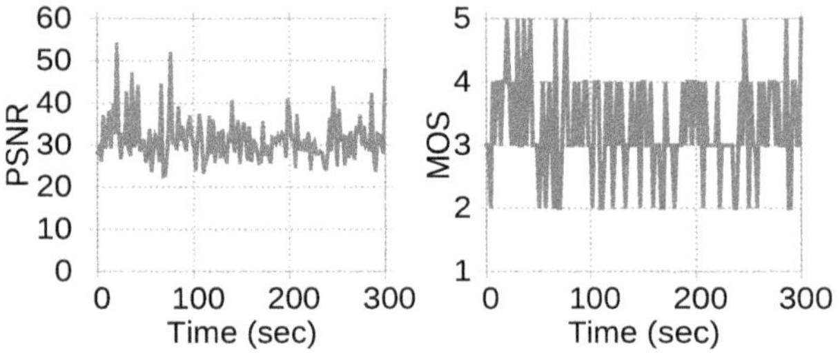

(a) PSNR. (b) Mean opinion score.

Figure 18: Subchannel classification accuracy in fast varying spectrum context.

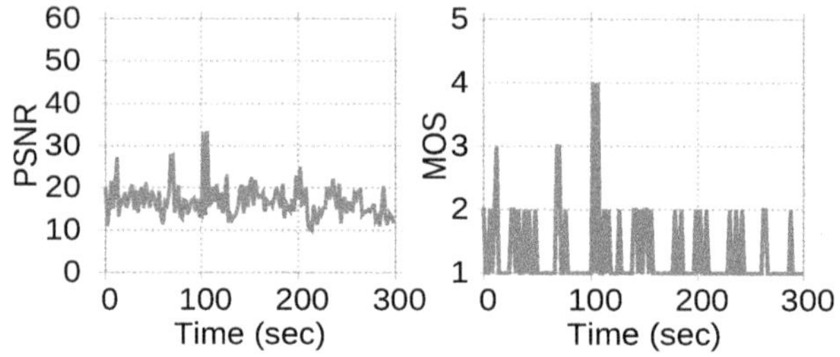

(a) PSNR. (b) Mean opinion score.

Figure 19: Audio quality when the target piconet implements the countermeasure approach.

audio stream without encryption. (3) We then synthesize the real packet loss trace with the simulated audio stream. If a packet is found loss in the real trace, the equivalent packet is dropped from the simulated audio stream. For each dropped packet, the previous packet (in the simulated audio stream) is replayed for loss concealment. (4) We use the peak signal to noise ratio (PSNR) to quantify the quality of the simulated audio stream, which should be equivalent to an eavesdropped audio file by BlueEar. As shown in Fig. 18(a), the PSNR is calculated every 2 seconds time window. (5) Finally, we map the PSNR values to mean opinion scores (MOS), as shown in Fig. 18(b), using the method proposed by [27] [16]. As in Fig. 18, MOS is categorized into five voice qualities, including excellent, good, fair, poor, and bad. We find that BlueEar can maintain a voice quality equal to or higher than fair in 81% of time.

8.3 Practical countermeasure

To counteract sniffing systems like BlueEar, we discuss a practical countermeasure, which can be implemented as a user-space script on the Bluetooth master, and requires no modifications to existing slaves. The key idea is to flip the status of a set of randomly selected good subchannels, thereby interfering the subchannel classifier, making it hard for the sniffer to learn the adaptive hopping sequence. Specifically, to comply with the FCC rule that requires Bluetooth to use at least 20 subchannels for hopping, the countermeasure randomly selects $n-20$ good subchannels to flip, where n is the total number of good subchannels. The subchannel map is updated every 200ms using the user-space script, which is composed using the interface provided by BlueZ –the open source Bluetooth stack. To evaluate the performance of the proposed countermeasure, we conduct the following experiment. The setup of this experiment is similar to the setup of the previous experiment presented in section 8.2 except that the target piconet implements the countermeasure approach.

Fig. 17 and 19 evaluate the effectiveness of the countermeasure. As expected, the average PSNR is about 15 due to high packet loss rate caused by the countermeasure, as in Fig. 19(a). As a result, the lower PSNR rates degrade the quality of the eavesdropped audio to poor in 95% of the time, as shown in Fig. 19(b).

9. CONCLUSION

This paper presents BlueEar, the first Bluetooth packet sniffer that only uses cheap, Bluetooth-compliant radios. Bluetooth has a dual-radio architecture, where two radios are coordinated by a suite of novel algorithms to eavesdrop on an indiscoverable Bluetooth device, relieving the need of expensive specialized radios adopted by commodity sniffers. Extensive experiments show that BlueEar can maintain a high packet capture rate higher than 90% in dynamic settings. We discuss the privacy implications of BlueEar, and propose a practical countermeasure that can reduce the packet capture rate of the sniffer to 20%.

10. ACKNOWLEDGMENTS

This work was supported in part by U.S. National Science Foundation under grant CNS1423221. We would like to thank the anonymous reviewers and our shepherd, Jeremy Gummeson, for their insightful feedback.

11. REFERENCES

[1] Android auto. https://www.android.com/auto/.

[2] Bluetooth technology website. https://www.bluetooth.com/.

[3] Busting the bluetooth myth – getting raw access. http://www.remote-exploit.org/content/busting_bluetooth_myth.pdf.

[4] Carplay – apple. http://www.apple.com/ios/carplay/.

[5] Gnuradio. https://gnuradio.org/.

[6] Ubertooth. http://ubertooth.sourceforge.net/.

[7] Adafruit. Bluefruit le sniffer. https://www.adafruit.com/products/2269.

[8] A. Cidon, K. Nagaraj, S. Katti, and P. Viswanath. Flashback: Decoupled lightweight wireless control. In *Proceedings of the ACM SIGCOMM 2012 Conference on Applications, Technologies, Architectures, and Protocols for Computer Communication*, SIGCOMM '12. ACM, 2012.

[9] A. K. Das, P. H. Pathak, C.-N. Chuah, and P. Mohapatra. Uncovering privacy leakage in ble network traffic of wearable fitness trackers. In *Proceedings of the 17th Internation Workshop on Mobile Computing Systems and Applications*, HotMobile '16. ACM, 2016.

[10] S. R. Fluhrer and C. S. Inc. Improved key recovery of level 1 of the bluetooth encryption system. Cambridge University Press, 2002.

[11] FTE. Frontline test equipments. http://www.fte.com/.

[12] FTE. Fte comprobe bpa 600. http://www.fte.com/products/BPA600.aspx.

[13] FTE. Fte comprobe sodera. http://www.fte.com/products/sodera.aspx.

[14] S. Gollakota, F. Adib, D. Katabi, and S. Seshan. Clearing the rf smog: Making 802.11n robust to cross-technology interference. In *Proceedings of the ACM SIGCOMM 2011 Conference*, SIGCOMM '11, pages 170–181, New York, NY, USA, 2011. ACM.

[15] R. Gummadi, D. Wetherall, B. Greenstein, and S. Seshan. Understanding and mitigating the impact of rf interference on 802.11 networks. In *Proceedings of the 2007 Conference on Applications, Technologies, Architectures, and Protocols for Computer Communications*, SIGCOMM '07. ACM, 2007.

[16] C. heng Ke, C. kuen Shieh, W. shyang Hwang, and A. Ziviani. An evaluation framework for more realistic simulations of mpeg video transmission. *Journal of INFORMATION SCIENCE AND ENGINEERING 24, 425-440 (2008)*, 2008.

[17] M. Hermelin and K. Nyberg. Correlation properties of the bluetooth combiner generator. In *Proceedings of the Second International Conference on Information Security and Cryptology*, ICISC '99. Springer-Verlag.

[18] J. Huang, W. Albazrqaoe, and G. Xing. Blueid: A practical system for bluetooth device identification. In *INFOCOM, 2014 Proceedings IEEE*, 2014.

[19] J. Huang, G. Xing, G. Zhou, and R. Zhou. Beyond co-existence: Exploiting wifi white space for zigbee performance assurance. In *Network Protocols (ICNP), 2010 18th IEEE International Conference on*, pages 305–314, Oct 2010.

[20] T. Instruments. Sniffer firmware of cc2540. https://e2e.ti.com/support/wireless_connectivity/f/538/t/197748.

[21] T. Joachims. Making large-scale SVM learning practical. In B. Schölkopf, C. Burges, and A. Smola, editors, *Advances in Kernel Methods - Support Vector Learning*, chapter 11, pages 169–184. MIT Press, Cambridge, MA, 1999.

[22] C.-J. M. Liang, N. B. Priyantha, J. Liu, and A. Terzis. Surviving wi-fi interference in low power zigbee networks. In *Proceedings of the 8th ACM Conference on Embedded Networked Sensor Systems*, pages 309–322. ACM, 2010.

[23] Logitech. Logitec advanced 2.4 ghz technology. http://www.logitech.com/images/pdf/roem/Logitech_Adv_24_Ghz_Whitepaper_BPG2009.pdf.

[24] Y. Lu, W. Meier, and S. Vaudenay. The conditional correlation attack: A practical attack on bluetooth encryption. In *Proceedings of the 25th Annual International Conference on Advances in Cryptology*, CRYPTO'05. Springer-Verlag, 2005.

[25] Y. Lu and S. Vaudenay. Cryptanalysis of bluetooth keystream generator two-level e0. In *in Advances in Cryptology-ASIACRYPT 2004, Lecture Notes in Computer Science*. Springer, 2004.

[26] Y. Lu and S. Vaudenay. Faster correlation attack on bluetooth keystream generator e0. In *Advances on Cryptography - CRYPTO 2004, Lecture Notes in Computer Science*, 2004.

[27] A. N. Moldovan, I. Ghergulescu, and C. H. Muntean. A novel methodology for mapping objective video quality metrics to the subjective mos scale. In *Broadband Multimedia Systems and Broadcasting (BMSB), 2014 IEEE International Symposium on*, pages 1–7, June 2014.

[28] X. Pan, Z. Ling, A. Pingley, W. Yu, N. Zhang, and X. Fu. How privacy leaks from bluetooth mouse? In *Proceedings of the 2012 ACM Conference on Computer and Communications Security*, CCS '12. ACM, 2012.

[29] E. Researches. Ettus research. https://www.ettus.com.

[30] M. Ryan. Bluetooth: With low energy comes low security. In *Proceedings of the 7th USENIX Conference on Offensive Technologies*, WOOT'13. USENIX Association, 2013.

[31] Y. Shaked and A. Wool. Cracking the bluetooth pin. In *Proceedings of the 3rd International Conference on Mobile Systems, Applications, and Services*, MobiSys '05. ACM, 2005.

[32] B. SIG. Bluetooth core specification v4.0. https://www.bluetooth.org/.

[33] D. Spill and A. Bittau. Bluesniff: Eve meets alice and bluetooth. In *Proceedings of the First USENIX Workshop on Offensive Technologies*, WOOT '07. USENIX Association, 2007.

[34] Y. Yubo, Y. Panlong, L. Xiangyang, T. Yue, Z. Lan, and Y. Lizhao. Zimo: Building cross-technology mimo to harmonize zigbee smog with wifi flash without intervention. In *Proceedings of the 19th Annual International Conference on Mobile Computing & Networking*, MobiCom '13, pages 465–476, New York, NY, USA, 2013. ACM.

Characterizing and Improving WiFi Latency in Large-Scale Operational Networks

Kaixin Sui[†‡], Mengyu Zhou[†], Dapeng Liu[†‡], Minghua Ma[†‡],
Dan Pei[†‡]*, Youjian Zhao[†‡], Zimu Li[†], Thomas Moscibroda[§]
[†]Tsinghua University [§]Microsoft Research
[‡]Tsinghua National Laboratory for Information Science and Technology (TNList)

ABSTRACT

WiFi latency is a key factor impacting the user experience of modern mobile applications, but it has not been well studied at large scale. In this paper, we design and deploy WiFiSeer, a framework to measure and characterize WiFi latency at large scale. WiFiSeer comprises a systematic methodology for modeling the complex relationships between WiFi latency and a diverse set of WiFi performance metrics, device characteristics, and environmental factors. WiFiSeer was deployed on Tsinghua campus to conduct a WiFi latency measurement study of unprecedented scale with more than 47,000 unique user devices. We observe that WiFi latency follows a long tail distribution and the 90th (99th) percentile is around 20 ms (250 ms). Furthermore, our measurement results quantitatively confirm some anecdotal perceptions about impacting factors and disapprove others. We deploy three practical solutions for improving WiFi latency in Tsinghua, and the results show significantly improved WiFi latencies. In particular, over 1,000 devices use our AP selection service based on a predictive WiFi latency model for 2.5 months, and 72% of their latencies are reduced by over half after they re-associate to the suggested APs.

Keywords

Wireless Network; WiFi Latency; Measurement

1. INTRODUCTION

WiFi latency is a critical performance measure for modern real-time, interactive Internet applications, such as online gaming, web browsing, and live collaboration applications. These applications have strict requirements on end-to-end latency [28, 33, 53]. For example, [53] shows that 20 ms last-mile latency will be amplified into about two to three seconds of web page load time, so slow that is beyond 47% of web users' expectation [19]. While the latency on the wired Internet is relatively stable and well-engineered (*e.g.*, via CDN), the last-hop WiFi latency is often unpredictable and a dominating factor in the end-to-end latency. For example, our measurement results in §3.1 show that, while the median WiFi latency is as low as 3 ms, its 90th and 99th percentiles are around 20 ms and 250 ms, respectively.

Characterizing WiFi latency using WiFi-related metrics (*e.g.*, channel utilization) is a key first step towards mitigating these problems. Understanding the reasons for high WiFi latency occurrences can lead to better designs of wireless protocols/hardware as well as better diagnosis and improvements in operational WiFi networks. However, measuring and characterizing WiFi latency at large scale is challenging, and to the best of our knowledge, there exists no comprehensive attempt at this problem. The reasons are manifold. First, measuring WiFi latency directly in an enterprise- or campus-scale WiFi network is difficult because i) WiFi latency is not reported in commonly used wireless products; ii) sniffer-based measurement methods are too costly or inconvenient to deploy in large-scale networks; iii) methods based on modifying firmware or software of access points (APs) take significant time to be adopted in commercial deployments; and iv) vanilla measurement methods based on pings are influenced by the device's energy saving modes (§2.1). Secondly, while directly measuring WiFi latency is thus challenging, characterizing WiFi latency by means of reducing it to other more easily measurable WiFi-related metrics is also challenging. Specifically, it turns out that there is no simple correlation between WiFi latency and any other such readily available metric. Instead, as we show in this paper, WiFi latency is related to other radio parameters and metrics in subtle and non-linear ways, revealing a complex interplay between multiple WiFi metrics, protocol parameters and environmental factors.

To tackle these challenges, we design **WiFiSeer** (Fig. 1), a framework for *measuring* and *characterizing* WiFi latency at large-scale, as well as *improving* WiFi latency in large operational Enterprise Wireless Local Area Networks (EWLAN) [9, 10], such as in campuses, shopping malls, airports, and hotels.

WiFiSeer first makes use of a new ping based methodology, called `ping2` (§2.1), to measure the WiFi latency of devices connected to the EWLAN. At the same time, WiFiSeer periodically polls the readily available data using SNMP (Simple Network Management Protocol) to derive potential impacting factors of WiFi latency in the EWLAN. Data from `ping2` and SNMP are associated and form the WiFi latency dataset of WiFiSeer. In a one-week exemplary dataset of real deployment in the EWLAN of Tsinghua University (THU-WLAN), hundreds of millions of WiFi latency records are collected based on `ping2`. Each of these records associates a specific WiFi latency with 11 industry-standard radio factors (*e.g.*, channel utilization), 3 protocol factors (*e.g.*, channel number), and 6 environmental factors (*e.g.*, buildings) from the SNMP data (§2.2). More than 2,700 APs, 114 buildings, and more than 47,000 mobile devices are observed in the dataset.

*Dan Pei is the corresponding author.

MobiSys'16, June 25-30, 2016, Singapore, Singapore
© 2016 ACM. ISBN 978-1-4503-4269-8/16/06...$15.00
DOI: http://dx.doi.org/10.1145/2906388.2906393

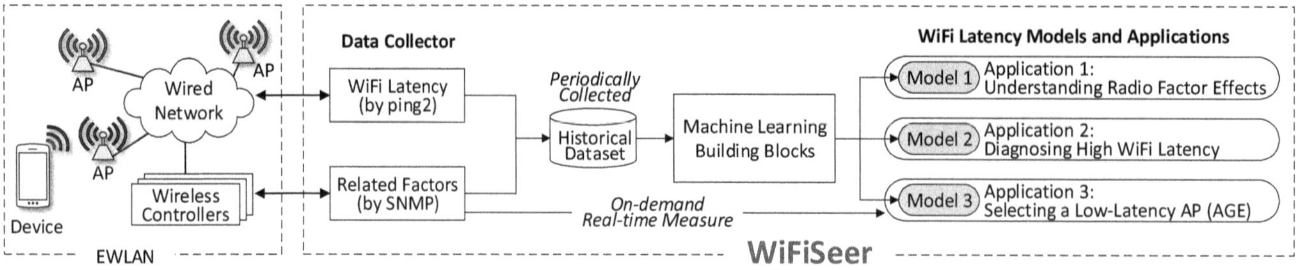

Figure 1: Overview of WiFiSeer.

The above large-scale dataset enables a panoramic view on the WiFi latency in the wild. First, some common perceptions about unsatisfying WiFi latency are quantitatively confirmed: i) WiFi latency follows a long tail distribution: its 50th, 90th and 99th percentiles are around 3 ms, 20 ms and 250 ms, respectively; ii) 75% of user devices experience at least one unsatisfying episode which has the average latency of over 20 ms for more than one minute in a week. Second, straightforward visual inspection also reveals some interesting observations (§3.2): i) the 5 GHz band is still largely underutilized and offers lower latency than 2.4 GHz; ii) the default RSSI-based band selection of devices is biased towards 2.4 GHz; iii) RSSI is not as highly correlated with WiFi latency as channel utilization for example.

In order to understand the reasons behind these observations and mitigate the high WiFi latency in operational networks, we model WiFi latency based on WiFi related factors, which are easily measurable, but interdependent, and related to WiFi latency in non-linear or even non-monotonic ways. WiFiSeer uses machine learning to provide modeling building blocks and then applies them to build three different models tailored for three different practical applications, which in turn enable us to make more interesting observations and insights.

In the first application, WiFiSeer correlates industry-standard radio factors (*i.e.*, easily measurable WiFi performance metrics) to WiFi latency. This model can help vendors and protocol designers to evaluate potential solutions. The model shows that the three most informative indicators for WiFi latency are channel utilization, the number of online devices, and the signal-to-noise-ratio (SNR), while the commonly considered RSSI used for AP selection is not. The model also describes that these metrics can relate to WiFi latency in non-intuitive and intricate ways.

In the second application, WiFiSeer provides a WiFi latency model to help operators diagnose high WiFi latency in operational EWLANs. Specifically, this model identifies where and when WiFi latency is high, and provides potential impact factors for these "bad apples". Based on the results of this application, we accordingly deployed two concrete mitigation approaches (adding a 5 GHz only SSID and dense AP deployment) in THU-WLAN, which turned out to be effective in practice (§5.2).

In the third application, WiFiSeer implements AGE (**A**ssociate to **G**ood **E**nterprise APs), a latency-oriented AP selection service composed of a helper app installed on user's devices and a centralized controller running a predictive model. AGE controller predicts the WiFi latency of APs near a device based on readily-available performance metrics and environmental factors. Then the AGE client app guides the device to associate to the AP with the lowest predicted latency. Deployment of AGE on over 1,000 Android devices for 2.5 months shows that after AGE re-associations, 72% of the latencies are reduced by more than half.

To summarize, our main contributions are:

- WiFiSeer framework is general enough to enable researchers or operators worldwide to study their own networks. It comprises a systematic methodology for modeling the complex relationships between WiFi latency and a diverse set of WiFi performance metrics, device characteristics, and environmental factors.
- We present an enterprise-scale measurement study of WiFi latencies, the largest reported so far, complementing prior WiFi studies that have focused on interference [51] and throughput [46]. Our results quantitatively confirm some anecdotal perceptions, disapprove some others (*e.g.*, the impact of RSSI on latency), and reveal some previously unknown insights (*e.g.*, AP selection mechanisms are inadequate and not collaborative). We believe these results have implications to all players in the mobile Internet ecosystem.
- We deploy three practical solutions for improving WiFi latency in an operational EWLAN. The results show significantly improved WiFi latencies.

The rest of the paper is organized as follows. §2 describes how WiFiSeer collects WiFi latencies and related factors. §3 shows a large-scale measurement study based on the dataset collected from THU-WLAN. §4 introduces how WiFiSeer builds comprehensive WiFi latency models using machine learning techniques. §5 presents three typical applications based on the models in §4 to characterize and improve WiFi latency in large-scale operational networks. §6 discusses several directions for extensions of WiFiSeer. §7 reviews related work and §8 concludes the paper.

2. DATA COLLECTION

In this section, we describe how WiFiSeer collects the dataset of WiFi latencies and related factors. The measurement studies (§3) and model building (§4) are both based on the dataset collected in this way.

2.1 Measuring WiFi Latency

In an operational large-scale EWLAN, systematically measuring WiFi latencies at low cost is challenging. First, WiFi latency is not readily available in common wireless products. For example, the APs of Cisco do not monitor WiFi latency in the SNMP data. Second, sniffer-based methods [31, 32, 47] require deploying extra wireless sniffers, and are thus inconvenient or too costly for a large EWLAN. Third, methods based on modifying the firmware or software of APs [12, 46, 51] cannot be used immediately because it takes a long time for vendors to adopt them in commercial products. Finally, the standard ping methods, issued from a mobile device to an AP (*e.g.*, as used in MobiPerf [39] and Speedtest [17]) or issued from an AP side to a mobile device, can in principle estimate WiFi latency [37], but in practice are unusable (see the evaluation of ping2 later) because they are impacted by the device's *energy saving modes* [6, 7, 14, 16], such as the low power suspend mode of the processor [48] and the power saving mode of the WiFi chip [35]. In particular, if the device is in the energy saving mode, the ping latency will be significantly inflated by the device wake-up time and is thus inaccurate. Because there lacks a feasible WiFi latency measurement tool, researchers and operators rarely know accurate WiFi latencies in an EWLAN.

Design of ping2: To obtain more accurate WiFi latency, we develop ping2, a ping based light-weight WiFi latency measurement tool. The key idea of how ping2 avoids the additional delay introduced by the energy saving mode is intuitive. As shown in Fig. 2, ping2 runs on a server on the wired network in the EWLAN, and sends two consecutive pings from the server to a user's device. The first ping is used to wake up the device. After the first ping is returned, the second ping is immediately issued. Since the device default active mode time (*e.g.*, about 200 ms for Android devices [36] and 100 ms for iPhone [35]) is usually longer than the RTT (*e.g.*, in Fig. 4, 98% of RTT is less than 200 ms, and 97% of that is less than 100 ms), the second ping, in most cases, avoids the device's energy saving mode, and is able to measure WiFi latency more accurately. Thus, the second ping (RTT 2 in Fig. 2) is deemed as the measured result by ping2. Note that the wired part latency (from the ping2 server to the AP) is negligible because the 99th percentile of wired part latency is less than 1 ms in THU-WLAN according to our measurement.

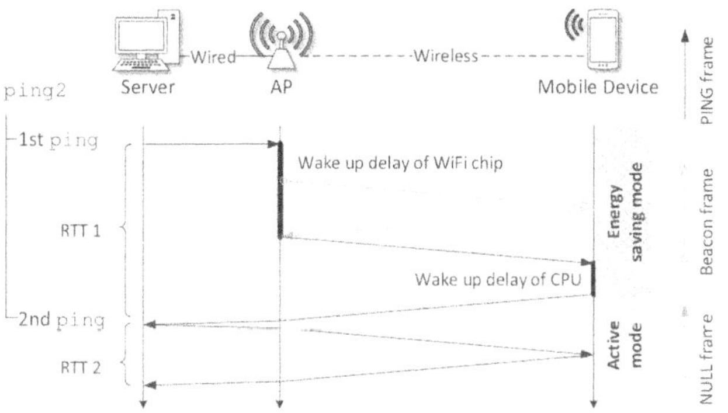

Figure 2: Time line of ping2.

We use ping2 to measure the WiFi latency of users' devices that connect to the EWLAN. In order to obtain a stable latency, we use ping2 to measure the latency of each device every 10 seconds and take the average of six measured results in a minute as one WiFi latency record in the dataset. The IP addresses of the connected devices are recorded by the EWLAN and can be obtained from the SNMP data. To reduce bandwidth cost, ping2 uses ping packets without any payloads.

Evaluation of ping2: We now evaluate ping2 in terms of its accuracy, server overhead, and battery overhead of users' devices. In order to validate the accuracy of ping2, we conduct controlled experiments on three different types of mobile devices in a small testbed. The testbed has an AP, a Linux server connected to the AP in a wired way, and three mobile devices including an Android smartphone (LG Nexus 5), a Windows tablet (Surface Pro 3), and a Linux laptop (Lenovo ThinkPad X1 Carbon). The testbed is set up in an isolated environment where almost no traffic is on the wireless channel we used. We restore the three devices to their factory settings such that the devices will not be waken up by additional installed softwares. Each time, we let only one mobile device connect to the AP via WiFi, and then use the following methods to measure WiFi latency in turn: M_1 uses ping2 to measure latency every 10 s; M_2 pings from the server to the mobile device every 10 s; M_3 pings from the mobile device to the server every 10 s; M_4 pings from the mobile device to the server every 1 ms; M_5 is MobiPerf, an app that is installed only for the smartphone and pings from the smartphone to the server every 0.5 s and uses the average of 10 pings as a latency result. We assume that WiFi latency remains the same during the experiment, and consider the result of M_4 as the ground truth of WiFi latency since the ping of that high frequency prevents devices entering energy saving mode [14, 16]. M_4 is a more general method to obtain the ground truth of WiFi latency than manually turning off the energy saving mode of devices, because the later depends on or may even not be supported by devices. We use each method to measure latency 120 times and show their CDFs in Fig. 3. Among these methods, M_1 (ping2) is the most similar to M_4 for different devices, which indicates that ping2 can measure WiFi latency more accurately. On the other hand, M_3 and M_5 introduce extra latency because if the device is in energy saving mode, it needs several milliseconds to wake up before sending the ping; M_2 is even worse because according to the power saving strategy, waking up a device from the AP side requires waiting for an AP beacon, which can be delayed for as long as a beacon cycle [29], *e.g.*, 100 ms in THU-WLAN.

In terms of server overhead, ping2 is extremely light-weight. We implement ping2 using C++ multithreading, and run it on an ordinary Linux server (with two Intel E5-2420 CPUs, 32 GB memory, and a gigabit ethernet card). At peak hour, ping2 is capable of measuring the WiFi latency of more than 15,000 online users' devices using less than 10% CPU utilization and 1MB/s bandwidth (also including the overhead of SNMP data collection).

In addition, ping2 introduces relatively low and occasional overhead on the batteries of users' devices. We conduct A/B tests on 6 different pairs of phones in our small testbed. For each pair, one is measured by ping2 and the other is not. To evaluate the worst case, that is, let ping2 wake up the phones from the energy saving mode as much as possible, we set all the phones to their factory settings and standby mode, so they are in energy saving mode in most cases during the test. We find that ping2 costs at most 7%–10% of the battery volume for different phones in a persistent test of 24 hours (Table 1). In practice, the impact of ping2 could be much less because users' phones themselves are not always in energy saving mode. Specifically, they are woken up periodically by the background traffic of mobile apps [49], such as the transmission of app logs and keep-alive packets. More importantly, ping2 does not have to run all the time. WiFiSeer only needs to periodically collect a dataset, *e.g.*, for a week every quarter, to build WiFi latency models.

In summary, ping2 is an accurate and low-cost tool for measuring WiFi latencies in a large EWLAN. It also is very general and can be plugged into an operational EWLAN without any modifications to the existing APs or users' devices.

Table 1: Maximum battery costs of ping2 in a persistent A/B test of of 24 hours.

ID	Brand	Model	Battery costs of ping2
1	Huawei	Honor 6	7%
2	Xiaomi	Mi 4	8%
3	Vivo	X5 Pro	8%
4	Oppo	R7	9%
5	Samsung	Galaxy Note 3	10%
6	Meizu	MX5	10%

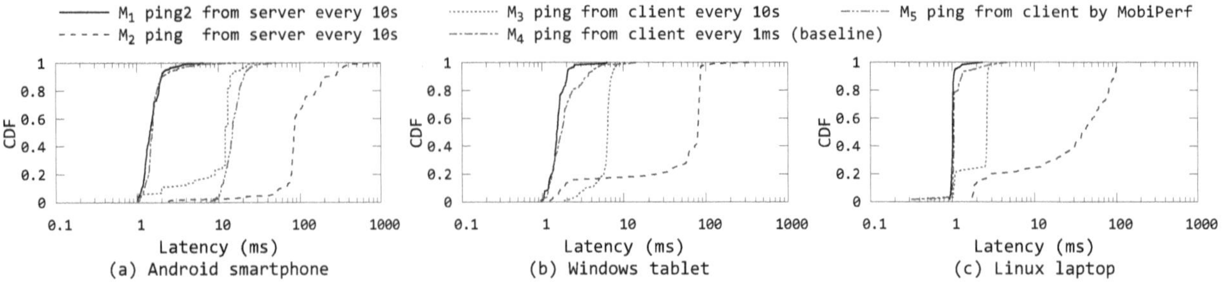

Figure 3: CDFs of latency measured by different methods. M_5 (MobiPerf) is only for the smartphone.

2.2 Collecting Related Factors

SNMP data is a commonly-used data source for monitoring large-scale EWLANs. Most vendors provide a large range of useful SNMP data on their wireless controllers. To avoid causing overload of the wireless controllers, WiFiSeer polls the SNMP data once per minute. The wireless performance related factors we collect are listed in Table 2. They generally fall into three broad categories: radio factors, protocol factors, and external factors. Table 2 also shows the value range of each factor observed in our dataset. The applications (§4.1) that each factor is used for are also marked.

Radio factors: Radio factors include typical universal wireless performance metrics of APs and user devices, for example channel utilization, interference utilization, receiver/transmitter utilization, and #devices (per radio).[1] See [4] for details of these factors. These radio factors describe the properties of the wireless environment and may fundamentally affect WiFi latency or be correlated to it.

Protocol factors: Protocol factors represent spectrum and frequency properties such as the 5 GHz band. Protocol factors can be described by radio factors. For example, the 5 GHz band has less devices and lower channel utilization. Thus, protocol factors can be deemed as specific collections of radio factors.

External factors: External factors include temporal and spatial factors as well as hardware characteristics of APs and user devices. They often affect WiFi latencies indirectly through radio factors. For example, the rush hour implies a high channel utilization and may cause high WiFi latencies. The five AP models are Cisco AIR-CAP{3602I-C, 702W-C, 3502E-C, 3702I-H, 3502I-C}-K9. The WiFi chip manufacturers are derived from the organizationally unique identifier (OUI) in the device's MAC address. The building type is derived from the usage of the building: classroom buildings, libraries, dormitories, cafeterias, gyms, administrative buildings, departments, hotels, elementary school, and others. Day of week and time of day are derived from the SNMP data timestamp. Some of these external factors, such as the AP models and the buildings, are specific to our THU-WLAN deployment.

Table 2: Wireless performance related factors.
For Application 2, factors of $\checkmark_1$ are used in the first stage of the model, and factors of $\checkmark_2$ are used in the second stage (§5.2).

ID	Radio factor	Value range	Used in app		
			1	2	3
1	Antenna gain	$\geq$ 0 dBm	✓		✓
2	Noise power	$\geq$ -128 dBm	✓		✓
3	Interference power	$\geq$ -128 dBm	✓	$\checkmark_2$	✓
4	Transmit power	$\geq$ -1 dBm	✓	$\checkmark_2$	✓
5	#Devices (per radio)	$\geq$ 0	✓	$\checkmark_2$	✓
6	Channel utilization	0 – 100%	✓	$\checkmark_2$	✓
7	Interference utilization	0 – 100%	✓	$\checkmark_2$	✓
8	Receiver utilization	0 – 100%	✓		✓
9	Transmitter utilization	0 – 100%	✓		✓
10	RSSI	$\geq$ -128 dBm	✓		✓
11	SNR	$\geq$ -128 db	✓		✓

ID	Protocol factor	Value range	1	2	3
12	Channel number	1, 6, 11, 13; 36, 149, 153, 157, 161, 165		$\checkmark_2$	✓
13	Band	2.4 GHz, 5 GHz		$\checkmark_2$	✓
14	Protocol	802.11a, b, g, n, ac		$\checkmark_2$	

ID	External Factor	Value range	1	2	3
15	AP model	5 models			✓
16	WiFi chip manufacture	152 manufactures			✓
17	Building	114 buildings		$\checkmark_1$	✓
18	Building type	10 types		$\checkmark_1$	✓
19	Day of week	Mon, Tue, ..., Sun		$\checkmark_1$	✓
10	Time of day	24 hours		$\checkmark_1$	✓

3. LARGE-SCALE MEASUREMENT STUDY

We have deployed all components of WiFiSeer in THU-WLAN. Tsinghua campus covers an area of about 4 km^2 with more than 53,000 students, faculties, and staff. More than 2,700 dual band Cisco APs governed by 14 Cisco 5508 wireless controllers provide a dual-band SSID "Tsinghua" in 114 buildings for WiFi access. We use WiFiSeer to collect one week of data of WiFi latency and related factors. Our dataset contains hundreds of millions of records (up to 500 GB) from more than 47,000 unique devices. To the best of our knowledge, this dataset thus represents a WiFi latency measurement of unprecedented scale. It provides us a unique opportunity to understand WiFi latency, and its relationship to a diverse set of related factors in the wild. There are several high-level findings that generalize beyond the scope of THU-WLAN: (1) WiFi latency has a long tail; (2) the 5 GHz band is largely underutilized and provides lower latency than 2.4 GHz; (3) AP selection mechanisms are inadequate and not collaborative; (4) Different WiFi chipsets differ greatly in their WiFi latency. We provide insights into these and other results in this section.

3.1 Distributions and Relationships

WiFi latency: Fig. 4 shows the distribution (CDF) of WiFi latency in THU-WLAN. While the median WiFi latency is low (about 3 ms), the 90th percentile is around 20 ms and the 99th percentile is even more than 250 ms. As mentioned in the introduction, this long tail is critical because it can lead to multiple seconds of application-level or user-perceived latency [15]. For example, according to [53], when last-hop latency increases only 10 ms,

[1]Channel utilization is the percentage of time used by all traffic of this channel; interference utilization is the part of channel utilization used by other 802.11 networks (*e.g.*, rogue APs [52]) on the same channel; receiver/transmitter utilization is the percentage of time the AP receiver/transmitter is busy operating on packets; #devices (per radio) is the number of devices connected to the specific band of the AP.

web page load time will increase hundreds of milliseconds; about 20 ms last-hop latency can result in about two to three seconds of page load time for popular websites (*e.g.*, Google and Yahoo), a time that is beyond 47% of users' expectation [19]. Because of this multifold amplification of WiFi latencies to user perceived latencies, the long-tail distribution we observe is alarming.

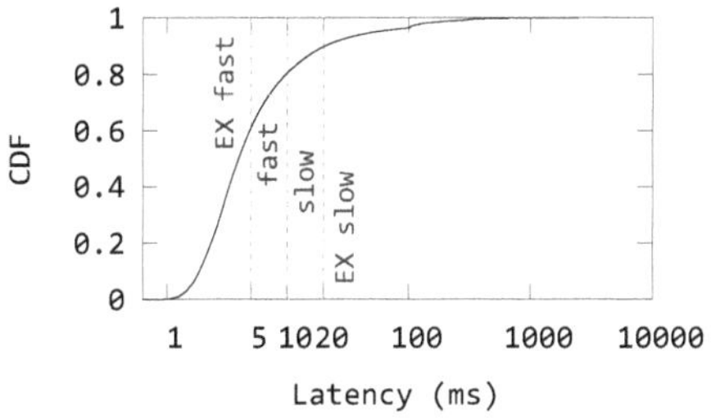

Figure 4: WiFi latency distribution.

For better conceptualization, we categorize WiFi latency into four classes based on the end-to-end latency requirements of Internet services (Table 3). With this classification, we see that in Fig. 4, about 20% of measured WiFi latencies belong to classes `slow` and `EX slow`. We also find that on Tsinghua campus, 75% of user devices experience at least one unsatisfying episode of `EX slow` WiFi latency for more than one minute in a week. The above results demonstrate that high WiFi latency not only exists but is also quite common in practice.

Table 3: Classes of WiFi latency.

WiFi latency class (`EX`: extremely)	Range	Referred Internet service end-to-end latency requirement
`EX fast`	< 5 ms	Online gaming [33]
`fast`	6 – 10 ms	Online collaborative show [28]
`slow`	11 – 20 ms	Quick Web surfing [53]
`EX slow`	> 20 ms	-

Related factors: Fig. 6 shows the distribution (left Y-axis) of some factors.[2] The numeric factors are binned by 1 unit (*e.g.*, 1% and 1 dBm). Our dataset includes a wide variety of factors (radio and environmental factors, protocol parameters, *etc.*). The results present a subset of these values that are of interest with regard to WiFi latency. For example, the median of interference power is less than -80 dBm; noise power is under -80 dBm in most cases; the median of #devices (per radio) is below 5; the median of channel, interference, and receiver/transmitter utilization is below 30%, 5%, and 10%, respectively; the median of RSSI and SNR of devices are -66 dBm and 29 db; 802.11n is the dominant protocol.

Relationship to WiFi Latency: To understand the qualitative relationship between WiFi latency and the above related factors, we also plot the average WiFi latency against (binned) values of each factor (right Y-axis of Fig. 6). The trends visually confirm that some factors, such as channel utilization, correlate with WiFi latency well. To quantify these relationships, we consider two common measures: the Kendall rank correlation coefficient (Kendall score for short) and the information gain. These two measures are complementary [41]. While the Kendall score quantifies the monotone relationships (increasing or decreasing), the information gain quantifies how well we can predict WiFi latency if we know a factor. Table 4 shows the results for the radio factors whose values are numeric. The factors are sorted in descending order of the absolute Kendall scores. We see that channel utilization is the most important factor, ranked first for both measures. Interestingly, we notice that these two measures can be conflicting for some factors. For example, RSSI is ranked high for the Kendall score, but its information gain is very low. It means that although RSSI negatively correlates well with WiFi latency, it does not help in predicting it. The reason for this counter-intuitive result is that 96% of RSSI values concentrate on the range between -85 dBm and -45 dBm, where WiFi latency does not change much with RSSI. These results demonstrate the complex relationships between WiFi latency and other diverse factors. We will show how to systematically model WiFi latency in §4.

[2] Due to the limitation of space, we only show 11 radio factors, 3 protocol factors, and one external factor (time of day) .

Table 4: Correlation and information gain.

Radio factor	Kendall score	Information gain
Channel utilization	0.886	0.1708
#Devices	0.799	0.0355
Interference power	0.489	0.0629
RSSI	-0.472	0.0008
Noise power	0.230	0.0336
Transmit power	-0.214	0.0047
Antenna gain	0.200	0.0081
Interference utilization	0.132	0.0462
SNR	-0.116	0.0020
Receiver utilization	0.075	0.0294
Transmitter utilization	-0.056	0.0588

3.2 Observations

Our dataset provides ample material to study WiFi latency. We make three important observations, the first one is specific to the measurement environment but also representative, and the other two are due to the protocol implementation.

5 GHz has lower latency: On Tsinghua campus, the average WiFi latency of 5 GHz is 35% lower than that of 2.4 GHz. Furthermore, Fig. 5(a) also shows that the WiFi latency distribution in 5 GHz is better. A potential reason is that only half as many devices use 5 GHz than 2.4 GHz, and thus channel utilization in 5 GHz is much lower (Fig. 5(b)). This observation is consistent with [26]. See §5.2 for how we improve WiFi latency using 5 GHz in THU-WLAN.

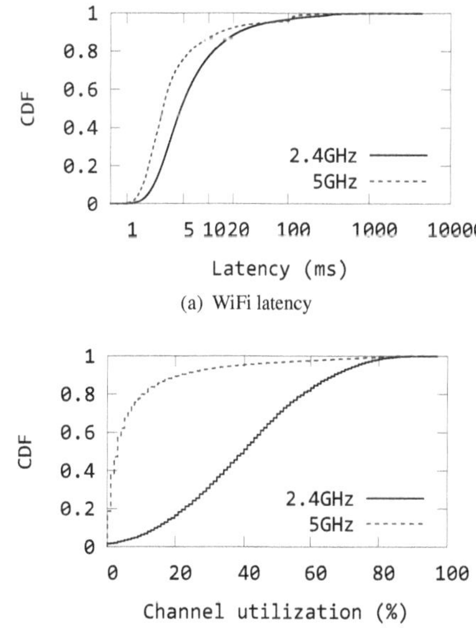

(a) WiFi latency

(b) Channel utilization

Figure 5: 5 GHz vs. 2.4 GHz.

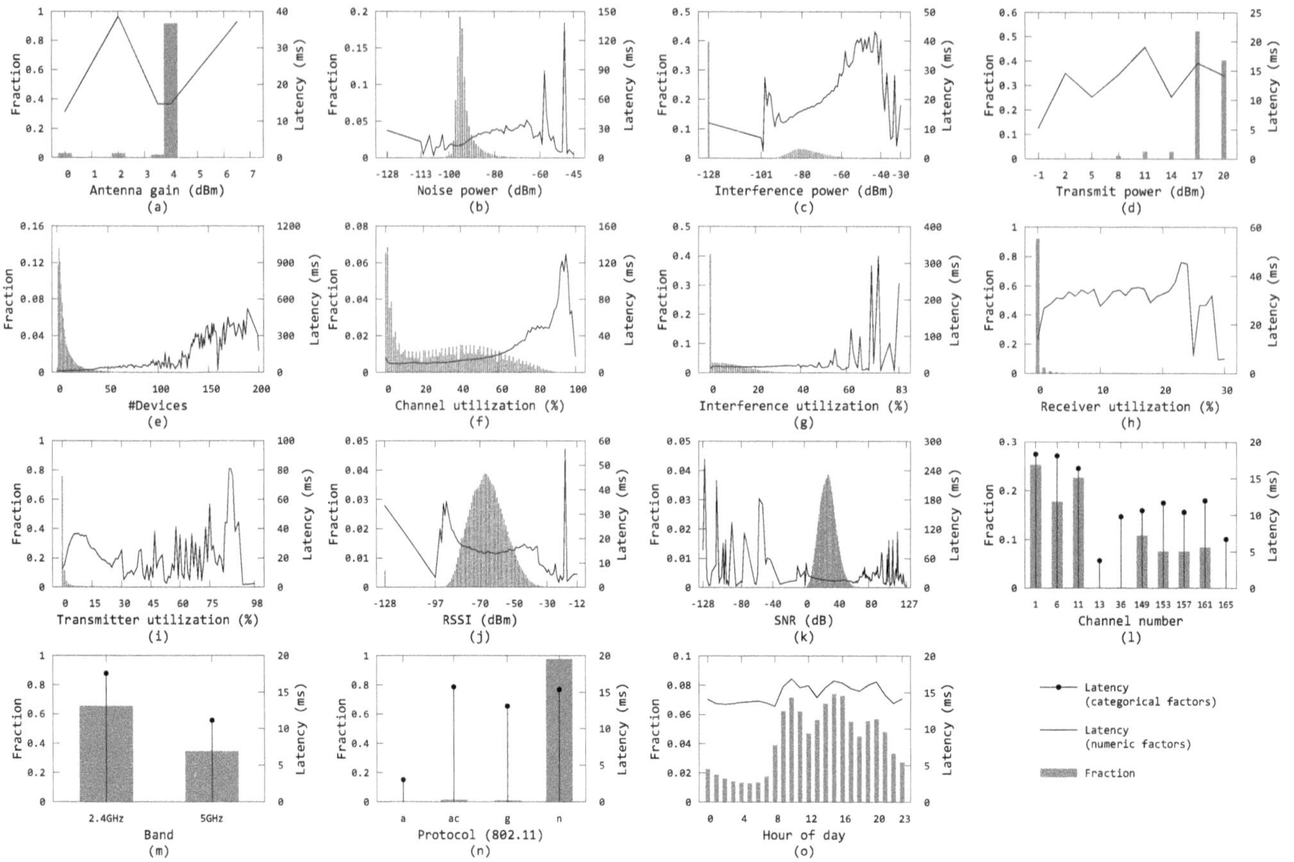

Figure 6: Distribution of factors, and their relationships with WiFi latency. Some peaks of latency are caused by the lack of enough latency data for corresponding factor values.

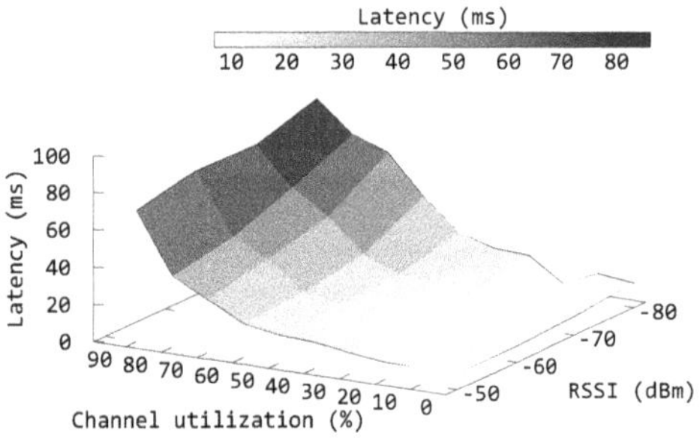

Figure 7: Joint effect of RSSI and channel utilization.

Table 5: Major WiFi chip manufacturers in Tsinghua.

WiFi chip manufacturer	#Devices	Latency (ms)		
		Mean	Median	90th-%ile
Intel	1153	9.63	3.53	15.15
Xiaomi	2626	11.58	3.8	16.56
Apple	21210	12.88	3.31	18.57
HonHai	848	13.75	3.36	18.84
Samsung	3735	14.52	4.02	20.08
Huawei	2536	17.16	4.54	27.21
Meizu	1061	43.83	4.28	131.3

AP selection mechanisms are inadequate and not collaborative: Given the above findings, we find that, surprisingly, dual-band devices (supporting both 2.4 GHz and 5 GHz) are 1.6× more frequent than single-band devices (supporting only 2.4 GHz), and over 50% of the dual-band devices connected to 2.4 GHz. A natural question is that since 5 GHz provides a lower WiFi latency, why are dual-band devices nevertheless connecting to 2.4 GHz? The reason is that the device AP selection heavily depends on RSSI, and since 5 GHz signals attenuate faster, devices are biased towards 2.4 GHz [26]. In contrast, RSSI is not a very important factor for WiFi latency: good RSSI does not guarantee low WiFi latency. For example, Fig. 7 shows that RSSI has a trivial effect on WiFi latency when channel utilization is low. Moreover, when channel utilization exceeds 50%, even high RSSI (*e.g.*, -50dBm) cannot achieve low latency. Interestingly, we also find that AP vendors such as Cisco provide a mechanism (which is also used in THU-WLAN) to direct dual-band devices to the 5 GHz band by delaying probe responses of 2.4 GHz to make 5 GHz more attractive [11]. However, our measurement shows that device vendors do not collaborate well with this ad hoc mechanism, because a user device can still discover the 2.4 GHz of APs by listening to their beacons, leading to crowded 2.4GHz and little-utilized 5GHz bands.

WiFi chipsets are not equal: Table 5 shows the WiFi latency of the major WiFi chip manufacturers that have more than 800 devices in our dataset, sorted by the mean of their WiFi latency. We notice that these manufacturers differ a lot in the tail part (90th percentile). It is interesting to note that in addition to radio factors, device factors also potentially impact WiFi Latency.

4. MODELING METHODOLOGY

The measurements in the previous section show that many factors impact WiFi latency. In this section, we present how WiFiSeer builds more comprehensive WiFi latency models based on machine learning for three representative applications (§6 discusses some other applications.).

4.1 Applications and Challenges

Applications: We begin by describing the model requirements of the three applications in WiFiSeer: (a) Application 1 is to systematically understand how radio factors affect WiFi latency in EWLAN, *i.e.*, which combination(s) of factors impact WiFi latency and how? (b) Application 2 is to help operators diagnose high WiFi latency in the EWLAN by locating where and when WiFi latency is high, and then identifying potential impact factors that operators can take action to improve. (c) Application 3 is to associate user devices to low-latency APs by predicting WiFi latency based on readily-available factors.

All the three applications need effective models to characterize the relationship between WiFi latency and different factors. However, they differ significantly in their requirements with respect to the models (Table 6). First, the model usages are different. The first two applications both aim at providing human-readable insights, thus they need the models to be intuitive enough to interpret rather than black boxes; in contrast, the third application merely needs the model to predict WiFi latency as accurately as possible. Secondly, the applications make use of different related factors. While Application 1 is interested in radio factors, Application 2 cares mostly about environmental factors such as temporal and spatial factors, since they provide specific locations and times for troubleshooting. Besides, because AP selection happens before a device connects to a certain AP, Application 3 cannot use factors that are only available after the connection is established. Finally, the applications focus on different WiFi latency ranges. Application 2 is to diagnose high WiFi latency, Application 3 seeks to find low WiFi latency APs, and Application 1 pays attention to both.

Motivated by these considerations, rather than building a single unified WiFi latency model, we argue that the model should be tailored for the specific application.

Challenges: However, modeling WiFi latency imposes several challenges: First, the relationships between WiFi latency and related factors are complex. As mentioned in §3.1, these relationships are non-linear, or even non-monotonic. As a result, simple approaches such as linear regression that assume a linear or monotonic relationship are unlikely to work. Secondly, various factors are naturally interdependent of each other. For example, Fig. 8 visually shows that SNR and RSSI are highly correlated; Fig. 5(b) shows that channel utilization is quite different in 2.4 GHz and 5 GHz. With such subtle interdependencies, the individual relationship could be a combined effect of several factors. Finally, the distribution of WiFi latencies is highly skewed. For instance, Fig. 4 shows that high WiFi latency is much rarer. Modeling such imbalanced data often has biases (*e.g.*, ignoring high WiFi latency), and thus are less representative [38].

4.2 Machine Learning Algorithms

To address the challenges outlined above, WiFiSeer uses supervised machine learning based methods to model WiFi latency. At a high level, we begin by categorizing WiFi latency into different classes (§3.1), and then build classification models to express the

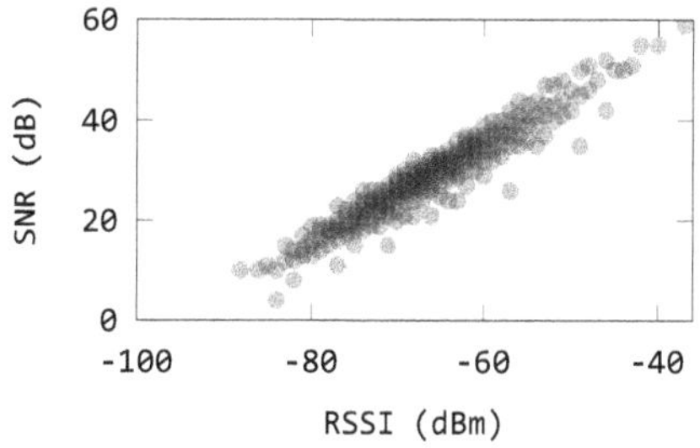

Figure 8: Interdependency between SNR and RSSI.

WiFi latency as a function of the related factors[3]. These models can be used to explain or predict WiFi latencies based on the related factors. All models are built offline using the dataset in §3.

We need to be careful when choosing machine learning algorithms. The algorithms should be able to not only tackle the complex relationship and the interdependencies, but also satisfy the different requirements of the applications (Table 6). We conducted some pilot experiments on commonly used machine learning algorithms, including k-nearest neighbor (KNN), supporting vector machine (SVM), naive Bayes, neural networks, decision trees, and random forests (see [13] for details). We use these algorithms to do binary classification on our dataset (`slow/EX slow` WiFi latency as one class and `fast/EX fast` WiFi latency as the other class). The dataset is undersampled to deal with the imbalanced class problem [38]. The main idea is to randomly remove a part of majority class data to make classes balanced. We evaluate the classification accuracy using precision-recall curves [38]. Fig. 9 shows that random forests outperform other algorithms by achieving higher recall ($\frac{\text{\# of reported true positives}}{\text{\# of true positives}}$) for the same precision ($\frac{\text{\# of reported true positives}}{\text{\# of reported positives}}$). As a result, we select random forests to build the predictive model for Application 3. In addition, we find that among these learning algorithms, decision trees have a unique advantage of being easy to interpret and also reasonably accurate. Thus, we select decision trees to build the descriptive models for Application 1 and Application 2.

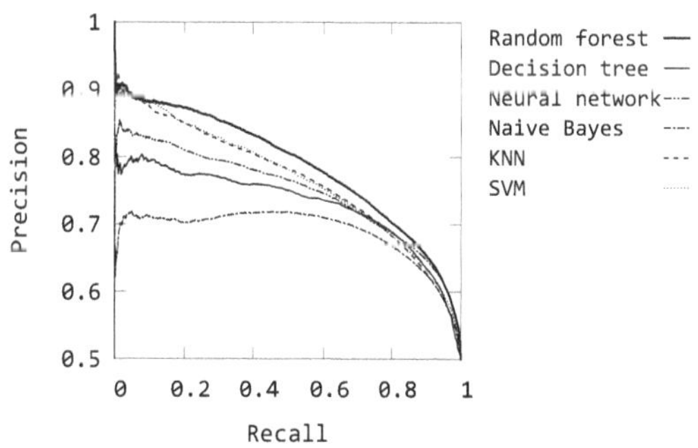

Figure 9: Comparing different machine learning algorithms (Y-axis starts from 0.5).

Table 7 summarizes the model and its configuration for each application. To determine a proper parameter setting for each model, we use 10-fold cross-validation to select the parameter setting that best achieves the goal of the model. We describe these models and how they are used for each application in §5.

[3]We also test regression models (*e.g.*, regression trees) in our pilot experiments, but its accuracy is low. Moreover, classification models are often more straightforward and usable for practitioners [24, 25, 54].

Table 6: Requirements of WiFi latency models for different applications.

	Application 1 Understanding effects of radio factors	Application 2 Diagnosing high WiFi latency	Application 3 Selecting a low-latency AP
Model usage	Intuitive descriptive model	Intuitive descriptive model	Accurate predictive model
Factors interested in (see Table 2)	Industry-standard radio factors	Environment-specific factors and factors actionable for operators	Factors that are available before devices connect to APs.
The WiFi latency interested in	Both high and low latency	High latency	Low latency

Table 7: Configurations and performance of WiFi latency models for different applications.

	Model 1 for Application 1	Model 2 for Application 2	Model 3 for Application 3
Modeling method	Decision tree	Decision trees	A random forest
Classification & Classes (see Table 3)	Multiclass classification: 1. `EX slow` 2. `slow` 3. `fast` 4. `EX fast`	Binary classification: 1. `EX slow` 2. `not EX slow`	Binary classification: 1. `slow/EX slow` 2. `fast/EX fast`
Factors used	Column 4 in Table 2	Column 5 in Table 2	Column 6 in Table 2
How to solve imbalanced data	Undersampling	Adjust the decision threshold	Undersampling
Model goal	Maximizing accuracy	Achieving acceptable precision of class 1 and maximize recall of class 1	Achieving high precision of class 2 and maximize recall of class 2
Performance	Accuracy = 0.42 (multiclass classification)	Precision = 0.59, recall = 0.64 (median)	Precision=0.76, recall=0.67

5. APPLICATIONS

Based on the three models we build in §4, WiFiSeer provides three applications to characterize and improve WiFi latency in large-scale operational networks.

5.1 App 1: Understanding Radio Factors

To understand the effects of the 11 radio factors on WiFi latency, we build a decision tree (Fig. 10) for the four WiFi latency classes. The specific configuration is shown in the second column of Table 7. The tree has an accuracy of 0.42, which is reasonable for multiclass classification [25]. Fig. 10 shows that among all the 11 radio factors, only 4 factors appear in the decision tree. Intuitively, because the decision tree puts important factors near the root to better classify the data, factors close to the root has more effect on WiFi latency than factors close to the leaves, than factors not appearing in the tree. In particular, we find that channel utilization and #devices (in the top three levels of the decision tree) are the two most important radio factors for characterizing WiFi latency. On the other hand, SNR and the transmit utilization only take effect on lower-level branches, *e.g.*, when channel utilization $> 47.5\%$ and #devices ≤ 11.5. Other radio factors that do not show up in the decision tree play a relatively less important role for WiFi latency.

The decision tree also shows the thresholds of how these radio factors affect WiFi latency. These thresholds quantitatively describe conditions in which typical wireless problems are likely to occur. The main takeaways are as follows:

First, for channel utilization, the `EX slow` class only appears when channel utilization $> 47.5\%$, and the `EX fast` class only appears when it $\leq 47.5\%$. Therefore, channel utilization greater than 47.5% can be deemed as the ***heavy load problem***. The decision tree suggests that the heavy load problem is a key cause of `EX slow` WiFi latency, and should be avoided if one wants to achieve `EX fast` WiFi latency. The threshold 47.5% quantitatively confirms previously suggested rules-of-thumb that channel utilization should be kept under 50% for good WiFi performance [5, 21].

Second, we observe that even when channel utilization is very low, a large #devices can still impact WiFi latency. For example, the leftmost `slow` node occurs where channel utilization is ≤ 22.5 and #devices > 35.5. Previous studies suggest that this is caused by the ***local contention problem***: a large number of concurrent senders increase the data collision probability and the backoff waiting time, and decrease the achievable channel utilization [27, 40]. Besides, each device has to wait for its turn to receive the data from the AP. The waiting time becomes long when the AP is connected by many devices.

Third, for SNR, we find that the split points of SNR nodes in the decision tree are from 21.5 dB to 25.5 dB. This suggests that SNR less than 20 dB is low, and could impact WiFi latency. Specifically, the ***fading and noise problem*** increases the bit error rate and thus increases the MAC layer frame retry times; or decreases the PHY rate and thus increases the transmission time, which both in turn inflate the WiFi latency.

The above observations and the tree model characterize how radio factors affect WiFi latency in a typical large-scale EWLAN, and can help further evaluations on the inherent trade-offs in the design of protocols and hardware.

5.2 App 2: Diagnosing High WiFi Latency

For diagnosing high WiFi latency, we consider a binary classification (`EX slow` and `not EX slow`) since the operators (*e.g.*, those we worked with) care more about `EX slow` cases. In the diagnosis, the time and place is important because operators need to know when and where high WiFi latency is likely to occur so that they can take further actions, such as troubleshooting in the field. However, since the decision tree does not guarantee that these factors appear, we use a two-stage method in Application 2.

We first split the data based on the combinations of temporal factors (time of day and day of week) and spatial factors (buildings and building types). In order to provide high-level results, we categorize the time of day into six meaningful intervals: morning (08:00 – 11:00), lunch (11:00 – 13:00), afternoon (13:00 – 17:00), dinner (17:00 – 19:00), evening (19:00 – 22:00), sleep (22:00 – 08:00); day of week into two types: weekdays and weekends. We define a *problem time and place* as any spatial-temporal combination whose 1) data is more than 0.1% of the total and

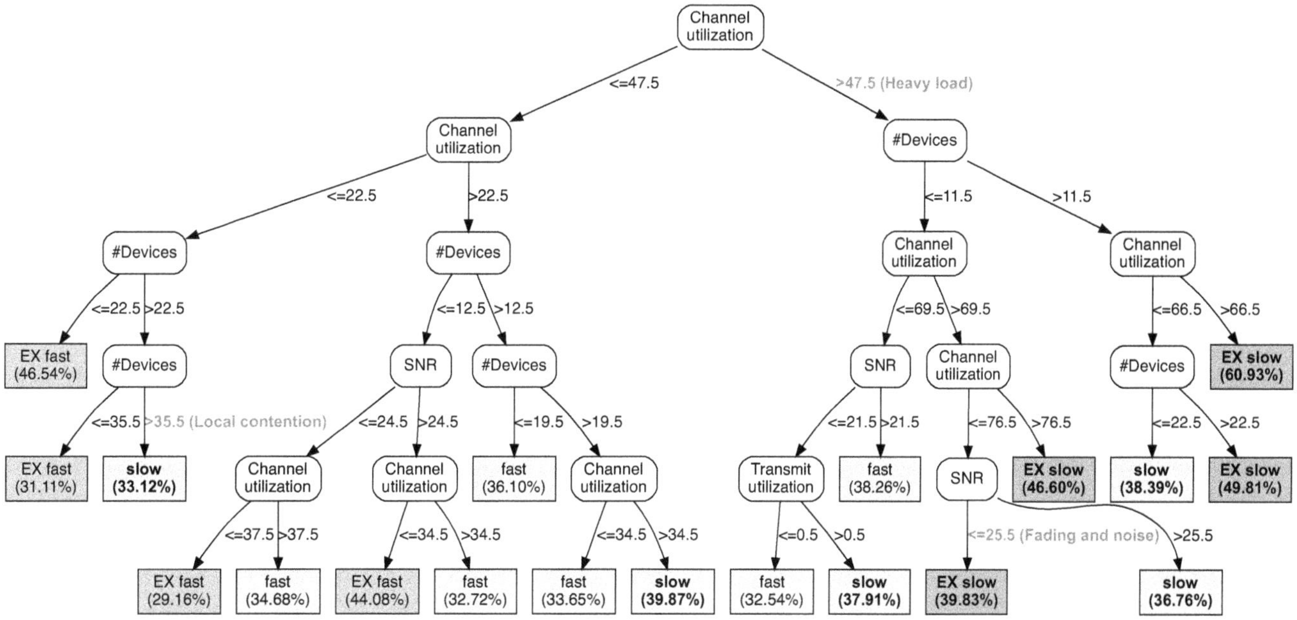

Figure 10: Decision tree for modeling the effects of radio factors on WiFi latency. The percent of the major class in the node is shown.

Table 8: Examples: problem time and places of 6Jiao.

Building-Building Type-Day-Time	%[EX slow]	%Data
6Jiao-Classroom-Weekday-Morning	36%	0.80%
6Jiao-Classroom-Weekday-Afternoon	35%	0.82%
6Jiao-Classroom-Weekday-Evening (Its decision tree is shown in Fig. 11)	51%	0.28%
6Jiao-Classroom-Weekend-Morning	33%	0.13%

2) %[EX slow] (percentage of EX slow) is significantly high ($\geq$1.5$\times$ the global %[EX slow] [41]). The global %[EX slow] is about 10% in THU-WLAN (Fig. 4). In this way, we found 92 problem time and places out of 1368 on Tsinghua campus. For example, Table 8 shows the problem time and places regarding a classroom building named 6Jiao (the sixth classroom building, also the largest one in Tsinghua).

Then, for each problem time and place, we build a decision tree (that is, 92 decision trees in total) based on factors that operators can possibly take action on to affect latencies. The specific configuration of the decision trees is shown in the third column of Table 7. Overall, the median precision and recall of those decision trees are 0.59 and 0.64, respectively.

A decision tree identifies a *high WiFi latency condition* as the combination of the factors and their values on the path from the root to an EX slow node. For example, Fig. 11 shows the decision tree of the problem time and place "6Jiao-Classroom-Weekday-Evening". The two high WiFi latency conditions, represented by two bold paths, are "channel utilization > 66.5% and #device > 13.5" and "50.5% < channel utilization $\leq$ 66.5% and #device > 41.5". As such, the operators should focus their efforts on investigating and solving the heavy load and local contention problems in the weekday evening of 6Jiao.

Table 9 shows the prevalent patterns of high WiFi latency conditions, that is, ignoring the specific factor values in the conditions. We see that high channel utilization, a large number of devices, and high interference power are the three dominant factors across the high WiFi latency conditions in THU-WLAN.

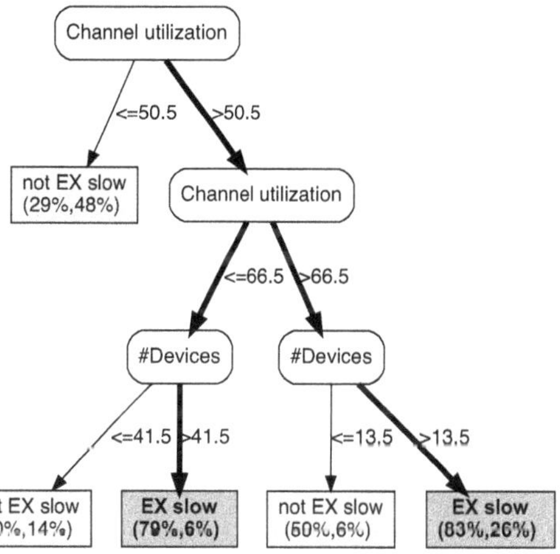

Figure 11: Decision tree for the problem time and place "6Jiao-Classroom-Weekday-Evening". A tuples in a leaf node means ($\frac{\text{EX slow data in the node}}{\text{data in the node}}$, $\frac{\text{data in the node}}{\text{data in the tree}}$). Bold paths represent two high WiFi latency conditions.

Table 9: Prevalent patterns of high WiFi latency conditions that appear in more than five problem time and places.

High WiFi latency condition pattern	Frequency
Channel utilization > x and #devices > y	21
Channel utilization > x	18
#Devices > x	11
Channel utilization > x and #devices $\leq y$	8
Channel utilization > x and y < #devices $\leq z$	8
#Devices > x and y < channel utilization $\leq z$	6
Interference power > x and #devices > y	6
Interference power > x and channel utilization > y and #devices $\leq z$	6

Practical solutions: To solve those common issues, we have deployed two solutions in practice to optimize the WiFi latency in THU-WLAN. First, we intend to guide more dual-band user devices to connect to the 5 GHz to avoid high WiFi latency conditions, because the 5 GHz band has fewer devices and lower channel utilization (Fig. 5(b)), and thus can provide lower latency (Fig. 5(a)). To this end, we add a 5 GHz only SSID "Tsinghua-5G" in addition to the original dual-band SSID "Tsinghua". This gives a chance for the owners of dual-band devices to manually select the 5 GHz band, which in turn solves the aforementioned problem that the default band selection of devices is biased towards 2.4 GHz. The number of user devices connected to "Tsinghua-5G" keeps growing and hit 6,000 at the end of Oct. 2015. We find that, on average, the WiFi latency of "Tsinghua-5G" is 22% lower than that of the original SSID "Tsinghua".

Second, we propose a dense AP deployment solution to avoid high WiFi latency conditions, and deploy this solution in Dorm#31. In particular, for 78 rooms from the 1st floor to the 4th floor in Dorm#31, we deploy *one AP in each room* in which live three students. Such dense deployment significantly reduces the number of devices per radio. Besides, the channel and the power of each AP are also well-engineered to mitigate the interference among APs, and no ethernet ports are available in the rooms so that the interference of rogue APs can be eliminated as much as possible. Compared with other dorms with regular AP deployment on Tsinghua campus — *e.g.*, Dorm#17 where two students live in a room and about *10 rooms share one AP* — the AP in Dorm#31 has fewer devices, less interference, lower channel utilization, and thus lower WiFi latency as shown in Fig. 12(a-d). On average, our dense AP deployment improved WiFi latency by 36%.

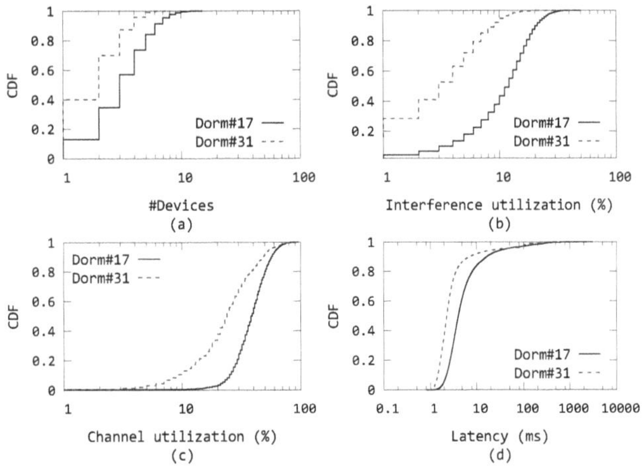

Figure 12: Dense AP deployment (Dorm#31) *vs.* regular AP deployment (Dorm#17).

5.3 App 3: Selecting a Low-Latency AP

An EWLAN often deploy many APs to improve WiFi availability and support device roaming. Therefore, a user device typically hears multiple APs in its vicinity [43], *e.g.*, user devices can hear on average 5 APs in THU-WLAN at the same time. However, deciding which AP to associate to for low latency is a challenging task because neither the device nor `ping2` can measure WiFi latency before the device associates to an AP. Thus, one needs to select a low-latency AP based on other WiFi metrics that are measurable and available before the connection being established, such as RSSI and channel utilization. However, the relationship between WiFi latency and WiFi metrics is complex (Fig. 6), and the default RSSI-based AP selection cannot assure low latency (§3.1). To solve this problem, WiFiSeer provides machine learning based latency-oriented AP selection, called **AGE** (**A**ssociating to **G**ood **E**nterprise APs), to help devices associate to low-latency APs nearby. AGE controls the AP association of user devices by a mobile app we developed, so that AGE can be easily deployed without any changes to device OS/drivers or AP firmware. AGE has already been deployed in THU-WLAN and is used daily by over 1,000 user devices. The deployment shows that AGE reduces WiFi latency substantially (shows later).

Design of AGE: Fig. 13 shows the high-level overview of AGE. It contains two main components: the AGE helper app installed on user devices to associate devices to the AP selected; the AGE controller which uses WiFi latency Model 3 (a random forest) to predict WiFi latencies of APs around a device based on readily-available WiFi factors from the SNMP data. Model 3 is built offline with the historical dataset (last column of Table 7). Its precision and recall are 0.76 and 0.67, respectively. Note that, to avoid battery overhead for devices, AGE does not use `ping2` to measure WiFi latency of devices. WiFiSeer only uses `ping2` for infrequent historical data collection, not for online AGE prediction.

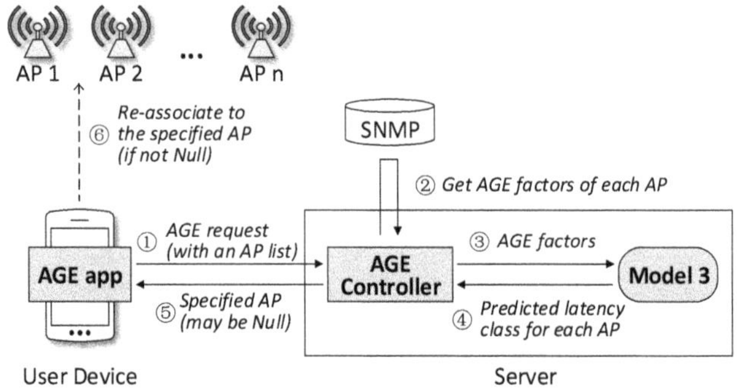

Figure 13: AGE overview.

In particular, AGE works as follows:

Step 1: When a device is connected to the EWLAN, the AGE app periodically[4] sends an AGE request with a list of nearby APs it scanned to the AGE controller.

Step 2: For the APs in the list, the AGE controller collects their related factors (last column of Table 2) from the SNMP data, called AGE factors here.

Step 3 & 4: Based on those AGE factors, Model 3 generates the likelihood that an AP is `fast/EX fast` or `slow/EX slow`. Then, the AP is classified as `fast/EX fast` or `slow/EX slow` if the likelihood is higher than 0.6; otherwise, the AP is deemed as `not sure`. We use 0.6 as the threshold because it best achieves the goal of Model 3 (Table 7) in offline 10-fold cross-validation.

Step 5: With the classification results of Model 3, the AGE controller decides whether the device should re-associate to another AP instead of the current one. Specifically, if the current connected AP is predicted as `slow/EX slow`, and there exists at least one nearby AP being predicted as `fast/EX fast`, the AGE controller will respond with the AP that has the highest likelihood of `fast/EX fast`; otherwise, the AGE controller returns `Null`.

Step 6: The AGE app re-associates the device to the specified AP (if not `Null`) by modifying the device WiFi configurations (*e.g.*, using the Android APIs [8]).

[4]For our deployment, the interval is set to 5 minutes when the device screen is on, and 20 minutes when it is off.

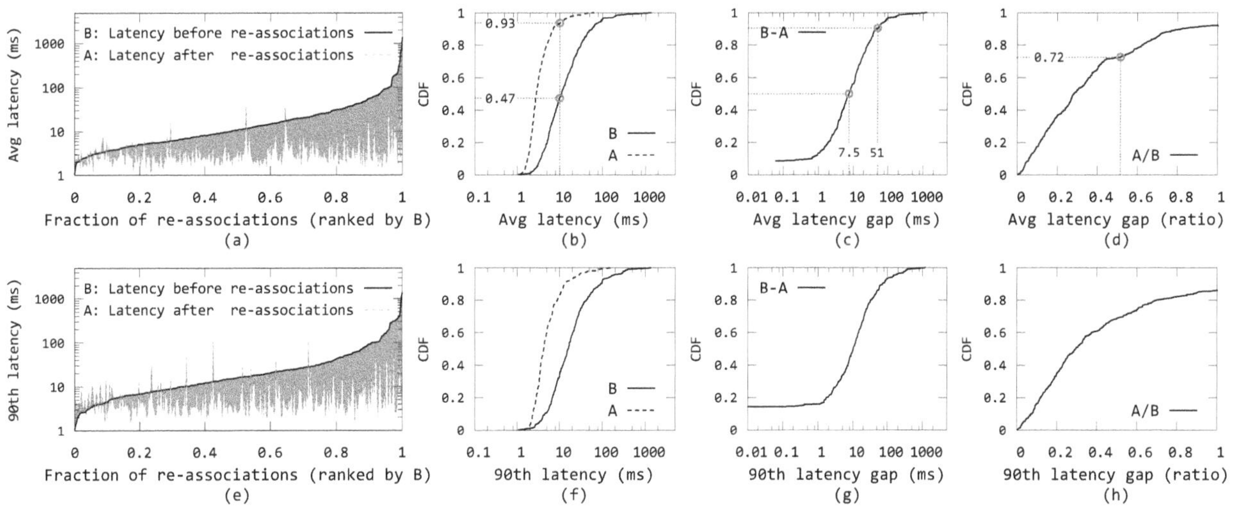

Figure 14: Comparison of WiFi latencies before (B) and after (A) AGE re-associations.

Large-scale deployment of AGE: We implemented the AGE app as a component of the Android version TUNet[5] as shown in Fig. 15. AGE automatically runs in the background, so users do not have to manually run it. 1165 devices have installed AGE since Sept. 2015, and have used it for 2.5 months.

To evaluate AGE, we measure the WiFi latency of these devices using `ping2` (This measurement is only for evaluation, it is not a part of the design of AGE). Fig. 14 shows the performance of AGE re-associations, that is, one-minute latency before and after devices re-associate to the APs suggested by AGE. For these re-associations, AGE significantly reduces both the average and the 90th percentile of WiFi latency. For example, focusing on the average latency in Fig. 14(a-d), 92% of the re-associations reduce the latency (green areas below the solid line in Fig. 14(a)); the fraction of `fast/EX fast` ($\leq$ 10 ms) has been improved from 47% before re-associations to 93% after re-associations (Fig. 14(b)); after re-associations, 50% of latencies are reduced by more than 7.5 ms and 10% of latencies are reduced by more than 51 ms (Fig. 14(c)), and relatively, 72% of the latencies are reduced by more than half (Fig. 14(d)). The results of the 90th percentile (Fig. 14(e-h)) are similar.

Our large-scale real-world deployment demonstrates that AGE is much more effective at selecting low-latency APs than the default AP selection of devices. Thus, AGE provides a promising framework for EWLANs to improve their WiFi latency.

6. DISCUSSION

Generality of WiFiSeer: WiFiSeer can be easily adopted by network operators in typical operational EWLANs. For the measurement part, WiFiSeer only uses traditional SNMP data and the light-weight `ping2` method, both of which are general methods for EWLANs. Furthermore, for the running of WiFiSeer, continuous running of data collection is not required by WiFiSeer. For modeling and the three applications, WiFiSeer takes advantage of widely used machine learning algorithms, which are well-known for being general and able to deal with diverse data. The three applications are independent of each other and thus can be run separately on demand.

[5]TUNet is a mobile app which can help users automatically login the captive portal of THU-WLAN. The version with AGE can be downloaded from [18].

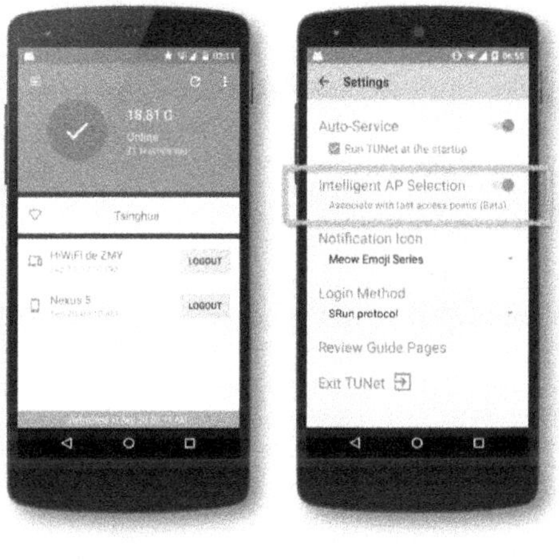

Figure 15: TUNet with the AGE app as a component.

Other WiFi latency related applications: The machine learning approaches in WiFiSeer can be used in other applications. For example in EWLAN optimizations, due to the lack of knowledge on how different actions will influence performance, operators face hard decisions on whether certain actions will work or not. In other words, it is difficult to estimate beforehand their impact on network performance. WiFiSeer can provide a predictive model to help operators estimate the performance improvement of different actions. Based on the operational experience, operators can roughly estimate the impact of an action on the radio factors. For example, adding an AP for client-concentrated areas reduces the number of devices of nearby APs by 20%. By using our model, the potential benefit on latencies can be predicted before taking any real-world actions. Thus, our modeling approach can also help operators make decisions to balance cost/benefit trade-offs.

Potential improvements of AGE: In the AGE deployment, we notice that some devices do not collaborate well with the AGE app. In particular, although AGE suggests re-associations, some devices may not authorize the AGE app to do this, or some devices will change back to the original APs after AGE re-associations because of the conflicts between the default device AP selection algorithm and AGE. It shows that AGE has the potential to bring more benefits if it can be implemented on device hardware/OS levels or in protocols as we discuss next.

Future 802.11k/v integration: The real-world deployment (§5.3) of AGE shows that EWLAN users could have a much better latency experience. The strategy of AGE can be an important complement to the traditional 802.11k/v protocol, which is designed to assist AP selection when devices roam. The current implementation of 802.11k/v only provides a way to exchange several data (*e.g.*, channel loads, neighbor reports, and link measurements) between APs and devices, but leaves the AP selection to the user devices. This task, however, is challenging as elaborated in §4.1. AGE can be integrated into 802.11k/v to systematically solve those problems, and make 802.11k/v more intelligent in the future. Still, for legacy EWLANs and user devices, where 802.11k/v is not supported, our application-level attempt is a viable way for WiFi latency optimization.

Other WiFi performance metrics beyond latency: Different mobile applications are often sensitive to different WiFi performance metrics, *e.g.*, latency we studied in this work, throughput, or both. Also, it is possible that the good conditions for latency could conflict with that for throughput. Therefore, a promising extension of AGE is to build predictive models not only for latency but also for other metrics, such as throughput or even application layer metrics (*e.g.*, web page load time). Then, according to user's preference, AGE can select the AP that has either reasonable performance for all those metrics or the best performance for the active application, *e.g.*, high throughput for online videos. We will explore this direction in our future work.

7. RELATED WORK

WiFi measurements: Analyzing packet traces is a costly way to monitor a wireless network. It is hard to modify the hardware of enterprise APs to capture and record wireless frame traces like WiSe [46] and PIE [51]. Additional hardware, *e.g.* extra sniffers in Jigsaw [32] and Wit [44], are also inappropriate for large scale measurements. Meraki [26] monitors the wireless link at large scale using the customized AP with dedicated radio hardware (*e.g.*, Meraki MR18). In contrast, within WiFiSeer framework, WiFi latency measurement method of `ping2` and traditional SNMP are low-overhead and deployable in large-scale EWLANs.

Modeling: There are some prior studies of modeling key performance indicators in different domains, such as video QoE [25, 41, 50] and web QoE [24]. They also take advantage of machine learning algorithms, such as decision trees, to model the complex relationships. However, machine learning building blocks cannot be set once and for all. In this paper, we explore how to tailor models for three different applications (§4).

AP selection: There are many methods for AP selection. Currently most devices only utilize part of the available information to make choices with simple assumptions of wireless performance. Preferential association to APs with stronger RSSI is a common approach [55], but stronger signal strength does not assure better performance [42]. Some implementations utilize more historical or actively measured client-side information besides RSSI [3, 45]. However, it is time-consuming, battery-draining and sometimes bothering for a user device to test each nearby AP only by itself [1].

Some approaches exchange information of the wireless environment between the EWLAN and its clients — specifically, implementations of 802.11k/v [22, 23] standards. *E.g.*, Cisco enterprise APs can send neighbor AP report (defined in 802.11k, called "AP assisted roaming" by Cisco [2]) to 802.11k equipped iOS devices [20], which helps speed up scanning, reduces power consumption, and makes efficient use of air time. However, the information currently exchanged neither contains direct measurement of WiFi latency nor provides enough knowledge for 802.11k/v-capable devices to actually select best performing APs.

In addition, some work [30, 34, 43] attempts to associate a user device to multiple APs *simultaneously*. It requires the device to be equipped with more than one physical WiFi interface card or support virtual interfaces. Nevertheless, these solutions still need a way to decide which APs nearby have better performance. WiFiSeer provides a methodology for modeling and predicting WiFi performance, which is complementary to those solutions.

8. CONCLUSION

In this paper, we present WiFiSeer, a general and practical framework for measuring and characterizing WiFi latency in large-scale operational EWLANs. WiFiSeer was deployed in Tsinghua to conduct a WiFi latency measurement study of unprecedented scale. Our machine learning-based characterization results provide important insights to network operators and 802.11 protocol designers. Among commonly suspected reasons for unsatisfying WiFi latency, heavy traffic load, local contention, noise and fading, and interference are indeed quantitatively confirmed as top reasons, whereas RSSI (often used for AP selection) is not. Our machine learning based modeling reveals the complex but quantitative impacts of various factors on real-world WiFi latency, which are hard to obtain through theoretical analysis or simulations. The real-world performance gains resulting from two deployed mitigation approaches suggested by WiFiSeer highlight the promise of data-driven re-engineering of operational networks.

Our results also show that existing AP selection mechanisms are inadequate. Ad hoc solutions from AP and OS vendors do not collaborate with each other, resulting in poor utilization of available resources, *e.g.*, crowded 2.4 GHz and little-utilized 5 GHz bands. Through adaptively re-associating a device to better performing APs, our widely deployed AGE client greatly helps to mitigate these problems on Tsinghua campus. Encouraged by this result, we advocate that protocol designers, OS vendors, AP vendors, and researchers should work together to push 802.11k/v deployment, and to improve the methodologies, such as WiFiSeer, to generate better data-driven intelligence to drive the 802.11k/v protocols.

Acknowledgments

We thank our shepherd Kamin Whitehouse and the anonymous reviewers for their thorough comments and valuable feedback. We are grateful to Lab μ for their efforts on developing TUNet and for them allowing us to implement AGE as a component of it. We appreciate Weichao Li, Fan Ye, Hewu Li, and Chunyi Peng for their helpful suggestions, as well as Yousef Azzabi for his proofreading.

This work was partly supported by the Key Program of the National Natural Science Foundation of China under grant 61233007, the National Natural Science Foundation of China (NSFC) under grant 61472214 & 61472210 & 61033001 & 61361136003, the National High Technology Research and Development Program of China (863 Program) under grant 2013AA013302, the National Basic Research Program of China (973 Program) under grant 2013CB329105 & 2011CBA00300 & 2011CBA00301, the Tsinghua National Laboratory for Information Science and Technology key projects, the Global Talent Recruitment (Youth) Program, and the Cross-disciplinary Collaborative Teams Program for Science & Technology & Innovation of Chinese Academy of Sciences-Network and system technologies for security monitoring and information interaction in smart grid.

References

[1] 802.11 association process explained. https://documentation.meraki.com/MR/WiFi_Basics_and_Best_Practices/802.11_Association_process_explained.

[2] 802.11r, 802.11k, and 802.11w deployment guide, cisco ios-xe release 3.3: 802.11k assisted roaming. http://www.cisco.com/c/en/us/td/docs/wireless/controller/technotes/5700/software/release/ios_xe_33/11rkw_DeploymentGuide/b_802point11rkw_deployment_guide_cisco_ios_xe_release33/b_802point11rkw_deployment_guide_cisco_ios_xe_release33_chapter_010.html.

[3] Android framework classes and services. https://android.googlesource.com/platform/frameworks/base/. Accessed: 2015-01-23.

[4] Cisco snmp. http://tools.cisco.com/Support/SNMP/do/BrowseOID.do.

[5] Designing for voice / tech tools. http://wirelesslanprofessionals.com/wlw-010-designing-for-voice-tech-tools/.

[6] Edimax wifi adapter seems to go to sleep if not used. https://www.raspberrypi.org/forums/viewtopic.php?t=61665.

[7] Edison wifi delay and power saving. https://communities.intel.com/message/255890.

[8] enablenetwork of wifimanager in android. http://developer.android.com/reference/android/net/wifi/WifiManager.html#enableNetwork(int,boolean). Accessed: 2015-09-22.

[9] Ewlan market. http://www.delloro.com/news/enterprise-wireless-lan-market-to-expand-70-percent-by-2018.

[10] Ewlan overview. http://www.cisco.com/c/en/us/td/docs/solutions/Enterprise/Mobility/emob41dg/emob41dg-wrapper/ch1_Over.html.

[11] Load balancing and band select on the cisco wireless lan controller. https://supportforums.cisco.com/document/81896/load-balancing-and-band-select-cisco-wireless-lan-controller.

[12] Openwrt. https://openwrt.org/.

[13] Orange. http://docs.orange.biolab.si/reference/rst/index.html.

[14] Ping on mavericks on late 2013 macbook pro slow and variable compared to windows. http://apple.stackexchange.com/questions/110777/ping-on-mavericks-on-late-2013-macbook-pro-slow-and-variable-compared-to-windows.

[15] Round-trip time is important. https://marketo-web.thousandeyes.com/rs/thousandeyes/images/ThousandEyes_Use_Case_Enterprise_and_IT_Operations.pdf.

[16] Slow ping on raspberry pi. http://procrastinative.ninja/2014/11/19/slow-ping-on-raspberry-pi/.

[17] Speed test. http://www.speedtest.net/.

[18] Tunet. http://netman.cs.tsinghua.edu.cn/wp-content/uploads/2016/04/TUNet-Android-v3.2.4.apk_.zip.

[19] What is the business value of application speed and performance to you? https://s3.amazonaws.com/cisco-partnerpedia-production/product_files/78904/original/Speed_Matters.pdf.

[20] Wi-fi network roaming with 802.11k, 802.11r, and 802.11v on ios. https://support.apple.com/en-us/HT202628.

[21] Wi-fi tip: Channel utilization best practice. http://www.revolutionwifi.net/revolutionwifi/2010/08/wi-fi-tip-channel-utilization-best.html.

[22] Ieee standard for information technology– local and metropolitan area networks– specific requirements– part 11: Wireless lan medium access control (mac)and physical layer (phy) specifications amendment 1: Radio resource measurement of wireless lans. *IEEE Std 802.11k-2008 (Amendment to IEEE Std 802.11-2007)* (June 2008), 1–244.

[23] Ieee standard for information technology– local and metropolitan area networks– specific requirements– part 11: Wireless lan medium access control (mac) and physical layer (phy) specifications amendment 8: Ieee 802.11 wireless network management. *IEEE Std 802.11v-2011 (Amendment to IEEE Std 802.11-2007 as amended by IEEE Std 802.11k-2008, IEEE Std 802.11r-2008, IEEE Std 802.11y-2008, IEEE Std 802.11w-2009, IEEE Std 802.11n-2009, IEEE Std 802.11p-2010, and IEEE Std 802.11z-2010)* (Feb 2011), 1–433.

[24] BALACHANDRAN, A., AGGARWAL, V., HALEPOVIC, E., PANG, J., SESHAN, S., VENKATARAMAN, S., AND YAN, H. Modeling web quality-of-experience on cellular networks. In *MoBicom 2014*.

[25] BALACHANDRAN, A., SEKAR, V., AKELLA, A., SESHAN, S., STOICA, I., AND ZHANG, H. Developing a predictive model of quality of experience for internet video. In *ACM SIGCOMM Computer Communication Review* (2013), vol. 43, ACM, pp. 339–350.

[26] BISWAS, S., BICKET, J., WONG, E., MUSALOIU-E, R., BHARTIA, A., AND AGUAYO, D. Large-scale measurements of wireless network behavior. In *Proceedings of the 2015 ACM Conference on Special Interest Group on Data Communication* (2015), ACM, pp. 153–165.

[27] BONONI, L., CONTI, M., AND GREGORI, E. Design and performance evaluation of an asymptotically optimal backoff algorithm for ieee 802.11 wireless lans. In *System Sciences, 2000. Proceedings of the 33rd Annual Hawaii International Conference on* (2000), IEEE, pp. 10–pp.

[28] CHAFE, C., GUREVICH, M., LESLIE, G., AND TYAN, S. Effect of time delay on ensemble accuracy. In *Proceedings of the International Symposium on Musical Acoustics* (2004), vol. 31.

[29] CHANDRA, P., AND LIDE, D. *Wi-Fi Telephony: Challenges and solutions for voice over WLANs*. Newnes, 2011.

[30] CHANDRA, R., BAHL, P., AND BAHL, P. Multinet: connecting to multiple ieee 802.11 networks using a single wireless card. In *INFOCOM 2004. Twenty-third AnnualJoint Conference of the IEEE Computer and Communications Societies* (March 2004), vol. 2, pp. 882–893 vol.2.

[31] CHENG, Y.-C., AFANASYEV, M., VERKAIK, P., BENKO, P., CHIANG, J., SNOEREN, A. C., SAVAGE, S., AND VOELKER, G. M. Shaman automatic 802.11 wireless diagnosis system.

[32] CHENG, Y.-C., BELLARDO, J., BENKÖ, P., SNOEREN, A. C., VOELKER, G. M., AND SAVAGE, S. *Jigsaw: solving the puzzle of enterprise 802.11 analysis*, vol. 36. ACM, 2006.

[33] CLAYPOOL, M., AND CLAYPOOL, K. Latency can kill: precision and deadline in online games. In *Proceedings of the first annual ACM SIGMM conference on Multimedia systems* (2010), ACM, pp. 215–222.

[34] CROITORU, A., NICULESCU, D., AND RAICIU, C. Towards wifi mobility without fast handover. Usenix NSDI.

[35] DING, N., PATHAK, A., KOUTSONIKOLAS, D., SHEPARD, C., HU, Y. C., AND ZHONG, L. Realizing the full potential of psm using proxying. In *INFOCOM, 2012 Proceedings IEEE* (2012), IEEE, pp. 2821–2825.

[36] DING, N., WAGNER, D., CHEN, X., PATHAK, A., HU, Y. C., AND RICE, A. Characterizing and modeling the impact of wireless signal strength on smartphone battery drain. In *Proceedings of the ACM SIGMETRICS/International Conference on Measurement*

and Modeling of Computer Systems (New York, NY, USA, 2013), SIGMETRICS '13, ACM, pp. 29–40.

[37] GRIGORIK, I. *High Performance Browser Networking: What every web developer should know about networking and web performance.* " O'Reilly Media, Inc.", 2013.

[38] HE, H., GARCIA, E., ET AL. Learning from imbalanced data. *Knowledge and Data Engineering, IEEE Transactions on 21*, 9 (2009), 1263–1284.

[39] HUANG, J., CHEN, C., PEI, Y., WANG, Z., QIAN, Z., QIAN, F., TIWANA, B., XU, Q., MAO, Z., ZHANG, M., ET AL. Mobiperf: Mobile network measurement system. Tech. rep., Technical report, Technical report, Technical report). University of Michigan and Microsoft Research, 2011.

[40] JI, X., HE, Y., WANG, J., WU, K., YI, K., AND LIU, Y. Voice over the dins: improving wireless channel utilization with collision tolerance. In *Network Protocols (ICNP), 2013 21st IEEE International Conference on* (2013), IEEE, pp. 1–10.

[41] JIANG, J., SEKAR, V., STOICA, I., AND ZHANG, H. Shedding light on the structure of internet video quality problems in the wild. In *Proceedings of the Ninth ACM Conference on Emerging Networking Experiments and Technologies* (New York, NY, USA, 2013), CoNEXT '13, ACM, pp. 357–368.

[42] JUDD, G., AND STEENKISTE, P. Fixing 802. 11 access point selection. *ACM SIGCOMM Computer Communication Review 32*, 3 (2002), 31–31.

[43] KATEJA, R., BARANASURIYA, N., NAVDA, V., AND PADMANABHAN, V. N. Diversifi: Robust multi-link interactive streaming. CoNEXT.

[44] MAHAJAN, R., RODRIG, M., WETHERALL, D., AND ZAHORJAN, J. Analyzing the mac-level behavior of wireless networks in the wild. In *ACM SIGCOMM Computer Communication Review* (2006), vol. 36, ACM, pp. 75–86.

[45] NICHOLSON, A. J., CHAWATHE, Y., CHEN, M. Y., NOBLE, B. D., AND WETHERALL, D. Improved access point selection. In *Proceedings of the 4th international conference on Mobile systems, applications and services* (2006), ACM, pp. 233–245.

[46] PATRO, A., GOVINDAN, S., AND BANERJEE, S. Observing home wireless experience through wifi aps. In *Proceedings of the 19th annual international conference on Mobile computing & networking (MobiCom 2013)*, ACM, pp. 339–350.

[47] PAUL, U., KASHYAP, A., MAHESHWARI, R., AND DAS, S. R. Passive measurement of interference in wifi networks with application in misbehavior detection. *Mobile Computing, IEEE Transactions on 12*, 3 (2013), 434–446.

[48] PENG, G., ZHOU, G., NGUYEN, D. T., AND QI, X. All or none? the dilemma of handling wifi broadcast traffic in smartphone suspend mode. *Power (mW) 300*, 400, 500.

[49] QIAN, F., WANG, Z., GAO, Y., HUANG, J., GERBER, A., MAO, Z., SEN, S., AND SPATSCHECK, O. Periodic transfers in mobile applications: network-wide origin, impact, and optimization. In *Proceedings of the 21st international conference on World Wide Web* (2012), ACM, pp. 51–60.

[50] SHAFIQ, M. Z., ERMAN, J., JI, L., LIU, A. X., PANG, J., AND WANG, J. Understanding the impact of network dynamics on mobile video user engagement. In *The 2014 ACM international conference on Measurement and modeling of computer systems* (2014), ACM, pp. 367–379.

[51] SHRIVASTAVA, V., RAYANCHU, S. K., BANERJEE, S., AND PAPAGIANNAKI, K. Pie in the sky: Online passive interference estimation for enterprise wlans. In *NSDI* (2011), vol. 11, p. 20.

[52] SUI, K., ZHAO, Y., PEI, D., AND ZIMU, L. How bad are the rogues' impact on enterprise 802.11 network performance? In *Computer Communications (INFOCOM), 2015 IEEE Conference on* (April 2015), pp. 361–369.

[53] SUNDARESAN, S., FEAMSTER, N., TEIXEIRA, R., MAGHAREI, N., ET AL. Measuring and mitigating web performance bottlenecks in broadband access networks. In *ACM Internet Measurement Conference* (2013).

[54] WANG, X. S., BALASUBRAMANIAN, A., KRISHNAMURTHY, A., AND WETHERALL, D. How speedy is spdy. In *NSDI* (2014), pp. 387–399.

[55] XU, F., TAN, C. C., LI, Q., YAN, G., AND WU, J. Designing a practical access point association protocol. In *INFOCOM, 2010 Proceedings IEEE* (2010), IEEE, pp. 1–9.

ReCon: Revealing and Controlling PII Leaks in Mobile Network Traffic

Jingjing Ren
Northeastern University
Boston, USA
renjj@ccs.neu.edu

Ashwin Rao
University of Helsinki
Helsinki, Finland
ashwin.rao@cs.helsinki.fi

Martina Lindorfer
SBA Research
Vienna, Austria
mlindorfer@iseclab.org

Arnaud Legout
Inria
Sophia Antipolis, France
arnaud.legout@inria.fr

David Choffnes
Northeastern University
Boston, USA
choffnes@ccs.neu.edu

Abstract

It is well known that apps running on mobile devices extensively track and leak users' personally identifiable information (PII); however, these users have little visibility into PII leaked through the network traffic generated by their devices, and have poor control over how, when and where that traffic is sent and handled by third parties. In this paper, we present the design, implementation, and evaluation of *ReCon*: a cross-platform system that reveals PII leaks and gives users control over them without requiring any special privileges or custom OSes. *ReCon* leverages machine learning to reveal potential PII leaks by inspecting network traffic, and provides a visualization tool to empower users with the ability to control these leaks via blocking or substitution of PII. We evaluate *ReCon*'s effectiveness with measurements from controlled experiments using leaks from the 100 most popular iOS, Android, and Windows Phone apps, and via an IRB-approved user study with 92 participants. We show that *ReCon* is accurate, efficient, and identifies a wider range of PII than previous approaches.

1. INTRODUCTION

There has been a dramatic shift toward using mobile devices such as smartphones and tablets as the primary interface to access Internet services. Unlike their fixed-line counterparts, these devices also offer ubiquitous mobile connectivity and are equipped with a wide array of sensors (*e.g.,* GPS, camera, and microphone).

This combination of rich sensors and ubiquitous connectivity makes these devices perfect candidates for privacy invasion. Apps extensively track users and leak their personally identifiable information (PII) [17, 23, 27, 35, 58], and users are generally unaware and unable to stop them [21, 29]. Cases of PII leaks dramatically increased from 13.45% of apps in 2010 to 49.78% of apps in 2014, and the vast majority of these leaks occur over IP networks (less than 1% of apps leak data over SMS) [44].

MobiSys '16, June 25–30, 2016, Singapore.

ISBN 978-1-4503-4269-8/16/06...$15.00

DOI: http://dx.doi.org/10.1145/2906388.2906392

Previous attempts to address PII leaks face challenges of a *lack of visibility* into network traffic generated by mobile devices and the *inability to control* the traffic. Passively gathered datasets from large mobile ISPs [58, 60] provide visibility but give users no control over network flows. Likewise, custom Android extensions that are often integrated in dynamic analysis tools provide control over network flows but measurement visibility is limited to the devices running these custom OSes or apps [24], often requiring warranty-voiding "jailbreaking." Static analysis tools can identify PII leaks based on the content of the code implementing an app, but suffer from imprecision and cannot defend against dynamic code loading at run time.

We argue that improving mobile privacy requires (1) trusted third-party systems that enable auditing and control over PII leaks, and (2) a way for such auditors to identify PII leaks. Our key observation is that a PII leak must (by definition) occur over the network, so interposing on network traffic is a naturally platform-independent way to detect and mitigate PII leaks. Based on this insight, we propose a simpler, more effective strategy than previous approaches: interposing on network traffic to improve visibility and control for PII leaks.

Using this approach, we focus on the problem of identifying and mitigating PII leaks at the network level. We describe the design and implementation of a system to address this problem called *ReCon*, which detects PII leaks from network flows alone, presents this information to users, and allows users fine-grained control over which information is sent to third parties. We use machine learning and crowdsourcing-based reinforcement to build classifiers that reliably detect PII in network flows, even when we do not know a priori what information is leaked and in what format. To address flows using SSL or obfuscation, we describe techniques that allow our system to detect PII leaks in encrypted flows with user opt in, and adapt to obfuscation.[1]

By operating on network traffic alone, *ReCon* can be deployed in mobile networks [4], in home networks, in the cloud, or on mobile devices. *ReCon* is currently deployed using VPN tunnels to software middleboxes running on popular cloud platforms, because this allows us to immediately deploy to arbitrary mobile device OSes and ISPs.

Our key contributions are as follows:

[1] We support SSL decryption for controlled experiments and private *ReCon* instances, but disable them in user studies for privacy reasons.

- A study using controlled experiments to demonstrate how PII leaks from iOS, Android, and Windows Phone devices, motivating the need for (and potential effectiveness of) systems that identify PII leaks from network flows. We find extensive leaks of device identifiers (> 50% of the top 100 apps from all 3 OSes), user identifiers (> 14% of top 100 Android/iOS apps), locations (14-26% of top 100 Android/iOS apps) and even passwords (3 apps) in *plaintext traffic*.
- An approach for the detection and extraction of PII leaks from arbitrary network flows, using machine learning informed by extensive ground truth for more than 72,000 flows generated by mobile apps.
- A system that enables users to view PII leaks from network flows, provide feedback about relevant leaks, and optionally modify leaks.
- An evaluation of our system, showing it is efficient (classification can be done in less than one ms), and that it accurately identifies leaks (with 98.1% accuracy for the vast majority of flows in our dataset). We show that a simple C4.5 Decision Tree (DT) classifier is able to identify PII leaks with accuracy comparable to several ensemble methods atop DTs (AdaBoost, Bagging, and Blending) that take significantly more processing time (by a factor of 7.24).
- A comparison with three alternative techniques for detecting PII leaks using information flow analysis. We show that overall *ReCon* finds more PII leaks than all three approaches. Further, *ReCon* can leverage information flow analysis techniques to improve its coverage, as we demonstrate in §5.3.
- A characterization of our approach on traffic generated by user devices as part of an IRB-approved user study. We demonstrate that our approach successfully identifies PII leaks (with users providing 5,351 labels for PII leaks) and characterize how these users' PII is leaked "in the wild." For example, we find previously unreported sensitive information such as usernames and passwords (21 apps) being leaked in plaintext flows.

In the next section, we motivate our work using the results of controlled experiments identifying extensive information leakage in popular apps. We then describe the design (§3) and implementation (§4) of *ReCon*. We validate our design choices using controlled experiments in §5 and in §6 we show their relevance "in the wild" with a deployment of ReCon using an IRB-approved study with 92 participants. We discuss related work in §7 and conclude in §8.

The code and data from our controlled experiments are open-source and publicly available at:

`http://recon.meddle.mobi/codeanddata.html`

2. MOTIVATION AND CHALLENGES

In this section, we use controlled experiments to measure PII leakage with ground-truth information. We find a surprisingly large volume of PII leaks from popular apps from four app stores, particularly in plaintext (unencrypted) flows. Based on these results, we identify several core challenges for detecting PII leaks when we do not have ground-truth information, *i.e.*, for network traffic generated by arbitrary users' devices. In the next section, we describe how to automatically infer PII leaks in network flows when the contents of PII is not known in advance.

2.1 Definition of PII

Personally identifiable information (PII) is a generic term referring to "information which can be used to distinguish or trace an individual's identity" [38]. These can include geographic locations, unique identifiers, phone numbers and other similar data.

Central to this work is identifying PII leaked by apps over the network. In this paper, we define PII to be either (1) **Device Identifiers** specific to a device or OS installation (ICCID, IMEI, IMSI, MAC address, Android ID, Android Advertiser ID, iOS IFA ID, Windows Phone Device ID), (2) **User Identifiers**, which identify the user (name, gender, date of birth, e-mail address, mailing address, relationship status), (3) **Contact Information** (phone numbers, address book information), (4) **Location** (GPS latitude and longitude, zip code), or (5) **Credentials** (username, password). This list of PII is informed by information leaks observed in this study. While this list is not exhaustive, we believe it covers most of the PII that concerns users. We will update the list of tracked PII as we learn of additional types of PII leaks.

2.2 Threat Model

To improve user privacy, we should inform users of any PII that is exposed to eavesdroppers over insecure connections, and any *unnecessary* PII exposed to other parties over secure (*i.e.*, encrypted) connections. Determining what information is necessary to share remains an open problem that we do not solve in this work, so we consider the upper bound of all PII transmitted to other parties.

Specifically, we define a "leak" as any PII, as described in Section §2.1, that is sent over the network from a device to a first or third party over both secure (*i.e.*, HTTPS) and insecure (*i.e.*, HTTP) channels. We further define the following two threat scenarios:

Data-exfiltrating apps. In this scenario, the app developers either directly, or indirectly via advertising and analytics libraries, collect PII from the users' mobile devices, beyond what would be required for the main functionality of the apps. In this work, we do not establish whether a PII leak is required for app functionality; rather, we make all leaks transparent to users so they can decide whether any individual leak is acceptable.

Eavesdropping on network traffic. Here, the adversary learns PII about a user by listening to network traffic that is exposed in plaintext (*e.g.*, at an unencrypted wireless access point, or by tapping on wired network traffic). Sensitive information, such as passwords, are sent over insecure channels, leaving the users vulnerable to eavesdropping by this adversary.

ReCon addresses both scenarios by automatically detecting PII leaks in network flows, presenting the detected leaks to users and allowing them to modify or block leaks. Clearly, some information should never be sent over insecure channels. Thus, whenever *ReCon* detects a security critical leak, such as a password being sent over HTTP, we follow a responsible disclosure procedure and notify the developer.

2.3 Controlled Experiments for Ground Truth

Our goal with controlled experiments is to obtain ground-truth information about network flows generated by apps and devices. We use this data to identify PII in network flows and to evaluate *ReCon* (§5).

Experiment setup. We conduct controlled experiments using Android devices (running Android 5.1.1), an iPhone (running iOS 8.4.1) and a Windows Phone (running Windows 8.10.14226.359). We start each set of experiments with a factory reset of the device followed by connecting the device to *Meddle* [49]. *Meddle* provides visibility into network traffic through redirection, *i.e.*, sending all device traffic to a proxy server using native support for virtual private network (VPN) tunnels. Once traffic arrives at the proxy server, we use software middleboxes to intercept and modify the traffic. We additionally use SSLsplit [9] to decrypt and inspect SSL flows only during our controlled experiments where *no human subject traffic is intercepted.* Our dataset and the full details of our experiments are available on our project page at `http://recon.meddle.mobi/codeanddata.html`.

Manual tests. We manually test the 100 most popular free apps for Android, iOS, and Windows Phone from the *Google Play* store, the iOS *App Store*, and the *Windows Phone Store* on August 9, 2015 as reported by App Annie [2]. For each app, we install it, interact with it for up to 5 minutes, and uninstall it. We give apps permission to access to all requested resources (*e.g.,* contacts or location). This allows us to characterize real user interactions with popular apps in a controlled environment. We enter unique and distinguishable user credentials when interacting with apps to easily extract the corresponding PII from network flows (if they are not obfuscated). Specific inputs, such as valid login credentials, e-mail addresses and names, are hard to generate with automated tools [20]. Consequently, our manual tests allow us to study app behavior and leaks of PII not covered by our automated tests.

Automated tests. We include fully-automated tests on the 100 Android apps used in the manual tests and also 850 of the top 1,000 Android apps from the free, third-party Android market *AppsApk.com* [3] that were successfully downloaded and installed on an Android device.[2] We perform this test to understand how third-party apps differ from those in the standard *Google Play* store, as they are not subject to *Google Play*'s restrictions and vetting process (but can still be installed by users without rooting their phones). We automate experiments using *adb* to install each app, connect the device to the *Meddle* platform, start the app, perform approximately 10,000 actions using *Monkey* [11], and finally uninstall the app and reboot the device to end any lingering connections. We limit the automated tests to Android devices because iOS and Windows do not provide equivalent scripting functionality.

Analysis. We use *tcpdump* [10] to dump raw IP traffic and *bro* [5] to extract the HTTP flows that we consider in this study, then we search for the conspicuous PII that we loaded onto devices and used as input to text fields. We classify some of the destinations of PII leaks as *trackers* using a publicly available database of tracker domains [1], and recent research on mobile ads [22,34,43].

2.4 PII Leaked from Popular Apps

We use the traffic traces from our controlled experiments to identify how apps leak PII over HTTP and HTTPS. For our analysis we focus on the PII listed in §2.1. Some of this information may be required for normal app operation; however, sensitive information such as credentials should never travel across the network in plaintext.

Table 1 presents PII leaked by iOS, Android and Windows apps in plaintext. Device identifiers, which can be used to track user's behavior, are the PII leaked most frequently by popular apps. Table 1 shows that other PII—user identifiers, contacts, location, and *credentials such as username and password*—are also leaked in plaintext. Importantly, our manual tests identify important PII not found by automated tests (*e.g.,*, Monkey) such as user identifiers and credentials. Thus, previous studies based on automation underestimate leakage and are insufficient for good coverage of PII leaks.

Cross-platform app behavior. We observed that the information leaked by an app varied across OSes. Of the top 100 apps for Android, 16 apps are available on all the three OSes. Of these 16 apps, 11 apps leaked PII in plaintext on at least one OS: 2 apps leaked PII on all the three OSes, 5 apps leaked PII in exactly one OS, and the remaining 4 apps leaked PII in 2 of the OSes. A key take-away is that *PII analysis based only on one OS does not generalize to all OSes.*

Leaks over SSL. During our experiments, we observed that PII is also sent over encrypted channels. In many cases, this is normal app behavior (*e.g.,* sending credentials when logging in to a site, or sending GPS data to a navigation app). However, when such information leaks to third parties, there is a potential PII leak. We focus on the PII leaked to tracker domains [1], and find that 6 iOS apps, 2 Android apps and 1 Windows app send PII to trackers over SSL. The vast majority of this information is device identifiers, with three cases of username leaks. While SSL traffic contains a minority of PII leaks, there is clearly still a need to address leaks from encrypted flows.

Our observations are a conservative estimate of PII leakage because we did not attempt to detect obfuscated PII leaks (*e.g.,* via salted hashing), and several apps used certificate pinning (10 iOS, 15 Android, and 7 Windows apps) or did not work with VPNs enabled (4 iOS apps and 1 Android app).[3] Our results in §5.3 indicate that obfuscation is rare today, and our results above show that significant PII leaks are indeed visible in plaintext.

2.5 Summary and Challenges

While the study above trivially revealed significant PII leaks from popular mobile apps, several key challenges remain for detecting PII leaks more broadly.

Detection without knowing PII. A key challenge is how to detect PII when we do not know the contents of PII in advance. One strawman solution is to simply block all advertising and tracking sites. However, this is a blunt and indiscriminate approach that can disrupt business models supporting free apps. In fact, the developers of the top paid iOS app Peace (which blocks all ads) recently withdrew their app from the App Store for this reason [40].

Another strawman solution is to automatically (and/or symbolically) run every app in every app store to determine when PII is leaked. This allows us to formulate a regular expression to identify PII leaks from every app regardless of the user: we simply replace the PII with a wildcard.

There are several reasons why this is insufficient to identify PII leaks for arbitrary user flows. First, it is impractically expensive to run this automation for all apps in every app store, and there are no publicly available tools for doing this outside of Android. Second, it is difficult (if not impossible) to use automation to explore every possible code path that would result in PII leaks, meaning this approach would miss significant PII. Third, this approach is incredibly brittle – if a tracker changes the contents of flows leaking PII at all, the regular expression would fail.

These issues suggest an alternative approach to identifying PII in network flows: use machine learning to build a model of PII leaks that accurately identifies them for arbitrary users. This would allow us to use a small set of training flows, combined with user feedback about suspected PII leaks, to inform the identification of a PII leaks for a large number of apps.

Encoding and formatting. PII leaked over the network can be encoded using Unicode and other techniques like gzip, JSON, and XML, so a technique to identify PII in network flows must support a variety of formats. In our experience, it is relatively straightforward to extract the encoding for a flow and search for PII using this encoding. We support the encodings mentioned above, and will add support for others as we encounter them.

[2] 14 apps appear both in the AppsApk and Google Play stores, but AppsApk hosts significantly older versions.

[3] For more details, please see our tech report [52].

				# Apps leaking a given PII				
OS	**Store**	**Testing Technique**	**# of Apps**	**Device Identifier**	**User Identifier**	**Contact Information**	**Location**	**Credentials**
iOS	App Store	Manual	100	47 (47.0%)	14 (14.0%)	2 (2.0%)	26 (26.0%)	8 (8.0%)
Android	Google Play	Manual	100	52 (52.0%)	15 (15.0%)	1 (1.0%)	14 (14.0%)	7 (7.0%)
Windows	WP Store	Manual	100	55 (55.0%)	3 (3.0%)	0 (0.0%)	8 (8.0%)	1 (1.0%)
Android	AppsApk	Automated	850	155 (18.2%)	6 (0.7%)	8 (0.9%)	40 (4.7%)	0 (0.0%)
Android	Google Play	Automated	100	52 (52.0%)	0 (0.0%)	0 (0.0%)	6 (6.0%)	0 (0.0%)

Table 1: **Summary of PII leaked in plaintext (HTTP) by iOS, Android and Windows Phone apps.** *User identifiers and credentials are leaked across all platforms. Popular iOS apps leak location information more often than the popular Android and Windows apps.*

Encryption. Flows in the mobile environment increasingly use encryption (often via SSL). Sandvine reports that in 2014 in North American mobile traffic, approximately 12.5% of upstream bytes use SSL, up from 9.78% the previous year [54]. By comparison, 11.8% of bytes came from HTTP in 2014, down from 14.66% the previous year. A key challenge is how to detect PII leaks in such encrypted flows. *ReCon* identifies PII leaks in plaintext network traffic, so it would require access to the original plaintext content to work. While getting such access is a challenge orthogonal to this work, we argue that this is feasible for a wide range of traffic if users run an SSL proxy on a trusted computer (*e.g.,* the user's home appliance, such as a computer or home gateway) or use recent techniques for mediated access to encrypted traffic [48, 55].

Obfuscation of PII. The parties leaking PII may use obfuscation to hide their information leaks. In our experiments, we found little evidence of this (§ 5.3). In the future, we anticipate combining our approach with static and dynamic analysis techniques to identify how information is being obfuscated, and adjust our system to identify the obfuscated PII. For example, using information flow analysis, we can reverse-engineer how obfuscation is done (*e.g.,* for salted hashing, learn the salt and hash function), then use this information when analyzing network traces to identify leaked PII. In the ensuing cat-and-mouse game, we envision automating this process of reverse engineering obfuscation.

3. RECON GOALS AND DESIGN

The previous section shows that current OSes do not provide sufficient visibility into PII leaks, provide few options to control it, and thus significant amounts of potentially sensitive information is exfiltrated from user devices. To address this, we built *ReCon,* a tool that detects PII leaks, visualizes how users' information is shared with various sites, and allows users to change the shared information (including modifying PII or even blocking connections entirely).

The high-level goal of our work is to explore the extent to which we can address privacy issues in mobile systems at the network level. The sub-goals of *ReCon* are as follows:

- Accurately identify PII in network flows, *without* requiring the knowledge of users' PII *a priori.*
- Improve awareness of PII leaks by presenting this information to users.
- Automatically improve the classification of sensitive PII based on user feedback.
- Enable users to change these flows by modifying or removing PII.

To achieve the first three goals, we determine what PII is leaked in network flows using network trace analysis, machine learning, and user feedback. We achieve the last goal by providing users with an interface to block or modify the PII shared over the network. This paper focuses on how to address the research challenges in detecting and revealing PII leaks; as part of ongoing work outside the scope of this paper, we are investigating other UIs for modifying PII leaks, how to use crowdsourcing to help design PII-modifying rules, and how we can use *ReCon* to provide other types of privacy (*e.g.,* k-anonymity).

Figure 1 presents the architecture of the *ReCon* system. In the "offline" phase, we use labeled network traces to determine which features of network flows to use for learning when PII is being leaked, then train a classifier using this data, finally producing a model for predicting whether PII is leaked. When new network flows enter *ReCon* (the "online" phase), we use the model to determine whether a flow is leaking PII and present the suspected PII leak to the user via the *ReCon* Web UI (Fig. 2). We currently detect PII as described in the previous section, and will add other PII types as we discover them. Note that our approach can detect any PII that appears in network traffic as long as we obtain labeled examples.

We collect labels from users (*i.e.,* whether our suspected PII is correct) via the UI and integrate the results into our classifier to improve future predictions (left). In addition, *ReCon* supports a map view, where we display the location information that each domain is learning about the user (right). By using a Web interface, *ReCon* users can gain visibility and control into their PII leaks without installing an app. A demo of *ReCon* is available at `http://recon.meddle.mobi/DTL-ReconDemo.mp4`.

To support control of PII, *ReCon* allows users to tell the system to replace PII with other text (or nothing) for future flows (see the drop-down boxes in Fig. 2(a)). Users can specify blocking or replacement of PII based on category, domain, or app. This protects users' PII for future network activity, but does not entirely prevent PII from leaking in the first place. To address this, we support *interactive* PII labeling and filtering, using push notifications[4] or other channels to notify the user of leaks immediately when they are detected (as done in a related study [15]).

3.1 Non-Goals

ReCon is not intended as a blanket replacement for existing approaches to improve privacy in the mobile environment. For example, information flow analysis [24] may identify PII leaks not revealed by *ReCon.* In fact, *ReCon* can leverage information flow analysis techniques to improve its coverage, as we demonstrate in §5.3. Importantly, *ReCon* allows us to identify and block unobfuscated PII in network flows from arbitrary devices without requiring OS modifications or taint tracking.

The need for access to plaintext traffic is an inherent limitation of our approach. We discussed several ways to address encryption and obfuscation of PII in the previous section. If these should fail, we

[4]Push notifications require a companion app, and we currently support Android (we plan to release iOS and Windows versions soon).

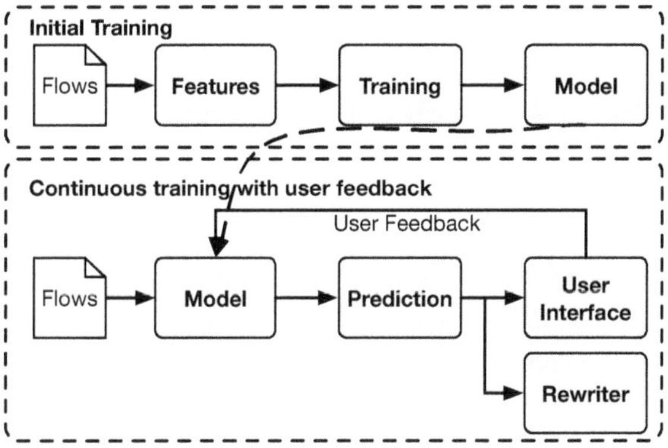

Figure 1: *ReCon* **architecture**. *We initially select features and train a model using labeled network flows (top), then use this model to predict whether new network flows are leaking PII. Based on user feedback, we retrain our classifier (bottom). Periodically, we update our classifier with results from new controlled experiments.*

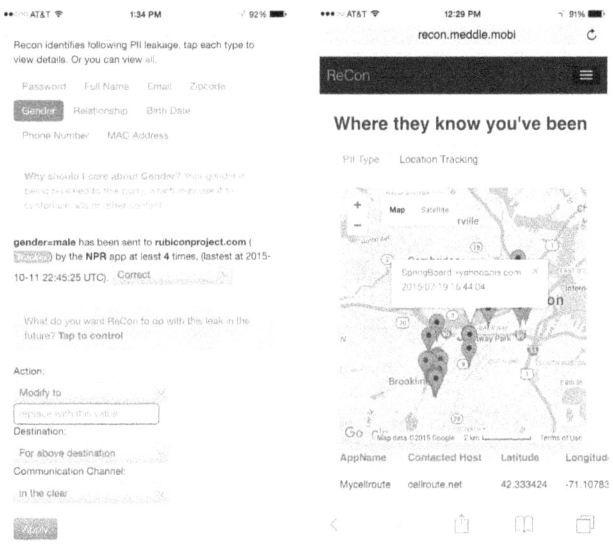

(a) PII leaks and actions (b) Map view of location leaks

Figure 2: **Screen capture of the** *ReCon* **user interface**. *Users can view how their PII is leaked, validate the suspected PII leaks, and create custom filters to block or modify leaks.*

can recover plaintext traffic with OS support for access to network traffic content as it appears before encryption or obfuscation. Of course, getting such support from an OS could be challenging. Alternatively, policymakers such as the FTC could intervene by barring developers from using techniques that explicitly eschew auditing tools such as *ReCon*, by citing it as a type of "deceptive business practice" currently disallowed in the US.

3.2 Deployment Model and User Adoption

Because *ReCon* needs access only to network traffic to identify and modify PII leaks, it admits a variety of deployment models, *e.g.*,, in the cloud, in home devices, inside an ISP, or on mobile devices. We are currently hosting this service on *Meddle* in a cloud-based deployment because it provides immediate cross-platform support with low overheads [49]. We are also in discussions with Telefonica to deploy *ReCon* on their Awazza [4] APN proxy, which has attracted thousands of users.

3.3 Protecting User Privacy

An important concern with a *ReCon* user study is privacy. Using an IRB-approved protocol [8], we encrypt and anonymize all captured flows before storing them. We have two deployment models: the first study (approval #13-08-04) captures all of a subject's Internet traffic and entails in-person, signed informed consent; the second study (approval #13-11-17) captures only HTTP GET/POST parameters (where most leaks occur) and users consent via an online form. The secret key is stored on a separate secure server and users can delete their data at any time.

We will make the *ReCon* source code publicly available. For those who want to run their own *ReCon* instance (*e.g.*, if they do not want to participate in our study), our system requires only that a user has root on a Linux OS. *ReCon* can be deployed in a single-machine instance on a home computer, as Raspberry Pi plugged into a home router, a dedicated server in an enterprise, a VM in the cloud, or in the device itself. One can also selectively route traffic to different *ReCon* instances, *e.g.*,, to a cloud instance for HTTP traffic and a trusted home instance or on-device software such as HayStack [51] to decrypt HTTPS connections to identify PII leaked over SSL.

4. RECON IMPLEMENTATION

We now discuss key aspects of our implementation. We then evaluate our design decisions in the following section, and finally demonstrate how they hold up "in the wild" via a user study with 92 participants. Table 2 presents a roadmap for the remainder of the paper, highlighting key design decisions, evaluation criteria, and results. The *ReCon* pipeline begins with parsing network flows, then passing each flow to a machine learning classifier for labeling it as containing a PII leak or not.

4.1 Machine Learning Techniques

We use the *weka* data mining tool [28] to train classifiers that predict PII leaks. We train our classifier by extracting relevant features and providing labels for flows that leak PII as described below. Our input dataset is the set of labeled flows from our controlled experiments in §2.3. To evaluate our classifiers, we use k-fold cross validation, where a random $(k-1)/k$ of the flows in our dataset are used to train the classifier, and the remaining $1/k$ of the flows are tested for accuracy. This process is repeated n times to understand the stability of our results (see §5).

Feature extraction. The problem of identifying whether a flow contains PII is similar to the document classification problem,[5] so we use the "bag-of-words" model [32]. We choose certain characters as separators and consider anything between those separators to be words. Then for each flow, we produce a vector of binary values where each word that appears in a flow is set to 1, and each word that does not is set to 0.

A key challenge for feature extraction in network flows is that there is no standard token (*e.g.*, whitespace or punctuation) to use for splitting flows into words. For example, a colon (`:`) could be part of a MAC address (*e.g.*, `02:00:00:00:00`), a time-of-day (*e.g.*, `11:59`), or JSON data (*e.g.*, `username:user007`). Further frustrating attempts to select features, one domain uses "`=>`" as a delimiter (in `username =>user007`). In these cases, there is no single technique that covers all flows. Instead, we use a number of different delimiters "`, ; / ( ) { } [ ]`" to handle

[5] Here, network flows are documents and structured data are words.

Section	Topic	Dataset	Key results
4.1	Implementation	Controlled exp.	Feature extraction and selection, per-domain per-OS classifiers
4.2	"	Controlled exp.	Automatically identifying PII in flows
5.2	Evaluation: ML techniques	Controlled exp.	Decision trees provide best trade-off for accuracy/speed, per-domain per-OS classifiers outperform general ones, feature selection balances accuracy and training time, heuristics for PII extraction are accurate
5.3	Evaluation: IFA comparison	Automated exp.	*ReCon* generally outperforms information flow analysis techniques, and can learn new association rules from them to further improve accuracy
6	Evaluation: "in the wild"	User study	*ReCon* is efficient, users labels confirm accuracy of *ReCon* even for apps not previously seen, retraining based on user labels substantially improves accuracy, significant amounts of sensitive information is leaked in plaintext from popular apps.

Table 2: **Roadmap for key topics covered in §4, §5 and §6.** *We train and test our classifier using 10-fold cross-validation, i.e., a random 9/10 samples for training and the remaining 1/10 for testing; we repeat this process 10 times to tune our parameters.*

the common case, and treat ambiguous delimiters by inspecting the surrounding content to determine the encoding type based on context (*e.g.,* looking at content-encoding hints in the HTTP header or whether the content appears in a GET parameter).

Feature selection. A simple bag-of-words model produces too many features to be useful for training accurate classifiers that make predictions within milliseconds (to intercept PII leaks in real time). To reduce the feature set, we assume that low-frequency words are unlikely to be associated with PII leaks, because when PII does leak, it rarely leaks just once. On the other hand, session keys and other ephemeral identifiers tend to appear in exactly one flow. Based on this intuition, we apply a simple threshold-based filter that removes a feature if its word frequency is too small. We select a reasonable threshold value empirically, by balancing accuracy and classification time for labeled data (discussed in §5.2.3). To avoid filtering PII leaks that occur rarely in our labeled data, we oversample rarely occurring PII leaks(so that their number occurrences is greater than the filter threshold). In addition, we randomize PII values (*e.g.,*, locations, device IDs) in each flow when training to prevent the classifier from using a PII value as a feature.

While the above filter removes ephemeral identifiers from our feature set, we must also address the problem of words that commonly appear. Several important examples include information typically found in HTTP flows, such as `content-length:`, `en- us`, and `expires`. We thus add stop-word-based filtering on HTTP flows, where the stop words are determined by term frequency—inverse document frequency (tf-idf). We include only features that have fairly low tf-idf values and that did not appear adjacent to a PII leak in a flow from our controlled experiments.

Per-domain-and-OS and general classifiers. We find that PII leaks to the same destination domain use the same (or similar) data encodings to transfer data over the network, but that this encoding may differ across different OSes. Based on this observation, we build per-domain-and-OS models (one classifier for each [destination domain, OS] pair) instead of one single general classifier. We identify the domain associated with each flow based on the *Host:* parameter in the HTTP header. If this header is not available, we can also identify the domain associated with each IP address by finding the corresponding DNS lookup in packet traces. We identify the OS based on the fact that different OSes use different authentication mechanisms in our VPN, and users tell us in advance which OS they are using. This improves prediction accuracy because the classifier typically needs to learn a small set of association rules. Further, per-domain-and-OS classifiers improve performance in terms of lower-latency predictions (§5.2.3), important for detecting and intercepting PII leaks in-band.

The above approach works well if there is a sufficiently large sample of labeled data to train to the per-domain per-OS classifier. For domains that do not see sufficient traffic, we build a (cross-domain) general classifier. The general classifier tends to have few labeled PII leaks, making it susceptible to bias (*e.g.,* 5% of flows in our general classifier are PII leaks). To address this, we use undersampling on negative samples, using 1/10 sampling to randomly choose a subset of available samples.

Note that we do not need to train classifiers on every domain in the Internet; rather, we train only on domains contacted by users' traffic. Further, we do not need every user to label every PII leak; rather, we need only a small number of labeled instances from a small number of users to identify PII leaks for *all* users whose traffic visits those domains.

Adapting to PII leaks "in the wild." A key challenge for any ML technique is identifying flows leaking PII that were never seen in controlled experiments. To mitigate this problem, we integrate user feedback from flows that we did identify using one of our classifiers. Specifically, when a user provides feedback that we have correctly identified PII, we can search for that PII in historical flows to identify cases *ReCon* missed due to lack of sufficient training data. Further, we can use these flows to retrain our classifier to successfully catch these instances in future network flows. We discuss the effectiveness of this approach in §6.

Any system that allows user feedback is susceptible to incorrect labels, *e.g.,* via user error or Sybil attacks. There are two ways to address this. First, we can simply train per-user classifiers, so any erroneous labels only affect the user(s) who provide them. Second, we can train system-wide classifiers if we can reliably distinguish good labels from bad ones. To this end, we envision using existing majority-voting algorithms and/or reputation systems [36].

4.2 Automatically Extracting PII

A machine learning classifier indicates whether a flow contains PII, but does not indicate *which content in the flow is a PII leak.* The latter information is critical if we want to present users with information about their leaks and allow them to validate the predictions.

A key challenge for extracting PII is that the key/value pairs used for leaking PII vary across domains and devices; *e.g.,* the key "device_id" or "q" might each indicate an IMEI value for different domains, but "q" *is not always associated with a PII leak.* While we found no solution that perfectly addresses this ambiguity, we developed effective heuristics for identifying "suspicious" keys that are likely associated with PII values.

We use two steps to automatically extract PII leaks from a network flows classified as a leak. The first step is based on the relative probability that a suspicious key is associated with a PII leak, calculated as follows:

$$P_{type,key} = \frac{K_{PII}}{K_{all}}$$

where *type* is the PII type (*e.g.,* IMEI, e-mail address), *key* is the suspicious key for that *type* of PII, K_{PII} is the number of times the key appeared in flows identified with PII leaks, and K_{all} is the number times the key appeared in all flows. The system looks for suspicious keys that have $P_{type,key}$ greater than a threshold. We set this value to an empirically determined value, 0.2, based on finding the best trade-off between false positives (FPs) and true positives (TPs) for our dataset. For users wanting more or less sensitivity, we will make this a configurable threshold in *ReCon* (*e.g.,* if a user wants to increase the likelihood of increasing TPs at the potential cost of increased FPs).

In the second step, we use a decision tree classifier, and observe that the root of each tree is likely a key corresponding to a PII value. We thus add these roots to the suspicious key set and assign them a large P value.

In the next section, we evaluate *ReCon* using controlled experiments on a pre-labeled dataset. This evaluation will only use the initial training phase. Next, we evaluate *ReCon* in the wild with a user study on our public deployment (§6). This evaluation will use both the initial training phase and the continuous training phase obtained from real users.

5. EVALUATION

This section evaluates the effectiveness of *ReCon* in terms of accuracy and performance. First, we describe our methodology, then we describe the results from controlled experiments in terms of classifier accuracy compared to ground truth and to information flow analysis. In the next section, we evaluate our system based on results from a user study.

Our key finding are: 1) we demonstrate that a decision-tree classifier is both accurate (99% overall) and efficient (trains in seconds, predicts in sub-milliseconds); 2) *ReCon* identifies more PII than static and dynamic information-flow analysis techniques, and can learn from the results of these approaches to improve its coverage of PII leaks. Note that this paper focuses on reliably identifying leaks and enabling control, but does not evaluate the control functionality.

5.1 Dataset and Methodology

To evaluate *ReCon* accuracy, we need app-generated traffic and a set of labels indicating which of the corresponding flows leak PII. For this analysis, we reuse the data from controlled experiments presented in §2.3; Table 3 summarizes this dataset using the number of flows generated by the apps, and fraction that leak PII. We identify that more than 6,500 flows leak PII, and a significant fraction of those flows leak PII to known trackers. The code and data from our controlled experiments are open-source and publicly available at `http://recon.meddle.mobi/codeanddata.html`.

Recall from §4.1 that we use k-fold cross-validation to evaluate our accuracy by training and testing on different random subsets of our labeled dataset. We tried both $k = 10$ and $k = 5$, and found these values caused only a small difference (less than 1%) in the resulting accuracy.

We use this labeled dataset to train classifiers and evaluate their effectiveness using the following metrics. We define a positive flow to be one that leaks PII; likewise a negative flow is one that *does not* leak PII. A false positive occurs when a flow does not leak PII but the classifier predicts a PII leak; a false negative occurs when a flow leaks PII but the classifier predicts that it does not. We measure the false positive rate (FPR) and false negative rate (FNR); we also include the following metrics:

- **Correctly classified rate** (CCR): the sum of true positive (TP) and true negative (TN) samples divided by the total number of samples. $CCR = (TN + TP)/(TN + TP + FN + FP)$. *A good classifier has a* CCR *value close to 1.*
- **Area under the curve** (AUC): where the curve refers to receiver operating characteristic (ROC). In this approach, the x-axis is the false positive rate and y-axis is the true positive rate (ranging in value from 0 to 1). If the ROC curve is $x = y$ ($AUC = 0.5$), then the classification is no better than randomly guessing. *A good classifier has a* AUC *value near 1.*

To evaluate the efficiency of the classifier, we investigate the runtime (in milliseconds) for predicting a PII leak and extracting the suspected PII. We want this value to be significantly lower than typical Internet latencies.

We use the *weka* data mining tool to investigate the above metrics for several candidate machine learning approaches to identify a technique that is both efficient and accurate. Specifically, we test Naive Bayes, C4.5 Decision Tree (DT) and several ensemble methods atop DTs (AdaBoost, Bagging, and Blending).

5.2 Lab Experiments

In this section, we evaluate the impact of different implementation decisions and demonstrate the overall effectiveness of our adopted approach.

5.2.1 Machine Learning Approaches

A key question we must address is which classifier to use. We believe that a DT-based classifier is a reasonable choice, because most PII leaks occur in structured data (*i.e.,* key/value pairs), and a decision tree can naturally represent chained dependencies between these keys and the likelihood of leaking PII.

To evaluate this claim, we tested a variety of classifiers according to the accuracy metrics from the previous section, and present the results in Fig. 3. We plot the accuracy using a CDF over the domains that we use to build per-domain per-OS classifiers as described in §4.1. The top two graphs (overall accuracy via CCR and AUC), show that Naive Bayes has the worst performance, and nearly all the DT-based ensemble methods have high CCR and AUC values. (Note that the x-axis does not start at 0.)

Among the ensemble methods, Blending with DTs and k-nearest-neighbor (kNN) yields the highest accuracy; however, the resulting accuracy is not significantly better than a simple DT. Importantly, a simple DT takes significantly less time to train than ensemble methods. For ensemble methods, the training time largely depends on the number of iterations for training. When we set this value to 10, we find that ensemble methods take 7.24 times longer to train than a simple DT on the same dataset. Given the significant extra cost with minimal gain in accuracy, we currently use simple DTs.

The bottom figures show that most DT-based classifiers have zero FPs (71.4%) and FNs (76.2%) for the majority of domains. Further, the overall accuracy across all per-domain per-OS classifiers is >99%. The domains with poor accuracy are the trackers `rlcdn.com` and `turn.com`, due to the fact their positive and negative flows are very similar. For example, in this case the key `partner_uid` is associated both with an Android ID value and another unknown identifier.

To provide intuition as to why DTs work well, and why PII leak detection presents a nontrivial machine-learning problem, we include several examples of DTs trained using our data. Some cases

	Manual tests			*Automated tests (Monkey)*	
OS (Store)	iOS (App)	Android (Play)	Windows (WP)	Android (Play)	Android (AppsApk)
Apps tested	*100*	*100*	*100*	*100*	*850*
Apps leaking PII	*63*	*56*	*61*	*52*	*164*
HTTP flows	14683	14355	12487	7186	17499
Leaking PII	845	1800	969	1174	1776
Flows to trackers	1254	1854	1253	1377	5893
Leaking PII to trackers	508	567	4	414	649

Table 3: **Summary of HTTP flows from controlled experiments.** *Manual tests generated similar numbers of flows across platforms, but Android leaked proportionately more PII. Collectively, our dataset contains more than 6500 flows with PII leaks.*

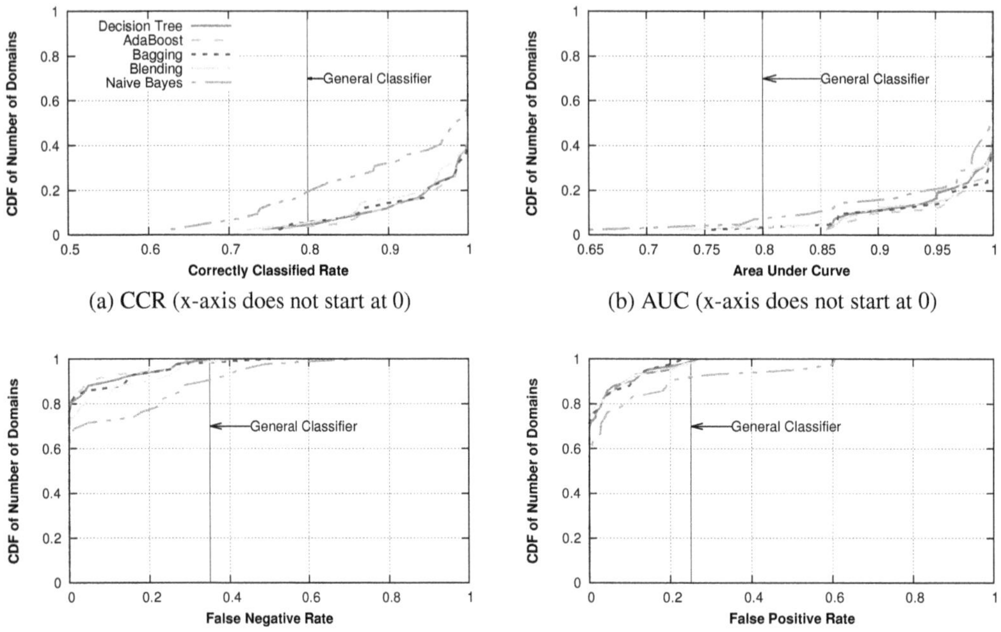

(a) CCR (x-axis does not start at 0)

(b) AUC (x-axis does not start at 0)

(c) FNR

(d) FPR

Figure 3: **CDF of per-domain-and-OS (PDAO) classifier accuracy, for alternative classification approaches.** *For the 42 PDAO classifiers, DT-based classifiers outperform Naive Bayes, and they exhibit good accuracy (high CCR and AUC, low FPR and FNR). The vertical line depicts accuracy when using one classifier across all domains, which leads to significantly worse performance.*

of PII leaks are simple: Fig. 4(a) shows that Android Advertiser ID is always leaked to the tracker `applovin.com` when the text `idfa` is present in network traffic. Other cases are not trivial, as seen in Fig. 4(b). Here, we find that `auid` is not always associated with an IMEI value, and the DT captures the fact that the IMEI will *not* be present for a `getImage.php5` request if the `urid` is present. Finally, Fig. 4(c) gives an example of a non-trival DT for a different type of PII—e-mail address. Here, the term `email` appears in both positive and negative flows, so this feature cannot be used alone. However, our classifier learns that the leak happens in a `/user/` request when the terms `session` and `deviceId` are not present.[6] Overall, 62% of DTs are the simple case (Fig. 4(a)), but more than a third have a depth greater than two, indicating a significant fraction of cases where association rules are nontrivial.

5.2.2 Per-Domain-and-OS Classifiers

We now evaluate the impact of using individual per-domain-and-OS (PDAO) classifiers, instead of one general classifier for all flows. We build PDAO classifiers for all domains with greater than 100 samples (*i.e.,* labeled flows), at least one of which leaks PII. For the remaining flows, there is insufficient training data to inform a classifier, so we create a general classifier based on the assumption that a significant fraction of the flows use a common structure for leaking PII.[7]

We evaluate the impact of PDAO classifiers on overall accuracy in Figure 3. The vertical lines in the subgraphs represent values for the general classifier, *which is trained using all flows from all domains*. The figure shows that >95% of the PDAO classifiers have higher accuracy than the general classifier. Further, the high-accuracy PDAO classifiers cover the vast majority of flows in our dataset (91%). Last, training PDAO classifiers is substantially less expensive in terms of runtime: it takes *minutes* to train PDAO classifiers for thousands of flows, but it takes *hours* to train general classifiers for the same flows.

[6]Note that in this domain `deviceId` is actually used for an app-specific identifier, not a device identifier.

[7]Note that once *ReCon* acquires sufficient labeled data (*e.g.,* from users or controlled experiments) for a destination domain, we create a PDAO classifier.

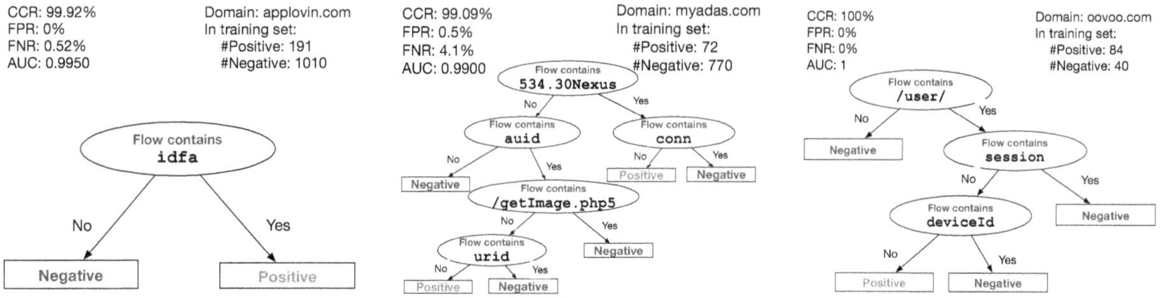

(a) Simple DT for device identifier (b) Non-trivial DT for device identifier (c) Non-trivial DT for e-mail address

Figure 4: **Example decision trees (DTs) for *ReCon*'s per-domain per-OS classifiers.** *The classifier beings at the root (top) node, and traverses the tree based on whether the term at each node is present. The leaves (boxes) indicate whether there is a PII leak (positive) or not (negative) for each path. The top right of each figure shows the number of positive/negative samples used to train each DT.*

5.2.3 Feature Selection

The accuracy of the classifiers described above largely depends on correctly identifying the subset of features for training. Further, the training time for classifiers increases significantly as the number of features increases, meaning that an efficient classifier requires culling of unimportant features. A key challenge in *ReCon* is determining how to select such features given the large potential set derived from the bag-of-words approach.

We use Figure 5 to illustrate this problem and how we address it. Here, we focus on statistics for the tracker domain `mopub.com` (266 flows out of 1,276 leak PII); other domains exhibited similar properties.

First, we focus on the threshold for including features in our training set. As described in § 4.1, we filter out features from words that appear infrequently. Fig. 5(a) shows the impact of this decision on training time, where the x-axis is the minimum number of appearances for a word to be included as a feature, and the y-axis is the time required to train a classifier on the resulting features. The figure shows that including all words (threshold = 1) significantly increases training time, but there is a minimal impact on training time if the threshold is greater than or equal to 20. The corresponding number of features decreases from 450 to 29 as the threshold for word occurrence increases from 1 to 99.

Picking the right number of features is also important for classifier accuracy, as too many features may lead to overfitting and too few features may lead to an incomplete model. We evaluate this using Fig. 5(b), where the x-axis is the number of features, the left y-axis is accuracy (the y-axis does not start at zero), and the right y-axis is training time. Even small numbers of features lead to high accuracy for this domain, but increasing the number of features beyond 250 does not improve performance (but does increase training time). We see a similar effect on the FP rate in Fig. 5(c).

While the training time may not seem high in this context, we note that this cost must be incurred for each domain and each time we want to update the classifier with user-labeled flows. With potentially thousands of flows and labels in a large-scale deployment, such training times can significantly affect the scalability and responsiveness of *ReCon*.

With this in mind, we propose the following strategies for picking threshold values. First, we can use the above analysis to find the best threshold, then periodically update this threshold based on new labeled data. Second, we can pick a fixed threshold based on the average threshold across all domains (word frequency = 21). We evaluated the impact of these two approaches, and found they were nearly identical for our dataset. This suggests that a fixed value is sufficient for our dataset, but we propose periodically updating this threshold by performing the above analysis daily or weekly as a low-priority background process.

5.2.4 PII Extraction Strategies

As discussed in § 4.2, we use two heuristics to identify key/value pairs that are likely to leak PII. We use our dataset to evaluate this approach, and find that the FP and FN rates are 2.2% and 3.5%, respectively. By comparison, a naive approach that treats each key/value pair equally yields FP and FN rates of 5.1% and 18.8%, respectively. Our approach is thus significantly better, and our FP and FN rates are low enough to correctly extract PII the vast majority of the time.

5.3 Comparison with IFA

Our labeled dataset in the above analysis may miss PII leaks that are obfuscated or otherwise hidden from our analysis. We now evaluate our approach by comparing with one that is resilient to such issues: information flow analysis (IFA). We experiment with three IFA techniques: (1) static IFA with FlowDroid [13], (2) dynamic IFA with TaintDroid [24] (via Andrubis [44]), and (3) AppAudit [59], which uses a combination of both static and approximated dynamic analysis. Each of these tools has limitations: some are very resource intensive and some pose restrictions on the type of apps they can successfully analyze.

Static IFA. FlowDroid detects PII leaks as data flowing between sensitive sources and sinks, which are configured via a list of Android API calls. However, the analysis is quite resource intensive: for 4.99% of apps, our available memory of 8GB was insufficient for analysis; for 17.24% of apps the analysis exceeded our analysis timeout of 30 minutes. The detected leaks are reported as paths between the API calls. Note that this approach can lead to false positives, since a detected leak may never be triggered during app execution.

Dynamic IFA. Andrubis is an app analysis sandbox that uses TaintDroid to identify PII leaks from Android apps during dynamic analysis. Andrubis installs each app in an emulated Android environment and monitors its behavior for 240 seconds. Besides calling all of the app's registered components and simulating common events, such as incoming SMS and location changes, it uses Monkey [11] to generate approximately 8,000 pseudo-random streams of user events. In addition to detailed analysis report

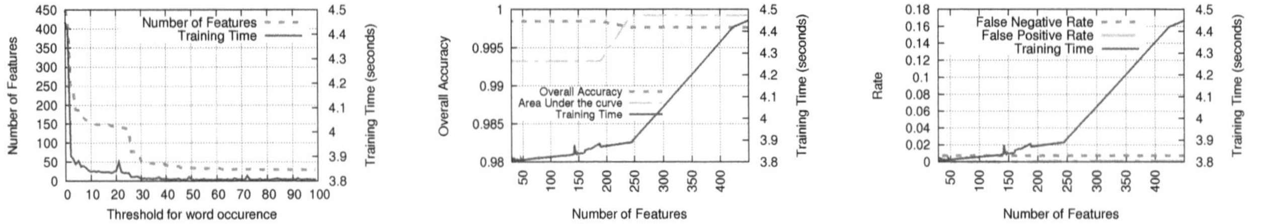

(a) #features changes as threshold changes (b) accuracy and training time over #features (y-axes do not start at 0) (c) false negative and false positive rate and training time over #features

Figure 5: **Feature selection** *for the tracker domain mopub.com. Using ≈200 features leads to high accuracy and low training times; however, adding more features increases training time with no benefit to accuracy.*

Approach	#apps leaking PII (#reports)	Device Identifier	User Identifier	Contact Information	Location	Credentials
FlowDroid (Static IFA)	91 (546)	51 (21.52%)	0(-)	9 (52.94%)	52 (64.20%)	×
Andrubis (Dynamic IFA)	90 (497)	78 (35.46%)	×	10 (62.50%)	3 (3.75%)	×
AppAudit (Hybrid IFA)	64 (620)	57 (24.05%)	×	3 (17.65%)	4 (4.94%)	×
ReCon	155 (750)	145 (61.18%)	6 (100%)	4 (23.53%)	29 (35.80%)	0 (-)
Union of all approaches	278 (750)	237	6	17	81	0

Table 4: **Comparison of *ReCon* with information flow analysis (IFA) tools.** *This comparison is based on automated tests for 750 Android apps (apps from the Google Play and AppsApk dataset for which we observed network flows). We present the number of Android apps detected as leaking PII (or in the case of FlowDroid, flagged as potentially leaking PII), as well as the percentage of leaking apps detected by each tool out of all leaking apps detected by any of the tested tools in each category (× means the tool does not track that type of information). User credentials were not leaked because our automation tools cannot input them.*

including all detected data leaks, it also provides the recorded network packet traces. However, this analysis fails for 33.73% of apps because they exceed the file size and/or API level limit of Andrubis.

Hybrid IFA. AppAudit flags functions that potentially leak PII through static analysis, then performs simulated dynamic analysis to filter out candidate functions to confirm PII leaks. It reports leaks to the network, file system and through SMS from sources such as the location, contacts and device identifiers. The analysis failed for 17.33% of apps. Note that AppAudit only approximates the execution of suspicious functions, and thus does not record any network packet traces.

Methodology and results. We use the 850 apps from *AppsApk.com* and the top 100 apps from *Google Play* from §2.3, and focus on the 750 apps that produced network traffic in our experiments. Since static and hybrid IFA approaches do not provide network flows, they only indicate whether an app will potentially leak a certain type of PII. To compare these techniques with dynamic analysis, we base our comparison on the *number of apps* that potentially leak a certain type of PII. Specifically, we flag an app as a leaking a certain type of PII if any of the tested tools detected an actual or potential PII leak in that category (this occurs for 278 apps). We further filtered out cases where dynamic analysis incorrectly flagged a PII leak.

Table 4 shows the number and percentage of apps that were flagged by FlowDroid, Andrubis, AppAudit and *ReCon*. FlowDroid mainly identified potential location and phone number leaks, while AppAudit mainly identified IMEI leaks. Andrubis performed well in detecting device identifiers (ICCID, IMEI, IMSI) and the phone number. *Importantly, ReCon identifies more PII leaks overall, and in more categories than IFA.*

The above results are encouraging for *ReCon*, and we further investigated mismatches between *ReCon* and TaintDroid results, since the latter provides network traces that we can process

	# leaks detected	Device Id.	User Id.	Con-tacts	Loca-tion	Cred-entials
		Type of PII being leaked				
Andrubis	plaintext	173	N/A	10	8	N/A
	obfuscated	124	N/A	16	0	N/A
	incorrect	140	N/A	24	6	N/A
	Total	457	N/A	50	14	N/A
ReCon	TP	146	17	7	35	0
	FN	27	0	0	0	0

Table 5: **Comparison with Andrubis (which internally uses TaintDroid), for Android apps only.** *Note that this table counts the number of flows leaking PII, not the number of apps. TaintDroid has a higher false positive rate than ReCon, but catches more device identifiers. After retraining ReCon with these results, ReCon correctly identifies all PII leaks. Further, ReCon identifies PII leaks that TaintDroid does not.*

via *ReCon*. Note, as the authors of TaintDroid themselves acknowledge [24], it may generate false positives (particularly for arrays and IMSI values), due to propagating taint labels per variable and IPC message. We thus manually inspected flows flagged as leaking PII, and discarded cases where the identified PII did not appear in plaintext network flows (*i.e.,* false positives). Table 5 shows the results of our analysis, grouped by PII type.

We use the plaintext leaks identified by Andrubis as ground truth, and evaluate our system by sending the Andrubis network traffic through *ReCon* trained with the pre-labeled dataset described in Section §5.1. The *ReCon* false positive rate was quite low (0.11%), but the false negative rate was relatively high (15.6%). The vast majority of false negative flows were Device ID leaks (124/457 are obfuscated and 140/457 are false positive reports from Andrubis). *Importantly, when we retrain ReCon's classifier with the Andrubis data, we find that all of the false negatives disappear.* Thus, *ReCon* is *adaptive* in that its accuracy should only improve as we provide it more and diverse sets of labeled data. In the next section we describe results suggesting that we can also use crowdsourcing to provide labeled data.

In addition, we can use network traces labeled by IFA to train *ReCon* classifiers even in the presence of PII obfuscation. This works because *ReCon* does not search for PII itself, but rather the contextual clues in network traffic that reliably indicate that PII leaking.

Finally, *ReCon* identified several instances of PII leaks that are not tracked by IFA. These include the Android ID, MAC address, user credentials, gender, birthdays, ZIP codes, and e-mail addresses.

6. RECON IN THE WILD

We now describe the results of our IRB-approved user study, where participants used *ReCon* for at least one week and up to over 200 days, interacted with our system via the UI, and completed a follow-up survey. Our study is biased toward flows from the US due to initial recruitment in the Boston area, but includes connections from users in 21 countries in four continents. While we cannot claim representativeness, we can use the user feedback quantitatively, to understand the impact of labeling on our classifiers. We also use the study qualitatively, to understand what PII was leaked from participant devices but not in our controlled experiments, and to understand users' opinions about privacy.

The study includes 92 users in total, with 63 iOS devices and 33 Android devices (some users have more than one device). In the initial training phase, we initialized the *ReCon* classifiers with the pre-labeled dataset discussed in §5. Then we use the continuous user feedback to retrain the classifiers. The anonymized results of PII leaks discovered from our ongoing user study can be found at `http://recon.meddle.mobi/app-report.html`.

Runtime. While the previous section focused on runtime in terms of training time, an important goal for *ReCon* is to predict and extract PII in-band with network flows so that we can block/modify the PII as requested by users. As a result, the network delay experienced by *ReCon* traffic depends on the efficiency of the classifier.

We evaluated *ReCon* performance in terms of PII prediction and extraction times. The combined cost of these steps is less than 0.25 ms per flow on average (std. dev. 0.88), and never exceeds 6.47 ms per flow. We believe this is sufficiently small compared to end-to-end delays of tens or hundreds of milliseconds in mobile networks.

Accuracy "in the wild." Participants were asked to view their PII leaks via the *ReCon* UI, and label them as correct or incorrect. As of Dec 8, 2015, our study covers 1,120,278 flows, 9,573 of which contained PII leaks that *ReCon* identified. Of those, there are 5,351 TP leaks, 39 FP leaks and 4,183 unlabeled leaks. Table 6 shows the results across all users. *The users in the study found few cases when ReCon incorrectly labeled PII leaks.* The vast majority (85.6%) of unlabeled data is device identifiers, likely because it is difficult for users to find such identifiers to compare with our results.

Impact of user feedback on accuracy. To evaluate the impact of retraining classifiers based on user feedback, we compare the results without user feedback (using our initial training set only) with those that incorporate user feedback. After retraining the classifier, *the false positive rate decreased by 92% (from 39 to 3), with a minor impact on false negatives (0.5% increase, or 18/5,351).*

Retraining classifiers. As discussed in §4.1, we retrain *ReCon* classifiers periodically and after collecting sufficient samples. We provide options to set the frequency of retraining and the retraining process is relatively low cost. In our experience, retraining the general classifier once a day or once a week is sufficient to retain high accuracy. This is a process that occurs in the background, takes little time per domain (0.9 s per domain on average), and is easily parallelized to reduce retraining time.

User survey. To qualitatively answer whether *ReCon* is effective, we conducted a survey where we asked participants, "Have you changed your ways of using your smartphone and its applications based on the information provided by our system?" Of those who responded to the voluntary survey, a majority (20/26) indicated that they found the system useful and changed their habits related to privacy when using mobile devices. This is in line with results from Balebako et al. [15], who found that users "do care about applications that share privacy-sensitive information with third parties, and would want more information about data sharing."

In terms of overhead, we found that a large majority of users (19/26) observed that battery consumption and Internet speed were the same better when using *ReCon*. While the remaining users observed increased battery consumption and/or believed their Internet connections were slower, we do not have sufficient data to validate whether this was due to *ReCon* or other factors such inherent network variations or increased user awareness of these issues due to our question.

PII leak characterization. We now investigate the PII leaked in the user study. As Table 6 shows, the most commonly leaked PII is device identifiers, likely used by advertising and analytic services. The next most common leak is location, which typically occurs for apps that customize their behavior based on user location. We also find user identifiers commonly being leaked (*e.g.*, name and gender), suggesting a deeper level of tracking than anonymous device identifiers. Depressingly, even in our small user study we found 171 cases of credentials being leaked in plaintext (102 verified by users). For example, the Epocrates iOS app (used by more than 1 million physicians and health professionals) and the popular dating app Match.com (used by millions, both Android and iOS were affected) leaked user credentials in plaintext. Following responsible disclosure principles, we notified the app developers. The Epocrates app was fixed as of November, 2015 (and the vulnerability was made public [6] after we gave them time to reach out to users to convince them to upgrade), and Match.com fixed their password exposure in January, 2016 without notifying us or the public. These results highlight the negative impact of closed mobile systems—even basic security is often violated by sending passwords in plaintext (21 apps in our study).

We further investigate the leaks according to OS (Table 6).[8] We find that the average iOS user in our study experienced more data leaks than the average Android user, and particularly experienced higher relative rates of device identifier, location, and credential leaks.

We investigated the above leaks to identify several apps responsible for "suspicious" leaks. For example, the ABC Player app is inferring and transmitting the user's gender. Last, All Recipes—a cookbook app—is tracking user locations even when there is no obvious reason for it to do so.

7. RELATED WORK

Our work builds upon and complements a series of related work on privacy and tracking. Early work focused on tracking via Web browsers [7, 53]. Mobile devices make significant PII

[8]Note that these results are purely observational and we do not claim any representativeness. However, we did normalize our results according to the number of users per OS.

	Leak Type	total	correct	Feedback on leaks wrong	no label/unknown
iOS	Device ID.	3229	12	35	3182
	User ID.	655	216	2	437
	Contact Info.	6	3	1	2
	Location	4836	4751	0	85
	Credential	36	30	0	6
Android	Device ID.	399	2	0	397
	User ID.	31	30	0	1
	Contact Info.	8	8	0	0
	Location	238	227	0	11
	Credential	135	72	1	62

Table 6: **Summary of leaks predicted by OS.** *We observe a higher number of leaks for iOS because the number of iOS devices (63) is more than the number of Android devices (33).*

available to apps, and early studies showed PII such as location, usernames, passwords and phone numbers were leaked by popular apps [57]. Several efforts systematically identify PII leaks from mobile devices, and develop defenses against them.

Dynamic analysis. One approach, dynamic taint tracking, modifies the device OS to track access to PII at runtime [24] using dynamic information flow analysis, which taints PII as it is copied, mutated and exfiltrated by apps. This ensures that all access to PII being tracked by the OS is flagged; however, it can result in large false positive rates (due to coarse-granularity tainting), false negatives (*e.g.,* because the OS does not store leaked PII such as a user's password), and incur significant runtime overheads that discourage widespread use. Running taint tracking today requires rooting the device, which is typically conducted only by advanced users, and can void the owner's warranty. Other approaches that instrument apps with taint tracking code still either require modifications to platform libraries [16], and thus rooting, or resigning the app under analysis [50], essentially breaking Android's app update and resource sharing mechanisms. When taint tracking is performed as part of an automated analysis environment, user input generation is crucial to improve coverage of leaks. Tools such as Dynodroid [47], PUMA [30], and A3E [14] automatically generate UI events to explore UI states, but require manual input for more complex user interactions, *e.g.,* logging in to sites [20]. Finally, taint tracking does not address the problem of which PII leaks should be blocked (and how), a problem that is difficult to address in practice [34]. Nevertheless, automated dynamic analysis approaches are complementary to *ReCon*: as we demonstrated in §5.3, *ReCon* can learn from PII leaks identified through dynamic information flow analysis.

Static analysis. Another approach is to perform static analysis (*e.g.,* using data flow analysis or symbolic execution) to determine *a priori* whether an app will leak privacy information [12, 13, 19, 23, 25, 31, 37, 39, 46, 59, 61–63]. This approach can avoid run-time overhead by performing analysis before code is executed, but state-of-the-art tools suffer from imprecision [18] and symbolic execution can be too time-intensive to be practical. Further, deploying this solution generally requires an app store to support the analysis, make decisions about which kinds of leaks are problematic, and work with developers to address them. Static analysis is also limited by code obfuscation, and tends not to handle reflection and dynamically loaded code [64]. A recent study [44] finds dynamically loaded code is increasingly common, comprising almost 30% of goodware app code loaded at runtime.

New execution model. Privacy capsules [33] (PC) are an OS abstraction that prevent privacy leaks by ensuring that an app cannot access untrusted devices (*e.g.,* a network interface) after it accesses private information, unless the user explicitly authorizes it. The authors show the approach is low cost and effective for some apps, but it is currently deployed only as a prototype extension to Android and requires app modifications for compliance.

Network flow analysis. *ReCon* analyzes network flows to identify PII leaks. Previous studies using network traces gathered inside a mobile network [26, 58], in an ISP [45], and in a lab setting [41] identified significant tracking, despite not having access to software instrumentation. In this work, we build on these observations to both identify how users' privacy is violated and control these privacy leaks *regardless of the device OS or network being used.*

PrivacyGuard [56], AntMonitor [42] and HayStack [51] use the Android VPNService to intercept traffic and perform traffic analysis. A limitation of these approaches is they rely on hard-coded identifiers for PII, or require knowledge of a user's PII to work. Further, these approaches currently work only for the Android OS. In contrast, *ReCon* is cross-platform, does not require a priori knowledge of PII, and is adaptive to changes in how PII leaks.

8. CONCLUSION

In this paper we presented *ReCon*, a system that improves visibility and control over privacy leaks in traffic from mobile devices. We argued that since PII leaks occur over the network, detecting these leaks at the network layer admits an immediately deployable and cross-platform solution to the problem. Our approach based on machine learning has good accuracy and low overhead, and adapts to feedback from users and other sources of ground-truth information.

We believe that this approach opens a new avenue for research on privacy systems, and provides opportunities to improve privacy for average users. We are investigating how to use *ReCon* to build a system to provide properties such as k-anonymity, or allow users to explicitly control how much of their PII is shared with third parties—potentially doing so in exchange for micropayments or access to app features.

9. ACKNOWLEDGEMENTS

We thank the anonymous reviewers and our shepherd, Ben Greenstein, for their feedback. We also thank our study participants, and for contributions toward early work in this area from Justine Sherry, Amy Tang, and Shen Wang.

The *ReCon* project is supported by the Data Transparency Lab. The research leading to these results has also received funding from the FFG – Austrian Research Promotion under grant COMET K1 and from u'smile, the Josef Ressel Center for User-Friendly Secure Mobile Environments. Ashwin Rao was partially supported by a research grant from Nokia.

10. REFERENCES

[1] Ad blocking with ad server hostnames and ip addresses. `http://pgl.yoyo.org/adservers/`.

[2] App Annie App Store Stats. `http://www.appannie.com/`.

[3] AppsApk.com. `http://www.appsapk.com/`.

[4] AwaZza. `http://www.awazza.com/web/`.

[5] Bro: a System for Detecting Network Intruders in Real-Time. `https://www.bro.org`.

[6] Epocrates upgrade message. `https://www.epocrates.com/support/upgrade/message-full`.

[7] Lightbeam for Firefox. http://www.mozilla.org/en-US/lightbeam/.
[8] Meddle IRB consent form. https://docs.google.com/forms/d/1Y-xNg7cJxRnlTjH_56KUcKB_6naTfRLqQlcZmHtn5IY/viewform.
[9] SSLsplit - transparent and scalable SSL/TLS interception. http://www.roe.ch/SSLsplit.
[10] Tcpdump. http://www.tcpdump.org/.
[11] UI/Application Exerciser Monkey. https://developer.android.com/tools/help/monkey.html.
[12] Y. Agarwal and M. Hall. ProtectMyPrivacy: Detecting and Mitigating Privacy Leaks on iOS Devices Using Crowdsourcing. In *Proc. of MobiSys*, 2013.
[13] S. Arzt, S. Rasthofer, C. Fritz, E. Bodden, A. Bartel, J. Klein, Y. Le Traon, D. Octeau, and P. McDaniel. FlowDroid: Precise Context, Flow, Field, Object-sensitive and Lifecycle-aware Taint Analysis for Android Apps. In *Proc. of PLDI*, 2014.
[14] T. Azim and I. Neamtiu. Targeted and Depth-first Exploration for Systematic Testing of Android Apps. In *Proc. of OOPSLA*, 2013.
[15] R. Balebako, J. Jung, W. Lu, L. F. Cranor, and C. Nguyen. "Little Brothers Watching You:" Raising Awareness of Data Leaks on Smartphones. In *Proc. of SOUPS*, 2013.
[16] J. Bell and G. Kaiser. Phosphor: Illuminating Dynamic Data Flow in Commodity JVMs. In *Proc. of OOPSLA*, 2014.
[17] T. Book and D. S. Wallach. A Case of Collusion: A Study of the Interface Between Ad Libraries and Their Apps. In *Proc. of ACM SPSM*, 2013.
[18] Y. Cao, Y. Fratantonio, A. Bianchi, M. Egele, C. Kruegel, G. Vigna, and Y. Chen. EdgeMiner: Automatically Detecting Implicit Control Flow Transitions through the Android Framework. In *Proc. of NDSS*, 2015.
[19] X. Chen and S. Zhu. DroidJust: Automated Functionality-aware Privacy Leakage Analysis for Android Applications. In *Proc. of WiSec*, 2015.
[20] S. R. Choudhary, A. Gorla, and A. Orso. Automated Test Input Generation for Android: Are We There Yet? In *Proc. of the IEEE/ACM International Conference on Automated Software Engineering (ASE)*, 2015.
[21] S. Consolvo, J. Jung, B. Greenstein, P. Powledge, G. Maganis, and D. Avrahami. The Wi-Fi Privacy Ticker: Improving Awareness & Control of Personal Information Exposure on Wi-Fi. In *Proc. of UbiComp*, 2010.
[22] J. Crussell, R. Stevens, and H. Chen. MAdFraud: Investigating Ad Fraud in Android Applications. In *Proc. of MobiSys*, pages 123–134. ACM, 2014.
[23] M. Egele, C. Kruegel, E. Kirda, and G. Vigna. PiOS: Detecting Privacy Leaks in iOS Applications. In *Proc. of NDSS*, 2011.
[24] W. Enck, P. Gilbert, B.-G. Chun, L. P. Cox, J. Jung, P. McDaniel, and A. N. Sheth. TaintDroid: An Information-Flow Tracking System for Realtime Privacy Monitoring on Smartphones. In *Proc. of USENIX OSDI*, 2010.
[25] C. Gibler, J. Crussell, J. Erickson, and H. Chen. AndroidLeaks: Automatically Detecting Potential Privacy Leaks in Android Applications on a Large Scale. In *Proc. of TRUST*, 2012.
[26] P. Gill, V. Erramilli, A. Chaintreau, B. Krishnamurthy, D. Papagiannaki, and P. Rodriguez. Follow the Money: Understanding Economics of Online Aggregation and Advertising. In *Proc. of IMC*, 2013.
[27] M. C. Grace, W. Zhou, X. Jiang, and A.-R. Sadeghi. Unsafe Exposure Analysis of Mobile In-app Advertisements. In *Proc. of WiSec*, 2012.
[28] M. Hall, E. Frank, G. Holmes, B. Pfahringer, P. Reutemann, and I. H. Witten. The WEKA Data Mining Software: An Update. *ACM SIGKDD Explorations Newsletter*, 11(1):10–18, 2009.
[29] S. Han, J. Jung, and D. Wetherall. A Study of Third-Party Tracking by Mobile Apps in the Wild. Technical Report UW-CSE-12-03-01, University of Washington, 2012.
[30] S. Hao, B. Liu, S. Nath, W. G. Halfond, and R. Govindan. PUMA: Programmable UI-automation for Large-scale Dynamic Analysis of Mobile Apps. In *Proc. of MobiSys*, 2014.
[31] S. Hao, B. Liu, S. Nath, W. G. Halfond, and R. Govindan. PUMA: Programmable UI-Automation for Large-Scale Dynamic Analysis of Mobile Apps. In *Proc. of MobiSys*, 2014.
[32] Z. Harris. Distributional structure. *Word*, 10(23):146–162, 1954.
[33] R. Herbster, S. DellaTorre, P. Druschel, and B. Bhattacharjee. Privacy capsules: Preventing information leaks by mobile apps. In *Proc. of MobiSys*, 2016.
[34] P. Hornyack, S. Han, J. Jung, S. Schechter, and D. Wetherall. "These Aren't the Droids You're Looking For": Retrofitting Android to Protect Data from Imperious Applications. In *Proc. of ACM CCS*, 2011.
[35] M. Huber, M. Mulazzani, S. Schrittwieser, and E. Weippl. Appinspect: Large-scale Evaluation of Social Networking Apps. In *Proc. of ACM COSN*, 2013.
[36] S. Jagabathula, L. Subramanian, and A. Venkataraman. Reputation-based worker filtering in crowdsourcing. In *Advances in Neural Information Processing Systems*, pages 2492–2500, 2014.
[37] J. Jeon, K. K. Micinski, and J. S. Foster. SymDroid: Symbolic Execution for Dalvik Bytecode. Technical Report CS-TR-5022, University of Maryland, College Park, 2012.
[38] C. Johnson, III. US Office of Management and Budget Memorandum M-07-16. http://www.whitehouse.gov/sites/default/files/omb/memoranda/fy2007/m07-16.pdf, May 2007.
[39] J. Kim, Y. Yoon, K. Yi, and J. Shin. SCANDAL: Static Analyzer for Detecting Privacy Leaks in Android Applications. In *Proc. of MoST*, 2012.
[40] H. King. No. 1 paid app on iTunes taken down by developer. http://money.cnn.com/2015/09/18/technology/peace-ad-blocking-app-pulled/index.html, September 2015.
[41] B. Krishnamurthy and C. Wills. Privacy Diffusion on the Web: A Longitudinal Perspective. In *Proc. of ACM WWW*, 2009.
[42] A. Le, J. Varmarken, S. Langhoff, A. Shuba, M. Gjoka, and A. Markopoulou. AntMonitor: A system for monitoring from mobile devices. In *Proc. of Wrokshop on Crowdsourcing and Crowdsharing of Big (Internet) Data*, 2015.

[43] I. Leontiadis, C. Efstratiou, M. Picone, and C. Mascolo. Don't kill my ads! Balancing Privacy in an Ad-Supported Mobile Application Market. In *Proc. of ACM HotMobile*, 2012.

[44] M. Lindorfer, M. Neugschwandtner, L. Weichselbaum, Y. Fratantonio, V. van der Veen, and C. Platzer. Andrubis - 1,000,000 Apps Later: A View on Current Android Malware Behaviors. In *Proc. of BADGERS*, 2014.

[45] Y. Liu, H. H. Song, I. Bermudez, A. Mislove, M. Baldi, and A. Tongaonkar. Identifying personal information in internet traffic. In *Proceedings of the 3rd ACM Conference on Online Social Networks (COSN'15)*, Palo Alto, CA, November 2015.

[46] L. Lu, Z. Li, Z. Wu, W. Lee, and G. Jiang. CHEX: Statically Vetting Android Apps for Component Hijacking Vulnerabilities. In *Proc. of ACM CCS*, 2012.

[47] A. Machiry, R. Tahiliani, and M. Naik. Dynodroid: An Input Generation System for Android Apps. In *Proc. of the Joint Meeting on Foundations of Software Engineering (ESEC/FSE)*, 2013.

[48] D. Naylor, K. Schomp, M. Varvello, I. Leontiadis, J. Blackburn, D. R. López, K. Papagiannaki, P. Rodriguez Rodriguez, and P. Steenkiste. Multi-context TLS (mcTLS): Enabling secure in-network functionality in TLS. In *Proc. of ACM SIGCOMM*, 2015.

[49] A. Rao, A. M. Kakhki, A. Razaghpanah, A. Tang, S. Wang, J. Sherry, P. Gill, A. Krishnamurthy, A. Legout, A. Mislove, and D. Choffnes. Using the Middle to Meddle with Mobile. Technical report, Northeastern University, 2013.

[50] V. Rastogi, Z. Qu, J. McClurg, Y. Cao, Y. Chen, W. Zhu, and W. Chen. Uranine: Real-time Privacy Leakage Monitoring without System Modification for Android. In *Proc. of SecureComm*, 2015.

[51] A. Razaghpanah, N. Vallina-Rodriguez, S. Sundaresan, C. Kreibich, P. Gill, M. Allman, and V. Paxson. Haystack: In Situ Mobile Traffic Analysis in User Space. *arXiv preprint arXiv:1510.01419*, 2015.

[52] J. Ren, A. Rao, M. Lindorfer, A. Legout, and D. R. Choffnes. ReCon: Revealing and controlling privacy leaks in mobile network traffic. *CoRR*, abs/1507.00255, 2015.

[53] F. Roesner, T. Kohno, and D. Wetherall. Detecting and Defending Against Third-Party Tracking on the Web. *Proc. of USENIX NSDI*, 2012.

[54] Sandvine. Global Internet Phenomena Report. `https://www.sandvine.com/downloads/general/global-internet-phenomena/2014/1h-2014-global-internet-phenomena-report.pdf`, 1H 2014.

[55] J. Sherry, C. Lan, R. A. Popa, and S. Ratnasamy. BlindBox: Deep packet inspection over encrypted traffic. In *Proc. of ACM SIGCOMM*, 2015.

[56] Y. Song and U. Hengartner. PrivacyGuard: A VPN-based Platform to Detect Information Leakage on Android Devices. In *Proc. of ACM SPSM*, 2015.

[57] The Wall Street Journal. What They Know - Mobile. `http://blogs.wsj.com/wtk-mobile/`, December 2010.

[58] N. Vallina-Rodriguez, J. Shah, A. Finamore, H. Haddadi, Y. Grunenberger, K. Papagiannaki, and J. Crowcroft. Breaking for Commercials: Characterizing Mobile Advertising. In *Proc. of IMC*, 2012.

[59] M. Xia, L. Gong, Y. Lyu, Z. Qi, and X. Liu. Effective Real-time Android Application Auditing. In *IEEE Symposium on Security and Privacy*, 2015.

[60] N. Xia, H. H. Song, Y. Liao, M. Iliofotou, A. Nucci, Z.-L. Zhang, and A. Kuzmanovic. Mosaic: Quantifying Privacy Leakage in Mobile Networks. In *Proc. of ACM SIGCOMM*, 2013.

[61] L. K. Yan and H. Yin. DroidScope: Seamlessly Reconstructing the OS and Dalvik Semantic Views for Dynamic Android Malware Analysis. In *Proc. of USENIX Security*, 2012.

[62] Z. Yang, M. Yang, Y. Zhang, G. Gu, P. Ning, and X. S. Wang. AppIntent: Analyzing Sensitive Data Transmission in Android for Privacy Leakage Detection. In *Proc. of ACM CCS*, 2013.

[63] Y. Zhang, M. Yang, B. Xu, Z. Yang, G. Gu, P. Ning, X. S. Wang, and B. Zang. Vetting undesirable behaviors in Android apps with permission use analysis. In *Proc. of ACM CCS*, 2013.

[64] Y. Zhauniarovich, M. Ahmad, O. Gadyatskaya, B. Crispo, and F. Massacci. StaDynA: Addressing the Problem of Dynamic Code Updates in the Security Analysis of Android Applications. In *Proc. of ACM CODASPY*, 2015.

CASE: Comprehensive Application Security Enforcement on COTS Mobile Devices

Suwen Zhu
Stony Brook University
suwzhu@cs.stonybrook.edu

Long Lu
Stony Brook University
long@cs.stonybrook.edu

Kapil Singh
IBM Research
kapil@us.ibm.com

ABSTRACT

Without violating existing app security enforcement, malicious modules inside apps, such as a library or an external class, can steal private data and abuse sensitive capabilities meant for other modules inside the same apps. These so-called "module-level attacks" are quickly emerging, fueled by the pervasive use of third-party code in apps and the lack of module-level security enforcement on mobile platforms.

To systematically thwart the threats, we build CASE, an automatic app patching tool used by app developers to enable module-level security in their apps built for COTS Android devices. During runtime, patched apps enforce developer-supplied security policies that regulate interactions among modules at the granularity of a Java class. Requiring no changes or special support from the Android OS, the enforcement is complete in covering inter-module crossings in apps and is robust against malicious Java and native app modules. We evaluate CASE with 420 popular apps and a set of Android's unit tests. The results show that CASE is fully compatible with the tested apps and incurs an average performance overhead of 4.9%.

1. INTRODUCTION

Mobile operating systems, including Android and iOS, enforce application-level sandbox, which assigns each app a separate security identity and maintains proper isolation among apps. While effectively mitigating attacks among apps, the existing sandbox becomes useless in face of the emerging *in app threats*, whereby a module of an app, such as a third-party library or an external class, adversely affects the rest of the app or manipulates the underlying OS. For instance, a recent study [21] found that, in both Android and iOS apps, some popular advertisement libraries turned rogue and have been stealing user private information. Another report [1] revealed that more than 18,000 Android apps covertly upload SMS messages from mobile devices to remote servers, unbeknown to users and even app developers, caused by a widely used in-app payment library. In-app threats also lead to the formation of mobile botnets and use native code for hiding the malicious activities [12].

We refer to this type of attacks as "*module-level attacks*", where a module can be as small as a class inside an app. Such attacks are hardly detectable because they do not violate the existing security enforcement mechanisms on mobile platforms, which operate at the application level and cannot distinguish app modules. Module-level attacks are also difficult to prevent. App developers often have to blindly trust external code and libraries included in their apps due to the incapability of imposing separate security restrictions on them. These attacks have been quickly emerging and evolving as the integration of external SDKs and libraries becomes nearly universal in mobile app development.

Previous research studied certain instances of module-level attacks, but failed to cover the entire class of attacks. Some of the proposed solutions isolate a particular type of malicious module, such as advertisement or JNI libraries [18, 16, 20], in ways inapplicable to other types of malicious modules. Other solutions introduce component-awareness to the Android permission checks [23] but cannot control interactions among components. Besides, the proposed mitigations only apply to coarse-grained app modules, such as a compilation unit. They also require changes to Android OS, which impedes wide adoption in the largely fragmented Android market.

To fully prevent module-level attacks, we propose CASE (Comprehensive Application Security Enforcement), an automatic app patching tool for app developers to enable module-level security in their apps built for COTS Android devices (*i.e.*, no OS or middleware changes are needed). CASE's enforcement recognizes app modules at a very fine granularity: *a class for Java code or a JNI library for native code*. In patched apps, each app module can have its own security identity and developer-defined security policies are enforced on a per-module basis, for example, "module A cannot access or reflect on any field or method of module B" or "module A cannot use permission P assigned to the app", where A can be defined in an untrusted library, B can be a sensitive class, and P can be solely intended for a special module's use. To the best of our knowledge, this fine-grained module-level enforcement is the first of its kind. It is essential to stop the emerging module-level attacks.

Realizing this enforcement requires mediation of all the possible channels via which a module may interact with another module or the underlying system. Realizing this mediation in a complete, robust, and efficient fashion is quite challenging given the design requirement that, the mediation must operate purely in user space to avoid modifying Android framework or OS. This requirement not only rules out OS-level support but also attracts potential manipulations and evasions by malicious code in apps, such as a rogue library. To overcome these challenges, we first design a novel module-level mediation scheme for Android apps, namely *dual-layer interception*, which checks all cross-module interactions unexpected to developers. We then propose two self-protection mech-

MobiSys'16, June 25 - 30, 2016, Singapore, Singapore

ISBN 978-1-4503-4269-8/16/06...$15.00

DOI: http://dx.doi.org/10.1145/2906388.2906413

anisms for the user-space mediation, namely *native-safe pages* and *concealed handler*, which together prevent the most powerful attack permitted in our threat model—arbitrary native code trying to bypass the mediation.

We build CASE as an automatic app-patching tool that developers can simply drop in their toolchain. CASE takes a compiled app as input, along with a developer-supplied policy describing (dis)allowed inter-module crossings. It then inserts the core mediation library into the app and rewrites the app's boot routine so that during runtime the mediation and its self-protection mechanisms are properly initialized prior to app execution. It finally signs the patched app with a developer key and produces a releasable package. The whole process happens without any developer assistance, such as code annotation or design refactoring, which usually limits adoption in practice and is error-prone. Since CASE operates directly on compiled apps without requiring changes to app design, not only app developers but also IT administrators and security-savvy app users can employ CASE to protect apps from module-level attacks (discussed in § 5).

We evaluate CASE in terms of its deployment cost and compatibility, security and robustness, and runtime overhead, using 420 popular apps and a set of unit tests. CASE has successfully prevented all the disallowed inter-module crossings in these tests. On average, CASE delays app launch by 0.174 seconds, increases memory usage by 1.19MB, and slows down app execution by 4.93%. The results indicate that CASE is complete, robust, and efficient for defending module-level attacks in real-world.

In summary, this work makes the following contributions:

- A study of the emerging module-level attacks, identifying the demands and challenges for defenses;
- Three novel techniques to achieve complete, robust, and efficient mediation of inter-module crossings in user-space for Android apps, which defends against the module-level attacks in their most powerful forms;
- A drop-in tool that app developers can easily adopt in their toolchain to enable module-level security enforcement in new or existing apps.

The rest of the paper is organized as follows: we discuss the module-level attacks and explain the defense challenges in §2; we explain the design of CASE in §3, centering around the three core techniques; in §4 we share our implementation experience and insights; we report the analysis and evaluation of CASE in §6; we contrast the related works in §7 and conclude the paper in §8.

2. BACKGROUND

2.1 Example Attacks

We use CamX, a hypothetical camera app, as an example to illustrate module-level attacks and the lack of defense. CamX, in addition to capturing photos, provides three value-adding features: image filters, cloud backup, and social network integration. Instead of implementing these features by herself, CamX's developer imports a 3rd-party Java class that encapsulates the image filters, along with a JNI library, and uses the SDKs provided by the cloud and social-network vendors (*e.g.*, Dropbox and Facebook).

Module-level Attacks: As increasingly observed in reality [21, 1, 12], external modules included in apps can be tainted or malicious. Assuming the image filter class in CamX is harmful, it can freely access other modules as well as the system resources meant for these modules. For example, manipulating the integrated SDKs, the harmful class can steal users' files in the cloud storage or manipulate their social network accounts. It can also abuse the camera or Internet access granted to the app. Leveraging its JNI library, a malicious module can theoretically access any user-space data or code loaded in the app's memory space.

In general, module-level attacks can happen in two forms: module-to-module and module-to-system. The first form involves a module stealing data or abusing code of another module. For instance, the malicious image filter class in CamX can use Java reflection to stealthily invoke the file download APIs in the cloud SDK or read the objects that record user profiles inside the social network SDK. The malicious class may also invoke the Android framework APIs for accessing the Internet or the camera. The second form involves a module directly accessing system-managed resources, including virtual memory, file systems, and the app runtime. For instance, a malicious JNI library can scan memory and files for sensitive data. It also can interfere with the execution of the app's Java code by manipulating the virtual machine.

Although gradually gaining attention among app developers and users, module-level attacks remain largely unstoppable because the existing security mechanisms on mobile platforms treat apps as the minimum security entities and cannot regulate or recognize app modules.

2.2 Defense: Requirements and Challenges

Defending against the emerging module-level attacks demands a new layer of security enforcement, on top of the conventional per-app enforcement, that acts on individual modules inside apps. To support modules of various sizes and types, the new enforcement has to allow modules to be defined at a fine granularity, such as a Java class. It must intercept and mediate all instances of the module-to-module and module-to-system interactions in an app that may lead to module-level attacks. The enforcement should not require changes to mobile OS or middleware, which are known to severely slow down and limit real-world adoption, needless to say enlarging the already bloated system software layer on mobile platforms. While operating in the user space, the enforcement needs to protect itself against malicious modules (either Java or native code) running inside same apps.

To meet the above requirements, a potential module-level security enforcement must overcome the following challenges:

($C1$) **Intercept cross-module interactions completely and practically:** There are two typical approaches to security interception: dynamically monitoring applications at a privileged software layer (*e.g.*, inside the language runtime or OS), or statically instrumenting applications' code. However, neither meets the aforementioned requirements. The first approach enjoys a full view and control of application execution, but it requires changes to system software. The second approach, though only modifying applications, cannot provide complete interception, particularly in cases where malicious code use obfuscation techniques to confuse and evade static instrumentation. Therefore, a new interception mechanism is needed for capturing all cross-module interactions, such as a reflective field read or an API invocation. However, the language runtime or OS does not explicitly track these interaction, and worse, malicious modules may obscure them.

($C2$) **Prevent implicit module crossing:** Though not ubiquitous used, native code (in the form of JNI libraries) is commonly found in popular Android apps [20]. Such code can directly access the virtual memory of the containing app, including the regions where the language runtime (*e.g.*, Dalvik VM) saves its internal data, such as the class definitions and the raw representations of objects. Therefore, malicious native code can stealthily manipulate other app modules via direct memory access. For instance in CamX, to access the Java object storing the session key in the social network SDK, the malicious JNI code can locate the raw object in memory and then retrieve its sensitive data fields. Such cross-module access is implicit in that it happens at the virtual memory level without involving the Dalvik VM. Although implicit module crossing in itself represents a security violation (*i.e.,* abusing VM's internal data), preventing it is challenging as it requires protection over VM's memory regions against malicious code running in the same process at the same privilege level as the VM.

($C3$) **Protect interception mechanism in user space:** A malicious module may attempt to subvert the user-space interception mechanisms in the following ways. First, it may tamper with the "hooks" that the interception mechanism places in memory, such as those in the Global Offset Tables (GOTs) and the function preambles. The hooks redirect code executions to security checks before allowing them to enter any sensitive routines (*e.g.,* accessing a protected module). If malicious code reverts or removes the hooks, it bypasses the security checks entirely. Second, a malicious module may locate the sensitive routines in memory and directly invoke them, evading any hooks and security checks. Third, even if the hooks are protected and the sensitive routines are hidden, a malicious module may direct code executions to the locations immediately following the successful checks, as if the executions underwent the hooks and passed the security checks. Therefore, a robust interception mechanism needs to protect its own data and code (*e.g.,* hooks and security checks) from app code sharing the same memory space.

3. ENABLING MODULE-LEVEL SECURITY

3.1 CASE Overview

To stop the emerging module-level attacks, we build CASE, which enables security regulations on individual modules inside Android apps. CASE is intended primarily for app developers' use. It enforces developer-supplied security policies that describe (dis)allowed cross-module interactions. CASE identifies app modules at the granularity of a class (Java code) or a JNI library (native code). CASE mediates both module to module (*e.g.,* reading a member field of a different class) and module-to-system (*e.g.,* making a direct system call) access during an app execution. Rather than modifying the Android Framework or OS, CASE retrofits the module-level security enforcement into apps via automatic app patching. This design has two main advantages: first, it makes CASE compatible with all COTS Android devices and thus is *readily deployable*; and second, it minimizes developers' assistance and thus is *easily adoptable* (*i.e.,* developers only need to provide desired policies without having to modify app code or understand the enforcement mechanism).

Threat Model: We adopt a threat model that is both realistic and permissive in the context of defending module-level attacks. We trust the OS as it is locked via hardware features on COTS mobile devices. Although malicious apps may in theory comprise the OS by exploiting rare vulnerabilities, such apps are out of scope for this work because module-level attacks become pointless in these apps. On the other hand, we assume the existence of the most powerful app-level adversaries. The adversaries can gain full control over one or more modules in an app and aim at: (*i*) penetrating into a sensitive module in the app; (*ii*) abusing the privileges and resources granted to the entire app. Tainted or malicious modules can contain arbitrary Java and native code, which is loaded inside the same app VM and process as the targeted modules as well as CASE.

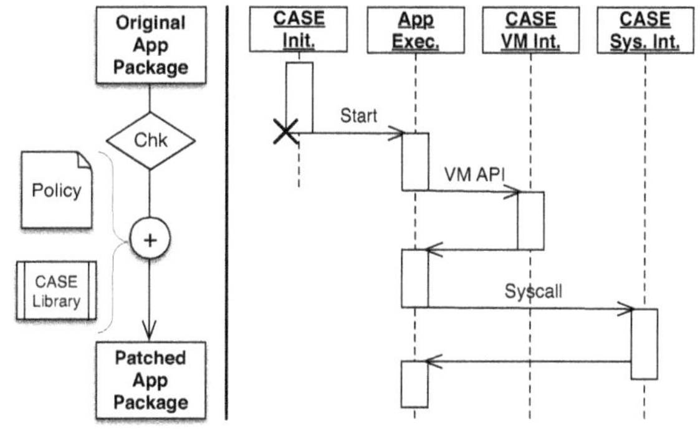

Figure 1: CASE workflow: static patching phase (left) and dynamic enforcement phase (right)

Workflow: CASE consists of two main components, an automatic app patcher and a runtime enforcement library, which function in the app building phase and app execution phase, respectively (Figure 1). In the first phase, the CASE patcher, streamlined in the app building toolchain, takes as input the compiled app executable and the developer-supplied policies. The patcher checks the native library, if any, in the executable for disallowed instructions (explained in § 3.4). It then injects the policies and the CASE enforcement library into the app package. Subsequently, the patcher rewrites the app boot routine so that the self-initialization of the enforcement library is always performed prior to the original startup sequences of the app. The patcher finally signs the app using the developer's key and produces a releasable app package.

The second phase starts when the patched app is launched and CASE's self-initialization is triggered. The initialization sets up the interception mechanism for cross-module interactions (§ 3.3). Additionally, it enables the protection measures for the interception mechanism to prevent evasions and tampering by malicious modules in the app (§ 3.4 and 3.5). During the app execution, the enforcement library monitors every cross-module interaction that warrants a check as described by the policies. It denies any forbidden module crossings and alarms the app user of the event.

3.2 Overall Design and Rationale

CASE addresses the open problem of "*completely and robustly mediating cross-module interactions*". We achieve *completeness* using a mechanism called the *dual-layer interception*. It was driven by our observation that, module crossings can happen at two orthogonal layers: (*i*) the VM layer where the module-to-module interactions happen; (*ii*) the system call layer where the module-to-system interactions happen. Module-to-module interactions trigger the VM internal functions in charge of class resolution or JNI transition; similarly, module-to-system interactions trigger system calls. By interposing a set of selected VM internal functions and system call interfaces, the dual-layer interception monitors all module crossings encountered during an app execution. Without requiring any support from the VM or the OS, the CASE enforcement library realizes the function interposition via in-memory code patching and GOT hooking. The details about the set of interposed functions and the interposition techniques are explained in § 3.3.

To ensure the *robustness* of the interception against malicious modules, we introduce two protection measures, namely the *native-safe pages* and the *concealed handler*. The former prevents evasion of the interception and the latter protects the interception mechanism against tampering.

To evade dual-layer interception, a sophisticated malicious module may perform implicit module crossing by sidestepping the VM or the regular system call interface, and therefore, avoids the interposed functions. Specifically, malicious native code can directly locate and parse the raw presentation of a Java object in memory, and in turn, manipulate the member fields or methods in a VM-agnostic fashion. The malicious module can also make implicit system calls by locating and jumping to the system call entry points without explicitly invoking the interposed system call wrappers. We design the native-safe pages to prevent implicit module crossing. The key rationale behind the design is that implicit module crossing cannot succeed without direct memory access to VM's internal data or system call entry points. The native-safe pages are regular memory pages with special page-level protection attributes dynamically set by the CASE enforcement library. Allocating VM's internal data in the native-safe pages prevents direct access by app code. Keeping system call wrappers and entry points in the native-safe pages hides them from direct execution.

In addition to evasion, tampering is the other way to bypass the interception. Since operating in user space, a malicious module may directly abuse CASE's internal data and code. For instance, it can try to overwrite memory data critical to the interception, including the policy rules and internal states. It may also try to manipulate CASE's interception routines, such as bypassing the security checks. To prevent potential subverting of CASE, we introduce two security properties, namely *interception integrity* and *interception invisibility*, which apply to CASE's internal data and code, respectively. The intuition is that no tampering is possible if malicious code cannot modify the internal data or observe (find in memory) the internal code.

To achieve interception integrity, the CASE enforcement library write-protects the memory pages for its static data and function hooks (both GOTs and patched code) during the self-initialization phase. Malicious code cannot override this page protection thanks to the system call interception. To achieve interception invisibility, CASE uses a novel invocation mechanism for stealthily invoking its interception routines. The mechanism, called the *concealed handler*, repurposes the standard POSIX signal handling to hide sensitive code in user space memory while allowing other code to invoke the hidden code without knowing its address. Using the concealed handler, CASE hides its interception routines and other internal code that app code must not directly call or partially execute.

Next, we delve into the detailed design and usage of CASE's three core techniques: the dual-layer interception, the native-safe pages, and the concealed handler. We explain how they tackle the major challenges associated with enforcing module-level security in user space (§ 2.2).

3.3 Dual-layer interception

A key insight that inspired the dual-layer interception is that, despite their large variety, inter-module crossings in apps take place at either of the two software boundaries: the boundary between two modules (*e.g.,* when accessing data or code in a object of a different class) and the boundary between a module and the underlying OS (*e.g.,* when accessing IPC, network, or hardware sensors), as illustrated in Figure 2. To capture all inter-module crossing that warrant security checks, the dual-layer interception covers a set of selected functions located at either the language runtime layer or the system call layer. We refer to the set of functions as *MinSet* (Table 1). Derived from our manual examination of all Dalvik internal APIs for class and JNI management, *MinSet* represents the minimum set of functions that either module-to-module or module-to-system crossings have to trigger.

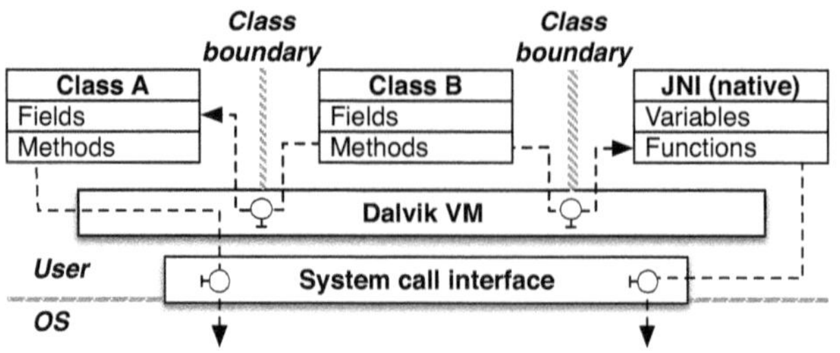

Figure 2: The dual-layer interception

Table 1: Functions in *MinSet*

Function	Library	Purpose
ioctl	libc	IPC interception
open	libc	file system isolation
link	libc	file system isolation
unlink	libc	file system isolation
connect	libc	socket access
dlopen	linker	self-protection
dlclose	linker	self-protection
dlsym	linker	self-protection
mmap	libc	self-protection
mremap	libc	self-protection
munmap	libc	self-protection
mprotect	libc	self-protection
fork	libc	process management
execve	libc	process management
dvmPlatformInvoke	libdvm	JNI interception
*Method_invokeNative	libdvm	reflection interception
*Constructor_constructNative	libdvm	reflection interception
*Field_getField	libdvm	reflection interception
*Field_setField	libdvm	reflection interception
*Field_getPrimitiveField	libdvm	reflection interception
*Field_setPrimitiveField	libdvm	reflection interception
dvmLookupClass	libdvm	class managing
loadClassFromDex0	libdvm	class managing
dvmFindPrimitiveClass	libdvm	class managing
findMethodInListByDescriptor	libdvm	class managing
findMethodInListByProto	libdvm	class managing
dvmFindVirtualMethodByName	libdvm	class managing
dvmFindStaticField	libdvm	class managing
dvmFindInstanceField	libdvm	class managing
sigaction	libc	self-protection

* denoting the common prefix "Dalvik_java_lang_reflect_".

At the system call layer, *MinSet* contains the system call wrappers that apps use for accessing system-managed resources, including `open` for file systems and sensors, `ioctl` for driver-exposed interfaces and Binder IPC, `socket` and `connect` for sockets and network. Intercepting these system calls allows for full mediation of a module's access to system-managed resources. In addition, *MinSet* also contains a few system calls that are not directly related to enforcing security policies but critical for preventing attacks against CASE. These include `mmap` and `mprotect` for memory management and protection (*e.g.,* write-protecting trampoline code, GOTs, and policy rules), and `sigaction` for exclusively handling the sensitive signals as the concealed handler requires (§3.5). Unlike the previous works that intercept system calls enforcing security policies [25], our interception is immune from malicious native code running in the same process. Besides, it also mediates module-to-module interactions, which no previous work has achieved.

At the language runtime layer, *MinSet* contains selected APIs from two Android runtime libraries, namely the Dalvik VM (`libdvm`) and the dynamic linker and loader (`linker`). The selected internal APIs in `libdvm` are used by the VM whenever an object's member fields and methods are being accessed or when a JNI library is being invoked. Intercepting these APIs allows for security checks on all kinds of module-to-module interactions inside apps. On the linker's side, *MinSet* contains APIs for dynamically loading executables and looking up symbols in loaded executables, such as `dlopen` and `dlsym`. Intercepting the linker APIs is necessary for covering newly loaded modules and securing loaded modules, including the CASE enforcement library.

CASE additionally employs standard function interception methods, namely GOT hooking and dynamic binary patching. The former is used whenever applicable whereas the latter is needed when an interception target is a private API or does not have an exported symbol (*i.e.,* the target does not have any GOT entry). Although these interception methods have been widely used, they are intrinsically vulnerable in adversarial environments as the one CASE faces (*e.g.,* sharing a memory space with untrusted or malicious native code). Our key contribution to the interception methods lies in the self-protection techniques that make them robust against powerful adversaries (*e.g.,* malicious code running inside the same process).

The dual-layer interception overcomes the challenge $C1$, acting as the underpinnings to enable CASE's complete module-level security mediation.

3.4 Native-safe pages

A malicious module may bypass the dual-layer interception via implicit module crossing, whereby it interacts with the OS or another module without using or triggering the functions in *MinSet*. For instance, a malicious module can directly initiate a system call by jumping to the system-entering instructions (*e.g.,*`SYSENTER` and `SWI`) inside the system call wrappers in `libc`. It may also directly read and parse the VM's internal data in memory without using any VM APIs, and in turn, inspect another module. In general, implicit module crossing is possible because native code in apps can execute arbitrary instructions and has unchecked access to an app's entire user-space memory. Benign apps never need to carry out implicit module crossing.

To prevent implicit module crossing, we introduce the native-safe pages. By converting the memory pages where the system call wrappers and the VM internal data reside into the native-safe pages, the CASE enforcement library ensures that apps' native code cannot directly execute or access the system call wrappers and the VM internal data. The native-safe pages are built on the basic page-level memory protection without affecting app's normal functioning. They switch to enforcement mode only for the duration of JNI execution and remain in permissive mode (*i.e.,* no performance overhead) otherwise. CASE supports two types of native-safe pages (Figure 3):

Native-safe pages for system call wrappers: These pages store and protect the default system call wrappers. Since they are frequently accessed, keeping them locked and only unlock them for each permitted call can cause significant app delays, even if the enforcement is not always-on (*i.e.,* only in effect during app native code execution). Instead of repeatedly locking and unlocking these pages, our design only performs a single page protection adjustment at each switch between the permissive mode and the enforcement mode. In permissive mode, these pages are unlocked and freely accessible. When entering the enforcement mode (*i.e.,* switching to JNI execution), CASE locks these pages (*i.e.,* set the `PROT_NONE` bit) and duplicates these pages at a hidden and random location in memory[1], as shown in Figure 3. Every subsequent system call by the app triggers a page fault, which is transparently handled by the concealed handler (§ 3.5), where the call undergoes the security checks and, if passed, is forwarded to the hidden system wrappers. This design takes advantage of the self-contained and location-independent nature of the system call wrappers (*i.e.,* they do not reference external code or data via relative offsets, and therefore, can function normally when relocated to different memory locations.)

Obviously, the security of this optimization hinges on the confidentiality of the duplicated wrappers' locations in memory, which is assured as follows. First, as part of the interception invisibility enabled by the concealed handler (§ 3.5), the CASE enforcement library's internal code and data, including the whereabouts of the duplicated system call wrappers, are kept secure and secret from app code. Second, the hidden pages are surrounded by guard pages that prevent brute-force memory searches by malicious native code. Without requiring memory locks, the hidden pages remain unreachable for all but the checked invocations of system call wrappers. This design achieves efficient mediation and protection of the system call interface.

Using duplicated, hidden system call wrappers also solves two additional issues, namely cyclic page lock and thread unsafety, that we would run into if we simply lock the wrappers. First, without duplicated wrappers, no user-space code, including the CASE enforcement library, can make system calls once the native-safe pages for the system call wrappers have been locked. As a result, CASE cannot call `mprotect` to unlock any native-safe pages when needed, leaving the app execution in a cyclic lock. Second, without duplicated wrappers, CASE needs to unlock the native-safe pages for each checked system call, which exposes the pages and the system call interfaces to all concurrent threads of the app that may execute malicious native code.

Native-safe pages for VM internal data: These pages store and protect the internal data of the VM, including the class hierarchies and the raw object pools (Figure 3). They ensure that the resident data are only accessible to the intended code, namely the VM's internal APIs. Similar to their counterparts for system call wrappers, the native-safe pages for VM data are only effective when JNI code is running and use the basic page-level memory protection but in a different fashion. These pages are locked prior to any JNI code execution, which should never directly access data on these pages. They are unlocked when the app execution switches from JNI back to Java code.

However, this intuitive form of protection can break normal app executions when the VM happens to access its data during a page lockdown. We observe that, the VM may access a locked data page only when a Java thread is running concurrently with the thread that triggered the page lock and is running JNI code. CASE avoids this adverse impact on the VM by interleaving the native and Java threads. The interleaved executions start when a VM thread encounters a page fault due to the locked native-safe pages. CASE immediately suspends the VM thread and let the active native thread(s) continue. After the native threads return or 100 microseconds (*i.e.,* tuned to Linux's `DEF_TIMESLICE`) expire, whichever comes first, CASE suspends all native threads, unlocks the native-safe pages, and resumes the previously suspended VM thread. It repeats the preemption and switches back and forth between Java

[1]It duplicates the virtual memory mappings rather than the content.

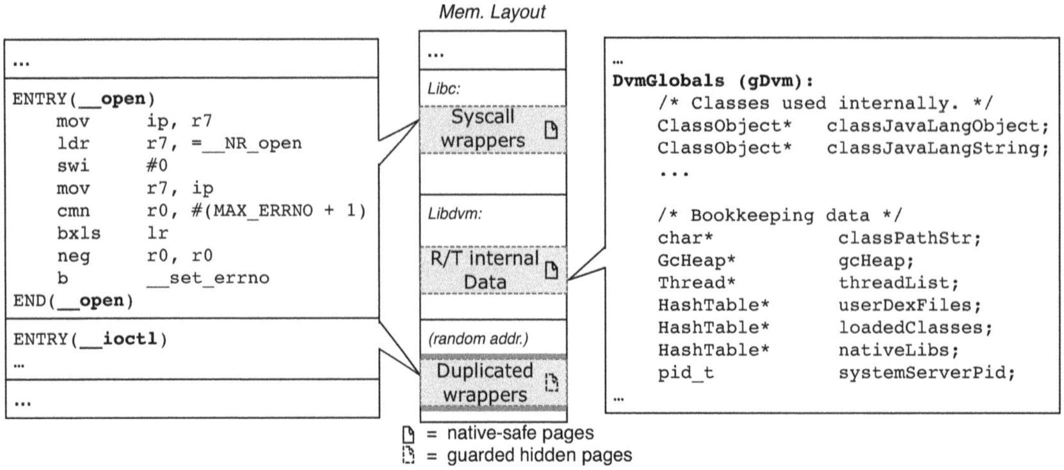

Figure 3: The native-safe pages for system call wrappers and the internal data of the runtime

and native threads until the JNI execution finishes or the app enters the single-thread execution. CASE carries out the thread interleaving and scheduling purely in the user-space by using the `SIGSTOP` and `SIGCONT` signals. It identifies the correct instances to raise these signals by monitoring an app's thread creation and JNI invocation, a capability enabled by the dual-layer interception (*i.e.,* it covers the related system calls and the JNI bridge APIs). Note that the interleaved execution rarely happens in practice as normal apps' JNI code are usually single-threaded and invoked synchronously by Java code. We tested 20 popular apps from Google Play that use JNI and found none of them triggering the interleaved execution.

With the aforementioned properties, the native-safe pages stop both forms of implicit module crossing in apps and overcome challenge $C2$.

3.5 Concealed handler

The two security properties, interception integrity and invisibility, guarantee CASE's robustness against tampering. Interception integrity is straightforward and achieved by write-protecting the memory pages for CASE's static data and code. In comparison, interception invisibility is challenging because it requires the interception routines to be hidden and protected from app code, despite the shared memory address space. CASE achieves interception invisibility via the concealed handler.

Using the standard POSIX signals, the concealed handler enables blind invocation and orderly execution of its (sensitive) code—untrusted code running in the same process can invoke the concealed handler without knowing its address in memory or influencing its execution. Since the concealed handler's code or data are undiscoverable in memory, malicious code cannot invoke it partially (*e.g.,* jumping to the middle of the function) or out-of-order (*e.g.,* ROP-style execution), nor access its associated data. In general, the concealed handler can be used by many user-space security enforcement or monitoring systems to create invisible yet invokable sensitive routines.

To create a concealed handler that encapsulates the sensitive routines, the CASE enforcement library first allocates two memory pages at random locations (one for code and one for data) during its initialization phase. It then loads a master dispatch function, the sensitive routines, and their associated data to these pages. Next, the dispatch function is registered as the handler for `SIGSEGV` (*i.e.,* for page faults). In theory, any standard signal suffices, but having the master function handle the page fault signal allows for tight integration with the native-safe pages. No pointers to these pages are saved in use-space memory as they may leak the hidden locations. Only the OS knows the address to the master dispatcher as the registered signal handler. The system call interception prevents app code from reading or changing the handler.

CASE's concealed handler contains the sensitive routines essential to its enforcement mechanism, including the resolver for the hidden system call wrappers and the native thread orchestrator, as discussed below.

System call wrapper resolver: Resolving the addresses of hidden system call wrappers takes place in a transparent fashion: the caller is neither aware of the indirection (*i.e.,* the system call is serviced by a duplicated wrapper) nor able to extract the address of the hidden system call wrapper. As shown in the example trampoline in Figure 4, when the native-safe pages are in permissive mode, the load instruction loads the address of the original wrapper into the `r7` register (Line m). The register is then used as the control flow transfer target (Line j), which happens after a successful security check. The system call interposition finishes as if the native-safe pages do not exist. In contrast, when the native-safe pages are in the enforcement mode, the load instruction on Line n causes a page fault because the native-safe pages for the original system call wrappers are now locked. The page fault instantly triggers the concealed handler. Next, the wrapper resolver in the concealed handler is activated, which looks up the address of the duplicated wrapper from its secret table stored in the hidden data page. It then loads the secret address of the hidden wrapper into `r7` and finally returns the control back to the trampoline. The trampoline continues from the fault instruction (Line n), and if the security check succeeds, jumps to the address saved in `r7` (Line j), which now points to the hidden wrapper. It is worth noting that, the caller as well as the trampoline are not aware of the system call redirection and wrapper resolution process. The design of the trampoline allows for transparent system call redirection and resolution, which happen only when the native-safe pages are locked. The secret value cannot leak because it is saved only in `r7` between Line m and j, where no return or indirect jump exists that may be exploited.

Native thread orchestrator: This routine is triggered when a page fault occurs on the native-safe pages where the VM internal data are stored. The orchestrator first checks if the page fault is caused by apps' native code, and if so, terminates the thread and raises an alert (*i.e.,* app's code should never directly access the VM internal data). If the fault occurs on a VM thread, the orchestrator performs

```
    ENTRY(__open_trampoline)
    ...
    /*load original wrapper*/
m:  ldr     r7, =__open
n:  ldr     r7, [r7]
    ...
    /*perform checks*/
    ...
    /*if checks passed*/
j:  mov     r7, ip
    ...
    END(__open_trampoline)
```

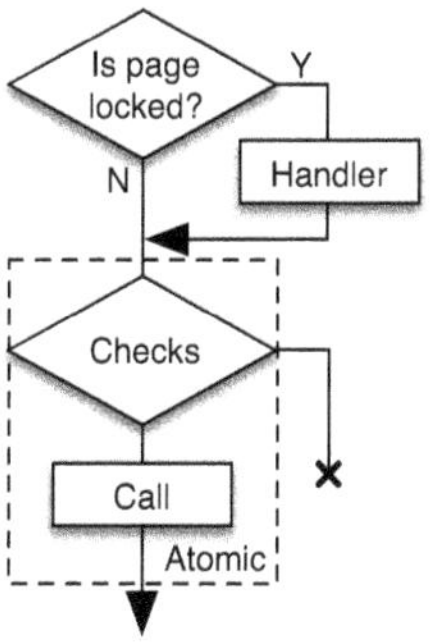

Figure 4: An example system call trampoline, showing the transparent and blind invocation of the wrapper resolution routine (not shown) in the concealed handler.

the thread interleaving as described in § 3.4. The reason for placing the orchestrator in the concealed handler is two-fold. First, the orchestrator needs to perform the sensitive operations (*e.g.,* unlocking the native-safe pages), which are disallowed by the dual-layer interception if performed outside of the concealed handler. Second, the sensitive code in the orchestrator must be protected from abuse by malicious code.

The concealed handler enables the interception invisibility for CASE and, together with the interception integrity measures, solves challenge $C3$.

4. IMPLEMENTATION HIGHLIGHTS

Due to the space constraints, we only highlight the major implementation details that are necessary for others to reproduce and expand our system.

CASE injection & initialization: CASE is mostly written in C with a few helper classes in Java (*e.g.,* the call stack dumper for Java code). It is compiled into a JNI library along with a few Dalvik class files. Our automatic app patcher employs the widely used Apktool to inject CASE into an app. The patcher first adds (or rewrites) a subclass of the `android.app.Application` in the app. The subclass is automatically invoked by the OS to initialize the app itself as well as additional VM instances, if any, created during the app execution (*e.g.,* an `isolatedProcess` or a remote service). The `Application` subclass initializes CASE by setting up the dual-layer interception, the native-safe pages, and the concealed handler prior to app code execution. This way, we can ensure that CASE is always invoked at app entry point and protect CASE from attacks at the initialization phase. If the app contains native code, the patcher then verifies that the code does not use system call instructions. The verification runs conservatively on ambiguous instruction sets (*e.g.,*`x86`) in favor of soundness: any legitimate instruction sequence that starts with a system call instruction and proceeds to an indirect control transfer is deemed as dangerous and triggers an alert. The patching process is fairly straightforward and does not modify the original app code, and therefore, does not cause compatibility issues or broken apps. The patched app can run on all the Android versions that the app originally targets.

Since app developers are our main target as the users of CASE, we allow app developers to provide their own key to sign the app after the rewriting process. As app developers are expected to have a good understanding of their own app, as well as the expected functionality of the untrusted or potentially vulnerable modules, they are capable of making reasonable policy rules. We also assume that the app developers are able to appropriately handle resource access denial, for example, by either notifying the device users or by silently terminating the app. Although the app needs to be repackaged if its security policies are updated, we believe such updates occur far less often than app update itself, and would not bring noticeable overhead to app's updating process.

Function call interception: CASE uses two standard dynamic function call interception techniques, namely GOT hooking and binary patching. The basic functioning of both techniques are well known. However, we gained new insights into using the techniques on Android for enforcing security policies.

Our prototype uses GOT hooking for intercepting invocations of system call wrappers. The technique is particularly convenient to implement on Android, whose dynamic linker resolves all GOT entries ahead of time (*i.e.,* no support for lazy binding) and locks the memory pages afterwards. Therefore, CASE overwrites all the GOT entries that correspond to the functions in $MinSet$ at once during the CASE initialization phase without having to force the linker to resolve the symbols. We also patch any newly loaded libraries by monitoring all `dlopen` system calls. Since all system calls are exported and resolved from GOT at the time of use, we can easily achieve complete mediation.

On the other hand, since there are no centralized function pointer tables for VM-level APIs, we choose binary patching to intercept VM-level APIs in $MinSet$. Although not as easy to implement, the binary patching technique offers two unique benefits over the GOT hooking technique. First, it is quick to apply and takes effect globally inside a process. For example, patching VM APIs only takes a linear memory copy (*i.e.,* overwriting the old code page with a branch instruction to the trampoline) and does not involve any table lookups or per-function treatment as GOT hooking does. It is effective on all upcoming API calls regardless of the calling module. Second, it can intercept calls to private functions (in this case, private VM APIs), which are not exported to GOT at all. These functions exist because they are supposed to be only used by the Dalvik VM internally (*i.e.,*`libdvm.so`). External API calls are secured by the native-safe pages.

Native-safe pages: The native-safe pages store the security-critical resources that do not have any dominant accessors, including system call wrappers and the VM's internal data. The implementation of the native-safe pages can directly influence the security and robustness of the entire CASE system. The location of the native-safe pages for the system call wrappers have to remain undecidable by adversaries. It is known that, even if ASLR is present, the memory pages allocated using `mmap` are typically continuous in virtual memory and thus deterministic. CASE forces `mmap` to allocate a randomly located page sequence by providing a random base address in user space and then verifying the allocation result. In addition, CASE makes the first and the last page in the sequence non-accessible and uses them as guard pages to prevent linear memory search by malicious code.

The system call wrappers that are not security-sensitive, but are located on the same memory pages as functions in $MinSet$, have to be handled carefully. We do not monitor these functions, but since these pages will be locked at the time the execution enters native threads, we copy them into the native-safe pages as well. We silently forward the non-sensitive system calls to their counterparts in the native-safe pages without performing any policy checks. In addition, the native-safe pages for the internal runtime data have to cover not only the data regions of `libdvm` (*e.g.,*`.data` and `.bss`) that are page aligned, but also the heap area for the VM's book-keeping data that is pre-allocated by the Zygote process and not mixed with apps' data.

Concealed handler: The concealed handler ensures the hidden functions and data are not referenced by any user-space pointers. The hidden code and data pages required by the concealed handler are allocated during the initialization phase in a similar fashion as the native-safe pages for system call wrappers. All global data items used by concealed handler are organized into an array, which is always allocated at the beginning of the hidden data page. The data are referenced via relative offset to the array's starting address, which is also the base address of the hidden data page. This implementation detail allows for efficient address resolution and easy data access. Before being mapped to the hidden code page, the concealed handler's code is localized with the hardcoded array address adjusted to the address of the hidden data page. Therefore, during runtime, concealed handler's code always finds its data via simple array indexing.

CASE registers the concealed handler as the handler for the relevant signals, (*e.g.*, `SIGSEGV`, `SIGSTOP`, and `SIGCONT`). The original handlers are saved, and can invoked by the concealed handler when a signal is not meant to be handled by CASE. This is critical for preserving Dalvik's signal handling chains. When a signal is raised as a result of CASE's enforcement, concealed handler parses the `ucontext` object on the stack, which describes the execution context when the fault occurred, including the instruction pointer, the register values, *etc.* The concealed handler uses the instruction pointer to determine which routine should handle the signal. It may also receive implicit parameters from the registers and return values back by overwriting the registers (*e.g.*, passing the address of a hidden system call wrapper via the register). All the routines in the concealed handler are kept short and do not perform asynchronous operations or raise signals, a requirement imposed by the OS on signal handlers.

5. DISCUSSION

Policy Specification: This paper focuses on proposing the new module-level enforcement mechanism while leaving the formal specification and automatic generation of policies for future work. However, for the sake of demonstration, we include below a basic language specification that we currently use to compose policies for CASE:

```
Rule::= {Sub Op Obj Cond}
Sub ::= class_ID|JNI_lib_name
Op  ::= read|write|execute
Obj ::= {sys_resource|vm_resource} x Mod
Mod ::= scope_modifier
Cond::= runtime_conditions
```

We designed CASE's policy specification to be comprehensible and easy to use for intended users, namely app developers. They can define policies to restrict untrusted modules in two simple steps: (1) identifying the modules with the class names or executable names; (2) choosing the accessible resources and the access conditions for the modules. For example, an app developer can define a policy that allows a third-party library in her app (*i.e.*, `Sub = com.example.lib.*`) to send/receive SMS to/from a particular number (*i.e.*, `Obj = SMS, Mod=Number:1234567, Op = read & write`). The policy can also require user's presence at the moment of the SMS access (*i.e.*, `Cond=User_Active & App_Foreground`). This policy prevents an untrusted library, which only needs limited SMS capability (e.g., for user registration), from stealthily sending SMS to unexpected numbers (*e.g.*, a premium number) or reading SMS meant for other apps (*e.g.*, a 2nd-factor authentication code). We note that, to define policies, app developers do not need any knowledge about how the untrusted modules work but just a high-level understanding of the modules' expected behaviors. Developers should have this high-level understanding of the modules because they have chosen to use the modules in their apps. Furthermore, with the help of a simple policy generator[2], app developers would not need to understand the policy syntax or write raw policies. Instead, the tool would assist developers via GUI to choose modules, resource types, access scope, and conditions, and eventually create policy stubs based on developers' selections. Therefore, we do not expect policy definition would prevent app developers (or users), including those with little security expertise, from making use of CASE to protect their apps.

Porting CASE to ART: We used Dalvik as the reference VM for implementing CASE because it was the default Android runtime when our project started. Although ART has replaced Dalvik in recent Android releases, we confirmed that the Dalvik-based design of CASE applies to ART as well and porting CASE to ART does not involve design changes. This is because, despite the major difference introduced by the ahead-of-time compilation, the two runtimes largely share the same in-VM interfaces for class and object management and use the same JNI bridge, which allows the dual-layer interception, the native-safe pages, and the concealed handler to remain effective for ART.

Alternative Usages: While it is mainly designed for app developers, CASE can be alternatively used by the IT administrators and end users to enforce module-level security policies on apps that, for instance, using apps containing untrusted or unwanted modules. Although it is challenging for average users to identify app modules and define proper policies, we believe that tech-savvy users and IT administrators should be able to describe modules using packages names and class names (i.e., easily retrievable and human readable) without understanding app designs or needing developer assistance. However, when not used by app developers, CASE cannot produce app packages signed by the original app developer keys, which may cause inconvenience to automatic app updates.

Memory Layout Disclosure: The effectiveness of the native-safe pages and the concealed handler partly relies on the confidentiality of app memory layout. There have been known channels through which the memory layout of a process can be observed or inferred. Our design considers and blocks these channels. For instance, certain system calls take user-space addresses as parameters, and when receiving an inaccessible address, they return a error code rather than triggering a page fault. By employing the dual-layer interception, CASE prevents attackers from exploiting these system calls to bypass guard pages that surrounding hidden pages. Similarly, CASE blocks direct access to the `/proc/self/maps` files by JNI code, preventing memory mapping disclosures.

6. ANALYSIS AND EVALUATION

We conducted a series of experiments to evaluate CASE in terms of its completeness and robustness, compatibility with COTS apps, and runtime overhead. Our experiments involved the following sets of apps and test inputs:

($S1$) a set of 420 apps, selected from the 50 most downloaded apps across 26 function categories from Google Play and HiAPK (a top alternative Android market), excluding games and apps that do

[2]Building this tool should only involve straightforward development effort and is out of the scope of this paper.

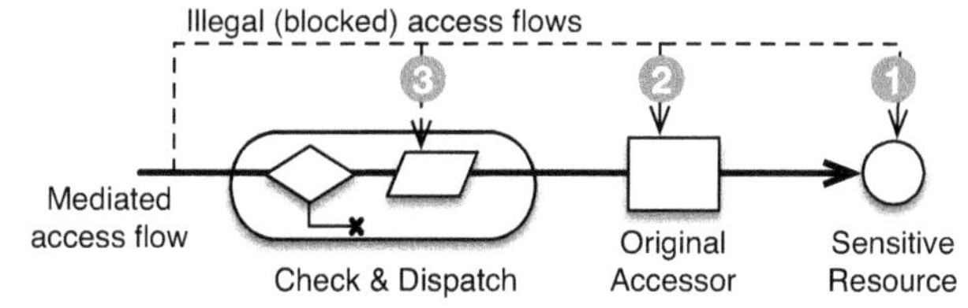

Figure 5: Potential evasion or tampering of CASE

not use any sensitive permission (*i.e.,* an indicator of low security relevance);

($S2$) a set of 20 apps randomly drawn from $S1$ for semi-manual, in-depth study and tests;

($S3$) a set of in-house and Android's unit tests for stress and coverage testing.

We first analyzed the *completeness and robustness* of CASE's enforcement (§ 6.1). We then examined CASE's *deployment cost and compatibility* by exercising our automatic app patcher against $S1$ and subsequently testing the patched apps (§ 6.2). The results show that patching CASE into legacy and COTS apps is fast, effortless, and free of compatibility issues. We finally measured the *runtime overhead* of CASE in three settings: enforcing generic security policies on a large number of apps in $S1$; enforcing app-specific policies (*i.e.,* manually tailored for each app) on the 20 apps in $S2$; and stress testing the critical paths of CASE using $S3$ (§ 6.3).

The results indicate that CASE is efficient for practical use. All experiments were conducted on an LG Nexus 5 phone running Android Kitkat.

6.1 Security Analysis

For benign apps, it is safe to assume that their code follows a regular pattern. This indicates that the app code solely relies on system calls for accessing system-managed resources, and the Dalvik VM for Java-level cross-class interactions. We propose *dual-layer interception* to monitor app's sensitive operations by intercepting APIs at two layers, namely the system call wrappers and the interfaces exposed by the Dalvik VM. We identified a minimum set of functions that cover all cross-boundary interactions. This way, we could effectively and completely mediate all security-critical activities on both layers.

In addition to the comprehensive security enforcement, CASE defends against the most powerful adversaries at app-level, who may attempt either bypassing security checks or tampering with the CASE enforcement mechanism itself. The adversaries are allowed to deploy malicious code, either in Java or in native form, in enforced apps alongside CASE. Figure 5 generalizes possible evasions into three types. We show that CASE is designed to provide countermeasures to all of them and achieve robustness.

First, malicious native code may attempt to directly access the sensitive resources (①) without invoking the typical resource accessors. For example, it may perform system calls using embedded assemblies rather than the `libc` wrappers; it may also locate the VM's internal data items in memory (*e.g.,* class table) and manipulate the raw data without calling VM APIs. **Countermeasure**: CASE forbids embedded system call instructions in apps. This is checked by the automatic patcher at app rewriting phase. For sensitive VM data, we allocate *data native-safe pages* to hold these data. The native-safe pages are hidden at random memory location, and protected with guard pages to prevent memory scan. We allow the native-safe pages to be accessible when Java threads are running, since code compiled from high-level languages (*i.e.,* Java) can not directly access virtual memory. When native threads starting, we immediately lock the pages and prevent access to VM data.

Second, malicious code may try to bypass the function interception by directly invoking the resource accessors (②). For example, native code can invoke the system call wrappers or VM-level APIs via function pointers or indirect jumps. **Countermeasure**: CASE disables the default system call wrappers while native code is running. Even if malicious native code can acquire the function pointers to the system call wrappers, directly invoking them will cause a page fault. Similarly, we use *code native-safe pages* to keep a hidden copy of system call wrappers. Only legitimate system calls that go through our trampolines are redirected to these code native-safe pages. On the other hand, although the VM-level APIs are not protected as the system call wrappers, we lock the memory pages that hold VM internal data essential to these APIs. Any unchecked invocation of such APIs eventually will hit the locked data native-safe pages and fail.

Third, sophisticated malware may launch control-flow attacks against the trampolines (③), where intercepted calls to functions are checked for policy compliance and dispatched to the original accessors if the check passes. For example, malware may perform ROP-style tricks that coerce the control flow to jump to the middle of a trampoline right after the checkpoint, continue on the affirmative branch, and later return to the malicious code when the resource access finishes. **Countermeasure**: CASE ensures the atomicity of its security checks and trampolines. For system calls, we design the *concealed handler* mechanism to only expose the address of the hidden system call wrappers if the execution arrives at the trampolines via the first instruction and goes through the entire check. For VM APIs, the data native-safe pages remain locked during the entire execution of native code, which strictly blocks any access to the VM's internal data by native code.

6.2 Deployment Cost and Compatibility

The automatic app patcher was designed to minimize the efforts and cost associated with deploying CASE in practice. It helps developers to enforce fine-grained policies and least-privilege principle among different modules in their apps without having to implement the complex enforcement mechanisms by themselves. To measure the performance of the app patcher, and more generally, the overhead and compatibility of CASE's rewriting approach, we ran the patcher through the 420 apps in $S1$. We used a set of generic policies that reflect some common security needs of most apps, rather than specifically defining a policy for each app:

($P1$) `com.package execute (dlopen)x(Path: /system/lib/) always`

($P2$) `com.package.module read|write (File-sys)x(Path:$APPHOME/module/) always`

($P3$) `com.package.main read (Location)x( NULL) always`

($P4$) `com.package read|write (Internet)x( IP:xxx.xxx.xx.xxx) always`

($P5$) `com.package.module1 read (fieldID)x (com.package.module2) module1==module2`

On average, each app takes 6.34 seconds to be patched and the size of the app executable increases by 65.58 KB or 4.22%. Such costs are generally affordable given that the patching process happens only once per app install in an offline fashion and today's mobile devices are usually equipped with ample storage.

6.3 Runtime Overhead

The runtime overhead of CASE-enabled apps include the approach-intrinsic overhead and policy-specific overhead. The former is universal to all CASE-enabled apps whereas the latter depends on the nature and complexity of enforced security policies.

Table 2: Unit testing results

Operation	Number of runs	Crossed interface	Intercepted API	Per-operation time (ms) original app	Per-operation time (ms) CASE-enabled app	Per-operation time (ms) overhead	Per-operation overhead (%)
Open a file	1,000	module-to-system	open	0.310512	0.314719	0.004207	1.35%
Modify the value of a global variable in another package	100,000	module-to-module	setField	0.021202	0.022097	0.000895	4.22%
Query 200 contacts	500	module-to-module	ioctl	38.181994	38.920963	0.738970	1.94%
Network access	10,000	module-to-system	connect	0.080651	0.087197	0.006546	8.12%

Table 3: End-to-end performance tests on $S2$

	Package name	**Activity**	**Original app (ms)**	CASE-**enabled app (ms)**	**Overhead (ms)**	**Overhead**
1	com.jb.mms	.ui.MainPreference, .ui.NotifyPreference	400.00	408.00	8.00	2.00%
		.ui.ComposeMessageActivity	356.00	370.00	14.00	3.93%
2	com.facebook.orca	.auth.LoginScreenActivity, .auth.SilentLoginActivity	978.00	1,018.00	40.00	4.09%
		.threadlist.ThreadListActivity, .creation.CreateThreadActivity	962.00	1,037.00	75.00	7.80%
3	com.fsck.k9	.activity.MessageList	312.00	318.00	6.00	1.92%
4	com.snda.inote	.activity.NoteViewActivity, .activity.NoteEditActivity	1,266.00	1,287.00	21.00	1.66%
5	com.yelp.android	.ui.activities.ActivityNearby, .ui.activities.ActivityBusinessListResults	333.33	357.00	23.67	7.10%
6	wind.android	.setting.activity.MoreAppSettingctivity, .setting.activity.SystemSettingActivity	352.00	370.00	18.00	5.11%
7	com.symantec.android.spot	.ui.EulaActivity	473.00	492.00	19.00	4.02%
8	com.corewillsoft.usetool	.chrome.browser.ChromeTabbedActivity	360.00	376.00	16.00	4.44%
9	com.zhangdan.safebox	.activities.MainActivity	584.00	632.00	48.00	8.22%
		.activities.card.AddCreditCardActivity, io.card.payment.CardIOActivity	902.00	908.00	6.00	0.67%
10	com.tecace.cameraace	com.android.camera.CaptureActivity	244.44	248.89	4.45	1.82%
		com.tecace.photogram.PEffectActivity	774.00	782.00	8.00	1.03%
11	com.piriform.ccleaner	.ui.activity.CleanActivity, .ui.activity.CleanCacheActivity	234.00	266.00	32.00	13.68%
		.ui.activity.AppManagerActivity	166.00	178.00	12.00	7.23%
12	com.gemini.calendar	.Month	236.25	242.50	6.25	2.65%
13	cn.ecook	.MainTab, .ui.SearchUser	730.00	796.00	66.00	9.04%
14	com.hotelvp.tonight	.activities.CityListActivity	260.00	280.00	20.00	7.69%
15	cn.dict.android.pro	.activity.UserGuidanceActivity, .activity.TranslationActivity	556.00	605.00	49.00	8.81%
16	com.fstop.photo	.ListOfFoldersActivity	840.00	882.00	42.00	5.00%
17	com.jiubang.go.backup.ex	.recent.summaryentry.SingleInfomation-ViewActivity, .BackupProcessActivity, .ReportActivity	806.00	850.00	44.00	5.46%
		.RestoreProcessActivity, .ReportActivity	300.00	326.00	26.00	8.67%
18	com.tvkdevelopment.nobloat	.activities.BackedUpApps	412.00	414.00	2.00	0.49%
		.activities.Blacklist	408.00	432.00	24.00	5.88%
19	org.mightyfrog.android. simplenotepad	.FolderView, .NoteEditor, .Checklist	366.00	382.00	16.00	4.37%
20	com.qo.android.am3	com.quickoffice.mx.FileSystemListActivity, com.quickoffice.mx.FileListActivity, com.quickoffice.mx.SaveFileAsActivity	390.00	434.00	44.00	11.28%
		Average	14,001.02	14,691.39	690.37	4.93%

First, we measured the approach-intrinsic overhead in the same experiment setup as the compatibility test, where the 420 patched apps in $S1$ were automatically exercised with the generic policies enforced. The average delay in cold app startup is 0.174 seconds (a 17.6% slowdown). The timed period starts from the moment when the app launch intent is sent out to the moment when the default activity-ready Logcat message is captured. The slowdown is a result of loading the CASE library and initializing the enforcement mechanisms. The absolute delay is hardly noticeable in practice and varies marginally across different apps. The increases in peak CPU `utime` and peak CPU `stime` are 4.47% and 9.01%, respectively. They represent the worst case CPU utilization increases in user and kernel modes. The increased memory utilization, 1.19MB on average (`Uss`), matches with the sizes of CASE library and the native-safe pages. To measure CASE's impact on battery consumption, we conducted two drain tests on a fully charged battery: the first test repeatedly ran the unpatched apps in $S1$ till the battery died and the second test did the same but on the patched apps in $S1$. The first test lasted 5.52h while the second test lasted 5.19h (20 minutes 2 seconds less), indicating a 6.43% battery overhead of CASE.

Our second experiment consists of a series of stress testing. We created a set of unit tests (Table 2), each repeatedly carrying out a critical operation that CASE intercepts. The unit tests contain common security checks of different types to simulate the enforcement of comprehensive security policies. Compensating the previous end-to-end overhead evaluation, these unit tests offer insights into CASE's worst-case overhead associated with enforcing certain class of policies listed in $P1$ through $P5$. The results are shown in Table 2. The average per-operation overhead is less than 3.91%, which is unnoticeable in practice because the absolute delays are at the microsecond scale and not accumulative. Moreover, we notice that such overhead is negligible in the much longer end-to-end operations (*e.g.,* accessing files after obtaining the descriptor).

Third, to determine the end-to-end operation overhead of CASE, we performed semi-manual experiments on a sufficient yet manageable size of apps. For each app in $S2$, we exercised the selected features of the app in order to measure the relative delays caused by CASE's security enforcement. The tested features were selected based on the consideration that they should start from a user input event and proceed nonstop (*i.e.,* no further user input or asynchronous wait is needed) till the end marked by certain detectable UI changes. For instance, a testing feature of Yelp is the search of nearby restaurants. It begins with a touch event on the search button, then proceeds to read the GPS data and query the remote server, and eventually displays the search result in a list view.

Fully executing such a feature serves as an end-to-end test of CASE's enforcement overhead. It also allows for semi-automatic and precisely timed tests: we first identify a feature's triggering UI (*e.g.,* a button) and the terminating UI (*e.g.,* a result view); with this input, our UI automator then carries out the feature and times its execution in two separate runs—one on the original version and the other one on the CASE-enabled version of the app. The relative increase in the time spent for executing a feature quantifies CASE's end-to-end performance overhead. Table 3 shows the end-to-end testing results on the apps in $S2$. Across all the 20 apps, CASE incurred an average enforcement overhead of 4.93% (Table 3).

7. RELATED WORK

To mitigate threats imposed by malicious or vulnerable apps, several solutions have been proposed to enhance Android app security. These solutions either extend the underlying Android framework or instrument the app to include inline mediation hooks.

OS-level protection: MockDroid [3] and DeepDroid [22] mock sensitive data items when apps are not allowed to access them. AirBag [24] provides a virtualized app runtime environment that mediates apps' access to system resources. [4] prevents privilege escalation attacks by validating all inter-app communication (ICC) against app permissions. FlaskDroid [5] and SEAndroid [19] mediate component interactions for security enforcement. TaintDroid [9] and AppFence [11] dynamically track sensitive information within an application to detect privacy violations. ASM [10] and ASF [2] extend Android security with programmable interfaces and multilayer access control. All these works introduce new app protection and security enforcement capabilities to the Android OS. In comparison, CASE addresses a different line of threats, namely the module-level attacks. It enables fine-grained class-level security mediation for the first time, without modifying the OS.

App-level protection: Different Inline reference monitors (IRMs) were proposed to control app's access to sensitive APIs through bytecode rewriting [7, 8, 13] or native code interposition [25]. Similar to CASE, they do not require modifications to the Android framework or OS, but unlike CASE, their mediation may be circumvented by malicious code using reflections or native code. DeepDroid [22] and FireDroid [17] use `ptrace` to monitor an app's behavior. However, these solutions require mobile devices to be unlocked and rooted, which severely limits their practical deployment and arguably weakens device security. AppCage [26] creates app-level sandboxes to constrain app code. While it does not require OS changes or root privileges, its enforcement applies to individual apps and cannot recognize app modules.

Component-level protection: There have been some proposals to split monolithic apps into mutually distrusting components [18, 20, 23] to administer independent security policies for these components. AdSplit [18] isolates advertisement libraries into separate processes and maintain UI consistency. Similarly, NativeGuard [20] runs JNI libraries in separate processes in isolation to the containing app. These process-based isolations work well on independent libraries, but they are too rigid and coarse to be applied to libraries or external code that are closely integrated with apps. Moreover, they suffer from high IPC overheads while requiring stubs to be created for each component. Another relevant body of research, including Apex [14], CRePE [6] and Saint [15], enables configurable and contextual security policies for regulating an app's interaction with other apps and its access to system-managed resources. In comparison, CASE recognizes app modules and allows security policies to be defined and enforced at module level—a currently missing security capability essential for defending against the module-level attacks. Aurasium [25] intercepts resource-accessing system calls via GOT hooking. CASE's dual-layer interception also intercepts system calls, though for a different purpose. In addition, CASE's interception covers the VM-level APIs, captures inter-module crossings, and more importantly, is protected by the native-safe pages and the concealed handler and is robust against malicious Java and native code.

8. CONCLUSION

We have presented the design, implementation and evaluation of CASE, a system that for the first time enables fine-grained module-level security in Android apps. The enforcement does not require any changes in the OS and is robust against malicious Java and native code, thanks to the three novel core techniques: dual-layer interception, native-safe pages, and concealed handler. We implemented a prototype of CASE for Android. Our evaluation against

420 real apps shows that CASE effectively and efficiently enforces module-level security policies, and is suitable for quick and wide adoption to defend against the emerging module-level attacks.

9. ACKNOWLEDGMENT

We thank the anonymous reviewers for their insightful comments. We thank our shepherd, Ardalan Amiri Sani, for his guidance on the final paper revisions. This project was supported by the National Science Foundation (Grant#: CNS-1421824) and the Office of Naval Research (Grant#: N00014-15-1-2378). Any opinions, findings, and conclusions or recommendations expressed in this paper are those of the authors and do not necessarily reflect the views of the National Science Foundation or the Office of Naval Research.

10. REFERENCES

[1] Chinese taomike monetization library steals sms messages. http://researchcenter.paloaltonetworks.com/2015/10/chinese-taomike-monetization-library-steals-sms-messages/.

[2] Michael Backes, Sven Bugiel, Sebastian Gerling, and Philipp von Styp-Rekowsky. Android security framework: Extensible multi-layered access control on Android. In *ACSAC*, 2014.

[3] Alastair R. Beresford, Andrew Rice, Nicholas Skehin, and Ripduman Sohan. MockDroid: Trading privacy for application functionality on smartphones. In *HotMobile*, 2011.

[4] Sven Bugiel, Lucas Davi, Alexandra Dmitrienko, Thomas Fischer, Ahmad-Reza Sadeghi, and Bhargava Shastry. Towards taming privilege-escalation attacks on Android. In *NDSS*, 2012.

[5] Sven Bugiel, Stephan Heuser, and Ahmad-Reza Sadeghi. Flexible and fine-grained mandatory access control on Android for diverse security and privacy policies. In *USENIX Security*, 2013.

[6] Mauro Conti, Vu Thien Nga Nguyen, and Bruno Crispo. CRePE: Context-related policy enforcement for Android. In *ISC*, 2011.

[7] Benjamin Davis and Hao Chen. RetroSkeleton: Retrofitting Android apps. In *MobiSys*, 2013.

[8] Benjamin Davis, Ben Sanders, Armen Khodaverdian, and Hao Chen. I-ARM-Droid: A rewriting framework for in-app reference monitors for Android applications. 2012.

[9] William Enck, Peter Gilbert, Seungyeop Han, Vasant Tendulkar, Byung-Gon Chun, Landon P. Cox, Jaeyeon Jung, Patrick McDaniel, and Anmol N. Sheth. TaintDroid: An information-flow tracking system for realtime privacy monitoring on smartphones. *ACM Trans. Comput. Syst.*, 2014.

[10] Stephan Heuser, Adwait Nadkarni, William Enck, and Ahmad-Reza Sadeghi. ASM: A programmable interface for extending Android security. In *USENIX Security*, 2014.

[11] Peter Hornyack, Seungyeop Han, Jaeyeon Jung, Stuart Schechter, and David Wetherall. These aren't the droids you're looking for: Retrofitting Android to protect data from imperious applications. In *ACM CCS*, 2011.

[12] Trend Micro Inc. Library file in certain android apps connects to c&c servers. http://blog.trendmicro.com/trendlabs-security-intelligence/library-file-in-certain-android-apps-connects-to-cc-servers/, 2012.

[13] Jinseong Jeon, Kristopher K. Micinski, Jeffrey A. Vaughan, Ari Fogel, Nikhilesh Reddy, Jeffrey S. Foster, and Todd Millstein. Dr. Android and Mr. Hide: Fine-grained permissions in Android applications. In *ACM SPSM*, 2012.

[14] Mohammad Nauman, Sohail Khan, and Xinwen Zhang. Apex: Extending Android permission model and enforcement with user-defined runtime constraints. In *ACM ASIACCS*, 2010.

[15] Machigar Ongtang, Stephen McLaughlin, William Enck, and Patrick McDaniel. Semantically rich application-centric security in android. In *ACSAC*, 2009.

[16] Paul Pearce, Adrienne Porter Felt, Gabriel Nunez, and David Wagner. AdDroid: Privilege separation for applications and advertisers in Android. In *ACM ASIACCS*, 2012.

[17] Giovanni Russello, Arturo Blas Jimenez, Habib Naderi, and Wannes van der Mark. FireDroid: Hardening security in almost-stock Android. In *ACSAC*, 2013.

[18] Shashi Shekhar, Michael Dietz, and Dan S. Wallach. AdSplit: Separating smartphone advertising from applications. In *USENIX Security*, 2012.

[19] Stephen Smalley and Robert Craig. Security Enhanced (SE) Android: Bringing flexible MAC to Android. In *NDSS*, 2013.

[20] Mengtao Sun and Gang Tan. NativeGuard: Protecting Android applications from third-party native libraries. In *ACM WiSec*, 2014.

[21] Symantec. Ad library behind pulled ios apps also used in android development. http://www.symantec.com/connect/blogs/ad-library-behind-pulled-ios-apps-also-used-android-development, 2015.

[22] Xueqiang Wang, Kun Sun, Yuewu Wang, and Jiwu Jing. DeepDroid: Dynamically enforcing enterprise policy on Android devices. In *NDSS*, 2015.

[23] Yifei Wang, Srinivas Hariharan, Chenxi Zhao, Jiaming Liu, and Wenliang Du. Compac: Enforce component-level access control in Android. In *ACM CODASPY*, 2014.

[24] Chiachih Wu, Yajin Zhou, Kunal Patel, Zhenkai Liang, and Xuxian Jiang. AirBag: Boosting smartphone resistance to malware infection. In *NDSS*, 2014.

[25] Rubin Xu, Hassen Saidi, and Ross Anderson. Aurasium: Practical policy enforcement for android applications. In *USENIX Security*, 2012.

[26] Yajin Zhou, Kunal Patel, Lei Wu, Zhi Wang, and Xuxian Jiang. Hybrid user-level sandboxing of third-party Android apps. In *ACM ASIACCS*, 2015.

Targeted Mimicry Attacks on Touch Input Based Implicit Authentication Schemes

Hassan Khan, Urs Hengartner, Daniel Vogel
Cheriton School of Computer Science, University of Waterloo, Canada
{h37khan, urs.hengartner, dvogel}@uwaterloo.ca

ABSTRACT

Touch input implicit authentication ("touch IA") employs behavioural biometrics like touch location and pressure to continuously and transparently authenticate smartphone users. We provide the first ever evaluation of targeted mimicry attacks on touch IA and show that it fails against shoulder surfing and offline training attacks. Based on experiments with three diverse touch IA schemes and 256 unique attacker-victim pairs, we show that shoulder surfing attacks have a bypass success rate of 84% with the majority of successful attackers observing the victim's behaviour for less than two minutes. Therefore, the accepted assumption that shoulder surfing attacks on touch IA are infeasible due to the hidden nature of some features is incorrect. For offline training attacks, we created an open-source training app for attackers to train on their victims' touch data. With this training, attackers achieved bypass success rates of 86%, even with only partial knowledge of the underlying features used by the IA scheme. Previous work failed to find these severe vulnerabilities due to its focus on random, non-targeted attacks. Our work demonstrates the importance of considering targeted mimicry attacks to evaluate the security of an implicit authentication scheme. Based on our results, we conclude that touch IA is unsuitable from a security standpoint.

1. INTRODUCTION

Implicit authentication (IA) employs behavioural biometrics to continuously and transparently recognize and validate the identity of smartphone users. Several biometrics have been proposed such as device usage behaviour [7, 31], gait behaviour [6, 19], keystroke behaviour [9, 13] and touch input behaviour ("touch IA") [4, 8, 11, 12, 14, 20, 21, 33, 34]. Touch IA schemes rely on the finger movement patterns that are generated when people use their device normally: no special gestures are required. Previous work suggests not only do they provide lower detection delay compared to other behavioural biometrics, but they are secure since studies suggest less than 5% of random mimicry attackers would be successful at bypassing them [4, 12, 14]. Consequently, these touch IA schemes have been called *"... the more natural, unobtrusive future of smartphone biometrics"* [24]. Researchers have proposed to use touch IA as a middle ground for users who do not configure any authentication mechanism due to usability issues [33] or as a second line of defense if primary authentication is compromised [14, 20, 33]. Touch IA is even under consideration as a candidate behavioural biometric in the active authentication project of DARPA [5].

The accuracy evaluation in existing touch IA proposals follows a conventional methodology for classifier evaluation. Touch data is collected from users and a classifier is trained for each user by employing a subset of their data as positive training samples and other users' data as negative samples. To calculate accuracy statistics, the remaining data from other users is used as synthetic attack data. Using random attackers who have no knowledge of their victims' behaviour fails to capture more realistic attack scenarios such as shoulder surfing and offline training where attackers have access to their victims' raw touch data. Only Bo et al. [4] and Frank et al. [14] acknowledge their evaluations omit these realistic attack scenarios. Both argue adversaries could not learn invisible features such as touch pressure and swipe acceleration only by shoulder surfing, and Frank et al. [14] rule out attacks using a victim's raw touch data because malware is needed to gather the data. These arguments have been considered *"sound without doubt"* by others [28] and to the best of our knowledge, these attacks have never been evaluated.

We argue that shoulder surfing and offline training are realistic for malicious insiders like friends, family, and colleagues – insiders that are recognized threats [23]. In a recent study on the security perceptions of IA, potential early adopters voiced their concern regarding shoulder surfing attacks [17]. Unlike random attackers, malicious insiders are able to observe their victims' behaviour, giving them with an advantage for shoulder surfing attacks. Moreover, an attacker may launch sophisticated mimicry attacks after gathering the victim's raw touch data by asking that victim to perform a task on the attacker's device. This eliminates the need for malware or sophisticated logging. Previous work provides no evidence that touch IA protects against these targeted mimicry attack scenarios.

We perform the first evaluation of targeted mimicry attacks on three diverse touch IA schemes: SilentSense [4], Touchalytics [14], and Li et al. [20]. These schemes have hundreds of citations and media coverage [24]. We collect

MobiSys'16, June 25-30, 2016, Singapore, Singapore
© 2016 ACM. ISBN 978-1-4503-4269-8/16/06...$15.00
DOI: http://dx.doi.org/10.1145/2906388.2906404

raw touch data from 55 users and multi-angle video of 9 users during the data collection step. We recruit 32 attackers and motivate them to launch shoulder surfing and offline training attacks on selected victims. For shoulder-surfing attacks, the attacker studies videos of the victim to observe their touch behaviour before launching a mimicry attack. For offline training attacks, we develop a feedback and training app, `Mimicker`, that analyses and visualizes a victim's raw touch data to train attackers.

Our results show it is surprisingly easy to bypass touch IA schemes. For 128 unique victim-attacker pairs, we observe a bypass success rate of 84% for shoulder-surfing attacks, much higher than the 5% rate using the random attacker model [4, 14, 20]. Furthermore, among successful attackers, 90% only shoulder surfed for two minutes or less and 70% successfully mimicked in their first attempt. Similarly, for 128 unique victim-attacker pairs, we record a bypass rate of 86% for offline training attacks using `Mimicker` with over 80% of successful attackers bypassing IA on their first attempt. Additional experiments show that for shoulder surfing attacks, an attacker has about 70% chance of success without any knowledge of the underlying features of the touch IA scheme. With offline training, the attacker does not need to know the exact IA scheme used by the victim because schemes have many overlapping features. An attacker can train using one scheme, and bypass other schemes with a 76% bypass success rate. These targeted mimicry attacks not only require fewer resources, but are significantly more devastating compared to a non-targeted generic attack [28]. Our findings provide strong evidence to reconsider the evaluation strategy of IA proposals and question the security of touch IA in general. Our main contributions are:

1. We provide the first ever evaluation of targeted mimicry attacks on touch IA schemes and show their susceptibility to these attacks.
2. We show the accepted assumption that shoulder surfing attacks on touch IA are infeasible due to the hidden nature of some features is incorrect.
3. We outline a method and provide the necessary apparatus for malicious insiders to perform offline training attacks without installing a malicious app on their victims' devices.
4. We release shoulder surfing videos, training models, and our open source `Mimicker` Android app for researchers to replicate our experiments and extend our methodology to other IA domains[1].

2. THREAT MODEL AND ATTACKS

We use the standard threat model used for touch IA schemes [4, 20, 33]. An adversary attempts to gain unauthorized access to a victim's device, which employs a touch IA scheme to continuously authenticate the device user. The victim has either not configured a primary authentication scheme (such as a PIN) or the adversary has bypassed it completely through known mechanisms like shoulder surfing or smudge attacks [2]. Furthermore, the adversary is aware of the presence of a touch IA scheme on the victim's device.

Accuracy numbers reported in the IA literature evaluate this threat model against a random attacker model. This means that data from random attackers with no knowledge of their victims' behaviour is used as synthetic attack data. While this tests scenarios where attackers have possession of a stranger's device, it does not cover attacks by malicious insiders seeking to mimic their victim's behaviour. Smartphone users are concerned about insider threats from friends, family members, and colleagues [23]. IA evaluations should also consider this threat. We evaluate two malicious insider mimicry attacks: shoulder surfing and offline training.

Shoulder surfing attacks: Malicious insiders may observe their victims' interactions. It is impractical for users to conceal all touch input behaviour by shielding the device screen or holding the device at extreme angles. While the "invisible nature of features" argument [4, 14] is true for a subset of features such as touch pressure, it may not hold for features such as touch location and swipe duration. Thus, adversaries may attempt to mimic these observable features. It is unclear whether mimicking observable features by shoulder surfing provides an advantage.

Offline training attacks: Malicious insiders can gain access to the raw touch data of their victims through various techniques. Since any foreground app is able to capture touch input events, malicious insiders can recommend an instrumented app from the official app store to their victims, which in turn collects and transmits raw touch data to the malicious insiders. Malicious insiders may ask their victims to visit a webpage where HTML5 `TouchEvents` are used to skim raw touch data. TapPrints uses similar methods to infer tap locations and corresponding keystrokes by sensing the accelerometer and gyroscope sensors in the background [22]. Finally, malicious insiders have the convenient option of obtaining the raw touch data of their victims by asking them to perform a task (e.g., read an article or view photos) on the insiders' device. This eliminates the need to install or access anything on the victims' devices. Once the insiders gain access to the raw touch data, they can use it to train and mimic their victims' behaviour.

3. BACKGROUND

Before we describe the three touch IA schemes evaluated in our work, we review metrics used in the IA literature when reporting accuracy statistics. A *true accept* (TA) is when an access attempt by a legitimate user is granted; a *false reject* (FR) is when an access attempt by a legitimate user is rejected by the IA scheme. A *true reject* (TR) is when an access attempt by an adversary is rejected; a *false accept* (FA) is when an access attempt by an adversary is granted by the IA scheme. *Equal Error Rate* (EER) is the operating point where the rate of false accepts equals the rate of false rejects.

With these metrics in mind, we now describe and justify the three IA schemes we evaluated.

3.1 Touchalytics [14]

Touchalytics extracts 31 features from the raw touch data of a swipe. These features capture a user's behaviour using four features for the swipe location, three features for the swipe direction, nine features for the velocity and acceleration of the swipe, six features for the duration and the length of the swipe, four features for the curvature of the swipe, three features for the orientation of the finger and the device, and the touch area and the touch pressure at the midpoint of the swipe. An evaluation of Touchalytics on a

[1] https://crysp.uwaterloo.ca/software/mimicker

dataset of 41 participants shows that with the SVM or the kNN classifier it provides an EER of 4% for a window of eight swipes. We chose Touchalytics because in addition to its low EER, to the best of our knowledge, it captures touch input behaviour using the most extensive feature set.

3.2 LXG [20]

LXG[2] derives following features from a swipe gesture: (1) coordinates of the first touch point; (2) touch area at the first touch point; (3) moving direction at the first touch point; (4) moving distance; (5) duration; (6) average moving direction; (7) average moving curvature; (8) average touch area; and (9) max-area portion. The authors also evaluate the tap gesture but they propose using it only as an auxiliary gesture due to its high EER. The authors evaluate LXG with the SVM classifier and they create separate training models for each of the four swipe directions. Their evaluation on a dataset of 75 participants indicates that LXG provides an EER of 8% with a window of eight swipes. We selected LXG because its small feature set complemented our selection of Touchalytics and enabled us to evaluate the impact of feature set size on the training effort of the attackers.

3.3 SilentSense [4]

SilentSense uses a combination of the touch input behaviour and the device's reaction to the touch input to create a model of touch behaviour. SilentSense uses four touch features: the touch pressure, the finger area, the duration, and the location of the swipe; and two device reaction features: the device vibration and the device rotation using the accelerometer and gyroscope sensors, respectively. For the scenarios where users are walking, the micro-movement patterns are adjusted using four walking features. However, since an attacker can choose to stay stationary during the attack, we omit the walking scenario and the corresponding features from our lab-based evaluations. This omission does not impose non-trivial restrictions on the attackers. An evaluation of SilentSense shows that with an SVM classifier on a dataset of 100 users, it achieves an EER of 1% with a window of three swipes. We chose SilentSense due to its low EER and its use of micro-movement features in addition to the touch features.

4. VICTIM DATA COLLECTION

We collected a dataset of raw touch data and video recordings of "victims." Raw touch data is used to train IA classifiers and train attackers for offline mimicry attacks. Video recordings are used for shoulder surfing mimicry attacks. Existing raw touch datasets [14, 33] do not contain accelerometer and gyroscope data, nor do they have accompanying video recordings. Note that we received approval from our university's IRB for all experiments involving human participants.

4.1 Data collection

We implemented two Android apps to collect raw touch data using the same tasks as Touchalytics [14]: a Wikipedia app collects up and down swipes while users read articles of their choice; and a "spot the differences" app collects left and right swipes while users navigate between two slightly different illustrations. Each participant used these apps on a LG Nexus 5 device while in our lab. No directions were given beyond explaining the basic tasks of reading articles and finding differences. Each participant interacted until at least 150 swipes in each direction were logged, the minimum number of training samples required by the IA schemes.

Logged data: For every touch interaction, we record-ed: time stamp in milliseconds; touch point x and y coordinates; touch pressure; area covered by the finger on the screen; finger orientation; screen orientation; rotation values from the gyroscope sensor across three axes; and acceleration values from the accelerometer sensor across three axes. Accelerometer and gyroscope data were collected in a separate thread up to 100Hz.

Videos for shoulder surfing attacks: We captured video of nine participants while they used the data collection apps. At least ten swipes in each direction were captured in two views, above the device and from the side. Each had an unobstructed view of the participant's finger on the touch screen. All videos were shot in 1080p format (1920x1080 pixels) with a frame rate of 29 FPS. The smartphone occupied 4-5% of the video frame. Given the open-ended task, the videos were between 23 and 44 seconds (avg 31 secs).

Data statistics: We recruited 55 participants (a subset of these also participated in the attacks experiment). On average, the participants took 26 minutes to submit data. In total, we logged about 35,000 swipes comprising over 1.1 million touch points, and over 2.5 million accelerometer and gyroscope sensor readings.

4.2 Parameter value selection

We fix two tunable parameters in our experiments, operating threshold and window size. Operating threshold defines the desired values for negatively correlated FA and FR entries. By increasing the operating threshold, FRs can be decreased at the cost of increased FAs (and vice versa). Theoretically, at lower false accept rates (FAR), it should be difficult to launch successful mimicry attacks. Therefore, we set FAR for an arguably higher false reject rate (FRR) of 20% with corresponding FARs of 0.4% for Touchalytics, 4% for LXG, and 0.2% for SilentSense (see §4.3). The effect of the operating threshold is further investigated in §8.3. Window size defines the number of swipes used to calculate a user's authentication score. Larger window sizes increase confidence against classification scores at the cost of increased detection delay. We set the window size to eight swipes since the IA schemes we evaluate provide reasonable accuracy at eight swipes or less (see § 3).

4.3 Evaluation baseline

To establish a baseline, we use our dataset to evaluate the three touch IA schemes against the random attacker model. We construct non-overlapping training and test sets for each user using negative instances from other users' data. Half of the data is used for training, and the remaining for testing. Figure 1 shows the ROC curves that plot true accept rate (TAR) against FAR using an SVM classifier. The ROC curves show an EER of 4% for Touchalytics, 9% for LXG, and 3% for SilentSense. These low EERs are very similar to the rates reported in the original papers and establish the efficacy of these schemes against the random attacker model.

[2]LXG are the initials of the last names of the authors.

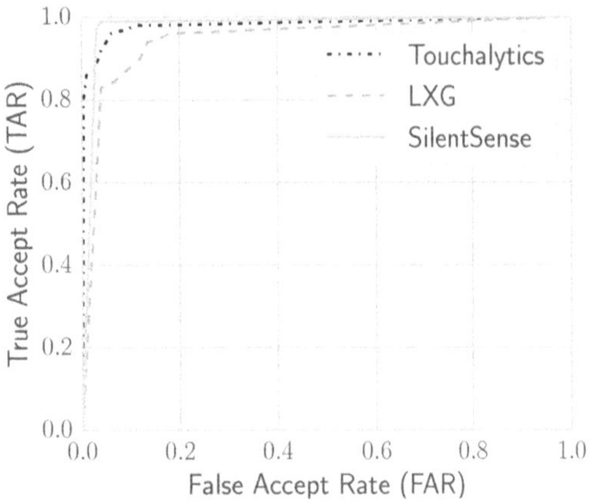

Figure 1: Accuracy of the IA schemes against the random attacker model with a window size of eight swipes.

5. ATTACK DESIGN

In this section, we describe apps and tasks used for offline training attacks and for attack evaluation.

5.1 `Mimicker` for offline training attacks

Our `Mimicker` app trains an attacker to mimic a victim's behaviour using feedback and visualizations generated from that victim's raw touch data. The three main components of `Mimicker` are the target swipe selection module, the training interface, and the feedback module. The target swipe selection module chooses an optimal *target swipe* from actual victim swipes. The training interface displays the target swipe so the attacker can swipe along a similar path (the *mimic swipe*). If the mimic swipe is rejected by the IA scheme, the feedback module displays instructions about a single behavioural aspect to bring the mimic swipe closer to the target swipe (e.g., move start point towards right). The attacker continues adjusting their swipe based on these instructions until their mimic swipe is accepted.

Target swipe selection: Any victim's swipe classified as a true accept can be used as a target swipe. However, our goal is to present the attackers with an optimal swipe to increase their chances of success. We do this by selecting a victim's true accepted swipe with the highest similarity score with the rest of the victim's true accepted swipes. This simple heuristic provides an advantage to the attackers since their mimicry attempts can focus on the hypothesis space with the maximum concentration of true accepted swipes (i.e., the victim's most typical swipes). The target swipe selection module accomplishes this as follows: It creates a dataset, D, with positive samples from the victim's swipes and negative samples from other users' swipes. It uses the kNN classifier ($k = 5$) to find a subset of true accept swipes, S_{TA}, from D. For $n = |S_{TA}|$, it identifies the n nearest neighbours from D for every swipe that belongs to S_{TA}. The similarity score is the number of swipes in the n nearest neighbours that belong to S_{TA}. The similarity score of each swipe is recorded in the similarity rank table and the swipe with the highest similarity score is returned as the target swipe. We also evaluate using non-optimal target swipes in §8.4.

Training interface: Figure 2a provides a screenshot of the `Mimicker` user interface. The target swipe is displayed in green and the last mimic swipe is displayed in black. If the mimicry attempt is successful, "Accepted" is displayed at the top in green, otherwise the instruction from the feedback module is displayed in red. In the upper-left, the success or failure of recent attempts are displayed at swipe- and window-level. The success criteria for window-level are defined in §6.

Feedback module: The feedback module is responsible for comparing the mimic swipe with the target swipe to generate feedback for the attackers. The most obvious way to achieve this is to give feedback based on the classifier feature with the largest difference between target swipe and mimic swipe. However, this would not consider that some features are easier to mimic (e.g., first touch location is easier to mimic compared to midpoint velocity). To address this, the feedback module selects the first feature with absolute difference greater than a threshold from feature categories ordered by ease of adjustment: swipe location, swipe length, swipe duration, touch pressure, touch area, device rotation, device vibration, and swipe curvature. The feedback module focuses on features that are more adjustable for attackers and can be visualized or explained in simple instructions. Some features, like 50%-percentile pairwise velocity and median velocity at the last three points are hard to adjust for and difficult to comprehend. We acknowledge this means our bypass success rates form a lower bound by focusing on low-effort attackers.

5.2 Apparatus for attack evaluation

Personal data on smartphones can be broadly categorized as textual (e.g. emails, texts) and multimedia (e.g. images, videos). Our attack tasks reflect these categories. To further simulate a realistic mimicry attack scenario, the attacker has to multi-task by searching for interesting data while mimicking the victim. We introduce two tasks that capture the multi-tasking nature of real-world mimicry attacks. For attacks on textual data, the attacker is presented with a browser like interface with a collection of paragraphs from Wikipedia where each paragraph discusses a different topic. A question precedes the paragraphs and the attacker has to swipe up or down to find the paragraph that contains the answer to the question and then find the answer within that paragraph. For multimedia data, the attacker is provided with several feline images along with a numeric label for each image in an image viewer app. The attacker is then provided with a description of a feline (e.g., a white kitten) and is asked to swipe left or right to report the numeric label of the image that matches the description. While the attacker has to tap the target app icon to launch it, we do not consider the tap gesture since it provides too few features to be discriminative and has a high EER [14, 20].

At launch time, the apps are trained using the SVM classifier on the victim's training model constructed using positive samples from the victim and negative samples from other users. The apps provide no feedback for individual swipes; however, in case of a reject, the apps display a popup to inform the attackers of their failure (simulating the point when an explicit authentication method should appear in a deployed IA scheme). If the attackers are successful, the apps allow them to complete the task. Finally, the apps record the raw touch, accelerometer and gyroscope data of the attackers along with the result of their mimicry attempt.

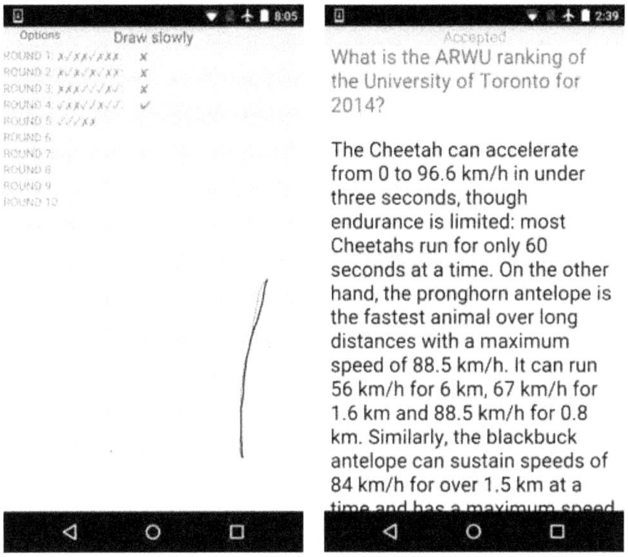

(a) Tracing phase (b) Pseudo-attack phase

Figure 2: Screenshot of `Mimicker` interface.

6. ATTACK PROTOCOL

We now describe the protocol used to conduct attacks. The attack protocol was shaped by a pilot study with three volunteers from our lab. Relevant results from the pilot with subsequent changes to the final protocol are noted where applicable.

6.1 Participant recruitment and motivation

We recruited participants to be attackers in September of 2015 through a university-wide mailing list and using Craigslist and Kijiji under the "other jobs" section. The title of the advertisement was "Participate in a research study on mimicry attacks on a novel authentication scheme for smartphones" and it stated adults who owned and used a smartphone for over six months could participate. Each participant completed a demographic survey and was invited to our lab for the study.

In a real attack, malicious adversaries are motivated to snoop the devices of their victims to find valuable information. For our experiments, we motivate participants to mount best effort attacks with performance-based monetary rewards. All participants were paid \$10, but they could earn another \$6 based on performance. If they mounted a successful mimicry attack on the chosen victim in their first attempt, they received \$0.75. If they mounted a successful attack on the second or subsequent attempt, they received \$0.50.

6.2 Study procedure

The procedure began with each participant submitting raw touch data using the collection apps described in §4.1. This data forms a baseline to measure adjustments made by the participant during the attacks. The experimenter then briefed the participant (using a script and visual aids) with an explanation of touch IA, comprehensible features of their target IA schemes, the apparatus, tasks, and the performance based rewards. We investigate the scenarios where the attackers have limited knowledge of touch IA in §8.2.

Each participant mounted shoulder surfing and offline training attacks as explained below. Attack type order was counterbalanced across participants. For each attack type, the participant was assigned four victims to mimic up and left swipes. In the pilot study, each attacker was assigned only two victims and mimicked four swipe directions, but there were no significant differences in attack success. By reducing to up and left swipes, we could double the number of victims for each attacker. Testing more attacker-victim pairs is most relevant to our work, and up and left swipes are predominant directions for viewing new content. All eight victims assigned to an attacker were unique to avoid carry-over effects.

The four victims for each attack type were split into two groups: two were protected using either Touchalytics or LXG, and two were protected using SilentSense. We decided to assign either Touchalytics or LXG to make it easier for the attackers to remember their target IA schemes' features. The assignment of Touchalytics or LXG, and the order of the target IA schemes, were both counter balanced across the attackers. Attackers trained and mounted their attack on one victim swipe direction at a time using the assigned touch IA scheme and attack type. Swipe direction and the corresponding attack task order was counterbalanced.

Shoulder surfing attacks: The shoulder surfing attack had two parts: watching videos of the victim and attacking by mimicking the victim's swipes while completing the attack tasks (see §5.2). The attacker was shown the victim's shoulder surfing video clips on a 50" television. The attacker was not allowed to hold a device while watching the clips. They were informed about the camera angles and told they could watch the clips from either angle as many times as they wanted. Once the participant indicated they were prepared, the video was closed and they were given the device to mimic the victim's swipes while performing the attack task. Participants were told that if their attack failed, they could watch the clips again before mounting another attack. In §8.1, we evaluate a scenario where the attack occurs one week after shoulder surfing.

Offline training attacks: The offline training attack had two parts: training using the `Mimicker` app and attacking by mimicking the victim's swipes while completing an attack task. Training and attack were performed on two different LG Nexus 5 devices to simulate switching to a victim's device in a real attack.

Training was completed in two phases, a *tracing phase* (Figure 2a) with feedback and the target swipe and a *pseudo-attack phase* (Figure 2b) with only feedback overlaid on the attack task. The participant was informed that they had to bypass the IA scheme for two consecutive windows during each training phase before proceeding to the actual attack. If they were not successful, they had to continue the current training phase for at least ten windows before given another opportunity to bypass the IA scheme. During the attack, no feedback was provided. Attackers had to set the device down in between the tracing and pseudo-attack phases.

The pseudo-attack phase was introduced after the pilot study where 25% of the attacks failed despite successful completion of training. This appeared to be caused by the abrupt change between the tracing phase and the attack task: the attackers did not always memorize the location

Gender:	56% Male
	44% Female
Occupation:	31% Employed
	63% Grad student
	6% Undergrad student
Age group:	41% 18 - 25 years
	31% 26 - 30 years
	28% 31 - 35 years
IT experience:	53% Studied/worked in IT

Table 1: Demographics of the participants (n=32).

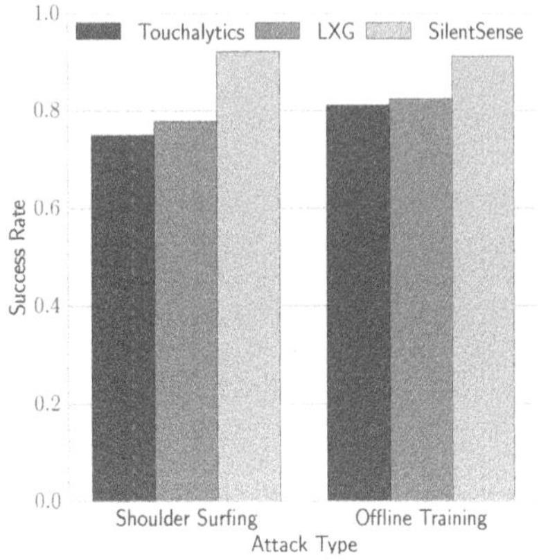

Figure 3: Bypass success rate for the three IA schemes across all attacker-victim pairs.

of the target swipe during training since `Mimicker` displayed the swipe; switching the device after training disrupted their device holding posture; and, unlike training, the attacks involved performing a task in addition to mimicking. The pseudo-attack phase increases training quality for attackers: we argue that a real attacker can leverage similar training mechanisms by approximating the task they plan to attack. For the purpose of our experiment, no feedback was provided for one window (*experiment window*) between the two phases to measure the efficacy of introducing the pseudo-attack phase.

7. EVALUATION

The study was completed by 32 participants (demographics provided in Table 1). In total, 512 attacks were logged (256 for each attack type), which were mounted by 256 unique attacker-victim pairs in up and left directions. We logged 3656 mimic swipes for shoulder surfing and 2984 mimic swipes for offline training attacks. During training, 17,064 swipes were logged.

7.1 Attacker success

We measure the efficacy of attacks on IA schemes through the bypass success rate at the victim-level and the TRR at the window-level. The bypass success rate is defined as the ratio of successful attacks to all attacks of a particular attack type or a particular direction.

Figure 3 shows bypass success rate against each IA scheme for both attack types across all attacker-victim pairs. For shoulder surfing attacks, 75%, 78%, and 92% of the attacks successfully bypassed against Touchalytics, LXG, and SilentSense, respectively. For offline training attacks, 81%, 82%, and 91% of the attacks successfully bypassed against Touchalytics, LXG, and SilentSense, respectively. An independent samples t-test for bypass success rates between shoulder surfing and offline training attacks for each scheme indicates no significant differences. We note that the bypass success rate may be over-reported due to naturally occurring false accepts; however, for the random attacker model, our chosen operating threshold has negligible FAR. Compared to the random attacker model (Figure 1) at a FRR of 20%, we observe about 20,000%, 2000%, and 45,000% increase in FAR for Touchalytics, LXG, and SilentSense, respectively.

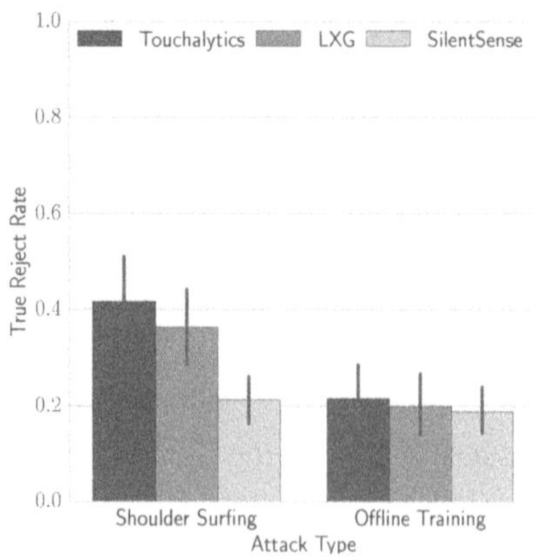

Figure 4: Average within window TRR for the three IA schemes across across all attacker-victim pairs. Error bars represent 95% confidence intervals.

To understand the performance of each scheme against mimicry attacks at the window-level, we calculate the average TRR across each attack window for all victim-attacker pairs for both attack types in Figure 4. Figure 4 shows that significantly lower TRRs are observed for offline training attacks for Touchalytics (t = *2.12*, p = *0.03*) and LXG (t = *3.28*, p = *0.001*). Lower TRRs are expected for offline training attacks because the attacks were mounted after the attackers received training. On the other hand, there are no significant differences between shoulder surfing and offline training attacks for SilentSense (t = *0.56*, p = *0.57*). Since the device reaction features of SilentSense rely on the device holding posture, the attackers were able to observe and mimic it during shoulder surfing. Consequently, the attackers performed better for SilentSense for shoulder surfing attacks when compared with the other schemes.

In terms of swipe direction, the bypass success rate for shoulder surfing attacks was 86% and 82% for up and left swipes. For offline training attacks, the bypass success rates were 85% and 87% for up and left swipes. An independent samples t-test indicates no significant differences between attack type for up (t = *-0.36*, p = *0.71*) and left swipes (t = *1.03*, p = *0.3*).

Note that IA provides continuous authentication so attackers must continue mimicking a victim swipe after swipe. While our experiments require attackers to bypass their victim only once, after learning their victims' behaviour and bypassing IA for one window, they can mimic the behaviour on subsequent windows. This is shown in offline training,

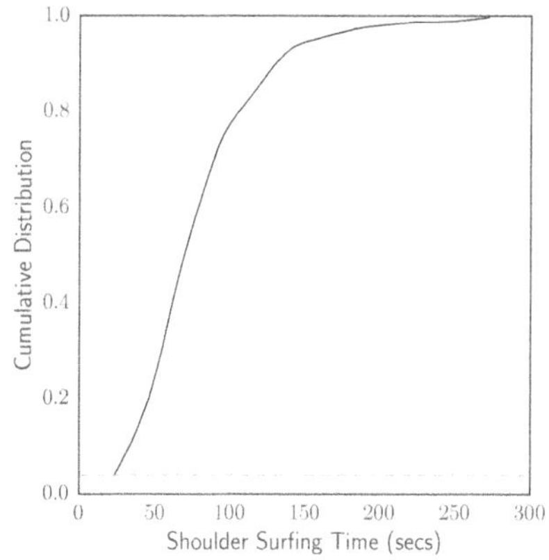

Figure 5: Shoulder surfing time for successful attacks.

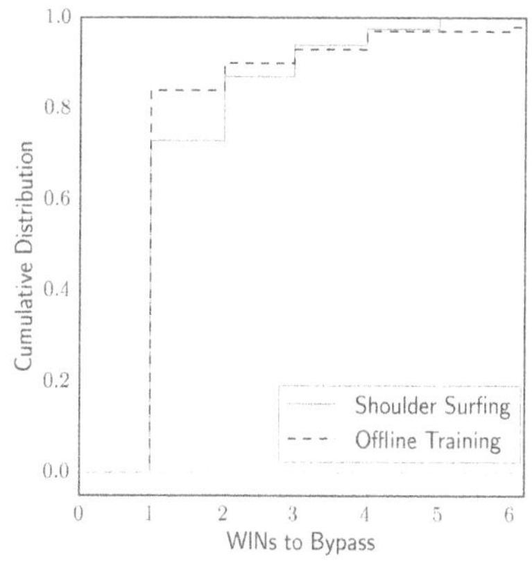

Figure 7: Windows until bypass for successful attacks.

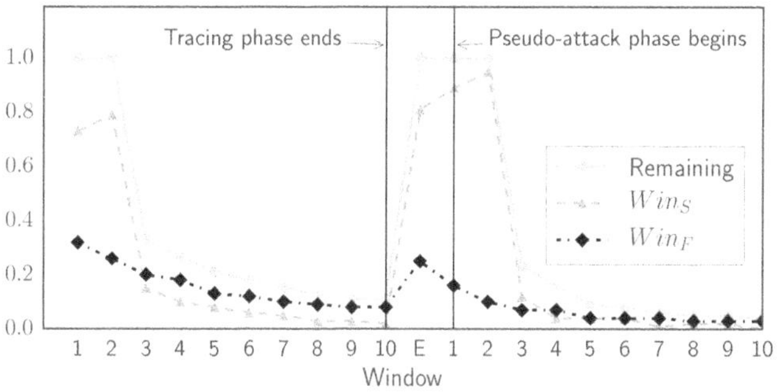

Figure 6: Proportion of attacker-victim pairs who required training for a window (Remaining) and their distribution across successful (Win_S) and failed (Win_F) windows. Window ('E') is the experimental window.

where attackers must bypass IA for three consecutive windows (two pseudo-attack windows and one attack window).

7.2 Attacker effort

To estimate attacker effort, we define three measures: shoulder surfing time (i.e., time spent viewing videos) captures attack preparation effort for shoulder shoulder surfing attacks; the number of windows used during training captures attack preparation effort for offline training attacks; and the number of windows until bypass (number of attempts required to mount a successful attack) captures attack execution effort for both types of attacks.

Shoulder surfing time: Figure 5 shows the cumulative distribution of time spent shoulder surfing before successful attacks. For 15% of successful attacks, the attackers were able to estimate the victims behaviour by observing them only for half a minute. Similarly, 40% and 90% of the successful attackers required less than a minute and less than two minutes of shoulder surfing time. These results indicate attackers require trivial shoulder surfing time for successful attacks.

Number of training windows: Figure 6 shows the proportion of remaining attacker-victim pairs who still required training in a particular window and their distribution across successful (Win_S) and failed windows (Win_F). Recall that our protocol requires attackers to successfully mimic two consecutive windows in each phase. This means that 100% of all attackers will have at least two training windows in both phases in addition to the experiment window between the two phases. As an example for interpreting Figure 6, consider window 3 of the tracing phase. Here 33% of attacker-victim pairs remain because they were unsuccessful at mimicking the target swipe in both window 1 and window 2. Moreover 15% of attacker-victim pairs were successful at mimicking the target swipe while 19% failed in window 3.

Overall, 67% and 77% attacker-victim pairs only required two windows to complete the tracing and the pseudo-attack phase, respectively. A consistent decrease in the proportion of remaining attacker-victim pairs and Win_F from window 3 to window 7 in the tracing phase shows that `Mimicker` feedback was effective. However, after window 7, only 4% are able to successfully complete the training. Some attacker-victim pairs were unable to complete training after ten windows: 11% did not proceed past the tracing phase and 4% did not proceed past the pseudo-attack phase.

Regarding the efficacy of our pseudo-attack training phase, observe that the special experiment window ('E') with only the attack task and no feedback has a 25% increase in Win_F. This window simulates the same abrupt jump from training to attack, and the result is the same as the 25% attack failure rate in the pilot. However, attacker-victim pairs corrected their behaviour when they received feedback: Win_F drops to 16% in Window 1 then to 10% in Window 2.

Number of windows until bypass: Figure 7 shows the cumulative distribution of the number of windows until bypass. This captures the attack execution effort in terms of number of attempts to successfully mount each type of attack. Recall attackers were allowed to retry in case of a failed attack attempt and they could optionally shoulder surf or retrain before their next attempt. For the shoulder surfing attacks, about 73% of the successful attackers only required a single window and 93% required three windows or less to bypass the IA scheme. For offline training attacks, about 85% of the successful attackers bypassed the IA scheme in their first attempt and 90% required two attempts or less to gain access to the victim's device. There were no significant differences across the number of attempts to bypass for IA schemes or attack types.

Attacker effort and success: For shoulder surfing attacks, a Pearson correlation test indicates a slightly negative correlation between success rate of an attacker (the ratio of successful attacks among all attacks of a particular attack

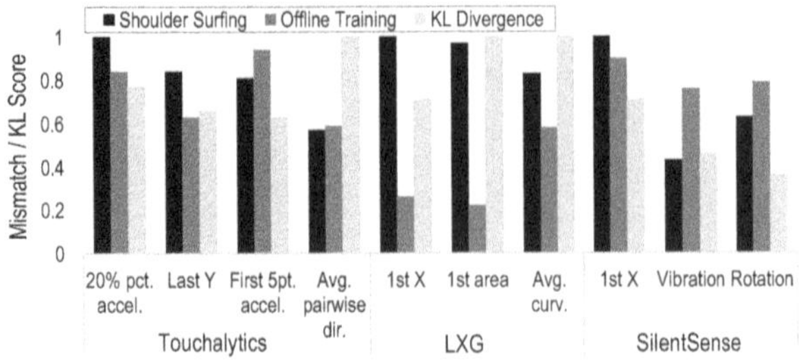

(a) Difficult to mimic features

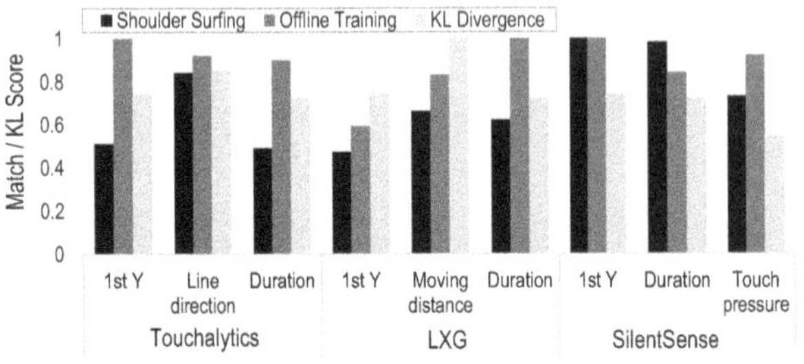

(b) Easy to mimic features

Figure 8: Difficult and easy to mimic features across failed and successful attempts, respectively.

type or direction executed by this attacker) and the amount of time they shoulder surfed *(r = -0.07)*. We also observe a negative correlation between the success rate and the number of retries *(r = -0.19)* for the shoulder surfing attacks. These results indicate that the failed attempts are not due to the lack of effort by the attackers. A similar analysis cannot be performed for offline training attacks since `Mimicker` requires the attackers to attempt training for at least ten windows before giving up and only the attackers who successfully complete training mount attacks.

7.3 Difficult or easy to mimic features

To measure how difficult or easy it was for the attackers to mimic IA schemes, we calculate mismatch and match scores for individual features for successful and failed attempts, respectively. We first calculate the absolute differences between individual features of the target and mimic swipes. The target swipe is explicit in offline attacks, but not when shoulder surfing. For shoulder surfing, the victims' swipe that is the nearest neighbour of the mimic swipe is selected as the target swipe. Mismatch and match scores are calculated by computing the normalized distribution of the occurrence of features in the top three most divergent and similar features, respectively. The Kullback-Leibler (KL) divergence [18] score for features is also calculated for the attacker-victim pairs on the raw input data from the device usage dataset. The KL divergence score provides a baseline for feature similarity and indicates the extent of adjustments made by the attackers for a feature. A higher KL divergence score indicates that the feature values are different across the participants.

Figure 8 shows features with high match or mismatch scores (features with low scores omitted due to space constraints). Features related to swipe curvature, velocity, and acceleration have higher KL divergence and mismatch score for both attack types (see Figure 8a). `Mimicker` does not provide feedback for acceleration or velocity related features since they are hard to comprehend, so we cannot fully conclude they are hard to mimic for offline training attacks. However, we can conclude these features are difficult to mimic for shoulder surfing attacks.

Figure 8b shows that swipe duration and touch pressure are easier to mimic. Some location based features (first and last touch coordinates) fall in both difficult and easy to mimic feature groups, especially for shoulder surfing attacks. We suspect that this is because some attackers are more critical observers than others.

Figure 8a shows that for almost all the features, the mismatch score is lower for offline training attacks. Since `Mimicker` provides feedback, attackers know how to adjust their behaviour to improve performance. This is quite pronounced for the location-related features such as '1st X', '1st Y', and 'Last Y' because `Mimicker` renders the target swipe.

There is an anomaly between LXG and SilentSense mismatch scores for the '1st X' location feature for offline training attacks. We suspect the higher mismatch score for SilentSense is due to its small feature set size and low KL divergence scores for vibration and rotation features. This indicates an overlap in behaviour across participants, increasing the chance that '1st X' is in the top three mismatched features.

8. DISCUSSION

In this section we discuss constrained attack scenarios and the effect of key parameters.

8.1 Basic shoulder surfing attacks

In our evaluation of shoulder surfing attacks, we assume attackers can record a video of their victims and watch it immediately before launching the attack. We were curious about the performance of a basic shoulder surfing attack using direct observation with hand written notes and a delay between observation and attack. To investigate this scenario, we repeated the shoulder surfing portion of the experiment with ten of the participant attackers, but inserted a one week delay between watching the videos and the attack. Each attacker viewed shoulder surfing videos of one victim they did not encounter in the main experiment. They were encouraged to make notes. One week later, the attacker returned to mount the attack on the victim. They were encouraged to consult their notes.

Table 2 compares mean bypass success rates across attackers for shoulder surfing attacks with delay and without delay (taken from their performance in the main experiment). Delayed attacks had a bypass success rate of 80%, 90%, and 90%, which an independent samples t-test did not find significantly different compared to attacks without delay. To gain insight into what attackers felt was important and what features they were mimicking, the notes were collected and their content categorized. Eight attackers drew the device screen with the corresponding location and curve of the swipe. Six of these attackers also noted the holding posture of the victims by drawing the holding hand and the location of the fingers of their victims. Two attackers wrote textual notes (such as: *"right bottom on the edge"*), seven noted the swipe speed (five noted it as slow/medium/fast; one marked a location on a continuous scale from slow to fast, and one wrote

Attack follow up	Success Rate		
	Touchalytics	LXG	SilentSense
Immediate	80%	90%	95%
Delayed	80%	80%	90%

Table 2: Effect of introducing one week delay between shoulder surfing and the attacks.

"one-mississippi"). Three attackers noted of the swiping finger or thumb of the victim. This small experiment suggests basic shoulder surfing is surprisingly effective, even when behavioural characteristics are mimicked at a coarse level.

8.2 Attacks with limited knowledge

In our evaluation, we assume the attacker has full knowledge regarding the victim's IA scheme. We were curious how performance is affected if the attacker has limited knowledge about the IA scheme or its features. In a scheme-oblivious offline attack scenario, the attacker has the victim's raw data and a training app like `Mimicker`, but they do not know the exact IA scheme used by the victim (e.g., whether it is Touchalytics or LXG). For the feature-oblivious shoulder surfing attack scenario, the attacker has no knowledge of any of its features. We evaluate the performance of attacks for these scenarios using the data from our main evaluation.

8.2.1 Scheme-oblivious offline attacks

We simulate this attack scenario by mounting attacks on a different IA scheme than the one used for offline training. For example, if an attacker trained and successfully attacked a victim using `Mimicker` for LXG, would the attacker have been successful if they trained for LXG but that victim actually used Touchalytics? We accomplish this by replaying attack swipes logged during successful attacks in the main experiment on the same victim protected with a different IA scheme. Note there is some inherent overlap in schemes since they share some features, or capture touch behaviour across limited dimensions like location, pressure, area and speed. However, the specific model built by the scheme classifier could still be very different.

Table 3 shows that after training on Touchalytics, bypass success rates increased by 3% when the victim was actually protected by LXG and decreased by 8% when they used SilentSense. After training for LXG, bypass success decreased by 6% for Touchalytics and 11% for SilentSense. Finally, after training SilentSense, bypass success decreased by 17% for Touchalytics and 14% for LXG. There appears to be a greater drop when attackers train on Touchalytics/LXG and attack SilentSense (and vice versa). This is due to less overlap between Touchalytics/LXG and SilentSense (more touch features in the former, more device reaction features in the latter). Overall, 70% or higher bypass success rate for scheme-oblivious attacks indicates attackers may not even need to know the exact scheme used by their victims.

8.2.2 Feature-oblivious shoulder surfing attacks

We evaluate the success rate for feature-oblivious shoulder surfing attacks with an experiment using ten participants from our data collection (they were not attackers in the main experiment). The main experiment shoulder surfing attack protocol was followed except attackers were provided no details about touch IA and were simply told they would

Training Scheme	Scheme for Attacks		
	Touchalytics	LXG	SilentSense
Touchalytics	81%	84%	73%
LXG	76%	82%	71%
SilentSense	75%	78%	92%

Table 3: Bypass success rates for offline training attacks when attack attempts are replayed for different schemes.

	FRR			
	20%	25%	30%	35%
Shoulder surfing	84%	81%	78%	77%
Offline training	86%	85%	83%	83%

Table 4: Bypass success rates for the attackers for different operating thresholds.

attack a device protected using a scheme that employs the touch input and device holding behaviour.

The results show a bypass success rate of 60%, 50% and 80% for Touchalytics, LXG, and SilentSense, respectively. Unsuccessful attackers were briefed on the features after they ended their attempted attacks. These attackers viewed the videos again and mounted attacks on the victims they failed to mimic. For these retry attempts after a briefing, bypass success rates were 75%, 80% and 85% for Touchalytics, LXG and SilentSense, respectively. These results indicate that attackers have a 50% or higher chance of defeating these schemes without any knowledge of the underlying features, but the chances of success increase with feature knowledge.

8.3 Effect of operating threshold

In the main experiment, we chose a FRR of 20%, which created FAR of 0.4%, 4%, and 0.2% for Touchalytics, LXG and SilentSense, respectively. To understand the effect of different operating thresholds on mimicry attacks, we evaluate attacks efficacy at FRRs from 20% to 35% and corresponding FARs. Note that a FRR of 35% is impractical since the IA scheme would reject the device owner for a third of their swipes making it quite unusable. We perform an offline evaluation by replaying the attack data through the IA schemes with different operating thresholds and log the bypass success rates for each threshold. A limitation with this simulated evaluation is that offline attackers are likely to perform better if they trained at the tested FRR. However, these results do provide a lower bound for bypass success rate.

The results in Table 4 show only a 7% decrease in success rate when the FRR is increased from 20% to 35% for shoulder surfing attacks. For offline attacks, the decrease in success rate is only 3%. There is a sublinear decrease in bypass success rate for a linear increase in FRRs, which is similar to the sublinear increase in FAR for linear increase in FRR (see Figure 1). We believe the lower relative decrease in the bypass success rate for offline training attacks is a result of the low intra-window TRR (see Figure 4).

8.4 Effect of different target swipes

The `Mimicker` target swipe selection module selects the 'best' swipe from a set of 150 swipes of the victim (§5.1). We were curious how an attacker's bypass success rate was affected if they could not collect a large number of their victim's swipes and had to train using a suboptimal target swipe. To evaluate this, ten volunteers from the main experiment participated in a smaller experiment spanning three ten-minute sessions of offline training attacks, with each session spaced one week apart (to mitigate carry over effects). Each attacker was assigned two victims; one victim was protected with LXG and the other with SilentSense. For each session, the attackers performed offline training attacks using the best, average, and worst swipes (the order was counter balanced across attackers). The best, average and worst swipes correspond to the top, middle and bottom locations of the similarity rank table, respectively (see §5.1). These well defined categories of swipes avoided a possible confound when randomly picking a target swipe.

The bypass success rates for the best, average and worst target swipes for LXG were 90%, 100% and 60%, respectively. For SilentSense, the bypass success rates were 100%, 100% and 80% for best, average, and worst swipes, respectively. A one way between subjects ANOVA score indicates a significant effect of target swipe on the intra-window TRR for the three target swipe types $(F(2, 27) = 9.18, p = 0.0009)$. Post hoc comparisons using the Tukey HSD test indicated that the mean for the intra-window TRR for the best $(M = 0.05, SD = 0.07)$ and average $(M = 0.02, SD = 0.04)$ swipes were significantly different than the worst swipe $(M = 0.47, SD = 0.44)$. However, the intra-window TRR for the best swipe did not significantly differ from the average swipe. These results indicate that while there is a reasonable chance ($\geq$ 70%) of success using any true accepted swipe as the target swipe, attackers can increase their chances of success by collecting more raw data to mine for an optimal target swipe.

8.5 Attacker- or victim-bound success?

Previous work has shown the performance of a generic attack against touch IA schemes is victim dependent [28], meaning some victims are easier to attack than others. We investigate if the same is true for mimicry attacks. A Kruskal-Wallis test comparing bypass success rates found no significant effect across victims, indicating no victims were easier to bypass than others. The same test was used to compare bypass success rates across attackers. No significant effect was found, indicating no attackers were better at mounting attacks than others.

9. LIMITATIONS

Like most human subjects studies, the scope is limited to people willing to participate. We discuss more specific limitations below.

We used similar devices for data collection and attacks. If an attacker collects a victim data using a device with a different form factor than the victim's device, a transformation would need to applied to the features.

We used the same tasks to collect victim data and evaluate attacker performance. This setup represents a resourceful adversary able to obtain a victim's data using an app similar to the target. Even if an adversary used apps with different input behaviour, the results will likely be similar (previous work reports 5-8% increase in EER due to significantly different apps [16]).

The participants who volunteered for the additional experiments (reported in §8) did not receive remuneration for their participation. Consequently, these participants may had less motivation, which may have affected their performance.

We omitted difficult to comprehend features from briefings and the feedback module of ***Mimicker****.* We note that dedicated attackers may have increased their chances of success by training on the omitted features. However, our experimental setup demonstrates the vulnerability of these schemes against relatively effortless attacks.

Our protocol trained an attacker to mimic their victim's swipes one direction at a time excluding multi-touch gestures like pinch to zoom [12]. This simplified the attack tasks and expedited attacker training.

It might be difficult for the attacker to mimic multi-touch gestures or multiple swipe directions simultaneously. However, swipe is the predominant form of gesture and an attacker can view content using one directional swipe for most target applications (email and messaging apps using up swipes while gallery app using left swipes). Due to their infrequent use, Touchalytics also ignores multi-touch gestures. While efficacy of mimicry attacks on multi-touch gestures is an open research question, we do not address it in this paper to conform to our realistic attack scenario. In terms of mimicry attacks on multiple swipe directions, given the trivial shoulder surfing and offline training time required, the attacker can leverage `Mimicker` or observational notes to train for different directions in real-time to mount these attacks.

10. RELATED WORK

Since the focus of our work is targeted mimicry attacks on touch IA, we do not discuss spoofing attacks on physiological biometrics (such as fingerprint and facial recognition). In this section, we discuss attacks on behaviour-based authentication systems.

Generative algorithms based attacks employ general population statistics and have been proposed for handwriting recognition, keystroke and touch IA. For handwriting recognition, Ballard et al. [3] show that a generative model based on concatenative synthesis exceeds the effectiveness of forgeries rendered by skilled humans. Serwadda and Phoha [27] analyze keystroke data from over 3000 PC users to observe statistical traits and then feed it to their generative algorithm to increase the EER of a keystroke classifier from 28% to 84%. More related to our work is a generative algorithm based attack on touch IA by Serwadda and Phoha [28]. They show that a robotic device equipped with generic traits across touch data poses a major threat to touch IA schemes as it increases their EER from 5% to 50%. While, unlike the targeted attacks discussed in this work, an attacker mounting their generic attack does not require shoulder surfing or the collection of the raw data of the victims, the attacker requires a mechanical robot to mount the attack, which may be impractical or suspicious in a work environment. Furthermore, the evaluations of the generic attack show that it failed for up to 40% of the victims because their touch behaviour was distinct. Targeted mimicry attacks can be leveraged to target any victim with more devastating effect.

Crowd sourcing based targeted mimicry attacks have been demonstrated for speaker and gait verification systems. Panjwani and Prakash [25] propose a method to crowdsource search for candidate mimics for speakers in a given target population. They show that while the probability of finding a successful match is only 3%, MTurk workers are easier and cheaper to locate and recruit than mimicry artists. Gafurov et al. [15] used a database of 760 gait sequences from 100 subjects to show that while trained forgery attacks were unsuccessful for the gait biometric, closest matching subjects from the database could be used to increase the EER up to 80%. Given that an inter-user overlap exists across touch behaviour [28], similar crowd sourcing attacks might be possible on touch IA schemes. However, our evaluations show that the attackers can effortlessly adjust their behaviour to mimic their victims thereby eliminating the need to locate and recruit users with similar touch behaviour.

Shoulder surfing attacks have been evaluated for IA proposals that employ cognitive abilities [1] and eye movement patterns [10]. Shoulder surfing attacks have also been evaluated for explicit authentication schemes that employ user defined touch gestures [26, 29, 30]. These research endeavors indicate that shoulder surfing attacks are not a threat for their respective proposals. We suspect that user defined gesture based schemes are resilient because of the smaller intra-user divergence for a gesture. We evaluate touch IA and show its vulnerability to shoulder surfing attacks.

Finally, targeted mimicry attacks that train the attackers to mimic their victims have been demonstrated for handwriting and keystroke biometrics. For handwriting recognition, Ballard et al. [3] show that some users – who are better forgers than others – can be trained using a naive method to successfully attack the handwriting biometric. Tey et al. [32] use the keystroke data of the victim to train attackers to mimic two keystroke features on PCs. Their evaluations show that with the full knowledge of the keystroke patterns of the victims, 14 of their best attackers (out of 84 attackers) were able to achieve a 99% bypass success rate. While our offline training attacks are inspired by the work of Tey et al., we perform the first ever evaluation of offline training attacks on touch IA.

11. CONCLUSION & FUTURE WORK

We evaluate two simple attacks by malicious insiders that effectively circumvent touch IA; showing for the first time that it is unsuitable from the security standpoint. We show that the widely accepted assumption that shoulder surfing attacks on touch IA are infeasible due to the hidden nature of many touch input features is incorrect. We also demonstrate how dedicated attackers can use an app like `Mimicker` to train themselves to mimic victims offline with very high success. Moreover, mimicry attacks appear practical even if the attacker has limited knowledge of the victim's IA scheme or limited logged examples of the victim's touch behaviour.

As future work, an extended evaluation of offline training attacks considering all features (including difficult to comprehend features) is a logical next step for evaluating mimicry attack efficacy. A more hopeful focus for future research is the identification of a set of mimicry-resilient features that bolster IA security.

12. ACKNOWLEDGMENTS

Thanks to the anonymous reviewers and Jakob Eriksson for their valuable comments. We thank Google and NSERC for their support. We also thank members of the CrySP lab for submitting raw data and permitting us to make videos for shoulder surfing attacks.

13. REFERENCES

[1] A. Al Galib and R. Safavi-Naini. User authentication using human cognitive abilities. In 18th International Conference on Financial Cryptography and Data Security. Springer, 2015.

[2] A. J. Aviv, K. Gibson, E. Mossop, M. Blaze, and J. M. Smith. Smudge attacks on smartphone touch screens. In 4th Usenix Conference on Offensive Technologies. Usenix Association, 2010.

[3] L. Ballard, D. Lopresti, and F. Monrose. Forgery quality and its implications for behavioral biometric security. IEEE Transactions on Systems, Man, and Cybernetics, 37(5):1107–1118, 2007.

[4] C. Bo, L. Zhang, X.-Y. Li, Q. Huang, and Y. Wang. Silentsense: silent user identification via touch and movement behavioral biometrics. In 19th Annual International Conference on Mobile Computing & Networking. ACM, 2013.

[5] Board Agency Announcement. DARPA-BAA-13-16 Active Authentication. https://www.fbo.gov/utils/view?id=0a869cb811991d73b143bd5e050d1a4b, Mar. 2016.

[6] M. Boyle, A. Klausner, D. Starobinski, A. Trachtenberg, and H. Wu. Poster: Gait-based smartphone user identification. In 9th International Conference on Mobile Systems, Applications, and Services. ACM, 2011.

[7] S. Buthpitiya, A. K. Dey, and M. Griss. Soft authentication with low-cost signatures. In International Conference on Pervasive Computing and Communications. IEEE, 2014.

[8] A. De Luca, A. Hang, F. Brudy, C. Lindner, and H. Hussmann. Touch me once and I know it's you!: Implicit authentication based on touch screen patterns. In Annual Conference on Human Factors in Computing Systems. ACM, 2012.

[9] B. Draffin, J. Zhu, and J. Zhang. Keysens: Passive user authentication through micro-behavior modeling of soft keyboard interaction. In Mobile Computing, Applications, and Services. Springer, 2014.

[10] S. Eberz, K. B. Rasmussen, V. Lenders, and I. Martinovic. Preventing lunchtime attacks: Fighting insider threats with eye movement biometrics. In 22nd Annual Network & Distributed System Security Symposium, 2015.

[11] T. Feng, Z. Liu, K.-A. Kwon, W. Shi, B. Carbunar, Y. Jiang, and N. Nguyen. Continuous mobile authentication using touchscreen gestures. In Symposium on Technologies for Homeland Security. IEEE, 2012.

[12] T. Feng, J. Yang, Z. Yan, E. M. Tapia, and W. Shi. TIPS: Context-aware implicit user identification using touch screen in uncontrolled environments. In 15th Workshop on Mobile Computing Systems and Applications. ACM, 2014.

[13] T. Feng, X. Zhao, B. Carbunar, and W. Shi. Continuous mobile authentication using virtual key typing biometrics. In 12th International Conference on Trust, Security and Privacy in Computing and Communications. IEEE, 2013.

[14] M. Frank, R. Biedert, E. Ma, I. Martinovic, and D. Song. Touchalytics: On the applicability of

touchscreen input as a behavioral biometric for continuous authentication. IEEE Transactions on Information Forensics and Security, 8(1):136–148, 2013.

[15] D. Gafurov, E. Snekkenes, and P. Bours. Spoof attacks on gait authentication system. IEEE Transactions on Information Forensics and Security, 2(3):491–502, 2007.

[16] H. Khan and U. Hengartner. Towards application-centric implicit authentication on smartphones. In 15th Workshop on Mobile Computing Systems and Applications. ACM, 2014.

[17] H. Khan, U. Hengartner, and D. Vogel. Usability and security perceptions of implicit authentication: Convenient, secure, sometimes annoying. In 11th Symposium on Usable Privacy and Security, 2015.

[18] S. Kullback and R. A. Leibler. On information and sufficiency. The Annals of Mathematical Statistics, 22(1):79–86, 1951.

[19] J. R. Kwapisz, G. M. Weiss, and S. A. Moore. Cell phone-based biometric identification. In 4th IEEE International Conference on Biometrics: Theory Applications and Systems. IEEE, 2010.

[20] L. Li, X. Zhao, and G. Xue. Unobservable reauthentication for smart phones. In 20th Annual Network & Distributed System Security Symposium, 2013.

[21] C.-C. Lin, C.-C. Chang, and D. Liang. A novel non-intrusive user authentication method based on touchscreen of smartphones. In International Symposium on Biometrics and Security Technologies. IEEE, 2013.

[22] E. Miluzzo, A. Varshavsky, S. Balakrishnan, and R. R. Choudhury. Tapprints: your finger taps have fingerprints. In 10th International Conference on Mobile Systems, Applications, and Services. ACM, 2012.

[23] I. Muslukhov, Y. Boshmaf, C. Kuo, J. Lester, and K. Beznosov. Know your enemy: the risk of unauthorized access in smartphones by insiders. In 15th International Conference on Human Computer Interaction with Mobile Devices and Services. ACM, 2013.

[24] New Scientist. Touchscreen phones know it's you from taps and swipes. http://www.newscientist.com/article/dn24193-touchscreen-phones-know-its-you-from-taps-and-swipes.html, Mar. 2016.

[25] S. Panjwani and A. Prakash. Crowdsourcing attacks on biometric systems. In 10th Symposium On Usable Privacy and Security. Usenix Association, 2014.

[26] N. Sae-Bae, K. Ahmed, K. Isbister, and N. Memon. Biometric-rich gestures: a novel approach to authentication on multi-touch devices. In Annual Conference on Human Factors in Computing Systems. ACM, 2012.

[27] A. Serwadda and V. V. Phoha. Examining a large keystroke biometrics dataset for statistical-attack openings. ACM Transactions on Information and System Security, 16(2):8, 2013.

[28] A. Serwadda and V. V. Phoha. When kids' toys breach mobile phone security. In 20th ACM Conference on Computer & Communications Security. ACM, 2013.

[29] M. Shahzad, A. X. Liu, and A. Samuel. Secure unlocking of mobile touch screen devices by simple gestures: you can see it but you can not do it. In 19th Annual International Conference on Mobile Computing & Networking. ACM, 2013.

[30] M. Sherman, G. Clark, Y. Yang, S. Sugrim, A. Modig, J. Lindqvist, A. Oulasvirta, and T. Roos. User-generated free-form gestures for authentication: Security and memorability. In 12th Annual International Conference on Mobile Systems, Applications, and Services. ACM, 2014.

[31] E. Shi, Y. Niu, M. Jakobsson, and R. Chow. Implicit authentication through learning user behavior. In Information Security. Springer, 2011.

[32] C. M. Tey, P. Gupta, and D. GAO. I can be you: Questioning the use of keystroke dynamics as biometrics. In 20th Annual Network & Distributed System Security Symposium, 2013.

[33] H. Xu, Y. Zhou, and M. R. Lyu. Towards continuous and passive authentication via touch biometrics: An experimental study on smartphones. In 10th Symposium On Usable Privacy and Security. Usenix Association, 2014.

[34] X. Zhao, T. Feng, and W. Shi. Continuous mobile authentication using a novel graphic touch gesture feature. In 6th International Conference on Biometrics: Theory, Applications and Systems. IEEE, 2013.

Privacy Capsules: Preventing Information Leaks by Mobile Apps

Raul Herbster
MPI-SWS

Scott DellaTorre
University of Maryland

Peter Druschel
MPI-SWS

Bobby Bhattacharjee
University of Maryland

Abstract

Preventing the leakage of user information via untrusted third-party apps is a key challenge in mobile privacy. We propose and evaluate *privacy capsules (PCs)*, a platform execution model for mobile apps that prevents the flow of private information to untrusted parties by design. With PCs, apps execute in two sequential phases. In the *unsealed* phase, the app has no access to sensitive input but full access to untrusted network resources. In the *sealed* state, the untrusted app has access to sensitive input, but can no longer communicate with untrusted resources. Privacy capsules are implemented by the mobile platform, are language independent, and require few changes to apps. Using a prototype PC implementation in Android, we show that PCs have low performance and energy overhead, and are suitable for a large class of apps.

1. INTRODUCTION

Mobile apps on major platforms provide a dizzying array of functionality, and form the basis for the success of these platforms. Users buy relatively inexpensive, often free, apps that cater to the necessities (schedule, online access, health monitoring) to entertainment (games, music) and beyond. The spectrum of functionality available on these devices also make them a repository of sensitive personal information, which is either explicitly added by the user (credit cards, passwords) or inferred from sensor readings (location, activity), and is often available to downloaded apps.

Prior work has shown that many third-party apps access information for which they do not have a legitimate need; some forward information to providers without the user's knowledge or consent. Egregious examples, such as flash light apps that access and upload user's location, phone number and contacts, are relatively easy to flag as malware [4] and have been the subject of popular press articles [6]. However, the problem is typically more subtle: Felt et al. [20] found that one third of 940 apps on the Android Market requested more permissions than needed. Enck et al. [19] analysed 30 popular Android applications and found that half of them send users' location to advertising servers, and two thirds handle private data in a suspicious manner.

ACM acknowledges that this contribution was authored or co-authored by an employee, contractor or affiliate of a national government. As such, the Government retains a nonexclusive, royalty-free right to publish or reproduce this article, or to allow others to do so, for Government purposes only.

MobiSys'16, June 25-30, 2016, Singapore, Singapore

DOI: http://dx.doi.org/10.1145/2906388.2906409

Beyond malware, even benign apps that are poorly designed or have bugs pose a threat to user privacy. A typical class includes apps that use insecure network protocols for service requests: according to one source, 92% of the top 500 Android applications available in app stores (Amazon and Google Play) use insecure protocols and/or leak sensitive information in other ways [3]. Documented bugs [7] have leaked plain text chat logs and passwords for hundreds of millions of users.

There are two primary techniques for restricting app behavior. The first, which is widely deployed, is for the app to pre-declare the set of resources it requires. Resource access is often coupled with user consent at the time of first use. In practice, this form of coarse-grained access control has proven to be ineffective. Most users are unsure whether an app legitimatately requires a particular resource; when faced with a choice to either approve access or forego the use of the app, they tend to approve [21, 23]. Further, the temporal granularity over which access is granted is coarse-grained, e.g., once access to location is granted, an app can query present location anytime until the access is explicitly revoked. Finally, even if an app must access a set of resources, there is no way to prevent unwanted information flow among those resources; for instance, if an app requires access to current location and network, platform access control cannot prevent the app from forwarding the current location to any network peer.

The second approach, still within the research domain, seeks to address app misbehavior using more fine-grained access control [26], or information flow control (IFC) [9, 19]. Fine-grained access control can minimize or prevent illegitimate resource accesses, but cannot detect or prevent illegitimate flows. Solutions relying on IFC can detect and prevent illegitimate flows, but have high performance and energy overhead, and suffer from false positives [25].

We propose **Privacy capsules (PC)**: a low-overhead technique that provides containment of sensitive information. By design, the containment properties of PCs are trivially simple to prove. PCs' run-time efficiency and containment guarantees come at a cost: PCs require applications to be structured in a particular manner, and may preclude certain classes of applications.

PCs are implemented as part of the mobile platform and enforce a two-phase execution model:

- An app's execution starts in the *unsealed state*, where it can freely access untrusted resources but has no access to private information.
- Once the app explicitly chooses to switch to the *sealed state*, it can access private information but can no longer access untrusted resources. The app cannot return to the unsealed state, but only terminate and restart (in the unsealed state).

A platform policy specifies what information is considered private. By construction, the PC execution model prevents the flow of private data to untrusted channels, i.e., it is impossible for the app to leak private information[1].

PC apps must be written to conform to this execution model. We believe this approach is viable because for many classes of applications, especially those that implement a service-query model, the required changes are minor, especially for newly developed apps. The containment guarantees provided by the PC model provides adoption incentives to both platform providers, app developers, and users. The platform will guarantee that apps, no matter how poorly designed or malicious, cannot leak private information; app developers do not have to secure their back end storage or audit their designs against attacks or misconfiguration, and users no longer have to trust apps, or debate privacy and access settings.

To enable rich functionality without compromising privacy, PCs provide additional mechanisms to enable legitimate flows of private information: sealed repositories, sealed channels, and selective declassification.

- Using a *sealed repository (SR)*, an app in sealed state can store private information persistently across executions. Data stored in an SR is encrypted with a user- and app-specific key that is never revealed by the platform, and therefore cannot be leaked by the app. An SR can reside in untrusted storage, such as the provider's Cloud.
- Using a *sealed channel (SC)*, live voice/video/chat data can be exchanged among instances of an app in sealed state on different users' devices. App instances and participating users are authenticated, and information in the channel is encrypted with keys that are never revealed to the app.
- Finally, apps may effect legitimate flows of private information to third parties using *selective declassification (SD)*. With SD, specific information can be disclosed to a specific third party with the user's express consent.

Using these mechanisms, we describe the design of three prototype PC-compliant apps, each of which represent a class of apps. A *train scheduling and ticketing* app represents apps that serve maps, event/transportation schedules, and product catalogs, and allow users to browse/purchase items. A *wellness* app represents the class of apps that monitor health and fitness sensors, analyze and tabulate data, and enable the sharing of selected data with friends, coaches, or health care providers. Finally, we present a *live chat* app, which represents the class of apps focused on communication with other users.

The rest of this paper is organized as follows. We discuss background and related work in Section 2. Section 3 presents the design of privacy capsules. Section 4 presents guidelines for developing PC-compliant apps and sketches our PC-compliant sample apps. An experimental evaluation follows in Section 5, and we conclude in Section 6.

[1]Our prototype does not account for timing attacks, but such attacks could be mitigated using randomization and other well-known techniques.

2. BACKGROUND AND RELATED WORK

Personal mobile devices can capture a continuous record of their users' location, activity, and audiovisual environment, and are commonly used to store schedules, passwords, banking records, and other sensitive information. The primary mechanism for ensuring user privacy and security is an audit by the platform provider, which usually ensures that gross malware is culled from the app marketplace.

Unfortunately, privacy leaks via apps are common and come in three flavors: *Incidental* privacy leaks occur as a side effect of the app's operation. For instance, an app that queries a database on a provider's site for information related to the user's current location or interests leaks information to the provider as part of each query. *Accidental* privacy leaks occur due to app bugs and vulnerabilities that expose the user's private information to network eavesdroppers, attackers, or other apps. Finally, a *malicious* leak occurs when an app deliberately and needlessly forwards private information to third parties. All three types of privacy leaks are amplified when the app requests and is granted access to private information that is not required to implement its documented functionality.

In this section, we survey the commonly used mechanisms, both deployed and in research, that have been developed to address privacy leaks.

2.1 Mobile platform permission systems

Mobile platforms including Android, iOS, and Windows Phone control the resources each third-party app can access. Users are asked to grant an app access to resources like the network, camera, microphone, location provider, calendar, contacts, etc., either at installation time or upon first access. Prior work has shown that users tend to approve most requests, presumably because they are unable to judge whether an app has a legitimate need for a resource, and may not be fully aware of the risks [21].

Several prior works aim to improve the permission system found in mobile platforms. Stowaway [20] analyzes an app statically to determine the set of resources it actually needs from its API usage. Bartel et al. [14], Au et al. [11] and Atzeni et al. [10] propose similar approaches. Dr. Android [26] provides more fine-grained access control for Android, for instance, by distinguishing read and write access to a resource, but still relies on correct decisions taken by lay users.

AppGuard [12], Aurasium [36], and NativeGuard [34] rely on inlined reference monitors to enforce more fine-grained access control policies than the platform. In these solutions, accesses to resources are dynamically monitored and the policies enforced. The user is notified whenever a certain application does not follow policy. In AppGuard, the policies are defined by the user. Aurasium monitors the calls between the app and the OS. It defines a fixed set of policies; for instance, calls to functions like `ioctl()`, `open()`, `fork()`

and `dlopen()` are considered as potentially risky. NativeGuard verifies if the native libraries follow the permission initially defined by the developer as part of the manifest file.

2.2 Information flow control

Information flow control (IFC) [32] has been used to enforce data confidentiality and integrity in different environments [15, 16, 18, 37], including mobile [19, 24, 30]. Unlike access control, IFC can track the flow of private information through an app. For instance, IFC can prevent an app from sending the user's private information to the network, even though it has access to both resources.

TaintDroid [19] uses fine-grained taint tracking to detect private data leakage in Android apps. It is a considerable advance over Android's permission control, but does not consider implicit/indirect flows, which arise from the program's control flow [27]. Moreover, TaintDroid incurs considerable performance and energy overheads. Some forms of IFC can be enforced using static analysis([30], [24]); while efficient, these tools can identify a relatively small class of information leakage, and are constrained to apps where the source code (and all libraries) are available for analysis.

SpanDex [17] relies on runtime techniques to mitigate leaks of specific private information like passwords through implicits flows in mobile apps. ReCon [31] uses machine learning to identify personally identifiable information (PII) in network traffic, enabling users to detect and manage potential privacy leaks by mobile apps. ReCon must be trained to identify specific PII and is subject to classification accuracy. The system can be deployed either as part of the mobile platform, or as a trusted middlebox with access to cleartext network traffic.

2.3 Sandboxing approaches

Sandboxing is a well-known technique for isolating the execution of untrusted programs, and can be used to control app access to sensitive information and resources. Sandboxing has been proposed for social networks [33, 35] and for mobile platforms [29].

Lee et al. [29] propose πBox, a sandbox technique for Android where apps can establish connections outside the sandbox through restricted storage and communication channels, preventing apps from exposing data via world-readable files. This approach does not prevent the application from accessing sensitive data from sensors, or from leaking it to the application provider.

In contrast to prior work, PCs enforce a simple execution model for untrusted apps, which rules out privacy leaks by design. Enforcing the PC execution model does not require expensive runtime intervention like taint tracking. Instead, PCs intercept untrusted apps' I/O operations and modify them according to the rules for the app's current sealing state.

3. DESIGN

Privacy capsules are implemented by a trusted mobile platform. The platform includes the OS, and a set of basic services, such as a location provider, a Contacts application, and a GUI, all of which are also assumed to be trusted.

Execution model: The PC execution model is depicted in Figure 1. The execution of an app starts in the unsealed state, where it has access to public inputs and untrusted resources. Later in its execution, the app process may switch to sealed state, where it has access to private inputs and trusted resources, but can no longer write to untrusted channels. Once in sealed state, the process cannot return to unsealed state, only terminate.

All sensor data (health/fitness, inertial, camera, microphone), geolocation, GUI inputs, phone status, databases (e.g,. contacts, calendars) are private by default. Public files, network connections, and interprocess communication (IPC) with untrusted processes in unsealed state are considered untrusted channels.

The main components of PCs are the following:

Key manager: The PC key manager maintains, for each app and user, a set of cryptographic keys used to encrypt data in sealed repositories and channels. Apps can request keys be created and select keys for use with a specific repository or channel. Apps refer to keys using handles, but cannot access the keys.

Sealed respositories (SR): In sealed mode, an app process may read and write an SR, allowing the app to persistently store data across executions. Data stored in an SR is encrypted with a user-specific key maintained by the PC key manager. SRs may reside in untrusted storage, like the Cloud.

Sealed channels (SC): An SC allows an app process in sealed mode to communicate with instances of the same app executing on other users' devices. The communicating apps are authenticated by the PC platforms, and communication is encrypted with a channel-specific key. Apps using a SC retain access to GUI events, and the device's microphone and camera. SCs are designed to enable person-to-person communication apps.

Selective declassification: An app process in sealed mode can disclose a particular data item to a particular third party with the user's express consent. To allow the user to determine the nature of the information disclosed, PCs track the type and provenance of all input data. When an app asks for selective declassification, the PC platform presents the user with the origin and type of the information to be disclosed and asks for confirmation.

The PC execution model ensures that no private data can flow to untrusted channels or parties, except via selective declassification.

PC-compliant apps can be installed and executed alongside ordinary apps on the same platform. We envision that users may continue to use ordinary apps from their bank, employer, or other reputable providers they trust. However, privacy conscious users would insist on PC-compliance for apps from less well-known providers, and for apps that require access to sensitive information (health, financial, private communication, etc.)

3.1 Threat model

The mobile platform, including the PC implementation, the OS, and platform apps, are trusted[2]. Attacks against these components are out of scope. We believe these assumptions are reasonable because (i) reputable platform providers

[2]When sealed channels are used, the mobile platforms on all communicating devices are trusted.

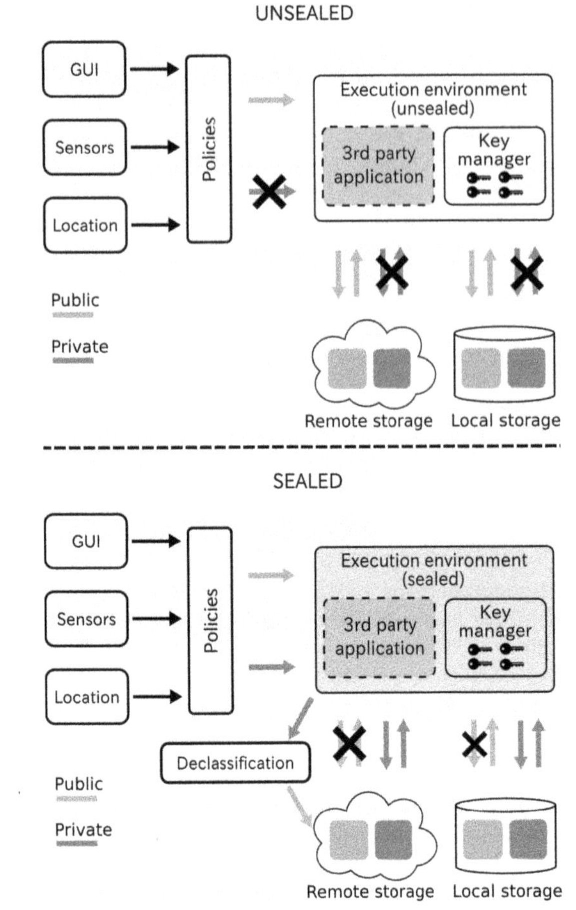

Figure 1: Privacy Capsules execution model

	App State	
	Unsealed	Sealed
Platform, Sys. Events		
App launch/fg/bg events	allow	allow
GUI events	deny	allow
All other sys. events	deny	allow
Device Sensors		
Sensor	deny	allow
Display	allow	allow
Audio	deny	allow
Microphone	deny	allow
Camera	deny	allow
Precise location	deny	allow
Public location	allow	allow
Device/network status	deny	allow
System Services		
Calendar read/write	deny	allow
Contacts read/write	deny	allow
Phone calls/SMS	deny	deny
Files/network		
Open/Close streams	allow	deny
Read streams	allow	allow
Write streams	allow	deny
PC Key Management		
Create/set keys	allow	deny
Cryptographic key access	deny	deny
PC sealed repository/channel		
SC/SR creation	allow	deny
SR/SC read/write	deny	allow

Table 1: Default PC policy for apps in sealed and unsealed states

have an interest in protecting users' privacy and the integrity of their platform, and (ii) while technically sophisticated users may compromise ("jail-break") their platform, compromising the integrity of PCs will only place their own privacy at risk.

By design, the guarantees provided by PCs hold regardless of app bugs, vulnerabilities, or deliberate misbehavior. For this work, it is assumed that apps do not exploit timing channels to leak private information. We believe that timing channels can be thwarted by shaping app I/O operations in the PC platform. However, a closer analysis and prevention of timing channels in the context of PCs remains the subject of future work.

3.2 State-dependent access restrictions

PCs prevent illicit information flows by mediating I/O operations depending on app's current state. Table 1 lists relevant operations and their state-dependent restrictions.

In the unsealed state, an app process has full access to untrusted channels like network connections and files, and the public location as defined by the location policy (see Section 3.4). The process can open but not read or write sealed repositories, sealed channels, and sources of private data, including sensors and GUI events. The process can interact with other processes in unsealed state only, and may receive a limited set of system event types that are not privacy sensitive. Finally, the process can instruct the PC key manager to create keys, and to select keys for use with specific sealed repositories and channels.

In the sealed state, the process has access to all private inputs, system events, databases, and status information, as well as sealed repositories/channels, but it can no longer write to untrusted channels. The process can interact with other processes in sealed state only. To prevent an app from leaking private information, the process can no longer open new files, network connections, or input devices, create nor select keys. These events can be observed by untrusted parties and could be exploited to encode private information as part of a covert channel (see Section 3.5).

Access to APIs for cellular voice calls or simple text messages (SMS) is prohibited in sealed mode, because it is difficult to effectively prevent leakage of private information via these technologies. However, PC-compliant apps for VoIP or secure messaging (chat) can be implemented, as shown in Section 4.5.

3.3 App launch

When a user or an app in unsealed state launches a PC-compliant app, the new app process starts in unsealed state. The new process can switch to sealed state when ready.

In Android, apps can launch other apps through events called *Intents*, which may pass arguments from the launching app to the launched app. Therefore, when an app process in sealed state launches an app, PC needs to ensure that no private information is leaked. In general, an app in sealed state may launch another app only if the launched app is a trusted platform app, the launched app is PC-compliant and forcibly started in sealed state, or the arguments passed in the intent are selectively declassified.

3.4 Location policy

Privacy capsules require no app-specific policies, and no user-specific policies with one exception: A user may wish to select a location privacy policy. The device's current location as defined by latitude/longitude is considered private, like any other sensor input. However, the location policy may define a *public geofence*, which is available to apps in unsealed state. The public geofence is the current location expressed as a geographic region at a particular political/administrative level. The top levels are world, continent, country. For a location in the US, the lower levels are state, county or independent city, municipality, ZIP code, street, address. An example location policy might say that the current location at the state level is public, and can be accessed by apps in unsealed state.

PCs automatically maintain a public geofence according to the location policy in effect. When the device moves out of the region covered by the current public geofence, PCs conservatively switch to the next higher level (e.g., from state to country). The user is notified of the change and has the option to adjust the public geofence manually. To avoid leaking information about the user's current location (i.e., somewhere at the geofence boundary) to unsealed apps, automatic changes to the public geofence are delayed randomly.

Apps in unsealed state may invoke a trusted map application to request the user to specify a location, e.g., a destination to be used for a navigation or travel booking application. The PC platform makes this input available to the app after generalizing the location to the same political/administrative level as the current public geofence.

3.5 Sealed repositories (SR)

Sealed repositories allow apps to store private information (profiles, logs, keys, accumulated sensor information) across launches. An SR can be stored as a local file on the device, or on a Cloud provider via HTTPS. Data stored in an SR is encrypted with a cryptographic key created and stored on behalf of the app by the PC key manager. The key itself is never revealed to the app; as a result, the app can read and write an SR whenever it is in sealed mode, but it cannot reveal its content to a third party.

An SR must be created and opened while the app is in unsealed mode. Creating or opening binds the name of a file-backed SR, and the URL and HTTPS GET/POST arguments for a Cloud-backed SR. Requiring creation and opening in unsealed mode ensures that no private information can be encoded in the set of SRs, their names, URLs, or GET/POST arguments, which can be observed by third parties; however, apps may still negotiate app-specific authentication without involving the platform. Once in sealed mode, the platform uses a well-known API (GET/POST/REST) to communicate over the channel created by the app.

SRs must be read sequentially, in their entirety, and only once per execution to prevent an app from encoding private information in its pattern of access.

3.6 Sealed channels (SC)

Sealed channels enable communication among instances of an app that execute on different users' devices, and support typical communication apps like messaging, chat, video calls, or multiuser games. When combined with appropriate key management as in Persona [13], SC can even be used to support private online social networks.

An SC must be set up in unsealed mode. When an app requests an SC, the PC platform launches the contacts app to have the user select participants. (Since the app is in unsealed state, it has no access to the contents of the contacts database). Using the public keys in the contacts database, the platform then authenticates the selected participants and establishes a shared session key. When the app instances on the participating devices switch to sealed state, they can access the SC.

Note that sealed mode app instances can freely share information. This is necessary as the participants wish to exchange video, audio, text typed on the keyboard, or other GUI events. To prevent such app instances from sharing other information like user's sensor inputs, locations, databases (e.g., calendar, contacts), or sensitive device state, an app with an active SC is denied access to private inputs other than GUI events, camera, and microphone.

3.7 Selective declassification

In some cases, users wish to deliberately disclose some private information to a particular third party. For instance, a user of a purchasing app who wishes to purchase an item needs to disclose to the vendor their choice of item, typically along with a name, shipping address, or payment information. As another example, a user of a fitness/health app wishes to disclose some of her sensor data to a coach or health care provider.

Selective declassification allows an app in sealed mode to declassify information with the express consent of the user. For this purpose, the trusted platform requires the user to confirm the declassification of a specific data item to a specific third party.

Users must be able to verify what information they are asked to declassify. For this purpose, the PC platform signs all private input data consumed by PC-compliant apps with its provenance metadata. Sensor data is signed with its type, sensor, and time of capture. GUI input is signed with the GUI mask and time at which it was entered.

Apps are allowed to declassify only information that corresponds directly to a set of signed input data items. This restriction ensures that an app cannot trick the user by encoding additional, private information in the data to be declassified, e.g., using steganography[3].

Finally, when an app requests declassification, the platform displays the metadata of the information to be declas-

[3]We considered allowing declassification of arbitrary data by presenting the user with the union of the metadata of all inputs consumed by the app. This approach is safe in terms of information flow because the metadata covers all inputs that could be reflected in the to-be-declassified data. However, in general the union of the metadata lacks specificy, which may make it difficult for users to make informed decisions about declassification.

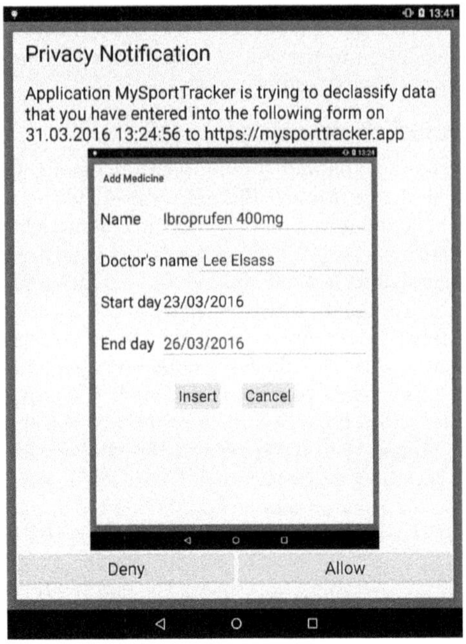

Figure 2: Example disclosure dialogue

sified, along with the specific third party to which the app wishes to declassify. The third party may be a provider identified by an authenticated HTTPS domain (via a secure connection), a specific person identified by a public key (via a file encrypted with that public key), or another app (via an intent). Only if the user confirms is the information declassified and encrypted for the third party.

Figure 2 shows an example declassification confirmation dialog for information about medication that was previously entered by the user. In the case of sensor information, the displayed metadata identifies the sensor, the resolution, and the period covered by the data.

Unlike existing permission systems, selective declassification enables users to decide on a case-by-case basis whether specific information identified by its metadata should be disclosed to a specific third party. The app remains untrusted, but the user implicitly entrusts the third party with the declassified information.

Generalized Declassification.

Both Sealed Channels and Selective Declassification are examples of declassification whereby users' input is required to explicitly allow specific information to be declassified to a known destination. More generally, we envision a declassfication architecture for PCs that uses a standalone key distribution infrastructure to disseminate Attribute-based keys corresponding to device resources (similar to the key management in [13]). Sealed channels and selective declassification allow us to demonstrate the utility of PCs and implement useful classes of applications; generalized declassification remains a topic of future work.

4. DEVELOPING APPS WITHIN PCS

To be able to run inside a privacy capsule and benefit from its privacy guarantees, apps must conform to the PC execution model. In this section, we present the PC API, and discuss guidelines for developers who wish to write PC-compliant apps. We also describe three PC-compliant apps we implemented: a train timetable app, a health/fitness app, and a simple text chat.

4.1 Privacy capsules API

The privacy capsules API is summarized in Table 2. The API calls are grouped into three categories. The basic API provides operations for creating and selecting keys, for creating and opening file-based SRs, and for swiching to the sealed state. The HTTP connection API provides means for creating and opening HTTP-based SRs, and for declassification into HTTP connections. The secure channels (SC) API provides means to establish a sealed channel (SC). With the exeption of the SC API, which is currently available only in Java, APIs are also available for C programs.

4.2 Guidelines for developing PC apps

Next, we give general guidelines for developing PC-compliant apps. A key question for the developer of a PC-compliant app is how to split the apps's functionality between the unsealed and sealed states. At a high level, functions that require communication with untrusted third parties require unsealed state, while functions that depend on private data require sealed state. Moreover, the two states must occur sequentially and only one transition is allowed, from unsealed to sealed state. Depending on the nature of an app, this constraint, which ensures that no private information can flow to untrusted channels, may require some care. Following, we discuss common patterns of app information flow, and how to accomplish them in a PC-compliant manner.

Maintaining private information across launches: Many apps store private information like the user's search and activity history, personal profile, authentication credentials, etc., persistently across app launches. In many cases, the information is stored in the Cloud on the app provider's site. PC-compliant apps can store such information in a sealed repository, accessed from sealed state.

Sensitive database queries: A large class of apps provide maps and directions, transportation scheduling and ticketing, discovery of nearby resources, shopping, and may include advertising components. Such apps typically query a Cloud database, where the queries depend on private data like the user's location, destination, history, profile, and interests. Privacy-preserving, PC-compliant versions of such apps maintain a cache of the database on the local device, and resolve queries locally from the cache. In unsealed state, the app updates its cache from the Cloud, along with new tips, advertisements, or promotions pushed by the Cloud provider. Once in sealed state, the app resolves user queries and performs ad selection from the local cache.

Purchase transactions: Apps that perform reservation or purchase transactions must necessarily disclose some private information, like the product ID, name, shipping address, or payment details, to the vendor. PC-compliant apps use selective declassification to disclose such specific information to a particular vendor from the sealed state, with the user's express consent.

Health/Fitness/Nutrition advice: Apps that allow users to seek advice from health care providers, fitness

Seal/Unseal API

Function	Description	Java (class `PrivacyCapsulesService`)
Seal	Seals the app	`boolean seal()`
Get seal status	Checks if app is sealed	`boolean isSealed()`
Key creation	Creates a key and returns a handle	`long createKey()`
Set key	Associates a key with the given SR file descriptor	`long setKey(FileDescriptor, long)`
Associate handle with name	Associates a handle (long) with a textual name	`boolean setHandlePair(long,byte[])`
Retrieve handle by name	Retrieves handle associated with given name	`long retrieveHandlePair(byte[])`

HTTP Connection

Function	Description	Java (package `java.net.*`)
Open connection	Opens a HTTP connection with a remote SR	`HttpURLConnection URL#openConnection(long)`
Open connection for data disclosure	Opens a PC HTTP connection for selective data disclosure	`HttpURLConnection URL#openDisclosureConnection(long)`

Secure Channels

Function	Description	Java (class `PrivacyCapsulesService`)
Open SC	Shows a dialog with existing contacts; opens a SC and returns a file descriptor associated with each selected contact.	`ParcelFileDescriptor[] createSecureChannel()`
Get SC input stream	Returns the input stream associated with a SC	`getSecureChannel[Client/Server] Input(ParcelFileDescriptor)`
Get SC output stream	Returns the output stream associated with a SC	`getSecureChannel[Client/Server] Output(ParcelFileDescriptor)`

Table 2: Summary of privacy capsules API

coaches, or nutrition advisers necessarily release private information (e.g., health and fitness sensory data, nutrition/activity logs) to third parties. PC-compliant apps use selective declassification to disclose such specific information to a particular provider from the sealed state, with the user's express consent.

Live communication with other users: Communication applications like voice/video calling and chat necessarily require live communication with the participants of the call. PC-compliant apps set up a sealed channel in unsealed mode, and use the channel from a restricted sealed state that grants access to GUI events, camera, and microphone.

Social networking: Many apps have a social networking component, where private information is made available selectively to specific groups of other users. While we have not yet experimented with such apps, we believe that a generalized form of declassification based on attribute-based key management can support such apps.

Sensor matching: Apps like "bump" [2, 5] require accelerometer, location and clock readings to be compared between different devices. In our prototype, such apps can be implemented by selectively declassifying the sensor inputs to a Cloud-based matching service. In future work, we plan to add support for privacy-preserving sensor matching using multiparty secure computation, as in [8].

Next, we describe three PC-compliant apps we developed. Each sample app represents a large class of similar apps. Designing and implementing these apps did not present any difficult challenges related to the PC execution model. With the PC execution flow in mind, it was possible to quickly design the apps.

4.3 DB train timetable app

We implemented a train timetable app that replicates the functionality of a proprietary app offered by the German railway company DB (Deutsche Bahn). Our app relies on DB's Cloud backend service, which offers an open Web API.

In normal operation, the DB app queries the DB backend and returns a travel plan to the user, which reveals the user's point of departure (often the current location), destination and time of travel to the DB backend service. Users also have a ticketing option, which submits the user's name and payment details to the DB backend as part of a transaction, and returns an online ticket. The DB app supports an offline mode, where the timetable is cached on the device and the app resolves information queries from the cache.

Our PC-compliant version of the app instead follows the execution flow shown in Figure 3. In the unsealed state, the app updates its local cache of the timetable and realtime information from the DB backend, for the region indicated by the user's public geofence. Once in sealed state, the app accesses an SR storing the user's profile and payment details, and receives GUI input from the user about particular connections. It then queries the relevant information from the locally cached database. A similar approach is taken in PlaceLab [28].

If the user wishes to purchase a ticket, the app requests selective declassification of the connection details, along with personal and payment details obtained from the SR. If the user approves, the details are sent to the DB backend as part of a ticketing transaction.

Without the ticketing option, which we have not yet implemented, the app consists of 1417 lines of Java code. Compared to a conventional implementation of the app that has

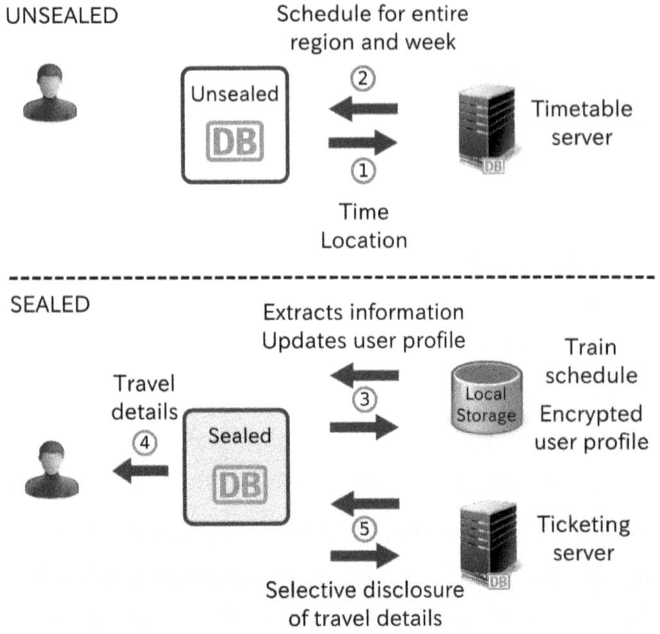

Figure 3: PC-compliant DB app

an offline mode, only a few lines of additional code are necessary. This code uses the PC API to open an SR, switch to sealed mode, and request selective declassification when issuing a ticketing transaction.

Maintaining a local copy of the database for a region corresponding to the user's current public geofence requires some additional bandwidth. As we will show in Section 5.4, the required bandwidth is low in practice.

4.4 Health/Fitness app

We built a simple wellness/fitness app that monitors a Bluetooth connected wearable fitness sensor (Polar H7 heart rate sensor), and allows users to enter additional information (medications, meals). Users can send some of their data to a coach. We also built a simple app for the coach, who can receive fitness data from users and respond with fitness and nutrition advice. A simple, untrusted web backend service supports a REST API to store encrypted user data and to exchange encrypted data among users and coaches.

The fitness app, in unsealed state, opens an SR used to store the user's profile information and personal health record (PHR), which consists of sensor data and data logged by the user. Then it switches to sealed mode, where it reads out sensors, accepts input from the user, and adds data to the PHR. When the user wishes to send data to a coach, the app requests selective declassification of the corresponding data. If the user approves, the data is encrypted for the coach and sent to the backend service.

The coach's app, in unsealed mode, downloads encrypted user data from the backend. Then, it switches to sealed mode, where it can retrieve its keys from an SR containing the coach's profile data, and decrypts the user data. Once the coach has entered her response, the apps asks for selective declassification of the response.

The apps consist of a library with common procedures (5378 lines of Java code), the client's app (3127 lines of Java code) and the coach's app (314 lines of Java code). There is little code specific to the use of PCs. Usage of the selective declassification API required 202 lines of Java code. Listing 1 shows how to selectively disclose data through a HTTP connection using the PC API.

Listing 1: Example of data declassification through PC HTTP connections

```
...
  PrivacyCapsulesService pcService =
PrivacyCapsulesService.from(getActivityContext());
  long handle = pcService.createKey();
  URL url = new URL("http://example.com/service");
  HttpURLConnection con =
      (HttpURLConnection) url.openDisclosureConnection(handle);
  conn.setRequestMethod("POST");
  ...

  if (pcService.seal()) {
    /* Get account from the contacts database */
    /* Get password from GUI */
    List<NameValuePair> params = new ArrayList<NameValuePair>();
    params.add(new BasicNameValuePair("account", account));
    params.add(new BasicNameValuePair("password", password));

    OutputStream os = conn.getOutputStream();
    BufferedWriter writer =
        new BufferedWriter(new OutputStreamWriter(os,"UTF-8"));
    writer.write(getQuery(params));
    ...
  }
...
```

4.5 Messaging app

We built a simple messaging app that allows the live exchange of text messages among users. In unsealed mode, the app sets up a secure channel, which causes the platform to launch the contacts app to allow the user to select the participants. Once in sealed mode, the app has access to the GUI and sealed channel and can exchange messages with the participants.

The app has around 600 Java lines of code and very few lines are specific to the use of PCs. As shown in Listing 2, the traditional calls to establish a socket (line #3) and to obtain the socket's input and output streams (#8) are replaced by the PC secure channels API.

5. PERFORMANCE EVALUATION

In this section, we describe a prototype implementation of privacy capsules in Android, and present experiments to evaluate the performance of PCs.

5.1 Prototype

The PC prototype has components in both the Android kernel and the Android framework. In the Android kernel, we added a syscall to support the PC API. Moreover, we added a kernel module (`pc_module.ko`), which contains 3990 lines of code and provides the core of the kernel PC implementation. It intercepts all I/O syscalls of PC-encapsulated processes by changing the syscall table to refer to the PC kernel module [22].

The kernel module also performs the cryptographic operations, and uses AES-128 to encrypt/decrypt the blocks of data. The handle:file mapping is stored by the PC kernel implementation as a system protected file and the key is re-

Listing 2: Creating a secure channel and obtaining its input/output streams

```
...
  PrivacyCapsulesService pcService =
PrivacyCapsulesService.from(getActivityContext());
  final ParcelFileDescriptor[] contactsFd =
        pcService.createSecureChannel();
  pcService.seal();
  connected = true;
  while (connected) {
    try {
      if (pcService != null) {
        if (contactsFd[0] != null) {
          OutputStream outputStream =
new ParcelFileDescriptor.AutoCloseOutputStream(contactsFd[0]);
          BufferedWriter bWriter =
new BufferedWriter(new OutputStreamWriter(outputStream)),true)
          PrintWriter out = new PrintWriter(bWriter);
          ...
        }
        ...
      }
...
```

covered every time it is required to perform cryptographic operations.

In the Android framework, 3846 lines of code were added to provide a Android system service (PrivacyCapsulesService), notification support for declassification and location policies, permission control, system services control and a Java API for accessing the features provided by PC.

Changes to the existing Android permission system are another part of the prototype. Android has several different permissions that are granted to the application, which are specified in a manifest XML file by the developer. Permissions are managed at two levels: user space permissions and kernel space permissions. For user space, every time the application needs to access a certain resource associated with a specific permission, Android checks if the application has been granted the proper rights to do so. This is implemented in the Android framework. For kernel space, the system associates each permission (for example, GPS access) to a system group. Therefore, only those applications that belong to a particular group (for instance, the gps_access group), can access the resource. The PC implementation makes changes to the permission system to deny apps in unsealed state access to sensitive resources, i.e. calendar, contacts and sensors.

5.2 Experimental platform

The evaluation was performed on a rooted Nexus 9 device (volantis), with Linux Kernel 3.10 (android-tegra-3.10-lollipop-release) and Android 5.1 (AOSP for volantis). The Nexus 9 is a 2.3 GHz dual-core 64-bit Denver tablet, with 2 GB LPDDR3-1600 RAM and 16 GB flash storage.

The Nexus 9 has an ARM V8 CPU with cryptography extension, including SIMD instructions that speed up algorithms such as AES and SHA. To make use of these capabilities, we enabled the following kernel configuration options: CONFIG_CRYPTO_HW, CONFIG_ARM64_CRYPTO, CONFIG_CRYPTO_AES_ARM64_CE, CONFIG_CRYPTO_AES_ARM64_CE_CCM, CONFIG_CRYPTO_AES_ARM64_CE_BLK. For experiments with the Health/Fitness app, we used a Dell Intel®Core™3.20GHz desktop with a i5-3470 CPU and 8 GB of main memory as the backend server. The mobile devices connected to the server via our institute's Wi-Fi network.

5.3 Privacy capsules overheads

We begin with an evaluation of performance overheads of the PC execution model, and the crypto overheads associated with sealed repositories.

In the first experiment, we compare the latency of reading/writing data in different configurations: a plain file in unmodified Android; a plain file with PCs in unsealed state, and a sealed repository in sealed state. Figures 5 and 4 show the results for read and write operations, respectively, of sizes 1, 4K and 10K bytes, with whiskers indicating standard deviation. In each case, an existing file of 1MB size was read or overwritten.

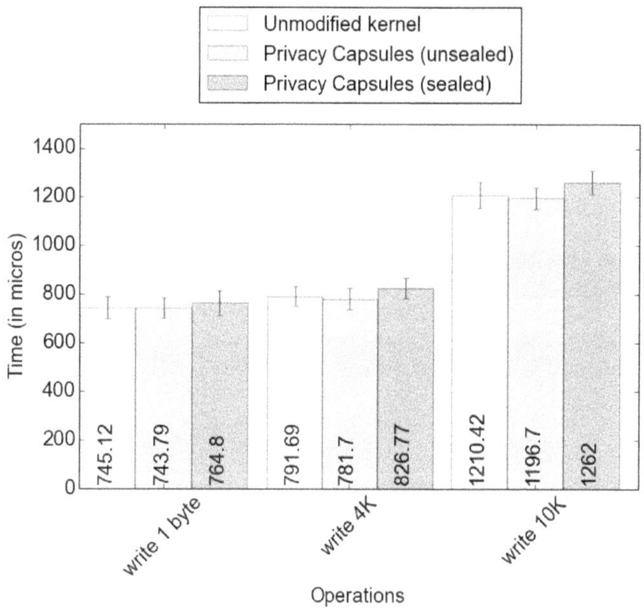

Figure 4: Write overheads

The latency differences between the unmodified Android system and privacy capsules in unsealed state is small, within a standard deviation. This shows that PC's overhead for intercepting I/O operations directly in the kernel is negligible, as expected.

The overheads for read/write operations to SRs are higher, due to the required data encryption. The overhead for write operations is very low, 2.6% for 1 byte, 4.4% for 4K byte, and 4.2% for 10Kbyte writes. Read operations are very fast in our experiments, because they are served from Linux's buffer cache after the first iteration of the experiment. As a result, the overheads are larger, 55% for 1 byte, 319% for 4K byte, and 286% for 10Kbyte reads.

In the second experiment, we compare the performance of two versions of a simple demo app. The two versions are functionally equivalent, but one is PC-compliant, while the other executes on plain Android. The PC-compliant version opens an existing SR and select a key for it, creates a new SR and selects a key for it, then switches to sealed state. In sealed state, it reads the existing SR, writes the new SR, then terminates. The plain Android version opens

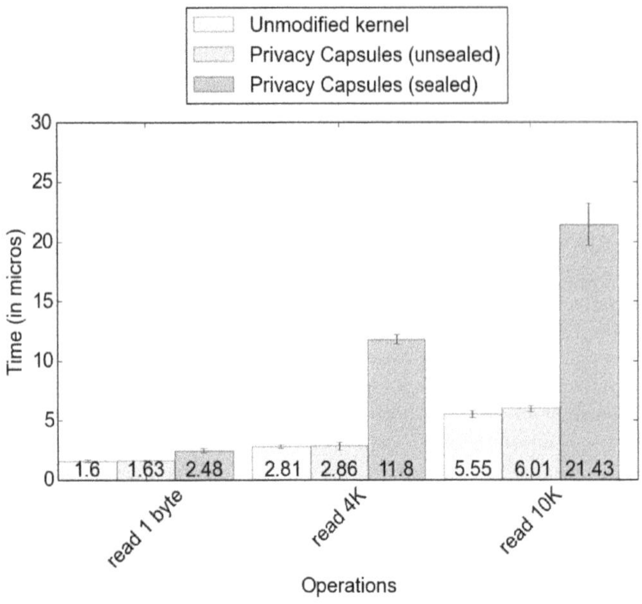

Figure 5: Read overheads

an existing file and reads it, creates a new file and writes it, then terminates. The SRs and files are 1MB in size.

Figure 6 shows the execution time of the two versions. The values were obtained using traceview [1]. The overhead of the PC-compliant version is about 1%.

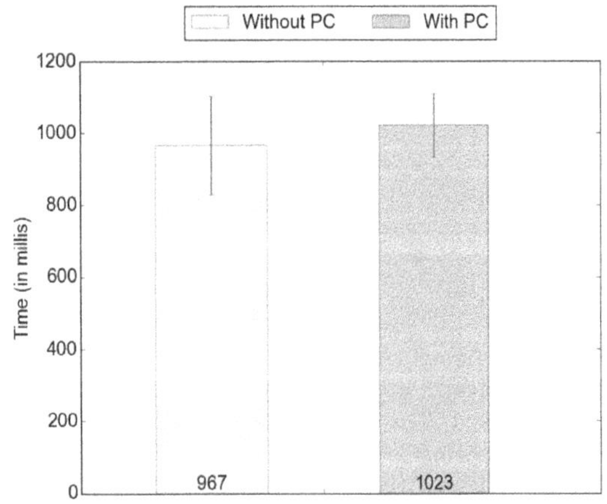

Figure 6: Runtime for two versions of the demo app

We also performed experiments with the sample apps described in Section 4. Latency overheads due to the use of PCs were small enough to remain unnoticeable to the user in all cases.

5.4 Train app: Bandwidth and storage usage

The train timetable app is an example of a class of apps that provide information about a particular geolocation or trajectory from a database. Implementing such apps in a privacy-preserving manner requires that queries about specific locations are performed on a locally cached copy of the database. Minimally, a portion of the database must be cached that is sufficiently large to absorb all queries within the user's public geofence.

The storage and bandwidth requirements for maintaining such a local copy depend on the size and update rate of the database, as well as the size of the user's public geofence. Here, we measure these requirements for the DB train app we built.

Towards this end, we collected data from the Deutsche Bahn (DB) online train schedule system. DB is the largest rail transport company in Central Europe. We fetched the timetable on Dec 5, 2014. It includes 5374 stations, is 12.2MB large, and changes every six months.

The DB systems also publishes real-time updates like platform changes, delays, and cancellations. The updates consist of text messages stating a delay (e.g., "+2min", "appr. +50min", "Train cancelled") and a reason (e.g., "Platform changed", "Technical failure", "Delay from previous trip", "Person on the tracks", "Delay of a preceding train", "Waiting for an incoming train").

We fetched realtime data through the DB Web API for all the stations during the period from 7pm, Mon, 8 December, 2014 to 5:51pm, Wed, 10 December 2014. Of our 144623151 queries, 365843 (or .25%) failed with an HTTP status 404 (not found) or 408 (timeout); as a result, we may have missed a small proportion of realtime updates. The data collected is likely to be typical for weekdays under normal conditions. We expect that volume could be considerably higher in case of a strike, accident, or extreme weather conditions.

We checked how much of the realtime data change over time. Therefore, we considered all changes in the field "delay" and "reason" as updates. Figure 8 shows cumulative distributions of the realtime update volume over time for all German states, and Figure 7 shows the same for the main stations of selected German cities (population in parentheses): Saarbrücken (177,201), Frankfurt am Main (701,350), Berlin (3,562,166) and Hamburg (1,751,775). The figures cover the 24 period within our data collection period that had the highest volume of realtime updates.

We observed many cases of realtime updates that report a delay of zero minutes and a reason of "No delay" for a particular train service. These updates seems redundant, but account for a significant proportion of the updates, ranging from 16.4% for the state of Hamburg to 78% for the state of Sachsen (Saxony).

Given this data, we can estimate the additional bandwidth requirements for a privacy-preserving DB train scheduling app that maintains a cached copy of the timetable and real-time updates relevant to the user's current public geofence. Maintaining the timetable requires up to 12.2 MB twice per year, assuming conservatively that the entire table changes. The resulting bandwidth requirement is negligible.

If a user's public geofence is set to "Germany", maintaining a local cache of realtime updates requires on average 6211 KB for a 24 hour period, which is also negligible. Reducing the public geofence to the state level reduces the bandwidth requirement to between 19 KB/24 hours for Bremen (state with least volume) and 1138 KB/24 hours for North Rhine-Westphalia (state with most volume). Reducing the public geofences further to the city level reduces the bandwidth requirement to between 7.92 KB/24 hours for Saarbrücken (city with lowest volume) and 60.34 KB/24 hours for Frankfurt am Main (city with highest volume).

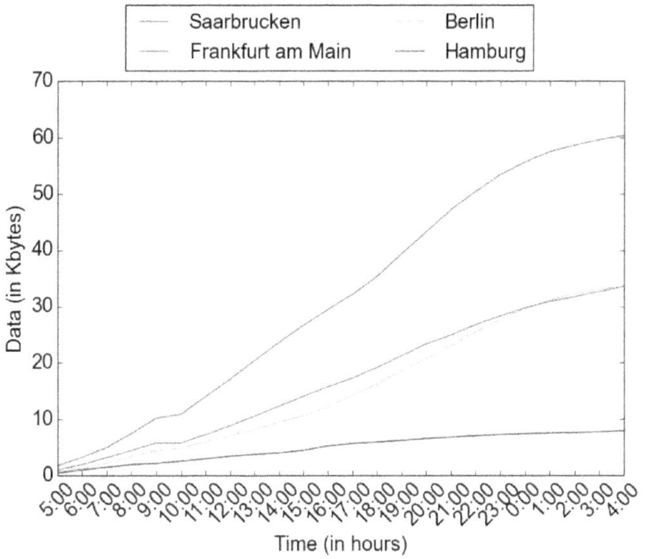

Figure 7: Cumulative DB realtime data by city

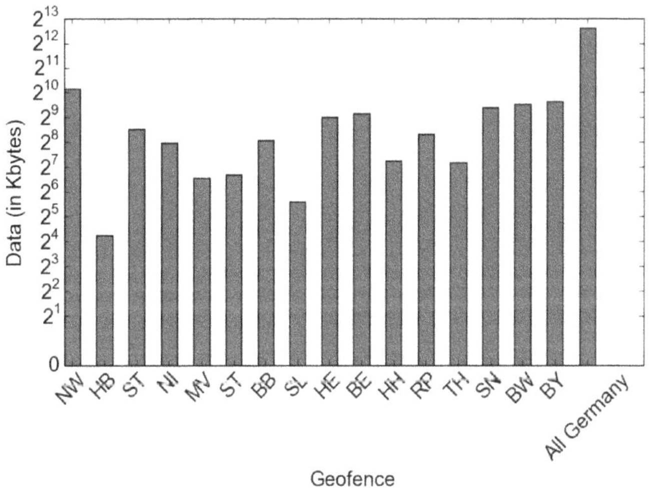

Figure 8: DB realtime data over 24 hours, by state

We conclude that the bandwidth requirements for maintaining a local cache of timetable and realtime updates for a train schedule app is neglibigle, even when the user's public geofence is at the level of a large country in Europe. Given these very low traffic volumes, even unusual events (strike, weather) that cause the volume to increase by one or two orders of magnitude would be of little concern. Note that the use of a public geofence larger than country would make no difference in this case, as the scope of the DB system and app is limited to a country.

6. CONCLUSIONS

We presented the design of privacy capsules, an execution platform for mobile apps that prevents privacy leaks by design. We have implemented a prototype implementation in Android and experimented with three example applications, representing common application classes. Runtime overhead is very low, and the app changes required to program apps within the privacy capsules execution model are moderate.

7. ACKNOWLEDGMENTS

We would like to thank the anonymous reviewers and our shepherd Landon Cox for their helpful feedback. This research was partially supported by the European Research Council (ERC Synergy imPACT 610150), the German Science Foundation (DFG CRC 1223), and by the United States National Science Foundation (award numbers: IIS-0964541 and CNS-1314857.)

8. DEDICATION

We dedicate this paper to the memory of Scott DellaTorre.

9. REFERENCES

[1] Android traceview tool. http://developer.android.com/tools/help/traceview.html. Accessed: 08.12.2015.

[2] Meet Bump, the App Store's Billionth Download. http://www.pcworld.com/article/163840/article.html. Accessed: Apr 11, 2016.

[3] MetaIntell identifies enterprise security risks, privacy risks and data leakage in 92% of top 500 android mobile applications. http://www.businesswire.com/news/home/20140122006295/en/MetaIntell-Identifies-Enterprise-Security-Risks-Privacy-Risks#.VLeLfnWx15Q. Accessed: Jan 15, 2015.

[4] Mobile malware stealing data from legitimate apps. http://www.alphr.com/news/security/389716/mobile-malware-stealing-data-from-legi timate-apps. Accessed: Nov 22, 2015.

[5] Review: Bump, the One Billionth iPhone App. http://www.pcmag.com/article2/0,2817,2345899,00.asp. Accessed: Apr 11, 2016.

[6] The Top Ten Mobile Flashlight Applications Are Spying On You. Did You Know? http://www.cyberdefensemagazine.com/the-top-ten-mobile-flashlight-applications-are-spying-on-you-did-you-know/. Accessed: Aug 31, 2015.

[7] UNH cyber forensics group reveals smartphone app issues affecting 968 million. http://www.unhcfreg.com/#!UNH-Cyber-Forensics Group-Reveals-Smartphone-App-Issues-Affecti ng-968-Million/c5rt/376C3F2A-18F6-41E9-9A42-D05AAD8E2DCA. Accessed: Jan 15, 2015.

[8] Aditya, P., Sen, R., Joon Oh, S., Benenson, R., Bhattacharjee, B., Druschel, P., Wu, T., Fritz, M., and Schiele, B. I-Pic: A Platform for Privacy-Compliant Image Capture. In *Proceedings of the 14th Annual International Conference on Mobile Systems, Applications, and Services* (New York, NY, USA, 2016), MobiSys '16, ACM.

[9] Arzt, S., Rasthofer, S., Fritz, C., Bodden, E., Bartel, A., Klein, J., Le Traon, Y., Octeau, D., and McDaniel, P. FlowDroid: Precise Context, Flow, Field, Object-sensitive and Lifecycle-aware Taint Analysis for Android Apps. *SIGPLAN Not. 49*, 6 (June 2014), 259–269.

[10] Atzeni, A., Su, T., Baltatu, M., D'Alessandro, R., and Pessiva, G. How dangerous is your android app?: An evaluation methodology. In *Proceedings of the 11th International Conference on Mobile and Ubiquitous Systems: Computing, Networking and Services* (ICST, Brussels, Belgium, Belgium, 2014), MOBIQUITOUS '14, ICST (Institute for Computer Sciences, Social-Informatics and Telecommunications Engineering), pp. 130–139.

[11] Au, K. W. Y., Zhou, Y. F., Huang, Z., and Lie, D. PScout: Analyzing the Android Permission Specification. In *Proceedings of the 2012 ACM Conference on Computer and Communications Security* (New York, NY, USA, 2012), CCS '12, ACM, pp. 217–228.

[12] Backes, M., Gerling, S., Hammer, C., von Styp-Rekowsky, P., and Maffei, M. Appguard - real-time policy enforcement for third-party applications. Tech. Rep. A/02/2012, Saarland University, http://www.infsec.cs.uni-saarland.de/projects/appguard/android_irm.pdf, July 2012.

[13] Baden, R., Bender, A., Spring, N., Bhattacharjee, B., and Starin, D. Persona: An online social network with user-defined privacy. *SIGCOMM Comput. Commun. Rev. 39*, 4 (Aug. 2009), 135–146.

[14] Bartel, A., Klein, J., Le Traon, Y., and Monperrus, M. Automatically securing permission-based software by reducing the attack surface: An application to android. In *Proceedings of the 27th IEEE/ACM International Conference on Automated Software Engineering* (New York, NY, USA, 2012), ASE 2012, ACM, pp. 274–277.

[15] Bichhawat, A., Rajani, V., Garg, D., and Hammer, C. Information flow control in webkit's javascript bytecode. In *Principles of Security and Trust*, M. Abadi and S. Kremer, Eds., vol. 8414 of *Lecture Notes in Computer Science*. Springer Berlin Heidelberg, 2014, pp. 159–178.

[16] Cheng, W., Ports, D. R. K., Schultz, D., Popic, V., Blankstein, A., Cowling, J., Curtis, D., Shrira, L., and Liskov, B. Abstractions for Usable Information Flow Control in Aeolus. In *Proceedings of the 2012 USENIX Conference on Annual Technical Conference* (Berkeley, CA, USA, 2012), USENIX ATC'12, USENIX Association, pp. 12–12.

[17] Cox, L. P., Gilbert, P., Lawler, G., Pistol, V., Razeen, A., Wu, B., and Cheemalapati, S. Spandex: Secure password tracking for android. In *Proceedings of the 23rd USENIX Conference on Security Symposium* (Berkeley, CA, USA, 2014), SEC'14, USENIX Association, pp. 481–494.

[18] Efstathopoulos, P., Krohn, M., VanDeBogart, S., Frey, C., Ziegler, D., Kohler, E., Mazières, D., Kaashoek, F., and Morris, R. Labels and Event Processes in the Asbestos Operating System. In *Proceedings of the Twentieth ACM Symposium on Operating Systems Principles* (New York, NY, USA, 2005), SOSP '05, ACM, pp. 17–30.

[19] Enck, W., Gilbert, P., Chun, B.-G., Cox, L. P., Jung, J., McDaniel, P., and Sheth, A. N. TaintDroid: An Information-flow Tracking System for Realtime Privacy Monitoring on Smartphones. In *Proceedings of the 9th USENIX Conference on Operating Systems Design and Implementation* (Berkeley, CA, USA, 2010), OSDI'10, USENIX Association, pp. 1–6.

[20] Felt, A. P., Chin, E., Hanna, S., Song, D., and Wagner, D. Android permissions demystified. In *Proceedings of the 18th ACM Conference on Computer and Communications Security* (New York, NY, USA, 2011), CCS '11, ACM, pp. 627–638.

[21] Felt, A. P., Ha, E., Egelman, S., Haney, A., Chin, E., and Wagner, D. Android permissions: User attention, comprehension, and behavior. In *Proceedings of the Eighth Symposium on Usable Privacy and Security* (New York, NY, USA, 2012), SOUPS '12, ACM, pp. 3:1–3:14.

[22] Garfinkel, T. Traps and pitfalls: Practical problems in system call interposition based security tools. In *In Proc. Network and Distributed Systems Security Symposium* (2003), pp. 163–176.

[23] Gerber, P., Volkamer, M., and Renaud, K. Usability versus privacy instead of usable privacy: Google's balancing act between usability and privacy. *SIGCAS Comput. Soc. 45*, 1 (Feb. 2015), 16–21.

[24] Gibler, C., Crussell, J., Erickson, J., and Chen, H. AndroidLeaks: Automatically Detecting Potential Privacy Leaks in Android Applications on a Large Scale. In *Proceedings of the 5th International Conference on Trust and Trustworthy Computing* (Berlin, Heidelberg, 2012), TRUST'12, Springer-Verlag, pp. 291–307.

[25] Henderson, A., Prakash, A., Yan, L. K., Hu, X., Wang, X., Zhou, R., and Yin, H. Make it work, make it right, make it fast: Building a platform-neutral whole-system dynamic binary analysis platform. In *Proceedings of the 2014 International Symposium on Software Testing and Analysis* (New York, NY, USA, 2014), ISSTA 2014, ACM, pp. 248–258.

[26] Jeon, J., Micinski, K. K., Vaughan, J. A., Fogel, A., Reddy, N., Foster, J. S., and Millstein, T. Dr. Android and Mr. Hide: Fine-grained Permissions in Android Applications. In *Proceedings of the Second ACM Workshop on Security and Privacy in Smartphones and Mobile Devices* (New York, NY, USA, 2012), SPSM '12, ACM, pp. 3–14.

[27] King, D., Hicks, B., Hicks, M., and Jaeger, T. Implicit flows: Can't live with 'em, can't live without 'em. In *Proceedings of the 4th International Conference on Information Systems Security* (Berlin, Heidelberg, 2008), ICISS '08, Springer-Verlag, pp. 56–70.

[28] LaMarca, A., Chawathe, Y., Consolvo, S., Hightower, J., Smith, I., Scott, J., Sohn, T., Howard, J., Hughes, J., Potter, F., Tabert, J., Powledge, P., Borriello, G., and Schilit, B. Place lab: Device positioning using radio beacons in the wild. In *Proceedings of the Third International Conference on Pervasive Computing* (Berlin, Heidelberg, 2005), PERVASIVE'05, Springer-Verlag, pp. 116–133.

[29] Lee, S., Wong, E. L., Goel, D., Dahlin, M., and Shmatikov, V. πBox: A platform for privacy-preserving apps. In *Proceedings of the 10th USENIX Conference on Networked Systems Design and Implementation* (Berkeley, CA, USA, 2013), nsdi'13, USENIX Association, pp. 501–514.

[30] Lu, L., Li, Z., Wu, Z., Lee, W., and Jiang, G. CHEX: Statically Vetting Android Apps for Component Hijacking Vulnerabilities. In *Proceedings of the 2012 ACM Conference on Computer and Communications Security* (New York, NY, USA, 2012), CCS '12, ACM, pp. 229–240.

[31] Ren, J., Rao, A., Lindorfer, M., Legout, A., and Choffnes, D. ReCon: Revealing and Controlling PII Leaks in Mobile Network Traffic. In *Proceedings of the 14th Annual International Conference on Mobile Systems, Applications, and Services* (New York, NY, USA, 2016), MobiSys '16, ACM.

[32] Schwartz, E. J., Avgerinos, T., and Brumley, D. All You Ever Wanted to Know About Dynamic Taint Analysis and Forward Symbolic Execution (but Might Have Been Afraid to Ask). In *Proceedings of the 2010 IEEE Symposium on Security and Privacy* (Washington, DC, USA, 2010), SP '10, IEEE Computer Society, pp. 317–331.

[33] Singh, K., Bhola, S., and Lee, W. xbook: Redesigning privacy control in social networking platforms. In *Proceedings of the 18th Conference on USENIX Security Symposium* (Berkeley, CA, USA, 2009), SSYM'09, USENIX Association, pp. 249–266.

[34] Sun, M., and Tan, G. NativeGuard: Protecting Android Applications from Third-party Native Libraries. In *Proceedings of the 2014 ACM Conference on Security and Privacy in Wireless & Mobile Networks* (New York, NY, USA, 2014), WiSec '14, ACM, pp. 165–176.

[35] Viswanath, B., Kiciman, E., and Saroiu, S. Keeping information safe from social networking apps. In *Proceedings of the 2012 ACM Workshop on Workshop on Online Social Networks* (New York, NY, USA, 2012), WOSN '12, ACM, pp. 49–54.

[36] Xu, R., Saïdi, H., and Anderson, R. Aurasium: Practical Policy Enforcement for Android Applications. In *Proceedings of the 21st USENIX Conference on Security Symposium* (Berkeley, CA, USA, 2012), Security'12, USENIX Association, pp. 27–27.

[37] Zeldovich, N., Boyd-Wickizer, S., Kohler, E., and Mazières, D. Making Information Flow Explicit in HiStar. In *Proceedings of the 7th USENIX Symposium on Operating Systems Design and Implementation - Volume 7* (Berkeley, CA, USA, 2006), OSDI '06, USENIX Association, pp. 19–19.

Regulating ARM TrustZone Devices in Restricted Spaces

Ferdinand Brasser
Technische Universität Darmstadt
ferdinand.brasser@trust.cased.de

Daeyoung Kim
Rutgers University
daeyoung.kim@cs.rutgers.edu

Christopher Liebchen
Technische Universität Darmstadt
christopher.liebchen@trust.cased.de

Vinod Ganapathy
Rutgers University
vinodg@cs.rutgers.edu

Liviu Iftode
Rutgers University
iftode@cs.rutgers.edu

Ahmad-Reza Sadeghi
Technische Universität Darmstadt
ahmad.sadeghi@trust.cased.de

ABSTRACT

Smart personal devices equipped with a wide range of sensors and peripherals can potentially be misused in various environments. They can be used to exfiltrate sensitive information from enterprises and federal offices or be used to smuggle unauthorized information into classrooms and examination halls. One way to prevent these situations is to regulate how smart devices are used in such restricted spaces. In this paper, we present an approach that robustly achieves this goal for ARM TrustZone-based personal devices. In our approach, restricted space hosts use remote memory operations to analyze and regulate guest devices within the restricted space. We show that the ARM TrustZone allows our approach to obtain strong security guarantees while only requiring a small trusted computing base to execute on guest devices.

CCS Concepts

•Security and privacy → Mobile platform security; •Networks → Mobile and wireless security;

Keywords

ARM TrustZone; Restricted spaces; Mobile device security

1. INTRODUCTION

Personal computing devices, such as phones, tablets, glasses, watches, assistive health monitors and other embedded devices have become an integral part of our daily lives. We carry these devices as we go, and expect them to connect and work with the environments that we visit.

While the increasing capability of smart devices and universal connectivity are generally desirable trends, there are also environments where these trends may be misused. In enterprise settings and federal institutions, for instance, malicious personal devices can be used to exfiltrate sensitive information to the outside world. In examination settings, smart devices may be used to infiltrate unauthorized information [5], surreptitiously collude with peers [40] and cheat on the exam. Even in less stringent social settings, smart devices may be used to record pictures, videos or conversations that could compromise privacy. We therefore need to regulate the use of smart devices in such *restricted spaces*.

Society currently relies on a number of ad hoc methods for policy enforcement in restricted spaces. In the most stringent settings, such as in federal institutions, employees may be required to place their personal devices in Faraday cages and undergo physical checks before entering restricted spaces. In corporate settings, employees often use separate devices for work and personal computing needs. Personal devices are not permitted to connect to the corporate network, and employees are implicitly, or by contract, forbidden from storing corporate data on personal devices. In examination settings, proctors ensure that students do not use unauthorized electronic equipment. Other examples in less formal settings include restaurants that prevent patrons from wearing smart glasses [37], or privacy-conscious individuals who may request owners to refrain from using their devices.

We posit that such ad hoc methods alone will prove inadequate given our increasing reliance on smart devices. For example, it is not possible to ask an individual with prescription smart glasses (or any other assistive health device) to refrain from using the device in the restricted space. The right solution would be to allow the glass to be used as a vision corrector, but regulate the use of its peripherals, such as the camera, microphone, or WiFi. A general method to regulate the use of smart devices in restricted spaces would benefit both the *hosts* who own or control the restricted space and *guests* who use smart devices. Hosts will have greater assurance that smart devices used in their spaces conform to their usage policies. On the other hand, guests can benefit from and be more open about their use of smart devices in the host's restricted space.[1]

Prior research projects (*e.g.*, [15, 27, 39, 42, 48, 49]) and enterprise mobile-device management (MDM) solutions to address this problem (*e.g.*, Samsung Knox [52], Microsoft Intune [38] and Blackberry EMM [13]) have typically assumed that guest devices are benign. These solutions outfit the guest device with a security-enhanced software stack that is designed to accept and enforce policies supplied by restricted space hosts. A host must trust the software running on a guest device to correctly enforce its policies, and generally has no means to obtain guarantees that a guest device is policy-compliant. Clearly, malicious guest devices with a suitably-modified software stack can easily bypass policy enforcement.

Our vision is to enable restricted space hosts to enforce usage policies on guest devices with provable security guarantees. Simultaneously, we also wish to reduce the amount of trusted policy-enforcement code (*i.e.*, the size of the security-enhanced software stack) that needs to execute on guest devices. To that end, this paper offers a number of advances:

[1] We only consider overt use of guest devices. Covert use must still be addressed using other methods, such as physical checks.

MobiSys'16, June 25-30, 2016, Singapore.
© 2016 ACM. ISBN 978-1-4503-4269-8/16/06...$15.00
DOI: http://dx.doi.org/10.1145/2906388.2906390

① **Use of trusted hardware.** We leverage the ARM TrustZone [3] on guest devices to offer provable security guarantees. In particular, a guest device uses the ARM TrustZone to produce *verification tokens*, which are unforgeable cryptographic entities that establish to a host that the guest is policy-compliant. Malicious guest devices, which may have violated the host's policies in the restricted space, will not be able to provide such a proof, and can therefore be apprehended by the host. Devices that use the ARM TrustZone are now commercially available and widely deployed [9], and our approach applies to these devices.

② **Remote memory operations.** We use host-initiated remote memory operations as the core method to regulate guest devices. In this approach, a host decides usage policies that govern how guest devices must be regulated within the restricted space. For example, the host may require certain peripherals on the guest device (*e.g.,* camera, WiFi or 3G/4G) be disabled in the restricted space. The host sends these policies to the guest device, where a trusted policy-enforcement mechanism applies these policies by reading or modifying device memory.

The principal benefit of using remote memory operations as an API for policy enforcement is that it considerably simplifies the design and implementation of the policy-enforcement mechanism, while still offering hosts fine-grained control over guest devices. Remote memory operations also give hosts that use our approach the unique ability to scan guest devices for kernel-level malware. Combined with the ARM TrustZone, which helps bootstrap trust in the guest's policy-enforcement code, our approach offers hosts an end-to-end assurance that guest devices are policy-compliant.

③ **Secure device checkpointing.** The downside to enforcing policies by modifying device memory is that changes to the guest device are ephemeral, and can be undone with a simple reboot of the guest device. We therefore introduce *REM-suspend*, a secure checkpointing scheme to ensure that a guest device remains "tethered" to the host's policies even across device reboots and other power-down events.

④ **Vetting for guest device privacy and security.** The advances above benefit hosts, but guests may be uncomfortable with the possibility of hosts accessing and modifying raw memory on their devices. If access to raw guest device memory is not mediated, malicious hosts may be able to use this access to compromise the guest's privacy and security. For example, the host can read sensitive and private app data from devices and install malicious snooping software (*e.g.,* keyloggers) on the guest device. We therefore mediate the host's access to the guest device by introducing a vetting service. The vetting service is trusted and configurable by guests, and allows them to check the safety of the host's memory operations before performing them on the devices. The vetting service ameliorates guests' privacy and security concerns and restricts the extent to which hosts can control their devices.

We built and evaluated a prototype to show the benefits of our approach. We show that a small policy-enforcing code base running on guest devices offers hosts fine-grained policy-based control over the devices. We also show that a vetting service with a few simple sanity checks allows guests to ensure the safety of the host's remote memory operations.

2. RESTRICTED SPACES

We provide an overview of the restricted space model, motivate some features of our enforcement mechanism, and describe our threat model. Because our mechanism relies on the ARM TrustZone, we begin by introducing its features.

2.1 Background on the ARM TrustZone

The TrustZone is a set of security enhancements to chipsets based on the ARM architecture. These enhancements cover the processor, memory and peripherals. With TrustZone, the processor executes instructions in one of two security modes at any given time, a *normal world* and a *secure world*. A third *monitor mode* facilitates switching between the normal and the secure worlds. The secure and normal worlds have their own address spaces and different privileges. The processor switches from the normal world to the secure world via an instruction called the secure monitor call (`smc`). When an `smc` instruction is invoked from the normal world, the processor context switches to the secure world (via monitor mode) and freezes execution of the normal world.

The ARM TrustZone partitions memory into two portions, with one portion being exclusively reserved for the secure world. It also allows individual peripherals to be assigned to the secure world. For these peripherals, hardware interrupts are directly routed to and handled by the secure world. While the normal world cannot access peripherals or memory assigned to the secure world, the secure world enjoys unrestricted access to all memory and peripherals on the device. It can therefore access the code and data of the normal world. The secure world can execute arbitrary software, ranging from simple applications to an entire operating system (OS).

A device with ARM TrustZone boots up in the secure world. After the secure world has initialized, it switches to the normal world and boots the OS there. Most TrustZone-enabled devices are configured to execute a *secure boot* sequence that incorporates cryptographic checks into the secure world boot process [3, §5.2.2]. For example, the device vendor signs the code with its private key, and the vendor's code in the boot ROM verifies this signature using the vendor's public key. These checks ensure that the integrity of the boot-time code in the secure world has not been compromised, *e.g.,* by reflashing the image on persistent storage. Most vendors lock down the secure world via secure boot, thereby ensuring that it cannot be modified by end-users. This feature allows hosts to trust software executing in the secure world and treat it as part of the trusted computing base (TCB). In this paper, we assume that guest devices use secure boot.

2.2 Entering and Exiting Restricted Spaces

Check-in. When a guest enters a restricted space, he checks in each of his devices during entry (Figure 1). During check-in, the guest device communicates with the host's policy server for the following tasks:

① **Authentication.** The first step is for the host and the guest to mutually identify each other. We assume that both the guest and the host have cryptographic credentials (*e.g.,* public/private key pairs) that are validated via a trusted third party, such as a certifying authority. The host and the guest mutually authenticate each other's credentials in the standard way, as is done during SSL/TLS handshakes.

The host's policies are enforced by a mechanism that executes in the secure world of the guest device. We rely on TrustZone's secure boot sequence to prevent unauthorized modifications to this code. Note that the end-user's usual work environment on the device, *e.g.,* the traditional Android, iOS or Windows environment with apps, executes in the normal world (and is untrusted). We expect the secure world software running the mechanisms proposed in this paper to be created and distributed by trusted entities, such as device vendors, and execute in isolation on guest devices.

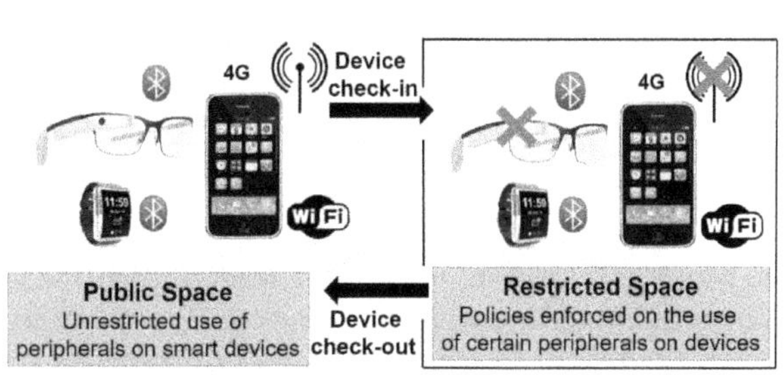

Restricted space model. Guests "check-in" their personal devices when entering restricted spaces. During check-in, hosts inspect, analyze and modify the configurations of these devices in accordance with their usage policies. In this example, the host restricts the use of the camera on the smart glass, and the 4G data interface on the smart phone. However, the glass and watch can continue to use Bluetooth pairing, while the phone can connect to the host's access points using WiFi. When guests leave the restricted space, they "check-out" their devices, restoring them to their original configurations.

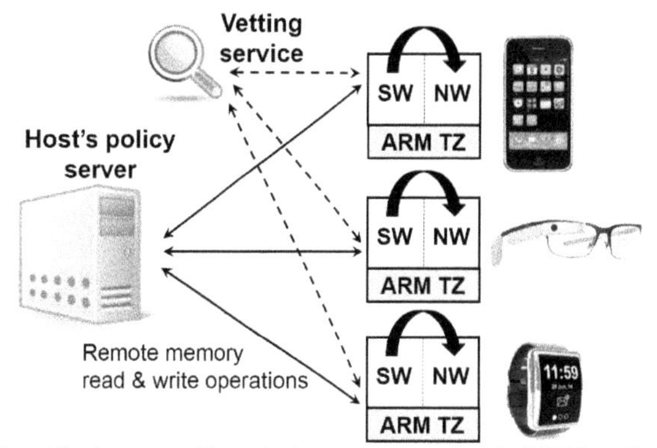

Guest device setup. Guest devices are equipped with ARM TrustZone and execute components of the policy enforcement mechanism in the secure world (SW). The details of this mechanism appear in Section 4. At check-in, the host's policy server leverages the secure world to remotely inspect and modify normal world (NW) memory.

Figure 1: An overview of the entities of our restricted space model and the setup of guest devices.

② **Host remotely reads guest state.** The host requests the guest device for a snapshot of its normal world memory and CPU register state. The secure world on the device fulfills this request (after it has been cleared by the vetting service) and sends it to the host. The secure world also sends a cryptographic checksum of this data to prevent unauthorized modifications during transit.

The host uses raw memory pages from the device in two ways. First, it scans memory pages to ensure that the normal world kernel is free of malicious software. A clean normal world kernel can bootstrap additional user-level security mechanisms, *e.g.,* an antivirus to detect malicious user-level apps. Second, it extracts the normal world's configuration information. This includes the kernel version, the list of peripherals supported, memory addresses of various device drivers for peripherals and the state of these peripherals *e.g.,* whether a certain peripheral is enabled and its settings. The host can also checkpoint the configuration for restoration at check-out.

The host terminates check-in at this point if it finds that the guest device is malicious or runs a kernel version that it cannot reconfigure. The action that the host takes depends upon the specific setting. For example, in a federal building, the device owner may be asked to quarantine the device outside the restricted space or enclose it in a physically-secured Faraday cage. In less stringent settings, the host may blacklist the device's MAC address and prevent it from connecting to any local resources in the restricted space. Note that benign end-users may not have willingly installed malware on their devices. A failed check-in has the desirable side-effect of allowing such end-users to detect that their device is infected.

③ **Host remotely modifies guest state.** The host modifies the guest device to conform to its restricted usage policies. The host's restrictions on a guest device depend on what it perceives as potential risks. Cameras and microphones on guest devices are perhaps the most obvious ways to violate the host's confidentiality because they can be used to photograph confidential documents or record sensitive meetings. Networking and storage peripherals such as WiFi, 3G/4G, Bluetooth and detachable storage dongles can work in concert with other peripherals to exfiltrate sensitive information. Dually, guest devices can also be used to infiltrate unauthorized information into restricted spaces, *e.g.,* students can cheat on exams by using their devices to communicate with the outside world.

The host controls peripherals on guest devices by creating a set of updates to the device's normal world memory and requesting the secure world to apply them. For example, one way to disable a peripheral is to unlink its driver from the device's normal world kernel (details in Section 3). The secure world applies these updates after using the vetting service to ensure the safety of the requested updates.

We assume that it is the host's responsibility to ensure that the memory modifications are not easily bypassable. For example, they may be undone if the user of the guest device directly modifies kernel memory, *e.g.,* by dynamically loading kernel modules or using /dev/kmem in the normal world. The host must inspect the guest device's snapshot for configurations that lead to such attacks, and disallow the use of such devices in the restricted space.

In steps ② and ③, the secure world performs the host's read and write operations only if they are approved by the vetting service. Guests configure the vetting service to suit their security and privacy goals. If the vetting service deems an operation unsafe, device check-in is aborted and the device is left unmodified. The guest cannot use the device in the restricted space because its security and privacy goals conflict with the host's usage policies.

④ **Host obtains verification token from guest.** After the guest device state has been modified, its secure world produces a verification token to be transmitted to the host. The verification token is a cryptographic checksum over the memory locations that were modified. The token is unforgeable in that only the secure world can re-create its value as long as the host's memory updates have not been altered, and any malicious attempts to modify the token can be detected by the secure world and the host.

The check-in steps above bear some resemblance to TPM-based software attestation protocols developed in the trusted computing community [51]. Like TPM measurements, which attest the software stack or properties of dynamic data structures [50], verification tokens attest that a guest device's state complies with the host's policies. Both TPM measurements and verification tokens are grounded in a hardware root of trust. However, unlike traditional software attestation, which has largely been restricted to passive checks of a remote machine's state, verification tokens attest to the integrity of the host's remote modifications of the guest device.

Like in software attestation, a correct verification token attests the state of the guest device only at the instant at which it was produced by the secure world. To ensure that the guest device remains policy-compliant, the host can request the device to send it the verification token at any point when the device is in the restricted space. The secure world on the device computes this token afresh, and transmits it to the host,[2] which compares this freshly-computed token with the one obtained during check-in. It uses this comparison to ensure that the guest has not altered the normal world memory updates from the previous step. The verification token incorporates a host-supplied challenge to ensure that the guest device cannot simply replay old tokens. As we demonstrate in Section 6, verification tokens are only a few hundred bytes in size and can be computed by the secure world in just a few milliseconds. Thus, hosts can request guest devices to send verification tokens at frequent intervals, thereby increasing confidence that the guest device was continuously policy-compliant.

The verification token is ephemeral, and can be computed afresh by the guest only within an expiration period. The token expires upon device check-out or if the device is powered off, thereby ensuring that end-users cannot undo the host's memory updates by simply rebooting the device. In Section 4.4, we describe *restricted space-mode (REM) suspend*, a special protocol that suspends the device while allowing the verification token and the host's memory updates to persist.

Check-out. Once checked-in, the guest device are free to avail of the facilities of the restricted space under the policies of the host. For example, in Figure 1, the smart glass and watch can pair with the smart phone via Bluetooth, while the smart phone can use the host's WiFi access point. When the guest checks-out, two tasks must be accomplished:

① **Host checks guest state.** The host requests the guest to send the verification token to ensure that the device is policy-compliant. The token may not match the value obtained from the device at check-in if the host's memory modifications have been maliciously altered or if the end-user chose to consciously bypass REM-suspend and reboot the device. It is not possible to differentiate between these cases, and the host's policy to deal with mismatches depends upon the sensitivity of the restricted environment. For example, in a federal setting, detailed device forensics may be necessary. As previously discussed, hosts can request the verification token from the device at any time when it is in the restricted space. Hosts use this feature to frequently check the verification token to narrow the timeframe of the violation.

② **Restoring guest state.** To restore the state of the device, the end-user simply performs a traditional device reboot. The host only modifies the memory of the device, and not persistent storage. Rebooting therefore undoes all the memory modifications performed by the host and boots the device from an unmodified version of the kernel in persistent storage. Alternatively, the host can restore the state of the device's peripherals from a checkpoint created at check-in. The main challenge here is to ensure consistency between the state of a peripheral and the view of the peripheral from the perspective of user-level apps. For example, when the 3G interface is disabled, an app loses network connectivity. However, because we only modify memory and do not actually reset the peripheral, the 3G card may have accumulated packets, which the app may no longer be able to process when the kernel state is restored. Mechanisms such as shadow drivers [59] can possibly enable such "hot swaps" of kernel state and avoid a device reboot.

[2]This assumes that the host's policy still allows communication between the host and the guest. If all of the guest's peripherals are disabled, the host must physically access the guest to visually obtain the fresh token.

2.3 Threat Model

We now summarize our threat model. From the host's perspective, the guest device's normal world is untrusted. However, the host trusts device manufacturers and vendors to equip the secure world with TrustZone's secure boot protocol. This allows the host to establish trust in the secure world, which contains the policy-enforcement code. It is the host's responsibility to inspect the normal world memory snapshot to determine whether it is malicious, contains known exploitable vulnerabilities, or allows guests to bypass its memory modifications. From the guest device's perspective, the host may attempt to violate its security and privacy by accessing and modifying normal world memory. The guest relies on the vetting service, which it trusts, to determine the safety of the host's remote memory operations. Guests must keep their devices powered-on or use REM-suspend to ensure that verification tokens persist during their stay in the restricted space.

Out-of-Scope Threats. The guest device's normal world may contain zero-day vulnerabilities, such as a new buffer overflow in the kernel. The host may not be aware of this vulnerability, but a malicious guest may have a successful exploit that allows the host's policies to be bypassed. While such threats are out of scope, the host may require the guest's normal world to run a fortified software stack (*e.g.,* Samsung Knox [9] or MOCFI [23]) that implements defenses for common classes of attacks. The host could check this requirement during the inspection phase. A malicious guest device may also launch a denial-of-service attack, which will prevent the host from communicating with the secure world on the guest device. Such attacks can be readily detected by the host, which can prevent the device from checking-in. We also do not consider physical attacks whereby an adversarial guest attempts to bypass the host's memory updates by modifying the contents of the device's memory chip using external methods.

We restrict ourselves to guest devices that use the ARM TrustZone. It may still be possible for hosts to enforce usage policies on non-TrustZone devices using other means (see Section 7). However, it is not possible to provide strong security guarantees without trust rooted in hardware. While such "legacy" devices are still pervasive today, modern devices are outfitted with the TrustZone, and data from Samsung [9] indicates that millions of ARM TrustZone devices are already deployed. We hypothesize that in the future, hosts will have to contend with fewer legacy guest devices than they do today.

Finally, we only consider overt uses of guest devices in restricted spaces. Covert uses, where a guest stealthily smuggles a device into the restricted space without check-in and carefully avoids an electronic footprint (*e.g.,* by shielding the device from the host's WiFi access points), must still be addressed with traditional physical security methods.

3. REMOTE MEMORY OPERATIONS

We now discuss how hosts can use remote memory read and write operations to analyze and control guest devices. Our goal is to describe the power of remote memory operations as an analysis and control API. The discussion below is therefore intentionally broader than the features that we implemented in our prototype (a description of which appears in Section 6).

Analysis of Guest Devices. Hosts analyze memory snapshots of a guest's normal world kernel to determine its configuration and scan it for kernel-level malware (also called *rootkits*).

① **Retrieving configuration information.** When a guest device first checks-in, the host must determine the configuration of the device, so that it can suitably tailor further analysis of the device. The host determines the kernel version by inspecting code pages, thereby also allowing it to check if the guest has applied recommended security patches. To ensure that the normal world is free of malicious kernel code, the host compares a hash of each kernel code page against a whitelist, *e.g.,* of code pages in approved Android distributions [35, 54]. Additionally, the host must ensure that the kernel is configured to disallow well-known attack surfaces, *e.g.,* access to /dev/kmem and dynamic module loading. Finally, the host identifies addresses at which functions of a peripheral's driver are loaded, where they are hooked into the kernel and the addresses that store memory-mapped peripheral settings. To do so, it uses the recursive memory snapshot traversal technique described below. The host uses this information to design the set of memory updates that reconfigure the device to make it policy-compliant.

② **Detecting malicious data modifications.** Rootkits achieve malicious goals by modifying key kernel data structures [11, 43, 44]. The attack surface exposed by kernel data structures is vast. For instance, a rootkit could inject a device driver in kernel memory and modify kernel function pointers to invoke methods from this driver. Other examples of data structures that can be misused include process lists, entropy pools used by the kernel's random number generator, and access control structures [11, 43].

We now describe a generic approach, developed in prior work [10, 16, 21, 28, 44], that hosts can use to detect such malicious data modifications by analyzing the normal world's memory snapshot. The main idea is to recursively traverse the memory snapshot and reconstruct a view of the kernel's data structures, and use this view to reason about the integrity of kernel data. We assume that the host has access to the type declarations of the data structures used by the guest device's normal world kernel, *e.g.,* the sizes, layouts, and fields of every data structure. The host obtains this information from trusted repositories using the kernel version, extracted as discussed earlier.

Snapshot traversal starts from well-known entrypoints into the system's memory, *e.g.,* the addresses of the entities in System.map. When the traversal process encounters a pointer, it fetches the memory object referenced by the pointer and recurses until all objects have been fetched. This traversal process works even if the guest device uses address-space layout randomization (ASLR) techniques to protect its normal world, as is done on modern Android, iOS and Windows devices. Having reconstructed a view of kernel data structures, the host can then determine whether they have been maliciously modified. For example, it could check that function pointers in the kernel point to functions defined in the kernel's code space [44]. Similarly, the host can check that the kernel's data structures satisfy invariants that typically hold in an uncompromised kernel [10]. Prior research projects have explored in-depth the full power of memory snapshot analysis for rootkit detection [10, 16, 21, 28, 44]. We do not further elaborate on these rootkit detection policies because they are orthogonal to our focus. Our own prototype implementation only showcases a simple rootkit detection policy that ensures the integrity of the normal world's system call table. However, our design allows hosts to implement any of the complex rootkit detection policies described in prior work.

Analysis of memory snapshots is a powerful approach for hosts to obtain strong assurances about guest devices. A rootkit-infected OS kernel can be reliably diagnosed *only by externally observing its code and data, e.g.,* using memory snapshots as already discussed. Prior techniques that enforce policies on guest devices by using security-enhanced, policy-enforcing normal world kernels (*e.g.,* [13, 15, 27, 38, 39, 42, 48, 49, 52]) can also benefit from our approach to establish normal world kernel integrity to hosts. Although recent work [62] has explored cache-only normal-world rootkits on ARM TrustZone devices (which do not leave a memory footprint), the large majority of known rootkits operate by modifying kernel memory and can be detected via memory snapshot analysis.

We have restricted our discussion and our prototype implementation to analyzing the normal world's kernel memory snapshot. In theory, it is possible for a host to also request and analyze the normal world's user-space memory, *e.g.,* for malicious apps that reside in memory or on the file system. However, in practice, user-space memory may contain sensitive information stored in apps, which guests may be unwilling to share with hosts. For example, guests can configure their vetting service to mark as UNSAFE host requests to fetch user-space memory pages, as we do in our prototype (see Section 5).

To ensure user-space security, hosts can leverage the normal world kernel after establishing that it is benign, *e.g.,* using the snapshot traversal methods described above. The host can require the normal world kernel to execute a mutually-agreed-upon anti-malware app in user-space. At check-in, the host scans the process list in the device's kernel memory snapshot to ensure that an anti-malware is executing. This app can check user-space memory and the file-system for malicious activity. At check-out, it can ensure that the same app is still executing by comparing its process identifier to the value obtained at check-in,[3] thereby ensuring that the anti-malware app was active for the duration of the guest's stay.

Control over Guest Device Peripherals. Hosts control the availability and configuration of peripherals on guest devices via remote memory updates to the devices. After analyzing the guest's memory snapshot, hosts prepare a set of memory updates to control various peripherals on guest devices. These updates are used to simply uninstall peripherals that may be misused violate the host's policies. Our overall approach to controlling peripherals is to update peripheral device drivers. On modern OSes, each peripheral has an interface within the kernel. This interface consists of a set of function pointers that are normally set to point to the corresponding functions within the peripheral's device driver, which communicates with the peripheral.

We adopted two broad strategies to update device drivers:

① **Nullifying interfaces (Figure 2(a)).** This approach simply sets the function pointers in the peripheral's interface to NULL. If the kernel checks these pointers prior to invoking the functions, it will simply return an error code to the application saying that the device is not installed. This approach has the advantage of only involving simple writes to the kernel (NULL bytes to certain addresses), which can easily be validated as safe if the guest so wishes. However, we found in our evaluation (Section 6) that this approach can crash the device if the kernel expects non-NULL pointers.

② **Dummy drivers (Figure 2(b)).** In this approach, the host writes a dummy driver for the peripheral and links it with the kernel in place of the original driver. If the dummy driver simply return a

[3]The security of this scheme is based on the fact that PIDs on UNIX systems are, for all practical purposes, unique on a given system. For example, while they can be recycled, it requires a large counter to wrap around.

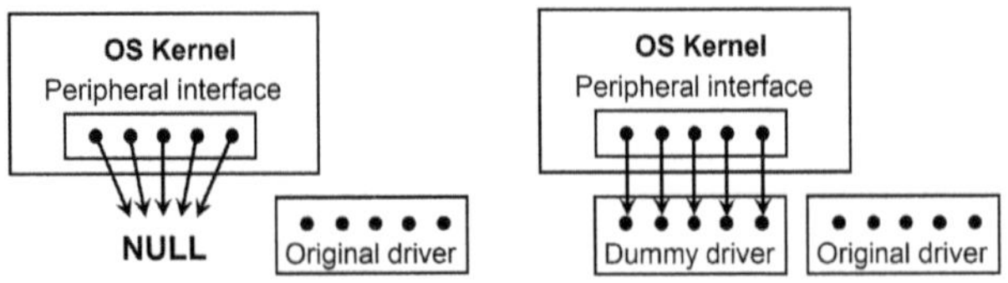

(a) NULLifying the interface **(b) Installing a dummy driver**

Each device driver exposes an interface and is linked to the kernel via function pointers. Part (a) shows how to uninstall the peripheral by making the kernel's device interface point to NULL bytes. Part (b) shows how to uninstall the peripheral by unlinking the original driver and instead linking a dummy driver.

Figure 2: Uninstalling peripheral device drivers using remote write operations to kernel memory.

suitable error code rather than communicating with the peripheral, it has the effect of uninstalling the peripheral. The error code is usually bubbled up to and handled by user apps. Some apps may not be programmed to handle such errors, so an alternative approach could be for the dummy driver to return synthetic peripheral data instead of error codes [12]. Dummy drivers also offer fine-grained peripheral control. For example, with 3G/4G, it may be undesirable to simply uninstall the modem to disable voice messaging because it also prevents the guest from making emergency calls. The host can avoid this by designing a dummy driver that allows calls to emergency numbers alone, while disabling others. In this approach, the host introduces new driver code into the guest. From the guest's perspective, this code is untrusted and must be safety-checked by the vetting service.

For the above approaches to be effective, the guest must not have access to certain attack vectors that can be used to bypass the host's memory updates. The onus of ensuring these attack vectors are precluded resides with hosts, who must carefully design their policies to analyze guest device memory snapshots. For example, the analysis must ensure that the /dev/kmem interface is not available to guests, that dynamic module loading is disallowed, and that peripheral registers are not mapped into user-space memory using the mmap interface. Likewise, the snapshot analysis must carefully account for all the interfaces exported by peripheral device drivers and aliases to the functions implemented in them to ensure that an unlinked driver is no longer reachable from any paths in the normal world kernel.

4. POLICY ENFORCEMENT

We now present the design of our policy enforcement mechanism, which executes in the guest's secure world. The host must establish a channel to communicate with the guest's secure world. This channel must be integrity-protected from adversaries, including the guest's untrusted normal world. One way to set up such a channel is to configure the secure world to exclusively control a communications peripheral, say WiFi, and connect to the host without involving the normal world. Thus, the secure world must also execute the code necessary to support this peripheral. For peripherals such as WiFi, this would require several thousand lines of code from the networking stack to run in the secure work.

Our design aims to minimize the functionality that is implemented in the secure world. In our design, the normal world is assigned all peripherals on the guest device and therefore controls all external communication from the device. It establishes the communication channel between the secure world and the host. All messages transmitted on the channel are integrity-protected by the message sender using cryptographic checksums. The secure world

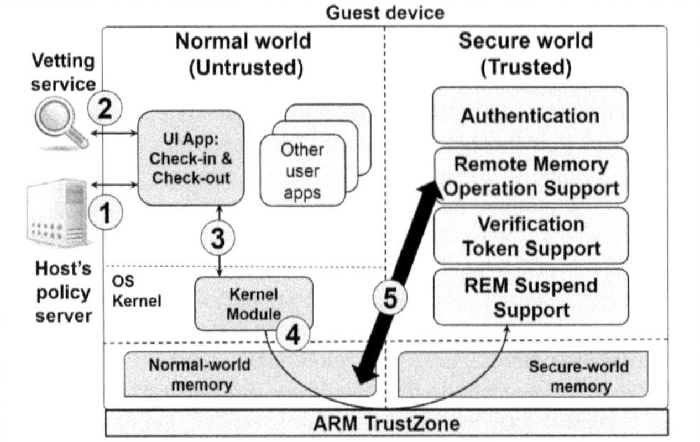

① The host communicates with the UI app on the guest and sends requests to perform remote memory operations. ② The UI app uses the vetting service to determine the safety of the request. ③ If determined to be safe, the UI app forwards this request to the supporting kernel module. ④ The kernel module invokes the secure world by performing a world switch. ⑤ The secure world performs the requested memory operations on the normal world memory on behalf of the host. The components in the normal world (the UI app and kernel module) are untrusted. We rely on ARM TrustZone's secure boot to establish trust in the secure world.

Figure 3: Guest device setup showing components of the policy enforcement mechanism.

itself provides support for just four key operations: mutual authentication (Section 4.1), remote memory operations (Section 4.2), verification tokens (Section 4.3), and REM-suspend (Section 4.4).

Guest devices are therefore set up as shown in Figure 3. Within the normal world, the end-user's interface is a user-level app (called the UI app) that allows him to interact with the host for device check-in and check-out. The app interacts with the components in the secure world via a kernel module. The host sends a request to perform remote memory operations on the guest device to the app. The app determines the safety of this request using the vetting service (Section 5), and forwards the request to the kernel module, which invokes smc to world switch into secure world. The components of the secure world then perform the request and communicate any return values to the host via the UI app. All messages include a message-authentication code computed using a key established during the mutual authentication step.

We do not place any restrictions on how the host and guest device communicate. Thus, the host's policy server could be hosted on the cloud and communicate with the guest device over WiFi or 3G/4G. Alternatively, the host could install physical scanners at a kiosk or on the entry-way to the restricted space. Guest devices would use Bluetooth, NFC, or USB to pair with the scanner and use it to communicate with the host.

The core mechanisms that run in the secure world of the guest device have two key features. They are *policy-agnostic* in that the same mechanisms can be used to enforce a variety of host policies. The narrow read/write interface is also *platform-agnostic*, and allows the same mechanisms to work irrespective of whether the normal world runs Android, iOS or Windows. This approach shifts complex device analysis and policy formulation tasks to the hosts. Hosts would naturally need to have separate modules to analyze and formulate memory updates for various normal world OSes.

4.1 Authentication

The host and guest device begin by mutually authenticating each other (Figure 4). We assume that both the host and the guest de-

Let host's public/private keypair be PubKeyH, PrivKeyH.
Let guest's public/private keypair be PubKeyG, PrivKeyG.

1. **Guest → Host**: PubKeyG, Certificate(PubKeyG)
2. **Host → Guest**: PubKeyH, Certificate(PubKeyH)
3. Guest and host verify Certificate(PubKeyH) and Certificate(PubKeyG)
4. **Host → Guest**: M, $\mathsf{Enc}_{\mathsf{PrivKeyH}}(M)$ (*i.e.,* host signs M), where M is $\mathsf{Enc}_{\mathsf{PubKeyG}}(k_s$, timestamp)
5. Guest verifies host's digital signature, decrypts M to obtain k_s, and checks timestamp

Figure 4: Mutual authentication and establishment of k_s.

vice have public/private key pairs with digital certificates issued by a certifying authority. The guest device stores its private key PrivKeyG in its secure world, thereby protecting it from the untrusted normal world.

Authentication is akin to SSL/TLS handshakes. The host and the guest exchange public keys and validate the certificates of these keys with the issuing authority. The host then computes a session key k_s, which is then transmitted to the client over a secure channel. Note that k_s is only used to protect the integrity of messages transmitted between the guest and the host and not their secrecy. The key k_s is stored in secure world memory, and is invisible to the normal world. It persists across REM-suspends of the guest device, but is erased from memory if the device is rebooted.

As with SSL/TLS, the ability of this protocol to resist man-in-the-middle attacks depends on the host and guest device's ability to validate each other's public keys. We assume that device vendors would provision PubKeyG for individual devices and register them with a certifying authority. Hosts register PubKeyH in much the same manner as is done for Web services today. While there is a case to be made that the certifying authority model has its limitations in the era of the Web and smart devices [17], we note that our use of authentication is entirely standard—to validate the host's and guest device's identities and to establish a session key k_s. Thus, we think that the other parts of our policy enforcement mechanism will work as-is with alternative authentication schemes, *e.g.,* those that use identity-based encryption.

4.2 Remote Reads and Writes

Remote Reads. During check-in the host typically requests the guest to send raw memory pages from the normal world for analysis. The UI app receives this request and performs a world switch to complete the request. The world switch suspends the UI app and transfers control to the secure world. Each request is a set (or range) of virtual memory addresses of pages that must be sent to the host. The host also includes a message-authentication code, a SHA1-based HMAC in our case, with the request. The HMAC is computed on the body of the request using the key k_s negotiated during authentication.

The secure world checks the integrity of the request using the HMAC. This step is necessary to ensure that the request was not maliciously modified by the untrusted components in the normal world. The secure world then translates each virtual page address in the request to a physical page address by consulting the page table in the normal world kernel. In this case, the page table will correspond to the suspended context in the normal world, *i.e.,* that of the UI app, into which the running kernel is also mapped. It then creates a local copy of the contents of this physical page from the normal world, and computes an HMAC over the page (again using k_s). The page and its HMAC are then copied to a buffer in the normal world, from where they can be transmitted to the host by the UI app. The host checks the HMAC and uses the page for analysis. This process could be iterative, with the host requesting more pages from the guest device based upon the results of the analysis of the memory pages received up to that point.

Both the host and the secure world are isolated from the normal world, which is untrusted. We only rely on the normal world kernel to facilitate communication between the host and the secure world. Moreover, both the host and the secure world use HMACs to protect the integrity of messages transmitted via the normal world. The normal world may drop messages and cause a denial-of-service attack; however, such attacks are outside our threat model (see Section 2.3). The host can therefore reliably obtain the memory pages of the normal world to enable the kinds of analyses described in Section 3. Communication between the host and the secure world is not confidential and is therefore not encrypted.[4] Thus, a malicious normal world kernel can potentially snoop on the requests from the host to fetch pages and attempt to remove the infection to avoid detection. However, this would have the desirable side-effect of cleaning the guest device at check-in.

Remote Writes. The host reconfigures the guest by modifying the running state of the normal world kernel via remote memory updates. The host sends the guest a set of triples $\langle vaddr_i, val_i, old\text{-}val_i\rangle$ together with an HMAC of this request. The normal world conveys this message to the secure world, which verifies its integrity using the HMAC. For each virtual address $vaddr_i$ (which refers to a memory location in the virtual address space of the UI app) in the request, the secure world ensures that the current value at the address matches $old\text{-}val_i$. If *all* the $old\text{-}val_i$ values match, the secure world replaces their values with val_i; else the *entire* operation is aborted.

Because the normal world is frozen during the course of this operation, the entire update is atomic with respect to the normal world. When a remote write operation succeeds, the secure world computes and returns a verification token to the host. If not, it returns an ABORT error code denoting failure.

The host's memory update request is aborted if the value stored at $vaddr_i$ does not match $old\text{-}val_i$. This design feature is required because the host's remote read and write operations do not happen as an atomic unit. The host remotely reads pages copied from the normal world's memory, analyzes them and creates remote write request using this analysis. During this time, the normal world kernel continues to execute, and may have updated the value at the address $vaddr_i$.

If the memory update is aborted, the host repeats the operation until it succeeds. That is, it refetches pages from the guest, analyzes them, and creates a fresh update. In theory, it is possible that the host's memory updates will abort *ad infinitum.* However, for the setting that we consider, aborts are rare in practice. This is because our write operations modify the addresses of peripheral device driver hooks. Operating systems typically do not change the values of device driver hooks after they have been initialized at system boot.

In theory, a remote memory write can also abort if the virtual address $vaddr_i$ referenced in the request is not mapped to a physical page in memory, *i.e.,* if the corresponding page has been swapped out to persistent storage. In practice, however, we restrict remote writes to kernel data pages that are resident in physical memory, as is the case with device drivers and pages that store data structures

[4]The host and guest could communicate over SSL/TLS, but this channel on the guest ends at the UI app, which runs in the normal world.

of peripherals. Thus, we do not observe ABORTs due to a failure to resolve $vaddr_i$s.

It is possible to completely avoid such problems by designing the both the read and write operations to complete within a single world switch. During this time, the normal world remains frozen and cannot change the view of memory exported to the host. The read and write operations will therefore happen as an atomic unit from the normal world's perspective. However, in this case, the secure world must have the ability to directly communicate with the host. As previously discussed, we decided against this design because it has the unfortunate consequence of bloating the functionality to be implemented in the secure world. Thus, we make the practical design tradeoff of minimizing the functionality of the secure world while allowing the rare remote write failure to happen.

Note that our approach uses virtual addresses in remote memory operations. In doing so, we implicitly trust the integrity of page tables in the normal world kernel, which are used to translate these virtual addresses to physical ones. Recent work has demonstrated address-translation redirection (ATRA) attacks that work by maliciously modifying page table entries and the page table base register [31]. An ATRA attack effectively hides malicious code and data modifications by creating shadow pages containing unmodified code and data, and maliciously modifying page table entries to redirect requests from a security monitor to these shadow pages. On ARM TrustZone devices, it is possible to defend against such attacks by ensuring that all normal world page table updates are shepherded by the secure world. This is implemented by modifying the normal world kernel to invoke the secure world (via smc) for page table updates, and implementing a suitable security policy within the secure world to ensure the integrity of these updates [9, 24]. We have not implemented this defense in our prototype and doing so will require additional code in the secure world. However, we note that such a defense is already implemented as part of the secure world in Samsung Knox [9]. We hypothesize that a solution that integrates our approach with Knox will therefore be robust against ATRA attacks.

4.3 Verification Tokens

The host receives a verification token from the secure world upon successful completion of a remote write operation that updates normal world memory. A verification token $\mathsf{VTok}[r]$ is the following value: $r||\mathit{MemState}||\mathsf{HMAC}_{k_s}[r||\mathit{MemState}]$ where *MemState* is $\langle vaddr_1,\ val_1\rangle||\ldots||\langle vaddr_n,\ val_n\rangle$, the set of $vaddr_i$ modified by the remote write, and the new values val_i at these locations. The token $\mathsf{VTok}[r]$ is parameterized by a random nonce r. This nonce can either be provided by the host together with the remote write request, or can be generated by the secure world.

Verification tokens allow the host to determine whether the guest attempted to revert the host's memory updates, either maliciously or by turning off the guest device. To do so, the host obtains a verification token $\mathsf{VTok}[r_{checkin}]$ upon completion of check-in, and stores this token for validation. During checkout, the host requests a validation token $\mathsf{VTok}[r_{checkout}]$ from the guest over the same virtual memory addresses. The secure world accesses each of these memory addresses and computes the verification token with $r_{checkout}$ as the nonce. The host can compare the verification tokens $\mathsf{VTok}[r_{checkin}]$ and $\mathsf{VTok}[r_{checkout}]$ to determine whether there were any changes to the values stored at these memory addresses.

The nonces $r_{checkin}$ and $r_{checkout}$ ensure the freshness of the tokens $\mathsf{VTok}[r_{checkin}]$ and $\mathsf{VTok}[r_{checkout}]$. The use of k_s to compute the HMAC in the verification token ensures that the token is only valid for a specific device and for the duration of the session, *i.e.,* until check-out or until the device is powered off, whichever comes earlier. Because k_s is only stored in secure world memory, it is ephemeral and unreadable to the normal world. Any attempts to undo the host's memory updates performed at check-in will thus be detected by the host.

4.4 Restricted Space Mode (REM) Suspend

If a guest device is rebooted, the host's updates to device memory are undone and k_s is erased from secure world memory, thereby ending the session. However, it is sometimes necessary to suspend the device in the restricted space, *e.g.,* to conserve battery power. We design REM-suspend to handle such cases and allow the session key k_s to persist when the device is woken.

The ARM TrustZone allows a device to be configured to route certain interrupts to the secure world [3]. We route and handle power-button presses and low-battery events in the secure world by prompting the user to specify whether to REM-suspend the device. When a guest device is checked into a restricted space, we configure the default power-down option to be REM-suspend; the default reverts to the traditional power-down sequence when the device checks out. The user can consciously choose to bypass REM-suspend, in which case the device shuts down the traditional way, thus ending the session. The same happens if the device shuts down due to other causes, *e.g.,* power loss caused by removing the device's battery.

When the guest device REM-suspends, the secure world checkpoints normal world memory, which contains the host's updates, and the key k_s, which are both restored when the device is woken up. The main challenge is to protect the confidentiality of k_s. The device user is untrusted, and can read the contents of persistent storage on the device; k_s must thus be stored encrypted with a key that is not available to the device user.

To achieve this goal, we leverage a feature referenced in the ARM TrustZone manual [3, §6.3.1], which provisions a device with a statistically-unique one-time programmable secret key that we will refer to as $\mathsf{K_{Dev}}$. $\mathsf{K_{Dev}}$ is located in an on-SoC cryptographic accelerator, and accessible only to secure world software [3, §6.3.1]. $\mathsf{K_{Dev}}$ cannot be read or changed outside the secure world, other bus masters or the JTAG [32]. $\mathsf{K_{Dev}}$ allows confidential data to be encrypted and bound to the device, and has previously been referenced in other research [7, 18, 46, 53]. Note that $\mathsf{K_{Dev}}$ is not the same as PrivKeyG, the device's private key.

In REM-suspend, the secure world first checkpoints normal world memory and CPU registers, and suspends the execution of the normal world. It sets a bit $\mathsf{B_{REM}}$ to record that the device is REM-suspended. It stores the checkpoint and $\mathsf{B_{REM}}$, together with an HMAC of these values under k_s on the device's persistent storage. It also stores to persistent storage the value of k_s encrypted under $\mathsf{K_{Dev}}$. The untrusted device user does not know $\mathsf{K_{Dev}}$, and therefore cannot forge the encrypted value of k_s or retrieve the cleartext value of k_s. The HMACs under k_s protect the integrity of the normal world checkpoint and $\mathsf{B_{REM}}$. An alternative way to protect the integrity of the normal world checkpoint and $\mathsf{B_{REM}}$ is to store them in the replay-protected memory block (RPMB), a trusted storage partition available on many mobile devices that come equipped with a embedded multi-media storage controller. The RPMB offers integrity-protection for stored data, ensures data freshness by protecting against replay attacks, and has been leveraged in recent work [46]. However, even with this alternative the confidentiality of k_s needs to be protected by encrypting it using $\mathsf{K_{Dev}}$.

When the device is woken up, the secure world uses $\mathsf{B_{REM}}$ to check if the device is REM-suspended. If so, it uses $\mathsf{K_{Dev}}$ to retrieve k_s, verifies the integrity of the normal world checkpoint and $\mathsf{B_{REM}}$

using their HMACs, and starts the normal world from this checkpoint. The device resumes execution under the same session and continues to produce verification tokens if requested by the host.

The original ARM TrustZone manual [3] described K_{Dev} in the context of a hypothetical device, and K_{Dev} is not part of the core specification of the TrustZone architecture. As such, it is not clear how many deployed devices support K_{Dev}; for example, it is not supported by the TrustZone-enabled board that we used for our prototype implementation. Many emerging ARM TrustZone-based security solutions [18, 46, 53] rely on the existence of K_{Dev}, and it is likely that future revisions of the TrustZone architecture will incorporate such a key. The REM-suspend protocol can be used on any device that supports K_{Dev} or a cryptographic key with similar properties, *i.e.,* a hardware-provisioned key only accessible from the secure world. Note that guest devices that do not support such a key can still be restricted using our approach. However, the only shortcoming is that without REM-suspend, a power-down event will undo the memory updates requested by the host, and clear k_s, thereby terminating the session with the host.

5. GUEST PRIVACY AND SECURITY

We built a vetting service trusted by guests to determine the safety of a host's request. We built it as a cloud-based server, to which the guest device forwards the host's memory updates together with a copy of its normal world memory image (via the UI app). We assume that the device and the vetting service have authenticated each other as in Figure 4 or use SSL/TLS to obtain a communication channel with end-to-end confidentiality and integrity guarantees. It may also be possible to implement vetting within the secure world itself. However, we chose not to do so to avoid bloating the secure world.

The vetting server checks the host's requests against its safety policies and returns a SAFE or UNSAFE response to the device. The response is bound with a random nonce and an HMAC to the original request in the standard way to prevent replay attacks. The secure world performs the operations only if the response is SAFE. Guests can configure the vetting server with domain-specific policies to determine safety. Our prototype vetting service, which we built as a plugin to the Hex-Rays IDA toolkit [1], analyzes memory images and checks for the following safety policies. Although simple and based on conservative whitelisting, in our experiments, the policies could prove safety without raising false positives.

- **Read-safety.** For each request to read from address $vaddr_i$, we return SAFE only if $vaddr_i$ falls in a pre-determined range of virtual addresses. In our prototype, acceptable address ranges only include pages that contain kernel code and kernel data structures. The vetting server returns UNSAFE if the read request attempts to fetch any addresses from kernel buffers that store user app data, or virtual address ranges that lie in app user-space memory.

- **Write-safety.** Our prototype currently only allows write requests to NULLify peripheral interfaces or install dummy drivers that disable peripherals. We use the following safety policy for dummy drivers. For each function f implemented in the dummy driver, consider its counterpart f_{orig} from the original driver, which the vetting service obtains from the device's memory image. We return SAFE only if the function f is identical to f_{orig}, or f's body consists of a single return statement that returns a *valid* error code (*e.g.,* -ENOMEM). We define an error code as being valid for f if and only if the same error code is returned along at least one path in f_{orig}. The intuition behind this safety check is that f does not modify the memory state of the device or introduce new and possibly buggy code, but returns an error code that is acceptable to the kernel and client user apps. For more complex dummy drivers that introduce new code, the vetting service could employ a traditional malware detector or more complex program analyses to scan this code for safety.

We implemented the above safety policies in a 190-line Python plugin to the IDA toolkit. In the following section, we report the performance of the vetting server as it established the safety of various host requests to uninstall guest device peripherals. Although we have only explored the simple safety policies discussed above, the vetting service can implement more complex policies, and we plan to experiment with such policies in future work. For example, although our read-safety policy ensures that only kernel code and data pages can be sent to the host, even these pages may compromise the guest's privacy. The buffer cache and various buffers used by the networking stack reside in kernel data pages, and may store sensitive user information. A more nuanced read-safety policy would identify which memory addresses store such data and mark as UNSAFE any host requests to fetch data from those addresses. Note that implementing more complex vetting policies will increase the code-base of the vetting service, which the guest trusts. However, this complexity does not affect the size of the TCB running on the guest device.

6. IMPLEMENTATION AND EVALUATION

We implemented our policy enforcement mechanism on a i.MX53 Quick Start Board from Freescale as our guest device. This board is TrustZone-enabled and has a 1GHz ARM Cortex A8 processor with 1GB DDR3 RAM. We chose this board as the guest device because it offers open, programmable access to the secure world. In contrast, the vendors of most commercially-available TrustZone-enabled devices today lock down the secure world and prevent any modifications to it. A small part of main memory is reserved for exclusive use by the secure world. On our i.MX53 board, we assigned the secure world 256MB of memory, although it may be possible to reduce this with future optimizations. The normal world runs Android 2.3.4 atop Linux kernel version 2.6.35.3.

We built a bare-metal runtime environment for the secure world, just enough to support the components shown in Figure 3. This environment has a memory manager, and a handler to parse and process commands received from the host via the normal world. To implement cryptographic operations, we used components from an off-the-shelf library called the ARM mbed TLS (v1.3.9) [2]. Excluding the cryptography library, our secure world consists of about 3,500 lines of C code, including about 250 lines of inline assembly. The secure world implements all the features described in Section 4, except for one minor deviation in the implementation of the REM-suspend protocol. The i.MX53 does not support K_{Dev}, so our prototype implements REM-suspend assuming that such a key is available and can be fetched from hardware.

Figure 5 shows the sizes of various components. We used mbed TLS's implementation of SHA1 and HMACs, RSA and X509 certificates. As shown in Figure 5, the files implementing these components alone comprise only about 4,000 lines of code. In addition to these secure world components, we built the kernel module and the UI app (written as a native daemon) for the normal world, comprising 165 lines of code. We implemented a host policy server that authenticates guest devices, and performs remote memory operations. We conducted experiments to showcase the utility of remote reads and writes to enforce the host's policies on the guest. The guest and the host communicate over WiFi.

Component Name	LOC
Secure World (TCB)	
Memory manager	1,381
Authentication	1,285
Memory ops. & verif. tokens	305
REM-suspend	609
SHA1+HMAC	861
X509	877
RSA	2,307
Normal World	
Kernel module	93
UI app	72

Figure 5: Sizes of components on the guest.

Peripheral uninstalled	Approach used (from Figure 2)	Device used	Bytes added or modified	Vetting time (sec.)	Verification token (bytes)
USB (webcam)	NULLification	i.MX53	104	-	260
USB (webcam)	Dummy driver	i.MX53	168	2.22	388
Camera	NULLification	Nexus	140	-	332
Camera	Dummy driver	Nexus	224	2.19	500
WiFi	Dummy driver	Nexus	152	5.58	356
3G (Data)	Dummy driver	Nexus	192	2.15	436
3G (Voice)	Dummy driver	Nexus	124	2.15	300
Microphone	Dummy driver	Nexus	164	2.27	380
Bluetooth	Dummy driver	Nexus	32	2.52	116

Figure 6: Peripherals uninstalled using remote write operations to a guest device.

Guest Device Analysis. To illustrate the power of remote memory read operations to perform device analysis, we wrote a simple rootkit that infects the guest's normal world kernel by hooking its system call table. In particular, it replaces the entry for the close system call to instead point to a malicious function injected into the kernel. The malicious functionality ensures that if the process invoking close calls it with a magic number, then the process is elevated to root. Although simple in its operation, Petroni and Hicks [44] show that over 95% of all rootkits that modify kernel data operate this way.

We were able to detect this rootkit on the host by remotely reading and analyzing the guest's memory pages. We remotely read pages containing the init, text and data sections of kernel memory. Our analyzer, a 48 line Python script, reads the addresses in the system call table from memory, and compares these entries with addresses in System.map. If the address is not included, *e.g.,* as happens if the entry for the close system call is modified, it raises an error. For more sophisticated rootkits that modify arbitrary kernel data structures, the host can use complex detection algorithms [10, 16, 44] based on the recursive snapshot traversal method outlined in Section 3.

For the above experiment, it took the secure world 54 seconds to create an HMAC over the memory pages that were sent to the host (9.2MB in total). It takes under a second to copy data from the normal world to the secure world and vice versa. It may be possible to accelerate the performance of the HMAC implementation using floating point registers and hardware acceleration, but we have not done so in our prototype.

Guest Device Control. We evaluated the host's ability to dynamically reconfigure a guest device via remote memory write operations. For this experiment, we attempted to disable a number of peripherals from the guest device. However, the i.MX53 board only supports a bare-minimum number of peripherals. As proof-of-concept, we therefore tested the effectiveness of remote writes on a Samsung Galaxy Nexus smart phone with a Texas Instruments OMAP 4460 chipset. This chipset has a 1.2GHz dual-core ARM Cortex-A9 processor with 1GB of RAM, and runs Android 4.3 atop Linux kernel version 3.0.72. This device has a rich set of peripherals, but its chipset comes with TrustZone locked down, *i.e.,* the secure world is not accessible to third-party programmers. We therefore performed remote writes by modifying memory using a kernel module in its (normal world) OS. Thus, while remote writes to this device do not enjoy the security properties described in Section 4, they allow us to evaluate the ability to uninstall a variety of peripherals from a running guest device.

Figure 6 shows the set of peripherals that we uninstalled, the method used to uninstall the peripheral (from Section 3), the device on which we performed the operation (i.MX53 or Nexus), and the size of the write operation, *i.e.,* the number of bytes that we had to modify/introduce in the kernel. We were able to uninstall the USB on the i.MX53 and the camera on the phone by NULLifying the peripheral interface. For other peripherals, we introduced dummy drivers designed according to the safety criterion from Section 5. We also used dummy drivers for the USB and the camera to compare the size of the write operations. In this case, the size of the write includes both the bytes modified in the peripheral interface and the dummy driver functions. For the 3G interface, we considered two cases: that of disabling only 3G data and that of only disabling calls. Our experiment shows it is possible to uninstall peripherals without crashing the OS by just modifying a few hundred bytes of memory on the running device.

For each uninstalled peripheral, Figure 6 shows the time taken by the vetting service to determine the safety of the write operation (using the policy from Section 5). Our vetting service runs on a quad-core Intel i5-4960 CPU running at 3.5Gz, with 16GB of memory. Figure 6 also shows the size of the verification token generated by the secure world for the write operation. The size of the verification token grows linearly with the size of the write operation, but is just a few hundred bytes in all cases. On the i.MX53, it took the secure world under 6 milliseconds to generate the verification tokens. This shows that it is practical for the host to request the guest device to resend the verification token at periodic intervals during its stay in the restricted space.

Installing a dummy driver disables the peripheral, but how does it affect the user app that is using the peripheral? To answer this question, we conducted two sets of experiments involving a number of client user apps that leverage the peripherals shown in Figure 6. In the first set of experiments, which we call the *passive setting*, we start with a configuration where the client app is not executing, replace the device driver of the peripheral with a dummy, and then start the app. In the second set of experiments, called the *active setting*, we replace the peripheral's device driver with the dummy as the client app that uses the peripheral is executing.

Figure 7 shows the results of our experiments. For both the passive and active settings, we observe that in most cases, the user app displays a suitable error message or changes its behavior by displaying a blank screen or creating an empty audio file. In some cases, particularly in the passive setting, the app fails to start when the driver is replaced, and the Android runtime displays an error that it is unable to start the app.

7. RELATED WORK AND ALTERNATIVES

TrustZone Support. A number of projects have used TrustZone to build novel security applications. TrustDump [58] is a TrustZone-based mechanism to reliably acquire memory pages from the normal world of a device (Android LiME [26] and similar acquisition tools [25, 57, 60] do so too, but without the security offered by TrustZone). While similar in spirit to remote reads, Trust-

USB	*MobileWebCam*	*Camera ZOOM FX*	*Retrica*	*Candy Camera*	*HD Camera Ultra*
Passive	AppErrMsg	AppErrMsg	AndroidErrMsg	AppErrMsg	AndroidErrMsg
Active	AppErrMsg	AppErrMsg	AppErrMsg	AppErrMsg	AppErrMsg
Camera	*Camera for Android*	*Camera MX*	*Camera ZOOM FX*	*HD Camera for Android*	*HD Camera Ultra*
Passive	AndroidErrMsg	AppErrMsg	AppErrMsg	AndroidErrMsg	AndroidErrMsg
Active	BlankScreen	AppErrMsg	AndroidErrMsg	BlankScreen	BlankScreen
WiFi	*Spotify*	*Play Store*	*YouTube*	*Chrome Browser*	*Facebook*
Passive	LostConn	LostConn	LostConn	LostConn	LostConn
Active	LostConn	LostConn	LostConn	LostConn	LostConn
3G (Data)	*Spotify*	*Play Store*	*YouTube*	*Chrome Browser*	*Facebook*
Passive	LostConn	LostConn	LostConn	LostConn	LostConn
Active	LostConn	LostConn	LostConn	LostConn	LostConn
3G (Voice)	*Default call application*				
Passive	AppErrMsg: Unable to place a call				
Active	AppErrMsg: Unable to place a call				
Microphone	*Audio Recorder*	*Easy Voice Recorder*	*Smart Voice Recorder*	*Sound and Voice Recorder*	*Voice Recorder*
Passive	AppErrMsg	AppErrMsg	AppErrMsg	AppErrMsg	AppErrMsg
Active	EmptyFile	EmptyFile	EmptyFile	EmptyFile	EmptyFile

We use *Passive* to denote experiments in which the user app was not running when the peripheral's driver was replaced with a dummy, and the app was started after this replacement. We use *Active* to denote experiments in which the peripheral's driver was replaced with a dummy even as the client app was executing. ① AppErrMsg denotes the situation where the user app starts normally, but an error message box is displayed within the app after it starts up; ② BlankScreen denotes a situation where the user app displayed a blank screen; ③ LostConn denotes a situation where the user app loses network connection; ④ EmptyFile denotes a situation where no error message is displayed, but the sound file that is created is empty; ⑤ AndroidErrMsg denotes the situation where the user app fails to start (in the passive setting) or a running app crashes (in the active setting), and the Android runtime system displays an error.

Figure 7: Results of robustness experiments for user apps.

Dump's focus is to be an alternative to virtualized memory introspection solutions for malware detection. Unlike our work, TrustDump is not concerned with restricted spaces, authenticating the host, or remotely configuring guest devices.

Samsung Knox [9] and SPROBES [24] leverage TrustZone to protect the normal world in real-time from kernel-level rootkits. These projects harden the normal world kernel by making it perform a world switch when it attempts to perform certain sensitive operations to kernel data. A reference monitor in the secure world checks these operations, thereby preventing rootkits. In our work, remote reads allow the host to detect infected devices, but we do not attempt to provide real-time protection from malware. Our work can also leverage Knox to enhance the security of the normal world (Section 2.3).

While we have leveraged TrustZone's ability to isolate secure world memory from the normal world, TrustZone supports additional features that can be used to explore alternative designs. One such feature is TrustZone's support for peripheral reassignment between the normal and secure worlds. Using this feature, a host could require all of a guest device's restricted peripherals to the trusted secure world during check-in. The secure world implements the equivalent of dummy drivers that control and therefore restrict peripherals.

The above design is a viable alternative that we plan to explore in future work. In our current design, we chose to explore the benefits and limits of remote memory operations because it allowed us to satisfy our goal of minimizing the size of the TCB on guest devices. The alternative design described above would require additional driver code to execute in the secure world. That said, even this design alternative can leverage some of the ideas from our current work. For example, peripherals assigned to the secure world at check-in can be reassigned to the normal world via a device reboot. A protocol based on REM-suspend can be used to save peripheral assignment state upon power-down events, and restore the peripheral assignment upon power-up in guest devices that support K_{Dev}.

TrustZone has also been used to improve the security of user applications. Microsoft's TLR [53] and Nokia's ObC [33] use TrustZone to provide a secure execution environment for user apps, even in the presence of a compromised kernel. Other applications include ensuring trustworthy sensor readings from peripherals [36], securing mobile payments (*e.g.,* Apple Pay and Samsung Pay), mobile data billing [47], attesting mobile advertisements [34], and implementing the TPM-2.0 specification in firmware [46].

Enterprise Security. With the growing "bring your own device" (BYOD) trend, a number of research projects and enterprise MDM products (*e.g.,* [13, 38, 52]) have developed security solutions that enable multiple persona (*e.g.,* [6, 15, 27]) or enforce mandatory access control policies on smart devices (*e.g.,* [15, 27, 55, 61]). Prior work has also explored context-based access control and techniques for restricted space objects to push usage policies onto guest devices (*e.g.,* [19, 39, 41, 42, 48, 49]).

These projects tend to use one of two techniques. One is to require guest devices to run a software stack enhanced with a policy enforcement mechanism. For instance, ASM [27] introduces a set of security hooks in Android, which consult a security policy (installed as an app) that can be used to create multiple persona on a device. Each persona is customized with a view of apps and peripherals that it can use. Another approach is to require virtualized guest devices [4, 6, 20, 22]. In this approach, a trusted hypervisor on the guest device enforces isolation between virtual machines implementing different persona.

The main benefit of these techniques over our work is the greater app-level control that they provide. For example, they can be used to selectively block sensitive audio and blur faces by directly applying policies to the corresponding user apps [30, 49]. These techniques are able to do so because they have a level of semantic visibility into app-level behavior that is difficult to achieve at the level of raw memory operations.

On the other hand, our approach enjoys two main benefits over prior work. First, our approach simplifies the design of the trusted policy-enforcing code that runs on guest devices to a TCB of just a few thousand lines of code. In contrast, security-enhanced OSes and virtualized solutions required hundreds of thousands of lines of trusted policy-enforcement code to execute on guest devices. Prior research has investigated ways to reduce the TCB, *e.g.,* by creating small hypervisors [56]. However, the extent to which such work on small hypervisors applies to smart devices is unclear, given that any such hypervisor must support a variety of different virtualization modes, guest quirks, and hardware features on a diverse set of personal devices.

The second benefit of our approach is that it provides security guarantees that are rooted in trusted hardware. Prior projects have generally trusted guest devices to correctly implement the host's policies. This trust can easily be violated by a guest running a maliciously-modified OS or hypervisor. It is also not possible for a host to obtain guarantees that the policy was enforced for the duration of the guest's stay in the restricted space. We leverage the TrustZone to offer such guarantees using verification tokens and REM-suspend.

Other Hardware Interfaces. Hardware interfaces for remote memory operations were originally investigated for the server world to perform remote DMA as a means to bypass the performance overheads of the TCP/IP stack [8, 29]. This work has since been repurposed to perform kernel malware detection [45] and remote repair [14]. These systems use a PCI-based co-processor on guests via which the host can remotely transfer and modify memory pages on the guest.

On personal devices, the closest equivalent to such a hardware interface is the IEEE 1394 (Firewire), which is available on some laptops. However, it is not currently available on smaller form-factor devices. Another possibility is to use the JTAG interface [32], which allows read/write access to memory and CPU registers via a few dedicated pins on the chipset. However, the JTAG is primarily used for debugging and is not easily accessible on consumer devices. One drawback of repurposing these hardware interfaces is that they cannot authenticate the credentials of the host that initiates the memory operation. Moreover, to use these hardware interfaces on guest devices, the host needs physical access to plug into them. Thus, these interfaces are best used when the guest can physically authenticate the host and trust it to be benign.

8. CONCLUDING REMARKS

This paper develops mechanisms that allow hosts to analyze and regulate ARM TrustZone-based guest devices using remote memory operations. These mechanisms can be implemented with only a small amount of trusted code running on guest devices. The use of the TrustZone allows our approach to provide strong guarantees of guest policy-compliance to hosts. Our vetting service allows guests to identify conflicts between their privacy goals and the hosts' usage policies.

While this paper demonstrates technical feasibility of our approach, questions about its adoptability in real-world settings remain to be answered. For example, we can imagine our solution to be readily applicable in settings such as federal or corporate offices and examination halls, where restricted spaces are clearly demarcated and the expectations on guest device usage are clearly outlined. Will it be equally palatable in less stringent settings, such as social gatherings, malls or restaurants? A meaningful answer to this question will require a study of issues such as user-perception and willingness to allow their devices to be remotely analyzed and controlled by hosts. We hope to investigate these and other issues in follow-on research.

Acknowledgments. We thank the MobiSys reviewers, our shepherd Ardalan Amiri Sani, Trent Jaeger, Xinyang Ge, Giuseppe Petracca, and Santosh Nagarakatte for their comments on drafts of this paper. Daeyoung Kim, Vinod Ganapathy and Liviu Iftode were supported in part by the US National Science Foundation grants CNS-1441724, CCF-1408803, CNS-1117711, and CNS-0952128. Ferdinand Brasser, Christopher Liebchen and Ahmad-Reza Sadeghi were funded by the German Science Foundation (DFG) as part of project S2 within CRC 1119 CROSSING, European Union's Horizon 2020 research and innovation program under grant agreement number 643964 (SUPERCLOUD), and the Intel Collaborative Research Institute for Secure Computing.

REFERENCES

(All URLs verified in April 2016.)

[1] Hex-rays software: About IDA. https://www.hex-rays.com/products/ida/index.shtml.

[2] SSL Library ARM mbed TLS/PolarSSL. https://tls.mbed.org.

[3] ARM security technology – Building a secure system using TrustZone technology, 2009. ARM Technical Whitepaper. http://infocenter.arm.com/help/topic/com.arm.doc.prd29-genc-009492c/PRD29-GENC-009492C_trustzone_security_whitepaper.pdf.

[4] VMware news release — Verizon Wireless and VMware securely mix the professional and personal mobile experience with dual persona Android devices, October 2011. http://www.vmware.com/company/news/releases/vmw-vmworld-emea-verizon-joint-10-19-11.html.

[5] N. Anderson and V. Strauss. Cheating concerns force delay in SAT scores for South Koreans and Chinese. In *Washington Post*, October 30, 2014.

[6] J. Andrus, C. Dall, A. V. Hof, O. Laadan, and J. Nieh. Cells: A virtual mobile smartphone architecture. In *ACM Symposium on Operating Systems Principles*, 2011.

[7] N. Asokan, J-E. Ekberg, K. Kostiainen, A. Rajan, C. Rozas, A.-R. Sadeghi, S. Schulz, and C. Wachsmann. Mobile trusted computing. *Proceedings of the IEEE*, 102(8), August 2014.

[8] The InfiniBand Trade Association. The InfiniBand^{TM} architecture specification. http://www.infinibandta.org.

[9] A. Azab, P. Ning, J. Shah, Q. Chen, R. Bhutkar, G. Ganesh, J. Ma, and W. Shen. Hypervision across Worlds: Real-time kernel protection from the ARM TrustZone secure world. In *ACM Conference on Computer and Communications Security*, 2014.

[10] A. Baliga, V. Ganapathy, and L. Iftode. Detecting kernel-level rootkits using data structure invariants. *IEEE Transactions on Dependable and Secure Computing*, 8(5), 2011.

[11] A. Baliga, P. Kamat, and L. Iftode. Lurking in the shadows: Identifying systemic threats to kernel data. In *IEEE Symposium on Security & Privacy*, 2007.

[12] A. Beresford, A. Rice, N. Skehin, and R. Sohan. MockDroid: Trading privacy for application functionality on smartphones. In *ACM HotMobile*, 2010.

[13] Blackberry. Enterprise mobility management – Devices, Apps, Content. Productivity Protected. http://us.blackberry.com/enterprise/solutions/emm.html.

[14] A. Bohra, I. Neamtiu, P. Gallard, F. Sultan, and L. Iftode. Remote repair of operating system state using backdoors. In *International Conference on Autonomic Computing*, 2004.

[15] S. Bugiel, S. Hauser, and A.-R. Sadeghi. Flexible and fine-grained mandatory access control on Android for diverse security and privacy policies. In *USENIX Security Symposium*, 2013.

[16] M. Carbone, W. Cui, L. Lu, W. Lee, M. Peinado, and X. Jiang. Mapping kernel objects to enable systematic integrity checking. In *ACM Conference on Computer and Communications Security*, 2009.

[17] J. Clark and P. C. van Oorschot. SoK: SSL and HTTPS: Revisiting past challenges and evaluating certificate trust model enhancements. In *IEEE Symposium on Security & Privacy*, 2013.

[18] P. Colp, J. Zhang, J. Gleeson, S. Suneja, E. Lara, H. Raj, S. Saroiu, and A. Wolman. Protecting data on smartphones and tablets from memory attacks. In *ACM International Conference on Architectural Support for Programming Languages and Operating Systems*, 2015.

[19] M.J. Covington, P. Fogla, Z. Zhan, and M. Ahamad. A context-aware security architecture for emerging applications. In *Annual Computer Security Applications Conference*, 2002.

[20] L. P. Cox and P. M. Chen. Pocket hypervisors: Opportunities and challenges. In *ACM HotMobile*, 2007.

[21] W. Cui, M. Peinado, Z. Xu, and E. Chan. Tracking rootkit footprints with a practical memory analysis system. In *USENIX Security Symposium*, 2012.

[22] C. Dall and J. Nieh. KVM/ARM: The design and implementation of the Linux ARM hypervisor. In *ACM International Conference on Architectural Support for Programming Languages and Operating Systems*, 2014.

[23] L. Davi, A. Dmitrienko, M. Egele, T. Fischer, T. Holz, R. Hund, S. Nurnberger, and A.-R. Sadeghi. MoCFI: Mitigating control-flow attacks on smartphones. In *Network & Distributed Systems Security Symposium*, 2012.

[24] X. Ge, H. Vijayakumar, and T. Jaeger. SPROBES: Enforcing kernel code integrity on the TrustZone architecture. In *IEEE Mobile Security Technologies Workshop*, 2014.

[25] Google. Using DDMS for debugging. http://developer.android.com/tools/debugging/ddms.html.

[26] A. P. Heriyanto. Procedures and tools for acquisition and analysis of volatile memory on Android smartphones. In *11th Australian Digital Forensics Conference*, 2013.

[27] S. Heuser, A. Nadkarni, W. Enck, and A.-R. Sadeghi. ASM: A programmable interface for extending Android security. In *USENIX Security Symposium*, 2014.

[28] O. S. Hofmann, A. M. Dunn, S. Kim, I. Roy, and E. Witchel. Ensuring operating system kernel integrity with OSck. In *ACM International Conference on Architectural Support for Programming Languages and Operating Systems*, 2011.

[29] Mellanox Technologies Inc. Introduction to InfiniBand, September 2014. http://www.mellanox.com/blog/2014/09/introduction-to-infiniband.

[30] S. Jana, D. Molnar, A. Moshchuk, A. Dunn, B. Livshits, H. J. Wang, and E. Ofek. Enabling fine-grained permissions for augmented reality applications with recognizers. In *USENIX Security Symposium*, 2013.

[31] D. Jang, H. Lee, M. Kim, D. Kim, D. Kim, and B. Kang. ATRA: Address translation redirection attack against hardware-based external monitors. In *ACM Conference on Computer and Communications Security*, 2014.

[32] Joint Test Action Group (JTAG). 1149.1-2013 - IEEE Standard for test access port and boundary-scan architecture, 2013. http://standards.ieee.org/findstds/standard/1149.1-2013.html.

[33] K. Kostiainen, J. Ekberg, N. Asokan, and A. Rantala. On-board credentials with open provisioning. In *ACM Symposium on Information, Computer and Communications Security*, 2009.

[34] W. Li, H. Li, H. Chen, and Y. Xia. AdAttester: Secure online advertisement attestation on mobile devices using TrustZone. In *ACM MobiSys*, 2015.

[35] L. Litty, A. Lagar-Cavilla, and D. Lie. Hypervisor support to detect covertly executing binaries. In *USENIX Security Symposium*, 2008.

[36] H. Liu, S. Saroiu, A. Wolman, and H. Raj. Software abstractions for trusted sensors. In *ACM MobiSys*, 2012.

[37] M. McGee. New website tracks "Glasshole-Free Zones," businesses that have banned Google Glass. In *Glass Alamanac (*http://glassalmanac.com*)*, March 2014.

[38] Microsoft. Microsoft Intune: Simplify management of apps and devices. https://www.microsoft.com/en-us/server-cloud/products/microsoft-intune/.

[39] M. Miettinen, S. Heuser, W. Kronz, A.-R. Sadeghi, and N. Asokan. ConXsense – Context profiling and classification for context-aware access control. In *ACM Symposium on Information, Computer and Communications Security*, 2014.

[40] A. Migicovsky, Z. Durumeric, J. Ringenberg, and J. Alex Halderman. Outsmarting proctors with smartwatches: A case study on wearable computing security. In *International Conference on Financial Cryptography and Data Security*, 2014.

[41] M. Ongtang, S. McLaughlin, W. Enck, and P. McDaniel. Semantically-rich application-centric security in Android. In *Annual Computer Security Applications Conference*, 2009.

[42] S. Patel, J. Summet, and K. Truong. Blindspot: Creating capture-resistant spaces. In *Protecting Privacy in Video Surveillance*, 2009.

[43] N. Petroni, T. Fraser, A. Walters, and W. A. Arbaugh. An architecture for specification-based detection of semantic integrity violations in kernel dynamic data. In *USENIX Security Symposium*, 2006.

[44] N. Petroni and M. Hicks. Automated detection of persistent kernel control-flow attacks. In *ACM Conference on Computer and Communications Security*, 2007.

[45] N. L. Petroni, T. Fraser, J. Molina, and W. A. Arbaugh. Copilot: A coprocessor-based kernel runtime integrity monitor. In *USENIX Security Symposium*, 2004.

[46] H. Raj, S. Saroiu, A. Wolman, R. Aigner, J. Cox, P. England, C. Fenner, K. Kinshumann, J. Loeser, D. Mattoon, M. Nystrom, D. Robinson, R. Spiger, S. Thom, and D. Wooten. fTPM: A firmware-based TPM 2.0 implementation, November 2015. Microsoft Research Technical Report 2015-84.

[47] H. Raj, S. Saroiu, A. Wolman, and J. Padhye. Splitting the bill for mobile data with SIMlets. In *ACM HotMobile*, 2013.

[48] N. Raval, A. Srivastava, K. Lebeck, L. P. Cox, and A. Machanavajjhala. MarkIt: Privacy markers for protecting visual secrets. In *ACM International Joint Conference on Pervasive and Ubiquitous Computing UPSIDE Workshop*, 2014.

[49] F. Roesner, D. Molnar, A. Moshchuk, T. Kohno, and H. J. Wang. World-driven access control for continuous sensing. In *ACM Conference on Computer and Communications Security*, 2014.

[50] A.-R. Sadeghi, C. Stuble, and M. Winandy. Property-based TPM virtualization. In *Information Security Conference*, 2008.

[51] R. Sailer, X. Zhang, T. Jaeger, and L. van Doorn. Design and implementation of a TCG-based integrity measurement architecture. In *USENIX Security Symposium*, 2004.

[52] Samsung. KNOX workspace supported MDMs. https://www.samsungknox.com/en/products/knox-workspace/technical/knox-mdm-feature-list.

[53] N. Santos, H. Raj, S. Saroiu, and A. Wolman. Using ARM TrustZone to build a Trusted Language Runtime for mobile applications. In *ACM International Conference on Architectural Support for Programming Languages and Operating Systems*, 2014.

[54] A. Seshadri, M. Luk, N. Qu, and A. Perrig. SecVisor: A tiny hypervisor to provide lifetime kernel code integrity for commodity OSes. In *ACM Symposium on Operating Systems Principles*, 2007.

[55] S. Smalley and R. Craig. Security enhanced Android: Bringing flexible MAC to Android. In *Network & Distributed Systems Security Symposium*, 2013.

[56] U. Steinberg and B. Kauer. NOVA: A microhypervisor-based secure virtualization architecture. In *European Symposium on Computer Systems*, 2010.

[57] A. Stevenson. Boot into recovery mode for rooted and un-rooted Android devices. http://androidflagship.com/605-enter-recovery-mode-rooted-un-rooted-android.

[58] H. Sun, K. Sun, Y. Wang, J. Jing, and S. Jajodia. TrustDump: Reliable memory acquisition on smartphones. In *European Symposium on Research in Computer Security*, 2014.

[59] M. M. Swift, M. Annamalai, B. N. Bershad, and H. N. Levy. Recovering device drivers. *ACM Transactions on Computer Systems*, 24(4), 2006.

[60] J. Sylve, A. Case, L. Marziale, and G. G. Richard. Acquisition and analysis of volatile memory from Android smartphones. *Digital Investigation*, 8(3-4), 2012.

[61] X. Wang, K. Sun, Y. Wang, and J. Jing. DeepDroid: Dyanmically enforcing enterprise policy on Android device. In *Network & Distributed Systems Security Symposium*, 2015.

[62] N. Zhang, H. Sun, K. Sun, W. Lou, and Y. T. Hou. CacheKit: Evading memory introspection using cache incoherence. In *IEEE European Symposium on Security and Privacy*, 2016.

Author Index

www.ingramcontent.com/pod-product-compliance
Ingram Content Group UK Ltd.
Pitfield, Milton Keynes, MK11 3LW, UK
UKHW051412290926
15471UKWH00009B/1561

9 781450 346085